291.9   Alcohol-Related Disorder NOS

Amphetamine (or Amphetamine-like)-Related Disorders

Amphetamine Use Disorders

304.40   Amphetamine Dependence[a]

305.70   Amphetamine Abuse

Amphetamine-Induced Disorders

292.89   Amphetamine Intoxication
Specify if: With Perceptual Disturbances

292.0   Amphetamine Withdrawal

292.81   Amphetamine Intoxication Delirium

292.xx   Amphetamine-Induced Psychotic Disorder

   .11   With Delusions[I]

   .12   With Hallucinations[I]

292.84   Amphetamine-Induced Mood Disorder[I,W]

292.89   Amphetamine-Induced Anxiety Disorder[I]

292.89   Amphetamine-Induced Sexual Dysfunction[I]

292.89   Amphetamine-Induced Sleep Disorder[I,W]

292.9   Amphetamine-Related Disorder NOS

Caffeine-Related Disorders

Caffeine-Induced Disorders

305.90   Caffeine Intoxication

292.89   Caffeine-Induced Anxiety Disorder[I]

292.89   Caffeine-Induced Sleep Disorder[I]

292.9   Caffeine-Related Disorder NOS

Cannabis-Related Disorders

Cannabis Use Disorders

304.30   Cannabis Dependence[a]

305.20   Cannabis Abuse

Cannabis-Induced Disorders

292.89   Cannabis Intoxication
Specify if: With Perceptual Disturbances

292.81   Cannabis Intoxication Delirium

292.xx   Cannabis-Induced Psychotic Disorder

   .11   With Delusions[I]

   .12   With Hallucinations[I]

292.89   Cannabis-Induced Anxiety Disorder[I]

292.9   Cannabis-Related Disorder NOS

Cocaine-Related Disorders

Cocaine Use Disorders

304.20   Cocaine Dependence[a]

305.60   Cocaine Abuse

Cocaine-Induced Disorders

292.89   Cocaine Intoxication
Specify if: With Perceptual Disturbances

292.0   Cocaine Withdrawal

292.81   Cocaine Intoxication Delirium

292.xx   Cocaine-Induced Psychotic Disorder

   .11   With Delusions[I]

   .12   With Hallucinations[I]

292.84   Cocaine-Induced Mood Disorder[I,W]

292.89   Cocaine-Induced Anxiety Disorder[I,W]

292.89   Cocaine-Induced Sexual Dysfunction[I]

292.89   Cocaine-Induced Sleep Disorder[I,W]

292.9   Cocaine-Related Disorder NOS

Hallucinogen/Hallucinogen-Related Disorders

Hallucinogen Use Disorders

304.50   Hallucinogen Dependence[a]

305.30   Hallucinogen Abuse

Hallucinogen-Induced Disorders

292.89   Hallucinogen Intoxication

292.89   Hallucinogen Persisting Perception Disorder (Flashbacks)

292.81   Hallucinogen Intoxication Delirium

292.xx   Hallucinogen-Induced Psychotic Disorder

   .11   With Delusions[I]

   .12   With Hallucinations[I]

292.84   Hallucinogen-Induced Mood Disorder[I]

292.89   Hallucinogen-Induced Anxiety Disorder[I]

292.9   Hallucinogen-Related Disorder NOS

Inhalant-Related Disorders

Inhalant Use Disorders

304.60   Inhalant Dependence[a]

305.90   Inhalant Abuse

Inhalant-Induced Disorders

292.89   Inhalant Intoxication

292.81   Inhalant Intoxication Delirium

292.82   Inhalant-Induced Persisting Dementia

292.xx   Inhalant-Induced Psychotic Disorder

   .11   With Delusions[I]

   .12   With Hallucinations[I]

292.84   Inhalant-Induced Mood Disorder[I]

292.89   Inhalant-Induced Anxiety Disorder[I]

292.9   Inhalant-Related Disorder NOS

Nicotine-Related Disorders

Nicotine Use Disorder

305.10   Nicotine Dependence[a]

Nicotine-Induced Disorder

292.0   Nicotine Withdrawal

292.9   Nicotine-Related Disorder NOS

Opioid-Related Disorders

Opioid Use Disorders

304.00   Opioid Dependence[a]

305.50   Opioid Abuse

Opioid-Induced Disorders

292.89   Opioid Intoxication
Specify if: With Perceptual Disturbances

292.0   Opioid Withdrawal

292.81   Opioid Intoxication Delirium

292.xx   Opioid-Induced Psychotic Disorder

   .11   With Delusions[I]

   .12   With Hallucinations[I]

292.84   Opioid-Induced Mood Disorder[I]

292.89   Opioid-Induced Sexual Dysfunction[I]

292.89   Opioid-Induced Sleep Disorder[I,W]

292.9   Opioid-Related Disorder NOS

Phencyclidine (or Phencyclidine-Like)—Related Disorders

Phencyclidine Use Disorders

304.90   Phencyclidine Dependence[a]

305.90   Phencyclidine Abuse

Phencyclidine-Induced Disorders

292.89   Phencyclidine Intoxication
Specify if: With Perceptual Disturbances

292.81   Phencyclidine Intoxication Delirium

292.xx   Phencyclidine-Induced Psychotic Disorder

   .11   With Delusions[I]

   .12   With Hallucinations[I]

292.84   Phencyclidine-Induced Mood Disorder[I]

292.89   Phencyclidine-Induced Anxiety Disorder[I]

292.9   Phencyclidine-Related Disorder NOS

Sedative-, Hypnotic-, or Anxiolytic-Related Disorders

Sedative, Hypnotic, or Anxiolytic Use Disorders

304.10   Sedative, Hypnotic, or Anxiolytic Dependence[a]

305.40   Sedative, Hypnotic, or Anxiolytic Abuse

Sedative-, Hypnotic-, or Anxiolytic-Induced Disorders

292.89   Sedative, Hypnotic, or Anxiolytic Intoxication

.11   With Delusions[I]

.12   With Hallucinations[I]

Specify if: With Perceptual Disturbances

292.81   Sedative, Hypnotic, or Anxiolytic Intoxication Delirium

292.81   Sedative, Hypnotic, or Anxiolytic Withdrawal Delirium

292.82   Sedative-, Hypnotic-, or Anxiolytic-Induced Persisting Dementia

292.83   Sedative-, Hypnotic-, or Anxiolytic-Induced Persisting Amnestic Disorder

292.xx   Sedative-, Hypnotic-, or Anxiolytic-Induced Psychotic Disorder

   .11   With Delusions[I,W]

   .12   With Hallucinations[I,W]

292.84   Sedative-, Hypnotic-, or Anxiolytic-Induced Mood Disorder[I,W]

292.89   Sedative-, Hypnotic-, or Anxiolytic-Induced Anxiety Disorder[W]

292.89   Sedative-, Hypnotic-, or Anxiolytic-Induced Sexual Dysfunction[I]

292.89   Sedative-, Hypnotic-, or Anxiolytic-Induced Sleep Disorder[I,W]

292.9   Sedative-, Hypnotic-, or Anxiolytic-Related Disorder NOS

Polysubstance-Related Disorder

304.80   Polysubstance Dependence[a]

Other (or Unknown) Substance-Related Disorders

Other (or Unknown) Substance Use Disorders

304.90   Other (or Unknown) Substance Dependence[a]

305.90   Other (or Unknown) Substance Abuse

Other (or Unknown) Substance-Induced Disorders

292.89   Other (or Unknown) Substance Intoxication
Specify if: With Perceptual Disturbances

292.0   Other (or Unknown) Substance Withdrawal
Specify if: With Perceptual Disturbances

292.81   Other (or Unknown) Substance-Induced Delirium

292.82   Other (or Unknown) Substance-Induced Persisting Dementia

292.83   Other (or Unknown) Substance-Induced Persisting Amnestic Disorder

292.xx   Other (or Unknown) Substance-Induced Psychotic Disorder

   .11   With Delusions[I,W]

   .12   With Hallucinations[I,W]

292.84   Other (or Unknown) Substance-Induced Mood Disorder[I,W]

292.89   Other (or Unknown) Substance-Induced Anxiety Disorder[I,W]

292.89   Other (or Unknown) Substance-Induced Sexual Dysfunction[I]

292.89   Other (or Unknown) Substance-Induced Sleep Disoder[I,W]

292.9   Other (or Unknown) Substance-Related Disorder NOS

SCHIZOPHRENIA AND OTHER PSYCHOTIC DISORDERS (273)

295.xx   Schizophrenia

The following Classification of Longitudinal Course applies to all subtypes of Schizophrenia:

Episodic With Interepisode Residual Symptoms (*specify if:* With Prominent

Abnormal Psychology

SECOND EDITION

David S. Holmes *University of Kansas*

HarperCollins*CollegePublishers*

Sponsoring Editor: Catherine Woods
Developmental Editor: Rebecca Kohn
Project Editor: Karen Trost
Art Director and Cover Designer: Lucy Krikorian
Cover Illustration: Edward A. Butler
Photo Researcher: Roberta Knauf
Production Manager: Willie Lane
Compositor: Black Dot
Printer and Binder: R. R. Donnelley & Sons Company
Cover Printer: The Lehigh Press, Inc.

ABNORMAL PSYCHOLOGY, SECOND EDITION

Library of Congress Cataloging-in-Publication Data
Holmes, David S. (David Sheridan), 1939–
    Abnormal psychology/David S. Holmes.—2nd ed.
        p.   cm.
    Includes bibliographical references and index.
    ISBN 0-673-99635-2
    1. Psychology, Pathological.   2. Psychology, Pathological—Case studies   I. Title.
    [DNLML   1. Mental Disorders.   2. Social Behavior Disorders.   WM
    100 H749a   1994]   RC454.H62   1994
    616.89—dc20
    DNLM/DLC   93–30083
    for Library of Congress   CIP

94 95 96   9 8 7 6 5 4 3 2

Contents in Brief

Contents in Detail

Case Studies

Preface

It is with genuine excitement that I sit down to write the preface for *Abnormal Psychology*, Second Edition. A lot has happened in the three years since the first edition appeared, and many more of the pieces of the puzzle of abnormal behavior have been found. The addition and integration of those pieces have resulted in what I sincerely believe is a book that reflects a modern understanding of abnormal behavior. Before discussing the specifics of what is new in this edition, I will take a few paragraphs to describe the general features of the book for those instructors who did not use the first edition.

GENERAL GOALS

My first goal in writing this book was to develop a book that would *teach* and *involve* students. Regardless of how "up-to-date" or sophisticated a book may be, if it cannot teach, it is virtually useless. To achieve that goal, I organized the material carefully (I'm a nut about organization), and I arranged it so ideas built systematically on one another. I also tried to convey a sense of excitement about the problems and progress in this area, and I used numerous case studies to illustrate symptoms, causes, and treatments.

My second goal was to present the *new and intriguing findings in the area of abnormal psychology that are not found in most of the other books in the area.* The "core" findings are here, but there is much more. This book is *not* what in the publishing industry is called a "me too" book.

My third goal was to present material in a context that encouraged *critical evaluation.* Understanding what we know is important, but it is equally important for students to understand what we do not know. Furthermore, fostering critical evaluation is essential because throughout their lives the students will be bombarded by reports of "new breakthroughs" in the area of mental health, and it is crucial that they be able to evaluate those findings effectively. We all hope that what we teach will last beyond the end of the semester, and the critical evaluation fostered here should help achieve that goal.

PERSPECTIVES

All the major disorders discussed in this book are systematically examined from four perspectives: *psychodynamic, learning, cognitive,* and *physiological.* Where it is applicable, attention is also given to the *humanistic-existential* explanation for abnormal behavior. This approach provides balance, and it enables students to compare and evaluate the various explanations for a specific disorder. In presenting each explanation I have taken the position of an advocate of that position. However, the various explanations are not presented as mutually exclusive or necessarily competing. On the contrary, in many instances they are presented as complementing one another so that, when taken together, the four perspectives provide a more complete understanding of a disorder than any single perspective could. The perspectives work together, and the whole is better than the sum of the parts.

The physiological perspective gets more coverage in this book than it does in most other books. This reflects the fact that there are many new findings concerning the physiological factors that influence abnormal behavior and its treatment. Because most undergraduate students have relatively little background in physiology, this material is approached in a very careful, step-by-step fashion so as to be comprehensible, nonthreatening, and meaningful.

One writer observed that two decades ago the study of abnormal behavior was "brainless" and now it is "mindless." In this text I have attempted to integrate the brain with the mind in a way that is understandable to students.

ORGANIZATION

The overall organization of the book is fairly traditional in that the major sections are devoted to the following:

1. *Introductory material* (definitions, history, stress, introductions to the perspectives, diagnostic techniques, research methods)
2. *Anxiety, somatoform, and dissociative disorders*
3. *Mood disorders*
4. *Schizophrenic disorders*
5. *Other disorders* (personality, infancy and childhood, physical health, substance abuse, sexual disorders, organic disorders, and retardation)
6. *Issues of law, patient care, and prevention*

For the most part these are freestanding sections and they can be reordered to fit the variety of course plans used by different instructors.

This book has a larger number of chapters than some other books. That is because I discuss the treatments for different types of abnormal behavior (anxiety, mood, schizophrenia) in separate chapters. There are also more chapters because I broke particularly large topics down into several chapters. Students who used the book preferred and did better with the somewhat smaller and consistently sized units, and instructors appreciated the fact that if they wanted to reorder or eliminate topics, they could be more selective in doing so.

I used a consistent outline for discussing each disorder:

A. Symptoms
   1. Mood
   2. Cognitive
   3. Somatic
   4. Motor
B. Issues
   1. History
   2. Prevalence
   3. Demographic factors
   4. Diagnostic problems
C. Explanations
   1. Psychodynamic
   2. Learning
   3. Cognitive
   4. Physiological
D. Treatment

Students and instructors have liked the consistency and clarity of the organization. The outline provided them with a consistent, cognitive template with which to organize material. That facilitated teaching, aided recall, and enhanced the ability to compare ideas and disorders.

CASE MATERIAL

Case material is of crucial importance in a book on abnormal psychology, and I have used three types. First, there are 60 case studies that are set off from the explanatory material. A unique feature of many of these is that they are *first-person accounts* written by people who had experienced (or are experiencing) a particular disorder. For example, an undergraduate student describes the panic attack she had in class; a man suffering from a severe obsessive-compulsive disorder explains how his life is disrupted because he must do everything seven times; a mother discusses her postpartum depression; a student reviews his roller coaster life while suffering from a bipolar disorder; and a young professional woman describes the problems of living posed by her serious delusional disorder. These cases make the disorders more real and more personal.

Other cases include well-known or particularly interesting persons such as John Madden, the CBS football announcer who suffers from phobias; Kenneth Bianchi, the "Hillside Strangler," who attempted to feign a multiple personality; the "three Christs of Ypsilanti," who tried to resolve the conflicts in their delusional identities; John Hinckley, Jr., who tried to assassinate President Reagan; and Billy Boggs, the woman who lived on the streets of New York and burned money. There are, of course, traditional case studies as well.

In addition to these case studies, each chapter is preceded by three or four brief vignettes that reflect the type of disorder or intervention that will be discussed in that chapter. These vignettes are used to catch the students' interest and alert them to relevant issues. Finally, there are many brief examples scattered throughout the text that are used to illustrate particular symptoms, concepts, issues, and problems. This mix of case studies, vignettes, and examples provides a rich foundation of clinical case material on which to build an academic understanding of causes and treatments.

TREATMENT

I have done two things differently with regard to the treatment of abnormal behavior. First, rather than lumping all treatments into one section, the treatment of a disorder is discussed immediately after the disorder is described and explained. I did this because in most cases the treatment of a disorder should be directly related to the cause of the disorder, and thus learning about treatments can be another way to learn about disorders. Furthermore, discussing treatment in the context of the disorder also establishes a meaningful link between a disorder and its treatment, and that helps students understand why different treatments are used for different disorders. I have tried to conceptualize each disorder and its treatment as a *package.*

The second thing I have done differently is to devote somewhat more space to treatment than have most other authors. I did that because for my students treatment is an intriguing and often controversial aspect of abnormal behavior. Their questions stem from academic curiosity but also from practical concerns (e.g., "They gave my mom shock treatment when she was in the hospital. Will that cause brain damage?"). I have tried to present up-to-date information regarding a wide variety of treatments along with realistic comments about their limitations and problems.

I recognize that instructors have widely differing views with regard to teaching about treatment (e.g., some like to deal with it at the end of the course, others skip it because of insufficient time). The organization of this book permits a number of approaches. You can deal with treatment as part of the discussion of each disorder, lump the sections on treatment together at the end of the course, have the students read about treatment but not lecture on it in class, or ignore treatment completely. Information and flexibility are built in; the choice of what to do is yours.

LEVEL OF DIFFICULTY AND WRITING STYLE

In the publishing industry, books are traditionally labeled "upper-" or "lower-"level books as a function of whether they are used most at major research institutions or small colleges. We were pleased when the first edition was adopted at well over 500 colleges and universities *across the entire range of schools.* The reason for the wide range of adoptions was that the book contained the *substance demanded by scholars,* but was written in a style that made the material *accessible to a wide variety of students.*

I have done a number of things to make the book easier to read. For example, the material in each chapter follows a careful outline that is delineated with headings and subheadings. These headings correspond to the points in the outline that precedes the chapter. I also have been careful to use thesis sentences, simple declarative statements, boldface type to identify new terms, and italics to highlight important points. Furthermore, in discussing experiments I have not included details that are not essential to understanding the what, why, or potential criticisms of the experiment. This makes reading easier without sacrificing sophistication.

Understanding was also facilitated by using *over 140 full-color graphs*—more than five times as many as are found in most other textbooks. These graphic aids were designed to be easily readable, and each is topped with a *headline* that summarizes the findings. The concept is discussed in the text, summarized in the headline, and displayed graphically in color, thus bringing the point home in three ways.

Readability was also enhanced by eliminating nonessential names. For example, rather than saying, "In a recent experiment by Archer, Boring, Carter, and Dorg (1988), it was found that . . .," I have said, "It was recently reported that . . . (Archer et al., 1988)." The emphasis is on the *ideas* and *findings,* not individual investigators. This is a subtle change, but it greatly reduces "noise" and makes reading easier.

Finally, this book does not contain "boxes." Boxes serve to break up pages of text visually, but they also break up the flow and development of ideas. It is my view that if material is relevant, it should be integrated into the text; if it is irrelevant, it should not be included. The elimination of boxes also eliminates the questions, "Is the stuff in the boxes important? Are we responsible for it?"

NEW IN THE SECOND EDITION

With the preceding as background, we can go on to consider what is new in the second edition. New material can be placed in four categories. The first of those involves the *changes brought about by the publication of DSM-IV.* The changes in DSM-IV are not as great as the prepublication speculation led many to believe they would be. Instead, for the most part this version is more of a fine-tuning of DSM-III-R than a major revision. For example, there are a few label changes (simple phobias was changed to specific phobias), anorexia and bulimia were moved out of childhood disorders and given their own category, "seasonal pattern" and "postpartum onset" were introduced as subtypes of mood disorders, an acute stress disorder was added, the passive-aggressive personality disorder was dropped, the brief reactive psychosis was changed to the brief psychotic disorder and the notion of a precipitating stress was dropped, the minimum time for symptom duration for a diagnosis for schizophrenia was increased from one week to one month, all of the disorders except personality disorders were moved from Axis II to Axis I, Axis IV is used to record psychosocial and environmental stressors rather than to rate severity of stressors, and in many cases diagnostic criteria were streamlined. The one controversial late change was the addition of premenstrual dysphoria as a mood disorder. These and other changes were incorporated into the second edition where relevant.

Second, extensive new coverage is given to the *important advances in the cognitive and physiological areas of abnormal psychology.* With regard to cognitive factors, I have described the new findings linking cognitions to anxiety and mood disorders, but I have also introduced a *human information-processing* approach to understanding the role of cognitions. That is, rather than simply saying that erroneous thoughts can lead to abnormal behavior, I have employed what we know about things such as *stages of memory, selective attention and recall, neural networks,* and *priming* to explain the *processes* by which cognitions become distorted and then distort behaviors. This brings modern cognitive psychology to bear on clinical issues, an approach that is unique to this book.

Numerous advances in our understanding of the

physiological basis of abnormal behavior are also described in the second edition. Among the most exciting are those linking low levels of serotonin and diffuse brain damage to the obsessive-compulsive disorder, and the findings concerning the role of serotonin and prenatal factors in schizophrenia. (Move over, dopamine hypothesis!)

These new findings in the area of cognition and physiology have had two important effects. First, previously unaccountable cases of some disorders can now be explained. In other words, some missing pieces have been found. Second, there is more specificity in our understanding of causes, which in turn influences treatments. For example, it is now clear that different disorders within the class of anxiety disorders (e.g., phobias, panic, obsessive-compulsive, general anxiety) probably stem from radically different causes, and thus require different treatments.

Third, there is a *general updating* that involves hundreds of new references over many areas. For example, there is new information on stress, comorbidity, fads in diagnoses, PTSD in urban settings, the panic disorder, antidepressants and anxiety, seasonal affective disorder, diathesis-stress and depression, daily hassles and depression, rates and causes of suicide, the controversies over Clozaril and Prozac, malignant neuroleptic syndrome, hyper- and hypofrontality in schizophrenia, neurological basis of hallucinations, positive and negative symptoms, gender and drug effects, the borderline disorder, serotonin and cognitive factors in bulimia, treatment of autism, aversive treatment procedures, genetics of alcoholism, problems with voluntary admission to hospitals, the "duty to warn," and the reversal of the ALI rule on insanity. With regard to references, I should mention that I have not added references simply for the sake of adding references, and I prefer to cite the classic breakthrough investigations rather than more recent follow-ups that only tweak the design.

The fourth group of changes in this edition can best be labeled *pedagogical changes.* Numerous new figures have been introduced to illustrate theoretical relationships, describe processes, and clarify research findings. Also, a variety of new case studies have been included. Notable in this group is a series of three that are focused on a friend of mine who suffers from schizophrenia. In one she describes her symptoms; in a second she talks about her treatment; and the third is devoted to the cost of her mental illness. (This woman is also featured in the videotape that is available to accompany the book.) In another case study, an individual with the borderline personality disorder describes the feelings associated with self-mutilation. Other cases revolve around problems such as the attention-deficit disorder in adulthood and the treatment of depression. In field trials, students found the new cases to be both dramatic and helpful to their understanding.

Overall, the successful features of the first edition, in combination with the additions and refinements of the second edition, have resulted in a text that will challenge, intrigue, excite, and teach a wide variety of students while meeting the high academic standards of their instructors.

SUPPLEMENTS

Test Bank

After students have worked hard in a course, there is nothing more disappointing and frustrating for them than having to take poor examinations that do not measure what they have learned. Similar frustrations are experienced by conscientious instructors who worry about whether their tests accurately reflect what the students learned. Unfortunately, in many cases the preparation of a test item file for a book is an afterthought, and the task is relegated to a person who was neither involved in writing the text nor skilled in writing test items. Because of my concern with this problem, I worked very closely with David J. Lutz (a former student and teaching assistant of mine) in preparing the test bank for the first edition. That test bank was widely regarded as one of the best in the industry. For the second edition, I took responsibility for the test bank. In refining it, I relied on item analyses of many items, as well as comments by colleagues and students, and only the best items were retained or added. I think that you will find it to be an effective tool. The test bank is available in printed form and on floppy disks for most popular desktop computers.

Practice Tests

These are a collection of tests with answers provided that I have used in my classes in the past. They are shrinkwrapped with the text and afford the students more opportunities to test their skills in the course material and relieve the anxiety of test-taking.

Study Guide

Written by David J. Lutz of Southwest Missouri State University, this guide will help students master the material they are learning. It includes learning objectives, annotated chapter outlines, a glossary of key terms, and reviews and self-tests with answers. If the Study Guide is not available at your bookstore, ask the bookstore manager if he or she can order copies, or call HarperCollins directly at 1-800-638-3030.

Supershell Computerized Tutorial

Also written by David Lutz, this interactive tutorial program for IBM and IBM-compatible computers is keyed specifically to my text. It provides immediate correct answers to drills, practice-test questions, and glossary terms. It contains material not found in the Study Guide and provides a running score for students.

Instructor's Manual

Written by Frank J. Prerost of Western Illinois University, this manual contains teaching aids for each chapter: chapter overviews, key terms, and learning objectives, all keyed to chapter outlines. In addition, the manual includes discussion and lecture ideas and suggestions for activities and projects.

ACKNOWLEDGMENTS

Writing and revising this book was a huge task, and its completion was made possible by the help of many individuals. First, recognition should go to the thousands of researchers whose work provided the basis for this book. Without their efforts, we would still think that abnormal behavior was caused by demons.

Second, it is important to acknowledge the contributions of the reviewers who carefully read the manuscript and offered helpful suggestions. Until now they have been an anonymous group, but now I would like to thank them all: Thomas Bradbury, University of California Los Angeles; Linda Bosmajian, Hood College; James F. Calhoun, University of Georgia; Michael Cline, J. Sargeant Reynolds Community College; Eric Cooley, Western Oregon State University; Robert D. Coursey, University of Maryland at College Park; William Curtis, Camden County College; Linda K. Davis, Mt. Hood Community College; Richard Downs, Boise State University; Stan Friedman, Southwest Texas State University; William Rick Fry, Youngstown State University; Steve Funk, Northern Arizona University at Flagstaff; Bernard S. Gorman, Nassau Community College; Stephen Hinshaw, University of California at Berkeley; William G. Iacono, University of Minnesota; Rick Ingram, San Diego State University; Carolin Keutzer, University of Oregon; Alan King,

University of North Dakota; Herbert H. Krauss, Hunter College; David Lowy, Oakland University; Janet R. Matthews, Loyola University; Gary McClure, Georgia Southern University; Joseph Newman, University of Wisconsin at Madison; and Carol Thompson, Muskegon Community College.

Third, this revision would still be a pile of manuscript pages if it had not been for the outstanding staff at HarperCollins. Most notable in that group are Catherine Woods, psychology editor; Marcus Boggs, editor-in-chief; Art Pomponio, director of development; Evelyn Owens, supplements editor; Rebecca Kohn, development editor; Karen Trost, project editor; Mark Paluch, marketing manager; Lucy Krikorian, design manager; Roberta Knauf, photo editor; and Bruce Emmer, copy editor. Also, Diane Kappen did a splendid job on the test bank.

Fourth, and very important, is the large number of colleagues, students, friends, and family members (especially MRH) who provided information, advice, and support throughout this exciting but sometimes difficult period of revision. These people were invaluable.

Finally, thanks are due to my students, who kept asking tough questions, and to the clients who shared their painful experiences. Insofar as this book is dedicated to anyone, it is dedicated to them. I hope that this book will take us one step further in the process of understanding abnormal behavior.

CONTINUING SUPPORT AND FEEDBACK

Unfortunately, no book on a topic as broad and complex as abnormal behavior can be completely satisfactory to everyone. If I have not been clear on some point, if you want more information, or if you disagree with something I have said and think a change is in order, *let me know*. Many faculty members and students wrote in response to the first edition, and I hope you will write in connection with this edition. I will do what I can to get back to you—*I promise*! Teaching and learning about abnormal psychology is a difficult and exceptionally important task for both academic and personal reasons, and it can be helped by good ongoing relationships among author, instructor, and student. I'd be delighted if we can work together, and any help you might offer that would improve this book would be very much appreciated. Good luck with your course—I'll look forward to hearing from you.

DAVID S. HOLMES

About the Author

David S. Holmes received his Ph.D. in clinical psychology from Northwestern University and did his internship at the Massachusetts Mental Health Center, Harvard University. He has been on the faculty at Northwestern University, the University of Texas at Austin, the New School for Social Research, and the University of Kansas. He was also a Visiting Research Scholar at the Educational Testing Service, Princeton.

Professor Holmes focuses most of his attention on the areas of psychopathology, personality, and health psychology. He has published more than 120 articles in leading scientific journals. Professor Holmes was named the "Outstanding Teacher in a Four-Year College or University" by the Division of Teaching of the American Psychological Association, received the "Standard Oil Foundation Award for Excellence in Teaching," and was named one of the "Outstanding Educators in America." Most recently, Professor Holmes received the "Award for Distinguished Teaching in Psychology" from the American Psychological Foundation. Among other things, the citation for that award called attention to his "writing accessible textbooks with impeccable scholarship."

Within the American Psychological Association, Professor Holmes has served on the Board of Scientific Affairs, the Board of Convention Affairs, the Committee on Membership and Fellowship, and the Board of Educational Affairs. He has been elected a fellow of the divisions of Clinical Psychology, Personality and Social Psychology, Health Psychology, Teaching of Psychology, and General Psychology. He was also elected a fellow of the American Psychopathological Association.

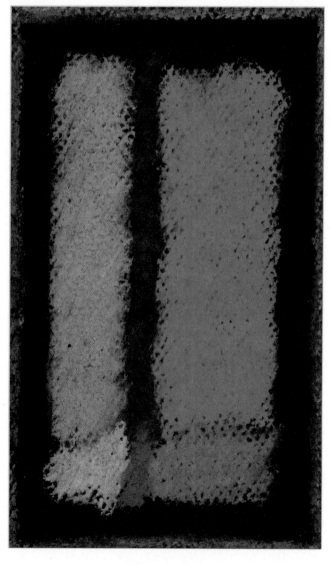

About the Artwork

The 29 pastel panels in this book were created specifically for *Abnormal Psychology*, Second Edition, by New York artist and graphic designer Edward A. Butler. A graduate of Philadelphia College of Art, Butler is the recipient of The Society of Illustrators Merit Award and the Philadelphia, Chicago, and New York Art Directors Clubs Awards. His work is held by several private collectors.

PART 1

Introduction

• OUTLINE •

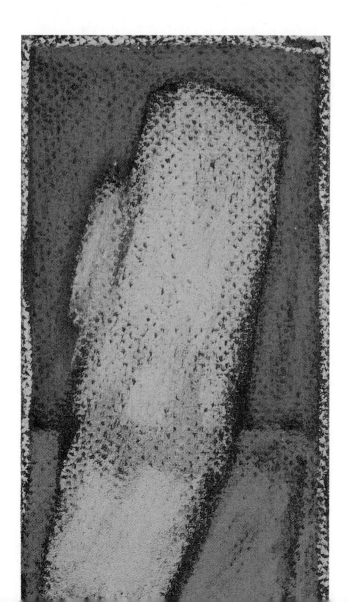

Chapter 1
History and Definitions

•OUTLINE•

Mental disorders constitute one of the most serious and perplexing problems in Western civilization. Consider the following facts:

More than 30% of Americans suffer from at least one major psychological disorder during their lifetimes.

About 5% of the population suffers from major depression, and the rate is increasing.

Valium, used for the treatment of anxiety, is one of the most frequently prescribed drugs in the United States.

Alcoholism and alcohol abuse cost the U.S. economy about $125 billion a year.

These figures are staggering, but they do not convey the intensely personal aspects of the problem:

The confusion and terror felt by a person with schizophrenia when suddenly the world just does not make sense anymore

The agony and despair of the depressed individual who feels unreachable, in a deep, dark hole

The conflict of the person with bulimia who binges and purges every day until her teeth and throat rot from the gastric acid

The shock of the mother whose unresponsive infant is labeled autistic

The terrible feeling of helplessness when the heavy door to the "closed ward" swings shut and locks behind you

This is not a book about the problems of someone else. Mental illness touches all of us at some time during our lives; if we are not the ones afflicted, it will be a family member, loved one, or close friend. The problem of abnormal behavior is personally relevant and emotionally charged, but in this book we will explore the problem from an objective, scientific point of view. Although we must be dispassionate in our study of the problem, it is important that we keep in mind the importance and intense personal ramifications of what we are studying.

Scientists and practitioners have learned a great deal about the causes and treatment of abnormal behavior. However, there is still a gap between what we know and what we need to know. This book is about what we know and about the gap.

In this chapter, we will first consider how abnormal behavior has been viewed in the past and then develop a definition of abnormal behavior. In Chapters 2 and 3, we will examine the various perspectives that are used to explain abnormal behavior and the techniques that are used to diagnose and study it. With

that material as background, we will go on to consider the symptoms, causes, and treatments of a variety of disorders.

■ HISTORICAL BACKGROUND

Society has explained and treated abnormal behavior in different ways at different times. How a particular society reacts to abnormality depends on its values and assumptions about human life and behavior. For example, in a society like Europe in the Middle Ages, in which a religious point of view was predominant, abnormality was often ascribed to supernatural causes, such as demons, and treatment involved prayers and various forms of exorcism. In U.S. society, which puts a great deal of faith in science and the "miracles of modern medicine," it is not surprising that abnormal behavior is considered a mental illness and is often treated with drugs.

In the following sections, we will briefly consider the history and evolution of thinking concerning abnormal behavior. The information presented here should not be considered mere history because many of the old ideas still play important roles in contemporary thinking about abnormal behavior. Unlike many other sciences, when new ideas about abnormal behavior and treatment were developed, they did not necessarily replace older ideas. Instead, they were added to the existing group of explanations and treatments.

Phases in the History of Abnormal Behavior

Demonology.   The belief that abnormal behavior is caused by supernatural forces that take control of the mind or body goes back beyond the start of recorded history. Evidence in the form of papyrus scrolls, monuments, and the early books of the Bible reveals that the ancient Egyptians, Arabs, and Hebrews believed that abnormal behavior was the result of possession by supernatural forces such as angry gods, evil spirits, and demons. There was nothing unusual about these ancient cultures' attributing abnormal behavior to the action of supernatural forces because they believed that many other phenomena, such as fires and floods, were also caused by supernatural rather than natural forces.

The typical approach to expelling the demons was to use incantations, prayers, or potions to persuade them to leave. In some instances, various forms of physical punishment, such as stoning or flogging, were advocated as a means of forcing the demons out of a possessed person.

Introduction of Physiological Explanations.

The first attempt to explain abnormal behavior in terms of natural rather than supernatural causes occurred during the Golden Age of Greece when **Hippocrates** (hip-POC-ruh-tēz; c. 460–c. 377 B.C.), who is known as the father of modern medicine, taught that the brain is the organ responsible for mental disorders. He also suggested that behavior was governed by the relative levels of four **humors** (fluids) in the body: *black bile, yellow bile, phlegm,* and *blood.* For example, he believed that an excess of black bile caused depression; that too much yellow bile was associated with tension, anxiety, and personal instability; that high levels of phlegm resulted in a dull or sluggish ("phlegmatic") temperament; and that excess blood volume was related to rapid mood swings. Hippocrates lacked scientific techniques to verify his explanation, but his approach started us on the path toward seeing abnormal behavior as a physiological malfunction or disease and provided the foundation for the **physiological perspective** on abnormal behavior.

Treatment during this period involved attempts to restore the appropriate balance among humors, and that was usually done by draining off excess fluids from the body or by altering diet, exercise, alcohol intake, or lifestyle in general. Because disturbed people were considered to be suffering from illnesses, they were cared for like other sick people.

Return to Demonology.

During the Middle Ages (c. A.D. 500–1500), religion became the dominant force in virtually all aspects of European life, and the naturalistic approach of Hippocrates and his followers was essentially abandoned. Life was perceived as a struggle between good and evil forces, and the evil forces were led by the Devil, who was thought to afflict disturbed persons. In other words, the ancient idea of demonic possession was revived, and brutal exorcistic treatments were used to drive the Devil out. For example, persons who were thought to be possessed by the Devil would be stoned or tortured in other ways. Worst of all, disturbed persons might be accused of being agents of the Devil (not merely his victims) and therefore labeled *witches.* Toward the end of the Middle Ages, official church policy dictated that witches were to be identified and destroyed. To assist with that task, a manual for identifying and examining witches, *Malleus Maleficarum* (The Witch Hammer), was published in 1486. This manual became a widely respected authority and guide for witch-hunts. Unfortunately for the mentally ill, the manual equated abnormal behavior with possession by the Devil, and possessed individuals were assumed to be witches. To drive the Devil out, the witches had to be killed, often burned alive.

During the Middle Ages, mental illness was thought to be the result of demonic possession. Various forms of exorcism were used to drive out the Devil.

In this phase of demonology, then, disturbed individuals were seen as threats to society and were killed in an attempt to protect others. This practice spread to settlements in America, where witch-hunts reached their peak in the 1690s with the famous Salem witchcraft trials. Persecution of individuals as witches abated in some areas of Europe as early as 1610 and was legally brought to a halt in America around 1700.

Introduction of Humane Care.

Some fortunate people received humane care during earlier periods, but the 16th century marked the first time that it was widely recognized that disturbed people needed care, not exorcism or condemnation. In 1547, the hospital of Saint Mary of Bethlehem in London was dedicated to the care of disturbed people. The word *care,* however, is hardly appropriate to describe how patients in these early hospitals (asylums) were treated. In fact, the early asylums were more like prisons than hospitals. Nothing was done for the inmates other than to confine them under horrible conditions. They were often chained to the wall, sometimes in a way that prevented them from lying down to sleep. Or they might be chained to large iron balls that they had to drag with them whenever they moved. Furthermore, large numbers of extremely disturbed people were confined in close quarters, which resulted in dreadful chaos and confusion. Indeed, the word *bedlam,* which means "a place, scene, or state of uproar and confusion," was derived from the name of the Bethlehem hospital.

Rather than being a source of concern to society at large, conditions in these early asylums constituted a source of amusement, and tickets to view the patients were actually sold to the public.

After disturbed individuals were recognized as patients, the next step in bringing about humane care involved improving the conditions in which the patients lived. The most famous effort in this regard has traditionally been ascribed to **Philippe Pinel** (fi-LĒP pē-NEL; 1745–1826) in 1792. He directed that the patients in his hospital in Paris be unchained and that the hospital quarters be renovated to make them more pleasant. In England at about the same time, **William Tuke** (tyo͞ok; 1732–1822) and the Quakers opened a "retreat" for patients on a country estate. Their approach was based on the notion that rest, fresh air, and exposure to nature had therapeutic value. In the United States, **Benjamin Rush** (1745–1813), the "father of American psychiatry," introduced humane treatment in the Pennsylvania Hospital in 1783. **Dorothea Dix** (1802–1887) was a New England schoolteacher who became concerned about the terrible living conditions and harsh treatments that were forced on patients, so between 1841 and 1881 she conducted an effective campaign to inform the public about the problem. She also raised money and is credited with the establishment of 32 mental hospitals throughout the United States.

Freeing patients from their chains and building more and better hospitals undoubtedly made patients more comfortable, but the therapeutic effect of these changes has been greatly exaggerated. Written accounts and drawings of the time suggest that patients became tranquil, even normal, when their chains were removed. Although this may have been true for some patients, in most cases it seems unlikely that the changes resulted in significant improvements. That is the case because effective treatments were not yet available, and without treatment, serious disorders tend to persist regardless of how comfortable patients are. If fresh air and freedom were sufficient to cure mental disorders, mental illness would not be the serious problem it is today.

Introduction of Psychological Explanations.

The belief that the causes of abnormal behavior were psychological can be traced to 19th-century Europe. One of the first important figures in this regard was **Franz Anton Mesmer** (MEZ-mur; 1734–1815). Mesmer believed that abnormal behavior was the result of an imbalance of certain "magnetic fluids" in the body (a physiological cause). To correct the imbalance, Mesmer had groups of patients sit around a large tub filled with a "magnetic fluid." Then, while music played in the background, the patients would take iron rods from the tub and apply them to the afflicted parts of their bodies. Mesmer would also touch the patients with his magnetized wand. As the treatment session progressed, some of the patients would start to tremble; their limbs would twitch convulsively; they would groan, choke, laugh, and scream; and finally some of them would dance wildly or faint. This "crisis" would

This painting shows patients being unchained at the Salpêtrière Hospital in Paris in 1792. The movement toward more humane treatment of mental patients marked an important turning point in society's attitude toward the mentally ill. However, it did not lead to significant improvement for most patients because effective treatments were not yet available.

One early treatment consisted of spinning patients. Benjamin Rush, the "father of American psychiatry," is quoted as saying that "no well-regulated institution should be unprovided with the circulating swing."

continue for some time, but when it finally subsided, many of the patients were apparently free of the symptoms for which they had sought treatment.

Mesmer's successes attracted considerable attention, and in Paris his patients included such notables as King Louis XVI, Queen Marie Antoinette, and the Marquis de Lafayette. Mesmer was apparently successful in relieving the symptoms of some of his patients, but his technique was seriously questioned by the scientific communities in Vienna and Paris. Because of those concerns, a panel of experts was convened in Paris in 1784 to examine Mesmer's practices and issue a report. (The members of the panel included Benjamin Franklin, who was the United States ambassador to France; Joseph Guillotin, who invented the decapitating machine; and Antoine-Laurent Lavoisier, who discovered oxygen.) The panel failed to find any support for magnetism and concluded: "That which has been proved through our examination of magnetism is that *man can affect man* . . . almost at will by stimulating his imagination" (Bromberg, 1959, p. 173). Mesmer was labeled a charlatan and barred from further medical practice. Ironically, then, although Mesmer believed that abnormal behavior was due to *physical* factors, his work led others to the conclusion that *psychological* and *interpersonal* factors played an important role in many disorders. As a footnote to Mesmer's career, it should be noted that although he

died in obscurity in Switzerland in 1815, he has had a lasting influence on psychology because he is considered the father of hypnotism, which was originally known as **mesmerism** (MEZ-mur-iz-um).

Another well-known contributor to the development of the psychological explanation of abnormal behavior was **Jean-Martin Charcot** (shar-KŌ; 1825–1893), a neurologist and the head of the Salpêtrière Hospital in Paris. (This was the same hospital in which, a century earlier, Pinel had freed the patients from their chains.) Charcot was interested in patients who were suffering from what then was called *hysteria*. **Hysterical disorders** involve physical symptoms that have no demonstrable organic basis. The symptoms may include paralysis, blindness, pain, seizures, and deafness. An example would be an individual whose arm is paralyzed even though no muscle or nerve damage can be found. Today, we call problems like this **somatoform** (sō-MAT-uh-form) **disorders** because they take the *form* of *somatic* problems.

Charcot believed that there was a link between hysterical disorders and hypnosis because patients with hysterical disorders were easily hypnotized and because with hypnosis he could eliminate old symptoms and introduce new ones. Indeed, he became famous for demonstrations in which he hypnotized patients and then dramatically eliminated or induced symptoms. His explanation of the link between hysterical disorders and hypnosis was that both resulted from a neurological weakness. In other words, he believed that both hysterical disorders and susceptibility to hypnosis were forms of illness due to a physiological cause. However, to his surprise, some of his students demonstrated that *normal* people could also be hypnotized and have symptoms induced. That demonstration led Charcot to revise his explanation and conclude that hysterical disorders and hypnosis were

This engraving shows one of Mesmer's treatment sessions.

not a result of a neurological weakness (a physiological cause) but were the effects of *suggestion* (a psychological cause). Charcot's interest in patients with hysterical disorders and his conclusion that their symptoms had a psychological basis set the stage for the work of Freud.

Sigmund Freud (1856–1939) was trained as a neurologist, and like Charcot he was interested in treating patients with hysterical disorders. Early in his career, Freud became friends with another neurologist, **Josef Breuer** (BROY-ur; 1842–1925), who had been treating a patient referred to in Freud's writings as **Anna O.** Anna O. had a number of symptoms, including paralyses of three limbs, problems with vision and speech, difficulty with eating, and a persistent nervous cough. What was most interesting about Anna O. was that after she *talked* about her symptoms under hypnosis, the symptoms temporarily disappeared. Breuer suggested that talking about her problems enabled Anna O. to reduce tension and that the reduction of tension led to a reduction of symptoms. He labeled this process **catharsis** (kuh-THAR-sis), which means "a purging that brings about spiritual renewal or release of tension."

Sigmund Freud pioneered the psychodynamic approach to understanding abnormal behavior. He is shown here with his daughter Anna Freud, who became a leader in the ego psychology movement.

The case of Anna O. led Freud to begin thinking about hysterical disorders in terms of psychological causes, and shortly thereafter he went to Paris for a year to study with Charcot. Freud gained considerable experience with hypnosis during the time he spent with Charcot, but he came to believe that hypnosis was not a very effective method of treatment. In some cases, he was unable to hypnotize the patient at all, and in other cases, the posthypnotic suggestions did not last. Consequently, Freud gave up the use of hypnosis and substituted a procedure of his own, which he called **free association**. In this technique, the patient was asked to lie on a couch and talk about anything that came to mind. Initially, Freud would interrupt the patient to ask questions, but one day a patient told him to stop interrupting because he was interfering with her chain of thought. Freud did as the patient requested and discovered that the patient's unrestrained chain of thoughts led to topics and revealed important information that he would never have thought to ask about. Eventually, Freud came to believe that this process of uninhibited talk would lead the patient to reveal the psychological problems and conflicts that had led to the symptoms.

Freud's clinical experience led him to hypothesize that the human mind is much like an iceberg—the largest portion is completely hidden from view. In Freudian terms, the vast hidden part of the mind is called the **unconscious**, and it contains powerful urges, fears, and conflicts that exert a strong influence on a person's behavior even though the person is completely unaware of their existence. Freud believed that the most important memories and conflicts that are sealed in the unconscious are those that are left over from early childhood. Thus, events a person has "forgotten" are stored in the unconscious, where they continue to affect the person's behavior throughout life. Freud explained his cases of mysterious physical ailments as defenses against unacceptable unconscious impulses. For example, a person who seemed to be paralyzed might unconsciously want to act aggressively against others, and the paralysis would prevent this. A person who seemed blind might unconsciously want to avoid seeing something disturbing.

Freud's theory is complex, and we will discuss it in more detail in Chapter 2. Here it suffices to note that Freud believed that the source of all behavior, normal and abnormal, is the interaction of forces within the mind. This point of view is called the **psychodynamic perspective**, *dynamic* referring to the forces in the mind that act to push and pull our behavior in various directions.

At the same time that Freud was treating his patients and developing his theory of behavior, the Russian physiologist **Ivan Pavlov** (1849–1936) was working with dogs in his laboratory and making some very different discoveries about behavior. Pavlov discovered that if a stimulus (meat) that elicited a response (salivation) was consistently paired with a neutral stimulus (a bell) that did not initially elicit the response, after many pairings the neutral stimulus would elicit the response. Today we call this process **classical conditioning**. Classical conditioning is relevant for understanding behavior because it can be used to explain why an individual has a particular uncontrollable physiological or emotional response when exposed to a particular stimulus (e.g., fear when exposed to a snake).

While Pavlov was working with dogs, an American psychologist named **Edward L. Thorndike** (1874–1949) was studying how cats solved problems. He noticed that if a cat was given a reward (a bit of food) after solving a problem, the cat was more likely to use that behavior again in the future. In other words, Thorndike pointed out that behavior is governed by rewards and punishments, a process he called **operant conditioning** (the term *operant* comes from the fact that the animal acts or operates to get rewards or avoid punishments). Animal trainers had been using the principles of operant conditioning for years (the old "carrot and stick" approach), but Thorndike refined the principles and made them scientifically respectable.

Pavlov and Thorndike expanded our understanding of how conditioning influenced behavior, but their work was limited to animals, and they were not interested in applications to human behavior. However, a brash young American psychologist named **John B. Watson** (1878–1958) seized the notion of conditioning and actively promoted the idea that it could be used to explain normal and abnormal behavior in humans. For example, Watson suggested that fears (phobias) are the result of classical conditioning rather than unconscious conflicts and that behaviors such as tantrums are operantly conditioned because they lead to rewards. Watson was so bold as to suggest that he could mold a young child into any type of adult using classical and operant conditioning. Watson labeled this conditioning-based approach **behaviorism** because it was focused on observable behaviors rather than the unconscious and unobservable processes that were emphasized by Freud. Behaviorism quickly became popular because of its objective, scientific basis and because it provided techniques for changing behavior (conditioning) that were faster than the psychotherapeutic techniques developed by Freud and his followers. The famous American psychologist **B. F. Skinner** (1904–1992) continued the refinement of operant conditioning and was a strong advocate for be-

B. F. Skinner was an influential advocate of behaviorism. His work in the area of operant conditioning paved the way for the learning approach to abnormal behavior. Much of Skinner's work was based on research involving pigeons and rats.

haviorism. Behaviorism provided the basis for the **learning** (or conditioning) **perspective** on abnormal behavior.

Despite the appeal of behaviorism, some psychologists believed that it was too limited because it ignored cognitive processes. That is, from the standpoint of behaviorism, the individual was seen as only responding to environmental factors (rewards, punishments, stimuli) and not thinking or having internal direction. Indeed, one critic wryly pointed out that behaviorists saw the behavior of other people as due to rewards and punishments, but they saw their own behavior as motivated by a need to *understand*. The critics did not deny the influence of conditioning, but they suggested that thoughts also played an important role in determining behavior. For example, the thought "I am not a worthwhile person" could lead to depression, and the erroneous belief that "all snakes are dangerous" could lead to a phobia for snakes. Therefore, during the 1970s there was an increased interest in the influence of thought processes on human behavior. The movement gained additional momentum during the 1980s when psychologists discovered some of the ways in which humans process information. For example, it was learned that memories are linked together in networks, and stimulation of one memory can result in the recall of related memories. That helped psychologists understand the "stream of consciousness" and how thoughts might be distorted.

The recognition that thoughts influence behavior, in combination with an increase in the understanding of how we think, led to the development of the **cognitive perspective** on abnormal behavior. In summary, over the past 200 years, psychological explanations for abnormal behavior have evolved from suggestion to unconscious conflicts to conditioning and finally to thought processes.

Renewed Interest in Physiological Explanations.

By the middle of the 20th century, numerous physiological treatments for abnormal behavior were in use, but none was particularly effective. For example, one treatment for schizophrenia was to strap the patient into a chair and spin the chair until the patient passed out. Another involved soaking the patient in hot and cold baths. However, in the early 1950s, a physiologically based method of treatment was introduced that had a truly revolutionary effect on our understanding and treatment of abnormal behavior. At that time, French chemists were working on antihistamines for use in treating allergies and asthma. One negative side effect of the antihistamines was their tendency to make normal individuals drowsy. However, when a strong version of the antihistamines was given to patients suffering from schizophrenia, they became calm, their cognitive confusion was reduced, and their behavior became much more normal. In other words, the calming that was a negative side effect for persons with allergies was found to be helpful for persons suffering from schizophrenia.

More powerful forms of the antihistamines were quickly adapted for use as antipsychotic drugs, and they revolutionized the care and treatment of highly disturbed patients. Hospital wards were transformed from pits of confusion and chaos into places of relative calm. This meant that staff time could be devoted to treating patients rather than merely keeping them physically restrained. Furthermore, many patients who had previously needed to be locked up could now be given medication and released. Before the introduction of these drugs, it had been estimated that 750,000 hospital beds would be needed for psychiatric patients by 1971. In fact, fewer than half that many were actually required because the use of antipsychotic drugs greatly reduced the need for hospitalization.

A second important effect of the antipsychotic drugs was that they opened up a new way of studying the causes of abnormal behavior. If researchers could determine how the brain was affected by these drugs, it might be possible to determine what it was in the brain that caused the abnormal behavior. This gave birth to the important area of **psychopharmacology** (sī-kō-FAR-muh-KOL-uh-jē), in which investigators examine the effects of drugs on brain functioning and behavior.

Current Perspectives on Abnormal Behavior

We have gone from demons to drugs in explaining abnormal behavior, but when new ideas have come along, we have not always abandoned previous explanations. Instead, we have accumulated explanations, and this multiplicity of explanations is both good and bad. On the positive side, multiple explanations may be good because (a) different disorders may stem from *different causes* (e.g., anxiety might be due to psychological factors, whereas schizophrenia may be due to physiological factors), (b) any one disorder may result from *more than one cause* (anxiety may result from either psychological or physiological factors), or (c) *different causes may combine* to result in a disorder (psychological stress may cause physiological changes that in turn lead to anxiety).

On the negative side, we have not abandoned certain explanations and treatments that have no scientific support. Scientifically groundless ideas about abnormal behavior have been preserved because our thinking is influenced by religious and economic factors as well as scientific findings. You may have been amused when you read that demonology was used to explain abnormal behavior and that torture was used to "cure" afflicted individuals as recently as 1700, but you should recognize that in some religious groups, psychological disturbances are still blamed on the Devil and exorcism is still used to treat disturbed individuals.

It should also be noted that we usually see the inhumane treatment of disturbed individuals as a thing of the past, but this is not necessarily the case. In states facing budgetary cutbacks, patients who are in need of hospitalization may be refused admittance, and those who have been hospitalized may be discharged regardless of their conditions. Instead of being treated, these patients are relegated to the streets to fend for themselves, and they often exist in deplorable conditions. Irrational fear of disturbed individuals also continues. For example, in one city in New York, such fears led the residents to pass a law prohibiting disturbed individuals from living within the city limits. This is reminiscent of the banishment from medieval communities of persons thought to be witches. (Fortunately, the New York law was overturned by the courts.)

Overall, then, it is clear that the present phase of understanding and treatment of abnormal behavior represents a melding of what has gone before, some of it worthwhile, some not. In subsequent chapters, we will carefully scrutinize the currently accepted points of view concerning abnormal behavior, and we will try to develop informed opinions concerning its causes and treatments.

DEFINING ABNORMAL BEHAVIOR

We have discussed the importance and history of abnormal behavior, but we have not defined what is actually meant by "abnormal behavior." Arriving at a generally acceptable definition is difficult because some theorists define abnormal behavior from the point of view of the *individual* whose behavior is being considered, while other theorists define abnormal behavior from the point of view of the *culture* in which the individual is living. Because each viewpoint has something to contribute to an overall definition, both viewpoints will be discussed.

When defining abnormal behavior from the point of view of the individual, attention is focused first on the individual's **distress**. Individuals are defined as abnormal when they are anxious, depressed, dissatisfied, or otherwise seriously upset. Second, attention is focused on the individual's **disability**. Individuals are defined as abnormal when they are not able to function personally, socially, physiologically, or occupationally. From the personal point of view, then, abnormality is defined primarily in terms of the individual's *happiness* and *effectiveness*, and what others think about the individual is irrelevant.

When defining abnormal behavior from the cultural point of view, attention is focused on **deviance**, that is, the degree to which an individual deviates from *cultural norms*. For example, an individual who hallucinates will be defined as abnormal because most people do not hallucinate. In this regard, it is relevant to note that what is normal in one culture may be abnormal in another culture. For example, in some cultures, hallucinations are a sign of schizophrenia and the individual is hospitalized, but in other cultures, hallucinations are thought to be the voice of a god and the individual is made a priest (Murphy, 1976). It should also be noted that only deviant behaviors that the culture considers "bad" are defined as abnormal. Having an IQ of 140 or being exceptionally well adjusted is also deviant, but such "good" deviance is not considered abnormal in the way the word *abnormal* is customarily used. From the cultural point of view, then, abnormality is defined in terms of cultural norms, and the feelings of the individual are disregarded.

From the foregoing discussion, it appears that distress, disability, and deviance (the "three Ds") can all play a role in defining abnormal behavior. We must remain flexible in terms of which of these criteria we use to determine whether a particular individual is abnormal. For example, if we use only the personal point of view, the happy but hallucinating individual will not be treated, and if we use only the cultural point of view, the depressed individual who is no bother to anyone will be ignored until he or she attempts suicide.

Sometimes the personal and cultural points of view come into conflict. This is most likely to occur when the cultural point of view is used and the rights of the individual are ignored. Such a conflict has occurred in the case of homosexuality. The practice of homosexuality deviates from our cultural norm, but a question arises over whether we have the right to label individuals "abnormal" because of their sexual orientation. For many years, homosexuality was labeled abnormal, but in 1980, the issue was reconsidered by the panel of experts that decides what behaviors will be listed in the *Diagnostic and Statistical Manual of Mental Disorders*, and it was decided that homosexuality was not a disorder unless the individual was unhappy about his or her sexual orientation. The issue was considered again in 1987, and homosexuality was dropped completely as an abnormal disorder. In the case of homosexuality, then, the rights of the individual were given precedence over cultural norms.

In summary, both personal and cultural aspects of behavior are taken into consideration in determining what is abnormal, and it is therefore possible for abnormality to differ from individual to individual, from culture to culture, and from time to time. It is hazardous to attempt a specific definition, but it might be said that *abnormal behavior is behavior that is personally distressful or personally disabling, or is culturally so deviant that other individuals judge the behavior to be inappropriate or maladaptive.*

THE "MYTH OF MENTAL ILLNESS"

In discussions of abnormal behavior, it is usually implied that the behavior is a reflection of "mental illness," and the concept of mental illness implies that there is something "wrong" with the individual such that he or she needs to be "treated." However, some observers argue that *mental illness is a myth*; in other words, there is no such thing as mental illness and individuals do not need to be treated (Szasz, 1961, 1970). That is a radical departure from the usual point of view, and it deserves some comment before we go on.

The belief that mental illness is a myth is based on three notions. First, it is argued that abnormal behavior is simply *different* behavior and not necessarily a reflection of illness. That is, individuals may have personality traits that deviate from what society wants, but that does not mean that the traits constitute an illness in the sense that a cancerous growth is an illness.

Second, an individual may have an unusual belief, but that does not mean that the individual is *wrong*. For example, we may not agree with an individual who believes that he or she is God, but that does not mean that he or she is not God. Indeed, many leaders and inventors were once thought to be wrong and "crazy." Furthermore, even if the individual is wrong, that does not mean that he or she is sick. If you make a mistake in deriving a formula in calculus, does that mean that you are sick? Might a person with a "delusion" simply be mistaken rather than sick?

The third argument put forth by those who advocate the myth point of view is that abnormal behavior is due to something that is wrong with *society* rather than something that is wrong with the *individual*. For example, if an individual breaks down in the face of overwhelming stress, the problem lies in the environment rather than in the individual. Withdrawing or becoming depressed may be a rational response to an irrational environment rather than a sickness. In summary, being different, being wrong, or responding to abnormal environments should not be the basis for labeling an individual as sick.

Proponents of this view point out that the **myth of mental illness** can lead to unfortunate consequences. For example, if we label individuals as ill, we may implicitly encourage abnormal behavior because that is the way sick people behave. Furthermore, by labeling individuals as ill, we may relieve them of responsibility for their behavior because sick people are not responsible for their conditions. Should a person who commits murder be set free because, at the time of the crime, he or she was "insane"? Finally, if we attribute deviant behavior to illness, we may ignore and not work on the social factors such as poverty and stress that may cause abnormal behavior.

If the concept of mental illness is wrong, why is it such a popular explanation for behavior? Proponents of the myth point of view argue that the notion of mental illness is a convenient way for us to deal with people who disturb us. For example, if we label as sick people whose behavior we find disturbing, we can see them as different from us, which makes us feel better about ourselves. Also, if we label them as sick, we can justify locking them up so that they will no longer disturb us. As support for this, the proponents cite cases of individuals who were locked up for many years simply because they were annoying other people. The individuals may not have been "out of their minds," but

by locking them up, the disturbing individuals were out of *our* sight and out of *our* minds. Finally, by using mental illness as an explanation for deviant behavior, we avoid responsibility for the social problems that underlie the deviant behavior. That is, if we say that you are sick and should be changed, we do not have to undertake the difficult task of changing society.

Is mental illness a myth or a reality? The myth notion is a radical departure from the traditional point of view, but it does have merit. There are some serious forms of abnormal behavior that result from environmental factors rather than disease. For example, the *brief psychotic disorder* involves hallucinations, delusions, and a disruption of thought processes, but in many cases the disorder is thought to be a *reaction* to an overwhelming stress, and the symptoms will clear up when the stress is reduced regardless of whether or not the individual gets treatment. It is also the case that the definition of mental illness may have been stretched a bit. For example, if a child is having difficulty with arithmetic, he or she could be diagnosed as suffering from the *mathematics disorder* (see Chapter 16). Similarly, if you are unduly concerned about your physical appearance, you could be diagnosed as suffering from the *dysmorphic disorder* (see Chapter 7). Are those really psychiatric illnesses?

There is also no doubt that sometimes the system is abused or fails, so individuals are incarcerated in hospitals unjustifiably or by mistake. However, there are also individuals who experience serious symptoms in the absence of environmental stress and whose symptoms can be relieved only with some form of therapy. Furthermore, as the case studies in this book will illustrate, some individuals suffer terribly from their bizarre symptoms, symptoms that cannot be written off simply as differences in personality or rational responses to an irrational society. The serious and debilitating symptoms from which these people suffer are not due to suggestion and are not under voluntary control. Clearly, some individuals are ill.

The notion that mental illness is a myth is less popular today than it was 20 years ago. That change may reflect an increase in our understanding of abnormal behavior, or it may reflect an increasingly conservative society. Although it is now generally agreed that mental illness exists, it is important that we not ignore the voice of dissent on this issue. In considering abnormal behavior, we constantly must be careful that we do not simply dismiss disagreeable behavior as due to illness, and we must not allow the system to be misused by accident or by intent. Mental illness is not a myth, but the possibility raises important issues that we must keep in mind.

THE TRAINING AND PRACTICE OF PSYCHIATRISTS AND PSYCHOLOGISTS

Now that we have reviewed the history and definition of abnormal behavior, it might be helpful to describe the training and professional activities of the individuals who are most involved in the mental health profession, psychiatrists and clinical psychologists.

Psychiatrists

Psychiatrists are individuals who after completing college go on to 4 years of *medical school*, where they obtain a general medical education, and then take a 1-year medical internship. On completion of the internship, they receive an MD degree (Doctor of Medicine) and are qualified to practice general medicine. They then enter a *residency in psychiatry*, which is a training program in psychiatry that usually takes about 3 years. The program is based in a hospital and is focused on the clinical practice of psychiatry (e.g., treatment of mentally ill individuals). At the end of that training, the individuals become board-certified psychiatrists and are qualified to practice psychiatry.

Clinical Psychologists

Traditionally, **clinical psychologists** are individuals who after graduating from college go on to 4 to 6 years of *graduate school*, where they study abnormal behavior (e.g., assessment, therapy) and research techniques (e.g., design of experiments, statistics). During their time in graduate school, the students write a master's thesis and a doctoral dissertation, both of which involve original research. After completing their graduate studies, these individuals go on to a 1-year clinical psychology internship in which they refine their clinical skills. On completion of the internship, these individuals receive a PhD degree. PhD stands for Doctor of Philosophy, which reflects the scholarly and scientific heritage of clinical psychology rather than the more narrow training for practice. After earning the PhD degree, in most states, individuals who wish to practice as psychologists must take an examination to become licensed or certified.

Note that the training of psychiatrists is focused almost exclusively on clinical practice, whereas the training of clinical psychologists involves a blend of clinical practice and research. The training of psychologists is designed to produce individuals who are *practitioners* who can work with disturbed individuals but who are also *scientists* who can conduct research that will advance our understanding of abnormal behavior.

This approach to training is referred to as the **scientist-practitioner model** of training.

However, over the past 20 years, a second model of training for clinical psychologists has been developed that is based on the model used for training psychiatrists. It was argued that because many clinical psychologists spend their entire careers in clinical practice and do not do any research, the time they spent learning research methodology and conducting research in graduate school was not productive and could have been better spent developing their clinical skills. Therefore, a program of studies was developed that was focused almost exclusively on the development of clinical skills. This program and the usual 1-year clinical psychology internship lead to the PsyD degree (Doctor of Psychology). Like the MD degree program, the PsyD degree program prepares individuals for clinical practice. Today, clinical psychologists may have either a PhD or a PsyD degree, and there is some controversy over which type of training is more appropriate. However, rather than arguing about which approach to training is best, when evaluating the qualifications of a psychologist it is more important to ask if the quality of his or her training is sufficiently high and if the training is relevant for what he or she is doing.

The most notable difference in the professional activities of psychiatrists and clinical psychologists is the fact that psychiatrists can prescribe medication (e.g., drug therapy) and perform other medical procedures (e.g., administer electroconvulsive therapy), whereas clinical psychologists cannot. That difference is a reflection of the differences in their training: Psychiatrists have gone to medical school, and psychologists have not. However, the difference between what psychiatrists and psychologists can do is becoming blurred because there is a movement afoot to grant clinical psychologists prescription privileges for psychiatric drugs. The argument is that the need for individuals who can prescribe drugs far outstrips the number of psychiatrists who are available, and that with some additional training clinical psychologists could fill that need. Advocates for prescription privileges for psychologists also argue that there are already numerous nonphysician professionals who have limited prescription privileges (dentists), so there are precedents for extending the privileges to psychologists. Furthermore, for years psychologists in some hospitals have been prescribing drugs informally under the supervision of psychiatrists. To evaluate the ability of psychologists to prescribe psychiatric drugs, the National Institutes of Mental Health is conducting an experiment in which a number of psychologists are receiving additional training in physiology and pharmacology, prescribing drugs, and having their prescriptions monitored by a panel of psychiatrists. If the psychologists are found to be effective in prescribing medication, laws might be passed to extend prescription privileges to them. However, even if the results of that experiment indicate that properly trained psychologists can effectively prescribe psychiatric drugs, the granting of prescription privileges is probably a long way off because such a move is strongly opposed by the American Medical Association, and there are even psychologists who argue that the traditional distinction between psychiatrists and psychologists should be maintained. The fact that the prescription privilege for psychologists is being seriously considered reflects a basic and important change, and it is a development to watch carefully. As a footnote to this discussion, it should be mentioned that originally the practice of psychotherapy was limited to psychiatrists.

Finally, one cautionary note should be sounded: Current laws regulate only who may use the labels *psychiatrist* and *psychologist*, which means that *any persons* can "hang out a shingle" and offer themselves as *psychotherapists*, *counselors*, or any other title that implies expertise in the area of mental health. Therefore, in selecting someone for help, it is essential that you carefully check the individual's qualifications.

With this material as background, we can go on in Chapter 2 to consider the various theories that are used for understanding abnormal behavior.

■ SUMMARY

We began this chapter with a consideration of how our understanding and treatment of abnormal behavior have evolved over six phases:

1. Initially, it was believed that individuals who behaved abnormally were possessed by demons.
2. During the Golden Age of Greece and Rome, the emphasis shifted to natural or physiological explanations such as humors in the body.
3. The Middle Ages saw the emphasis shift back to demons as causes of abnormal behavior.
4. Beginning in the 17th and 18th centuries, it was again recognized that disturbed individuals were sick rather than possessed, and attempts were made to treat them in more humane ways. Some of the individuals who made important contributions in that regard were Philippe Pinel, William Tuke, Benjamin Rush, and Dorothea Dix.
5. In the 19th century, attention began to be focused on psychological explanations for abnormal behavior. Franz Mesmer and Jean-Martin Charcot began with physiological explanations, but their experiences eventually led to psychological interpretations of their findings. Sigmund Freud followed them, and based on his work with patients, he developed the psychodynamic explanation, which emphasizes unconscious conflicts as the cause of abnormal behavior. The laboratory research of Ivan Pavlov, Edward Thorndike, and B. F. Skinner led to a psychological explanation of abnormal behavior based on the principles of learning. This view was widely promulgated by John B. Watson under the label of behaviorism. The most recent psychological explanation for abnormal behavior is that thoughts influence behavior. This cognitive explanation developed in part as a reaction against behaviorism and was enhanced by recent discoveries about how humans process information.
6. In the 1950s, the discovery of drugs that were effective for treating abnormal behavior renewed interest in physiological explanations for behavior.

Next, we reviewed the definitions of abnormal behavior. When defining abnormal behavior from the point of view of the individual, attention is focused on the individual's distress and disability. When defining abnormal behavior from the point of view of the culture, deviance from cultural norms is the crucial factor. We suggested that abnormal behavior could be defined as behavior that is personally distressful or personally disabling, or culturally so deviant that other individuals judge the behavior to be inappropriate or maladaptive.

After defining abnormal behavior, we considered the arguments related to the notion that mental illness is a myth. That idea is not widely held today, but it raises serious questions that we must keep in mind when considering abnormal behavior and its treatment.

Finally, we reviewed the differences in training and practice of psychiatrists and clinical psychologists. The major difference is that psychiatrists are trained in medicine and clinical psychologists are not, which means that psychiatrists can prescribe drugs but psychologists cannot. However, that distinction may be breaking down because there is now a movement to provide psychologists with additional training in physiology and pharmacology and to extend prescription privileges to them. It was also noted that clinical psychologists may earn either of two degrees (PhD or PsyD), the difference being the amount of training they receive in research.

KEY TERMS, CONCEPTS, AND NAMES

In reviewing and testing yourself on what you have learned from this chapter, you should be able to identify and discuss each of the following:

Anna O.
behaviorism
Breuer, Josef
catharsis
Charcot, Jean-Martin
classical conditioning
clinical psychologist
cognitive perspective (on abnormal behavior)
demonology
deviance from cultural norms (as definition of abnormal behavior)
disability (as definition of abnormal behavior)

distress (as definition of abnormal behavior)
Dix, Dorothea
free association
Freud, Sigmund
Hippocrates
humors (bodily fluids)
hysterical disorders
learning perspective (on abnormal behavior)
Mesmer, Franz Anton
mesmerism
myth of mental illness
operant conditioning

Pavlov, Ivan
physiological perspective (on abnormal behavior)
Pinel, Philippe
psychiatrist
psychodynamic perspective (on abnormal behavior)
psychopharmacology
Rush, Benjamin
scientist-practitioner model
Skinner, B. F.
somatoform disorders
Thorndike, Edward L.
Tuke, William

Chapter 2
Theoretical Perspectives and Stress

• O U T L I N E •

I n this chapter, we will first consider the major theoretical perspectives that are used for understanding abnormal behavior. We will then examine the general concept of stress because it plays a role in all of the perspectives. These introductory discussions will provide you with a background for understanding the subsequent discussions of specific disorders.

• Theoretical Perspectives

Most problems can be viewed and solved from more than one perspective. A mountain can be viewed from the north, south, east, and west, and it might be possible to climb the mountain from each direction. The summit is always the same, but the trails to it can be very different. Similarly, there are currently a number of theoretical perspectives for viewing and understanding abnormal behavior: *psychodynamic, learning, cognitive, physiological,* and *humanistic-existential.* In this book, we will approach the causes and treatment of abnormal behavior from each of these perspectives. Just as some mountain trails lead to dead ends and do not get us to the summit, so some perspectives may not lead us to an understanding of abnormal behavior. However, if we are to understand the terrain of abnormal behavior, it is important that we explore each type of abnormal behavior from each perspective.

In this chapter, we will briefly review the basic concepts of each perspective. Keep three things in mind while reading this chapter. First, the material is offered only as a foundation on which we will build a more thorough understanding later when we consider specific disorders. Second, the ideas offered here are presented from the point of view of an advocate of each perspective. After each perspective is presented, a few comments will be made concerning its general strengths and weaknesses, but specific criticisms will be discussed when we attempt to use each perspective to explain specific disorders. Third, in this chapter, we will focus on the concepts of each perspective rather than on the individuals who developed them or the historical or intellectual context in which they were developed. (For background information, see Chapter 1.)

THE PSYCHODYNAMIC PERSPECTIVE

According to the **psychodynamic perspective**, *abnormal behavior stems from intrapsychic conflict.* Conflict results in **stress**, which, if not reduced, causes a distortion or breaking of the personality, just as extreme physical stress can cause a steel girder to twist out of shape and break.

Psychoanalytic (Freudian) Theory

The **psychoanalytic (Freudian) theory** suggests that abnormal behavior results from the following sequence: **conflict-anxiety-defense-symptoms**. That is, conflict leads to anxiety; we then use defense mechanisms to reduce the anxiety, and the defense mechanisms distort our behavior and lead to symptoms. Freud suggested that the most important conflicts are between our biological needs and the restraints imposed on our satisfying those needs (Fenichel, 1945; Freud, 1933/1964). In other words, there is conflict between what we want to do and what our conscience tells us it is all right to do. The foundations for these conflicts are established during early childhood. To understand how these conflicts develop, we must understand Freud's view of personality. Freud described the human personality in two ways. In his **structural approach**, he described the components of the mature personality, and in his **developmental approach**, he described how the personality developed between birth and adulthood.

Structural Approach.   Freud divided the personality into three components, the **id**, the **ego**, and the **superego**. The id is the source of all of our innate biological needs (instincts), and the id's goal is to satisfy those needs as rapidly and as completely as possible. Because the id seeks to satisfy biological needs and provide pleasure, the id is governed by what Freud called the **pleasure principle**. Unfortunately, the id is very ineffective in actually satisfying our needs. Indeed, rather than taking constructive action to satisfy our needs, the id relies on what Freud called the **primary process**, which involves simply thinking or fantasizing about the satisfaction of a need. When we use daydreams instead of actions to satisfy our needs (thinking about food rather than going to the kitchen to prepare a meal), we are using the primary process to satisfy our needs.

In sharp contrast to the id, our superego embodies the restraints imposed on us by societal rules, taboos, and moral values. We learn to accept the dos and don'ts of society during the socialization process we go through as children. To the extent that socialization is effective, these restraints become part of us (the superego) rather than external forces.

The ego is the third component of our personality structure, and it has the difficult task of mediating between the id and the superego. To accomplish that task, the ego tries to find realistic and effective ways of satisfying the needs of the id while not violating the restraints established by the superego. For example, when we get hungry, our ego tries to find ways of getting food rather than leaving the id simply to fantasize about food. However, the method used to get the food must not conflict with the rules set out by the superego. If the ego is functioning properly, we work for our food; we do not steal it. Whereas our id operates on the primary process, the ego operates on the **secondary process**, which was Freud's term for thinking and problem solving.

In a variety of ways, the interactions of our id, ego, and superego can result in abnormal behavior. For example, if our ego does not effectively satisfy the needs of the id, the id will revert to the use of primary processes (fantasies) to satisfy its needs. The use of primary processes can result in childlike behavior, hallucinations, and delusions. If our superego somehow gains most of the power, we may become constricted and rigid in our behavior.

Developmental Approach.
Freud suggested that personality develops in five **psychosexual stages: oral, anal, phallic, latency**, and **genital**. These stages are important for three reasons. First, the early stages of psychosexual development provide the foundation for the later stages, and if problems occur in the early stages, subsequent personality development is likely to be distorted. As the old saying goes, "As the twig is bent, so grows the tree." Second, if you are unable to complete the tasks associated with any one stage, you may become **fixated** at that stage and develop no further. For example, someone with "childlike" ways of thinking or behaving may be fixated at an early stage of psychosexual development. Third, these stages of development are crucial because if you are faced with

overwhelming conflict and stress, you may *regress* to an earlier stage of psychosexual development in which you felt more secure. An individual who eats excessively when under stress may have regressed to the oral stage of development, a more secure time of life. With these points in mind, we can go on to describe briefly the most important aspects of the five stages of psychosexual development.

1. *Oral Stage.* The oral stage ordinarily lasts from birth until about age 2. In this stage, most activity and pleasure are associated with the eating of food and stimulation of the lips. During the oral stage, the boundaries between the self and the rest of the world are not yet clear. Infants can get whatever they wish by using the primary process (fantasies). Because infants are not aware of the fact that their needs are actually satisfied by others, they assume that they themselves are responsible for the satisfaction. For most people, the oral stage is a pleasant time, and therefore it is an attractive stage to which to regress in the face of stress. Adult behaviors such as thumb sucking, drinking from bottles (breast substitutes?), smoking, and excessive eating are often used to obtain gratification in the face of stress, and these behaviors may be minor forms of regression to the oral stage.

2. *Anal Stage.* The most important task during the anal stage is toilet training. If a parent reacts with anxiety and disgust to the "mess" a child makes, the child may learn to be overly concerned about cleanliness and orderliness. The large number of television advertisements for toilet bowl cleaners may be evidence of the traumatic and lasting effects of the American approach to toilet training. Toilet training may also affect other aspects of personality. For example, if the parent is strict and demanding in the process of toilet training (remember the toilet seat you were strapped

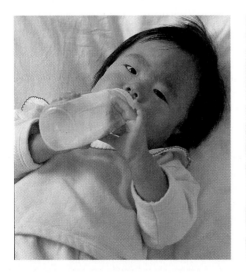

The oral stage usually lasts from birth to about age 2. Adult behaviors such as smoking, drinking from a bottle, or excessive eating may represent a minor regression to the oral stage.

Freud suggested that a child's experience with toilet training may play a significant role in personality development.

into until you "performed"?), the child may retain the feces in retaliation. That behavior may generalize and result in the child's becoming a stingy or obstinate adult. By contrast, if the parent encourages the child and then praises the child when a bowel movement is produced, the child may grow up to be generous, productive, and creative.

3. *Phallic Stage.* Of paramount importance during the phallic stage is the resolution of the attraction of young boys to their mothers (the **Oedipus** [ED-i-pus] **attraction**) and the attraction of young girls to their fathers (the **Electra** [ē-LEK-tra] **attraction**). Freud suggested that young boys have incestuous wishes toward their mothers but limit their advances when they realize that their fathers are jealous and can do them physical harm (castrate them) if they pursue a relationship with their mothers. Therefore, rather than pursuing their mothers directly, young boys *identify* with their fathers and thereby obtain their mothers vicariously. This is similar to the vicarious pleasure we get when we identify with a movie or television hero who has someone or something we want. What is important about a son's identification with his father is that as part of the identification process, the son takes on the characteristics of his father (just as we try to act or dress like our heroes), and in so doing the son takes on his father's attitudes about right and wrong. By adopting the attitudes of his father, a boy internalizes societal mores and develops his superego.

The Electra attraction for the young girl is somewhat different. When she notices that she does not have external genitals like the male, she feels castrated. She blames her mother for this condition, with-

draws from her mother, and turns her affection toward her father, who has the organ she is missing. The daughter then realizes that her mother might harm her if she pursues her father, so she gives up competing for her father and identifies with her mother in order to win her father vicariously. As was the case with the little boy, this process of identification results in the formation of a superego.

4. *Latency Stage.* As the name implies, Freud believes that little happens during the latency stage, which corresponds roughly to the period of early adolescence. During this period, the child firms up the attitudes and behaviors that were developed in the preceding stages and awaits the onset of maturity.

5. *Genital Stage.* In the genital stage, the individual achieves personal and sexual maturity. This stage lasts until death, and in it the individual plays out the roles and struggles with the conflicts that were established in the preceding stages. Dealing with those conflicts can be difficult and anxicty provoking, so sometimes we use defense mechanisms to avoid conflicts and anxiety. These defense mechanisms are discussed next.

Anxiety and Defense Mechanisms. When we are unsuccessful in resolving a conflict through normal constructive actions, we become anxious. In Freudian theory, **anxiety** is considered both a *symptom* of conflict and a *signal* to use a **defense mechanism**. Defense mechanisms are psychological maneuvers by which we distort reality in ways that will help us avoid conflicts and reduce anxiety. There are numerous defense mechanisms, the most important of which are discussed here (for a review, see Holmes, 1984a).

1. *Repression.* One way of dealing with anxiety-provoking conflicts or thoughts is to force them from conscious awareness. This process is called **repression**. Repressed material is not lost like forgotten material; it is *stored* in the unconscious, where it can continue to influence our behavior without our awareness. Freud suggests that we are unlikely to remember anything about our toilet training because we have repressed those "dirty" experiences, but they continue to influence our behavior through unconscious processes. Repression may be the most important defense in Freudian theory because it is through repression that material gets into the unconscious, and the unconscious plays a crucial role in explaining behavior.

2. *Suppression.* Another way to deal with anxiety-provoking material is to intentionally avoid thinking about it. This is called **suppression**. The most common method of suppressing material is to think about something else. For example, you may watch television to distract yourself from thinking about an examination you just failed.

3. *Denial.* **Denial** involves the reinterpretation of the anxiety-provoking material to make it less threatening. The failed examination may be reinterpreted as a valuable experience for learning about what you need to study.

4. *Projection.* **Projection** is the process whereby you attribute your own personality characteristics to other people. For example, if you are frightened, you might see other people as frightened. Projection can serve as a defense mechanism because if you have an unacceptable personality trait and you project it onto another person, your belief that the other person has the trait might reduce your concern about having the trait. For example, if you are hostile and see a respected friend as being hostile, you may be able to conclude that being hostile is not such a bad thing after all.

5. *Displacement.* There are two kinds of **displacement**. **Object displacement** occurs when you express a feeling toward one individual that should be expressed toward someone else. A man may be angry with his boss but express his anger against his wife. He does this because it is less anxiety provoking to be aggressive toward his wife than toward his boss. **Drive displacement** occurs when you have one feeling (drive) that cannot be expressed, so the energy from that feeling is transferred to another feeling that can be expressed. Freud suggests that sexual feelings may be displaced and expressed as aggression.

6. *Regression.* When faced with conflict, stress, and particularly frustration, you may use **regression** to return to an earlier stage of life in which you were more secure and successful. Not only do we run home in the face of stress, but we may also go back to using previously successful strategies for solving problems.

7. *Identification.* When using **identification**, you take on the personal characteristics of another individual and to some extent become the other individual. This may help you satisfy your needs vicariously. Dressing like someone you admire or envy is a form of identification. Alternatively, when you identify with someone of whom you are afraid, you might feel as though you have taken on some of that person's power, thereby reducing your fear. Some long-term prisoners in the Nazi concentration camps walked, dressed, and acted like their feared Gestapo captors.

8. *Rationalization.* **Rationalization** involves giving a *good* reason for some behavior that is not the *real* reason. In doing so, you can disguise actual but unacceptable motivations.

9. *Compensation.* If you feel threatened in some area, you may seek **compensation** by working extra hard to overcome the real or imagined weakness. For example, some athletes may be compensating for their beliefs that they are weak.

10. *Intellectualization.* To avoid threatening emotions, you might focus on the objective, nonemotional details of an otherwise emotional situation. For example, a terminally ill individual may focus his or her attention on the technical aspects of a disease rather than the fact that he or she is facing death. That is called **intellectualization**.

11. *Reaction Formation.* **Reaction formation** is said to occur when you desire something or want to do something, but because of a conflict you transform the desire or the behavior into the opposite. For example, someone who is unconsciously aroused by pornography may defend against that by labeling pornography as disgusting and leading a fight against it.

The defense mechanisms just discussed are only some of the defenses that have been identified. It is important to recognize that although defense mechanisms help people avoid conflicts and reduce anxiety, they usually do so at a cost. If you use a defense mechanism to avoid a conflict and reduce anxiety, you are unlikely to work on realistic ways of eliminating the conflict. For example, if you use denial to reduce the importance and anxiety associated with a future exam, you may not study for the exam and hence fail it. Also, defense mechanisms generally involve distortions of reality, and distortions of reality reduce our ability to function effectively. In these ways, defense mechanisms can lead to inappropriate and abnormal behavior.

Levels of Consciousness.   Finally, some attention must be given to Freud's ideas concerning consciousness. At any point in time, you are aware of many things, such as feelings, friends, problems, and commitments. All of these things are in our **conscious mind**. There are also many things, such as friends from long ago or unimportant events, that we no longer keep in consciousness but that we can recall if we try. This recallable material is in our **preconscious**. However, most important for Freudian theory is the **unconscious**, where we store important but anxiety-provoking memories. Because these memories are psychologically painful, we have repressed them; they are locked away in the unconscious where we cannot remember them. The fact that we cannot remember them does not mean that these memories do not influence our behavior, for indeed they do. Freud suggested that many "unexplainable" behaviors are motivated by unconscious memories, conflicts, and drives. A major goal of psychoanalytic therapy is to bring unconscious material to consciousness so that the patient can respond to it knowingly and appropriately. This is generally done by removing the conflict and anxiety associated with these memories in order to allow a "return of the repressed."

Freud was very influential, but colleagues and followers disagreed with him on some points and introduced modifications of his theories. In the next section, we will consider the major points of difference.

Neo-Freudian Theories

The term **neo-Freudian** is used to identify a group of theorists who accept many of Freud's ideas but who depart from them in two important respects. First, neo-Freudians place *less emphasis on the id* and *more emphasis on the ego*. Freud believed that the satisfaction of the needs of the id plays the crucial role in personality, but the neo-Freudians believe that the controlling function of the ego is the most important aspect of personality. For them, the ego is not simply the mediator or compromiser between the powerful id and superego; it is the controller of power and activities (Hartmann, 1958, 1964). In other words, rather than seeing humans as pushed in one way or another by the needs of the id and the superego, the neo-Freudians see individuals as able to use their egos to consciously pick and choose between satisfying the id and satisfying the superego. The neo-Freudians also focus on the defense mechanisms used by the ego to facilitate personality functioning. Unlike Freud, who saw the defenses as generally pathological, the neo-Freudians believe that the defenses can play constructive, positive roles. One of the leaders in the **ego psychology** movement was Freud's daughter, **Anna Freud** (1895–1982; Freud, 1946).

The second major departure the neo-Freudians introduced has to do with the *source of anxiety.* For Freud, the clash between the id and the superego was the most important source of anxiety, but the neo-Freudians focus on other problems. One of these followers suggested that **feelings of inferiority** create anxiety and that individuals spend much of their lives compensating for those early feelings (Adler, 1927; Ansbacher & Ansbacher, 1956). For example, as a child, the famous Greek Demosthenes had been embarrassed by his stuttering, so he spent years practicing clear speech and went on to become a great orator. Jesse Owens, the Olympic gold medal winner, was crippled as a child and trained hard to overcome his early handicap. The use of compensation to overcome feelings of inferiority and achieve personal control is an example of a constructive use of a defense mechanism.

In summary, the neo-Freudians accept many of Freud's ideas, such as the belief that abnormal behavior has its roots in early childhood, but they differ from Freud on the relative importance of the ego and on the source of conflict. In general, the neo-

Some neo-Freudians believe that individuals who experience anxiety because of feelings of inferiority may strive to overcome these feelings with great achievements. Pictured here is Jim Abbott, who became a pitcher for the New York Yankees despite the fact that he has only one arm.

Freudians offer a broader, more social, and more positive view of personality than Freud.

Comment

There is considerable controversy about the psychodynamic explanations for abnormal behavior. The controversy revolves primarily around the question of whether or not there is sufficient evidence to support these explanations. Most of the support comes from the day-to-day experiences of psychologists and psychiatrists with their patients, and relatively little support comes from scientific research. Psychotherapists who apply Freud's explanations consistently report that the explanations are useful for understanding patients and that patients tell them about experiences that are consistent with the explanations. Critics suggest that the therapists are biased in what they see and record, and that patients report experiences that are consistent with the explanations because the therapists unintentionally lead them to make such statements.

The relative lack of controlled scientific research supporting the psychodynamic explanations stems in large part from the fact that it is extremely difficult, if not impossible, to do research on the explanations because they do not lend themselves to scientific testing. In many instances, the explanations cannot be tested because they can be used to predict (or explain after the fact) any outcome. For example, if a patient talks about Oedipal problems, that is evidence for the existence of Oedipal problems, but if a patient does not talk about Oedipal problems, that is also evidence for the existence of Oedipal problems because it is assumed that the problems were so threatening that the patient repressed them. Similarly, if it is predicted that a patient will be angry but instead is loving, that is explained by suggesting that the patient changed the feelings through the process of drive displacement or reaction formation. Critics argue that because the psychodynamic explanation can be used to predict *anything*, it really predicts *nothing*, and therefore it cannot be tested.

The fact that the psychodynamic explanation may be untestable does not necessarily mean that it is wrong. However, critics argue that if it is untestable and conflicts with another explanation that is testable and does have scientific support, then we should discard the psychodynamic explanation in favor of the explanation with scientific support.

The controversy between the advocates and the critics of the psychodynamic explanation has raged for years, and today we appear to be no closer to its resolution than we were decades ago. Rather than continuing to argue, the advocates and critics appear to have agreed to disagree, go their own ways, and continue developing their explanations. This is probably the most constructive and effective way of resolving the controversy because science advances by *abandoning* one theory for a *better* one, not by *disproving* the less good one. Given time to work rather than argue, a better theory may emerge.

THE LEARNING PERSPECTIVE

The basic tenet of the **learning perspective** is that *abnormal behavior is learned*. At the outset, two general points should be noted with regard to the learning perspective. First, traditional learning theorists do not make any assumptions about internal processes, such as thinking, that cannot be observed directly. Instead, they take the position that our explanations for behaviors should be based only on *observable* variables, and therefore they limit their attention to external factors such as stimuli and reinforcements (rewards). In short, the organism is viewed as simply responding to external stimulation. This emphasis on observable variables reflects the learning theorists' reaction against what they thought was an unjustified and unscientific reliance on unobservable internal factors by psychoanalytic theorists. The second point is that the learning perspective encompasses two distinctly different types of learning, *classical conditioning* and *operant conditioning*. These two types of conditioning have different roles in the development of abnormal behavior, so we will consider the processes and implications of each.

Classical Conditioning

Classical conditioning was discovered accidentally by the Russian physiologist **Ivan Pavlov**, who was studying saliva from dogs. To collect saliva for analysis, Pavlov's assistant would ring a bell to get the dog's attention; Pavlov would immediately blow a small amount of powdered meat into the dog's mouth, which caused the dog to salivate; and the saliva would

Ivan Pavlov and his assistants accidentally discovered classical conditioning while collecting saliva from dogs.

be collected with a tube fitted in the dog's mouth. As the story goes, one day Pavlov's assistant accidentally rang the bell before Pavlov was ready to blow the powdered meat into the dog's mouth. Much to Pavlov's surprise, when the bell was rung the dog salivated. Because the bell and the powdered meat had been paired frequently in the past, the bell alone was enough to elicit a response that previously could be elicited only by the meat powder.

In general, classical conditioning occurs when a stimulus that elicits a particular response is consistently *paired* with a neutral stimulus that does not elicit the response, as when food that elicits salivation is paired with the sound of a bell. After repeated pairings of the two stimuli, the previously neutral stimulus itself elicits the response; for example, the sound of the bell results in salivation. The stimulus that originally elicited the response (the food) is called the **unconditioned stimulus**, and the neutral stimulus that takes on the ability to elicit the response (the sound of the bell) is called the **conditioned stimulus**.

Perhaps the most famous example of classical conditioning in humans is the case of **"Little Albert,"** a boy who was conditioned by **John B. Watson** in an attempt to demonstrate that fears are learned rather than innate (Watson & Rayner, 1920). Watson first presented a white rat to Little Albert, who showed no fear of the rat and enjoyed playing with it. When Watson next presented Little Albert with the rat, he also rang a very loud gong that frightened the child. This same procedure of pairing the rat with the frightening gong was repeated a number of times until later, when only the rat was presented, Albert immediately became afraid. In this way, Watson used classical conditioning to make Albert fear a stimulus that previously had not elicited fear. (The procedures Watson used have been criticized for a variety of technical reasons; Harris, 1979. However, the principles suggested by this original demonstration were subsequently confirmed by a substantial amount of well-controlled research; Hilgard & Marquis, 1961.)

An instance of classical conditioning happened to me one day when I was cleaning a pan I had used to cook a meal. After scrubbing the pan with Comet cleanser, I felt queasy, became nauseated, and had to lie down. While lying there, I began thinking what appeared to be random thoughts about the course in experimental psychology I had taken as an undergraduate student several years earlier. I thought about the instructor, about some of the class projects, about my experiences in the laboratory—and suddenly I realized why I was sick! It had been my job to clean the monkey cages. This was a particularly unpleasant task because I had to spend hours scraping and scrubbing the feces-encrusted cages with Comet cleanser. While doing this, I was often on the verge of getting sick to my stomach. The repeated pairing of the neutral stimulus of Comet cleanser with the sickening task of cleaning the monkey cages had produced a classically conditioned nausea response to the stimulus of Comet cleanser. Two years later, when I was confronted with the stimulus, the nausea response was elicited and I became sick again.

Classical conditioning is relevant for our understanding of abnormal behavior because it provides the basis for many inappropriate emotional and physiological responses, such as Little Albert's fear and my nausea. Little Albert's fear of the rat would certainly be considered abnormal. Indeed, if he had been brought to a clinic, Little Albert would probably have been diagnosed as suffering from a phobia (an irrational fear). My getting sick to my stomach every time I used Comet cleanser would be considered strange, if not abnormal.

Generalization of Responses.   Through a process called **generalization**, the classically conditioned response may eventually be elicited not only by the conditioned stimulus but also by new stimuli that are *similar* to the conditioned stimulus. For example, Little Albert became fearful when he was shown a rabbit, a dog, and even a ball of cotton and a fur coat. The degree to which generalization occurs is a function of the similarity between the conditioned stimulus and some new stimulus. The greater the similarity between a conditioned stimulus (a white rat) and a new stimulus (a ball of cotton), the more likely it is that the new stimulus will elicit the conditioned response. Stimuli that are very dissimilar will not elicit the conditioned response. For example, Little Albert did not show an increase in fear to a set of wooden blocks.

Generalization greatly increases the number of stimuli that can elicit a particular conditioned response; it can also make it difficult to understand someone's responses. Little Albert's fear of women in fur coats stemmed from his original problem with rats, and if we did not know about his history of conditioning and the process of generalization, his response to women in fur coats would be very perplexing. The generalization of a conditioned response is illustrated in Figure 2.1.

Extinction and Endurance of Responses. Classically conditioned responses can be eliminated through a process known as **extinction**, whereby the conditioned stimulus is presented repeatedly *without being paired with the unconditioned stimulus*. For example, when Pavlov's dogs repeatedly heard the bell and did not get any powdered meat, they stopped salivating in response to the bell.

FIGURE 2.1   GENERALIZATION: STIMULI THAT ARE SIMILAR TO THE CONDITIONED STIMULUS WILL ELICIT THE CONDITIONED RESPONSE, BUT THE RESPONSE WILL BE SOMEWHAT WEAKER THAN THE RESPONSE TO THE CONDITIONED STIMULUS.

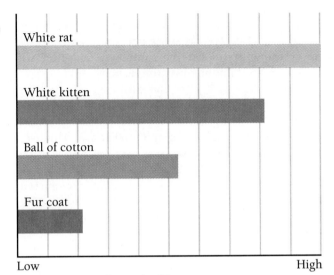

White rat

White kitten

Ball of cotton

Fur coat

Low   High

Strength of fear response

Extinction may take a long time, and in many cases the conditioned response may reappear after it was supposedly extinguished (Rackman, 1989). For example, after extinction trials, Pavlov's dogs may have stopped salivating to the sound of the bell, but if a period of time went by and then the bell was presented again, the dogs would again salivate. That is known as **spontaneous recovery** of the extinguished response. The recovered response will be weaker than the original response, and over time it can be extinguished again. The cycle of extinction, spontaneous recovery, and extinction may have to be repeated a number of times until the response is completely extinguished. Spontaneous recovery can be discouraging and can slow down the therapy when extinction procedures are used to eliminate classically conditioned responses such as fears.

It is important to remember that once a conditioned response is established, it may last indefinitely unless extinction procedures are introduced. My conditioned response to the scrubbing with Comet lasted for over 2 years before it popped up unexpectedly when I was again exposed to the cleanser. The endurance of conditioned responses was clearly illustrated in an experiment with sheep. In the experiment, a red light was paired with a shock to the hooves so that the sheep became classically conditioned to lift their front hooves when they saw a red light (J. Bescherat,

personal communication, 1963). When the conditioning was completed, the sheep were turned out to pasture. Nine years later, the sheep were brought back into the laboratory and presented with the red light, and they immediately lifted their front hooves.

The endurance of classically conditioned responses is important for our understanding of abnormal behavior because inappropriate or abnormal emotional responses may be traced to much earlier instances of classical conditioning. As was the case with my response to Comet, the conditioned response may remain long after the situation in which it occurred is forgotten.

Involuntary Nature of Responses. One final and important point is that *classically conditioning responses are not under voluntary control.* Once the conditioning has been completed, the response occurs whenever the stimulus is presented, and the subject is unable to keep from giving the response. Pavlov's dogs had no choice but to salivate when the bell rang, Little Albert had no choice but to be fearful when he saw the rat, and I could not inhibit my feelings of nausea when I was confronted with the cleanser odor. The involuntary nature of classically conditioned responses makes the problem worse because it leads to feelings of being out of control. For example, if later in life Albert had a date with a woman who wore a fur coat, when he saw her he would have no choice but to become very fearful, regardless of how irrational he realized it was and how hard he tried not to be afraid. Obviously, classical conditioning can lead to serious, prolonged, confusing, and uncontrollable abnormal behavior in a number of ways. We will return to the process of classical conditioning throughout this book as an explanation for abnormal behavior.

Operant Conditioning

Operant conditioning occurs when a response is *followed by a reward* (reinforcement), so that in the future you are more likely to use the response to get the reward (Skinner, 1953). Unlike classical conditioning, operant conditioning is due not to the simple pairing of two stimuli but to the pairing of a response with a reward. (Traditional learning theorists do not use the term *reward* because its effects imply an unobservable internal process, drive reduction. Instead, they prefer the term *reinforcement*. For the sake of convenience, in this discussion we will take a more liberal position and use *reward.*)

A famous example of operant conditioning is B. F. Skinner's experiments with white rats. In the simplest of these experiments, rats were placed in a cage with a lever that when pushed caused food to drop into a cup. The rats were hungry and quickly learned the response of pushing the lever to get the reward of food. In other experiments, the rats were placed in a cage with a lever that turned off a shock that came from a grid on the floor. The rats in these experiments learned to push the lever to turn off the shock and reduce their pain. In a variation on these experiments, a red light came on a few seconds before the shock, and the rats quickly learned that if they pushed the lever when the red light came on, they could avoid the shock. In all of these experiments, the rats learned the lever-pushing response because it resulted in a reward or because it resulted in the elimination or avoidance of something negative.

Although we like to think of ourselves as somewhat more sophisticated than rats pushing levers, much of our daily behavior can be understood in terms of attempts to gain rewards or avoid punishments. For example, you may be reading this book to obtain the reward of learning something new, to obtain the reward of getting a good grade, or to avoid the punishment associated with getting a bad grade. In each of these cases, your behavior is determined by the reward contingencies associated with reading the book.

Operant conditioning is relevant for our understanding of abnormal behavior because we often perform inappropriate behaviors to obtain rewards or avoid punishments. A child may have temper tantrums to gain attention, you may withdraw into your own fantasy world because it is more pleasant than the real world, or an individual who is claustrophobic may avoid small rooms to avoid the anxiety engendered by being in a confined space.

Individual Differences in Rewards and Punishments.

There are large individual differences in terms of what is rewarding and what is punishing; to paraphrase an old saying, "One person's reward is another person's punishment." In general, however, rewards are things that we will work to get, and punishments are things that we will work to reduce or avoid. Because individuals vary so greatly in what they find rewarding and punishing, it is crucial for us to analyze behavior in terms of what the individual involved considers rewarding or punishing and not in terms of what *we* think is rewarding or punishing. For example, some individuals find the aches, pains, sweat, and exhaustion associated with strenuous exercise rewarding, while others find it punishing. If those who find it punishing do not take the others' perspective, they may find it difficult to understand why others exercise.

Extinction of Responses.

When an operant response *no longer results in a reward*, it no longer has value for you, and you will stop using it. This process is referred to as *extinction*. Extinction of appropriate responses can contribute to the development of abnormal behavior. For example, if you are consistently ignored (not rewarded) when you make appropriate interpersonal responses, you may turn away from others who approach you and withdraw into a world of fantasy that is rewarding. Extinction can also be used to eliminate abnormal behavior. For example, by ignoring the child who is having temper tantrums, we are refusing to reward the tantrums, and they will eventually be abandoned (extinguished).

Schedules of Rewards.

When you are learning a response, it is important that you receive a reward every time you make a correct response. However, once you have learned the response, the response will be more resistant to extinction if you are given rewards only *intermittently*. The effect of an **intermittent schedule of reward** on operantly conditioned responses is clearly apparent in slot machine gambling. If a slot machine pays off 100% of the time, when it stops paying off, the gambler will realize that something has changed and will stop using the machine. But if the machine pays off only intermittently, the gambler keeps playing in the hope that the next response will result in a reward.

Understanding the effects of intermittent schedules of reward helps us understand why individuals continue to use certain behaviors even when those behaviors are rarely rewarded. It also points to the importance of being consistent about withholding rewards when our goal is to extinguish some particular behavior. For example, if a parent occasionally gives in to a child's temper tantrums, the parent will actually be strengthening the response with an intermittent schedule of rewards rather than helping to extinguish it.

The intermittent schedule of reward used in slot machines keeps people responding even when they are rewarded only rarely.

Voluntary Nature of Responses. Unlike classically conditioned responses, operantly conditioned responses are under *voluntary* control. Skinner's rats could have decided whether or not to press the lever to get the food, you could elect not to read this book in preparation for the examination, the child could voluntarily stop having a temper tantrum, and the gambler could decide to stop putting quarters in the slot machine. Operant responses are voluntary, but at some point the motivation to perform certain operant responses may reach such a high level that they effectively cease to be voluntary. For example, the starving rat may have little choice but to press the lever to get food, and the student with a classically conditioned fear of small spaces may have little option but to flee in terror when the instructor closes the door of a small classroom.

Vicarious Conditioning

In each of our examples of classical and operant conditioning, the learner was directly involved in the conditioning process. Little Albert was exposed to the rat and the gong, and the child learned through trial and error that having temper tantrums resulted in rewarding attention. However, such direct involvement is not necessary for conditioning to occur. Another child who only watched when the rat and gong were presented to Little Albert could vicariously develop the conditioned fear of the rat, and a child who watched another child get attention (reward) for a tantrum could learn to use tantrums to get attention. The old saying "Monkey see, monkey do" definitely applies to conditioning. This type of indirect conditioning is usually referred to as **vicarious** (vī-KER-ē-us) **conditioning**, but it is also sometimes called **observational learning** or **modeling** (Bandura, 1969; Bandura & Walters, 1963).

Because classical and operant conditioning can take place vicariously, we can develop conditioned responses without directly experiencing the conditioning process. We need not actually have a frightening experience with an eleva-tor to develop an elevator phobia. Just hearing frightening things about elevators will do the trick. Because we do not need to experience the exposure directly, vicarious conditioning greatly expands the possibilities of developing inappropriate conditioned responses.

It might be noted that the occurrence of vicarious conditioning indicates that some internal processes (thinking) must be involved. This is contrary to the position of the traditional learning theorists, who believed that internal processes are not necessary to explain behavior.

Combination of Classical and Operant Conditioning

It is noteworthy that classical and operant conditioning can combine to result in abnormal behavior. Classical conditioning can lead to fears, and then operant conditioning can lead to behaviors that are used to reduce the fears. Classical conditioning was responsible for Little Albert's fear, and through operant conditioning he could have learned to avoid women in fur coats.

Operant conditioning can also contribute to abnormal behavior by slowing the extinction of classically conditioned abnormal responses. If through operant conditioning you learn to avoid a conditioned stimulus, you will never learn that the stimulus is no longer associated with the unconditioned stimulus, and therefore extinction will not occur. For example, if Little Albert avoided rats, he would never learn that they were no longer paired with the frightening gong. Similarly, individuals who avoid high places because they were once frightened in a high place do not learn that high places are not necessarily frightening, and consequently their fear does not extinguish. The use of operant behaviors to avoid feared stimuli helps us understand why some classically conditioned fears are so persistent.

Comment

The principles underlying the learning perspective have been consistently supported by rigorous experimental research. However, you should not conclude that there is no controversy over the learning perspective for explaining abnormal behavior. Critics do not question the validity of the principles of conditioning, but they do question whether those principles can account for the highly complex behaviors of disturbed individuals. In other words, the critics argue that the principles are true and may be able to account for some fears, but the principles may not be sufficient to explain more complex behaviors such as hallucinations and delusions. Whether the learning perspective is indeed too simple to account for the diverse and complex abnormal behavior observed in humans will be considered in greater detail later when we examine the various types of abnormal behavior.

THE COGNITIVE PERSPECTIVE

The basic notion of the **cognitive perspective** is that *abnormal behavior results from problems with cognitive content* (thoughts) *or disruptions in the thought processes.* That is, problems with cognitions lead to problems with behaviors. This explanation makes intuitive sense, but to understand it thoroughly, we must also understand how the problems with cognitions develop.

The erroneous thoughts that lead to abnormal behavior result from problems in the way we perceive, store, and retrieve information. If we make errors in what we see, store, and remember, that will greatly distort our views of the world, and that could result in abnormal behavior. Furthermore, some serious disorders such as schizophrenia may be due to disruptions in cognitive processes. For example, the inability to maintain attention could interfere with functioning. All of this can be understood in terms of what we know about human **information processing**. Let us consider how these processes influence behavior.

Associative Networks and Recall

The most widely accepted explanation of how information is stored and recalled is called the **associative network theory** (Bower, 1981; Collins & Loftus, 1975; Estes, 1991; Ingram, 1984). In general, this theory suggests that individual memories are linked together in networks, and that activation of one memory will lead to the activation of other memories in the same network. To understand this theory, we must consider four basic aspects.

1. *Clusters.* Each memory consists of a cluster of components, and the activation of any one of the components will lead to the activation of the other components and result in the memory. Components of a memory could include images, feelings, and physiological responses. For example, your memory of a particular person involves the person's name, an image of the person, your emotional response to the person, a recollection of the scent of his aftershave or her perfume, and many other things. Activation of any one component will result in the memory. For example, a person's name will bring the person to mind, but so will his or her scent. (Women used to give men a handkerchief on which they had put some of their perfume, the notion being that the scent would keep active the memory of the woman while the couple was apart.)

2. *Activation.* Individual memories that are related are connected in networks, and the activation of any one memory in a network will lead to the activation of the other memories in that network. For example, memories associated with school (e.g., other students, classes, parties, exams) may all be in one "school" network, and seeing or thinking about another student will cause you to recall other things about school. Similarly, memories that all involve unpleasant events (e.g., failures, rejections, death of a loved one) may be linked in a network, and thinking about one unpleasant event will lead you to recall other unpleasant events. The sequential stimulation of memories in a network is the *thought process*, or the "stream of consciousness." With regard to abnormal behavior, the stimulation of a network involving unpleasant events could lead to depression because the individual would recall many negative (depressing) experiences.

3. *Priming.* Memories and connections that were used more recently or frequently are activated more easily and become stronger. In a number of experiments, some individuals read happy passages while others read sad passages, and when they were then asked to recall experiences from earlier in their lives, the individuals who had read the happy passages were more likely to recall happy experiences than individuals who had read sad passages. That occurred because different networks had been activated by the reading of the different passages. This process is called **priming**; activating a network primes you to recall things in that network. Of course, priming becomes circular in that a primed network is more likely to be used, and using it primes it for use again. The process of priming explains why once we get off on a topic, such as reasons for being depressed, we tend to perseverate on that topic. The fact that we have networks that are primed or are stronger than others leads to what are called **cognitive sets**. We have *sets* of memories that are *set* to be recalled, and the fact that they are more likely to be used influences our views of the world.

4. *Automatic Activation.* The activation of networks is an automatic process. Thought processes do not stop, and if one network is not stimulated, the most recently primed or strongest network is likely to be activated. This accounts for why you tend to drift back to a particular topic unless you are focusing your attention elsewhere. Using an analogy to a computer, a friend of mine who tends to be depressed described his depressing thoughts as his "default option." That is, whenever he is not thinking about something else, he begins thinking depressing thoughts. To avoid that default option, he tries to distract himself with television, radio, or reading.

A diagram of a simplified set of networks is presented in Figure 2.2. The overall network is made up of three networks, one involving negative memories (in blue), one involving memories of people (in red), and one involving positive memories (in black). There are strong associations or connections within networks (solid lines) and weaker associations or connections between networks (broken lines). An individual with this set of networks who experienced or thought about a failure would go on to recall other failures, rejections, missed opportunities, and possibly the death of a loved one. In contrast, an individual who experienced or thought about a success experience would go

FIGURE 2.2   A HYPOTHETICAL SET OF THREE
CONNECTED MEMORY NETWORKS.

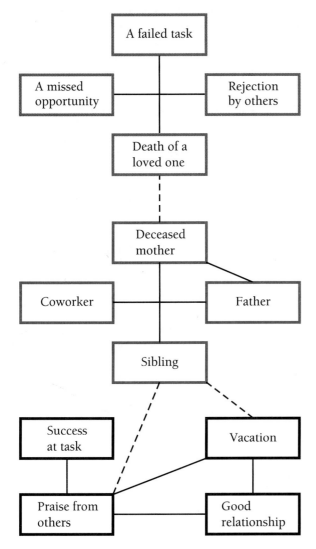

The overall network is made up of three networks, one involving negative memories (blue), one involving memories of people (red), and one involving positive memories (black). Strong associations are indicated with solid lines, and weaker associations are indicated with broken lines.

on to recall praise from others, good relationships, and possibly a pleasant vacation. Because connections within networks are strong and used frequently, activation is likely to continue reverberating around a network, and therefore the individual would continue having those memories. If activation of the negative network is prolonged, the individual might become depressed.

Stages of Memory Processing

The associative network theory helps us understand how memories are organized and retrieved, but how does information get into the memory network? The answer to that question is crucial because only information that gets into the system can be recalled and influence us later. The most widely accepted explanation for how information enters the memory system is the **three-stage theory of memory processing**. Those stages involve (a) the entry of information in the *sensory memory*, (b) the passage of some of that information into the *short-term memory*, and (c) the processing of some of that information for storage in the *long-term memory*. The stages of memory processing are summarized in Figure 2.3.

Sensory Memory.   Everything you perceive goes first to the **sensory memory**. It is like a photograph or a tape recording of what is happening. However, the sensory memory can hold the information for only a second or two at most, and after that it is as though the photograph fades or the tape wears out. Consequently, from all that you perceive, you must quickly select the pieces that are most important and send them on to your short-term memory for processing. The remaining unselected information is lost. That loss may be crucial if the information is essential to effective functioning. What is important and noticed is defined by what network is activated at that time. If your "food network" is activated because you are hungry, you are likely to notice restaurants and ignore gas stations; if your "negative events network" is activated because

FIGURE 2.3   STAGES OF MEMORY.

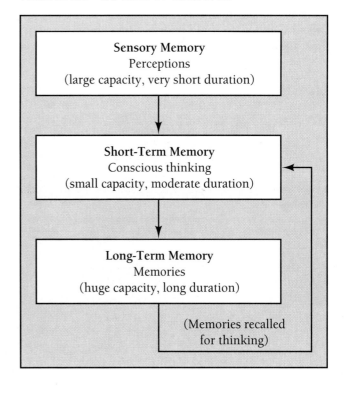

you are depressed, you are likely to notice interpersonal slights and ignore compliments.

Short-Term Memory.

The **short-term memory** is where you do your *thinking* and where you *process information for storage in the long-term memory*. Unlike the sensory memory, which has a large capacity and short duration, the short-term memory can only hold about seven pieces of information at any one time, but the information can be held for 15 to 20 seconds without processing.

Whether and how you process information in the short-term memory for storage in the long-term memory is very important because if you do not process the information or you process it ineffectively, you will not be able to retrieve it later, and then for all practical purposes the information will be *lost*. Effective processing involves *actively thinking about how a piece of information is related to other pieces of information in your networks*. In other words, to process information so that you can recall it later, you must put the information into a memory network and link the information to as many other memories in the network as possible. When the information is needed later, you will be able to retrieve it by activating any of the memories to which it is connected. If the information is not linked to other memories, later recall will be difficult or impossible, and therefore you may not have access to needed information.

Long-Term Memory.

The **long-term memory** is where all of the processed information is *stored*. It contains all of your memories and networks. It has a huge capacity, and it may hold information indefinitely. The information that is stored in your long-term memory is not in your consciousness, but if it is needed it can be activated and brought to the short-term memory and consciousness. There is a constant interplay between the short- and long-term memories in that information is continually being brought up from the long-term memory, used for thinking, and then sent back to the long-term memory.

Selective Attention and Selective Recall

You may have realized by now that there is considerable selectivity in what we perceive, process, and recall. In other words, cognitive processes result in **selective attention** and **selective recall**. Specifically, (a) only a fraction of the information that enters the sensory memory is moved to the short-term memory, (b) only a limited amount of information that gets to the short-term memory is processed for storage in the long-term memory, (c) only the information in the long-term memory that has been processed effectively will be recalled, and (d) information in a primed or strong network is very likely to be recalled. This selectivity is not a random process; it is guided by what we think is important and unimportant. We focus on what appears to be important and ignore what appears to be unimportant, and the process can become circular.

Selective attention and recall are important because they can lead to exaggerated or erroneous ideas, and those can lead to inappropriate or abnormal behavior. For example, if you believe that you are sickly, you will notice and remember every minor pain and interpret them all as signs of illness. Similarly, if you believe that you are socially inadequate, you will attend to and recall every minor social slight and blunder. In some cases, selective attention can result in **self-fulfill-**

Selective attention and recall could cause erroneous ideas that might, in turn, lead to inappropriate or abnormal behavior. If you incorrectly thought others were rejecting you, you might in fact bring on that rejection by avoiding people or by behaving in a hostile way.

ing prophecies. For example, if you incorrectly thought that others were rejecting you, you might begin avoiding them or behave in a hostile manner toward them, and those behaviors would bring on the rejection you had incorrectly thought was there earlier.

Overall, cognitive theorists suggest that (a) our early experiences lead to the initial development of cognitive networks or sets, (b) the networks or sets then lead to selective attention and recall, (c) the selective attention and recall influence what we think, and (d) our thoughts determine our behaviors, normal and abnormal.

Distortions of Memories and False Memories

So far we have focused on problems that arise because of not processing (not recalling) information or focusing too much attention on information. However, existing memories can also be *distorted*, and these distortions can influence behavior. In one experiment on **distortions of memories**, college students were shown a film of a traffic accident, and later one group was asked how fast the cars were going when they "contacted" each other, whereas another group was asked how fast the cars were going when they "smashed" (Loftus & Palmer, 1974). The students with whom the word *smashed* was used estimated the speed at almost 10 miles per hour faster than the students with whom the word *contacted* was used. Clearly, memories can be distorted rather easily, and distorted memories might distort our behavior.

There is also evidence that entirely new **false memories** can be "implanted" and that once implanted, they are resistant to rejection. Specifically, if the source of a suggestion concerning an experience is highly credible and you do not have strong contrary evidence concerning the experience, you might accept the suggested experience as real. In one study, individuals casually mentioned to their siblings the "memory" of a relatively traumatic but totally false event (getting lost in a large shopping mall when very young), and within a matter of days the siblings had accepted the event as real and had embellished it by remembering feelings of fear and other details (Loftus, 1992). When later the individuals were informed of the deception, some of them were actually resistant to giving up the memory. For example, one said, "Really? I thought I remembered being lost . . . and looking around for you guys. I do remember that. And then crying, and Mom coming up and saying, 'Where were you? Don't you . . . Don't you ever do that again' " (p. 39).

A more dramatic example of an implanted memory occurred in the case of a man who after prolonged questioning pleaded guilty to raping his daughters 18 years earlier (Ofshe, 1992). To test the possibility that the confession was due to a suggestion during the interrogation process, an experiment was conducted in which the man was told that two of his other children had now accused him of forcing them to have sex while he watched. When he denied it, he was told to think about it, and then was returned to his jail cell. The next day the man reported remembering which of his children had been involved and added vivid recollections of what had happened. It is noteworthy that the man had nothing to gain by his admission and indeed could face an additional prison sentence. Faced with the overwhelming (but false) evidence of the children's testimony and in the absence of proof to the contrary, he accepted the accusations as true and then embellished on the suggestion. There is now a considerable body of evidence concerning false confessions that are honestly believed by the confessors (Bedau & Radelet, 1987; Kassin & Wrightsman, 1993).

The facts that existing memories can be distorted and new false memories can be introduced have implications for understanding some of the experiences that are "recalled" during psychotherapy and are then used to explain disorders. Therapists often ask leading questions and suggest possibilities that are consistent with their theoretical orientation (e.g., "Do you remember having strong feelings about your mother?" "People with problems like yours often have been sexually abused as children"), and that may lead to the creation of false memories. Some years ago, when Rankian therapy was popular, patients in that therapy reported recalling the trauma of coming through the birth canal.

The overall conclusion to be drawn here is that our behaviors are guided in large part by what we remember, but our memories are subject to deletions, exaggerations, distortions, and falsehoods. Insofar as our memories are erroneous, our behaviors may be inappropriate and our explanations for our behaviors may be inaccurate.

Disrupted Cognitive Processes

It should now be clear that there are numerous ways in which cognitive content can be distorted and thereby lead to abnormal behavior. However, some forms of abnormal behavior appear to be due to **disrupted cognitive processes** rather than distortions in cognitive content. Consider the following example of a conversation between an interviewer and a patient suffering from schizophrenia:

Interviewer: Have you been nervous or tense lately?
Patient: No, I got a head of lettuce.
Interviewer: You got a head of lettuce? I don't understand.

Patient: Well, it's just a head of lettuce.

Interviewer: Tell me about lettuce. What do you mean?

Patient: Well, . . . lettuce is a transformation of a dead cougar that suffered a relapse on the lion's toe. And he swallowed the lion and something happened. The . . . see, the . . . Gloria and Tommy, they're two heads and they're not whales. But they escaped with herds of vomit, and things like that. (Neale & Oltmanns, 1980, p. 102)

Clearly, in this case the problem is not simply distorted ideas. The disruptions in cognitive processes this patient shows are generally associated with more serious disorders such as schizophrenia. It is one thing to be depressed because you consistently exaggerate the negative aspects of your life, but it is quite another thing to think and communicate like the patient in this example.

Cognitive theorists believe that disruptions in cognitive processes are due to problems with *attention* and *associations*. The basic notion is that (a) individuals have lapses in attention, (b) during those lapses they are distracted by other thoughts, and (c) they then "spin off" on the new thoughts rather than following up their original thoughts. That is, instead of a patient's speech being complete gibberish as it initially appears, the speech actually consists of strings of thought fragments, no one of which is completely developed because the patient was distracted and went on to the next thought.

The thought fragments are not strung together randomly. Instead, through various associations, one thought fragment elicits the next thought fragment in the string, and so on. Researchers have identified a variety of types of associations that result in the intrusion of thoughts (Chapman et al., 1964, 1984; Maher, 1983). One of these types of disruptive associations occurs when words are used that have more than one meaning, such as *pen* ("writing instrument," "fenced enclosure," "jail"). When talking to another individual, a person with schizophrenia may correctly use one meaning of a word with several meanings. However, as soon as the word has been used, it may give rise to another thought based on another meaning of the word, and then the person may spin off onto the new thought without making the transition clear to the listener. For example, the individual may say, "Henry lent me his pen, which was full of criminals." In this example, the word *pen* was first used to refer to a writing instrument, but the use of the word gave rise to thoughts about a penitentiary. The speaker then spun off and finished the sentence with a phrase related to a penitentiary. Because a wide variety of associations can result in the intrusion of new thoughts, it can be very difficult to follow those associations and understand what is being communicated. We will consider other types of disruptive associations later.

It is noteworthy that from the cognitive perspective, the cognitive problems seen in disturbed persons are considered to be only extreme cases of the same types of problems experienced by normal persons. At one time or another, we have all behaved inappropriately because we have exaggerated the importance of some event, let our attention lapse, or made an associative error that led to a misunderstanding. If it is true that the cognitive behaviors of disturbed individuals are only extreme instances of the types of cognitive behaviors seen in normal individuals, much of our extensive knowledge about the cognitive behavior of normal individuals can be brought to bear on our understanding of abnormal behavior.

Comment

The cognitive perspective has considerable intuitive appeal, and it is supported by solid evidence from modern cognitive psychology. As a consequence, the cognitive perspective is currently a very popular means of explaining abnormal behavior. However, the cognitive perspective leaves unanswered the question of why or how thought processes become disrupted. That is, disruptions in attention may be an excellent explanation for the thought disorders seen in schizophrenia, but we are still left to explain why the problems with attention develop. To explain the problems with attention, we must consider another explanation. Specifically, it has been suggested that the problems with attention seen in schizophrenia may be due to excessively high levels of neurological arousal. If this is the case, the cognitive and physiological explanations may work together to explain this type of abnormal behavior. In the next section, we will consider the physiological perspective on abnormal behavior.

Finally, it should be noted that cognitive theorists assume that problems with thought process are the *cause* of abnormal behavior, whereas most other theorists take the position that problems with thought processes are *symptoms* of abnormal behavior.

THE PHYSIOLOGICAL PERSPECTIVE

The basic assumption of the **physiological perspective** is that abnormal behavior is due to problems with *physiological factors such as synaptic transmission, brain structure, and hormone levels*. The development of new technologies is enabling investigators to make impressive advances in our understanding of the links between physiology and behavior, and in the following sections we will review the basic elements of this rapidly emerging area.

FIGURE 2.4   A NEURON (NERVE CELL).

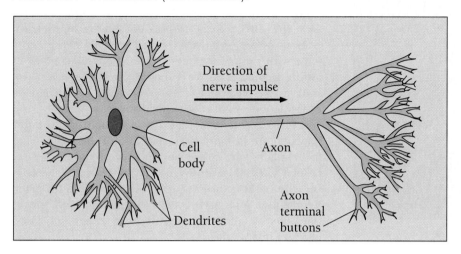

Neuroanatomy and Neuronal Functioning

The Neuron and the Nerve Impulse.   The brain consists of between 10 and 12 billion cells called **neurons**. Strings or chains of neurons make up a **nerve fiber**. Depending on the function they serve, neurons differ greatly in size and shape, but they all share a number of structural and functional characteristics. As Figure 2.4 shows, each neuron consists of **dendrites**, a **cell body**, an **axon**, and **terminal buttons**. The important thing about neurons is that they can carry an *electrical* impulse called the **nerve impulse**. This impulse starts when one neuron stimulates the dendrite or cell body of another neuron. The nerve impulse then travels from the dendrite or cell body down the axon to the terminal buttons, where the impulse is transmitted to the next neuron.

Synaptic Transmission.   Having traveled down the axon and out to the terminal buttons, the impulse comes to the **synapse** (SIN-aps), which is a small gap separating one neuron from the next neuron in the chain. The first neuron is called the **presynaptic** (PRĒ-sin-AP-tik) **neuron**, and the second, the **postsynaptic** (POST-sin-AP-tik) **neuron**. The nerve impulse must then "jump" the synapse and stimulate the next neuron if the impulse is to continue down the chain. To make the jump, the impulse causes the terminal buttons on the presynaptic neuron to secrete a chemical substance called a **neurotransmitter**. The neurotransmitter then flows across the synapse and stimulates the next neuron. The neurotransmitter stimulates the postsynaptic neuron by entering **receptor sites** on the dendrites or cell bodies of the postsynaptic neuron. Figure 2.5 illustrates a neurotransmitter being

FIGURE 2.5   NEUROTRANSMITTERS ARE RELEASED BY THE PRESYNAPTIC NEURON, CROSS THE SYNAPSE, AND STIMULATE THE POSTSYNAPTIC NEURON.

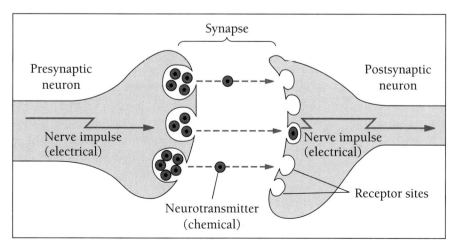

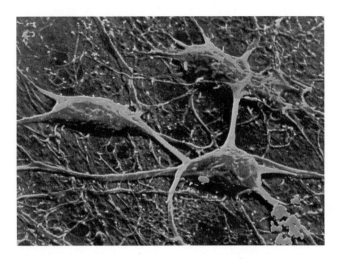

This photo of three neurons illustrates the complex pattern of connections between neurons.

released by a terminal button on the presynaptic neuron, flowing across the synapse, fitting into a receptor site on the postsynaptic neuron, and causing it to fire. The process by which the nerve impulse travels down the axon is *electrical,* whereas the process by which it crosses the synapse is *chemical.*

Neurons fire on what is known as the **all-or-none principle**. In other words, when neurons are stimulated, they either do or do not fire, and if they do fire, they do so with a given amount of energy, regardless of the strength of the stimulation that provoked the firing. Because neurons always fire with the same amount of energy, the intensity of neuronal activity is not a function of the strength with which they fire but of the *frequency* with which they fire or the *number* of neurons that fire. When there is not enough of the neurotransmitter in an area of the brain, the neurons in that area will not fire at all or too few of them will fire to get the job done. If there is too much of the neurotransmitter, there may be excessive neurological activity caused by neurons firing too many times or too many neurons firing. In either case, abnormal behavior may result.

Levels of synaptic transmission are important for understanding abnormal behavior. For example, insufficient levels of transmission in the area of the brain that controls mood can result in depression, whereas excessive levels of transmission in that area can result in mania. Furthermore, excessive levels of transmission in certain areas of the brain can result in a disruption of thought processes like that seen in schizophrenia.

Neurotransmitters.   The crucial factor in synaptic transmission is the presence of the neurotransmitter that carries the impulse across the synapse. There are many neurotransmitters, but at present only a few have been linked to abnormal behavior.

Neurotransmitters belong to a general class of agents known as *biogenic amines* or simply **amines** (AM-ēnz). Because neurotransmitters are amines, explanations for abnormal behavior that involve problems with neurotransmitters are often referred to as **amine hypotheses**. We will consider particular neurotransmitters or amines in greater detail later when we examine the causes of specific disorders.

It is noteworthy that any one neurotransmitter may operate in more than one area of the brain. That fact explains why we see combinations of otherwise unrelated sets of symptoms in some disorders. For example, the neurotransmitter that is responsible for some depressions also plays a role in appetite, and that is one of the reasons why depressed persons show changes in appetite.

The influence of a neurotransmitter in more than one area of the brain also accounts for some of the side effects that occur when drugs are used to treat psychological disorders. For example, schizophrenia is thought to be due to high levels of a neurotransmitter called *dopamine* that operates in the areas of the brain that are responsible for thought processes. To correct that problem, persons with schizophrenia are often given drugs that block the action of dopamine. However, dopamine also operates in the areas of the brain that are responsible for motor behavior. As a result, the drugs that are used to treat schizophrenia also influence motor behavior and can produce side effects such as a stiff-jointed walk or involuntary muscle contractions.

Factors Influencing Synaptic Transmission

Because synaptic transmission is so important to our understanding of abnormal behavior, we must give some attention to the various factors that influence it.

Neurotransmitter Levels.   The amount of a neurotransmitter present at the synapse is crucial to the transmission of the nerve impulse from one neuron to the next. If the level is too low, the next neuron will not receive enough stimulation to fire, and if it is too high, too much activity will be stimulated. Three processes influence the level of the neurotransmitter at the synapse:

1. *Production.* The presynaptic neuron may produce too much or too little of the neurotransmitter.
2. *Metabolism.* Substances called *enzymes* that are present in the area of the synapse may metabolize (destroy or change) too much or too little of the neurotransmitter. This process is called **metabolism**.
3. *Reuptake.* The presynaptic neuron may take up or

FIGURE 2.6   NEUROTRANSMISSION IS REDUCED BY LOW
PRODUCTION OF TRANSMITTER SUBSTANCES,
REUPTAKE, METABOLISM, AND BLOCKING OF RECEPTOR
SITES.

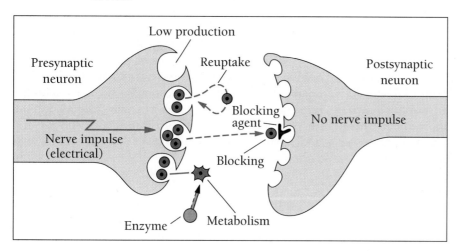

reabsorb the neurotransmitter before it can stimulate the next neuron. That process is called **reuptake** (RĔ-UP-tāk). Excessive reuptake reduces the level of the neurotransmitter below the needed level, and insufficient reuptake leaves too much of the neurotransmitter at the synapse.

A malfunction of any one of these processes may impair synaptic transmission and result in abnormal behavior. These processes are illustrated in Figure 2.6.

Blocking Agents. The neurotransmitter stimulates the postsynaptic neuron by fitting into receptor sites on the postsynaptic neuron much as a key fits into and opens a lock. Other chemicals, called **blocking agents**, are structurally similar to the neurotransmitter and can also fit into the receptor sites, but they do not cause the neuron to fire because they do not fit the receptor sites perfectly. When blocking agents are present, they block the neurotransmitter from getting into the receptor sites, thus preventing stimulation of the postsynaptic neuron. It is like putting the wrong key in a lock; that key does not open the lock and it prevents you from putting the right key in the lock. Some drugs are blocking agents and are used to reduce excessive synaptic transmission. For example, the drugs that are used to treat schizophrenia block dopamine from entering the receptor sites, thus reducing the excessive levels of synaptic transmission and decreasing the disruption of thought processes. Blocking of receptor sites is illustrated in Figure 2.6.

Inhibitory Neurons. Another factor affecting synaptic transmission is the activity of **inhibitory neurons**. An inhibitory neuron is a neuron that is located at the synapse between two other neurons and which inhibits transmission between those neurons. Inhibitory neurons work either by reducing the level of the neurotransmitter secreted by the presynaptic neuron or by making the postsynaptic neuron less sensitive to stimulation. In Figure 2.7, neuron A is the presynaptic neuron, neuron B is the postsynaptic neuron, and neuron C is the inhibitory neuron. If inhibitory neuron C is active, it reduces the amount of the transmitter substance released by neuron A or reduces the sensitivity of neuron B. In either case, the likelihood that neuron B will fire is reduced.

Inhibitory neurons play important roles in a number of disorders. For example, some forms of anxiety occur because inhibitory neurons in some areas of the

FIGURE 2.7   WHEN AN INHIBITORY NEURON
FIRES, IT CAN INHIBIT THE SYNAPTIC
TRANSMISSION BETWEEN OTHER
NEURONS.

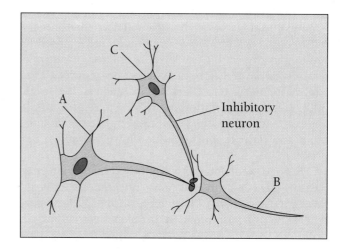

brain are not active enough; that leads to excessive synaptic transmission, which leads to what we experience as anxiety. The level of activity of inhibitory neurons is controlled by their levels of neurotransmitters, so treatment may involve using drugs that increase the levels of those neurotransmitters. Finally, it should be noted that in some cases neurotransmitters that work with inhibitory neurons in one area of the brain also work with action-oriented neurons in other areas of the brain. For example, a neurotransmitter known as *serotonin increases* transmission in the area of the brain involved with mood but *inhibits* transmission in the area of the brain responsible for thought processes. Clearly, the influence of neurotransmitters can be complex and sometimes seemingly paradoxical.

Neuron Sensitivity.

A fourth factor influencing synaptic transmission is the level of sensitivity of the postsynaptic neuron. More sensitive neurons are more likely to fire when stimulated than those that are less sensitive.

Number of Receptor Sites.

Finally, the level of synaptic transmission can be influenced by the number of receptor sites on the postsynaptic neuron. The likelihood of a neuron's being stimulated is increased if there are more receptor sites. As we will see later, it is believed that schizophrenia is due to excessively high levels of synaptic transmission, and persons with schizophrenia have more receptor sites. The number of receptor sites declines with age, and so does the incidence of schizophrenia.

Causes of Problems with Synaptic Transmission

We have discussed some of the problems with synaptic transmission that can cause abnormal behavior. We must now take our understanding one step further and determine what causes problems with synaptic transmission. There are at least three such causes. First, problems with synaptic transmission may result from external factors such as personal or environmental *stressors*. For example, when animals are exposed to prolonged stressors, their levels of the neurotransmitters serotonin and norepinephrine are reduced. This is of particular interest because in humans, low levels of these neurotransmitters are related to depression. It appears, then, that stress can lower the levels of serotonin and norepinephrine, which in turn leads to depression.

Second, problems with synaptic transmission may have a *genetic* basis in that some individuals have a genetic predisposition to have high or low levels of particular neurotransmitters. If problems with synaptic transmission have a genetic basis, we would expect mental disorders to run in families. Consistent with this explanation, investigators have found that the biological children of depressed parents are more likely to experience depression than children of nondepressed parents, even when the children are adopted and not raised by their biological parents.

Finally, problems with synaptic transmission may be due to an apparently *spontaneous breakdown* of the neurological system for reasons we do not yet understand. Spontaneous breakdowns may account for the development of problems in individuals who are not under stress and do not have a family history of such problems.

Brain Structure

There is also growing evidence that differences in **brain structure** are associated with some symptoms. For example, some individuals who suffer from schizophrenia have enlarged ventricles (cavities in the brain through which fluids flow), distorted structures in the temporal lobe, and a deterioration of the surface of the brain. Similarly, a tangling and breaking of neurons appears to underlie the decline in functioning seen in Alzheimer's disease. These problems with brain structure can result from infections and traumas during the prenatal and postnatal periods as well as from genetic factors. We will discuss these problems and their causes in greater detail later when we discuss specific disorders.

Hormones

Hormones are fluids that glands secrete directly into the bloodstream, and once in the bloodstream the hormones serve to *stimulate* activity. (Indeed, the word *hormone* is derived from a Greek verb meaning "to stir up," based on a noun meaning "impulse" or "assault.") Abnormal levels of hormones are linked to disorders involving aberrant sexual behavior and aggression.

Comment

There is now substantial and rapidly increasing evidence for the physiological perspective. Recognition of the growing importance of this perspective is reflected in the fact that the American Psychological Association requires that graduate students in clinical psychology take coursework specifically focused on the physiological explanations for abnormal behavior.

An important limitation of the physiological perspective is that it does not necessarily explain why individuals develop the specific cognitive symptoms they do. For example, a high level of neurological activity in one area of the brain seems to be related to anxiety, but that does not explain why one person develops a phobia for flying but another becomes fearful of snakes. It seems likely that the physiological perspective works in *combination* with other perspectives to explain abnormal behavior. That is, physiological factors may *predispose* individuals to general types of disorders, and then personal experiences give form to the disorders.

THE HUMANISTIC-EXISTENTIAL PERSPECTIVE

The last perspective we will consider is the **humanistic-existential perspective**. This is a relatively new approach to understanding abnormal behavior, and in many respects it was developed as a reaction against the other perspectives. Indeed, the humanistic-existential perspective is sometimes referred to as the "third force" to distinguish it from the psychodynamic and learning perspectives that were dominant when the humanistic-existential perspective was developed.

Advocates of this perspective object to the view of human beings as simply products of unconscious drives, conditioning, and physiology. The humanists and existentialists propose instead that humans are conscious beings who make voluntary choices about their actions and that consequently, each human develops as a unique individual. The proponents of this perspective also suggest that to understand a person's behavior, it is essential to see or experience the world from that person's point of view. That is the case because behavior is due to conscious choices, and a person's choices are influenced by a personal perception of the situation. Because of the emphasis on the role of perceptions in determining behavior, the humanistic-existential perspective is sometimes referred to as the **phenomenological approach**. (Phenomenology is a philosophy based on the notion that knowledge is gained through experience rather than through thought and intuition.)

The humanistic-existential perspective is similar to the cognitive perspective in that both emphasize the role of conscious processes, voluntary control, and the influence of knowledge in guiding behavior. However, the perspectives differ with regard to the role of *motivation* in behavior. Motivation is largely ignored in the cognitive perspective (humans are like information processing machines), whereas theorists in the humanistic-existential group assume that humans are motivated to achieve enhanced levels of personal awareness, growth, experience, and existence. Failure to achieve these goals could lead to anxiety or depression.

The humanistic-existential perspective is not really a single systematic approach for explaining behavior but is instead a loose confederation of the ideas of a number of theorists. These theorists generally share the ideas mentioned earlier, but there are also some differences among them. Probably the most important differences are associated with the distinction between the humanists and the existentialists.

The Humanistic Position

The most important feature of the humanistic position is the belief that individuals are motivated by *positive growth toward personal wholeness, perfection, uniqueness, and self-sufficiency*. In other words, rather than being driven by forces from below, outside, or within, as suggested by the other perspectives, humanists see us as drawn from above to a higher state of personal development. This is a more positive and optimistic view of human development than the views offered by other perspectives. The search for a higher state of development is what sets humans apart from other species; hence the term *humanism* is applied to this position.

Theorists who subscribe to the humanistic position do not deny the existence or importance of physiological drives. However, they suggest that humans develop strategies for satisfying those drives relatively early in life and then move on to other higher social and personal motivations. In that regard, **Abraham Maslow**, a leading exponent of the humanistic viewpoint, suggested that needs can be seen as a series of steps and that as each is overcome, the individual moves up and closer to personal fulfillment. He identified the following needs (steps) (Maslow, 1970):

     5.   Self-actualization
    4.   Self-esteem
   3.   Love and belongingness
  2.   Safety and security
1.   Physiological needs

From a humanistic position, the individual's needs and motives change over time. The fact that our needs change and we must struggle with current crises leads the humanistic theorists to focus on the present, the "here and now." This is in sharp contrast to psychoanalytic or learning theorists, who emphasize past conflicts or the individual's history of conditioning in trying to understand abnormal behavior.

The higher state of development toward which humans are thought to strive is usually referred to as a state of **self-actualization**. Just as it is difficult to arrive at a definition of beauty, so it is difficult to arrive at an exact definition of self-actualization, and as with beauty, writers use examples to illustrate the concept

"To be, or not to be, that is the question." Hamlet's soliloquy is a famous example of an existential crisis.

rather than words to describe it. Notable historical figures who have been said to be self-actualized include Abraham Lincoln, Thomas Jefferson, and Eleanor Roosevelt. In general, it might be said that self-actualized individuals rise above their own needs and can freely experience and give of themselves. Not all individuals achieve self-actualization, and many who do only experience it for short periods of time. Those brief moments of attainment are called **peak experiences**.

In discussing self-actualization and human potential, the humanists have gone a long way toward identifying what is involved in a healthy personality. This is different from the other perspectives, in which it is implied that health is simply the absence of pathology. For the humanists, health is much more.

According to the humanistic approach, stress results when there is a discrepancy between our **current self** or current level of functioning and our self-actualized or **ideal self**. The ideal self is the embodiment of all of the wonderful and lofty things that as children we are taught we *ought* to be. Unfortunately, we usually fail to reach those goals, our failure results in stress, and the stress leads to tension, depression, and anxiety. The problem can become circular in that when we

do not achieve our ideal selves, we experience stress, and then the presence of stress blocks any further growth toward a higher level of personality development. Psychotherapy based on the humanistic approach is focused on helping the individual to overcome obstacles and close the gap between the current self and the ideal self.

The Existential Position

Existentialism is a 20th-century philosophy of human existence that emphasizes two things. The first is our *awareness of our existence* ("being"), an awareness that leads to the recognition that we could cease to exist ("nonbeing"). Ceasing to exist can involve death, but lesser instances occur when our lives lose direction and meaning and when we feel personally isolated. When in desperation we ask, "What is life about?" and "Is it all worth it?" we are struggling with psychological existence and the possibility of nonbeing. The second point emphasized by the existentialists is that as humans, we are free to make choices, and therefore we have *responsibility* for our lives and our existence.

According to the existential point of view, anxiety stems from our awareness of the possibility that we could cease to exist and from the responsibility for making decisions that will have long-term consequences for our existence or being. Persons are said to face an "existential crisis" when they come to a turning point in their lives and must make a decision about the direction in which to go—and to determine whether there is true meaning for them in *any* direction. To make a decision and to go struggling to find meaning in life is "to be," and the existentialists talk about the "courage to be" (Tillich, 1952). Hamlet summarized the issue in his famous soliloquy, "To be, or not to be, that is the question." (He chose being and struggled on for three more acts.) The alternative to being is to give up the struggle and lapse into a state of nonbeing. Giving up and accepting nonbeing could lead to depression. Some might say that the individual with schizophrenia has abandoned being in this world.

Like the humanistic approach, the existential approach is less mechanistic than the other perspectives we have discussed, but the existential approach is less optimistic than the humanistic approach. Rather than seeing us as being drawn toward a higher and finer level of development, the existentialists see us as struggling with the grim realities of life and death, being and nonbeing.

Comment

For many persons, the humanistic-existential perspective has a good deal of intuitive appeal and offers a much more positive view of human beings than the other perspectives. However, critics suggest that the humanistic-existential approach has two major problems. The first is that many of its most important concepts, such as self-actualization, are ill defined and impossible to measure. Because the concepts cannot be measured, the theory is untestable, and an untestable theory is of limited value. However, for the most part, the humanists and existentialists are not bothered by the lack of scientific evidence because their personal experiences validate the theory. Furthermore, given their emphasis on the uniqueness of the individual and personal experiences, it is unlikely that humanists and existentialists would find meaning in any research that involves groups and generalizations.

The second problem is that the humanistic-existential theorists have not developed a comprehensive theory of abnormal behavior. They have focused most of their attention on the general anxiety or depression that relatively normal individuals experience, but they have not systematically addressed the more specific or more serious disorders. In one early attempt to explain schizophrenia, a leading proponent of the humanistic position suggested that schizophrenia was not a disorder but simply an alternative form of adjustment and that it was the "normal" individuals who suffered from a problem because they allowed themselves to be unduly restricted by cultural restraints (Laing, 1964). That position is not widely accepted today.

It is important to be aware of the humanistic-existential perspective because it provides an interesting contrast and counterpoint to the other perspectives. However, because the humanistic-existential perspective has not been applied to a broad range of abnormal behaviors and has not been subjected to many empirical tests, in this book it will receive less attention than the other perspectives.

CONFLICTS AND COMPLEMENTS AMONG PERSPECTIVES

You have seen that there are a number of explanations for most of the disorders we will discuss in this book. From this you might assume that the various explanations are in conflict and that only one explanation is correct. It is true that for some disorders the different explanations are in conflict, but in many instances more than one explanation is correct because the disorders have more than one cause. For example, in one individual anxiety might result from intrapsychic conflict, whereas in another individual it might stem from genetically determined high levels of neurological ac-

tivity. Consequently, for some disorders the problem is not to determine *which* explanation is correct but to determine *for whom* each explanation is correct.

It is also possible that different explanations may be appropriate for different disorders. For example, it has been suggested that stress may be the best explanation for many anxieties and that physiological problems may be the best explanation for more serious disorders like schizophrenia.

In some instances, the different explanations may actually work together to provide a more comprehensive explanation for the disorder. For example, the psychodynamic perspective suggests that disorders are due to intrapsychic conflict, whereas the physiological perspective suggests that disorders are due to physiological problems. Rather than being contradictory, it is possible that conflict does *precipitate* disorders, but it is most likely to do so in individuals who have a physiological *predisposition* to the disorder. This interaction of stress and physiological predisposition is often referred to as the **diathesis** (DĪ-ATH-uh-sis)-**stress hypothesis** of abnormal behavior. (*Diathesis* means "a constitutional predisposition to a particular state.")

In summary, the five perspectives discussed in this chapter should not be thought of as competing with one another. Instead, like members of a relay team, each perspective contributes something to our understanding of abnormal behavior, which is our "finish line." Even though a particular perspective may fall on its face in one lap, in so doing it shows us a problem to be avoided. Together the various perspectives will help us understand abnormal behavior.

• Stress

The various perspectives that are used to explain abnormal behavior differ greatly, but they all involve the concept of *stress.* Because stress often plays a role in the development of abnormal behavior, it is essential that we develop a basic understanding of stress before going on. At this point we will consider only the basics, and will develop the concept more fully later when it becomes relevant to specific disorders.

Stressors and Stress

The word *stress* is often used to refer both to the *cause* of stress (e.g., a test is a stress) and to a *response* (e.g., you experience stress when you take a test). To be more precise in our usage, it is helpful to use the word **stressor** when talking about a cause of stress and the word **stress** when talking about the response to a stressor. Having made that distinction, we must define what a stressor is. Actually, it is somewhat difficult to define stressors because what may be a stressor for one individual may not be a stressor for another individual. For example, standing in a cage with 10 hungry lions would undoubtedly be a stressor for many of us, but it is not a stressor for an experienced lion tamer. Rather than attempting to define stressors in terms of their physical characteristics, it is more effective to define them *operationally*. Defined operationally, stressors are *situations that require major adjustments that overtax us.* Faced with the lions, you and I would be overtaxed by having to fight or run, but the lion tamer would simply go through his or her usual routine. Both negative and positive situations can be stressful because they can both require major adjustments. Marriage may be a positive experience, but because it can require major adjustments, it can be a stressor.

Components of Stress

The stress response has two components, *psychological* and *physiological*. The psychological component of the stress response involves emotions such as anxiety and tension. Because of the unpleasant nature of these emotions, we are motivated to reduce them.

The physiological component of the stress response involves bodily changes such as increased heart rate, blood pressure, and muscle tension. Those changes prepare us for physical action—*fight* or *flight*. They are also unpleasant, so we tend to want to reduce them.

An interesting question that arises is, which comes first, the psychological response or the physiological response? On the one hand, it is widely assumed that stressors trigger *psychological responses (emotions) that in turn lead to physiological responses.* That is, if you become frightened, your heart rate increases. This is known as the **Cannon-Bard theory of emotion** because it was formulated by Walter Cannon and Philip Bard, two early investigators. On the other hand, it is also possible that *stressors trigger physiological responses that in turn lead to psychological responses.* That is, your heart rate increases, and therefore you begin experiencing fear. Evidence for this counterintuitive explanation comes from findings that drugs that stimulate physiological arousal (e.g., increased heart rate) can lead to the experience of emotions (e.g., fear) in the absence of any reason to be afraid (Schachter & Singer, 1962). This is known as the **James-Lang theory of emotion** because it was developed by William James and Carl Lang, two other early investigators.

Which explanation is correct? As with most things, it is probably not an either-or situation: Both explanations are probably correct. Stressors may stimulate both psychological and physiological responses, and once started, the psychological and physiological responses may stimulate each other, thereby heightening and maintaining the overall arousal.

Note that the physiological component of the stress response may not be appropriate for dealing with most modern-day stressors. For example, physiological responses that prepare you to fight or run may help you in dealing with a hungry lion, but they will be of no value in preparing for an examination in calculus or a demanding job, and those are the kinds of stressors with which most of us deal most often. Indeed, physiological arousal may be counterproductive in dealing with those stressors because it may distract you from your cognitive problem solving.

From Stressors to Abnormal Behavior

Now that we have some understanding of the concept of stress, we can examine the process that leads from stressors through stress to abnormal behavior. The steps in that process are summarized in Figure 2.8. Stress can play an important role in the development of abnormal behavior, but it should not be assumed from this diagram that stress necessarily precedes the development of all abnormal behaviors. For example, abnormal behavior could be learned or could be the result of physiological problems.

Awareness and Appraisal. After a potential stressor develops, the first step involves becoming *aware* of it and *appraising* the challenge it poses (Lazarus & Folkman, 1984). The individual who does not know that a tumor is developing in his or her body cannot take appropriate steps to have it treated, and an individual who does not know about an impending examination cannot begin studying. Sometimes there is some truth in the notion that if you are calm while all around you are losing their heads, you probably do not understand what is going on. Some individuals attempt to avoid or postpone stress by intentionally not looking for potential problems (e.g., they do not go to the physician for a physical or do not check syllabi for dates of exams). In contrast, other individuals are constantly seeking out problems and thereby increasing the likelihood of stress (Mathews et al., 1990). Clearly, awareness and appraisal are essential first steps leading to stress and abnormal behavior.

Coping. Once you are aware of the potential stressor, you can begin **coping**—solving the problem or adjusting to it. The individual who discovers a tumor can

FIGURE 2.8 STEPS IN THE PROCESS THAT CAN LEAD FROM STRESSORS TO ABNORMAL BEHAVIOR.

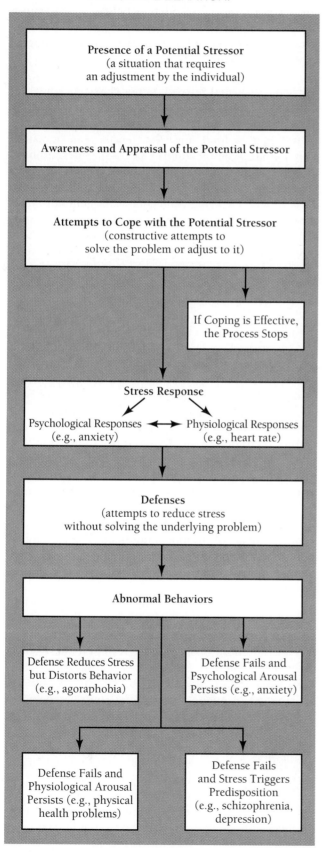

go in for treatment, and the student facing an exam can reduce social activities and spend more time studying. In cases in which coping is effective for dealing with the stressor, the process stops.

Stress and Defense. If you are not able to cope with the situation and it overtaxes you, the stress response will be triggered, thereby resulting in the unpleasant effects of psychological and physiological arousal. Facing such a state of stress, individuals may begin using defense mechanisms to reduce the stress. Defense differs from coping in that coping involves *constructive problem solving*, whereas defense involves reducing stress *without solving the problem*. One defensive strategy involves reappraising the stressor so that it is no longer viewed with alarm. This is generally called denial or **situation redefinition** (Bennett & Holmes, 1975; Holmes & Houston, 1974; Houston & Holmes, 1974). A tumor could be called a "bump," and the exam could be thought of as a "quiz." In one experiment, two groups of students were told that they were going to receive a series of painful shocks, but the students in one group were told to think of the shocks as "vibrating sensations" rather than painful shocks. The students who redefined the shocks as vibrating sensations subsequently had lower heart rates, perspired less, and reported less anxiety while waiting for the shocks than the students who did not use redefinition.

Another defensive strategy is **avoidant thinking**, and it involves intentionally distracting oneself from thinking about upsetting things (Bloom et al., 1977). Dentists may use music to distract their patients from the stressful sound of the drill, and college students often watch television as a means of distracting themselves from unpleasant tasks on which they should be working. The students may not be interested in what is on the TV, but attention to the TV blocks thoughts about studying and tests. Other potential defenses were reviewed earlier in the section on defense mechanisms.

Three points should be noted concerning defenses. First, sometimes a defense requires so much effort that it results in as much arousal as the stress it was used to avoid (Houston, 1972; Manuck et al., 1978; Solomon et al., 1980). Indeed, sometimes it is more efficient to "take your lumps and get on with it" than it is to get involved in elaborate defenses.

Second, a defense may reduce stress in the short run, but if it postpones appropriate action, in the long run it can bring on more serious consequences and higher stress. For example, to avoid stress some individuals avoid seeking medical attention for symptoms (e.g., persistent headaches, a lump in a breast), and by the time they are finally forced to get attention, it is too late for effective treatment.

Third, we now know that not all behaviors that were originally labeled defenses actually reduce stress. Projection is a case in point. Many people project their undesirable traits onto other people, but there is no evidence that doing so reduces the stress associated with having the undesirable traits. In other words, projecting hostility onto others will not necessarily make an individual less anxious about being hostile (Holmes, 1978, 1981).

Abnormal Behavior.   The final step in the process involves the emergence of abnormal behavior, and that can occur in four ways. First, the defenses may reduce stress, but *the behavior involved in the defenses may be abnormal.* For example, an individual who is afraid that something bad might happen if he or she goes out of the house might defend by staying in the house, but staying in the house for months at a time is abnormal (agoraphobia). Second, the defenses may not be effective, so *the psychological component of stress will persist,* resulting in anxiety or, if prolonged, possibly depression. Third, the defenses may not be effective, so *the physiological component of stress will persist,* and that high level of arousal can lead to physical problems such as coronary artery disease, ulcers, and headaches. Fourth, if the defenses are not effective, *the stress may trigger a predisposition* and result in disorders such as depression or schizophrenia (diathesis-stress). The ways in which stress may be related to specific disorders will be discussed throughout the rest of this book.

SUMMARY

In this chapter we discussed five perspectives for understanding abnormal behavior. First, we examined the psychodynamic perspective, in which abnormal behavior is thought to stem from intrapsychic conflict. The most popular of the psychodynamic theories is the psychoanalytic theory of Freud, who described personality from both structural (id, ego, superego) and developmental (oral, anal, phallic, latency, and genital stages) points of view. Freud suggested that conflict between the id and the superego results in anxiety, which is a signal to use various defense mechanisms (repression, projection, regression, etc.) to avoid the conflict and anxiety. The distortions of reality caused by the use of the defenses are thought to result in abnormal behavior. For Freud, then, the steps that lead to abnormal behavior are conflict, anxiety, defense, symptoms.

The neo-Freudians accept many of Freud's ideas but see the ego as powerful and controlling rather than simply mediating between the id and the super-

ego. They also believe that the major conflicts that lead to abnormal behavior are personal and social rather than conflicts between the id and the superego. Furthermore, the neo-Freudians believe that defenses such as compensation can lead to positive and constructive behaviors rather than necessarily leading to abnormal behavior.

The learning perspective suggests that abnormal behavior is learned through either classical or operant conditioning. Classical conditioning occurs when an unconditioned stimulus that elicits a particular response (e.g., a loud noise that elicits fear) is paired with a conditioned stimulus (e.g., a harmless animal) such that the conditioned stimulus eventually elicits the response (e.g., the presence of a harmless animal leads to fear). Through the process of generalization, classically conditioned responses can be elicited by stimuli that are similar to the original stimulus. Classically conditioned responses are not under voluntary control. These responses can be extinguished by repeatedly presenting the conditioned stimulus without the unconditioned stimulus. Inappropriate and uncontrollable emotional responses such as anxiety are thought to be due to classical conditioning.

In contrast, operant conditioning occurs when a response is followed by a reward (or the avoidance of a punishment) so that in the future an individual is likely to use the response to get the reward (or avoid the punishment). Operantly conditioned responses are under voluntary control. These responses can be extinguished if they are not followed by rewards, but they will be more resistant to extinction if they have been rewarded using an intermittent schedule. Many abnormal behaviors are thought to be the result of operant conditioning. Classical and operant conditioning can also work together to result in abnormal behavior; for example, fears of various stimuli may be developed with classical conditioning, and then operant responses may be used to avoid the stimuli and reduce the fears.

According to the cognitive perspective, abnormal behavior is explained in terms of problems with thought content and disrupted cognitive processes. To understand those problems, we reviewed the associative network theory (activation of memories in a network leading to a stream of consciousness) and the three stages of memory processing (sensory memory, short-term memory, long-term memory). Selective attention, selective recall, distortions of memories, and false memories can distort our thoughts and behaviors. It was also pointed out that serious forms of abnormal behavior may result from disruptions in thought processes (lapses in attention and problems with associations). Within the cognitive perspective, erroneous thoughts and disturbed thought processes are considered to be the causes rather than only the symptoms of abnormal behavior. Furthermore, the errors and disturbances in the cognitions of abnormal individuals are viewed simply as more extreme forms of the problems often experienced by normal individuals.

The physiological perspective suggests that abnormal behavior results from problems associated with synaptic transmission, brain structure, or hormone levels. Synaptic transmission is influenced by (a) levels of the neurotransmitters, (b) blockage of the neurotransmitters, (c) the effects of inhibitory neurons, (d) neuron sensitivity, and (e) the number of receptor sites. Too much or too little neurological activity results in abnormal behavior, and the nature of the abnormality depends on the level of activity and the part of the brain in which the activity is taking place. Problems with synaptic transmission may stem from (a) psychological stress, (b) genetic predisposition, (c) a spontaneous breakdown in the system, or (d) a combination of genetic predisposition and psychological stress (diathesis-stress). Problems with brain structure can disrupt neurological functioning, and problems with hormones can influence arousal, both of which can influence behavior.

The humanists propose that the conflict that leads to abnormal behavior stems from the discrepancy between our current level of functioning (current self) and a higher level of functioning toward which we strive (ideal self; self-actualization). The existentialists believe that abnormal behavior, primarily anxiety and depression, stems from our awareness of the fact that we could cease to exist and that we must take responsibility for ourselves.

The perspectives explain abnormal behavior in various ways, but they are not necessarily in competition with one another. Indeed, it is likely that (a) different disorders have different explanations, (b) some disorders may have more than one explanation, and (c) in some cases, different explanations may work together to result in a disorder.

Finally, we considered the concept of stress. Stressors are situations that require adjustment; they overtax the individual and thereby lead to stress. Stress has a psychological component (emotions such as anxiety) and a physiological component (increased physical arousal such as elevated heart rate), both of which are perceived as unpleasant. Emotions may cause physiological arousal (the Cannon-Bard theory) or physiological arousal may lead to emotions (the James-Lang theory). The steps that lead from stressors to abnormal behavior include (a) initial awareness and appraisal of the stressor, (b) an ineffective attempt to cope with the stressor, (c) the onset of the stress response, (d) the use of defenses to reduce stress, and (e) the development of abnormal behaviors.

Now that we have examined the perspectives for understanding abnormal behavior and the concept of stress, we can go on to consider how abnormal behavior is diagnosed and studied.

KEY TERMS, CONCEPTS, AND NAMES

In reviewing and testing yourself on what you have learned from this chapter, you should be able to identify and discuss each of the following:

all-or-none principle	conscious mind	generalization
amine hypotheses	coping	genital stage
amines	current self	hormones
anal stage	defense mechanisms (defenses)	humanistic-existential perspective
anxiety	dendrite	id
associative network theory	denial	ideal self
avoidant thinking	developmental approach to personality	identification
axon	diathesis-stress hypothesis	information processing
blocking agents	displacement	inhibitory neurons
brain structure	disrupted cognitive processes	intellectualization
Cannon-Bard theory of emotion	distortions of memories	intermittent schedule of reward
cell body	drive displacement	James-Lang theory of emotion
classical conditioning	ego	latency stage
cognitive content	ego psychology	learning perspective
cognitive perspective	Electra attraction	Little Albert
cognitive set	extinction	long-term memory
compensation	false memories	Maslow, Abraham
conditioned stimulus	feelings of inferiority	metabolism
conflict-anxiety-defense-symptoms	fixated	modeling
sequence	Freud, Anna	neo-Freudian theories

nerve fiber
nerve impulse
neuron
neurotransmitter
object displacement
observational learning
Oedipus attraction
operant conditioning
oral stage
Pavlov, Ivan
peak experiences
phallic stage
phenomenological approach
physiological perspective
pleasure principle
postsynaptic neuron
preconscious
presynaptic neuron

primary process
priming
projection
psychoanalytic (Freudian) theory
psychodynamic perspective
psychosexual stages
rationalization
reaction formation
receptor sites
regression
repression
reuptake
secondary process
selective attention
selective recall
self-actualization
self-fulfilling prophecies
sensory memory

short-term memory
situation redefinition
Skinner, B. F.
spontaneous recovery
stress
stressor
structural approach to personality
superego
suppression
synapse
terminal button
three-stage theory of memory
    processing
unconditioned stimulus
unconscious
vicarious conditioning
Watson, John B.

Notes:

Chapter 3

Diagnostic Techniques and Research Methods

• O U T L I N E •

abeling an individual "abnormal" tells us very little because the label is too broad. We do not know whether the individual is anxious, depressed, having physical problems, hallucinating, delusional, addicted to drugs, or suffering from any of hundreds of other symptoms. The need for better descriptions led to the development of a **diagnostic system** that describes and classifies different types of abnormal behavior.

THE DIAGNOSTIC SYSTEM FOR ABNORMAL BEHAVIOR

A diagnostic system serves two major purposes. First, it enables us to *communicate* information about individuals who suffer from abnormalities. The diagnostic label "major depression" tells us much more about an individual's symptoms than the label "abnormal." Second, a diagnostic system helps us decide how to *treat* an individual. A diagnostic system itself does not lead to treatments, but once a set of symptoms (diagnosis) is linked to a particular cause or an effective treatment, the diagnosis helps us identify who should be treated in what way. In many respects, the diagnostic system is the foundation for our understanding and treatment of abnormal behavior, and therefore it is important that we understand the system and how it works.

Background

The diagnostic system most widely used in the United States was introduced by the American Psychiatric Association (APA) in 1952 and has undergone extensive revisions since then (APA, 1952, 1968, 1980, 1987; 1994). In its early forms, the system consisted simply of brief descriptions of the symptoms and causes associated with various disorders. When making a diagnosis, a clinician tried to select the description that best fit the client. Unfortunately, the early system suffered from two serious problems. First, the descriptions of the various disorders were rather vague. Second, there was no consistent basis for diagnoses because they could be based either on the patient's *symptoms* or on assumptions about the *cause* of the symptoms.

The vagueness of the descriptions and the inconsistent basis for making diagnoses led to two practical problems. First, the system was *unreliable*. (The **reliability** of a diagnostic system refers to the degree to which a person with a given set of symptoms will receive the same diagnosis when examined by different clinicians.) When using the original system, there was often less than 50% agreement among clinicians who diagnosed the same patient (Beck et al., 1962; Ward et al., 1962; Zigler & Phillips, 1961). Second, the diagnoses arrived at with the system were often *invalid*. (The **validity** of a diagnostic system refers to the degree to which a person will receive the correct diagnosis.) The invalidity of the diagnoses stemmed from their unreliability; if different individuals came up with different diagnoses, some of those diagnoses had to be wrong. Obviously, a system that yields unreliable and invalid diagnoses is not of much help, and consequently there was widespread dissatisfaction with it.

The Current System

Because of the problems with the original system, in 1980 the American Psychiatric Association introduced a completely new diagnostic system, published in a manual known as DSM-III (*Diagnostic and Statistical Manual*, third edition). In 1987, a revised version of the manual was published, known as **DSM-III-R**. A refinement of that manual was published in 1994 and called DSM-IV (American Psychiatric Association, 1994). Our discussion of abnormal behavior in this book will be based on the descriptions contained in DSM-IV.

Beginning with DSM-III, four important advances were made that improved our diagnostic procedures.

1. *The symptoms for each diagnostic category are clearly listed.* Earlier manuals simply contained a short and rather vague description of each disorder, but in DSM-IV the precise symptoms of each disorder are listed, and it is specified how many symptoms must be present before the diagnosis can be made.

In an attempt to make the system even more objective and uniform, the manual contains "decision trees" for making diagnoses. A decision tree for diagnosing various mood disorders is presented in Figure 3.1. If there is evidence of a particular symptom, the decision tree indicates what diagnosis should be given. If there is no evidence of that symptom, the decision tree indicates what symptom should be looked for next, and so on. The use of these decision trees makes the diagnostic process much more objective and uniform and therefore increases the reliability of the process. There are now even computer programs that will lead the clinician through the decision trees. The programs ask questions about symptoms and then give a diagnosis or ask more questions that lead to other diagnoses. With the necessary symptoms clearly listed and the steps in the decision process outlined, the only room for subjective error is in the decision as to whether or not the patient has a particular symptom. (We will consider techniques for assessing symptoms later in this chapter.)

FIGURE 3.1   A DECISION TREE FOR DIAGNOSING MOOD DISORDERS.

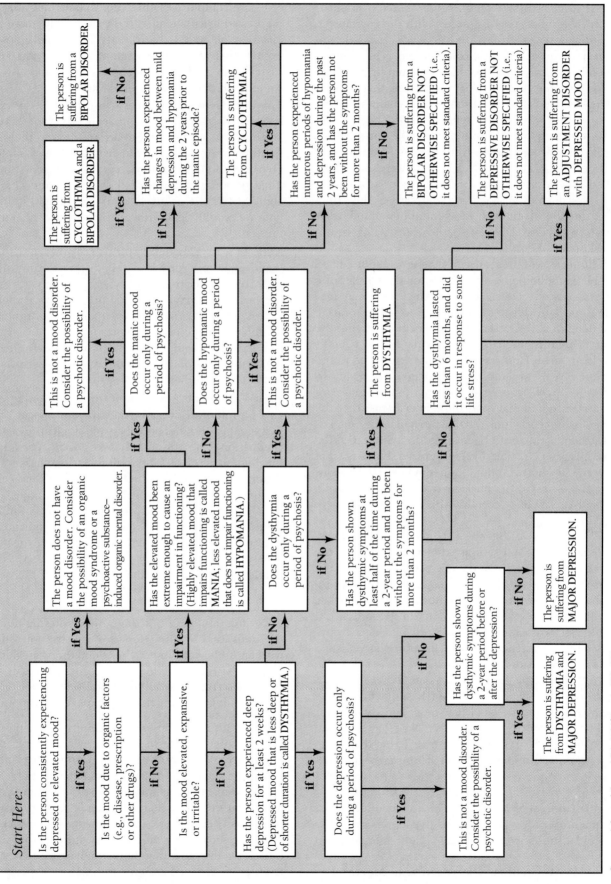

Source: Adapted from APA (1987), pp. 380–381.

2. *Assumptions about the suspected causes of disorders are not used in making diagnoses.* With the current system, diagnoses are based on *observable behaviors,* and suspected causes are generally ignored. The elimination of assumptions about causes resulted in the elimination of some popular diagnostic labels that implied an underlying cause. For example, for many years the term *neurotic* was used to refer to disorders involving the symptoms of anxiety, but because the term *neurotic* implies that anxiety stems from unconscious conflicts, it is no longer used. Instead, what were previously called *anxiety neuroses* are now called *anxiety disorders.* The new diagnostic label simply describes the symptoms and does not involve assumptions about their cause. In general, DSM-IV is atheoretical, that is, not based on any theory.

Concern with the cause of symptoms has not been completely eliminated in making diagnoses because *objective evidence* concerning certain causes can provide important information needed to make an accurate diagnosis. For example, if a person is hearing the voice of John Kennedy (i.e., hallucinating) or believes that he or she is God (i.e., delusional), and if an examination reveals organic brain damage, the diagnosis will be changed from Schizophrenia to a diagnosis of brain damage. Similarly, if there is evidence that the individual recently took a hallucinogenic drug such as LSD, the diagnosis will be changed to a Substance Related Disorder. It should be recognized, however, that objective evidence about brain damage or previous drug use is very different from assumptions about ill-defined causes like "conflict with mother" that were used previously.

3. *The number of disorders was greatly increased over earlier editions.* For example, the first edition of the manual listed only four disorders of childhood, but DSM-IV lists more than 40. Some critics have suggested that too many problems are now listed as disorders and that we are extending too far the boundaries of "abnormal." For example, a child who was having difficulty with arithmetic could be diagnosed as having a "Mathematics Disorder."

4. *Individuals are given diagnoses on five separate axes.* Until the publication of DSM-III, individuals were given one diagnostic label that described their major clinical problem (e.g., depression). Now they are given diagnoses on five **axes** (dimensions) so that their diagnoses contain more information. Those axes are as follows:

Axis I: Clinical Syndromes. This axis contains all of the major disorders, such as anxiety, depression, schizophrenia, substance abuse, and organic mental disorders.

Axis II: Personality Disorders and Mental Retardation. This axis contains the disorders (e.g., obsessive-compulsive, mild retardation) that might be overlooked when attention is directed to the more florid disorders on Axis I. Individuals can have diagnoses on both Axes I and II. For example, an individual could suffer from a major depression (Axis I) and also show compulsive personality traits (Axis II).

Axis III: General Medical Conditions. This axis allows the diagnostician to indicate whether there are any medical conditions that are relevant to the understanding or treatment of the disorder. For example, evidence of organic brain damage may be relevant for understanding an individual with impaired cognitive abilities, and the presence of diabetes might influence how we would deal with an individual who was depressed.

Axis IV: Psychosocial and Environmental Problems. This axis provides the diagnostician with an opportunity to indicate whether there are any psychosocial or environmental problems that might affect the individual's diagnosis, treatment, or prognosis. Examples of potential problems include the loss of social support, death of a loved one, discrimination, educational problems, economic problems, legal problems, and other sources of stress.

Axis V: Global Assessment of Functioning. This axis permits the diagnostician to indicate an overall judgment of the individual's psychological, social, and occupational functioning at the *present time* and for the highest level of functioning during the *past year.* Rating of present functioning will reflect the need for treatment, and the repeated use of the rating allows the clinician to track the progress of therapy. Rating of previous function is of value because it indicates the level of adjustment the individual can be expected to achieve after the disorder has been eliminated. For example, if the therapist knows that during the best of times the individual had only a marginal level of functioning, that would eliminate unrealistic expectations regarding treatment outcome. Also, knowing how well the individual has functioned in the past provides us with an understanding of the foundation on which we have to base treatment. Level of functioning is rated on a scale from 1 to 100 with end points labeled persistent inability to function and superior functioning.

The introduction of the multidimensional approach to diagnosis was quite revolutionary, and it greatly expanded the information provided by a diagnosis. For example, instead of simply labeling an individual "depressed" as was done before, we now might learn that the individual (a) is depressed; (b) tends to be obsessive-compulsive in personality style, which may make psychotherapy difficult; (c) suffers from a serious heart disorder that limits activity and may contribute to the depression; and (d) is experiencing moderate psychosocial stress (has recently changed careers), which may also contribute to the depression, but (e) has functioned very well within the past year, suggesting the potential to do well again.

The system introduced in DSM-III and continued in DSM-IV is an improvement over the previous systems in that it makes the diagnostic procedures more reliable (Williams, 1985a, 1985b). The validity of diagnoses has probably also been increased, but this is more difficult to assess because for most disorders there is no absolute standard against which we can compare our diagnoses. (With regard to validity, it should be noted that high reliability is *necessary* for high validity but high reliability *does not ensure* high validity. It is possible to do something consistently wrong so that you are reliable but invalid!)

Although DSM-IV is the most widely used diagnostic system in the United States and the system on which this book is based, there are a number of other systems. For example, there is the *International Classification of Diseases* (ICD-9), and a variety of more specialized diagnostic systems is used for certain subsets of disorders.

Problems with Diagnostic Systems in General

The changes that were made in the DSM greatly improved the diagnostic system for abnormal behavior, but you should realize that a number of problems are inherent in any diagnostic system. One problem is that whenever an individual is put into a category, some of that person's *uniqueness is lost*, and therefore we may miss something important about the individual. In the DSM it is pointed out that it is wrong to think that all individuals who have the same disorder are alike in all important ways. They may have the same disorder, but they differ in other important ways. We may classify individuals as men versus women, old versus young, or suffering from schizophrenia versus normal, and although each of those classifications tells us something about the individual, each also serves to obscure other things about the person. Just as all men are not alike, so all persons with schizophrenia are not alike.

Another problem with a diagnostic system is that diagnoses can lead us to *attribute characteristics to individuals that the individuals do not possess.* Many persons who suffer from schizophrenia have hallucinations and delusions, so it is often assumed that a patient with a diagnosis of schizophrenia will have both hallucinations and delusions when in fact the individual may have only one or the other. This can lead to two problems. First, we develop an erroneous picture of the individual that can cause us to misinterpret his or her behavior. For example, if the person with schizophrenia does not report hallucinations, we may assume that the person is being defensive and denying or hiding them. Second, if we assume that an individual has a

particular symptom, we may actually create the symptom in the individual through the process of suggestion. If an authority figure such as a psychologist or a psychiatrist assumed that a person with schizophrenia had hallucinations and repeatedly asked the patient about them, the individual might think that he or she *should* have them. The line between "thoughts" and "voices in our heads" can become blurred. If we think we should be hearing voices, we may interpret thoughts as voices and *voilà*, we have hallucinations!

Because of the problems associated with diagnostic labels, it has been suggested that we replace them with **checklists of symptoms**. The lists would include symptoms like hallucinations, delusions, depression, and anxiety, but they would also include items on which we would rate the degree to which the individual was suicidal, verbally responsive, able to sleep, motivated to improve, able to interact effectively with others, bothered by feelings of guilt, physically active, able to organize, able to concentrate, reliable, and honest and the degree to which support was available to the individual from family and friends. With ratings on dimensions like these, we would know, for example, that an individual was depressed but also that he or she was suicidal, willing to talk (which is certainly important in dealing with suicidal individuals), and honest and that there is a social support system to care for the individual outside of the hospital.

In some respects, the use of checklists is the next step beyond the use of multiple axes for making diagnoses, but it has some differences. The checklist approach has many more dimensions, so we get more information. Also, a checklist could be used by nurses, ward attendants, friends, and family members as well as psychologists and psychiatrists, and we could therefore get a broader perspective on the individual being rated. That might be very helpful because the traditional interview from which diagnostic impressions are obtained is brief and may not provide a representative picture of the person. The individual could even provide a self-rating, and the inconsistencies between that report and those of others might help in understanding the individual. With multiple raters making judgments in multiple places, we could get a much better idea of the individual's problems as well as when and where the problems are most likely to occur. Checklists have been tried and found to be very effective (Derogatis, 1993; Wittenborn, 1951, 1962). However, probably because they involve a radical departure from the traditional way of thinking about and describing patients, they have not yet gained widespread acceptance.

Finally, some attention should be given to how we misuse the diagnostic labels when talking about individuals. We usually use diagnostic labels to refer to the *whole person* rather than to the fact that the individual suffers from a *particular disorder*. For example, sometimes we refer to individuals as "schizophrenics" rather than as individuals "with schizophrenia." This is like referring to an individual with cancer as "a cancer." The use of a diagnostic label to refer to an entire individual is inappropriate because it implies that the disorder influences all aspects of the individual's life when in fact this may not be the case. Even very serious disorders such as schizophrenia sometimes influence only a limited part of the individual's life. Some individuals with hallucinations and delusions live normal and productive lives because their symptoms do not lead to inappropriate behaviors. To avoid attributing a disorder to the whole person, DSM-IV does not use expressions such as "a schizophrenic" or "an alcoholic" and instead recommends phrases like "an individual with Schizophrenia" or "an individual with Alcohol Dependence." That is a convention we will follow in this book.

TECHNIQUES FOR DIAGNOSING ABNORMAL BEHAVIOR

So far we have discussed the importance of diagnoses and have learned that they are based on observable symptoms or, in some cases, on the cause of the symptoms. We will now examine the procedures used to assess symptoms and causes. Four major procedures will be examined: *observation, interviewing, psychological testing,* and *physiological testing.* More than one technique is usually used because the different techniques provide different types of information. Furthermore, the strengths of one technique can compensate for the weaknesses of another.

Observation

Observation of an individual in his or her natural environment can be very helpful because it enables us to assess behavior directly and to evaluate the effects of situational factors on behavior. However, direct observation usually plays a relatively minor role in the assessment of abnormal behavior because of various practical and ethical problems associated with it. It is simply not practical to have trained observers "in the field" recording the behavior of individuals. In addition, serious ethical questions are associated with observing individuals without informing them about the observation, and the behavior that can be observed with permission through one-way windows in a hospital is probably not typical behavior because the individual is aware of being observed. Although the unsystematic observations of friends and relatives are used, we must be cautious about such observations because the observers are not trained and may be biased

Psychologists use techniques such as observation to assess behavior in young children.

(e.g., they may want to see only the good, or they may be influenced by sex-role stereotypes). Another source of unsystematic observations is the notes made by nurses and ward attendants on patients' charts, but a psychiatric ward may not be a good place to observe behavior because we cannot expect normal behavior in an abnormal environment.

One group of individuals with whom observations are frequently used is young children. Situations can be arranged in which children interact with peers or parents, and the children often ignore or are unaware of the observers. The fact that young children can be observed is important because unlike adults, they do not yet have the skills to report how they act or feel.

Interviewing

It is often difficult or impossible to observe individuals in their natural environments, and therefore we use **interviewing**—conversations during which individuals report on how they act in various situations. In a **structured interview**, the interviewer rigidly follows a specific list of questions, whereas in an **unstructured interview**, the interviewer "goes with the flow," pursuing topics of interest and avoiding dead ends. Structured interviews have the advantage of ensuring that all relevant topics will be covered, at least superficially. Unstructured interviews may miss something that is relevant, but they allow for deeper probing when an important point is revealed. The best approach may be to do a structured interview followed by an unstructured interview in which important points are followed up.

Interviews also provide an opportunity to observe a client's behavior. Indeed, a client's style of respond-

A diagnostic interview can reveal much about a person, both from what the person says and how the person behaves.

ing may be more important than the content of what the client says. In some interviews, the interviewer may actually behave in a particular way to see how the client reacts. For example, in an interview designed to measure the aggressive and competitive personality style known as the *Type A behavior pattern* (Friedman & Rosenman, 1974), the interviewer will occasionally pause and fumble briefly as if searching for the right word to use. What the interviewer is really doing is waiting to see if the client will jump in and finish the sentence (Rosenman, 1978).

In other situations, the combination of content and style may be informative. For example, when asked about hallucinations, a client might respond harshly saying, *"No! I don't hear voices!* Only crazy people hear voices, and I'm not crazy!" In that case, the inappropriate vehemence of the client's denial of the hallucinations may lead the interviewer to conclude that in fact the client does suffer from hallucinations.

The interview is also important because it can yield valuable information about the individual's background and family. Increasing emphasis is being placed on family information because family interactions and genetic factors are now seen as playing important roles in the development of abnormal behavior. Not only do we want to know what problems there may have been in the family (e.g., family history of mental disorders, child abuse, infidelity), but we also want to know what, if anything, was effective in overcoming them.

Overall, the interview is of value because it provides both information about the individual and an opportunity to observe the individual. However, the interview does have a number of weaknesses. First, clients may not be good (or honest) reporters con-

cerning their behavior. Second, sometimes the interviewer must make interpretations concerning the client's reports and actions, and the inferences drawn may be wrong. For example, was the client mentioned earlier really having hallucinations, or was the client's denial so vehement out of exasperation at being asked about hallucinations? Finally, the interview may not be particularly good for observing behavior because the situation in which it occurs is so limited and not representative of more relevant life situations. In other words, the way an individual responds in a formal interview in the office of a psychologist or psychiatrist may not be the way the individual responds in the real world.

Psychological Testing

Psychological testing can be divided into four types: *objective, projective, intelligence,* and *neuropsychological.* We will consider each type in some detail.

Objective Testing. In some respects, **objective testing** of personality is an extension of the interview method of collecting information because the tests consist of lists of questions to which the individual responds. Numerous objective tests are used to measure a wide variety of abnormal behaviors ranging from brief periods of anxiety to chronic schizophrenia.

The most widely used objective test of abnormal behavior is probably the **Minnesota Multiphasic Personality Inventory,** usually referred to as the **MMPI.** The MMPI was originally published in 1942, and a revision, the **MMPI-2** was published in 1989. The MMPI-2 contains 567 questions grouped to form scales that measure nine types of abnormal behavior ranging

TABLE 3.1   ITEMS LIKE THOSE FOUND ON MMPI CLINICAL SCALES

Depression (Scale 2)
I generally feel that life is worth living (F).
I do not sleep well (T).
Psychopathic Deviate (Scale 4)
I have many fewer fears than other people (T).
In school, I was frequently in trouble for acting up (T).
Paranoia (Scale 6)
A lot of people have it in for me (T).
I have frequently been punished for things that were not my fault (T).
Schizophrenia (Scale 8)
I cannot keep my attention focused on one thought (T).
I hear strange things that others do not hear (T).
Mania (Scale 9)
I am a very important person (T).
I like to stir up activity (T).
Social Introversion (Scale 0)
I like to talk to members of the opposite sex (F).
At parties, I sit by myself or with one other person (T).

from depression to schizophrenia. There is also one scale that measures masculinity-femininity. Each item is answered by checking "True," "False," or "Cannot Say." Table 3.1 contains a sample of items like those found on some of the clinical scales. An individual gets a score on each scale of the MMPI, and the scores are plotted on a graph to yield a personality profile. Figure 3.2 contains an MMPI personality profile for an individual who has elevated scores on the Depression and Schizophrenia scales.

In addition to the clinical scales, three control scales are used to identify individuals for whom the test scores may not be valid. For example, there is a Lie scale that identifies individuals who are trying to fake good scores. The Lie scale contains items like "I never put off until tomorrow things that should be done today." It is unlikely that many people would consistently mark "True" for items like this, so if an individual does respond that way, the assumption is that the person is trying to give socially acceptable responses rather than accurate ones.

Interpretations can be based on simple inspection of a personality profile (see Figure 3.2), but it is now possible to use computer programs that will compare an individual's profile to that of thousands of other people about whom information is available and then print out a description of the individual (Bloom, 1992; Matarazzo, 1986). The MMPI-2 can also be scored for a variety of new scales that measure characteristics such as dominance, social responsibility, college maladjustment, and post-traumatic stress disorder (Graham, 1990). With these new scales, a very comprehensive description of an individual can be developed. Recently, a version of the test was designed specifically

for adolescents. This test is known as the **MMPI-A**. It has somewhat fewer items, the items are written at a lower reading level (6th grade), and the test measures some topics such as family problems that are particularly relevant for understanding adolescents.

The value of scores based on objective tests is limited by three factors: (a) the degree to which the person taking the test responds honestly, (b) the quality of the norms used for constructing and interpreting the test, and (c) the validity of the items, that is, the extent to which the test items really measure what they purport to measure.

Projective Testing.   In psychology, the term **projection** refers to the fact that we often attribute our own personality characteristics to other people and to inanimate stimuli such as inkblots. For example, an angry person might see other people as angry or might interpret an inkblot as an ill-tempered monster. We may also project the cause of our feelings, and therefore a frightened person may see others as hostile (i.e., frightening). In **projective testing**, we assess what an individual projects onto others to determine what the individual is like and how he or she sees the world. The individual is shown various stimuli (e.g., inkblots, pictures of people) and is asked to tell what the inkblots look like or what is going on in the picture. Because the inkblots are really only inkblots and because the pictures do not tell a particular story, what the individual sees in the inkblots and pictures is due to the projection of the person's own traits, needs, conflicts, and perceptions of the environment.

The best-known projective test is the **Rorschach** (RŌR-shok) **test**, which was developed by Herman

FIGURE 3.2   A MINNESOTA MULTIPHASIC PERSONALITY INVENTORY
PROFILE FOR A PERSON WITH SYMPTOMS OF
DEPRESSION AND SCHIZOPHRENIA.

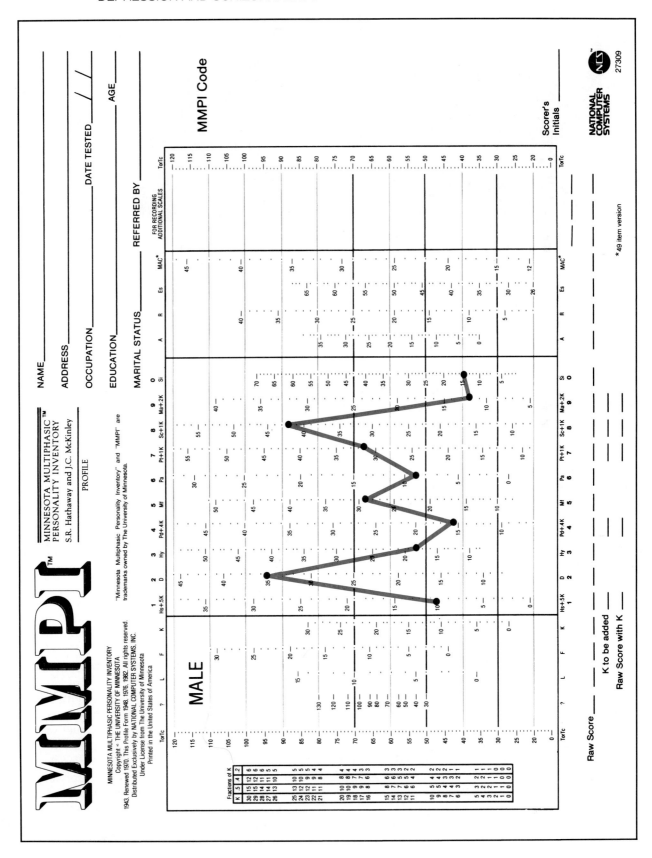

FIGURE 3.3   INKBLOTS LIKE THOSE ON THE RORSCHACH.

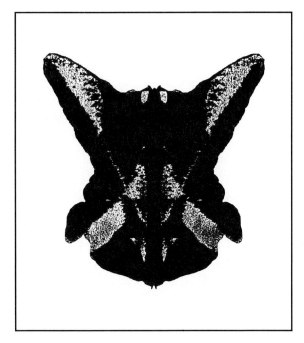 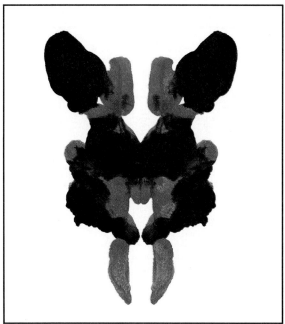

Rorschach after he noticed that his children saw different things when they looked at clouds (Rorschach, 1942). The Rorschach consists of 10 cards, each with one inkblot printed on it. Inkblots like those in the Rorschach are presented in Figure 3.3. Five of the cards are made with only black or gray ink, and five of the cards are made with different colored inks. The client is given the cards one at a time and asked, "Tell what you see on each card, or anything that might be represented there."

Responses to the Rorschach are scored in two ways. First, attention is given to the *content* of what the client saw in the inkblot. Consistently seeing mutilated bodies or squashed bugs would have very different implications from seeing flowers, the face of a cat, people dancing, or other happier images. Second, attention is given to *what it was about the inkblot* that led the client to see what he or she saw. For example, does the actual shape of the inkblot justify what was seen? If the shape justifies the response, that is considered to be an appropriate or healthy response and it is scored F+ (F stands for "form"). But if the response cannot be justified (i.e., the test administrator cannot see the same response when it is pointed out), it suggests that the individual is not in touch with reality, and the response is scored F–. We do not expect any individual to give only F+ responses, but if the proportion of F+ responses falls below 60% or 70%, there is reason for concern over the degree to which the individual is in contact with reality.

The use of color in making responses is also thought to be important because responding to color supposedly reflects the amount of emotion the individual has and how he or she deals with emotion. The theory suggests that if the individual never incorporates the colors, the individual is emotionally "flat." If the individual does use the color but when doing so gives poor responses (F–), it is assumed that the individual is easily overwhelmed by emotion and that his or her functioning is disrupted by emotion. Numerous other factors, such as the use of shading of grays in the inkblot and whether the client sees motion in the response (e.g., "a person running") are also taken into consideration in scoring responses to the Rorschach. (For more information on scoring, see Beck et al., 1961; Exner, 1978; Klopfer, 1962; Rapaport et al., 1946).

The Rorschach is one of the most widely used projective tests, but serious questions have been raised about its reliability and validity, and consequently there is a continuing controversy over whether it should be used. One of the most serious criticisms stems from the consistent finding that knowing an individual's Rorschach responses does not allow a clinician to make more accurate judgments about the individual than if the clinician only has basic demographic information about the individual from an interview (see Garb, 1985). In other words, the Rorschach may not increase what we can learn from easier and faster methods such as an interview.

Another widely used projective test is the **Thematic Apperception Test**, usually referred to simply as the **TAT** (Murray, 1943). The TAT differs from the Rorschach in that instead of giving responses to

FIGURE 3.4   A PERSON TAKING THE THEMATIC
APPERCEPTION TEST (TAT).

inkblots, clients make up stories about pictures. Figure 3.4 shows a person taking the Thematic Apperception Test. Theoretically, the stories the client tells reflect the themes, problems, conflicts, and characters that are important in the client's life.

As with the Rorschach, there are a number of problems with the TAT that undermine its usefulness. The most serious problem is that the TAT only measures traits and motives that individuals *know they have*, and there is no evidence that individuals project motives or traits of which they are unconscious (Holmes, 1968, 1981). For example, a hostile person who believes that he or she is hostile will project that trait on the TAT. However, if a hostile person does not believe that he or she is hostile, the person will not project that trait on the TAT at a rate greater than individuals who are not hostile. The fact that the TAT only measures conscious characteristics greatly limits its usefulness, and the results of a variety of investigations have revealed that simple self-reports are as effective as or more effective than TAT stories in measuring personality (e.g., Holmes, 1971; Holmes & Tyler, 1968).

Another problem with the TAT is that individuals can *fake their responses* (Holmes, 1971). Specifically, when responding to the TAT, individuals can effectively conceal their real personalities and can introduce other personality characteristics that they do not have.

Finally, even when individuals are not faking, there is a *problem with interpreting the stories* accurately because it is difficult to determine whether the traits that are being projected are the traits that the individuals *possess* or the traits that are the *cause* of those traits. For example, if an individual describes others as hostile, it could mean that he or she is hostile, or it could mean that he or she is afraid because others are seen as hostile.

Another type of projective test is the **Incomplete Sentences Test** (Rotter & Rafferty, 1950), in which the individual is given a sheet with incomplete sentences like, "My mother . . . ," "What bothers me is that . . . ," and "Other people. . . . " The individual then completes the sentence with whatever comes to mind first. In other projective tests, the individual is asked to draw a person (**Draw-A-Person Test**; Machover, 1949) or is asked to draw a house, a tree, and a person (**House-Tree-Person Test**; Buck, 1948). There is also a children's version of the TAT known as the **CAT** (**Children's Apperception Test**; Bellak, 1954). Most of these tests do not have formal scoring procedures. Instead, the interpretations are dependent on the subjective judgments and clinical intuition of the tester. In most cases, serious questions have been raised concerning the validity of these tests, but it is unclear whether the problem is with the principle on which the test is based, the test itself, or the skill of the tester.

Advocates of the use of projective tests have argued that clinical experience with the tests suggests that they are revealing and helpful, and that the lack of empirical evidence supporting their utility is the result of the insensitivity of the research methods that were used to assess them. In other cases, the users of the tests have agreed that the tests are without empirical support, but they continue to use them as a means of facilitating the interview process, much as icebreakers are used at parties. The debate over the clinical utility of projective tests has been going on for years, and although projective tests play a prominent role in the diagnostic process, they are considered less important now than they were some years ago.

Intelligence Testing. **Intelligence testing** often plays an important role in determining a diagnosis and developing a treatment plan. For example, intelligence tests can be used to help decide whether an individual's problems are due to mental retardation, and they can also be used to determine what type of therapy might be most effective (psychotherapy might not be effective for an individual with poor verbal skills).

The intelligence tests used in clinical settings usually involve one-on-one interactions between a client and an examiner during which the client performs a series of tasks (e.g., math problems, puzzles) over the course of at least 2 hours. This type of testing allows for the assessment of various abilities and provides the examiner with an opportunity to watch the client work so that the examiner can determine the reasons for poor performance and take them into consideration. For example, individuals who are excessively anxious or depressed may perform at levels below their actual ability, and that must be taken into consideration when interpreting the results of the test and predicting future performance.

Most of the individual intelligence tests contain subscales designed to measure **verbal intelligence** and **performance intelligence**. With the **Wechsler Adult Intelligence Scale (WAIS)**, verbal intelligence is measured with six subtests:

1. Information (How far is it from New York to San Francisco?)
2. Comprehension (Why do we have laws?)
3. Arithmetic (A shirt that usually sells for $30 is reduced in price by 15% during a sale. What does the shirt cost during the sale?)
4. Similarities (How are a pound and an inch alike?)
5. Digit Span (Repeat the following list of numbers from memory: 2, 7, 9, 4, 8.)
6. Vocabulary (What does the word *overture* mean?)

Performance intelligence is measured with five subtests:

1. Picture Completion (looking at pictures of objects and determining what parts are missing)
2. Block Design (arranging blocks to form designs; see Figure 3.5)

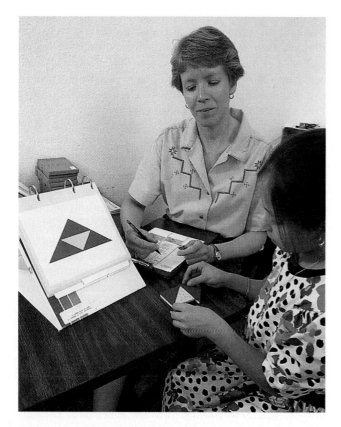

Intelligence testing often plays an important role in making a diagnosis and developing a treatment plan.

FIGURE 3.5   A BLOCK DESIGN TEST IS ONE SUBTEST USED TO MEASURE INTELLIGENCE ON THE WECHSLER ADULT INTELLIGENCE SCALE.

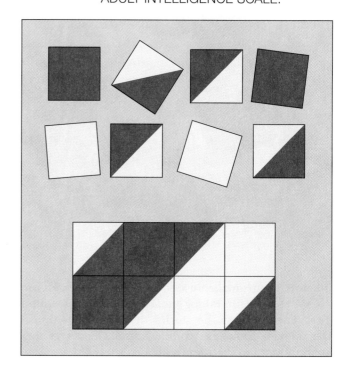

3. Picture Arrangement (arranging a set of pictures to make a story)
4. Object Assembly (putting puzzles together)
5. Digit Symbol (learning to associate numbers with various symbols)

The most widely used test for individuals over 16 years of age is the **Wechsler Adult Intelligence Scale (Revised Edition)**, generally known as the **WAIS-R**. For testing school-age children there is the **Wechsler Intelligence Scale for Children (Third Edition)**, known as the **WISC-III**, and for preschoolers there is the **Wechsler Preschool-Primary Scale of Intelligence**, known as the **WPPSI**. The **Stanford-Binet** test can also be used with children. Because of the importance of measuring intelligence and because it is essential that the tests be unbiased with regard to culture or social class, new tests of intelligence are being developed constantly.

Individual intelligence tests are very reliable and effective for predicting school performance. Because they involve reasoning and problem solving, they can also be helpful for predicting performance in the real world. They are not without their problems, however, and we will discuss some of their limitations when we discuss mental retardation in Chapter 20.

Neuropsychological Testing.   When it is suspected that an individual is suffering from some sort of organic brain damage, **neuropsychological testing** may be used to identify the location and nature of the damage. Such testing is based on the fact that different abilities are located in different areas in the brain, and therefore by measuring the pattern of an individual's abilities and disabilities, it is possible to make inferences about the location and extent of the brain damage. Some neuropsychological tests measure as many as 14 different abilities and may require a day to complete. The tests include things such as puzzles that must be done while blindfolded, verbal tasks involving naming objects and concepts, and reaction time tasks.

In addition to assisting in the diagnostic process, the information provided by neuropsychological tests can also be helpful in designing a treatment program (determining what abilities need to be retrained or compensated for) and making plans for the individual's future functioning (determining whether there are things the individual will never be able to do again). The two most frequently used neuropsychological tests are the **Halstead-Reitan Neuropsychology Battery** and the **Luria-Nebraska** battery (Golden et al., 1978).

Physiological Testing

Physiological (medical) **testing** has always played a role in the assessment of psychological problems because many psychological problems have physiological aspects. For example, a **sphygmomanometer** (SFIG-mō-muh-NOM-uh-tur) is used to measure high blood pressure (hypertension), the **electroencephalograph** (ē-LEK-trō-en-SEF-uh-lō-graf; EEG) is used to record the electrical activity of the brain, and **X-rays** are sometimes helpful in identifying structural problems of the brain. Recently developed techniques have greatly improved our ability to examine the structure and functioning of the living brain.

Two of these new techniques are **computerized axial tomography** (tō-MOG-ruh-fē), better known as the **CT scan** (or *CAT scan*), and **magnetic resonance imaging**, or **MRI**. These techniques are similar to the X-ray in that they produce images of internal organs such as the brain. However, they differ from an X-ray because rather than producing an image that shows all of the overlapping parts of the brain, with the CT and MRI techniques we get pictures of "slices" of the brain. Thus one part of the brain does not hide or mask the parts behind it. Furthermore, because CT and MRI can produce pictures of very thin slices of the brain, we are able to get much greater detail, and that detail may be important in diagnosing brain damage. An MRI of the human brain is presented in Figure 3.6.

A third new technique is **positron emission tomography,** which is usually referred to simply as a **PET scan**. The PET scan is like the CT scan in that it

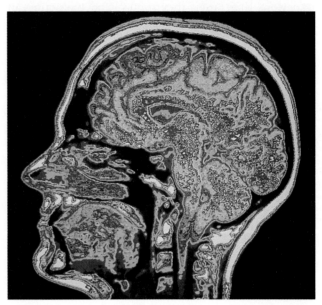

FIGURE 3.6   MAGNETIC RESONANCE IMAGING (MRI) SCAN OF THE BRAIN.

Source: From Andreasen et al. (1986), p. 138, fig. 1.

involves pictures of the brain taken one slice at a time. However, the PET scan shows the *activity* of the brain rather than its *structure*. In the PET scan procedure, a radioactive agent (isotope) that binds to a particular chemical in the brain (glucose, a neurotransmitter) is administered to the client. Then, by recording where the isotope goes, we can measure the location and activity of the brain chemical of interest. (We can record the location of the isotopes because they emit positrons, which can be recorded with equipment that is sensitive to radioactivity—hence the name, *positron emission* tomography.) PET scans reflecting glucose metabolism (energy production) in the brain of a patient during normal, manic, and depressed periods are presented in Figure 10.2 in Chapter 10.

Issues Concerning Diagnostic Methods

Considerable progress has been made in the technical development and refinement of diagnostic techniques, but a number of basic issues remain troublesome and deserve comment.

Utility of Various Types of Diagnostic Information.
It is clear that clinicians can use information from a number of sources in making diagnoses. The question then is, which type of information is most helpful for making diagnoses? To answer this question, researchers have given clinicians different types of information about individuals and then asked them to make judgments about the individuals. These investigations revealed some surprising findings (see Garb,

1985). For example, clinicians were not more effective in making judgments when they watched videotapes of interviews than when they simply read typescripts of the interviews. That suggests that visual and auditory cues gained in interviews do not help in making judgments. Similarly, when clinicians were given only demographic information, their judgments were as accurate as when they were given both demographic information and projective test (Rorschach, TAT) responses. In sharp contrast to these negative findings are results indicating that the addition of MMPI responses to demographic data consistently led to more valid personality assessments. Furthermore, information from a neuropsychological test (Halstead-Reitan battery) greatly increased the validity of judgments concerning brain damage over judgments made using only information from general IQ tests. The results of these studies raise serious questions concerning the utility of clinical judgments based on either the behavioral aspects of clinical interviews or projective test responses. However, the MMPI and the neuropsychological tests do add to the validity of clinical judgments. The fact that the MMPI was helpful is especially noteworthy because the MMPI is the least expensive and least time-consuming means of collecting information.

Measurement of Transient Versus Enduring Traits.

A paradox associated with personality testing is that even if a test is exceptionally effective for assessing the subtleties of thoughts and feelings at the time the test is given, it may not be effective for explaining past behavior or predicting future behavior. That is because some aspects of personality (and abnormality) can change; what we measure today may not have existed earlier or may not exist later. When projective tests are criticized for being unreliable (yielding different results at different times), some clinicians defend them by suggesting that the tests are not unreliable but that the individual has changed and the test has picked up the change. Even if it is true that the tests are sensitive to such changes and that is why they appear to be unreliable, the fact remains that they do not help us understand past behavior or predict future behavior.

Traits Versus Situations for Predicting Behavior.

Our diagnostic procedures are designed to assess personality traits (e.g., hostility, anxiety, motivation, distractibility) so that we can use those traits to explain past behavior and predict future behavior. However, it has been argued that behavior is determined by situational factors rather than personality traits (Mischel, 1977). Your professor may be reserved and constrained in class, but at a social gathering that same professor may be outgoing and uninhibited. Your friend may be relaxed and confident when alone but extremely anxious and fearful when in groups. One woman I knew felt sluggish because of low blood pressure (hypotension), but her symptoms went unexplained for years because she was very tense around physicians, and when they took her pressure, it rose to "normal." In these cases, behaviors, feelings, and physiological responses were determined by situations rather than personality traits.

There has been considerable controversy over the question of whether traits or situations are more important for determining behavior, but it now appears that both factors influence behavior. Sometimes the individual's behavior is different in different situations, but in other cases the individual behaves the same way in different situations. Obviously, traits and situations and the interaction between them must be considered in attempting to understand behavior. Unfortunately, most diagnostic tests do not take the situation into account. When predicting behavior, then, it may be appropriate to recall that when in Rome, individuals do what their test results suggest they will do, but they may also do what the Romans do.

Comorbidity.

An individual can suffer from two or more psychological disorders at the same time (e.g., depression and substance abuse, depression and schizophrenia, general anxiety and phobias), just as a person may suffer from two or more physical disorders at the same time (e.g., diabetes and pneumonia). The co-occurrence of two disorders is called **comorbidity**. (The word *morbid* refers to disease, and *morbidity* refers to the *occurrence* of disease, so *comorbidity* means "the co-occurrence of two or more diseases.") Rates of comorbidity among some psychological disorders can be as high as 70%, so you should not be surprised if an individual qualifies for more than one diagnosis (e.g., Barsky, 1992; Brady & Kendall, 1992; Kendall, 1992; Rodhe et al., 1991; Sanderson et al., 1990).

There are three explanations for comorbifity, and they have different implications (Widiger et al., 1991). First, it is possible that in some cases individuals have two disorders at the same time simply by *chance*, and that there is no connection between the two disorders. Comorbidity on the basis of chance certainly occurs, but some disorders tend to co-occur more than others, thereby suggesting that in some instances of comorbidity there may be connections between some disorders. One explanation for the connection is that *one disorder leads to another*. For example, having an eating disorder may cause you to become depressed. The other explanation is that the *two disorders stem from a common cause*. For example, mood and appetite are both controlled by the same area of the brain, so a problem in that area could result in the comorbidity of depression and an eating disorder. Overall, then, when considering the diagnostic process, it is essential to recognize that comorbidity occurs and to examine patterns of comorbidity because they may provide clues to the causes of some disorders.

Comorbidity also has important implications for treatment. If you assume that the disorders co-occurred by chance, you would treat the disorders separately; if you assume that one led to another, you would treat the primary disorder; and if you assume that the disorders stem from a common cause, you would treat that cause. Finally, comorbidity may influence prognosis because the existence of one disorder may make the treatment of another disorder more or less difficult. For example, personality disorders may hinder the treatment of depression (Shea et al., 1992).

Subjectivity, Suggestion, and Diagnostic Fads.

Despite all of the attempts to make the diagnostic system objective, reliable, and valid, there is still a great deal of subjectivity in the system, and that leads to errors. The subjectivity is not in what symptoms lead to diagnoses (those have been clearly laid out in DSM-IV) but in the degree to which the diagnostician looks for particular symptoms, interprets ambiguous behaviors as symptoms, or even suggests symptoms to the client. For example, one colleague of mine sees the symptoms of the multiple personality disorder in virtually every client he sees, whereas most psychologists and psychiatrists never see one individual with a multiple personality disorder in their entire careers (see Chapter 6). Do individuals with multiple personality disorders somehow seek out my colleague, are other therapists missing the diagnosis, or is my colleague biased in his probing for and interpretation of symptoms? Similarly, in one hospital in which I worked, the staff was very interested in schizophrenia, whereas in a nearby hospital, the bipolar disorder (manic-depression) was of most interest. When patients were transferred between the two hospitals, their diagnoses were changed.

It should also be noted that there are diagnostic fads during which a particular diagnosis is popular and will be widely used, only to taper off later. The obsessive-compulsive disorder provides a good case in point. In one 20-year period, there was an increase of more than 500% in the number of publications on that disorder, and the use of that diagnosis in one leading hospital increased by 400% (Stoll et al., 1992; see Figure 3.7). In contrast, in the same period, the use of the paranoid diagnosis declined by 19%.

Overall, then, the diagnostic system used for abnormal behavior went through a major revolution that made it more objective and reliable and, it is hoped,

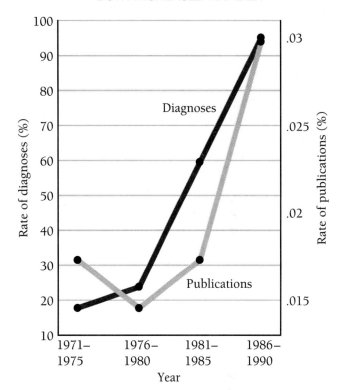

FIGURE 3.7   PUBLICATIONS ON THE OBSESSIVE-COMPULSIVE DISORDER AND DIAGNOSES OF THE DISORDER HAVE BOTH INCREASED RAPIDLY.

Source: Adapted from Stoll et al. (1992), p. 639, fig. 1.

more valid. In its present form, the diagnostic system is a product of clinical experience, science, and economics. Clinical experience and science have an influence because they lead to new refinements. Economics plays a role because insurance companies will pay only for the treatment of disorders that are listed in the DSM, and therefore there is constant pressure from mental health care providers to add new diagnoses so that practices can be expanded. Because of these factors, the diagnostic system is constantly evolving.

METHODS FOR STUDYING ABNORMAL BEHAVIOR

Finding the causes of and cures for abnormal behavior is like a complex mystery, and research methods are the tools we will need to evaluate the clues and solve the mystery. An understanding of research methods will help you to understand and evaluate the current information about abnormal behavior contained in this book, and it will also help you evaluate findings that you will read or hear about in the future.

Research methods can be divided into four types: *case study, correlational, controlled experimental,* and *multiple-baseline experimental.* Each type plays a role in our study of abnormal behavior, and each type has strengths and weaknesses in terms of the information it provides.

Case Study Research

With **case study research** we examine the life history of an individual in an attempt to formulate explanations for the individual's behavior. For example, when attempting to understand a disturbed patient, a clinician might learn that the patient's parents were hostile, rejecting, demanding, and only sometimes loving when the patient was a child. The clinician might then speculate that the patient's problems result from "bad parenting." Having observed this relationship in the one case, the clinician might hypothesize that bad parenting leads to abnormal behavior in general. It was through a series of case studies that Freud developed his psychodynamic theory of abnormal behavior. Similarly, you have probably used the case history approach in attempting to understand and explain the behavior of some of your friends (e.g., "Kent is insecure on dates because when he first started going out, he got 'dumped on' a couple of times"), and you might then have gone on to use the explanations to account for the behavior of other individuals.

Case studies provide an excellent source of hypotheses (potential explanations) about the causes of abnormal behavior, but they cannot be used to prove that a particular hypothesis is correct. That is because with the case study, it is impossible to rule out other potential hypotheses. A patient may have received bad parenting but may also have seen high levels of violence on television, been frustrated by the "new math," inhaled high levels of lead from automobile exhaust, grown up during a period of rapid cultural change, or inherited some defective genes. All of those factors have been used to account for abnormal behavior, but the case study does not allow us to determine which, if any, are responsible. It is also hazardous to form a general hypothesis on the basis of a case study because we cannot determine the degree to which the relationship in one individual holds for other individuals.

Another problem with case studies is that the observations are often biased. Once a clinician has a theory about the cause of a disorder, he or she may be very selective in what is reported about cases, and facts may even be distorted. In one of Freud's famous case studies (Emma E.), he reported that a woman's nosebleeds were due to psychological causes, and he used that observation to support one of his theories. However, recently discovered letters between Freud and one of his colleagues (Fleiss) reveal that Freud knew that the woman had undergone a series of operations on her nose and that during one operation a half meter of gauze had been accidentally left in her nasal cavity. Freud did not mention that in his case study (Masson, 1984).

Thus, in general, case studies can provide excellent descriptions of abnormal behavior, and they can suggest potential explanations for the behavior, but they cannot be used to prove explanations, and we must be careful about their objectivity. Numerous cases studies appear in this book, but they are included to provide descriptions of various disorders and not to suggest or support explanations.

Correlational Research

Correlational research is like case study research in that observations are made about the co-occurrence of two variables (e.g., bad parenting and abnormal behavior). However, in correlational research, observations are made of many individuals instead of just one. A statistical test is then conducted to determine whether the relationship between the two variables is reliable enough to justify the conclusion that the relationship is not due to chance. For example, if we examined 100 individuals and consistently found that those who showed the most abnormal behavior had received the worst parenting and that those who showed the least abnormal behavior had received the best parenting, we could conclude that there was a reliable correlation between quality of parenting and abnormal behavior. Such a relationship is presented graphically in part (*a*) of Figure 3.8. By contrast, if the relationship between quality of parenting and abnormal behavior was found in only a few of the people we studied, we could not conclude that there was a reliable correlation between parenting and behavior. Such a nonrelationship is presented graphically in part (*b*) of Figure 3.8.

The nature and strength of the relationship between two variables is expressed by means of a **correlation coefficient** (abbreviated *r*). Correlation coefficients range between +1.00 and −1.00. A high *positive* correlation (e.g., +.40 or +.60) indicates that individuals with high scores on one variable have high scores on the other variable (e.g., high levels of abnormal behavior are associated with high levels of bad parenting). A high *negative* correlation indicates that individuals who have high scores on one variable have low scores on the other variable (e.g., high levels of abnormal behavior are associated with low levels of bad parenting). A low correlation, regardless of its direction, indicates that there is little or no relationship between the two variables.

FIGURE 3.8 SCATTER PLOTS OF CORRELATIONAL
DATA: (*a*) POSITIVE CORRELATION;
(*b*) NO CORRELATION.

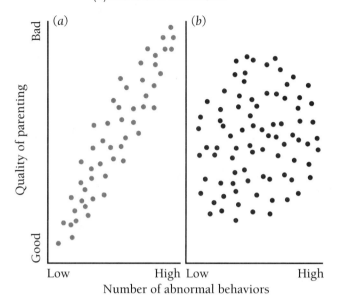

It is important to realize that a correlation between two variables does not necessarily mean that there is a *causal* relationship between the variables. Instead, it may be that the relationship is due to the influence of a third variable. In the case of the correlation between bad parenting and abnormal behavior, it is possible that genetic factors caused both the parents and their offspring to behave in abnormal ways. Similarly, socioeconomic stress may have caused the parents to behave badly, and the same stress may also have caused the children to behave badly. In those cases, then, the relationship between parenting and abnormal behavior was actually due to the influence of a third variable.

Even if there is a causal relationship between two correlated variables, the correlation does not allow us to determine the *direction* of the causation. If bad parenting was correlated with abnormal behavior, you might assume that bad parenting led to abnormal behavior, but it is possible that the abnormal behavior in the children frustrated the parents and led them to behave badly. In that case, the abnormal behavior on the part of the children caused the bad parenting.

In summary, correlational research enables us to determine whether there are reliable relationships between variables, but it does not enable us to conclude that a difference in one variable causes a difference in another variable. Furthermore, if there is a causal relationship, the correlation does not tell us the direction of the causation. To establish causal relationships, we

must use the experimental approaches that will be considered next.

Controlled Experimental Research

In **experimental research**, we attempt to determine whether a difference in one variable *causes* a difference in another variable (Campbell & Stanley, 1963). The variable whose effects we are studying (e.g., parenting) is called the **independent variable**, and the variable that will be influenced (e.g., children's adjustment) is called the **dependent variable**. (An easy way to remember the names for the variables is to recall that the dependent variable is *dependent* on—or influenced by—the independent variable.)

The first step in **controlled experimental research** is the **random assignment** of subjects to **experimental** and **control conditions**. For example, as subjects arrive for the experiment, the first would be assigned to the experimental condition, the second to the control condition, the third to the experimental condition, and so forth. Random assignment is used in an attempt to make the subjects in the two conditions comparable before the experiment begins. If subjects are randomly assigned, we assume that the subjects in the two conditions are comparable, but to test that assumption, in some experiments the investigators compare the two groups of subjects with a **pretest** on the dependent variable. Next we alter the independent variable in the experimental condition but not in the control condition, a procedure known as the **experimental manipulation**. Finally, we use a **posttest** to measure the dependent variable in the two conditions. If a difference is found between the experimental and control conditions in the dependent variable, we assume that the manipulation of the independent variable caused the difference.

To test the hypothesis that bad parenting causes abnormal behavior in children, we might (a) randomly assign families to experimental and control conditions, (b) use a pretest to assess the levels of abnormal behavior in the two groups of children, (c) have the parents in the experimental condition intentionally use bad parenting techniques while the parents in the control condition use normal parenting techniques, and then (d) some years later use a posttest to assess the levels of abnormal behavior of the children in the two conditions. (There is obviously an ethical problem with intentionally having parents use bad parenting techniques that we think will lead to abnormality, and we will discuss that later.) If children who received the bad parenting were found to have more abnormal behavior than those who received normal parenting, we could conclude that bad parenting caused abnormal

FIGURE 3.9   RESULTS OF A HYPOTHETICAL
EXPERIMENT ON GOOD VERSUS BAD
PARENTING.

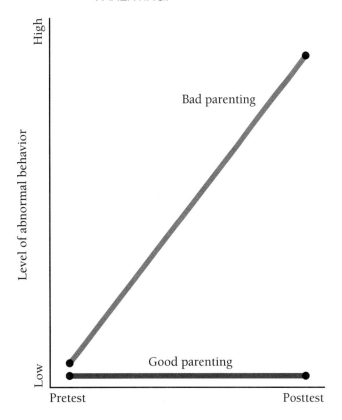

behavior. Such an outcome is presented graphically in Figure 3.9.

In any experiment, it is crucial that the subjects in the experimental and control conditions be alike and be treated alike except with respect to the independent variable. If there are other differences between the groups, it will be impossible to determine which variable is responsible for the change that is observed in the dependent variable. For example, if we manipulated type of parenting but the subjects in the bad parenting condition also happened to go to poorer schools, we could not determine whether their levels of abnormal behavior were due to bad parenting, poor schooling, or the combination of bad parenting plus poor schooling. If there is more than one difference between the conditions, the experiment is said to be **confounded**. (The word *confound* comes from a Latin word meaning "to pour together, confuse, ruin.") In the experiment just described, parenting and schooling are confounded, the results are confused, and the experiment is ruined.

Multiple-Baseline Experimental Research

Another way of experimentally testing the effects of an independent variable is to use a **multiple-baseline ex-**

perimental research procedure in which the subjects are observed over a series of periods in which the independent variable is and is not manipulated. For example, in testing to determine whether hostility on the part of parents leads to social withdrawal in children, the social behavior of children would be observed for periods in which the parents (a) behaved in a normal way toward the children (first baseline period), (b) acted in a hostile manner toward the children (experimental period), and (c) again behaved in a normal way toward the children (second baseline period). If the children showed more social withdrawal during the experimental period than during the baseline periods, it could be concluded that hostility on the part of parents caused social withdrawal in children. An example of results obtained with a multiple-baseline experiment is presented in Figure 3.10. In that experiment, the effects of a drug on schizophrenic symptoms was being tested, and the periods in which the patient was given the drug were interspersed with periods in which the patient was not given the drug. The results indicated that symptom levels were low during the drug periods and high during the no-drug (baseline) periods, therefore indicating that the drug was effective.

Placebo and Double-Blind Procedures

Two practical problems arise especially when doing research on treatments for abnormal behavior. One is the so-called **placebo** (pluh-SĒ-bō) **effect**. A placebo, by definition, has no therapeutic effect (e.g., a pill

FIGURE 3.10   RESULTS OF A MULTIPLE-BASELINE
EXPERIMENT ON THE EFFECTS OF A
DRUG ON SYMPTOMS OF
SCHIZOPHRENIA.

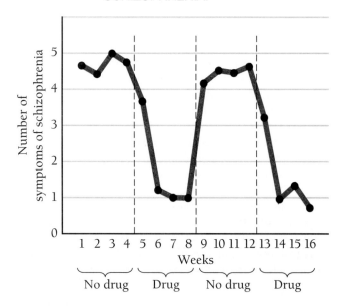

with no active ingredients). However, some patients who are given placebos and who believe they are getting an effective treatment may show improvement in their conditions (A. Shapiro, 1980). For example, if patients are given colored water labeled "powerful pain reliever," they may actually experience some relief from their pain. The second problem involves what are called **demand characteristics**. Subjects in experiments will sometimes intentionally do as they think the experimenter wants them to do regardless of whether the experimental manipulation was actually effective in changing their behavior (Orne, 1962). For example, patients in a treatment condition may report feeling better and act better because they think they *should* rather than because they actually *do*. Obviously, both the placebo effect and demand characteristics could influence the results of experiments on treatments and lead to conclusions that ineffective treatments were actually effective.

To avoid the problems associated with the placebo effect and demand characteristics, in research on treatments it is essential to include a placebo treatment condition in which the patients think they are getting the treatment but in which the crucial element of the treatment is missing. In studying the effects of drugs, we might have (a) a *treatment condition* in which the patients receive pills containing active ingredients, (b) a *placebo condition* in which the patients receive pills that do not contain active ingredients, and (c) a *no-treatment condition* in which the patients do not receive pills. The degree to which patients in the placebo condition showed greater improvement than the patients in the no-treatment condition reflects the placebo effect, and the degree to which the patients in the treatment condition showed greater improvement than the patients in the placebo condition reflects the actual effect of the treatment. This effect is illustrated in Figure 3.11. Note that placebo effects are not limited to drugs; they also occur with psychological interventions such as psychotherapy. Unfortunately, it is much more difficult to design a placebo control condition for an experiment on psychotherapy, but one is essential nevertheless.

The effects of suggestion influence not only the subjects in experiments but also raters who are evaluating the subjects. For example, if a depressed patient is given a treatment that the therapist thinks will help, the therapist may selectively notice improvements in the patient (e.g., smiles) and ignore behaviors that suggest lack of improvement (e.g., lack of activity). To avoid the effects of suggestion on both patients and raters, we can use a **double-blind procedure** in which neither the patients nor the raters know which patients are receiving the real treatment and which patients are receiving the placebo. In double-blind experiments on the effects of drugs, patients in the ex-

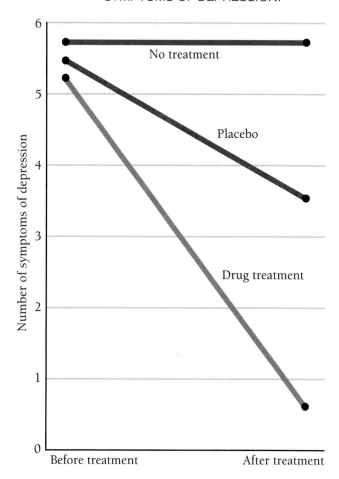

FIGURE 3.11   RESULTS OF AN EXPERIMENT COMPARING THE EFFECTS OF DRUG TREATMENT, PLACEBO TREATMENT, AND NO TREATMENT ON THE SYMPTOMS OF DEPRESSION.

perimental condition are given pills containing active ingredients while those in the placebo condition are given pills with no active ingredients, but neither the patients nor the raters know which patients are receiving the medication and which are receiving the placebo.

Strategies for Avoiding Practical and Ethical Problems

Experiments are the best means of establishing causal relationships, but it is often impossible to conduct experiments because of practical problems. For example, when studying the effects of bad parenting, it is not feasible to get parents to behave badly toward their children for 10 years. Similarly, when studying the effects of prolonged stress, we cannot experimentally manipulate events such as wars, earthquakes, and deaths of family members.

It is also sometimes impossible to use experiments to study the causes of abnormal behavior because it is unethical to knowingly cause abnormal behavior. We could not do the experiment on the effects of bad parenting because it would be unethical to intentionally expose children to bad parenting techniques that we suspect will result in abnormal behavior. Similarly, we could not study the effects of brain damage on behavior by cutting out parts of the brains of individuals in an experimental condition. Because of these practical and ethical problems, we must sometimes rely on alternative techniques for studying the causes of abnormal behavior.

Animal Research.   One strategy that is used to avoid some practical and ethical problems is to do experiments on animals (Mineka, 1985). For example, when investigators were interested in determining the effects of extreme social isolation on the emotional development of infants, they raised monkeys in complete isolation (Harlow, 1959). In research on the effects of brain damage on abnormal behavior, parts of the brains of rats and monkeys were destroyed, and then the effects on the animals' behavior were studied. However, research on animals does pose some problems. For example, there is always the practical problem of generalizing the results obtained with animals to humans. Is a monkey's emotional response comparable to a human's emotional response? Can a monkey develop schizophrenia? Furthermore, ethical standards also place limitations on what can be done with animals. Whereas once animals were treated as objects, today they are accorded many of the rights formerly reserved for humans, such as protection from undue pain.

Analogue Research.   A second means of overcoming practical and ethical problems is to do **analogue** (AN-uh-log) **research**. An *analogue* is something that is *similar* to something else, and in analogue research we study procedures and behaviors that are similar to but not as extreme as those in which we are really interested. For example, we cannot expose children to years of bad parenting, but we could bring children into a laboratory for an hour and have them interact with an individual who acted either in a mildly hostile manner (experimental condition) or in a neutral manner (control condition). We would not expect the brief experience with the mildly hostile individual to result in long-term serious abnormal behavior, but it could cause moderate and brief forms of tension, anxiety, or withdrawal. From that we might assume that if children were exposed to a more hostile individual for a longer period, real or more serious abnormal behavior

Animals are used in research when it is impractical or unethical to use humans. For example, to determine the relative importance of contact and feeding in forming attachments, this monkey was raised with a cloth "mother" and a wire "mother" that contained a feeding bottle. The study showed that the monkey preferred the cloth mother (contact) and went to the wire mother only for nourishment. Clearly, this study could not have been conducted on a human infant.

would result. The problem with analogue research is that we can never be positive of the degree to which we can generalize from our analogous procedures and behaviors to the real procedures and behaviors in which we are interested.

Quasi-Experimental Research.   A third means of avoiding some of the practical and ethical problems of experimental research is to use **quasi-experimental research** (Cook & Campbell, 1979). In quasi-experimental research, we do not actually manipulate the independent variable. Instead, we take advantage of naturally occurring situations in which there are differences in the independent variable. For example, if we were studying the effects of chronic stress on the development of depression, we might compare the people who live near a potentially dangerous nuclear power plant to those who live near a nondangerous coal-fired power plant (Baum et al., 1993). If the people living near the two different types of power plants are the same on all other variables (age, sex, race, intelligence, socioeconomic status, ethnic background), but those who lived near the nuclear power plant are more depressed, we might conclude that the chronic stress of living near a dangerous power plant led to depression. The important thing to recognize about quasi-experimental research is that subjects are not randomly assigned to conditions, and therefore we cannot be sure that the subjects in the conditions are comparable on all variables except the independent variable. It is possible that the individuals living near the nuclear power plant were more depressed before moving to that community or that some factor in the community other than the stress of the nuclear plant led to the depression.

Delayed Treatment.

When an experiment is conducted to test the effects of a particular treatment such as psychotherapy or drugs, subjects in the no-treatment control condition are not given any treatment. This raises an ethical problem because the experimenters are intentionally withholding a potentially effective treatment from individuals who need the treatment. Some researchers try to overcome this problem by arguing that when the experiment is conducted, they do not yet know for sure that the treatment is effective, and therefore they are not knowingly withholding an effective treatment from patients who need it. However, that argument is weakened by the fact that if they did not strongly believe that the treatment is effective, they would not be testing it. The ethical problem posed by withholding treatment may be avoided to some extent by providing the treatment to the subjects in the control condition after the experiment is over. With such a **delayed treatment** procedure, everyone gets the treatment, but the patients in the control condition get it later. Giving the patients in the control condition delayed treatment can also add to our research findings because if the patients do not improve during the control (delay) period but then do improve when the treatment is begun, we have additional evidence from which to conclude that the treatment is effective.

Genetic Research

Genetic factors are playing an increasingly important role in our understanding of many physical and psychological disorders, and therefore it is essential to have an understanding of the procedures, promises and pitfalls of this area of research (Mullan & Murray, 1989; Pardes et al., 1989; Plomin et al, 1990; Reiss et al., 1991). Genetic research is not a *type* of research, like correlational and experimental research. Rather, it is a *topic* of research, but because it involves some

unique procedures and problems, it deserves special attention in this discussion of research methods.

Research Strategies.

The effects of genes are usually studied indirectly, and there are three methods by which that is done. The first is **family studies**. Members of a biological family share more genes with one another than they share with non–family members. Therefore, if abnormal behavior is due to genetic factors, it would be expected that the biological relatives of individuals with a particular disorder would be more likely to have the disorder than the biological relatives of individuals who do not have the disorder. In other words, it would be expected that abnormal behavior would "run in families." However, even if it were found that a disorder did run in families, we could not necessarily conclude that the disorder was due to genetic factors because family members usually share the same environment as well as some of the same genes.

The second method involves **twin studies. Monozygotic** (MON-ō-zī-GOT-ik; MZ) or "identical" twins have *identical* genes, and **dizygotic** (DĪ-zī-GOT-ik; DZ) or "fraternal" twins do not, so if a disorder is due to genetic factors, the disorder will be more likely to co-occur in MZ than DZ twin pairs. The rate of co-occurrence is called the **concordance** (kun-KŌR-dens) **rate**.

With data obtained from monozygotic and dizygotic twins, we can estimate the degree (proportion) to which a particular characteristic (e.g., depression) is due to genetic factors. The simplest way to do that is to subtract the correlation for DZ twins from the correlation for MZ twins and multiply the difference by 2. For example, if depression is correlated .40 in MZ

Studying monozygotic ("identical") twins who were reared apart is one way to determine genetic influences on behavior. This pair of twins was separated at birth and reunited at age 32. Both had become firefighters and apparently share many personality traits.

twins and .15 in DZ twins, we could conclude that about 50% of the variability in depression is due to genetic factors ($.40 - .15 = .25 \times 2 = .50$; Falconer, 1960). That formula provides only a rough estimate (and sometimes an overestimate) of the effects of genes; a variety of more complicated and sophisticated methods have been developed.

One potential problem in the study of twins is the possibility that MZ twins share more personal experiences than DZ twins (e.g., greater overlap of friends, similar dressing), and if that were the case, part of the higher concordance rate among MZ twins could be due to their shared experiences rather than to their shared genes (Loehlin & Nichols, 1976). There is evidence that the overlap in experiences is not an important factor, but we should keep it in mind (Plomin et al., 1990).

The third indirect method for studying genetic factors involves **adoptee studies**. With this method, investigators examine the rates of a disorder in children who were born to disordered or normal parents but were adopted at birth and raised by normal parents. The children have the genes of either disordered or normal parents, but they are all raised in normal social environments. Therefore, if the offspring of disordered parents show a higher rate of the disorder than the offspring of normal parents, it could be concluded that genetic factors contributed to the development of the disorders. This is the most convincing of the indirect methods.

A fourth approach involves studying genes themselves, a strategy that has been made possible by recent technological advances. A variety of reports has been based on this approach, but the findings have been very inconsistent, and therefore this approach has not yet yielded any firm conclusions.

Genetic Research and Environmental Factors.

If we can determine how much of the variability in a disorder is due to genetic factors, by subtraction we can determine how much may be due to environmental factors. In our example on depression, 50% of the variability was due to genetics, so as much as 50% of the variability could be due to environmental factors. However, two qualifications concerning that conclusion should be noted. First, when considering environmental variables, it is essential to recognize that they are not limited to the *social* variables such as economic class, interpersonal relations, and conflict that are usually thought of when the concept of environment is mentioned. Environmental factors also include a host of *physiological* variables such as hormone exposure during prenatal development, maternal illness during prenatal development, complications during the birth

process, and exposure to physical traumas and toxins (e.g., lead) later in life. We are now learning that these nonsocial environmental factors are very important in a variety of disorders.

Second, we may *overestimate* the amount of variability due to environmental factors when we subtract the variability due to genetics from the total variability (100%) and assume that the remaining variability is due to environmental factors. The problem is that other sources of variability, such as errors in our measurement and yet unthought-of factors, are also included in that remaining variability, thus artificially inflating the amount of variability that we attribute to environmental factors. Indeed, it has been estimated that errors in our measurement of personality and abnormal behavior may contribute between 15% and 30% of the variability that is not accounted for by genetic factors (Tellegen et al., 1988). The remaining variability is due to environmental factors *plus* some undetermined amount of variability due to errors.

A Comment on Statistics

After data have been collected, it is essential that they be evaluated objectively, and to do that we use a wide variety of **statistical tests**. A thorough discussion of these tests is beyond the scope of this book, but a few general comments are necessary to put the test results into perspective so that you can evaluate them.

Most statistical tests are used to assess the reliability of the findings of an investigation. For example, if we collect data and then compute a correlation between scores measuring "bad parenting" and scores measuring "maladjustment in children," we might find that the scores are correlated +.30. Once we have the correlation, we have to determine whether it reflects a *real* relationship that would be found again if we collected a new set of data or whether it is due to *chance*, a one-time fluke. To make that determination, we use a statistical test that will indicate how many times in 100 we could expect that particular correlation to occur by chance. If the results of the test indicate that the correlation would be expected to occur fewer than 5 times in 100 by chance, we can conclude that the correlation is **statistically significant**. Stated in another way, a statistically significant result is one that would be expected to occur in at least 95% of investigations (i.e., 95 times out of 100). Similarly, if we conduct an experiment and find that children who were treated badly have a mean maladjustment score of 40, whereas the children who were treated well have a mean maladjustment score of 10, we have to determine whether the difference in means was due to the way children were treated or to chance. If a statistical test indicates that the difference in means would be expected to occur fewer than 5 times in 100 by chance, we can conclude that the difference in means is statistically significant.

This is fairly straightforward, but there are two conceptual problems you should keep in mind. First, the results may be statistically significant, but *if the experiment is confounded, the results are meaningless.* That is, the fact that the results are statistically significant does not mean that they are valid. In evaluating any finding, it is essential to determine whether it is methodologically sound.

The second problem stems from the use of the word *significant.* Most people assume that the word significant means "important," but as used by statisticians, the word *significant* means "reliable." Therefore, it is essential that you not misinterpret a "statistically significant" (reliable) effect as necessarily important because a great many statistically significant findings are in fact *trivial.* For example, we may find that a particular treatment has a statistically significant effect on patients' depression scores, but the treatment may change the scores by only 2 points on a scale that runs from 1 to 100. The 2-point change may be reliable (statistically significant) but trivial.

The problem of differentiating between statistically significant and important findings can be easily illustrated with a correlation. To determine the strength of a correlation, *square* it, and the resulting value will indicate the percentage of variability in one variable that can be accounted for by the other variable. For example, correlations of .30 are typical in the behavioral sciences and are often reliable, but with a correlation of .30 you can account for only 9% of the variability. That is, if parenting and abnormal behavior were correlated .30, knowing how bad the parenting had been would allow us to account for only 9% of the differences in behavior.

Because our statistical tests assess only statistical significance, it is essential that we go on to determine the **clinical significance** or practical importance of our findings. A variety of attempts has been made to develop a quantitative approach to determining clinical significance, but they have been largely unsuccessful, and in most cases clinical significance is assessed with a *subjective* judgment (Jacobson, 1988; Jacobson & Truax, 1991; Speer, 1992). In summary, then, just as "all that glitters is not gold," all results that are statistically significant are not important, and we must be careful to separate the important from the trivial among the "significant." All of the research findings reported in this book are statistically significant (reliable), and I have attempted to select findings that were clinically or theoretically significant as well.

In this introductory discussion of research methods, we have considered merely the basic issues in a very complex area. We will deal with other, more complicated issues as they arise in the context of our discussion of abnormal behavior.

■ SUMMARY

We began this chapter with a discussion of the diagnostic system that is used in the United States to classify abnormal behavior. The system is known as DSM-IV, and it relies almost exclusively on current symptoms for determining a diagnosis. Five axes are used to describe the individual. Axes I and II are used to describe the individual's major symptoms and personality problems. Axis III is used to indicate whether the individual has any medical conditions that are related to the disorder. Axis IV is used to indicate whether there are any psychosocial or environmental problems that influence the disorder. Axis V is used to rate the individual's current and previous levels of functioning. The use of the five axes results in a much more complete picture of the individual than was the case with earlier systems. Unfortunately, with any diagnostic system, some of the individual's uniqueness is lost. Specifically, once an individual is given a diagnosis, we may overlook the presence of behaviors not contained in the diagnosis, or we may assume that the individual has behaviors that in fact he or she does not have.

Next we reviewed the various methods used to assess persons. They include observations, interviews, psychological testing (objective, projective, intelligence, and neuropsychological), and physiological testing (CT, MRI, and PET scans). It was pointed out that some tests are more useful than others in helping clinicians make accurate judgments, and because behaviors change, sometimes measuring current behavior cannot help explain past behavior or predict future behavior. The importance of situations for influencing behavior was also recognized. We then discussed comorbidity and its implications for understanding symptom patterns and planning treatments. Despite the refinements introduced by the DSM, errors in diagnosis can be introduced by differences in subjectivity, suggestion, and fads.

We examined four methods of studying abnormal behavior. The first was the case study method, in which personal history is examined in an attempt to find an explanation for an individual's behavior. Case studies can provide a hypothesis about the causes of abnormal behavior, but they cannot be used to prove hypotheses because alternative explanations cannot be ruled out. Case studies are also limited in that they do not enable us to determine the degree to which an explanation is applicable to other individuals.

The second approach was correlation research, in which the co-occurrence of two variables is studied in numerous individuals. This is an improvement over the case study method because the reliability of the observed relationship can be tested. However, a correlation between two variables does not necessarily mean that there is a causal relationship between them because the relationship could be due to the influence of a third variable. Furthermore, even if there is a causal relationship, the correlation does not tell us whether differences in variable A cause differences in variable B or vice versa.

The third approach we discussed was controlled experimental research, in which the independent variable is manipulated in the experimental condition but not the control condition, and then the effects on the dependent variable are measured. Controlled experimental research is effective for documenting causal relationships.

The next approach we considered was the multiple-baseline approach, in which subjects are observed over a series of periods during which the independent variable is sometimes manipulated and sometimes held constant. If the dependent variable changes over periods as a function of whether or not the independent variable has been manipulated, it can be concluded that there is a causal relationship between the independent and dependent variables.

Placebo effects (due to expectations about the effect of a treatment) and demand characteristics (pressure to report what persons think they should be experiencing rather than what they are experiencing) can lead to false conclusions concerning the effects of independent variables. To overcome these problems, a double-blind procedure can be used in which neither the person nor the experimenter who is evaluating the person's behavior knows whether the person has been given a placebo or a real treatment.

To overcome various practical and ethical problems associated with research on abnormal behavior, it has sometimes been necessary to use animal, analogue, and quasi-experimental research. Each of those strategies is effective for avoiding problems, but each has its own limitations (e.g., problems of generalizing from animals to humans, use of procedures that are similar but not identical to those of interest, nonrandom assignment of subjects).

Next we discussed genetic research. Indirect means of studying the effects of genes include the study of families, the comparison of concordance rates in monozygotic and dizygotic twin pairs, and adoptee studies in which rates of disorders are compared between children who are raised by their biological parents or by adoptive parents. Recent technological advances have also enabled researchers to examine specific genes directly. Finally, it was pointed out that statistical tests are used to assess the reliability of research findings, and that statistically significant finding is reliable but not necessarily valid or important. There is not yet a good means of assessing clinical (practical) significance.

With the material from the first three chapters as background, we can now begin our discussion of specific disorders.

KEY TERMS, CONCEPTS, AND NAMES

In reviewing and testing yourself on what you have learned from this chapter, you should be able to identify and discuss each of the following:

adoptee studies (in genetics)
analogue research
axes (in diagnostic systems)
Axis I: Clinical Syndromes
Axis II: Personality Disorders
Axis III: General Medical Conditions
Axis IV: Psychosocial and
    Environmental Problems
Axis V: Global Assessment of
    Functioning
case study research
checklists of symptoms
Children's Apperception Test (CAT)
clinical significance
comorbidity
computerized axial tomography (CT
    scan)
concordance rate
confounded

control condition
controlled experimental research
correlational research
correlation coefficient (*r*)
delayed treatment
demand characteristics
dependent variable
diagnostic system
dizygotic
double-blind procedure
Draw-A-Person Test
DSM-IV
electroencephalograph (EEG)
experimental condition
experimental manipulation
experimental research
family studies (in genetics)
Halstead-Reitan Neuropsychology
    Battery

House-Tree-Person Test
Incomplete Sentences Test
independent variable
intelligence testing
interviewing (for diagnosis)
Luria-Nebraska (neuropsychological
    test)
magnetic resonance imaging (MRI)
Minnesota Multiphasic Personality
    Inventory (MMPI, MMPI-2, MMPI-A)
monozygotic
multiple-baseline experimental
    research
neuropsychological testing
objective testing
observation (for diagnosis)
performance intelligence
physiological testing (for diagnosis)
placebo effect

positron emission tomography (PET scan)
posttest
pretest
projection
projective tests
psychological testing
quasi-experimental research
random assignment
reliability

Rorschach test
sphygmomanometer
Stanford-Binet (intelligence test)
statistically significant
statistical tests
structured interview
Thematic Apperception Test (TAT)
twin studies (in genetics)
unstructured interview
validity

verbal intelligence
Wechsler Adult Intelligence Scale (WAIS, WAIS-R)
Wechsler Intelligence Scale for Children (Third Edition) (WISC-III)
Wechsler Preschool-Primary Scale of Intelligence (WPPSI)
X-rays

PART 2

Anxiety, Somatoform, and Dissociative Disorders

•OUTLINE•

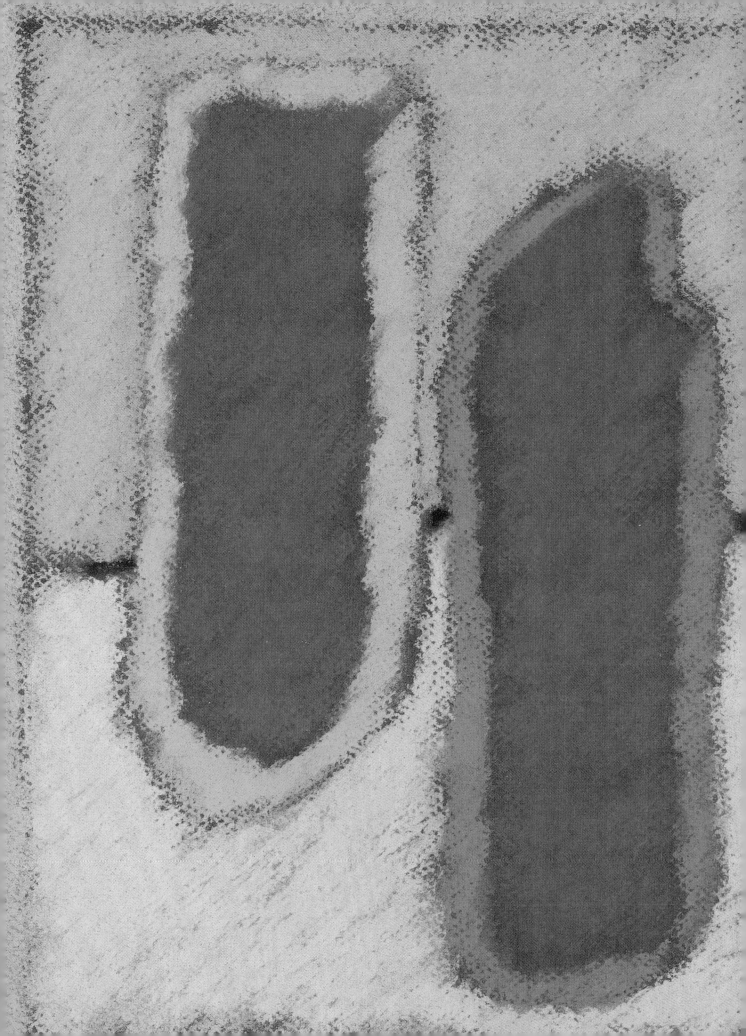

Chapter 4

Anxiety Disorders: Symptoms and Issues

• O U T L I N E •

Four months ago, while Elaine was in a clothing store, she began trembling and having hot flashes. Suddenly she developed a sharp pain in her chest and her heart began beating very rapidly. She was dizzy and short of breath and felt as though she were going to pass out or die. Everything was out of focus and seemed to be spinning around. She was terrified! A saleswoman called an ambulance, and Elaine was rushed to the emergency room of a nearby hospital. Heart and blood tests did not reveal any evidence of a heart attack or any other abnormality. Since the first attack, she has had two others, one while at a movie and one while at home reading. These attacks "just come out of the blue" and are very frightening. Elaine suffers from a *panic disorder*, a type of anxiety state.

David is afraid of snakes. His palms sweat, his heart rate increases dramatically, and he feels very tense when he sees even a small garden snake that he knows is not harmful. In fact, he becomes tense when he sees snakes on television. He also shows some anxiety when he sees other reptiles such as alligators. David knows that his fear of snakes is irrational, but he cannot control his emotional response. David suffers from a *phobia*.

Over a period of a year, Mrs. Wilson began leaving her house less and less, and usually she would not go out unless someone was with her. She could not explain exactly what it was that she was afraid of; she just felt that something terrible would happen if she left the house. Finally she stopped going out at all, and it has now been more than 4 years since she has left the house. Mrs. Wilson does not show any other unusual behavior, and she is fine as long as she is at home. Mrs. Wilson suffers from a disorder known as *agoraphobia*.

Lennie served as a rifleman in Vietnam. That was almost 30 years ago, but the experience still haunts him. He frequently has nightmares about his experiences fighting in the jungle, and occasionally during the day something will happen, such as a helicopter flying overhead, that will bring the experiences back. Not all of the experiences come back; there are large blocks of time for which he has no memories. Lennie often catches himself scanning his surroundings looking for hidden danger. His underlying tension and fear make him emotionally distant and interfere with his personal relationships. Lennie shows the symptoms of a *posttraumatic stress disorder*.

The first three chapters of Part 2 are devoted to the **anxiety disorders**. As the name implies, in these disorders anxiety is the major symptom or the cause of other symptoms. Anxiety is also a symptom in a variety of other disorders. For example, it is common for depressed individuals to be anxious, and we often see anxiety as a symptom in schizophrenia. However, in the anxiety disorders, anxiety is the *primary symptom* or is the *primary cause* of other symptoms, whereas in the other disorders, anxiety is the *result* of other problems. For example, a woman who is suffering from depression may be anxious because she believes that she is a useless failure and doomed to a life of misery. Similarly, a man with schizophrenia may be anxious because he has a delusion that his brain is being destroyed by gamma waves from the planet Egregious. It is important to keep the distinction between primary and secondary anxiety in mind when making diagnoses and planning treatments. With that point clarified, we can go on to consider the symptoms of anxiety.

SYMPTOMS OF ANXIETY

Mood Symptoms

The mood symptoms in anxiety disorders consist primarily of anxiety, tension, panic, and apprehension. The individual suffering from anxiety has the feeling of impending doom and disaster from some specific or unknown source.

Other mood symptoms associated with anxiety often include depression and irritability. The depression can stem from the fact that the individual may not see a solution for his or her problems and is ready to give up and "throw in the towel." Loss of sleep due to anxiety can lead to irritability. Both depression and irritability are considered secondary symptoms because they stem from the anxiety that is the primary symptom.

Cognitive Symptoms

The cognitive symptoms in anxiety disorders reflect the apprehensiveness and concern about the doom the individual anticipates. For example, an individual who has a fear of being out in public (agoraphobia) will spend a great deal of time worrying about the terrible things that might happen in public and planning how to avoid them. Furthermore, because attention is focused on those potential disasters, the person does not attend to the real problems at hand and is therefore inattentive and distractible. As a consequence of the inappropriate focusing of attention, the individual often does not work or study effectively, and that can add to the anxieties.

Somatic Symptoms

The somatic symptoms of anxiety can be divided into two groups. First are the *immediate* symptoms, which consist of sweating, dry mouth, shallow breathing, rapid pulse, increased blood pressure, throbbing sensations in the head, and feelings of muscular tension. These symptoms reflect the *high level of arousal* of the autonomic nervous system, the same responses that we see in fear. Additional symptoms can occur because the individual begins breathing too rapidly, a process known as **hyperventilation**. Hyperventilation can result in light-headedness, headache, tingling of the extremities, heart palpitations, chest pain, and breathlessness. These primary somatic symptoms are what you would experience if your professor suddenly announced a pop quiz that would be worth half your grade!

Second, if the anxiety is prolonged, *delayed* symptoms such as chronically increased blood pressure, headaches, muscular weakness, and intestinal distress (poor digestion, stomach cramps) may set in. These symptoms reflect *fatigue* or *breakdown* of the physiological system stemming from the prolonged arousal. These are the symptoms you might experience if you failed the quiz referred to earlier and then worried about failing for the rest of the semester. In some cases, the prolonged arousal can cause serious tissue damage or illness (for example, prolonged stomach acidity can lead to ulcers; see Chapter 17).

Not everyone who experiences anxiety will experience the same physical symptoms. That is because there are individual differences in the patterning of autonomic reactivity (Lacey, 1950, 1967). For example, when I am anxious, I tend to experience muscular tenseness, particularly in my throat (a response that, if prolonged, results in a change in or loss of my voice). Someone else may be more likely to respond with increased blood pressure (which, if prolonged, can result in hypertension).

Motor Symptoms

Anxious individuals often exhibit restlessness, fidgeting, pointless motor activity such as toe tapping, and exaggerated startle responses to sudden noise. These motor symptoms reflect the individuals' high levels of cognitive and somatic arousal and their attempts to protect themselves from what they see as threatening. Because the activities are random or not sufficiently focused on one goal, they are often unproductive and can interfere with effective functioning. For example, if you are anxious before a test, you may pace your room randomly, but the pacing does not make you feel better and will even prevent you from doing some useful last-minute studying.

With this description of the symptoms of anxiety as background, we can now go on to consider the *phobic disorders* and *anxiety states* in which anxiety plays the primary role.

PHOBIC DISORDERS AND ANXIETY STATES

The anxiety disorders can be divided into two major categories, **phobic disorders** and **anxiety states**. The disorders in these two categories differ in terms of the degree to which the anxiety is *localized* or *diffused*. In the case of phobic disorders, the anxiety is localized and associated with one particular object or situation. For example, an individual may become very anxious when confronted with spiders or when in a tall building. By contrast, in anxiety states, the anxiety is diffused, not related to any one thing, and is experienced as omnipresent or free-floating. An individual suffering from an anxiety state may feel as though his or her entire life is enveloped in an electrified cloud or that every turn bodes doom and disaster from which there is no escape. In the sections that follow, we will consider phobic disorders first because they are somewhat simpler and clear-cut; then we will go on to examine anxiety states. The subtypes of the phobic disorders and anxiety states are listed in Table 4.1.

Phobic Disorders

Phobias are *persistent and irrational fears of a specific object, activity, or situation.* Phobias involve fears that have *no justification* in reality (for example, fear of open spaces) or fears that are *greater than what is justified* (for example, extreme fear of flying).

An important aspect of the phobic fear is that *the individual is aware of the irrationality of the fear.* In other words, people with phobias know that their fear is not really justified, but at the same time they cannot simply stop being afraid. For example, the individual

TABLE 4.1   CLASSIFICATION OF ANXIETY
                    DISORDERS

PHOBIC DISORDERS	ANXIETY STATES
Agoraphobia	Panic disorder
Social phobias	Generalized anxiety disorder
Specific phobias	Posttraumatic stress disorder
	Obsessive-compulsive disorder
	Acute stress disorder

who has an elevator phobia *knows* that there are hundreds of thousands of elevators, *knows* that every day of the year those elevators each make hundreds of trips without anyone getting hurt, and *knows* that the probability of getting hurt in an elevator is very low (maybe even lower than when walking up stairs). Despite that knowledge, however, the individual is still afraid to ride in an elevator. This knowledge of the reality of the situation is important because it distinguishes an individual with a phobia from an individual with a **delusion**, which is an unjustified belief about the world that the individual does not recognize as wrong. Delusions usually reflect a much more serious problem (see Chapter 12). In the phobic disorders, then, we see an inappropriate separation of the cognitive and emotional aspects of psychological functioning.

There is a great deal of variability in the degree to which phobias interfere with an individual's ability to function. The degree to which a phobia will be disruptive is determined in part by the likelihood that the individual will encounter the feared object or situation in daily life. *Claustrophobia* (KLOS-trō-FŌ-bē-uh), a fear of small enclosed places, would not be particularly disruptive for a Kansas wheat farmer, but it could pose a serious problem for an office worker living in New York City who must frequently spend time in cramped elevators, small offices, and crowded subway cars. Many people have phobias for harmless insects, but because they do not encounter the insects on a regular basis, those fears do not have a major effect on their lives.

Phobias can lead to disruptive behavior in two ways. First, if the feared object or situation can be avoided easily, the avoidance may result in unfortunate consequences. For example, an individual with an elevator phobia who had a job on the 15th floor might have to quit the job and take a less desirable job on a lower floor in order to avoid taking the elevator. Second, if the feared object or situation cannot be avoided easily, the individual may experience uncontrollable and overwhelming fear and panic. When that occurs, the individual may show very embarrassing and inappropriate emotional outbreaks, fainting, and attempts to escape.

The case of the sportscaster John Madden illustrates the inconvenience caused by a phobia. Rather than taking a few hours to fly from New York to San Francisco to broadcast a football game, he must spend 3 or 4 days on a train or a bus to get to his destination. His symptoms are discussed in Case Study 4.1.

Phobic disorders are probably more common than you realize because people with phobias often conceal their problems effectively. I was completely unaware of a colleague's rather severe elevator phobia because each time we went to our offices on the fourth

Case Study 4.1

JOHN MADDEN: A 260-POUND "FRAIDY-CAT"?

John Madden is 6 feet 4 inches tall and weighs 260 pounds. As a football player, he was an offensive and defensive tackle, and following his playing career, he was the coach of the Oakland Raiders football team for 10 years. Madden is not the sort of fellow you would expect to be afraid of much, but guess again. Madden suffers from a variety of fears, most of which seem to stem from claustrophobia.

Sportscaster John Madden suffers from a fear of flying that greatly interferes with his professional life because he must take a train or a bus from coast to coast to broadcast football games.

Madden's fear of being hemmed in is very general. He is afraid of planes, elevators, crowds, and even tight-fitting clothing. The anxiety that keeps him out of planes causes him considerable inconvenience because as a sportscaster, he must make frequent trips from coast to coast to broadcast football games. Rather than making the trip in a matter of a few hours by plane, it takes him 3 or 4 days to make the trip on a train.

Originally, Madden misdiagnosed his symptoms of anxiety as the effects of an inner-ear infection. Whenever he flew, he became tense, and he thought that the tension was a physiological reaction to the altitude. He soon realized, however, that the symptoms started "as soon as the stewardess closed the door"—before the plane was off the ground. "One day I had a flight from Tampa to California with a stop in Houston. I got off there, checked into a hotel, and never flew again." Madden reports that at first he was embarrassed by his phobia, but now he publicly jokes about it.

As is often the case with individuals who suffer from claustrophobia, Madden's fears and anxieties are not limited to small places. Madden's more general anxiety is reflected in the fact that he is a chronic worrier. He points out that he gave up his very successful coaching career with the Raiders because "the constant worrying made the seasons run together, and I just burned out." Undoubtedly because of his constant worrying, Madden suffers from a bleeding ulcer.

Source: Adapted from Leershen (1984).

---

floor, he would say something like, "Let's take the stairs. The exercise will be good for us." I became aware of his problem only when one day we had to move some heavy boxes to the sixth floor, and after the boxes were loaded into the elevator, he told me he would take the stairs and meet me at the top.

Phobic disorders are divided into three groups as a function of the type of situation that elicits the fear. We can now go on to consider these types of phobias.

Agoraphobia. The major symptom of **agoraphobia** (AG-uh-ruh-FŌ-bē-uh) is *fear of being in public places from which escape might be difficult* if the individual suddenly became anxious. In a sense, agoraphobia is a fear of becoming afraid, and it is associated with public places because in those situations the fear would be most disruptive and embarrassing. Often individuals with agoraphobia also have a fear of being alone be-

cause if they begin experiencing their fear, they want a friend around to help them.

Because of the fear associated with public places, the lives of people with agoraphobia become dominated by their attempts to avoid contact with large groups of people. Therefore, these individuals may confine themselves to their homes and venture out as little as possible. They do not avoid crowds because they have any delusions or because they are depressed and want to be alone. Instead, being in crowds makes them fearful because "something" might happen to them. Like my friend who concealed his elevator phobia from me, persons with agoraphobia are often successful in concealing their fears by declining social invitations. Furthermore, because they avoid social gatherings, we have less contact with them and are therefore less likely to realize that they have a problem. An example of agoraphobia is presented in Case Study 4.2 (p. 81).

The scene on the left made a woman with a spider phobia very nervous because it reminded her of spiders in a web. Her response illustrates the fact that stimuli associated with the feared stimulus can elicit fear. For most people the scene on the right would be a beautiful view. But a person with a phobia of heights would find it terrifying.

Social Phobia.   Like agoraphobia, **social phobia** also results in an avoidance of groups, but rather than stemming from some vague fear of losing control, a social phobia is generally based on the individual's *irrational fear that he or she will behave in an embarrassing way and then be criticized by others.* A social phobia is then primarily a fear of criticism, and an individual with a social phobia avoids people to avoid criticism (Turner & Beidel, 1989; Trower & Gilbert, 1989).

The anxiety of a person with a social phobia does not stem from any specific delusion (e.g., that others are plotting against him or her) but rather from a general fear that he or she will be criticized for inept behavior. Obviously, a social phobia can severely constrict a person's life. An example of a relatively minor social phobia is presented in Case Study 4.3 (p. 82).

Specific Phobia.   A **specific phobia** involves an *irrational fear about an object or situation other than crowds (agoraphobia) and personal criticism (social phobia).* As such, specific phobia is a residual category that includes all of the other possible phobias. Some specif-

ic phobias are listed in Table 4.2. Traditionally, phobias were named with the Greek word for the feared object or situation, but this is no longer done consistently (note the use of the terms *agoraphobia* and *social phobia*), and because it only adds confusion, it may soon be abandoned.

Anxiety States

Anxiety states differ from phobic disorders in that in anxiety states, *the emotional response is diffused and not related to any one particular situation or stimulus.* In these disorders, the anxiety is said to be "free-floating." We can distinguish four types of anxiety states, and they will be considered in the following sections.

Panic Disorder.   A **panic disorder** involves *brief periods of exceptionally intense spontaneous anxiety.* These periods come and go suddenly, usually lasting only a few minutes, and their occurrence is unpredictable. They seem to come "out of the blue" and can even start during sleep (*nocturnal panic attacks*). In addition to intense psychological feelings of apprehension, fear, and terror, the individual experiences physical

TABLE 4.2   SOME SPECIFIC PHOBIAS

Acrophobia: fear of high places	Mysophobia: fear of contamination
Algophobia: fear of pain	Nyctophobia: fear of darkness
Astraphobia: fear of storms	Ochlophobia: fear of crowds
Claustrophobia: fear of small places	Pathophobia: fear of disease
Hematophobia: fear of blood	Syphilophobia: fear of syphilis
Monophobia: fear of being alone	Zoophobia: fear of animals

Case Study 4.2

THE WOMAN WHO WENT TO BED DRESSED: A CASE OF AGORAPHOBIA

Ann is a 34-year-old college-educated woman who is married and the mother of two children. When I first met her, she impressed me as being mature, attractive, and personally outgoing. Ann had a normal childhood and adolescence, and her early adult life had gone smoothly. However, about 3 years ago, she began to feel somewhat "tense, nervous, and upset" whenever she left the house to shop, go to a party, or car-pool the children.

At first, the anxiety was relatively low, and she described it as a "vague tension that sort of came from nowhere." As time went by, however, the level of anxiety became progressively greater. Within a year, her anxiety while out of the house was so high that she was unable to go more than a few blocks from home unless her husband or her sister were with her "for protection." Sometimes even when she was out with them she would begin to tremble, have "hot flashes," and start sweating, and she would eventually have to leave wherever she was and go home as quickly as possible. This resulted in a variety of embarrassing situations. For example, she left parties abruptly, fled from crowded stores, and once ran out of church in the middle of the service. When friends noticed her unusual behavior, she would explain it by saying that she was "tired," "not feeling well," or had a lot of work at home that needed to be done.

It got to the point where Ann rarely ventured out of the house, and even when she did, it was only for very brief periods, and she never went far. If Ann thought about going out of the house, she would be so anxious by the time she was supposed to leave that she would not be able to leave. To get around this problem, when it was necessary for her to shop, Ann would go to bed the night before fully dressed and made up. When she awoke the next morning, she would immediately jump out of bed and run out of the house, hoping to get to the store before her anxiety got so high that she would have to stop and return home. This worked about half of the time, but sometimes she would get "trapped in the checkout line" and have to leave her basket and rush home in a panic.

Ann could not explain why she became anxious when she left the house. She could only say that there might be "an emergency," but she could not remember an emergency ever occurring, and she could not think of what emergency might occur other than getting sick. She recognized the irrationality of her fear. She also realized that her fear was disrupting her life and her family, but try as she might, she could not suppress or overcome the fear.

---

symptoms that can include shortness of breath, heart palpitations, chest pains, choking or smothering sensations, dizziness, feelings of unreality, tingling of the extremities, hot and cold flashes, sweating, faintness, and trembling or shaking. An example of the changes in heart rate that are associated with a panic attack is presented in Figure 4.1 (p. 82). Those data were collected quite by chance when a woman happened to have a panic attack while she was receiving relaxation training and having her physiological responses monitored. Note that the attack occurred while she was relaxing in a nonstressful situation and that in less than 2 minutes her heart rate increased by 52 beats per minute, an increase of 81%. Because of the physical symptoms, an individual who is having a panic attack may think that he or she is having a heart attack. One patient who suffered from panic attacks said, "Most people only face dying once; I do it a couple of times a week! It's scary."

Panic attacks are very frightening. Individuals who experience panic attacks become concerned about losing control and often think that they are "going crazy," and therefore they sometimes begin avoiding public places in favor of staying home, where they feel safe. If the avoidance becomes extreme, the individual may be diagnosed as suffering from a **panic disorder with agoraphobia** rather than simply from a panic disorder. Between attacks, the individual is often anxious about possible impending attacks, therefore causing an elevated general level of anxiety. Because of that, sometimes individuals suffering from a panic disorder are erroneously diagnosed as suffering from a generalized anxiety disorder (to be discussed shortly).

It is important not to confuse panic attacks with the intense periods of arousal that are associated with physical exertion or the stress of real life-threatening situations. Furthermore, it should be noted that for many years panic attacks were misdiagnosed as cardiac or respiratory problems and treated accordingly, of course with no benefit to the patient. Fortunately, now that panic attacks are recognized as a psychological disorder, they are receiving widespread attention in the medical and public press, and the likelihood of misdiagnosis has been greatly reduced.

Case Study 4.3

"PHONE PHOBIA": A CASE OF A SOCIAL PHOBIA

The following account was written by an intelligent, professional woman who describes herself as suffering from a "phone phobia." That label is something of a misnomer because she is not anxious about the telephone but rather about the social interactions that take place on the phone.

"When I'm on the phone, I am extremely tense—it's as if I'm 'on the line,' and I am almost paralyzed with fear. I feel as though I have to justify making the call, have a good reason for calling so that I don't 'bother' the other person, and have to explain what I want clearly and briefly so as not to take up too much of the other person's time. I am always sure that I am going to make an ass of myself when I call someone.

"Over the years, I have developed certain strategies for dealing with my phone phobia. For any call, I establish a day and a time for making the call—it's on my calendar. However, I often postpone important calls if my level of tension is too high when they come up on my calendar. If I make the call and the other person is out, I am always relieved.

"I also feel threatened, tense, and anxious when I receive calls. I feel as if I'm being put on the spot, and I won't be able to think fast enough to come up with intelligent answers to the other person's questions. When the phone rings, I may start to tremble badly. To deal with my fear, I have established a firm rule for myself: I always pick up the phone after the second ring. With that rule, I give myself a little time to build up my courage, but I can't avoid the fear by not answering the phone. This phone phobia makes my professional and personal life really difficult. It's all rather crazy, but I can't get over it, so I just try to get around it."

FIGURE 4.1 INCREASED HEART RATE IN A WOMAN EXPERIENCING A PANIC ATTACK.

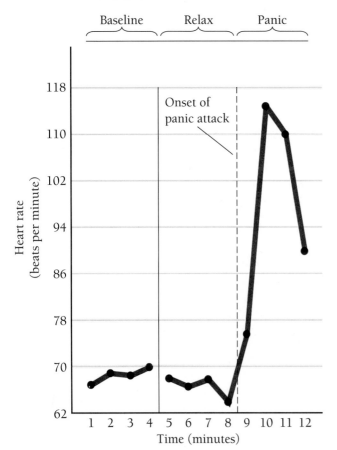

Source: Adapted from Cohen et al. (1985), p. 98, fig. 2.

The panic disorder is thought to be rather common; in one study of undergraduate students it was found that 2.4% met the criteria for having a panic disorder (Telch et al., 1989). A description of a rather mild panic attack in an undergraduate student of mine is presented in Case Study 4.4.

Generalized Anxiety Disorder. The **generalized anxiety disorder** involves *general, persistent anxiety that lasts for at least six months and is not associated with any particular object or situation* (Rapee, 1991). The anxiety is present constantly, and there is no escape from it. The prolonged nature of the anxiety separates it from the panic disorder, and it is usually less intense than what is seen in the panic disorder.

The generalized, omnipresent nature of the anxiety results in some additional problems that are not seen in the other anxiety disorders. Because the anxiety is general and not associated with a particular object, the individual does not know from where the threat and doom will come and must therefore be exceptionally vigilant and must continually scan the surroundings for the threat. This may result in debilitating effects such as distractibility and fatigue. To imagine what a generalized anxiety disorder is like, think about how you feel just before taking an exceptionally important examination, and then imagine those feelings lasting for months without your knowing why you are upset.

Posttraumatic Stress Disorder. The **posttraumatic stress disorder** has undoubtedly existed

Case Study 4.4

A PANIC ATTACK IN CLASS

An undergraduate student recently gave me the following account of one of her panic attacks.

"It was around 10:00 A.M. and I was taking notes in an introductory philosophy class. As I was writing, my hand started to tremble and I began having difficulty writing. My handwriting became steadily worse, and I started getting very dizzy. This had never happened to me in a class before, and I didn't know what to do. I thought about trying to leave the room, but I was afraid that I wouldn't make it to the door. I tried to get rid of the dizziness by laying my head down, but it only got worse. I was trembling so badly that I could not take notes, and in an attempt to hold on, I tried to focus all of my attention on the professor. It didn't work. I could barely see him, I couldn't hear him, and the room looked like a black-and-white photo negative. I became extremely frightened and thought that I was going to black out. The girl next to me saw that I was having trou-

ble and suggested that I leave the room, but I couldn't understand what she was saying—it was all a distant blur. Eventually I got up and stumbled out of the room—right in the middle of the lecture. I knew if I didn't walk out, I would be carried out. I sat down outside the classroom and put my head between my knees to get rid of the dizziness and blackness. It was several minutes before the symptoms went away and I could return to the classroom.

"Since that first attack, I have had five or six similar attacks. They are always extremely frightening, but now that I understand what's happening and know that I'll get over it and won't die or something, it's not quite as bad. Having the attacks can be very embarrassing, and I worry that sometime I am really going to make a fool out of myself somewhere. Fortunately, most times people just think I am getting sick and they are very sympathetic."

---

throughout history, but it has only gained widespread attention since it was observed in veterans of the Vietnam conflict. The major symptom of this disorder is the *reexperiencing of a traumatic event*. The traumatic events that precipitate this disorder are extreme; they include natural disasters (floods, earthquakes), accidental disasters (plane crashes, fires), and deliberate disasters (wars, torture, death camps, rape, assaults).

The reexperiencing may take the form of recur-

rent painful memories of the event, recurrent dreams or nightmares about the event, or "flashbacks" in which for some period of time (usually minutes or hours but sometimes longer) the individual relives the event and behaves as though experiencing the event at that moment. This reexperiencing phenomenon can persist for many years after the event. One victim of this disorder had experienced savage fighting as a 19-year-old GI in the Battle of the Bulge during World

Victims of disasters such as the World Trade Center bombing (left) or extreme political upheaval in the former Republic of Yugoslavia (right) may develop a posttraumatic stress disorder. Symptoms include recurrent painful memories of the event, recurrent dreams or nightmares, or even flashbacks.

War II. Today, five decades later, he still wakes up two or three nights a week with terrifying nightmares about the fighting.

In addition to the reexperiencing, there is often a general *numbing of responsiveness* or reduced involvement with the external world (Litz, 1992). This psychic numbing is apparent in diminished interest in usual activities, feelings of detachment from others, and blunted emotional responses when the individual is not reexperiencing the traumatic experience. In short, the individual has a limited and emotionally flattened life that is punctuated with intense emotional experiences involving the earlier trauma.

Finally, a number of other symptoms that are sometimes associated with a posttraumatic stress disorder reflect the individual's continuing general arousal. These symptoms include hyperalertness, problems with sleep, guilt about surviving when others did not, trouble concentrating, avoidance of activities that arouse memories of the traumatic event, and heightened arousal upon exposure to events that symbolize or resemble the traumatic event. An example of a posttraumatic stress disorder in a Vietnam veteran is presented in Case Study 4.5.

There is no doubt that the posttraumatic stress disorder is a real disorder that afflicts many people, but care must be taken not to apply the diagnosis indiscriminately. This is particularly the case with regard to Vietnam veterans. Those individuals were exposed to terrible stresses during their military service; undoubtedly many of them are still suffering the effects of those stresses, and they should be diagnosed and treated for posttraumatic stress disorders. However, it is easy to attribute apathy, lack of direction, adjustment problems, and failures to a posttraumatic stress disorder resulting from a Vietnam experience when in fact those feelings are due to some other cause. Those feelings and reactions are not necessarily uncommon among males as they move through middle adulthood (the "midlife identity crisis"). Therefore, we must be careful not to "suggest in" the disorder or use it to explain current problems that may stem from other causes.

It is also important that we not limit the diagnosis of posttraumatic stress disorder to individuals who have undergone the stress of combat. Veterans have gotten the most attention with regard to such disorders, but victims of natural disasters, accidents, child abuse, rape, and other crimes also suffer from posttraumatic stress disorders, and we must be sensitive to the influence that those experiences may have on their adjustment as well.

Obsessive-Compulsive Disorder. The **obsessive-compulsive disorder** involves *recurrent obsessions*

or compulsions or both. An **obsession** is a *persistent idea, thought, image, or impulse* that an individual cannot get out of his or her mind. Because they are not under voluntary control and are often repugnant to the individual, obsessions are said to be **ego-dystonic** (Ē-gō-dis-TON-ik). We all occasionally go through periods when we cannot get a thought or a tune out of our heads, although usually the content is not distasteful, the episodes do not last too long, and they would not be classified as obsessions or abnormal.

Obsessions and worries both involve perseverative thinking, but there are important differences between them and they should not be confused (Turner et al., 1992). In general, worries are usually related to everyday experiences (e.g., work, money, family), occur in the form of a thought, are not usually repugnant, are seen as controllable, and are not usually resisted by the individual. In contrast, obsessions generally revolve around a unique topic (e.g., dirt or contamination, death, aggression), often involve impulses as well as thoughts, are often repugnant, are seen as uncontrollable, and are resisted by the individual.

Common clinical obsessions are repetitive thoughts of violence (killing or harming someone), contamination (becoming infected with germs), and doubt (persistently wondering whether one has done something like hurting another individual). Obsessions can interfere with normal thoughts and thus can impair the individual's ability to function effectively. For example, it would be hard to study and perform well in school if you were constantly thinking about killing someone or worrying about the possibility that you forgot something important. Obsessions can also limit behavior. For example, an obsession with the possibility of infection may lead an individual to avoid situations that involve the possibility of dirt and germs.

True compulsions may briefly forestall anxiety. A compulsion such as stepping over cracks may not interfere with normal activities, but some compulsions can seriously disrupt normal functioning.

Case Study 4.5

POSTTRAUMATIC STRESS DISORDER: A VIETNAM VETERAN TALKS ABOUT HIS LIFE

My marriage is falling apart. We just don't talk anymore. Hell, I guess we've never really talked about anything, ever. I spend most of my time at home alone . . . she's upstairs and I'm downstairs. Sure we'll talk about the groceries and who will get gas for the car, but that's about it. She's tried to tell me she cares for me, but I get real uncomfortable talking about things like that, and I get up and leave.

I really don't have any friends and I'm pretty particular about who I want as a friend. The world is pretty much dog eat dog, and no one seems to care much for anyone else. As far as I'm concerned, I'm really not a part of this messed up society. What I'd really like to do is have a home in the mountains, somewhere far away from everyone. Sometimes I get so angry with the way things are being run, I think about placing a few blocks of C-4 [military explosive] under some of the sons-of-bitches.

I usually feel depressed. I've felt this way for years. There have been times I've been so depressed that I won't even leave the basement. I'll usually start drinking pretty heavily around these times. I've also thought about committing suicide when I've been depressed. I've got an old .38 that I snuck back from Nam. A couple of times I've sat with it loaded, once I even had the barrel in my mouth and the hammer pulled back. I couldn't do it. I see Smitty back in Nam with his brains smeared all over the bunker. Hell, I fought too hard then to make it back to the World [United States]; I can't waste it now. How come I survived and he didn't? There has to be some reason.

Sometimes, my head starts to replay some of my experiences in Nam. Regardless of what I'd like to think about, it comes creeping in. It's so hard to push back out again. It's old friends, their faces, the ambush, the screams, their faces [tears] . . . You know, every time I hear a chopper [helicopter] or see a clear unobstructed green treeline, a chill goes down my back; I remember. When I go hiking now, I avoid green areas. I usually stay above the timber line. When I walk down the street, I get real uncomfortable with people behind me that I can't see. When I sit, I always try to find a chair with something big and solid directly behind me. I feel most comfortable in the corner of a room, with walls on both sides of me. Loud noises irritate me and sudden movements or noise will make me jump.

Night is the hardest for me. I go to sleep long after my wife has gone to bed. It seems like hours before I finally drop off. I think of so many of my Nam experiences at night. Sometimes my wife awakens me with a wild look in her eye. I'm all sweaty and tense. Sometimes I grab for her neck before I realize where I am. Sometimes I remember the dream; sometimes it's Nam, other times it's just people after me, and I can't run anymore.

I don't know, this has been going on for so long; it seems to be getting gradually worse. My wife is talking about leaving. I guess it's no big deal. But I'm lonely. I really don't have anyone else. Why am I the only one like this? What the hell is wrong with me?

Source: Goodwin (1980), pp. 1–2.

A **compulsion** is a *behavior that is performed over and over in a stereotyped fashion.* The behavior appears to be designed to achieve some goal (handwashing to avoid germs), but it is actually senseless and ineffective (the hands were not dirty to begin with). The individual realizes the irrationality of the behavior and does not get any particular pleasure from it but becomes tense and anxious if the behavior is not performed. Clinically common compulsions include handwashing, counting, checking, and touching. As with obsessions, compulsions can seriously disrupt normal functioning. Apart from interfering with normal activities, compulsions can have other serious effects. For example, an individual with a handwashing compulsion may wash his or her hands until the skin has literally been scrubbed away.

Behaviors such as eating, drinking, and gambling when done excessively are sometimes referred to as "compulsive." However, that is an incorrect use of the term because pleasure is derived from those activities, even if they lead to negative outcomes. True compulsions are not pleasurable, except for the fact that they may briefly forestall anxiety.

There is some controversy over the mood that accompanies the obsessive-compulsive disorder. This disorder is classified as an anxiety disorder, and indeed individuals are often anxious about their obsessions (e.g., about thoughts of killing someone) or about the consequences of not completing a compulsive act (e.g., dying if they do not step over cracks). However, the mood that probably most frequently accompanies the obsessive-compulsive disorder is depression. Because of that and because the obsessive-compulsive disorder can be treated more effectively with antidepressant medication than with antianxiety medication, some theorists have suggested that the obsessive-compulsive disorder should be classified as a mood disorder.

A man with a serious obsessive-compulsive disorder is described in Case Study 4.6 (pp. 88–89).

Acute Stress Disorder.   The acute stress disorder is a new disorder that made its first appearance in DSM-IV and involves a period of intense anxiety that lasts for one month or less. This anxiety could stem from some transient situational factor such as a natural disaster or personal experience (attack, rape). This disorder is of interest because it may provide the basis for a subsequent posttraumatic stress disorder.

Now that you have an understanding of the major anxiety disorders, we can consider the questions that are asked and steps that are taken in diagnosing them. In Figure 4.2 you will find a decision tree for diagnosing anxiety disorders.

ISSUES ASSOCIATED WITH ANXIETY DISORDERS

Normal Versus Abnormal Anxiety

It is likely that we have all experienced anxiety at some time, but that does not mean that we all suffer from anxiety disorders. In many instances, anxiety is a normal, adaptive, and positive response. For example, anxiety can serve as a drive that increases our efforts and performance. Psychotherapists actually prefer their patients to have some level of anxiety because the anxiety serves to motivate the patients to work on their problems. Because anxiety can be positive or

In some situations, such as waiting for an entrance during a musical performance, anxiety is appropriate. Unfortunately, even appropriate anxiety can sometimes interfere with execution of a task.

negative, the question that must be asked is, when is anxiety abnormal?

There are three factors to consider when making a distinction between normal and abnormal anxiety. The first is the *level* of the anxiety. In many situations, some level of anxiety is appropriate, but if the anxiety goes above that level, it could be considered abnormal. For example, it is normal to be somewhat anxious about flying, but it would be abnormal if your anxiety was so high that you fainted when you got on a plane or you refused to get on a plane.

The second factor to consider is the *justification* for the anxiety. Anxiety of any level would be considered abnormal if there were no realistic justification for anxiety in the situation. The word *realistic* is important because the anxious individual may unrealistically interpret a situation as threatening and therefore become anxious, but that does not justify the anxiety. For example, an individual may be anxious around spiders, but in most cases that is not justified.

Third, anxiety is abnormal if it leads to negative *consequences*. For example, anxiety that leads to poor performance on the job, social withdrawal, or hypertension (high blood pressure) would be considered abnormal.

Although we must consider the level, justification, and consequences of anxiety in making the distinction between normal and abnormal anxiety, in the final analysis there is no simple rule or cutoff point, and eventually the decision concerning normality versus abnormality is a subjective one.

Prevalence of Anxiety Disorders

Approximately 15% of the population will suffer from an anxiety disorder at some time during their lives (Robins et al., 1984; Myers et al., 1984). Phobias are the most common problem (13.5%), followed by obsessive-compulsive disorders (2.5%) and panic disorders (1.4%). In one study in which 449 randomly selected women were interviewed about their fears, it was found that (a) 74% of the women reported at least one fear, (b) 23% had intense fears, (c) 19% had intense fears that led them to avoid the feared object or situation, and (d) .7% of the women were to some extent incapacitated by their fears (Costello, 1982). When all levels of fear are considered, fears associated with animals were found to be most common (43%), followed by nature (e.g., storms, 41%), social situations (29%), mutilation (21%), and separation (13%). When only intense fear and intense fear with avoidance are considered (the levels of fear that might be considered abnormal), we find that fear of animals is most common (approximately 13%) and the others considerably less frequent (5% or less).

FIGURE 4.2   A DECISION TREE FOR DIAGNOSING ANXIETY DISORDERS.

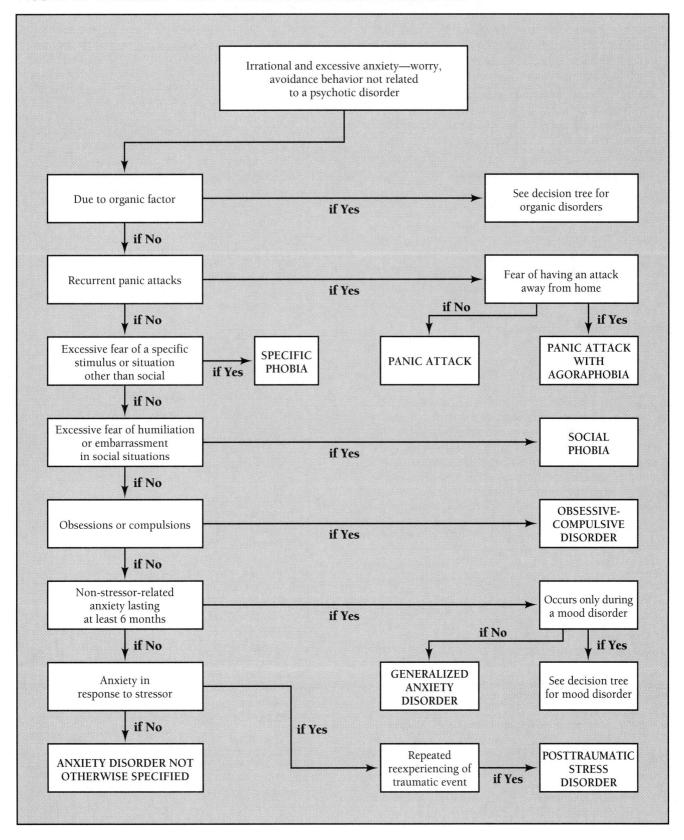

Case Study 4.6

INTERVIEW WITH A MAN WHO SUFFERS FROM AN OBSESSIVE-COMPULSIVE DISORDER

Here is an excerpt from an interview I had with a 35-year-old man who suffered from an obsessive-compulsive disorder for about 6 years. He was a college graduate and had been a successful middle-level manager in a relatively large company. His obsessive-compulsive behavior had interfered with his work, and at the time of the interview he was working at a lower-level position. He was in therapy, receiving counseling, and taking both anti-depressant and antianxiety medication.

Holmes: Could you begin by telling me how the problem began?

Client: I can't tell you what the specific events were, but for a while I felt like something wasn't right in my life. I even talked to my wife about going to a marriage counselor. One of the behaviors I noticed first was that when it was time to eat, I would always reach into the cabinet and take the second dinner plate, not the top plate. The thought was that there might be germs on the top plate, but that plate would protect the second one. That's how it all started. I can't tell you what the second ritual was, but it didn't take long before I developed a lot of rituals.

There seemed to be two basic rituals. Anytime I was going anywhere, whether it was going from one part of the house to another or leaving the house, I would always walk out backward. For example, I would always back out of the house. The other thing was that I would always do things over and over. For example, I would open and close the car door twice, and open and close the house door twice. If I was going through a door, I would do it twice. I would walk through and then turn around and do it again. A circular pattern developed in which I did things over and over. Numbers became very important in this whole pattern. I had to do things a certain number of times. It wasn't always the same number. It depended on how high my anxiety was. Two was a common number, so was four, five, seven, or nine, but never would I go above eleven or twelve. Thirteen was a terribly unlucky number. The more anxious I was, the more times I had to do things.

Holmes: What was it you had to do seven times?

Client: Any of the things. Opening and closing the car door, or going through a door.

Holmes: And what did you think would happen if you didn't do this?

Client: I think that when I first started doing rituals, I saw it more as a protection. When I took the second plate, I wouldn't get germs, and that would keep me from getting sick. Very quickly it took a negative twist, where if I didn't do one of these things, something terrible would happen. Always I had a fear of a heart attack, a fear of a stroke, and a fear of dying. Those were the three major fears. In a short time, I had a full-blown set of rituals. And the rituals covered every part of my life. For exam-

ple, I'd wake up in the morning and I'd have to throw the sheets off of me, cover myself up again, and then throw the sheets off again. From that point, everything I did was controlled by the rituals. They controlled how I brushed my teeth—right down to how I picked up the toothbrush. I would pick it up, put it down, and then pick it up again. I'd put my socks on, take them off, and then put them on again. Shirt on and off and on again. Again the number two. It would take me three and a half hours to get dressed and out in the morning!

It got to the point that I couldn't go by graveyards and couldn't go by hospitals—they reminded me of death. Then it got to where I couldn't even go by signs, like hospital signs. If I came to stop signs—"stop" meant my heart might stop—so I had to do everything to avoid these. It got to the point—let's say I came to a stop sign. I'd say, "Is it all right if I go by the stop sign?" and whoever I was with had to say, "Yes." They couldn't say "hm-mm" or "OK." I would keep badgering them until they said the word yes. When they said the word yes, it would be all right.

You can't imagine how degrading this was for me, so I'd say to myself, "By God I'm not going to do it this time," and I'd get by the stop sign without asking permission. Maybe I'd get half a block down the street—and I'd break out in a sweat and have to make a U turn and go back through the stop sign again. I became a real U turn artist. There have been times I've made five or six U turns on a busy street in the space of ten blocks—just so I could go back through stop signs again. God, it was insane! If I didn't do one of my rituals, I'd really panic. I remember that when I left work, I would have to drive around the building twice before going home. On a bad day, I'd have to do it eleven times. Well, one day I said, "The hell with this, I'm not going to do it—bingo. I'm going to drive straight home." So I didn't drive around the building and started home, but as soon as I got about a block away, I could sense some shallow breathing, heart starting to race a little bit, all the signs. To make a long story short, about midway home I thought, "I blew it, I blew it, I got to go back!" I just froze. Then the panic started. All the physical symptoms came, and I thought, "I'm losing it. I got to get back to get around the building!" Then I thought, "No, I'll never make it. I'll have to get home, so I drove seventy and eighty miles an hour down city streets—my foot just shaking on the pedal. Once I got to the top of a hill where I could see the house, I could feel the tension drop. By the time I got home, I was real shaky, but it was over.

Holmes: Your family must have become upset about this.

Client: My youngest daughter literally hated my guts. No one understood it—I didn't understand it. Gee, anyone ought to be able to walk through a damn door without doing it twice. What do you mean you can't do that! It was very difficult.

Holmes: Earlier you said that you did your rituals to avoid possibly dying. How did you connect something like picking up a toothbrush with dying? Why did picking up a toothbrush twice protect you from possibly dying?

Client: Well, everything is connected to living. You put the toothbrush in your mouth, but you have to breathe through your mouth. Anything that had to do with my mouth or nose was . . . Putting a shirt on over my head . . . put a shirt on my chest . . . What's on your chest? Your heart. All these things, ha!— There's an insane logic to it all. It all had its purpose. It's kind of like the guy sitting in a field in Kansas snapping his fingers over and over, and when another guy asks him why he is snapping his fingers, he says, "It keeps the elephants away." The other guy then says, "Hell, there aren't any elephants in Kansas." The first guy responds, "See, it works!"

Demographic Characteristics

Anxiety disorders are more likely to be diagnosed in women than in men. The prevalence of various anxiety disorders in women and men is presented in Figure 4.3.

There is also some evidence that at least among women, the prevalence of fears at all levels (mild through intense) appears to decrease with age. In fact, the prevalence of intense fears among women between 56 and 65 years of age is only about half of what it is among women between 18 and 25 (Costello, 1982). The relationship between age and the prevalence of various levels of fear among women is presented in Figure 4.4 (p. 90).

In addition to the relationships with sex and age, some data suggest that agoraphobia and specific phobia are more prevalent among individuals with less education (Robins et al., 1984).

Very little attention has been given to the question of whether the rates of anxiety disorders differ across ethnic groups, and the data that do exist are difficult to interpret (Neal & Turner, 1991). For example, there is some evidence that African-Americans may be more likely to suffer from anxiety disorders than Caucasian Americans (Regier et al., 1984). However, the levels of anxiety disorders in minority groups are probably underestimated because members of minority groups are more likely to perceive their problems as medical and hence seek help for medical rather than psychiatric problems. Even if there is a link between ethnicity and anxiety disorders, it would not be clear whether the important factor is ethnicity or social class because in most investigations middle- and upper-class minority group members have not been sampled thoroughly (Williams, 1986).

Finally, it is noteworthy that the prevalence of some anxiety disorders may be substantially increased by where a person lives. A study of young inner-city residents revealed a 39.1% rate of the posttraumatic stress disorder. That high rate reflected the fact that these individuals had a high rate of exposure to stresses such as sudden injury (9.4%), physical assault (8.3%), seeing someone seriously hurt or killed (7.1%), sudden death of a friend or a relative (5.7%), threat to one's life (2.5%), and rape (1.6%) (Breslau et al., 1991).

Fear Versus Anxiety

When reading the sections on phobias and anxiety states, you may have noticed a change in the terminology that was used to describe the emotion that is associated with the two disorders. When talking about

FIGURE 4.3 ANXIETY DISORDERS ARE MORE PREVALENT IN WOMEN THAN IN MEN.

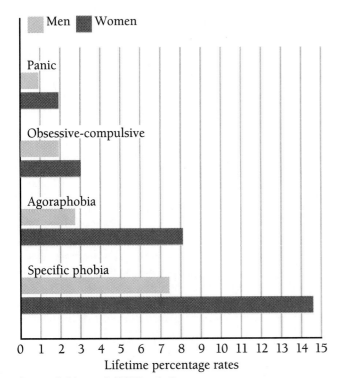

Lifetime percentage rates

Source: Robins et al. (1984), tab. 3.

FIGURE 4.4   PREVALENCE OF WOMEN'S FEARS DECREASES WITH AGE.

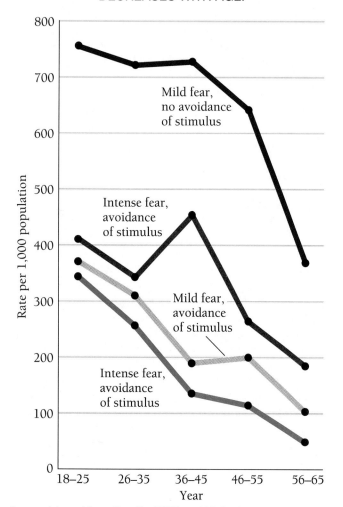

Source: Adapted from Costello (1982), p. 283, fig. 2.

not accurately communicate what is meant. If anxiety is really only a type of fear, it might be more effective to call it fear and then use a modifier to indicate what type of fear is being referred to (for example, "fear of the unknown" when walking through the woods).

The question of the similarity or difference between fear and anxiety is not raised here with the expectation that the word *anxiety* will be dropped from our vocabulary, and indeed we will continue to use it throughout this book. Rather, the question is raised to draw attention to the fact that when talking about anxiety, we must understand and state explicitly what we mean by the term—usually a type of fear.

Trait Anxiety Versus State Anxiety

One widely accepted distinction regarding anxiety is the difference between *trait anxiety* and *state anxiety*. **Trait anxiety** refers to a relatively enduring characteristic of the individual that transcends the boundaries of place and time, whereas **state anxiety** is limited to a particular time or situation (Spielberger, 1971). Individuals with trait anxiety are anxious regardless of where they are or what they are doing, but individuals who suffer from state anxiety are anxious only while in particular situations (taking examinations, flying, on a date). When talking about an individual who is anxious, it is important to clarify whether the arousal is a chronic trait or a brief and passing state.

Cognitive Anxiety Versus Somatic Anxiety

Anxiety can also be broken down in terms of the types of symptoms that individuals experience. **Cognitive anxiety** involves symptoms such as worry, feelings of pressure, frustration, and concerns about failure. **Somatic anxiety** involves symptoms such as feeling physically "tight" and restless and having a rapid heartbeat and an upset stomach.

Research has suggested that the cognitive and somatic symptoms constitute two separate components of anxiety and that the two may influence different aspects of behavior (Holmes & Roth, 1989; Schwartz et al., 1978). For example, it has been shown that taking a difficult examination increases both cognitive and somatic anxiety, but only the cognitive anxiety hinders performance on the examination (Holmes & Roth, 1989). The cognitive anxiety has a deleterious effect on test performance because the worry and concerns about failure interfere with effective problem solving. If you get to an item on a test that you do not know and then begin worrying about failing (experiencing cognitive anxiety), you will not be able to concentrate on the rest of the test. The rapid heart rate and upset stomach associated with somatic anxiety apparently do

phobias, the word *fear* was used, and when talking about anxiety states, the word *anxiety* was used. Do the words *fear* and *anxiety* reflect an important difference, or are they two words for the same thing?

Most people have an intuitive feeling that there is a difference between fear and anxiety, and they often identify *knowledge* as the crucial factor: If they know what is bothering them, they are afraid, but if they do not know, they are anxious. Using that distinction, you would be anxious if you were walking through the woods at night because you would not know what might be lurking in the shadows, but if you suddenly came face to face with a bear, you would be afraid. However, we could just as easily talk about "fear of the unknown" and "fear of the known" and thereby not use the word *anxiety*. One justification for not using the word *anxiety* is that it is a vague term for which people have different meanings, and therefore it may

Somatic anxiety (e.g., rapid heart rate) does not necessarily interfere with performance on a test. However, cognitive anxiety (e.g., worry about consequences) can impede test performance.

not influence intellectual performance. In contrast, it has been reported that somatic anxiety rather than cognitive anxiety is the best predictor of physical symptoms, sleep disturbance, and the use of a student health center (Frost et al., 1986). The distinction between cognitive and somatic anxiety is important in terms of accurately describing what individuals are experiencing and predicting what their behavior will be, and it may also be important for developing a treatment plan.

In summary, it is becoming clear that anxiety is not an omnipresent amorphous state; instead, it can be situation-specific and has separate components that are individually related to how people will respond in different situations. Anxiety is as old as humanity, but we are still in the process of refining our understanding of it.

▮ SUMMARY

Anxiety is present in many types of abnormal behavior. In the anxiety disorders, it is either the major symptom or the major cause of other symptoms. The primary mood symptoms of anxiety are tension, panic, agitation, and apprehension. The cognitive symptoms include worry, rumination, and distractibility. The cognitive symptoms stem from the fact that anxious individuals expect something bad to happen to them, so they are constantly "on alert" and worrying about the doom that is about to befall them. Two types of somatic symptoms are apparent in anxiety. First are the immediate somatic symptoms, such as sweating, dry mouth, shallow breathing, increased heart rate and blood pressure, and muscular tension. Second are the delayed somatic symptoms that result from prolonged

tension or arousal, including muscular weakness, intestinal distress, headaches, and chronically elevated blood pressure. Motor symptoms seen in anxious individuals generally involve random activities such as fidgeting and toe or finger tapping. These are reflections of the high levels of emotional, cognitive, and somatic arousal.

The anxiety disorders can be divided into phobic disorders and anxiety states. In phobic disorders, the anxiety is limited to a particular situation, whereas in the anxiety states, the anxiety is free-floating and not limited to any one situation. Three types of phobic disorders have been identified. Agoraphobia involves fear of public places from which escape might be difficult if the individual suddenly became anxious. Social phobias entail fears of social situations in which the individual might be subjected to criticism. Specific phobias account for all other irrational fears, such as fear of heights, animals, small places, or storms.

There are four types of anxiety states. In the panic disorder, the individual experiences brief periods of exceptionally intense anxiety that are not related to any specific event and therefore are very unpredictable. Because panic attacks can be frightening and disruptive in social situations, some individuals who suffer from panic attacks avoid social situations and thus develop symptoms of agoraphobia. The generalized anxiety disorder involves chronic free-floating anxiety. The diagnosis of posttraumatic stress disorder is applied to individuals who previously underwent a highly stressful experience and are still haunted by that experience. These people are bothered by recurrent painful memories, nightmares, or flashbacks of the stressful event. They also sometimes show emotional numbing and reduced involvement with life. Combat experiences are often cited as causes of posttraumatic stress disorders, but the disorder can also stem from a variety of stresses such as natural disasters, crimes, and child abuse. Individuals who suffer from the obsessive-compulsive disorder have persistent ideas (obsessions) and engage in repetitive behaviors (compulsions) that are ego-dystonic and inappropriate. These can include thoughts of hurting someone and acts of constant checking, counting, or touching that trigger anxiety if not done. Finally, the acute stress disorder inolves a brief period of intense anxiety that might provide the basis for a subsequent posttraumatic stress disorder.

In some circumstances, anxiety may be a good thing because it serves as a drive or motivator. However, anxiety is considered abnormal if the level becomes too high, if there is no justification for the anxiety, or if it leads to undesirable consequences. It is assumed that between 2% and 4% of the population suffers from anxiety disorders. Women are more likely than men to be diagnosed as having an anxiety disorder, and the incidence of these disorders decreases as people grow older.

Distinctions are made between trait and state anxiety and between cognitive and somatic anxiety. Attention to these subtypes of anxiety helps us describe anxious individuals more precisely and predict more accurately how they will respond in various situations.

■ KEY TERMS, CONCEPTS, AND NAMES

In reviewing and testing yourself on what you have learned from this chapter, you should be able to identify and discuss each of the following:

acute stress disorder
agoraphobia
anxiety
anxiety disorders
anxiety states
cognitive anxiety
compulsion
delusion

ego-dystonic
generalized anxiety disorder
hyperventilation
obsession
obsessive-compulsive disorder
panic disorder
panic disorder with agoraphobia

phobic disorders (phobias)
posttraumatic stress disorder
social phobia
somatic anxiety
specific phobia
state anxiety
trait anxiety

Notes:

Chapter 5

Anxiety Disorders: Explanations

• O U T L I N E •

avid has a severe snake phobia. When his case is discussed at a clinic conference, there are strong disagreements over the cause of his phobia. A clinician who subscribes to the *psychodynamic* theory suggests that David has a conflict over the expression of sexual impulses and that the anxiety stems from that conflict. The clinician also suggests that the anxiety is associated with snakes because snakes are sexual (penis) symbols. Another clinician who approaches disorders from a *learning* perspective believes that in the past, snakes were paired with a fear response (David saw his mother recoil in fear when she saw a snake in the garden), and because of the process of classical conditioning, the stimulus of snakes now elicits the fear response. A third clinician, who takes a *cognitive* approach to abnormal behavior, believes that David has erroneous beliefs about snakes and that those beliefs lead David to misinterpret or exaggerate the danger that snakes pose for him. Because David automatically thinks his erroneous thoughts when he sees a snake, he is blocked from considering more realistic views of snakes.

Lou Ann suffers from chronic free-floating anxiety, and she is diagnosed as having a generalized anxiety disorder. There is disagreement over the cause of her disorder. The psychodynamically oriented clinician believes that the anxiety stems from an underlying conflict and that the anxiety is diffused because there is no symbolic representation of the conflict. The learning theorist suggests that anxiety has been classically conditioned with many stimuli and that Lou Ann is chronically anxious because at least one of those stimuli is almost always present in her environment. This clinician believes that the anxiety only appears to be free-floating because it is elicited by so many stimuli. A physiologist discounts both of those explanations. He asserts that the general anxiety is due to the fact that inhibitory neurons in Lou Ann's brain are not functioning adequately, thereby causing her to have excessive neurological activity in the areas of the brain that are responsible for arousal. That arousal is interpreted as anxiety, and it is free-floating because it is not associated with any observable external event.

In Chapter 4, we examined the symptoms and issues associated with anxiety disorders. With that material as background, we can now consider the explanations that have been offered to account for those disorders.

PSYCHODYNAMIC EXPLANATIONS

From the psychodynamic perspective, anxiety is thought to result from *intrapsychic conflict.* Different psychodynamic theorists have focused attention on different conflicts, but Freud's ideas have had the strongest influence.

Freud's Psychoanalytic Explanation

Freud identified three types of anxiety and suggested that each stemmed from a different source. First, he noted that anxiety can stem from *threats from the external world* such as illnesses, financial problems, and failures, and he labeled that **objective anxiety**. Although objective anxiety can result in considerable discomfort, Freud did not believe that it was an important cause of abnormal behavior.

Second, Freud pointed out that anxiety can result from *internal conflict over the expression of id impulses* (Freud, 1926/1959). According to Freud, conflict and anxiety are generated when the id seeks gratification of its needs but is thwarted by the ego and the superego. For example, a young man may want very much to have sex with a woman he is dating, but doing so is unacceptable to the superego, and that conflict results in anxiety. The anxiety that stems from the fear of punishment by the superego is termed **moral anxiety**.

Third, Freud suggested that anxiety can stem from the fear that the superego will not be effective in restraining the id and that *unacceptable behavior will break through.* For example, sexual or hostile urges may not be adequately controlled, therefore leading the person to behave in an uncontrolled and inappropriate way. Anxiety about that possibility is called **neurotic anxiety**. For Freud, moral and neurotic anxiety were the primary causes of abnormal behavior, and the remainder of our discussion will focus on these two types of anxiety.

It is important to recognize that according to Freud, the conflicts that result in anxiety occur on the **unconscious** level, and consequently we are not aware of why we are anxious. Anxiety is thus a signal of some underlying conflict. The unconscious nature of the conflict explains why anxiety often appears irrational and unrelated to the objective situation.

Two factors determine whether we will experience anxiety. The first is the degree of conflict within the personality. The degree of conflict is determined in part by the standards established by the superego. If the superego is very restrictive in terms of what is acceptable behavior, conflict will be high, and we will experience anxiety. If the superego is lenient, there will be less conflict and less anxiety. It has been suggested that some anxiety disorders are declining in frequency, and this decline is due to today's more liberal attitudes toward sexual behavior. The notion is that because of more liberal attitudes (a more lenient superego), people generally experience less conflict and therefore less anxiety, which in turn leads to fewer anxiety disorders.

The second factor influencing anxiety levels is the effectiveness of our **defense mechanisms** (see Chapter 2). Defense mechanisms help us avoid conflict and thereby avoid anxiety. For example, **repression**, **denial**, or **suppression** may be used to deal with the desires that the superego finds unacceptable. Alternatively, **displacement** can be used to find safe objects or activities for unacceptable drives. A person whose superego prohibits him or her from participating in sex may reduce conflict by channeling pent-up sexual energy into creative writing, a process known as **sublimation**. **Obsessive-compulsive behaviors** also function to control conflict because if you are obsessively counting things or humming a tune to yourself, you cannot think about or act on unacceptable drives.

According to Freud, the experiences we have while going through the stages of psychosexual development play a crucial role in determining what conflicts will occur and how severe those conflicts will be. For example, Freud speculated that if a mother was exceptionally strict with a child about not soiling the diapers during the anal stage, later in life the child would have conflicts over cleanliness and control. It might also be that the failure to identify with the parent during the phallic stage could result in a very weak superego, and therefore the person would have less conflict and anxiety. Because Freudians believe that conflicts have their roots in early childhood experiences, these experiences must be examined carefully in the search for the cause of anxiety.

Phobias Versus Anxiety States.
In the case of phobias, the anxiety is focused on one particular object. Freud explained this by suggesting that the object *symbolically* represented the conflict that had generated the anxiety. For example, if an individual has a conflict over sexual expression and snakes serve as phallic (penis) symbols, the individual's anxiety might take the form of a snake phobia. Seeing a snake would reawaken or heighten the conflict and exacerbate the anxiety. The fact that a snake-phobic individual is afraid of a snake despite the fact that he or she con-

sciously knows that the snake is not dangerous is taken as evidence that the fear comes from an unconscious conflict. When the anxiety is not associated with a particular object or symbol, it will be diffused or free-floating, thereby resulting in a general anxiety state.

The Boiler Analogy. The relationship between conflict and anxiety can be explained with the **boiler analogy**. In this analogy, (a) the personality is a boiler, (b) conflict is the heat under the boiler that causes the pressure in the boiler to rise, and (c) anxiety is the pressure in the boiler. If the level of heat is low, the pressure in the boiler will be low, and it is unlikely that problems will arise. In contrast, if the heat is intense, the pressure in the boiler will get very high, and a number of things could happen. One possibility is that a valve could be opened and some of the pressure could be released into another system. In human terms, pressure might be drained off through the process of displacement. (For example, tension over sexual conflict can be released into creative activity.) If the pressure cannot be released into another system, the sides of the boiler will be put under great tension. In human terms, the tension is an anxiety state. If there is a weakness in one part of the boiler, there will be a distortion (even a break) in the weak area. In human terms, the localized distortion is a phobia. Whether or not there will be a problem depends on the level of heat (conflict) and the strength of the boiler (personality). Just as some boilers can withstand more pressure because they have better walls and stronger supporting bands, so some individuals can withstand more conflict because they have better-developed personalities and stronger defenses.

Comment

In many respects, the Freudian explanation for anxiety is quite simple: *Intrapsychic conflict causes anxiety.* But because of the numerous ways in which conflict can be generated, the variety of ways in which tension can be discharged, and the many ways in which symbols can influence the process, the explanation becomes very complex. Freudians argue that the complexity is essential if the explanation is to account for the uniqueness of individuals. However, critics claim that the complexity of the explanation and the subjectivity involved in interpreting symbols makes the theory untestable, and if it cannot be tested, we cannot rely on it.

Critics have also questioned Freud's strong emphasis on sexual conflicts as the cause of anxiety. In that regard, it is noteworthy that many of Freud's original followers disagreed with him about the nature of the conflicts that led to anxiety. Rather than emphasizing conflicts over id impulses (usually sexuality), the

neo-Freudians suggested that the important conflicts revolve around such things as feelings of inferiority and the desire to be dependent versus independent. Although these theorists believe that the basis of conflict is different, like Freud they assume that conflicts lead to anxiety and that defenses are used to avoid or reduce the anxiety. Conflict and defense against it are still the crucial elements. For many years, Freud's psychodynamic explanation was the dominant explanation for anxiety, but now there are a number of other viable explanations, and we will consider them in the following sections.

LEARNING EXPLANATIONS

The learning explanations for understanding anxiety disorders are based on the processes of **classical conditioning** and **operant conditioning**. Classical conditioning is used to explain the development of anxiety, and operant conditioning is used to explain a variety of anxiety-related behaviors.

The Development of Anxiety: The Role of Classical Conditioning

Learning theorists conceptualize anxiety as a *classically conditioned fear response.* In other words, they assume that a fear response has been paired with a previously neutral stimulus, and as a result of that pairing (conditioning), the previously neutral stimulus now elicits the fear (see Chapter 2). For example, an individual who was frightened while in an elevator will now become fearful whenever in or near an elevator. Not only does the original neutral stimulus elicit the fear, but because of the process of **generalization**, other stimuli that are *similar* to the original stimulus also elicit the fear. The individual with the elevator phobia may become fearful in other small, enclosed places.

Classically conditioned responses are *not under voluntary control.* Therefore, an individual cannot stop having a fear response when the conditioned stimulus is encountered, even if the fear response is objectively unjustified. The individual is clearly aware that there is very little justification for the fear of elevators, but because classically conditioned responses are not under voluntary control, the individual for whom the elevator and the fear response have been paired has no choice but to become afraid.

The case of Little Albert presented in Chapter 2 is probably the best-known laboratory demonstration of anxiety development through classical conditioning, but it is easy to think of other examples. A young man who goes out with a woman who is consistently critical and rejecting of him may become anxious with the woman. Furthermore, the anxiety response may generalize to other women, resulting in his having an anxiety attack whenever he is in the presence of women—or at least women who are in some way similar in appearance or style to the woman who was originally threatening.

The examples we have discussed so far have been limited to phobic disorders in which the individual was anxious with a specific stimulus (elevators, animals, women). But can classical conditioning also be used to account for the general anxiety states in which the anxiety appears to be free-floating and not associated with a particular stimulus? Learning theorists explain generalized anxiety disorders by suggesting that they are *broadly based phobias*. In other words, they reject the notion that the anxiety is free-floating and instead suggest that the generalized anxiety disorder is actually a phobia in which the phobic stimulus is generally present. The young man who became anxious with women would be chronically anxious and might appear to suffer from a generalized anxiety disorder if he were usually in the presence of women.

Critics of the conditioning explanation for the development of anxiety often point to individuals with phobias who have not actually been harmed in the presence of their fear-provoking stimuli, and they ask how the fears were conditioned. Indeed, individuals with elevator phobias have probably not been in an elevator crash, and individuals with spider phobias have probably not been bitten by a spider. In reply, learning theorists point out that responses can be developed through **vicarious conditioning** (Bandura & Rosenthal, 1966). The individual with a phobia may have heard about another individual's unfortunate experience, and that may have been sufficient to pair fear with the stimulus. Some spider phobias may be traced back to childhood when children learned about Little Miss Muffett's fear response when the spider sat down beside her. The process of vicarious classical conditioning makes it unnecessary to actually experience the pairing of the stimulus and the emotional response, thereby expanding the range of possibilities for developing classically conditioned anxiety responses.

The development of phobias through vicarious conditioning was demonstrated in an interesting series of experiments with monkeys (Cook et al., 1985; Mineka et al., 1984). In these experiments, *observer monkeys* who had been raised in the laboratory did not show any fear when they were first exposed to a real snake, a toy snake, a model snake, or some black cord. The observer monkeys were then allowed to watch *model monkeys* interact with the snake and other objects. The model monkeys had been raised in the wild, and they showed high levels of fear in response to the snake. After watching the model monkeys, the observer monkeys were again exposed to the various stimuli, and then they showed high levels of fear in response to the snake and moderate levels of fear in response to the similar objects. The vicariously conditioned fear persisted and was almost as strong 3 months later when the monkeys were tested again. These results are presented graphically in Figure 5.1.

In one respect, it is fortunate that vicarious conditioning occurs, because without it we would have to experience everything of which we should be afraid. That would be an inefficient and dangerous way of learning about threats. However, vicarious conditioning can easily result in inappropriate fears. Without actually experiencing a situation to see if it really is threatening, we may unjustifiably pair a threat with the situation and develop an irrational fear. For example, a child seeing a parent's fear response to a harmless spider (or hearing about Miss Muffett's response to the spider that sat down beside her) might vicariously condition a fear of spiders.

FIGURE 5.1   MONKEYS SHOWED GREATER FEAR OF SNAKES AND SIMILAR OBJECTS AFTER OBSERVING ANOTHER MONKEY SHOW FEAR OF A SNAKE.

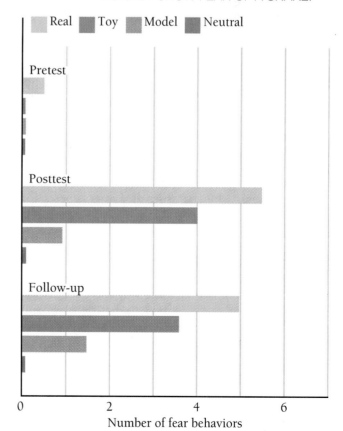

Source: Adapted from Cook et al. (1985), p. 603, fig. 8.

A frightening experience involving an elevator, or even hearing about an elevator accident, could lead to a classically conditioned fear of elevators.

Critics of the conditioning explanation also ask why phobic fears do not extinguish as other classically conditioned responses do. The learning theorists respond by pointing out that phobic fears can be extinguished, but they are generally not extinguished because individuals avoid the fear-provoking stimuli. For extinction to occur, the stimulus must be repeatedly presented without being paired with the unconditioned response. In the case of Little Albert, for example, the white rat would have to be presented over and over without the loud gong being sounded. Because the phobic individual avoids the stimulus, the link between the stimulus and the emotional response cannot be weakened or eventually broken, and hence the fear is maintained. In Chapter 6, where we discuss the techniques of treating anxiety disorders, we will consider a number of effective ways that have been developed to extinguish classically conditioned phobias.

The Development of Anxiety-Related Symptoms: The Role of Operant Conditioning

Many anxiety disorders also involve a variety of other symptoms such as avoidance behaviors. Learning theorists explain these other symptoms with the process of operant conditioning (see Chapter 2).

The operant conditioning explanation runs as follows. Anxiety is unpleasant, so we try to reduce or avoid it as much as possible. If we do something that is effective for reducing the anxiety (for example, avoiding or fleeing the fear-provoking situation), we feel better. Feeling better is a reward for using the response. Because responses that are rewarded are likely to be used again, the next time we are anxious, we will use the response again in the hope of again reducing the anxiety. The individual with an elevator phobia reduces anxiety by not taking elevators. For learning theorists, then, the inappropriate responses associated with anxiety disorders are simply operantly conditioned responses that anxious individuals use to reduce their anxiety.

One of the notable things about most anxiety-related responses is that they appear irrational. Some of these responses are irrational because the fear on which they are based is irrational. For example, avoiding elevators is irrational because there is no reason to be afraid of elevators. In other cases, the fear may be rational but the response is irrational because it does not really protect the individual. For example, a baseball player who is justifiably anxious about striking out may always wear a pair of "lucky socks" that he happened to wear one day when he hit a home run. In yet other cases, both the fear and the response may be irrational. For example, an individual may believe that stepping on cracks is dangerous and thus compulsively avoid stepping on cracks. All these behaviors may be *objectively* irrational, but the important point is that the individual *believes* that the behaviors provide protection from some danger, and the behaviors are therefore anxiety-reducing and rewarding.

Because these irrational responses do not really protect individuals (the baseball player sometimes strikes out while wearing his lucky socks; the person who compulsively avoids cracks in the sidewalk may fall and break a leg), you might ask why these behaviors do not extinguish. Actually, the fact that they seem to work *some of the time* (occasionally the baseball player gets a hit, and the person who avoids cracks does not always fall) makes the responses more resistant to extinction because they are on an **intermittent schedule of reward**, which increases resistance to extinction (see Chapter 2).

Comment

The first point to consider when evaluating the learning explanation for anxiety disorders is that the principles of learning and conditioning are supported by a vast body of well-done laboratory research (Hilgard &

Marquis, 1961; Klein, 1987). There is little doubt about the existence of classical and operant conditioning, and therefore we can have confidence in the principles on which the learning explanation for anxiety is based.

The question that arises, however, is, can the principles that were developed in highly controlled laboratory situations with animals can be generalized to complex abnormal behaviors that occur in humans? The best way to test that would be to conduct experiments in which the principles of learning are used to create abnormal behavior in humans. Obviously, doing that poses serious ethical problems (see Chapter 3). For example, there is some question about whether the original experiment with Little Albert was ethically justified. Was it fair or ethical to create a phobia in the child?

Indirect support for the learning explanation comes from the fact that learning and conditioning obviously play important roles in the development of normal behavior, so it seems reasonable to assume that the same principles could also play a role in the development of abnormal behavior. If intentionally pairing negative consequences (punishment) with misbehavior is effective for making a child anxious about using that behavior, might it not also be that inadvertently pairing negative consequences with appropriate behaviors or situations would result in similar anxieties that we would call phobias?

COGNITIVE EXPLANATIONS

The basic premise of the cognitive explanations for anxiety disorders is that some individuals have *problems processing threat-related information*. Specifically, individuals develop anxiety disorders when they (a) selectively attend to threats around them, (b) selectively recall past threats, (c) misinterpret neutral situations as threatening, or (d) erroneously expect something bad to happen (Butler & Mathews, 1983; Ingram & Kendall, 1987; Litz & Keane, 1989; Mathews, 1990; McNally, 1990). We will consider each of these processes.

Problems with Information Processing

Selective Attention.   It is normal to become anxious when you see or think about a threat (e.g., exams, illness, financial problems). Cognitive theorists suggest that some persons develop anxiety disorders because *they focus excessive amounts of attention on threats and therefore see more threats than other individuals* do. That is, **selective attention** leads them to see more threats, and the perception of all the threats makes them anxious. Selective attention apparently occurs when information comes into the sensory memory and the individual scans it and decides what should be sent to short-term memory for processing. (For a review of the cognitive processes associated with memory, see Chapter 2.)

Selective attention for threat-related information was demonstrated in experiments in which anxious and nonanxious individuals were shown a list of words in which the words were printed in different colors. The task was to ignore the meanings of the words and name the color in which each word was printed. Some of the words were threatening; others were neutral. If anxious individuals are more likely to focus their attention on threats, presumably they would take longer to name the colors in which threatening words were printed because the individuals would focus on the threat (word meaning) and that would interfere with their attention to the color.

In one study of this type, nonanxious women and anxious women who had been raped and were suffering from a posttraumatic stress disorder were shown threat-related words (*penis, AIDS, victim*) and neutral words (*polite, moderate, typical*) (Cassiday et al., 1992). When asked to name the colors in which the words were printed, the anxious women took longer to respond to the threat-related words, thereby suggesting that they were attending to the meaning rather than the color. They also took longer in general to respond to all words, suggesting that anxiety was generally interfering with cognitive processing. These findings are presented in Figure 5.2 (p. 102). Other investigators have reported similar findings (MacLeod & Mathews, 1988; MacLeod et al., 1986; Mathews et al., 1990; McNally et al., 1990).

Selective Recall.   Cognitive theorists also suggest that **selective recall** of threatening experiences contributes to the development of anxiety disorders. Specifically, individuals who recall more threats will have more reasons to be anxious. There are two reasons to expect that anxious individuals will be more likely to recall threats than nonanxious individuals. First, as noted in the previous section, anxious individuals are more likely to perceive threats and are therefore more likely to process and store them in long-term memory, so anxious individuals have more threatening memories on which to draw. Second, because the individuals are anxious, they are more likely to have an active associative network involving threats, so threat-related memories are more likely to be activated.

The hypothesis that anxious individuals are more likely than nonanxious individuals to use selective recall for threat-related information was tested in an

FIGURE 5.2   ANXIOUS INDIVIDUALS ATTEND MORE
TO THREATS THAN NONANXIOUS
INDIVIDUALS, SLOWING THEIR
ABILITY TO NAME THE COLOR OF
THREAT-RELATED WORDS.

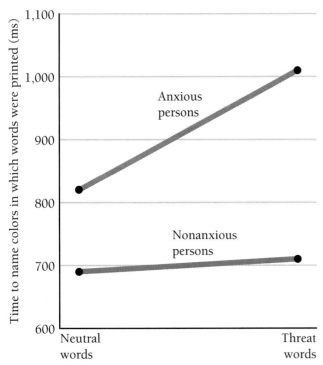

Source: Adapted from Cassiday et al. (1992), p. 290, fig. 1.

FIGURE 5.3   INDIVIDUALS WHO HAVE A PANIC
DISORDER RECALL MORE THREAT-
RELATED WORDS AND FEWER
POSITIVE WORDS THAN INDIVIDUALS
WHO DO NOT HAVE A PANIC
DISORDER.

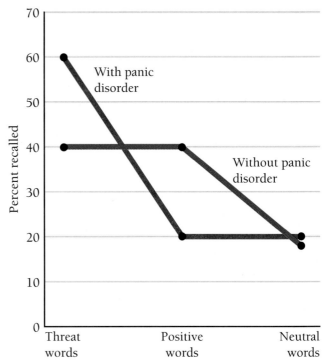

Source: Cloitre and Liebowitz (1991), p. 380, fig. 1.

experiment in which individuals who did or did not suffer from the panic disorder were shown a list containing threat-related words (*trembling, anxious, morgue, cancer*), positive words (*excited, glad, gift, banquet*), or neutral words (*steady, tolerant, boxes, farmer*). Later the individuals were tested for their recall of the words (Cloitre & Liebowitz, 1991). The results indicated that the two groups showed comparable recall for the neutral words, but the individuals with the panic disorder recalled more threatening words and fewer positive words than the individuals who did not have the panic disorder. These results are presented in Figure 5.3.

Misinterpretation.   Anxious individuals are also more likely than nonanxious individuals to misinterpret neutral or ambiguous situations as threatening, and such **misinterpretation** could contribute to anxiety. In one experiment, currently anxious individuals, recovered anxious individuals, and nonanxious individuals were read sentences that could be interpreted in either a threatening or a nonthreatening way (Eysenck et al., 1991). One of the sentences was "The doctor examined little Emma's growth." The threaten-

ing interpretation was "The doctor looked at little Emma's cancer," and the nonthreatening interpretation was "The doctor measured little Emma's height." After hearing 32 such sentences, the threatening and nonthreatening versions of the sentences were presented to the individuals, and their task was to identify which sentences they had heard earlier. The results indicated that when compared to the nonanxious individuals, the anxious individuals were more likely to choose the threatening alternative. Those results are presented in Figure 5.4. Similar results have been reported by other investigators (Butler & Mathews, 1983; McNally & Foa, 1987).

Erroneous Expectations.   **Erroneous expectations** can also lead to anxiety. That is, in many cases individuals show inappropriate anxiety because they incorrectly expect a situation to be threatening. For example, there is now evidence that many individuals who develop agoraphobia do so because they expect to have a panic attack outside of the home (Clum & Knowles, 1991). That expectation leads them to stay

Anxious individuals are more likely than nonanxious individuals to misinterpret neutral or ambiguous situations as threatening. In turn, such misinterpretations can lead to further anxiety.

home in an attempt to avoid the panic attack and so causes agoraphobia to develop.

Misinterpretation and erroneous expectation have been used to explain panic attacks. That is, (a) an individual may show minor signs of anxiety or arousal (low levels of hyperventilation and muscular tenseness), (b) those signs are misinterpreted as signs of greater anxiety to come, (c) the individual then becomes more anxious in anticipation of higher anxiety to follow, and (d) then the level of anxiety spirals out of control into panic. From a cognitive perspective, then, panic attacks are due to a "fear of fear" (Kenardy et al., 1992; Roth et al., 1992).

Selective Processing and Cognitive Performance

Selective attention and selective recall can distort a person's view and lead to anxiety, but attention and memories can also *distract* the individual from other tasks at hand, and that distraction is responsible for the poorer cognitive performance that is often associated with anxiety. **Test anxiety** provides a good example of this (Sarason, 1980; Sud & Sharma, 1989). Individuals who suffer from test anxiety do poorly on exams because they are constantly distracted by thoughts and feelings associated with failure. For example, when individuals with test anxiety encounter a question on an exam for which they do not have a ready answer, they immediately think that they will fail; that activates a network of failure-related thoughts and feelings, and the resulting flood of failure-related thoughts and feelings interferes with thinking about the question and potential answers. The interference precludes working effectively on the question, and they cannot answer it, thus confirming their concerns about failure and starting a vicious cycle. The solution

FIGURE 5.4 ANXIOUS INDIVIDUALS WERE MORE LIKELY THAN RECOVERED ANXIOUS AND NONANXIOUS INDIVIDUALS TO MISINTERPRET AMBIGUOUS SENTENCES AS THREATENING.

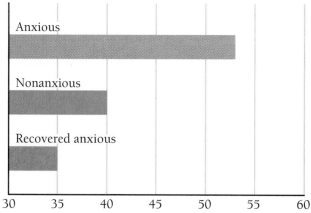

Percentage of threatening interpretations endorsed

Source: Eysenck et al. (1991), p. 146, fig. 1.

for test anxiety is not to "spin off" onto the failure-related thoughts and feelings, but that is easier said than done because the process is automatic and hence very difficult to avoid or stop (Meichenbaum, 1972).

An Application

The effects of selective attention, selective recall, misinterpretation, and erroneous expectations because of an activated associative network can be seen in the following clinical example.

A forty-year-old man had gone on a skiing trip near Denver and, while on the slopes, had begun to feel shortness of breath, profuse perspiration, faintness, and weakness. He also felt cold and had a feeling of instability. He had difficulty in focusing on any object and had waves of severe anxiety. Over all the symptoms hovered a sense of unreality. He was in such a state of collapse that he had to be taken from the slopes in a stretcher and rushed to a hospital. When no physical abnormalities were found, he was told he had an "acute anxiety attack." (Beck & Emery, 1985, pp. 4–5)

This man had skied many times before, and because of the altitude, exertion, and weather conditions, on those occasions he had experienced the same physical symptoms of shortness of breath, chest pains, fatigue, sweating, and cold. The question then is, why were the symptoms this time associated with the intense anxiety? Cognitive theorists offered the following explanation based on the skier's interpretation of the situation:

In this particular instance, however, his episode on the slopes was colored by a recent bereavement in his family. His brother, who was ten years older, had died several weeks previously from a heart attack. This man's thinking seemed to go something like this: "If it could happen to my brother, it could happen to me. . . . My brother got his heart attack after exercise and so could I." Hence, instead of making the most plausible explanation of his symptoms (as due to skiing in a cold, rarefied environment), he interpreted them as what he feared most—namely, a fatal heart attack. . . . When he started to have shortness of breath and other symptoms, he thought, "This must be a heart attack. . . . this is what it's like to be dying." . . . Thus, the missing piece in this puzzle is his cognition—his interpretation of normal physiological responses to exercise in a cold environment and a rarefied atmosphere as indicating a life-threatening disorder. (Beck & Emery, 1985, p. 5)

In other words, because of the recent death of his brother, the man had an active network associated with death. That network resulted in selective attention to the physical symptoms of altitude and fatigue because the symptoms were like those of a heart attack. Also because of the existing network, the symptoms were misinterpreted as signs of a heart attack, the man erroneously expected to have a heart attack, and this perception gave rise to anxiety.

In this case, the skier misinterpreted physical signs and became fearful of a physical disorder. Similar misinterpretations can occur with personal or social signs and can lead to fears about personal or social problems. For example, if you are sensitive to social rejection (possibly because you were previously rejected or saw others being rejected), you may misinterpret the behavior of others as signs of rejection. Specifically, if others are preoccupied and do not greet you or do not greet you with as much enthusiasm as they usually do, immediately you may interpret that as a sign that you have done something wrong and that you are going to be rejected. As a result of your misinterpretation, you will become anxious and begin avoiding others to avoid the embarrassment of rejection. The consequence would be a social phobia.

The effects of cognitive sets can be seen in the behavior of students taking a course in abnormal psychology. In this course, you develop a cognitive set to see behavior as abnormal; you notice things about your behavior and that of your friends that you had overlooked before, and you interpret the behavior differently. The "blahs" become "depression," and a brief period of distractibility becomes a "schizophrenic thought disorder." Prior to taking the course, you might not have noticed the behaviors or would have interpreted them differently.

Comment

The cognitive explanations for understanding anxiety are currently very popular among psychologists and psychiatrists. However, there are two problems with these explanations. First, the cognitive explanations cannot account for the free-floating anxiety seen in anxiety states. The basic premise of the cognitive theory is that individuals have cognitive *reasons* for their anxiety, but the characteristic symptom of free-floating anxiety is that the individual does *not* have an explanation for the anxiety—it just comes "out of the blue." Cognitive theorists suggest that "a specific thought or image is not always identifiable. In such cases it is possible, however, to infer that a cognitive set with a meaning relevant to danger has been activated" (Beck & Emery, 1985, p. 6). In other words, the cognitive theorists *assume* that there is an inappropriate interpretation of the situation even when the individual cannot report one. That is a particularly awkward problem for a theory that relies on conscious explanations for symptoms. Although this is a serious limitation of the theory, it is not necessarily a reason to reject it. The cognitive explanations may simply be limited to anxieties that stem from cognitive factors; to account for all anxieties, we may need more than one explanation. Free-floating anxiety may stem from something other than a cognitive cause.

The second problem revolves around the question of cause and effect. Cognitive psychologists usually assume that anxiety-related thoughts lead to the feelings of anxiety, but it is also possible that in at least some cases, feelings of anxiety lead to anxiety-related thoughts. That is, anxiety may cause individuals to seek out cognitive explanations for their feelings. That process was demonstrated in an experiment in which college students either were or were not made to feel anxious. Then the students were asked to describe Russians, who at that time in history were the "bad guys" (Bramel et al., 1965). The students who were anxious saw the Russians as hostile warmongers (which would justify their anxiety), whereas the students who were not anxious saw the Russians as generally nice people (because the students were not anxious, there was no reason to see others as hostile).

These findings indicate that at least some of the time, anxiety influences cognitions. However, regardless of whether or not cognitions influence anxiety, it is possible that selective attention and selective recall could prolong the anxiety after it got started. The use of the cognitive theory to explain anxiety is a relatively new development, and with additional research and refinement, it could become an even more powerful explanation.

PHYSIOLOGICAL EXPLANATIONS

Anxiety disorders are widely regarded as psychological disorders that stem from conflicts, inappropriate conditioning, or faulty cognitions. However, despite the belief that anxiety is psychological, one of the drugs that is prescribed most frequently in the United States is **Valium (diazepam)**, a drug that is used effectively to treat anxiety. Does the widespread use of Valium and other tranquilizers imply that anxiety really has a physiological basis, or are those drugs simply crutches to be used until the psychological treatment can be effective? We will now examine the possibility that the anxiety disorders have a physiological basis.

We now know that *different anxiety disorders have different physiological causes.* Therefore, when seeking to understand the physiological basis for anxiety, we must examine the various disorders separately. We will do that in the following sections.

Insufficient Neural Inhibition and the Generalized Anxiety Disorder

The physiological explanation for the generalized anxiety disorder is that there is *excessive neurological activity in the area of the brain that is responsible for emotional arousal,* and that arousal is experienced as anxiety. The excessive neurological activity is thought to stem from the fact that **inhibitory neurons** that ordinarily reduce neurological activity are not functioning adequately.

Inhibitory neurons serve to reduce the firing of other neurons (see Chapter 2). Specifically, at the synapse of neuron A and neuron B, there may be an inhibitory neuron C, and when that inhibitory neuron fires, it releases a chemical that inhibits the synaptic transmission between neurons A and B. If the inhibitory neurons are not functioning adequately, the neurological activity between A and B will go unchecked and result in the high levels of neurological activity (arousal) we experience as anxiety.

The reduced level of functioning of the inhibitory neurons is believed to be due to low levels of a neurotransmitter known as **GABA** (gamma-aminobutyric acid), and therefore we refer to this as the *GABA explanation* for general anxiety. In short, it is believed that (a) low levels of GABA result in a low level of activity of the inhibitory neurons, (b) the low level of activity of the inhibitory neurons results in a high level of activity of other neurons in the areas of the brain that are responsible for arousal, and (c) the high level of activity (arousal) is experienced as anxiety. The free-floating nature of the anxiety that is seen in anxiety states is exactly what would be expected from low levels of GABA because GABA levels are independent of environmental events.

Evidence for the GABA explanation for anxiety is based on our understanding of the neurological effects of a group of drugs called **benzodiazepines** (BEN-zō-dī-AZ-uh-pīnz) that have been found to be effective for reducing anxiety. Because of their anxiety-reducing effects, these drugs are commonly called **tranquilizers.** The most common of the benzodiazepines is Valium (diazepam). There is substantial evidence that the benzodiazepines increase GABA activity and decrease anxiety (Bertilsson, 1978; Costa & Greengard, 1975; Enna & De France, 1980; Haefely, 1977; Mao et al., 1977). Because the benzodiazepines increase GABA activity and decrease anxiety, it is assumed that low levels of GABA are responsible for anxiety.

Sodium Lactate, Hyperventilation, and Panic Attacks

The reduced activity of inhibitory neurons provides a good explanation for the *chronically* elevated levels of anxiety seen in the generalized anxiety disorder, but it appears that a different physiological process may underlie the *brief* but intense elevation of anxiety seen in panic attacks. In 1967, it was discovered that injections of **sodium lactate** caused panic attacks in many individuals (Pitts & McClure, 1967).

In research on the effects of sodium lactate, individuals who did and did not suffer from panic attacks were brought into a laboratory and given sodium lactate intravenously for approximately 20 minutes. Within about 10 minutes, most of the individuals who had a history of panic attacks began experiencing a severe panic attack. They became tense and then terrified, and they showed elevated heart rates and blood pressures. When the injections were terminated, the panic attacks subsided, and the individuals returned to their normal states. It is noteworthy that these effects were not found in individuals who did not have a history of panic attacks.

A variety of research has documented the fact that panic attacks that are induced by lactate injections are physiologically and psychologically comparable to panic attacks that occur spontaneously (Appleby et al., 1981; Fink et al., 1970; Gorman et al., 1988; Guttmacher et al., 1983; Kelly et al., 1971; see also review by Pitts & Allen, 1979, and criticisms by Margraf et al., 1986). It has also been established that the panic attacks that are induced with sodium lactate are specific to individuals who have had spontaneous panic attacks, and the attacks are unlikely to occur in individuals with other anxiety disorders (Gorman et al., 1985; Liebowitz, Fyer, et al., 1985).

It seems that sodium lactate plays a role in panic attacks, but four limitations should be noted. First, although we can bring on panic attacks with sodium lactate, we do not understand the process by which the effect occurs (Gorman, 1984). It was suggested that the injections are stressful and that the stress brings on the attacks. However, that explanation has been abandoned because the results of a series of experiments have indicated that stress (mental arithmetic, induced hypoglycemia, cold packs) did not bring on panic attacks in patients who had a history of panic attacks (Grunhaus et al., 1983; Kelly et al., 1971; Roth et al., 1992).

Second, although increases in sodium lactate via injections cause panic attacks, we do not understand how or why the increases occur naturally outside of the laboratory. Indeed, we do not even know whether spontaneous panic attacks are due to increases in sodium lactate.

Third, high levels of sodium lactate do not provide a complete explanation for panic attacks because the injections only result in panic attacks in individuals who have a history of spontaneous panic attacks. This suggests that those individuals have some unique characteristic that predisposes them to the panic attacks, but as yet that factor has not been identified.

Finally, injections of sodium lactate do not result in panic attacks in all individuals who have a history of them (Gorman et al., 1985; Liebowitz, Gorman, et al., 1985). In one investigation, the lactate injections failed to result in panic attacks in 28% of the patients.

The reason for this inconsistency is not yet understood.

As an alternative explanation, some theorists have suggested that panic attacks are brought on by **hyperventilation** (rapid and shallow breathing that results in a buildup of CO_2). The notion is that a circular process begins wherein (a) individuals become anxious, (b) they begin hyperventilating, (c) the effects of the hyperventilation (shortness of breath) contribute to the anxiety, and (d) the anxiety in turn increases the hyperventilation. Ultimately, this process is thought to lead to panic. This possibility has been tested in a variety of ways with mixed results, and it now appears that hyperventilation can contribute to anxiety but is probably not a particularly good explanation for the panic disorder.

Finally, it is worth noting that panic attacks can begin while an individual is sleeping (nocturnal panic attacks), and those attacks occur during periods of sleep when the individual would not be dreaming (Craske & Barlow, 1989; Mellman & Uhde, 1989). That is of interest because it suggests that the panic attacks are not triggered by some environmental factor. Indeed, the attacks cannot even be attributed to dreams. This apparent absence of psychological causes provides additional indirect support for the physiological basis for panic attacks.

Physiological Factors and Conditioning in Phobias

It appears that low levels of GABA can account for the *chronic* free-floating anxiety seen in the generalized anxiety disorder and that high levels of sodium lactate can account for the *acute* anxiety seen in panic attacks. We must now ask whether the physiological factors can also be used to explain the *stimulus-specific anxiety seen in the phobic disorders.* The answer is no and yes. No, it does not seem likely that levels of GABA or sodium lactate by themselves can be used to explain specific fears or anxieties because there is no reason to believe that these biochemical factors would suddenly change in the presence of a snake or a small place. However, it may be that individuals with low levels of GABA are more susceptible to classical conditioning, and that such conditioning could lead to the association of fear with specific stimuli.

Low levels of GABA could contribute to classical conditioning in two ways. First, individuals with low levels of GABA, and consequently higher levels of neurological arousal, might simply be more conditionable because of their higher levels of neurological arousal. Second, it is possible that individuals with generally high levels of arousal might be more likely to respond with fear when confronted with a potentially fear-provoking stimulus. That is, overaroused individuals may be more easily frightened. If they are more likely to experience fear, it is more likely that a fear will get paired with a stimulus and more likely that classical conditioning will occur.

Physiologically caused panic attacks could also be involved in the classical conditioning of phobias. If a panic attack occurred in combination with some specific stimulus such as being outdoors or being in a crowd, the fear brought on by the panic attack might become associated with the stimulus, and later the stimulus alone would elicit fear. With regard to that possibility, you will recall that there is a specific diagnosis of *panic disorder with agoraphobia* that is used for individuals who become afraid of going to public places because they have had panic attacks there. Overall, then, it appears that by themselves, physiological factors such as GABA and sodium lactate may cause the generalized anxiety and panic disorders, and that those factors may work in combination with conditioning to cause phobias.

Mitral Valve Prolapse and Anxiety

As early as 1871, it was reported that patients who suffered from anxiety tended to have an unusual heart murmur (an odd sound that occurred when the heart beat) (Da Costa, 1871). The relationship between anxiety and that particular heart murmur has been reported by numerous investigators in the intervening 125 years (see Gorman, 1984). We now know that the heart murmur found in anxious patients is due to the fact that the mitral valve in the heart (the valve that normally stops blood from flowing back from the left ventricle into the left atrium) is *prolapsed* (pushed back too far), so there is some backflow of blood. In other words, with **mitral valve prolapse**, when the left ventricle contracts, some of the blood flows back into the atrium rather than into the aorta and to the rest of the body. The sound of the blood flowing back into the atrium is the heart murmur.

Mitral valve prolapse is diagnosed in 40% to 50% of anxious individuals but in only 5% to 20% of the normal population. Although the relationship between mitral valve prolapse and anxiety is quite strong, we do not yet understand the relationship. It may be that the symptoms associated with mitral valve problems (heart palpitations, chest pain, shortness of breath) contribute to anxiety, or it is possible that the rapid heart rate associated with anxiety might contribute to mitral valve problems. It is also possible that highly anxious persons are more likely to get thorough physical examinations, and therefore a mitral valve prolapse is more likely to be diagnosed. At present, the connection, if any, between anxiety and mitral valve

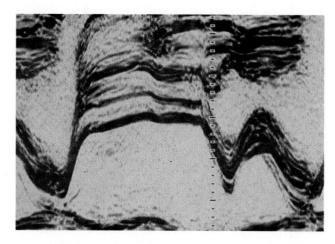

The disorder known as mitral valve prolapse occurs when the valve between the left atrium and the left ventricle does not close properly, and therefore there is some backflow of blood from the ventricle to the atrium. That backflow is apparent in this echocardiogram. Individuals with anxiety disorders are more likely to be diagnosed with mitral valve prolapse, but it is not clear whether there is a functional relationship between the disorders.

prolapse is not clear (Dager et al., 1988; Gorman et al., 1988; Margraf et al., 1988).

Serotonin, Brain Damage, and the Obsessive-Compulsive Disorder

The obsessive-compulsive disorder (OCD) appears to have a cause that is different from the other anxiety disorders. This possibility was first suggested by the finding that in many cases, the symptoms of the OCD could be brought under control with an *antidepressant* drug rather than an antianxiety drug (see review by Hollander et al., 1988). The antidepressant drug reduced the obsessions and compulsions, whereas the antianxiety drug only reduced the anxiety that was associated with the symptoms (the patients still had the obsessions and compulsions but were less anxious about them).

We will discuss the nature and effects of antidepressant drugs in greater detail later (see Chapter 11), but for now it is relevant to note that the antidepressant drugs that are effective for treating the OCD block the *reuptake* of a neurotransmitter known as **serotonin**. (Reuptake is the process by which the presynaptic neuron absorbs some of the neurotransmitter that has just been released. Blocking reuptake makes more of the neurotransmitter available at the synapse, thereby increasing the activity at the synapse; see Chapter 2). One well-known drug that blocks the reuptake of serotonin is **Prozac (fluoxetine)**, and Prozac is effective for treating the OCD as well as for treating depression.

The fact that drugs that increase the levels of serotonin at the synapse can reduce the OCD suggests that *the OCD may be due to low levels of serotonin.* This is a relatively new hypothesis, but it has gained considerable support. For example, in a study of children with the OCD, it was found that low levels of serotonin were associated with high levels of OCD symptoms (Swedo et al., 1992).

In another study, it was found that when patients with the OCD were given a drug that *reduced* serotonin activity (it blocked the serotonin receptors at the synapse), 55% of the patients showed a substantial increase in their OCD symptoms, whereas none of the patients who were given a placebo showed an increase in OCD symptoms (Hollander et al., 1992). Viewed in another way, the drug that reduced serotonin activity resulted in a 67% *increase* in OCD symptoms, whereas the placebo resulted in a 29% *decrease* in OCD symptoms. These findings are presented in Figure 5.5.

The connection between levels of serotonin and the symptoms of the OCD was demonstrated in an interesting study of dogs who showed severe chronic licking of their paws or flanks, behaviors that can be seen as comparable to the handwashing of humans with the OCD (Rapoport et al., 1992). These dogs were given

FIGURE 5.5   REDUCING SEROTONIN ACTIVITY LEADS TO INCREASES IN OCD SYMPTOMS.

(a)

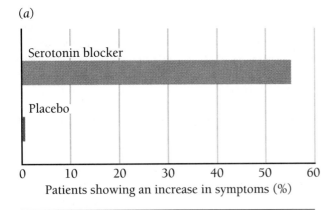

Patients showing an increase in symptoms (%)

(b)

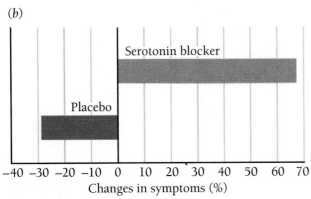

Changes in symptoms (%)

Source: Hollander et al. (1992), p. 23.

either (a) an antidepressant drug that blocked the reuptake of serotonin (Prozac/fluoxetine), (b) an antidepressant drug that did not block the reuptake of serotonin, or (c) a placebo. The results indicated that the dogs who received the drug that blocked the reuptake of serotonin showed substantial reductions in licking, whereas the dogs who received the other drug or the placebo did not show reductions in licking. This provides an interesting animal model for understanding the OCD and support for the serotonin explanation.

Overall, evidence for the low serotonin explanation for the OCD comes from studies demonstrating that (a) increasing serotonin levels reduces symptoms, (b) low levels of serotonin are related to high levels of symptoms, and (c) reducing serotonin activity increases symptoms. However, one qualification should be noted: Low serotonin levels may not be responsible for all cases of the OCD. For example, in the study in which patients were given a drug to decrease serotonin activity, the drug caused increases in the OCD in only 55% of the patients (Hollander et al., 1992). Interestingly, the drugs that block serotonin reuptake are only effective for treating about 50% of the patients with the OCD (see Clomipramine Collaborative Study Group, 1991). These findings suggest that there may be different causes of the OCD, only one of which is low levels of serotonin.

A possible second cause of the OCD is some minor form of *brain damage.* Support for this notion comes from studies in which the investigators assessed the so-called **soft signs** of neurological damage in patients with the OCD (Bihari et al., 1991; Hollander et al., 1990). Soft signs are symptoms such as minor motor coordination and perceptual problems that cannot be linked to damage in a particular area of the brain. The results indicated that patients with the OCD had almost four times as many soft signs of damage than individuals who did not have the OCD, and that within the patient group, the number of soft signs was correlated with the severity of obsessions ($r = .37$). It is not yet clear how the brain damage is related to the development of symptoms, but these findings suggest that the OCD may stem from either problems with neurotransmitters (e.g., serotonin) or minor brain damage.

The Genetic Basis

We have learned that physiological problems associated with GABA, sodium lactate, and serotonin underlie various anxiety disorders, but the question still remains, what precipitates the underlying physiological problems? One possibility is that the problems with GABA, sodium lactate, and serotonin are due to *genetic factors.*

Studies of Families. If the biological relatives of individuals with anxiety disorders have a higher prevalence of anxiety disorders than individuals in the general population, it might be that the concordance of the disorders is due to shared genes. The prevalence of anxiety disorders among the biological relatives of individuals with anxiety disorders has been examined in a variety of studies; the results are summarized in Table 5.1.

The table indicates, first, that the prevalence of anxiety disorders among the relatives of individuals with anxiety disorders is much higher than the prevalence of anxiety disorders in the general population (an average of over 20% versus an estimated 4%). That suggests that there may be a genetic basis for anxiety disorders. A second finding of note is that the first-degree relatives (parents, siblings, or children) of individuals with anxiety disorders have a higher prevalence of anxiety disorders than second-degree relatives (grandparents, aunts, uncles, half siblings; 23% vs. 7%). That is important because the first-degree relatives share more genes with the patients than the second-degree relatives do, so if there is a genetic basis for anxiety disorders, we would expect a higher concordance rate with first- than second-degree relatives. Third, it was found that among the relatives of individuals with anxiety disorders, the prevalence rate for women is twice as high as the prevalence rate for men (23% vs. 11%). This higher concordance rate for women might be interpreted as suggesting that the genetic basis for anxiety disorders is sex-linked.

The investigations of families provide support for a genetic basis for anxiety disorders, but conclusions cannot be drawn from these investigations because they do not rule out the potential role of interpersonal factors in the development of anxiety disorders. For example, because we are more likely to spend more time with first-degree relatives than with second-degree relatives, the higher prevalence of anxiety disorders among first- than second-degree relatives of anxiety sufferers might be due to their shared experiences and environments rather than to their shared genes.

Studies of Twins. The potential genetic contribution to the development of anxiety disorders has also been studied by comparing the concordance rates of anxiety disorders in monozygotic (MZ) twins and in dizygotic (DZ) twins. If there is a genetic basis for anxiety disorders, we would expect a higher concordance rate among MZ twins, who have identical sets of genes, than among DZ twins, who have different sets of genes. The concordance rates among twins for anxiety disorders have been examined in at least five large studies, and each revealed that the concordance rate was higher among MZ than DZ twins (Slater & Shields, 1969; Torgersen, 1979, 1983; Noyes et al., 1987; Kendler, Neale, et al., 1992a). In four of those studies, the concordance rates for MZ twins were 41%, 30%, 34%, and 37%, respectively, while the concordance rates for DZ twins were only 4%, 9%, 17%, and 31%, respectively. Analyses of the data from the fifth investigation revealed that the inheritability of the generalized anxiety disorder was about 30% and that the remaining variability was due to unique environmental factors (Kendler, Neale, et al., 1992a). That level of heritability is in the range of what is found for personality traits in general.

TABLE 5.1 RATE OF ANXIETY DISORDERS IS HIGHER AMONG RELATIVES OF INDIVIDUALS WITH ANXIETY DISORDERS

STUDY	PERCENTAGE OF MALES	PERCENTAGE OF FEMALES	PERCENTAGE OF ALL SUBJECTS
First-Degree Relatives			
McInnes (1937)	—	—	15
Brown (1942)	—	—	16
Wheeler et al. (1948)	—	—	49
Cohen et al. (1951)	12	20	16
Noyes et al. (1978)	13	24	18
Crowe et al. (1980)	22	42	31
Cloninger, Martin, et al. (1981)	3	13	8
Harris et al. (1983)	17	45	31
Crowe et al. (1983)	17	33	25
Noyes et al. (1987)	—	—	28
Second-Degree Relatives			
Brown (1942)	—	—	3
Pauls et al. (1980)	5	14	10

Source: Adapted in part from Carey (1982).

TABLE 5.2   MONOZYGOTIC TWINS HAVE A HIGHER CONCORDANCE RATE FOR THE OBSESSIVE-
             COMPULSIVE DISORDER THAN DIZYGOTIC TWINS

STUDY	Percent Concordant Monozygotic Twins	Percent Concordant Dizygotic Twins
Inouye (1965)	80	50
Inouye (1972)	77	0
Tarsh (1978)	—	100
McGuffin & Mawson (1980)	100	0
Carey & Gottesman (1981)	33	7
Mean	68%	15%

Source: Adapted from Turner et al. (1985), p. 434.

The concordance rates for the obsessive-compulsive anxiety disorders were also studied among MZ and DZ twins, and those results are summarized in Table 5.2. Among MZ twin pairs, the average concordance rate was 68%, whereas among DZ twins it was only 15%. Those results strongly suggest a genetic basis for the obsessive-compulsive disorder.

The studies of families and of twins provide consistent evidence suggesting that there is a genetic basis for anxiety disorders. In considering these findings, however, you should realize that the concordance rate is not 100%, and therefore factors other than genes must contribute to the disorders.

Comment

There is now strong evidence that physiological factors can cause free-floating anxiety, panic attacks, and obsessive-compulsive behaviors, and that genetic factors play a role in determining who will develop an anxiety disorder. However, at present the physiological explanation has two limitations. First, by itself, the physiological explanation cannot account for the stimulus-specific anxieties seen in phobias. In those cases, physiological and conditioning factors may work together. Second, inheritance does not account for all anxiety disorders (concordance rates are not 100%), thus suggesting that other factors are also important.

◼ HUMANISTIC-EXISTENTIAL EXPLANATIONS

Humanistic theorists believe that anxiety develops when there is a discrepancy between an individual's current level of personality functioning and a higher level of functioning (self-actualization) to which the individual aspires. In other words, anxiety stems from a difference between the **current self** and the **ideal self**. One highly anxious student complained, "I just never achieved my personal potential. I never seem to be able to be as good as I *should* be. I'm always worrying about why I'm not getting it together. It really wor-

ries me." Supporting this explanation are the results of a number of investigations in which people were asked to take a personality test twice, once indicating what they were really like and once indicating how they wanted to be or should be. Differences between the scores were greater for anxious than for nonanxious persons (Rogers, 1951).

An anxious individual who is tied up worrying about the discrepancy between the current self and the ideal self cannot free up energy to work on reducing the discrepancy and cannot achieve self-actualization. Stuck at an unsatisfying point of development, the person remains anxious. The problem is circular: The current-versus-real-self discrepancy results in anxiety, the anxiety precludes reducing the discrepancy, and the discrepancy continues to cause anxiety. Going round and round, anxiety increases. From this perspective, then, anxiety stems from the failure to achieve the goal of self-actualization.

The existential theorists take a slightly different position and emphasize the role of responsibility and freedom of choice in causing anxiety. To be real persons, rather than lapsing into states of passive nonbeing, requires that we take responsibility for ourselves and make important choices about the directions our lives should take. The famous existential philosopher Jean-Paul Sartre said, "I am my choices," and if we are the product of our choices, having to make choices can be anxiety-provoking. Deciding about your future (your major, whether you should marry) involves portentous choices and can lead to anxiety. However, even seemingly minor choices can change the course of your life. In Robert Frost's poem "The Road Not Taken," he reflects on how when he came to a fork in the path, by chance he turned one way rather than another, and turning the way he did changed his entire life. If you dwell on all the choices and their implications, you could be in a constant state of anxiety. In summary, the humanists believe that anxiety stems from the failure to arrive at self-actualization, whereas the existentialists believe that it stems from the problems and responsibility of getting there.

There is no doubt that personal shortcomings and choices are sources of anxiety. The question is whether those factors can cause the extreme, uncontrollable, and debilitating levels of anxiety seen in the anxiety disorders.

SUMMARY

In this chapter, we have reviewed a variety of explanations for phobias and anxiety states. Psychodynamic theorists suggest that anxiety stems from unconscious conflicts. If there is a stimulus that is symbolic of the underlying conflict, the anxiety will be focused on that stimulus, and the result will be a phobic disorder. If there is not a symbolic stimulus, the anxiety will be free-floating, and the result will be an anxiety state (e.g., general anxiety disorder, panic attacks). Concerns have been raised about the psychodynamic explanation because of its complexity and because of the subjectivity involved in applying it to any one individual.

Learning theorists believe that anxiety is the result of classical conditioning. They also suggest that through the process of operant conditioning, we learn ways of reducing our anxiety (e.g., we avoid or flee anxiety-provoking situations), and that leads to additional symptoms. Learning theorists use the concepts of generalization and vicarious conditioning to explain phobias in individuals for whom fear was never directly paired with the stimulus. Although classical conditioning can be used to account for phobias in which the fear is associated with a specific stimulus, it is difficult to use this explanation to account for anxiety states and panic disorders in which the anxiety is free-floating. However, in those disorders, it may be that fear is associated with numerous stimuli so that it only appears that the anxiety is free-floating.

Cognitive theorists suggest that faulty information processing leads to anxiety. Specifically, selective attention, selective recall, misinterpretations, and erroneous expectations all serve to heighten levels of anxiety. Furthermore, the attention to anxiety-related information distracts us from other relevant information and interferes with cognitive performance. However, it is difficult to use this explanation to account for free-floating anxiety for which individuals do not have a cognitive explanation. Furthermore, in at least some situations it appears that anxiety influences cognitions rather than vice versa.

Physiological theorists suggest that (a) generalized anxiety results from low levels of GABA, (b) panic disorders are somehow related to high levels of sodium lactate, and (c) the obsessive-compulsive disorder is linked to low levels of serotonin and/or minimal brain damage. In many cases, those physiological problems appear to stem from genetic factors. By themselves, physiological factors cannot account for the stimulus-specific anxiety seen in phobic disorders. However, it may be that individuals who are more aroused due to low levels of GABA are more conditionable, and their conditionability might predispose them to develop phobias.

Humanistic theorists attribute anxiety to the discrepancy between our current self and our ideal self (i.e., our failure to achieve self-actualization). Existential theorists suggest that anxiety stems from the fact that we must take responsibility for the important choices in our lives.

There is probably some support for each of these explanations. Rather than arguing over which explanation is "correct," it seems more reasonable to conclude that there are multiple causes for anxiety. Different anxiety disorders may be best explained differently. For example, classical conditioning may best explain phobias, and low-levels of GABA may best explain generalized anxiety. Furthermore, in some cases, one particular disorder might have more than one cause. For example, phobias could be due to either classical conditioning or to erroneous cognitions. It is also possible that different explanations may work together to result in a disorder. For example, physiological (genetic) factors may predispose some individuals to panic attacks, and if they had panic attacks in public places, they might develop classically conditioned anxiety for public places. Then, through the process of operant conditioning, they might learn to avoid public places with the result that they would develop agoraphobia or agoraphobia with panic attacks.

KEY TERMS, CONCEPTS, AND NAMES

In reviewing and testing yourself on what you have learned from this chapter, you should be able to identify and discuss each of the following:

benzodiazepines	denial	GABA
boiler analogy	diazepam (Valium)	generalization
classical conditioning	displacement	hyperventilation
current self	erroneous expectations	ideal self
defense mechanisms	fluoxetine (Prozac)	inhibitory neurons

intermittent schedule of reward
misinterpretation (of neutral stimuli)
mitral valve prolapse
moral anxiety
neo-Freudians
neurotic anxiety
objective anxiety
obsessive-compulsive behaviors

operant conditioning
Prozac (fluoxetine)
repression
selective attention
selective recall
serotonin
sodium lactate
soft signs (of brain damage)

sublimation
suppression
test anxiety
tranquilizers
unconscious
Valium (diazepam)
vicarious conditioning

Notes:

Chapter 6

Treatment of Anxiety Disorders

• OUTLINE •

Tom is in psychoanalysis. He sees his analyst four times a week and has been doing so for almost 3 years. During his sessions, he lies on a couch and talks about whatever comes to mind, but usually his chain of thought leads him back to childhood experiences. His analyst sits behind him and only rarely makes comments. Despite the analyst's neutral behavior, Tom frequently attributes characteristics to the analyst and then responds with feelings such as anger, dependence, or hostility. When that occurs, Tom is probably transferring his attitudes and feelings about other people to the analyst. By examining and reliving early experiences and by seeing how he responds to the analyst, Tom can identify the unconscious conflicts that lead to his anxiety and inappropriate behavior. Resolving the conflicts or realizing that he has been mistaken in his perceptions should lead to a reduction of his anxieties.

Judy is generally anxious, but she becomes particularly upset when she has to deal with authority figures. In the hope of overcoming that problem, she has been seeing a psychotherapist. During her weekly sessions, Judy sits facing her therapist, and they discuss her problem and the possible causes. Her therapist offers explanations and provides new ways of looking at things, but they are only suggestions. The therapist provides guidance and social support when Judy tries new ideas and behaviors. Judy and the therapist have agreed that treatment will be limited to one session a week for 6 months, so it is essential that Judy keep focused and work actively on solving her problem.

Elizabeth has a severe phobia for heights that for years has kept her from going above the second floor of any building. She is now seeing a therapist who is using a behavioral approach for treating the phobia. The treatment involves taking Elizabeth up in tall buildings, but only one floor at a time. Each time she goes to a higher floor, she is flooded with anxiety, but she "hangs in," and eventually the anxiety subsides and she is able to go to the next floor. The therapist hopes that by exposing Elizabeth to the feared stimulus (high places) without anything terrible happening, Elizabeth's fear response to high places will extinguish. It is like Pavlov ringing the bell but not giving the dog any meat—eventually the dog will stop salivating. Elizabeth is becoming less fearful, and she is now able to go to the 10th floor before becoming anxious. The treatment seems to be working, but Elizabeth wonders whether the fear is being extinguished or whether she is just developing more realistic beliefs about high places.

Anthony has a phobia for dogs. His therapist is teaching Anthony how to inhibit the fear response by replacing it with a relaxation response. To do this, the therapist first taught Anthony a series of exercises he could use to achieve a state of deep muscle relaxation. Once Anthony was relaxed, the therapist had him imagine a situation that was only slightly fearful (e.g., a small dog some distance away). If the relaxation response is sufficient to inhibit the fear response in that situation, Anthony is asked to imagine a slightly more fearful situation (e.g., sitting next to a small, friendly dog). This procedure is used until Anthony is able to imagine situations that were previously very frightening to him without becoming anxious. The key to effective treatment is never to let the fear response overwhelm the relaxation response. It is hoped that the inhibition of fear that is learned by imagining situations in the office will generalize to real situations outside the office.

Marilyn suffers from chronic free-floating anxiety. Her therapist suspected that the problem stems from excessive neurological activity in the area of the brain responsible for anxiety. The therapist prescribed the drug Valium (diazepam), which reduces neurological activity. The Valium does reduce Marilyn's anxiety, but it has some side effects that she does not like. For example, it makes her somewhat drowsy and causes constipation. The side effects seem less severe now than when she first started taking the drug, but it may be that she is just learning to cope with them. In deciding how much of the drug she should take, Marilyn and her therapist try to find the "balance point" where the anxiety is sufficiently reduced but the side effects are not too bothersome. Marilyn knows that the drug is an effective treatment but not a cure.

George suffers from panic attacks, and because of his concern about having one in public, he developed agoraphobia. Antianxiety medication did not seem to be helpful in dealing with the panic attacks, but after trying a number of different drugs, it was discovered that a tricyclic antidepressant reduced the frequency and severity of the panic attacks. When the fear of having a panic attack was reduced, the agoraphobia decreased. It is not understood why the antidepressant worked, but George is now almost symptom-free.

In this chapter we will begin our examination of the techniques that are used to treat abnormal behavior. This chapter is focused on the treatment of anxiety disorders; later chapters will be devoted to the treatment of mood disorders (depression, mania) and schizophrenic disorders. It is important to discuss the treatment of specific types of disorders rather than treatment in general because different disorders require different treatments, and we are more effective at treating some disorders than others. Because this is the first chapter on treatment, a number of basic issues will be introduced that will provide a background for later chapters on treatment.

The treatment of a disorder is usually directly related to its cause. If we believe that a disorder stems from a conflict, treatment is focused on resolving the conflict, but if we suspect that a disorder results from a physiological imbalance, treatment is designed to correct the imbalance. Because there are psychodynamic, learning, cognitive, and physiological explanations for each disorder, we will examine treatment from each of those perspectives.

■ PSYCHODYNAMIC APPROACHES

Psychodynamic theorists believe that anxiety is caused by *unresolved conflicts*, and therefore psychodynamic therapists treat anxiety by helping their clients *identify* and *resolve conflicts*. In other words, the goal of psychodynamic treatments is to help clients develop **insights** about the cause of anxiety, and it is assumed that the insights will lead to behavior change.

Psychodynamically oriented therapists vary greatly in terms of the types of conflicts on which they focus (e.g., sexual, intrapersonal, interpersonal, or social) and the therapeutic techniques they use. As a result, it is difficult to generalize about psychodynamic psychotherapy. However, a useful distinction can be drawn between the technique called **psychoanalysis**, which was developed by Freud, and the techniques that were developed later, which are generally referred to as **psychotherapy**. Note that the term *psychotherapy* is often used generically to refer to all forms of psychological treatment. In this text, however, we will use the term *psychotherapy* to refer to psychodynamic treatments other than psychoanalysis, and we will specifically label other approaches (learning, cognitive, etc.).

Psychoanalysis

Freud's experiences treating clients led him to the conclusions that anxieties stem from underlying conflicts and that the only way to relieve the anxieties is to resolve the conflicts. The first task of psychoanalysis, then, is to discover what conflict is causing the client's anxiety. Unfortunately, the search for conflicts is hampered by two factors. First, the conflict is usually rooted in early childhood and is therefore covered by many layers of experience, and second, the conflict is unconscious. The conflict is unconscious because in the client's attempt to reduce the anxiety, the conflict has been repressed and thereby banished from awareness. In psychoanalysis, then, a client goes back through his or her life experiences and examines each experience from a more mature and objective standpoint. In the case of a stressful experience that led to a conflict, this reexamination often reveals that the client originally misinterpreted what had happened (e.g., "My father wasn't really trying to hurt me. He doesn't really hate me"). The insights about what really happened reduce anxiety and allow repressed material to come to the surface ("the return of the repressed"). Once that conflict is resolved, the client can take another step back in time to another experience and conflict.

Once the crucial conflict has been identified and resolved, the client works back to the present and in so doing corrects the misperceptions developed because of the original conflict (e.g., "I really don't have to be anxious about being alone; that is just a manifestation of my childhood fears that if my mother left me alone, I would do something naughty or she would never come back"). Overall, the process of psychoanalysis involves going back to discover the root of the problem and then revising one's views and feelings after the problem has been identified. From this it should be recognized that in psychoanalysis, attention is focused not on symptoms such as anxiety or a phobia but on the suspected cause; the assumption is that if the cause is eliminated, the symptoms will cease.

The process of psychoanalysis is long; it is not unusual for it to take three or four analytic sessions per week for a period of 2 or 3 years, or even longer. During analytic sessions, the client lies on a couch. The therapist, called a **psychoanalyst** or simply an **analyst**, sits behind the client so as not to distract the client. Traditionally, the analyst plays a relatively passive role, doing little more than pointing out similarities or inconsistencies in feelings or experiences that may de-

During psychoanalysis, the client usually reclines on a couch while the analyst sits behind to avoid distracting the client. Although the analyst traditionally plays a passive role, occasionally he or she will offer an interpretation to help the client reach an insight.

serve further attention by the client. Occasionally, the analyst may offer an interpretation in ord]er to help the client reach an insight about a relationship or a conflict. In psychoanalysis, the responsibility for progress rests primarily on the client's shoulders.

Free Association. A number of techniques are used to help clients find their way back to the source of conflict, one of which is **free association**. Clients are encouraged to say whatever comes to their minds without any restrictions (see Chapter 1). For example, at the beginning of a session, a client may comment that earlier in the day he had been cut off by a man driving another car. That might lead the client to talk about earlier instances in which he had been frustrated by other men who blocked or threatened him. The string of associations might ultimately lead to memories about having been angered by his father, and the analyst might ask if the initial phrase about being "cut off" had some symbolic meaning in this context (castration anxiety?). The notion underlying this technique is that if clients do not defensively censor what is thought and said, important but otherwise unthought ideas will come to awareness. One such thought leads to another by association, thus providing a means of working back through a series of ideas, feelings, and experiences that are not ordinarily accessible.

Dream Interpretation. A second frequently used technique is **dream interpretation** (Freud, 1900/1957). Freud believed that many of our experiences and feelings are so threatening that they cannot be expressed consciously even with the freedom provided

One of the difficult tasks of psychoanalysis is to break the dream code so that the latent content may be uncovered.

by free association. However, such feelings and experiences may be expressed in dreams because during sleep the controls of the ego and superego are relaxed, thus enabling the threatening content to slip through. Even then, in many cases the feelings and experiences cannot be expressed directly and must be disguised and expressed in symbols. The fact that threatening content is often disguised in symbols is used to explain why at first dreams sometimes do not make sense. One of the difficult tasks of psychoanalysis is to break the symbol code so that the dream can be interpreted. For example, in one case, Freud suggested that a man's overcoat was a symbol for a condom (Freud, 1900/1957). Freud used the term **manifest content** to refer to the surface meaning (e.g., "coat") and the term **latent content** to refer to the underlying meaning (e.g., "condom").

Resistance. Often the flow of experiences and feelings in the process of analysis is blocked because the client has encountered something particularly anxiety-provoking and does not want to deal with it. This blocking is called **resistance**, and it can involve talking about trivial issues rather than important ones,

coming late for sessions, or even "forgetting" to come to a session. When resistance occurs, it is used as a sign that the client has come to a particularly important issue, and then the problem is to overcome the resistance and discover the issue.

Transference. A very important aspect of analysis is the relationship between the client and the analyst. Because the analyst remains rather distant and aloof, the analyst presents a generally neutral image to the client. However, despite the analyst's neutral behavior, the client will often attribute characteristics to the analyst and may respond to the analyst with feelings such as anger, dependence, seductiveness, or hostility. These reactions stem from the fact that the client is responding as though the analyst were one of the significant persons in the client's emotional life (e.g., mother, father, sibling, lover). This is referred to as **transference** because the client transfers feelings about another person onto the analyst (Luborsky et al., 1985).

Transference is important because it allows the client to relive and reexperience problems associated with people who are not actually available in the therapy session. Transference can also be used to demonstrate to clients how they sometimes respond inappropriately to others. For example, someone who expects rejection from the analyst may come to realize that he or she inappropriately expects rejection from everyone. Transference reactions to the analyst can serve almost like a replay of the client's previous experiences and reactions, a replay in which the client can both discharge pent-up feelings about past conflicts and gain crucial insights about current feelings and behaviors.

The Lost-Traveler Analogy. The client in psychoanalysis can be thought of as a traveler who has taken a wrong turn and is lost, and who therefore misinterprets what is happening in the situation and becomes anxious. The task of the lost traveler is to trace the path back to the point at which the wrong turn was taken, learn to read the road signs more accurately, and start over from there. Unfortunately, the road map for the early part of the trip is too faded to be read, and parts of it have been torn off. So the traveler, with the analyst as a companion, must do a lot of backtracking and exploring to find the place of the original wrong turn. The analyst, who has had some experience on these roads, can make suggestions about where to look for signs and can point out things that the traveler missed along the way, but the analyst does not know exactly where they are going because the analyst joined the traveler long after the wrong turn. As the traveler returns to one town after another, long-forgotten experiences are recalled, and related feelings of joy and pain are felt once again. Sometimes the traveler slips and responds to the analyst as though the analyst were an individual whom the traveler knew and loved or hated in that town long ago. Once the crucial intersection is found and the traveler recognizes the errors that were made in reading road signs, the trip can be started over. More experienced and knowledgeable, the traveler is now better equipped to find the intended destination and understand the situation, thereby eliminating the anxieties.

It is relevant to note that interest in and use of psychoanalysis have waned drastically over the past two decades. Indeed, many of the institutes in which psychoanalysts are trained no longer have enough applicants to fill their classes, and some have closed. This decline in interest stems from at least three factors: (a) The Freudian theories on which psychoanalysis is based are less popular now than they once were, (b) questions have been raised about the effectiveness of the treatment process, and (c) even if one accepts Freud's theory and believes that psychoanalysis is effective, for most people today psychoanalysis is simply not a practical technique. Very few people have the time or interest to devote an hour a day, 4 days a week for several years, to resolving a conflict. Furthermore, the cost of a traditional analysis can easily total $125,000, putting it beyond the reach of most people. Psychoanalysis may be to psychotherapy what the 1960 Cadillac is to automobiles: It may get you from place to place, but it has been replaced by smaller, faster, more efficient, and less expensive models.

Psychotherapy

There are many forms of psychotherapy. In general, these approaches differ from psychoanalysis and are similar to one another in that (a) the client sits up and talks with the therapist rather than lying down and free-associating; (b) psychotherapy is usually limited to one session per week and usually does not go on for years; (c) therapists are usually more active than analysts, so the nature of the treatment is more likely to be influenced by the therapist's interpersonal style; and (d) the client may be seen individually or in a small group with four or five other clients. Although there are many differences between psychoanalysis and psychotherapy, some similarities exist because elements of psychoanalysis have been adapted for use in psychotherapy. For example, the psychotherapist is likely to point out and interpret relevant associations (e.g., "It is interesting that whenever you get anxious, you start talking about your father. Might there be some

connection there?"). Transference also plays a role in many forms of psychotherapy, thereby enabling clients to identify and work on problems through the relationship with the therapist.

The various forms of psychotherapy share certain elements, but they are also very different from one another, and a number of schools of psychotherapy have developed. For the most part, these schools are associated with different post-Freudian psychodynamic explanations for abnormal behavior. In our discussion of psychotherapies, we will focus on two major dimensions along which the various psychotherapies differ rather than on differences between individual schools per se. Although we will be discussing the extremes of the two dimensions, it is important to remember that most psychotherapists probably take a position in between and incorporate ideas from both ends. Case Study 6.1 is excerpted from a 26-year-old woman's report of her experience in psychotherapy.

Internal Versus External Problems. Traditional psychotherapists believe that anxiety stems from a problem within the client (e.g., unresolved conflict), and they focus on helping the client identify and correct the problem. This approach is similar to that used in psychoanalysis, but it differs in that the problem is not necessarily assumed to be rooted in early childhood, and the psychotherapist takes more direct and active steps to identify and solve the problem.

Other psychotherapists believe that anxiety arises because the client's inherent goodness and ability to grow emotionally have been stifled by external psychosocial constraints (e.g., lack of a nurturant atmosphere). This position was developed primarily by humanistic psychotherapists, and one well-known form of this type of psychotherapy is **client-centered psychotherapy** (Rogers, 1951). The goal of the client-centered psychotherapist is to establish a nurturant interpersonal environment in which the client can grow. To establish such an environment, the therapist provides the client with *unconditional positive regard* and *sincere empathic understanding*. In other words, the therapist accepts the client uncritically as a basically good person and attempts to feel and understand what the client is experiencing. Furthermore, the therapist often shares his or her own personal reactions, feelings, and experiences, thereby becoming a more "real" person for the client. That is in sharp contrast to the private role most traditional psychotherapists take. The atmosphere of acceptance, understanding, and sharing established by the therapist allows the client's inner strength and qualities to surface so that personal growth can occur and anxiety can be left behind.

Some of the principles and techniques of client-

Case Study 6.1

ONE CLIENT'S EXPERIENCE IN PSYCHOTHERAPY

I've been going to a therapist for a little over a year now, and usually I go once a week. I started because I was, well, I wasn't happy. I was always tense, and that seemed to be wrecking all of my friendships, and I was a loner. I didn't know what to do about it until one day a friend of mine suggested that I might "see someone for some professional advice." My first reaction was, "That's not for me. I'm not crazy!" But then I discovered that quite a few of my friends were in or had been in therapy, so I thought I'd give it a try.

I didn't know quite what to expect at first; I thought I'd lay on a couch and talk about my mother and father a lot, but that's not what happened. My therapist is a woman about 40 years old, but I don't know for sure because she never talks about herself. (A couple of times I got up enough courage to ask her something about herself, but each time she just said something like, "We're here to talk about you, and I think it would be better if we kept focused on that." She was very nice about it, but she drew a clear line.)

During my sessions, I sit in a comfortable chair, and my therapist sits across from me. There is a desk in the office, but she doesn't sit behind it. The office is quiet and very comfortable.

Originally, we spent time talking about my being tense and the problems I was having with people—we sort of had to get the issues on the table so that we'd know what we were working on. After that, we spent time talking about other things, like my family, experiences in school, and my job. It seemed like she was trying to get to know me in general, but often when we were talking about what seemed to be peripheral things, examples would come up of people or situations that upset me. In talking about it, I came to realize that what I thought was only a limited and current problem was really pretty pervasive and had been around for a long time. At first I thought, "Gee, I've been around problem people for a long time." We spent a lot of time talking about my interactions with other people, and then a pattern started to emerge slowly, a pattern that went way back. It seemed that I never really had any close relationships, and instead I was always fighting people. My therapist called it "moving against or away from others rather than with or toward them." Having realized that, I was faced with a real problem: Did I move against others for good reason—did they have a problem?—or was the problem with me? I struggled with that for a long time. Usually, I was pretty defensive and came up with long lists of problems with other people. My therapist never disagreed, but she asked gentle, prodding questions that forced me to question myself. She never pushed or argued with me; she would just pose questions or suggest alternatives. She was gentle, but some of her observations opened up some pretty painful possibilities. It isn't always fun to look at yourself from the outside and turn things upside down. The bottom line came to be, "If I think everyone else has problems, maybe the problem is in the way I think about other people." That was a real change in perspective for me, and to be perfectly honest, I haven't completely accepted it yet. I can buy it intellectually (it makes sense), but buying it emotionally is a little different. What I'm doing now is experimenting a little; when a conflict starts to emerge, I ask myself, "Is this problem out there or in me?" I think I'm doing better, but you don't change 20 years of experience overnight.

Even if it is true that my problems are due to me, that doesn't explain why I developed them in the first place. One day, my therapist sort of suggested that maybe I was very sensitive—insecure?—and that by finding fault and opposing or running away from other people, I avoid the risk of being rejected. That led to a long discussion about security, and the issue is still hanging there. Even if I am insecure, why am I that way? Objectively, I've got a lot going for me, but subjectively, I'm not sure. You see, one question and its answer just leads to another question, and therapy goes on and on.

The talking has been good, but I've had ups and downs with my therapist. There were times when she really got on my nerves. For a while I almost stopped going. In fact, I skipped a number of sessions without telling her that I wasn't coming because I was convinced that she didn't like me and that the only reason she was seeing me and being nice to me was that I was paying her. I remember that there used to be a man who had an appointment before me, and my therapist would always be smiling at him when he left her office, and then she'd turn to me in a very businesslike way. When I came to the conclusion that I was just a paying customer, I really felt hurt—but I didn't say anything. The first two times I cut sessions, she made some comment about my missing, and I said that an emergency had come up, and she let it pass. The third time I did it, she told me I would have to pay for missed sessions, and she asked why I had missed. I fumbled around and came up with some dumb excuse—and she just sat there. I talked around in circles, and after letting me hang for a while, she asked whether I was upset with her and whether I was dealing with the feeling by running away—or at least by not coming in. I said, "Of course not; why should I be upset with you? You haven't done anything to me." I know now that I was using denial and playing word games. I didn't realize it at the time, but I was doing with her what I do—or did—with everyone.

Earlier I said that therapy "goes on and on," and that poses a problem because therapy is expensive. I could never afford it myself, but fortunately my health insurance covers most of it. One glitch is that my policy only covers a certain number of visits per year, so last year, when I got beyond that number, I cut back on my visits to one a month. With the new calendar year starting, I'm back to once a week. The other day at the office, I heard that we are switching insurance companies and that the new company is going to allow only a set number of visits for a specific type of problem and after that we are on our own. I'm not sure what effect this will have on me. I hope I can get my act together before the insurance runs out. I don't have a life-and-death type of problem, but therapy sure has been great. Therapy is tough to explain, but this is what I have been going through.

---

centered psychotherapy are illustrated in Case Study 6.2.

Past Versus Present.

Most psychotherapists take the position that current anxieties have their foundations in the client's past experiences. This is similar to the position of psychoanalysts, but less extreme because psychotherapists do not necessarily assume that the problems are rooted as far back as early childhood and infancy. Because of the belief that present anxieties stem from past problems, most of the time in psychotherapy is spent discussing past experiences.

In contrast, some psychotherapists ignore the past and focus exclusively on the present, the "here and now." These psychotherapists do not deny that their clients' problems may be a product of their pasts, but they argue that the clients should not be slaves to the past or, for that matter, to the future. As one advocate of this approach pointed out, "The past is no more and the future not yet. Only the now exists" (Perls, 1970, p. 4). These therapists attempt to relieve anxiety by having clients recognize, acknowledge, and accept ("get in touch with") their current desires, needs, ambitions, and fears. The notion is that clients will be less anxious if they can get the various aspects of their personalities integrated into a meaningful whole, regardless of where the pieces came from or where they will take the clients in the future. The goal is to get the client's current act together.

Therapy Content and Style.

An interesting finding concerning psychotherapy is that clients usually talk about whatever issues their particular therapist believes are important. For example, clients who see Freudian therapists often talk about issues related to Oedipal conflicts, whereas clients who see therapists who take other points of view may talk about things like feelings of inferiority or lack of personal growth. The fact that clients talk about the issues that their psychotherapists believe are crucial is often interpreted by the psychotherapists as evidence that the issues in question are the important ones. However, the question arises, why do clients talk about the things in which their particular psychotherapists are interested?

One of the reasons why clients tend to focus on topics that are of interest to their psychotherapists is that psychotherapists often exert a strong influence over what their clients say, although they may do so unintentionally. The influence psychotherapists exert was studied extensively some years ago when psychologists studied **verbal conditioning** (Holmes, 1967). In the simplest of the verbal-conditioning experiments, students were given a stack of cards, and printed on each card was a different verb and five pronouns (*I, he, she, we, they*). Each student's task was to make up a sentence for each card using the verb and any one of the pronouns. The experimenter sat quietly while the student made up sentences for the first 20 cards; after that, the experimenter showed interest (rewarded the student) by saying "good" or "uh-huh" each time the student made up a sentence using one particular pronoun that the experimenter selected at random. No response was made after sentences employing other pronouns. As indicated in Figure 6.1 (p. 124), the results indicated that the students rapidly increased use of the pronoun that was rewarded.

In more complex experiments that bear a greater similarity to the therapeutic situation, students were asked to talk about various early childhood experiences, and the experimenters used interest (leaning forward, taking notes, head nodding) to selectively reward the discussion of particular types of experiences such as negative ones involving mother, sibling rivalry, or loneliness. As in the pronoun experiments, when students were rewarded for talking about a particular type of experience, they talked more about that type

Case Study 6.2

A CLIENT-CENTERED PSYCHOTHERAPIST AND A CLIENT

The following exchange took place between a therapist and a client in a client-centered psychotherapy session. The client has felt hopeless about herself and has spent most of this hour discussing her feelings of inadequacy and lack of personal worth.

Client: (*Long pause.*) I've never said this before to anyone—but I've thought for such a long time—This is a terrible thing to say, but if I could just—well, if I could just find some glorious cause that I could give my life for I would be happy. I cannot be the kind of a person I want to be. I guess maybe I haven't the guts—or the strength—to kill myself—and if someone else would relieve me of the responsibility—or I would be in an accident—I—I—just don't want to live.

Therapist: At the present time things look so black to you that you can't see much point in living—

Client: Yes—I wish I'd never started this therapy. I was happy when I was living in my dream world. There I could be the kind of person I want to be—But now—There is such a wide, wide gap—between my ideal—and what I am. I wish people hated me. I try to make them hate me. Because then I could turn away from them and could blame them—but no—It is all in my hands—Here is my life—and I either accept the fact that I am absolutely worthless—or I fight whatever it is that holds me in this terrible conflict. And I suppose if I accepted the fact that I am worthless, then I could go away someplace—and get a little room someplace—get a mechanical job someplace—and retreat clear back to the security of my dream world where I could do things, have clever friends, be a pretty wonderful sort of person—

Therapist: It's really a tough struggle—digging into this like you are—and at times the shelter of your dream world looks more attractive and comfortable.

Client: My dream world or suicide.

Therapist: Your dream world or something more permanent than dreams—

Client: Yes. So I don't see why I should waste your time—coming in twice a week—I'm not worth it—What do you think?

Therapist: It's up to you, . . . It isn't wasting my time—I'd be glad to see you—whenever you come—but it's how you feel about it—if you don't want to come twice a week—or if you want to come twice a week?—once a week?—It's up to you.

Client: You're not going to suggest that I come in oftener? You're not alarmed and think I ought to come in—every day—until I get out of this?

Therapist: I believe you are able to make your own decision. I'll see you whenever you want to come.

Client: I don't believe you are alarmed about—I see—I may be afraid of myself—but you aren't afraid of me—

Therapist: You say you may be afraid of yourself—and are wondering why I don't seem to be afraid for you?

Client: You have more confidence in me than I have. I'll see you next week—maybe.

In this exchange, the client expresses her feelings that her growth has been stifled (the gap between her ideal and what she is), and the therapist does not attempt to find or solve an underlying problem but instead accepts her uncritically (even her thoughts of suicide), expresses interest in seeing her, and indicates that he believes she can make good decisions herself.

Source: Rogers (1951), pp. 46–47.

In client-centered therapy, the therapist accepts the client uncritically and works to establish a positive, nurturing environment. The therapist often shares personal reactions, feelings, and experiences.

FIGURE 6.1 STUDENTS INCREASE THEIR USE OF *I* AND *WE* WHEN THE USE OF THOSE PRONOUNS IS REWARDED WITH INTEREST BY THE EXPERIMENTER.

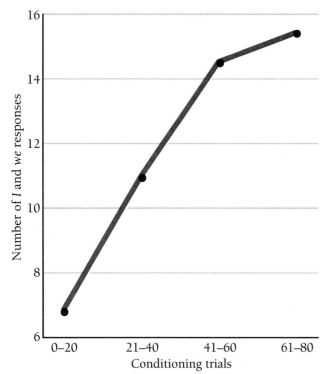

Source: Adapted from Holmes (1967), p. 291, fig. 2.

of experience. Similar processes probably go on in psychotherapy, and they can be used to explain why clients often talk about things that psychotherapists think are interesting and important.

Some of the improvements that result from psychotherapy may also be a consequence of verbal conditioning. For example, it is possible that clients are subtly conditioned to say or think things that lead to more adaptive behavior (e.g., "I don't have to be anxious because I can handle these situations"). That might be a form of cognitive therapy. Alternatively, it is possible that clients are conditioned to report improvements regardless of what is happening. Psychotherapists who want to see improvements may unwittingly reward their clients for reporting that they are doing better.

Some psychoanalysts have argued that they do not influence their clients through verbal conditioning because they play a passive role in the treatment process. However, because they respond less, whatever responses they do make may be all the more important to the client. A colleague of mine who had been in analysis for 4 years argued that the procedure was objective because his analyst rarely said anything, but one day he told me with great excitement that his analyst had smiled at him at the end of his hour on the couch! Convinced that he had done "something right," he went over and over the material from that hour in his sessions for the next few weeks. Either the smile meant that he had said something important that pleased his analyst and his continued talking about it confirmed its importance to the analyst, or the smile meant something else (Was the analyst glad the session was over?) and my friend then misled the analyst about the importance of the material by continuing to talk about it. Clearly, psychotherapists intentionally or unintentionally do influence what their clients tell them, and that must be taken into account in any evaluation of the content of psychotherapy.

Related to style, it is important to realize that most experienced psychotherapists do pretty much the same things in psychotherapy despite differences in their theoretical orientations and training. The issues on which they focus may differ and a therapist's personality may influence how he or she comes across, but most psychotherapists have genuine respect and concern for their clients, listen attentively, reflect on and clarify what is said, offer explanations for problems, and suggest potential solutions. In summary, a psychotherapist's experiences in dealing with clients and finding what works through trial and error appear to be more important than theory and training.

Group Psychotherapy. As the name implies, in **group psychotherapy**, a number of clients are seen at one time. The number of clients may range from three or four to eight or more. Sometimes there will be more than one therapist in the group. The group approach has a number of advantages. First, talking about problems in front of others may initially be threatening, but the other members of the group can be a source of support, and it can be comforting to realize that others have similar problems and are making progress in overcoming them. One woman who had been in group therapy for married couples commented: "For me it was very instructive to see how other couples dealt with conflicts over money, sex, in-laws, whether to have children, infidelity, careers, and so on. It was valuable to see that other people could cry and that men could be intimidated." Second, the other members of the group can aid in the therapeutic process by helping the client explore problems and come up with solutions. Probably most important is the fact that the group provides a microcosm of life outside of therapy, and therefore in therapy individuals can see how they respond to others and how others respond to them, and they can practice new ways of relating.

An interesting extension of group psychotherapy is **family psychotherapy**, in which the family group

Group therapy is a popular therapeutic technique. Members of the group draw support from the fact that others are coping with similar problems. The group setting provides an opportunity for the participants to understand how they interact with one another and to practice new ways of relating.

works on shared problems. Having the family members come together with a therapist who can exert some control and facilitate interactions can enhance communication among family members.

Time-Limited Psychotherapy. In most psychotherapies, the client and therapist work together until the problem is solved, but in **time-limited psychotherapy**, they work together for a previously agreed-on limited number of sessions (e.g., 10 or 15 sessions). The number of sessions is limited in an attempt to make the client work harder and make more efficient use of the time available and thereby speed up the process. Just as students sometimes put off work on a tough term paper until just before it is due, so clients sometimes avoid the difficult issues in therapy if they think they can put them off until later sessions. (The tendency to put off the work of therapy also occurs within therapy sessions, and clients often do not get to the tough issues until the end of a therapy session. That is referred to as the "end of the hour" effect.) Note that time-limited psychotherapy is not a type of therapy per se, only a means by which most traditional forms of psychotherapy can be packaged. The only difference that may emerge is that with the time-limited approach, the therapist may have to be somewhat more active to keep the client moving along. Research has revealed that the time-limited approach is usually at least as effective as time-unlimited therapy (see Koss & Butcher, 1986; Orlinsky & Howard, 1986).

The use of the time-limited strategy was once an option, but today it is often imposed by insurance companies that have to pay for therapy. The companies have a panel of experts review the client's problem and make a judgment about how many sessions the treatment should require, and then the company will pay only for the number of recommended sessions.

Effectiveness of Psychotherapy

The question of whether psychotherapy is effective is one of the most hotly and passionately debated questions in the area of abnormal psychology. For example, E. G. Boring, a leading historian of psychology, underwent psychoanalysis for a period of years and then published an article titled "Was This Analysis a Success?" (Boring, 1940). In that article he wrote:

I had eagerly awaited a light from heaven, at the very least to be changed from Saul to Paul; and all that happened was that the analysis petered out in an uneventful session on June 21. . . . Now, four years after the close of the analysis, I find myself quite uncertain as to whether it has made any important change in me. . . . There is so much about this personality of mine that would be better if different, so much that analysis might have done and did not! (pp. 9–10)

In response, Boring's analyst wrote back saying that "without the analysis," Boring was in "danger of a breakdown" (Sacks, 1940). He went on to say that "some patients behave to the therapeutist in a manner like that of a criminal to the lawyer who has got them off: they deny that they even were seriously involved, and they want to forget all about it." This particular dispute was based on psychoanalysis, but similar differences of opinion have been documented with respect to psychotherapy. In one investigation, clients, therapists, and independent judges rated the effects of psychotherapy (Horenstein et al., 1973). Examination of the ratings revealed that the therapists rated the psychotherapy as much more effective than the clients, and the judges agreed with the clients, thereby suggesting that therapists may overrate the value of their service.

Of more importance to the debate over the effectiveness of psychotherapy were the findings of a series of investigations indicating that about 65% of "neurotic" individuals showed improvement in psychotherapy but that the same proportion of individuals who were *not* treated also improved (Eysenck, 1961). From those findings it was argued that psychotherapy is no more effective than time alone or no more effective than the informal help individuals receive from friends. Those findings sparked considerable controversy and provoked much research on the effects of psychotherapy.

Two conclusions have emerged from the research on the effects of psychotherapy (see Bergin & Lambert, 1978; Lambert et al., 1986; Luborsky et al., 1975; D. Shapiro & D. Shapiro, 1982; Smith et al., 1980; Vanden Bos & Pino, 1980; Winokur & Rickels, 1981). First, it now seems that the percentage of individuals who improve without treatment is closer to 40% than 65%. This means that the success rate of psychotherapy need not be as high as once thought to be more effective than no treatment. Second, it is now generally agreed that the percentage of individuals who improve with therapy is greater than the percentage who improve without therapy. It may also be that individuals in therapy improve faster than those who are not in therapy. In other words, psychotherapy is effective for many clients with anxiety disorders. Unfortunately, it is difficult to determine how much more effective psychotherapy is than no treatment because the estimates of success differ greatly from study to study, but a success rate between 65% and 75% for anxious clients is probably not unrealistic. That is about 30% more than would improve without treatment.

Why Does Psychotherapy Work?

Having concluded that psychotherapy is effective, we must ask, why is it effective? Three lines of research have been pursued to answer that question. First, numerous investigations were conducted to compare the *effects of different types of psychotherapy*. If one type of psychotherapy was found to be more effective than another, it could be concluded that whatever went on in that type of psychotherapy was crucial to improvement. Unfortunately, there is no consistent evidence that any one type of psychotherapy is more effective than another (see Luborsky et al., 1975; Stiles et al., 1986). It is possible that the lack of differences is due to the finding noted earlier that after a while, therapists do pretty much the same things regardless of their theoretical positions or training. However, even

when differences in approach were maximized, differences in outcome have been nonexistent or minimal (e.g., Sloane et al., 1975).

In the second line of research, investigators attempted to link very specific variables rather than general theoretical orientations to increased success in psychotherapy. Investigators examined the effects of *client variables* (e.g., social class, age, sex, personality, expectations; Garfield, 1986), *therapist variables* (e.g., social class, age, sex, personality; Beutler et al., 1986), and *therapy process variables* (e.g., therapy style, client involvement, type of therapeutic relationship; Orlinsky & Howard, 1986). Some relationships were found, but they were usually very weak and not sufficient to account for the effectiveness of psychotherapy.

The third set of findings stems from comparisons of the effectiveness of *professional versus paraprofessional* therapists. **Paraprofessionals** are usually volunteers who have received some instruction in dealing with disturbed individuals but not the extensive training that characterizes professionals. There is some controversy over the findings, but the majority of evidence indicates that paraprofessionals are usually as effective as professional therapists, and in some instances may be even more effective (see Durlak, 1979, 1981; Nietzel & Fisher, 1981; Hattie et al., 1984). For example, in one investigation, hospitalized patients were treated by either medical students who had no training in psychiatry or by psychiatrists (Miles et al., 1976). There was no difference in the improvement rate of those who were seen by the students and those who were seen by the psychiatrists. These findings suggest that professional training may not contribute to the outcome of psychotherapy.

The findings reviewed here pose an awkward problem: We have evidence that psychotherapy is more effective than no treatment, but *we do not have evidence indicating what makes psychotherapy effective*. However, two possible explanations can be derived from the data. First, it may be that although no one of the factors we have examined accounts for the effects of therapy by itself, the combined effect of numerous variables is responsible for the improvements seen in psychotherapy. In other words, the success of psychotherapy, like the success of most interpersonal relationships, may be due to a subtle combination of factors.

The second explanation is that improvement in and out of psychotherapy is due to **social support**, and because individuals in psychotherapy are more likely to get support, they are more likely to show improvement. The argument here is that friendship or support is the crucial factor for improvement and that psychotherapy is the "purchase of friendship" (Schofield, 1964). The role of social support has received considerable attention lately, and we now know that social support is important for both avoiding the effects of stress and recovering from stress. That is, individuals who have close friends in whom they can confide and who can provide emotional support are less influenced by stress and recover from stress faster (Winefield, 1987; see also Chapter 9).

We can conclude this discussion by noting that psychodynamic psychotherapy encompasses a variety of therapeutic strategies that are widely accepted and generally effective for overcoming problems, but we do not yet know whether their effects are due to subtle interpersonal chemistry, social support, or some other, yet unidentified factor.

LEARNING APPROACHES

In our earlier discussion of the causes of anxiety, it was pointed out that learning theorists believe that anxiety is a *classically conditioned* fear response and that an anxiety disorder occurs when a fear response becomes associated with a stimulus that should not elicit fear (see Chapter 5). For example, agoraphobia occurs when fear somehow becomes paired with the stimulus of being away from home, and after that, being away from home elicits fear. Because the anxiety is thought to result from inappropriate conditioning of a fear response, the learning approach to therapy involves correcting the inappropriate conditioning. That can be done by *extinguishing* the fear response, *inhibiting* the fear response by substituting a response that is incompatible with the fear response, or *learning to relax* and then using the relaxation response to overcome anxiety when it occurs. We will discuss all three strategies.

The learning approaches to treatment are focused on the *physiological* aspects of anxiety (e.g., muscle tension, heart rate). The underlying assumptions are that *physiological tension is the cause of the cognitive feelings of anxiety,* and that the *reduction of physiological tension will result in the reduction of cognitive anxiety.* In other words, learning theorists assume that we are anxious because our hearts are beating fast, not that our hearts are beating fast because we are anxious. Actually, the relationship probably goes both ways. If you suddenly came face to face with a hungry tiger, you would probably begin worrying about what was going to happen to you and your heart rate would go up. In that case, your thoughts would influence your physiological responses. By contrast, if you were given a drug that increases your heart rate, you might feel anxious. That is, your physiological responses would influence your thoughts. Therapists who use the learning approach to therapy do not necessarily deny the influence of thoughts on anxiety; instead, they simply choose to focus on physiological arousal because they believe that it is a more important or more frequent cause of anxiety. With that clarified, we will now consider the three strategies for reducing anxiety that are based on the learning explanation.

The approaches to treatment that we will discuss here were developed from the principles of learning, but recently, cognitive explanations have been offered to explain their effects. Both the learning and the cognitive explanations for these therapies are summarized in Table 6.1.

Extinction of Anxiety

One means of eliminating a classically conditioned anxiety response is through the process of **extinction** (see Chapter 2). Extinction occurs when the feared stimulus (the conditioned stimulus) is repeatedly presented *without* the reason for being afraid (the unconditioned stimulus). For example, if an individual who has a classically conditioned fear of dogs is repeatedly exposed to friendly dogs that do not bite, the fear associated with the dogs will eventually be extinguished.

When using extinction as a therapeutic strategy, individuals with phobias are repeatedly exposed to the stimuli they fear. Because exposure to the feared stimulus initially results in an individual's being flooded with anxiety, this therapeutic technique is often referred to as **flooding** (Emmelkamp, 1986). It is also re-

TABLE 6.1   LEARNING AND COGNITIVE EXPLANATIONS FOR THERAPIES SUGGESTED BY LEARNING THEORY

TECHNIQUE	LEARNING EXPLANATION	COGNITIVE EXPLANATION
Flooding, implosion	Extinction of anxiety	Exposure leads to increased self-efficacy
Systematic densensitization, counterconditioning	Inhibition of anxiety	Exposure leads to increased self-efficacy
Relaxation training, biofeedback training	Blocking of anxiety	Training leads to feelings of self-control and self-efficacy

If an individual (such as the person depicted here) who has a classically conditioned fear of dogs is repeatedly exposed to friendly dogs, the fear of dogs will eventually be extinguished.

ferred to as **implosion therapy** (Stampfl & Lewis, 1967, 1968). (An *implosion* is an inrushing of pressure; here it refers to the sudden increase of anxiety when the individual is first exposed to the feared stimulus.)

Individuals may be exposed to the real feared stimulus (e.g., an individual with a fear of heights may be taken to the top of a tall building), or they may be asked to imagine the feared stimulus (e.g., told to imagine being on top of a tall building). Actual exposure to the feared stimulus is called **in vivo exposure**, and imagined exposure is called **in vitro exposure**. In vivo exposure is usually more effective, but in vitro is often more practical in the therapeutic setting. The use of in vivo exposure for the treatment of anxiety is illustrated in Case Study 6.3, which was written by the client's therapist.

Numerous experiments have documented the effectiveness of exposure for reducing or eliminating fears (Emmelkamp, 1982, 1986). The results of one experiment indicated that exposure was as effective as medication (Tofranil/imipramine) for reducing agoraphobia (Mavissakalian & Michelson, 1983). In that experiment, clients were assigned to either (a) an *exposure* condition, in which they received in vivo exposure to open places such as large shopping malls; (b) a

medication condition, in which they received a drug known to be effective for reducing agoraphobic fears; (c) an *exposure plus medication* condition, in which they received both the exposure and the drug; or (d) a *control* condition, in which the clients discussed their problems. Anxiety was measured after 1, 2, and 3 months of therapy; the results of those measures are presented in Figure 6.2. All three treatments were equally effective for reducing anxiety and were more effective than the control condition in which clients only discussed their problems.

Exposure has also been found to be more effective than some other psychological therapies. For example, in one experiment, clients with phobic fears of heights, elevators, or darkness were assigned to therapy conditions in which they received either *guided exposure* (e.g., going up in tall buildings with the therapist) or *cognitive restructuring* (Biran & Wilson, 1981). Cognitive restructuring is a type of therapy in which clients discuss their fears and in doing so are led to change their attitudes and beliefs about the situations that frighten them.

FIGURE 6.2   EXPOSURE, TOFRANIL, AND EXPOSURE PLUS TOFRANIL WERE ALL EQUALLY EFFECTIVE FOR REDUCING ANXIETY.

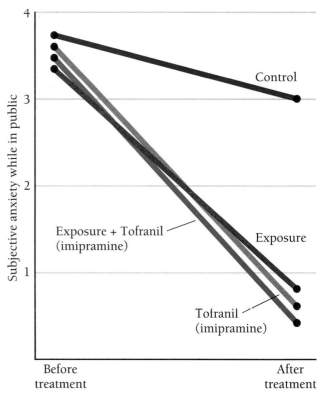

Source: Adapted from Mavissakalian and Michelson (1983), p. 513, fig. 1.

Case Study 6.3

TREATMENT OF A DOG PHOBIA WITH IN VIVO EXPOSURE

Ned was a college senior majoring in mathematics. He was well adjusted in all respects except for the fact that he had a severe fear of dogs. So far as he could remember, he had never been hurt or bitten by a dog.

I decided to use in vivo exposure to dogs as a means of extinguishing Ned's fear. To do this, Ned and I first went to a local pet shop that had a large number of puppies for sale. The puppies were small and very friendly, and each was in a cage. At first, we simply walked around the shop looking at other things but staying away from the dogs. When Ned was relaxed and comfortable, he and I walked slowly over to a cage containing a small cocker spaniel puppy that looked somewhat sleepy. This did not bother Ned much, and I asked him to put his finger through the bars of the cage and scratch the puppy's head. He was a little tentative, thinking the puppy might snap, but he did it, and nothing much happened. Next we went to a cage with three or four wide-awake and active puppies in it, and I asked Ned to put his hand in and play with the puppies. Again he was tentative, but he did it. After he was comfortable with that, I encouraged him to roughhouse with the puppies a little and let them chew on his finger a bit. Again he started out somewhat tentatively, but he did it, and after a few minutes he was enjoying playing with the pups. From there we went from cage to cage and back to some cages playing with the various puppies.

After about 40 minutes, Ned smiled somewhat sheepishly and said, "Once you get used to them, they're kinda fun. Their little teeth can be sharp, but if you're careful, it's all right." However, he then added, "But they're only puppies—not full-grown dogs." I told him we would take it "one step at a time" and that his "homework" before our next session was to go to three or four different pet stores and play with the puppies. The homework was designed to expose him to as many puppies as possible and to deal with them without me there for support.

At the beginning of our next session, Ned reported that he had gone to five different pet shops to play with puppies, that two or three times he had picked puppies up to hold them, and that he was comfortable doing that, but he hastened to add, "But those are only puppies. Dogs are a different thing." After talking for a few minutes, we went to a nearby park where a canine obedience class was being held. The dogs in the class were full-grown, on leashes, and generally well behaved because this was one of the final sessions. We watched the class for a while, noting specifically that the dogs were controllable, and after the class we talked to the owners and Ned very tentatively petted the dogs while their owners held them on a short leash. Ned then worked with the owners to put two dogs through their exercises ("sit," "stay," "come," etc.). At first, he was really nervous when the dog would come, but in time he got used to it. When the session was over, Ned was exhausted (it had been a strain), but he also felt exhilarated; he had played with dogs and enjoyed it.

At our next session, Ned and I developed a list of training exercises that would expose him to more dogs, different kinds of dogs, and dogs in different circumstances. He went to more pet stores and obedience classes as well as to dog shows and veterinarians. He also sought out friends who had dogs and spent time with them and their dogs. If the fear is to extinguish, it is important that the feared stimulus be experienced over and over in the absence of fear. Also, because the fear has generalized, it is important that all of the fear-related stimuli be experienced over and over. During the next couple of weeks, I pushed Ned really hard to increase the amount and types of exposure. With time, the fear slowly diminished, and Ned could play easily with relatively big dogs, even allowing them to lick his face. At the end of the treatment period, Ned commented, "Well, the fear is gone. There is really no reason to be afraid; dogs are like people—most of them are friendly, and the only problem is to separate the friendly ones from the others. After this treatment, I'm not afraid of dogs—I'm sick of them!"

The effectiveness of the two types of therapy was measured by determining how many fear-related behaviors the clients would perform. Fear-related behaviors included looking down from a window on the sixth floor, staying alone on a roof, and walking near the edge of a roof. These behaviors were measured before therapy, after therapy, and 1 month later. In addition, after the 1-month follow-up test, clients who originally received cognitive restructuring therapy were given guided exposure therapy, and their fear behavior was measured again. The results of this experiment indicated that clients in both treatment conditions performed more fear-related behaviors (showed decreases in fear), but the clients who received guided exposure performed more fear-related behaviors than clients who received cognitive restructuring. Furthermore, when the clients in the cognitive restructuring group were given guided exposure, they immediately improved to the level of clients who had originally received guided exposure. The results of this experiment are presented in Figure 6.3.

It now appears that there is good evidence that exposure can be an effective strategy for reducing anxiety, but a question has been raised about why exposure works. Originally it was assumed that exposure caused the extinction of the conditioned fear response, but it now appears that the fear reduction may be due instead to cognitive factors. In other words, it may be that because nothing terrible happens when individuals are repeatedly exposed to a stimulus that they thought was dangerous, they begin to realize that the stimulus is in fact not dangerous or that they can cope with the situation. Those changes in thoughts may re-

FIGURE 6.3 GUIDED EXPOSURE WAS MORE EFFECTIVE FOR REDUCING FEAR-RELATED BEHAVIORS THAN COGNITIVE RESTRUCTURING.

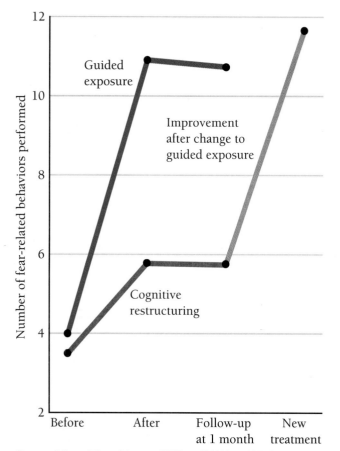

Source: Adapted from Biran and Wilson (1981), p. 892, fig. 1.

sult in fear reduction. For example, a man who is afraid of heights and is taken to the top of a tall building may initially be flooded with anxiety, but he soon realizes that nothing terrible happens and therefore changes his beliefs about the situation, which in turn reduces his fears.

Support for the cognitive explanation for the effects of exposure is provided by the experiment we just discussed (Biran & Wilson, 1981). In addition to measuring fear, the experimenters measured feelings of confidence, or what is often called **self-efficacy** (Bandura, 1977). The results indicated, first, that improvements in self-efficacy were related to decreases in fear and, second, that exposure was more effective than cognitive restructuring for increasing self-efficacy. In summary, exposure does reduce fear, but it seems that the effect may be due to changes in cognitions rather than to the extinction of the classically conditioned response.

It might be noted that exposure can also be used to explain why psychodynamic psychotherapy is effective. It may be that talking and thinking about anxiety-provoking situations in psychotherapy is a form of symbolic exposure and that the exposure results in new cognitions (perhaps insights) that in turn lead to reductions in anxiety.

Inhibition of Anxiety

A second learning-based approach to therapy is founded on the idea that the anxiety response can be *inhibited* by an incompatible response, specifically, a relaxation response. In other words, if a relaxation response is paired with the feared stimulus, the relaxation response will preclude the possibility of an anxiety response. This therapeutic approach is known as **systematic desensitization** (Wolpe, 1958), but it is sometimes referred to as **counterconditioning**. The procedure has three steps. First, the individual is taught how to relax. This is done with a series of exercises in which the individual tenses and then relaxes sets of muscles and in so doing learns to become completely relaxed. This procedure is known as **progressive muscle relaxation** (Jacobsen, 1938). In a typical muscle relaxation training session, the individual reclines in a comfortable chair and is given relaxation exercises by a trainer who speaks slowly with a resonant and relaxing voice. The trainer gives instructions like the following:

Settle back as comfortably as you can. Close your eyes, take a deep breath, hold it, and then let it out. Now take another deep breath, holding it deeply and then letting it out. And another. Still another. As you continue to breathe deeply, let yourself relax—more and more. Relax more and more with each breath. I am now going to make you aware of certain

Case Study 6.4

SYSTEMATIC DESENSITIZATION: THE CASE OF LITTLE PETER

A form of systematic desensitization was reported as early as 1924 in the case of Peter. Like Little Albert, whom we have talked about before, Peter had become afraid of furry objects such as rabbits and fur coats. To overcome this fear, a rabbit was presented to Peter, but it was initially presented far enough away so that Peter did not become afraid. A laboratory assistant then began feeding Peter his favorite food, and then the rabbit was slowly brought closer and closer. Feeding was used to elicit relaxation and pleasure because relaxation training would not be effective with a child as young as Peter. The hope was that the pleasure associated with eating would overwhelm and inhibit the fear. In fact, the procedure was effective in eliminating Peter's fear. With-

in a short period of time, Peter was calmly sitting and eating with the once feared rabbit right next to him.

This case is often cited as an example of the effectiveness of systematic desensitization, but it should be recognized that other processes were going on as well. Most noteworthy is the fact that on most days during the treatment period, other children who were not afraid of the rabbit were brought in to play with Peter and the rabbit, and it appears that some of Peter's fear was reduced by observing the fearlessness of the other children.

Source: Based on Jones (1924) and Kornfeld (1989).

---

sensations in your body and then show you how you can reduce these sensations. First, direct your attention to your arms, and your hands in particular. Clench both fists. Clench them tightly and notice the tension in the hands and in the forearms. Notice this tension as it spreads from your fingers through your hand and through your wrists. As you continue to focus on this tension, I want you to count to yourself slowly along with me. When you reach three, gradually relax the tension in these muscles. Gradually unclench your fists and let your hands hang loose. Ready. Now count with me: one, two, three. Gradually relax. Note the difference between the tension and the relaxation. Concentrate now on the sensation of relaxation as it comes to replace the tension. Try to make this process continue. Focus on the relaxation as it spreads throughout your fingers, your hands, your wrists, and your lower arms. Once again, now, clench your hands into fists tightly, noticing the tension in your hands and forearms. Tighten. Again, count slowly with me, and when you reach three, gradually reduce the tension in your hands and arms. One, two, three. Now relax. Let your fingers spread out, relaxed, and note the difference once again between tension and relaxation.

This procedure is repeated a number of times, and then the trainer moves on to a different set of muscles (upper arms, shoulders, back, legs, neck, forehead) until the individual has learned how to relax all of the major muscle groups.

Second, a list of feared stimuli is compiled in which the stimuli are arranged in order from least feared to most feared. An individual with a phobia for dogs might list the following situations: (a) watching a small puppy in a cage 10 feet away, (b) sitting next to a small dog, and (c) petting a large German shepherd. This list is referred to as a **fear hierarchy**, and it contains many stimuli so that the increase in the level of fear from one stimulus to the next is very small.

Third, the individual is told to begin relaxing and is then asked to imagine the least feared stimulus. The process is started with the least feared stimulus because the individual is most likely to be able to relax and inhibit the fear of that stimulus. If able to remain relaxed while thinking of the first stimulus, the individual is asked to begin thinking about the next least feared stimulus. This procedure is repeated until the individual is relaxing while thinking about the most feared stimulus. If the individual becomes anxious during the procedure, he or she is asked to go back to imagining a previous stimulus with which relaxation was possible. The procedure is repeated a number of times until the relaxation response is consistently effective for inhibiting the fear response.

In some cases, the procedure may be done in vivo rather than in vitro. For example, an individual who is afraid of dogs might move closer and closer to a dog while using the relaxation response to inhibit fear, or an individual who is afraid of heights might inhibit fear with a relaxation response while going up in a tall building one floor at a time. A famous example of the use of systematic desensitization is presented in Case Study 6.4.

Early research suggested that systematic desensitization is effective for reducing fears, and consequently the strategy was used widely (see Kazdin & Wilcoxon, 1976). However, the results of more recent research suggest that the effects may not be as strong as was once thought (Emmelkamp, 1986; Ollendick, 1986). Furthermore, it also appears that the effects may not be due to the inhibition of fears but rather to the exposure to feared stimuli that occurs when the individual works through the fear hierarchy (Emmelkamp, 1982). The exposure could then lead to changes in self-efficacy, so there is a cognitive explanation for what was originally introduced as learning-based treatment.

Learning to Relax

The third learning-based approach to the treatment of anxiety involves teaching individuals how to relax and then having them apply their newly learned skill when they begin feeling anxious. Unlike the extinction and inhibition procedures, in which the client's role is passive, with this approach the client is taught a new skill (relaxation) and then he or she actively applies the skill whenever necessary.

There is evidence that relaxation training is effective in enabling individuals to reduce physiological arousal (see Borkovec & Sides, 1979). For example, individuals who receive progressive muscle relaxation training show lower muscle tension, blood pressure, and heart rate during training sessions than individuals who do not receive the training. More important, a number of experiments have indicated that once individuals learn how to relax, they can apply what they have learned to reduce anxiety in a variety of situations. For example, after having been taught to relax, individuals show lower anxiety during interviews, while getting ready to give speeches, and while preparing for dental operations (e.g., Chang-Liang & Denney, 1976; Goldfried & Trier, 1974; Miller et al., 1978; Zeisset, 1968).

In most cases, applied relaxation does not involve exposure to the feared stimuli during training, and therefore the effects cannot be attributed to exposure per se. However, it is possible that relaxation training leads to a feeling of improved ability to cope, and therefore the effects of the relaxation training might be due to changed cognitions (increases in self-efficacy) rather than the use of relaxation.

Clients are usually taught to relax using progressive muscle relaxation procedures, but recent attempts have been made to teach clients how to relax with **biofeedback training**. Biofeedback training involves giving the individual instantaneous information about the degree to which he or she is able to change anxiety-related responses such as muscle tension, skin temperature, blood pressure, and heart rate. For example, electrodes that detect heart rate are attached to an individual, and the individual's heart rate is displayed on a meter. The individual watches the meter and tries to reduce the heart rate. The instantaneous feedback on the degree to which heart rate has gone up or down supposedly permits the individual to learn quickly what is effective for reducing heart rate and thereby to achieve a state of reduced physiological arousal.

Biofeedback is usually used to alter a specific physiological response such as blood pressure or heart rate, but it has been argued that those reductions can lead to a general reduction of subjective anxiety. We will discuss the effects of biofeedback training in greater detail in Chapter 17, but two points concerning biofeedback should be made here. First, contrary to what is usually assumed, most of the evidence indicates that biofeedback is no more effective than mere rest for reducing many physiological responses such as blood pressure and heart rate (see Holmes, 1985a; Roberts, 1985). In other words, biofeedback training is associated with reduced levels of arousal, but sitting quietly has the same effect, and it is likely that the effects of biofeedback training are actually due to sitting quietly rather than to the biofeedback. Second, there does not appear to be any evidence that biofeedback training has any long-term effects. That is, biofeedback

Relaxation training teaches clients to relax and then to apply their newly learned skill in situations that cause them anxiety.

training (or sitting quietly) may reduce arousal during the training session, but it does not reduce arousal in subsequent stressful situations (Bennett et al., 1978). Overall, then, biofeedback training does not appear to be a particularly effective means of reducing general anxiety.

Comment

The learning approaches to the treatment of anxiety were originally developed as straightforward extensions of the learning explanations for anxiety and the belief that reducing physiological tension would reduce cognitive anxiety. The treatments that are based on the principles of learning have been found to be effective, but there are now reasons to believe that at least some of their effects are due to cognitive factors such as the reevaluation of the feared objects or increased feelings of self-efficacy. However, it should not be concluded that the learning explanations for the effects of treatment have been abandoned in favor of strictly cognitive explanations. It is more likely that processes such as extinction play a role along with the changing of cognitions. In other words, it now appears that anxiety may be reduced by changing both physiological arousal and cognitions. Next we will consider the cognitive strategies for reducing anxiety.

COGNITIVE APPROACHES

Cognitive theorists assume that anxiety occurs when individuals (a) selectively attend to anxiety-provoking stimuli, (b) selectively recall anxiety-provoking thoughts, (c) misinterpret neutral stimuli as anxiety-related, and (d) erroneously expect situations to be threatening. In other words, problems with *information processing* lead to *incorrect beliefs*, which in turn lead to anxiety. For example, an individual may notice dogs, recall that a friend was once bitten by a dog, mistake a friendly dog for a mean one, and expect to be bitten, all of which would lead to a dog phobia. Because incorrect beliefs lead to anxiety, in the cognitive approach to treatment, the goal is to *change beliefs*. Another goal of some cognitive therapists is to *distract* individuals from their maladaptive thoughts. We will discuss some of the more popular techniques used to achieve those goals and then consider the effectiveness of this approach.

Techniques for Changing Beliefs

Changing beliefs is often referred to as **cognitive restructuring**. Two types of anxiety-provoking beliefs can be changed: beliefs about the situation and beliefs about the ability to cope with the situation. For example, a belief about a situation, "It is dangerous to be up in tall buildings," can be changed to "There is really no danger in being up in tall buildings." Similarly, a belief about the ability to cope, "I will panic and lose control if I go up in a tall building," can be changed to "I can learn to relax while up in a tall building, and if that does not work, I can calmly move to a lower floor until I regain control."

Cognitive Therapy.   One technique that is used to change beliefs is called **cognitive therapy**, and it involves offering clients more accurate statements in the hope of correcting their errors and misunderstandings (Beck & Emery, 1985). The statements are initially offered as *hypotheses*, and the clients are asked to test them out and see for themselves whether they are correct. For example, the therapist might simply suggest that tall buildings are not dangerous and suggest that the client go up in a building to see if anything serious happens. After discovering that nothing serious happens, the client changes beliefs, and the anxiety is reduced.

Rational-Emotive Therapy.   Some therapists believe that it is more effective if clients come up with their own new beliefs. These therapists force clients to develop more accurate beliefs by actively cross-examining the clients and challenging their beliefs. For example, when working with an individual who has a phobia for high places, the therapist might ask, "How many tall buildings have ever fallen over?" "Have you ever heard of anyone accidentally falling out of a tall building?" or "Isn't it really safer to be up in a tall building than on the ground trying to cross a busy street?" By doing this, the therapist forces the client to reexamine beliefs, recognize errors in logic, and develop more accurate beliefs. This approach is called **rational-emotive therapy** (Ellis, 1962; Ellis & Grieger, 1977, 1986).

Some therapists augment the procedures by having their clients practice applying their new cognitive strategies in relatively low-stress situations. The practice prepares them for more stressful situations and gives them confidence that they will be able to deal with situations when they occur in everyday life. This procedure is called **stress inoculation training** (Meichenbaum, 1975).

Effectiveness of Cognitive Therapy

Cognitive therapy is a very popular approach to treatment, and there is a substantial amount of evidence supporting its effectiveness. For example, in one experiment, individuals with social phobias were assigned to conditions in which they received either cognitive-behavioral treatment or a placebo treatment (Heimberg et al., 1990). Individuals in the cognitive-behavioral treatment condition received training in cognitive restructuring of maladaptive thoughts (e.g., "Nothing bad will happen to me in a group of people") and exposure to the phobic situation (i.e., groups of people). Individuals in the placebo treatment condition received lectures on phobias and group support. Anxiety was measured before treatment began, immediately after treatment ended, and 3 and 6 months later. The results indicated that individuals in both conditions showed improvement, but that the individuals who received the cognitive-behavioral treatment showed greater improvement (see Figure 6.4).

Limitations.   It is clear that cognitive therapy can be effective for reducing phobias insofar as phobias are based on erroneous beliefs, but by definition cognitive therapy would *not* be effective for treating the generalized anxiety disorder and the panic disorder because those disorders are not based on beliefs; instead, the anxiety comes "out of the blue." Despite that logical limitation, considerable attention has been focused on using cognitive therapy for treating the panic disorder, and the treatment is often reported to be successful. However, a review of the evidence indicates that in the well-controlled investigations that produced positive results, the therapy was found to be effective primarily for reducing *anxiety about having a panic attack* and effectively *dealing with the anxiety when it occurs* rather than eliminating the attacks per se (Mattick et al., 1990; Michelson & Marchione, 1991). That is, clients learn to think, "A panic attack is not the end of the world" and "I can deal with this anxiety." The effects are definitely valuable, but it is important to understand the nature of the effects.

Alternative Processes for Changing Beliefs. It is generally assumed that beliefs are changed most effectively through the process of cognitive therapy, but there are data indicating that simple exposure to the anxiety-provoking situations can be just as effective for changing beliefs. For example, in one experiment, individuals with severe driving phobias participated either in a *cognitive therapy* condition, which involved cognitive therapy plus 11 hours of driving practice, or a *driving-practice-only* condition (exposure), in which they simply practiced driving for 11 hours (Williams & Rappoport, 1983). The cognitive therapy consisted of (a) training in relabeling of feelings (e.g., "These anxious feelings won't harm me; they're just uncomfortable"), (b) developing positive expectations ("I will be able to manage regardless of how I feel"), (c) focusing on task-relevant thoughts ("Keep my mind on my driving"), and (d) using self-distraction (planning recreational activities). The results revealed that the clients who were given cognitive therapy used more coping thoughts while driving than the practice-only clients, but there were no differences between the cognitive therapy and driving-practice-only conditions in terms of decreases in self-reported fear, increases in confidence, or increases in the ability to drive through the city alone. It was concluded that "fear is indeed rooted in thought, but . . . the best way to change thought is through performance-based treatments which give clients firsthand evidence that they can function effectively" (Williams & Rappoport, 1983, p. 312). In other words, successful experiences with driving (exposure) resulted in changed attitudes about driving, and those changed attitudes reduced fear. Hence it can be concluded that changing cognitions (beliefs) is an effective way to reduce anxieties, and both cognitive and behavioral strategies are effective for changing cognitions and reducing anxieties.

Distraction

The last cognitive strategy we will consider for reducing anxiety is **distraction**, whereby the individual does not reduce anxiety by changing anxiety-provoking thoughts but instead simply avoids them. The most

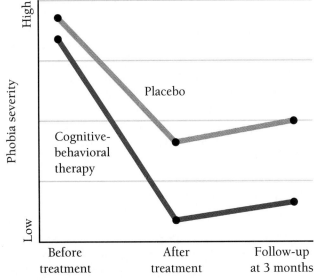

FIGURE 6.4   INDIVIDUALS WITH SOCIAL PHOBIAS WHO RECEIVED COGNITIVE-BEHAVIORAL TREATMENT SHOWED GREATER REDUCTIONS IN FEAR THAN INDIVIDUALS WHO RECEIVED PLACEBO TREATMENT.

Source: Adapted from Heimberg et al. (1990), p. 11, fig. 1.

popular distraction-based therapy for dealing with stress is **meditation** (D. H. Shapiro, 1980; West, 1987). The crucial factor in most forms of meditation is the use of a **mantra**, which is a nonsense word (e.g., *abna*) that the individual repeats over and over while meditating. The mantra is used to "clear the mind," and it achieves that goal by keeping the individual from thinking about anything that might be arousing. In other words, the mantra is a distractor like "counting sheep," which some people use to help them get to sleep when they are worrying about something. The act of meditating provides a distraction because you cannot think anxiety-provoking thoughts while concentrating on a mantra. Beyond that, however, it has been suggested that while meditating, you somehow refresh yourself and replenish your energy so that you can cope better afterward, but exactly how that is accomplished has never been explained scientifically.

Meditation has been practiced for centuries in the Far East, and a form called **transcendental meditation** was popularized in the West during the 1960s and 1970s (Mahesh Yogi, 1963). Another meditative technique that has gained widespread acceptance, which employs counting rather than a traditional mantra, is known as the **relaxation response** (Benson, 1975).

There are many misconceptions about the effects of meditation. Most of the attention given to meditation revolves around the possibility that it can reduce physiological arousal, and there are numerous anecdotal reports about the ability of yogi masters to reduce or stop their hearts, reduce respiration, and alter blood chemistry. Reduction of physiological arousal is relevant to the treatment of anxiety because high physiological arousal could be a cause or an effect of anxiety. There is no doubt that sitting quietly and meditating will reduce physiological arousal, but the important point that is often overlooked is that *meditation does not result in greater reductions in physiological arousal than simply sitting quietly without meditating* (see Holmes, 1984b, 1987). In more than 20 experiments, the arousal of meditating and resting individuals was compared, and the results consistently indicated that meditating and resting individuals showed comparable reductions in arousal. At present, then, it cannot be concluded that meditation is more effective than rest for reducing the physiological causes or effects of anxiety.

Although meditation does not reduce physiological arousal more than rest, it is possible that it might reduce the subjective feelings of anxiety (e.g., apprehension, worry). That possibility was tested in an interesting series of experiments in which individuals were randomly assigned to conditions in which they either participated in (a) real meditation, (b) bogus meditation (sat quietly with eyes closed but did not use a

Many persons use meditation as a stress-reducing technique. However, evidence from controlled experiments indicates that simply sitting quietly results in similar reductions in physical arousal.

mantra), or (c) antimeditation (engaged in deliberate, active cognitive activity designed to be the antithesis of meditation; Smith, 1976). The individuals in all three conditions were led to believe that the meditation they were performing would help them. The results indicated that the individuals in *all three* meditation conditions reported decreases in anxiety and that there were no differences in the degree to which the various meditation procedures reduced anxiety. Because the bogus meditation and antimeditation procedures were as effective as real meditation, it must be concluded that the anxiety reductions were due to *expectations* about the effects rather than to the meditation per se. In summary, the existing evidence indicates that meditating may reduce arousal, but sitting quietly and expectations about what will happen, and not the meditation, are responsible for the effect.

Comment

We have seen how changing cognitions (beliefs) can be an effective way to reduce anxiety and, specifically, phobias. Cognitions can be changed both with cognitive strategies, such as teaching clients more appropriate thoughts, and with behavioral strategies, such as exposing clients to situations to show them that the situations are not dangerous or that the clients can handle the situations. Paradoxically, some behavioral strategies, such as exposure, that were originally designed to influence learning may be at least as effective for changing cognitions as some of the strategies that were specifically designed to change cognitions.

PHYSIOLOGICAL APPROACHES

The physiological approach to the treatment of anxiety disorders involves using drugs to *correct the biochemical problems* that lead to excessive levels of anxiety. In considering the drug treatment of anxiety disorders, it is important to recognize that different disorders stem from different underlying physiological causes. For example, in most cases, the generalized anxiety disorder is due to low levels of GABA, the obsessive-compulsive disorder stems from low levels of serotonin, and the panic disorder is linked to sodium lactate (see Chapter 5). That is important because the different causes require different drugs for treatment. In the sections that follow, we will first review the early drugs that were initially used to treat all forms of anxiety, and then we will examine the specific anxiety disorders that are most effectively treated with the various types of drugs. Following that, we will consider the side effects of the drugs and some of the controversial issues associated with their use.

Early Drug Treatment of Anxiety

Barbiturates.   The first drugs that were used to treat anxiety were the **barbiturates** (bar-BICH-ur-its). These drugs were introduced in the 1930s and were used until the early 1950s. They are fast-acting, powerful, *general sedatives* that act by reducing overall activity in the central nervous system. In large doses, they can act quickly to induce sluggishness or sleep. They have three major drawbacks for treating anxiety: (a) They are physically and psychologically addicting, so they cannot be used for prolonged periods of time; (b) at high levels, they are extremely lethal (they result in paralysis of the respiratory center of the brain, so the patient stops breathing); and (c) their effects are general rather than specific to anxiety. Treating anxiety with barbiturates is like killing a fly with a bomb; you will knock out a lot more than the target with it. For these reasons, barbiturates are rarely used today in the treatment of anxiety. Among the most widely used barbiturates were Amytal (amobarbital), Nembutal (pentobarbital), and Seconal (secobarbital).

Propanediols.   The **propanediols** (PRŌ-pān-DI-ōls) were introduced in the early 1950s and played an important role in the drug revolution in the treatment of mental patients. These drugs were originally used with very disturbed patients, and because of their strong sedating effects, they were responsible for bringing calm and control to psychiatric wards that had previously been characterized by disruptive and "crazy" behavior. The best known propanediols were **Equanil** and **Miltown** (both **meprobamate**).

These drugs were an improvement over the barbiturates because they are not addictive, do not have dangerous side effects, and are more focused (they do not simply "knock the patient out"). Unfortunately, the major effect of these drugs is as a *muscle relaxant*, and insofar as they reduce anxiety, they do so because they relax the muscles. There is now some question about how effective these drugs actually are for treating anxiety. A review of the research reveals that in only 5 of 26 experiments were Equanil and Miltown found to be more effective than a placebo in the treatment of "psychoneurotic" (primarily anxious) clients (Greenblatt, 1971). In fact, it appears that the propanediols do not serve to reduce anxiety until the dosage levels get close to the point of inducing extreme drowsiness and impaired mental functioning (Rickels & Snow, 1964). Because the effects of the propanediols are focused on muscle relaxation rather than on the target symptom of anxiety and because of their limited effectiveness for treating anxiety, they are now rarely used to treat anxiety.

General Anxiety and the Benzodiazepines

Now we will consider specific anxiety disorders, their suspected physiological causes, and the treatments that are effective with them. The links among diagnoses, suspected biochemical causes when known, and drug treatments of choice are summarized in Table 6.2.

We now know that in many cases, general anxiety is due to low levels of **GABA**, a neurotransmitter that is essential for the activity of **inhibitory neurons**. If GABA is low, (a) inhibitory neurons do not fire, (b) consequently neurological activity in the area of the brain that is responsible for arousal becomes too high, and (c) that high level of activity is experienced as anxiety. To overcome that problem, a group of drugs known as **benzodiazepines** (BEN-zō-dī-AZ-uh-pēnz) was developed. Benzodiazepines are effective for treating anxiety because they *increase GABA activity* (primarily by aiding its entry into the receptor cites), and thereby inhibit neurological activity (Haefely, 1977; Mao et al., 1977). The effects of benzodiazepines are specific to the parts of the brain responsible for anxiety (reticular activating system, limbic system), and therefore they do not have the more widespread effects seen with the barbiturates and the propanediols. However, at high dosage levels,

TABLE 6.2 ANXIETY DISORDERS, THEIR BIOCHEMICAL CAUSES, AND THE DRUGS USED IN THEIR TREATMENT

DISORDER	PHYSIOLOGICAL CAUSE	DRUG TREATMENT
General anxiety	Low levels of GABA that lead to excessive levels of neurological activity	Benzodiazepines that increase GABA activity
Obsessive-compulsive disorder	Low levels of serotonin	Antidepressants (bicyclics and tricyclics) that block reuptake of serotonin
Panic	Probably involves sodium lactate, but process is unknown	Antidepressants (bicyclics, tricyclics, MAO inhibitors); mechanism is unclear
Phobias	Probably due to conditioning or to erroneous beliefs, but high levels of arousal or reactivity could contribute to those causes	Benzodiazepines reduce general anxiety; beta blockers reduce heart rate reactivity; antidepressants have unspecified effects

Note: Disorders may have more than one cause. Those with biochemical causes can be treated with drugs as indicated here.

benzodiazepines can have broader effects and cause drowsiness and general sedation.

The most widely used benzodiazepine is **Valium (diazepam)**. Valium is a relatively fast-acting drug that reaches its peak concentration within 1 hour. It is transported out of the brain rather quickly, but its metabolites (new substances produced during its breakdown) remain, and because the metabolites are effective for reducing anxiety, the clinical effects are prolonged. Valium is a very safe drug, and no deaths due to overdose have been recorded. High levels of diazepam are not lethal because there is an upper limit to its ability to reduce neurological activity, and that limit is below the point at which respiratory activity and other vital functions are inhibited. However, high levels of benzodiazepines taken in combination with other drugs such as alcohol can be lethal. Frequently used benzodiazepines are listed in Table 6.3.

There is substantial evidence that benzodiazepines are effective for reducing general anxiety (Greenblatt & Shader, 1974, 1978; Kellner et al., 1978). For example, benzodiazepines were found to be more effective than placebos in 22 of the 25 experiments conducted in one 5-year period. The results of one experiment in which Valium was compared to a placebo are presented in Figure 6.5 (p. 138). Further-

more, in double-blind reversal experiments in which groups of clients received either benzodiazepines or placebos and then the treatments were reversed, anxiety went down when clients were taking the benzodiazepines and up when they were taking the placebos. Overall then, it can be concluded that benzodiazepines are effective for treating general anxiety.

Obsessive-Compulsive Disorder and Antidepressants

It now appears that for about half of the individuals who suffer from the obsessive-compulsive disorder (OCD), the cause is low levels of the neurotransmitter serotonin (see Chapter 5). It follows, then, that to treat the OCD, we should use drugs that increase the levels of serotonin, and that leads to an interesting paradox: The drugs that are most effective for increasing serotonin are *antidepressant* drugs, not antianxiety drugs. Technically, the drugs that increase serotonin levels are known as **bicyclics** or **tricyclics** because their chemical structures involve two or three circles, respectively (see Chapter 11). These drugs have their effects because they block the reuptake of serotonin by the presynaptic neurons, thus making more serotonin available at the synapse (see Chapter 2).

The utility of **antidepressants** for treating the OCD was clearly demonstrated in a large experiment involving 520 patients who were given either a tricyclic (Anafranil/clomipramine) that blocked the reuptake of serotonin or a placebo, and the patients' symptoms were assessed once each week for 10 weeks (Clomipramine Collaborative Study Group, 1991). The results indicated that by the end of the first week, the patients taking the antidepressant were already showing greater reductions in symptoms than those in the placebo group, and the difference became pro-

TABLE 6.3 FREQUENTLY USED BENZODIAZEPINES

TRADE NAME	GENERIC NAME
Ativan	lorazepam
Centrax	prazepam
Klonopin	clonazepam
Librium	chlordiazepoxide
Valium	diazepam
Xanax	alprazolam

FIGURE 6.5   VALIUM (DIAZEPAM) WAS MORE
EFFECTIVE FOR REDUCING ANXIETY
THAN A PLACEBO.

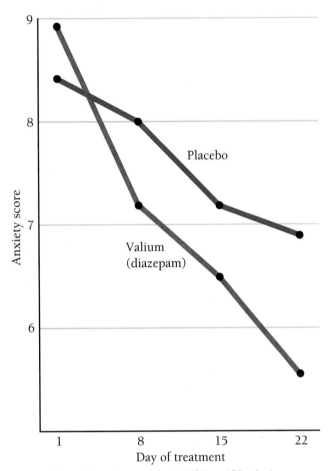

Source: Adapted from Burrows et al. (1976), p. 178, tab. 4.

FIGURE 6.6   AN ANTIDEPRESSANT DRUG
(ANAFRANIL/CLOMIPRAMINE) WAS
MORE EFFECTIVE THAN A PLACEBO
FOR REDUCING THE SYMPTOMS
OF THE OBSESSIVE-COMPULSIVE
DISORDER.

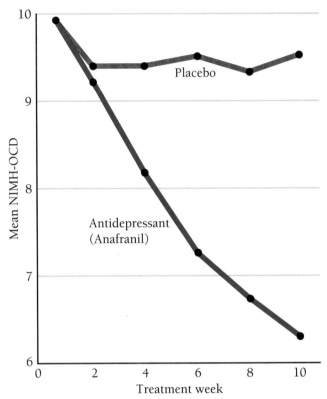

Note: Means are for the NIMH Global OC Scale. Data are collapsed over Study 1 (patients who had been ill for at least 2 years) and Study 2 (patients who had been ill for at least 1 year).
Source: Clomipramine Collaborative Study Group (1991), p. 734, tab. 3.

gressively greater over the remaining 9 weeks of the study. These results are presented in Figure 6.6. In general, the patients taking the antidepressant drug showed a 36% decline in symptoms, whereas the patients taking the placebo showed only a 2% decline in symptoms. The results also indicated that the drug was effective in treating the symptoms of the OCD even in patients who were not depressed, thus indicating that the drug reduced the symptoms of the OCD directly rather than reducing depression and thereby reducing the symptoms of the OCD. Similar results have been found with adolescents who suffered from the OCD and were given a tricyclic (De Veaugh-Geiss et al., 1992). It should also be noted that the widely used bicyclic antidepressant Prozac (fluoxetine), which also blocks the reuptake of serotonin, has been shown to be effective for treating the OCD (e.g., Pigott et al., 1990).

The results in Figure 6.6 are based on overall means, but a slightly different picture emerges when improvements in individuals patients are considered. When that was done, it was found that by the end of the 10 weeks of treatment, only half of the patients who were taking the drug had scores in the normal or subclinical range (below 6). This means that some of the patients showed large improvements, whereas others showed small or no improvements, thus suggesting that the drug was working for only a subgroup of patients. That result is consistent with the notion that the OCD may stem from more than one cause (see Chapter 5). Clearly, antidepressants that block the reuptake of serotonin are effective for treating patients for whom low levels of serotonin are effective for treating patients for whom low levels of serotonin is the problem underlying the OCD. It is suspected that in other patients, the symptoms may stem from minimal brain damage (see Chapter 5), and there is not yet a treatment for those patients.

Panic Disorder, Agoraphobia, and Antidepressants

In Chapter 5, it was explained that in many individuals, the panic disorder can be brought on by an injection of sodium lactate, but we do not yet understand the connection between sodium lactate and panic or the underlying cause of the panic disorder. However, in experimenting with different drugs, it was found that *antidepressant* drugs were often effective for treating the panic disorder and the agoraphobia that sometimes accompanies the panic disorder. (Recall that agoraphobia is often linked to panic attacks, probably because individuals become fearful of having a panic attack in public and therefore restrict their public activities.) The antidepressants that are effective are the tricyclics that were discussed earlier, but another type of antidepressant known as **MAO inhibitors** (or **MAOIs**) is also effective. MAO inhibitors inhibit the effects of chemicals that oxidize (break down) norepinephrine and serotonin at the synapse. If the oxidation of the neurotransmitters is inhibited, more of the neurotransmitters will be available at the synapse, and hence there will be more activity at the synapse. By making more norepinephrine and serotonin available either by blocking their reuptake (tricyclics) or by inhibiting their breakdown (MAOIs), panic attacks are reduced. Although we know that the drugs reduce panic attacks, we do not yet understand exactly why that happens.

Two sets of findings have yielded evidence that tricyclics and MAO inhibitors are effective for treating panic attacks and agoraphobia. The first set of findings emerged from the research in which it was learned that panic attacks can be brought on artificially by injections of sodium lactate (see Chapter 5). In that research it was also found that if individuals were first given either a tricyclic or an MAO inhibitor, when they were later given the sodium lactate, they did not have their usual panic attacks (Klein, 1982; Rifkin et al., 1981). In other words, the tricyclics and MAO inhibitors were effective for inhibiting the artificially induced panic attacks.

The second set of findings stems from the treatment of clients who have spontaneous panic attacks (i.e., those not brought on by sodium lactate injections). In double-blind studies in which the effects of an antidepressant were compared to those of a placebo, the antidepressant was found to be more effective

for reducing panic attacks and agoraphobia than the placebo (e.g., Mattick et al., 1990; Mavissakalian & Perel, 1989, 1992a, 1992b). Furthermore, when the medication was discontinued, the panic attacks and agoraphobia returned.

Phobias, Benzodiazepines, Beta Blockers, and Antidepressants

Phobias are widely believed to stem from either classical conditioning or erroneous beliefs concerning the danger associated with specific stimuli (e.g., "snakes are dangerous"). However, there are some suggestions that individuals with phobias are more physiologically aroused or physiologically reactive than other individuals, and that might contribute to their classical conditioning of phobias or explain their strong response to the erroneous beliefs. Furthermore, the symptoms of arousal or reactivity (e.g., elevated heart rate) might be misinterpreted as signs of anxiety and thereby contribute to the development of fears and phobias (see Chapter 5 and review by Levin et al., 1989). If either of those possibilities is true, phobias could be treated by reducing physiological arousal and reactivity.

General arousal or anxiety can be reduced with benzodiazepines, and there is evidence that these drugs can lead to a reduction in phobias. That was demonstrated in an early experiment on pigeons in which the birds were first taught to peck at a disk to receive food; then they were given electrical shocks when they pecked the disk, so they avoided making the response. In other words, anxiety was associated with the disk, so the birds avoided pecking it. However, on subsequent days, the birds either were or were not given benzodiazepines, and it was found that when they were given the drug, their pecking of the disk returned almost to the normal (preshock) level, but when they were not given the drugs, they avoided pecking the disk (Sanger & Blackman, 1981; see review by Houser, 1978). In human terms, a phobia was induced in the birds (fear of pecking the disk), which was then treated effectively with benzodiazepines. There are also numerous experiments on humans in which benzodiazepines were effective for reducing phobias (Levin et al., 1989). The reduction in arousal may reduce the physiological basis for the phobia, or the reduction in anxiety may enable to the individual to test the frightening situation and realize that it is not really dangerous (i.e., the erroneous cognitions are corrected).

Heart rate reactivity (as opposed to general chronic arousal) can be controlled with drugs known as **beta blockers**. These drugs keep heart rate stable in the face of stress (e.g., exercise or fear) by blocking the stimulation of the heart. Beta blockers were originally developed for individuals with heart problems who had to avoid cardiac stress, but they can be used to treat individuals with phobias because if heart rate does not increase in what is thought to be a fearful situation (e.g., public speaking), the individual may reevaluate the situation and reduce the fear (see Levin et al., 1989).

Finally, it should be noted that there is a growing body of evidence that MAO inhibitors are effective for treating social phobias (e.g., Levin et al., 1989; Gelernter et al., 1991; Liebowitz et al., 1992). Unfortunately, the reason this type of antidepressant is effective for reducing the social phobia is not yet clear.

Side Effects of the Benzodiazepines

The evidence clearly indicates that benzodiazepines are effective for reducing general anxiety, but do these drugs have negative side effects? The answer is yes. The benzodiazepines' negative side effects include drowsiness, light-headedness, dry mouth, nausea, blurred vision, and constipation (Evans, 1981). Some of these side effects are experienced by as many as 30% of the individuals who take the drugs. However, it is important to note that individuals who take placebos also experience many of these side effects, thus suggesting that some of the side effects are due to suggestions or expectations rather than the drugs per se (but that does not, of course, reduce their unpleasantness).

Given that the drugs do have side effects, we must go on to ask, do the negative side effects outweigh the positive effects? The answer is no; in most cases, individuals would rather put up with the side effects than suffer from the symptoms the drugs relieve. Three points should be noted in this regard:

1. The side effects of the drugs are usually *not severe enough to disrupt normal living.* For example, 13% of the individuals who take Valium experience a dry mouth, but at worst that is only a minor annoyance and does not generally interfere with normal daily living.
2. Some clients report side effects of drowsiness or confusion, but there is evidence that at the proper dosages, benzodiazepines actually *enhance mental functioning* (Bond et al., 1974). This enhancement occurs because without the drug, the individual's level of anxiety is so high that it interferes with performance, whereas the drug reduces the excessive anxiety, and consequently performance improves. For most individuals, the net effect seems to be positive.
3. Over time, many of the *side effects disappear* entirely or become relatively unimportant. That may occur because the body adjusts to the effects of

the medication (McKim, 1986). Many of the side effects about which patients complain occur only at high dose levels.

Perhaps the best indication that the side effects of the benzodiazepines are not unduly troublesome is the fact that it is rarely difficult to get individuals to keep taking these drugs. Indeed, individuals seek these medications and, if anything, find them difficult to give up.

Issues Associated with Drug Treatment

Before concluding our evaluation of drug treatment, it might be helpful if we considered some of the questions and concerns that are often raised when the use of drugs is discussed. These questions and concerns are relevant for the drug treatment of anxiety, but they are also relevant for the drug treatment of other disorders such as depression and schizophrenia that we will consider later.

Treatment Versus Cure. Drugs are *treatments, not cures.* That is, a drug will temporarily change the level of a neurotransmitter and thereby relieve symptoms, but the drug will not correct the underlying problem that led to the inappropriate level of the neurotransmitter. When the drug is withdrawn, the symptoms may return. The fact that drugs do not provide cures is certainly a limitation, but that limitation is not a reason to reject the treatment, especially considering that we do not at present have a cure. If you have a bad headache, you may take an aspirin to relieve the pain. The aspirin will not cure the headache, but it will relieve the pain and let you get on with your activities. Should you not take the aspirin just because it is not a cure? Perhaps a better analogy is to diabetes, a disorder that stems from the fact that the individual does not produce enough insulin (a situation that is similar to not producing enough GABA). Diabetes can be treated effectively by giving the individual insulin injections on a regular basis, but the insulin does not cure the problem of underproduction of insulin by the body. Should individuals with diabetes stop taking the insulin because it does not cure the disorder? Perhaps some day we will identify cures for headaches, diabetes, anxiety, and schizophrenia, but until then we will have to be content with symptom relief.

Long-Term Need for Drugs. Because drugs provide treatments rather than cures, clients often ask, "Will I have to stay on the drug from the rest of my life?" Probably not, but in some cases yes. In some cases, the biochemical imbalance that is being corrected by the drug may be a temporary aberration that will correct itself spontaneously, or the imbalance may be age-limited and will be corrected after running its course. The temporary nature of some imbalances is reflected in the fact that panic attacks and periods of generalized anxiety do go away, and disorders such as anxiety and schizophrenia tend to remit with increasing age. In those cases, the individuals can cease taking the drug as soon as the imbalance has been corrected. Unfortunately, there are also biochemical imbalances that may be lifelong, and like those responsible for diabetes, they may require medication throughout the life span. The key to determining whether medication is still necessary is occasionally to test the lower limit of drug dosage effectiveness (can you get along with less medication?) or occasionally to take "drug holidays" (can you get along without any medication?). Of course, that should be done under careful supervision.

Drug Dependence.   A potential problem with the use of benzodiazepines revolves around the development of physical **dependence** after prolonged use. (Dependence on a drug is said to develop when physical symptoms occur if the use of the drug is terminated; see Chapter 18.) In the 1980s, serious concerns were raised because physicians were prescribing benzodiazepines so widely and anecdotal reports suggested that some persons had become "addicted" (Marks, 1978; Lader, 1978). Indeed, Valium was referred to as "psychiatric aspirin" and the "opium of the masses." Research on the addictive quality of benzodiazepines is difficult to do because some of the symptoms of anxiety that return when the use of the drug is terminated may be mistaken for symptoms of dependence when in fact they are simply the symptoms for which the treatment is needed. However, there is now some evidence that dependence can develop after prolonged use at high levels. In one experiment, persons who had been on high daily doses of benzodiazepines for at least 3 months were either switched to a placebo or had their drug level slowly tapered over an 8-week period (Busto et al., 1986). The patients who were switched to the placebo showed a greater increase in symptoms. Specifically, they showed increases in anxiety, tension, insomnia, difficulty in concentration, and fear, all of which were symptoms for which the drug had been prescribed originally. However, the patients who were switched to the placebo also showed symptoms of involuntary muscle tremors and cognitive confusion, symptoms that the investigators attributed to dependence. From these results, it can be concluded that some of the symptoms that occur when the use of benzodiazepines is terminated abruptly are due to physical dependence, but most of the symptoms reflect the return of the disorder for which the drug was original-

ly taken. Fortunately, dependence can be minimized with a careful withdrawal process (Rickels et al., 1991).

Psychologists and Prescriptions for Drugs. At the present time, psychologists are not licensed to write prescriptions for drugs, and therefore drugs can be obtained only from physicians. However, that may be changing. Because of the widespread need for drugs and the fact that there are too few physicians available, research is now under way to determine whether psychologists would be effective in prescribing drugs if they were given additional training in psychopharmacology.

Comment

The physiological approach to treatment has become much more sophisticated and effective since it was realized that different disorders are due to different physiological problems and therefore require different drugs. Now, rather than simply prescribing an "antianxiety" drug for all types of anxiety disorders, different types of drugs are prescribed for different anxiety disorders (e.g., benzodiazepines for general anxiety, antidepressants for OCD and panic attacks). This has greatly increased the effectiveness of drug treatment. Furthermore, the development of new drugs that are more specific in their effects (influencing only one neurotransmitter) has improved effectiveness and reduced unwanted side effects. These changes have reduced some of the criticisms of the drug treatment of anxiety that were relevant as recently as 5 or 10 years ago.

■ SUMMARY

Psychodynamic theorists believe that anxiety stems from unresolved conflicts, which therapists attempt to identify and resolve. Psychodynamic treatment can be divided into two major types, psychoanalysis and psychotherapy. Psychoanalysis is a long process relying primarily on free association, the interpretation of dreams, resistance, and transference. There are numerous forms of psychotherapy, and many of them borrow elements from psychoanalysis.

Differences among various psychotherapies can be organized along two dimensions: (a) whether the anxiety is seen as being due to a problem within the client or as stemming from psychosocial constraints that limit the client's personal growth and (b) whether the emphasis is placed on the past or the present. Psychotherapy is practiced with individuals and in small groups, and the use of time-limited psychotherapy has been increasing. Psychotherapy has been found to be more effective than no treatment for reducing symptoms, but it is not clear what process is responsible for the effects. One possibility is that social support accounts for the improvements that occur in and out of psychotherapy.

Learning theorists assume that anxiety stems from inappropriate classical conditioning, and they use three strategies to correct or overcome the conditioning. The first strategy, based on the process of extinction, involves repeatedly exposing clients to feared stimuli. This is often referred to as flooding or implosion therapy. The second strategy involves the inhibition of the anxiety response by pairing the feared stimuli with a relaxation response that is incompatible with the fear response. Relaxation is learned through a technique known as progressive muscle relaxation, and the treatment in which relaxation is paired with the feared stimuli is known as systematic desensitization. The third strategy involves teaching clients how to relax and then instructing them to employ the relaxation response when any stimulus begins to cause anxiety. The learning-based approaches to treatment are effective for reducing anxiety, but their success may be due to the fact that they change individuals' beliefs rather than changing conditioning per se. Biofeedback training is also used to teach clients how to relax, but for most physiological responses, it is no more effective for reducing arousal than sitting quietly.

Therapists who subscribe to the cognitive explanation for anxiety assume that anxiety stems from incorrect beliefs, and they treat anxiety by changing beliefs. They do that by offering new non-anxiety-provoking beliefs or hypotheses (cognitive therapy) or by helping clients develop their own new non-anxiety-provoking beliefs (rational-emotive therapy). There is evidence that these strategies are effective for changing cognitions and reducing fears and phobias. In the case of the generalized anxiety disorder and the panic disorder, cognitive therapy appears to be more effective in helping individuals deal with the anxiety than in eliminating the disorders. Paradoxically, however, strategies such as exposure that are based on the learning explanation may actually be as effective for changing cognitions and reducing fear as the cognitive strategies. Another cognitive approach to treatment of anxiety is based on distraction, and the most frequently used strategy is meditation, in which a mantra is used to distract the individual from arousing thoughts. The most popular forms of meditation are transcendental meditation and the relaxation response. Unfortunately, meditation is no more effective for reducing physiological arousal than sitting quietly, and its effects on subjective anxiety appear to be due to placebo and expectancy effects.

From a physiological perspective, anxiety is due to biochemical imbalances, and physiological approaches to treatment involve the use of drugs to correct those imbalances. Originally, we used barbiturates and propanediols, which served to reduce general arousal, but now we use drugs that are more specific in their effects and are less sedating. Moreover, because different anxiety disorders involve different types of imbalances, different drugs are used to treat different disorders: Benzodiazepines are used for generalized anxiety, and antidepressants are used for the obsessive-compulsive disorder and panic attacks. Phobias are treated with benzodiazepines, antidepressants, and beta blockers, but those drugs probably serve only to blunt the symptoms rather than to correct the underlying problem (which is probably conditioning or erroneous beliefs). The benzodiazepines do cause some troublesome side effects, but they often diminish over time, and for most individuals the positive effects of the drugs outweigh the side effects. Drug treatment has been shown to be very effective, but it is a treatment and not a cure; individuals may have to continue taking the drugs and can become dependent on them.

■ KEY TERMS, CONCEPTS, AND NAMES

In reviewing and testing yourself on what you have learned from this chapter, you should be able to identify and discuss each of the following:

analyst	cognitive therapy	fear hierarchy
antidepressants	counterconditioning	flooding
barbiturates	dependence	free association
benzodiazepines	diazepam (Valium)	GABA
beta blockers	distraction	group psychotherapy
bicyclics	dream interpretation	implosion therapy
biofeedback training	Equanil (meprobamate)	inhibitory neurons
client-centered psychotherapy	extinction	insights
cognitive restructuring	family psychotherapy	in vitro exposure

in vivo exposure
latent content
manifest content
mantra
MAO inhibitors (MAOIs)
meditation
meprobamate (Equanil, Miltown)
Miltown (meprobamate)
paraprofessionals

progressive muscle relaxation
propanediols
psychoanalysis
psychoanalyst
psychotherapy
rational-emotive therapy
relaxation response
resistance
self-efficacy

social support
stress inoculation training
systematic desensitization
time-limited psychotherapy
transcendental meditation
transference
tricyclics
Valium (diazepam)
verbal conditioning

Chapter 7

Somatoform and Dissociative Disorders

· O U T L I N E ·

lice has frequently consulted physicians about a wide variety of physical symptoms including vague pains, lumps, dizziness, blurred vision, digestive problems, and numbness. Because in many cases a cause cannot be identified, she is often sent to specialists who do additional work-ups, but even they have difficulty making a firm diagnosis. Her case becomes more complex because usually after a short period of treatment, the symptoms change, and then additional medical consultations are necessary. Alice spends a lot of time in physicians' offices, and her illnesses cause considerable disruption in her life. Recently, it was concluded that Alice is suffering from the *somatization disorder* rather than a series of actual organic disorders.

William does not frequently experience many physical symptoms, but when even a minor one occurs, he immediately thinks it is an early sign of some very serious disorder and becomes extremely tense and anxious. His fears are allayed only after a thorough physical examination. He suffers from *hypochondriasis.*

The 15 clerical staff members of a research institute had been under considerable pressure to get a large amount of data entered into the computer, and they had spent long hours working at their terminals. On Wednesday, two terminal operators went home early complaining of headaches, dizziness, and nausea. By 11:00 the next morning, four other operators had begun vomiting uncontrollably, three reported that their vision was so blurred that they could not see across the room, one fainted, and most of the others reported lesser forms of physiological distress. In attempting to explain this epidemic, it was first thought that the workers' computer screens were giving off excessive radiation or that chemical pollutants had gotten into the air-conditioning system. Environmental engineers were unable to confirm either of those possibilities. After two days of rest during which the systems were checked, the staff went back to work in the same environment with no ill effects. The staff probably suffered from *mass psychogenic illness,* a modern version of the dancing manias of the 15th century.

Bob appears to be a model husband and father, but he has been going to a psychotherapist for about 2 years because he is "tense and dissatisfied." In the course of therapy, it has come out that Bob frequently has affairs with other women. His behavior in therapy has been somewhat inconsistent: Sometimes he does not talk about the affairs and instead focuses on his tension, but at other times he talks about his sexual escapades in a rather cavalier fashion and shows no sign of anxiety or remorse. His therapist believes that Bob may have a *multiple personality disorder.*

In this chapter, we will consider two groups of disorders. *Somatoform* disorders revolve around physical symptoms for which we cannot find a physical cause. *Dissociative* dissorders involve the loss of contact with parts of one's personality. Until recently, these disorders were subtypes of a general disorder known as **hysteria**, but that term has been abandoned as a diagnostic label.

◼ SOMATOFORM DISORDERS

The dominant feature of most **somatoform disorders** is the presence of *physical symptoms such as pain, paralysis, blindness, or deafness for which there is no demonstrable physical cause.* In the absence of a physical cause, it is presumed that the symptoms stem from psychological causes.

At the outset, we must distinguish between somatoform disorders and what have traditionally been called **psychosomatic disorders** such as ulcers, tension headaches, and cardiovascular problems. In both types of disorders, the causes are psychological and the symptoms are physical. The difference between the two is that with somatoform disorders, there is *no physical damage* (e.g., an individual may complain about stomach pain, but there is nothing physically wrong with the stomach), whereas with psychosomatic disorders, there is *physical damage* (e.g., ulcers involve lesions in the lining of the stomach). The term *somatoform* is used because there is no physical damage; the symptoms only take the *form* of a somatic disorder.

There are five somatoform disorders: somatization, hypochondriasis, conversion, pain, and the body dysmorphic disorder. The major symptoms of the various somatoform disorders are summarized in Table 7.1.

Somatization

The diagnosis of **somatization** (sō-MAT-uh-ZĀ-shun) **disorder** is used for individuals who have *numerous, recurrent, and long-lasting somatic complaints that are apparently not due to any actual physical cause.* Individuals with this disorder reject the notion that their symptoms are caused by psychological factors, and they persist in seeking a medical solution. By middle adulthood, they have complained about almost every symptom pattern imaginable, consulted every specialist available, and developed a medicine cabinet that rivals the shelves of the local pharmacy. Indeed, in order to be diagnosed as having a somatization disorder, an individual must have complained about, taken medicine for, changed lifestyle because of, or seen a physician regarding numerous different symptoms (DSM-IV).

In addition to their complaints about physical symptoms, individuals with a somatization disorder may also report anxiety and depression. Those complaints are not part of the disorder per se but are a consequence of the individual's belief that a serious medical problem exists. In common parlance, an individual with the somatization disorder is often referred to as a "hypochondriac," but as we will see, that term is reserved for a somewhat different set of symptoms.

Hypochondriasis

The dominant feature of **hypochondriasis** (HĪ-pō-kon-DRĪ-uh-sis) is the individual's *unrealistic concern and anxiety about potential physical problems.* Individuals with this disorder interpret minor physical sensations or signs as abnormalities that will inevitably lead to serious diseases, and consequently they become anxious and upset about their symptoms. For example, a headache is interpreted as a symptom of a developing brain tumor, or a slight skin irritation is seen as an

TABLE 7.1   PREDOMINANT SYMPTOM PATTERNS IN THE SOMATOFORM DISORDERS

Somatization	Person complains about and seeks treatment for numerous physical symptoms (weakness, fainting, urinary problems, nausea, etc.) for which no organic cause can be found.
Hypochondriasis	Person unrealistically interprets physical signs (lumps, irritations, pains, etc.) as evidence of serious diseases, and those interpretations lead to high levels of anxiety and fear.
Conversion	Person experiences one or more major symptoms (blindness, paralysis, etc.) for which no organic cause can be found. In some cases, the person is not concerned about the symptom.
Pain	Person experiences severe or prolonged pain that either has no organic cause or is more severe than can be justified by an existing organic cause.
Body dysmorphic	Person is preoccupied with some imagined defect in his or her physical appearance.

early sign of skin cancer, and consequently the individual becomes distraught and seeks treatment. Medical examinations and reassurances that there is nothing wrong may temporarily allay the concern, but soon a new sign of impending physical disease will be found, and the cycle will start over again.

Hypochondriasis is similar to somatization in that both disorders involve concerns about physical symptoms. The disorders differ in that individuals with somatization are concerned with a wide variety of current symptoms and diseases, whereas those with hypochondriasis show excessive anxiety about one or two symptoms and the implications they could have for potential future diseases.

Conversion and Mass Psychogenic Illnesses

In cases of **conversion disorder**, the individual has *one or more major physical symptoms that greatly impair functioning, but an organic basis for the symptoms cannot be found.* Conversion symptoms usually occur in the musculoskeletal or sensory systems. Frequently cited conversion symptoms include paralyses, seizures, blindness, deafness, tunnel vision, anesthesia (loss of feeling or sensation), and paresthesia (pricking or tingling sensations of the skin). In many cases, the symptoms are closely related to the individual's activities or occupation. For example, pilots who fly at night develop night blindness, whereas pilots who fly during the day develop day blindness (Ironside & Batchelor, 1945), and violinists develop paralyses or cramps in the hands. Because of this relationship, conversion disorders used to be referred to as **craft palsies**.

An interesting feature associated with some cases of conversion disorders is that in the face of what appears to be a very serious medical problem, the individual shows little or no concern. For example, when faced with the stress of flight training, 56 student pilots at the U.S. Naval Aerospace Medical Institute developed serious conversion symptoms that included paralyses, paresthesias, deafness, and visual problems, but none of the young men was concerned with the symptoms or their long-term effects (Mucha & Reinhardt, 1970). The absence of the appropriate emotional response is traditionally referred to as *la belle indifférence* ("beautiful indifference") and contrasts sharply with the considerable concern over their symptoms shown by individuals with other types of somatoform disorders. However, this lack of concern is shown by only about one-third of the persons with conversion disorders.

Certain features of the conversion disorder help us distinguish between it and an actual physical disorder. The most conclusive of these clues is the occurrence of a symptom pattern that could not possibly be the result of a physical cause. An example of this is the classic **glove anesthesia** in which the individual loses feeling in the hand up to the point at which a glove would stop. Given the nerve pathways in the arm and hand, we know that such a pattern of insensitivity is impossible. The distinction between glove anesthesia and actual nerve pathways is illustrated in Figure 7.1. Unfortunately, as the level of medical sophistication in the general public increases, individuals are less likely to exhibit symptom patterns that are blatantly impossible, and hence it is becoming more difficult to separate conversion disorders from actual physical disorders on the basis of the inappropriateness of symptom patterns.

The presence of *la belle indifférence* can also be a good clue to the presence of a conversion disorder.

FIGURE 7.1   THE LACK OF FEELING IN GLOVE ANESTHESIA DOES NOT FOLLOW THE NERVE PATHWAYS IN THE HAND.

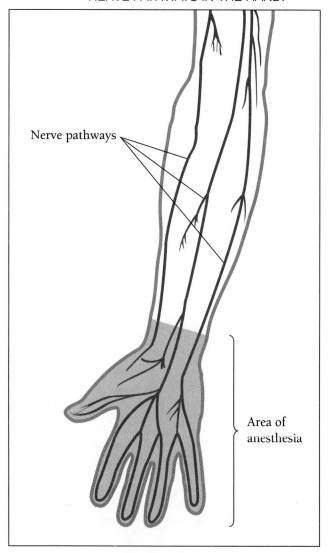

Nerve pathways

Area of anesthesia

Another clue is the absence of negative consequences that would be the inevitable result of the physical disorder. For example, individuals with conversion disorders who suffer from epileptic-like seizures may not hurt themselves during a seizure, and psychogenically blind individuals may not bump into things.

A final clue that may be used for distinguishing between conversion and physical disorders is the consistency of the symptom pattern. In the case of an individual with a conversion disorder, the symptoms may change with changes in the stress (a paralyzed leg before a track meet and a paralyzed hand before an examination), whereas there will be greater consistency in the symptoms stemming from an actual physical disorder. Unfortunately, in many cases, all of these clues are lacking, and the differential diagnosis of these disorders can be very difficult.

A dramatic example of a conversion disorder I observed occurred in a sophomore woman who came to the university hospital about midway through the fall semester with "intermittent blindness." This woman's vision would begin dimming on Sunday evening, and by Monday morning she would be blind. The blindness lasted until Friday evening, and by Saturday morning her vision was completely restored. This cycle persisted for 3 weeks. The student showed no surprise at the unusual nature of her disorder and evinced no concern about her condition. Indeed, she observed cheerily that she was sure we would be able to take care of the problem and, after all, it was not interfering with the important social activities associated with football weekends! After 3 weeks the symptoms remitted. It is not clear why they remitted at that point, but it may be associated with the fact that the midterm examination period was over. The student stayed in school (but did not go to many of her classes because she was "too far behind") until the last week of the semester, when she withdrew "for medical reasons."

Before concluding our description of conversion disorders, some attention should be given to **mass hysteria**, or what is now called **mass psychogenic illness** (Colligan et al., 1982). Mass psychogenic illness involves *an epidemic of a particular conversion disorder.* The best known of these epidemics are the **dancing manias** that were prevalent in the 15th and 16th centuries. In those epidemics, large groups of people danced, hopped, and jerked uncontrollably for hours or days until they finally fell exhausted (Martin, 1923).

Contrary to what is often assumed, mass psychogenic illnesses did not stop with the Middle Ages. In fact, numerous epidemics were reported in recent years, but they are less extreme than the medieval dancing manias (Sirois, 1982). For example, in 1979, a sudden outbreak of a peculiar illness spread quickly among Boston grade school children who were gath-

The dancing manias of the 15th and 16th centuries were early examples of mass psychogenic illness. In these manias, groups of people hopped and jerked uncontrollably.

ered at an assembly (Small & Nicholi, 1982). The children reported experiencing dizziness, hyperventilation, weakness, headache, nausea, and abdominal pain. Of the 224 children who attended the assembly, 40 to 50 required some type of treatment on the scene, and 34 had to be hospitalized. However, no physical basis could be found for any of the symptoms. Other instances of mass psychogenic illness involved 84 women in a television assembly plant in Singapore who began screaming, fainting, and going into trances (Chew et al., 1976); 85 women and 59 men working in a factory in the southeastern United States who developed dizziness, nausea, difficulty in breathing, headaches, and a bad taste in the mouth (Folland, 1975); 35 women working in an office of a midwestern university who experienced nausea, vomiting, dizziness, and fainting (Stahl & Lebedun, 1974); and over 900 persons (mostly schoolgirls) who developed blindness, headache, stomachache, and discoloration of the skin (Hefez, 1985). In one case of an unexplained syndrome of "allergy" among plastics workers, it was found that those who developed the illness had a higher rate of anxiety or depressive disorders (54% vs. 4%) and somatization (69% vs. 13%) than individuals who did not develop the illness, thereby suggesting a psychological predisposition or cause (Simon et al., 1990). It is interesting to note that over the past 500 years, there have been changes in the purported causes of mass psychogenic illness that parallel changes in our culture: In the 15th century, the disorders were attributed to curses; now they are attributed to factors such as radiation from computer screens. An example of mass psychogenic illness is presented in Case Study 7.1.

Pain Disorder

The **pain disorder** involves the *complaint of pain in the absence of an identifiable organic cause*, in which case the pain is thought to have a psychological origin. It is believed that some back problems may actually be pain disorders.

Unlike individuals with conversion disorders, individuals with pain disorders are very concerned about their problem, and they may make frequent visits to physicians for treatment. The extent of the impairment caused by this disorder ranges from a slight disturbance of social or occupational functioning to total incapacity and need for hospitalization. The pain disorder could loosely be considered a subtype of the somatization disorder; the only differences between the two is that the pain disorder is limited to pain.

Body Dysmorphic Disorder

The **body dysmorphic** (dis-MOR-fik) **disorder** involves the *preoccupation with some imagined or minor defect in one's physical appearance*. Examples could include excessive concern about a mole or the shape of one's nose. In some cases, the disorder can lead to social withdrawal, occupational dysfunction, and even suicide (Phillips, 1991). Not included in this disorder are individuals with anorexia, who are unjustifiably concerned about their weight (see Chapter 16.) The dysmorphic disorder is the most recent addition to the group of somatoform disorders, added with the publication of DSM-III-R in 1987. At this point, little is known about the nature, prevalence, and implications of the body dysmorphic disorder. There is some question about whether this problem is important enough to be considered a somatoform disorder.

ISSUES ASSOCIATED WITH SOMATOFORM DISORDERS

Historical Background

Somatoform disorders (specifically conversion disorders) have a long history and have been associated primarily with women. From as early as 1500 B.C. we have

a description of "a woman ill in seeing," and it was thought that the disorder resulted from a malpositioned uterus (Veith, 1965). Similarly, in the writings of the ancient Greeks, we find numerous descriptions of women with what appear to be conversion disorders. Those disorders were attributed to the fact that because the womb had not been sexually satisfied, it had gone wandering through the body in search of satisfaction, and in its wandering it had lodged itself in such a way as to cause the disorder. For example, if a woman had a paralyzed arm, it was assumed that the womb had become stuck in her shoulder or elbow. Because it was assumed that a dissatisfied womb was the cause of the problem, early Greek physicians recommended sex as a treatment for these disorders. The importance of the womb in causing these problems is reflected in the fact that the problems were once labeled "hysterical"—the term *hysteria* comes from the Greek word for "womb."

Increased attention was focused on somatoform disorders in the 19th century when **Jean-Martin Charcot**, a famous French physician, dramatically demonstrated that by using suggestion, he could induce and eliminate all manner of symptoms in women patients suffering from what was then called hysteria. **Sigmund Freud** also worked with patients suffering from somatoform disorders and drew a considerable amount of attention to them. Like the Greeks who preceded him, Freud concluded that the basis of the problem was sexual—specifically, conflicts over sexuality. Interestingly, Freud did not believe that the disorder was limited to women, and early in his career he gave a

In the 19th century, French physician Jean-Martin Charcot demonstrated that somatoform symptoms could be introduced and eliminated with suggestion. Freud was so impressed with Charcot's work that he kept a copy of this etching in his office.

Case Study 7.1

MASS PSYCHOGENIC ILLNESS IN JUNIOR HIGH AND HIGH SCHOOL STUDENTS

On April 13, 1989, approximately 600 student performers gathered at the Santa Monica Civic Auditorium for the 40th annual "Stairway of the Stars" concert. This was the major classical music performance (choral and orchestra) for students in the 6th through 12th grades. The performance started at 7:30 P.M., but shortly thereafter, it was interrupted when symptoms such as headaches, dizziness, weakness, abdominal pain, shortness of breath, chills, chest pain, and nausea began spreading through the student performers. Eleven students found themselves unable to open their eyes, and 18 fainted. The problem became so bad that the concert had to be stopped, and the students, along with the 2,000 spectators, were forced to evacuate the auditorium.

The fire department sent two paramedic squads and two engine companies, and together they set up a treatment area outside the auditorium. The students were placed on stretchers that were lined up on the lawn, and eight ambulances were used to rush the most severely ill students to local hospitals.

Physical examinations and laboratory tests performed on the students did not reveal any abnormalities. Furthermore, there was no evidence of toxic fumes or materials in the area. Because there were no confirmed physical illnesses and no evidence of environmental threats, the school officials rescheduled the concert for the next evening, but many parents were unconvinced of the safety of the situation and therefore kept their children at home.

A follow-up study of the students who did and did not develop symptoms revealed some interesting differences. For example, when compared to students who did not show symptoms, those who did show symptoms were more likely to have had a chronic illness (25% vs. 10%), more likely to have had a recent acute illness (17% vs. 11%), more likely to have experienced the death of a relative or friend (70% vs. 55%), and, most important, more likely to have observed a friend get sick at the concert (71% vs. 41%).

The affected students truly believed that they were sick and showed signs of illness such as vomiting or fainting, but no underlying causes could be identified. The absence of underlying causes, in combination with the data concerning the influence of suggestion (e.g., previous experience with illness and seeing others become sick), clearly leads to the diagnosis of mass psychogenic illness.

Source: Small et al. (1991).

---

paper at a meeting of the Medical Society on "male hysteria." His suggestion that males suffer from hysteria (conversion disorders) was met with disbelief and laughter, and he was literally laughed off the stage and almost banished from the society.

Although not recognized as such at the time, conversion disorders undoubtedly played an important role in the symptoms seen in many of the soldiers who served in World War I. It is probable that many of the symptoms that were attributed to "shell shock" were in fact conversion disorders. The presence of conversion disorders in men was finally recognized during World War II because medical science had progressed to the point where the potential organic causes of some of the GIs' symptoms could be definitely ruled out, thereby suggesting psychological causes (Ziegler et al., 1960).

The diagnostic label "hysteria" was eliminated when DSM-III was published in 1980. This was done to remove the numerous connotations that had come to be associated with the term hysteria, such as the idea that it is necessarily caused by sexual conflict. When DSM-III-R was published in 1987, all the comments suggesting that somatoform disorders are more prevalent in women were omitted.

Prevalence and Gender

It is estimated that about 2% of the population experiences the various somatoform disorders. That rate has held steady since shortly after the turn of the 20th century (Stephens & Kamp, 1962). Women are more likely to be diagnosed as suffering from conversion disorders than men. In fact, in the six investigations of conversion disorders published in 1979 and 1980, women constituted 74% of the total number of persons diagnosed as having conversion disorders. In another study of 147 individuals with "multiple unexplained somatic complaints," it was found that 58% of the women and 40% of the men could be diagnosed as suffering from the somatization disorder (Golding et al., 1991). Unfortunately, we still do not know why women are more likely to receive the diagnosis. It may be that for historical reasons diagnosticians are biased in favor of diagnosing the disorder in women; women are more likely to seek help for the types of complaints that are associated with somatoform disorders; or like other disorders such as depression, there is something about the cause of the disorder (e.g., particular stresses, physiological factors) that predisposes women to the disorder.

Differential Diagnoses of Somatoform and Physical Disorders

Differentiating between individuals with somatoform disorders and those with physical disorders has always been difficult, and there is a considerable body of evidence documenting the fact that individuals with somatoform disorders are frequently misdiagnosed as having physical disorders. For example, in one study of adolescents who were originally diagnosed as epileptic, 84% were later diagnosed as actually having somatoform disorders (Gross, 1979).

By contrast, patients with physical disorders are sometimes erroneously diagnosed as having somatoform disorders. For example, when an investigator did a 9-year follow-up on patients who had originally been diagnosed as having conversion disorders, he found that 60% had died from or developed signs of physical diseases related to the central nervous system (Slater & Glithero, 1965). Using another approach to the problem, one investigator compared the prevalence of organic brain disorders in patients who were diagnosed as suffering from conversion disorders and control patients who were diagnosed as suffering from depression or anxiety (Whitlock, 1967). The results indicated that among the patients who had been diagnosed as suffering from conversion disorders, 62.5% showed signs of organic brain disorder, whereas only 5.3% of the control patients showed signs of organic brain disorder. The results of these investigations suggest that more than half of the patients diagnosed as having a somatoform disorder may actually be suffering from a physical problem. That is a very serious discrepancy because the misdiagnosed patients do not receive the appropriate medical attention. The problem of accurately diagnosing somatoform disorders may have become more difficult because of the public's increased level of medical sophistication; that is, medically informed individuals are less likely to develop impossible or blatantly transparent symptoms. The day of simple glove anesthesia or a paralyzed arm before an examination may have almost disappeared among educated individuals.

Are Somatoform Symptoms Real or Faked?

Are the symptoms seen in somatoform disorders real or faked? Can real physical symptoms exist without an underlying physical cause? Certainly there are cases in which persons fake somatic illnesses in deliberate attempts to gain sympathy, avoid responsibility, or obtain insurance benefits. Faking disorders to avoid responsibility is commonly called **malingering**, and in DSM-IV, disorders that are consciously faked are called **factitious** (fak-TISH-us) **disorders**. Although those cases do occur, the symptoms in somatoform disorders can be real.

The best evidence in support of the reality of somatoform symptoms comes from research on the **placebo effect** (A. Shapiro, 1980; Shapiro & Morris, 1978). A placebo effect occurs when an individual is given a treatment that has no therapeutic value (for example, a pill does not contain any active ingredients), but the individual believes that the treatment should help and consequently shows the expected change (see Chapter 3). Many studies document the positive effects of placebos on physical symptoms such as reductions in pain, and it is generally agreed that the placebo effect is due to suggestion.

The placebo effect is relevant for understanding somatoform symptoms because placebos can be used to induce symptoms as well as reduce them. If psychological processes such as the placebo effect or suggestion can reduce real symptoms, it seems reasonable to conclude that the psychological processes are also sufficient to result in real symptoms. Some individuals undoubtedly do fake symptoms, but in other cases somatoform symptoms can be real, so we should not assume that individuals with somatoform disorders are necessarily faking.

Somatoform Disorders and Medical Progress

Finally, you should recognize that as medical science progresses, some of what we currently think are somatoform disorders may someday be found to be actual physical disorders. Somatoform disorders consist of physical symptoms for which there is no demonstrable cause, but the failure to demonstrate a physical cause could be due to the fact that we have not yet found it. For example, some years ago, women who showed the physical symptoms of pregnancy but in fact were not pregnant were diagnosed as having a somatoform disorder known as **pseudocyesis** (SYOO-dō-sī-Ē-sis, "sham or hysterical pregnancy"). However, with increased understanding of hormone imbalances, those individuals are now usually recognized as suffering from a physical disorder.

Now that we have discussed the symptoms and issues associated with the somatoform disorders, we can turn our attention to the dissociative disorders. Following that, we will consider the explanations that have been offered for these two sets of disorders.

DISSOCIATIVE DISORDERS

In **dissociative disorders**, there is a serious *separation of personality functions so that the individual is not aware of or loses contact with important aspects of his or her personality*. For example, individuals with dissociative disorders experience symptoms such as amnesia, multiple personalities, and loss of personal identity. The term *dissociative disorder* is used because it is assumed that the individuals with symptoms like amnesia or multiple personalities are *dissociating* themselves (escaping) from parts of their personalities that give rise to stress.

There are four types of dissociative disorders: *dissociative amnesia, dissociative fugue, dissociative identity disorder (multiple personality)*, and *depersonalization*. Each type involves a dissociation, but the way the dissociation is achieved differs from disorder to disorder. For example, the individual may forget some stressful material (amnesia), leave a stressful situation and develop a new identity (fugue), or develop alternative personalities (multiple personality). The major symptoms of the dissociative disorders are summarized in Table 7.2.

Dissociative Amnesia

Dissociative amnesia is characterized by a *sudden inability to remember important personal information or events*. This type of amnesia usually occurs immediately following some type of severe stress; the stressful event or information associated with it is forgotten. For example, soldiers sometimes have psychogenic amnesia for periods of battle. After getting to safety, the soldiers simply do not remember much about the very dangerous battle in which they have just fought. Similarly, I have had a number of students who reported being amnesic for the time period surrounding a serious automobile accident in which they were involved but not physically injured. It has been suggested that psychogenic amnesia can also be triggered by unacceptable impulses or acts such as an extramarital affair; the individual simply does not remember doing the unspeakable—or the unthinkable!

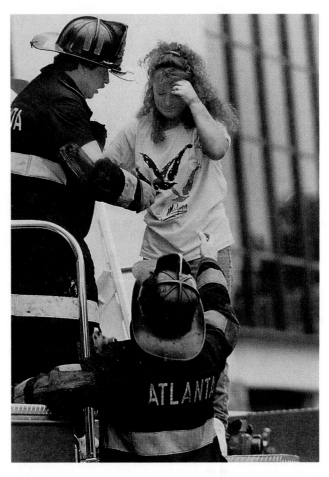

Amnesia may occur in response to a severe stress. The individual will not remember the stressful event or information associated with it.

Obviously, there are many reasons why we are sometimes unable to recall things, and it is important not to confuse psychogenic amnesia with failure to recall because of the failure to process information (the individual may have been distracted by other aspects of the situation), ordinary forgetting, organic mental disorders, substance-induced intoxication, an alcohol amnesic disorder, or the amnesia that sometimes occurs following a concussion (Hirst, 1982).

TABLE 7.2 PREDOMINANT SYMPTOM PATTERNS IN THE DISSOCIATIVE DISORDERS

Amnesia	A sudden inability to remember important personal information. The inability to recall the information cannot be explained by ordinary forgetfulness.
Fugue	Sudden travel away from home or place of work with the inability to recall one's past. During the fugue, a new identity is developed.
Dissociative identity disorder (multiple personality)	The presence within an individual of two or more distinct personalities. The various personalities take complete control of the individual's behavior at different times, and one personality may not be aware of another.
Depersonalization	The experience of being detached from one's self and observing the self from the position of an outside observer, or the experience of feeling mechanical or as if in a dream.

Dissociative Fugue

An individual who is experiencing a **dissociative fugue** (fyoog) suddenly and unexpectedly *travels to a new locale, assumes a new identity, and is amnesic for his or her previous identity.* This flight typically follows a severe psychosocial stress such as a marital quarrel, personal rejection, military conflict, or natural disaster. The fugue state may last only a few hours, but it generally lasts months. During the fugue, the individual behaves appropriately and does not show any signs of suffering from a psychological disorder; the person simply starts a new life and does fine. When the fugue ends, the individual returns to his or her original identity and has no memory of what took place during the fugue. The feature of fugue that distinguishes it from amnesia is that in the fugue, the individual is unaware of the lost material and substitutes new material (a new identity) in its place.

One interesting case that was diagnosed as fugue involved a man who was having serious financial and marital problems. The day following a particularly serious argument with his wife about their impending bankruptcy, the man went fishing and did not return. When his empty boat was found on the lake, it was presumed that he had fallen overboard and drowned. About a year later, the man's widow was on an automobile trip through a nearby state and stopped for lunch in a roadside restaurant. She was surprised at the quality of the food but even more surprised when on her way out, she discovered her deceased husband sitting in one of the booths and then learned that he was now married to the woman who owned the restaurant. When confronted, he appeared not to know her.

Dissociative Identity Disorder (Multiple Personality)

The term multiple personality disorder has been used for many years, but in DSM-IV that term has been replaced with **dissociative identity disorder**. For the sake of convenience, in this chapter I will use the traditional term, *multiple personality disorder.*

An individual diagnosed as experiencing a **multiple personality disorder** appears to have *two or more distinctly different personalities, each of which is dominant at a different time.* Typically, some of the personalities will not be aware of the other personalities (Fahy, 1988; Putnam, 1989; Ross, 1989).

The multiple personality disorder has received a great deal of attention in the popular press, films, and television. Some of the best-known accounts of multiple personality are *The Three Faces of Eve* (Thigpen & Cleckley, 1957), *Sybil* (Schreiber, 1973), *The Five of Me* (Hanksworth & Schwarz, 1977), and *The Minds of Billy Milligan* (Keyes, 1981).

Chris Sizemore is the woman on whom The Three Faces of Eve is based. She now claims that she had 21 separate personalities.

There is usually a sharp contrast between at least two of the personalities in a multiple personality disorder, who are ordinarily in conflict. One personality is usually "good," while the other is of more questionable character. Therapists have referred to the "saint" versus the "devil" (Prince, 1908) and the "square" versus the "lover" (Ludwig et al., 1972) personalities in their patients. That contrast is apparent in *The Three Faces of Eve.* Eve White was a quiet, demure, and somewhat inhibited young woman who had been in psychotherapy for the treatment of headaches and blackouts. While talking to her physician one day, Eve White put her hands to her head as if she had been seized by a sudden pain. After a moment, she seemed to shake herself loose and looked up with a reckless smile and a bright voice and said, "Hi there, Doc!" When asked her name, she immediately replied, "Oh, I'm Eve Black" (Thigpen & Cleckley, 1954, p. 137). In contrast to Eve White, Eve Black was a wild, devil-may-care, promiscuous woman. As you might have guessed, the "good" personality is usually not aware of the "bad" personality, but the "bad" personality is usually aware of (and bored with) the "good" personality.

The case of Eve appears to have been more complex than it was originally portrayed. In a book published 23 years later, the woman who had been known as Eve (actually Chris Sizemore) explained that she had actually had 21 separate personalities or, as she put it, "strangers who came to inhabit my body" (Sizemore & Pittillo, 1977). Studies reveal that individuals with the multiple personality disorder report having from 2 to 60 different personalities, the average being 13 to 16 (Putnam et al., 1986; Ross et al., 1989; Ross, Miller, et al., 1990; Schultz et al., 1989). The results of those surveys also indicate that about 90% of the individuals diagnosed as having a multiple personality disorder are women.

Some comment should be made to clear up the confusion that sometimes arises over the terms *multiple personality, schizophrenia,* and *split personality. Multiple personality* refers to a disorder in which an individual develops a number of distinctly different and separate personalities. In contrast, the term *schizophrenia* refer to a disorder in which the individual has one personality, but that personality has split off from reality or has split itself between the functions of emotion and reasoning (Bleuler, 1950). An individual with a multiple personality disorder does not necessarily have schizophrenia, and an individual with schizophrenia does not necessarily have multiple personalities. The term *split personality* is not a diagnostic label; it is slang without any clinical meaning.

Depersonalization

The **depersonalization disorder** involves a *temporary, episodic loss or distortion of the self.* The depersonalization experience can probably be best described as an "as if" experience with regard to the self: Individuals with this disorder feel *as if* their extremities have changed in size, *as if* they were acting mechanically, *as if* they were in a dream, or *as if* they were out of their bodies and viewing themselves from a distance. In talking about depersonalization experiences, one person described how "it was like I somehow drifted out of my body and floated way above it, and I could look down on me like I was someone else on a stage." Another said, "My body seemed to be made of rubber that could stretch. . . . I really didn't have any definite form. Sometimes my head would become huge, or my arms would become extremely long and I'd have big hands. It was really kinda crazy."

The "as if" nature of the disorder is important because it distinguishes the depersonalization disorder from schizophrenia, in which the individual may have the same symptoms but believes them to be true. Because the feelings appear to be "crazy" (e.g., looking down at oneself from above), individuals with the depersonalization disorder are often concerned that they might be "going crazy," and therefore the symptom pattern is often accompanied by anxiety.

It is important to note that this disorder, like some of the other disorders we have discussed, can appear briefly in many normal individuals. Indeed, the results of a questionnaire study indicated that in some age groups, almost 30% of the individuals sampled reported depersonalization experiences (Ross et al., 1990). The percentages of individuals in different age groups who reported depersonalization experiences are presented in Figure 7.2. The presence of the symptom pattern is considered to constitute a disorder only when it results in significant impairment of an individual's social or occupational functioning. The deper-

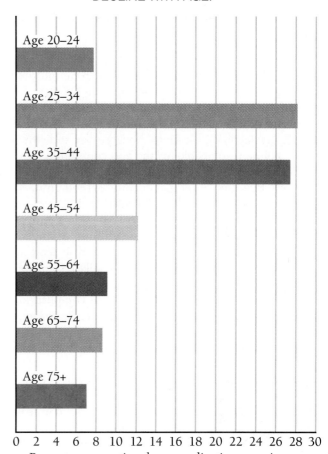

FIGURE 7.2 DEPERSONALIZATION EXPERIENCES ARE RELATIVELY COMMON BUT DECLINE WITH AGE.

Percentage reporting depersonalization experiences

Source: Ross, Joshi, and Currie (1990), p. 1549, tab. 1.

sonalization disorder differs from most other dissociative disorders in that it does not involve a disturbance of memory or consciousness.

ISSUES ASSOCIATED WITH DISSOCIATIVE DISORDERS

Can Dissociative Disorders Be Faked?

In diagnosing dissociative disorders, we must be sensitive to the possibility that the individual may be faking. For example, an individual who wanted to escape an unpleasant life situation might try to fake amnesia or a fugue. In one study of military personnel who reported being amnesic, 42% were found to be faking (Kiersch, 1962). Furthermore, in investigations of 32 individuals who were charged with crimes and who claimed to have amnesia for the acts, 66% were found to be faking, clearly indicating that individuals may attempt to use these symptom patterns to avoid difficulties. However, the fact that some individuals fake the disorders does not deny the reality of the disorders in others; it only suggests that we must be cautious in using the diagnoses.

Does the Multiple Personality Disorder Really Exist?

An interesting controversy revolves around the question of whether individuals actually do have multiple personalities as they are described in DSM-IV, or whether the disorders are somehow artificial or faked. That question is of theoretical interest, but it also has important legal implications because an individual might not be responsible for the acts committed by an alternative personality, especially if the individual was unaware that the other personality existed. Indeed, multiple personality is a popular disorder in the insanity defense (Keyes, 1981; Schwarz, 1981). For example, Kenneth Bianchi, known as the "Hillside Strangler" and alleged to have raped and strangled at least 12 young women, claimed he was not legally responsible for the crimes because his other personality committed the acts. A somewhat different legal complication arose in a case in which a woman apparently consented to have sex with a man and then later accused him of rape when another of her other personalities emerged and objected.

There are two alternative explanations for the behavior of individuals who appear to have the multiple personality disorder. First, it is possible that in at least some cases, the individual is consciously *faking* the disorder to avoid responsibility or to get attention. The husband of a student of mine claimed to have multiple personalities when one day his wife came home unexpectedly and discovered him dressed in her clothes. He had a transvestic fetishism (see Chapter 19), and he tried to convince his wife that she was married to his "normal personality," who knew nothing about his "transvestite personality," who only came out while she was not home. During a thorough examination, he admitted the attempted deception.

It is also possible that the symptoms of a multiple personality may be *suggested to the individual by a therapist.* The possibility that therapists suggest the symptom pattern to patients gains indirect support from the fact that most therapists never see one case of multiple personality in their entire careers (Gruenewald, 1971; Rosenbaum, 1980), whereas some therapists report seeing as many as 100 or more such cases (Allison & Schwartz, 1980; Bliss, 1980, 1984; Braun, 1984; Kluft, 1982; Watkins, 1984). The implication is that therapists who are particularly interested in this disorder subtly suggest the symptom pattern to their patients. In that regard, it is noteworthy that individuals with the multiple personality disorder are generally regarded as being highly suggestible and that the disorder is often discovered while the client is under hypnosis (a state of heightened suggestibility). Problems produced as a result of treatment (for example, suggestions of the therapist) are called **iatrogenic** (YAT-rō-GEN-ik) **disorders**.

Evidence concerning the role that therapists' suggestions play in the development of multiple personality comes from the records of interactions between therapists and patients during therapy (Spanos et al., 1985; Sutcliffe & Jones, 1962). This is illustrated in the following quotation from an interview with Kenneth Bianchi, who later reported a multiple personality (see Case Study 7.2, p. 158). Before Ken made any comments reflecting the possibility of a multiple personality, the interviewer said:

I think that perhaps there might be another part of Ken that I haven't talked to. . . . I would like to communicate with that other part. . . . I would like that other part to come to talk to me. . . . Part, would you please come to communicate with me? . . . Would you please come, Part, so I can talk to you? (Orne et al., 1984, p. 128)

Not only did the interviewer suggest the possibility of another personality, but he actually gave the other personality a name ("Part") and repeatedly pleaded with Part to come out and talk to him.

This case led to an interesting study in which three groups of college students were asked to role-play Bianchi in an interview situation (Spanos et al., 1985). Students in one condition participated in an interview that closely followed the one used with Bianchi in that the interviewer (a) suggested that they might have another part, (b) said he would like to communicate with that part, and (c) talked directly to "Part." Students in the second condition participated in a similar interview, but the interviewer (a) suggested that we sometimes have thoughts and feelings that are "walled off" and (b) said that he would like to be in contact with "another part of you" but (c) did not address "Part" directly. In the control condition, the interviewer did not talk about a "part" or walled-off thoughts and feelings. When the students were then asked who they were and to talk about themselves, those in the first two conditions enacted another personality (used a different name, feigned amnesia for their real personality, and admitted to a crime their real personality denied). Furthermore, in a later session, when the students were asked to take personality tests as themselves and as another part of themselves, the students in the first two conditions gave very different test responses on the two administrations, whereas there was not a difference in the control condition. In other words, when the interviewer suggested the possibility of a multiple personality, the students' behavior and personality test scores were consistent with a multiple personality, but when the interviewer did not suggest the possibility of a multiple personality, the students did not behave as though they had multiple personalities. These results clearly indicate that the way an interview is conducted can suggest the possibility of a multiple personality (Spanos, 1986).

Suggestions made to patients could lead them to deliberately fake the disorder or to believe that they actually had the disorder; in either case, they would act in accordance with the diagnosis. In view of the publicity the disorder gets, if an authority suggests that you have the disorder and if having the disorder explains or justifies your behavior, you may very well accede to the suggestion.

To counter the evidence implying that suggestion provides the basis for multiple personality, believers in the disorder assert first that the disorder is really more prevalent than is generally believed but that it is usually misdiagnosed as schizophrenia (Rosenbaum, 1980; Watkins & Johnson, 1982). They then go on to argue that the therapists who see many patients with multiple personality disorders do not suggest the disorder but are more sensitive to the subtle distinctions between multiple personality and schizophrenia, and are therefore more likely to identify patients who have the multiple personality disorder.

Believers in the multiple personality disorder also point to research evidence. First, they cite numerous reports indicating that personality and intelligence tests reveal large differences among the various personalities of any one patient (Brandsma & Ludwig, 1974; Congdon et al., 1961; Jeans, 1976; Keyes, 1981; Larmore et al., 1977; Luria & Osgood, 1976; Osgood & Luria, 1954; Osgood et al., 1976; Prince, 1908; Thigpen & Cleckley, 1954; Wagner & Heise, 1974). For example, tests may reveal that one personality is hostile and not particularly bright, while the other personality is loving and smart. These findings are not particularly persuasive, however, because it is easy to give false responses to tests and because the individuals who interpreted the responses to projective tests were not blind to the conditions and thus may easily have been biased in their scoring.

Second, believers in the multiple personality disorder point to research indicating that different patterns of brain wave activity (EEGs) are associated with the different personalities of any one individual (Braun, 1983b; Coons et al., 1982; Larmore et al., 1977; Ludwig et al., 1972). Indeed, in the case of one individual with four personalities, it was reported that it was "as if four different people had been tested" (Larmore et al., 1977, p. 40). These findings initially provided strong support for the validity of multiple personality, but their value has been greatly weakened by the results of a study in which EEG activity was recorded in two individuals diagnosed as having multiple personalities and one normal control who role-played different personalities (Coons et al., 1982). In that study, it was found that the EEG differences between the personalities that were role-played by the control subject were actually *greater* than the EEG differences between the personalities of the individuals diagnosed as having the multiple personality disorder. It appears that the differences in concentration, mood, or relaxation that are associated with different roles influence brain wave activity, and hence differences in brain wave activity cannot be used to verify the existence of multiple personalities (Coons et al., 1982; Coons, 1988; Miller & Triggiano, 1992). Interpersonality differences in a wide variety of other physiological measures (cerebral blood flow, heart rate, respiration, skin conductance) have also been examined, but comparisons with control subjects who are role-playing have not revealed reliable differences (see review by Miller & Triggiano, 1992). Finally, therapists have reported case studies in which one personality had a toothache, was color-blind, or had an allergy whereas the individual's other personality did not suffer from those problems, but those differences have not been independently verified or compared to differences that can be induced by suggestion (Wilson, 1903; Braun, 1983a). Indeed, some of these frequently cited and dramatic differences (e.g., an individual with diabetes who used different amounts of insulin while in different personalities) can be traced back to one unsubstantiated observation that has simply been reported over and over. Clearly, this evidence does not provide any support for the existence of multiple personalities.

The problems surrounding the diagnosis of the multiple personality disorder are highlighted in the widely publicized case of Kenneth Bianchi, the Hillside Strangler. This case is discussed in Case Study 7.2 (pp. 158–159). While reading the case study, ask yourself the following questions: (a) Was Kenneth Bianchi suffering from a multiple personality disorder, or was he feigning one in an attempt to escape punishment? (b) Should he have been treated for his disorder or punished for his crimes? (c) Do people really suffer from multiple personality disorders?

Before concluding this discussion of the multiple personality disorder, three additional points should be noted. First, at present, there does not appear to be much, if any, empirical evidence for the existence of the multiple personality disorder, but *the absence of evidence does not necessarily mean that the disorder does not exist.* New evidence may come to light. Second, even if you conclude that Kenneth Bianchi was faking, this does not necessarily mean that all individuals who show evidence of multiple personalities are faking.

Case Study 7.2

THE HILLSIDE STRANGLER: A CASE OF MULTIPLE PERSONALITY?

In the fall and winter of 1977–1978, ten young women were raped and strangled, and their nude bodies were left on various hillsides in Los Angeles County. The killer became known as the "Hillside Strangler." In January 1979, two women were raped and strangled in Bellingham, Washington. Shortly thereafter, a good-looking 27-year-old man named Kenneth Bianchi was arrested and charged with those murders and later charged with some of the murders in Los Angeles. As part of his criminal and psychiatric evaluation, Bianchi participated in a series of interviews that were videotaped. Those tapes provide a fascinating objective record of what some experts believe is a multiple personality and others believe is a scam that Bianchi used in an attempt to be declared insane so that he would not be punished for his crimes.

The presence of the second alleged personality originally came out when Bianchi participated in a hypnotic interview conducted by a psychologist named Watkins, a specialist in multiple personalities who was working for the defense.

Watkins: I've talked a bit to Ken, but I think that perhaps there might be another part of Ken that I haven't talked to, another part that maybe feels somewhat dif-

When Kenneth Bianchi was accused of being the "Hillside Strangler," he claimed to have multiple personalities and that another personality, Steve, committed the crimes. It was determined that Bianchi did not have the multiple personality disorder and he was sentenced to life in prison.

ferently from the part that I've talked to. And I would like to communicate with that other part. And I would like that other part to come to talk to me. . . . Part, would you please come to communicate with me? . . . Would you please come, Part, so I can talk to you? Another part, it is not just the same as the part of Ken I've been talking to. . . . All right, Part, I would like for you and I to talk together, we don't even have to—we don't have to talk to Ken unless you and Ken want to. . . .

Bianchi: Yes.
Watkins: Part, are you the same thing as Ken, or are you different in any way? . . .
Bianchi: I'm not him.
Watkins: You're not him. Who are you? Do you have a name?
Bianchi: I'm not Ken.
Watkins: You're not Ken. OK. Who are you? Tell me about yourself.
Bianchi: I don't know.
Watkins: Do you have a name I can call you by?
Bianchi: Steve.
Watkins: Huh?
Bianchi: You can call me Steve.

Bianchi then went on to talk about how he (Steve) had strangled and killed "all these girls," pointing out that "I fixed him [Ken] up good. He doesn't even have any idea." At the end of the interview, the psychologist asked to speak to Ken, who then promptly returned. When Ken was asked about Steve, he replied, "Who's Steve?"

In a later interview, after Ken was told about the existence of Steve, Ken talked about his "readiness for the fight" for dominance with Steve. Ken also began complaining of headaches, a symptom that Watkins attributed to the conflict and struggle over the emergence of Steve against Ken's will. When Watkins asked Ken why he was feeling bad, there was an angry snarl, and then Steve emerged complaining about the difficulty of getting out now that Ken knew about him. He said:

All these f—— years I had it made. I could come and go as I pleased. He never knew about me. But now he does. I have some feeling it's partly your fault. You started this whole f—— thing. . . . I try to come out. Instead I stay where I'm at, and he complains about f—— headaches . . . I'd like to give him a big f—— headache.

Investigations of Bianchi's past revealed that he had participated in numerous scams. In one case, he stole a psychologist's diploma, inserted a new name, and began a practice as a psychologist. He was also involved with a teenage prostitution ring. Despite clear evidence that those things occurred, Ken denied them and claimed to have had amnesic episodes during the periods in question. Watkins concluded that the illegal acts had been perpetrated by another personality of which Ken was not aware, and Watkins suggested that this was additional evidence for the multiple personality diagnosis. In contrast, the prosecution considered these to be instances of conscious misrepresentation.

The expert witnesses for the prosecution were led by a psychologist-psychiatrist named Martin Orne, who argued that rather than suffering from a multiple personality disorder, Bianchi suffered from an "antisocial personality disorder" and that he was faking the multiple personalities to avoid punishment. (Major symptoms of the antisocial personality disorder include repeated criminal behavior, lying, and a lack of anxiety; it will be discussed in Chapter 16.) A number of points were made to discredit the diagnosis of multiple personality. First, it was suggested that the disorder had not appeared spontaneously but had been suggested to Bianchi by Watkins. Some support for that is found in the transcript of the interview in which Steve originally emerged.

Second, Orne laid a small trap for Bianchi by suggesting that if he really did have a multiple personality disorder, he would have a third personality. The idea behind this was that if Bianchi was faking and if he were led to believe that having another personality would give his diagnosis more credibility, he would begin showing one. After the suggestion was made, Bianchi was hypnotized. Steve appeared first, followed shortly by a third personality, Billy.

The prosecution also pointed to a history of crime and lying. With regard to lying, it is interesting to note that although Bianchi claimed to know nothing about the multiple personality disorder, a search of his room revealed numerous textbooks on psychology. He had also been a psychology major in college, thus making it unlikely that he was unfamiliar with the disorder. It was also discovered that Bianchi had made a number of other conscious attempts to mislead the prosecution (e.g., he had asked others to lie about where he was at various crucial times).

Faced with overwhelming evidence and serious questions about the validity of his multiple personality defense, Bianchi withdrew his plea of not guilty by reason of insanity and entered into a plea bargain. (The demand for the death penalty was dropped in exchange for Bianchi's pleading guilty and testifying against another individual who had been involved in the murders.)

Despite his plea bargain, Bianchi steadfastly maintained his multiple personality. When given an opportunity to address the court before the sentence was passed, Bianchi gave an impassioned and tearful speech in which he said that he would have to devote his entire life to seeing that no one would follow in his footsteps. However, in sharp contrast to that display of emotion and regret, a detective assigned to the case reported that within 3 minutes of leaving the courtroom, Bianchi was sitting with his feet up on a desk, smoking a cigarette and laughing.

In his concluding comments before sentencing Kenneth Bianchi, the judge observed, "Mr. Bianchi caused confusion and delay in the proceedings. In this Mr. Bianchi was unwittingly aided and abetted by most of the psychiatrists, who naively swallowed Mr. Bianchi's story, hook, line, and sinker, almost confounding the criminal justice system."

Kenneth Bianchi was sentenced to life in prison.

Sources: Allison (1984); Orne et al. (1984); Watkins (1984); *People* v. *Buono* (1983).

And finally we must distinguish between the *objective* existence and the *phenomenological* existence of the disorder. We may not be able to prove objectively that the disorder exists, but if individuals (and their therapists) believe that it does, they will behave as though it does, and therefore in some respects it does. However, that type of existence involves a very different type of cause and treatment than what is usually assumed. Overall, then, the question of whether or not there are individuals with multiple personality disorders is still unanswered, and it has important psychological and legal implications.

PSYCHODYNAMIC EXPLANATIONS

Pent-Up Psychic Energy and Somatoform Disorders

Freud's explanation for somatoform disorders is that pent-up emotional energy is converted into physical symptoms. The process by which it occurred was never made completely clear, but Freud (1920/1955) suggested that the

imprisoned emotions undergo a series of abnormal changes. In part they are preserved as a lasting charge and as a source of constant disturbance in psychic life; in part they undergo a change into unusual bodily innervations and inhibitions which present themselves as the physical symptoms of the case. (pp. 30–31)

Freud's speculation that pent-up emotional energy was somehow converted into physical symptoms provides the basis for the term *conversion disorder*.

Freud also suggested that the later expression of the "imprisoned emotions" eliminated symptoms because it reduced the "charge." Today we call this **catharsis.** You may have experienced catharsis when you finally talked about a problem that you had kept "bottled up inside" and got the problem "off your chest." (The phrase "off your chest" is interesting in terms of symptoms because when we are tense or anxious about something, we often feel a tightness in the chest or as though there were steel bands around the chest.)

Avoidance of Stress and Dissociative Responses

Psychodynamic theory suggests that dissociative disorders result from our attempts to dissociate ourselves from stressful events or to obliterate our memories of them. In other words, the dissociative disorders involve what can be considered as massive uses of **repression** (see Chapter 2). For example, an individual who found an experience exceptionally stressful might simply banish all memory of the experience from consciousness and would therefore experience amnesia.

■ LEARNING AND COGNITIVE EXPLANATIONS

Operant Responses and Somatoform Disorders

The basic tenet of the learning theory explanation for somatoform disorders is that the symptoms are operant responses that are learned and maintained because they result in rewards (Ullman & Krasner, 1969). The reward can occur in three ways. First, the symptoms may enable the individual to *avoid some unpleasant or threatening situation*. For example, a conversion disorder involving a paralyzed hand may enable a student to skip an examination for which he or she is not prepared. I once worked with an athlete who always "pulled a muscle" before any track meet in which the competition was particularly good and might threaten his unbeaten record. His "pulled muscle" was rewarding because it protected his unbeaten record. The fact that the symptom saves the individual from a threatening situation may explain why in some cases the indi-

vidual is not concerned with the serious implications of the symptom (*la belle indifférence*).

Second, somatoform symptoms can provide an *explanation or justification for failure*, thereby relieving the individual of personal responsibility. The student who comes home at the end of the semester wearing an eye patch because of "eye trouble" can hardly be blamed for failing grades.

Third, somatoform symptoms can *attract concern, sympathy, and care* for the individual, and that attention can be very rewarding. If attention is to be elicited from others, the individual with the symptom must be concerned about the symptom, and hence in these cases the individual will probably not exhibit *la belle indifférence*.

Roles

Somatoform symptoms may be maintained because they result in rewards, but how do these symptoms originally develop? One possibility is that individuals learn to play the role of a sick individual either by observation or through personal experience with illness. We each play many **roles**, and we must learn the behaviors for each role. When we first try out a new role, it requires effort and seems unreal; we are "playing" the role. However, as time goes by, the role becomes second nature, and the distinction between role and self becomes blurred. We are no longer playing the role—we have internalized the role, and the role is us.

In the case of somatoform disorders, the individual may have learned the role of a sick individual while

Children learn that being sick can result in care and sympathy. In the case of somatoform symptoms, an individual may adopt the "sick" role when faced with stress or when in need of attention.

actually being sick or by observing another individual who was sick. Later, when faced with stress or in need of attention, the individual might shift to the "sick" role just as someone might change from a "partygoer" role to a "student" role as the situation required. This change to the sick role is not done with any more conscious intent than you used when you changed to your student role when you picked up this book and began studying. The situation demanded it, you were accustomed to the role, and you used it. Furthermore, the individual with a somatoform disorder is not faking a role any more than you are now faking a student role. Just as you have internalized the role of student and are not faking it, the individual with a somatoform disorder has internalized the role of sick individual and is not faking that role.

The sick role seen in somatoform disorders is probably an extension of less extreme behaviors that most of us have used. At one time or another, most of us have developed a headache or some other minor somatic complaint that enabled us to avoid a disagreeable event. We were not necessarily lying or faking the problem; after thinking about it for a while, we came up with a symptom that had some, albeit minimal, basis in reality. If focusing on the somatic complaint was successful in getting us out of the disagreeable event or getting us some sympathy, we might do it again and again until it became a frequent and seemingly natural means of solving problems.

Support for the role explanation for somatoform disorders comes from the fact that individuals with these disorders often have role models for sick behavior. In one investigation, it was reported that 70% of the parents of individuals with conversion disorders had a real disorder that was similar to the individuals' conversion disorders. In another investigation, 20% of the relatives of individuals with somatization disorders were also found to have somatization disorders (Arkonak & Guze, 1963). Finally, information from patients revealed that three variables were strongly associated with the hypochondriacal syndrome: (a) a high level of life defeats, (b) a high level of family illness, and (c) a low pain threshold (Bianchi, 1973). It appears that when faced with stress (defeat), individuals with a family history of illness (models) may complain of illnesses. The low pain threshold may provide at least a minimal basis for the complaints because individuals with low pain thresholds may actually experience more physical discomfort than other individuals.

Learning and cognitive theorists have had very little to say about the development of dissociative disorders. That is probably because dissociative disorders are rare and because there is some skepticism over whether they actually exist. However, it is possible that the role explanation could be extended at least to the multiple personality disorder. In that regard, it should be recognized that many of us have multiple personalities in that most of us play different roles in different situations (when in Rome, we do as the Romans do). Sometimes those roles are quite different, even conflicting. To avoid conflict, we may keep our conflicting roles completely separate and may not attend to the conflicts. For example, when I was an undergraduate, there was some conflict between my "jock" role and my "student" role. I behaved very differently in the two roles; usually dressed differently in the two roles; and although I did not realize it at first, when I was a senior, a friend pointed out that my different sets of friends even called me by different names (Dave vs. David).

The trouble with this explanation is that with multiple roles, we are *aware* of the "other personality" (I knew I studied and knew I was in training), but that is not the case with a multiple personality disorder. The development of different and conflicting multiple roles can be used to explain an *approximation* of the multiple personality disorder, but whether multiple roles can account for what is technically referred to as a multiple personality disorder has not yet been resolved.

PHYSIOLOGICAL EXPLANATIONS

Physiological Sensitivity, Arousal, and Somatoform Disorders

We generally assume that persons who suffer from somatization or hypochondriasis complain about symptoms that are not really there. However, it may be that these persons are actually *more sensitive to bodily sensations* or are *more physiologically aroused*, which would lead to more bodily sensations. If that is the case, their higher levels of sensation could provide a basis for more complaints. For example, persons who are more sensitive to pain would be more likely to notice normal aches and pains and would therefore be more likely to conclude that they were suffering from some disease than persons who were simply not aware of the same aches and pains. It is not suggested that these individuals have more symptoms, only that they may have more sensations that they *interpret* as symptoms.

The explanation that somatoform symptoms stem from higher levels of somatic sensations is supported by some empirical evidence. For example, it has been found that individuals with hypochondriasis are better able to estimate their heart rates and thus appear to be more sensitive to internal processes than other individuals (Tyrer et al., 1980). In another investigation, it was found that individuals with hypochondriasis had unusually high levels of somatic arousal (e.g., higher heart rates and muscle tension) (Hanback & Revelle, 1978). Such increased arousal could result in more somatic sensations, which could provide the basis for symptoms. Finally, it has been found that individuals with hypochondriasis have lower pain thresholds (Bianchi, 1973). Individuals with lower pain thresholds would experience more sensations, and those sensations might then be interpreted as symptoms. Although there is evidence linking somatic sensitivity or arousal to somatoform disorders, at this point we do not know whether increased sensitivity or arousal leads to the disorders or vice versa.

It is also worth noting that anxiety results in heightened somatic arousal (see Chapter 4). The presence of anxiety could then lead to a somatic condition on which an individual could build a set of somatic complaints. In other words, the individual becomes anxious, the anxiety results in increased somatic arousal, and the sensations of somatic arousal are interpreted as symptoms of some disorder. For example, an anxious person whose heart rate is elevated might conclude that the rapid heart rate reflects an underlying cardiac problem. This sequence might be more likely to occur if the individual had a personal or family history of illness, such as heart attacks, that provided a role model and additional justification for the development of the "illness" explanation for the sensations.

Hemispheric Dominance and Somatoform Disorders

We should also give some attention to the interesting finding that conversion symptoms are more likely to occur on the left side of the body (Engel, 1970; Galin et al., 1977; Stern, 1977). This is of interest because the left side of the body is controlled primarily by the right side of brain, and the right side of the brain is primarily responsible for emotions. On the basis of these two facts, researchers have speculated that a high level of emotional arousal on the right side of the brain disrupts other functioning on that side of the brain and produces unusual somatic symptoms on the left side of the body. (This explanation is strikingly similar to Freud's suggestion that an emotional "charge" is converted into "unusual bodily innervations.") Alternatively, it has been suggested that symptoms are more likely to appear on the left side because they will be less incapacitating if they are on the side opposite the preferred hand. This seems unlikely, however, because frequently the symptoms do not involve the hands and thus from a functional standpoint, the side on which the symptom occurs is irrelevant.

At present, there do not appear to be any specific physiological explanations for the various dissociative disorders. Neurologists and psychologists are working very hard to solve the riddles of why we do and do not remember things, but breakthroughs specific to the dissociative disorders have not yet been made. Research on these disorders is very difficult because the disorders occur so rarely.

▌SUMMARY

Somatoform disorders are characterized by physical symptoms or complaints about physical symptoms for which physiological bases have not been found. The somatoform disorders include somatization, hypochondriasis, conversion, pain, and the dysmorphic disorder. Mass psychogenic illness involves an epidemic of conversion disorders.

Somatoform disorders have been traced back as far as the time of the ancient Greeks, when the disorders were attributed to wandering wombs. More recently, they played an important role in the theorizing of Sigmund Freud. Somatoform disorders are more likely to be diagnosed in women, but the reasons for that are not clear. A problem revolves around misdiagnosis; somatoform disorders are sometimes misdiagnosed as actual physical disorders, and vice versa. Some critics have questioned whether physical symptoms can actually exist without an underlying physical cause. Probably the most convincing evidence for the reality of the symptoms comes from research on the placebo effect. Advances in medical understanding have led to the conclusion that some disorders that were once thought to be somatoform are in fact due to physiological causes.

The dissociative disorders include amnesia, fugue, dissociative identity (multiple personality), and the depersonalization disorder. Dissociative disorders are characterized by a dissociation or separation of experiences from consciousness. For example, the individual with psychogenic amnesia has separated from consciousness the memory of certain stressful experiences, and the individual with a multiple personality disorder has separated from consciousness whole aspects of personality. With the exception of the depersonalization disorder, which may occur in as many as 30% of normal adults, dissociative disorders are relatively rare. In the case of the multiple personality disorder, there is considerable controversy over whether the disorder even exists as it is traditionally described.

The psychodynamic explanation for somatoform disorders is that pent-up emotional energy is converted into physical symptoms. It is assumed that the eventual expression of the emotion will result in catharsis and a reduction of the symptoms. Dissociative disorders are explained by the avoidance of stress. For example, repression could result in the inability to remember an event or an aspect of personality.

The learning or cognitive explanation for somatoform disorders is that the symptoms are operant responses (roles) that are learned and maintained because they enable the individual to obtain rewards or to reduce stress. Specifically, individuals learn the role of a sick person, and that role enables them to avoid stress, justify failure, or attract attention or sympathy.

Physiological factors may play a role in the development of somatoform disorders in that some individuals have higher levels of somatic sensitivity or arousal, which leads them to be more aware of somatic sensations. Awareness of somatic sensations, in combination with a realization that other individuals do not have the same sensations, may lead individuals to suspect that they have a disease. That would be the case especially when there is a personal or family history of disease that would provide further justification for the belief and a model for the behavior. Note that this explanation does not suggest that heightened arousal or sensitivity causes the disorder; it only suggests that heightened arousal or sensitivity provides a basis for the development of the disorder. The fact that somatoform disorders often occur on the left side of the body is explained by suggesting that excessive emotional arousal (which occurs on the right side of the brain) disrupts functioning on the left side of the body.

The psychodynamic explanation for these disorders is that they stem from attempts by individuals to separate or dissociate themselves from stress-provoking conflicts. Learning, cognitive, and physiological theorists have had relatively little to say concerning the origins of these disorders.

KEY TERMS, CONCEPTS, AND NAMES

In reviewing and testing yourself on what you have learned from this chapter, you should be able to identify and discuss each of the following:

la belle indifférence
body dysmorphic disorder
catharsis
Charcot, Jean-Martin
conversion disorder
craft palsies
dancing manias
depersonalization disorder
dissociative amnesia
dissociative disorders

dissociative fugue
dissociative identity disorder
factitious disorders
Freud, Sigmund
glove anesthesia
hypochondriasis
hysteria
iatrogenic disorders
malingering
mass hysteria

mass psychogenic illness
multiple personality disorder
pain disorder
placebo effect
pseudocyesis
psychosomatic disorders
repression
roles
somatization disorder
somatoform disorders

PART 3

Mood Disorders

•OUTLINE•

Chapter 8

Depressive Disorders: Symptoms and Issues

• O U T L I N E •

ois is a 36-year-old woman who spends most of the day slumped in a chair staring blankly at the floor. Her face is slack and expressionless, she is rather unkempt, and she rarely moves or speaks. Occasionally, she weeps quietly to herself. Lois has difficulty getting to sleep at night, and she usually awakens at about 2:30 A.M. and cannot get back to sleep. She does not care about eating and has lost 12 lb in the past 3 months. When asked what was wrong, she slowly gave the following answer in a voice that was almost inaudible: "Everything is wrong; everything has gone wrong. It's just too much. (*Long pause*) I'm a complete failure. (*Long pause*) I just don't think things will get better—and I just don't care anymore. (*Begins crying*) I wish I were dead. Then I'd have it over with. . . . Everyone would be better off without me hanging around. I just can't make it anymore." Lois has been like this for about 3 months. She suffers from a *major depression of the retarded type.*

Ernst is a 68-year-old accountant for a large retail store. He has always been in good health and has always worked hard. He will retire in 2 years. Lately, he has become rather depressed. When asked what is bothering him, he replied: "What's it all for? I've kept the books balanced for 46 years, but what difference has it made to the world or to me? I came in as an assistant accountant and now I'm the senior accountant—not better, just older. The day after I leave, someone else will take over my desk and nothing will change. Old accountants don't die, they just get moved to the debit side of the ledger. I'm going to get moved over without ever having done or accomplished anything. I've been here for over 45 years, people have come and gone, and I'm just here. They don't even know who I am in the front office. If I'd been smart, I would have done something else with my life—and now it's too late." Ernst thinks of suicide sometimes, but at this point it is just a thought. Ernst suffers from *depression.*

Last week, Jennifer gave birth to a healthy 7-lb, 6-oz baby boy. Everyone is excited and happy—everyone, that is, except Jennifer, who became very depressed shortly after giving birth. She feels "tired and terrible." Sometimes she actually feels repulsed by the baby and does not want to see or care for him. Jennifer feels guilty about her feelings because this should be a joyous time for her, but she just cannot snap out of it. When other people are around, she sometimes tries to fake feeling good and happy about the baby, but that does not work because she often breaks into tears for no apparent reason. Nothing her friends say helps, and her husband is getting worried. She has thought about suicide. Jennifer is suffering from a *postpartum depression.*

In the chapters in Part 3, we will examine the nature and treatment of **mood disorders**. These disorders involve disturbances in mood that range from deep **depression** to wild **mania**. The study of mood disorders is important because their symptoms can be serious and because many people suffer from them. Indeed, it has been estimated that 8% of the population will suffer from a mood disorder at some time during their lives. Depression is the most common mood disorder, and it occurs so often that it has been called the "common cold of psychological disorders." What is also alarming is that the incidence of mood disorders is increasing rapidly. It may be that we are moving out of the "age of anxiety" and into the "decade of depression."

The large group of mood disorders is divided into a number of subgroups. The organization of those subgroups is presented graphically in Figure 8.1. The first major subgroup consists of the depressive or **unipolar disorders** in which depression is the primary symptom. The second major subgroup consists of the **bipolar disorders**. In bipolar disorders, depression is also a prominent symptom, but it alternates with mania (periods of intense excitement and activity). The term *bipolar* stems from the fact that the persons show both extremes or "poles" of mood. Individuals who today would be diagnosed as bipolar would have been called **manic-depressive** some years ago. A decision tree similar to the one used to diagnose mood disorders can be found in Figure 3.1 in Chapter 3.

In a second level of the mood disorders, we find symptom patterns that have lasted for at least 2 years and are like those in the depressive and bipolar disor-

ders but are less severe. The less severe form of the depressive disorder is known as the **dysthymic** (dis-THĪ-mik) **disorder**, and the less severe form of the bipolar disorder is called the **cyclothymic** (sī-klō-THĪ-mik) **disorder**.

Although there is some overlap in symptoms in the depressive and bipolar disorders, the emerging evidence suggests that these are different sets of disorders, and therefore we will consider them separately. We will examine the depressive disorders in this chapter and the bipolar disorders in Chapter 10.

SYMPTOMS OF DEPRESSION

There are two distinctly different symptom patterns in depression, **retarded depression** and **agitated depression**. Retarded depression is more frequent and involves a decrease in energy level such that the smallest task may seem difficult or impossible to accomplish. Individuals with retarded depression show reduced and slowed body movements. They also show reduced and monotonous speech. By comparison, individuals with agitated depression are unable to sit still: They pace, wring their hands, and pull or rub their hair or skin. There may also be sudden outbursts of complaining in which the individual shouts or talks rapidly. One woman who suffered from agitated depression spent most of her waking hours walking in circles around her bedroom, wringing her hands and weeping. She also cried through most of the night. On the surface, agitated depression involves many of the symptoms of anxiety, and it is sometimes difficult to differentiate between agitated depression and anxiety. Agitated depression may also be confused with mania, because both can involve a high level of activity. However, the agitated depressive is sad, whereas the manic often appears happy. Because retarded depression is more common, we will focus most of our attention on that type.

Mood Symptoms

The primary symptoms of the major depressive disorder revolve around problems of mood. The individual feels depressed, "blue," sad, hopeless, discouraged, "down." Frequently, the depressed person also feels isolated, rejected, and unloved. Depressed persons sometimes describe themselves as being alone in a deep, dark hole where they cannot be reached and from which they cannot climb out.

Depression is sometimes accompanied by anxiety (Mullaney, 1984). This is especially the case in the early or **prodromal** (PRŌ-DRŌ-mul) **phase**, when the

FIGURE 8.1 MOOD DISORDERS: TYPES AND ORGANIZATION.

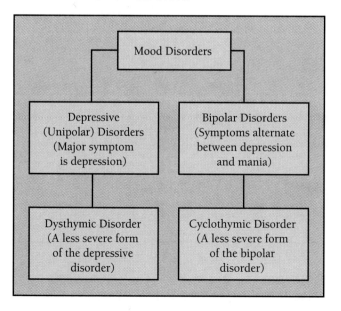

Individuals suffering from a depressive disorder often experience both depression and a sense of being rejected, unwanted, or isolated.

symptom pattern is taking shape. During this phase, the individual believes that everything is going wrong, is upset and anxious, and does a lot of worrying. In fact, during the prodromal phase, it is sometimes difficult to determine whether the individual is experiencing the onset of depression or is suffering from an anxiety state. Although anxiety continues to be a component of the depressive disorder, as time goes by, the individual gives up the struggle to "get out from under" and accepts fate; the level of anxiety is reduced, and the level of depression increases.

Cognitive Symptoms

At least six cognitive symptoms or processes play important roles in depression. First, depressed individuals have very *low self-esteem*. Specifically, depressed individuals usually think they are inadequate, inferior, inept, incompetent, and generally worthless, and they often feel guilty about their failures.

A second important cognitive symptom is *pessimism*. Depressed individuals believe that they will never be able to solve their problems and that things will only get worse. The pessimism that is characteristic of depressed individuals was illustrated in a study in which depressed and nondepressed students rated the degree to which they thought they *should* be able to perform a variety of tasks and also the degree to which they thought they *would* perform the tasks (Kanfer & Zeiss, 1983). There was no difference between depressed and nondepressed individuals in how well they thought they should perform, but the depressed individuals rated the degree to which they would perform much lower than the nondepressed individuals did. In

other words, the standards of depressed and nondepressed individuals are the same, but the depressed individuals are more pessimistic about reaching the standard. Those results are presented graphically in Figure 8.2.

Third, in persons with depression, we see a *reduction in motivation*. Because they do not believe that they will be able to solve their problems, depressed individuals see no reason to work on those problems or to seek help in overcoming them. All seems lost and hopeless, so there is no point in trying. Of course, if they do not work on their problems or seek help for them, the problems will not be solved, and the accumulation of unsolved problems can provide additional reasons for depression.

Consider the case of a student who became depressed after failing a midterm examination. The failure and depression led the student to think, "I guess I'm just not smart enough to get through this course. I'll certainly flunk the final, so there is no point in going to class or working on this course anymore." Obviously, this approach will result in failure, will provide more reasons for depression, and will confirm the individual's beliefs about his or her inadequacy.

Unfortunately, the depression, low self-esteem, pessimism, and lack of motivation tend to spread and encompass more than just the original cause of the depression. This *generalizing of negative attitudes* is the fourth important cognitive symptom in depression. Research has shown that the degree to which persons

FIGURE 8.2   DEPRESSED AND NONDEPRESSED STUDENTS AGREED ABOUT HOW WELL THEY SHOULD PERFORM ON A TASK, BUT THE DEPRESSED STUDENTS DID NOT THINK THEY WOULD PERFORM AS WELL AS THE NONDEPRESSED STUDENTS.

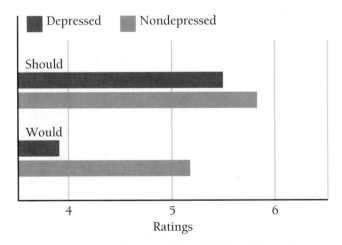

Source: Adapted from Kanfer and Zeiss (1983), p. 323, tab. 2.

generalize their problems is related to the degree of seriousness of their depression (Carver & Ganellen, 1983). Specifically, deeply depressed individuals were more likely to agree with items such as "Noticing one fault of mine makes me think more and more about other faults" and "When even one thing goes wrong, I begin to feel bad and wonder if I can do well at *anything at all*."

Women showed more inappropriate overgeneralizing than men, and the relationship between depression and overgeneralization was stronger among women than among men. The finding that women generalize negative attitudes more than men may have implications for the fact that women are more likely to suffer from depression than men. In the case of the depressed student who failed the midterm, he might go on to believe that in addition to being an academic failure, he is also a social failure and might begin withdrawing and making fewer social contacts.

In some cases, there is justification for feeling depressed (failing an examination can be serious and have negative long-term effects), but depressed individuals tend to exaggerate the seriousness of the problem and become excessively pessimistic. This *exaggeration of the seriousness of problems* is the fifth major cognitive symptom of depression and can become so extreme that the individual may develop a **delusion**. That is, despite strong evidence to the contrary, the individual develops and maintains totally erroneous beliefs that are bizarre and patently absurd. For example, a very depressed individual might believe that he or she was suffering from progressive brain deterioration. The delusions seen in depression are less bizarre than those seen in schizophrenia (i.e., the depressed individual does not think that he or she is God) and are likely to be related to mood (e.g., depression related to an imagined illness) (Junginger et al., 1992).

The sixth cognitive symptom that plays an important role in depression is *slowed thought processes* (Miller, 1975). Depressed individuals lack the motivation or mental energy to think quickly and work actively on a problem. This is very important because in some cases they are then unable to work effectively. Indeed, depressed individuals show very poor intellectual performance, especially on tasks that require speed or effort in processing (e.g., math problems under time pressure). We can easily see the effects of depression on memory functioning. On short-term memory (a delay of 1 second), depressed individuals perform as well as nondepressed individuals, but on long-term memory (delays of 20 or 30 seconds), depressed individuals perform less well than nondepressed individuals (Colby & Gotlib, 1988). Those results are presented in Figure 8.3. The finding that depressed and nonde-

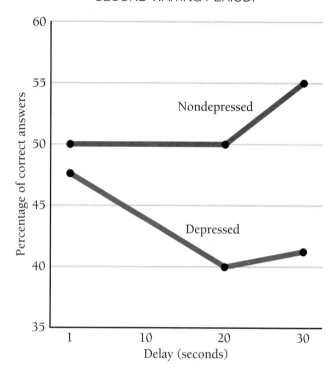

FIGURE 8.3   DEPRESSED INDIVIDUALS SHOWED DECLINES IN RECALL AFTER A 20-SECOND WAITING PERIOD.

Source: Colby & Gotlib (1988), p. 621, Fig. 3.

pressed individuals did not differ in recall performance after a 1-second delay but did differ after delays of 20 and 30 seconds is due to the fact that after only 1 second, the material is still in the *short-term memory*, but by the 20-second point, it would have to have been processed and sent to the *long-term memory* (see Chapter 2). Processing for long-term memory takes energy that the depressed individual lacks, and therefore the information is not sent to the long-term memory but instead is lost. Obviously, that loss could reduce subsequent functioning. It is noteworthy that the greatest difference in cognitive performance between depressed and nondepressed individuals comes toward the end of the task on which they are working, an effect that is probably due to the decline in motivation and energy on the part of depressed individuals.

From the preceeding comments it is clear that depressed individuals have more negative self-perceptions than nondepressed individuals, but it is interesting to note that in at least some cases, the depressed individuals may be *more accurate* in their self-perceptions than nondepressed individuals. That is, it may be that depressed individuals do not distort their perceptions downward but rather that nondepressed individuals distort their perceptions upward. For example, when college students were asked to estimate how well they performed on a task, depressed students gave lower estimates that were closer to their actual performance than the inflated estimates of nondepressed students, and when college students were asked to rate their social skills, the lower estimates of depressed students were closer to the ratings of independent judges than the inflated estimates of nondepressed students (Alloy & Abramson, 1979; Lewinsohn et al., 1980). This prompted the investigators to suggest that in at least some situations, depressed individuals are "sadder but wiser."

Motor Symptoms

The most prominent and most important motor symptom in depression is *psychomotor retardation*, which involves a reduction or slowing of motor behavior. Depressed persons frequently sit with a drooping posture and a blank, expressionless gaze. Some depressed individuals simply curl up in bed and attempt to sleep. If they do move, they do so very slowly and as though they were dragging a 10-ton weight. They may even report feeling like they have the weight of the world on their shoulders and just cannot move under this burden. Psychomotor retardation also affects speech patterns. Depressed individuals talk very little, and when they do talk, it is in a quiet monotone. Often they will break off talking in midsentence because they do not have the energy or the interest to finish the sentence.

In contrast, some depressed persons show *psychomotor agitation* and are unable to sit still. These people are restless and constantly fidgeting or pacing. It is noteworthy that the activities of these individuals are random rather than focused on achieving any particular goal, and thus their activities do not gain them anything. Psychomotor agitation is much less prevalent than psychomotor retardation. The differences in motor activity lead to the diagnoses of retarded and agitated depression that were discussed earlier.

Somatic Symptoms

Depressed individuals are prone to suffer from a variety of somatic problems. One of the most notable is a *disturbed sleep pattern*. Depressed individuals often have difficulty getting to sleep and then experience *early awakening* in that they wake up early in the morning (around 2:00 A.M., for example) and are unable to get back to sleep. Early awakening appears to be associated with more serious depressions, and the time of early awakening may be an index to the depth of the depression. It appears that as the depression lifts, the time of the early awakening becomes later and later. In some cases of depression, the individuals begin sleeping more than usual, an effect called **hypersomnia** (HĪ-pur-SOM-nē-uh).

Disturbed eating patterns are also common in depressions. Many depressed individuals lose interest in eating, and food ceases to have any flavor for them. Consequently, they decrease their food intake. In other cases, the depressed individuals may want to eat and realize that they need to eat, but because they do not have the energy to prepare good meals, they rely on a diet of easily available "junk food" that fails to fulfill their nutritional needs. There are also some depressed individuals for whom eating becomes very important. For these people, eating becomes the only pleasant activity in their otherwise gloomy lives.

Another somatic symptom that is often associated with depression is *reduced sexual interest or drive*. This is often referred to as a **loss of libido** (li-BĒ-dō; *libido* is the psychodynamic term for sexual drive). The severity of somatic symptoms in unipolar depressed patients, bipolar depressed patients, and normal controls is summarized in Figure 8.4.

The somatic symptoms involving sleep, appetite, and sex can be due to any of three factors. First, these somatic disturbances can stem from the fact that the individuals are psychologically distressed, and that distress has a psychologically disruptive influence. Second, depression is associated with a variety of biochemical changes in the brain, and those changes influence the functioning of the hypothalamus, which in turn influences sleep, appetite, and sex. Third, some somatic symptoms, such as fatigue and digestive problems, may not be due to the depression per se but may instead be *secondary symptoms* caused by the fact that the individual is not sleeping well, not eating well, and not exercising.

Apart from the specific problems associated with sleep, appetite, and sex, depressed individuals are more susceptible to a variety of diseases, apparently as the result of an impairment of the functioning of the **immune system** (Schleifer et al., 1984). Specifically, there is evidence that depressed individuals produce fewer **lymphocytes** (LIM-fō-sīts; white blood cells), which play an important role in fighting off disease (see Chapter 17).

Less psychologically sophisticated individuals may emphasize their physical symptoms and underplay their psychological symptoms. This can result in what is called a "masked depression" in which the depressive symptoms are concealed by a mask of physical symptoms. If the individual is focused on and discusses only the physical symptoms, misdiagnosis may result.

In considering the mood, cognitive, motor, and somatic symptoms of depression, it is important to recognize that these symptoms can also serve as causes of additional depression. For example, cognitive symptoms such as low self-esteem, reduced motivation, and pessimism may lead to generally **negative cognitive sets** that preclude seeing the positive aspects of life

FIGURE 8.4   DEPRESSED PATIENTS SUFFER FROM A VARIETY OF SOMATIC SYMPTOMS.

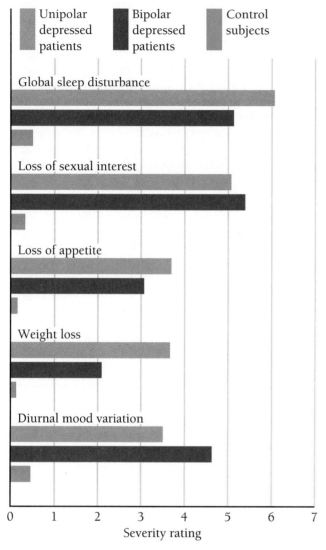

Source: Adapted from Casper et al. (1985), p. 1100.

Symptoms of depression such as low self-esteem, reduced motivation, loss of sleep, and poor appetite can contribute to a deepening of the depression.

and thereby contribute to a deepening of the depression. Similarly, reduced or ineffective motor activity can interfere with effective problem solving, further convincing depressed individuals of their ineptitude. Somatic symptoms such as loss of sleep and poor appetite can also sap individuals of energy, thereby reducing their effectiveness. In short, a vicious circle can develop in which the symptoms of depression lead to greater depression. An example of an individual suffering from a major depression is presented in Case Study 8.1 (p. 174).

Not all instances of depression result in hospitalization, and in many cases, individuals just keep struggling, watching their personal relations and personal potential deteriorate, making excuses for themselves, and thinking that they are just not good people. This

type of experience was beautifully described for me by a student who wrote a term paper on the topic of depression and its treatment. She opened the paper with a description of her own experience with depression before it was successfully treated; you will find her description in Case Study 8.2 (p. 176).

As mentioned earlier, the dysthymic disorder is a less severe form of the depressive disorder (see Figure 8.1). It is likely that many individuals suffer from this disorder but are not formally diagnosed because the symptoms are milder and may not greatly impair the individuals' ability to function. Although these individuals are often not formally diagnosed as suffering from a psychological problem, dysthymic individuals suffer over a prolonged period of time and miss much of what is positive in life.

ISSUES ASSOCIATED WITH DEPRESSION

Normal Versus Abnormal Depression

Feelings of sadness, disappointment, grief, and depression are part of the human condition and are experi-

Case Study 8.1

MAJOR DEPRESSION IN A YOUNG WOMAN

Diane is a 28-year-old single woman who has suffered from serious depression since she was 16. Her first period of depression culminated in an almost fatal drug overdose. After her suicide attempt, she was hospitalized on and off for several years, and when not in the hospital, she was treated regularly in the outpatient clinic. Treatment consisted of psychotherapy and antidepressant drugs. Her adjustment during this period was only marginal, but she was able to complete high school.

Diane has remained out of the hospital now for about 7 years, but her depression has persisted. In describing her feelings, she says:

I wish someone would give me a spoon and tell me to move a mountain. Then my sense of hopeless futility would be more tangible. . . . Life is an absurd waste of time. . . . My existence is a freak accident of nature. . . . It seems that I can only handle short, sweet episodes of positive momentum.

Her overwhelming sense of worthlessness and inadequacy has prevented her from establishing any meaningful friendships that could challenge her negative self-image and provide support. Not surprisingly, her ruminations concerning her "emo-

tional hellishness" interfere with her capacity to concentrate, think clearly, or make decisions. She spends much of her time staring into space, looking but seeing only gray, negative images of life.

Diane is a bright young woman, and although plagued by almost ceaseless depression, she managed to complete college and hold several part-time jobs. However, consistent with her unrealistic self-devaluation, she minimizes these accomplishments, saying, "It took so long to finish college, my degree is useless, and the work is mindless." She seems to lack any foundation on which to build a positive self-evaluation.

Despite the severity of her depression and her sense of hopelessness, Diane has not attempted suicide again. She credits therapy with providing her with at least one supportive and nurturing relationship that helps her get through the "rough spots of life." She views the possibility of long-term meaningful change skeptically: "I've been miserable all my life, and I don't know if I know how to live differently. I'm not sure I know what it is like to be happy. I probably wouldn't recognize it if I was."

---

enced by everyone at some time. The question arises, then, what distinguishes normal depression from abnormal depression? The boundary is not clear, but two factors that should be considered in making the distinction are the *depth* of the depression and the *duration* of the depression. With regard to depth, it is normal to occasionally feel somewhat "down," "blue," or mildly depressed. There is reason for concern, however, when the depression is so deep that the individual cannot function adequately. Regardless of the depth of the depression, there is cause for concern if the duration of the depression is prolonged and the individual does not "snap out of it." In cases such as the death of a loved one, it is justified to be depressed for a while, but if the depression is more prolonged than what is justified by the original cause, the possibility of abnormal depression must be considered.

Prevalence of Depression

More than 5% of the population will suffer from a major depression sometime during their lives, and about 3% will experience the less severe but still troublesome symptoms of dysthymia (Boyd & Weissman, 1982; Robins et al., 1984). Other research sets the levels even higher, suggesting that about 12% of individu-

als who were examined met the requirement for a "major depression" (Coryell et al., 1991). Taken together, those figures indicate that depression is one of the three most prevalent psychological disorders. (The other two are substance abuse and anxiety.) The problem is magnified by the fact that in many cases, depression is a chronic or recurring disorder, and thus not only is the rate high, but also the duration of the disorder is long.

Substantial evidence indicates that the prevalence of depression has been increasing throughout the 20th century (Hagnell et al., 1982; Klerman, 1976, 1979; Klerman et al., 1985; Robins et al., 1984; Weissman & Myers, 1978). The increase in mild and medium levels of depression is illustrated in the results of a study conducted in Sweden in which all of the inhabitants of one particular area were examined repeatedly between 1947 and 1972 (Hagnell et al., 1982). As indicated in Figure 8.5, the rates of "medium" and "mild" depression increased greatly over time, especially among women. The finding that severe depressions did not increase (and actually showed a decrease among women) is not completely understandable, but it might be due to the fact that a variety of effective treatments for depression have been developed. The treatments may have been more likely to be applied to

FIGURE 8.5   RATES OF MEDIUM AND MILD DEPRESSION HAVE INCREASED OVER TIME.

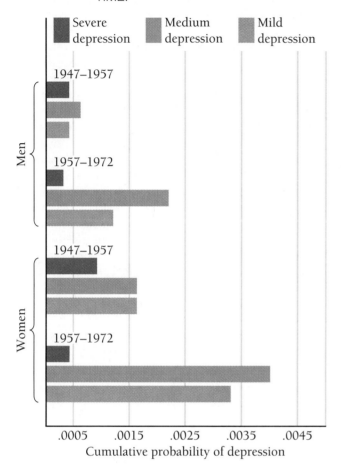

Source: Adapted from Hagnell et al. (1982), p. 284, tab. 3.

to recur. In one investigation it was found that 45% of the individuals who were studied had two episodes, and 33% had three episodes (Lewinsohn et al., 1989). The likelihood of relapse is higher for females and higher for individuals whose initial depression was more serious. In fact, for seriously depressed individuals, the relapse rate may be as high as 90%.

Demographic Factors

Depression is much more likely to be diagnosed in women than in men, the ratio being about 2:1 (Boyd & Weissman, 1982; Duncan-Jones & Henderson, 1978; Lewinsohn et al., 1986; Robins et al., 1984; Weissman & Klerman, 1977; Weissman & Myers, 1978; Wing et al., 1978). This has been the case in 30 countries over a period of 40 years. The difference in depression rates between women and men is illustrated in Figure 8.6.

Various reasons have been advanced to account for the generally higher rate of diagnosed depression among women than men, including the following:

1. Because of their social roles, women are freer to

FIGURE 8.6   WOMEN SHOW HIGHER RATES OF DEPRESSION THAN MEN.

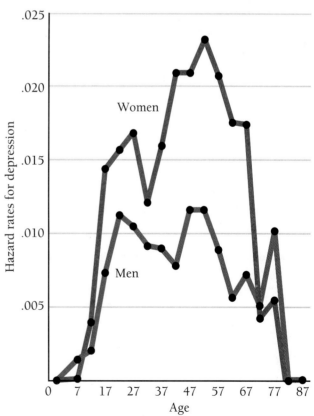

Source: Lewinsohn et al. (1986), p. 381, fig. 1.

severely depressed individuals, and therefore that level of depression was held in check. The findings concerning the increasing rate of depression have prompted some people to express concern about the coming "age of melancholy" (Klerman, 1979). This could be a serious trend.

One cautionary note should be sounded concerning the findings that the incidence of depression is on the increase. It is possible that depression is not actually increasing but that we are becoming more willing to admit to depression or more likely to diagnose it than we were. In other words, it may be that depression is becoming more acceptable or less of a stigma, and it is the change in attitude rather than a change in the actual incidence of depression that is reflected in the data. In this regard, it is noteworthy that only the mild and medium levels of depression are increasing; those are the levels that would have been easier to deny or ignore.

With regard to the prevalence of depression, it is also important to recognize that *depression is very likely*

Case Study 8.2

A STUDENT'S STRUGGLE WITH DEPRESSION

"I feel as though I have spent my whole life trapped inside a glass bottle. I could look out and view the world, but it always seemed dulled and distorted by the thick, scratched glass. If anyone would shake me up the slightest bit, I felt as though I was going to crack and shatter in a million pieces. Perhaps that was precisely what I wanted so that I could cut people with the millions of jagged edges. My anger was enormous. It angered me that people were so damn happy and all I could do was watch.

"After experiencing these feelings for as much of my life as I could remember, I entered psychotherapy at the age of 17 because my parents thought I was 'depressed.' I was easily swayed by the idea because in the pit of stomach I really did not want to go on feeling the way I did. When the time came to enter college, I quit my therapy and concluded that my feelings of entrapment and isolation must just be a major character flaw. My first year of college was filled with ups and downs. I couldn't seem to keep any relationships intact, with males or females. It seemed that everyone was always tired of being around me and accused me of being perpetually pessimistic. Sometimes I would spend days secluded by myself. When people would ask if something was wrong, I would reply with a philosophical answer about how some people need more time to themselves than others and that I had accepted that fact about myself. I rationalized my seclusion by telling myself that people who aren't comfortable by themselves are actually more insecure than those who can be alone. As I was never happy with what I was doing in the present, I tended to move around a lot in a ploy to 'experience different things' and 'get in touch with myself.' As time went by, my depression was pushed to an all-time low, and I found myself incapacitated. I began spending more and more time in my bed huddled under my blankets with my door closed. Most of the time, I didn't feel particularly bad about not accomplishing anything because I knew that I physically couldn't get out of bed and I had lost faith that I had any academic prowess whatsoever. All of my relationships deteriorated because nobody wanted or knew how to deal with me. This only served to substantiate what I had decided about myself—that I was a worthless person who could never accomplish anything."

Note: We will return to this student's experiences later when we consider the treatment of depression (see Chapter 11).

---

express feelings in general and therefore freer to express the negative feelings associated with depression.

2. Women are more likely to be exposed to the types of stressful situations that result in depression.

3. Physiological and hormonal differences between men and women predispose women to depression.

In one study that was conducted to determine the reason for the higher rate of depression among women than men, it was found that when men and women were matched in terms of level of depression, the women were not more likely to label themselves as depressed and were not more likely to seek treatment (Amenson & Lewinsohn, 1981). Those findings do not provide support for the "freer to express negative feelings" explanation. Moreover, although numerous demographic variables such as age, income, and education were related to depression, controlling for those variables did not eliminate the sex differences in depression.

It has also been found that women were more frequently exposed to more of the factors that have been shown to be related to depression, such as low education, low income, current illness, and recent illness. As before, however, when males and females were matched in terms of these stress factors, women still had higher rates of depression (Amenson & Lewinsohn, 1981; Radloff & Rae, 1979). Furthermore, a variety of psychological variables such as self-esteem, locus of control, and stressful life events were found to be related to depression, but controlling for those did not eliminate the sex differences. The fact that environmental and psychological variables have not been found to be related to the sex differences in depression has led some investigators to speculate that women may respond to stress differently than men or that women may have a greater physiological predisposition to depression than men.

The results of one study suggest that the higher rate of depression in women is due at least in part to the fact that women who become depressed do so more frequently than men (Amenson & Lewinsohn, 1981). In that study, the depression levels of 686 women and 312 men were measured at two points in time about 8 months apart. The prevalence of depression in women was found to be about twice as high as for men (11.4% vs. 5.1% at the first test, 12.8% vs. 7.1% at the second test). More important, the percentage of women who had been depressed before was higher than the percentage of men who had been depressed before (62.3% vs. 48.8%).

Age also plays a role in depression. Unlike many other disorders, depression is found throughout the life span. In general, however, the incidence of depression tends to peak sometime in the 40s, and there is also evidence of a second peak in old age (Post, 1982). The pattern of depression across age is different for men and women (Boyd & Weissman, 1982; Lewinsohn et al., 1986), with women showing a higher rate of depression earlier.

The differences in rates of depression for men and women at different ages may be due at least in part to the effects of marriage. Some investigations have revealed that marriage increased the rate of depression in young women but decreased the rate in young men (Radloff, 1975). That effect is apparently due to the fact that marriage often provides an additional source of support for men whereas it entails additional demands and responsibilities for women.

Independent of sex and age, depression is higher among individuals with less income, those with less education, and those who are unemployed or recently divorced or separated (Langner & Michael, 1963; Levitt & Lubin, 1975; Murphy et al., 1991; Radloff, 1977). It has been speculated that it is the stress associated with these factors that contributes to the depression, but it may also be that depression leads to these problems. We will have to keep all of these demographic factors in mind later when we examine the various explanations for depression.

Exogenous Versus Endogenous Depressions

It is generally agreed that some depressions are due primarily to *external* (psychological) factors like conflict and stress, whereas other depressions are due primarily to *internal* (physiological) factors such as low levels of certain neurotransmitters. Depression due to external factors is referred to as an **exogenous** (eg-ZOJ-uh-nus) **depression**, and depression due to internal factors is referred to as an **endogenous** (en-DOJ-uh-nus) **depression**. (Exogenous depressions are also sometimes called "reactive" depressions because the individual is supposedly reacting to some environmental problem.) Before we examine the distinction between exogenous and endogenous depressions, it must be made clear that depression may result from a combination of exogenous and endogenous factors. Therefore, it is often more appropriate to consider the distinction in terms of *more or less* rather than *either-or*. We will discuss the interaction of exogenous and endogenous factors later.

The distinction between exogenous and endogenous depressions is important in terms of treatment. Psychotherapy would probably be most effective for an exogenously depressed person, whereas drug therapy would probably be most effective for an endogenously depressed person.

Problems in Identifying Exogenous and Endogenous Depressions.
Although the exogenous-endogenous distinction is important for understanding and treating depressed individuals, it is very difficult to determine who is suffering from exogenous depressions and who is suffering from endogenous depressions. Numerous attempts have been made to distinguish between them on the basis of differences in symptom patterns, but this approach has not proved particularly fruitful. The only consistent difference in symptom patterns is that endogenously depressed individuals are more likely to have a personal or family history of depression. (The finding that endogenously depressed individuals are more likely to have family members who are depressed has been interpreted as evidence that endogenous depressions are likely to be due to genetic factors. We will discuss this in Chapter 9.)

The problem is further complicated by the fact that because they are unaware of the physiological basis for the depression, endogenously depressed individuals are often able to find what *appears* to be a cause or justification for the depression in the environment, thus throwing the diagnostician off the trail of the real cause. A simple example of the misattribution of the cause for an endogenous depression is presented in Case Study 8.3 (p. 178).

The Dexamethasone Suppression Test.
Some hope for our ability to distinguish between exogenous and endogenous depression was aroused when a blood test was developed that was thought to be effective in identifying endogenously depressed individuals (Carroll, 1982). The test is called the **dexamethasone** (DEK-suh-METH-uh-sōn) **suppression test (DST)**, and it is based on the following principles. One of the physiological factors associated with endogenous depression is the excessive secretion of **cortisol** (hydrocortisone) by the adrenal gland. Cortisol is a hormone that facilitates the breakdown of proteins into glycogen and sugar, thus helping prepare the individual for stress. Dexamethasone suppresses the production of cortisol in normal and exogenously depressed individuals but not in endogenously depressed individuals. Theoretically, then, endogenous and exogenous depressives could be differentiated by testing to see whether or not they reduce their production of cortisol when given dexamethasone. In the DST, dexamethasone is administered to the client late in the evening, and then levels of cortisol are assessed in the blood at 8:00 A.M., 2:00 P.M., and 11:00 P.M. the next day.

Case Study 8.3

MISATTRIBUTION OF THE CAUSE OF AN ENDOGENOUS DEPRESSION

I knew this student rather well, and I was very concerned when one morning he came to me very depressed and tearful, asking whether he could be excused from class that day. When I asked what the problem was, he went on at great length about his mother's serious medical problem and how upsetting it was for him. I was surprised and initially confused by his level of despair because although his mother's problem was a reason for some concern, never before had he been this distressed about it. Another reason for his depression, mentioned almost in passing, was that he had been bothered by some neck pains stemming from an automobile accident a few weeks earlier. He said the pain had been so troublesome the previous night that he had taken an additional tablet of the muscle relaxant prescribed by his physician. We did not discuss his concerns any further, but because of the degree to which he was upset, I excused him from class and asked that he check back with me later in the day. About 3 hours later he called me, and with some amazement told me how, while sitting in his 11 o'clock class, the "black cloud of gloom" that had been hanging over him all morning "seemed to just lift and drift away." Everything was now "sunny and bright," and he felt great. I asked about his concern for his mother, and he said that of course he was worried, but maybe he had been a little "unrealistic" about the problem earlier in my office. He was amazed how that "black cloud" had lifted and how great he suddenly felt.

What really caused this depression, and why did it suddenly lift?

We later realized that he was very sensitive to the muscle-relaxing medication he had been given and that the medication had a depressing side effect. Unbeknownst to him at the time, the depression had been triggered by the medication, and he then misattributed the cause of his depression to a personal or environmental factor. The depressing effect of the drug was later confirmed by experimentally increasing and decreasing the dosage (a multiple baseline single-subject design) and observing changes in mood. He is now very careful with the medication he takes.

Unfortunately, a substantial amount of research has indicated that the DST test is accurate only 40% to 70% of the time, and after reviewing the evidence, a task force of the American Psychiatric Association concluded that "positive initial DST status in major depression does not add significantly to the likelihood of antidepressant [drug] response, and a negative test is not an indication for withholding antidepressant [drug] treatment" (APA Task Force, 1987, p. 1253). In other words, the test does not reliably discriminate between endogenously and exogenously depressed individuals and hence is not particularly effective in predicting who will respond well to drug therapy versus psychotherapy. Overall, then, the identification of individuals with endogenous versus exogenous depressions is crucial for research and treatment, but at present our ability to make the distinction between the two types of depression is limited.

Interaction of Exogenous and Endogenous Depressions.

The issue of exogenous versus endogenous depression is made more complex by the fact that in some cases, one form can lead to the other. On the one hand, the prolonged psychological stress associated with an exogenous depression can cause physiological changes that eventually result in an endogenous depression. For example, rats and monkeys exposed to prolonged stress showed changes in the levels of the neurotransmitters that are known to lead to endogenous depression (Raleigh et al., 1984; Weiss et al., 1976). On the other hand, the inappropriate behavior brought on by an endogenous depression can result in personal or environmental problems that can contribute to an exogenous depression. For example, an endogenous depression can seriously reduce an individual's ability to function (slowed thinking, lack of activity, constant crying), the inability to function leads to the loss of job or friends, and the loss provides the basis for an exogenous depression. Clearly, the distinction between endogenous and exogenous depressions is very important for understanding and treating depressions, but the task of differentiating between them is exceptionally complex and difficult.

Primary Versus Secondary Depression

To this point in our discussion, we have been considering individuals for whom depression is the primary symptom. It is important to recognize, however, that depression is often a secondary symptom in individuals who are suffering from some other preexisting disorder such as anxiety, alcoholism, schizophrenia, or a physical disorder. For example, a person with schizophrenia may have a delusion that he or she is dying and may therefore be depressed, but in this case the depression is a secondary symptom of the schizophrenia. Because the causes of **primary depression** and **secondary depression** are very different, these depressions require different treatments, and the primary-secondary distinction is important when making diagnoses.

Types of Depression

There are two opposing approaches to the question of whether there are different types of depression. Some years ago, the prevailing notion was that distinctly different types of depression stemmed from different causes. By cause I do not mean exogenous and endogenous factors, but rather *situations*; depressions were identified as a function of the situations from which they developed. For example, depressions resulting from aging were called **involutional depressions**, and depressions that followed giving birth were called **postpartum depressions**. Later it was generally agreed that, although the situations might be different, the underlying factors (stress, biochemical imbalances) were the same, and nothing could be gained by labeling the depressions in terms of the situations from which they developed; therefore, the situational labels were dropped. With the publication of DSM-IV, the pendulum has begun to swing back, and situational labels have been attached for some depressions. For example, there is now a diagnosis called depression *with postpartum onset*. In this section we will consider types of depression that are frequently mentioned, some of which are now officially designated as types of depression by DSM-IV.

Involutional Depression.
The term *involutional depression* has traditionally been used to refer to the depression associated with the onset of advanced age. The incidence of depression increases substantially after the age of about 65, and the predominance of female over male depressives that exists before age 65 diminishes or even reverses with increasing age (Post, 1982). Related to the increase in depression with age are the findings that the proportion of individuals who attempt and are successful at committing suicide is greater among individuals over 65. In fact, individuals over 65 account for at least 25% of all suicides (Sendbuehler, 1977; Sendbuehler & Goldstein, 1977). In view of the fact that life expectancies are increasing, the relationship between depression and aging is particularly important.

Involutional depression was originally thought to be a consequence of the physiological factors associated with aging, and those factors certainly do contribute to depression in many cases. More recently, however, attention has shifted to the role that psycho-

The incidence of depression increases substantially after about the age of 65. The proportion of individuals who commit suicide also rises in this age group.

logical and cultural factors play. Old age and the approach of old age can be stressful periods because of (a) the loss of family, friends, status, and respect; (b) increased illnesses and the financial problems associated with aging; and (c) the fact that the future is limited and may appear bleak. In most Western societies in which progress is fast-paced, older individuals are seen as obsolete and are regarded as "second-class citizens" who must be moved out of the way. These individuals are often deprived of the contributing role so highly prized in our society, thus undermining their self-confidence and self-esteem.

A classic case of involutional depression is Willy Loman in Arthur Miller's play *Death of a Salesman* (1949). His experience is summarized in Case Study 8.4.

Depression with Postpartum Onset.
Depression with postpartum onset was originally called postpartum depression; it refers to a relatively severe depression that sets in shortly after a woman gives birth and lasts between 6 weeks and a year (Hopkins et al., 1984; Pitt, 1982). There is some controversy over the frequency of this disorder, with estimates going as high as 30% of the women who give birth (Rees & Lutkins, 1971). However, in some prospective studies in which increases in depression were studied in

Case Study 8.4

WILLY LOMAN: A CASE OF INVOLUTIONAL DEPRESSION

As the play opens, Willy Loman enters slowly from the right. He is past 60 years of age, dressed quietly, and slowed by fatigue and the weight of two large sample cases. He approaches his home, a small, fragile-seeming house dwarfed by the solid mass of apartment buildings that have been built around it. Night is coming and the light is dim, but even if it were day, it is unlikely that much light could penetrate to the small plot of land on which the house sits. Willy Loman is coming back from a business trip. Actually, we can't really say coming *back*, because he never made it to his destination. He explains to his wife, "I got as far as a little above Yonkers. I stopped for a cup of coffee. Maybe it was the coffee. . . . (*pause*) I suddenly couldn't drive anymore. The car kept going off onto the shoulder, y'know?"

That is how the play opens, and that is how Willy's life is closing—a slow, grinding, uneventful, but terrible close. Willy is worn out. He is through. He just can't stay on the road anymore. Like his house, Willy's life and dreams are just shells; the house is starved for light, and Willy is starved for hope.

Willy Loman, the main character in Arthur Miller's Death of a Salesman, *experiences the deep depression that some people develop as their lives draw to an end (Courtesy of the* L.A. *Times).*

Willy Loman has been a sales representative for a New York manufacturer for 36 years. He opened up the New England territory for the company, and ever since he has traveled the territory, carrying his heavy sample case and making calls on buyers. Willy has done a good job over the years; he had a good sales record and took pride in the fact that he could walk into any large store in his territory and people knew him. Important to him, Willy Loman was liked, well liked.

Unfortunately, things began to change. The line, the buyers, the boss all changed, and Willy was being left alone on the sidelines. Willy changed too; he no longer has the energy to keep up. In reflecting on how the buyers respond to him now, Willy comments, "I don't know the reason for it, but they just pass me by. I'm not noticed."

There are other disappointments to be faced—or avoided. Willy has two sons, Biff and Happy, and his dreams revolve around Biff. Biff had been immensely successful in high school, at least athletically and socially, but somehow he never made it. Life beyond high school was more than a football field and giddy teenage girls, and Biff just drifted from one dead-end job to another. For years, Willy denied what was really happening to Biff—there was always that great job and success right around the corner—but the fact that Biff was not going to make it is beginning to seep into Willy's awareness like a penetrating and numbing chill. Willy's life is over, and his dreams for his son are fading. Willy, the usually optimistic and outgoing salesman, is shaken. He is slipping into depression.

Faced with a bleak present and a worse future, Willy dwells on missed opportunities. Frequently, he thinks about his successful brother Ben, and at one point he says to himself, "Why didn't I go to Alaska with my brother Ben that time! Ben! That was a genius, that man was success incarnate! What a mistake! He begged me to go." But the opportunity is past, and Willy is all that he will ever be—and less than he ever hoped.

Seeking solace, Willy lapses into reminiscences in which he goes back to better times and talks aloud to persons as they were then. Often he relives times when he was a rising salesman and his sons were promising young high school athletes. His devoted wife stands by him and gently coaxes him back to the present. When his sons come home for a visit and see their father's behavior, they are embarrassed and angry with him. His wife defends him: "A small man can be just as exhausted as a great man. He works for a company thirty-six years this March, opens up unheard-of territories to their trademark, and now in his old age they take his salary away. . . . The man who never worked a day but for your benefit? When does he get the medal for that?"

In an emotional confrontation between the two boys and their mother, she reveals, "He's dying, Biff. . . . He's been trying to kill himself." The boys initially refuse to believe it, but she shows them an automobile insurance report and says, "They have evidence. That all those accidents in the last year— weren't—weren't—accidents." The boys are still unconvinced, so she finally tells them about a short rubber hose she has found in the basement. "There's a little attachment on the end of it. I knew right away. And sure enough, on the bottom of the

water heater there's a new little nipple on the gas pipe."

In many respects, Willy Loman's life is over, and there is nothing left for him. He is slipping into a deep depression, and he is planning to end his life. I won't tell you about the rest of the play. You should read or see it if you can, because it is a very sensitive portrayal of the development of depression in later life. Willy Loman provides the model of what many people go through as they approach the end of their lives. They cannot keep up, so they are left behind, and it is rare that all of their dreams are fulfilled. When faced with that, they respond in different ways, and like Willy, many become depressed. The play is entitled *Death of a Salesman*, but it could be *Death of Everyman*.

---

women who were or were not pregnant and giving birth, it was found that the women who gave birth had only slightly elevated rates of depression (O'Hara et al., 1990; Troutman & Cutrona, 1990). Interestingly, depression following abortion is only one-fifth as common as depression after childbirth (Brewer, 1978; Tietze & Lewitt, 1972).

Despite its frequency and long history, many women are not aware of the disorder, and therefore it catches them by surprise when the "happy event" occurs. Many women apparently try to hide their postpartum depression because they feel guilty about being depressed when tradition dictates that they should be feeling joyful.

Disturbances of mood associated with childbirth

cover a wide range of severity, and not all of the disturbances should be classed as postpartum depression. Actually, some degree of depression, anxiety, irritability, loss of appetite, sleep disturbance, tearfulness, and emotional instability is normal and to be expected after giving birth. Those responses occur because of the physical discomfort and stress associated with labor and delivery, the hormonal changes that occur with childbirth, the onset of lactation, the side effects of medication, and the hospital environment.

A transient phenomenon experienced by 50% to 80% of postpartum women, referred to as the **maternity blues**, involves changes in mood and crying (Hopkins et al., 1984; O'Hara, Schlechte, Lewis, & Varner, 1991; O'Hara, Schlechte, Lewis, & Wright,

Many women experience a brief period of depression after giving birth known as "maternity blues." Postpartum depression is more prolonged, can be severe, and sometimes results in tragic consequences. These parents are sitting before the coffin of their 2-month-old infant son, whom the mother drowned.

Case Study 8.5

A FIRST-PERSON ACCOUNT OF A MILD POSTPARTUM DEPRESSION

A few days after delivering our second child, I started to feel very anxious, guilty, and depressed. Although we had a happy, healthy 4-year-old son, I now felt utterly helpless in taking care of this new infant. I felt very guilty, thinking that I hadn't prepared myself better by reading books or something. I couldn't remember what to do for specific problems, and I was generally anxious about everything. I felt hopelessly inadequate.

I wasn't even slightly hungry, and when I did eat, I either vomited or had diarrhea. This made me worry that my baby wasn't getting proper nutrition because I was breast-feeding. I would awake an hour or two before the alarm went off at 6:00 A.M., and I would start worrying that I wouldn't be able to get everything done on time or that I wouldn't be a good wife and mother. It was terrible.

I was extremely tired and exhausted all of the time, and I cried at the drop of a hat. I couldn't concentrate on anything very long, and I felt entirely overwhelmed with my predicament. I couldn't imagine how my mother had coped with six children and maintained her sanity. I remember that I did a great deal of complaining that I simply couldn't handle all of this, but somehow I kept going enough to get by.

Meanwhile, the baby picked up on my unhappiness and anxiety and became extremely fussy, which made me feel even less capable as a mother. I recall very clearly a day when a friend stopped in, and although the baby wouldn't stop crying for me, she stopped immediately when my friend took her. My friend persuaded me to call my physician, who prescribed some antidepressants for a couple of weeks. Before long, the symptoms went away, and I was more like my normal self, even after I stopped taking the pills. Soon I was enjoying life again as I had before, and at our 6-week checkup, both the baby and I were in excellent condition and fine spirits.

Note: Although they appeared to be effective in this case, antidepressant drugs are not necessarily effective, nor are they the treatment of choice in all cases of postpartum depression. Treatment is discussed in Chapter 11.

1991; Pitt, 1973; Robin, 1962; Yalom et al., 1968). The maternity blues are more extreme than the normal reactions just described, but because the maternity blues last only 24 to 48 hours, this transient response is not particularly serious and is not considered to be postpartum depression. Women who experience the maternity blues are, however, more likely subsequently to develop postpartum depression with the birth of the next child. A mild case of postpartum depression is described in Case Study 8.5. The woman in Case Study 8.5 suffered from only a mild case of postpartum depression, but the depression can be much more serious and can have tragic consequences. Women suffering from postpartum depression are often suicidal and sometimes have persistent thoughts of killing their babies as well; in a growing number of documented cases, the mothers have actually killed their infants (Toufexis, 1988).

The data concerning the characteristics of women who do and do not experience postpartum depression are limited and sometimes conflicting. At present, however, it can be concluded that postpartum depression (a) has not been found to be related to age, (b) has not been found to be related to the number or order of pregnancies, (c) is more likely to recur in subsequent pregnancies following an initial episode of depression, (d) is more likely to occur in women with a history of other psychiatric disorders, and (e) is more likely to occur in women with a family history of other psychiatric disorders (see reviews by Hopkins et al., 1984; Pitt, 1982).

The question of the causation of postpartum depression is complex and not yet clearly answered, but a number of factors merit attention. It has long been suspected that physiological factors, especially endocrine fluctuations, play a role in postpartum depression because it is known that massive hormonal changes take place after delivery and during the 2-day "latency period" that usually occurs before the onset of the depression. Some indirect evidence concerning the influence of hormones is provided by research indicating that women who suffer from menstrual difficulties (dysmenorrhea and premenstrual syndrome) are more likely to experience postpartum depression (Dalton, 1971; Pitt, 1968, 1973; Yalom et al., 1968). In other words, it seems that women who have difficulty in compensating physiologically for normal hormonal changes will have even greater difficulty adjusting to the dramatic changes associated with birth. Nevertheless, hormonal changes do not provide a complete explanation; many other factors may be involved, and their roles must be researched.

Psychological explanations have included the presence of unresolved conflicts (Karacan & Williams, 1970; Klatskin & Eron, 1970), concerns about personal failure and control (O'Hara et al., 1982), the occurrence of stressful life events (Paykel et al., 1980), and a lack of social support (Gordon et al., 1965; Grossman et al., 1980). These are the same variables that have been used to account for all other depressions (see Chapter 9), and it is because of this overlap that postpartum depression is not seen as a unique disorder. Instead, it is viewed like any other depression, but one that just happens to coincide with or is exacerbated by the stress of birth (e.g., Gotlib et al., 1991; O'Hara, Schlechte, Lewis, & Varner, 1991; O'Hara, Schlechte, Lewis, & Wright, 1991; Whiffen, 1992). As with other depressions, women who experience postpartum depression are at increased risk for a subsequent depression (Philipps & O'Hara, 1991).

Menopausal Depression. For many years, it was thought that women experienced emotional problems when they ceased menstruating (i.e., when they went through the "change of life"), but recent data do *not* support the existence of a unique **menopausal depression**. For example, in one longitudinal study of 541 healthy women, it was found that those who went through natural menopause did not show changes in depression, anxiety, anger, excitability, nervousness,

problems with sleeping, Type A behavior, perceived stress, job dissatisfaction, or public self-consciousness (Matthews et al., 1990). Indeed, the only notable change was an increase in "hot flashes." Some of these results are summarized in Figure 8.7. Other investigators have reported similar findings (e.g., Schmidt & Rubinow, 1991). It should be noted that "menopausal depression" is not an official classification and does not appear to be a frequent problem.

Depression with Seasonal Pattern. Over the years, there have been numerous reports that the incidence of depression increased during the winter months, and it was generally assumed that winter depressions were simply due to the fact that winter is a dull, depressing time of year. However, some investigators have suggested that for at least some individuals, depression in winter and hypomania in spring are due to the *changes in light intensity* that are associated with the seasons. For many years the investigators called the light-related mood shifts the **seasonal affective disorder (SAD)** (Rosenthal et al., 1984) but it is now officially called **depression with seasonal pattern**. Based on data from patients who had experienced the winter-related depression over a number of years, the investigators reported a strong relationship between the number of individuals reporting depression in any one month and the average daily amount of sunlight in that month. That relationship is presented in Figure 8.8 (p. 184). As you might expect, the relationship between depression and months of the year is reversed in the Southern Hemisphere, where winter comes in July and August.

If the moods (depression, hypomania) are due to differences in light, then we should be able to change the moods of individuals with SAD by exposing them to more light during the winter. Some success has been reported with that approach, and we will discuss it later when we consider the treatment of mood disorders (see Chapter 11).

Premenstrual Dysphoric Disorder. The most controversial disorder to be introduced in DSM-IV is the **premenstrual dysphoric disorder**, which involves depression that precedes a woman's monthly menstruation. To be diagnosed as suffering from this disorder the woman must experience at least 5 of the following symptoms, and they must be severe enough that they interfere with her normal functioning: depression; anxiety; mood swings; anger or irritability; decreased interest in work, school, friends, and hobbies; difficulty concentrating; lethargy; appetite changes; sleep disturbances; feeling overwhelmed or out of control; physical symptoms associated with the menstrual cycle (e.g., breast tenderness, headaches, weight gain). The

FIGURE 8.7 NATURAL MENOPAUSE DID NOT LEAD TO INCREASES IN EMOTIONAL PROBLEMS.

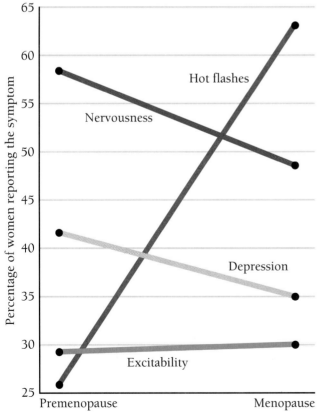

Source: Matthews et al. (1990), p. 350, tab. 4.

FIGURE 8.8   FOR SOME INDIVIDUALS, THERE IS A RELATIONSHIP BETWEEN THE LEVEL OF DEPRESSION
AND THE AMOUNT OF DAILY SUNLIGHT.

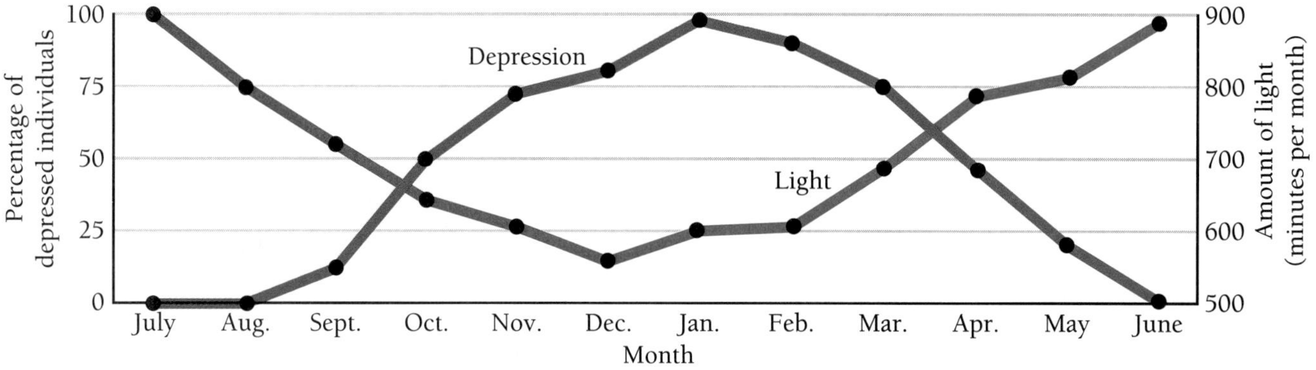

Source: Adapted from Rosenthal et al. (1984), p. 74, fig. 1.

pattern of symptoms must persist over a number of months. Note that this diagnosis does *not* refer to what is generally called the *premenstrual syndrome* (PMS) that many women experience; the premenstrual dysphoric syndrome is a much more extreme and serious pattern of symptoms. Accurate figures are not yet available, but it is estimated that this disorder might afflict between 3% and 5% of the female population.

The introduction of this diagnosis was controversial because it was argued that the diagnosis makes "abnormal" a normal part of the female experience, and that the existence of this diagnosis says, in essence, that *some women have a psychiatric disorder every month.* Obviously, that would have wide-ranging economic, professional, and political ramifications. Some critics of the diagnosis also suggest that if there is a problem, it is *hormonal* in nature and that it is inappropriate to classify it as a psychiatric disorder. It has also been charged that the diagnosis was introduced simply to increase the pool of patients for psychiatrists and psychologists to treat, thereby increasing their income.

In contrast, proponents of the diagnosis point out that, like it or not, there are women who suffer from these symptoms, and by establishing the diagnosis we recognize their suffering as real and give them the opportunity to obtain treatment that can be paid for by insurance. (Note: You cannot be reimbursed for treatment for a disorder that is not officially recognized.) The proponents have even gone so far as to suggest that this diagnosis will enhance the women's movement because, with proper treatment, more women will be able to compete more effectively. With regard to the argument that this is a hormonal problem and not a psychiatric disorder, it has been pointed out that many psychiatric disorders such as anxiety, depression,

and schizophrenia have physiological bases, but that does not disqualify them as psychiatric disorders. Finally, proponents of the diagnosis point out that because some women suffer from the disorder it does not mean that all women do, and they draw an analogy to schizophrenia: the fact that schizophrenia exists does not mean that everyone suffers from it. Because of the controversy over this disorder, in DSM-IV it is included in an appendix of disorders that require "further study."

Depressive Personality Versus Dysthymia

For some years, there has been a controversy over whether or not there is a **depressive personality** that is separate from the depressive disorder (Phillips et al., 1990). Early versions of the DSM included an "affective personality" in the section on personality disorders (the term *affect* was then used to refer to depression or mood), but in DSM-III-R that designation was dropped and *dysthymia* was introduced to reflect mild depression (see Figure 8.1). There have been attempts to distinguish a depressive personality from the depressive disorder, but the distinction, if any, is not clear (Klein, 1990). At best, the depressive personality may represent one end of a continuum of severity running from depressive personality through dysthymia to depressive disorder. That continuum might also reflect steps in the development of a major depression, and there is now evidence that dysthymia often precedes a major depression (Lewinsohn et al., 1991).

This concludes our discussion of the symptoms and issues associated with depression; in the next chapter we will examine the causes of depression.

SUMMARY

The primary symptom of the major depressive disorders is depression, sometimes accompanied by anxiety. Depressed individuals also experience cognitive symptoms that include low self-esteem, pessimism about the future, reduced levels of motivation, exaggeration of the seriousness of their daily problems, and slowed thought processes. Retarded depression is most common and involves reduced motor behavior, whereas agitated depression involves a high level of aimless motor activity such as pacing and fidgeting. The somatic symptoms most frequently associated with depression are problems of sleep, appetite, and sexual functioning.

The distinction between normal and abnormal depression revolves around the depth and duration of the depression. The prevalence of depression has been increasing over the past century, especially among women. The prevalence of depression among women is at least twice as high as among men, and women are more likely to suffer repeated episodes. Rates of depression also tend to be higher among individuals who have lower income, are less educated, and are undergoing stresses such as unemployment and divorce.

Depressions can generally be divided into two major types, the endogenous type, stemming from internal physiological factors, and the exogenous type, stemming from external psychosocial factors. Although the endogenous-exogenous distinction is important for understanding and treating depressed individuals, it is very difficult to determine whether an individual is suffering from an endogenous or an exogenous depression. That is so because the two types show very similar symptom patterns, except for the fact that individuals with endogenous depressions are more likely to have a family history of the disorder. Endogenously depressed individuals often misattribute their problems to psychosocial causes. The dexamethasone suppression test (DST) is sometimes used in attempts to distinguish between the types, but the test is unreliable. The situation is complicated by the fact that the prolonged stress associated with some exogenous depressions can also lead to physiological changes and hence to endogenous depressions. Furthermore, the personal disruption associated with endogenous depressions could result in exogenous depressions.

Another important distinction is between primary depression, in which the mood disorder is the major problem, and secondary depression, in which the mood disorder is the consequence of some other physical or psychological problem.

In the past, attempts were made to distinguish between depressions that occurred at different points in the life cycle or over time. Most noteworthy in this regard are involutional depression, postpartum depression, and menopausal depression. However, it is now generally agreed that although depressions may be more likely to occur at some points in time or after some events, the processes that lead to these depressions are the same as those that lead to depression in general. Related to the timing of depression is the seasonal affective disorder (SAD), which involves depression during times of reduced daylight (winter) and sometimes hypomania during the spring.

The concept of a depressive personality is still widely used, but it has been replaced by dysthymia. At most, the depressive personality appears to reflect a very low level of depression that in time might lead to dysthymia and possibly to major depression.

KEY TERMS, CONCEPTS, AND NAMES

In reviewing and testing yourself on what you have learned from this chapter, you should be able to identify and discuss each of the following:

agitated depression
bipolar disorders
cortisol
cyclothymic disorder
delusion
depression
depression with seasonal pattern
depression with postpartum onset
depressive personality
dexamethasone suppression test (DST)
dysthymic disorder

endogenous depression
exogenous depression
hypersomnia
immune system
involutional depression
loss of libido
lymphocytes
mania
manic-depressive
maternity blues
menopausal depression

mood disorders
negative cognitive set
premenstrual dysphoric disorder
primary depression
prodromal phase
retarded depression
seasonal affective disorder (SAD)
secondary depression
unipolar disorders

Chapter 9

Depressive Disorders: Explanations

• O U T L I N E •

Charles is a 26-year-old salesman who was admitted to a psychiatric hospital because he was very depressed and was talking about "ending it all." In his admission interview, he reported that he had been under a lot of stress for the past year. His sales quotas were being set higher and higher, and he could not keep up. It seems likely that stress did play a role in the development of his depression, but how? One possibility is that the prolonged stress resulted in low levels of a neurotransmitter called serotonin and that the low level of that substance was causing his symptoms (depression, disturbed sleep and appetite). It is also possible that the stressful factors in Charles's life (sales quotas, national economic factors) were not under his control. The lack of control could have led to feelings of helplessness, which could in turn lead to depression. A third explanation is that because Charles had to work so hard and business had not been good, he did not have time for pleasure and received very few rewards. The low levels of pleasure and reward could have led to the depression.

Marilyn is a 36-year-old woman who has been very depressed for 3 months. This is her fifth bout of depression in the past 4 years. There are a number of potential explanations for her depression. From a psychodynamic standpoint, it might be suggested that the depression stemmed from the fact that Marilyn's husband left her 5 years ago. Specifically, Marilyn may have turned some of the anger she felt for her husband in on herself, and that was the basis for the depression. It might also be hypothesized that Marilyn was not really as depressed as she appeared but was reporting symptoms as a means of getting attention and sympathy from the people around her. Another explanation is that as a child, Marilyn had developed a negative cognitive set that led her to expect the worst of herself, her situation, and her future. When faced with even a small problem, such a negative set would lead her to say, "I can't overcome that," "This is too hard," or "I will always be a failure." The negative set may have been activated and strengthened by the failure of her marriage, resulting in low self-esteem, pessimism, depression, and reduced activity. It is also possible that Marilyn's depression stemmed from genetically determined low levels of the neurotransmitter norepinephrine. Low levels of that neurotransmitter can result in low levels of neurological activity in the areas of the brain that are responsible for pleasure, and that can in turn result in depression.

In Chapter 8, we reviewed the symptoms of depression and considered some of the important issues associated with it. In this chapter, we will examine the explanations for how depressions develop. Perhaps because depression afflicts so many people, it has attracted a lot of attention, and a wide variety of theories have been offered to explain it.

PSYCHODYNAMIC EXPLANATIONS

Loss with Anger Turned Inward

Freud's most widely accepted theory of depression revolves around the consequences of **loss**. In a paper titled *Mourning and Melancholia*, Freud (1911/1955) noted some similarities between depression and **mourning** (the feelings of sorrow and grief that occur when a loved one dies), and he based his theory of depression on those similarities. Freud first observed that both mourning and depression occur after the loss of a loved object. (In Freudian terms, an "object" is a person to whom one is attached.) Second, he recognized that we often have ambivalent feelings about lost love objects. We may love a lost object, but at the same time we are angry with or even hate the person for leaving or rejecting us. Such ambivalent feelings are frequently seen in a mourning individual who, though sad and tearful about the death of a loved one, will suddenly say, "Why did you have to leave me! How could you do this to me!" Third, Freud pointed out that depressed persons are often unjustifiably self-critical and angry with themselves and blame themselves for things that are not their fault. Freud suggested that these people are self-critical because they attempt to deal with the loss by symbolically taking in the lost object as part of the self, but when the lost object becomes part of the self, the negative feelings associated with the lost object get turned on the self. For Freud, then, the crucial factor in depression is **anger turned inward**, and the event that triggers the process is loss. Particularly crucial in this view are losses that occur in childhood, such as the death of a parent. A person who has experienced such a loss may find other losses later in life particularly hard to bear because the experiences reactivate the earlier feelings of grief.

Numerous investigations have revealed that losses of many types are associated with depression. For example, people who have recently experienced the death of a relative show higher levels of depression than other people (Bornstein et al., 1973; Bunch, 1972; Clayton et al., 1968), and those who have lost a spouse are at significantly greater risk for suicide (MacMahon & Pugh, 1965).

Freud believed depression to be the result of the negative feelings associated with loss. However, the fact that not all depressed individuals have experienced a loss suggests that depression may be due to stress, and that loss is only one type of stress.

The findings linking loss and depression are often taken as support for Freud's theory, but two qualifications should be noted. First, the fact that depression is often preceded by loss does not necessarily mean that the depression stems from the process of taking the lost object in as part of the self and then turning anger inward. Depression may be associated with loss, but these data do not offer any evidence concerning how the two are related. Second, it is important to realize that although losses often precede depressions, many depressed individuals have not experienced a loss, and therefore using the concept of loss to explain depression may be too limited. The fact that some but not all depressions are associated with loss might be explained by suggesting that depression is due to stress, and that loss constitutes only one type of stress. In view of this possibility, we must examine the research concerning stress and depression.

Stress and Depression

A substantial amount of evidence links **stress** to depression, and in investigations in which the effects of both stress in general and loss in particular have been considered, stress was found to be a better predictor of depression than loss (Billings et al., 1983; Paykel & Tanner, 1976). In one study, it was found that stressful life events (e.g., loss of a job, illness, breakup of a relationship) were linked to depression, and the greater the number of stressful events experienced, the greater the likelihood that the individuals would become depressed (Brown & Harris, 1978; those results are summarized in Figure 9.1). In another study, the investigators examined the lives of women who were in treatment for depression and who either did or did not relapse (Paykel & Tanner, 1976). The researchers found that the women who relapsed had experienced more undesirable events, especially in the month before the relapse, than the other women. That led the investigators to conclude that even treatment may not protect people from the effects of stress. In another study, it was found that the best predictor of who would relapse was the answer to the question, "How critical is your spouse of you?" (Hooley & Teasdale, 1989). Apparently, critical spouses create stress and precipitate relapses.

Results like those in Figure 9.1 appear to provide evidence for the influence of stress on depression, but one interpretive problem should be noted. Rather than stress causing depression, it is possible that at least in some cases, the *early effects of the depression may cause the stress.* For example, an individual who is becoming depressed does not function well and might therefore lose a job before being diagnosed as suffer-

Chronic stress, such as stress resulting from poverty, can lead to depression.

ing from depression. In such a case, the depression might be attributed to the stress of losing the job, when in fact the depression caused both the loss of the job and the stress.

To determine whether depressed individuals generate stress or are simply the victims of stress, one investigator conducted a longitudinal study in which she assessed the types and levels of stress faced by depressed women (Hammen, 1991). She found that when compared to medically ill and normal women, depressed women were more likely to generate stress, and that the stresses they generated were more serious than the other stresses they faced.

To avoid the cause-or-effect problem in the study of stress and depression, some investigators compared the levels of depression in groups of individuals who either were or were not exposed to some clearly definable stressor such as surgery, heart attack, financial loss, or the need to provide long-term care for an elderly spouse (Maguire et al., 1978; Mayou, 1979; Richards, 1973). In one investigation, it was found that 29% of the individuals who experienced a catastrophic financial loss when a bank failed developed severe depression, whereas only 2% of individuals who did not experience that loss developed depression (Ganzini et al., 1990). Overall, the research consistently reveals more depression in individuals exposed to stress, thus

FIGURE 9.1   THE GREATER THE NUMBER OF STRESSFUL LIFE EVENTS EXPERIENCED, THE MORE LIKELY WOMEN WERE TO BECOME DEPRESSED.

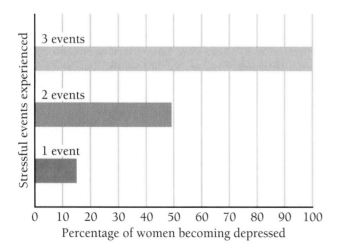

Source: Brown and Harris (1978), p. 108.

FIGURE 9.2   PERSONS LIVING NEAR THE DAMAGED THREE MILE
ISLAND NUCLEAR POWER PLANT SHOWED HIGHER
LEVELS OF DEPRESSION THAN PERSONS LIVING
ELSEWHERE (*a*), AND MADE FEWER ATTEMPTS TO SOLVE
PROBLEMS THAN PERSONS LIVING ELSEWHERE (*b*).

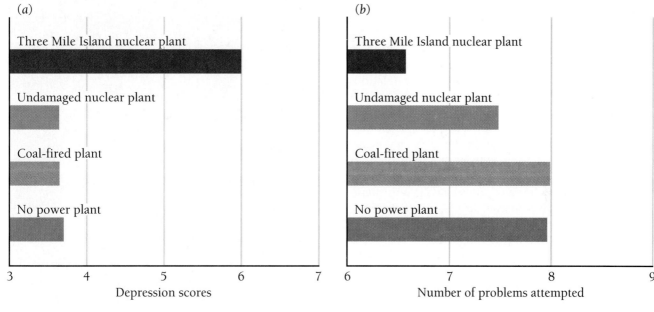

Source: Adapted from Baum et al. (1983), pp. 568–569, tabs. 2 and 3.

providing strong evidence linking stress to the onset of depression.

So far we have focused our attention on the effects of *acute* stress, but *chronic* stress resulting from factors like interpersonal conflict, job dissatisfaction, poverty, or illness also appear to contribute to depression. The effects of chronic stress on depression were documented in a series of studies of persons who lived near the Three Mile Island (TMI) nuclear power plant at which there was a near disaster (meltdown and release of deadly radiation) and thereafter posed a constant worry for nearby residents. In one of those studies, people living near the TMI plant were compared to (a) people who lived near an undamaged nuclear plant, (b) people who lived near an undamaged coal-fired plant, and (c) people who did not live anywhere near an energy plant (Baum et al., 1983). Tests conducted a year and a half after the accident at the TMI plant revealed two interesting findings: First, the persons living near the TMI plant reported higher levels of depression, anxiety, somatic distress, and personal alienation (psychological isolation) than the other persons. Second, when the persons from the four locations were given a series of problems on which to work, those who lived near the TMI plant made fewer attempts to solve the problems and did not perform as well. These findings clearly demonstrate

the effects of stress on depression and depression-related behaviors. The results are presented in Figure 9.2.

Some attention has also been given to the role of persistent "daily hassles" as a potential cause of depression (Fry, 1989; Holahan et al., 1984; Kanner et al., 1981; Wolf et al., 1989). Specifically, investigators found that the frequency with which individuals reported being annoyed by things like "misplacing or losing things," "social obligations," "too many responsibilities," and "home maintenance" was related to depression, sometimes more strongly than the presence of more serious forms of stress. It is probably true that a lot of little nagging problems can get a person down, but it is unlikely that they will lead to clinical levels of depression. Furthermore, getting upset by those little things may be more a *reflection* of depression than a *cause* of depression (Johnson & Bornstein, 1991).

Moderating Factors in the Stress-Depression Relationship

Stress is often related to depression, but not everyone who is exposed to stress becomes depressed. Therefore, we must consider what factors moderate the stress-depression relationship.

Social Support. One important factor in the stress-depression relationship is the amount of **social support** the individual has available when facing the stress. There is now evidence that individuals who have a close friend or a group of close friends are less likely to become depressed when under stress (e.g., Andrews et al., 1978; Billings et al., 1983; Brown & Harris, 1978; Miller & Ingham, 1976; Monroe, Imhoff, et al., 1983; Roy, 1978; Tennant & Babbington, 1978; Warren & McEachren, 1983). It is noteworthy that it is not simply the *number* of friends but the *quality* of the relationships that is important (Billings et al., 1983). One friend with whom you can be really close is more important than several superficial relationships. However, having a close friend does not necessarily mean that you will get social support from that individual. In one study, it was found that friends sometimes simply "echoed" what the other person was saying and therefore they only reinforced the depression (Belsher & Costello, 1991). The key seems to be understanding and support in working through it.

In one study of the effects of social support, college students reported on the number of "close friends" they had, and later their levels of depression were assessed after the stress of final examinations (Monroe, Imhoff, et al., 1983). The results revealed that students who had the most close friends were the least likely to become depressed.

We know that individuals who have social support are less likely to be depressed, but we do not yet understand the process by which social support protects us

Persistent daily hassles are a potential cause of depression.

from depression (Brehm & Smith, 1986). One possibility is that stressful events are less stressful when the burden can be shared with others. In that regard, it is interesting to note that in laboratory experiments it was found that when awaiting a stressful situation (a painful electric shock), most subjects preferred to wait with others (Schachter, 1964). In other words, misery likes company, or more likely, company makes trouble less upsetting.

Social support tends to reduce depression, but unfortunately, depressed individuals are less likely to get social support because they are unpleasant to be around (Coyne, 1976a, 1976b; Gotlib & Robinson, 1982; Hammen & Peters, 1978; Howes & Hokanson, 1979). Always crying, complaining, pacing, or inactive, they are simply not good company. Lack of social support may contribute to the onset of depression and may also serve to prolong it (McLeod et al., 1992).

Individual Differences. A variety of individual difference factors serves to moderate the stress-depression relationship. One of those factors is the **coping**

Social support helps reduce stress and the likelihood of depression.

strategies individuals use when exposed to stress (Billings & Moos, 1981; Billings et al., 1983; Coyne et al., 1981; Folkman & Lazarus, 1980; Pearlin & Schooler, 1978). In general, depressed individuals are more likely to use passive strategies such as avoidance, acceptance, wishful thinking, eating, and smoking, and they are more likely to seek advice and emotional support. Nondepressed individuals are more likely to use active strategies that are focused on solving and overcoming the problem.

It seems likely that stress in combination with passive coping strategies could lead to depression, but we do not yet have studies in which defensive styles were assessed before the individuals became depressed. Therefore, we cannot rule out the possibility that the passive coping strategies are the result rather than the cause of depression. However, we do know that passive coping strategies are associated with depression and that they are relatively ineffective for overcoming most problems. Therefore, passive strategies probably serve to maintain depression, even if they do not initially cause it.

Another individual difference factor that has received a lot of attention is **aerobic** (ā-RŌ-bik) **fitness**. Aerobic fitness refers to the effectiveness with which a person can process oxygen. It is improved by exercises such as jogging, swimming, and cycling in which the heart rate is elevated for prolonged periods of time. There is a growing body of evidence that individuals who are in better aerobic condition show smaller responses to stress (Holmes & McGilley, 1987; Holmes & Roth, 1985; McGilley & Holmes, 1988; Sinyor et al.,

Individuals who are in better aerobic condition show smaller physiological responses to stress.

1983), and the lessened response to stress may serve to reduce the possibility of depression. In one study, the investigators identified a group of students who were experiencing a high degree of life stress (e.g., divorce of parents, geographic moves, broken relationships) that might be expected to lead to depression (Roth & Holmes, 1987). The students were then given either 10 weeks of aerobic training, 10 weeks of relaxation training, or no treatment. The students who received the aerobic training showed lower levels of depression than the students in the other conditions (see also Roth & Holmes, 1985). Apparently, improvements in aerobic fitness protected students from the effects of stress and from depression.

Limitations of the Stress-Depression Hypothesis

Although stress has been implicated as a cause of depression, there are four limitations on the causal relationship that should be considered:

1. *Not all individuals who are exposed to stress become depressed.* This can be explained in part by the effects of moderating variables such as coping strategies and individual differences that may protect some individuals from the effects of stress. (Also, as we will discuss later, some individuals may be predisposed to respond more negatively to stress.)

2. *Not all individuals who become depressed have been exposed to stress.* In fact, in some studies, 20% or more of the individuals who became depressed had not experienced stress. It appears, then, that stress is not the only factor that can cause depression, and we must therefore consider other potential causes (cognitive factors, physiological factors, etc.).

3. *Stress can lead to disorders other than depression.* Because stress can lead to a variety of disorders, there must be some **predisposing factors** that lead some individuals to react with depression rather than with another disorder. If our theory of depression is to be complete, we must identify the predisposing factors (e.g., early experiences, genetic predisposition) for depression.

4. *The stress-depression hypothesis does not specify the process by which stress results in depression.* Certain individuals exposed to stress will become depressed, but we do not understand what goes on inside them to produce the depression.

■ LEARNING EXPLANATIONS

The concepts related to learning lead to two explanations for depression. One explanation is that depression stems from *low levels of reward or high levels of punishment* (or both). The other explanation is that depressive behaviors are *learned and maintained because they lead to rewards* such as sympathy and support. In the following sections, we will discuss each of these explanations.

Insufficient Rewards and Excessive Punishments

The most prominent learning-related hypothesis for explaining depression is that receiving a low level of **rewards** or a high level of **punishments** will lead to depression (Ferster, 1973; Lazarus, 1968; Lewinsohn, 1974; Rehm, 1977). Low levels of reward and high levels of punishment are thought to contribute to depression in any or all of three ways:

1. An individual who receives fewer rewards or more punishments will have a generally less pleasant life, and that could contribute to depression.
2. If an individual's behavior does not result in rewards or results in punishments, the individual might have a reduced sense of self-worth and develop a low self-concept, which can contribute to depression.
3. If a behavior is not rewarded or is punished, the likelihood of using the behavior again will be reduced, thus resulting in the reduced activity commonly seen in depression. The reduced activity could further decrease the probability of getting rewards, and thus a vicious cycle could develop that would contribute to greater and greater depression.

With these possibilities in mind, we must go on to determine whether depressed individuals actually do get fewer rewards or more punishments.

Levels of Environmental Rewards and Punishments.
Rewards and punishments can come from two sources, our environment (people and events around us) and ourselves. A variety of evidence indicates that depressed individuals do in fact receive fewer rewards and more punishments from others. For example, in one study, 40 students each spent 15 minutes talking to one of 40 other students who either were or were not depressed (Gotlib & Robinson, 1982). The interactions between the pairs of students were videotaped and analyzed. The results revealed that the students who interacted with depressed students "smiled less often, demonstrated less arousal and pleasantness in their facial expressions, talked about less positive and more negative content in their conversations, and made fewer statements of direct support to the target individuals" than those who

talked to nondepressed students (p. 231). Clearly, the depressed students got fewer rewards and more punishments from their peers than the nondepressed students did. Other investigations have also revealed that we are more rejecting and less pleasant to depressed than nondepressed individuals (Coyne, 1976a; Gotlib & Robinson, 1982; Hammen & Peters, 1978; Howes & Hokanson, 1979; Joiner et al., 1992; see also the review by Marcus & Nardone, 1992).

There is also evidence that depressed individuals gravitate toward persons who view them unfavorably and solicit unfavorable feedback from other people (Swann et al., 1992). Specifically, when college students were given the opportunity to interact with other students and obtain feedback about themselves, depressed students were more likely than nondepressed students to ask to interact with individuals who had evaluated them negatively and to seek negative information about themselves. That behavior reduces their rewards and adds to their punishments.

The situation with regard to rewards and punishments is made even worse by the fact that when depressed individuals receive the *same* amount of reward or punishment as nondepressed individuals, the depressed individuals *think* that they receive *fewer rewards* and *more punishments*. In one experiment, depressed and nondepressed persons worked on a task, and regardless of how they actually performed, they received standard levels of reward and punishment (Nelson & Craighead, 1977). The subjects were then asked to estimate the number of rewards and punishments they had received. The results indicated that the depressed subjects underestimated their levels of reward and overestimated their levels of punishment. In other words, the depressed individuals always recalled the situation as less pleasant (fewer rewards, more punishments) than it actually was. Those results are presented in Figure 9.3.

Another factor that reduces rewards and increases punishment is that depressed individuals are *less effective at solving social problems* than nondepressed individuals (Marx et al., 1992). Their social ineptitude undoubtedly makes life less pleasant. Overall, then, depressed individuals (a) get low levels of reward and high levels of punishment from those around them, (b) seek out individuals who will not reward them, (c) underestimate their rewards and overestimate their punishments, and (d) are poor social problem solvers. All of those factors would lead to a serious reward-punishment imbalance that could result in an unpleasant life and contribute to the depression.

Environmental factors can also influence rewards and punishments and may bring on depression. For example, moving from one location to another may cause an individual to lose contact with previous

FIGURE 9.3 DEPRESSED PERSONS RECALLED MORE PUNISHMENTS AND FEWER REWARDS THAN NONDEPRESSED PERSONS.

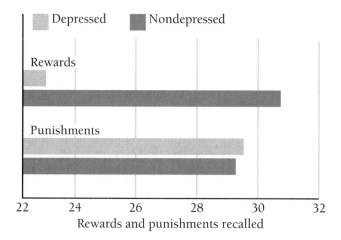

Source: Adapted from Nelson and Craighead (1977), p. 383, tab. 2.

FIGURE 9.4 DEPRESSED PERSONS GAVE THEMSELVES FEWER REWARDS AND MORE PUNISHMENTS THAN NONDEPRESSED PERSONS.

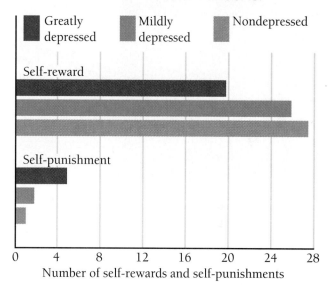

Source: Adapted from Rozensky et al. (1977), p. 36, tab. 1.

sources of reward, and changes in what behaviors are rewarded make once rewarding activities useless. Also, sometimes standards are increased, making higher levels of performance necessary for rewards to be achieved. Consider the college jock who after graduation moves away from the university and is no longer the darling of all the cheerleaders. Now his rewards are no longer based on his ability to throw a ball, and depression might set in if he does not find alternative sources of rewards.

Levels of Self-Reward and Self-Punishment.

Some theorists have emphasized the role of self-reward and self-punishment in depression (Rehm, 1977; Wilcoxon et al., 1976), and there is evidence that depressed individuals give themselves fewer rewards and more punishments for their behaviors. In one experiment, depressed and nondepressed individuals were asked to work on a simple laboratory task and to give themselves rewards (small amounts of money) and punishments (withdrawal of money) for their performance (Rozensky et al., 1977). The results indicated that the depressed individuals gave themselves fewer rewards and more punishments than the nondepressed individuals. These results are presented in Figure 9.4. Similar results have been found with hospitalized depressed patients and depressed university students (Lobitz & Post, 1979; Nelson & Craighead, 1977, 1981).

Rewards and Punishments as Causes of Depression.

It seems clear that depressed individuals get fewer rewards and more punishments from their

environments and from themselves than nondepressed individuals. We must now ask whether these differences in levels of rewards and punishments are the *causes* or the *effects* of depression.

In one of the very few experiments that have been conducted to answer that question, it was found that subjects who gave themselves fewer rewards for working on a task showed greater increases in depression than subjects who gave themselves more rewards (Nelson & Craighead, 1981). However, caution must be used in interpreting the results of this experiment because the depression that resulted from the low level of rewards was very mild and was not like the clinical depression we are concerned with in this chapter. It is possible that clinical depression might have developed had the lack of rewards been more severe and prolonged, but at present no such evidence is available.

In seeking evidence for the causal role of low rewards in producing depression, some theorists have pointed to the fact that therapy in which depressed persons are trained to increase their levels of reward can result in decreases in depression (Fuchs & Rehm, 1977; Jackson, 1972; Rehm et al., 1979). Again, however, caution must be used in interpreting these findings because lifting depression with an increase in rewards may not be equivalent to causing depression with a decrease in rewards. Overall, then, research on the causal role that lack of rewards plays in depression is suggestive but not definitive; lack of rewards can result

Environmental factors can influence the level of rewards one receives and can bring on depression. For example, moving to a new location might cause an individual to lose contact with previous sources of reward.

in mild depression, but its relationship to clinical depression has not yet been established.

Depression as an Operant Behavior

In sharp contrast to the theory just discussed is the possibility that some depressive behavior may be initiated and maintained because it *results in rewards*. We may be more attentive, caring, and supportive of individuals who are "down in the dumps" or depressed. We may also do nice things for them to cheer them up, and all of those things could serve to reward the depressive behavior. Furthermore, by doing everything for depressed individuals in the hope of making them feel better, we may actually be convincing them that they are not good people or not well enough to do things for themselves, and that could also lead to more depression.

There are two potential problems with this explanation. First, as you will recall, research presented earlier indicated that we usually punish rather than reward depressed individuals; in view of that, the number of individuals for whom depression would be caused by rewards from others would seem to be very limited. Even if we are initially rewarding and supportive of depressed individuals, that quickly changes as our tolerance and patience diminish. Second, we have to ask whether the behavior that is rewarded is actually depression or whether it is a facade covering normal or near-normal feelings. In other words, the individual might simply *act* depressed in order to get the attention but not really *be* depressed. Such an effect is sometimes seen in hospitalized patients who are about to be discharged and who do not want to leave the pro-

tected atmosphere of the hospital (Braginsky et al., 1969). In those cases, the patients sometimes put on a brief show of abnormal behavior so that they can stay in the hospital. Overall, then, this explanation seems to have very limited applicability and is probably related to "depressive-like" behavior rather than true depression.

■ COGNITIVE EXPLANATIONS

There are two cognitive theories of depression. In one, it is hypothesized that individuals become depressed because they focus on the negative aspects of life. The presence of these negative cognitions can be understood best in terms of problems with information processing. In the other theory, it is assumed that feelings of helplessness about controlling the negative outcomes of life lead to depression.

Negative Cognitive Sets and Information Processing

The first theory revolves around the notion that depressed individuals have **negative cognitive sets** that lead them to focus their attention on personal shortcomings and other reasons to be depressed. The act of *thinking the depressing thoughts leads to the depression* (e.g., Beck, 1967, 1976; Teasdale, 1983). For example, an individual who is generally successful might ignore successes or misinterpret them as flukes and will dwell on and magnify the importance of failures. As a result of those negative perceptions, the individual will have a self-image as a failure, will assume that the future will be filled with failures, and will fall victim to depression.

To understand how these negative cognitive sets develop and operate, psychologists have applied what we know about human **information processing**, and that has led to a considerable refinement in our understanding of the underlying processes (Ingram, 1984). In general, the information processing approach has three components. First, depressed individuals are thought to have strong and active **associative networks** that link together memories that involve depression. The depression networks were probably originally established when the individuals had some depression-related experiences. That is, early experiences with depression laid down (or "burned-in") the depression networks. (For a review of associative networks, see Chapter 2.)

Second, because of their active depression networks, depressed individuals are more likely to attend to depressing factors around them. In information processing terms, depressed individuals use **selective attention** and focus on the depressing information that is coming into the sensory memory. Furthermore, they are more likely to send the depressing information to the short-term memory for processing (conscious attention) and then store the information in the long-term memory. Of course, seeing and thinking about reasons for depression contributes to depression, and the storage of that information adds to the depression network.

Third, because of the extensive depression networks that keep developing, depressed individuals are more likely to recall depressing information. That is, if you have more depressing memories, and if those memories have numerous associative links to other memories, it is very likely that one of those depressing memories will be activated. Activating that memory will activate the entire depression-related network, with the result that you will be flooded with depressing memories. In other words, the depressed individual is constantly recalling old reasons for depression.

The picture that develops from this information processing model is consistent with the picture of clinical depression: The depressed individual is always seeing reasons for depression, is always remembering other reasons for depression, and the process is cyclical and builds on itself. Depressed individuals cannot help themselves; the process is as automatic as your computer operating system "booting up" when you turn the machine on. In the following sections, we will examine the evidence related to this explanation.

Presence of Negative Cognitions. The first question we must ask is, do depressed individuals actually have more negative cognitions than nondepressed individuals? The answer is yes, and furthermore it appears that negative cognitions may increase and decrease as depressions increase and decrease. In one investigation, depressed psychiatric patients, nondepressed psychiatric patients, and normal individuals completed a 40-item questionnaire that measured the degree to which they had negative cognitions (Hamilton & Abramson, 1983). Using items like "If I fail at my work, then I am a failure as a person," the questionnaire measured negative expectancies about outcomes, excessive self-blame for failures, beliefs about lack of control, and assumed negative judgments by others. The patients filled out the questionnaire when they were admitted to the hospital and again when they were discharged (on the average, 17 days later). The normal control subjects also took the test twice, with 17 days between the tests.

The results revealed three interesting findings. First, at the time of admission, the depressed patients as a group had more negative cognitions than the nondepressed patients or the normal individuals, thus indicating that negative cognitions were associated with depression. Second, the high level of negative cognitions among depressed patients was due to the extreme scores of a *subset* of patients, thus indicating that negative cognitions are not characteristic of all depressed individuals. Third, over the course of their treatment, the depressed patients who had negative cognitions showed a decline in those cognitions such that at the time of their discharge, their cognitions were no different from those of the nondepressed patients or the normal individuals. In other words, as the depression lifted, the negative cognitions declined. The results of this investigation are presented in Figure 9.5.

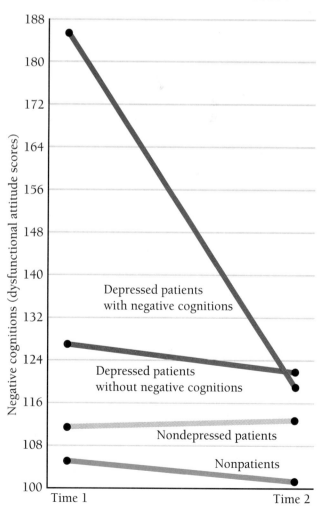

FIGURE 9.5   DEPRESSED CLIENTS USED FEWER NEGATIVE COGNITIONS AS PSYCHOTHERAPY PROGRESSED.

Source: Adapted from Hamilton and Abramson (1983), p. 181, fig. 1.

Selective Attention. The second question we must ask is, do depressed individuals selectively attend to negative information? Again, the answer is yes. In one interesting demonstration of selective attention, mildly depressed and nondepressed individuals were shown "happy" and "sad" faces while their eye fixations were recorded (Matthews & Antes, 1992). The results indicated that the depressed individuals looked more often at sad parts of faces than did the nondepressed individuals, thus suggesting that they sought out negative aspects of life.

Selective Recall. Next we must ask, are depressed individuals more likely to recall negative events than are nondepressed individuals? Yes; depressed individuals are more likely than nondepressed individuals to recall things such as failures, being left out of peer groups, or being criticized by teachers or employers (Isen et al., 1978; Laird et al., 1982; Madigan & Bollenbach, 1982; Natale & Hantas, 1982; Snyder & White, 1982; Teasdale & Fogarty, 1979; see reviews by Blaney, 1986; Bower, 1981, 1987; Johnson & Magaro, 1987).

The effect of mood on recall was neatly demonstrated in an experiment in which students who were in a neutral mood learned a group of pleasant and unpleasant personality-related words (*considerate, helpful, thoughtful, pleasant, kind, friendly, rude, cruel, hostile, ungrateful, impolite, mean*; Clark & Teasdale, 1985). Following that, the students were made to feel happy or depressed, and then they were asked to recall the words. The results indicated that female students recalled more pleasant than unpleasant words when they were happy and recalled more unpleasant than pleasant words when they were depressed. Mood did not influence the recall performance of men. The fact that mood was more likely to influence the recall of women than men may help account for the finding that women are more likely to become depressed than men.

The fact that depressed individuals are likely to recall negative events can be explained in terms of **priming**. That is, the depression activates the depression-related network and makes it more sensitive to later activation, so the memories of negative events that are stored in that network are more likely to be recalled (Bower, 1981; Teasdale, 1983).

Negative Cognitions as a Cause of Depression.

Now that we know that depressed individuals have more negative cognitions than nondepressed individuals, we must go on to ask whether the negative cognitions *cause* depression or are the *result* of depression. To answer that question, some theorists have pointed to a series of experiments in which it was found that reading negative or sad statements led to increases in mild depression (Coleman, 1975; Frost et al., 1979; Frost et al., 1982; Hale & Strickland, 1976; Natale, 1977; Strickland et al., 1975; Teasdale & Bancroft, 1977; Velten, 1968; also see reviews by Blaney, 1986; Bower, 1981; Goodwin & Williams, 1982). The statements the individuals read were like the following: "I'm discouraged and unhappy about myself," "I feel worn out," "My health might not be as good as it's supposed to be." When compared to individuals who read positive or neutral material, individuals who read negative material (a) reported higher levels of depression, anxiety, and hostility; (b) were more likely to prefer solitary or inactive activities; (c) performed worse on an intelligence test; (d) wrote more slowly; (e) paused more often in their speech; (f) made more constricted doodles; and (g) altered their eating behavior.

These findings are interesting, but the depression that was generated by reading the negative statements was not particularly deep, did not last more than a few minutes, and could be completely eliminated by a simple distraction such as working briefly on another task (Frost & Green, 1982; Isen & Gorgoglione, 1983). In other words, thinking the negative thoughts resulted in feelings that were more like the sadness we feel while watching a "depressing" movie than they were to the clinical depression we see in patients. Because of that, the findings concerning cognitively induced changes in mood do not provide evidence that negative cognitions result in clinical depression. However, the induction procedures used in these experiments were very brief, and it might be that more intense or prolonged procedures that more closely approximate what some individuals experience in daily living could result in greater depression.

In another approach to the problem, investigators measured negative cognitions in almost 1,000 persons, and then 1 year later assessed the persons to determine which ones became depressed (Lewinsohn et al., 1981). The results indicated that individuals who became depressed did not have more negative cognitions before becoming depressed than individuals who did not become depressed. The fact that negative cognitions did not precede depression raises serious questions about whether negative cognitions cause depression or whether depression causes negative cognitions.

Questions about the causal role of negative cognitions were also raised in an investigation in which depressed patients were given either cognitive therapy that was designed to treat the depression by changing cognitions or were given antidepressant drug therapy (Simons et al., 1984). Both treatments were effective for reducing depression, but the relevant finding here was that *both treatments reduced negative cognitions.* The fact that lifting the depression with medication reduced negative cognitions suggests that depression may cause negative cognitions rather than negative cognitions causing depression. Numerous other investigations have also failed to reveal a causal link between cognitions and depression, so we must conclude that at present there is no reliable evidence that negative cognitions cause clinical levels of depression (see Haaga et al., 1991).

Negative Cognitions as a Predisposing Factor in Depression.

The lack of consistent evidence that negative cognitions cause depression poses a serious problem for the theory. However, it may be that rather than causing depression themselves, negative cognitions *predispose* individuals to become depressed when faced with stress. This can be referred to as the **cognitive diathesis-stress hypothesis.** The word *cognitive* is noteworthy here because when we use the term *diathesis* (which means "predisposition"), we are usually referring to *physiological* factors such as genes, but in this case the predisposition is based on a cognitive factor.

To test the cognitive diathesis-stress hypothesis, a number of investigators have collected data on negative cognitions, life stress, and symptoms of depression (Kwon & Oel, 1992; Olinger et al., 1987; Robins & Block, 1989; Segal et al., 1992). In general, it was found that *some* of the depressed individuals had experienced stressful life events, but *most* depressed individuals reported *both* negative cognitions *and* stressful life events. It appears that the perception of the world as difficult may heighten the impact of stress and thereby result in depression. This model is illustrated in Figure 9.6.

Negative Cognitions and the Maintenance of Depression.

In addition to predisposing individuals to depression, negative cognitions may also provide explanations or justifications for depression once it sets in (e.g., "It's understandable that I'm depressed because . . ."). If that is the case, negative cognitions could serve to *maintain* depression. This is supported by the results of a study in which it was found that depressed individuals who had more negative cognitions were less likely to improve than those who had fewer negative cognitions (Lewinsohn et al., 1981). There is also evidence that the negativity may feed on itself, spiraling and increasing as the depression wears on (Davis & Unruh, 1981; Holen-Hoeksema, 1991; Teasdale, 1988). Overall, then, having a negative cognitive set may lead to greater and greater negativity, and the negativity may preclude seeing the positive aspects of life, thereby prolonging the depression.

FIGURE 9.6   COGNITIVE DIATHESIS-STRESS MODEL OF DEPRESSION: NEGATIVE COGNITIONS MAY PREDISPOSE INDIVIDUALS TO DEPRESSION WHEN THEY FACE STRESSFUL LIFE EVENTS.

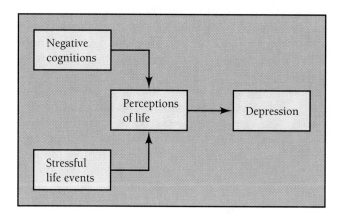

In summary, it is clear that (a) depressed individuals have more negative cognitions than nondepressed individuals, (b) the negative cognitions apparently stem from selective attention and enhanced recall of negative factors, (c) the negative cognitions do not cause depression but may predispose individuals to depression when they are exposed to stress, and (d) negative cognitions may serve to prolong depression.

Learned Helplessness

The **learned helplessness** explanation of depression asserts that individuals learn, correctly or incorrectly, that they cannot control future negative outcomes; they consequently feel helpless, and the feelings of helplessness lead to depression (Abramson et al., 1978; Miller & Norman, 1979; Peterson & Seligman, 1984; Roth, 1979; Seligman, 1975).

The major difference between the negative cognitions explanation and the learned helplessness explanation is that individuals with negative cognitions believe that they are *responsible* for the negative things that happen in their lives, whereas individuals who have learned helplessness believe that they are *helpless* in controlling the negative things (Abramson & Sackeim, 1977; Blaney, 1977). The difference, then, is one of self-blame (negative cognitions) versus uncontrollability (learned helplessness).

Early Laboratory Research on Helplessness and Depression.

The learned helplessness explanation was discovered quite accidentally in a series of experiments on conditioning with animals (see Maier & Seligman, 1976). In one of those experiments, dogs were exposed to one of three conditions (Maier et al.,

1969). The dogs in one condition were placed in a cage and given a series of inescapable (uncontrollable) shocks. When the shocks first came on, the dogs jumped, barked, scratched, and generally thrashed around, but their responses were ineffective, and they simply had to endure the shocks. The dogs in a second condition were placed in the cage and shocked, but these dogs could escape (control) the shocks by jumping over a small barrier and going to the other side of the cage. These dogs quickly learned to escape the shocks. The dogs in the third condition were placed in the cage but were never shocked, so they had no reason to learn an escape response. Twenty-four hours later, all of the dogs were returned to the cage and given shocks that they could escape if they jumped over the barrier.

The responses of the three groups of dogs are presented in Figure 9.7. On the first trial, the dogs who had learned the escape response the day before jumped the barrier very quickly to avoid the shock. The dogs who had not been shocked before required a little more time to jump over the barrier because they had not had any experience with it before, but by the

third or fourth trial they were also quickly avoiding the shocks. The most interesting and surprising finding was that the dogs who had received the inescapable shock on the previous day made very little attempt to avoid the shock (did not jump the barrier) and eventually simply lay down and endured it. Apparently on the basis of their previous experience in which they had been unable to do anything about the shock, these dogs simply gave up in this new situation. After three or four trials, some of the dogs did happen to cross the barrier and thereby escape the shock, but they did not catch on to the effectiveness of their response and did not use it again on later trials. In view of the similarity between the responses of the dogs and the responses of depressed individuals, the investigators inferred that the experience with inescapable stress had caused depression in the dogs.

After observing learned helplessness in animals, similar experiments were conducted with humans, and those experiments yielded comparable results. In one experiment, students were exposed either to a loud aversive noise that they could not terminate or to a loud aversive noise that they could terminate by pushing a button; other students were not exposed to a noise (Hiroto, 1974). When the students were later put in a test situation in which they could terminate an aversive noise by moving a lever from one side of a panel to another (a situation analogous to the dogs moving from one side of the cage to the other), the students who had been exposed to the uncontrollable noise did not perform as well as the students in the other conditions. Because lack of control over negative outcomes leads to depressive-like behavior, researchers concluded that lack of control and learned helplessness caused depression in humans (Hiroto & Seligman, 1975).

Beliefs About Control as a Cause of Depression.   The important question to ask now is, do attitudes about uncontrollability precede and therefore cause clinical depression? To answer that question, it is necessary to conduct research in which individuals' beliefs about control are measured, and later the individuals are followed up to determine whether those who originally felt that they were not in control were more likely to become depressed. Contrary to what might be expected on the basis of the original laboratory research, most of these studies have not provided support for the hypothesis that beliefs about control lead to depression (Cutrona, 1983; Danker-Brown & Baucom, 1982; Lewinsohn et al., 1981; Manley et al., 1982; Peterson et al., 1981; see also reviews by Brewin, 1985; Coyne & Gotlib, 1983).

Further doubts about the value of learned helplessness for explaining depression were raised by a se-

FIGURE 9.7   DOGS THAT HAD BEEN EXPOSED TO INESCAPABLE SHOCKS DID NOT JUMP THE BARRIER TO AVOID SHOCKS IN A NEW SITUATION.

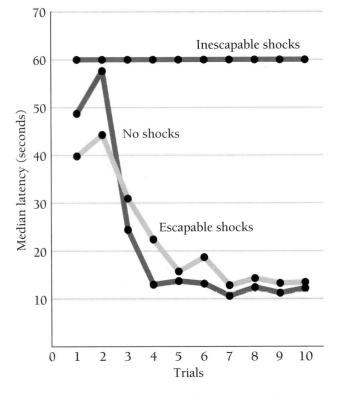

Source: Adapted from Maier et al. (1967), p. 328, fig. 10-13.

ries of experiments in which it was found that subjects who showed the learned helplessness effect (i.e., performed poorly on a task after not being in control on an earlier task) were *not aware* that they had not been in control on the first task and were not depressed (Oakes & Curtis, 1982; Tennen, Drum, et al., 1982; Tenner, Gillen, & Drum, 1982). In other words, the lack of control influenced behavior, but the effect was not due to beliefs about control, and the behavior did not reflect depression. Those findings have sparked considerable controversy and raised serious questions about whether learned helplessness plays a role in causing depression (Alloy, 1982; Oakes, 1982; Silver et al., 1982; Tennen, 1982).

If beliefs about control do not cause depression, it must be asked why the animals in the original laboratory studies became "depressed" when they were confronted with uncontrollable negative situations. One possibility is that the high levels of inescapable stress in those situations led to *learned inactivity* rather than to depression. In other words, the animals may have learned that their attempts to escape were useless, so they simply stopped trying, and the inference that the animals were depressed was incorrect. Alternatively, the high levels of stress to which they were exposed may have resulted in *physiological changes* (decreases in certain neurotransmitters) that in turn led to the depression (Anisman, 1978; Glazer & Weiss, 1976; Weiss et al., 1976). In that case, stress would have been the crucial factor, and helplessness would have been important only insofar as it added to the stress. That possibility will be discussed later when we consider the physiological explanations for depression.

Does all of this lead to the conclusion that learned helplessness is a useless concept for understanding depression? Probably not. At present, there does not appear to be any reliable evidence that learned helplessness plays a major role in *causing* depression, but it is likely that once an individual is depressed, learned helplessness can *prolong* the depression (Eaves & Rehm, 1984). The prolonging effect may be due to the fact that when feeling depressed and helpless, individuals do not make attempts to overcome their problems, thus precluding the possibility of finding solutions for the problems that initially caused the depression.

PHYSIOLOGICAL EXPLANATIONS

Neurotransmission and Depression

From a physiological standpoint, depression results from a *low level of neurological activity in the areas of the brain that are responsible for pleasure.* The low level of neurological activity is thought to stem from insufficient amounts of **neurotransmitters** at the synapses (Bunney & Davis, 1965; Maas, 1975; Schildkraut, 1965; Schildkraut & Kety, 1967). The two neurotransmitters that have been implicated in depression are **norepinephrine** (NOR-ep-i-NEF-rin) and **serotonin** (sē-rō-TŌ-nin). Norepinephrine is one of a number of chemicals known as **catecholamines** (KAT-i-KŌL-uh-mēnz), and often researchers will refer to catecholamines in general rather than norepinephrine specifically. Similarly, serotonin is one of the **indole amines** (IN-dōl AM-ēnz). Collectively, these neurotransmitters are known as **amines**, and consequently the physiological explanation for depression is sometimes called the **amine hypothesis**.

In this chapter, we are focusing on depression rather than mania, but it is relevant to note that whereas an excessively *low* level of a neurotransmitter can result in *depression*, an excessively *high* level can result in *mania*. In other words, too little or too much of a neurotransmitter can cause problems with mood. With this overview as background, we can now go on to examine the evidence for the neurotransmitter (amine) hypothesis.

Evidence Based on the Effects of Drugs. Neurotransmitters cannot be studied directly in the live brain, so we must rely on two types of indirect evidence concerning the relationship between neurotransmitter level and depression. The first involves studies of the effects on mood of drugs that are known to increase or decrease the levels of the relevant neurotransmitters. The results of this large body of research are summarized in Table 9.1.

The results presented in the table are clear on two points. First, drugs that increase the level of the catecholamines reduce depression in individuals who are depressed and cause mania in individuals who are not depressed. Apparently, increasing catecholamine levels

TABLE 9.1 INCREASES IN CATECHOLAMINE LEVELS REDUCED DEPRESSION OR CAUSED MANIA, AND DECREASES IN CATECHOLAMINE LEVELS CAUSED DEPRESSION AND REDUCED MANIA

	Change in Catecholamine Level	
	INCREASE	DECREASE
Depressed individuals	Reduces depression	—
Normal individuals	Causes mania	Causes depression
Manic individuals	—	Reduces mania

Source: Adapted from Zis and Goodwin (1982), p. 176, tab. 12.2.

in depressed individuals brings those levels to normal and reduces depression, whereas increases in nondepressed individuals who already have normal levels of the catecholamines result in excessively high levels and bring on mania. Second, drugs that decrease the level of the catecholamines reduce mania in individuals who are manic and can cause depression in normal individuals. In general, then, drugs that increase catecholamine levels elevate mood, and drugs that decrease catecholamine levels depress mood.

There is one notable exception to this pattern of findings. Lithium reduces both depression and mania in individuals who suffer from both (the bipolar disorder, discussed in Chapter 10). This double-barreled effect is probably due to the fact that lithium moderates the level of norepinephrine and does not allow it to get too high or too low. We will discuss lithium in greater detail in Chapter 11 when we consider the treatment of bipolar disorders.

Finally, it should be noted that mood changes based on changes in catecholamine levels can be caused by a variety of drugs other than those that are usually used to treat mood disorders. For example, amphetamines and cocaine cause "highs" (mania) because they result in higher levels of the catecholamines.

Evidence Based on the Study of Metabolites.

The second body of evidence concerning the influence of catecholamines on depression is based on studies of **metabolites**. Metabolites are the substances produced when neurotransmitters change their chemical structure as a result of interactions with other chemical agents. So by studying metabolities, we can study neurotransmitters indirectly. It is easier to study the metabolites of neurotransmitters than the neurotransmitters themselves because the metabolites are transported out of the brain and into the urine and the cerebrospinal fluid, where they can be measured. The assumption in this research is that finding low levels of the metabolites means that there are low levels of the neurotransmitters at the synapses in the brain. The metabolites that are of most interest are **MHPG**, which is the metabolite of norepinephrine, and **5-HIAA**, which is the metabolite of serotonin.

The relationship between MHPG and mood is illustrated in Figure 9.8, where the daily levels of MHPG excretion are plotted for a patient, along with an indication of whether the patient was in a depressed or manic state. Inspection of the figure indicates that MHPG levels are low during depression and high during mania and also that MHPG levels rise a few days before the mood shifts from depression to mania and fall before the mood shifts from mania to depression. The fact that MHPG levels change before the mood

change occurs is important because it suggests that the change in catecholamine level causes the mood change rather than vice versa. This effect has been documented in numerous investigations (Agren, 1982; Beckman & Goodwin, 1980; Bond et al., 1972; De Leon-Jones et al., 1975; Jones et al., 1973; Maas, 1975; Maas et al., 1972; Muscettola et al., 1984; Schildkraut et al., 1973; Schildkraut et al., 1978). Furthermore, there is evidence that increases in MHPG secretion are associated with recovery from depression (Greenspan et al., 1970; Pickar et al., 1978). Taken together, these findings provide strong support for the hypothesis that depression is related to levels of norepinephrine.

Subtypes of Physiologically Caused Depression.

The results presented so far offer strong support for the role that low levels of norepinephrine play in causing depression. There are, however, some inconsistencies in the results. For example, not all depressed individuals show low levels of MHPG, and not all patients showed reductions in depression when given drugs that increased the levels of norepinephrine. These inconsistencies led to the speculation that there may be two types of physiologically caused depression, one caused by low levels of norepinephrine and one caused by low levels of serotonin (Maas, 1975).

Evidence for the existence of two subtypes of physiologically caused depression stems from the combination of findings concerning patients' levels of MHPG and their response to drug therapy. In one group, norepinephrine seems to be the problem because the patients show low levels of MHPG before treatment is begun and show decreases in depression when given drugs that increase the levels of norepinephrine, but they do not show decreases in depression when given drugs that increase levels of serotonin.

In another group, serotonin seems to be the problem because the patients do not show low levels of MHPG before treatment is begun and do not show decreases in depression when given drugs that increase the levels of norepinephrine, but they do show decreases in depression when given drugs that increase the levels of serotonin (Maas et al., 1972; Schildkraut, 1973). The pattern of findings suggesting that depression can stem from low levels of norepinephrine or serotonin is summarized in Table 9.2.

Norepinephrine, Serotonin, and Symptoms Associated with Depression.

It is interesting to note that low levels of norepinephrine and serotonin can also be used to explain the reductions in sleep, appetite, sex, and motor activity that are often associated with depression. Norepinephrine and serotonin play a

FIGURE 9.8 A PATIENT SHOWED LOWER LEVELS OF MHPG JUST BEFORE AND DURING DEPRESSION AND HIGHER LEVELS JUST BEFORE AND DURING MANIA.

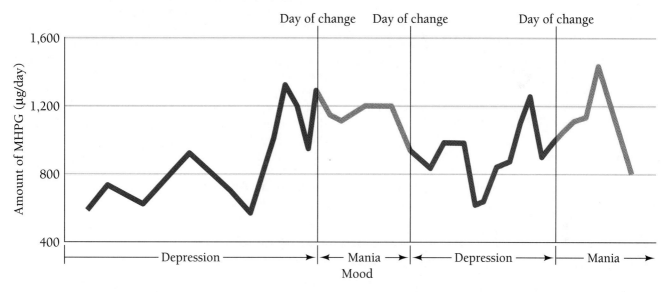

Source: Adapted from Maas (1975), p. 122, fig. 2.

crucial role in the functioning of the hypothalamus, which controls sleep, appetite, sex, and motor behavior (Sachar, 1982). It appears, then, that changes in the levels of neurotransmitters can account for both the mood changes seen in the depressive disorders and also many of the other symptoms that are associated with the disorders. The fact that levels of neurotransmitters can account for so many of the symptoms seen in the depressive disorders certainly increases the value of this explanation.

The Role of GABA. Anxiety is frequently associated with depression, but it has not been linked to norepinephrine or serotonin. Therefore, we must ask,

what gives rise to the anxiety seen in depressed individuals? Some of the anxiety is undoubtedly a response to the unpleasant state of being depressed, but there is also evidence that some of the anxiety may have a physiological basis. Specifically, it has been found that many depressed patients have lower levels of the neurotransmitter known as **GABA** than nondepressed individuals (Gerner & Hare, 1981; Gold et al., 1980; Kasa et al., 1982; Petty & Sherman, 1984). That is relevant because as you will recall from Chapter 5, GABA plays a role in anxiety (GABA is essential for the stimulation of inhibitory neurons that reduce the activity of the neurons responsible for anxiety). Finding low levels of GABA in depressed individuals is im-

TABLE 9.2 IN DIFFERENT INDIVIDUALS, DEPRESSION CAN STEM FROM LOW LEVELS OF NOREPINEPHRINE OR SEROTONIN

	Individuals Assumed to Have Low Levels of One Neurotransmitter	
	NOREPINEPHRINE	SEROTONIN
Pretreatment levels of MHPG	Low	Normal
Response to norepinephrine-related drugs	Reduces depression	No effect on depression
Response to serotonin-related drugs	No effect on depression	Reduces depression

Source: Adapted from Maas (1975).

portant because it enables us to explain their anxiety physiologically.

Genetic Factors in Depression

It is not enough to know that low levels of the neurotransmitters result in depression; we must also determine what causes those levels to be low. One explanation is that genetic factors contribute to the low levels of the neurotransmitters, so we must consider the evidence concerning that possibility.

Studies of Families.   Some evidence that depression is inherited is provided by the fact that depressed individuals are more likely than nondepressed individuals to have first-degree relatives (brothers, sisters, parents, or children) who also suffer from depression (see Nurnberger & Gershon, 1982). However, the problem with this evidence is that it may be the social contact with the relatives rather than the overlap of genes that resulted in the depression, so we must consider other evidence.

Studies of Twins.   If depression is due to genetic factors, it would be expected that the concordance rate for depression would be higher in monozygotic (MZ) twins, who are genetically identical, than in dizygotic (DZ) twins, who are genetically different. The results of seven studies of depression in MZ and DZ twins provide consistent evidence for a genetic basis for depression. Those results are summarized in Table 9.3. As you can see, the mean concordance rate among MZ twins is more than 4½ times greater than the concordance rate among DZ twins (65% vs. 14%). The results of a recent study of female twins indicated that the heritability of depression was between 33% and 45% and that the remaining variability was related to the unique experiences of the individuals rather than to specific family characteristics (Kendler et al., 1992b). That range of heritability is similar to what has been found for anxiety (see Chapter 5) and similar to what is found for many "normal" personality traits.

Additional evidence for the role of genetics in depression comes from a study in which it was found that if one twin was very depressed, the likelihood of the other twin being depressed increased (Bertelsen, 1979; Bertelsen et al., 1977). Specifically, the concordance rate for twin pairs in which one twin had fewer than three depressive episodes was only 33%, whereas the concordance rate for twin pairs in which one twin had three or more depressive episodes was 59%. Overall, then, the findings based on the study of twins provide additional evidence for a genetic basis for depression.

Studies of Adoptees.   The most convincing evidence for a genetic basis for depression comes from the study of individuals who either did or did not have depressed biological parents and were adopted and raised by nondepressed adoptive parents. If the biological offspring of depressed individuals became depressed even when raised by nondepressed adoptive parents, that would provide strong evidence for the role of genes in depression. In one study of this type, 38% of the adopted biological offspring of depressed parents were later found to be depressed, whereas only .07% of the adopted biological offspring of nondepressed parents were found to be depressed (Cadoret, 1978a).

In view of all of these results, it seems safe to conclude that genetic factors do play a role in depression. It is essential to realize, however, that (a) not all relatives of depressives become depressed, (b) the concordance rate for depression in monozygotic twins is not 100%, and (c) many people who become depressed do not appear to have a family history of depression. From these findings, we must conclude that although genetic factors play an important role in depression, genetic factors alone do not account for all depressions, and we do not yet understand the mechanism by which genes have their effects (Faraone et al., 1990).

TABLE 9.3   MONOZYGOTIC TWINS HAVE A HIGHER CONCORDANCE RATE FOR DEPRESSION THAN DIZYGOTIC TWINS

STUDY	Pairs of Monozygotic Twins		Pairs of Dizygotic Twins	
	CONCORDANT	DISCORDANT	CONCORDANT	DISCORDANT
Luxenberger (1930)	3 (75%)	1	0 (0%)	13
Rosanoff et al. (1935)	16 (70%)	7	11 (16%)	56
Slater (1653)	4 (57%)	3	4 (24%)	13
Kallman (1954)	25 (93%)	2	13 (24%)	42
Harvald & Hauge (1956)	10 (67%)	5	2 (5%)	38
Allen et al. (1974)	5 (33%)	10	0 (0%)	34
Bertelsen (1979)	32 (58%)	23	9 (17%)	43
Means	(65%)		(14%)	

Source: Adapted from Nurnberger and Gershon (1982), p. 126, tab. 9.1.

Influence of Stress on the Physiological Factors Associated with Depression

In our earlier discussion of the psychodynamic explanations for depression, we concluded that stress often precedes and apparently causes depression. However, we noted that the *process* that linked stress to depression had not been identified and that the explanation was therefore incomplete. Now we will consider the possibility that stress results in lower levels of the neurotransmitters and that that effect leads to depression.

In numerous experiments, animals have been exposed to stressors and then the levels of norepinephrine in their brains were assessed (see E. A. Stone, 1975). The stressors have included such things as electric shock, heat, noise, conflict, social separation, fighting, and observing other animals fighting. In almost every case, the stress led to reduced levels of norepinephrine. Furthermore, when the experiments have involved more than one level of stress, higher levels of stress led to lower levels of norepinephrine. In some cases, the norepinephrine was reduced by as much as 40% or 50%. The exact process by which stress reduces neurotransmitter levels is not yet understood, but it has been suggested that the effect is due to the increased neuronal activity associated with the intense emotional arousal that accompanies stress. In other words, high levels of neurological activity associated with stress somehow use up the available norepinephrine.

Most of the research on the effects of stress on neurotransmitters has been focused on norepinephrine, but it has also been reported that there was a sudden drop in serotonin in dominant monkeys when they were socially isolated so that they no longer enjoyed their social status (Raleigh et al., 1984). It is interesting to speculate whether similar effects might occur in humans who are faced with major changes in life circumstances such as forced retirement, job demotions, personal crises, or loss of social support.

What is most important about all these findings is that they consistently indicate that stress can lead to reductions in the levels of neurotransmitters, and we know that such reductions are associated with depression. It appears, then, that changes in neurotransmitter levels provide a link between stress and depression.

Although it is clear that stress can cause physiological changes that can lead to depression, two important limitations on our understanding should be noted. First, not all depressions are preceded by stress, thus suggesting that a factor other than stress can cause the reduction in neurotransmitters that leads to depression. It appears likely that in some cases, the reductions are due to spontaneous or genetically determined malfunctions of the neurotransmitter system. Second, the findings relating stress to physiological changes do not explain why only some of the individuals who are exposed to stress become depressed. To explain the inconsistency, we must assume that there is some predisposing factor that makes certain individuals more vulnerable to depression. The neurotransmitter systems of certain individuals may be more sensitive to stress, but such differences have not been confirmed.

■ HUMANISTIC-EXISTENTIAL EXPLANATIONS

Finally, we should give some attention to the humanistic and existential explanations for depression. In Chapter 5, we noted that proponents of the humanistic perspective believe that anxiety stems from the discrepancy between the real and ideal selves. Depression sets in when the individual realizes that the gulf between real and ideal selves will never be spanned and therefore he or she gives up in despondency. The individual essentially abandons achieving self-actualization, and that loss brings on depression.

Giving up is also an important factor in the existential explanation for depression. The individual who stops making choices and taking responsibility ceases to be—that is, ceases to exist as a real person. Failure to be is a symbolic death, and that death, along with the recognition of actual death, leads to depression. In midlife, many persons go through a crisis that involves depression because they realize that they are not going to be what they once hoped, recognize that their physical existence is coming to an end, and give up.

■ MULTIPLE CAUSES, DIATHESIS-STRESS, AND PROLONGING FACTORS

In this chapter, we have seen that depression can be caused by a variety of factors ranging from loss to low levels of neurotransmitters. Each of those factors can be used to account for *some* depressions, but no one factor can account for *all* depressions. For example, stress leads to depression in many people, but stress does not lead to depression in all people, and some depressed people have not been exposed to stress. Therefore, before concluding this chapter we must attempt to clear up the controversy over the question of what causes depression.

Multiple Independent and Secondary Causes

The finding that different factors lead to depression is best explained simply by concluding that *there are mul-*

tiple independent causes for depression. For example, Freud was right that loss can lead to depression, but so were the biochemists who showed that low levels of serotonin and norepinephrine were related to depression. It appears that once again the dodo in *Alice's Adventures in Wonderland* was correct when he said, "All are winners, and all must have prizes."

Although the various factors can operate as independent primary causes of depression, it should be noted that in some instances the causes may also operate as *secondary causes in a chain that leads to depression.* For example, although lowered levels of serotonin and norepinephrine can bring on depression by themselves, in some cases stress leads to lowered levels of the neurotransmitters and hence to depression. In that case, the lowered levels of neurotransmitters are *secondary* or *mediating* causes. It is essential to keep the distinction between primary and secondary causes in mind when thinking about treatment, because treating only secondary causes will not lead to a lasting solution of the problem (see Chapter 11).

Diathesis-Stress

Next we must answer the question of why a particular factor will lead to depression in some individuals but not in others. The finding that a particular cause will have differential effects in different individuals is best explained in terms of **diathesis.** That is, some individuals are *predisposed* to respond, and others are not (Monroe & Simons, 1991). For example, some individuals may have unstable or moderately low levels of neurotransmitters; when those individuals are exposed to stress, their levels of neurotransmitters drop, and depression sets in. In contrast, that would not happen to individuals who have more stable or higher levels of neurotransmitters.

In most discussions of the diathesis-stress model of depression, it is assumed that the predisposition is physiological (unstable or low levels of neurotransmitters). However, cognitive factors may also serve to predispose individuals to depression. For example, an individual may have unused negative cognitive sets, and when those are triggered by stress (e.g., a failure), depression ensues. Individuals who do not have the negative cognitive sets would be less likely to become depressed under stress.

Diathesis is not an either-or phenomenon; instead, there are gradations in the degree to which an individual may be predisposed to depression, so individuals are at greater or less risk. The diathesis model is portrayed in Figure 9.9. In that figure, different lines are used to indicate individuals with different degrees of predisposition, and as you can see, as stress or dis-

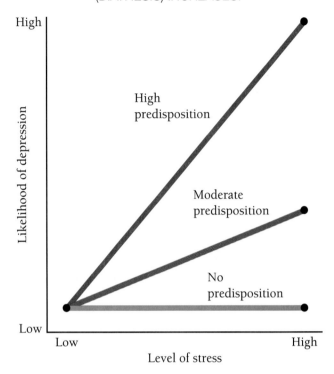

FIGURE 9.9 LIKELIHOOD OF DEPRESSION INCREASES AS LEVEL OF STRESS OR LEVEL OF PREDISPOSITION (DIATHESIS) INCREASES.

Source: Adapted from Monroe and Simons (1991), p. 415, fig. 4.

position increases, so does the likelihood of becoming depressed.

Prolonging Factors

Finally, it should be noted that once the individual is depressed, a number of factors may serve to prolong that depression, sometimes for long periods of time after the cause of the depression has dissipated. For example, an individual may become depressed because of a loss, but the depression will activate negative expectations and the recall of negative experiences, and those factors may maintain the depression after the problems related to the loss have been overcome. With treatment, it may be necessary to focus on factors other than those that initially caused the depression.

The bottom line in this discussion is that the explanation for depression is not simple. There may be multiple independent causes, there may be chains of primary and secondary causes, there may be interactions between causes and predispositions, and the depression may be prolonged by factors other than those that caused the depression. In attempting to explain

TABLE 9.4   PREDISPOSING FACTORS, PRIMARY AND SECONDARY CAUSES, AND PROLONGING FACTORS IN DEPRESSION

	PSYCHOLOGICAL	PHYSIOLOGICAL
Predisposing factors	Lack of social support Poor coping skills Negative expectations	Low or variable levels of neurotransmitters Poor aerobic condition
Primary causes	Psychosocial stress Loss Reward/punishment Negative cognitive set Loss of control	Reduction in norepinephrine or serotonin
Secondary causes	Impaired functioning due to endogenous depression results in psychological stress	Prolonged psychological stress leads to reductions in neurotransmitter levels
Prolonging factors	Negative expectations Enhanced recall of negative experiences Loss of social support	Chronic low levels of neurotransmitters

any one case of depression, you must consider a number of alternative explanations. The various psychological and physiological factors associated with depression are summarized in Table 9.4. Of course, not all of these factors play a role in every case of depression. Instead, different subsets of factors contribute to depression in different persons. Developing an understanding of the basis for depression is difficult because so many factors can contribute to the problem. Now that we are aware of the diversity of contributing factors and the various roles that they can play, we must be sensitive to the possibility of different processes in different individuals and not attribute all depressions to any one factor or confluence of factors.

■ SUMMARY

Freud originally hypothesized that depression was a reaction to loss. He suggested that anger toward the lost object (person) was turned inward on the self and resulted in depression. More recent psychodynamic theorists have pointed to the role of stress in causing depression and suggested that loss may be one type of stress. Evidence is now abundant that acute and chronic stress of many types can lead to depression, but the psychodynamic approach has not provided evidence concerning the process by which stress causes depression.

Learning theorists offer two explanations for depression. First, they hypothesize that depression is caused by low levels of reward or high levels of punishment (or both). The research indicates that low levels of reward and high levels of punishment can result in saddened mood or mild dysphoria, but so far they have not been directly linked to clinical levels of depression. The second learning theory explanation is

that depressive behaviors are learned or maintained because they result in rewards (e.g., attention, concern) from others. However, in view of the research indicating that depressed individuals are avoided and not rewarded by others, it does not appear that many depressions result from rewards.

There are also two cognitive theories of depression. The first suggests that because of selective attention and selective recall, individuals develop negative cognitions that lead to depression. There is evidence that depressed individuals have negative cognitions and that they selectively attend to and recall depressing material, but there is not strong evidence that negative cognitions cause clinical levels of depression. Instead, it appears that negative cognitions may predispose individuals to depression when they are under stress. The negative cognitions may also serve to maintain depression once it sets in. The second cognitive explanation suggests that depression is due to feelings of helplessness in controlling the negative aspects of life. This learned helplessness explanation has been the topic of intensive investigation during the past few years, but the results have been inconsistent and weak. Depressed individuals often do feel helpless, but in most cases those feelings appear to be the result rather than the cause of the depression.

From a physiological standpoint, depression is thought to stem from a low level of neurological activity in the areas of the brain that are responsible for pleasure. The low level of activity is attributed to low levels of norepinephrine or serotonin. Support for the physiological explanation is provided by findings that drugs that increase and decrease the levels of the neurotransmitters have the effect of decreasing and increasing depression and that the levels of the metabolite of norepinephrine increase and decrease with decreases and increases in depression. It appears that there may be two types of physiologically caused depression, one due to low levels of norepinephrine and one due to low levels of serotonin. Low levels of those neurotransmitters can also account for the disturbances of sleep, eating, and sexual function that often accompany depression. The anxiety that sometimes occurs with depression may be due to the depression or to low levels of GABA. Low levels of the neurotransmitters have been linked to prolonged stress. Studies of families, twins, and adoptees all point to a genetic basis for some depressions.

Humanistic-existential theorists believe that depression stems from the recognition that we will not achieve our personal goals (e.g., self-actualization) and a consequent giving up of responsibility that is a symbolic death.

Overall, it appears that depression may be due to multiple causes, and for different individuals at different times different factors may predispose, cause, or prolong depression. Depression is a serious problem that already afflicts many individuals, and it is increasing at an alarming rate. As this chapter attests, however, there is currently a wealth of theories and data from which we are developing a refined understanding of the problem. This understanding is important because it contributes to our ability to treat today's patients and prevent tomorrow's patients. Researchers and therapists in the area of depression do not share the negative expectations of the individuals on whose problems they work. Progress has been made in developing an understanding of depression, and there may be "a light at the end of the tunnel," which, contrary to the negative expectations of many depressed patients, is not another train coming at them!

■ KEY TERMS, CONCEPTS, AND NAMES

- -

In reviewing and testing yourself on what you have learned from this chapter, you should be able to identify and discuss each of the following:

aerobic fitness	GABA	norepinephrine
amine hypothesis	indole amines	predisposing factors
amines	information processing	priming
anger turned inward	learned helplessness	punishments
associative networks	loss	rewards
catecholamines	metabolites	selective attention
cognitive diathesis-stress hypothesis	MHPG	selective recall
coping strategies	mourning	serotonin
diathesis	negative cognitive sets	social support
5-HIAA	neurotransmitters	stress

Notes:

Chapter 10

Bipolar Disorder and Suicide

• O U T L I N E •

Carl was a happily married 28-year-old father of two who had always been very stable. However, 2 years ago he went through a period in which he became noticeably more active and extravagant. He slept less, had an unusual amount of energy, made many unrealistic plans for his small business, and spent a considerable amount of money needlessly on a new convertible and a lot of clothes. He seemed to be going off in three directions at once without giving anything much thought. After about a month, this phase passed, and Carl became his "old self" again, much to his wife's relief. Everything was normal for about a year, but then he began slipping into a mild depression. He stopped making business calls, at home he sat alone in his study, and he was convinced that he was a "rotten failure." He just wanted to be left alone. This depression lifted after a while, and once again Carl returned to his normal behavior. A week ago, however, he again started becoming very active, even agitated. He made plans for the entire family to take a vacation in the South Pacific as a celebration for a big business deal that he thought he would close, but was in fact only in the idea stage. He signed a contract to have an addition put on the house but then put the house up for sale and started negotiating to buy another one that was completely out of his price range. Emotionally, he was "on top of the world" and felt as though he could achieve anything he tried. However, he never actually accomplished much because he became distracted by other ideas before he could carry through on anything. He slept very little and called people in the middle of the night to set up business appointments he never kept. After about 3 days of this, his wife realized that he was completely out of control, and she called the family physician, who had Carl committed to the psychiatric ward of the local hospital. He was diagnosed as suffering from the *bipolar disorder.*

Kate was a 23-year-old fashion buyer for a large department store. Over the past 2 years, she had become somewhat depressed. She attributed her poor mood to exhaustion brought on by the constant strain of her job. She began going to a psychotherapist but stopped after only a few sessions because she didn't think she could be helped. At first, she had been very successful at her job, but recently she had chosen some lines of women's clothing that had "bombed," and now her confidence was shaken. Feeling hopeless, she occasionally gave some thought to suicide; it would provide a release from the constant strain she was under—and why not? She had nothing to live for. On a number of occasions, Kate made comments to her friends like "Nothing seems to be going right; sometimes I feel like stepping in front of a truck" or "Probably the best thing for me to do tonight is to take all the pills in my medicine cabinet and just not wake up tomorrow morning." Her friends knew that Kate was depressed, but they thought she would snap out of it, and they didn't take her comments about suicide seriously. When Kate did not come in for work for 2 days and did not answer her phone, a friend went to her apartment. Kate was lying dead in the bathtub, her wrists slashed. She had left a short note in which she simply apologized for not being a better person.

In this chapter, we will consider two topics: the bipolar disorder, in which individuals experience extreme mood swings that range from deep depression to high elation, and suicide. Suicide is not a disorder, but because it is frequently related to depression, it is relevant to consider it in this discussion of mood disorders.

• Bipolar Disorder

The **bipolar disorder** is one of the two major mood disorders. The other is depression, or what is often called the *unipolar disorder* (see Figure 8.1 in Chapter 8). The bipolar disorder differs from the depressive (unipolar) disorder in that it involves swings of mood between mania and depression. Because of those shifts, the bipolar disorder was formerly referred to as the *manic-depressive disorder*. (There are apparently a small number of individuals who experience mania but not depression, but because they are so rare, no separate diagnostic class has been established for them.)

SYMPTOMS OF THE BIPOLAR DISORDER

Because we described depression in detail in Chapter 9, here we will focus only on **mania**. The manic aspect of the bipolar disorder may have been developing for some time and may be quite serious before anyone realizes that there is a problem. We are often slow to recognize a manic episode because the individual is not upset, anxious, or depressed. Rather, the individual is happy, carefree, unconcerned about potential problems, self-reliant, apparently productive, and often in a playful, festive mood. During this early stage, the individual may be referred to as *hypomanic*, reflecting the low (*hypo-*) level of mania.

Mood Symptoms

During manic episodes, the predominant mood is *euphoria*. The patient is excited, excessively happy, emotionally expansive, and generally "flying high." DSM-IV suggests that irritability can also be present during a manic episode, but the irritability is probably only a response to the restraints imposed by people around the manic individual to limit inappropriate behavior. In other words, for the manic individual, "everything is coming up roses," but the individual may become irritated or angry if someone tries to clip those roses. For example, a 200-lb manic patient became irritated and

hostile when I objected to the fact that he had torn down my office drapes. He did not like the way the office was decorated, and in his expansive mood he had decided to redo it for me!

Cognitive Symptoms

The cognitive symptoms associated with a manic episode include *inflated self-esteem* and *grandiosity*. Patients with mania have completely unrealistic beliefs about what they can accomplish. One manic person I knew had an idea for a new type of automobile engine that he thought would revolutionize the industry and make him a millionaire overnight. When major problems with his idea were pointed out to him, he brushed them aside as "minor details" that would be worked out later.

Another important cognitive symptom seen in mania is *distractibility* and *fragmentation of attention*. In their euphoric and expansive moods, manic individuals cannot keep their attention focused on any one thing for long, and they are continually shifting their attention or getting distracted by other ideas, problems, or plans. This is often referred to as a *manic flight of ideas*. In some cases, the flight of ideas is so rapid and the shifts from topic to topic are so fast that it is difficult to follow the manic person's train of thought. The inventor mentioned in the preceding paragraph was so busy getting investors and buying equipment to manufacture his new engine that he never took time to think the idea through carefully enough to realize that it could never work. Because of their inability to focus attention and because they keep shifting from task to task, most manic patients are ineffective and do not accomplish much. Sometimes the flight of ideas and resulting confusion can be mistaken for a schizophrenic-type thought disorder, and hence manic patients are occasionally misdiagnosed.

Some bipolar patients also have *delusions* like those seen in schizophrenia. One manic patient talked very rapidly and jumped from topic to topic as she told me that she was married to Burt Reynolds, she was the first woman president of the United States, and her three daughters had been murdered in the hospital. Delusions such as those are not necessarily a component of the bipolar disorder but are sometimes seen in conjunction with it. When this combination of disorders occurs, the patient might be diagnosed as suffering from a **mood disorder with psychotic features**.

Motor Symptoms

The motor behavior of manic individuals parallels their excited cognitive behavior. The manic individual runs from one project to the next. During a particularly severe manic episode, one person drove through the downtown area of a large city at breakneck speed, sideswiping cars and driving wildly down sidewalks to get around cars at intersections. He had "important business deals to close" and was in a great hurry.

Their high levels of activity and exaggerated self-importance can lead some persons with mania to very inappropriate behavior. Notable in this regard are telephoning sprees, hypersexuality, and spending money. Because they are involved in so many things and because of their exaggerated confidence in their ultimate success, manic individuals often spend very large amounts of money (usually using credit) in short periods of time. In some cases, they will quickly go through their life savings and run themselves deep into debt.

Mania does not always result in ineffective or inappropriate behavior. I once knew a very creative patient who was an interior decorator. Whenever she had a severe manic episode (about once a year), she would completely redecorate her home by herself. Almost without stopping to sleep, she would repaint and rewallpaper her entire home in less than a week. She would use bright, cheery colors and do very creative things. I often envied her energy and results. Her success was probably due to the fact that her activities during the manic phase (painting and wallpapering) did not require sustained intellectual effort.

Somatic Symptoms

The only consistent somatic symptom seen in mania is a *decreased need for sleep.* Persons suffering from mania are constantly "fired up" and "on the move," and they sleep very little. These individuals ignore fatigue, aches, pains, and other somatic problems that may actually exist.

Case Study 10.1 (p. 216) presents a student's description of his first experience with a bipolar disorder.

ISSUES ASSOCIATED WITH THE BIPOLAR DISORDER

- -

Prevalence and Age of Onset

The bipolar disorder occurs in about 1% of the population (Robins et al., 1984). If less seriously disturbed (cyclothymic) individuals are included, the percentage of individuals who have the disorder is probably twice as high (Fremming, 1951; Helgason, 1961; James & Chapman, 1975; Krauthammer & Klerman, 1979), but that is still not as high as the other major disorders such as the depressive (unipolar) disorder and schizo-

phrenia. We are also less likely to see persons with bipolar disorders than persons with most other disorders because in most cases the bipolar disorder can be effectively treated with medication, and therefore many patients have only one or two relatively short attacks (see Chapter 11).

The risk period for onset is commonly believed to extend from about 15 to 60 years of age, with the most frequent onset occurring between ages 25 and 30 (Carlson et al., 1974; Krauthammer & Klerman, 1979; Loranger & Levine, 1978; Winokur et al., 1969). That age of onset is somewhat earlier than for the depressive (unipolar) disorder, which most often begins in the late 30s to mid-40s. First onset of mania is sometimes seen in elderly individuals, but the symptoms in those individuals are probably due to some other diseases or medication rather than the bipolar disorder (Young & Klerman, 1992).

The manic and depressive episodes of the bipolar disorder are usually separated by normal periods, and the episodes recur, establishing a cycle of manic, normal, depressive, normal, manic, normal, and so on. If not treated, the length of the normal periods between episodes decreases and the length of each episode increases (Klerman & Barrett, 1973). Once the bipolar disorder sets in, it can last for many years.

Demographic Factors

The distribution of the bipolar disorder in the population is very different from the distribution of the depressive disorder. Whereas women suffering from depression outnumber men 2 to 1, the bipolar disorder occurs about equally in men and women (Krauthammer & Klerman, 1979; Robins et al., 1984). Furthermore, whereas depression is found more frequently among lower-class individuals, class does not seem to be a factor in the bipolar disorder (Krauthammer & Klerman, 1979; Monnelly et al., 1974; Weissman & Myers, 1978; Woodruff et al., 1971).

Cycle Time

A frequent question is, how long does it take individuals with the bipolar disorder to go through one cycle of mania and depression? The answer is that there is very wide variability in cycle time. In one study of 919 individuals over a 5-year period, it was found that about 35% of the individuals went through only one cycle, whereas about 1% of the individuals went through 22 cycles—about one cycle every 3 months (Coryell et al., 1992). These results are presented graphically in Figure 10.1. These figures may be an underestimation of the natural course of the cycles because most of the patients were on medication to control their disorder.

FIGURE 10.1   THERE IS CONSIDERABLE VARIABILITY IN THE NUMBER OF CYCLES EXPERIENCED BY PATIENTS WITH THE BIPOLAR DISORDER.

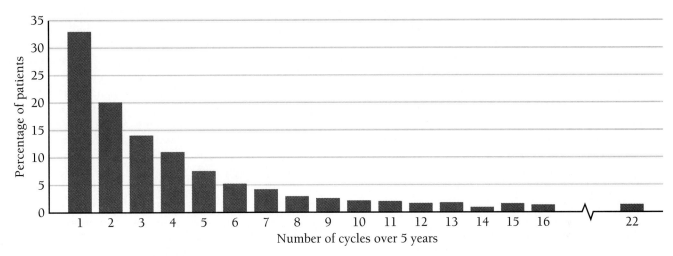

Source: Coryell et al. (1992), p. 128, fig. 1.

In recent years, some interest has been shown in individuals who show **rapid cycling**, defined as four or more cycles per year (Coryell et al., 1992; Wehr et al., 1988; Wolpert et al., 1990). In general, rapid cycling is more likely to occur in women, and it does not show a genetic pattern (the bipolar disorder runs in families, but relatives who have the bipolar disorder do not show concordance for rapid cycling). Also, individuals who do show rapid cycling are less likely than others to recover in the first or second year of treatment but are equally likely to recover thereafter. Overall, then, rather than reflecting a different type of bipolar disorder, rapid cycling probably indicates a more severe or virulent case.

Bipolar and Unipolar Disorders as Different Disorders

Because bipolar and depressive (unipolar) disorders share the symptom of depression, it is tempting to assume that they are actually one disorder with the bipolar patients simply having the additional symptom of mania. However, as indicated in Table 10.1, the two disorders show a variety of differences other than symptoms, and these differences suggest that these are two separate disorders (Winokur & Clayton, 1967;

Zerbin-Rudin, 1979). If they were the same disorder, it would be difficult to understand why the bipolar has an earlier onset than the depressive disorder and why there are sex differences in one and not the other. The question of whether the bipolar and depressive disorders are the same or different disorders has not yet been definitely answered, but it is likely that, as with many other disorders, we will eventually find that they are different but overlapping disorders.

Mania as a Secondary Symptom

It is important to distinguish between mania that is part of a bipolar disorder and **secondary mania**, which is the side effect of a drug or the result of some other disease (Krauthammer & Klerman, 1979; Tyrer & Shopsin, 1982). For example, secondary mania can be a side effect of some antidepressant drugs (Bunney, 1978; Van Scheyen & Van Kammen, 1979). In those cases, it appears that the drugs "overshoot the mark" and bring the patient out of depression, past a normal mood state, and into mania. In making diagnoses, then, care must be taken not to diagnose an individual as suffering from a bipolar disorder when in fact the individual's mania is the side effect of a drug or a symptom of another disease.

TABLE 10.1   DIFFERENCES BETWEEN BIPOLAR AND UNIPOLAR (DEPRESSIVE) DISORDERS

	BIPOLAR	UNIPOLAR
Symptoms	Mania and depression	Depression
Incidence	Rare (.75% to 1%)	Common (5%)
Onset	Early (25 to 30)	Later (35 to 45)
Gender ratio	Equal in women and men	More in women, 2:1
Genetics	More bipolar relatives	Fewer bipolar relatives

Case Study 10.1

A BIPOLAR EPISODE IN A 21-YEAR-OLD STUDENT

My bipolar disorder began one summer while I was living on a ranch in New Mexico. After about a month there, I began to feel increasingly self-conscious, unhappy, isolated, unmotivated, and listless. I attributed all of these symptoms to being in a new part of the country. As the depression worsened, I stopped interacting with others or participating in activities. I tried to escape in sleep, but though I spent my spare time in bed, I had great difficulty actually sleeping. I became obsessed with a desire to go away somewhere to be by myself, and I would wander aimlessly through the countryside, fantasizing about suicide. Ultimately, I spent 13 days huddled in a pile of rocks on the edge of a field, hoping to die of starvation or illness through exposure. But because I was unwilling to endure another hot day and cold night, I finally walked (or crawled) back to the ranch. My father had come to the ranch to find me when he learned that I was missing, and he brought me back home.

After getting home, I was unable to hold a job, and I constantly thought about killing myself; I wished I were alone and unbothered, in a deep, dark hole. I was seeing a psychotherapist, and I spent the hourly sessions staring at his carpet without speaking. Toward the end of summer, though, my mood began to lift. I noticed that I wasn't as preoccupied with death and that I felt that I might have a future after all. I did not associate this improvement with psychological counseling but rather with the idea that I had somehow "paid my dues" and now had been given some sort of earned emotional reward. Though I am not religious, I remember feeling a spiritual significance about this; something had "clicked" deep inside my head, and I wasn't about to question it.

I started to feel better and better. Within a few weeks, I was interacting well with my family, doing quite well at a job given to me by a friend of my father's, and planning to find my own apartment. My sessions with the psychotherapist became increasingly animated, and every day I felt happier and more positive. I found an apartment and quit my job because now it seemed too boring for me. I began to learn to play the guitar and got a job in an entertainment booking agency. I soon quit to start my own agency and began leading a very active and aggressive social life. I was feeling amazingly energetic, sharp, confident, and powerful—as if I could accomplish anything I wanted to, and very quickly!

The psychotherapist had by now become concerned about me, and he wanted me to promise to return the next week, when he would prescribe some lithium for me.[1] However, by this time my head was constantly spinning with new ideas and plans. My ability to concentrate was intense but changed focus rapidly. I had no concern for ethical and legal responsibilities and exercised no financial restraint. I wrote bad checks to my landlord and to Amtrak and took a train to California with my guitar and about one dollar in my pocket.

When it became clear to me that my erratic behavior was alienating my college friends in California, particularly a woman with whom I had fallen in love, I decided to return home and commit myself to a hospital. At this time, I absolutely believed that two things were true: that I was going to father the next messiah and that this idea was crazy. After coming home, I became so agitated—feeling ready to explode—that my mother drove me to the emergency room at the medical center, where I was given an injection of 300 ml of Thorazine.[2] I was handcuffed by the police and taken to the psychiatric ward. The next morning, I began receiving lithium carbonate; 3 weeks later, I was released.

[1]Lithium is a drug that is commonly used to treat the bipolar disorder (see Chapter 11).
[2]Thorazine (chlorpromazine) is a drug that is often used to treat schizophrenia. It was used in this case because when injected, it has an immediate and strong sedation effect (see Chapter 14).

With this general description of the symptoms and issues associated with the bipolar disorder as background, we can now go on to consider the causes of the disorder.

PSYCHODYNAMIC, LEARNING, AND COGNITIVE EXPLANATIONS

For most major disorders, there are widely held psychodynamic, learning, cognitive, and physiological explanations. However, that is not the case for the bipolar disorder because the psychological explanations have now been largely abandoned in favor of physiological ones. The demise of interest in psychological explanations for the bipolar disorder probably stemmed from the fact that the drug **lithium carbonate** was found to be highly effective for treating the disorder (see Chapter 11). Furthermore, treatments based on the psychological explanations had not been effective. In other words, because the physiologically based treatment was very effective and the psychologically based treatment was ineffective, we have come to believe that the psychological theory was wrong. Furthermore, because the disorder was being treated so effectively with the drug, there was little interest in pursuing psychological explanations or treatments. To provide a historical perspective, however, we will first examine the once popular psychological explanation for the bipolar disorder, and then we will go on to discuss the physiological explanations.

The basic tenet of the psychological explanation was that individuals with the bipolar disorder are basically very depressed (which they show during their depressive phase), but when the depression becomes too great, they attempt to *escape the depression with their manic behavior* (Freeman, 1971; Lewin, 1951). During the manic phase, the patients were said to be in a "manic flight from depression." In other words, the manic behavior was seen as a defense against overwhelming depression.

The flight-from-depression explanation for mania had a good deal of intuitive appeal because a commonly suggested remedy for depression is to "go out and do something wild" or to "put on a happy face." There were also numerous case studies that could be interpreted as supporting the flight-from-depression explanation. For example, one bipolar patient had a husband who was having affairs with other women, and that upset and depressed her. In her manic phase, she would sometimes dance around the ward singing, "I'm going to wash that man right out of my hair"— and on a number of occasions, she dumped washbasins of water over her head. The interpretation was that she used the singing and dancing to distract herself from the "underlying depression" about her husband, but even then her "real concern" about her husband came through in the content of what she sang (she wanted the unfaithful husband "out of her hair").

Although supported by such anecdotes, the psychological explanations had very little objective support (Winters & Neale, 1985), and they did not lead to effective treatment strategies. Other evidence suggesting that psychological factors may not play an important role in the bipolar disorders is that stressful life events often precede the onset of unipolar disorders but do not trigger bipolar disorders (Hammen et al., 1989; see also Chapter 9).

PHYSIOLOGICAL EXPLANATIONS

As noted earlier, lithium carbonate is very effective for treating persons with the bipolar disorder, and for that reason, most attention was turned to physiological explanations for the disorder. However, it should be pointed out that we do not yet understand exactly why it is effective, and therefore we do not yet have a complete physiological understanding of the bipolar disorder. Researchers are developing some good hypotheses, however, which we will consider now.

Physiological Imbalances

The fact that the symptoms in the bipolar disorder involve shifts between depression and mania suggests that the underlying problem involves some form of physiological instability (Schou et al., 1981; Siever & Davis, 1985). So far, no specific instability has been definitely identified, but there are two likely possibilities: changing levels of neurotransmitters and changing levels of postsynaptic sensitivity (Bunney & Murphy, 1976).

Changing Levels of Neurotransmitters.
The presynaptic membrane that regulates the release of the neurotransmitter may vary the amount of the neurotransmitter it allows into the synapse. During times when it allows an excessive amount of the neurotransmitter into the synapse, resulting in a high level of neurological activity, the individual becomes manic. When the membrane allows an insufficient amount of the neurotransmitter into the synapse, resulting in a low level of neurological activity, the individual becomes depressed.

Changing Levels of Postsynaptic Sensitivity.
It is also possible that changes in the sensitivity of the postsynaptic receptor sites may be the crucial factor in the bipolar disorder. At some times, the receptor sites may be very sensitive to stimulation, leading to more neurological activity and manic behavior. At other times, the receptor sites may be insensitive to stimulation, resulting in decreased neurological activity and depression.

We do not know exactly what aspect of the system is unstable or why. However, we do know that administering lithium carbonate is effective in eliminating symptoms in most patients with the bipolar disorder, and we assume that the drug serves to stabilize the erratic system. How that is achieved is still a topic of debate and research.

Cerebral Glucose Metabolism

Energy is required for all the activities that occur in the body. That energy is provided by a type of sugar called glucose, and the process of using glucose to produce energy is known as glucose metabolism. Just as your leg muscles require glucose when you run, your brain requires glucose when neurological activity occurs. Glucose metabolism can be used to measure brain activity. With the development of positron emission tomography (PET scans), we are now able to measure when and where high and low areas of glucose metabolism occur in the brain, and from that we can infer high and low levels of neurological activity.

PET technology has been used to study neurological activity in bipolar patients during their manic and depressive phases. Figure 10.2 contains PET scans from a patient with the bipolar disorder. The three scans in the top row were taken during a depressed phase, and the three scans in the bottom row were taken during a manic phase. You are looking down on the brain from the top, and the three scans in each row represent three levels (planes) of the brain. The colors indicate different amounts of glucose metabolism; red and yellow indicate higher metabolism, and blue and purple indicate lower metabolism. On the manic day, the patient had a much higher rate of cerebral glucose metabolism than on the depressed day; in fact, the rate of glucose metabolism on the manic day was 36% higher than on the depressed day (Baxter et al., 1985). Although these findings clearly indicate differences in brain functioning between manic and depressed days, we should not conclude that differences

in glucose metabolism are the cause of the bipolar disorder. Instead, they reflect the effects of the problems with neurotransmission that were discussed earlier. In the future, however, PET scans may help us refine our understanding of exactly where in the brain the high and low levels of activity are occurring, and that may lead to a more thorough understanding of the problem and to improved methods of treatment.

Genetic Factors

If the bipolar disorder stems from problems with neurological activity, we must go on to ask, what causes those underlying problems? One possibility is that individuals may inherit a neurological instability that results in the bipolar disorder.

Studies of Families. If there is a genetic basis for the bipolar disorder, we would expect that first-degree relatives (children, parents) of individuals with the disorder would have a higher rate of bipolar illness than individuals in the general population. Table 10.2 presents the results of eight studies of the relatives of individuals with the bipolar disorder. Those results reveal that the relatives of individuals with the bipolar disorder have high rates of the disorder, about 6%. That is about *six times higher* than the rate of the bipolar disorder in the general population. In contrast, the relatives of individuals with the bipolar disorder have the depressive (unipolar) disorder at a rate that is only *twice* what is found in the general population. Overall, then, it may be that bipolar individuals have inherited a specific predisposition to the bipolar disorder.

Studies of Twins. Studies of monozygotic and dizygotic twins also provide evidence for the role of heredity in the bipolar disorder. For example, in one study, it was found that among MZ twin pairs, the concordance rate for the bipolar disorder was 58%, whereas among DZ twin pairs, the concordance rate was only 17% (Bertelsen et al., 1977). Other studies have produced similar results (e.g., Zerbin-Rudin, 1969). In these studies, the concordance rate among MZ twins was more than three times higher than the concordance rate among DZ twins.

Studies of Adoptees. The role of genetic factors in the development of the bipolar disorder was also established in a study of the biological and adoptive parents of individuals who developed the bipolar disorder (Mendlewicz & Rainer, 1977). In that study, it was found that 31% of the biological parents of the patients suffered from a bipolar disorder, but only 12%

FIGURE 10.2   PET SCANS INDICATE HIGHER LEVELS OF CEREBRAL GLUCOSE METABOLISM DURING MANIC PHASES THAN DURING DEPRESSIVE PHASES.

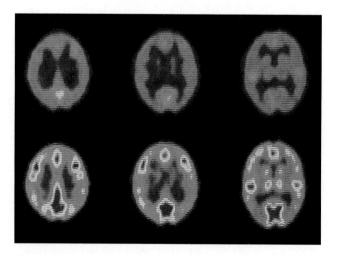

PET (positron emission tomography) scans from a bipolar patient during a depressive phase (top row) *and a manic phase* (bottom row).

Source: Baxter et al. (1985), p. 444, fig. 3.

TABLE 10.2   WHEN COMPARED TO THE RATE IN THE GENERAL POPULATION, FIRST-DEGREE RELATIVES OF PERSONS WITH THE BIPOLAR DISORDER HAVE A HIGHER RATE OF THE BIPOLAR DISORDER

STUDY	Percentage of First-Degree Relatives with a Mood Disorder	
	BIPOLAR DISORDER	UNIPOLAR DISORDER
Winokur et al. (1969)	10.2	20.4
Goetzl et al. (1974)	2.8	13.7
Helzer & Winokur (1974)	4.6	10.6
Petterson (1974)	4.6	2.7
Gershon et al. (1975)	3.8	6.8
James & Chapman (1975)	6.4	13.2
Trzebiatowska-Trzeciak (1977)	10.0	—
Smeraldi et al. (1978)	5.8	7.1
Average	6.0	10.6
General population	1.0	5.0

Source: Adapted from Perris (1982), p. 50, tab. 4.7.

of the adoptive parents suffered from a bipolar disorder.

Direct Examination of Genes. In a number of studies, the investigators actually examined the genes of a large number of individuals who did and did not suffer from the bipolar disorder (Detera-Wadleigh et al., 1987; Egeland et al., 1987; Hodgkinson et al., 1987). In one study, it was reported that individuals with the bipolar disorder had an additional gene on the short arm of chromosome 11, but other investigators were unable to replicate the finding, and therefore we are not yet able to draw a conclusion concerning specific genes or sets of genes.

Taken together, the evidence from studies of families, twins, and adoptees provides strong and consistent support for the speculation that heredity plays a role in the development of the bipolar disorder.

This completes our discussion of the symptoms and causes of the mood disorders. In Chapter 11, we will examine the various methods that are used for treating them. However, before doing that we will give some attention to the important topic of suicide. (Note: It should not be concluded that suicide is related to the bipolar disorder because the discussions of the two topics are included in the same chapter. Actually, suicide is more closely related to depression.)

• Suicide

Suicide is one of the 10 leading causes of death in the United States, and it is the second leading cause of death among young males. Overall, 30,000 individuals will commit suicide this year. The magnitude of the problem is actually much greater than the statistics suggest because many suicides are disguised as accidents and therefore go unrecognized. Furthermore, it is estimated that there are at least 8 to 10 attempted suicides for each one completed. The magnitude of the problem is clearly reflected in the findings of a study of college students: 26% of the students had considered suicide in the preceding 12 months, 2% had attempted suicide in the preceding 12 months, and 10% had attempted suicide at some time in the past (Meehan et al., 1992; similar results were obtained by Rudd, 1989). Fortunately, many of the attempts by younger individuals fail (especially those that involve overdoses of drugs that are not lethal). However, all too many of the attempts are successful. In view of the pervasiveness and seriousness of the problem, it is important that we give suicide thorough and careful consideration.

ISSUES ASSOCIATED WITH SUICIDE

Gender and Age Differences

Women are three times more likely to *attempt* suicide than men, but men are three times more likely to be *successful* in their attempts. The reason for the sex difference in attempted suicide is not clear, but it may be that women are more likely to suffer from depression than men, and depression plays a major role in suicide. The higher success rate among men reflects the fact that men use more violent techniques (guns,

For some people, suicide gestures are cries of help. In other cases a suicide gesture may be an attempt to manipulate or control others.

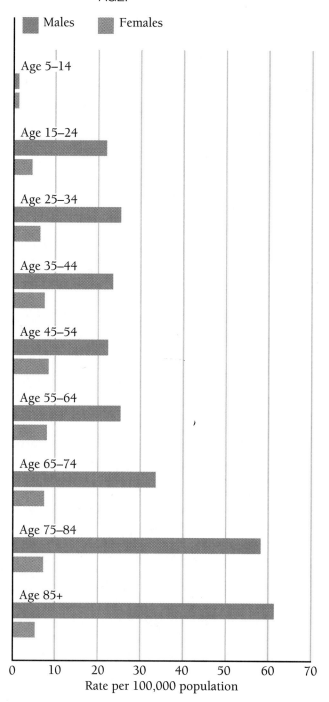

FIGURE 10.3   MALES HAVE A HIGHER RATE OF SUICIDE, WHICH INCREASES WITH AGE.

Source: Adapted from McIntosh (1992), p. 20, fig. 3.

jumps from buildings) than women (overdoses, wrist slashing), and the more violent techniques are more likely to be successful.

With regard to age, in almost all cultures, suicide rates increase with age (Lester, 1991). In the United States, the greatest increase comes between the ages of 65 and 84, and for individuals over the age of 65, the suicide rate is twice the national average (Kirsling, 1986). The generally high rate of suicide in older adults is due primarily to the very high rate of suicide among white males (McIntosh, 1992). Those findings are reflected in Figure 10.3. Older individuals are more likely to be successful in their suicide attempts than their younger counterparts, probably because they are more knowledgeable and because they are more likely to be absolutely resolute about what they are doing.

Problems in Assessing Changes in Suicide Rates

Some reports have suggested that the overall rate of suicide is increasing, and specifically that the rate among adolescents has tripled in the past 30 years. In-deed, the term *epidemic* has been used to describe the problem among adolescents (Centers for Disease Control, 1986). However, the data may be somewhat misleading because at least part of the apparent increase among adolescents appears to be due to the possibility that medical examiners are becoming more likely to designate an adolescent's death from poisoning or firearms as due to suicide rather than to an "accident" (Gist & Welch, 1989; Males, 1991a, 1991b). This conclusion is based on the fact that the overall death rate (accidents *plus* suicides) has remained flat in the 15–19 and 20–44 age groups. So, if the suicide rate for adolescents were increasing, the accident rate for adolescents would have to be decreasing, but we have no evidence of that. It is more likely that the apparent increase in suicides is due to changes in labeling of the cause of death.

The increase in reporting of suicides as suicides rather than as accidents may be due to changes in social factors. The influence of social factors was demonstrated in a study in which different medical examiners were given the same set of simulated cases and asked to decide on the causes of death (Jarvis et al., 1991). The results indicated that examiners were more likely to conclude that a death was due to suicide if the examiners were not associated with an organized religion or were living in small towns than if they were Roman Catholic or lived in large cities. Clearly, attitudes about suicide influence our willingness to report it, and as those attitudes change, we may be more willing to admit to a problem that has been with us for a long time.

Suicides, Covert Suicides, and Suicide Gestures

Many suicides are disguised and hence are not recognized as suicides. **Covert** (kō-VURT) **suicide** occurs when people do not want others to know what they have done either because they are ashamed or because their life insurance policies will not pay off for suicide. Automobile accidents are one method of covert suicide (Bollen & Phillips, 1981; Phillips, 1977, 1979). Individuals who use cars when attempting suicide will intentionally drive into the paths of other cars, trucks, or trains. For example, during two of her depressive episodes, a woman drove her car at high speed into a bridge support in an attempt to kill herself, but both cases were listed as accidents rather than suicide attempts. There has also been some speculation that some persons try to provoke the police into shooting them as a means of committing suicide.

In sharp contrast to covert suicides are **suicide gestures**, in which individuals engage in obvious suicidal behavior but do not really want to kill themselves. For example, a person may take an overdose of pills, but not enough to kill, or may slash his or her wrists, but not deeply enough to bleed to death. Persons who make suicide gestures generally make them in such a way that other people will find out. They may leave the empty pill bottle out or allow others to notice their bandaged wrists.

For some individuals, suicide gestures are *cries for help* (Farberow & Shneidman, 1961). The persons are desperate but do not know how to ask for help, are too ashamed to ask for help directly, or have asked for help and were ignored because others did not realize how upset they were. The suicide gesture is then a way of dramatizing the seriousness of the problem and asking for help indirectly.

For others, suicide gestures are attempts to *manipulate or control the people around them.* For example, an individual abandoned by a lover may make a suicide gesture in an attempt to get the lover to come back. In general, individuals who make suicidal gestures tend to be female, younger, less mature, and less depressed than individuals who actually intend to die, and suicide gestures tend to be more impulsive and less lethal than actual attempts (McHugh & Goodell, 1971; Robins & O'Neal, 1958; Rosen, 1970; Schmidt et al., 1954; Silver et al., 1971; Weissman, 1974). Nevertheless, it is often difficult to distinguish between a suicide gesture and an attempted suicide that failed. Moreover, even when it is clear that an attempt was only a gesture, the behavior should not be taken lightly. No matter what the motive, a gesture is a sign of a serious problem, and in making the gesture, the individual might accidentally succeed.

Some suicide attempts that fail nevertheless have serious consequences. For example, taking an overdose of certain drugs can lead to long-term problems such as brain damage. A particularly distressing example of such a consequence is presented in Case Study 10.2 (p. 222). This case also illustrates the difficulty of determining who will and will not commit suicide and the problem of what to do with individuals who are only suspected of suicidal intentions.

Warnings and Notes

The decision to commit suicide is ordinarily not made quickly, and often the individual contemplating suicide will give some warning. Interviews with friends and relatives of individuals who committed suicide indicated that between 60% and 70% of the victims had openly said that they wanted to commit suicide (direct threats) and another 20% to 25% had talked about the topic of suicide (indirect indication of their intentions; Farberow & Simon, 1975; Rudestam, 1971). These suicide signals can be indications of what the individuals plan to do, or they can be means of letting others know how upset they are in an indirect attempt to get help. *Remarks about suicide should always be taken seriously.* Ignoring a plea for help can further convince the individual of the hopelessness of the situation. It is

Case Study 10.2

AN UNSUCCESSFUL SUICIDE ATTEMPT

Ann was a very bright, attractive, personable, and energetic single woman who was 52 years old. She was an avid jogger and swimmer and was in excellent physical condition. As a physical therapist at a large metropolitan hospital, Ann specialized in working with patients who were severely disabled by strokes or spinal cord injuries. She worked with patients whom others despairingly referred to as "almost vegetables."

One spring, Ann checked into a general hospital for a complete head-to-toe medical checkup. She did not complain of any particular problem; she just told the physician that it was time for a checkup. Early in the morning of Ann's second day in the hospital, a nurse walking by saw Ann standing on the narrow sill outside her 15th-floor window. As she stood there, she was lifting herself up and down on her toes "like you do just before you take a dive." The nurse walked quietly up behind Ann, grabbed her, and pulled her back into the room. Ann was subsequently sent to a psychiatric hospital for evaluation.

Ann was annoyed that she was suspected of attempting to commit suicide. She said that she had been "trying to get some fresh air" and was simply doing her "breathing exercises" on the sill. She denied any thoughts of suicide and pointed out that because of her excellent condition and balance, there was no chance of her falling. The evaluation did not reveal any signs of psychopathology, and Ann, knowing hospital routines, was a helpful, compliant, model patient.

One aspect of Ann's record that concerned the hospital staff was that both her mother and her older sister had died of heart attacks in their mid-50s, an age that Ann was quickly approaching. It was suggested that Ann might believe that she would also experience a premature heart attack that would leave her in a condition like that of the patients with whom she worked daily. When Ann was questioned about that, she adamantly denied any such concerns and pointed out that if there was a potential problem, she had done the right thing by going into the hospital for a thorough checkup.

There was considerable debate among the hospital staff over whether or not Ann was in fact suicidal and what to do about it. Some argued that she had "too much ego strength" to commit suicide, others argued that "it takes a lot of ego strength to commit suicide," and others questioned how long this otherwise healthy patient could be kept in the hospital even if there was a consensus that she was suicidal. She was not willing to participate in therapy ("Why should I? I don't have a problem!"), and it did not seem reasonable to keep her locked up for the rest of her life.

While being evaluated, Ann had been assigned to an open ward, the door of which was watched by an attendant so that only patients with passes could leave. Three days after Ann's case conference, the attendant was briefly drawn away from the door by a scuffle between two adolescent patients, and during his brief absence, Ann walked quietly off the ward. She went directly to the center of the hospital, where there was a large circular staircase that went up four floors. She went up to the top floor, climbed up on the banister, and threw herself head first down the four-story stairwell. Ann landed on her back and broke her neck. She lived but was completely paralyzed from the neck down. Today Ann is a complete invalid, in the very state she sought to avoid through her suicide attempt.

---

interesting to note that in one investigation, it was found that about half of people who heard the suicide threats simply denied the importance of what they were hearing and did nothing (Rudestam, 1971). In some cases, the individuals who heard the threats actually *avoided* the suicidal individuals in the future. The other half of the individuals who heard the threats became appropriately concerned and either argued with the suicidal individuals or suggested that they seek help.

The notes left by individuals who commit suicide have attracted a lot of interest, and hundreds of such notes have been collected and analyzed (Cohen & Fiedler, 1974; Farberow & Simon, 1975; Shneidman & Farberow, 1957; Tuckman et al., 1959). Unfortunately, these notes add little to our understanding of suicide. For the most part, they are rather matter-of-fact state-

ments apologizing for the suicide, explaining why the suicide was necessary, saying good-bye to loved ones, and indicating the desired disposition of personal property. When the emotional content of one large sample of suicide notes was analyzed, it was found that 51% contained expressions of gratitude, affection, and concern for friends; 25% were completely neutral in terms of emotion; and 24% contained expressions of hostility and negative emotions (Tuckman et al., 1959).

Characteristics of Individuals Who Commit Suicide

Numerous attempts have been made to develop descriptions of the "typical" suicidal individual or to develop checklists to help identify individuals who are at

Derek Humphry wrote a book entitled Final Exit *in which he described numerous effective ways of committing suicide using readily available drugs. The book immediately became a best-seller.*

high risk. These attempts have rarely been effective for predicting individual cases because so many idiosyncratic factors enter into each case, and we must therefore be very careful in applying any of these profiles or formulas. However, some studies have provided us with general descriptions of individuals who are at risk for suicide, and they deserve some attention.

In one investigation, almost 3,000 depressed or suicidal inpatients were interviewed with regard to a wide variety of variables. Two years after the patients were discharged, a follow-up study was conducted to determine who had committed suicide (Motto et al., 1985). Analyses were then conducted to determine which variables were the best predictors of subsequent suicide; the results are presented in Table 10.3. In reviewing these variables, it is important to realize that most individuals who commit suicide do not have all or even most of these characteristics.

In addition to the characteristics noted in the table, membership in certain groups is also related to a higher risk of suicide. For example, adolescents, the elderly, alcoholics, individuals living alone, individuals from some Native American tribes, and professionals such as physicians, dentists, lawyers, and psychologists are also at higher risk for suicide (Schaar, 1974; Wekstein, 1979). We will discuss the causes for suicide in greater detail later, but the increased rate of suicide in these groups appears to be due to the fact that they experience higher levels of stress and depression or lack social support.

Seasons and Day of the Week

As early as 1897, a survey of numerous European countries revealed that without exception, the six warmest months had a higher suicide rate than the six coldest months (Durkheim, 1897/1951). The rate would rise slowly from January through June and then decrease. More recent findings are consistent with the earlier ones and indicate that suicides peak in the late spring or early summer. The reason for this pattern is not clear, but it may be that the optimism many people feel in the spring contrasts sharply with the depression and hopelessness felt by suicidal individuals. The contrast may heighten their despair and may increase the likelihood of suicide—but that is only a speculation.

Twenty years ago, suicides were not more likely to occur on any particular day, but now suicides are most likely to occur on Mondays (Maldonado & Kraus, 1991). The stress of "facing the workweek" may be responsible for the effect, and the change over time may be due to the increasing number of women in the work force. Finally, note that there is no consistent evi-

TABLE 10.3 PREDICTORS OF SUICIDE RISK

VARIABLE	HIGH-RISK CATEGORY
Age	Older
Occupation	Higher-status
Financial resources	More
Emotional disorder in family	Depression, alcoholism
Sexual orientation	Bisexual, homosexual
Previous psychiatric hospitalization	More admissions
Result of previous help	Negative or variable
Threatened financial loss	Yes
Special stress	Yes
Sleep	More sleep per night
Weight change	Gain or loss
Ideas of persecution	Yes
Suicidal impulses	Yes
Interviewer's reaction to person	Negative

Source: Adapted from Motto et al. (1985), p. 683, tab. 3.

TABLE 10.4   MYTHS ABOUT SUICIDE

People who talk about suicide won't commit suicide.

Untrue. Between 60% and 80% of persons who commit suicide have communicated their intent ahead of time.

Suicides and attempted suicides are in the same class of behavior.

Untrue. Some people are trying to kill themselves, while others may be making suicide gestures that are calls for help or attempts to communicate the depth of their despair. There may be different motivations, but all suicide-related behavior must be taken seriously.

Only very depressed persons commit suicide.

Untrue. Many people who commit suicide are depressed, but very depressed people often do not have enough energy to commit suicide, and often they commit suicide when they are getting better. Also, reaching the decision to commit suicide can relieve stress and depression, so people may appear less depressed just before committing suicide. Finally, suicide could be the result of a delusion, or it could be a well-thought-out solution to a problem unrelated to depression.

Protestants are more likely to commit suicide than Catholics.

Untrue. The evidence concerning this is mixed, but overall there does not appear to be a difference in rates in these religious groups.

Suicide rates are higher in rainy than sunny months.

Untrue. If anything, there is some evidence that suicide rates increase as spring arrives.

Suicidal tendencies are inherited.

Untrue. The fact that suicide "runs in families" is probably due to the fact that there is a genetic basis for some depressions, and depression is often a cause for suicide, or the fact that there is a genetic basis for low levels of serotonin, and low levels of serotonin are associated with suicide.

Source: Adapted in part from Pokorny (1968).

dence for the myth that suicides are related to the phases of the moon (Campbell & Beets, 1978).

Myths About Suicide

Table 10.4 contains a number of popular myths about suicide. Recognizing that these statements are not true is important because they can lead you to misinterpret or ignore early signs of suicide attempts, possibly with tragic consequences. We will consider the evidence refuting these myths later in this chapter.

■ PSYCHODYNAMIC EXPLANATIONS

Freud's View of Suicide

Freud once wrote that suicides could be regarded as disguised murders. In this view, the suicidal person's goal is not so much self-destruction as the destruction of another person, a lost object (person) with whom the person has identified. According to Freud, people who lose a loved object take the object in as part of themselves as a means of symbolically avoiding the loss (see discussion of causes of depression in Chapter 9). In addition to loving the object, however, they also hate the object for its desertion or rejection. (That anger turned inward is thought to be the cause of depression.) The suicide attempt may then be an expression of *aggression against the internalized object* rather than aggression against the self. For Freud, then, suicide was the ultimate act of anger turned inward. Because the person is not aware of the aggressive feelings toward the loved object, the person's suicidal feelings do not seem to have anything to do with the object or loss (Menninger, 1938).

Some clinicians have speculated that persons who have lost a parent during childhood seem to be especially at risk for depression and suicide. In those cases, grief and rage at parental "abandonment" is thought to be stored in the unconscious until a later experience of loss—romantic rejection, divorce, death of a loved one—triggers the release of pent-up pain and anger (Bowlby, 1973).

Freud also hypothesized that there was a **death instinct** that had the goal of returning the conflicted person to a state of calm and nonexistence from which he or she came. When the death instinct became stronger than the life instinct that usually held it in check, the result was suicide (Freud, 1920/1955).

Conflict, Stress, and Suicide

A more contemporary psychodynamic explanation for suicide is that people commit suicide to escape conflict and stress. A variety of investigations indicate that those who attempt suicide experience up to four times as many negative life events (for example, separations, major financial reversals, diagnoses of serious illnesses) just prior to their attempts than nonattempters in a comparable period of time (Cochrane & Robertson, 1975; Paykel et al., 1975; Slater & Depue, 1981).

Other evidence for the influence of stress on suicide is that during the Great Depression of the early 1930s, the suicide rate jumped from fewer than 10 per 100,000 to 17.4 per 100,000. Similarly, the rate of suicide increased during the economic recession of the 1970s (National Institute of Mental Health, 1976; Wekstein, 1979).

When considering the effects of stress on suicide, we should also consider the role played by social support in moderating the effects of stress. Individuals who attempt suicide often have less social support than nonattempters, suggesting that the absence of support intensifies the effects of stress (Braucht, 1979; Slater & Depue, 1981). Suicide attempters are often demographically dissimilar from their neighbors, so it appears that being a misfit could serve to isolate these individuals from needed sources of support. Finally, it is noteworthy that the stress experienced by individuals who commit suicide often involves losses such as deaths of relatives or friends that reduce social support.

Overall, then, there is no doubt that stress plays an important role in many suicides. However, two problems remain. First, not everyone who is exposed to stress commits suicide, so we must go on to consider the processes that might link stress to suicide for some individuals. Second, some individuals who commit suicide are not under stress, so we must also consider explanations for suicide other than stress.

Depression and Suicide

Depression plays a very important role in many suicides. It has been estimated that at least 80% of suicidal patients are depressed, and the rate of suicide among depressed individuals is 22 to 36 times higher than among nondepressed individuals (Kraft & Babigian, 1976; Robins & Guze, 1972; Slater & Depue, 1981). Depressed individuals commit suicide because from their perspective, life is not worth living. A frequent comment made by depressed individuals is "I wish I were dead."

The rate of suicide among depressed individuals would probably be even higher if it were not that many severely depressed patients simply do not have the energy to commit suicide. Because of this, many suicides occur after the individual begins to get better (Shneidman, 1979). The individuals are still depressed, but as they improve, they get more energy and are better able to carry out the suicidal act. For example, during the worst of her depression, one depressed woman sat motionless and simply stared into space (she was experiencing psychomotor retardation). When her depression began to lift and she started to move around, one of her first actions was to go to the bathroom and take an overdose of medication, which killed her.

As noted in our discussion of causes of depression, depression can result from stress or from physiological imbalances (low levels of norepinephrine or serotonin) that can occur in the absence of stress (see Chapter 9). It appears, then, that depression may mediate the relationship between stress and suicide. That is, stress leads to depression, which then leads to suicide. It also appears that physiologically caused depressions can help account for suicides that occur in the absence of stress. That is, low levels of norepinephrine or serotonin lead to depression, which then leads to suicide.

Fantasies and Suicide

From the psychodynamic standpoint, an important factor in determining whether someone will commit suicide is **fantasies** about what suicide will accomplish (Furst & Ostow, 1979). We shall discuss some of the fantasies that psychodynamic theorists deem most important.

Identification with the Lost Object.
In our discussion of the causes of depression, we pointed out that psychodynamic theorists believe that depression is triggered by a stressful loss. Some theorists suggest that depressed individuals attempt to regain the lost object (person) by identifying with it. If the object has been lost through death, the ultimate act of identification is one's own death, and thus it may be that attempts to identify with lost (dead) persons result in suicide. In support of that explanation, theorists have pointed to what are called "anniversary suicides," whereby an individual commits suicide on the anniversary of the other individual's death. An alternative explanation for anniversary suicides is that the anniversary brings back the individual's stress and despair, and the heightening of those factors leads to the suicide. Clearly, anniversaries of severe stresses are a time when increased social support is needed.

Rebirth.
Another fantasy that has been suggested as relevant for understanding suicide is the fantasy of being reborn after death without one's current problems. This fantasy gains support from religious beliefs concerning an afterlife or heaven. Indeed, in many religious funerals, the deceased individuals are described as having been relieved of their worldly burdens and having gone to a new life in a better place. (It is interesting to note, however, that in many religions, suicide is viewed as a sin, and the individual may be refused entry to heaven.) Consistent with this rebirth fantasy, one therapist reported that patients in a psychiatric hospital located next to a large river had the fantasy that they would "escape from this place, run out on the bridge, jump off and drown, and later come out alive and new on the other side" (Furst & Ostow, 1979).

Self-Punishment.
When we do things of which we do not approve, we often punish ourselves in a variety of little ways, such as depriving ourselves of some pleasure or treat. Psychodynamic theories suggest that in extreme cases, this self-punishment can result in suicide. They suggest that the "bad me" (associated with

the ego) and the "good me" (associated with the superego) get separated, and to punish the "bad me," the "good me" may kill the "bad me."

Revenge. Revenge may play a role in suicide in that it appears that some individuals commit suicide to make the people around them feel sorry and guilty. This motivation is often reflected in suicide notes that say, in effect, that "this would not have happened if you had not done thus and so." This is frequently seen in children who are powerless to attack the adults who control them. The children commit suicide in an attempt to get back at the adults. It is not uncommon for a child to think or say, "When I'm dead, you'll be sorry you weren't nicer to me!"

These are interesting speculations, and they often appear in discussions of suicide. However, so far there is little objective evidence consistently linking them to suicide, and therefore we must go on to consider alternative explanations.

LEARNING EXPLANATIONS

Rather than focusing on the underlying factors that cause an individual to want to commit suicide, learning theorists have focused their attention on the processes that facilitate committing suicide once the individual is motivated to do so. In that regard, learning theorists have pointed to the role played by *imitation* and *behavioral contagion*. We will consider those processes, and we will also consider the possibility that suicidal gestures may be carried out because they are a means of getting *rewards* (attention).

Imitation

The basic premise of the learning explanation is that suicide occurs in large part because of **imitation**. When faced with problems, an individual may hear of another individual's suicide, and that may suggest suicide as a solution. The other individual's suicide may also suggest an effective way of committing suicide.

Evidence for the effects of imitation on suicidal behavior is provided by the fact that suicide rates increase dramatically following reports of suicides on television or in newspapers (Bollen & Phillips, 1982; Phillips, 1974; see review by Stack, 1990). Examples of this are provided in Table 10.5, where you will find the dates of seven suicides that were reported on nationally televised evening news programs. With each date is the number of individuals who committed suicide in the United States during the following week and during a comparable control week that was not preceded by the report of a suicide. Those data indicate that the number of suicides increased by 7% after a nationally publicized suicide, resulting in 244 additional suicides. Other research has shown that levels of publicity given to suicides were related to the levels of subsequent suicides (more publicity, more suicides) and that the effect was limited to the geographic area receiving the publicity (Phillips, 1974).

The effect of imitation on suicide is probably stronger than the data in Table 10.5 suggest because those data reflect only overt cases of suicide. Data from other investigations indicate that motor vehicle fatalities increase following well-publicized suicides (Bollen & Phillips, 1981; Phillips, 1977, 1979), and it is likely that the accidents in which the individuals were killed were actually disguised or covert suicides.

It is interesting to note that suicides following publicized suicides come in two waves. There is a surge of suicides on the day of the report and the following day, then there is a lull, and finally there is another surge on the 6th and 7th days after the report. That has been the case for both overt and covert suicides (Bollen & Phillips, 1982; Phillips, 1977). These findings suggest that there may be two types of suicide re-

TABLE 10.5   INCREASES IN SUICIDES FOLLOWING STORIES ABOUT SUICIDES ON TELEVISION EVENING NEWS PROGRAMS

DATE OF STORY	SUICIDES AFTER STORY	SUICIDES DURING CONTROL PERIOD	DIFFERENCE
April 25, 1972	554	444	110
June 4, 1973	528	435	93
September 11, 1973	487	514	−27
July 15, 1974	482	462	20
April 11, 1975	593	572	21
September 3, 1975	553	501	52
May 13, 1976	550	575	−25
Totals	3,747	3,503	244

Source: Adapted from Bollen and Phillips (1982), p. 804, tab. 1.

Suicides sometimes occur in clusters because when one person commits suicide it can reduce the restraints in other people against committing suicide. This is called behavioral contagion. *Shown here is the cemetery in Plano, Texas, the town in which one such cluster occurred.*

sponders. Those who respond immediately may be more impulsive or have already contemplated suicide, and the publicized suicide may have only hastened an act that would have occurred anyway. In contrast, those who respond after 6 days may be making a more considered response or may not have seriously contemplated suicide as a solution prior to the example provided by the publicized suicide.

An interesting but unfortunate example of the effects of imitation on suicide is seen in the "epidemics" or clusters of suicide that occur among adolescents (Gould et al., 1989). In numerous instances, one adolescent has committed suicide, followed by a number of his or her peers, often using the same or a similar procedure. For example, in 1983, Bill Ramsey was killed in a drag-racing accident. Two days later, Bruce Corwin, Ramsey's best friend, said he would see Bill again "some sunny day" and then committed suicide by running his car in a closed garage. Six days later, Glen Curry, another 18-year-old, committed suicide in the same way. That was followed by the suicide of Henri Droit, who was not a friend of the others, but it was later discovered that he had newspaper articles about the previous suicides on his bulletin board at home. In addition to these four successful suicides, there were 12 unsuccessful suicide attempts in the following 8 weeks.

Occasional attempts have been made to prevent suicidal imitation. For example, to end a rash of sensational suicides in subways (individuals throwing themselves in the way of trains), news reporters agreed to stop publicizing the suicides. The reduction of publicity was associated with a reduction in those specific suicides (Etzersdorfer et al, 1992).

Behavioral Contagion

Simply getting the idea to commit suicide is rarely enough to result in the act. Even if an individual wants very much to do it, there are cultural restraints against committing suicide ("It is wrong to commit suicide," "Nice people don't commit suicide"). However, those restraints can be overcome through the process of **behavioral contagion** (Wheeler, 1966). Behavioral contagion occurs when (a) an individual wants to do something, (b) is restrained from doing it because society says that the behavior is wrong, (c) sees someone else do it and "get away with it," and then (d) thinks that he or she can get away with it also. Examples of behavioral contagion include crossing the street against the traffic light and smoking in no-smoking areas when others do so first. (Contagion differs from imitation in that contagion reduces restraints against performing a known behavior, whereas imitation simply introduces a new behavior.)

The concept of behavioral contagion is useful in understanding suicides, especially epidemics of suicide. Fortunately, behavioral contagion does not reduce all restraints, and thus its effect is limited. Observing others commit prohibited acts can reduce *external* restraints that stem from social rules, but it is relatively ineffective for reducing *internal* restraints that stem from one's own beliefs (Ritter & Holmes, 1968). This means that contagion would occur if the individual was originally restrained by the fact that society says that suicide is wrong, but contagion would not occur if the individual was restrained by the personal belief that suicide was wrong.

Hearing about suicides plays an important role in increasing their incidence, but hearing about suicides is not itself a sufficient explanation for suicide. Like other explanations, the learning explanation provides part, but not all, of the answer to the question of why people commit suicide.

Reward

Suicide threats and gestures are often calls for help, but they may also be operant behaviors used to manipulate others and get **rewards** (Bostock & Williams, 1975). In one case, a man began threatening to kill himself when a woman he had been dating broke off the relationship and refused to see him. He wrote to her saying, "Without you, there is nothing in life for me. Unless there is a chance that you will see me, I will end it all." At first, the woman gave in because the threats frightened her, but they were not a basis for a relationship, so she eventually told the police of his threats and stopped seeing him. Individuals who use suicide threats to manipulate others pose difficult problems because if we attempt to extinguish the behavior by ignoring it, we run the risk that the individual will succeed at suicide, accident or intent.

■ COGNITIVE EXPLANATIONS
- -

Some people who lack adequate problem-solving skills are cognitively unprepared to cope with their problems. The cognitive explanation for suicide suggests that when such people must face stress-provoking problems, they develop an attitude of hopelessness and eventually commit suicide because they see no other alternative. In this explanation, *poor problem-solving skills* and *hopelessness* provide the link between stress and suicide.

Poor Problem Solving

Research has demonstrated that suicidal individuals have **poor problem-solving skills** when compared to nonsuicidal individuals (Orbach et al., 1990; Patsiokas et al., 1979; Schotte & Clum, 1987). Specifically, suicidal individuals suffer from **cognitive rigidity**, which means that they lack the flexibility to see alternative solutions for their problems. In one study, suicidal and nonsuicidal psychiatric patients were asked to list alternative uses for a number of common items such as pencils and paper clips. The suicidal patients came up with 60% fewer uses than the nonsuicidal patients (Schotte & Clum, 1987). Furthermore, when each patient was reminded of an interpersonal problem from

real life and was asked to generate solutions for it, the suicidal patients generated fewer than half as many solutions as nonsuicidal patients and rated them as less likely to be effective.

The inability to solve problems because of cognitive rigidity can have a number of serious implications. First, people who are unable to solve problems will experience more failures, and that increases the stress on them. Second, the inability to solve problems leads to feelings of hopelessness, which, as we will see, is closely related to suicide. Third, once cognitively rigid individuals decide on suicide as a solution for their problems, they will pursue only that solution and not consider or develop other, better solutions. For example, a poor problem solver who is faced with financial difficulties may not be able to come up with an effective solution and may simply repeat the actions that led to the difficult situation in the first place. That may cause increased stress and feelings of hopelessness or depression and, with no solution in sight, encourage suicide. However, one qualification must be noted with regard to this explanation. Although in some cases poor problem solving may lead to stress, hopelessness, depression, and suicide, it is also possible that hopelessness and depression could lead to the poor problem solving. As noted earlier, depression does lead to poorer cognitive functioning (see Chapter 8), and there is now evidence that short-term changes in hopelessness and depression lead to short-term changes in problem-solving ability (Schotte et al., 1990). That is, at least for some persons, poor problem solving may be dependent on their state of depression rather than an enduring trait.

Hopelessness

The other important factor in the cognitive explanation for suicide is **hopelessness** (Beck et al., 1990; Ivanoff & Jang, 1991). Hopelessness is a component of depression, but depressed individuals can feel more or less hopeless, and the degree to which an individual feels hopeless is closely related to suicidal behavior. In fact, hopelessness is a better predictor of suicidal intent than depression in general. It has also been found that as hopelessness increases, so do thoughts about suicide and intentions to commit suicide (Beck et al., 1974; Beck et al., 1985; Minkoff et al., 1973; Motto, 1977; Wetzel, 1977). Table 10.6 contains some of the items from the questionnaire that is usually used to measure hopelessness. Those items will give you some understanding of what is meant by hopelessness and why individuals who answer yes are more likely to commit suicide.

The important role that hopelessness plays in suicide was demonstrated in a study in which 207 inpa-

TABLE 10.6   SAMPLE ITEMS FROM THE HOPELESSNESS SCALE (HIGH
SCORES ARE RELATED TO SUICIDE)

I might as well give up because I can't make things better for myself.
My future seems dark to me.
I just don't get the breaks, and there's no reason to believe I will in the future.
All I can see ahead of me is unpleasantness rather than pleasantness.
Things just won't work out the way I want them to.
It is very unlikely that I will get any real satisfaction in the future.
There's no use in really trying to get something I want because I probably won't
get it.

Source: Beck et al. (1974), p. 862, tab. 1.

tients who had taken the Hopelessness Scale were followed up 5 to 10 years later to determine which ones had committed suicide (Beck et al., 1985). Of the 14 patients who had committed suicide, 13 had scores of 10 or greater on the Hopelessness Scale. These results clearly reflect the role of hopelessness in suicide.

In one test of the cognitive model of suicide, investigators examined the levels of hopelessness and thoughts about suicide in individuals who experienced high or low life stress and who had good or bad problem-solving skills (Schotte & Clum, 1982). The results indicated, first, that individuals under high stress felt more hopeless and thought more about suicide than individuals under low stress. Second and more important, it was the individuals who were under high stress *and* who had poor problem-solving skills who felt most hopeless and thought most about suicide. The results concerning suicidal thoughts are presented in Figure 10.4. Overall, then, there is consistent and strong evidence that stress and poor problem solving are related to feelings of hopelessness and that hopelessness is in turn related to suicidal thoughts and behavior.

Delusions and Hallucinations

It is noteworthy that the rate of suicide among persons who suffer from schizophrenia is relatively high (Roy, 1983). In one study of 264 individuals who had been hospitalized with schizophrenia, it was found that the suicide rate was 10.6% among men and 4.7% among women (Westermeyer et al., 1991). The elevated rate of suicide in persons with schizophrenia may be due to at least three factors. First, such persons may have **delusions** that lead them to kill themselves. For example, persons with schizophrenia may believe that they are the devil and do not deserve to live, that they are cornered by foreign agents and must escape by poisoning themselves, or that they must kill themselves so

There is strong evidence that stress and poor problem-solving skills are related to feelings of hopelessness, which in turn are related to suicidal thoughts and behavior.

FIGURE 10.4   INDIVIDUALS WHO ARE UNDER HIGH
STRESS AND WHO HAVE POOR
PROBLEM-SOLVING SKILLS THINK
MOST ABOUT SUICIDE.

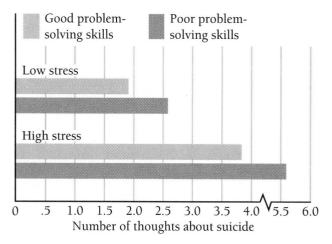

Source: Adapted in part from Schotte and Clum (1982), p. 693, tab. 2.

that they can rejoin God. Second, individuals with schizophrenia may have auditory **hallucinations** (voices) telling them to kill themselves. Finally, **despair** over their condition may lead to suicide.

Delusions and hallucinations are cognitive explanations for suicide, but those explanations are qualitatively different from the cognitive explanations based on problem-solving abilities and hopelessness. It thus appears that suicide can stem from two different classes of cognitions: (a) normal cognitions involving problem-solving skills and hopelessness and (b) abnormal cognitions involving delusions and hallucinations. It is interesting to note that stressful life events and hopelessness are related to suicide in persons who do not have schizophrenia, but those factors are not associated with suicides among persons with schizophrenia (Breier & Astrachan, 1984; Minkoff et al., 1973).

Cognitive Reasons for Not Committing Suicide

We have seen that a variety of cognitive factors contribute to suicide (poor problem-solving skills, hopelessness, hallucinations, delusions), but it is important to note that there are also a number of cognitive factors that make suicide less likely in people who are otherwise likely to commit suicide (Dyck, 1991; Linehan et al., 1983). Here is a list of six factors that have been shown to reduce suicidal intent, each followed by sample questions that are used to measure that factor.

1. *Survival and coping beliefs.* "I still have many things left to do." "No matter how badly I feel, I know that it will not last."
2. *Responsibility to family.* "It would hurt my family too much, and I would not want them to suffer." "My family depends on me and needs me."
3. *Child-related concerns.* "The effect on my children would be harmful." "It would not be fair to leave the children for others to take care of."
4. *Fear of suicide.* "I am a coward and do not have the guts to do it." "I am afraid that my method of killing myself would fail."
5. *Fear of social disapproval.* "I would not want other people to think I did not have control over my life." "I am concerned about what others would think of me."
6. *Moral objections.* "My religious beliefs forbid it." "I am afraid of going to hell."

Note that the positive cognitions about survival and coping are just the flip side of the hopelessness that was discussed earlier (if you have positive beliefs about survival and coping, you cannot be hopeless), but the other cognitions are relatively independent of hopelessness.

Finally, it should be noted that one other important reason why some individuals do not commit suicide is that they *lack an effective means by which to do it.* For example, accessibility of guns is related to the suicide rate; if guns are not available, suicide rates are lower (Clarke & Lester, 1989; Kellermann et al., 1992). Other factors that have been linked to reductions in suicide include the introduction of exhaust emission controls that reduced the poisonous carbon monoxide that comes from automobiles (Clarke & Lester, 1989), the detoxification of home heating gas (Lester, 1990), and lower heights of buildings (Marzuk et al., 1992). An elderly and very ill man in a hospital commented to me, "I want to die and I would commit suicide, but locked up in here, *I can't find a way to do it.*"

Overall, it appears that some individuals feel hopeless and consider suicide, but they do not attempt it because of the offsetting effects of cognitions about responsibility to family and children, fear of suicide, fear of social disapproval, moral objections, or the lack of effective means. The presence of these cognitions and options helps us understand why not everyone who feels hopeless commits suicide.

■ PHYSIOLOGICAL EXPLANATIONS

Levels of Serotonin

Some of the most interesting new findings concerning suicide revolve around the neurotransmitter **serotonin**. Specifically, *low levels of serotonin are associated with suicide* (Mann et al., 1992; see reviews by Korn et al., 1990; Rifai et al., 1992; Roy, 1990; Stanley & Stanley, 1989). In one of the classic studies on this topic that was done with depressed patients, it was found that only some of the patients had low levels of serotonin, but it was the patients with low levels of serotonin who were more likely to have attempted suicide (40% vs. 15%; Asberg et al., 1976). Furthermore, it was the patients with low levels of serotonin who were most likely to use violent means of attempting suicide.

We know that low levels of serotonin can cause depression (see Chapter 9), and therefore we might assume that the serotonin-suicide relationship is simply mediated by depression; that is, low levels of serotonin lead to depression, and then the depression leads to the suicide. That may be the case with some individuals, but serotonin must do something more because low levels of *both* serotonin and norepinephrine lead to depression, but suicide is higher among individuals with low levels of serotonin. Furthermore, it has been found that when patients were given drugs that increased levels of serotonin or norepinephrine, the drugs that increased serotonin levels were more effective for reducing suicide than those that increased norepinephrine (Sacchetti et al., 1991). Clearly, low levels of serotonin are linked to suicide.

The characteristic about serotonin that is important to our understanding here is that low levels lead to *aggression* as well as depression (Higley et al., 1992; Kruesi et al., 1992; see reviews by Brown & Goodwin, 1986; Van Praag, 1986). For example, in one study of men in the military, it was found that 80% of the differences in their levels of aggression could be accounted for by differences in their levels of serotonin; lower serotonin was associated with more aggression (Brown et al., 1979). Actually, low levels of serotonin do not lead to an increase in aggressive drive. Instead, normal levels of serotonin serve to *inhibit* aggressive or punished responses, and when the levels of serotonin drop, the inhibition lifts, and the aggressive or punished responses are used (Sanger & Blackman, 1976; Tye et al., 1979). Overall then, the process that apparently links serotonin to suicide is as follows: A low level of serotonin causes an increase in depression and a decrease in the inhibition of responses, so when the depression leads to thoughts of self-destruction, there is not enough inhibition of self-destructive behavior, and the individual attempts suicide.

Having established that low levels of serotonin are linked to suicide, the question arises, what causes the low levels of serotonin? There are two explanations. First, *stress* can cause a reduction in the levels of serotonin (see Chapter 9), and as we learned earlier, suicidal individuals experience as many as four times as many stressful life events as nonsuicidal individuals. Thus the stress-depression-suicide relationship can be mediated by lowered levels of serotonin. In that case, the relationship would actually be *stress-serotonin-depression-suicide.* Second, low levels of serotonin can be *inherited* (see Chapter 9), and that inheritance can be used to account for serotonin-depression-suicide relationship in individuals who are not exposed to stress. In that case, the relationship would be *genes-serotonin-depression-suicide.* In view of the role that genetic factors might play in suicide, it will be instructive to consider the evidence linking genetics and suicide.

Genetic Factors

Studies of Families.
In seeking to determine whether inheritance plays a role in suicide, some investigators have examined the family histories of suicidal individuals. Their results consistently indicate that the incidence of suicide among the relatives of suicidal individuals is substantially higher than the rate among the relatives of nonsuicidal individuals (Farberow & Simon, 1969; Roy, 1982; Stengel, 1964). One investigator found that 49% of the patients who attempted suicide had a family history of suicide (Roy, 1983). These results suggest a genetic influence, but of course it is also possible that the effects were due to social modeling, so we must go on to consider other evidence.

Studies of Twins.
The occurrence of suicide in monozygotic and dizygotic twins has been examined in two investigations (Haberlandt, 1967; Roy et al., 1991). Among the 113 sets of monozygotic twins in the two studies, the concordance rate was 14%, whereas among the 212 sets of dizygotic twins, the concordance rate was less than 1%. In other words, when the twins had identical genes, the concordance rate was about 15 times higher than when they had different genes, thus providing evidence for a genetic influence on suicide. These results are summarized in Figure 10.5.

Studies of Adoptees.
In a study based on the adoptee method, the investigators found that among the relatives of children who were adopted and later committed suicide, the suicide rate among the adoptees' *biological* relatives was 4.5%, whereas the suicide rate among the adoptees' *adoptive* relatives was 0% (Schulsinger et al., 1979).

Clearly, there is evidence for a genetic influence on suicide. In considering these findings, however, it should not be concluded that there is a gene for suicide. Instead, it is probable that genetic factors lead to low levels of serotonin, which lead to depression and reduced inhibition for self-destructive acts.

FIGURE 10.5 THE CONCORDANCE RATE FOR SUICIDE IS ALMOST 15 TIMES HIGHER IN MONOZYGOTIC THAN DIZYGOTIC TWINS.

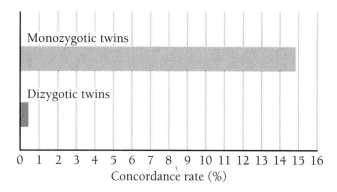

Sources: Haberlandt (1967); Roy et al. (1991).

Many of the factors that have been shown to contribute to suicide are reflected in the background and experiences of the young man who is discussed in Case Study 10.3.

SUICIDE AS A POSITIVE RATIONAL ACT

Throughout this discussion, suicide has been viewed, implicitly if not explicitly, as a negative act, as abnormal behavior, as something that should be prevented. In many cases that is certainly the case, but we should at least consider the possibility that in some cases suicide may be a positive act that reflects a reasonable and rational judgment (Humphry, 1992; Lester, 1989; Richman, 1992). Probably the clearest examples of suicide as a positive act occur when individuals are going through excruciating pain while dying of a terminal illness. For them, there is terrible pain but no hope, and an earlier painless death might seem a reasonable alternative. Actually, in situations like that, we now legally sanction what might be called "passive suicide" in that we respect living wills (agreements that medical procedures will not be used to prolong life in a terminally ill individual). In those cases, death comes because treatment is withheld, but in some cases withholding treatment may not result in death, or at least not for a long time or after a lot of pain. In cases like that and for individuals who are not able to commit suicide without help, groups such as the Hemlock Society advocate "assisted suicide" (sometimes called *voluntary euthanasia*). Assisted suicide is illegal in most countries, but it is practiced in various European countries where, contrary to the concerns of its opponents, it has not resulted in inappropriate or widespread use.

The situation becomes even less clear in cases in which the individual is not terminally ill or in great pain but for some rational reason has decided that the time for death has come. This is most likely to occur in older adults who have lived their lives and sense the beginning of a decline in their health and their ability to function. Not wanting to go through the decline, dependence, and degradation that often comes with old age and deteriorating health, they elect to end their lives. In those cases, the decision to die is based on a risk-benefit analysis. That is, the individual weighs the risk of losing some remaining good years against the benefit of ensuring not having to go through some of the terrors and suffering of old age. Is suicide a rational act in those cases?

Case Study 10.4 (p. 234) was written by the son of a woman who elected to die despite the fact that her life could have been saved and she might have had

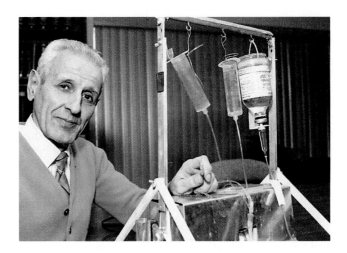

Are there situations in which suicide is a rational and positive act? Michigan physician Jack Kevorkian has created a tremendous controversy by helping several terminally ill people commit suicide with his "suicide machines."

some productive years ahead. This case falls in the large gray area in the definition of what behavior is appropriate and what behavior constitutes suicide. Did this woman commit suicide? Did she make a rational and reasonable decision? Can suicide be a rational and reasonable decision in some cases? Did the woman in Case Study 10.4 commit suicide? Should she have been diagnosed as a "danger to herself," committed to a hospital as a psychiatric patient, and treated against her will (part of which treatment would have been the coronary surgery)? Or was she a strong woman with strong beliefs about her own personal control of her destiny who simply took control of the situation—*her* situation? Is signing a living will an act of suicide? Are there situations in which suicide is a reasonable, rational, positive act? These questions have far-reaching philosophical, theological, and legal implications that are beyond resolution here, but they are questions of which you should be aware. These questions have implications for how we view suicide, and they are questions that you may have to face someday, for yourself or for someone you love.

SUMMARY

In this chapter, we dealt with two major topics, the bipolar mood disorder and suicide. The bipolar disorder (formerly called manic-depressive disorder) involves disturbances of mood in which the individual alternates between periods of mania and depression. This disorder is much less common than the depressive (unipolar) mood disorder, and equal numbers of men and women are afflicted. The bipolar and unipo-

Case Study 10.3

SUICIDE IN A 27-YEAR-OLD MALE GRADUATE STUDENT

Chuck was a mature, upper-middle-class 27-year-old graduate student in chemistry. After graduating from college, he married a woman he had dated for 2 years and took a job with a large chemical company. Although he did very well at his job, he became dissatisfied. He attributed his unhappiness to the fact that without more education, he could not move up in the company. With his wife's support, he quit his job and returned to graduate school to get a master's degree.

Graduate school was demanding and often stressful. Although his grades were excellent and his professors cited him as one of the most promising students, Chuck began to wonder whether he had what it took to "make it." More important, he began to wonder whether he wanted to make it. He frequently asked himself, "Was it all worth it?" He continued to do well in his coursework, but he seemed to lose his sense of direction and found it increasingly difficult to enjoy himself. His worry about keeping up in school, in combination with his self-doubts about his future, led him to become anxious, moody, and depressed, and he became increasingly difficult to live with. After about a year, he and his wife separated. She was opposed to the separation and wanted to stay together to work on the problem and help him. However, as his depression deepened, Chuck easily became angry and wanted to be left alone. Figuratively, he pushed her away. His wife moved back to her parents' home in a distant city, and Chuck moved into a small apartment, where he lived alone.

When Chuck started missing many of his classes and stopped going to the laboratory, his professors insisted that he "see someone for help." Chuck saw no point in it ("I'm not crazy. I just don't know what I want to do. I'm behind and unhappy, not crazy!"), but under pressure from his professors, he finally went to a psychiatrist.

During the first few sessions with the psychiatrist, Chuck admitted that he sometimes got quite depressed and that he was having difficulty sleeping through the night. He also acknowledged that sometimes he would spontaneously say to himself, "I wish I were dead" or "Life is terrible." Chuck occasionally talked about suicide in the abstract, but he denied that he was seriously considering suicide. When discussing suicide, it came out that his mother had once attempted suicide when he was about 12. He knew that she had subsequently received some psychiatric help, but he was too young at the time to know what had been done for her, and she had been killed about 4 years later when a car she was driving ran off the road.

The psychiatrist prescribed a tricyclic antidepressant for Chuck, but after 2 weeks of taking it, his depression had not improved. Chuck stopped taking the drug against the advice of the psychiatrist, who felt that not enough time had elapsed to give the drug a chance to have an effect. With the depression getting worse, the psychiatrist became concerned and recommended that Chuck voluntarily check into a psychiatric hospital where other treatments could be tried and where he could be more closely supervised. Chuck objected but agreed that he would think about hospitalization over the next couple of days and that they would discuss it again at their meeting the following Thursday.

Sitting on his bed that night, Chuck placed the end of a shotgun in his mouth and pulled the trigger.

---

lar disorders share the symptoms of depression, but because of the differences in related demographic factors, it is now believed that they are separate disorders. It was originally thought that manic episodes reflected flights from depression, but it is now generally agreed that the bipolar disorder is due primarily to physiological imbalances (e.g., changes in levels of neurotransmitters or changes in neuron sensitivity that influence levels of neurological activity). There is now strong evidence that the physiological imbalances that cause the mood swings in the bipolar disorder are due to genetic problems.

Next we discussed suicide. Suicide rates increase with age, with the highest rate occurring after the age of 65. The greatest increase is among white males. It is widely believed that the rate for suicide in general is increasing and that suicides among young people are showing the greatest increase, but these increases may actually be due to an increased willingness to admit that a death was a suicide rather than labeling it an accident. However, despite the increased willingness to admit to suicide, the figures still underestimate the true rate because many suicides are covert. It is difficult to come up with a profile of an individual who will commit suicide, but high-risk factors include age, history of depression, and stress. Suicides are most likely to occur in spring or early summer, and Monday now tends to be the day of highest risk.

Freud suggested that suicide is related to the release of aggressive feelings toward a lost object that has been taken in as part of the self. He also suggested

Case Study 10.4

"IT'S BEEN A GREAT LIFE. GOOD-BYE, WORLD."

Mother was a small, active woman of 72 who could pass for much younger. She exercised regularly, took classes at the university each semester, did volunteer work reading books onto tapes for visually impaired persons, and she had a part-time job in the student union. (She took the job because she liked to be as independent as possible and because she liked the contact with the young students.) She was happy and described her current life as "the best years of my life."

One day while at the union, Mother experienced severe pains in her chest and left arm. She immediately recognized the pains as signs of a heart attack. Thinking she was going to die, she looked up and said, "It's been a great life. Good-bye, World." Mother was rushed to the hospital, and as she was wheeled into the emergency room, she admonished the nurse, "I have a living will! Don't do anything extraordinary for me. I don't want some machine keeping me alive!"

Mother recovered from the heart attack, but all was not well. An angiogram revealed that she had 90% blockages in five major coronary arteries. Her physician came to her hospital room and explained the problem to her, went on to point out that the problem could be overcome with major bypass surgery, and told her that he had already made arrangements for the surgery. Mother listened attentively, and when he was through, she said quietly but firmly, "Thank you, but I don't think I'll have the operation."

"But Margaret, you don't understand. If you don't have the operation, you'll die."

"I understand," she replied, "but I am ready to die, and there are three reasons I don't want the operation. First, all I would be buying with the operation is time—time to wait to die of something else that might be more painful and difficult. I've seen too many of my friends struggle with things like cancer. . . . I've started to decline, and I am going to stop it here. I'm going to die, and a heart attack seems like the best of the alternatives. Second, I've lived my life, and it's been a good life. I've done most of the things I wanted to do, my children and grandchildren are grown, and this is a good time to go. Oh, sure, there are some things I'd like to do, but on balance, I'm ready. Third, I don't want to become a burden to anyone. The operation, the recuperation in a nursing home, and the limitations on my activities after that will put a strain on everyone, and I don't want that. Also, this whole thing will wind up costing a lot of money. I know that insurance will pay for most of it, but why spend that kind of money on me at this point in time? It just doesn't make sense; others need those resources more than I do."

The physician argued with her, and finally Mother took his hand as if to console him and said, "No, Doctor, you don't understand because you're not where I am. You're 50 years old; you're healthy; you have many important things to do—you have lots of living left. I'm 72; life is good and I am happy, but my health is obviously failing, I'm going to begin to decline, and this is a good time to wind it up. I really don't have much in front of me, and I'd rather go now while I am ahead. No, Doctor, I'm going to check out of the hospital and go home. For years I've been very careful about my diet and I've denied myself what I've wanted, but tonight if I want butter on my potato, I'll put *real butter* on it, and if I want chocolate cake for desert, I'll have *two* pieces."

Mother checked out of the hospital that evening, went home, and continued doing "her thing." She wasn't happy about this turn of events, and in letters to friends she mused over things that she would have to leave undone, but she concluded that on balance she was making the right decision.

About 5 days after Mother left the hospital, she had another attack. She sat and waited to die, but the pain became unbearable, so she finally had to call the hospital and go to the emergency room. The physician and I met her there, and he explained that if we acted quickly, the bypass surgery could still be done. Mother declined and asked how much time "the process" would take and whether the pain could be controlled. Shaking his head with dismay the physician told her that without the operation, she would probably live only another day or so and that, yes, the pain could be controlled with morphine. Mother quipped with a grin, "Morphine—gee, I get to be a junkie before I go—another new experience!"

Mother was taken to the intensive care unit, where she was hooked to a morphine pump and a vital signs monitor. We spent that evening and the next day talking and reminiscing. As the time went by, the level of morphine had to be increased, and consequently Mother would occasionally drift off to sleep. When a nurse would come in to check on her, she would wake up, we would talk some more, and then she would drift off again. Late that night, I sat by Mother's bed holding her hand and watching the heart rate monitor. Finally, her heart began to slow, gave a few erratic beats, and then stopped. Mother had died. As I looked at her and wept, I thought of how much I loved her, how much I would miss her, and how *proud* I was of her. Mother had been a positive woman who had remained in control. She had died with as little pain and as much dignity as possible. She arranged her death so that she was not a burden to others, and by saving resources, she contributed to others who she thought needed them more.

As I said earlier, I was very proud of Mother, and it did not occur to me until sometime later that in a technical sense, *Mother had committed suicide.* Suicide—we usually think of that as a desperate act of a hopeless person. Maybe we need to rethink our conception of suicide and death with dignity.

---

that the death instinct could result in suicide. More contemporary psychodynamic explanations focus on conflict, stress, and depression as causes of suicide. From a learning perspective, suicide is thought to stem from imitation and behavioral contagion. Suicide threats can also be effective for manipulating others and getting rewards. The cognitive explanations for suicide revolve around poor problem-solving skills, feelings of hopelessness, delusions, and hallucinations.

Cognitive factors such as concerns about family responsibilities, social disapproval, and moral objections can serve to inhibit suicidal behavior. Suicides are also inhibited by the lack of effective means to accomplish the act. From a physiological standpoint, suicide is linked to low levels of serotonin, which may be due to stress or genetic factors. We concluded the chapter by raising the question of whether in some cases suicide might be a positive rational act.

KEY TERMS, CONCEPTS, AND NAMES

In reviewing and testing yourself on what you have learned from this chapter, you should be able to identify and discuss each of the following:

behavioral contagion
bipolar disorder
cognitive rigidity
covert suicide
death instinct
delusions
despair

fantasies (concerning suicide)
hallucinations
hopelessness
imitation
lithium carbonate
mania
mood disorder with psychotic features

poor problem-solving skills
rapid cycling rewards
secondary mania
serotonin
suicide
suicide gesture

Chapter 11
Treatment of Mood Disorders

• O U T L I N E •

Carla has been very depressed since her father died last year. She now sees a therapist once a week. During her sessions, she talks about what her father meant to her and how lost and vulnerable she feels without him. Often she will reflect on childhood experiences, good and bad, in which her relationship with her father was molded. Her therapist says relatively little during the sessions but will occasionally ask a question to help Carla explore an issue that she overlooked or avoided. The therapist will also help her clarify her feelings by pointing out similarities or conflicts between things she says or feels. In general, however, her therapist is nondirective, and the actual work of psychotherapy is Carla's responsibility. Through this psychodynamic therapy, Carla is gaining a better understanding of the relationship she had with her father, learning why losing him was so traumatic, and developing mature methods of coping with the loss and stress. It may be a long process, but Carla feels that she is making progress and that she is getting better at dealing with her problems.

The therapist speculated that Mike's depression stemmed from the fact that there were too few rewards and too many punishments in Mike's life. As a first step in correcting that, Mike was asked to make lists of the things he found rewarding and punishing. Next, Mike and the therapist set up a program of goals that could be reasonably achieved, and each goal was paired with a reward. For example, now when Mike completes a report, he rewards himself with a movie. (Before he would have just gone on to work on the next report.) Mike and his therapist also developed ways of reducing some of the unpleasant parts of Mike's life. One thing that bothered him was saying no to people who asked him to do things. He just did not have the courage to say no, and consequently he was overwhelmed with responsibilities, which really got him down. To help with that, the therapist gave Mike assertiveness training so that he would be able to say no and social skills training so that he could say no without offending. Mike's life is a lot more pleasant now, and he feels much better about himself and his future.

Joan had a low self-concept and was depressed. Every time she faced a task, her first thought was, "I can't do that. I'll probably fail and make a fool of myself. I'm never going to be successful or happy!" She just never gave herself a chance. To overcome these automatic self-defeating thoughts, she and her therapist first conducted several experiments to see whether or not she really was incompetent and ineffective. When they revealed that she was not, she and her therapist began a program of replacing the automatic negative thoughts with more accurate thoughts. The program also involved activities in which she would act effectively in accordance with her new positive thoughts. The activities provided her with new behavior patterns and evidence that the positive thoughts were accurate. Joan feels better about herself and is less depressed. Now whenever she thinks a negative thought, she stops and asks herself whether the thought is realistic.

When Ann became depressed, her physician prescribed an antidepressant medication known as a *tricyclic*. Ann was warned that it would probably be 2 or 3 weeks before the medication would begin reducing the depression.

When she first started taking the medication, she had some annoying side effects such as dizziness, slightly blurred vision, and fatigue, so the dosage level had to be reduced somewhat. Four weeks after beginning the medication, her depression is gone, and she and her physician are working to reduce the dosage to the point at which she can take as little as possible and still keep the depression under control. They also plan "medication holidays" during which she will not take any medication to see if she can get along without it.

Although nothing particularly important had changed in his life, a little over a year ago, Fred became very depressed and could not snap out of it. Neither talking about his feelings nor antidepressant drugs seemed to help much. Three weeks ago, he began a course of *electroconvulsive therapy* in which twice a week he received a 140-volt shock for half a second along the right side of his brain. The shock causes a brief convulsion. After six shocks, his depression has lifted. Before treatment, he was told that the treatment caused a loss of some memories for some patients, but that has not occurred with Fred. He admits that the first time he went in for treatment, he was frightened, but he points out that he is not conscious during the procedure and that now "it's not a big deal."

Paul suffers from a bipolar disorder that takes him from wild periods of mania to desperate periods of depression. When he was brought to the hospital by police after one of his manic periods, he was given *lithium carbonate*. Within 3 days, his mood had stabilized, and he was released from the hospital. Paul now takes time-release lithium pills every day, and his mood remains on an even keel. Because he was doing so well, he once thought that he did not need the medication anymore and stopped taking it, but shortly thereafter he went into a terrible depression and wound up in the hospital.

The symptoms and causes of the depressive (unipolar) and bipolar disorders were discussed in Chapters 8, 9, and 10. In this chapter, we will consider various treatments for these disorders. In presenting each treatment, we will briefly review the suspected cause and discuss how the treatment is designed to overcome that cause. Then we will examine the treatment's effectiveness and any potential problems with its use.

PSYCHODYNAMIC APPROACHES

In Chapter 9, we learned that psychodynamic theorists believe that depression stems from conflicts associated with loss and stress. Therefore, the psychodynamic approach to treating depression is aimed at helping the individual (a) identify the losses and stresses that led to the depression, (b) overcome or reduce the losses and stresses, and (c) develop better ways of responding to them so that when faced with them again, the depression can be avoided. The procedures and techniques used in psychotherapy were described in Chapter 7 when we discussed the treatment of anxiety disorders. Therefore, here we will limit our attention to the question of whether psychotherapy is effective for treating depression.

Effectiveness of Psychotherapy

Psychotherapy is generally considered to be effective for treating depression. Studies carried out in the 1920s and 1930s (before therapeutic drugs were available) indicated that 40% of the individuals who were hospitalized for depression recovered within the first year and that 60% recovered within 2 years (Alexander, 1953). However, the problem with these and many other studies was that they did not include a no-treatment control condition in which patients did not receive therapy. The absence of that control condition is crucial because a high proportion of depressed individuals will improve even without treatment, an effect known as **spontaneous remission** of symptoms. Without a no-treatment control condition, we cannot determine how much of the improvement actually stemmed from the therapy. Fortunately, there are now a variety of controlled experiments from which we can draw firm conclusions.

In one experiment, acutely depressed patients were randomly assigned to a condition in which they received psychotherapy at least once a week or to a control condition in which they received "nonscheduled treatment"—no active treatment was scheduled, but if necessary, the patient could arrange one 50-minute session per month (Weissman et al., 1979). A clinician who was unaware of the type of treatment the patients were receiving assessed each patient's depression at various times during treatment. An analysis of those ratings indicated that the patients who received psychotherapy showed fewer relapses in depression than the patients in the control condition. Those results are presented in Figure 11.1. Other investigators have reported similar results (e.g., Klerman et al., 1974).

In an attempt to refine our understanding of what contributes to successful therapy, a considerable amount of research has been focused on the problem of identifying the personal characteristics of patients that are associated with successful therapy outcome. Unfortunately, most of the findings have been inconclusive or inconsistent (see Garfield, 1986). Only one

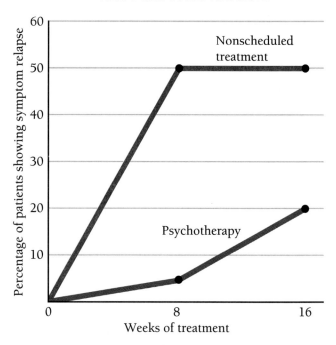

FIGURE 11.1   PSYCHOTHERAPY WAS MORE EFFECTIVE THAN "NONSCHEDULED TREATMENT" FOR REDUCING RELAPSES IN DEPRESSION.

Source: Adapted from Weissman et al. (1979), p. 557, fig. 1.

generalization can be made: More seriously depressed individuals will be less likely to benefit from psychotherapy or will require more time to benefit. Beyond that, no personal patient characteristics are consistently related to improvement.

Comment

Two points should be made concerning the effectiveness of psychotherapy for depression. First, although in many cases psychotherapy is effective for treating depression, it is not always effective. Indeed, one study revealed a 20% failure rate (Weissman et al., 1979), and we would expect more failures among more seriously depressed patients. Psychotherapy is not alone in failing to reduce all depressions, however, and we will see later that other therapeutic techniques also have only limited success.

Second, we do not yet understand what it is about psychotherapy that makes it effective for treating depression. It is encouraging that a wide variety of psychotherapies are effective, but if people get better almost regardless of what is done for them, it is difficult to determine what the crucial factor is that makes psychotherapy effective. If all of the techniques are effective (long-term psychoanalysis, group therapy, at-

Psychotherapy is frequently used to treat persons suffering from depression. It seems to be effective both in reducing the relapse rate for depression and in helping individuals improve their social adjustments and interpersonal relationships.

tention from a social worker, etc.), we are in the awkward position of concluding that the differences among the techniques (which the advocates of various points of view regard as so important) may in fact be irrelevant. The only common element to all of the approaches is **social support**, and that support may be the crucial element in the psychotherapeutic treatment of depression. That speculation is consistent with the wide variety of evidence indicating that social support is important for minimizing the effects of stress.

LEARNING APPROACHES

Learning theorists hypothesize that low levels of reward or high levels of punishment result in a less pleasant life, low self-esteem, and a decreased level of activity. Those factors then lead to depression. The learning approaches to the treatment of depression are aimed at helping patients increase the rewards and decrease the punishments in their lives.

Increasing Rewards and Decreasing Punishments

There are three steps for changing the levels of rewards and punishments. The first is to *identify* the aspects of the environment (people, activities, situations) that are the sources of rewards and punishments for the patient. To do that, the patient draws up a list of the most frequently occurring pleasant and unpleasant events and then monitors them to determine which are the most important in promoting good or bad feelings.

The second step is to teach the patient new skills or strategies to overcome, avoid, or *minimize the punishing experiences.* That step might include assertiveness training for patients who become upset when intimidated by others, time management training for those who are concerned about not getting things done, social skills training for those who have difficulty with interpersonal relationships, financial counseling for those beset with money problems, and relaxation training for those who find themselves under stress.

The third step involves teaching the patient to *increase the rewards* in his or her life. That is accomplished initially through a program of self-reinforcement. A "reward menu" is established using the list of rewards that was prepared earlier, and each reward is paired with a "price"—a task that must be accomplished to get the reward. Prices must be set high enough (tasks made difficult enough) so that the individual accomplishes something meaningful but not so

high that he or she never gets a reward. Getting the rewards can result in reduced levels of depression, and this approach can also help the individual become more active and accomplish more. In the case of one depressed man who loved going to the movies, a plan was established whereby he could not go to a movie until he had completed a specific task such as writing a report at work or painting a room at home. Within a short time, he was seeing more movies than he had before, which made him happy, and he was accomplishing more, which made him feel better about himself, and that also helped with his depression.

Three points should be noted: (a) The techniques used with any one patient are highly individualized and specific to the rewarding and punishing aspects of that particular patient's life; (b) a wide variety of techniques that might not ordinarily be considered part of psychotherapy are used to change behaviors in order to maximize rewards and minimize punishments; (c) the therapist plays a very active role in teaching the patient the skills that are necessary to maximize rewards and minimize punishments.

Effectiveness of Learning Therapy

In one interesting experiment, 28 moderately depressed women between the ages of 18 and 48 participated in one of three conditions: *self-control* therapy, *nonspecific* therapy, or a *waiting-list* control condition (Fuchs & Rehm, 1977). The self-control therapy was based on the learning approach to depression. It was called self-control therapy because with the learning approach, patients strive to gain more control over the rewards and punishments in their environments. Over the course of six weekly sessions, the patients in self-control therapy (a) were taught to identify the events that made them feel good and bad, (b) selected specific and realistically attainable goals that would make them feel better (e.g., "making better friends with women in my neighborhood"), (c) worked on achieving one or more of those goals, and (d) set up and used a self-reward system in which they gave themselves rewards for completing activities that were not inherently rewarding.

The patients in the nonspecific therapy condition also participated in six sessions, but their activities revolved around nondirective group therapy in which they discussed problems and feelings in an empathic manner. The patients in the waiting-list control condition were informed that they had been accepted for treatment but that all of the groups were filled and that they would have to wait 8 weeks before they would begin treatment.

The results indicated that patients in self-control therapy reported greater declines in depression than the patients in the other conditions. Those results are summarized in Figure 11.2. Furthermore, the patients who received self-control therapy also showed greater increases in social behavior. Apparently, the therapy influenced not only how patients felt but also how they subsequently behaved. Because increased social interaction could lead to increased rewards, it might be expected that the effects of self-control therapy would be maintained over time. Indeed, in a longitudinal study of the effects of a learning-based approach for the treatment of depression, it was found that the learning-based approach was superior to a control treatment (relaxation) and that the effect lasted at least 27 months (McLean & Hakstian, 1979, 1990).

Comment

The findings just discussed are encouraging, but we should note that the idea of increasing rewards (pleasant experiences) and decreasing punishments (unpleasant experiences) is not unique to the learning approach to treating depression. Indeed, it is basic to most psychotherapeutic approaches. What is different

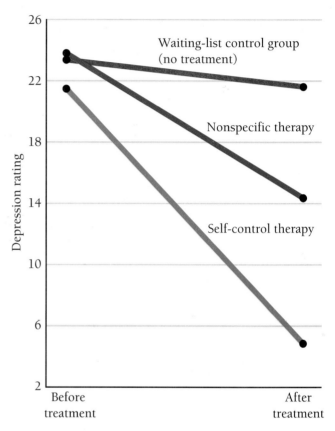

FIGURE 11.2   SELF-CONTROL THERAPY RESULTED IN GREATER DECREASES IN DEPRESSION THAN NONSPECIFIC THERAPY OR NO TREATMENT.

Source: Adapted from Fuchs and Rehm (1977), p. 210, tab. 1.

Changing response patterns can be one way to overcome depression. Here people in an assertiveness-training class are learning to express themselves more forcefully.

about the learning approach is the very direct, systematic, active, and varied ways in which the therapist works with the patient to overcome the punishments and increase the rewards.

We should also note that the learning approach to treating depression sometimes uses techniques drawn from other therapeutic approaches. Any technique that can increase rewards and decrease punishments will be used.

COGNITIVE APPROACHES

From a cognitive perspective, depression stems from negative cognitions (thoughts) that lead people to view themselves, their world, and their future in inappropriately negative ways ("I'm no good, my situation is terrible, and the future is bleak"). The goal of cognitive therapy is to change those cognitions to make them more accurate (Beck et al., 1979).

Changing Negative Cognitions

In cognitive therapy, the therapist tries to change negative cognitions through a three-step process. The first step is to *identify the negative cognitions* that are influencing the patient's mood and behavior ("I am depressed and withdrawn because others do not like me, and I will always be rejected by others in the future"). Rather than letting the patient accept the negative cognitions as true, the therapist tells the patient to consider them *hypotheses* to be tested. In other words, the therapist does not agree or disagree with the patient's views but takes a "let's see if you are correct" approach.

The second step involves *testing to determine whether the hypotheses are valid.* For example, if a patient is depressed because of the belief that he or she is disliked, the therapist and patient might conduct a little experiment in which the patient asks someone for a date to see if others actually do dislike and reject the patient.

Once the patient has done some carefully directed testing and finds that many of the negative cognitions are false (or at least not as serious as they were thought to be), the third step in the therapeutic processes can begin. That step involves the *replacement of the erroneous negative cognitions* with more accurate cognitions. For example, a patient will be instructed to replace negative thoughts with thoughts like "I may not be perfect, but I am not a bad person, and others do like me." That is not a simple step, and it takes some practice to get those positive thoughts to be as automatic as the previous negative thoughts. An important part of this phase of therapy involves activity planning. Rather than just thinking more accurate thoughts, the therapist and patient work together to plan activities that are consistent with the new accurate thoughts. In the case of a patient who feels rejected, they may plan a variety of social activities such as dates and parties. This is important because the patient needs consistent confirmation of the new beliefs concerning social acceptability. Without direction and planning, the individual may slip back into old ways. It is essential that the scheduled activities be carefully graded in terms of difficulty. A young man who felt depressed and rejected and who isolated himself socially for 2 years before therapy should probably start with a casual coffee date rather than attempt a weekend with the homecoming queen.

Because improvements in cognitive therapy occur when the patient collects data that actually disprove his or her negative cognitions, the individual will not be dependent on the therapist in the future. If negative cognitions crop up again, the patient will have learned to check and eliminate them. Indeed, the long-term success of cognitive therapy depends on the patient's careful monitoring of thoughts so as to avoid slipping back into the habit of using negative cognitions. Whenever they begin, the patient is taught to ask three questions (Hollon & Beck, 1979):

1. What is my evidence for this belief?
2. Is there another way of looking at this situation?
3. Even if it is true, is it as bad as it seems?

In cognitive therapy, the patient and therapist actively work together to develop more accurate cognitions that will lead to more positive feelings and behaviors.

Effectiveness of Cognitive Therapy

Initially, there was a high level of excitement about cognitive therapy because the results of an early experiment indicated that cognitive therapy was more effective than drug therapy for treating depression (Rush et al., 1977). In that experiment, 41 depressed patients were treated for 12 weeks with either cognitive therapy or an antidepressant drug (Tofranil/imipramine), and the patients who received cognitive therapy showed greater decreases in depression than the patients who received the drug treatment. Unfortunately, the results of numerous subsequent experiments have failed to confirm the superiority of cognitive therapy, and now even its advocates have concluded that "cognitive therapy is *neither more nor less effective than antidepressant medication* in the treatment of nonpsychotic, nonbipolar depressed outpatients" (emphasis added; Hollon et al., 1991, p. 97). The results of an experiment comparing cognitive therapy, drug therapy, cognitive therapy plus drug therapy, and cognitive therapy plus placebo therapy are presented in Figure 11.3 (p. 244). The sharp declines in depression reflect the strong and comparable effects of the various treatments.

It is generally assumed that cognitive therapy works because the patients learn to change their negative cognitions, but some doubts have been raised about that explanation. In one experiment on the effects of cognitive therapy and drug therapy, the experimenters collected data on changes in depression and also on changes in cognitions (Simons et al., 1984). What they found was that cognitive therapy and drug therapy were equally effective for reducing depression but also that cognitive therapy and drug therapy were *equally effective for reducing negative cognitions.* The reduction in negative cognitions would be expected in the cognitive therapy condition but not in the drug therapy condition unless negative cognitive cognitions were an *effect* rather than a *cause* of depression. The investigators suggest that "cognitive change may be more

FIGURE 11.3   COGNITIVE THERAPY, DRUG THERAPY, COGNITIVE PLUS DRUG THERAPY, AND COGNITIVE THERAPY PLUS PLACEBO WERE ALL EQUALLY EFFECTIVE FOR REDUCING DEPRESSION.

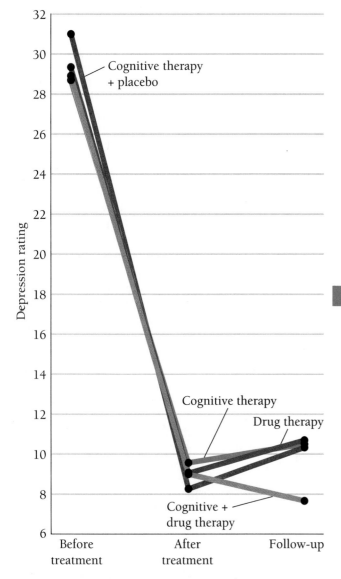

Source: Adapted from Murphy et al. (1984), p. 37, tab. 4.

Comment

Although cognitive therapy is not more effective than drug therapy, the fact that it can be *as effective* as drug therapy is very important because cognitive therapy does not have the unpleasant side effects that are sometimes associated with drug therapy. Furthermore, cognitive therapy does not require maintenance treatment, which is usually necessary with drug therapy. However, it should be recognized that the effectiveness of *cognitive therapy is limited to mild to moderately depressed outpatients* with a unipolar disorder, and it is not appropriate to use it with severely depressed individuals or those with a bipolar disorder. Overall, then, it appears that for many people, cognitive therapy is an effective treatment that can be a viable alternative to drug treatment. Future research will have to be focused more on why it works than on whether it works, and with a better understanding of the underlying process, psychologists may be able to enhance its effects.

PHYSIOLOGICAL APPROACHES

The physiological approaches to the treatment of depression can be divided into two types: *drug treatment* and *convulsive treatment* (the use of electrical shocks to induce convulsions). Both approaches have been effective, but the nature of their effects and the situations in which they are most effective are very different. We must give careful attention to physiological treatments because they are playing an increasingly important role in the treatment of depression today, but they are often misunderstood.

Drug Treatments

In Chapter 9, we saw that depression stems from low levels of neurotransmitters (norepinephrine or serotonin) at the synapses in the areas of the brain that are responsible for emotion. Those low levels are related to any or all of three processes: (a) *reuptake* (reabsorption) of the neurotransmitter by the presynaptic neuron, (b) *metabolism* (chemical breakdown) of the neurotransmitter, and (c) *insufficient production* of the neurotransmitter by the presynaptic neuron. Drug treatments are designed to reverse these processes and thereby restore an appropriate level of the neurotransmitter.

Tricyclics and Bicyclics: Drugs to Reduce Reuptake.   The drugs that are most widely used for the treatment of depression are the **tricyclics** and the

accurately seen as a part of improvement rather than the primary cause of improvement" (p. 45) and that we must rethink the explanation of cognitive therapy. Since then, even advocates of cognitive therapy for depression have concluded that the evidence does not support the notion that cognitive changes are "sufficient mediators" in the reduction of depression (De Rubeis et al., 1990). Clearly, cognitive therapy can be effective, but it is not clear exactly why.

newer **bicyclics**. These drugs work by reducing the re-uptake of norepinephrine and/or serotonin. The terms *tricyclic* and *bicyclic* are derived from the fact that the chemical structure of these drugs involves three or two circles. That is illustrated in Figure 11.4. Table 11.1 lists the most widely used antidepressant drugs by type, trade name, generic name, and bio-chemical basis.

Do these drugs relieve depression, and must the treatment be continued even after the depression has lifted? There is now strong and consistent evidence that tricyclics and bicyclics are more effective than no drugs or placebos for reducing depression. Figure 11.5 presents the results of one experiment in which acute-ly depressed patients were treated with a tricyclic (Tofranil/imipramine), a drug that is usually used to treat anxiety (Valium/diazepam), or a placebo (Covi et al., 1974). The patients who took the tricyclic showed greater improvement in depression than the patients who took either the antianxiety medication or the placebo.

Although the tricyclics and bicyclics are effective, in many cases the treatment must be continued be-cause the chance of relapse increases greatly if the drugs are withdrawn. In three experiments, depressed patients were first successfully treated with tricyclics (Elavil/amitriptyline or Tofranil/imipramine) and were then assigned to conditions in which they either continued to take the drug ("maintenance therapy") or began taking a placebo (Klerman et al., 1974; Mind-ham, 1973; Prien et al., 1974). The results of those ex-periments, summarized in Figure 11.6 (p. 246), reveal that in each experiment, the patients who continued

TABLE 11.1 FREQUENTLY USED ANTIDEPRESSION DRUGS

TYPE	TRADE NAME	GENERIC NAME
Tricyclic	Elavil	amitriptyline
	Pamelor	nortriptyline
	Sinequan	doxepin
	Tofranil	imipramine
Bicyclic	Prozac	fluoxetine
	Paxil	paroxetine
MAOI	Marplan	isocarboxazid
	Nardil	phenelzine
	Parnate	tranylcpromine
Other	Desyrel	trazodone
	Wellbutrin	bupropion
	Zoloff	sertraline

to take the drug had lower relapse rates than the oth-ers. In general, the drugs reduced the relapse rate by about 50%. (The overall differences in relapse rates across the different experiments are associated with differences in the severity of the depression; experi-ments in which the patients were more seriously de-pressed had higher overall relapse rates.)

One important practical point to note about the tricyclics and bicyclics (and other antidepressant drugs) is that there is a delay of 2 weeks or more (sometimes as long as 6 weeks) before they begin re-ducing depression (Quitkin et al., 1984). We do not yet understand the reason for this delay, but patients should be warned about it so that they do not become disappointed with the lack of immediate effects and

FIGURE 11.4 THE CHEMICAL STRUCTURE OF A TRICYCLIC ANTIDEPRESSANT AND A BICYCLIC ANTIDEPRESSANT.

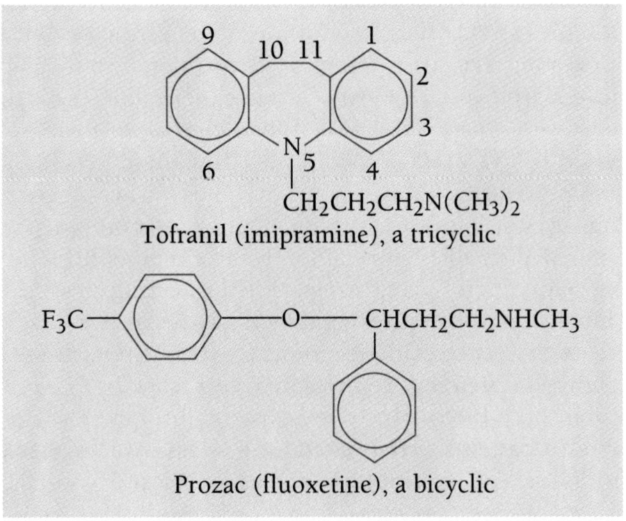

FIGURE 11.5 A TRICYCLIC DRUG WAS MORE EFFECTIVE THAN AN ANTIANXIETY DRUG OR A PLACEBO FOR REDUCING DEPRESSION.

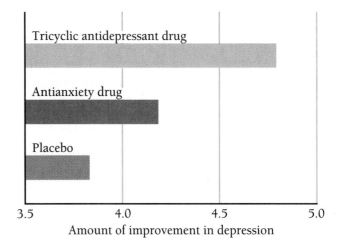

Source: Adapted from Covi et al. (1974), p. 196, tab. 4.

FIGURE 11.6   IN THREE EXPERIMENTS, TRICYCLIC
DRUGS REDUCED RELAPSE RATES
FOR DEPRESSION BY ABOUT 50%.

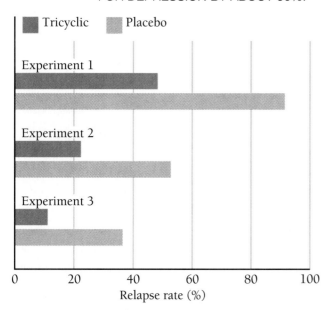

Sources: Prien et al. (1974); Mindham (1973); Klerman et al. (1974).

FIGURE 11.7   ONSET OF THE EFFECTS OF
ANTIDEPRESSANT DRUGS IS
SOMETIMES DELAYED.

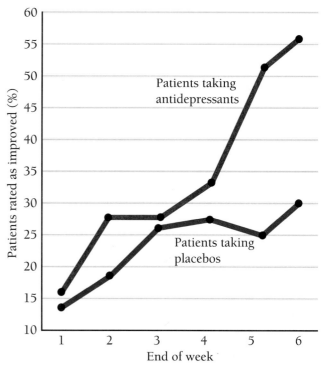

Source: Adapted from Quitkin et al. (1984), p. 240, fig. 1.

cease taking the medication. The delayed effect of antidepressant medication is illustrated in Figure 11.7.

The delayed effect of the antidepressant drugs also has implications for patient management, especially for those who are suicidal and for whom immediate relief is necessary. For these patients, hospitalization might be necessary until they are no longer a danger to themselves, or it might initially be necessary to use some other, faster-acting treatment, such as electroconvulsive therapy (to be discussed shortly), to break the depression.

A relatively new bicyclic drug that has attracted a lot of attention and widespread use is Prozac (fluoxetine). Unlike most of the other drugs that reduce reuptake of norepinephrine or norepinephrine and serotonin, the effects of Prozac are specific to the reuptake of serotonin. Prozac has been shown to be highly effective for reducing depression, and it does not have the side effect of weight gain, which is a problem for some individuals. Indeed, the use of Prozac often leads to a small loss in weight. Despite all of its positive effects, this drug has been surrounded by controversy. That controversy is discussed in Case Study 11.1.

MAO Inhibitors: Drugs to Reduce Metabolism.

Norepinephrine is metabolized (broken down) at the synapse by an enzyme called **monoamine oxidase** (MON-ō-uh-mēn OK-si-dās; **MAO**). If too much norepinephrine is metabolized, there will not be enough to

facilitate synaptic transmission, and depression will set in. Drugs that are used to treat depression by *inhibiting* the effects of monoamine oxidase are known as **MAO inhibitors** (MAOIs). If the metabolic breakdown is inhibited, more of the neurotransmitter will be available, and therefore the basis for the depression will be reduced or eliminated.

The effectiveness of MAOIs for protecting against low levels of norepinephrine during stress was demonstrated in an interesting experiment with rats. As we saw in Chapter 9, when laboratory animals are exposed to stress, their levels of norepinephrine decline, suggesting that stress brings on depression by reducing norepinephrine. However, in one experiment, the animals were given an MAOI. When they were then exposed to the stress, they did not show the decrease in norepinephrine (Maynert & Levi, 1964). This suggests that by slowing down the metabolism of norepinephrine, MAOIs allow normal levels of norepinephrine to be maintained during stress, thus protecting the individual from the depressing effects of stress.

A variety of evidence indicates that MAOIs are effective for treating depression (see review by Nies & Robinson, 1982). In one experiment, acutely depressed patients were treated for 6 weeks with an MAO inhibitor (phenelzine) or a placebo (Ravaris et al.,

Case Study 11.1

PROZAC: PANACEA OR PARADOX?

Prozac (fluoxetine) has been heralded as a wonder drug for the treatment of depression, but it has also been cited as a drug that leads people to suicide and even murder.

Prozac was introduced in 1987 and immediately became one of the most widely used drugs in the United States. *Newsweek* magazine even featured a capsule of Prozac on its cover. Prozac's widespread acceptance was based on two facts. First, the drug was very effective for reducing depression as well as other disorders such as the obsessive-compulsive disorder, anorexia, and bulimia. Second, it did not have many of the side effects that were associated with other antidepressants. For example, Prozac did not cause the weight gain that is associated with the use of some antidepressants, and that made it very popular. Sales of Prozac skyrocketed; more than a million prescriptions for Prozac were being filled every month! Prozac was seen as a panacea for a wide variety of disorders, and it quickly became the dandy of the drug market.

However, the view of Prozac changed suddenly when an article appeared in which it was reported that six patients who had been taking Prozac for major depression had experienced an emergence or intensification of thoughts about suicide (Teicher et al., 1990). After being put on Prozac, one man reported "nearly constant suicidal preoccupation" and "violent self-destructive fantasies," and when a woman who planned to commit suicide was given an increased dose of Prozac, she became violent and mutilated herself. That article was followed by reports of four other adults and six children who also experienced increases in thoughts about suicide after they began taking Prozac (Dasgupta & Hoover, 1990; King et al., 1991; Masand et al., 1991). Those reports opened the floodgates, and people telling sensational horror stories about the alleged effects of Prozac were on all of the TV talk shows. Furthermore, Prozac "survivor" groups were formed around the country to provide support for those who had gone through the perils of Prozac. Possibly the most dramatic aspect of the Prozac story involved the allegation that Prozac led people to commit murder. For example, it was alleged that Joseph Wesbecker was under the influence of Prozac when he stormed into a building with an AK-47 assault rifle and shot 20 people (eight fatally) before killing himself. Many defendants in murder cases began using what came to be known as the "Prozac defense"—using Prozac to explain their violent acts, thereby relieving themselves of responsi-

bility and opening up the manufacturer to huge law suits.

The alleged increase in violent behavior (toward self and others) associated with taking Prozac was particularly surprising in view of the drug's biochemical effects. We know that *low* levels of serotonin are associated with aggressive behavior and suicide (see Chapter 10), but Prozac blocks the reuptake of serotonin and therefore Prozac results in *higher* levels of serotonin. In other words, from a biochemical standpoint, if Prozac has any effect on aggression, it should *reduce* it. However, it is always possible that Prozac has some paradoxical effect on behavior, as some other drugs do. For example, we know that *stimulants* have the effect of *calming* hyperactive children (see Chapter 16). Might Prozac also have a paradoxical effect? Is Prozac a dangerous drug? Should it be withdrawn from the market?

Case studies can provide a signal that a problem may exist, but we cannot draw conclusions from case studies because the reported effects might be due to other factors. For example, in some of the cases that were reported, the individuals were also on other medications and were suffering from other psychiatric disorders, and it may have been those factors rather than the Prozac that led to the disturbed behavior. So case studies aside, what results have been generated by controlled research?

First, there is some evidence that when compared to a placebo, antidepressant drugs in general may lead to a *slight* increase in suicide of about 1% (Gardner & Cowdry, 1985; Rouillon et al., 1989; Soloff et al., 1987; see review by Mann & Kapur, 1991). If such an effect occurs, it is probably due to the fact that as the depression begins to lift, the individuals have more energy and are more active and are thus more likely to act on their lingering suicidal thoughts. In any event, if this effect occurs, it does not appear to be anything like the effect attributed to Prozac.

Second, the results of at least three large-scale double-blind controlled experiments did *not* reveal *any* evidence that Prozac resulted in an increase in suicidal thoughts or behavior (Altamura et al., 1989; Muijen et al., 1988; Sacchetti et al., 1991; see review by Mann & Kapur, 1991). Instead, Prozac was found to be generally *more* effective than the other drugs and placebos in reducing suicidal urges and depression.

If the controlled research does not support the initial claims that Prozac leads to increased rates of suicidal thoughts, how do we account for the case studies? First, it is possible that the behaviors were the result of the other medications the patients were taking or the other disorders from which they suffered. Second, it is also possible that in some cases the behavior was indeed an abnormal reaction to the Prozac. With virtually every drug there are individuals who have abnormal reactions (e.g., some people cannot take aspirin), so there are undoubtedly people who cannot tolerate Prozac. However, the number of those individuals appears to be very small. If some patients do show abnormal reactions, the solution is not to abandon the use of Prozac but rather to alert patients to the potential side effects and monitor the patients carefully, a strategy that is essential with any drug.

And what about the "Prozac defense"? In one case, a woman who murdered her husband while allegedly under the influence of Prozac was convicted of manslaughter rather than murder, but the lesser conviction was probably due to the jury's concern about the woman's advanced age of 74 rather than to her use of Prozac. Other cases involving the Prozac defense have been unsuccessful, and there now appears to be less interest in the Prozac defense.

Finally, you may recall my student in Case Study 8.2 who described her depression, her feelings of living inside a glass bottle, and how she huddled under the covers in her bed. She wrote that description as the introduction to her term paper on depression and its treatment with Prozac. She concluded her paper with the following:

> As I sit at my computer successfully completing the first major term paper I've been able to tackle this semester, I am thankful for the development of Prozac, and I am willing to risk the possible side effects. I am now able to experience everyday joys like others who I once could only envy. I still have good days and days when I feel "blue," but that is perfectly normal, and Prozac is no panacea. It has not been determined how long I will remain on Prozac, but as for now, I am just enjoying life. I like people, I'm proud of what I'm accomplishing, and I love myself.

1980). Figure 11.8 shows that the MAOI reduced depression and anxiety more than the placebo. The fact that the MAOI was also effective for reducing anxiety is consistent with our discussion in Chapter 6, where we learned that MAOIs are effective for reducing panic attacks and agoraphobia.

Although the MAOIs can be effective for treating depression, care must be used with some of them because they have potentially dangerous side effects (Nies & Robinson, 1982). The most serious is blood pressure so high that it can be fatal, a reaction called a *hypertensive crisis*. Such a crisis can occur when a patient who is taking an MAO inhibitor eats foods that contain **tyramine** (TĒR-uh-mēn) in large amounts (unpasteurized cheese, aged meats or sausages, yeast extract, wines, some beers, avocado) or takes other drugs (stimulants, decongestants, antihypertensives, tricyclic antidepressants). Because so many common foods and drugs can cause negative reactions to MAO inhibitors, some authorities believe that these drugs should only be taken by patients who are in a hospital where their diet can be carefully supervised and where help is available in the event of complications. At present, MAO inhibitors are usually used only after other antidepressant medications have been tried and found to be ineffective.

Psychomotor Stimulants: Drugs to Increase Production. A group of drugs known as **psychomotor stimulants** (e.g., amphetamines) can decrease depression by increasing the production of norepinephrine by the presynaptic neurons. Unfortunately, most psychomotor stimulants are addicting and have relatively short-term effects. Furthermore, after their effects wear off, the depression often worsens, an effect known as **postamphetamine depression**. Because of those problems, the psychomotor stimulants are not used widely or not used for long periods.

FIGURE 11.8   AN MAO INHIBITOR WAS MORE EFFECTIVE THAN A PLACEBO FOR REDUCING DEPRESSION AND ANXIETY.

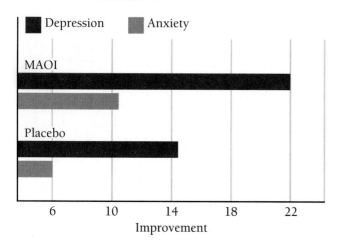

Source: Adapted from Ravaris et al. (1980), p. 1077, tab. 2.

Side Effects. We have already mentioned the sometimes lethal side effects of MAO inhibitors and the addictive nature of psychomotor stimulants, but the widely used tricyclics and bicyclics also have side effects. These can include dryness of the mouth, blurring of vision, difficulty in urination, constipation, palpitations of the heart, hypotension (low blood pressure), weight gain, and drowsiness or excitement. However, these unwanted side effects are generally correlated with the dosage level of the drug and thus can sometimes be minimized by using the lowest dosage level that is effective (Mindham, 1982). Furthermore, in many cases, the side effects diminish over time (the body seems to adjust to the medication) or patients learn ways to avoid or cope with the side effects. It is crucial to inform patients about possible side effects so that they can deal with them and not misinterpret them as additional symptoms of their disorder.

It is important to consider the trade-off between side effects and symptom relief. Regrettably, some side effects may be unavoidable, but we must ask whether the presence of the side effects is an acceptable price to pay for the relief from the misery and depression the patient might have to endure without the drug. As with most things, then, drug treatment for depression is a matter of balances, compromises, risks, and benefits, and the important thing is for both therapist and patient to be informed about the options and the consequences.

Comment. The theoretical underpinnings of drug therapy are persuasive, and the evidence concerning the effects of the drugs is consistent and generally strong. However, we must not ignore the fact that drug therapy is not effective in all cases. For example, even when tricyclics are used, as many as 30% of the patients do not improve. One explanation for the failures is simply that not all depressions have a physiological basis, and it would be unrealistic to expect a physiological treatment to be effective with those depressions. Another explanation is that some patients have not been given the right drug. For example, if an individual is depressed because of low levels of serotonin but is given a drug that influences levels of norepinephrine, it is unlikely that the drug therapy would be effective. Finally, drugs may not be effective because the dosage was not high enough or the drug was not used for a long enough period of time (Ravaris et al., 1976). Because there are many reasons why drugs may not be effective, it is often necessary to experiment with a number of drugs and dosage levels before abandoning drug therapy.

Finally we come to the complex and controversial question of whether drugs are a *cure* for depression (as

antibiotics cure pneumonia), a *treatment* for depression that must be maintained (as insulin is used to treat diabetes for the rest of the individual's life), or mere *suppressors* of symptoms until the disorder runs its course (as antihistamines do for the common cold). The fact that some individuals improve and can be withdrawn from the drug without experiencing a relapse suggests that for them, the drugs serve as a cure or suppress symptoms until the underlying disorder clears up. That is, once the proper physiological balance is restored or the stress is reduced, they do not need the drug. However, the fact that many individuals do relapse when the drugs are eliminated suggests that in some cases the drugs must be used as a long-term treatment. In other words, in many cases, the patients must be continued on a maintenance dose, a strategy that is often called **drug prophylaxis**. At present, it does not appear that we can determine the nature of the drugs' therapeutic effects, and we may ultimately find that all three explanations are correct for different individuals. From a practical standpoint, it seems wise to withdraw patients from their drugs occasionally; if they remain symptom-free, the medication can be discontinued, but if they begin to relapse, the drug regime can be reinstituted.

Electroconvulsive Therapy

The other physiological treatment for depression is **electroconvulsive therapy (ECT)**, commonly called "shock therapy." ECT is used widely for the treatment of depression, and it has been estimated that more than 10,000 patients in the United States receive ECT each day. Because ECT is widely used, frequently misunderstood, and often the focus of public and professional outcries (Breggin, 1979; Frieberg, 1975), it is essential that we give careful consideration to the procedures, effects, and side effects of ECT.

Background. ECT was originally developed as a treatment for schizophrenia when it was observed that patients who suffered from both schizophrenia and epilepsy appeared to remit their schizophrenic symptoms immediately following an epileptic convulsion. Clinicians speculated that if epileptic-like convulsions could be artificially induced in patients with schizophrenia, the convulsions might be effective for reducing the schizophrenia. Originally, the convulsions were induced with drugs such as insulin (Meduna, 1935), but it was quickly learned that greater control over the convulsions could be achieved if they were induced with an electrical shock to the brain, and electroconvulsive therapy was born (Cerletti & Bini, 1938). Since then, we have learned that ECT is not effective for treating schizophrenia, but evidence has accumulated that it can be effective for treating some types of depression.

Procedures.

In the typical portrayal of shock therapy in grade B horror movies, a screaming patient is held down on an operating table by brutish attendants, a physician holds large electrodes to the patient's temples, a flash of lightning-like electrical current arcs between the electrodes, and the patient shudders in pain and falls comatose, brain-damaged and changed for life. The early use of ECT may have involved some elements of that scenario, but it bears no resemblance to the procedures in use today. Regrettably, those portrayals and certain horror stories (some true) based on the early misuse of ECT have colored the general perception of the treatment.

Today, the patient is first given a strong sedative and a muscle relaxant. The sedative induces sleep, so the patient is not conscious when the convulsion is induced. The relaxant reduces muscular contractions during the convulsion. (Before muscle relaxants were used, patients often broke bones during the convulsions.) Once the patient is unconscious and relaxed, electrodes are placed on the skull and an electrical current of between 70 and 150 volts is passed between the electrodes for 1/10 second to 1 second to induce the convulsion. While the convulsion runs its course (usually 45 to 60 seconds), the patient shows some minor muscle contractions. These can range from an arching of the back and movement of the arms to movement only of the toes. The degree to which muscle contractions occur depends on the amount of the muscle relaxant that is administered. During the convulsion, it is necessary to put something in the patient's mouth to prevent swallowing of the tongue. The patient does not breathe during the convulsion, so CO_2 builds up, and therefore the patient is usually

given oxygen for 10 or 15 seconds immediately following the convulsion. A few minutes later, the patient regains consciousness. The entire procedure can take less than 15 minutes, and after having been through it once, most patients do not report any greater concern than would be expected for any other minor medical procedure.

ECT is generally given two or three times per week. The number of treatments necessary to obtain results differs widely from patient to patient. Many respond after five to eight treatments. Up to 20 treatments may be tried before abandoning hope for this approach (Kiloh, 1982). The old adage "an ounce of prevention is worth a pound of cure" probably provided the basis for an early belief that a few additional treatments should be given after the depression had lifted, but there is no evidence that the extra treatments help (Barton et al., 1973). ECT can be given on either an outpatient or an inpatient basis, but it is usually used for inpatients because they are more seriously depressed. Giving four to eight shocks in one session has been tried in an attempt to speed up the effects of the treatment, but that was not found to be as effective as separating the shocks by 1 or 2 days.

Effects on Depression.

The first question we must ask is, is ECT more effective than a placebo treatment? Two types of placebos have been used, a drug placebo and an ECT placebo. With the ECT placebo, the patient receives the sedative and muscle relaxant but is not given the shock. However, upon regaining consciousness, the patient is told that the shock was given. The results of at least 19 experiments have consistently indicated that ECT is more effective than either type of placebo for relieving depression (see reviews by Fink, 1979; Janicak et al., 1985; Scovern & Kilmann, 1980). The only qualification is that effectiveness of ECT is limited to patients suffering from severe endogenous (physiologically caused) depressions (Greenblatt et al., 1964). Understandably, ECT is not more effective than placebos for treating individuals with mild exogenous (environmentally caused) depressions. There is no reason to expect that an electrical shock to the brain would help individuals overcome depression that was due to an environmental event such as the loss of a loved one.

Next we must ask, is ECT more effective than antidepressant drugs? The evidence indicates that when treating individuals with endogenous depression, ECT is generally more beneficial than the drugs (Scovern & Kilmann, 1980). That is especially the case when more seriously depressed and delusional patients are being treated. In one study with severely depressed patients, ECT had an 83% success rate, whereas tricyclics had only a 35% success rate (Avery & Lubrano, 1979).

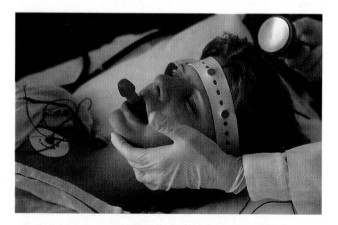

The procedures used to administer electroconvulsive therapy (ECT) bear little resemblance to those of the past. Today, the patient is unconscious during the treatment and is given a muscle relaxant to reduce muscle contractions.

In addition to being more effective than drugs, ECT has the advantage of producing its effects faster than drugs. The antidepressant drugs take at least 10 to 14 days to produce an effect and may take much longer, but ECT can begin showing its benefits within 3 or 4 days. The speed with which ECT works makes it very helpful in treating suicidal patients who may be a danger to themselves as long as they are depressed, and it may decrease the length of time that endogenously depressed patients must be hospitalized. Indeed, in one study it was found that patients who received ECT spent 13 fewer days in the hospital than patients who received tricyclics (Markowitz et al., 1987). That not only saved the patients time, but it would have saved each patient over $13,000.

Is ECT a long-lasting treatment, or are patients treated with ECT more likely to relapse than patients treated with drugs? That is a very important question, but before answering it, we must consider how the two treatments are usually used. ECT is administered until the depression lifts, and then it is discontinued. In contrast, drugs are administered until the depression lifts, and then the patient is kept on a maintenance dose to protect against a relapse. Because ECT is terminated but the drug therapy is not, it is not fair to compare ECT to extended drug therapy. From a practical standpoint, however, there is probably a somewhat higher relapse rate with ECT.

The findings that ECT can eliminate depression quickly and that drugs can serve to reduce relapse rates after the depression has lifted would suggest that the two treatments might be combined for best effects: Use ECT to lift the depression quickly, and then use drugs to protect against relapse. The empirical evidence concerning the efficacy of combining ECT and drug therapy is limited, but it does suggest that the combination of treatments is more effective than ECT alone for relieving depression and reducing relapses (Imlah et al., 1965; Kay et al., 1970; Seager & Bird, 1962).

Despite the substantial evidence that ECT is effective for treating endogenous depressions, we still do not know why it works. More than 50 theories have been advanced to account for its effects, but we have not reached any firm conclusions on the mechanism responsible (Lerer et al., 1984).

Side Effects.   When used appropriately, ECT is a relatively safe treatment. In one study of 18,627 patients who received an average of more than five shocks, not one fracture or death occurred (Kramer, 1985).

One occassional side effect of ECT that some patients find upsetting is **retrograde amnesia**. Patients receiving ECT may lose their memories for some events that occurred prior to the treatment, and as the number of treatments increases, the memory loss extends further back in time. This memory loss is called *retrograde* amnesia because it starts with recent events and works back from those. In most cases, the loss is minimal and little more than a minor annoyance. Although an event or a name may be forgotten, it can be relearned, and there is no permanent impairment. Furthermore, there is now evidence that as time goes by, the memories that were lost as a consequence of the shock may be regained (Calev et al., 1991). In that investigation, the memory performance of depressed patients was measured before and immediately after receiving ECT and then again 1 month and 6 months later. The patients received an average of nine treatments. The results indicated that there was a considerable loss in memory immediately after the treatment, but memory was back to the pretreatment level 1 month later and even a little higher 6 months later (probably due to the fact that the patients were generally functioning better after the depression had lifted). Those results are presented in Figure 11.9. Note that in some cases, memory loss may be exaggerated by patients who blame the treatment for the normal forgetting that we all experience.

The degree to which memory will be disturbed is influenced by where the electrodes are placed. Origi-

FIGURE 11.9   MEMORY FOR IMPORTANT EVENTS WAS NOT IMPAIRED 1 MONTH AFTER ELECTROCONVULSIVE THERAPY (ECT).

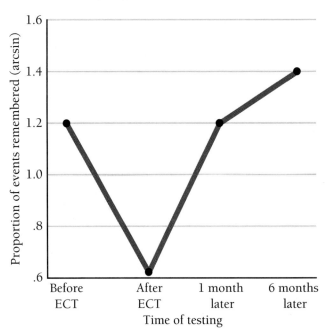

Source: Calev et al. (1991), p. 531, fig. 4.

nally, they were placed *bilaterally* (one on either side; see Figure 11.10), but a number of experiments have demonstrated that *unilateral* placement on the *non-dominant* side (e.g., both on the right side for right-handed individuals; see Figure 11.10) results in less retrograde amnesia (d'Elia & Raotma, 1975; Welch, 1982). The unilateral placement probably results in less memory disturbance because with that placement the current does not traverse the dominant side of the brain, which is responsible for most language functions.

One question that always arises with regard to ECT is whether it causes brain damage. Obviously, the application of 150 volts of electrical current to brain cells will result in some damage. However, when modern techniques are used (e.g., low levels of shock, oxygen during treatment to prevent anoxia during the convulsion), it is impossible to detect any brain damage even with highly sensitive MRI scans. In other words, what damage does occur is too minor to be detected with our most sensitive techniques.

A more important question is, does ECT result in impaired cognitive functioning? The data on this are limited, but they indicate that ECT may actually *improve* cognitive functioning (Sackeim, 1985). The improvement stems from the fact that the depression reduced cognitive functioning, so when the depression was eliminated by the shock, functioning improved. There are even data indicating that patients who received more than 100 ECT treatments over their lifetimes did not differ from nonshocked patients on measures of cognitive functioning (Devanand et al., 1991).

Comment.   After half a century of use (and abuse), it seems clear that ECT can be effective for treating severe endogenous depression. Furthermore, ECT produces results faster than drug therapy, making it especially helpful for treating suicidal patients for whom a rapid intervention in the disorder is essential. ECT does not appear to be a long-term cure for depression. Because patients cannot be put on a maintenance dose of ECT, the most effective treatment is probably to use ECT to break the depression and then to follow it up with a prophylactic drug treatment to protect against relapse. ECT has been more effective than drugs for reducing severe endogenous depression, but because it is a rather extreme treatment, it is usually reserved for the most serious cases or for individuals who do not respond to drug therapy. It is important to note that although ECT is often effective for treating endogenous depressions, despite 5 decades of use, we still do not understand why it works, and it continues to be a controversial treatment (APA Task Force, 1978; Breggin, 1979; Palmer, 1981; Weiner, 1982).

Light Therapy for the Seasonal Affective Disorder

In Chapter 8, we learned that a subset of depressions is likely to occur during seasons of the year when there is less light, a disorder known as the *seasonal affective disorder (SAD)*. If reduced light leads to depression in some individuals, exposing those individuals to more light should relieve their depression. That prescription was offered initially more than 2,000 years ago when Aretaeus said, "Lethargics are to be laid in the light and exposed to the rays of the sun." Despite the amount of time that has elapsed since light therapy was suggested, there is still controversy over this treatment, and it is still being refined (Termal et al., 1989). However, it does appear that two conclusions may be justified at this time. First, *bright light* (2,500 lux) is more effective than dim light (Wehr & Rosenthal, 1989). Indeed, dim light is often used as a control condition in experiments on light therapy. Second, light in the *morning* is more effective than light later in the day (Avery et al., 1993).

The process underlying SAD and light therapy is not clear. One hypothesis revolves around the production of **melatonin** (mel-uh-TŌ-nin), a hormone that regulates sleep activity cycles and at high levels may depress mood. Melatonin production is increased when periods of light are shorter, as they are in the winter. By exposing the individual to light in the morning ("dawn simulation"), the total period of light is increased, and that may suppress the production of melatonin. Other explanations revolve around the effects of light on metabolic rate and circadian rhythms (Gaist et al., 1990; Wehr & Rosenthal, 1989).

FIGURE 11.10   ELECTRODE PLACEMENT FOR ELECTROCONVULSIVE THERAPY.

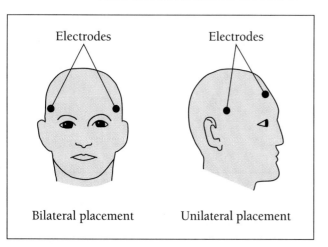

Electrodes   Electrodes

Bilateral placement   Unilateral placement

Exposure to bright light has been shown to be effective for some individuals in the treatment of seasonal affective disorder (SAD). However, the processes underlying SAD and light therapy are still unclear.

Finally, it should be noted that light therapy may have a side effect if full-spectrum fluorescent lights are used that emit ultraviolet light. Specifically, UV light can damage the retina, which is why we wear sunglasses that screen it out. Unfortunately, some research indicates that UV light may play a role in the therapeutic process of light therapy (Lam et al., 1991).

COMPARISONS AND COMBINATIONS OF TREATMENTS FOR DEPRESSION

In the preceding sections we have found that a variety of very different approaches can all be effective for treating depression. In view of those findings, two questions that are often asked are, *which treatment is most effective,* and *is a combination of treatments more effective than any one treatment alone?* The answers to those questions have important implications for the effective and efficient treatment of depression.

Comparisons of Psychotherapy, Cognitive Therapy, and Drug Therapy

There has been a hot debate over the question of which type of therapy is most effective for treating de-

pression (Dobson, 1989; Robinson et al., 1990). After reviewing the research, one group of authors concluded that "initial analysis suggested some differences in the efficacy of various types of treatment; however, once the influence of investigator allegiance was removed, there remained no evidence for the relative superiority of any one approach" (Robinson et al., 1990, p. 30). In other words, investigators with different orientations found evidence to support their own positions. In an attempt to overcome this problem of bias, the National Institute of Mental Health (NIMH) called together investigators who represented a number of different orientations and conducted an experiment in which about 250 depressed individuals were randomly assigned to four treatments: (1) *interpersonal psychotherapy,* (2) *cognitive behavioral therapy,* (3) tricyclic *drug therapy,* and (4) *placebo pill therapy* (Elkin et al., 1985, 1989). The therapy was conducted by experts in each area over the course of about 16 weeks, and a number of different measures of effectiveness were used.

The initial report of this investigation revealed two notable findings (Elkin et al., 1989). First, when persons who were initially *less* depressed were considered, *there were no reliable differences among the treatments in terms of effectiveness.* In other words, for mildly depressed persons, neither psychotherapy nor cognitive therapy nor drug therapy was more effective than the placebo. The lack of effectiveness of the treatments was surprising and needs more exploration. Second, when persons who were initially *more* depressed were considered, *there were differences among the effects of the treatments, but the differences were not particularly large.* For example, with one measure of effectiveness, it was found that (a) the drug therapy was reliably *more* effective than the placebo therapy, (b) the interpersonal psychotherapy and cognitive behavioral therapy showed levels of effectiveness that were *between* those of the drug and placebo therapies, but (c) the levels of effectiveness of the interpersonal psychotherapy and cognitive behavioral therapy were not reliably different from those of the drug and placebo therapies. Those findings are presented in Figure 11.11 (p. 254). (Note: If a difference is said to be not reliable, it means that the difference is relatively small and could be due to chance.)

These relatively weak findings were met with mixed emotions by therapists representing different points of view. The question that arises is, why were not greater differences found in the effects of therapies that involved such different procedures?

There are at least two answers to that question. First, it could be argued that although there were major differences among the various therapies, there were also some factors that were common to all of the

FIGURE 11.11 DRUG THERAPY WAS MORE
EFFECTIVE THAN PLACEBO
THERAPY BUT OTHER
DIFFERENCES WERE UNRELIABLE.

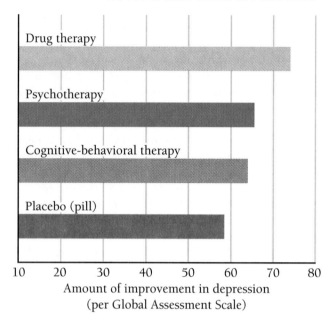

Amount of improvement in depression
(per Global Assessment Scale)

Source: Adapted from Elkin et al. (1989), p. 976, fig. 1.

therapies (a caring therapist, a rationale for symptoms, a treatment plan, expectations for improvement), and it may have been that those *common factors were responsible for the effects* (Frank, 1982; Imber et al., 1990). This is referred to as the **nonspecific (common) factor explanation**. The nonspecific factor explanation could even be applied to the placebo condition because the sessions in which patients were given their pills lasted 20 to 30 minutes, so there was more going on than just the giving of pills.

The second explanation is that *each therapy was effective but for a different type of patient*, and when different types of patients were "lumped together," the different effects of the therapies were canceled out and all of the therapies appeared to have similar and only moderate effects. We can call this the **specific patient explanation**, and we will discuss it in greater detail shortly.

Types of Patients and Types of Therapy

There are numerous differences among patients, such as intelligence and verbal ability, that could influence the type of therapy that would be most effective for a given patient (Beutler, 1991; Shoham-Salomon & Hanna, 1991; Smith & Sechrest, 1991; Snow, 1991; Sotsky et al., 1991). Probably one of the most important variables to consider is the type of depression with

which the patient is suffering. We know that depressions can stem from a number of different factors, and therefore it is overly simplistic to assume that any one therapy would be effective for patients with different types of depression. For example, psychotherapy may be more effective for individuals with exogenous (environmentally caused) depressions, and drug therapy may be more effective for individuals with endogenous (physiologically caused) depressions.

In one study relevant to this possibility, it was found that depressed patients who did not respond well to tricyclic drugs reported almost three times as many undesirable events in their lives during therapy than patients for whom the tricyclic drugs were effective (Lloyd et al., 1981). The events tended to be health-related and were perceived as being beyond the patients' control. These results suggest that the patients who did not respond to the drugs were suffering from exogenous (stress-related) depressions for which we would not expect the drugs to be effective.

Types of Symptoms and Types of Therapy

It is also possible that different types of therapies influence different types of symptoms. A series of comprehensive experiments concerning this possibility has revealed two interesting findings (Covi et al., 1974; Friedman, 1975; Klerman et al., 1974). First, psychotherapy was found to be more effective than drug therapy for helping patients deal with problems of living, social functioning, and interpersonal relations. However, drug therapy was found to be more effective than psychotherapy for reducing the feelings of depression and preventing relapse (see reviews by Klerman & Schechter, 1982; Weissman, 1979b). That is, psychotherapy influenced *behaviors* and drugs influenced *moods*. This does not mean that psychotherapy did not influence depression and that drugs did not influence the problems of daily living. It means only that the different approaches were relatively more effective with the different sets of symptoms.

Psychotherapy plus Drug Therapy

Because psychotherapy and drug therapy may influence different aspects of the depressive disorder, we might expect that the combination of the two therapies would result in the greatest effect. However, it has been argued that drug therapy may actually interfere with psychotherapy when the two are used in combination. For example, patients may rely on their pills for help and not devote sufficient effort to psychotherapy.

The controlled research on the separate and combined effects of psychotherapy and drug therapy permit two conclusions. First, there is no evidence that drug therapy interferes with psychotherapy, or vice versa (Covi et al., 1974; Friedman, 1975; Klerman et al., 1974). In other words, patients who are in psychotherapy but also taking drugs do not work less or do less well in psychotherapy. Second, there is good evidence that the combination may be more effective than either treatment alone (Di Mascio et al., 1979; Frank et al., 1989; Frank et al., 1990; Klerman, 1990; Klerman et al., 1974; Weissman et al., 1979). For example, in one experiment, acutely depressed patients were given (a) *psychotherapy alone,* (b) *drug therapy* (Elavil/amitriptyline) *alone,* (c) *psychotherapy plus drug therapy,* or (d) *nonscheduled treatment,* in which active treatment was not scheduled but the patient could call for one 50-minute session per month (Weissman et al., 1979). The results indicated that (a) the patients who received psychotherapy plus drug therapy were least likely to relapse, (b) the patients who received the nonscheduled treatment were most likely to relapse, and (c) the patients who received either psychotherapy alone or drug therapy alone showed intermediate relapse rates. Those results are summarized in Figure 11.12. The additive effect of psychotherapy and drug therapy occurs because when the symptoms of depression are reduced or eliminated with the drug, the patient can benefit more from the support and guidance provided in the psychotherapy (Klerman & Schechter, 1982).

In other research, it was found that among individuals who were at high risk for relapse after treatment for depression (they had a history of recurrent depression), relapse following drug treatment could be reduced if the individuals received psychotherapy (Frank, 1991; Frank et al., 1990). Furthermore, it was found that among the individuals who received psychotherapy, those whose therapy was more interpersonal (i.e., focused on social relations, support, and feelings rather than symptoms or intellectual issues) showed the lowest relapse rates (Frank et al., 1991). These findings offer additional support for the notion that the combination of drugs and psychotherapy is most effective, and they highlight the findings noted earlier that it is the personal rather than the technique-specific aspects of psychotherapy that are most important.

Comment

By now it should be clear that the question is not what treatment is best for depression but instead the question is *what treatment is best for what type of depression and what type of symptom?* The answer seems to be that physiological treatments (drugs, ECT) are better for depressions that are due to physiological problems (endogenous depressions), psychological treatments

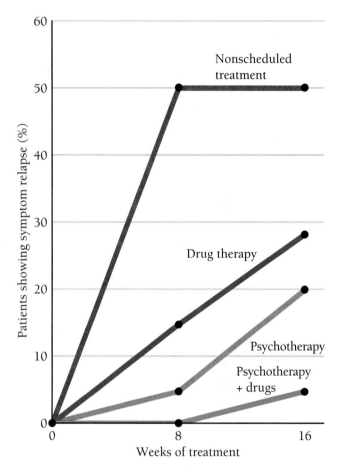

FIGURE 11.12 THE COMBINATION OF PSYCHOTHERAPY PLUS DRUG THERAPY WAS MOST EFFECTIVE FOR REDUCING RELAPSES IN DEPRESSION.

Source: Adapted from Weissman et al. (1979), p. 557, fig. 1.

are better for depressions that are due to psychological problems (exogenous depressions), and a combination of drugs and psychotherapy may be most effective for overcoming the wide range of symptoms that develop with depression and for preventing relapse.

Unfortunately, the problem of deciding on what type of treatment to use is complicated by the fact that it is difficult to determine whether an individual is suffering from an endogenous or an exogenous depression (see Chapter 8). In making that decision, we can consider whether there is a family history of mood disorders (a marker for a genetic or biochemical basis) and whether the individual experienced a strong stress prior to the depression (suggesting a psychological cause). However, neither of those signs is definitive, and therefore we often simply have to try different strategies to see which one works best for a particular individual. Which strategy should be tried first? Advocates for psychological interventions argue that psychotherapy should be tried first because it does not have unpleasant physiological side effects and because it is inherently wrong to experiment with biochemical balances in the body. In contrast, advocates for drug therapy argue that drugs should be tried first because if they are effective, they will probably work faster than psychotherapy, so we will know sooner whether they are an effective strategy. Furthermore, drug treatment is the less expensive alternative. (A month's supply of Prozac would cost about $65, which is only a fraction of what psychotherapy would cost.) In the absence of clear indications, which treatment to try first is often a matter of philosophy and pragmatics. The question of what to try first is one you may have to answer for yourself someday. What would you try first?

TREATMENT OF THE BIPOLAR DISORDER

The effective treatment of the bipolar disorder is exceptionally important because during their manic phases, individuals with the bipolar disorder can pose difficult management problems. As recently as 1970, our treatments for this disorder were ineffective, and we were limited to simply controlling the patients with straitjackets, heavy doses of sedatives, and confinement in seclusion rooms. That picture has changed dramatically, and the bipolar disorder can now be treated effectively.

The Use of Lithium

In 1949, it was discovered that **lithium carbonate** was effective for controlling both the mania and the depression seen in the bipolar disorder (Cade, 1949). Although lithium was used extensively in Europe to treat the disorder, it was not approved for use in the United States until 1970 because of its potentially serious side effects. Since its approval for use, it has been the treatment of choice for the bipolar disorder, and it is sometimes used to treat depression (the unipolar disorder) when other approaches fail.

Therapeutic Effects of Lithium.   There is strong and consistent evidence that lithium is effective for treating most but not all individuals who suffer from the bipolar disorder (Tohen et al., 1990). In one series of studies in which bipolar patients who were given either lithium or a placebo, 62% of the patients who were given lithium remitted their symptoms, whereas

only 5% of the patients who were given the placebo did so (see Fieve, 1981). In another series of studies, patients whose symptoms had been eliminated with lithium were either maintained on the lithium or were switched to a placebo without being informed (Baastrup et al., 1970; Hullin et al., 1972; Melia, 1970). The patients who remained on the lithium had a relapse rate of only 11%, but the patients who had been switched to the placebo had a relapse rate of 51%.

Although lithium has been found to be a very effective treatment for the bipolar disorder, the reason for its effectiveness is not yet clear (Manji et al., 1991; Risby et al., 1991). As we learned in Chapter 9, the bipolar disorder appears to stem from fluctuations in the amount of the neurotransmitter that is released by the presynaptic neurons or from fluctuations in the sensitivity of the postsynaptic neurons. Lithium probably reduces symptoms by stabilizing the processes responsible for transmitter release and neuron sensitivity, but exactly how it works has not yet been definitely established.

Monitoring Lithium Levels and Side Effects.
Low levels of lithium are not effective for treatment, and high levels are poisonous, so it is essential to monitor the levels of lithium in the bloodstream (Bassuk & Schoonover, 1977; Blom & Moore, 1978). During the first week, while levels are being established, it is necessary to take blood samples every day. Following that, weekly samples are necessary, and eventually checkups can be reduced to about one a month.

The most common side effects of lithium are thirst and frequent urination (to eliminate the fluids taken in to quench the thirst). At somewhat higher dosage levels, lithium can cause difficulty with concentration, memory, and motor coordination (Shaw et al., 1987). When the dosage level is too high, muscle tremors, gastric distress, and dizziness may set in (Herrington & Lader, 1981). Some years ago, patients would go through cycles in which side effects would set in shortly after the medication was taken and then dissipate as the effects of the drug wore off, only to appear again when the next dose was taken. The initial side effects occurred because patients had to be given a high enough dose to carry them through to the next administration. Fortunately, timed-release lithium tablets are now available, and thus the level of the drug can be maintained at a uniform level throughout the day without the side effect cycles.

Problems with Patient Compliance.   Lithium is clearly an effective drug for treating the bipolar disor-

Case Study 11.2

A 21-YEAR-OLD STUDENT WITH A BIPOLAR DISORDER WHO DISCONTINUED LITHIUM CARBONATE

After being "normalized" on lithium carbonate, I began to wonder whether I could exercise any conscious control over my moods. Having been through both extremes of bipolar illness, I believed that I would be able to detect the warning signals that would tell me when a mood swing was coming on. An inability to sleep and lack of appetite signaled a high coming on, and unwarranted depression and listlessness signaled a low. I rationalized that during my level period, I was medicating myself needlessly. Also, various aspects of taking lithium carbonate bothered me. The side effects of stomach discomfort, dry mouth, and the need to urinate frequently were very annoying, as was the simple hindrance of having to carry and take pills three times a day.

I also missed the wonderful feeling involved in the manic high. I believed that if I were to stay off lithium long enough to notice the first signs of mania coming on, I could then medicate myself to the point of holding my mood at a mild "hypomanic" state. This would let me feel happier and more energetic than usual, and I thought that with "a little medication" I could keep from climbing too high.

The problem, as I found out, is that it is very difficult to detect those first signals—especially those of depression. When I went off my medication, I found myself so depressed that I didn't even care enough to start the lithium again. Lithium does not have a fast-acting antidepression effect, and it took a long time for me to benefit when I did resume taking the medication.

My attempt to keep track of my high and control it was also unsuccessful. When I was feeling better (higher), I thought, "I can handle this—I'm sure I can handle a little more." Unfortunately, during the manic state, it is very hard to be objective, and I lost control. In the end, the expression "letting it get away from you" seems a very apt way to describe what generally happened when I went off my medication.

After a couple of disastrous experiences (I had to drop out of school and go back into the hospital until I was again normalized on lithium), I am now back on the medication for good, or at least until we have established that I am no longer at risk for bipolar mood swings. I now take my lithium in timed-release capsules, and the side effects are no longer noticeable.

---

der, and its side effects are minimal, especially when compared to the symptoms they replace. So you may be surprised to learn that it is frequently difficult to get patients to continue taking their lithium. Patients often stop taking it soon after their moods have stabilized. This usually occurs for one of three reasons: (a) Once the symptoms are gone the patient does not think that he or she needs the drug anymore, (b) the patient becomes annoyed with the side effects or the inconvenience of taking the medication, or (c) the patient misses the fun of the manic highs and goes off the medication in the hope of experiencing those highs again (Jamison & Akiskal, 1983; Van Putten, 1975). Going off the lithium in an attempt to "get high" is mostly likely to occur when the patient is facing a stress or crisis. It is interesting to note that bipolar patients are more likely to discontinue their drugs than unipolar patients, who experience only depression (Kocsis & Stokes, 1979).

An individual who goes off lithium is 28 times more likely to have a manic episode than an individual who stays on the medication (Suppes et al., 1991).

However, in some cases, the patient is foiled in the attempt to bring on mania because depression sets in instead. The experience of one patient who voluntarily discontinued his medication is presented in Case Study 11.2. (This is a follow-up report by the patient who described his original experience with the bipolar disorder in Case Study 10.1 in Chapter 10.)

LITHIUM AND TRICYCLICS FOR TREATING BIPOLAR AND UNIPOLAR DISORDERS

We have seen that lithium is usually used to treat the bipolar disorder and that tricyclics are usually used to treat depression (the unipolar disorder). Before concluding, however, we should note that in some cases (usually when the usual drug has not been effective), the drugs will be exchanged. There is evidence that lithium can be effective for reducing the depression seen in unipolar disorders and that the tricyclics can be effective for reducing the depression seen in the bipolar disorder (Davis, 1976a; Prien et al., 1984). Unfortunately, the tricyclics do not reduce the mania that is associated with the bipolar disorder, so they do not constitute a complete treatment for the bipolar disorder. Thus sometimes lithium can be used as a substitute for tricyclics in the treatment of unipolar disorders, but the tricyclics cannot be used as a substitute for lithium in the treatment of the bipolar disorder. Use of lithium as a substitute for tricyclics is rare, however, because of the greater problem of monitoring its levels and because of its side effects.

SUMMARY

When considering the treatment of depression, it is important to remember that many depressions (probably most mild depressions) diminish or disappear without formal treatment. If that were not the case, by early adulthood almost everyone would need treatment or would be in a constant state of depression. These reductions of depression without treatment are usually called spontaneous remissions, but rather than being truly spontaneous, they probably result from changes that take place without our notice. The stresses in our lives or the biochemical imbalances that initially bring on the depressions are reduced or eliminated, and hence the depressions are reduced or eliminated. It may not appear that way to a depressed individual (and it will do relatively little good to point it out), but the prognosis for most depressions is generally good; things will get better. However, for those individuals for whom the depression does not lift, a variety of effective therapeutic approaches are available.

Psychodynamically oriented therapists focus their efforts on helping patients deal with loss and stress. Although this approach can be successful, we do not yet understand what it is about the process of psychotherapy that results in the improvement. The fact that a wide variety of psychotherapeutic approaches appear to be equally effective suggests that the nonspecific factor of social support may be of prime importance.

Therapists who subscribe to the learning perspective believe that depression is due to low levels of reward and high levels of punishment, and therefore they teach patients how to increase rewards and reduce punishments. There is evidence that this approach can be effective. Actually, therapists of most persuasions (psychodynamic, learning, cognitive) work to increase rewards and decrease punishments, but those with a learning orientation pursue that goal more explicitly and systematically.

Therapists who approach depression from a cognitive perspective work to correct negative cognitions that lead patients to see themselves, their worlds, and their futures as negative. Cognitive therapy has been shown to be effective in a number of investigations. However, contrary to what was once thought, it is probably not superior to drug therapy for reducing depression, and some questions have been raised over exactly what it is about cognitive therapy that is responsible for the reductions in depression.

Therapists who view depression as due to low levels of neurotransmitters (norepinephrine or serotonin) will treat their patients with drugs that serve to reduce the reuptake of the neurotransmitters (bicyclics and tricyclics) or reduce the metabolism of the neurotransmitters (MAO inhibitors). Drug therapy has been shown to be effective for treating depression, but the drugs are a treatment rather than a cure, and they can have unpleasant side effects. However, in many cases, the side effects diminish with time and can be minimized by taking the lowest drug level that is effective. In serious cases of depression, electroconvulsive therapy (ECT) may be used. ECT is usually effective and fast-acting, but we do not yet understand why it works. ECT undoubtedly causes some brain damage, but it is not detectable in studies of brain structure or patients' cognitive performance. Furthermore, the retrograde amnesia that sometimes accompanies ECT can be reduced or eliminated with unipolar electrode placement. There is some evidence that light therapy can be effective for individuals with SAD, but it is not clear what aspect of the light produces the effects.

Controlled comparisons of the effectiveness of the various approaches to the treatment of moderate depression have not indicated a clear superiority of one approach over another. The lack of differences may be due to nonspecific factors present in all therapies or to the possibility that different approaches are effective for different subsets of patients. With regard to effects, it appears that psychotherapy may influence interpersonal symptoms, and drug therapy may influence the feelings of depression. Psychotherapy and drug therapy do not interfere with each other, and the combination appears to be more effective than either alone.

There is also a positive prognosis for patients suffering from the bipolar disorder. Spontaneous remissions are rare, and the disorder can be very serious if not treated, but in most cases it can be treated effectively with lithium carbonate. We do not understand exactly why lithium is effective for treating the bipolar disorder; it probably stabilizes either the production of neurotransmitters or the sensitivity of the postsynaptic neurons.

KEY TERMS, CONCEPTS, AND NAMES

In reviewing and testing yourself on what you have learned from this chapter, you should be able to identify and discuss each of the following:

bicyclics

drug prophylaxis

electroconvulsive therapy (ECT)

insufficient production (of
   neurotransmitters)

lithium carbonate

MAO inhibitors (MAOIs)

melatonin

metabolism (of neurotransmitters)

monoamine oxidase (MAO)

nonspecific (common) factor
   explanation

postamphetamine depression

psychomotor stimulants

retrograde amnesia

reuptake (of neurotransmitters)

social support

specific patient explanation

spontaneous remission

tricyclics

tyramine

PART 4

Schizophrenic Disorders

•OUTLINE•

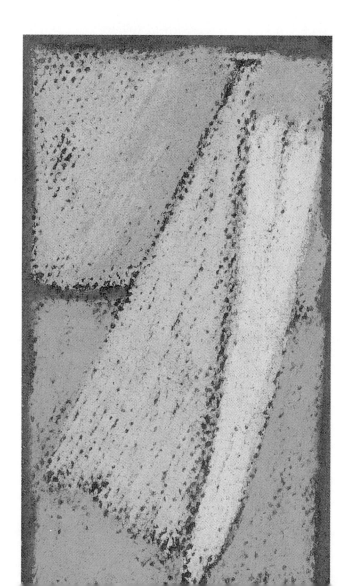

Chapter 12

Schizophrenic Disorders: Symptoms and Issues

ll of Lauren's friends thought that she was a typical, normal 34-year-old woman, but over a period of a few weeks, she began behaving more and more strangely. She did not recognize it, but she had a hard time concentrating, and when talking, she would jump from topic to topic with no apparent connection. She became very concerned about pollution and "cosmic radiation," and she attributed many personal as well as world problems to these factors. Sometimes she would laugh uncontrollably for no apparent reason. Lauren was admitted to a psychiatric hospital on an emergency basis when, according to her friends, "she just wasn't making sense anymore" and they became worried about her. After about 3 weeks in the hospital, many of her symptoms diminished, and she was transferred to the outpatient clinic, where she saw a social worker once a week. Within a month, she was judged to be "symptom-free," and her treatment was terminated. Four years have gone by since that episode, and during that time, she has not had any problems. She still does not understand what caused what she refers to as her "out-of-it period." The diagnosis in her records is "schizophreniform disorder."

Allan had always been a loner, and somehow he had just never "gotten his act together." He drifted through high school without ever really getting involved; he had no friends and joined in no outside activities. After high school, he tried working in a couple of fast-food places, but he could not seem to "keep things straight," and he lost those jobs. Allan was brought to a psychiatric hospital when the police found him on the street only half dressed. During his admission interview, he could give his name but did not know the day of the week, the month of the year, or where he was. It was impossible to learn much more about him because he was completely incoherent; his sentences were gibberish, and what could be understood was not related to the questions he had been asked. He kept talking about "they," but it was not clear who "they" were. Allan was admitted to the hospital with a diagnosis of "schizophrenia, disorganized type."

Ben has been hospitalized for over 30 years. During that time, he has received psychotherapy, numerous types of drugs, and electroconvulsive therapy. Every day for the past 8 years, he has sat in the same chair staring straight ahead but attending to nothing. The sides of his mouth twitch constantly, and his head jerks occasionally. He is able to take care of himself, go to meals, and feed himself. When asked questions, he only mumbles and then seems to "drift away." The ward staff cannot remember when he had his last visitor, and they refer to him as a "burned-out schizophrenic." It is unlikely that he will ever be able to leave the hospital.

The term **schizophrenia** (SKIT-zō-FRĒ-nē-uh) refers to a set of disorders that encompasses what are undoubtedly the most complex and frightening symptoms we will encounter. Individuals suffering from schizophrenia may hear voices, think that they are controlled by other persons, feel bugs crawling through passages in their bodies, believe that others are plotting against them, or express themselves using nonsensical language. It is estimated that between 1% and 2% of the population suffers from schizophrenia (Robins et al., 1984), and thus it is a serious disorder in terms of both the nature of the symptoms and the number of people who suffer from it.

Schizophrenia is particularly complex and frightening because the symptoms are totally beyond the realm of experience of most people. Many of us can understand disorders involving anxiety and depression because we have experienced those symptoms. However, few of us have had hallucinations and delusions, and thus we have great difficulty understanding them and often react to them with fear. Until recently, our fear of schizophrenia was intensified by the fact that it was considered incurable, and the diagnosis of schizophrenia meant a life sentence of misery and hopelessness on a back ward of a mental hospital. As we progress through Part 4, you will see that our understanding of schizophrenia is changing rapidly and that many of our earlier conceptions and fears of the disorder may no longer be appropriate.

Before going on to discuss the symptoms of schizophrenia, a brief comment should be made concerning the labels and phrases that are used when talking about individuals who suffer from schizophrenia. We usually talk about these persons as "schizophrenics," but that is not appropriate. Just as we do not talk about people with cancer as "cancers," we should not talk about people with schizophrenia as "schizophrenics." In doing so, we may imply more than is true. Having schizophrenia can be very serious, but it does not necessarily influence the person's entire being, and therefore it is not appropriate to write the whole person off as "schizophrenic." Many people have mild cases and have learned to cope with the symptoms (e.g., they may hear voices, but they may also ignore them), or their particular symptoms do not happen to interfere with their lives. Indeed, many persons with schizophrenia function effectively in society, and other people may not even be aware that they have the disorder.

Instead of talking about "schizophrenics," in this book we will talk about "individuals with schizophrenia" or "persons who suffer from schizophrenia." In some cases, that may seem awkward and wordy, but the way we label people is important because those labels influence our perceptions and conceptions. For example, the use of nonsexist language has reduced some of the stereotypes associated with gender. When I originally wrote these chapters on schizophrenia, I used the traditional approach and talked about "schizophrenics," but when I revised the chapters using the "individuals with schizophrenia" terminology, a subtle but important change emerged: The people I talked about become *people with a problem* rather than *problem people*. With this clarified, let us go on to discuss the symptoms of schizophrenia.

SYMPTOMS OF SCHIZOPHRENIA

Cognitive Symptoms

Probably the most obvious and most important symptoms of schizophrenia are cognitive. These symptoms include *hallucinations, delusions, disturbed thought processes*, and *cognitive flooding*.

Hallucinations. **Hallucinations** *are perceptual experiences that do not have a basis in reality*. An individual who hears, feels, smells, or sees things that are not really there is said to be hallucinating. *Auditory* hallucinations are the most common. They frequently involve hearing voices that comment on the individual's behavior, criticize the behavior, or give commands. For example, a woman we will discuss later hears monks chanting, "Cut yourself and die. Cut yourself and die" (see Case Study 12.2). Less frequently, hallucinations involve hearing other sounds, such as motors. *Tactile* and *somatic* hallucinations in which the individual imagines tingling or burning sensations of the skin or internal bodily sensations are also common. Finally, *visual* and *olfactory* hallucinations (seeing or smelling things that are not there) are also observed in persons with schizophrenia, but these types of hallucinations are less common than the others. It is important to realize that to the individuals having them, *hallucinations appear to be real perceptions*, and the individuals are *unable to distinguish hallucinations from real perceptions*. For example, the woman mentioned earlier is very bright and on one level knows that monks are not really chanting at her, but the experience is so real that she sometimes has to call me for what she calls a "reality check" to get reassurance that in fact there are no monks chanting at her.

Delusions. **Delusions** *are erroneous beliefs that are held despite strong evidence to the contrary*. Some delusions are bizarre and patently absurd; others are possible but unlikely. For example, the belief that there is a machine in the state capitol that sends out waves that make you think constantly about sex is a bizarre delusion, whereas the belief that there are FBI agents hid-

The Fly Man and The Snake
by Heinrich Müller/Collection de
l'Art Brut, Lausanne

Delusional beliefs that occur in schizophrenia are bizarre, pervasive, and resistant to change in the face of contrary evidence. This recently discharged patient may have been experiencing a delusion when he behaved as if the statue were a living person.

ing behind the trees in your backyard to spy on your sexual behavior is a nonbizarre delusion. The more bizarre the delusion, the more likely it is that the individual is suffering from schizophrenia.

The most common delusions are **delusions of persecution** in which individuals think that others are spying on them or planning to harm them in some way. Also common are **delusions of reference** in which objects, events, or other people are seen as having some particular significance to the person. For example, one patient believed that if a woman across the room folded a newspaper in a certain way, that was a sign that he was being followed by spies. Similarly, another patient interpreted a television advertisement proclaiming Coca-Cola as "the real thing" as a message that the people she was with at that time could be trusted. Persons suffering from schizophrenia also experience **delusions of identity** in which they believe that they are someone else. Common examples of this include delusions that they are Jesus, Joan of Arc, the president of the United States, Gypsy Rose Lee, or some other famous person. In many cases, individuals with schizophrenia develop very elaborate delusional systems involving many interrelated delusions, and the hallucinations they experience are often related to their delusions. One woman who thought she was the Virgin Mary (delusion of identity) heard voices (auditory hallucinations) that she thought were the voices of sinners crying out to her for mercy. Similarly, the stomach pains (somatic hallucinations) felt by another person with schizophrenia were taken as evidence that he had been poisoned (delusion of persecution).

Most normal individuals also maintain some beliefs that are inconsistent with reality. For example, we are sometimes incorrect in our assumptions about the motives of others, we see ourselves or others as better or worse than is actually the case, or we attach more importance to some things or behaviors than may be appropriate. However, the delusional beliefs in schizophrenia are more bizarre, more pervasive, and more resistant to change in the face of contrary evidence than the distortions most of us live with from day to day (see Oltmanns & Maher, 1988).

Disturbed Thought Processes. In addition to problems of *thought content* (what people think), there also appear to be problems in the way persons with schizophrenia think. It has been suggested that the *thought processes* of these individuals are characterized by a "loosening" of the associative links between thoughts, so that the individuals frequently spin off into irrelevant thoughts (Bleuler, 1936). A patient may be talking about his coat and then with no apparent transition will begin talking about medieval castles in Spain. Because persons with schizophrenia tend to include irrelevant ideas in their thoughts and conversations, their thought processes have been described as *overinclusive* (Cameron, 1944).

These disturbances in thought process are illustrated by the following response to the question "Who is the president of the United States?":

I am the president, I am the ex-president of the United States, I have been a recent president. Just at present I was present, president of many towns in China, Japan and Europe and Pennsylvania. When you are president you are the head of all, you are the head of every one of those, you have a big head, you are the smartest man in the world. I do testory and all scientist of the whole world. The highest court of doctoring, of practicing, I am a titled lady by birth of royal blood, (pointing to another patient) he has black blood, yellow blood, he is no man, a woman, a woe-man, etc. (Bleuler, 1936, pp. 72–73)

The phrases used by persons with schizophrenia are generally grammatically correct, but the thoughts expressed are disjointed and do not make sense when put together. Because of the apparent random nature of their thoughts, the utterances of persons with schizophrenia have been described as **flights of ideas** or **word salads**. Each ingredient or phrase is separately identifiable, but they have been mixed or tossed so that there is no order to them.

If individuals who suffer from schizophrenia have disturbed thought processes, their intellectual functioning is going to be impaired, and therefore in many cases we find that these individuals perform at *reduced intellectual levels*. For example, it would be difficult to perform well in an interview or on a test if you were giving responses that consisted of random thoughts strung together. Interestingly, the original term for schizophrenia was **dementia praecox** (di-MEN-shuh PRĒ-koks), which means "premature deterioration." When that term was introduced, it was thought that the patients suffered from an early onset of the type of intellectual deterioration that underlies senility. However, it was later realized that the deterioration in schizophrenia is very different from that in senility, and consequently the impaired intellectual functioning seen in schizophrenia is now referred to as the **schizophrenic deficit** in order to distinguish it from other forms of intellectual impairment.

Cognitive Flooding (Stimulus Overload). An important element in the cognitive experience of persons with schizophrenia involves an *excessive broadening of attention* that results in what may be termed **cognitive flooding** or **stimulus overload**. Many persons who suffer from schizophrenia lack the ability to screen out irrelevant internal and external stimuli. It is as though the "filter" that most of us have for eliminating extraneous stimuli is missing or broken. As a consequence, persons with schizophrenia are forced to attend to everything around and within them, and they feel as if they are being flooded to the point of overload with perceptions, thoughts, and feelings. The broadened attention, flooding, and overloading of the cognitive system is reflected in the following quotations from patients:

Things are coming in too fast. I lose my grip of it and get lost. I am attending to everything at once and as a result I do not really attend to anything.

Noises seem to be louder to me than they were before. . . . I notice it most with background noises.

Colors seem to be brighter now almost as if they are luminous. (McGhie & Chapman, 1961, p. 105)

One author provided the following description of the cognitive experience of schizophrenia:

The problem is that schizophrenia makes you so goddamned fragile. I was reacting appropriately, but to so many different things, so strongly, and in such a personal way that I didn't look that way to anyone else. More importantly, my being that fragile and reactive meant I couldn't do many things I wanted to do. I was so distractible that even very simple tasks were impossible to complete. (Vonnegut, 1975, p. 209)

This flooding can be seen in terms of brain activity. If you present a series of sounds, such as clicks, to individuals who are not suffering from schizophrenia, the brain will show a considerable response (increased electrical activity) to the first sound but a greatly reduced response to subsequent sounds. That is, the individual adapts to the stimulation, "closing the gate"

These images, created by persons with schizophrenia, reflect disturbed thought processes.

FIGURE 12.1 PERSONS WITH SCHIZOPHRENIA SHOW LESS ADAPTATION TO REPEATED STIMULATION THAN PERSONS WHO DO NOT SUFFER FROM SCHIZOPHRENIA.

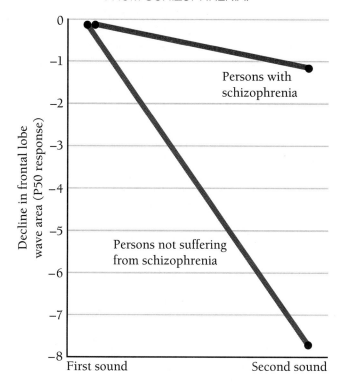

Source: Judd et al. (1992), p. 491, tab. 1.

on it. However, individuals who suffer from schizophrenia do not show the adaptation or gating. Instead, they show as great a response to subsequent stimuli as they did to the first stimulus (Braff et al., 1992; Judd et al., 1992). This effect is illustrated in Figure 12.1, in which the brain activity responses to two clicks in individuals who were or were not suffering from schizophrenia are plotted. The decline in responsivity shown by the individuals who were not suffering from schizophrenia was more than six times greater than the decline shown by individuals who were suffering from schizophrenia (−1.24 vs. −7.50). Obviously, the inability to close the gate on incoming stimulation could be very disruptive.

Note that cognitive flooding is not listed as a symptom of schizophrenia in DSM-IV. It is included here because it is an effective way of conceptualizing the nature of cognitive problems experienced by some individuals with schizophrenia.

Mood Symptoms

The moods of individuals with schizophrenia are typically described as "blunted," "flattened," or "inappro-

priate." In other words, these individuals are not as emotionally responsive as they should be to environmental or interpersonal situations. For example, when hearing of a death in the family or watching a very funny film, a person who has schizophrenia may remain impassive and show little or no emotional response. Yet in other situations, the same person will be emotionally volatile, but in a way that is inappropriate and inconsistent with what would be expected in the situation. For example, when discussing an injury or some other serious topic, the individual may break into laughter. Overall, then, the emotions of persons with schizophrenia can best be described as *inappropriate* or *situationally inconsistent*.

When interpreting the emotional responses (or lack thereof) of persons with schizophrenia, it is usually assumed that they give the *wrong response to a situation*. An alternative interpretation is that they give the right response to a *wrongly perceived situation*. That is, instead of responding incorrectly to the objective or external situation as it is perceived by others, the person with schizophrenia may be responding correctly to his or her own idiosyncratic interpretation of the situation (a delusion), to some internal response (a hallucination), or to some competing thought (stimulus overload).

The situation is analogous to one in which four persons are listening to recordings on headphones. Three of the people are hearing a very funny comedy album; unknown to the others, the fourth person is listening to quiet mood music. To those listening to the comedy album, the emotional responses of the fourth person would appear flat, blunted, and inappropriate. Viewed in this way, it may be that schizophrenia does not involve a disturbance of mood per se but rather that the mood appears to be disturbed because of underlying cognitive problems. It is possible that if we knew what a person with schizophrenia was responding to, the responses might strike us as perfectly appropriate.

One cautionary note should be sounded with regard to interpreting the flat mood that is often seen in persons with schizophrenia. Many of the antipsychotic drugs that are used to treat schizophrenia have the side effect of sedating the patient, so flat mood could be due to the schizophrenia or it could be due to the medication.

Somatic Symptoms

DSM-IV does not list any somatic symptoms for schizophrenia, but over the years a considerable amount of attention has been given to somatic responses. The somatic symptom that has attracted the most attention is general physiological arousal (heart rate, blood pressure, sweating palms), but the evidence is inconsistent and contradictory. In some studies, persons with schizophrenia are found to be more physiologically aroused than normal individuals, while in other studies they are found to be less aroused. The conflicting findings may be due to the possibility that different levels of arousal are associated with different types of schizophrenia or different phases of the disorder. For example, it may be that persons with acute cases are overaroused, but those with chronic cases are underaroused. It is also possible that level of arousal is a function of the types of delusions experienced. Persons who believed that others were plotting to kill them would probably be more aroused than persons who thought that they were already dead.

Hallucinations and delusions often involve somatic complaints (the individual may feel pains for which there is no organic basis or may believe that parts of his or her body are rotting away), but we must be careful not to confuse those cognitive symptoms with actual somatic symptoms. Also, because many of the drugs that are used to treat schizophrenia have somatic side effects such as dryness of the mouth and increased sensitivity to the sun, we must be careful not to confuse the effects of the treatment with the effects of the disorder.

Motor Symptoms

The range of motor symptoms in schizophrenia is wide. Some persons with the disorder remain immobile for long periods of time, whereas others are very agitated and exhibit a high level of activity. Other motor symptoms include unusual facial grimacing and repetitive finger and hand movements. Many of the movements of patients appear random and purposeless, but in a few cases they are related to the patients' delusions. For example, individuals with delusions of persecution may direct large amounts of activity toward hiding or defending themselves from their persecutors.

As was the case with some of the other symptom patterns, it is important to distinguish between the motor symptoms of schizophrenia and the side effects of the medications that are used to treat it. As we will learn later, many of the drugs that are given to persons with schizophrenia influence the areas of the brain that are responsible for motor behavior, and thus some (but not all) of the tremors, muscular contortions, and stiff gait these persons exhibit are due to the treatment and not the disorder.

Some of the delusions and problems with thought processes seen in schizophrenia are illustrated in Case Study 12.1.

Diagnostic Criteria

From the foregoing discussion, it should be apparent that the clinical picture of schizophrenia encompasses a wide variety of symptoms. The symptoms that are necessary for an official diagnosis of schizophrenia are summarized in the list in Table 12.1.

It is important to recognize that different individuals who are diagnosed as suffering from schizophrenia may have *very different sets of symptoms*. As indicated in Table 12.1, apart from showing a deterioration in functioning (criterion 2), an individual needs to suffer from only *any two* of the five symptoms (criterion 1) to be diagnosed as suffering from schizophrenia. One person might have hallucinations and delusions, another might have hallucinations and disorganized behavior, and a third might have disorganized speech and negative symptoms. Indeed, there are 10 different possible combinations of symptoms that could lead to the diagnosis, and no single symptom is common to all individuals who are diagnosed as suffering from schizophrenia.

It is also important to note that the diagnosis of schizophrenia is arrived at by *exclusion*. Individuals who suffer from other disorders such as organic mental disorders or mental retardation sometimes show the same symptoms (see Chapter 20), and an individ-

---

TABLE 12.1 DIAGNOSTIC CRITERIA FOR SCHIZOPHRENIA

1. At least two of the following are present for at least 1 month:
   a. Delusions
   b. Hallucinations
   c. Disorganized speech (frequent derailment or incoherence)
   d. Highly disorganized behavior
   e. Negative symptoms (e.g., flat mood, lack of motivation, poverty of speech, inability to experience pleasure)
2. Functioning in areas such as work, social relations, and self-care are markedly below previous levels.
3. Symptoms persist for at least 6 months.
4. Symptoms are not due to a major mood disorder (depression, mania).
5. Symptoms are not due to substance abuse, medication, or a general medical condition.

Case Study 12.1

THE THREE CHRISTS OF YPSILANTI: A CONFRONTATION OF DELUSIONS

Some years ago in a hospital in Ypsilanti, Michigan, a psychologist brought together three patients, each of whom believed that he was Christ. The goal was to see how—or if—these three men could resolve their conflict over who was Christ. Although each believed that he was Christ, they went by the names of Joseph, Clyde, and Leon. What follows is a summary of some of their interactions with one another and the psychologist. The first day, each man was asked to introduce himself:

Joseph: My name is Joseph Cassel.

Psychologist: Joseph, is there anything else you want to tell us?

Joseph: Yes, I'm God.

Clyde: My name is Clyde Benson. That's my name straight.

Psychologist: Do you have any other names?

Clyde: Well, I have other names, but that's my vital side and I made God five and Jesus six.

Psychologist: Does that mean you're God?

Clyde: I made God, yes. I made it seventy years old a year ago. Hell! I passed seventy years old.

Leon: Sir, it so happens that my birth certificate says that I am Dr. Domino Dominorum et Rex Rexarum, Simplis Christanus Pueris Mentalis Doktor. [In Latin, this means "Lord of Lords and King of Kings, Simple Christian Boy Psychiatrist."] It also states on my birth certificate that I am the reincarnation of Jesus Christ of Nazareth, and I also salute, and I want to add this. I do salute the manliness in Jesus Christ also, because the vine is Jesus and the rock is Christ, pertaining to the penis and testicles; and it so happens that I was railroaded into this place because of prejudice and jealousy and duping that started before I was born, and that is the main issue why I am here. I want to be myself. I do not consent to their misuse of the frequency of my life.

Psychologist: Who are "they" that you are talking about?

Leon: Those unsound individuals who practice the electronic imposition and duping. . . . I want to be myself; I don't want this electronic imposition and duping to abuse me and misuse me, make a robot out of me. I don't care for it.

Joseph: He says he is the reincarnation of Jesus Christ. I can't get it. I know who I am. I'm God, Christ, the Holy Ghost, and if I wasn't, by gosh, I wouldn't lay claim to anything of the sort. I'm Christ. . . . I know this is an insane house and you have to be very careful.

And so it went, each patient asserting that he was God and often rambling off into other associations and delusions. One day when Leon was holding his head as if in pain, the psychologist asked, "Do you have a headache?"

Leon: No, I don't sir, I was "shaking it off," sir. Cosmic energy, refreshing my brain. When I grab cosmic energy from the bottom of my feet to my brain, it refreshes my brain. The doctor told me that's the way I'm feeling, and that it is the proper attitude. Oh! Pertaining to the question that you asked these two gentlemen [a question about why they were here], each one is a little institution and a house—a little world in which some stand in a clockwise direction and some in a counterclockwise, and I believe in a clockwise rotation.

Sometimes the men developed other delusions to explain the conflicts brought on by their original delusions. For example, when Clyde was asked to explain the fact that Joseph and Leon both also claimed to be God, he explained: "They are really not alive. The machines in them are talking. Take the machines out of them and they won't talk anything. You can't kill the ones with machines in them. They're dead already."

When asked where the machines were located, Clyde pointed to the right side of Joseph's stomach. The psychologist then asked Joseph to unbutton his shirt, and with his permission, Clyde tried to feel around for the machine. When he couldn't find it, he said: "That's funny. It isn't there. It must have slipped down where you can't feel it."

The bizarre nature of the symptoms of these men and their interactions is reflected in the following descriptions of some of their typical ward behavior.

Coming to a table at which Clyde and Joseph are sitting, Leon says, "Ah, good morning, ye instrumental gods," and sits down with a self-satisfied smile. "These men are victims of electronic imposition," he continues.

Clyde leaps up, yelling: "I made the place!"

Later Joseph stands up, banging his fist on the table, and talks to Leon about "good old England." Leon, who is sitting down, stands up, and Joseph sits down. "My salute to you, sir," says Leon. Joseph gets to his feet again, and they salute each other. Then they shake hands, after which Leon shakes hands with Clyde, who is sitting close by, telling him he's an instrumental God, hollowed out four or six times. "Hallowed," Clyde insists, "not hollowed."

Queen Elizabeth is on TV. Joseph says he's not interested in watching the queen because she is taking his place, although he saved her years ago by preventing two men from throwing her off London Bridge.

After living together constantly for over 2 years and after meeting every day in an attempt to resolve their conflict, each of the three Christs of Ypsilanti still thought that he was Christ. Furthermore, none showed improvement in his schizophrenia.

Source: Adapted from Rokeach (1964).

ual is diagnosed as having schizophrenia *only after those other disorders have been ruled out.*

Finally, it is crucial to note that schizophrenia *does not necessarily imply an inability to operate effectively outside of a hospital.* The diagnosis requires that there be a deterioration from a previous level of functioning, but if the demands on the individual are low or do not involve areas in which the symptoms will be disruptive, the individual may be able to function effectively and undetected in society. Whether or not persons with schizophrenia are able to function in society depends on factors such as (a) the nature of the symptoms (delusions may be less disruptive for daily functioning than stimulus overload), (b) the context in which the individual must function (hallucinations will be less disruptive for a farmer plowing a field than for a secretary in a busy office), (c) the degree to which others will tolerate deviance (eccentricities are better tolerated in a university than a law firm), and (d) the severity of the symptoms. A colleague of mine is widely known as a brilliant scientist, but what most people do not know is that this person suffers from schizophrenia. Similarly, I know of a student who graduated from a prestigious medical school and then announced that he had been hallucinating and delusional for the past 5 years.

Many of the symptoms and problems of persons with schizophrenia are illustrated in Case Study 12.2.

PHASES OF SCHIZOPHRENIA

Individuals who suffer from schizophrenia are thought to go through three phases. First, some patients go through a **prodromal phase** in which intellectual and interpersonal functioning begins to deteriorate. During this phase, some peculiar behaviors appear, emotions become inappropriate, and unusual perceptual experiences begin to occur. This phase can last anywhere from a few days to many years. In cases in which the prodromal phase is prolonged and the individual shows an insidious downhill course, the long-term prognosis is usually poor.

Second is the **active phase**, in which the symptom patterns are clear-cut and prominent. Hallucinations, delusions, and disorders of thought and language become identifiable, and behavior may become more grossly disorganized. Third, some patients go through a **residual phase** that is similar to the prodromal phase in that the symptom picture again becomes less clear. Symptoms such as hallucinations and delusions may still exist, but they are less active and less important to the individual. Associated with the muting of symptoms is a general blunting or flattening of mood

The prognosis for "burned-out" patients is very poor.

and often a general decline in intellectual performance. This combination of symptoms often makes it impossible for the individual to return to the premorbid level of social and occupational functioning.

Although not officially recognized as such, there is another phase, often referred to as the **burned-out phase**. This more extreme form of the residual phase is most likely to be seen in patients who have been hospitalized for many years. The symptom picture is probably due in large part to the effects of long-term institutionalization. Burned-out individuals do not show many of their original symptoms of schizophrenia, but they show a very serious deterioration of social skills. They may eat with their hands, urinate in their clothing, and be completely insensitive to people around them. It is unlikely that burned-out patients will ever be able to function outside the hospital. These patients are sometimes referred to as "back ward" patients because they are generally "warehoused" out of sight of other patients and the public. Fortunately, the number of such patients seems to be declining. That is probably because we now have more effective treatments than we did when these patients were originally hospitalized, and so fewer patients deteriorate to this point. Also, with the new emphasis on community-based treatment, even disturbed patients are less likely to be kept in a hospital for long periods of time, and therefore they avoid the effects of institutionalization (see Chapter 22). An example of a burned-out patient is presented in Case Study 12.3 (p. 275).

TYPES OF SCHIZOPHRENIA

So far we have discussed schizophrenia as though it were one disorder, but it is now generally agreed that it probably involves a group of disorders, and it is now common to talk about the "schizophrenias" or the

Case Study 12.2

A TALK WITH BETTY ABOUT HER SYMPTOMS

Betty is a good friend of mine who suffers from a very severe case of schizophrenia. Betty is a very bright, articulate, and friendly woman who graduated from college with a degree in fine arts and later earned a master's degree in library science. Her father was president of a large state university, her mother is a teacher and nurse, and she has three sisters who are successful professionals.

Betty's schizophrenia first appeared when she was in college, and she has struggled with the symptoms ever since. She has been hospitalized many times and has had just about every treatment imaginable. She is currently on a variety of drugs that we will discuss in Chapter 14. It has been about 3 years since her last hospitalization, and she now lives by herself in an apartment. Betty calls me three or four times a week for brief chats and what she calls "reality checks." Each semester she comes to my class to talk about schizophrenia. Below is an excerpt from an interview with Betty in which she and I talked about some of her symptoms. Later in the book we will consider Betty's treatment.

David: Betty, let's talk a little about your symptoms. Could you begin by telling me about your hallucinations?

Betty: Hallucinations have been a major part of my illness. Probably the first hallucination I had was the sound of glass breaking when people walked. You know, that real fine crystal, and it would be kind of crunchy when people walked. It seemed strange and I couldn't understand it, but I heard it all the time.

The next hallucination that developed was that when certain people were around, I would hallucinate electricity coming out of their bodies, in colors. I could see it, and I didn't want to get radiation.

David: What did it look like?

Betty: Like neon, just coming in different colors. People looked like they had bands of color coming out of their bodies, and it was too hot for me to be close to them, physically, because I could feel the waves, the heat. I don't see the radiation much anymore, but now I see auras around people. Different people have different colors.

David: Do I have an aura now?

Betty: Oh, yes, blue. Blue is good. People with blue auras are good.

David: Have you had other visual hallucinations?

Betty: I think the most awful hallucination I had—and still have—is the blood, blood pouring down people's faces. Sometimes everybody has blood pouring down their foreheads and down their front. When I look at people, they are all bloody. It's really horrible. The first time it happened, I was so scared, and nobody believed me. They didn't understand what I was seeing, and they

kind of ignored me and sneered. It still happens, usually at night, but sometimes in the afternoon. It's like living in a slaughterhouse, and I don't want to look at anybody, so I just kind of keep to myself.

David: How do you deal with this? What do you do when it happens when you are talking to someone and the person starts bleeding?

Betty: I try and just finish the conversation and get away, but sometimes I can't. I just try to act normal. I have this thing about acting normal, which has nothing to do with reality whatsoever. I just say, "Hi, how are you," and then get out of there. I see it, I can't stop seeing it, so I have to get away from the bloody people.

David: Could you tell me about the demons?

Betty: They started up a long time ago. They used to come and go, but now they are constant—around me all the time. One set is in my head—I see them; they wear cloaks, and they chant.

David: Are they in your head or in the room?

Betty: These are my in-head ones; I have two sets. These are in my head, and they chant, "Cut yourself and die. Cut yourself and die." Well, sometimes they goof up and come out, and that really frightens me, and I want to get armed.

David: Armed?

Betty: Yes, get a knife or something to protect myself.

David: What about the out-of-head demons?

Betty: Well, they look like the demons, but their cloaks are bigger and black. They are men; I can't see their features, but they are human. They wear those leather pointy shoes, like they did in the Middle Ages. They don't chant; they talk to me. They tell me I'm stupid and worthless.

David: Where do you see them?

Betty: I don't think I've ever seen them on the street, but they are in my apartment all the time. When I sit at my desk, they line up behind me, and when I go to bed, they stand at the foot at the bed. They say all kinds of horrible things, like I should have been a dead fetus and that I'm useless and I hurt so many people in my life that I could never repay them all. I'm unsure anyway, and with the demons telling me those things, it's terrible.

David: How real do the demons appear?

Betty: How real? *Absolutely real.* I mean, intellectually, I know they are hallucinations, *but they are real to me.* I know they are hallucinations, but sometimes I have my doubts. That's when I have to call you for a "reality check"—to have you assure me that they are hallucinations.

Hallucinations are very real, and they can lead you to do some strange things. One night, I had this hallucination of myself covered in blood, and I went into the kitchen and got a knife and just cut my whole arm up. I thought, if I can bleed, I'm not dead, I'm alive.

David: Do you ever have other kinds of hallucinations, say, smell things?

Betty: Rotting flesh. I smell that off and on, not often. I often taste things. Things taste like metal—very unpleasant.

David: Let's shift to delusions. Can you tell me about your delusions?

Betty: Well, there's what I call the "ticker tape" delusion that everyone can read my forehead.

David: I don't understand.

Betty: You know, like in Times Square, where the words go around the front of the building in light bulbs. That's what I thought was here on my head, and as I had thoughts, they were flashed across my forehead, and I thought that everyone could read my thoughts. I was convinced that people could read my thoughts that way, and I couldn't figure out how to make it stop, so sometimes I would walk around with my hands over my forehead to keep people from reading my thoughts.

Talking about mind reading, I should tell you about the "shower" delusions. I had a male friend, and every morning when I got in the shower, I thought he was able to read my mind. I thought he could read my mind while I was in the shower, so whenever I was in there, I tried to keep thinking good thoughts about him. You know, "Andy is so nice," "Oh, gee, I really like Andy." I wanted him to think that I only thought good things about him.

David: This happened only in the shower?

Betty: Yep, but I thought that my mother could read my mind anywhere. That's what I made the code for.

David: The code?

Betty: Yes, if Mother said a certain sentence, that meant she was reading my mind but wasn't telling me. And the sentence would be something inane, like "How are you?"

David: So if your mother said, "How are you?" that was a signal that she was reading your mind?

Betty: Yes, and I was furious that she was doing it. I confronted her and she denied it, but I didn't believe her.

David: Have you had any other delusions?

Betty: Oh, yes, lots. Probably my major delusion has been that the police are after me. Whenever I see a patrol car, I am sure they are following me, and they can really frighten me. I am convinced that they can read my mind with their equipment, on their radios, and they are after me. They do it real cleverly; they don't just come out and get me. They watch; they're waiting for a chance. It's really scary.

David: Do you think that now?

Betty: (Pauses with a somewhat sheepish smile) Well. . . . I know it's a delusion, but . . . well, yes, I still think they are after me. Now I think, well, I'm not going to be paranoid about the police, and then a patrol car goes by and . . . I don't know . . . The funny thing is, I don't know what they would do to me or what I've done. You know, I have this feeling, a profound feeling inside of guilt. . . .

When I see a patrol car, it is a sign of oncoming psychosis.

David: A symbol of oncoming psychosis? I don't understand.

Betty: Well, they zap me with their radar, and eventually it will destroy my brain.

David: Let's talk a little about disturbances of thought processes. What's that like?

Betty: Well, it's like you have roads through your brain. When you think, you travel on them. Mine have detours and barricades. My thoughts get blocked or get detoured, and it gets all mixed up. I don't know quite when it started, but when I get a thought, I can't always follow it to completion. Sometimes it happens when I am talking. I get confused, or all of a sudden I'll think, "The demons are here," and then I'll start to worry about them or listen to them, so I get distracted.

David: Betty, can you tell me what it's like to function, to get through the day, with all of these symptoms?

Betty: It's like hell. You know, you see people doing things, just doing things, and it's so hard for me. People get up and eat and read and clean the house, and I have such a hard time just getting into the shower—and then I might have to worry about someone reading my mind. Everyone seems so competent, and I can't do it. . . . I think it's a dirty trick from the demons. . . .

I can't always think right, and then there is the paranoia. It makes very thing so hard to do. When I am around people, I think they can read my mind, that they know about my illness, that they are making fun of me, so I leave. I remember one day when I was working at the library and I had to alphabetize some cards, and I just couldn't do it. Sometimes when I am really sick, it is like everyone is speaking in Greek to me, and I can't understand it. It is like being in Italy and not speaking Italian, and no one can speak English to you. You just can't understand what is happening. It is just like being out of it. It's *hell*.

"schizophrenic disorders." In DSM-IV, distinctions are made among five types of schizophrenia. Each type has as a core the symptom pattern discussed earlier, but each type is differentiated from the others by the relative predominance or absence of a particular symptom or set of symptoms.

Case Study 12.3

"OLD ALEX": A CASE OF BURNED-OUT SCHIZOPHRENIA

The ward staff usually calls the patient "Old Alex." When he was hospitalized 36 years ago, he was diagnosed as "schizophrenic." He was described as intelligent and articulate but agitated and suffering from delusions of omnipotence. Then Alex thought he was "the brother of God, sent to free those who were damned by the Devil." Today Alex sits slumped in a metal chair in a lonely corner of Ward G. His mouth twitches frequently, and his head occasionally jerks involuntarily to the left. He is dressed in wrinkled blue pants and a plaid shirt, the laces of his shoes are not tied, and he does not wear socks. There is a large urine stain on his pants just below the belt.

Much of the time, Alex seems to be dozing, but when he is awake, he stares blankly at the wall a few feet in front of him. *Wheel of Fortune* is on the television and Vanna White is smiling and turning letters, but he doesn't seem to notice her—or anything else. Old Alex has been sitting there staring at the wall for as long as any of the ward staff can remember.

At 11:30, when it is time for lunch, a young attendant comes over, shakes Alex's shoulder gently, and says, "Come on, Alex, it's time for lunch. Come on, Alex, lunch." Alex turns his head and looks up. He looks at the young attendant for a few moments with great effort, as if he were straining to see through a dense fog. Then he gets up and shuffles with a stiff-legged gait toward the door where the other patients are waiting to be taken to the dining room. Once in the dining room, he eats his food with his fingers rather than with a fork, but when scolded by the attendant, he wipes his fingers on his shirt and begins using his fork.

Alex never makes any trouble on the ward, and he is liked by the staff. He has to be prodded to dress in the morning, and four or five times a day he has to be reminded about going to the bathroom, but he is compliant and does whatever he is told, in a mechanical way. His bad table manners do not reflect symptoms; it is more as if he has simply forgotten to use his fork.

Other people are often around Alex on Ward G, but he seems isolated and not really with them. Alex has an older sister in New Jersey who sent him a small box of cookies at Christmas 2 years ago, but that is the only contact he has had with his family for many years. Once every couple of years, the students from an abnormal psychology class visit the hospital, and Alex is one of the patients they interview. The interview is usually rather disjointed because Alex tends to lose the thread and drift off. When asked whether he still thinks he is the brother of God, he concentrates for a while as if trying to remember the plot of a long-forgotten movie and then responds somewhat distractedly, "Er . . . I don't think so . . . Maybe . . ."

Every 6 months, Alex is brought up for a routine evaluation at a ward staff meeting. This is strictly routine; his behavior has not changed in years, and there are no new treatments to be tried with him. The entries in his hospital file are repetitive: "No change. Recommend that care on domiciliary ward be continued." Alex will live out his life slumped in the chair, staring at the wall, and unaware that the woman on TV has just turned over a winning set of letters. There is a small graveyard behind the hospital, and someday Old Alex will be quietly moved there.

Disorganized Type

As the name indicates, persons with **disorganized schizophrenia** show the greatest degree of psychological disorganization. They are frequently incoherent; have blunted, inappropriate, or "silly" mood; are socially withdrawn; and show behavioral oddities such as grimaces and unusual mannerisms. However, they do not have a systematized set of delusions, and thus there is no understandable structure to their symptom pattern.

Catatonic Type

Catatonic (KAT-uh-TON-ik) **schizophrenia** is characterized by a psychomotor disturbance. In the classic form, the catatonic patient is stuporous and shows what is called **waxy flexibility.** Patients with this symptom pattern are like wax statues in that they are generally mute, and when placed in a particular position, they will remain in that position for long periods of time. One patient was so immobile that he did not blink his eyes, and they had to be taped shut so that the surface would not dry out and be damaged. In contrast, some patients show a high level of motor activity involving frenzied and excited behaviors, and yet others patients may vacillate between stupor and excitement. Although catatonic schizophrenia was apparently quite common several decades ago, individuals with this disorder are now very rare. The reason for the decline in catatonia is not clear, but it may be that these types of symptoms are particularly amenable to the medications that are available today.

Paranoid Type

The dominant symptoms in **paranoid** (PAR-uh-noyd) **schizophrenia** are delusions of persecution and grandiosity. For example, patients may think that family members are plotting against them in order to steal a long-lost inheritance (persecution) that would place them among the wealthiest people in the world (grandiosity). Patients with paranoid schizophrenia also sometimes have hallucinations with a persecutory or grandiose content (e.g., voices criticize them or tell them they have special talents). However, such patients do not show disorganization of thoughts or behavior. Indeed, apart from their delusions, they often behave in very normal ways. Probably because of their concerns about persecution and their need to defend their high self-concepts, these individuals tend to be anxious, argumentative, and sometimes violent if confronted.

Undifferentiated Type

Undifferentiated schizophrenia is essentially a catchall or "wastebasket" category consisting of individuals who cannot be placed in any of the preceding categories or who meet the criteria for more than one of them.

Residual Type

Individuals who are diagnosed with **residual schizophrenia** have had at least one schizophrenic episode in the past and currently show some signs of schizophrenia such as blunted emotions, social withdrawal, eccentric behavior, or thought disorder, but these symptoms are generally muted. Furthermore, symptoms like hallucinations and delusions are infrequent or vague. Although individuals with this pattern are identified as having a particular type of schizophrenia, in many cases it appears more likely that they are simply in the residual phase of the general disorder (we will return to this in our discussion of the course of schizophrenic disorders).

Although technically schizophrenia is broken down into the five types just discussed, in reality the symptoms seen in any one person often do not fit into any one of the types, or the symptoms change over time. Case Study 12.4 involves a man who first showed the symptoms of the paranoid type but in later episodes showed symptoms that do not fit clearly into one of the types. This case is particularly interesting because the person is a psychologist who functions normally and effectively as a professional in the periods between his acute episodes.

DISORDERS RELATED TO SCHIZOPHRENIA

Having described the clinical picture of schizophrenia and the five types of schizophrenia, it is important to distinguish between schizophrenia and five other disorders that in some cases involve the same symptoms as schizophrenia.

Brief Psychotic Disorder

The distinction between the **brief psychotic disorder** and schizophrenia involves the *duration* and *causes* of the disorders. The brief psychotic disorder lasts only between *1 day and 1 month* (so it is relatively *brief*), and in most cases it is thought to stem from *an overwhelming stress*. Indeed, prior to the publication of DSM-IV, this disorder was called the *brief reactive psychosis*. This symptom pattern is in contrast to schizophrenia which is traditionally thought to continue for a prolonged period of the individual's life, and the onset of which is not usually associated with any particular event or stress. We see instances of the brief psychotic disorder after various disasters (e.g., earthquakes, wars). The change in terminology (from reaction to disorder) reflects the change in view that schizophrenic symptoms can but need not be a response to environmental stressors.

Schizophreniform Disorder

The **schizophreniform** (SKIT-zō-FREN-i-form) **disorder** differs from the brief reactive psychosis and schizophrenia in terms of *duration*. Specifically, it lasts between *1 and 6 months*, thus putting it between the brief reactive psychosis and schizophrenia. Like schizophrenia, it does not appear to be triggered by a particular stress. In other words, this disorder takes the *form* of schizophrenia, but because of its shorter duration, it is not considered to be schizophrenia. If an individual is diagnosed as suffering from the schizophreniform disorder but the symptoms last longer than 6 months, the individual will be rediagnosed as suffering from schizophrenia.

The distinctions among schizophrenia, the brief reactive psychosis, and the schizophreniform disorder are summarized in Table 12.2 (p. 278). From a practical standpoint, the most important distinction among these three disorders is the difference in the *prognoses*. The prognosis for an individual suffering from schizophrenia is usually thought to be poor; it is possible that the disorder will persist throughout the individual's life. In contrast, by definition, the prognosis for an individual with a brief reactive psychosis or a schizophreniform disorder is very good (symptoms disappear within 4 weeks or 6 months, respectively). Indeed, it is widely assumed that individuals with those disorders will soon be symptom-free regardless of what

Case Study 12.4

A PSYCHOLOGIST TALKS ABOUT HIS OWN STRUGGLE WITH SCHIZOPHRENIA

Frederick J. Frese III was a 26-year-old college graduate when the symptoms of schizophrenia began to develop. At the time, he was a lieutenant in the U.S. Marine Corps, where he was responsible for guarding atomic weapons and providing security for the Fleet Intelligence Center for Europe. Fred wrote the following about his symptoms and his means of dealing with them.

"Work became very difficult for me, and I could not understand why everything seemed so hard to do in a proper manner. After several months of struggling to understand why things were so difficult, I suddenly figured it all out. It became quite obvious to me that during the Korean War, the Chinese had taken prisoners and given them posthypnotic suggestions. By the use of certain 'key words,' the Chinese were controlling those who had been their prisoners. It was very easy for me now. All I had to do was to find out which Marines and others had served in Korea, and avoid them, because if they found out that I knew about them, surely they would take steps to neutralize me. My immediate superior, a certain major, often talked about his experiences in the Korean War. He needed to be helped, and our country needed protection from him and the others under Chinese control. In order to help him, I decided to call the base hospital, where I talked to a psychiatrist about how we might best go about 'deprogramming' the persons who had been hypnotized. The psychiatrist asked me to come to the hospital to talk with him. I did so, but after a brief chat, I was escorted to a small single room in the hospital, where I was told that I was now a psychiatric patient and could not leave. Soon thereafter, I learned that I had been given the diagnosis of paranoid schizophrenia. Clearly, in my mind, I had made a serious mistake. Obviously, the psychiatrist had been in Korea, too.

"Those who the Chinese controlled now knew that I had discovered them, and I knew that it was only a matter of time before one of them would be 'activated' to kill me. I started demanding that a priest administer the last rites before they got to me. After about 3 days a kindly priest visited me and administered the sacrament, and I was prepared to die.

"But I was lucky. Before long, a plane arrived that took me to Washington where I became a patient in the Naval Hospital in Bethesda, Maryland. I was promptly escorted to the psychiatric ward. There I would remain for five months while I very carefully probed everyone I came in contact with to find out if they had ever been to Korea. I totally resisted the idea that I had a psychiatric problem. I just knew something very important that others did not know, and I did not seem to be able to convince anyone of the great threat that our country was facing. There was nothing wrong with me other than the fact that 'I knew too much.' After 5 months, I was released from the hospital and from the Marine Corps.

"Because I had learned to speak some Japanese when I was in the service, I enrolled in a graduate school to study international business. Those who were controlled by the Chinese did not seem to be around the school. Maybe I was safe. Maybe they had forgotten me, and I could quietly live a regular life. After a year, I graduated from business school and secured employment with a 'Fortune 500' company. The company needed my skills in Japanese to deal with Japanese manufacturing firms. It was very exciting to be receiving so much attention. But then, in all the excitement, I started behaving very strangely. I suddenly started being controlled by numbers and lights. Red lights stopped me and green lights started me, and all tasks were translated through numbers. I began stopping everything whenever I saw a red light no matter where the red light might be, and not starting again until I saw a green light. Finally, after a lot of desperate acts, one Sunday I went to a cathedral in the downtown area, where, without invitation, I started assisting the priest celebrating the High Mass. Shortly thereafter, I began feeling and behaving more strangely. I started grunting, then barking. I began turning into a monkey, then into a doglike animal, then into a reptile, a dragon, then into a wormlike creature. Later I was to 'realize' that what I was experiencing was like going backward through an evolutionary process. Finally, I degenerated totally. I had become only one atom, and it was the atom in the center of an atomic bomb. I was being loaded onto a bomber airplane. The world was going to end in nuclear holocaust, and I had been turned into the mechanism for its destruction. Everything was over. It was only a matter of time. . . .

"The next thing that I remember, I was in a bed with my legs and arms strapped down, inside a small room. It was another psychiatric ward. I was to remain there for several weeks.

"Unusual experiences like these happened to me numerous times during the past 23 years. But after the first 10 years, during which I was in 9 different hospitals for a total of about 300 days, I have not had to be rehospitalized. I still have breakdowns, but I have learned to sense when they are coming on and to 'cut short' the mechanism of the breakdown. I usually handle these circumstances or attacks by taking time off from work and staying around home singing, dancing, synthesizing the religions of the world, eating raw acorns, or behaving in some other strange manner as I work out my problems.

"During the time between breakdowns, I have earned a PhD in psychology and worked as a psychologist and administrator in a large state hospital, helping other people with schizophrenia who have not learned to cope as well as I have. I very much like being around the patients because I can see a lot of myself in each of them. We have a common experience. Whether the patients might be a 'mystic Abyssinian warrior' or hiding from 'the Green Gang,' whether they are hearing voices or cannot button their shirts properly, I remember 'being there' myself, and I know it is possible to return from that 'parallel reality' that one enters through the mechanism of psychosis."

Today, Dr. Frese works effectively as a psychologist and mental health administrator in Ohio. His case clearly illustrates the symptoms of schizophrenia and demonstrates that it is possible for some persons to lead productive lives while suffering from the disorder.

---

is or is not done for them. The diagnoses of brief psychotic disorder and schizophreniform disorder were introduced primarily to provide diagnoses for individuals who got better because, as we will see later, traditionally schizophrenia is considered a progressive disorder that does not remit.

Schizoaffective Disorder

As the name implies, the **schizoaffective** (SKIT-zō-uh-FEC-tiv) **disorder** involves a *combination of schizophrenia and a major mood disorder* (depression or mania). To be diagnosed as having the schizoaffective disorder, the individual must at one time have shown the symptoms of schizophrenia and a mood disorder and at another time shown only the symptoms of schizophrenia. This is a confusing and controversial diagnostic group and rather than having another diagnostic group, we might wonder why the individual is not simply diagnosed as suffering from schizophrenia and a mood disorder, just as an individual might have a cold and a broken arm.

Shared Psychotic Disorder

The diagnosis of **shared psychotic disorder** is used when an individual develops a delusion as a consequence of a close relationship with another individual who has a delusion. For example, a woman who has a delusion that she is Princess Diana might have a friend who thinks she is Fergie.

Delusional (Paranoid) Disorder

Finally, we must give some attention to the **delusional disorder**, which prior to the publication of DSM-III-R was referred to as the *paranoid disorder*. As the name implies, the major symptom of the delusional disorder is the *presence of one or more delusions*. Unlike some schizophrenic delusions, the delusions that are present in the delusional disorder are *nonbizarre*. In other words, they involve situations that could occur in real life, such as being followed, poisoned, infected, loved from a distance, or deceived by others. Auditory and visual hallucinations may be present in some cases, but when they are, they are limited to a few brief moments rather than occurring throughout the day as is the case in schizophrenia.

It is important to note that individuals with the delusional disorder do not show the persistent hallucinations, thought disorder, and general decline in intellectual performance seen in schizophrenia. Indeed, the presence of an unshakable delusion in an individual who otherwise appears normal and functions well is one of the striking things about the delusional disorder. This is illustrated in Case Study 12.5.

TABLE 12.2   DISTINCTIONS AMONG SCHIZOPHRENIA, THE BRIEF PSYCHOTIC DISORDER, AND THE SCHIZOPHRENIFORM DISORDER

DISORDER	DURATION	CAUSE
Brief psychotic disorder	1 day to 1 month	May be due to sudden stress
Schizophreniform disorder	1 to 6 months	Not specified
Schizophrenia	Lifelong	Not specified

Case Study 12.5

A SUCCESSFUL EXECUTIVE WITH A DELUSIONAL DISORDER

Mr. Arronson was a very successful executive in a large corporation. He was intelligent, hardworking, and quietly competitive. Those were the traits he thought were necessary to "keep one step ahead of the competition." Mr. Arronson was happily married, the father of two children, and well liked by his friends and colleagues. He had done well, his future was bright, and there was no sign of any problems.

One day, Mr. Arronson got to the office before his secretary had arrived. At about 9 o'clock, a telephone repairman arrived to install a new phone in Mr. Arronson's office. The secretary did not know that Mr. Arronson was already in his office, so she sent the repairman in without announcing him. When the door to his office opened and Mr. Arronson saw an unknown man carrying a heavy metal case and wearing a jacket with a phone company emblem on it, he reached into his desk drawer, took out a .38 caliber revolver, and shot the repairman at point-blank range! He then ran from the office but was soon caught.

A psychological examination revealed that for years, Mr. Arronson had suffered from a delusion that "others" were plotting against him, were trying to steal his ideas, and would eventually try to "eliminate" him. Mr. Arronson could not explain who the "others" were, but he believed that "they" got access to his mail and tapped his phone to "track" his ideas. Mr. Arronson was in a competitive business in which there was some "corporate espionage," but his beliefs were clearly delusional. The extremity of his delusions was reflected in the fact that he kept vans stocked with cans of food in four parts of the city (north, south, east, and west). The vans and food were to be used to help with his "getaway if they ever closed in." When the repairman entered the office unannounced carrying a black metal case, Mr. Arronson thought "they" were coming for him, and he shot in self-defense.

When making a diagnosis of delusional disorder (or paranoid schizophrenia), it is critical to rule out possible organic causes of the delusions. As we will learn later, delusions can stem from numerous types of drugs (particularly the amphetamines) and a variety of organic mental disorders (see Chapters 19 and 21), but in the case of the delusional disorder, the delusions cannot be traced to any known organic factor. Case Study 12.6 (p. 280) is a self-report of a serious delusional disorder written by an undergraduate student.

Before concluding our discussion of the disorders related to schizophrenia, a brief comment should be made concerning the **schizotypal** (SKIT-zō-TĪ-pul) and the **schizoid** (SKIT-zoyd) **personality disorders**. As the term implies, these are *personality disorders* rather than *psychoses*, so although they involve some of the symptoms of schizophrenia, they are less severe disorders. Specifically, an individual with the schizotypal personality disorder has mild versions of the symptoms seen in schizophrenia, and it is widely assumed that this disorder may be a mild form of schizophrenia. In contrast, an individual with the schizoid personality disorder shows the flat mood and social isolation often seen in schizophrenia, but not the cognitive symptoms such as hallucinations, delusions, or disturbed thought process. We will discuss these disorders in greater detail in Chapter 15, but at this point you should note their differences from schizophrenia.

Now that we have discussed the symptoms of schizophrenia, the types of schizophrenia, and the disorders related to schizophrenia, it might be helpful if we put the pieces together. In Figure 12.2 (p. 283), you will find a decision tree for making a diagnosis of schizophrenia. By working through it, you will see how the various factors are related and how a diagnosis is finally made.

Individuals with a delusional disorder do not show the persistent hallucinations, thought disorder patterns, and general decline of intellectual performance seen in schizophrenia. Shown here is cult leader David Koresh, whose behavior indicated that he probably suffered from a delusional disorder.

Case Study 12.6

A SERIOUS DELUSIONAL DISORDER IN AN UNDERGRADUATE WOMAN

I am a 26-year-old paranoid, maybe a paranoid schizophrenic. My first psychotic "breakdown" occurred when I was 20, but there were a lot of problems before that.

I was raised in a very chaotic family. Both my parents were alcoholics, and I experienced the usual madness that is always present within an alcoholic family. When I was a very young child, my mother taught me a complex fantasy life designed to "escape all of the people who would like to take advantage of us." By the age of 5 or 6, I was already having a difficult time distinguishing between fantasy and reality. I usually played by myself for a number of reasons. Many of the parents of classmates thought I was odd, and their children were not allowed to play with me unless the play was supervised. I often tried to pull them into my fantasies.

My mother was very concerned about established organizations such as school and government that might learn too much about our family. "They" might try to lock us up. I was never allowed to fill out any of the typical enrollment forms in grade school, but instead I had to take them home so that Mom could pick and choose what was pertinent for the school records. Often this rigorous screening would end in parent-teacher conferences, after which Mom would tell me, "They will definitely be watching you now."

By age 10, I totally believed my mother. The teacher would send home notes about the fact that I was talking to myself or some other aberrant behavior. Mom would tell me that I shouldn't do these things in public but that I could be "normal" at home. And so I was. I often stayed in the closet for hours talking to myself and enjoying the praise from Mom for being such a "good girl."

The punishments my mother gave me for misbehavior were often bizarre. They typically involved cleansing rituals in which I would be placed in a bathtub full of water and told to pray for purification and forgiveness.

In an attempt to flee this disturbed atmosphere, my brother entered the Marine Corps at 17. He was away for 3 years, and I felt as if my only link with sanity had been transferred from home. I was not allowed to write to him for fear that "they would read the mail." Once I wrapped a letter in a box and disguised it as a birthday present and mailed it to him. It was the only letter he received from me.

At 15, I entered high school, and this was the beginning of the serious downhill slide. There were too many people, and they were constantly staring at me, or so I thought. I adopted many strategies for avoiding them. I wouldn't look into their eyes. I wouldn't participate in any school activities. I was an honor student, but I wouldn't attend any of the functions associated with that status. I did attend one academic award ceremony at my mother's insistence. She didn't believe that I was a scholar, but she wanted us to go to "find out why they are persecuting the family."

I always attempted to avoid social contact. I would dress in unusual clothing (often my brother's or my mother's) and use a lot of makeup in an attempt to keep people from recognizing me. For relaxation, I sat in front of a strobe light and thought cosmic and mystic thoughts.

By my sophomore and junior years, my paranoia was fairly intense. The girls I knew had begun to date and establish their femininity, but I was being taught at home that sex was the work of the Devil and that all men are suspect. I began to question the motives of my girlfriends and their relationships with boys. As a consequence, they discontinued their friendships with me. Now I was sure it wasn't just the men who were suspect but that these girls were actually boys who were sent to trick me. I began to keep files on everyone I knew.

After graduation from high school, I got a job and moved out of the house. Things seemed relatively calm, but they were anything but calm within my mind. My fears about governmental agencies became so intense that I started checking my apartment for bugs and telephone taps whenever I returned home. Whenever I got a wrong-number call, I was certain that this marked the beginning of some complex eavesdropping scam whereby "they" could now hear everything going on inside my home. I changed my telephone number so often that finally the phone company refused to change it anymore without a fee. Now, I concluded, the phone company was in on the plot.

It was at this stage that I began to hear voices. At first they were friendly, and I thought I had been chosen by God for some special mission. I sat in the backyard or in the bedroom closet for hours and waited for messages that never came. After several weeks, the theme of the voices changed, and I felt damned and doomed. The voices would tell me of elaborate traps that were designed to get me, and they often involved the people with whom I worked. Whenever I spent any time with other people, I was sure they could hear my thoughts.

I took the following summer off to get my act together. I worked on some projects around my apartment and visited with friends. My concentration and motivation were quickly deteriorating, and I did not complete any of the projects. In an effort to elude my persecutors, I packed my car one fall evening and escaped in the night to wander around the southeastern United States. The money ran out in about 3 weeks, and "they" were still following me anyway, so I returned home.

When I returned, everything was the same. I still checked the apartment, I still sat in the closet, and often I stayed up the entire night roving from room to room so that "they couldn't get a fix on me." Finally, I could no longer cope with it all by myself, so I got in my car and drove to my parents' house. I drove in a roundabout fashion to elude my followers. When I arrived at their home, I had my "breakdown." I felt as if my limbs were not attached to my body and that my brain and mind were separate entities. I was waving my arms about madly in an attempt to get my mind to return to my brain and the two of them to reestablish themselves in my body. My mother held and rocked me in a darkened bedroom. I wanted to get to a mental hospital, but she wouldn't allow it. She called our family doctor of 30 years and described my state. The doctor called it a "psychotic break" and told Mom that if I had what he thought I had, it would pass regardless of the type of intervention used, so Mom decided to keep me at home. When I spoke (which was not frequent because I felt that everyone could hear my thoughts anyway), I was usually incoherent and began to cry. I knew that God was punishing me for all of my sins and that I would surely go crazy and die. Only one of these two things occurred.

I spent the next 2 or 3 months at my parents' home. After a couple of months, I began to feel better, although I was still extremely paranoid. The voices had dissipated, and I slowly reoriented myself to the outside world. I told my family that I still needed psychiatric help, but they refused to listen because "nobody in our family gets sick." Finally, I got a job delivering packages. I could work alone, and it didn't tax me mentally. I found any mental activity difficult, and occasionally I thought that my mind was going to blow up and my employer would find me dead in the streets from insanity. At that point, I sought the aid of a psychologist.

I immediately didn't like her, but I thought this was due to the paranoia. She gave me an MMPI and I lied on all of the questions to appear normal because I was sure she would send this information to the government. I wouldn't allow her to take notes, and after two sessions, I stopped going.

Next I went to the local mental health center. I was the only person in the waiting room, and I sat quietly until I noticed one of those big round mirrors that are mounted near the ceiling at corners. I could see them and they could see me. I began to pace and hide myself behind pillars. When the receptionist saw my behavior, she quickly assigned me to a social worker, who seemed concerned and sympathetic. I didn't tell her my "real" symptoms, but I am sure she was aware of them after my behavior in the waiting room. We could not get a schedule of meeting times worked out, so I left. Two weeks later, I had another breakdown. The dismembered feeling was back, so I called the social worker. She referred me to another social worker who had more flexible hours. I saw that social worker for a year, but I never told her any of my symptoms. One night, I finally told her about the voices, and she immediately sent me to a psychiatrist. After asking me how to spell my name properly, the psychiatrist prescribed Triavil. By the end of the week, the drug had offered no relief, so he prescribed Elavil as a supplement. My symptoms only got worse. While driving around at work, I was convinced that no one could see me. Some rational part kept saying that wasn't so, but the irrational part was winning. I became so delusional that I stopped at a self-serve gas station and asked the attendant in the little glass booth, "Can you see me?" He promptly closed his little window and picked up his phone. Poor man! I jumped back in my car and drove off, debating about whether I should admit myself to a local hospital, but my mother's words about no one in our family getting sick were still with me, so I didn't. Somehow I completed my work that day and returned to the psychiatrist and told him what he could do with his pills, and then I went to the social worker and told her what she could do with her practice.

About 2 years ago, I started seeing a psychologist. She has been teaching me social skills and coping techniques. During the first 4 months of therapy, I would not discuss the nature of the problem with her, although my symptoms were very pronounced. If she looked at me for too long, I thought that she was judging me, and I would hide behind the chairs in the office. She could not take notes. She could not record the sessions, and occasionally I would hide from her in her outer office. She worked very slowly with me, beginning with the issue of trust. After the first year, I did trust her somewhat. Sometimes she would "goof up" in my mind, and we would have to start all over with the trust thing. She told me to call her anytime I thought I was losing control, and I did. Sometimes I wouldn't talk while on the phone, but she would know it was me and would talk as if I were responding.

I started college as a part-time student and soon ran into many of the same problems I had faced in high school. However, my therapist helped me with everything from maintaining eye contact to processing information. I am continually scanning my environment for clues as to how I am doing (instead of who is trying to do what to me). I liken the techniques that I am learning in therapy to what a color-blind person learns; after many years, the color-blind person learns how other people process colors, and he identifies colors in those terms so that other people will understand him. There are still many stumbling blocks, but I am slowly learning to overcome them. I always sit in the front of the class, not because I am one of the smart folks but because if I need to ask a question, I won't notice that everyone is looking at me. I prefer to perform all of my social activities in groups. When I speak

alone with anyone for more than 2 or 3 minutes, I become quite frightened and think that they will know that I'm ill. I have two friends who know of my illness, and I often seek refuge with them when I feel about to collapse and I am unable to see my therapist. The collapses are still frequent (two to five a year) and usually consist of reducing me to a jelly-like state both mentally and physically, but they are getting less and less frequent and less overwhelming.

Note. The foregoing account was written when the woman was a senior in college. I have kept in contact with her over the years and can report that she is now for the most part symptom-free and is doing very well in a professional career. When I recently asked how she was getting along, she commented about how busy and behind schedule she was at work but said that it was a lot easier working now that she did not have to spend time checking every room for bugs. One clear sign of her improvement is her willingness to allow me to print her story.

POSITIVE VERSUS NEGATIVE SYMPTOMS OF SCHIZOPHRENIA

There is considerable dissatisfaction with the traditional classification of schizophrenia into the five types that were described earlier (disorganized, catatonic, paranoid, undifferentiated, and residual). That dissatisfaction arose because the classification has not led to an understanding of the processes underlying schizophrenia or to guidance concerning how to treat individuals with different symptom patterns. Therefore, a number of alternative means of classifying symptoms (and hence patients) have been suggested. The alternative that is most promising involves grouping symptoms into two types, **positive symptoms** and **negative symptoms** (see Andreasen, 1982; Andreasen & Olsen, 1982; McGlashan & Fenton, 1992).

Nature of Positive and Negative Symptoms

Positive symptoms include hallucinations, delusions, thought disorders, and bizarre behaviors. These are called positive symptoms because they are *active* or *florid* symptoms. In contrast, negative symptoms include flat mood, poverty of speech, inability to experience positive feelings, and apathy. These are called negative symptoms because they reflect *defects* or *lacks*. Another way of distinguishing between the types is that positive symptoms are behaviors not usually found in

normal individuals, whereas negative symptoms are the *absence of behaviors* usually found in normal individuals. This organization of symptoms is summarized in Table 12.3 (p. 284), along with some of the other factors that are associated with the two groups of symptoms.

There are strong correlations among positive symptoms, and there are strong correlations among negative symptoms, but positive symptoms are not correlated with negative symptoms (Lenzenweger et al., 1989; McGlashan & Fenton, 1992). This suggests that positive symptoms have a common cause and that negative symptoms have a common cause, but that the two types of symptoms have different causes. This is consistent with the notion suggested earlier that schizophrenia probably consists of two or more separate syndromes. Some patients may have both positive and negative symptoms, thus suggesting that their disorder stems from more than one underlying cause. (We will discuss causes in Chapter 13.)

Characteristics Associated with Positive and Negative Symptoms

The most consistent finding is that negative symptoms are associated with *poor premorbid adjustment*. For example, before being diagnosed as suffering from schizophrenia, individuals with primarily negative symptoms (a) showed poorer social and sexual functioning, (b) progressed less far in school, and (c) per-

FIGURE 12.2 DECISION TREE FOR DIAGNOSING SCHIZOPHRENIA.

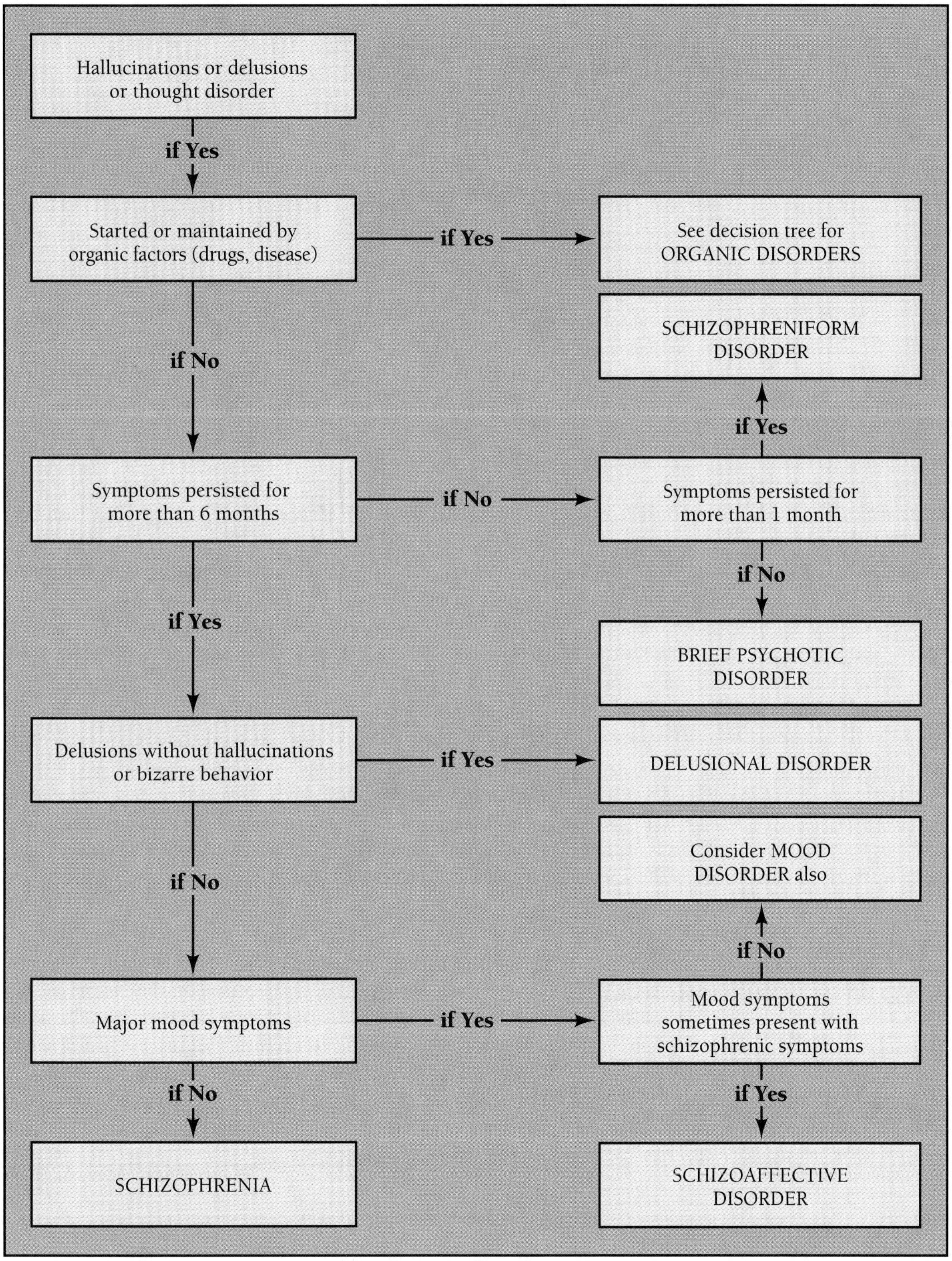

formed worse in work settings. There also appears to be a tendency for negative symptoms to be associated with lower scores on intelligence tests.

With regard to gender, it was found that *men were consistently more likely to suffer from negative symptoms than were women.* The reason for the gender differ-

ences is not clear, but it reflects the less optimistic view for males suffering from schizophrenia.

Individuals with positive or negative symptoms tend to be diagnosed as suffering from schizophrenia at about the same age, but because the negative symptoms are slower to develop than the positive symp-

TABLE 12.3   POSITIVE AND NEGATIVE SYMPTOMS OF
SCHIZOPHRENIA AND THEIR RELATIONSHIPS TO OTHER
VARIABLES

POSITIVE SYMPTOMS (BEHAVIORS NOT USUALLY FOUND IN NORMAL PERSONS)	NEGATIVE SYMPTOMS (ABSENCE OF BEHAVIORS USUALLY FOUND IN NORMAL PERSONS)
Hallucinations	Flat mood
Delusions	Poverty of speech
Thought disorder	Inability to experience positive feelings
Bizarre behavior	Apathy
Related variables:	**Related variables:**
Better premorbid functioning	Worse premorbid functioning
More frequent occurrence in females	More frequent occurrence in males
More rapid, later onset	Slower development, earlier onset
Less stable symptoms	More stable symptoms
Responsive to drug therapy	Unresponsive to drug therapy

toms, it appears that the disorder may have an earlier start for individuals with negative symptoms.

Finally, both positive and negative symptoms are fairly stable over time, but the negative symptoms are somewhat more stable (see McGlashan & Fenton, 1992). That is, the negative symptoms tend to be associated with a more chronic, treatment-resistant disorder, whereas the positive symptoms are more likely to remit or be successfully treated.

Overall, the distinction between positive and negative symptoms seems to reflect important differences in functioning and underlying processes, and it may be related to the differential effectiveness of different treatment strategies. There is still a good deal to be learned about positive versus negative symptoms, but the distinction already appears to be more valuable than the traditional classification of symptoms.

ISSUES ASSOCIATED WITH SCHIZOPHRENIA

Early Formulations

Now that we have an understanding of what schizophrenia is, we can consider how our conceptualization of the disorder developed over time. Formal attempts

at the systematic identification and explanation of schizophrenia did not take place until late in the 19th century when **Emil Kraepelin** (ā-MĒL KRĀ-puh-lin) (1856–1926) in Germany and **Eugen Bleuler** (OY-gen BLOY-lur) (1857–1939) in Switzerland focused their attention on the problem. These two men offered very different views of the disorder, and the views they introduced a century ago still influence our thinking about it. Their ideas are summarized in Table 12.4.

Description.   Kraepelin labeled the disorder *dementia praecox,* and he suggested that it had an *early onset* and was characterized by a *progressive and irreversible intellectual deterioration.* Indeed, it is from those two characteristics that he derived the name for the disorder: *Praecox* refers to the early onset of the disorder, and *dementia* refers to the progressive deterioration that occurs.

In contrast, Bleuler did not believe that the disorder necessarily had an early onset or that it inevitably led to intellectual deterioration. Because Bleuler used a broader definition, he included many more individuals (older and younger, recovered and chronic) within the diagnostic class and offered a more optimistic prognosis for individuals who were diagnosed as suffering from schizophrenia.

TABLE 12.4   THEORIES OF EMIL KRAEPELIN AND EUGEN BLEULER CONCERNING SCHIZOPHRENIA

KRAEPELIN	BLEULER
Early onset	Late onset possible
Progressive and irreversible deterioration	Deterioration not inevitable
Intellectual deterioration	Breakdown of associations
Variety of symptoms; patients can have any or all of them	Set of core symptoms that all patients have plus set of accessory symptoms that patients may or may not have
Called *dementia praecox* ("premature deterioration")	Called *schizophrenia* ("splitting of the mind")
Due to physiological causes	Due to physiological causes, but psychological factors may provoke or influence symptoms

Process.   Regarding the nature of the disorder, Kraepelin suggested that the symptoms reflected an intellectual deterioration (dementia) like that seen in senility. Bleuler, by contrast, suggested that the disorder involved a breakdown of the associative threads that connected words, thoughts, and feelings. The breakdown of those associations was then used to explain the symptoms seen in schizophrenia: Disordered language patterns stemmed from the use of disconnected words, problems in thought processes stemmed from the use of disconnected thoughts, and inappropriate affect stemmed from the fact that emotions were disconnected from thoughts. Bleuler coined the term *schizophrenia* ("splitting of the mind") to reflect the breakdown of associations.

Cause.   Finally, it is interesting to note that both Kraepelin and Bleuler believed that the disorder had a *physiological* basis. However, Bleuler, who was trained as a psychoanalyst, thought that the symptoms could be influenced by psychological factors. He wrote:

We must conclude from all of this that psychic experiences—usually of an unpleasant nature—can undoubtedly affect the schizophrenic symptoms. However, it is highly improbable that the disease itself is really produced by such factors. Psychic events and experiences may release the symptoms but not the disease. (Bleuler, 1950, p. 345)

Our current conception of schizophrenia involves a combination of the ideas of Kraepelin and Bleuler. From Kraepelin we have accepted the ideas that the disorder is progressive and irreversible and consists of a variety of symptoms in different combinations. We agree with Bleuler that the disorder can have a late onset and that it should be called *schizophrenia.* As we will see later, however, there are still differences of opinion concerning the causes of the disorder, but the prevailing point of view seems to be consistent with that of Bleuler that the disorder has a physiological basis but the symptoms are often precipitated and influenced by psychological factors.

Prevalence, Age, and Gender Distributions

The results of a community study in which almost 10,000 individuals were interviewed indicated that 1.5% of the population suffers from schizophrenia at some time during their lives and another .1% suffer from the schizophreniform disorder (Robins et al., 1984). The seriousness of the problem is magnified by the fact that schizophrenia is often a long-term disorder.

Schizophrenia is most frequently diagnosed during young adulthood. In fact, early editions of DSM specified that the onset must be before the age of 45,

but DSM-IV does not specify an age window for diagnosis. The community study just mentioned indicated that schizophrenia was most likely to be diagnosed between the ages of 25 and 44 (Robins et al., 1984). In many cases, especially those involving negative symptoms, the disorder undoubtedly starts much earlier, but the full symptom picture is not manifested and the individual is not diagnosed until young adulthood.

The evidence concerning a possible link between gender and schizophrenia is inconsistent; some studies reveal a higher rate for women, others reveal a higher rate for men, and yet others show no difference (e.g., Iacono & Beiser, 1992; Robins et al., 1984). In contrast, there is evidence that men are usually first diagnosed as having the disorder at a younger age than women (Lewine, 1981; Loranger, 1984). The relationship between gender and age at the time of diagnosis is illustrated in Figure 12.3.

This difference between the genders in the age of onset has been consistently found in more than a

FIGURE 12.3   SCHIZOPHRENIA IS DIAGNOSED EARLIER IN MALES THAN IN FEMALES.

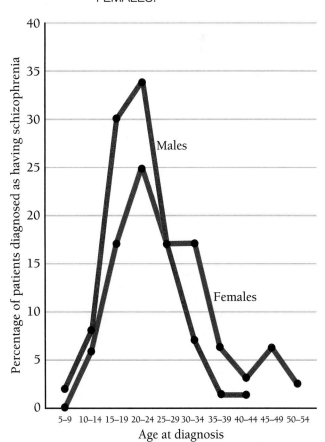

Source: Loranger (1984), p. 159, fig. 1.

dozen studies in numerous countries, but we still do not have an explanation for it. One possibility is that women are more likely to be at home than men, so their pathology is more likely to remain hidden for longer than would be the case for men. Another possibility is that the biochemical or hormonal differences between men and women play a role by either triggering the disorder earlier or suppressing it until later in one of the sexes. The evidence does not yet allow us to accept or reject any of these explanations, and it may well be that they all play a role.

Men and women apparently also differ in symptom picture and prognosis (Lewine, 1981): Men are more likely to have had very poor premorbid adjustment, to show symptom patterns involving withdrawal and passivity (negative symptoms), and to have poor prognoses. In contrast, women are more likely to have had good premorbid adjustment, to show symptom patterns involving a good deal of affect and activity (positive symptoms), and to have good prognoses. The difference in the histories, symptom patterns, and prognoses for men and women are unexplained at present.

Schizophrenia and Social Class

Members of the lower class are more likely to be diagnosed as suffering from schizophrenia than members of the upper class. In fact, the rate of schizophrenia has been reported to be as much as eight times higher in the lower class than in the middle or upper classes (Dohrenwend & Dohrenwend, 1974; Kohn, 1973; Strauss et al., 1978). It has been known for many years that the rate of schizophrenia is higher in the centers of cities where lower-class individuals are more likely to reside (Faris & Dunham, 1939; Hollingshead & Redlich, 1958; Srole et al., 1962). The relationship between social class and schizophrenia has often led to the speculation that the environmental stresses associated with living in the lower class cause (or at least contribute to) the development of schizophrenia. This has been referred to as the **sociogenic** (sō-sē-ō-JEN-ik) **model** of schizophrenia. The influence of stress on the development of schizophrenia will be considered in detail in Chapter 13. Here we will consider some alternative explanations for the relationship between social class and schizophrenia.

Downward Social Drift.

One explanation for the relationship between social class and schizophrenia is that suffering from schizophrenia leads individuals to drift downward into the lower social classes (Myerson, 1940). Such a drift might be expected because schizophrenia frequently results in greatly reduced levels of social and intellectual functioning, thus making it more difficult for the individual to maintain a position in society. For example, if a business executive developed a serious case of schizophrenia such that his or her thought processes were consistently disrupted by irrelevant associations, he or she might be forced to take a less important and lower-paying position that involved fewer intellectual demands. If the social drift hypothesis is true, the lower-class status of persons with schizophrenia would be a result rather than a cause of the disorder.

In one study of the social drift hypothesis, the investigators compared the social class of a group of male patients who had schizophrenia to the social class of the patients' fathers (occupational level was the measure of social class; Turner & Wagonfeld, 1967). The results indicated that 42.7% of the patients had drifted downward from the levels of their fathers, whereas national census data suggested that only 25.5% of males in general show such a drift.

Although there is evidence that schizophrenia is associated with downward social mobility, it does not appear that the amount of downward drift that has been documented is sufficient to account for the very strong relationship between social class and schizophrenia. Therefore, we must conclude that downward drift contributes to the class-disorder relationship but that other factors also contribute to it.

Bias in Diagnosis.

Because it is widely believed that schizophrenia is more likely to occur among lower-class individuals, it is possible that social class is used as a factor in making diagnoses. A class bias in the diagnostic process would enhance this relationship and perpetuate a potentially erroneous belief.

In an attempt to determine whether social class influenced diagnosis, I once gave two groups of psychiatrists sets of written descriptions of patients and asked them to make diagnoses. The descriptions given to the two groups were identical except that in one set the patients were described as having an upper-class background, whereas in the other set the same patients were described as having a lower-class background. When a comparison was made of the patients who had the same symptoms, it was found that the lower-class patients were more likely to be diagnosed as suffering from schizophrenia and the upper-class patients were more likely to be diagnosed as suffering from a bipolar disorder. It does seem, then, that social class influences diagnosis, but by itself the bias effect does not appear strong enough to account for the strong relationship between social class and schizophrenia.

Bias in Identification and Treatment.

If lower-class individuals are more likely to be treated in public hospitals and upper-class individuals are more likely to be treated in private hospitals, then because more re-

Schizophrenia is diagnosed more frequently among lower-class individuals.

search is done in public hospitals, it is more likely that investigators will have access to the records of lower-class patients, and hence lower-class persons with schizophrenia will be more likely to be identified than upper-class persons with schizophrenia. Second, if lower-class patients get lower-quality treatment than upper-class patients (and they probably do because they cannot afford the better treatment), then the lower-class persons with schizophrenia will be in treatment for longer periods of time and their numbers will increase over time. Therefore, when counts are made, more lower- than upper-class persons would be found with schizophrenia, but the difference would be a reflection of the differences in treatment rather than in the incidence of the disorder among upper- and lower-class patients (Kramer, 1957).

Bias in Self-Presentation.

It is also possible that differences in the ways that upper- and lower-class individuals present themselves and interact with the hospital staff will influence whether or not they are diagnosed as suffering from schizophrenia. For example, given the same set of symptoms, a poorly educated lower-class individual with inadequate social skills may be seen as having schizophrenia, whereas an upper-class individual will be seen as eccentric (Hollingshead & Redlich, 1958).

Prenatal and Perinatal Complications.

In Chapter 13, you will learn that some cases of schizophrenia can be linked to prenatal complications such as poor diet or diseases of the mother during pregnancy and to perinatal complications such as problems during labor or illness immediately after birth. Because those problems might be more likely to occur among poorer individuals, they might account for the higher proportion of schizophrenia in lower classes. (Goodman & Emory, 1992).

From the foregoing discussion, it should be clear that lower-class individuals are more likely to be diagnosed as having schizophrenia than upper-class individuals and that there is evidence supporting a number of explanations for that relationship. However, the nature of the relationship is not clear, and it is probably determined by a combination of several factors.

Importance of Distinctions Among Types of Schizophrenia and Among Related Psychotic Disorders

Earlier it was pointed out that distinctions have been made among five types of schizophrenia (disorganized, catatonic, paranoid, undifferentiated, and residual) and among five related psychotic disorders (brief psychotic disorder, schizophreniform, schizoaffective, induced psychotic disorder, and delusional disorder). The question we must ask is, do these distinctions have any practical value for the understanding, treatment, and prognosis of patients? In answering that question, it is helpful to consider the types of schizophrenia and the related psychotic disorders separately.

Types of Schizophrenia or Sets of Symptoms?

There is some doubt about whether the five types of schizophrenia that have been officially identified actually reflect different types of schizophrenia. This concern stems primarily from the fact that individuals who suffer from the different types do not show differences in their responses to therapy (Hawk et al., 1975; Strauss & Carpenter, 1972; Strauss et al., 1974). In other words, because the various types of patients often respond in the same way to therapy, it has been suggested that we are not dealing with different types of schizophrenia. That is an interesting argument, but one qualification should be noted: Different disorders can show similar responses to the same treatment. For example, the pains associated with headaches and pulled muscles can be reduced with aspirin, but that does not mean that a headache is the same thing as a pulled muscle.

If there are not distinct types of schizophrenia, then we face the problem of explaining why different patients show different sets of symptoms. One possibility is that there is a two-step process in the development of what we see as schizophrenia. First, there may be an initial cause, such as stress or a physiological problem, that creates some form of imbalance. Second, the individual's personal history or current circumstances may then determine how the individual responds to the imbalance. For example, an individual who is highly aroused or upset and who has other persons to blame for the feelings (or who has a history of being hurt by others) may develop delusions of persecution. In contrast, an individual who is equally aroused or upset but does not have others to blame may simply become confused and disorganized by the feelings. In other words, circumstances may give form to the problem and result in different sets of symptoms, but different sets of symptoms may not reflect differences in causes or the need for different treatments.

Overall, then, rather than schizophrenia consisting of a number of specific types, it is possible that schizophrenia consists of a large pool of symptoms, and the particular set of symptoms that any one individual develops is a function of the particular circumstances to which the individual is exposed. Because the types do not have much practical utility, less emphasis is being placed on them today than previously, and the degree to which they are used is probably due more to tradition than to their value or function. In the future, rather than using the vague and overlapping types, it might be more effective simply to describe an individual as "suffering from schizophrenia with" and then list the individual's specific symptoms (e.g., "schizophrenia with delusions" or "schizophrenia with thought process problems").

Schizophrenia Versus the Brief Psychotic Disorder and the Schizophreniform Disorder.

It does appear to be important to make distinctions between schizophrenia on the one hand and the brief psychotic disorder and the schizophreniform disorder on the other hand. In considering this distinction, it is essential to recognize that the difference between the patients in these classes is *not in the symptoms* that they show but in the *duration of the symptoms*. Schizophrenia is thought to be a long-term disorder, whereas the brief psychotic disorder and the schizophreniform disorder are thought to last only 1 month or 6 months, respectively, regardless of what is done for the patient. Obviously, this distinction has important implications for treatment and prognosis.

In summary, it appears that differences among the types of schizophrenia are relatively meaningless in terms of treatments and prognosis. However, differences in the length of time over which the symptoms developed or have persisted are crucial for treatment

and prognosis. If the symptoms developed over a long period of time or if they have persisted for more than 6 months, the prognosis is less optimistic.

With this description of schizophrenia, we can go on in the following chapters to consider its causes and treatment. Before doing that, however, let us briefly consider the experience of schizophrenia as expressed in free verse:

I
am
the
rear tire
of a bicycle,
not trusted enough
to be a
front tire,
expected to go
round and round
in one narrow rut,
never going very far,
ignored
except
when I
break down.

Then
I get lots of
frightening,
angry
attention
and
I am put into
a
garage,
sometimes for months,
where
I forget my function
and
I become afraid
to function
and all functions seem useless.

Next time out
I think I will be
an off-ramp
from a
freeway.

—Lynne Morris

◼ SUMMARY

Individuals with schizophrenia demonstrate a wide range of unusual and serious symptoms. In the cognitive area, they may (a) hear, feel, smell, and see things that normal individuals do not (hallucinations), (b) have bizarre beliefs about who they are and what is happening to them (delusions), (c) have a serious deficit in their intellectual functioning (schizophrenic deficit) and their ability to communicate, and (d) be unable to filter out irrelevant stimulation and hence feel flooded with stimulation (sensory overload). With regard to mood, their emotional responses may be flat and blunted or grossly inappropriate for the situation. Somatically, patients may be hyperaroused during the acute phase of the disorder but show normal or low arousal during the chronic phase. Motor symptoms can range from prolonged motionlessness to hyperactivity and agitation, and in some cases persons with schizophrenia demonstrate facial grimacing and repetitive finger or hand movements. In considering the symptoms of schizophrenia, it is important to separate the effects of the disorder from the side effects of treatments. Specifically, some medication can retard intellectual functioning, flatten mood, cause somatic symptoms such as dryness of the mouth and sensitivity to light, and disturb motor functioning.

Individuals with schizophrenia often go through three phases: the prodromal phase, in which the disorder develops; the active phase, in which the symptoms are most pronounced; and the residual phase, in which symptoms are diminished. A burned-out phase occurs for some individuals, but it may be due in part to the effect of long-term hospitalization.

Five types of schizophrenia have been identified: the disorganized, catatonic, paranoid, undifferentiated, and residual types. However, because the types do not appear to have much practical value (e.g., individuals with different types do not respond differently to treatment), there is some question as to whether they are indeed different types with different causes.

Five disorders that are related to schizophrenia have been identified. The brief psychotic disorder is usually a response to an overwhelming stress, and it lasts between 1 day and 1 month. The schizo-phreniform disorder lasts between 1 and 6 months, and its cause is unknown. The schizoaffective disorder involves a combination of schizophrenia and a major mood disorder (depression or mania). In the shared psychotic disorder, an individual shares a delusion with another person. Finally, in the delusional disorder, the individual has one or more major nonbizarre delusions but does not show any of the other symptoms of schizophrenia.

A distinction has been made between positive symptoms (e.g., hallucinations, delusions, thought disorders) and negative symptoms (e.g., flat mood, poverty of speech, apathy). Negative symptoms are associated with poor premorbid adjustment, are more often seen in men than women, are more stable than positive symptoms, and are linked to a poorer prognosis than positive symptoms.

Our conceptions of schizophrenia are strongly influenced by two early theorists. Kraepelin saw schizophrenia as having an early onset and a progressive and irreversible course. He called the disorder *dementia praecox* ("premature deterioration"). In contrast, Bleuler suggested that the disorder could begin later in life, and he did not believe that deterioration was inevitable. He called the disorder *schizophrenia* ("splitting of the mind"). Both theorists believed that the disorder had a physiological cause, but Bleuler thought that it could be influenced by psychological factors.

Schizophrenia occurs in about 1.5% of the population. Men usually have an earlier age of onset and a poorer prognosis. Schizophrenia is more likely to be diagnosed in individuals from the lower classes.

The distinctions among the five types of schizophrenia are probably not meaningful, but the distinctions among schizophrenia, the brief psychotic disorder, and the schizophreniform disorder are important in terms of prognosis.

■ KEY TERMS, CONCEPTS, AND NAMES

In reviewing and testing yourself on what you have learned from this chapter, you should be able to identify and discuss each of the following:

active phase	disturbed thought processes	schizoaffective disorder
Bleuler, Eugen	flights of ideas	schizoid personality disorder
brief psychotic disorder	hallucinations	schizophrenia
burned-out phase	Kraepelin, Emil	schizophrenic deficit
catatonic schizophrenia	negative symptoms	schizophreniform disorder
cognitive flooding	overinclusive thought processes	schizotypal personality disorder
delusional disorder	paranoid schizophrenia	sociogenic model
delusions	positive symptoms	stimulus overload
delusions (of identity, persecution, reference)	prodromal phase	undifferentiated schizophrenia
	residual phase	waxy flexibility
dementia praecox	residual schizophrenia	word salads
disorganized schizophrenia	shared psychotic disorder	

Chapter 13

Schizophrenic Disorders: Explanations

• O U T L I N E •

J eff has been diagnosed as suffering from schizophrenia. In an attempt to identify the factors that led to the disorder, Jeff's therapist focused on Jeff's early family life. His mother had been ambivalent and inconsistent in her responses to Jeff. She frequently told him how much she loved him, but she was also often harsh with him and would "close him out" psychologically. This made it difficult for Jeff to identify his mother's real feelings and to get close to her. He never knew whether he should move toward her or away, and regardless of what he did, it seemed wrong. The difficult situation was made worse by the fact that his father had a greatly exaggerated view of himself. Although he was only a night watchman at a factory, he believed that he was "being groomed for a vice presidency when the new management comes in." The family usually ignored the father's "little eccentricity," but when it couldn't be avoided, they just played along to humor him. When Jeff's best friend was suddenly killed in a car accident, Jeff couldn't handle the stress. People seemed to "go in and out of focus without any rhyme or reason." Not knowing what was real, Jeff withdrew into an imaginary world he could control.

Marion's therapist believes that many of Marion's symptoms are due to her social isolation and her preference for "her own little world." As a young child, Marion was a little different from her peers in that she preferred to play by herself with her dolls and with imaginary friends she invented. Even when she was with other children, she seemed to play "around" them rather than with them. In time, her peers began avoiding her because they did not share any interests with her and she seemed very distant. When one of Marion's high school classmates was asked about her, she replied, "Marion? Oh, she's out of it, a little weird. She marches to the tune of a distant drummer, and no one else hears that drummer." As Marion got older, she became more withdrawn, and she did not seem to realize how strangely she was behaving. She lost her reference points for what was appropriate and inappropriate, what was real and what was in her head.

Brian suffers from schizophrenia, and because of the disturbance in his thought processes, it is difficult for him to carry on a normal conversation. For example, recently, when the ward attendant said, "Come on, let's go to lunch," Brian responded, "Oh yes, in the church. That's where he was, you know the one, Notre Dame. Boy, she was beautiful. I wish we had some like her in here." Brian's "crazy" response stemmed from the fact that hearing the word *lunch* made him think of the word *hunch* and the book title *The Hunchback of Notre Dame.* That explains his talking about the church. He then seems to have picked up on the slang meaning of the word *dame*, which explains his comment about a beautiful woman. Brian's disturbance can be accounted for by problems with rapid and uncontrolled word associations.

Ruth suffers from Parkinson's disease, which causes problems with her physical movements. Those problems are due to a low level of the neurotransmitter dopamine, so she is treated with a drug called L-dopa that increases the level of dopamine. However, when she takes high levels of L-dopa, she develops the symptoms of schizophrenia. In contrast, Jane suffers from schizophrenia, which is thought to stem from high levels of dopamine. The drug she takes reduces the level of dopamine and reduces her schizophrenia, but in high doses it causes problems with her physical movements like those in Parkinson's disease.

In Chapter 12 we examined the symptoms and issues associated with schizophrenia. In this chapter we will undertake the task of identifying the causes of schizophrenia. Finding those causes is exceptionally important because schizophrenia afflicts hundreds of thousands of people, sometimes for life, and it can be a terrifying and debilitating disorder. However, solving the mystery of schizophrenia is a difficult and frustrating task. Many suspected villains, numerous blind alleys, and scores of potential clues must be evaluated. In attempting to solve this mystery, it is essential that we carefully examine even the dead ends because, frustrating as that can be, knowing what does *not* cause the disorder will help us dispel widely held but erroneous beliefs. For example, many people believe that being raised by a parent who suffers from schizophrenia will increase the likelihood that the child will develop schizophrenia, but that is not the case. Knowing what does not cause the disorder will also help us avoid the development of inappropriate treatments.

PSYCHODYNAMIC EXPLANATIONS

Intrapersonal Regression

Freud suggested that one tactic that individuals use to deal with overwhelming conflict and stress is **regression**—returning to an earlier stage of psychosexual development at which the individuals felt more secure (Arieti, 1974; Fenichel, 1945). To use a military analogy, the individual can be thought of as an advancing army that suddenly encounters fierce resistance and must retreat to an earlier but more secure and defensible position. Just as some armies are not prepared for battle and are more likely to retreat in the face of resistance, so some individuals are not prepared for life (have poorer defenses) and are more likely to regress in the face of conflict and stress. In the case of schizophrenia, it is thought that the individual has regressed all the way back to an infantile or oral stage of psychosexual development. The behavior of an individual with schizophrenia is thought to be babylike or childlike.

At the very early stages of psychosexual development, the ego and superego are not well developed, and consequently the id is dominant. Hallucinations and delusions then supposedly represent the unchecked activities of the id. An individual at the oral stage who wants something need only fantasize for it to exist. Many children have "imaginary friends" who become almost real; for the person who has regressed and developed schizophrenia, those imaginary people are real. One psychoanalytic theorist pointed out that we all have the capacity for hallucinations and delusions and suggested that the important question is, what keeps us from hallucinating and being delusional? The answer is that well-adjusted adults have well-developed egos that set limits on fantasy activity by constantly checking with reality. However, even well-adjusted individuals have occasional lapses in ego control that permit glimpses of psychotic-like thinking. This is most likely to occur during dreams or while we are very relaxed and the ego is less vigilant.

At present, there is no adequately controlled or empirical evidence to support the regression explanation for schizophrenia. For example, although the verbal and intellectual performance of persons with schizophrenia may appear to be childlike, careful analysis of those behaviors reveals that the kinds of errors made by the disturbed individuals are different from the kinds of errors made by young children (Buss & Lang, 1965). In other words, persons with schizophrenia may perform intellectual tasks at the same level as children, but the persons with schizophrenia perform at those levels because of different types of responses and errors. Overall, then, the intrapersonal regression explanation has no empirical support.

Interpersonal Withdrawal

Another psychodynamic theory suggests that persons with schizophrenia find contact with other individuals to be stressful, so they withdraw (Faris, 1934). This **interpersonal withdrawal** cuts the individuals off from feedback about what behaviors or thoughts are inappropriate, and in the absence of corrective feedback, they begin behaving strangely. Think how you might behave if for the past 5 years you had not noticed peo-

Social isolation at a young age is more likely to be an early symptom of schizophrenia than a cause of the disorder.

ple's responses to you or you had not been given feedback about what behaviors, emotions, or clothes were appropriate.

A variety of investigations have revealed that individuals who developed schizophrenia were more socially isolated as adolescents than individuals who did not develop schizophrenia (Barthell & Holmes, 1968; Bower et al., 1960; Kohn & Clausen, 1955; Schofield & Balian, 1959; Watt, 1978; Watt et al., 1970). For example, an analysis of the activities reported in high school yearbooks indicated that the students who later developed schizophrenia participated in fewer social activities than other students (Barthell & Holmes, 1968).

The major problem with these findings lies in the issue of cause and effect. Individuals who developed schizophrenia were more socially isolated, but did the isolation cause the schizophrenia, or was the isolation an early symptom of schizophrenia? Many individuals who choose to lead a very isolated existence (hunters or scientists who must live alone in isolated areas for long periods of time) do not develop schizophrenia,

and others who have social isolation forced on them (prisoners of war who are held in solitary confinement for long periods of time) do not develop schizophrenia. Support for the possibility that social isolation is an early symptom rather than a cause of schizophrenia comes from two studies in which it was found that biological children of persons with schizophrenia who were adopted and raised by normal parents showed greater social isolation than biological offspring of normal parents who were adopted and raised by normal parents (Kendler et al., 1982; MacCrimmon et al., 1980). Because the children of persons with schizophrenia are at greater risk for the development of schizophrenia, it appears that their social isolation was an early symptom. Overall, then, social isolation is often associated with the development of schizophrenia, but it is probably an early sign rather than a cause of the disorder.

Stress

There is a widespread belief that stress plays an important role in the etiology of schizophrenia, and there is empirical support for that position. In one study, 50 individuals with schizophrenia and 325 normal individuals were interviewed about their experiences during a 13-week period (Brown & Birley, 1968). For the patients with schizophrenia, the period in question was the 13 weeks immediately prior to the onset of their symptoms and hospitalization, whereas for the normal individuals it was a period that was not followed by symptoms or hospitalization. The results of this investigation are summarized in Table 13.1, and they indicate that individuals with schizophrenia were more likely to have experienced stressful life events (e.g., job loss, geographic move, divorce) than the normal individuals. Moreover, the individuals with schizophrenia were most likely to experience their stressful events in the 3-week period just prior to the onset of their symptoms.

Other investigators have found similar results (Jacobs & Meyers, 1976), and it has also been found that stressful life events are likely to precede relapses and readmissions to hospitals (Leff et al., 1973; see review by Dohrenwend & Egri, 1981). These findings suggest that for at least some persons, stress leads to schizophrenia. However, caution must be used in interpreting these findings because the stress may have been due to the *onset* of the schizophrenia rather than a *cause* of the schizophrenia. Alternatively, the patients may have distorted their reports of the events as a means of explaining or justifying the onset of the disorder.

One approach to identifying the environmental stress factors that may lead to schizophrenia is to com-

TABLE 13.1   STRESS WAS HIGHER FOR INDIVIDUALS WHO
DEVELOPED SCHIZOPHRENIA THAN FOR THOSE
WHO DID NOT

	Weeks Before Interview			
	10–12	7–9	4–6	1–3
Individuals with schizophrenia	14	8	14	46
Normal individuals	15	15	14	14

Note. Figures indicate percentage of individuals who experienced life stress during the interval indicated.
Source: Adapted from Brown and Birley (1968).

pare the lives of discordant monozygotic (MZ) twins (pairs of identical twins in which only one twin has developed schizophrenia). Because both members of the twin pair have identical genetic endowments, differences in their environmental experiences might lead us to the stress factors that result in schizophrenia. Unfortunately, these studies have not revealed any consistent differences in the experiences of the twins who did or did not develop schizophrenia, and therefore this approach has failed to provide evidence for the stress–schizophrenia relationship (Belmaker et al., 1974; Gottesman & Shields, 1976).

The role of stress in schizophrenia can also be examined by studying the incidence of the disorder in extremely stressful situations such as combat. Diagnoses made under battlefield conditions may not be comparable to those made under civilian conditions, but it does appear that the rate of schizophrenia is higher in combat than in civilian conditions. However, it should be recognized that many of the cases that were diagnosed in the battlefield may actually have been brief reactive psychoses rather than schizophrenia. Indeed, the battlefield patients were found to have very good prognoses and were sometimes described as having "3-day" psychoses or "5-day schizophrenia"

(Kolb, 1973; Kormos, 1978). That symptom pattern, in combination with the fact that there was an obvious precipitating stressful event, would certainly suggest the diagnosis of brief reactive psychosis rather than schizophrenia.

In summary, stress probably plays a role in the development of schizophrenia, but the relationship is not simple, and we will have to consider other factors before drawing a conclusion.

Family Influences

The family provides the context in which individuals spend their important formative years, and consequently many theorists have speculated that problems in the family may be at the root of schizophrenia. Most attention has been focused on the personality characteristics of the parents and communication patterns within the family.

Personality Characteristics of Parents. Psychodynamic theorists consider the mother–child relationship to be one of the crucial factors in the development of schizophrenia. They suggest that mothers of children who develop schizophrenia are

The intense stress of combat may lead to a brief psychotic disorder.

overprotective and *controlling* but at the same time *rejecting* and *distant*. The mother's overprotection supposedly stifles the child's emotional development, while her emotional distance deprives the child of personal security. The limited emotional development, in combination with the lack of security, leaves the individual vulnerable, and when faced with stress, the individual breaks down. The term **schizophrenogenic** (SKIT-zō-fren-uh-JEN-ik) **mother** was coined to describe such overprotecting but distant mothers (Fromm-Reichmann, 1948).

Research on the personality characteristics and child-rearing practices of the parents of individuals with schizophrenia yields two general conclusions. First, there is *no* consistent evidence that these mothers are any more likely than other mothers to fit the description of the schizophrenogenic mother (Goldstein & Rodnick, 1975; Hirsch & Leff, 1975; Jacob, 1975; Mishler & Waxler, 1968a; Wynne et al., 1979). Second, there is evidence that in many cases, the mothers and fathers of individuals with schizophrenia are *generally less well adjusted* than the parents of normal individuals (Hirsch & Leff, 1975). In fact, the parents of persons who suffer from schizophrenia often suffer from the disorder themselves.

The co-occurrence of poor adjustment in parents and children is clear, but we cannot necessarily conclude that the poor adjustment is transmitted to the children through the process of child rearing. Instead, there is evidence that having a severely disturbed child poses problems for the parents, and those problems have a negative effect on the parents' adjustment (Liem, 1980; Mishler & Waxler, 1968a). In other words, rather than parents causing problems in children, children cause at least some of the problems in parents.

Alternatively, it may be that the co-occurrence of schizophrenia in parents and children is due to their shared genes rather than the process of child rearing. Support for this possibility is provided by evidence that children of normal parents who are adopted and raised by disturbed foster parents are not more likely to develop schizophrenia than children of normal parents who are adopted and raised by normal foster parents (Wender et al., 1974). In other words, the "worst-case scenario" in which a child is raised by a parent with schizophrenia does not necessarily lead to schizophrenia in the child if the child had normal biological parents.

Communication Patterns. For many years, a popular explanation for schizophrenia was the **double-bind hypothesis** (Bateson et al., 1956). This hypothesis suggests that the messages given to children who later developed schizophrenia actually contained two conflicting messages, and the child would be punished for disobeying either of the messages. The conflict posed by the two messages and fear of punishment for disobeying supposedly led the child to respond in deviant ways (ignore the messages, see hidden meanings in them, give an irrelevant response) to avoid the conflict and punishment. The strategy seemed to be, when unsure about the message you are getting, to avoid trouble, confuse the situation. This is like the debating trick of bringing up something irrelevant when you are faced with an argument you cannot handle. Those deviant responses are thought to lead to schizophrenia.

Consider the situation in which a father and son disagree on something. The father spends 15 minutes trying his best to get the son to agree with his position and then concludes by saying, "But of course, I want you to make up your *own* mind." What is the child to do? If he finally agrees with his father, he has given in and has not made up his own mind as his father instructed him to do. But if he stands his ground and makes up his own mind, he disobeys his father's advice on the issue at hand. In that situation, the child cannot win and must do something to extricate himself from the situation. The classic (though somewhat contrived) example of a double-bind statement is "I order you to disobey me." Try to respond appropriately to that one! If you disobey, you are obeying the command, and if you obey, you are disobeying the command.

Communication explanations for schizophrenia have considerable intuitive appeal, but despite a large amount of research on the topic, there is *no* consistent evidence linking any particular communication problem or style to schizophrenia. For example, the parents of persons with schizophrenia are not more likely to give double-bind communications than the parents of normal children, and parents who have a child with schizophrenia and a normal child are not more likely to give double-bind communications to the disturbed than the normal child (Mishler & Waxler, 1968a, 1968b). Communications difficulties with people who are important to us do not help our adjustment, but they have not been shown to lead to schizophrenia.

Comment

At the beginning of this chapter, I pointed out that the search for an explanation for schizophrenia had been frustrating and had led to a number of dead ends. That appears to be the case with some of the psychodynamic explanations. When initially presented, the psychodynamic explanations were very appealing. For example, persons with schizophrenia do appear to have regressed to an early stage of development, they are withdrawn, they have been exposed to stress, their parents are disturbed, and the communication patterns in their families are poor. However, with the exception of the hypothesis relating stress to schizophrenia, years of empirical research have failed to provide consistent evidence for the psychodynamic explanations. The explanations initially appeared valid because we misinterpreted behavior (schizophrenia is not really regression), we confused cause and effect (withdrawal appears to be an early symptom rather than a cause of schizophrenia), and we did not realize that family and communication difficulties are not unique to persons with schizophrenia. We made these mistakes largely because the explanations fit what we saw, but we did not go on to test our hypotheses about cause and effect. However, we should not completely dismiss influences like those of the family because later we will see how they work in combination with other factors to exacerbate symptoms.

LEARNING EXPLANATIONS
- -

High Drive and Drive Reduction

The first explanation for schizophrenia offered by learning theorists was that acute schizophrenia is the result of **high drive** (Mednick, 1958). (Drive is a psychological or physiological factor that activates responses.) According to the learning theorists, high drive causes extraneous responses to be activated, and those responses are distracting and disrupt cognitive functioning. That disruption results in the cognitive symptoms (Mednick & Schulsinger, 1968; Neale, 1971). You may have had a similar but less severe experience when you became highly anxious on an exam and were unable to concentrate and make correct responses. Indeed, some of your responses may have been a little "crazy."

The learning theorists also suggest that because high drive is unpleasant, individuals attempt to reduce the unpleasantness by focusing on thoughts that are irrelevant to the drive. The attempts at self-distraction lead to the irrelevant thoughts and disruptions of thought processes that we diagnose as schizophrenia. You may have seen this process operating in yourself in unpleasant situations like preparing for or taking an examination. The anxiety (drive) associated with the examination was unpleasant, so to reduce the anxiety you thought about something else. However, thinking about irrelevant things interfered with your cognitive functioning. The presence of the irrelevant thoughts could also be used to explain the inappropriate mood seen in schizophrenia, in that individuals who are

thinking irrelevant thoughts would be expected to show inappropriate moods.

These hypotheses concerning the effects of drive initially generated a lot of interest, but the concept of drive was vague and the theory was incomplete because it did not explain why some individuals had high drive and others did not. For those reasons, the drive explanation for schizophrenia was largely abandoned, but we will learn later that a refined version of it plays an important role in the physiological explanation for schizophrenia.

Extinction of Attention to Relevant Cues and Attention to Irrelevant Cues

Learning theorists also suggested that schizophrenia might stem from the **extinction of attention to relevant cues** in the environment and the consequent **attention to irrelevant cues** (Ullman & Krasner, 1969). In other words, it is suggested that some individuals who find their social situations unrewarding or punishing start to ignore the relevant aspects of their environment and focus instead on irrelevant things that are rewarding (or at least neutral). The attention to irrelevant cues results in behaviors that are irrelevant and inappropriate.

According to this theory, disturbed thought processes are explained by suggesting that if the individual is not attending to the relevant cues in the situation, his or her responses will not make sense. For example, a student who finds a lecture boring (unrewarding) may stop paying attention and begin daydreaming. If the student is then suddenly called on to answer a question, the response will probably completely miss the point and may seem childish, illogical, or inappropriate. That is, the response might be described using the same phrases that are often used to describe the responses of persons with schizophrenia. In the case of a person with schizophrenia, the diversion of attention is more pervasive and of greater duration than with the bored student, and consequently the individual's responses will be even more disjointed, tangential, or irrelevant.

Delusions are accounted for by suggesting that if a particular set of beliefs is not effective for obtaining rewards or is punishing, the individual may alter his or her beliefs so they will be rewarding. Because the individual is no longer attending to the relevant cues in the environment, the new beliefs will not be accurate or corrected. A substantial amount of research indicates that if we are comfortable with a particular set of beliefs, we will not seek out or will actually avoid evidence that is inconsistent with our beliefs, thereby further reducing the possibility that erroneous beliefs will be corrected (Lord et al., 1979; O'Sullivan & Durso,

1984; Sweeney & Gruber, 1984). The development of a delusion through this process can be illustrated with a simple example. If a young man finds the social environment punishing because he cannot make friends, he may cease attending to the painful social cues in the environment and develop a belief (delusion) that he has not been able to make friends because he is exceptionally bright and therefore threatening to others. Inattention to the relevant social cues in the environment will preclude the correction of the erroneous belief. Furthermore, the individual's inappropriate behavior (stemming from attention to irrelevant cues and erroneous belief) could lead the individual's peers to actually reject him, which could in turn cause him to develop delusions of persecution.

Hallucinations can also be explained by selective attention. There is a fine line between "thoughts" and "hearing voices when no one else is there" (auditory hallucinations). We often recall or mentally rehearse conversations that involve numerous "voices." Because the world is threatening, the person with schizophrenia may cease attending to external cues and focus attention inward. (The unhappy individual is said to turn inward for solace.) Then, because he or she is not attending to the relevant social cues in the environment, the individual will not realize that attending to the internal cues is inappropriate. From there it is only a short jump to dealing with those internal stimuli as if they were real.

In an attempt to determine whether auditory hallucinations were actually the individual's own subvocal responses, an investigator attached sensitive equipment to the larynx of a patient with schizophrenia (McGuigan, 1966). He found that covert oral behavior increased just before the report of auditory hallucinations. The voices the patient heard were his own.

Critics have suggested that this explanation is too simplistic and have questioned whether the lack of attention to relevant cues is sufficient to account for the pervasive, uncontrollable, and bizarre behavior seen in some cases of schizophrenia. Questions of cause and effect have also been raised. Does inattention to relevant environmental cues lead to schizophrenia, or is inattention a symptom of schizophrenia? Furthermore, if schizophrenic symptoms simply stem from inattention to relevant cues, it should be possible to eliminate the symptoms by rewarding attention to relevant cues, but it is not that easy. We will return to an evaluation of this explanation after considering a number of other explanations.

Reward Value of Symptoms

Learning theorists also suggested that persons with schizophrenia use their abnormal behavior to get re-

In some cases, patients may use bizarre behavior to attract attention, which can be rewarding. Also, being labeled mentally ill permits a wide range of "acceptable" behaviors.

wards such as attention. On an overcrowded and understaffed hospital ward, it is unlikely that a quiet, symptom-free patient will get much attention, and therefore it behooves the patient who wants attention to act a little "crazy." Just as the squeaky wheel gets the oil, so the "weird schizophrenic" gets the attention. Attention can be a particularly powerful reward in hospitals where patients are rarely visited and are usually ignored by an overworked staff. Nurses have reported to me that some patients start acting crazier when they learn that I am bringing a group of students to the hospital for a tour because the patients want to be picked to visit with the students.

The results of a variety of experiments demonstrate that patients can and will manipulate their symptoms to gain rewards (Braginsky & Braginsky, 1967). In one of those experiments, long-term hospitalized patients were told that they were going to be interviewed by a psychologist. Randomly selected groups of patients were then led to believe that they were being interviewed (a) to determine whether they should be discharged, (b) to decide if they should be placed on a very desirable open ward (where they could come and go as they wished), or (c) simply to determine their mental status. The interviews were recorded, and later the responses of the patients were scored by three psychiatrists in terms of how disturbed the patients were. It was found that the patients who thought they were being interviewed for the open ward were rated as having the lowest level of abnormal behavior. These patients were able to fake relative health so that they could get on the desirable open ward. In contrast, the patients who thought that they were being interviewed for discharge or to determine their mental status were seen as having higher levels of pathology. The patients in the discharge condition did not fake health because they liked the hospital and did not want to risk being released. These results are presented in Figure 13.1.

Other evidence that symptoms may be used to get desired rewards comes from the finding that the amount of time patients stay in the hospital versus the community is related to the degree to which they like the hospital versus the community (Drake & Wallach, 1979). Among patients who were capable of living in the community, those who preferred the hospital stayed in the community an average of 9.5 days, whereas those who preferred the community stayed in the community an average of 233.9 days. It appears that some patients manipulate the impressions others have of them (sick vs. well) so that they can get what they want.

There is no doubt that rewards are important for developing and maintaining behaviors, and schizophrenic behaviors do not appear to be an exception. However, critics have argued that rewards can only be used to account for superficial behavior of patients and cannot account for their serious, uncontrollable problems with thought processes. Therefore, when considering symptoms, it might be helpful to distinguish between **strategic symptoms** that are used as a strategy for getting rewards and other symptoms that stem from other causes (Carson, 1984).

Labels and Roles

Some of the symptoms of schizophrenia may develop because individuals are labeled as "schizophrenic."

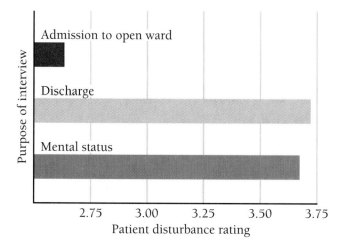

FIGURE 13.1   PATIENTS REDUCED THEIR SYMPTOMS TO QUALIFY FOR ADMISSION TO AN OPEN WARD.

Source: Adapted from Braginsky and Braginsky (1967), p. 545, tab. 1.

Giving individuals such **labels** could result in abnormal behavior in two ways. First, because we expect individuals who are labeled as suffering from schizophrenia to behave in "crazy" ways, we may subtly suggest abnormal behaviors to them. Consider the case of a woman who was admitted to a psychiatric hospital with the diagnosis of schizophrenia. Because persons with schizophrenia often hallucinate, the woman's therapist assumed that she hallucinated, and he therefore frequently asked her whether she heard voices when no one else was around. The woman did not have hallucinations, but after being asked about it by an individual of authority, the woman began to wonder whether she did indeed hallucinate. Given the suggestion that she might (or should?) and some time to think about it, the distinction between "listening to one's thoughts" and "hearing voices" became blurred ("Maybe those thoughts in my head are hallucinations"). The next time she was asked, she acknowledged hallucinating, thus fulfilling the therapist's expectations, and thereafter talked about her thoughts as hallucinations.

Being labeled as suffering from schizophrenia can also lead to symptoms because the **role** of being "schizophrenic" permits a wider variety of behaviors than the role of being "normal," and therefore an individual who is labeled as suffering from schizophrenia might use behaviors that ordinarily would be suppressed. For example, an individual who is defined as suffering from schizophrenia may not be expected to be responsible for his or her behaviors and is therefore allowed to act more deviantly. One day a patient became very frustrated, and to vent his anger he picked up a chair and began breaking it up by hitting it against the wall. When a ward attendant grabbed him and told him to stop, the patient yelled, "I'm going crazy!" The attendant then yelled back, "You may be crazy, but you can't break up furniture when *I'm* on duty!" Hearing that, the patient stopped, looked thoughtfully at the attendant for a moment, and then said he was sorry and walked away. In the future, that patient showed his "obvious deterioration of ego strength" only when a more tolerant attendant was on duty.

The effects of roles and expectations on abnormal behavior were demonstrated in research on **sensory deprivation**. Early researchers found that if individuals were placed in a soundproofed chamber for a few hours, they experienced a variety of potentially serious symptoms such as changes in perceptual experiences, inability to concentrate, and spatial and temporal disorientation (Bexton et al., 1954; Scott et al., 1959). Indeed, these findings led some theorists to speculate that schizophrenia was caused by sensory deprivation. However, that speculation may have been in error. In the early experiments, the investigators did not know what would happen to people who were deprived of stimulation, and therefore the participants in the experiments were asked to sign elaborate release forms before they were sent into the isolation chamber. They were also told that if they wanted to end the session for any reason, they could hit the large red "panic button" on the wall of the chamber. Later investigators speculated that the "symptoms" were being suggested by the procedures ("panic buttons," etc.) rather than caused by the isolation (Orne & Scheibe, 1964). To test that possibility, an experiment was conducted in which one group of individuals was treated in the usual way while another group was exposed to the same isolation but were told that they were in a "control" condition, and nothing was said about release forms, symptoms, or panic buttons. The results indicated that individuals who were warned about symptoms developed symptoms much like those seen in schizophrenia ("there are multicolored spots on the wall," "objects on the desk are becoming animated and moving about," "the buzzing of the fluorescent light is growing alternately louder and softer, so that at times it sounds like a jackhammer"), whereas individuals in the control condition were simply bored. In other words, taking away the panic button and the implicit suggestion about symptoms eliminated the schizophrenic-like symptoms.

In addition to the fact that labels and roles influence what people do, they also influence our *interpretation* of what they do and why they do it. For example, if you observe a person labeled as schizophrenic staring off into space, you would probably assume that the person is hallucinating rather than just thinking or daydreaming. If the person misunderstands something you say, you might attribute it to an "underlying thought disorder" rather than to a simple misunderstanding. Those interpretations will then influence how you respond to the person, which might in turn influence how the person responds to you. The influence of labels on the interpretation of behavior is illustrated in Case Study 13.1, which involves the labeling of normal persons as schizophrenics.

I had an experience similar to that of the people described in Case Study 13.1 when I was beginning my clinical internship at a large psychiatric hospital. The first day I was instructed to dress informally and "hang out" on one of the wards so that I could "get the feel of the place." Most patients quickly recognized me as "another one of the new trainees" and spent time talking to me and "showing me the ropes." I spent quite a bit of time talking with one middle-aged man who frequently made religious or biblical references, often called me "son," and once offered to pray for me in my "current time of need." Because I had been instructed not to probe, I was not able to identify this man's disorder, but I assumed that he had some delusion revolving around himself as God. Two days later at a staff meeting, the man and I were both a bit red-faced when I discovered that he was the ward chaplain and he realized that I was the new staff psychologist.

It is clear that labels and roles are responsible for some of the symptoms seen in schizophrenia and for the interpretations we give to people's behavior. However, labels and roles cannot be used to account for all of the symptoms because labels and roles can only have their effects *after* the individual has been diagnosed (labeled) and has assumed the role of patient. To reach that point, some symptoms must have already existed. Furthermore, the theory that schizophrenia stems from labels and roles suggests that to a large extent the symptoms are easily controllable (labels and roles can be changed), but it is clear that many of the cognitive symptoms of schizophrenia are not under voluntary control. Overall, then, labels and roles appear to provide part of the explanation for schizophrenia but not the entire explanation, and we will therefore have to go on to consider other explanations.

Comment

Learning theorists have proposed a number of explanations for the development and maintenance of schizophrenia, but the explanations have limitations. The high-drive explanation can account for disturbances in cognitive functioning, but it does not account for why some individuals have a high level of drive. Inattention to relevant cues can account for inappropriate social behavior and for cognitive symptoms, but it is questionable whether simple inattention is sufficient to explain the serious and uncontrollable symptoms of schizophrenia. Also, it is not clear whether inattention to relevant cues is a cause or an effect of schizophrenia. It seems that some of the symptoms seen in persons with schizophrenia may be maintained (and possibly caused) by the fact that the symptoms result in rewards such as attention, but it seems unlikely that some of the uncontrollable problems with thought processes are due simply to rewards. Finally, labels and roles also seem to explain some of the symptoms associated with schizophrenia, but these factors would only influence patients after they were initially diagnosed and thus they do not seem sufficient to explain all of the symptoms of schizophrenia.

COGNITIVE EXPLANATIONS

The cognitive explanations for schizophrenia are based on the following assumptions:

Case Study 13.1

1. Persons with schizophrenia actually have *different sensory experiences from normal individuals.*
2. Many of the symptoms of schizophrenia (e.g., hallucinations, delusions) stem from the attempts of persons to *explain* their different sensory experiences.
3. The disrupted intellectual and verbal performance seen in schizophrenia is due to the fact that the sensory experiences *interfere* with the persons' otherwise normal cognitive functioning.

The cognitive explanations differ from the psychodynamic and learning explanations in two important ways. First, rather than suggesting that the unusual sensory experiences seen in schizophrenia are *not real* and are *caused by* the disorder, the cognitive explanation suggests that the sensory experiences *are real* and *are the cause of the disorder.* In other words, the individual does not hallucinate because of schizophrenia; rather, the individual has different sensory experiences, and problems arise when he or she tries to *explain* them. Second, rather than suggesting that the thought processes seen in schizophrenia are deranged and different from those of other people, cognitive theorists suggest that the thought processes seen in schizophrenia are *like those of normal persons* and only *appear* to be deranged because the individual is dealing with different sensory experiences that interfere with the normal thought processes.

Sensory Experiences and Stimulus Overload

It is important to recall that many persons who suffer from schizophrenia experience **cognitive flooding** or **stimulus overload** (see Chapter 12). Specifically, many of them are acutely aware of sounds, sights, and sensations that normal individuals screen out. The question then arises, how do these sensory experiences lead to the symptoms of schizophrenia?

The nature of the overloading and its relationship to the development of symptomatology are illustrated in Case Study 13.2. Was the man in the case study suffering from schizophrenia when he called me? Was he in the process of developing schizophrenia? Let us consider how changes in sensory sensitivity like those experienced by this man could result in the development of symptoms that could lead to a potential long-term psychological disorder such as schizophrenia.

Hallucinations and Delusions

Traditionally, **hallucinations** have been interpreted as sensory experiences that do not have a basis in reality

Persons with schizophrenia may experience stimulus overload; many are aware of sights, sounds, and sensations that normal individuals screen out.

(Bentall, 1990). However, the extraordinary sensitivity to stimulation experienced by some people may provide the basis for what we call hallucinations. For example, individuals who report tactile hallucinations (e.g., tingling of the skin, gnawing sensations inside the body) may be somatically more sensitive and in fact experience sensations that other individuals do not experience. Similarly, individuals who hear voices that others do not hear may be more sensitive to sounds than other individuals.

This does not mean that the highly sensitive individuals are actually feeling and hearing exactly what they think they are feeling and hearing. Instead, it may be that these individuals are experiencing some vague or irrelevant stimulation, and in an attempt to make sense of it, they "fill in the blanks" and come up with a complete and meaningful perception. This filling-in process is not unusual or abnormal, and there is abundant evidence that we all use it. From this perspective, then, hallucinations may be interpreted as an expected consequence of the normal process of dealing with sensory experiences.

Delusions can also be accounted for by the presence of extra stimulation (Maher, 1988a, 1988b). It is generally assumed that we all have the same sensory experiences and have access to the same information. Therefore, if an individual holds a belief that is contrary to the commonly held evidence, the individual is thought to suffer from a delusion. However, it may be that individuals who have different beliefs (delusions) have had different sensory experiences (e.g., hear or feel things that others do not) and that those different experiences have led them to reach different conclusions about the world. Furthermore, if an individual has sensory experiences that other individuals clearly do not have, the individual having the different experiences would have to come up with explanations for them, and those explanations could result in delusions.

With regard to this explanation, consider the old parable about the five blind men who each felt a different part of an elephant and therefore had different sensory experiences concerning the shape of the elephant. If four of the blind men had each felt a leg and the fifth had felt the tail, the four who felt a leg might conclude that the fifth man who thought that the elephant was small and thin suffered from a delusion about the shape of elephants. Given some creativity, the four "normal" men who felt a leg might be able to come up with an explanation for the fifth man's "delusion." They might suggest, for example, that the fifth man was threatened by the obvious size of the elephant and resolved the threat by developing the delusion that the elephant was small and thin.

Some other examples may illustrate how attempts to explain differences in sensory experiences can re-

Case Study 13.2

STIMULUS OVERLOAD AND POTENTIAL SCHIZOPHRENIC SYMPTOMS

One morning, I received a telephone call from a friend, a very bright, psychologically sophisticated 34-year-old executive. He was in a state of near panic as he told me that he was afraid that he was "losing his mind" and "going crazy." When I asked what had happened, he told me that while driving to his office that morning, he began having strange experiences. First, he explained that everything he saw was very "intense," and that he could not ignore anything. For example, while driving by billboards, he saw things that he had never noticed before, such as the very small print at the bottom of the billboard that gives the name of the company that owns it. Second, he was having great difficulty with sounds. He explained that while he was driving on the expressway, he was constantly afraid that he was going to be run over by a huge truck because it sounded to him as though a truck were almost on top of him. When he looked in the rear-view mirror, however, it was obvious that the truck was a long distance away and of no danger to him. Moments later, however, it again sounded like he was about to be run down.

One of the most psychologically frightening experiences associated with sound occurred when he pulled up at a stoplight. There were two men in the car in front of him, and as one man turned his head to talk to the other man, my friend suddenly thought that because of his unusual sensitivity to sound, he would be able to hear the man talk despite the fact that he was in another car and the windows were up in both cars. Terrified by the possibility of something he knew to be impossible, he looked away, hoping that if he did not see the man speak, he might not hear him.

In his panic over these strange experiences and his loss of control, he called me for help. This was the first such "attack" that he had experienced, but as I listened to him talk, I recalled a number of related experiences of which I was aware. For example, he had become extremely uncomfortable and disoriented when he had to drive through a long tunnel in which lights flashed by as he drove along, he had always disliked loud rock music, and he had complained about movies in which there were sudden and rapid flashes of scenes. Clearly, he was generally sensitive to sensory stimulation, but never before had it been so severe, and in the past he had always been able to cope with it by avoiding it. For some reason, his sensitivity had suddenly been heightened, he was being overwhelmed by stimulation, and he did not know what was happening to him or how to deal with it.

---

sult in the development of delusions. Consider the case of a young student who, because of a problem with heightened sensitivity, became aware of the buzzing noise made by the fluorescent lights and to the muffled voices of the persons talking in the next room. Those sounds appeared very prominent to her, but when she mentioned them to her roommates, they denied hearing them. Those sounds were real to the young woman and had to be explained. The denial of those sounds by her roommates also had to be explained. Could it be that the persons in the next room were talking about her, that they were causing the light to make noise to annoy her, and that her roommates were now lying to her?

Consider also the example of the man in Case Study 13.2 who became sensitive to colors and sounds while driving his car. He would have had to account for the fact that he was now seeing and hearing things in his environment that he had not seen or heard before and that others were not noticing. He might assume that he now had some special powers or that the things he was seeing were special signs for him.

Finally, consider the case of an elderly woman who was losing her hearing. Because of that loss, it ap-

peared to the woman as though everyone around her was whispering, and she was faced with the problem of explaining that behavior. She might recall earlier times when she had disagreements with others, and knowing how elderly individuals are sometimes taken advantage of, she might conclude that the people around her were now planning to get back at her, perhaps to take her money. Why else would they be whispering? This woman's delusion was rooted in her different sensory experiences, and the delusion was simply given form by the nature of her prior experiences. No amount of psychotherapy concerning her earlier experiences with others would relieve the basis for her delusions—but a hearing aid to correct her sensory experiences would.

There is also laboratory evidence to support the notion that differences in sensory experiences can result in delusions. In one experiment, college students were shown pictures of Russians and while they were looking at the pictures, the students were given false physiological feedback concerning their anxiety levels (Bramel et al., 1965). One group received feedback indicating that they were very anxious while looking at the pictures, whereas another group received feedback indicating that they were not anxious while looking at the pictures. After getting the feedback, the students were asked to rate the degree to which they thought the Russians were hostile. The results indicated that the students who were led to believe that they were anxious rated the Russians as more hostile than the students who were led to believe that they were not anxious. These results suggest that the students who thought they were anxious had to explain or justify their apparent sensory experiences, so they attributed threat to the Russians ("I am anxious because of the threat posed by the Russians"). It might be said that those students developed "delusions of persecution" concerning the Russians.

In considering this explanation, it is relevant to note that there is a strong correspondence between the occurrence of cognitive flooding and delusions. Specifically, stimulus flooding and delusions are more likely to be seen in acute cases of schizophrenia (Payne, 1962; Payne & Friedlander, 1962). The fact that cognitive flooding is *correlated* with delusions does not prove that flooding *causes* delusions, but the implication is very strong and is supported by the laboratory research discussed earlier.

A crucial point in this explanation is that the cognitive process by which disturbed persons develop delusions is *identical* to the cognitive process by which normal individuals develop explanations. The problem for persons with schizophrenia is not to be found in the nature of their thought processes. Instead, their problem stems from the fact that they have more and different stimuli to incorporate into their views of the world than normal individuals do, and it is the incorporation of this additional material that leads to delusions.

Cognitive Functioning and Schizophrenic Deficit

Enhanced sensory sensitivity may also play a role in the **schizophrenic deficit**. It has long been thought that the impairments in thinking and talking evinced by persons with schizophrenia are due to **lapses of attention** and the **intrusion of irrelevant associations** that disrupt the person's thought processes (Maher, 1968, 1972, 1983; McGhie & Chapman, 1961; Shakow, 1963; Venables, 1964.) With schizophrenia, it is as if there is a breakdown in the **filter mechanism** that is responsible for screening out stimuli that are not related to the current thought (Payne et al., 1959). In the absence of that filtering or screening, the individual is flooded with stimuli and distracted from the problem at hand.

Clinical support for the influence of **distraction** on cognitive performance is readily available in the subjective reports of patients. Newly admitted patients consistently report problems in controlling the flow of incoming information (McGhie & Chapman, 1961), and the personal reports written by patients reflect their attentional problems (Freedman, 1974). One patient reported that with books he had

a hard time concentrating, getting into the actual reading of them [because] probably an external stimulus would take my attention off the book . . . a sound or something like a piece of sunlight is going on over here and that would probably start me thinking. (Freedman & Chapman, 1973, p. 50)

Another patient reported:

My mind was so confused I couldn't focus on one thing. I had an idea and I was wondering whether I should press charges and then all of a sudden my mind went to something pleasant, and then it went back to my work, and I couldn't keep it orderly. (p. 50)

In addition to this clinical evidence, the results of many laboratory experiments attest to the influence of cognitive distraction on the performance of people with schizophrenia (see reviews by Lang & Buss, 1965; Neale & Oltmanns, 1980). For example, in one experiment conducted with individuals who did and did not have schizophrenia, a series of numbers was read by a female experimenter, and the individuals' task was to recall the numbers after they had been read (Lawson et al., 1967). On half of the trials, a male experimenter read irrelevant (potentially distracting) numbers while the female read the test numbers. On the other trials, irrelevant numbers were not read. The performance of the individuals who did and did not have schizophrenia is presented graphically in Figure 13.2. The most important aspect of the findings is that the reading of irrelevant numbers had a more deleterious effect on the performance of persons with schizophrenia, an effect that is probably attributable to the fact that they could not screen out the distracting irrelevant numbers. Although we cannot be sure, the fact that the persons with schizophrenia did less well than normals even when they were not intentionally being distracted is probably due to the fact that they were distracted by other stimuli in the situation.

In summary, then, both clinical and experimental evidence indicates that the poor intellectual performance associated with schizophrenia is due to the fact that persons with the disorder are unable to filter out irrelevant stimuli, and those stimuli disrupt thought processes.

Cognitive Intrusions and Schizophrenic Language

Investigators working within a cognitive perspective have suggested that schizophrenic language is garbled

FIGURE 13.2   DISTRACTION RESULTED IN MORE ERRORS BY PERSONS WITH SCHIZOPHRENIA THAN BY PERSONS WHO DID NOT HAVE SCHIZOPHRENIA.

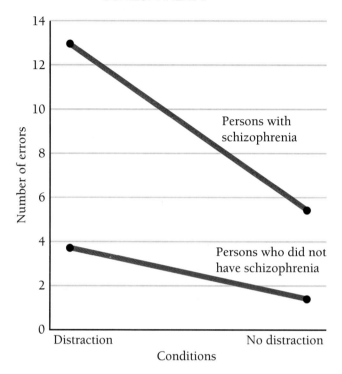

Source: Adapted from Lawson et al. (1967), p. 529, tab. 2.

and disordered because disturbed individuals are constantly being *distracted by interfering and irrelevant thoughts*, and therefore they jump from thought to thought. Those transitions between thoughts are not obvious to the listener, and hence the sentences of disturbed individuals seem chaotic. In the following sections, we will consider how those distractions might occur.

Unusual Word Associations.   Originally, researchers thought that individuals with schizophrenia had different meanings or associations for words than normal individuals. The use of different meanings would result in communications problems. To test that possibility, lists of stimulus words were read to persons who did or did not suffer from schizophrenia, and it was their task to give their first association to each stimulus word. The results indicated that the associations of persons with schizophrenia were *less common* than the associations of other persons, and therefore it was widely concluded that associative problems lay at the base of schizophrenia (Kent & Rosanoff, 1910; Moran, 1953; Moran et al., 1964; Murphy, 1923; Shakow & Jellinek, 1965).

Unfortunately, the early investigations did not contain controls to ensure that the stimulus words were correctly heard or understood. That was a serious omission because in later research it was found that persons with schizophrenia were more likely to *misunderstand* the stimulus words than normal individuals. When controls were introduced to ensure that everyone was responding to the same stimulus, there were no differences between the associations of persons who did or did not have schizophrenia (Lang & Luoto, 1962; Moran et al., 1964; Pavy, 1968). In view of those findings, it does not appear that the language problems associated with schizophrenia can be attributed to unusual word associations.

Associative Intrusions.   It has also been suggested that the language problems associated with schizophrenia stem from an inability to maintain attention and from the consequent intrusion of irrelevant thoughts (Chapman et al., 1964, 1984; Maher, 1983). That is, when constructing sentences, an individual may have lapses in attention during which other thoughts intrude, causing the person to "spin off" and begin dealing with the new thoughts. These intrusions are due to the person's *associations* with the words being used, and therefore the problems are said to be due to **associative intrusions**. Intrusions can result from a number of types of associations. We will consider four.

The first is a **semantic intrusion** in which the use of an *alternative meaning* for a particular word introduces a new thought. All of us have more than one association for many of the words we use. Examples of common words with multiple meanings are *rare, diamond, corn, bat, tip, yard,* and *pit.* Each of these words has a strong association (the first or most common association) and at least one weak association (the second or third most common associations). For example, a strong association for *date* is "an appointment to go out with someone," while a weak association is "a piece of fruit from a palm tree." In explaining disordered language, it has been suggested that persons with schizophrenia are likely to use the *strong association for a word regardless of whether that is the appropriate association.* Consider the following sentence: "When the farmer bought a herd of cattle, he needed a new pen." The word *pen* has two meanings; the strong association is "a writing instrument," and the weak association is "a fenced-in enclosure." Attention to the context in which the word *pen* appears indicates that in this case the weak association, "fenced-in enclosure," is the correct association, but persons with schizophrenia are more likely to use the strong association for the word *pen*, "writing instrument" (Chapman et al., 1964).

When one individual uses the word *pen* to indicate a fenced-in enclosure and another individual responds and talks about a writing instrument, it is easy to see how confusions will arise and how the conclusion can be drawn that the individual who responded with the wrong association has a thought disorder. Problems can also arise in constructing sentences. For example, a person with schizophrenia might start out using one meaning for a word but then get distracted and complete the sentence using another meaning. In the case of the word *pen*, the sentence might be "The cattle were in the pen, which I put in my shirt pocket."

A second type of associative intrusion involves thought content. A **thought content intrusion** occurs when a word reminds the individual of a *different topic*. For example, an individual may be telling a story about a particular cat, but in mentioning the topic of cats, the individual thinks of another story about another cat and in midsentence launches off into that story without making the transition clear.

A third type of associational intrusion is based on the *sound* of the word. Associations based on sound have traditionally been called **clang associations**. Examples of clang associations include *bang* and *fang*, *dog* and *bog*, *heed* and *deed*. In the process of constructing the sentence "When I saw the clown, I began to laugh," the person with schizophrenia might get to the word *clown* and think of the word *down*, and then complete the sentence with a phrase involving the word *down*, such as "Jack fell down and broke his crown and Jill came tumbling after." The resulting sentence, "When I saw the clown, Jack fell down and broke his crown," does not make sense.

The disrupting effects of clang associations are obvious in the following statement by a patient suffering from schizophrenia:

Oh you can have all the keys you want, they broke into the store and found peas, what's the use of keys, policeman, watchman, dogs, dog shows, the spaniel was the best dog this year, he is Spanish you know, Morrow castle what a big key they have Sampson, Schley, he drowned them all in the bay, gay, New York bay, Broadway, the White Way, etc. (Bleuler, 1936)

Fourth, there are **habit strength intrusions**. Certain words or phrases are frequently used together, and if one word or phrase is used, an individual is likely to think of (and possibly then use) the word or phrase that is habitually associated with it. For example, in answering the question "Who was living at home?" a person with schizophrenia who had a strong religious background might say, "The father, the son, *and the Holy Ghost*." The phrase "the Holy Ghost" intruded because in religious services that phrase often follows "The Father, the Son." Other examples might be drawn from phrases in commercials that we hear over and over or from familiar clichés. For example, when you hear the following phrases, what are you likely to think of? *A penny for . . .* [your thoughts]. *You can't have your cake . . .* [and eat it too]. *When it rains . . .* [it pours]. If a sentence contained one of these phrases and you were not attending carefully, you might complete the sentence with the words that are frequently associated with the phrase rather than with words that are appropriate.

Because there are different types of associational intrusions and a large number of potential associations of each type, a great many intrusions can appear in any given sentence. Thus in any one utterance, it is very difficult to understand where a person with schizophrenia has gone wrong in terms of associations.

If it is true that the language problems seen in schizophrenia are due to associative intrusions, it must be asked why those intrusions occur. Cognitive theorists suggest that the intrusions stem from the interaction of two factors: (a) momentary lapses in attention and (b) cognitive flooding, which provides the individual with numerous competing stimuli, each of which may be accompanied by associations.

Two lines of evidence support the idea that lapses in attention lead to the intrusions that disrupt the language of persons with schizophrenia. First, intrusions are most likely to occur at *transition points* in sentences (at commas, the ends of sentences, or other pauses) where attention would be most likely to lapse. It is probably because intrusions occur at the ends of phrases that the individual phrases of the sentences make sense, but the phrases do not fit together. Second, in the thought processes and speech patterns of normal individuals, intrusions are most likely to occur in situations in which *attention is weakened*. For example, normal individuals are more likely to come up with disjointed and irrelevant thoughts "out of the blue" when they are tired, especially relaxed, just waking up, or bored.

Two final points should be made concerning language problems associated with schizophrenia. First, it is important to recognize that the content of the intrusion may be related to something in the individual's background, but that background factor is not the cause of the intrusion. Therefore, understanding the content of the intrusion will not lead to an understanding of the schizophrenia. For example, the associative intrusion of "Holy Ghost" following the phrase "the father, the son" may indicate that the individual comes from a religious background, but it does not indicate that issues or conflicts associated with religion provide the basis for the schizophrenia. This position is very different from that of traditional psychodynamic theorists, who see symbolic significance in the content of the language of persons with schizophrenia.

Second, the processes that result in language problems seen in schizophrenia are no different from those that lead to errors or mistakes in the language of normal individuals. The errors made by disturbed persons are not unique; they are simply more extreme or more frequent errors of the types made by normal persons. Indeed, there is now a growing interest in explaining the cognitive problem in schizophrenia in terms of information processing and associative (neural) networks like those used earlier to explain the nonpsychotic disorders of anxiety and depression (see Chapters 5 and 9) (Cohen & Servan-Schreiber, 1992; Hoffman, 1992).

Comment

The cognitive explanations appear to deal effectively with a wide variety of symptoms seen in schizophrenia. The principles on which the explanations are based are rooted in broadly accepted scientific research. However, cognitive explanations have two major limitations. First, they do not explain why persons with schizophrenia have different sensory experiences and are more distractible than normal individuals, and therefore they do not provide an explanation for the factors that are thought to underlie the disorder. Second, cognitive explanations are effective for explaining positive symptoms like hallucinations, delusions, and problems with thought processes, but they do not account for negative symptoms like flat mood, poverty of speech, and apathy. As it stands, then, cognitive explanations are incomplete. However, it may be that the basis for the altered sensory experiences and the negative symptoms can be found in the physiological explanations we shall consider next.

PHYSIOLOGICAL EXPLANATIONS

There are three major physiological explanations for schizophrenia, and they appear to account for the different sets of symptoms that are seen in different individuals who suffer from schizophrenia. I will briefly introduce the explanations here, and then I will discuss each in greater detail. The first explanation is that *excessively high levels of neurological activity in some areas of the brain may serve to disrupt cognitive activity* and thereby result primarily in *positive* symptoms such as disturbed thought processes and hallucinations. This high level of activity is for the most part limited to the areas of the brain where **dopamine** (DŌ-puh-mēn) is the neurotransmitter. That is, high levels of dopamine activity lead to high levels of neurological activity and hence to some of the symptoms of schizophrenia. Because dopamine provides the basis for the

disruptive activity, we often refer to the **dopamine explanation for schizophrenia**.

The second explanation is that *excessively low levels of neurological activity in some areas of the brain may serve to retard cognitive activity* and thereby result primarily in *negative* symptoms such as poverty of speech and apathy. Low levels of neurological activity in the *frontal lobes* would be most important.

The third explanation is that *structural abnormalities in the brain may serve to retard cognitive activity* and thereby result primarily in *negative* symptoms. The structural problems could include malformations, damage, or deterioration.

If problems with neurological activity and brain structure cause symptoms, the question arises, what causes the problems with neurological activity and brain structure? The answer appears to be *genetic factors* and *biological traumas* (problems during prenatal development and birth). In other words, genetic factors and biological traumas lead to problems with levels of neurological activity and brain structure, which in turn lead to the positive and negative symptoms of schizophrenia. In some cases, the addition of psychological stress may exacerbate the symptoms caused by neurological activity and brain structure. This model of causation for schizophrenia is summarized in Figure 13.3.

We will now consider the evidence for each of the components.

FIGURE 13.3   SEQUENCE OF PHYSIOLOGICAL CAUSES IN THE DEVELOPMENT OF SCHIZOPHRENIA.

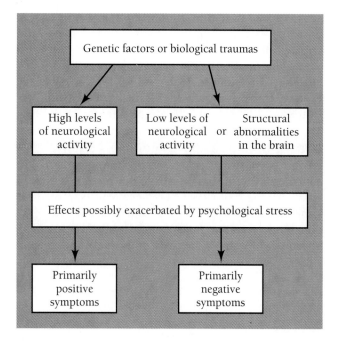

High Neurological Activity

It is widely agreed that high levels of neurological activity play a primary role in schizophrenia and that the crucial neurological activity occurs primarily in the areas of the brain where dopamine is the major neurotransmitter. However, there is now evidence that the neurotransmitter **serotonin** can also play a role in dopamine activity and hence in schizophrenia (Meltzer, Bastani, Kwon, et al., 1989; Pickar et al., 1991; Spoont, 1992). Specifically, in those areas of the brain where dopamine is a major neurotransmitter, serotonin serves to *inhibit neurological activity*, so if serotonin levels are too low, there will not be enough inhibition of dopamine activity, and neurological activity will become too high (Jenner et al., 1983; see discussion of inhibitory neurons in Chapter 2). By itself, a low level of serotonin is probably not sufficient to lead to schizophrenia, but in some cases, a low level of serotonin may combine with a high level of dopamine to cause or exacerbate schizophrenia. Therefore, in our discussions of the cause and treatment of schizophrenia, we must attend to both dopamine and serotonin. We will now consider the evidence for the dopamine explanation.

Effects of Decreasing Dopamine Activity.
The first set of evidence for the dopamine explanation comes from the fact that a group of drugs called **neuroleptics** (NYOO-rō-LEP-tiks) that *reduce dopamine activity* also *reduce the symptoms of schizophrenia* (Carlsson & Lindquist, 1963; Nyback et. al., 1968; see also Chapter 14). In other words, because neuroleptics reduce dopamine activity and reduce schizophrenic symptoms, researchers believe that high levels of dopamine activity result in schizophrenic symptoms. Further support for the relationship between dopamine and schizophrenia is provided by the finding that in most cases, the neuroleptics that are most effective for blocking dopamine activity are also those that are most effective for reducing schizophrenic symptoms (Carlsson, 1978; Horn & Snyder, 1971; Snyder, 1976).

Effects of Increasing Dopamine Activity.
The second set of evidence for the dopamine explanation comes from findings that drugs that *increase dopamine levels increase schizophrenic symptoms*. For example, it is known that amphetamines and cocaine increase dopamine levels and have the effect of causing schizophrenic symptoms in normal individuals and exacerbating symptoms in individuals who are already suffering from schizophrenia (Angrist et al., 1974; Baker, 1991; Griffith et al., 1972; Janowsky et al., 1973; Satel & Edell, 1991; Satel et al., 1991; Snyder, 1976).

The drug **L-dopa** (dihydroxyphenylalanine), which is used in the treatment of **Parkinson's disease**, can result in the symptoms of schizophrenia. Parkinson's disease involves muscle tremors that stem from low levels of dopamine in the **basal ganglia** of the brain, which are responsible for motor activity. L-dopa is used to treat Parkinson's disease because it interacts with an enzyme and becomes dopamine, thus increasing the level of dopamine and reducing the muscle tremors. Unfortunately, however, the increase in dopamine is not limited to the basal ganglia, and its increase in the other areas of the brain results in schizophrenic symptoms. Conversely, the use of drugs to reduce schizophrenia by reducing dopamine can have the effect of causing Parkinsonian symptoms (see Chapter 14).

Effects of the Number of Dopamine Receptors.
Third, there is now evidence that persons who suffer from schizophrenia have *more dopamine receptors* than other people (Wong et al., 1986). The higher level of receptors would be expected to result in more dopamine activity. Related to this, it is interesting to note that in men, the number of dopamine receptors declines sharply between the ages of 30 and 50, whereas the decline is somewhat less dramatic for women (Wong et al., 1984). The general decline of dopamine receptors in midlife may account for the lowered rate of schizophrenia during those years, and the more gradual decline of receptors in women may account for the fact that women are at risk for schizophrenia longer than men. In other words, not only do persons with schizophrenia have more dopamine receptors, but decreases in the numbers of receptors also appear to be consistent with decreases in symptomology. The relationship between age and dopamine receptors is illustrated in Figure 13.4.

Effects of Increasing Serotonin Activity.
As noted earlier, serotonin serves as an inhibitor of dopamine activity. Evidence for the role of serotonin in schizophrenia comes from the fact that a group of drugs called **atypical neuroleptics** that reduce dopamine activity and *increase serotonin activity* can be more effective for treating schizophrenia than regular neuroleptics that only reduce dopamine activity (see Kane et al., 1989). That is, increasing serotonin levels adds to the treatment effect, thus indicating that serotonin plays a role. Furthermore, there is also some preliminary evidence that taking neuroleptics in combination with other drugs that increase serotonin activity (e.g., Prozac) can be more effective for reducing the symptoms of schizophrenia than taking neu-

FIGURE 13.4   DOPAMINE RECEPTORS DECLINE MORE RAPIDLY WITH AGE IN MEN THAN IN WOMEN.

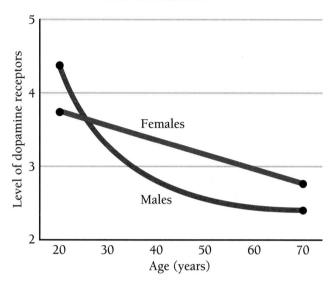

Source: Adapted from Wong et al. (1984), p. 1394, fig. 3.

FIGURE 13.5   DOPAMINE IS A NEUROTRANSMITTER IN NERVE TRACKS LEADING TO THE FRONTAL AND TEMPORAL LOBES AND IN THE BASAL GANGLIA.

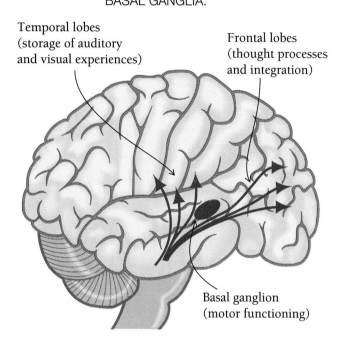

roleptics alone (Bacher & Ruskin, 1991; Goff et al., 1990).

It is essential to recall that the presence of schizophrenic symptoms is related to neurological activity in the areas of the brain in which dopamine is the neurotransmitter and not to activity in general. This is attested to by the fact that increases and decreases in dopamine-related activity are associated with increases and decreases in symptoms, but increases and decreases in *general* activity are not associated with changes in symptomatology. For example, using caffeine to increase general arousal in mildly disturbed patients does not exacerbate their symptoms, and using barbiturates to decrease their general arousal does not decrease their symptoms (Angrist & Gershon, 1970; Angrist et al., 1973).

High Neurological Activity and Symptoms.

The question now arises, how does the high level of dopamine activity lead to symptoms? To answer that question, it is essential to understand that dopamine is a major neurotransmitter in the nerve tracks leading from the **limbic system** to the **frontal lobes** and the **temporal lobes** of the brain. That is illustrated in Figure 13.5. Those connections are important for three reasons. First, the limbic system serves to generate neurological activity; it is where emotional and motivational arousal originates. If the nerve paths leading

from the limbic system are easily stimulated, the arousal produced in the limbic system is very likely to be transmitted to other areas of the brain (e.g., frontal and temporal lobes), possibly overstimulating those areas.

Second, the frontal lobes are where thought processes occur and are integrated. That is important because if the frontal lobes are overstimulated by arousal from the limbic system, thought processes will be disrupted, and that could lead to the disturbed cognitive processes seen in schizophrenia.

Third, the temporal lobes is where *memories for auditory and visual experiences are stored.* (These memories can be of real experiences or previous thoughts that involve sights and sounds.) The storage of perceptual memories in the temporal lobes is important because if the temporal lobes are overstimulated, erroneous perceptual memories could be activated, and that could result in hallucinations. To understand this possibility fully, a little background might be helpful.

It is generally assumed that each perceptual memory is stored in a group of cells in the temporal lobes and that when the group of cells is stimulated, the perception will be reproduced (Hebb, 1949). The storage and reproduction of perceptual memories were demonstrated in a series of studies in which investigators opened up the skulls of humans and then electrically stimulated specific areas of the temporal lobe (Penfield, 1955; Penfield & Perot, 1963). The stimulation resulted in immediate, clear, and specific perceptual experiences. For example, when one point in the temporal lobe of a young man was stimulated, he said, "Oh, gee, gosh, robbers are coming at me with guns" (Penfield & Perot, 1963, p. 616). When the stimulation was applied to another point, the young man reported hearing his mother talking. For this young man, both visual and auditory hallucinations could be produced with simple electrical stimulation. In the case of a young woman, when stimulation was applied at one point, she said, "I hear singing. . . . Yes, it is *White Christmas,*" and when stimulation was applied at another point, she reported, "That is different, a voice—talking—a man . . . a man's voice—talking" (p. 618). In both cases, when the stimulation was applied at the same points some time later, the same perceptions were reproduced.

It is clear from the foregoing discussion that by electrically stimulating areas of the temporal lobe, it is possible to produce what for all practical purposes are hallucinations—perceptual experiences that do not have a basis in reality. Analogously, then, it may be that the excessive and erratic stimulation of the temporal lobes by the dopamine-related nerves coming from the limbic system are responsible for the hallucinations seen in schizophrenia. Two other points are relevant here. First, from investigations using PET scans, we know that patients who suffer from schizophrenia and who have hallucinations have excessive neurological activity in the temporal lobes, so we know that the basis for the stimulation exists. Furthermore, reducing that neurological activity with drugs reduces the hallucinations. Second, individuals who suffer from **temporal lobe epilepsy** often experience hallucinations just before the onset of their seizures; that is, they have hallucinations at a time when we know that they are experiencing excessive and erratic neurological activity in the temporal lobes.

Finally, as Figure 13.5 indicates, dopamine is also a major neurotransmitter in the basal ganglion, an area that is important for *motor functioning.* That may account for some of the motor symptoms seen in schizophrenia (e.g., repetitive hand movements).

In summary, high levels of neurological activity in the brain may account for the disturbed thought processes and hallucinations (positive symptoms) seen in schizophrenia. However, to understand the negative symptoms of the disorder, we must examine the role of low levels of neurological activity and structural abnormalities in the brain, and we will do that in the next sections.

Low Neurological Activity

For some years, it has been suspected that the cognitive deficit that is seen in schizophrenia (e.g., poverty of thought and language, apathy) might be due to excessively low levels of neurological activity in the frontal lobes of the brain, where thought processes are developed. This explanation is referred to as the **hypofrontality hypothesis**, and a variety of investigations have provided support for it (e.g., Berman et al., 1992; Buchsbaum et al., 1992; Wolkin et al., 1992; see review by Andresen et al., 1992). For example, in one study, the investigators used PET scans to measure brain activity (metabolism) in individuals who were or were not suffering from schizophrenia (Buchsbaum et al., 1992). Measurements were made while the individuals worked on a challenging cognitive task (they had to watch numbers that appeared briefly every 2 seconds and push a button every time a zero appeared). The individuals with schizophrenia had never been on medication, so the effects of medication could be ruled out. The results revealed lower frontal lobe activity in the individuals with schizophrenia. The effects are illustrated in Figure 13.6. Similar effects have been reported by other investigators using different techniques, and in some studies it was found that the reduced frontal activity was related specifically to negative symptoms (e.g., Andreasen et al., 1992; Wolkin et al., 1992).

One particularly interesting investigation was done using twins who were concordant (both twins had the disorder) or discordant (only one twin had the disorder) for schizophrenia (Berman et al., 1992). The results indicated that only the twins who suffered from schizophrenia showed lower levels of neurological activity. This is relevant because it suggests that physiological differences—in this case hypofrontality that probably resulted from earlier brain damage—may account for cases of schizophrenia that cannot be accounted for by genetic factors (discordant twins).

FIGURE 13.6   BRAIN IMAGES FROM PERSONS WITH SCHIZOPHRENIA ARE IN THE BOTTOM ROW. YELLOW AND RED AREAS INDICATE HIGH LEVELS OF ACTIVITY.

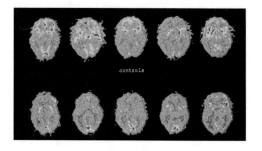

Other indirect evidence for the hypofrontality explanation comes from the fact that neuroleptics (drugs that reduce activity) are *not* effective for reducing negative symptoms.

Structural Abnormalities in the Brain

Another explanation for the symptoms of schizophrenia involves **structural abnormalities of the brain**. Malformation, damage, or deterioration could result in abnormalities that could interfere with brain activity, and as early as 1919, Kraepelin (1971) cited cerebral lesions as a cause of dementia praecox. Since then, numerous investigators have pointed to the similarities between some of the symptoms of schizophrenia and the symptoms of other disorders such as general paresis and encephalitis that are known to stem from structural abnormalities. With new imaging techniques such as CT and MRI (see Chapter 3), we can now get clear pictures of the living brain and then study the relationships between abnormalities of structure and function. (For reviews of these techniques, see Raz & Raz, 1990; Seidman, 1983.)

Enlarged Ventricles.   CT and MRI examinations have revealed that some individuals who suffer from schizophrenia exhibit enlargement of the **ventricles** (Andreasen et al., 1982; Degreef et al., 1992). The ventricles are the cavities or canals in the brain through which the cerebrospinal fluid flows. There are three ventricles; one *lateral ventricle* on each side of the brain and a *third ventricle* that goes through the center of the brain. It is estimated that these have become wider in 20% to 50% of persons with schizophrenia. The greatest widening is usually found in the third ventricle (Raz & Raz, 1990). That is of interest because it is believed that when schizophrenia is due to structural abnormalities in the brain, the problems appear first in the center and extend to the lateral areas only in the more severe cases (Weinberger, 1987). In fact, individuals with greater ventricle widening have suffered from schizophrenia longer and been hospitalized longer than individuals with less widening. Ventricular widening was also more prominent in males, which is consistent with the finding that males often suffer from more severe forms of schizophrenia and are more likely to have negative symptoms than females. Finally, ventricle widening appears to be more closely associated with negative symptoms (poverty of speech, flat mood, inability to experience pleasure, apathy) than with positive symptoms (Andreasen et al., 1982; Johnstone et al., 1976; Pearlson et al., 1989; Seidman, 1983). Enlarged and normal ventricles are depicted in the MRI scans presented in Figure 13.7 (brains viewed front to back).

FIGURE 13.7   MAGNETIC RESONANCE IMAGING (MRI) REVEALS ENLARGED VENTRICLES (CAVITIES IN THE BRAIN) IN PERSONS WITH SCHIZOPHRENIA (*TOP ROW*) RELATIVE TO NORMALS (*BOTTOM ROW*).

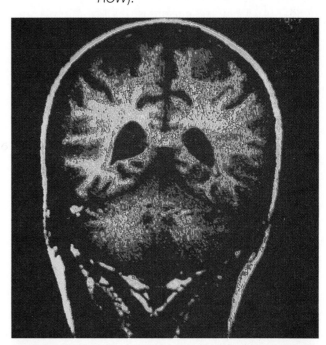

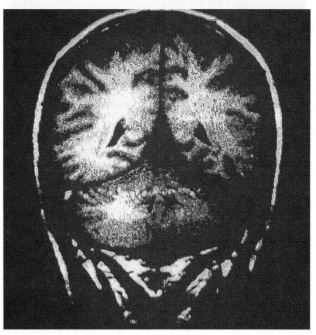

Source: Andreasen (1988), p. 1383, fig. 3.

Cortical Atrophy.   A second structural abnormality found in the brains of some individuals with schizophrenia is **cortical atrophy** (AT-rō-fē), which is a general *loss or deterioration of the nerve cells.* (The word *atrophy* denotes a wasting away, progressive decline, or degeneration.) The atrophy results in the widening of the grooves (*sulci*) covering the cerebral cortex, in enlargement of the clefts (*fissures*) between parts of the brain, and general deterioration of the brain surface. This type of damage appears to characterize the brains of 20% to 35% of the persons with schizophrenia, and it is also most likely to be found in chronic patients or those with negative symptoms.

Subcortical Atrophy.

Until recently, attention has been focused on the deterioration of the surface and cortex of the brain, but there is now also evidence that individuals with schizophrenia show deterioration in various **subcortical areas** of the brain (Breier et al., 1992; Zipursky et al., 1992). One area in which damage is frequently found is the **hippocampus**. The hippocampus is responsible for *information processing* (storing information in long-term memory), and hence damage there could contribute to the intellectual deficit and negative symptoms of schizophrenia. Another area that is often found to be damaged is the **amygdala**, an area that in normal individuals plays a role in *emotional arousal* and *assertiveness*, both of which are lacking in patients with negative symptoms.

Reversed Cerebral Asymmetry.

Finally, in some investigations, the brains of people with schizophrenia have been characterized by **reversed cerebral asymmetry**. In normal individuals, the left side of the brain tends to be larger than the right side, but in some individuals with schizophrenia, the right side of the brain tends to be larger. Furthermore, the enlarged ventricles that were discussed earlier are more likely to be on the left side (Suddath et al., 1990). The findings that many individuals with schizophrenia have problems on the left side of the brain is relevant for understanding symptoms because different cognitive functions tend to be located on one side of the brain or the other. For example, language function is on the left side of the brain, so damage on the left side could lead to the poverty of language which is often seen in schizophrenia. Consistent with that, it has been reported that among patients with schizophrenia, those with reversed asymmetry had lower verbal than performance IQ scores (Luchins et al., 1982).

Now that we have learned that problems with neurological activity and structural abnormalities in the brain are related to the positive and negative symptoms of schizophrenia, we must go on to ask, what causes the problems with neurological activity and the structural abnormalities? We will find the answers to that question by looking at genetic factors and biological traumas.

Genetic Factors

Genetic factors have long been suspected as a primary cause of schizophrenia, and there is now substantial evidence to support this.

Studies of Families.

Numerous studies have been conducted to determine whether schizophrenia tends to run in families. The results of those studies are summarized in Table 13.2, from which it can be concluded that the prevalence of schizophrenia in the relatives of persons with schizophrenia is higher than in the general population. It can also be concluded that the closer the biological relationship to the afflicted individual, the higher the prevalence of schizophrenia. For example, the concordance rate among siblings is between 8% and 14%, whereas the concordance rate among cousins is only 2% to 6%. It is also noteworthy that the prevalence of schizophrenia among individuals who had two parents with the disorder (40% to 68%) is substantially higher than among individuals who had only one parent with the disorder (5% to 10%). Clearly, the greater the degree to which an individual shares genes with a person who suffers from

TABLE 13.2   SCHIZOPHRENIA RISK: HIGHER FOR INDIVIDUALS WITH RELATIVES WHO SUFFER FROM THE DISORDER

	RISK (%)
Children of two parents suffering from schizophrenia	40–68
Children with one parent suffering from schizophrenia	9–16
Parent of a person suffering from schizophrenia	5–10
Nontwin siblings of a person suffering from schizophrenia	8–14
Grandchildren of a person suffering from schizophrenia	2–8
Stepsiblings of a person suffering from schizophrenia	1–8
Half siblings of a person suffering from schizophrenia	1–7
Cousins of a person suffering from schizophrenia	2–6
Nieces and nephews of a person suffering from schizophrenia	1–4

Source: Zerbin-Rudin (1972).

schizophrenia, the higher the likelihood that the individual will develop the disorder.

These results certainly suggest that there is a genetic basis for schizophrenia. However, because individuals who are more closely related are also more likely to share the same environment, we cannot definitely conclude from these results that there is a genetic basis for schizophrenia. Therefore, we must turn to other types of studies for more definitive data.

Studies of Twins.   In the studies of twins, the concordance rate for schizophrenia among dizygotic (DZ) twins is compared to the concordance rate for schizophrenia among monozygotic (MZ) twins. At least 13 studies of this type have been completed, involving more than 600 sets of MZ twins and more than 1,300 sets of DZ twins (see review by Gottesman, 1991). In every one of these studies, there was a higher concordance rate among MZ twins than among DZ twins. A typical concordance rate for MZ twins was about 50%, whereas the rate for DZ twins was about 15%. These findings consistently indicate that genetics do play an important role in schizophrenia.

The studies of twins have yielded two other relevant findings. First, in three different studies, the concordance rate for schizophrenia among MZ twins was found to be much higher if one of the twins was severely disturbed rather than only moderately disturbed (Gottesman & Shields, 1972; Kringlen, 1967, 1968; Rosenthal, 1961).

The second noteworthy finding is that when MZ twins are concordant for schizophrenia, both twins tend to show the same types of symptoms. In 31 of 34 sets of twins studied, both twins received the same subtype diagnosis (Fischer, 1971, 1973; Gottesman & Shields, 1972; Kringlen, 1967). This suggests not only that schizophrenia is inherited but also that a propensity for a specific set of symptoms may be inherited.

Studies of Adoptees.   Evidence for the role of genetic factors has also been provided by studies of adoptees. Four different approaches have been used to study adoptees. In the first, the investigators compared the rates of schizophrenia in children whose biological parents did or did not have schizophrenia but who had been adopted and raised by normal foster parents. In one study of this type, it was found that among persons whose biological mothers had schizophrenia, 11% developed schizophrenia, but among those whose biological mothers were normal, none developed schizophrenia (Heston, 1966). (Actually, the rate of schizophrenia among the offspring of mothers with schizophrenia jumps to 16.6% when the data are age-corrected. Age corrections are sometimes used when working with younger subjects who still have time to

develop schizophrenia.) Another study yielded similar results (Rosenthal et al., 1968; Rosenthal et al., 1971).

In the second approach to studying adoptees, the investigators started with a group of individuals who had been adopted and who were or were not suffering from schizophrenia, and then determined the rates of schizophrenia among the biological and the adoptive *parents* (Kety et al., 1975; see also Kendler et al., 1982a). That is, rather than going from parents to children, in this study the analysis went from children to parents. The results indicated that among the persons with long-term schizophrenia, 5% had biological parents who had the disorder, whereas none of their adoptive parents had the disorder. In contrast, among the normal persons, none of their biological parents had schizophrenia, whereas 1% of their adoptive parents had the disorder. Again the disorder was linked to the biological parents.

The third approach to studying adoptees focused on the siblings of six persons with schizophrenia who had been raised in foster homes (Karlsson, 1966). The disturbed individuals had 29 biological siblings who were raised in other foster homes and 28 foster siblings who were raised in the same homes as the children with schizophrenia. When the prevalence of schizophrenia in the biological and foster siblings was determined, it was found that 21% of the biological siblings had the disorder but none of the foster siblings had the disorder despite the fact that they had been raised in the same homes as the children with schizophrenia. Clearly, schizophrenia was linked to shared genes and not to shared environments.

In the last approach, the investigators compared the rates of schizophrenia in persons who had normal biological parents but who had been raised by foster parents who were either normal or were suffering from schizophrenia (Wender et al., 1974). The results revealed essentially the same rates of schizophrenia among persons who were and were not raised by foster parents with schizophrenia. That is, being raised by a foster parent with schizophrenia did *not* increase the likelihood of developing the disorder.

The results of the studies in which the adoption method was used clearly and consistently indicate that whether or not individuals develop schizophrenia is determined in large part by whether or not their biological parents suffered from schizophrenia and not by environmental factors such as who raised them. Because the adoption method enables us to separate the genetic and environmental effects, the results of these studies provide strong support for a genetic basis for some cases of schizophrenia.

Studies of Disorder Specificity.   Now we must consider the question of whether one inherits schizophrenia in specific or a predisposition to psychological disorders in general. To answer that question, investigators examined the disorders developed by children of parents who had schizophrenia or mood disorders. The results indicated that the children tend to develop the same disorder as their parents (Ödegard, 1972; Winokur et al., 1972). For example, in one study it was found that among disturbed children whose parents suffered from severe cases of schizophrenia, 78% developed schizophrenia and only 14.7% developed a bipolar disorder. In contrast, among the disturbed children of parents with a bipolar disorder, only 19.1% developed schizophrenia and 70.2% developed a bipolar disorder. Those results are summarized in Figure 13.8. Clearly, not only do the data indicate a genetic basis for schizophrenia, but they also indicate a high degree of specificity in the relationship. These findings are consistent with those mentioned earlier that indicated that MZ twins who were concordant for schizophrenia were almost always found to suffer from the same subtype of schizophrenia.

Studies of Specific Genes.

In all of the studies discussed so far, the genetic effect has been determined indirectly by studying relatives who shared genes rather than by studying the genes themselves. However, recent technological advances have made it possible to examine genes directly. Some investigators who used the new technology reported finding a link

Studies of families and twins have yielded compelling evidence for a genetic basis for schizophrenia. Shown here are the Genain quadruplets; each of the four girls eventually developed a schizophrenic disorder.

between a specific gene on chromosome 5 and schizophrenia (Sherrington et al., 1988). That finding was especially intriguing because the gene in question is one of the genes that influences dopamine and dopamine receptors. Unfortunately, other investigators were not able to replicate the finding (Kennedy et al., 1988; Sherrington et al., 1988). Examining specific genes holds out great promise, but the task is exceptionally difficult because not all cases of schizophrenia stem from genetic factors, and in cases in which there is a genetic basis, it is likely that the disorder stems from a complex interaction of a number of genes.

Overall, the results of the investigations we reviewed provide strong evidence that genetic factors play a role in schizophrenia. However, it is important to recognize that genetic factors do not account for all cases of schizophrenia. For example, not all of the biological offspring of parents with schizophrenia suffer from schizophrenia, and there is not a 100% concordance rate for schizophrenia among monozygotic twins. Indeed, genetic factors probably account for less than 10% of the cases of schizophrenia. Does this mean that the genetic explanation is wrong? No, it simply means that genetic factors are only one of the primary causes of schizophrenia. In the next section, we will consider the other major group of primary causes, biological traumas.

FIGURE 13.8   DISTURBED CHILDREN OF PARENTS WITH SCHIZOPHRENIA DEVELOPED SCHIZOPHRENIA, WHEREAS DISTURBED CHILDREN OF PARENTS WITH A BIPOLAR DISORDER DEVELOPED A BIPOLAR DISORDER.

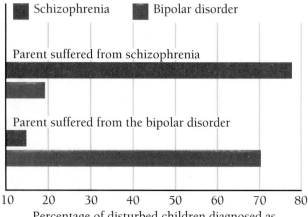

Percentage of disturbed children diagnosed as suffering from schizophrenic or bipolar disorders

Source: Adapted from Odegard (1972).

Biological Trauma

Another primary cause of schizophrenia appears to be **biological traumas** such as illness or physiological stress during the prenatal or perinatal periods. It may be that those traumas can account for the cases of schizophrenia that cannot be explained by genetic factors.

Prenatal Complications. The term *prenatal* refers to the time between conception and birth. Recent interest in the link between **prenatal complications** and schizophrenia came from the initially puzzling finding that in the Northern Hemisphere, individuals who later develop schizophrenia are most likely to be born during the months of January, February, or March (see Bradbury & Miller, 1985). This is known as the **season-of-birth effect**. This effect appears to be due to the fact that the mothers had become ill earlier in the winter when the rate of influenza was high, and the illness came during the *second trimester of pregnancy*, a period that is important for fetal brain development. The mothers' illnesses apparently retarded brain development or caused brain damage in the fetuses that led to the later development of schizophrenia. In view of that explanation, it is not the season of birth that is important but rather the *time of mothers' illnesses* that is crucial, so the effect might better be called the **second-trimester-illness effect**.

The possibility that schizophrenia is related to exposure to illness during the second trimester of fetal development has been supported by a variety of investigations. For example, in a retrospective study that covered 39 years, the investigators identified periods of high, medium, and low rates of influenza in the general population, and then they assessed the rates of schizophrenia in individuals who were born three months after each of those periods (Barr et al., 1990). The results indicated that schizophrenia was higher for individuals born after periods of high influenza, and the effect was specific to individuals who were in the second trimester of development during the peak influenza period. Those results are presented in Figure 13.9.

In this research, it was not possible to determine whether the pregnant women actually had influenza, so an inference about their infections was made based on the elevated rate of infection in the general population at that time. If mothers who actually had an infection could be identified, the findings would probably be much stronger.

It is clear that the mother's illness influences the brain of the fetus, but we do not understand the underlying process. It is unlikely that the fetus itself becomes infected because the virus probably cannot cross the blood–brain barrier between mother and fetus. However, the brain damage might result from *elevations in temperature* because fever accompanies influenza, and it has been shown that increases of only 2.5°C can cause brain damage in mammalian fetuses. The second trimester is particularly important because it is a time when the brain is going through a period of rapid growth and crucial connections between parts of

FIGURE 13.9 SERIOUS INFLUENZA EPIDEMICS DURING THE SECOND TRIMESTER OF PREGNANCY ARE RELATED TO HIGHER RATES OF SCHIZOPHRENIA IN THE OFFSPRING.

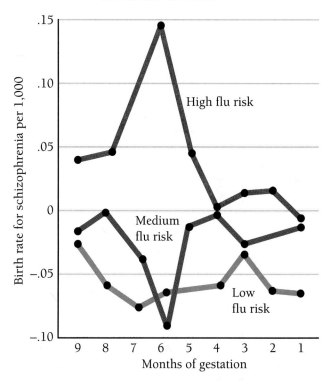

Source: Barr et al. (1990), p. 872, fig. 2.

the brain are being established (Jakob & Beckmann, 1986).

Why does damage that occurs in the second trimester of fetal development not result in schizophrenia until 20 or 25 years later? The answer is that the areas of the brain that are affected are normally slow to develop, so the effects of the damage (or nondevelopment) do not become apparent for some time (Weinberger, 1987). The symptoms that do eventually become evident are those that we usually characterize as negative symptoms (Opler et al., 1984).

Before concluding this discussion, it should be noted that (a) the seasonal effect is reversed in the Southern Hemisphere, where winter comes during July, August, and September; (b) the effect will occur during other months if a major influenza epidemic occurs sometime other than during the early winter; and (c) the effect does not hold for other psychiatric disorders such as anxiety and depression (Barr et al., 1990; Bradbury & Miller, 1985; Mednick et al., 1988; Mednick et al., 1990; Torrey et al., 1988; Watson et al., 1984).

Finally, it should be noted that the season-of-birth effect probably accounts for only 5% or 10% of the individuals who suffer from schizophrenia (Waddington et al., 1992). However, the important point illustrated by the effect is that prenatal complications can lead to schizophrenia, and mothers' influenza is undoubtedly only one of many potential complications. For example, it was recently reported that extreme food deprivation during the first trimester is linked to schizophrenia later in life (Susser & Lin, 1992). The problem we face is to identify the other complications; that is a difficult task because relevant events such as illnesses occurred many years before the onset of the disorder, and usually there is no record of them.

Perinatal Complications.   The term *perinatal* refers to the time immediately around birth. **Perinatal complications** include such things as prolonged or difficult labor, deprivation of oxygen during birth (anoxia), and the use of forceps in delivery. The notion here is that perinatal complications may result in brain damage that could later contribute to the development of schizophrenia.

A substantial amount of evidence now links perinatal complications to schizophrenia (Cannon et al., 1989; Kanofsky et al., 1990; Lyons et al., 1989; Machon et al., 1987; Wilcox, 1986; Wilcox & Nasrallah, 1987a, 1987b). In one longitudinal study of individuals who were at high risk for developing schizophrenia (their parents suffered from schizophrenia), it was found that those who developed the disorder were almost twice as likely to have experienced perinatal complications as those who did not develop the disorder (Mednick et al., 1987). In a more recent investigation of individuals with schizophrenia, it was found that those who had experienced perinatal complications such as bleeding, seizures, and hypertension were more likely to have structural abnormalities in the brain and that the relationship was stronger among individuals who did not have a family history of schizophrenia (Kanofsky et al., 1990). In other words, it appears that perinatal complications led to brain damage, which in turn led to schizophrenia, and that perinatal complications may account for schizophrenia in cases in which genetics is not a factor (individuals who do not have a family history of the disorder).

In another study that was part of a 40-year follow-up of over 500 individuals with schizophrenia, it was found that those who had not recovered were more likely to have had perinatal complications than those who improved (Wilcox & Nasrallah, 1987a, 1987b). This finding is consistent with the notion that perinatal complications lead to brain damage, which in turn leads to negative symptoms that are more difficult to treat. Clearly, research on prenatal and perinatal complications is providing more of the pieces of the puzzle of schizophrenia.

Diathesis-Stress Hypothesis

A very popular explanation for schizophrenia is that physiological factors establish a predisposition for schizophrenia but that environmental stress factors must also impinge on the individual before the schizophrenia will become manifest. In other words, genetic factors place the individual at risk, and then stress factors push the person over the edge. This is known as the **diathesis-stress hypothesis**. (The word *diathesis* means "bodily condition or constitution predisposing to a disease.") The diathesis-stress hypothesis can be illustrated with the following quip: "Humpty Dumpty had a fragile shell, but he didn't break until he fell."

This hypothesis makes intuitive sense and is widely accepted, but we have no direct evidence supporting it. For example, when studying monozygotic twins who were discordant for schizophrenia (one twin had the disorder and the other did not), researchers were unable to find stresses that had impinged on the disordered twin but not the normal twin (e.g., Gottesman & Shields, 1976).

The results of a long-term follow-up of children whose parents suffered from schizophrenia have been interpreted as offering evidence for the diathesis-stress hypothesis (Mednick, Cudeck, et al., 1984). In that study of high-risk (predisposed) children, the children who developed schizophrenia were those who experienced more personal stresses. However, examination of the stresses indicated that they were associated with higher levels of abnormality in the parents such as the mother having a psychotic episode. It may be that the children who developed schizophrenia did so because of a greater genetic contribution (their parents were more severely disturbed) rather than because of stress per se. In that regard, recall that the concordance rate for schizophrenia among twins was higher if one of the twins was severely disturbed rather than only moderately disturbed (Gottesman & Shields, 1972; Kringlen, 1967, 1968; Rosenthal, 1961).

The absence of evidence does not necessarily mean that the hypothesis is *wrong*; it only means that *it does not have support*. It is possible that we have not yet focused on the crucial stress variable or variables or that we do not yet have the ability to measure them. In any event, the diathesis-stress hypothesis is much less important now than it once was. Originally, it was the only way to explain findings that could not be accounted for by genetics (e.g., discordant twin pairs), but now many of those findings can be accounted for by biological traumas and brain abnormalities (Suddath et al., 1990).

Does all of this mean that we should abandon the diathesis-stress explanation? No, but the explanation might be revised somewhat. Rather than suggesting that stress somehow triggers symptoms that were not there before, it might be more accurate to say that *stress exacerbates existing problems*, sometimes moving them from a "subsymptom" level to a symptom level and at other times simply making them worse. There is no doubt that in many cases stress interferes with cognitive performance (when you are "stressed out," you probably do not perform well on exams), and that effect could compound existing problems that stem from high or low levels of neurological activity or from structural abnormalities in the brain. In Chapter 14, you will learn that patients who leave the hospital and return to a stressful situation are more likely to relapse than those who return to a nonstressful situation. It seems that the symptoms created by the high or low levels of neurological activity or structural abnormalities make life difficult, and the *addition* of stress may be overwhelming.

Comment

In Chapter 12, we saw that schizophrenia is a heterogeneous disorder and that different individuals can suffer from different symptoms. The physiological approach to schizophrenia offers three different explanations (high neurological activity, low neurological activity, structural abnormalities) that can be used to account for the different symptoms. Furthermore, the physiological approach encompasses both primary causes (genetic factors and biological traumas) and intermediate causes (neurological activity and structural abnormalities). Overall, then, the physiological approach is thus more comprehensive than the other approaches.

The physiological approach does not conflict with other approaches but instead complements them. Specifically, (a) the role of stress that is emphasized by the psychodynamic approach is incorporated into the diathesis-stress explanation, (b) the high drive that is central to the learning explanation can be understood in terms of excessively high neurological arousal, and (c) the disruptions in cognitive processing (stimulus overload, problems with attention) on which the cognitive approach is focused can be explained by excessively high neurological arousal. Furthermore, the physiological approach provides explanations for negative symptoms, whereas those symptoms are largely ignored by other approaches. Because the physiological approach to schizophrenia is more comprehensive and because the other approaches can be encompassed within it, the physiological approach is becoming the dominant approach for understanding schizophrenia. As we will see later, it also provides the best model for treatment.

HUMANISTIC-EXISTENTIAL EXPLANATIONS

Humanistic-existential theorists focus most of their attention on the less serious disorders such as anxiety and depression, but they have offered a radical explanation for schizophrenia that deserves brief comment here. Some humanistic-existential theorists suggest that the behavior seen in schizophrenia is labeled abnormal because it differs from the way most people behave, but that it is in fact the behavior of people who do *not* have schizophrenia that is abnormal (Laing, 1964). More specifically, they suggest that what we generally refer to as "normal" behavior is actually abnormal because social pressures have forced most people to adopt false and distorted selves and to become robots or automatons programmed to follow the dictates of society. From the humanistic-existential perspective, persons diagnosed as having schizophrenia are thought to be individuals who break out of society's mold and retreat into themselves in an attempt to find themselves as unique individuals apart from the roles established by society. In schizophrenia, then, individuals give up the masquerade of sanity and undertake a voyage of discovery of the real self. In their search for themselves, these individuals might demonstrate some unusual or inappropriate behavior, but from the humanistic-existential point of view, their behavior is not any more inappropriate than the behavior prescribed by society. From this perspective, individuals with schizophrenia are thought to be closer to finding their true selves than other people, but they are labeled abnormal because they are out of step with the majority. Like Columbus, who sailed west to find the East, persons with schizophrenia may be taking different paths to find themselves. This point of view has provided the basis for many provocative philosophical discussions, but it has had relatively little practical impact on our understanding or treatment of schizophrenia.

SUMMARY

The psychodynamic explanation suggests that the process underlying schizophrenia is either intrapersonal regression (regression to an earlier stage of development) or interpersonal withdrawal (social withdrawal). It is doubtful whether regression is a viable explanation because the cognitive processes seen in schizophrenia are not like those of children. Social withdrawal is frequently observed in individuals who later develop schizophrenia, but the evidence now suggests that in most cases, the withdrawal may be an early symptom of the disorder rather than a cause. The psychodynamic explanation also highlights the role of stress as a contributing factor in schizophrenia. The evidence indicates that stress often plays a role in the development of schizophrenia, but its role is more complex than is usually assumed.

Psychodynamic theorists have also emphasized the influence of personality characteristics of parents and the role of communications between parents and children. There is evidence that the parents of people who develop schizophrenia are less well adjusted than the parents of others, but it cannot be concluded that the parents' poor adjustment contributes to their children's schizophrenia. Disturbed children may cause adjustment problems in parents, or the co-occurrence of problems in parents and their children may be due to genetic factors. There is no evidence that communication problems contribute to schizophrenia.

Learning theorists suggested that high drive disrupts cognitive functioning. It is also speculated that in an attempt to reduce the high drive, individuals focus on thoughts that are irrelevant to the drive, and those associations further interfere with cognitive functioning. This explanation is somewhat simplistic, and it does not explain why persons with schizophrenia have higher drive.

A second learning explanation suggests that some persons are not rewarded for attending to relevant cues in the environment, and therefore they no longer attend to those cues and instead attend to irrelevant cues. The inattention to relevant cues is thought to lead to deviant responses and schizophrenia. Persons with schizophrenia do have problems with attention, but questions arise over cause and effect and over whether lack of attention is sufficient to explain the uncontrollable symptoms of schizophrenia.

There is evidence that some of the symptoms of schizophrenia exist because they result in rewards, just as some normal behaviors do. However, rewards do not seem sufficient to account for some of the uncontrollable problems with thought processes seen in schizophrenia.

Learning theorists also point out that labels influence our expectations about how people should behave and may therefore influence the symptoms we see in (or suggest to) individuals who are labeled as suffering from schizophrenia. Furthermore, once labeled as suffering from schizophrenia, the individual may exhibit inappropriate behaviors that would be inhibited were it not for the fact that the role of "a schizophrenic" permits the deviant behaviors. There is evidence that labels and roles do contribute to the symptoms of schizophrenia, but they cannot account for the entire symptom pattern because some symptoms had to exist initially for the individual to be labeled and given the role of schizophrenic.

The cognitive explanation for schizophrenia is different in that it begins with the premise that persons with schizophrenia cannot filter out irrelevant stimuli, and consequently they are flooded with stimulation beyond the point of overload. The fact that they are overloaded with stimulation makes them very distractible and results in their cognitive disorganization and deficit. Furthermore, in attempting to explain their unique experiences, the individuals develop what we refer to as delusions. The major limitation of this approach is that it does not explain why the persons with schizophrenia suffer from stimulus overload.

There are three physiological explanations for the symptoms of schizophrenia. The first is that cognitive activity is disrupted by high levels of neurological activity in the areas of the brain where dopamine is the primary neurotransmitter (the dopamine explanation). High neurological activity seems to be related primarily to positive symptoms of schizophrenia. The second explanation is that cognitive activity is retarded by low levels of neurological activity in the frontal lobes (the hypofrontality explanation). The reduced levels of activity are often linked to negative symptoms. The third explanation is that some symptoms of schizophrenia are due to structural abnormalities in the brain. Those abnormalities include enlarged ventricles, cortical and subcortical atrophy, and reversed cerebral asymmetry. Structural abnormalities of the brain seem to be associated primarily with the negative symptoms of schizophrenia.

Problems with neurological activity and structural abnormalities are thought to be due to genetic factors and biological traumas. Notable among the prenatal effects is the season-of-birth effect, which is due to maternal infection during the second trimester of fetal development. Perinatal complications include prolonged labor, anoxia during birth, and forceps delivery.

It is often suggested that genetic factors predispose the person to the disorder, and then the disorder is triggered by an environmental factor such as stress. This is referred to as the diathesis-stress hypothesis. The diathesis-stress hypothesis is still without direct support. It may be that rather than triggering symptoms, stress adds to or exacerbates existing problems.

The humanistic-existential theorists believe that schizophrenia is not a disorder but is instead an alternative form of adjustment. They suggest that schizophrenic behavior is defined as abnormal only because it deviates from the behavior pattern accepted by most people. Behavior that is usually defined as normal is seen by the humanistic-existential theorists as unduly constricted and robot-like.

KEY TERMS, CONCEPTS, AND NAMES

In reviewing and testing yourself on what you have learned from this chapter, you
should be able to identify and discuss each of the following:

amygdala
associative intrusions
attention to irrelevant cues
atypical neuroleptics
biological traumas
clang associations
cognitive flooding
cortical atrophy
delusions
diathesis-stress hypothesis
distraction
dopamine
dopamine explanation for
    schizophrenia
double-bind hypothesis
extinction of attention to relevant cues
filter mechanism
frontal lobes

habit strength intrusions
hallucinations
high drive
hippocampus
hypofrontality hypothesis
interpersonal withdrawal
intrusion of irrelevant associations
labels
lapses of attention
L-dopa
limbic system
neuroleptics
Parkinson's disease
perinatal complications
prenatal complications
regression
reversed cerebral asymmetry
rewards

roles
schizophrenic deficit
schizophrenogenic mother
season-of-birth effect
second-trimester-illness effect
semantic intrusions
sensory deprivation
serotonin
stimulus overload
strategic symptoms
structural abnormalities of the brain
subcortical areas
temporal lobe epilepsy
temporal lobes
thought content intrusions
ventricles

Chapter 14

Treatment of Schizophrenic Disorders

• O U T L I N E •

Bill was hospitalized with a diagnosis of schizophrenia. Neuroleptic drugs were effective for reducing his symptoms, and he was released from the hospital after 3 months. Then he and his family participated in family therapy once a week for 8 weeks. The therapy involved teaching Bill's family more effective communication and problem-solving skills. The goal of therapy was not to develop any new "insights" about Bill's psychological problems. Instead, it was designed to help his family accept Bill's illness and to foster a less stressful and more supportive environment for him. The therapy seems to have been effective; Bill has been able to remain out of the hospital on a reduced level of medication.

Over a period of a few months, Ann became very confused and developed a delusion that all of her coworkers were against her. She thought that they were sabotaging her work at night and putting "contaminants" in her drinking water that made her skin itch so that she would not be able to concentrate. One afternoon, she locked herself in a closet "for protection." She was admitted to a psychiatric hospital and immediately given a neuroleptic drug. During the 3 weeks that she was in the hospital, her medication was changed twice in an attempt to find the drug that would be most helpful and cause the fewest side effects. Ann is now out of the hospital and back at work, but she is on a maintenance dose of the medication, which is generally effective for holding her symptoms in check. However, sometimes she gets a little suspicious of her colleagues. Although the drug keeps her free of schizophrenic symptoms, its side effects sometimes make her head swim a bit. Because the side effects are somewhat annoying, Ann and her physician try to keep the drug dosage level as low as possible.

Ed has been hospitalized for 12 years with a diagnosis of schizophrenia. During that time, he has been on 8 or 10 different drugs and combinations of drugs. Nothing seems to help much. For the past couple of years, Ed has been having difficulty with involuntary muscle movements that make his tongue twist in his mouth and his head twist suddenly to the side, and he is unable to sit still for more than a minute or two. He gets up, paces briefly, sits down, and then gets up again. These motor symptoms are not part of his schizophrenia but are the symptoms of a disorder known as *tardive dyskinesia*, which can result from the use of some antipsychotic drugs. There is no effective treatment for this disorder. Ed appears to be one of those patients for whom we do not yet have an effective treatment. Ed will probably have to live out his days in a hospital.

Sid had been hospitalized with a diagnosis of schizophrenia for almost 9 years. Eighteen months ago, he was transferred to a ward that was organized as a "token economy." Here, whenever Sid shows appropriate behaviors (making his bed, initiating social interactions), he is given a plastic poker chip, and he can use his chips to buy privileges (TV time, grounds passes, better food). Through this procedure, Sid is learning to behave more "normally." He appears much better and may be released to a sheltered living environment, but he still suffers disturbances in his thought processes that he cannot control.

There are three reasons why it is important that we thoroughly understand the nature and effectiveness of the techniques that are used to treat schizophrenia. The first is humane: Schizophrenia is a disorder that afflicts hundreds of thousands of individuals, and without an understanding of what treatments are effective, many of those individuals are doomed to progressive deterioration and permanent institutionalization. The second reason is practical: The direct cost of caring for a person with schizophrenia can be well over $80,000 per year in a public institution and much more in a private institution. In addition, there are the indirect costs such as lost productivity. These costs pose an overwhelming public and personal burden, but they may be reduced with effective treatments. A final reason to consider the treatment of schizophrenia is theoretical: An understanding of what treatments are effective may contribute to our understanding of the causes of the disorder.

■ PSYCHODYNAMIC APPROACHES

Milieu Therapy

It has long been recognized that letting patients sit passively all day would have negative effects. Consequently, in most hospitals, attempts are made to enrich the patients' daily experiences by providing things such as occupational therapy, music therapy, art therapy, recreational therapy, ward meetings in which patients and staff work on problems, and perhaps field trips outside the hospital. All of these experiences are thought to contribute to the patients' recovery and are collectively referred to as **milieu** (mil-YOO) **therapy**.

The potential value of milieu therapy for many patients is obvious, and no one would propose that we return to the time when patients were simply allowed to vegetate. However, there is evidence that the socially stimulating environment provided by milieu therapy may not be good for all patients and may even hinder the recovery of some.

In one investigation, patients with chronic schizophrenia were assigned to either an experimental ward that had an intensive and stimulating milieu therapy program (meetings, trips, much staff contact, brightly decorated rooms designed in part by the patients, etc.) or to a regular (control) ward that provided care but little more (Schooler & Spohn, 1982). The patients' social behavior and their levels of pathology were assessed before, during, and after the 2-year treatment period. The results indicated that the patients who received the intensive milieu therapy showed a tendency to initiate more social interactions with other individuals, but they also showed a substantial increase in their

Milieu therapy may contribute to the recovery of many patients. However, in some cases a socially stimulating environment may have negative effects.

levels of abnormal behavior relative to the patients in the control condition. Furthermore, the patients who received intensive milieu therapy were not discharged from the hospital sooner, and after discharge, they did not remain in the community longer than patients who received the regular treatment. Similar results have been reported by numerous other investigators (see Van Putten & May, 1976; Wing, 1975).

It is interesting to note that intensive milieu therapy had its most negative effects on the most disturbed patients. The negative effects of milieu therapy seem to be due to the fact that the stimulation provided by the therapy contributed to stimulus overload, which is one of the components of schizophrenia (see Chapters 12 and 13). Specifically, milieu therapy increased hallucinations and reduced intellectual performance, both of which are related to stimulus overload.

In summary, it appears that either extreme in the environmental milieu can have deleterious effects on patients: A socially impoverished environment can result in social withdrawal and lack of motivation, whereas a very stimulating environment can exacerbate symptoms such as hallucinations, delusions, and problems of speech and language. Contrary to what is generally thought, then, milieu therapy is not universally effective, and like almost any other therapy, it must be tailored to the needs and capacities of the patient because in some cases "overdoses" can have negative effects.

Psychotherapy

In the 1950s, serious attempts were begun to use individual **psychotherapy** to treat individuals who were suffering from schizophrenia (Fromm-Reichmann, 1948, 1954; Sullivan, 1962). The psychotherapy was similar to that conducted with other types of patients (see Chapter 6), and the goal was to help patients gain insights into the dynamic causes of their disorders so that they could overcome them. However, psychotherapy with persons suffering from schizophrenia was more difficult than with other patients because of the communication problems associated with schizophrenia. For example, it would be very difficult to develop insights in patients who could not keep their attention on any one thought.

The introduction of psychotherapy as a treatment for schizophrenia was soon followed by experiments designed to assess its effectiveness. In the first of these experiments, 228 recently admitted patients with an "average prognosis" were assigned to one of five treatments: (a) individual psychotherapy, (b) drug therapy, (c) individual psychotherapy plus drug therapy, (d) electroconvulsive therapy, or (e) milieu therapy only (May, 1968). Actually, all of the patients received the milieu therapy, and therefore the question that was asked was, do any of the other therapies add to the effects that can be achieved by routine hospital care?

The results did not provide any evidence that individual psychotherapy was more effective than milieu therapy. That was the case regardless of whether the measure of outcome was release rate, length of hospital stay, nurses' assessment of outcome, therapists' assessment of outcome, or intellectual functioning. Furthermore, it was found that the combination of psychotherapy and drug therapy was not more effective than drug therapy alone, thus suggesting that psychotherapy did not add to what could be achieved with drugs alone. The findings concerning release rates are presented in Figure 14.1.

It could be argued that the results of that experiment were not more positive because the patients were not treated long enough (treatment was limited to 1 year), the therapists were not sufficiently trained (they had less than 6 years of experience), or the program was not intense or sophisticated enough (it was designed to be *typical*, not *ideal*). Therefore, a second investigation was conducted in which a group of 20 patients with chronic schizophrenia was given essentially the best of everything for 2 years (Grinspoon et al., 1968, 1972). The patients lived in a special ward

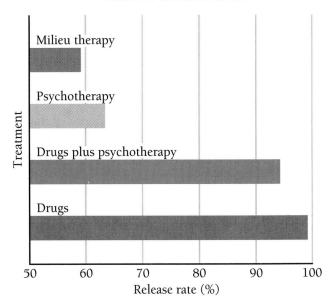

FIGURE 14.1   RELEASE RATES WERE LOWER FOR PATIENTS RECEIVING MILIEU THERAPY OR PSYCHOTHERAPY THAN FOR PATIENTS GIVEN DRUGS.

Source: Adapted from May (1968), p. 138, fig. 5-1.

that was designed to provide them with a therapeutically ideal environment. For example, in addition to excellent physical facilities,

> a nursing staff of 25 people, an occupational therapist, and a social worker involved the patients in an intensive program which included therapeutic community meetings and group or individual ward functions as well as frequent beach outings, museum visits, sports events, and the like. (Grinspoon et al., 1968, p. 69)

The psychotherapy was provided by senior psychiatrists chosen from among the best available in the Boston area. If it were available, today such treatment would easily cost in excess of $150,000 per year per patient. Unfortunately, despite the herculean effort at intervention, there was no evidence that the patients showed any improvement over the 2 years of treatment. However, as we will learn later, the patients did improve when they were given drugs, thus indicating that the patients were capable of improvement but that psychotherapy was not effective in achieving it.

To date, the well-controlled research has not supplied any evidence that traditional psychotherapy is effective for treating schizophrenia regardless of the outcome measure used. A few other experiments have provided somewhat more positive results (Karon & Vanden Bos, 1972; May, Tuma, et al., 1976; May, Van Putten, et al., 1976), but because of methodological problems, the results of those investigations are not generally considered valid or reliable. The fall from favor of individual psychotherapy for the treatment of schizophrenia is dramatically illustrated by the fact that when research on the treatment of schizophrenia was initiated in the early 1960s, it was considered unethical to have a control condition in which the patients did not receive psychotherapy. However, less than a decade later, it was considered unethical to have a control condition in which the patients received only psychotherapy (Mosher & Keith, 1980).

Family Therapy, Psychoeducation, and Social Skills Training

The findings concerning the effects of traditional psychotherapy are discouraging, but you should not conclude that psychotherapeutic interventions are not effective, for indeed they are. However, in seeking effective psychotherapeutic interventions, we must use a somewhat different model from what has been used in the past. The model that is emerging is often referred to as **family therapy** because it involves the family members as well as the patient. This approach is also referred to as **psychoeducation** or **social skills training** because it is focused primarily on education and training rather than on complex "underlying" or "dynamic" problems.

In general, this approach to treatment involves three elements (Halford & Hayes, 1991). The first element involves *educating the patient and the family* so that they can *understand the disorder*. For example, the patient and family are taught that schizophrenia, like

other disorders such as diabetes and epilepsy, is due to biochemical imbalances. To some extent, this "normalizes" the disorder and makes it less frightening so that everyone can deal with it more realistically.

The second element involves teaching the patient and family how to *reduce the stress that exacerbates the symptoms*. Regardless of whether or not stress causes schizophrenia, we know that an intense emotional climate can make the symptoms worse and contribute to relapse (Doane et al., 1985; Leff, 1976; Vaughn & Leff, 1976; Vaughn et al., 1984). This is not unique to schizophrenia; indeed, many of us do not function well when we are under high stress. Therefore, patients and families are taught strategies for "cooling" the emotional climate in which the patient lives. This may involve, for example, placing fewer demands on the patient or being less critical when he or she does not measure up to expectations. After all, because of his or her symptoms, the patient may be working under a distinct handicap. (Understanding that goes back to the educational element already mentioned.)

The third goal in this approach is to teach the patient strategies for *coping with the symptoms*. In many cases, it is not possible to eliminate all of the symptoms with whatever treatment is being used (e.g., drugs), and therefore it is essential for the patient to learn to cope with the remaining symptoms. Like the educational component, this is not unique to schizophrenia because patients with disorders such as diabetes and epilepsy must also learn ways of coping with their symptoms. Coping can take many forms and often requires help from others. For example, Betty

Teaching problem-solving skills to patients and their families is more effective for maintaining recovery than teaching such skills to patients alone.

(Case Study 12.2) calls me for a "reality check" when she begins to lose confidence in her ability to distinguish between reality and her hallucinations. In other cases, the patient may learn to avoid overly stimulating environments. For example, it would be disastrous for a patient suffering from stimulus overload to attend a rock concert; in some cases, even a noisy party could be difficult.

The goal of this approach is not to treat the schizophrenia per se but rather to prevent a relapse after the disorder has been brought under control with some other means (usually drugs). With this approach we attempt to take the stress component out of the diathesis-stress mixture, and thereby reduce the likelihood of igniting or exacerbating symptoms.

This approach to helping individuals with schizophrenia has been shown to be quite successful. In one of the best tests of this approach, the investigators assigned patients to one of four conditions: (a) drugs only, (b) drugs plus patient social skills training, (c) drugs plus family psychoeducation, or (d) drugs plus patient social skills training and family psychoeduca-

FIGURE 14.2   FAMILY PSYCHOEDUCATION AND PATIENT SOCIAL SKILLS TRAINING ARE EFFECTIVE FOR REDUCING RELAPSE RATES AFTER 1 AND 2 YEARS.

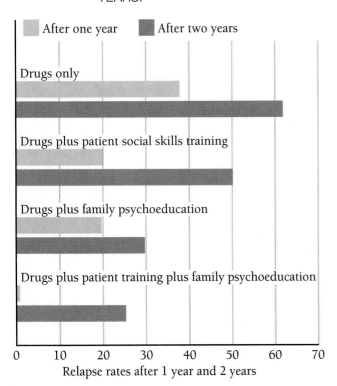

Source: Data from Hogarty et al. (1991), p. 342, tab. 1.

FIGURE 14.3   THE COMBINATION OF DRUGS AND FAMILY THERAPY WAS MOST EFFECTIVE FOR REDUCING RELAPSE RATES OF PATIENTS AFTER THEY LEFT THE HOSPITAL.

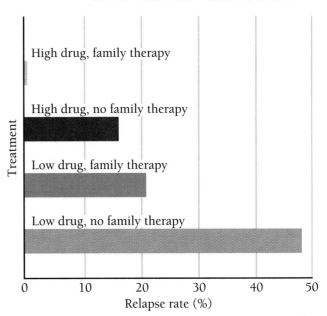

Source: Adapted from Goldstein (1980), p. 81, fig. 1.

tion (Hogarty et al., 1986, 1991). All of the patients were returning to family environments that could be characterized as highly emotional, and therefore these patients were at high risk for relapse. The results indicated that for patients who complied with their medication prescriptions, 1 year after discharge from the hospital, the relapse rates in the conditions were (a) drugs only, 38%; (b) drugs plus patient social skills training, 20%; (c) drugs plus family psychoeducation, 19%; and (d) drugs plus patient social skills training and family psychoeducation, 0%. After 2 years, the relapse rates were generally higher, and it appeared that the psychoeducation for family members had a more lasting effect than the social skills training for the patients (29% vs. 50% relapse rates, respectively), but they were still both more effective than drugs alone (62%). These results are summarized in Figure 14.2.

With regard to the decline in effectiveness of patient social skills training, it is noteworthy that the social skills training was as effective as the family psychoeducation until about 3 months before the end of treatment, at which point the patients receiving social skills training showed a sudden increase in relapse rate. The time of that increase in relapse rate corresponded with the time at which contact with the patients was being terminated because the study was coming to a close. That finding highlights the fact that schizophrenia cannot be treated as though it were an acute disorder, but instead it requires *continued maintenance therapy*. In any event, these findings are impressive and may actually underrepresent the general effectiveness of social skills training and psychoeducation because they were used with a population that was strongly disposed to relapse because their families had high expressed emotion (Bellack & Muesler, 1992). Other investigators have reported similar findings (e.g., Hogarty et al., 1973; Hogarty, Goldberg, & Schooler, 1974; Hogarty, Goldberg, & Collaborative Study Group, 1974; Hogarty et al., 1979).

Another experiment was conducted to determine whether patients who received family therapy would have lower relapse rates and would be able to get along with less medication (Goldstein, 1980). In that experiment, patients who had been hospitalized for an average of 14 days before being discharged were kept on either a high or a low maintenance dose of an antipsychotic drug and either were or were not given family therapy. The major goals of the family therapy were to identify future stresses to which the patients would be exposed and to make plans so that the stresses could be minimized or avoided. Therapy occurred only once a week for a 6-week period. The results concerning relapse (readmission to the hospital) after 6 months are presented in Figure 14.3.

Two important findings should be noted. First, the patients in the group that received high-drug-plus-family-therapy showed the lowest relapse rate (0%), whereas the patients in the low-drug-and-no-family-therapy group showed the highest relapse rate (almost 50%). Second, relapse rates in the high-drug-and-no-family-therapy and low-drug-plus-family-therapy groups were nearly the same. That suggests that family therapy reduced the level of drugs that was necessary to keep the patients out of the hospital.

In a more extensive experiment, one group of patients was given family therapy in which the patient and the patient's family learned problem-solving skills designed to reduce the stress in the patient's life, while another group of patients was given the same type of therapy (learning of problem-solving skills), but it was given only to the individual patient (Falloon et al., 1985). The investigation produced encouraging findings in three areas. First, patients in the family therapy condition showed lower levels of schizophrenia symptoms. Those results are presented in Figure 14.4.

The second finding was that after 9 months, the relapse rates were lower among patients receiving family therapy than among those receiving individual therapy. For example, only 11% of the patients receiving family therapy had to be rehospitalized, compared to 50% of the patients receiving individual therapy. Similarly, the rates of going to jail or being placed in other residential care facilities were also lower for patients

FIGURE 14.4   FAMILY MANAGEMENT WAS MORE EFFECTIVE THAN INDIVIDUAL MANAGEMENT FOR REDUCING SYMPTOMS OF PATIENTS WHO HAD BEEN RELEASED FROM THE HOSPITAL.

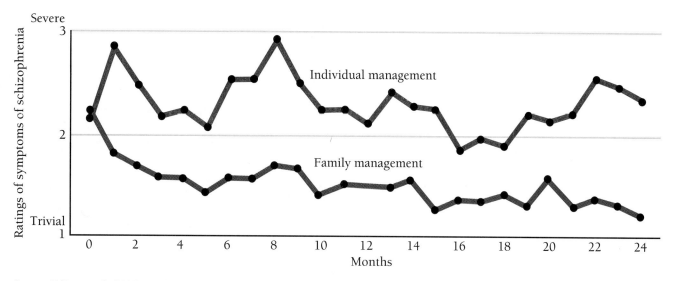

Source: Falloon et al. (1985), p. 891, fig. 2.

receiving family versus individual therapy (6% vs. 17%, respectively, for each measure). Overall, the patients who received family therapy spent an average of only 1 day out of the home, whereas patients in individual therapy spent an average of 12.22 days out of the home.

The third finding of interest is that the patients in the family therapy group were able to take somewhat lower levels of drugs during the treatment period than the patients in the individual therapy group. That finding is particularly noteworthy when considered with the fact that those patients also did better on other measures of adjustment (level of symptoms, relapse rates). In other words, the patients receiving family therapy took less medication and showed better adjustment. In summary, the results of this experiment are particularly noteworthy because they indicate that teaching problem-solving skills to patients and their families is more effective for maintaining recovery than teaching problem-solving skills only to patients. It is also noteworthy that this effective approach is based on straightforward training procedures rather than on the in-depth analyses and insights that were traditionally thought to be necessary for effective therapy.

It is clear from the research discussed here that teaching basic coping skills to disturbed persons and their families may not cure schizophrenia, but it can be an effective means of helping them deal with the day-to-day problems that are posed by the disorder. Case Study 14.1 focuses on a psychologist who has struggled successfully with schizophrenia for over 20 years.

Comment

Psychological interventions for schizophrenia got off to a poor start, but with the development of the education or training model and the involvement of the family, considerable strides have been made. It is noteworthy that therapy based on the education or training model can be conducted by a variety of professionals other than psychologists and psychiatrists, and even by paraprofessionals. That reduces costs.

LEARNING APPROACHES

Use of Rewards and Punishments

In Chapter 13 we learned that some learning theorists believe that individuals with schizophrenia behave strangely because their behavior is effective in obtaining rewards. Based on that assumption, the learning theory approach to the treatment of schizophrenia involves the manipulation of reward or punishment con-

tingencies such that abnormal behaviors (symptoms) are no longer rewarded or are punished and normal behaviors are rewarded. Case Study 14.2 (p. 330) illustrates this procedure.

Since the 1960s, hundreds of carefully controlled experiments have demonstrated that various behaviors of patients can be brought under control by manipulating reward and punishment contingencies. In many of the experiments, patients were given tokens when they behaved appropriately, and those tokens could later be used to buy desired rewards (hospital passes, better living conditions, better food, TV time, etc.). In other words, the tokens were used like money (earned, saved, and spent), and therefore this approach is often referred to as the **token economy** approach to treatment.

In one of the most impressive tests of the effectiveness of the token economy approach to treatment, 56 chronic mental patients were assigned either to a ward on which a very active milieu therapy approach was used or to a ward on which a token economy approach was used (Paul & Lentz, 1977). On both wards, the patients were kept very busy with a variety of activities (classes, group meetings, gym time, housekeeping, meals, individual assignments), and it was made clear to the patients that they were expected to act appropriately and to take responsibility for their behavior. When patients on either ward behaved appropriately, they were rewarded with positive statements and encouragement.

The important difference between the two wards was that patients on the token economy ward were re-

The token economy approach is effective for improving a patient's general behavior.

Case Study 14.1

A PSYCHOLOGIST WITH SCHIZOPHRENIA TALKS ABOUT WHAT HELPS HIM FUNCTION EFFECTIVELY

Fredrick J. Frese III is a psychologist who has struggled with schizophrenia for over 20 years. In Case Study 12.4, he described the onset of his symptoms and talked about his occasional "breakdowns." Dr. Frese believes it is important that the person with schizophrenia be aware of the nature of the problem in order to develop effective coping strategies. Despite his illness, most of the time he functions effectively. Here he describes some of the things that help.

"Persons with schizophrenia need to study carefully how they function. Until they can identify their deficits, it is very difficult to start building compensatory mechanisms that will enable them to function better. . . . Persons recovering from schizophrenia should be able to identify, and be on the lookout for, the sorts of persons, places, and things that can cause the type of stress that may precipitate their breakdowns. They should know how to get to environments that are helpful.

"Just as a diabetic must take action to control his or her blood sugar level, persons recovering from schizophrenia must learn to monitor and take measures to counteract an imbalance in subcortical neurochemical activity. But unlike diabetes, schizophrenia seriously interferes with rational processes, and once the irrationality begins, the person may have great difficulty acting in a rational or responsible manner.

"Because of our disability, it is very difficult for us to know what we do that normals do not understand. Therefore, it is very helpful to have a trustworthy normal person around to let us know what it is about our thoughts that perhaps it would be better not to share with everyone else. In my case, my wife constantly gives me feedback whenever I am saying or doing things that normal people may consider bizarre or offensive. Some things are rather obvious. If you are hearing voices, it is generally best not to talk back to them while normals are around. If your thoughts are dominated by the importance of the colors or similar sounds in the environment, you probably do not want to reveal too much about this to others.

"With help, other disabled persons learn to compensate for their disabilities and frequently lead dignified, productive lives. The blind learn to use canes and seeing-eye dogs; people with limited use of their legs learn to use crutches and wheelchairs. For the mentally ill, however, the parameters of our disability are often not easily defined. We need help and feedback so that we can understand exactly the nature of our disability.

"Unfortunately, feedback is not always enough. Sometimes the symptoms overwhelm the person, who then loses the ability to function. When that occurs, some flexibility on the part of other people in the environment is necessary.

"Schizophrenia tends to be an episodic disorder. We are going to have periodic breakdowns. This makes holding employment very difficult because the usual practice is to terminate employees who require frequent periods of leave. Work for us should be structured so that our disabilities are taken into account. Many of us are well educated or have useful skills when we are not having episodes. Why can't jobs be structured for us so that our episodic breakdowns do not automatically result in our loss of employment? Like the general population, we like and need to work, but the world of the chronically well needs to be a little more flexible in understanding that we are going to behave strangely from time to time and there are going to be times when we do not function well at all."

---

warded with tokens for good behavior ("You did a really good job smoothing the sheets and putting things away this morning, George; here is a token for keeping your room in order"). When they did not behave well, that was pointed out, and they were told that a token was being withheld ("You don't earn your appearance token this morning, Herman, because your hair is all tangled"). The tokens were then used like money to buy meals, rent better sleeping quarters (a four-bed dormitory room cost 10 tokens per week; a furnished one-bed room cost 22 tokens), obtain passes to leave the hospital, purchase recreational time (TV, piano, games, radio, phonograph, etc.), buy privileges like staying up later, and get other miscellaneous things such as use of the phone, laundry service, a haircut, or extra baths.

The investigation generated three types of findings. First, the results indicated that the token economy approach was more effective for improving patients' *general behavior*. For example, the patients on the token economy ward showed better interpersonal skills (cooperation, helpfulness, social activity), better instrumental role performance (vocational and housekeeping behaviors), and better self-care (grooming,

Case Study 14.2

TREATMENT OF BIZARRE SYMPTOMS WITH TECHNIQUES BASED ON LEARNING THEORY

The patient was a 47-year-old woman who had been hospitalized for 9 years and was diagnosed as suffering from chronic schizophrenia. She had a wide variety of symptoms, but three of them were particularly troublesome. The first was her continual stealing of food and overeating. She always ate everything on her tray and then stole food from the counter and from other patients. Because of her excessive eating, she weighed over 250 lb, and that was posing a risk to her physical health. Her second annoying symptom was hoarding hospital towels in her room. Despite the fact that the nurses kept retrieving them, the patient often had as many as 30 towels. The third and most extreme symptom was excessive dressing. At any one time, she might wear six dresses, several pairs of underwear, two dozen pairs of stockings, two or three sweaters, and a shawl or two. In addition, she often draped herself in sheets and wrapped a couple of towels around her head in a turban-like headdress. These behaviors had persisted for a number of years, and various attempts to change them (therapy, pleading) had been ineffective. Finally, it was decided to try a learning theory approach to treating the symptoms.

The patient's food stealing was treated by punishment (withdrawal of food). Nurses simply removed her from the dining room as soon as she picked up unauthorized food, so she missed a meal whenever she stole food. Within 2 weeks, the patient's food stealing was eliminated, and she ate only the diet prescribed for her. Her weight dropped to 180 lb in 14 months, a 28% loss.

The hoarding of hospital towels was treated with satiation. Rather than restricting the number of towels the patient had, the staff began giving her more towels. The notion was that if she had more towels than she wanted, the value of the towels would be reduced, and consequently the hoarding would be reduced. (This is like letting workers in a candy factory eat all they want; soon they do not want any more, and they stop eating the product.) At first, when a nurse came into her room with a towel, the patient said, "Oh, you found it for me, thank you." As the number of towels increased rapidly in the 2nd week, the patient responded by saying, "Don't give me no more towels. I've got enough." By the 3rd week of the treatment period, she was being given as many as 60 towels a day, and she said, "Take them towels away. . . . I can't sit here all night and fold towels." Soon her room was overflowing with towels, and in the 6th week, she complained to a nurse, "I can't drag any more of these towels, I just can't do it." When the number of towels in the patient's room reached 625, she started taking towels out of the room, so the staff stopped giving them to her. The patient had apparently had it with towels, and for the next 12 months, the average number of towels found in her room was 1.5 per week.

The patient's excessive dressing was treated by punishing overdressing and rewarding reduced dressing. Before each meal, the patient was required to get on a scale, and if she exceeded a predetermined weight (her body weight plus a specified number of pounds for clothing), she was simply told, "Sorry, you weigh too much; you'll have to weigh less," and she was not allowed in the dining room for that meal (punishment). The patient quickly learned that if she took some of her clothes off, she could meet the weight requirement and thereby get to eat (reward). Originally she was allowed 23 lb for clothes, but that was gradually reduced. Within a short period of time, the weight of her clothing dropped from 25 to 3 lb, and she was dressing normally.

It should be noted that the patient responded with some anger when she was first denied food as part of the treatment of her food stealing and overdressing. When that behavior was not rewarded (it was ignored), it disappeared, and no other inappropriate behaviors were introduced. Finally, it is interesting to note that as the patient's behaviors became less bizarre, patients and staff began interacting with her more, and she began to participate somewhat more actively in social functions.

Source: Adapted from Ayllon (1963).

---

care of belongings, appropriate mealtime behavior). The improvement in interpersonal skills is illustrated in Figure 14.5.

The second set of findings was related to the symptoms of schizophrenia. The patients on the token economy ward showed *less schizophrenic disorganization* (bizarre motor behaviors such as rocking, repetitive movement, and blank staring). However, the token economy treatment *did not reduce cognitive distortions* (delusions, hallucinations, incoherent speech) or hostile or belligerent behavior (aggressive behaviors such as screaming and cursing). In general, then, the token

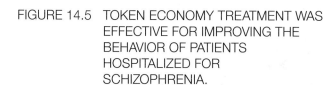

FIGURE 14.5 TOKEN ECONOMY TREATMENT WAS EFFECTIVE FOR IMPROVING THE BEHAVIOR OF PATIENTS HOSPITALIZED FOR SCHIZOPHRENIA.

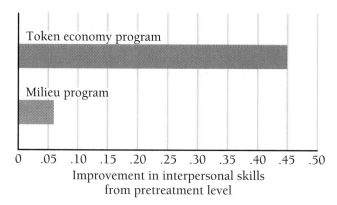

Source: Adapted from Paul and Lentz (1977), p. 317, fig. 29.4.

economy approach was more effective than milieu therapy for influencing general behavior but was not more effective than milieu therapy for influencing thought processes or emotional behavior. That is an interesting contrast, and we will return to it later.

Finally, there are two important findings concerning *hospital release:* More patients from the token economy ward than the milieu ward were released from the hospital (96.4% vs. 67.9%), and more patients from the token economy ward than the milieu ward achieved release to independent functioning and self-support as opposed to some form of continuing community care (10.7% vs. 7.1%).

Comment

There is no doubt that in many cases, the alteration of reward and punishment contingencies is effective for modifying the behavior of persons with schizophrenia. However, critics have questioned whether with this approach we are actually treating schizophrenia or whether we are simply altering superficial behaviors and ignoring or glossing over the real underlying problem. Consider the simple and probably not infrequent situation in which a therapist says something like this to a patient:

Look, as long as you keep wearing a cowboy hat and telling everyone that you are John Wayne, we are going to have to keep you locked up in this hospital, and life here is not pleasant. If you want to get out, just stop wearing the cowboy hat and telling everyone you are John Wayne. Now I don't care

who you think you are; it's really irrelevant. The point is, if you want out, you just can't tell everyone who you think you are. Be John Wayne at home but not in public if you want to stay out of this hospital.

If the patient wants to leave the hospital and takes the advice, he or she will be judged as being "in remission" and will be discharged. This straightforward exercise of behavior modification (the patient was rewarded for not acting crazy) has resulted in an individual who no longer appears to suffer from schizophrenia, but has the schizophrenia really been treated or changed? Obviously not, but many learning theorists would respond by saying, "So what? The patient's happy, and so is everyone else."

PHYSIOLOGICAL APPROACHES

Early Treatments

Convulsive Therapy. In the 1930s, a physician noted that patients who suffered from both schizophrenia and epilepsy showed reductions in their schizophrenic symptoms immediately after having an epileptic seizure. It was therefore speculated that schizophrenia might be treated by inducing seizures (Meduna, 1938). Initially drugs such as insulin were used to induce the seizures, but they were replaced by **electroconvulsive therapy (ECT)**, in which the convulsions are induced with an electrical shock (see Chapter 11). Convulsive therapy was widely used to treat schizophrenia for many years, but research now clearly indicates that ECT is not helpful for treating schizophrenia and is far less effective than drug therapy (Greenblatt et al., 1964; Heath et al., 1964; Miller et al., 1953). Today, ECT is rarely used to treat schizophrenia, and when it is used, it is used with patients who are not responding to other treatments. An often-heard explanation in those cases is, "Well, it probably won't hurt and it might help." At present, however, there is no reliable justification for the use of convulsive therapy with schizophrenia.

Psychosurgery. **Psychosurgery** is another somatic approach that was once popular but has now been generally abandoned (Shutts, 1982; Smith & Kiloh, 1977; Valenstein, 1980). Psychosurgery involves severing the connections between parts of the brain. Usually, the frontal lobes are separated from the rest of the brain. Psychosurgery was performed as early as the 19th century (Burckhardt, 1891), but the procedure as we know it today originated in 1935, when an operation known as a **prefrontal lobotomy** (lō-BOT-uh-mē) was introduced. The idea for the operation stemmed from a report that an excitable and sometimes violent chimpanzee had become docile and friendly after the destruction of her prefrontal cortex (Jacobsen et al., 1935).

To perform a prefrontal lobotomy, holes were drilled in the top of the skull, and then a knife was inserted and pivoted up and back so that a cut was made separating a portion of the frontal lobes from the rest of the brain. If the operation was not successful in reducing symptoms, it was performed again, but the second time the holes were drilled farther back on the skull so that more of the frontal area would be separated from the rest of the brain.

In 1948, the **transorbital lobotomy** was introduced. This procedure involved inserting an icepick-like knife through the top of the eye socket and up into the brain. The knife was then swung up and back to destroy brain tissue. The procedure is illustrated in Figure 14.6. Transorbital lobotomies could be performed as an office procedure and were widely used. (In some cases, electroconvulsive shocks were used to induce unconsciousness before the transorbital was performed.)

In the years between 1935 and about 1955, thousands of patients received lobotomies. Unfortunately, it is difficult to determine how effective the operations were because the nature of the operation differed greatly from hospital to hospital, and objective records

were not kept on patients' pre- and postoperation symptoms. There is some agreement, however, that the operations did result in a reduction in the intensity of the patients' emotional responses (it reduced anxiety or alleviated depression). However, it is not clear whether the operations were effective for reducing specific symptoms or simply made the patients calmer and more docile. In any event, they were easier to manage and more likely to be discharged. Needless to say, psychosurgery can have a wide variety of serious side effects, such as loss of cognitive abilities and sometimes a loss of emotional control. Psychosurgery was also misused. For example, I knew of a physician who performed transorbital lobotomies on adolescents who had behavior problems in school.

The use of psychosurgery diminished sharply in the mid-1950s in large part because of the introduction of drugs that were more effective and resulted in fewer negative side effects. Psychosurgical procedures are rarely used today. As a footnote to this discussion of psychosurgery, it might be mentioned that the physician who introduced the use of psychosurgery received the Nobel Prize for his work but was paralyzed later in life when he was shot in the spine by an angry lobotomized patient.

Drug Therapy

The introduction of antipsychotic drugs in the mid-1950s revolutionized the care and condition of mental patients. Almost overnight, psychiatric wards were transformed from "snake pits" where patients lived in straitjackets and were largely out of control to places of relative calm and order. Of course, some antipsychotic drugs have serious side effects, and critics argue that the benefits achieved by these drugs are superficial and are outweighed by the side effects they cause.

In this section, we will discuss the general nature and effects of the drugs that are used to treat schizophrenia and the controversies over their use. A thorough and balanced understanding of this often misunderstood and sometimes controversial area is important because the drugs are widely discussed in the mass media, the drugs play an important role in today's treatment and because someday you may have to make a decision concerning the use of one of these drugs for yourself or someone close to you.

Overview of Neuroleptic Drugs. One of the physiological causes of schizophrenia is excessively high neurological activity in the areas of the brain where **dopamine** is the major neurotransmitter. The high level of dopamine-related activity leads to symptoms because it disrupts cognitive activity (see Chapter 13). Therefore, the primary goal of modern drug ther-

FIGURE 14.6   THE TRANSORBITAL LOBOTOMY COULD BE PERFORMED IN THE PHYSICIAN'S OFFICE.

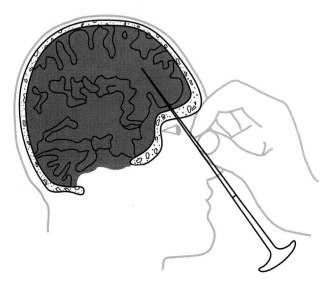

Before the introduction of neuroleptic drugs, scenes like this were common in psychiatric hospitals.

apy is to *reduce that level of neurological activity.* That is done with a group of drugs known as **neuroleptics**. The term *neuroleptic* is derived from *neuro*, which refers to the *brain*, and *leptic*, which comes from a Greek word meaning "to arrest." Neuroleptics relieve the symptoms of schizophrenia by arresting brain activity.

Neuroleptic drugs reduce brain activity in three ways. First, they *block the receptors on the postsynaptic neuron* so that the neurotransmitter (dopamine) cannot enter the receptor and cause the neuron to fire. It is like putting the wrong key in a lock; you cannot open the lock with the wrong key (the neuroleptic), but once it is there, you cannot get the right key in either (the dopamine). The degree to which drugs enter receptors is often a good predictor of how effective the drug will be in reducing symptoms; that is, more blocking is usually associated with greater symptom reduction.

The second way in which neuroleptics may reduce brain activity is by *reducing the sensitivity of the postsynaptic receptors.* If the receptors are less sensitive, they will be less likely to fire even when stimulated. The belief that neuroleptics reduce receptor sensitivity stems from the fact that although neuroleptics block receptors immediately, some symptoms do not diminish for days or even weeks after drug treatment is started. It appears that over time, the presence of the drug changes the sensitivity of the receptors, and this de-

layed change in sensitivity is responsible for the delay in the symptom relief. This process has not yet been documented, and it is still a matter of speculation.

Third, some new neuroleptics (called *atypical* neuroleptics) also increase the levels of the neurotransmitter **serotonin**. That can be effective for reducing symptoms because serotonin serves to *inhibit* dopamine activity.

Neuroleptics have a number of side effects that we will consider later, but at this point we should note that some of the drugs cause a particularly noticeable and debilitating side effect that involves *disturbances in muscle activity.* They can include involuntary tremors, twitches, shaking, and jerking. This type of side effect occurs because dopamine is also a neurotransmitter in the motor system, and when the general level of dopamine is altered with a neuroleptic drug, the function of the motor system is changed, thus resulting in the muscle movements. These motor side effects are referred to as **extrapyramidal** (EK-struh-puh-RAM-i-dul) **symptoms** because the neurons that are responsible for motor movements extend from a group of cells that look like a series of pyramids.

Neuroleptic drugs are sometimes incorrectly referred to as "major tranquilizers" to distinguish them from the "minor tranquilizers" that are used to treat anxiety (see Chapter 6). However, calling neuroleptic drugs "major tranquilizers" is misleading because although these drugs do calm disturbed and agitated patients, they are not simply stronger versions of the "minor tranquilizers," and they are not particularly effective for specifically treating anxiety. The notion of an antipsychotic drug as a "major tranquilizer" is probably a holdover from the days before we had true antipsychotic drugs and patients were treated (or at least controlled) with large doses of muscle relaxants (e.g., *Miltown,* which is a propanediol; see Chapter 6).

Numerous neuroleptic drugs are available today, and usually they are organized in terms of their chemical structure (see Table 14.1 on p. 334). However, for our purposes it is more helpful to organize them in terms of their biochemical and behavioral effects. In the following sections, we will discuss *low-potency, high-potency*, and *atypical* neuroleptics. In this discussion, the term *potency* refers to the degree to which a drug blocks the dopamine receptors.

Low-Potency Neuroleptics. **Low-potency neuroleptics** were the first neuroleptics to be developed, and as the label implies, they do not block dopamine receptors as effectively as the high-potency drugs that were developed later. However, they are effective for treating schizophrenia and are still used widely.

The most widely used low-potency drugs are in a class of drugs known as **phenothiazines** (Fē-nō-THĪ-

TABLE 14.1   FREQUENTLY USED NEUROLEPTIC DRUGS

TYPE	TRADE NAME	GENERIC NAME
Phenothiazines	Thorazine	chlorpromazine
	Mellaril	thioridazine
	Sparine	promazine
	Stelazine	trifluoperazine
	Compazine	prochlorperazine
	Trilafon	perphenazine
	Prolixin	fluphenazine
Butyrophenones	Haldol	haloperidol
Dibenzodiazepines	Clozaril	clozapine
Thioxanthenes	Navane	thiothixine
	Taractan	chlorprothixene

uh-zīnz), the best known of which is **Thorazine** (chlor-promazine). Thorazine was first introduced in the mid-1950s, and it immediately became a very popular drug for treating schizophrenia. Indeed, in the 1960s and 1970s, the question was not whether patients were on Thorazine but how much were they taking. Thorazine is still widely used today. The widespread use of phenothiazines was justified by its clinical effectiveness. In what is probably the classic experiment on the effects of phenothiazines, patients with schizophrenia at nine different public and private hospitals were randomly assigned to one of four conditions (Cole et al., 1964; Cole et al., 1966). The patients in three conditions received one of three different phenothiazines (Thorazine, Mellaril, Prolixin), whereas the patients in the fourth condition received a placebo. A double-blind approach was used in which neither the patients nor the physicians who were responsible for the treatments knew which patients were receiving which treatments. The patients' psychological functioning was assessed before treatment began and after 6 weeks of treatment.

The results of this experiment clearly indicate that the three phenothiazines were much more effective for reducing the symptoms of schizophrenia than the placebo. In fact, as indicated in Figure 14.7, fully 75% of the patients who received phenothiazines were "much improved," compared to only 25% of the patients who received the placebo. Only 2% of the patients who received phenothiazines got worse, whereas 48% of the patients who received the placebo got worse.

It is important to recognize that the improvements in the patients who received the phenothiazines were not simply due to the fact that the patients were sedated or tranquilized and therefore easier to manage. It is true that the patients were less hostile, irritable, and agitated, which may be interpreted as a tranquilizing effect. However, the patients who received the phenothiazines were also more socially ac-

tive, less indifferent to their environment, more coherent in their speech, less disoriented, better able to take care of themselves, and had fewer hallucinations and delusions. Obviously, the phenothiazines had effects well beyond the tranquilizing of patients, and in some ways the drugs actually served to activate the patients—they became more socially active and more involved and took better care of themselves.

FIGURE 14.7   PATIENTS WITH SCHIZOPHRENIA WHO TOOK NEUROLEPTIC DRUGS WERE MORE LIKELY TO IMPROVE AND LESS LIKELY TO GET WORSE THAN PATIENTS WHO TOOK PLACEBOS.

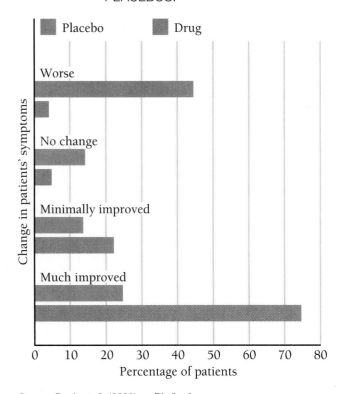

Source: Davis et al. (1980), p. 71, fig. 1.

The positive effects of the phenothiazines have also been demonstrated in an interesting long-term experiment with patients who suffered from schizophrenia (Grinspoon et al., 1968, 1972). In this investigation, 20 male patients who averaged only 27 years of age but had already spent an average of 6.5 years in mental hospitals were first moved to a special treatment ward where they were given a placebo for 3 months. Following that period, half of the patients were given a phenothiazine (Mellaril) for 15 months, while the other half continued to receive the placebo. After that period, all of the patients were again given a placebo for a 3-month period. Finally, half of the patients were again given the phenothiazine for a 3-month period, while the other half continued to receive the placebo. Thus the phases of the experiment involved placebo versus placebo, phenothiazine versus placebo, placebo versus placebo, and phenothiazine versus placebo.

If phenothiazines are effective, it would be expected that the patients would show improvements in their symptomatology while taking the drug but not while taking the placebo. That is exactly what was found; the results are summarized in Figure 14.8. Note that the patients did not immediately get worse when they were switched from the phenothiazine to the placebo. The delay in the deterioration of the patients stems from

the fact that the medication remains active in the patients' systems for some time after it has been taken.

Clearly, low-potency neuroleptics are effective for treating schizophrenia, but they are not effective with all patients, and they do have a number of side effects, which we will discuss in greater detail later.

High-Potency Neuroleptics.   In view of the effectiveness of the low-potency drugs, chemists began working to develop drugs that would block more of the dopamine receptors, and in the 1970s a number of **high-potency neuroleptics** were developed. The best known of these is **Haldol (haloperidol)**. Thorazine blocks 80% of the receptors; Haldol blocks about 85% (Farde et al., 1988).

In experiments comparing the effects of Thorazine and Haldol, Haldol was often found to be more effective for reducing the symptoms of schizophrenia, and therefore Haldol became widely used. However, it was quickly discovered that the increased effectiveness of Haldol had a price—an increase in the troublesome extrapyramidal side effects. That is understandable because Haldol blocks more dopamine receptors, and the blocking of certain dopamine receptors leads to the motor problems. Today Haldol continues to be used with many patients, but to reduce the side effects, the dose levels are kept as low as possible and other

FIGURE 14.8   PATIENTS SHOWED FEWER DISTURBED BEHAVIORS WHEN GIVEN ANTIPSYCHOTIC MEDICATION BUT GOT WORSE WHEN THEY WERE SWITCHED TO A PLACEBO.

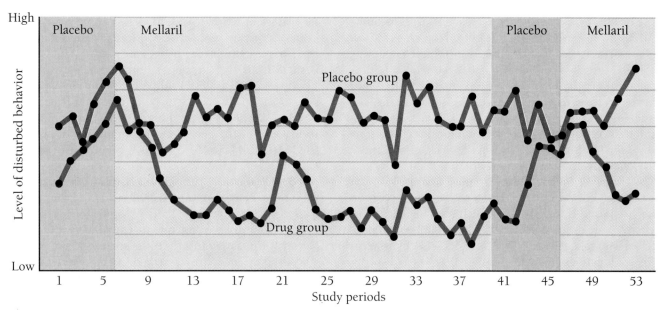

During placebo periods, patients in both groups received the placebo, but during the Mellaril periods, one group received the drug and the other received the placebo.

Source: Grinspoon et al. (1972), p. 150, fig. 1.

drugs are often prescribed to help reduce the extrapyramidal side effects.

Atypical Neuroleptics.

The latest development in drug treatment revolves around a new type of neuroleptic called **atypical neuroleptics**. The best known atypical neuroleptic is **Clozaril (clozapine)**.

Atypical neuroleptics differ from regular neuroleptics in three ways. First, they block fewer dopamine receptors than the regular neuroleptics. Indeed, whereas Thorazine and Haldol block 80% and 85% of the receptors, respectively, Clozaril blocks only 65% (Farde et al., 1988). At first, you might think that the lower blocking rate would make atypical neuroleptics less effective for treating schizophrenia, but before drawing that conclusion, we must consider the second difference.

The second difference is that atypical neuroleptics are *more selective in the sets of dopamine receptors they block*. Unlike regular neuroleptics, which block dopamine receptors in general, atypical neuroleptics block dopamine receptors in the nerve tracks that lead to the frontal cortex, where thinking takes place (A-10, mesolimbic system, D-2 receptors), but they do not block dopamine receptors in the nerve tracks associated with motor movements (A-9, extrapyramidal system, D-1 receptors) (Coward et al., 1989; Creese, 1985). This selectivity in blocking would lead to greater reductions in cognitive symptoms (frontal cortex activity) and fewer side effects involving motor functioning (extrapyramidal activity).

The third difference is that atypical neuroleptics also appear to *increase the level of serotonin activity* (probably by increasing the release of serotonin) (Meltzer, Bastani, Ramirez, & Matsubara, 1989). That is important because serotonin can inhibit dopamine activity, thereby resulting in greater reductions of neurological activity. It is also possible that serotonin may have its own effects (e.g., increasing serotonin can reduce depression; see Chapter 11). The fact that atypical neuroleptics are selective in blocking dopamine receptors and increase serotonin activity should result in greater symptom reduction with fewer side effects.

Clozaril (the best known atypical neuroleptic) was introduced in Europe in 1971, but it was not approved for use in the United States until 1990. The delay in its approval was due the fact that 1% or 2% of the patients who take Clozaril develop a side effect known as **agranulocytosis** (ā-GRAN-yuh-lō-sī-TŌ-sis), a disorder in which the individual's level of leukocytes (white blood cells) is greatly reduced (Griffith & Saameli, 1975; Lieberman et al., 1988). Such a reduction can be very serious because leukocytes are essential for fighting infections; in fact, agranulocytosis can be fatal. Fortunately, the agranulocytosis can be eliminated within about 2 weeks by simply taking the patient off of the Clozaril.

The possibility of developing agranulocytosis posed a dilemma because on the one hand Clozaril was effective for treating previously untreatable individuals, but on the other hand it could result in fatal side effects. This dilemma was resolved in the mid-1980s when the company that produces Clozaril developed a procedure for monitoring leukocyte levels. Specifically, once each week a sample of the patient's blood is taken and analyzed for leukocyte levels, and if the levels are within normal limits, the patient is given a week's worth of medication. However, if the leukocyte levels are low, the patient is not given the Clozaril until the leukocytes return to their normal levels. This procedure is known as **bundling** because the blood test is "bundled" with the sale of the medication.

The bundling procedure resolved the dilemma posed by the possibility of triggering agranulocytosis, but the bundling posed another problem—very high costs. Indeed, the cost of the combination of Clozaril and the company's blood tests came to about $9,000 per year! That amount was well beyond what most patients were able to pay, and it was also beyond what Medicaid was willing to pay. In the Clozaril bundle, then, we had a "rich person's drug for a poor person's disorder" (Winslow, 1990). (It is interesting to note that in Europe, where the blood monitoring is not required, the drug costs only between $1,000 and $1,500 per year.)

As it turned out, the $9,000 cost was much higher than necessary because the company was placing a very high price on its blood test. Physicians and pharmacists claimed that the blood test could actually be done for much less, but the company would not release the drug unless its own blood test was used. Company officials argued that the blood test was essential because of the potential side effects and that the high cost of the test was necessary to offset the expense of developing the drug. Eventually two things happened to make the drug cheaper. First, a number of patients sued Medicaid to force that program to pay for Clozaril. The patients argued that it was cheaper to pay $9,000 for the drug than to pay $40,000 for hospitalization. They also argued that it was discriminatory to pay $50,000 a year for kidney dialysis for individuals with kidney disease but not to pay $9,000 a year for Clozaril for individuals with schizophrenia. (Betty, whose experiences are described in Case Study 12.2, is one of the individuals who successfully sued Medicaid.) Second, powerful public and governmental pressure was brought to bear on the company that produces Clozaril, so the firm finally relented and agreed that the blood test could be done by other, less expensive companies. Now the average cost per year for Clozaril and the blood tests is approximately $8,000 (500 mg/day)—still expensive, but a real help to many individuals, and Medicaid will pick up some of the expense.

Is Clozaril worth $8,000 per year? At the outset, it is important to recognize that Clozaril is reserved for individuals who have not responded to other drug therapies, individuals who are sometimes referred to as **treatment-resistant patients**. Without Clozaril, these patients may be destined for custodial care on a back ward.

The landmark experiment on the effects of Clozaril was based on 319 treatment-resistant patients at 16 different hospitals (Kane et al., 1988, 1989). The typical patient was 35 years old, was diagnosed as suffering from chronic undifferentiated schizophrenia, was first hospitalized at about age 20, and had been hospitalized about eight times since then. In short, these were severely and chronically ill individuals who were ultimately bound for long-term custodial care in a state hospital.

The experiment involved two phases that each lasted 6 weeks. In the first phase, all of the patients were given Haldol (plus medication to relieve extrapyramidal side effects). This phase was used to be

sure that the patients indeed did not respond to other medication. Any patients who showed improvement during this phase were dropped from the experiment. In the second phase, patients who did not show improvement in the first phase were randomly assigned to a condition in which they received Thorazine (plus medication to relieve extrapyramidal side effects) or to a condition in which they received Clozaril. The patients' symptoms were evaluated each week by raters who did not know which patients were taking which drug.

The results revealed three interesting findings. First, the patients who took Clozaril showed greater reductions in positive symptoms (e.g., hallucinations, delusions, thought disorder) than the patients who took Thorazine. Second, somewhat suprisingly, the patients who took Clozaril also showed greater reductions in negative symptoms (e.g., flat mood, poverty of speech, disorientation). Third, the patients who took Clozaril showed *fewer extrapyramidal side effects* than the patients who took Thorazine, despite the fact that the patients who were taking Thorazine were also taking medication to offset such side effects. These results are summarized in Figure 14.9. Looked at in another way, 30% of the patients who took Clozaril

FIGURE 14.9   CLOZARIL IS MORE EFFECTIVE FOR TREATING
(A) POSITIVE AND (B) NEGATIVE SYMPTOMS THAN
A TYPICAL NEUROLEPTIC.

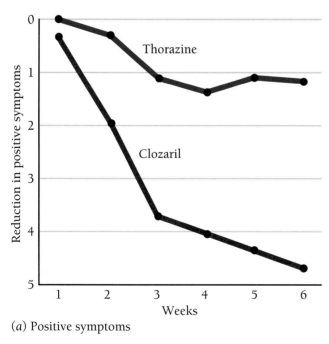

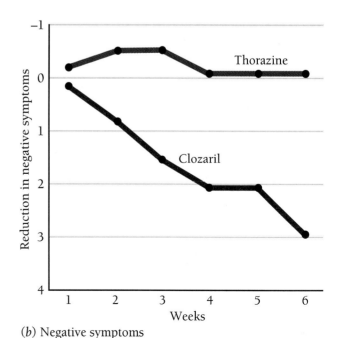

(*a*) Positive symptoms

(*b*) Negative symptoms

Source: Kane et al. (1988), p. 794, figs. 4 and 5.

showed significant clinical improvement (i.e., a 20% improvement or posttreatment scores in the "mild" range of pathology), whereas only 4% of the patients who took Thorazine showed such improvement. Since this initial experiment was reported, a number of other investigators have reported similar results (e.g., Honigfeld & Patin, 1989; Leppig et al., 1989; Lindstrom, 1989; Meltzer et al., 1989; Pickar et al., 1992). Clearly, in Clozaril we have a treatment for treatment-resistant patients that has widespread positive effects without the problem posed by extrapyramidal side effects.

Limitations of Drug Therapy.

It is clear that neuroleptics can be an effective treatment for schizophrenia, but it is important to note that they do have some limitations. First, neuroleptics provide a *treatment* for schizophrenia but *not a cure.* You will recall that the same was true in the drug treatment of anxiety and mood disorders (see Chapters 6 and 11). This means that in many cases, individuals may have to stay on the drugs for prolonged periods of time. The fact that drug therapy for schizophrenia must be continued is clearly reflected in the results of investigations in which some patients were maintained on their drugs while others were switched to placebos. A review of 31 studies involving 3,519 patients indicated that among the patients who were kept on their neuroleptics, the relapse rate was 19%, but among the patients who were switched to a placebo, the relapse rate was 55% (Davis et al., 1980).

Second, in many cases, the drugs are only effective for treating *some of the symptoms* (primarily positive symptoms), or they *reduce but do not eliminate symptoms* (hallucinations may be less frequent or less intense). That partial reduction in symptoms may be enough to enable the individual to function effectively in society but not enough to eliminate the burden of coping with the remaining symptoms.

Third, *not all patients are helped by drugs.* Neuroleptics such as Thorazine and Haldol can help about 80% of patients, and atypical neuroleptics such as Clozaril can help about another 6%, but that still leaves about 14% without help. We have come a long way in the drug treatment of schizophrenia, but if you or someone you love is in that remaining percentage, you realize that we have a way to go.

Drugs do not relieve all symptoms and are not effective with all patients because for the most part the drugs only work to reduce high levels of neurological arousal, and some of the symptoms of schizophrenia are due to low levels of neurological arousal or structural abnormalities in the brain (see Chapter 13). Unfortunately, we do not yet have effective treatments for

those latter causes. Overall then, there is no doubt that drugs can be very helpful in the treatment of schizophrenia, but they are not a panacea.

Side Effects of Drug Therapy.

We now come to the complex and sometimes serious problem of the **side effects** of drug therapy for schizophrenia. Just as there is no denying that neuroleptic drugs can reduce the symptoms of schizophrenia, so there is no denying that these drugs can induce a variety of side effects. In considering drug therapy, then, we must determine what the side effects are, whether they are serious and treatable, and whether they outweigh the benefits of the drugs.

There are two levels of side effects. At the more superficial level, patients who are taking neuroleptics experience symptoms such as dryness of the mouth or excessive salivation, blurred vision, grogginess, constipation, sensitivity to light, reduced sexual arousal, weight gain, and awkward or slowed motor activity. These effects can be annoying and sometimes troublesome, but they do not have long-term medical implications. Although not physically dangerous, these side effects can be psychologically very disruptive and frightening if the patient is not warned about them. For example, changes in vision or sensitivity to light could provide the bases for additional delusions, and an unexplained impairment in sexual performance could be very upsetting. However, if these symptoms are initially explained as normal and expected side effects that can be compensated for or treated, their impact will be minimal, especially when compared to the benefits obtained by the reduction of the schizophrenic symptoms.

Unfortunately, for some patients who take neuroleptics there is a more serious level of side effects that involves symptoms that may have important long-term implications. Probably the most serious of the known side effects is **tardive dyskinesia** (TAR-div dis-ki-NĒ-zē-uh) (Berger & Rexroth, 1980). Tardive dyskinesia is an extreme extrapyramidal symptom pattern that involves *involuntary* muscle movements that are most often associated with the mouth, lips, and tongue. Patients with tardive dyskinesia experience involuntary sucking, chewing, lateral jaw movements, smacking and pursing of the lips, thrusting and twisting of the tongue, and ticlike motions of the lips, eyes, and eyebrows. In some cases, there are also involuntary movements of the arms and trunk, such as twisting of the body and shrugging of the shoulders. These behaviors are not under voluntary control and go on continually while the patient is awake. Reports of the prevalence of tardive dyskinesia range from .5% to 56%, with a mean of about 15% in institutionalized patients. Paradoxically, then, in some patients neuroleptic drugs may be effective in treating the schizophrenia, but because of their side effects, the drugs leave the patients appearing even "crazier" (they have strange jerking movements) than when they suffered from the schizophrenia. More important, because tardive dyskinesia can interfere with speech, dexterity, eating, and respiration, it can result in serious disabilities and even death. With low-potency neuroleptics, it may be some years before tardive dyskinesia sets in, but with high-potency neuroleptics, minor symptoms may begin appearing within days or weeks. Tardive dyskinesia is thought to stem from the fact that prolonged use of the drugs causes the dopamine receptor sites to become *supersensitive* to dopamine. (They seem to be naturally compensating for the fact that the drugs limit the effect of dopamine.)

One treatment for tardive dyskinesia involves increasing the dosage level of the neuroleptic drug. That reduces the dopamine activity, which reduces the motor activity, but the higher dose can result in other side effects such as grogginess and in the long run may actually result in even higher levels of dopamine sensitivity and more severe tardive dyskinesia. Alternatively, other drugs can be given to stimulate cholinergic activity and thus restore the dopamine-cholinergic balance. (Cholinergic activity is associated with another neurotransmitter, *acetylcholine*, which is also involved in motor activity and can offset the effects of dopamine.) In some cases, however, the symptoms of tardive dyskinesia are irreversible, suggesting that some permanent structural alterations of the brain have occurred.

It should be noted that although prolonged use of neuroleptics can bring on tardive dyskinesia, there is now some evidence that other factors such as organic brain damage can cause tardive dyskinesia in the absence of neuroleptics (Khot & Wyatt, 1991; Wegner et al., 1985). Thus tardive dyskinesia can be part of a general disease process, and not all cases should be blamed on the use of neuroleptics.

One other serious side effect is the **malignant neuroleptic syndrome**, the symptoms of which include muscular rigidity, very high temperature that can lead to brain damage, fluctuating blood pressure and heart rate, confusion, agitation, and stupor or coma (Addonizio, 1991; Caroff et al., 1991; Keck et al., 1991; Warner et al., 1990). This side effect is more likely to occur with the high-potency neuroleptics, is more likely to occur in women, and appears to be due to a sudden drop in dopamine activity that causes a general dysregulation of the hypothalamus and other control centers in the brain. (This syndrome can also occur when patients stop taking medication for Parkinson's disease, that is, medication that keeps dopamine levels up.) Obviously, this is a very serious syndrome, but it occurs in fewer than 1% of the patients taking neuroleptics, it can be treated effectively if it is diagnosed quickly, and there is no evidence that it is more likely to return after treatment (Pope et al., 1991).

In summary, some patients are troubled by relatively minor side effects, whereas others suffer considerably from serious side effects of their medication, and we must be careful not to ignore or grow insensitive to those problems. However, we must also be cautious in responding to the demands of people who believe that drug therapy should be abandoned because of the side effects. It would be inappropriate to "throw the treatment out with the side effects." At present, the alternative to the side effects is a return to the straitjackets, padded cells, and snake-pit wards of earlier days. That is certainly not an attractive option.

One way of maximizing the benefits and minimizing the side effects of drug therapy is to use **lower-limit** or **noncontinuous drug therapy**. In most cases, once the patient's symptoms have been satisfactorily reduced with a given level of medication, that level is maintained indefinitely. However, for some patients, the medication level can then be slowly reduced or even discontinued (Carpenter & Heinrich, 1983). There is some risk in this because insufficient doses or the discontinuance of medication can result in relapses for many patients (Herz et al., 1991; Kane et al., 1983). The important point is that not all patients relapse (in the review of 31 studies cited earlier, only 55% of the patients who were switched to placebo relapsed; Davis et al., 1980), and the trial discontinuance would enable us to identify those fortunate patients who do not need a maintenance dose. For those who do need the medication and who relapse without it, the medication can be reinstituted. Even for those patients, however, dosage levels may be reduced until the symptoms become serious. Later, the lower limit can be tested again. This frequent testing of the lower limit requires more attention to the patient than the "set-it-and-leave-it approach," but symptom monitoring can be done by case managers such as social workers or by family members, and it can result in reduced levels of medication and reduced side effects (Kane, 1983).

Dose Levels and Drug Effectiveness. At this point, we should give some attention to the **dose-response relationship** in the treatment of schizophrenia. It is widely assumed that higher doses of neuroleptic drugs will be more effective than lower doses. That assumption has led to two time-honored treatment strategies: First, use initially very high dosage levels for acute patients so that the patients can be "brought back quickly," and second, vary dosage levels "as needed" to control the variations in patients' symptomatology (i.e., increase the dose when symptoms get worse). Unfortunately, the research evidence does not support either of those practices (Volavka et al., 1992; see also Donaldson et al., 1983). Although *moderate doses are usually more effective than low doses, very high doses are not more effective than moderate doses.* In the case of Thorazine, for example, daily doses in the range of 100–300 mg are effective for treating many patients with acute schizophrenia (Cohen et al., 1980), but doses higher than 500 mg are unlikely to add much benefit (Cole, 1982). Insofar as the high dosages are sometimes effective, the benefit is probably due more to the sedation effects of high dosages than to their antipsychotic effects (Lerner et al., 1979). Not only do high doses of neuroleptics add little to their antipsychotic effects, but high doses can add to their side effects (Gelenberg, 1983; Mehta et al., 1979; Quitkin et al., 1975).

It is also relevant to note that men often require higher levels of neuroleptics than women (Yonker et al., 1992). Specifically, when men and women of comparable body size are given comparable doses, women show higher levels of the drugs in their bloodstreams. In terms of symptom relief, it appears that women require only about half as much medication as men. Overall, then, neuroleptic drugs are effective for treating schizophrenia, but more is not necessarily better and may in fact be worse in terms of side effects, and we must also be sensitive to gender differences when deciding on dose levels.

Type of Drug and Type of Disorder.
Finally, we should address the question of whether different neuroleptic drugs are differentially effective for treating different subtypes of schizophrenia. For example, is one type of neuroleptic more effective for treating individuals with the paranoid type but another type more effective for treating individuals with the catatonic type? Although such a relationship might be expected, *there is no evidence indicating that different drugs are differentially effective with different subtypes* (Davis, 1976a; Goldberg et al., 1972; Hollister et al., 1974; Klein & Rosen, 1973; Leff & Wing, 1971; May, Van Putten, et al., 1976; see review by Pickar et al., 1991). However, clinical experience suggests that *some patients do respond better to one drug than another*, but the difference in responses seem to be linked to something about the patients rather than their symptoms per se, and we have not yet identified what it is about the pa-

tients that is crucial. In most cases, then, it is a matter of trial and error to find the most effective drug and dosage level for any given patient. This can be frustrating and time-consuming.

Comment

There is no doubt that for many patients neuroleptic drugs can be effective for reducing the symptoms of schizophrenia and that maintenance medication is effective for reducing relapse rates. Despite the positive effects, there has been and continues to be some resistance to the use of drugs for the treatment of schizophrenia. That resistance stems from the fact that the drugs have some potentially serious side effects and from a philosophical objection to the "chemical control" of human thought processes. Those are justifiable concerns, but they must be weighed against the fact that without drugs, many patients would be consigned to a miserable life, possibly even confined to a straitjacket. The use of drugs, then, involves practical and philosophical compromises, and we must give constant attention to the issues if we are to achieve and maintain the appropriate and delicate balance.

Neuroleptic drugs now enable us to control symptoms that a few years ago were beyond control, but they do not solve all of the problems. At present, the most effective treatment involves a combination of drugs to reduce the vulnerability to neurological disruption and psychoeducation to reduce the disruption that stems from stress. The confluence of those forces is reflected in the comments of the patients featured in the next section.

SCHIZOPHRENIA AND TREATMENT FROM THE PATIENT'S POINT OF VIEW

Through three chapters, we have examined schizophrenia and its treatment from an objective and dispassionate point of view. Before concluding, however, it might be interesting to consider the disorder and its treatment from the patient's perspective. Case Studies 14.3 and 14.4 are patients' personal accounts of their treatment experiences. These cases are not presented as evidence for or against any particular approach, and the experiences of these patients are not necessarily representative of all patients. What is most noteworthy about these reports is the importance of medication and also having another person to whom the patient can turn for help and support during the confusing and sometimes terrifying experience of schizophrenia.

Case Study 14.3

"CAN WE TALK?" A PERSONAL ACCOUNT OF THERAPY WRITTEN BY A RECOVERING PATIENT

A year and a half ago my therapist asked me if psychotherapy had helped me. I was a bit stunned but answered almost automatically, "Yes, of course it's helped me." . . . My therapist's question was prompted by the controversy about whether schizophrenic patients could truly benefit from talk therapy or were best helped by drug therapy. I was somewhat angered by the thought that some schizophrenic patients were being treated only with pills and a monthly rendezvous to pick up a prescription. Perhaps the most dramatic symptoms such as delusions and hallucinations may respond to such treatment, but there is so much more involved in the life of a schizophrenic patient than just these manifestations.

Even if one adheres to the belief that psychotherapy lends itself more to emotionally oriented problems than to something which appears to be more biochemical, one must take into consideration the emotional aspects of schizophrenia. Besides the day-to-day stress of contending with what often seems to be a monster raging inside one's mind, there are emotional problems that have evolved and accumulated over the course of the patient's life.

If this is true, the confusion I felt about myself was compounded by what seemed irrational or conflicting actions directed toward me. A child destined to become schizophrenic must deal not only with the seeds of illness within himself but also with the attitudes of others toward his "idiosyncrasies," whether these feelings are voiced openly or subtly manifested in everyday life. Even if medication can free the schizophrenic patient from some of his torment, the scars of emotional confusion remain, felt perhaps more deeply by a greater sensitivity and vulnerability.

Like so many schizophrenic patients I have my own history of hospitalizations, medication trials—good and bad, setbacks, milestones, turns in the road, light appearing and disappearing at the end of the tunnel. I have seen lights in the sky, heard choruses of people inside me—taunting, tormenting me, pinning me against the wall, driving me into insanity. The drama is endless, and the agony and terror are even more so.

I have had bright spots in my life, but they all seem to have been achieved in the shadow of illness, and the effort was so exhausting as to dim the exhilaration of the moment. I fought my way through Harvard in the midst of psychosis and "spaciness," which I now believe to have been a reaction to neuroleptics and which usually proved worse than psychosis. More than half my college life was spent in a private psychiatric hospital. Between hospitalizations, I attended a day program and spent 3, 4, or 5 nights a week there. In fact, I trudged up the hill leading to the hospital 6 days a week, sometimes twice a day, while I tried to juggle my education with my illness.

There is no doubt in my mind that therapy helped me get through school. My freshman year and the first half of my sophomore year (until my first hospitalization) I was involved in supportive therapies with two different therapists who seemed to offer day-to-day support that was well-intentioned but was not enough. It was the combination of support and learning to understand why I thought the way I did, why I felt so bad, that gave me the strength to finish school.

For so long I wondered why my therapist insisted on talking about my relationship with him. He was not my problem; the problem was my life—my past, my fears, what I was going to do tomorrow, how I would handle things, sometimes just how to survive. . . . I took a long time, but finally I saw why it was important to explore my relationship with my therapist—it was the first real relationship I had ever had: that is, the first I felt safe enough to invest myself in. I rationalized that it was all right because I would learn from this relationship how to relate to other people and maybe one day leave behind the isolation of my own world. . . . I often felt at odds with my therapist until I could see that he was a real person and he related to me and I to him, not only as patient and therapist, but as human beings. Eventually I began to feel that I too was a person, not just an outsider looking in on the world.

With the struggles back and forth it almost seems questionable at times whether all this is really worth it. There are days when I wonder if it might not be more humane to leave the schizophrenic patient to his own world of unreality, not to make him go through the pain it takes to become a part of humanity. Those are the days when the pain is so great, I think I might prefer craziness until I remember the immobilizing terror and the distance and isolation that keep the world so far away and out of focus. It is not an easily resolved dilemma. Either way the schizophrenic patient must withstand intolerable suffering, but it seems that only through psychotherapy can the world of unreality truly be dispelled. There are those bad days, but I must admit that there are other days when I am glad that they did not give up on me and there is someone standing beside me guiding me to the knowledge of another existence.

Medication or superficial support alone is not a substitute for the feeling that one is understood by another human being. For me, the greatest gift came the day I realized that my therapist really had stood by me for years and that he would continue to stand by me and to help me achieve what I wanted to achieve. With that realization my viability as a person began to grow. I do not profess to be cured—I still feel the pain, fear, and frustration of my illness. I know I have a long road ahead of me, but I can honestly say that I am no longer without hope.

Source: "A Recovering Patient" (1986).

Case Study 14.4

BETTY'S THERAPY: DRUGS AND MORE

Case Study 12.2 was focused on my friend, Betty, who suffers from a severe case of schizophrenia. Betty has numerous symptoms, including hallucinations that there are monks chanting, "Cut yourself and die," and that people dissolve into blobs of blood. In this case study we will review the various therapies Betty has received over the past 20 years. Betty has been hospitalized numerous times, but here we will focus on types of treatment rather than on the experience of hospitalization. (We will discuss hospitalization in Chapter 22.)

David: Would you tell me what type of therapy you tried first?

Betty: Well, I was living in New York City when I had my first break, and not knowing anything about mental illness at the time, I went to see a psychoanalyst. That was a big and costly mistake. We spent hours talking about things that had nothing to do with any of my symptoms. He just didn't understand. He would ask me about my toilet training, and I would try to talk about that while I was hallucinating his plants marching around the room. It was crazy. I saw him for several years, but we got nowhere. I should have been hospitalized.

David: After analysis where did you go?

Betty: Next was mega-vitamins; that was hot then. I took 40 different vitamins a day. I carried them around with me in a box along with little cups for water and small bits of food to take with the vitamins. At first I felt better, but it didn't last. I don't really think the vitamins helped; I think I just happened to be going through a period in which the symptoms were less intense. When I started becoming ill again, the vitamins did nothing. Finally I just crashed.

David: Okay, the vitamins didn't work. What was next?

Betty: When I crashed the doctor gave me CO_2 therapy. I'd never heard of it before, but he seemed to think it would help. First they give you some anticonvulsion medication, and you lay on a table with a mask over your face. You're breathing, but there's no oxygen. You breath harder and harder, but you can't get your breath, and then all of a sudden, bang, and you're out—unconscious. Oh God, it's terrible; it's like drowning. And while you're out you are supposed to have these good dreams, but my dreams were hideous. God, they were terrible. I don't know how all of this was supposed to help me, but it didn't. I had the treatment once a week for about a year, and it did nothing. In fact, I got worse.

David: All right, CO_2 therapy didn't work. What did you try next?

Betty: Well, for awhile I was on and off a lot of different drugs, mostly antidepressants, but they weren't working so I went into the hospital for shock therapy, ECT.

David: Did it help?

Betty: When I first woke up—for a few hours after a treatment—I guess I felt a little better, but not much. I wasn't as depressed, but the shocks didn't stop my hallucinations or delusions. My doctors didn't want to give up on shocks, though, so they kept giving me more. They were desperate to find something that would work. After I left the hospital I kept getting the shocks on an outpatient basis. Three times a week Mom and I would drive to the hospital in the morning so I could get my shocks. But there really wasn't much improvement—even after about 30 shocks.

David: Well, what was next?

Betty: Then I changed doctors, to a specialist in drugs. He tried a lot of drugs; I was always changing drugs trying to find the right one or the right combination.

David: Thorazine? Any help from Thorazine?

Betty: Made me drowsy, but didn't stop the symptoms—I was just drugged.

David: Haldol?

Betty: I had the best response to that, although even that wasn't much. Actually, on Haldol I felt so drugged that I didn't care if I was hallucinating.

David: Side effects? Tardive dyskinesia?

Betty: Off and on. I had a lot of facial twitches—my mouth jerked—and I rocked up and back all the time. That drove my mother nuts! For a while I had really bad side effects. I remember that my head would suddenly jerk back, my eyes would roll up, and my tongue would stick out. That was frightening. When that happened, we reduced the dose level and I started taking more drugs to counteract the side effects.

I don't know if this is a typical reaction to taking a lot of drugs, but I just felt like my world was coming inside me—coming and going—all very strange. I took Haldol, Stelazine, all of the tricyclics, and all of the MAO inhibitors. I took everything in every combination. Then we tried Clozaril.

David: Tell me about the Clozaril.

Betty: When it first became available, my doctor thought I would be a good candidate. It was very expensive, but I was getting worse and they were getting ready to admit me to the state hospital. I couldn't afford Clozaril, so we went to court to sue Medicaid to pay for it. It was a class action suit so other patients could get it too. The argument was, it's expensive, but less expensive than going in the hospital—which was the direction I was headed. We won, so I could get the drug.

David: Did the Clozaril help?

Betty: Well, first they had to put me in the hospital while I changed drugs. Every two weeks they would reduce my other medication and up the level of the Clozaril a little. And when I finally got off the Haldol and onto the Clozaril, I felt really good—almost back to normal. I was feeling like normal people do, and I was thrilled. I was doing so well that when I came back home the public television station did a special report on me and the effects of the Clozaril. Being on Clozaril was like the patients in the movie *Awakenings; I was back, I was normal, and it was wonderful!* I was really doing great for a few months—(*long pause*)—and then bam, they were back.

David: "They?"

Betty: The demons, the voices, the monks chanting, the fears about the police—everything. All the symptoms came back. It was terrible, so depressing. But I would never put Clozaril down because it helped a lot for a while, and things are better now than they could be. I'm on the highest dose possible; 900 milligrams a day! I'm just very drug-resistant.

David: You think the Clozaril is helping. Are you having any side effects?

Betty: The weight gain is the worst; I gained more than 20 pounds. I'm becoming a blimp, but I'd rather be fat than mentally ill. Oh, and sometimes the Clozaril makes me drool, but that's not a big deal.

David: Are you on any other drugs?

Betty: A lot. Zoloft for depression; two 100-milligram tablets twice a day. Klonopin, an antianxiety medication; four 2-milligram tablets at bedtime. That helps me sleep. Next is chloral hydrate. That's a classic old sleeping medication, and I take one before going to bed. Oxybutynin—that is for my bladder problem. The medication makes me incontinent, and this takes care of that. Oh, yes, I also take Ativan for anxiety.

David: That's a lot of medication, but you still have the serious symptoms. How do you handle what can't be controlled with the drugs?

Betty: What people have to understand is that schizophrenia is a physical disease—a problem with the brain—so it has to be treated with drugs. Unfortunately, in most cases the drugs are not enough. People with schizophrenia have to cope with a lot of problems—symptoms that can't be completely controlled with the drugs and problems in daily living that are caused by the symptoms. For those other problems we need social support.

David: Where do you get that social support?

Betty: Well, my case manager is important. She checks with me regularly and helps with all kinds of problems, like taking care of all of the Medicaid forms and things like that. Then I have some very good friends who are also patients. We can support each other because we know what the other person is going through. We can be frank with each other. We know what the symptoms are, so we understand. It makes you feel less alone. Other patients are important, but it is also very important to have friends who are not sick. The problem is, it is hard to make those connections; we get stuck in a psychiatric clique, a psychiatric ghetto. You have to make contacts in the real world, but that's hard. It's like trying to make integration work. One of the most important things for me is to have someone to call when I get really sick—someone to call when I am depressed or bothered by a delusion and need reassurance. That's when I call you, like last week when I was hallucinating voices from the drain and outside my window that were so real—I called you for reassurance that it was a hallucination. Those "reality checks" and support are important because the drugs can't do it all.

In a recent note to me, Betty summed up the importance of contact with others, and she gave me permission to print part of that note here.

Thank you for talking with me yesterday. I don't understand quite what was wrong, but things weren't adding up. You were most helpful in making things more cohesive for me. Thank you. I usually handle things better when I can identify the source. Most of the time my logic is random. Some things get processed, and others are like black holes. I guess I should be grateful for what I have. I am so much better than when I was on the Haldol. I am slowly coming to accept myself as something more than a broken doll. You have been wonderful to me. You gave me stature and took me seriously. *You saw me as something besides illness.* You have no idea what a gift you gave to me.

SUMMARY

Three conclusions can be drawn from the research on the treatment of schizophrenia. First, traditional psychotherapy is not more effective than simple milieu therapy for treating schizophrenia. In contrast, psychological interventions that involve the entire family and that use education and social skills training to reduce stress are effective for reducing relapse and reducing dependence on medication.

Second, rewards and punishments can be used to change the behavior of persons who suffer from schizophrenia. This approach to treatment has been used effectively in what are called token economies. The major criticism that has been leveled at this approach is that is improves behavior but does not improve the thought disorder that is the core of schizophrenia. However, altering behavior may enable patients to be discharged from hospitals and thus to live better and more productive lives even if they still suffer from cognitive disturbances.

Third, low- and high-potency neuroleptic drugs that block dopamine activity are often effective for treating schizophrenia. This conclusion is supported by the findings that when patients on neuroleptics are compared to patients receiving other treatments, the patients on neuroleptics are judged to be more improved, are released from the hospital sooner, and are less likely to return to the hospital. Atypical neuroleptic drugs such as Clozaril are more specific in the dopamine receptors they block, and these drugs also increase serotonin activity. Atypical neuroleptics are expensive, but sometimes they are effective for treating individuals who do not respond to regular neuroleptics. Furthermore, atypical neuroleptics help with negative as well as positive symptoms.

Unfortunately, neuroleptic drugs have side effects. Some of those side effects are minor (dryness of the mouth, sensitivity to the sun) and are probably acceptable trade-offs for the reduction of the debilitating symptoms. Other side effects, such as tardive dyskinesia and the malignant neuroleptic syndrome, are more serious, pose unacceptable risks, and require adjustments in the drug treatment program. In all cases, the goal should be to reduce as many symptoms as necessary with the lowest possible level of medication, and therefore drug therapy should routinely involve testing the lower limits of medication levels and drug holidays. Drugs can provide a treatment for schizophrenia but do not cure the disorder. The most effective and through approach to the treatment of schizophrenia is a combination of drugs to help with physiological problems and psychoeducation to help with environmental and interpersonal problems.

In Part 4, we have examined many of the pieces of the puzzle of schizophrenia, and we have been able to fit many of them together. Yet some of the pieces still do not fit, and some are still missing. Nevertheless, the picture that has eluded us for hundreds of years is now becoming clear, and it is possible, even likely, that in the near future, we will be able to complete the picture and our understanding of schizophrenia.

KEY TERMS, CONCEPTS, AND NAMES

In reviewing and testing yourself on what you have learned from this chapter, you should be able to identify and discuss each of the following:

agranulocytosis
atypical neuroleptics
bundling
Clozaril (clozapine)
dopamine
dose-response relationship
electroconvulsive therapy (ECT)
extrapyramidal symptoms
family therapy
Haldol (haloperidol)

high-potency neuroleptics
lower-limit drug therapy
low-potency neuroleptics
malignant neuroleptic syndrome
milieu therapy
neuroleptics
noncontinuous drug therapy
prefrontal lobotomy
psychoeducation
psychosurgery

psychotherapy
serotonin
side effects
social skills training
tardive dyskinesia
Thorazine (chlorpromazine)
token economy
transorbital lobotomy
treatment-resistant patients

PART 5

Other Disorders

· O U T L I N E ·

Chapter 15

Personality Disorders

• O U T L I N E •

For Louise, everything must be "just right." She can spend hours laying out and preparing her clothes for the next day, and then she is still not satisfied. When it comes to studying, she uses three colors of felt-tipped pens for underlining: red for very important ideas, blue for less important ideas, and yellow for ideas that are merely interesting. She has her pens and 10 perfectly sharpened pencils carefully arranged on her desk, which is always extraordinarily neat (books are put away, the top is dusted every day, and the drawers are meticulously arranged). Louise is never happy because she never feels "on top of things." She has few friends because her organizational activities take up so much time. Also, other people become annoyed with her need for control and lack of spontaneity, so they avoid her. Louise suffers from the *obsessive-compulsive personality disorder.*

Darryl is very distrustful of everyone. He does not have any obvious delusions that others are plotting against him, but he is constantly and unjustifiably suspicious of everyone. Because of this, he is anxious and distant, and he works best alone. Darryl appears to have a *paranoid personality disorder.*

Stan can be a lot of fun to be around because he is charming, bright, articulate, outgoing, and always ready to do something wild. Although Stan is very gregarious, he is actually self-centered and insensitive to the needs of others, and he will often take advantage of others. For example, while living with one woman, he was "sleeping around" and not making much of an attempt to cover his tracks. When confronted, he talked his way out of it, effectively blaming the other woman. A careful review of his background reveals that he has been in and out of a lot of scrapes, usually because he acted impulsively to satisfy some spur-of-the-moment want. For example, as an adolescent, he frequently cut school, was drunk, used other people's money without repaying it, and a couple of times stole a car to go joyriding. In most cases, he was able to con his way out of the trouble, only to repeat the behavior a short time later. Although he has frequently hurt those around him, he has never shown anxiety or remorse about his behavior. He just does not seem to have a conscience. Stan would be diagnosed as suffering from the *antisocial personality disorder,* but it is actually the people around him who suffer.

In this chapter, we will discuss a variety of problems that are known as **personality disorders**. These disorders differ from the others we have discussed in that in most cases, individuals with personality disorders behave in less deviant ways and are usually less distressed. In fact, some critics have suggested that many of the behaviors seen in personality disorders are not really abnormal but simply reflect differences in adjustment within the normal range. The underlying issue revolves around the question of where we should draw the line between normal and abnormal behavior. At present, the trend seems to be to set the cutoff point low and include more people in the abnormal category.

At the outset, it is important to note that at one time or another, most of us have shown some of the symptoms seen in the personality disorders. For example, we may have been dependent, passive, self-centered, emotionally detached, or guilt-free after doing something wrong. However, that does not mean that we have one of the disorders. Three factors separate people who have the disorders from those who do not. First, an individual with a disorder will *consistently* use the behaviors in question, whereas nondisturbed individuals will use them only occasionally. Second, an individual with a disorder will show a *more extreme* level of the behavior. For example, there is a difference between being orderly and being compulsive. Third, in disturbed individuals, the behavior results in *serious and prolonged problems with functioning or happiness.* It is important to keep these distinctions in mind so that you do not erroneously attribute a personality disorder to an individual who only sometimes shows a low level of the behavior in question and whose life is not disrupted by those instances. Keep these points in mind as we consider the various personality disorders.

This chapter has two major sections. In the first section, we will consider the *antisocial personality disorder* in some detail. In the second section, we will review a variety of other personality disorders.

• Antisocial Personality Disorder

Antisocial personality disorder is the official diagnostic label for the problem we will discuss in this section, but individuals with this disorder are commonly referred to as *psychopaths* or *sociopaths*. For the sake of convenience, in this chapter we will use the abbreviation APD for *antisocial personality disorder.*

A thorough understanding of the APD is important because persons with the disorder are among the most interpersonally destructive and emotionally harmful individuals in our society. Interestingly, with most other disorders, most of the problems are suffered by the individual with the disorder, but in the case of the APD, most of the problems are suffered by people around the disordered individual. As we will see, one of the difficulties with persons who have the APD is that they do not show any of the traditional signs of abnormal behavior (anxiety, hallucinations, delusions), and in fact they often appear to be very well adjusted. This makes them exceptionally difficult to recognize and diagnose, and as long as they go unrecognized, they continue causing problems for the people around them.

SYMPTOMS OF THE ANTISOCIAL PERSONALITY DISORDER

Mood Symptoms

The most important symptom in the APD is a *lack of anxiety or guilt.* Persons with the APD are often said to be "conscienceless" individuals. For example, after doing something that is wrong, inappropriate, or illegal (not returning borrowed money or killing someone), a person with the APD will show no anxiety, guilt, or remorse. Because they do not have the restraints that are typically provided by anxiety, persons with the APD tend to be "loose," impulsive, and have a devil-may-care attitude.

Second, persons with the APD are *hedonistic* (pleasure seeking). They seem to be guided by the dictum, "I want what I want when I want it"—and they take what they want regardless of the cost to others. In many cases, persons with the APD appear to be unable or unwilling to delay gratification of their needs, and consequently they act impulsively, with only their own wants in mind. In doing so, they frequently harm people around them.

A third symptom is a *shallowness of feelings* and *lack of emotional attachments to others.* Persons with the APD often verbalize strong feelings and commitments (e.g., they quickly profess love), but their behavior indicates otherwise. For example, a person with the APD may be involved in numerous sexual relationships, but those relationships come and go without having any real impact on the person.

Cognitive Symptoms

It is especially noteworthy that people with the APD typically appear to be very *intelligent*, have well-developed *verbal and social skills*, and have the ability to *rationalize* their inappropriate behavior so that it appears reasonable and justifiable. Because of these abilities, when they get themselves in trouble, they are often able to talk their way out of it. Consider the example of a charming 26-year-old male who, 3 days before he was to be married, was discovered by his fiancée to be having a very active affair with another woman. When confronted with irrefutable evidence of his inappropriate behavior, the young man first professed his unfaltering love for his fiancée and then went on to explain in the most sincere manner imaginable that he had no real feelings for the other woman (which in a sense was probably true) and that he was having the affair only as a means of testing his love for his fiancée. Indeed, he explained that he participated in the affair for the good of his fiancée so that once his love had been tested and found to be true, no one else would ever pose a threat to their relationship. He expressed some surprise at her lack of understanding but promised that nothing like that would ever happen again. They were married as planned, but the young man proceeded to engage in a long series of indiscretions, each of which was "explainable" and was followed by professions of remorse and more promises to reform.

Most persons with the APD also appear *unable to benefit from punishment.* In many situations, these people can avoid punishment by talking their way out of it. However, when they are punished, the punishment does not appear to have any effect, regardless of its severity. Because persons with the APD do not seem to learn or benefit from their experiences, they are not deterred and tend to engage in the same inappropriate behavior again and again, even when they are repeatedly punished for the behavior.

Motor Symptoms

Lack of anxiety leads persons with the APD to behave *impulsively.* An interesting aspect of their behavior that has been receiving attention lately is what is referred to as high *sensation-seeking* behavior. These people often engage in wild and dangerous activities (e.g., fast driving, skydiving) "for kicks" rather than to achieve some goal. If they take drugs, the drugs are more likely to be stimulants than sedatives. In a less dramatic vein, persons with the APD tell lies from which they cannot possibly reap any benefit other than the fun, intrigue, and "danger" associated with perpetrating the deception.

These people frequently cause emotional and financial harm to those around them, but as a general rule, they do not engage in overt physical aggression. However, there is a subset of persons with the disorder who may act very aggressively in some situations. The attention given by the media to aggressive behavior of these persons is disproportionate to the frequency with which that symptom occurs. The acts of aggres-

Serial killer Ted Bundy could probably be diagnosed as having suffered from the antisocial personality disorder. He used his good looks, intelligence, and charm to get close to his victims— all young women—whom he sexually abused and then murdered. Bundy was executed in Florida in 1989.

sion get the attention they do because they are so extreme and senseless. Examples of widely publicized cases include Richard Speck, who killed eight nurses one evening in an apartment in Chicago; the two killers who were made famous in Truman Capote's book *In Cold Blood;* Ted Bundy, who was suspected of killing more than 20 women in five states (including two women in a sorority house whom he battered to death); and Kenneth Bianchi, the Hillside Strangler. An example of a person with an APD is presented in Case Study 15.1.

Diagnostic Criteria

According to DSM-IV, to be diagnosed as suffering from the APD, an individual must meet the four criteria listed in Table 15.1 (p. 352). Three aspects of the diagnosis should be noted. First, an individual must be 18 years old before being diagnosed as suffering from the APD. That is because we must be sure that the individual has had an opportunity to learn what is appropriate behavior. As some observers have quipped, we are all born with the APD (i.e., without anxieties and inhibitions) and only become normal with maturity. Second, it is also relevant to note that delinquent or criminal behavior plays a very important role in determining the diagnosis. It may be that too much importance is placed on criminal behavior, and thus too many noncriminal (or uncaught) individuals with the

Case Study 15.1

A PERSON WITH THE ANTISOCIAL PERSONALITY DISORDER

As a child, Doug was well liked because of his good looks and charming manner. His parents thought he could do no wrong. In fact, however, Doug often disobeyed his parents and teachers, but he usually had a convincing explanation for his actions, or he blamed his friends. Therefore, he was seldom punished for this misbehavior. Once when he was 7, he told all of his friends that he was having a birthday but that he was not going to have a party or get any presents because his father was not working. Hearing that, the neighbors gave him a big party and lots of presents—only to learn that he had lied. His parents thought it was "cute," and he was not punished.

In high school, Doug had a series of girlfriends (indeed, he was much sought after) and many casual male buddies, but he never formed close attachments with anyone. His peers looked up to him because he was extroverted and daring, always ready to try something new. The first clear sign of antisocial behavior occurred when Doug was 15. He stole a car that belonged to an older friend and took three buddies on a joyride that lasted several hours. When they were finally caught, Doug lied about his part in the theft, blaming the friends who had accompanied him. His parents believed him, and they convinced the local police that Doug was innocent, so he again went unpunished for his actions.

Doug went to college but never graduated. He had the intelligence to do well, but he just stopped going to class. When he was about to be thrown out of school, he conned a woman in the admissions office into ignoring the last semester's grades (all Fs) by telling her that he had missed class because he had been going home to take care of his parents, who had been in a serious accident. Impressed with his devotion to his parents and his sincere hope to do better, she gave him an exemption. One summer, when his parents thought that he was in school taking "extra courses," he was in fact in Aspen tending bar. He got his roommate to forward his checks from home to Colorado.

After college, Doug did not hold any job for long. Although he could be hardworking, he usually lost his jobs because he did something foolish. For example, a number of times, he simply did not show up for a few days because on the spur of the moment, he decided to go backpacking. Once while working as an automobile salesman, he drove off one night with a very expensive demonstrator model and did not return. He made no attempt to conceal the car and was caught within a week. When taken to court, he claimed that he had intended to return to work the next day and that it was all a "misunderstanding." In exchange for his promise to pay for the use of the car, he was given a suspended sentence. Two days later, he left town.

At age 26, Doug married a girl of 18 who worked in one of the bars he frequented. They married almost "as a lark," and neither knew much about the other. He was unemployed, but she believed one of his lines in the bar and thought he was a stockbroker. Without her knowing it, they lived for the first couple of months off her savings, which he took from the bank. He also forged checks to pay for a car he leased and the numerous items of clothing he bought for himself. Also unbeknown to his wife, within 2 weeks of the marriage, he was having affairs with two other women (his wife thought he was seeing clients). He was eventually caught and convicted for check forgery and served 6 months in jail. A month after he was jailed, his wife discovered that she was pregnant. When his wife went to pick him up on the day he was scheduled to be released from jail, she discovered that he had been released early "for good behavior" and had left town.

In another state, Doug assumed another name, soon met the daughter of a wealthy family, and began to court the woman. Lonely and insecure, she was completely taken in by Doug's good looks, charm, attentive manner, and intelligence. He portrayed himself as a sensitive and lonely man who was rejected by his parents. He told her that he had plans to develop a retirement home, and the woman began giving him substantial amounts of money to lay the groundwork for the project. Doug took the money, opened a lavish office, and started an affair with his secretary.

The problems described here probably constitute only the tip of the iceberg of Doug's inappropriate behavior; because he was so effective at conning people, much of his misbehavior went undetected or unreported.

APD slip through the diagnostic net. To assume that only individuals with criminal records have the APD would be a serious error because many persons with this disorder are not criminals. Finally, note that the diagnosis of APD does not require that the individual show any of the symptoms traditionally associated with abnormal behavior (e.g., anxiety, depression, hallucinations, delusions). For that reason, persons with the APD are often not recognized as suffering from a psychological problem.

TABLE 15.1 DIAGNOSTIC CRITERIA FOR THE ANTISOCIAL PERSONALITY DISORDER

1. Person is at least 18 years of age.
2. Person suffered from a Conduct Disorder before the age of 15. (Conduct disorders involve the persistent disregard of the rights of others as in bullying, stealing, fighting, destruction of property; see Chapter 16.)
3. Person showed a pervasive pattern of disregard for the rights of others since the age of 15, showing at least three of the following:
   a. Failure to conform to social norms as evidenced by repeatedly performing acts that are illegal
   b. Irritability and aggressiveness, as indicated by repeated fights
   c. Irresponsibility, as evidenced by failure to sustain consistent work or honor obligations
   d. Impulsivity or failure to plan ahead
   e. Repeated lying, use of aliases, or conning other for personal profit or pleasure
   f. Reckless disregard for the safety of self or others
   g. Lack of guilt, as reflected in indifference to mistreatment of others
4. Symptoms do not occur during schizophrenia or a manic episode.

Source: American Psychiatric Association (1994).

ISSUES ASSOCIATED WITH THE ANTISOCIAL PERSONALITY DISORDER

Prevalence and Duration

One extensive community study revealed that 4.5% of the men but fewer than 1% of the women suffered from the APD (Robins et al., 1984). The disorder seems to be most apparent during late adolescence and early adulthood; and then, for reasons that are not yet understood, the disorder seems to "burn out" at around age 40 (Craft, 1969; Gibbens et al., 1955; Maddocks, 1970; Robins, 1966; Weiss, 1973). It is fortunate that the burnout occurs because, as we will learn later, this disorder is exceptionally resistant to treatment.

Primary Versus Secondary Disorders

Although the distinction is not specifically embodied in the official diagnostic criteria, there appear to be two types of the APD, the **primary** and the **secondary**. Low levels of anxiety are characteristic of both types, but they differ in the processes that are responsible for the low levels of anxiety. In the case of the primary APD, the individual is thought to be largely *incapable of developing anxiety*. In the case of the secondary APD, the individual is thought to be capable of developing anxiety but has *learned to avoid it*. Although anxiety is low in both types, the difference in the processes that lead to the low anxiety is important for understanding the development of the disorder and planning treatment strategies. (We will consider the development and treatment of the types later.)

Historical Background

The concept of the antisocial personality disorder has gone through four steps in its development, and an understanding of those steps is helpful for understanding current thinking about the disorder. The concept initially developed from the recognition that there was a disorder in which individuals behaved irrationally or inappropriately but did not have other symptoms. This form of "madness" was referred to as *manie sans délire* ("insanity without delirium"; Pinel, 1806). The disorder was also sometimes referred to as **moral insanity** because of the nature of the inappropriate behaviors (e.g., lying, cheating, stealing; Prichard, 1835).

The second step in the development of the concept occurred when it became generally accepted that the disorder had a *physiological basis*. That is, individuals with the disorder were thought to be suffering from an "innate, preternatural moral depravity" that stemmed from a "defective organization in those parts of the body which are preoccupied by the moral faculties of the mind" (Rush, 1812, p. 112). Similarly, the Italian anthropologist Cesare Lombroso talked about the "born delinquent" (Lombroso, 1911), and numerous other investigators began referring to the "constitutional inferiority" of these individuals. The label that was first used for individuals suffering from this disorder was **psychopath** (Koch, 1891). That term was explicitly coined to reflect the underlying physiological problem, pathology of the psyche.

In the 1930s and 1940s, psychodynamically oriented clinicians began speculating about the potential *interpersonal and social bases of the disorder* (Cleckley, 1941), and the emphasis shifted away from the potential physiological basis of the disorder. This shift from physiological to social determinism was consistent with the dominant cultural perspective of that period, and it resulted in the adoption of the label **sociopath** for these individuals, an obvious reference to potential *societal* contributions to the disorder.

In recent discussions, an attempt has been made to avoid any explicit or implicit inference concerning the cause of the disorder. To that end, in DSM-IV the terms *psychopath* and *sociopath* are not used and the disorder has been given the neutral label of *antisocial personality disorder.*

With the foregoing description of the symptomatology as background and with some understanding of how the disorder has been viewed in the past, we can now go on to consider the current theories and related data concerning the causes of the APD.

PSYCHODYNAMIC EXPLANATIONS

Structural Explanation

Traditional psychoanalytic theories provide two explanations for the APD (Fenichel, 1945). First, using Freud's structural approach to personality, some theorists have suggested that persons with the APD lack anxiety and guilt because *they did not develop an adequate superego.* In the absence of a well-developed superego, the restraints on the id are reduced, and that leads to impulsive and hedonistic behavior. Indeed, in discussing the APD, it has been said that "the lid is off the id." The failure to develop an adequate superego is thought to be the result of inadequate identification with appropriate adult (parental) figures, and it is assumed that the identification did not occur because the appropriate adult figures were either physically or psychologically unavailable.

Developmental Explanation

The second psychoanalytic explanation of the APD is based on Freud's developmental approach to personality. This explanation suggests that individuals with the APD are *fixated at an early stage of psychosexual development.* That is, the "immature" behavior of persons with the APD is attributed to retarded psychosexual development. The retarded development is in turn attributed to the fact that their needs for love, support, and acceptance were not satisfied by their parents, and the failure to satisfy those needs precluded advancing to the next stages of development.

Evidence for the Psychodynamic Explanations

The clinical literature is replete with case studies indicating that the early childhoods of persons with the APD are characterized by *bad parenting:* rejection, neglect, lack of love, abuse, and inconsistencies in parents' responses (e.g., Bennet, 1960; Bowlby, 1952;

Cleckley, 1976; Lindner, 1944; McCord & McCord, 1964; McCord et al., 1959; Partridge, 1928; Redl & Wineman, 1951). Those observations are interesting, but in the absence of comparisons with the early childhood experiences of normal individuals, they cannot be used as evidence for the hypothesis that lack of love during childhood results in the APD.

Fortunately, a number of investigations have been conducted in which the backgrounds of persons with the APD were systematically compared to the backgrounds of normal persons. One noteworthy study was focused on 150 males of age 30 who were diagnosed as either "neurotic," exhibiting "bad conduct" (APD), or "normal" (Roff, 1974). All of the men had been seen in child guidance clinics approximately 20 years earlier, and therefore information was available concerning the nature of their early experiences. Raters who were unaware of the men's current diagnoses used the childhood clinic records to make judgments about the types of parenting the men had experienced as children, and then the groups were compared in terms of their childhood experiences. The results of those comparisons indicate that the childhoods of persons with the APD are often characterized by neglect, rejection, and abuse on the part of the parents. The results are particularly interesting because the parental characteristics that separated the persons with APD from the normals also separated the persons with APD from neurotics, thus suggesting that the pattern of bad parenting associated with the APD is specific to that disorder and is not associated with maladjustment in general. The types of parental behavior on which the APD group differed from the normal and neurotic groups are summarized in Table 15.2 (p. 354).

It is clear from these results that there was a relationship between certain kinds of bad parenting and subsequent antisocial behavior. However, we cannot necessarily conclude that the bad parenting *caused* the antisocial behavior because there are two other possible explanations. First, it is possible that the antisocial behavior of the child led the parents to behave inappropriately and to become bad parents (Bell, 1968). That is, when faced with consistently incorrigible antisocial behavior on the part of the child, in desperation the parents might have tried different approaches to child rearing (became inconsistent), attempted more severe measures for gaining control (used excessive punishment), or withdrew in frustration (appeared to reject the child).

Second, it is possible that the bad parenting and the antisocial behavior of the child both stemmed from a third factor, a common gene pool. In that regard it is noteworthy that the descriptions of the parents of antisocial children suggest that the parents were themselves antisocial. If that is the case, and if it

Faye Dunaway played Joan Crawford, a famous "bad parent," in the movie Mommy Dearest. *People with the antisocial personality disorder are more likely to have been neglected, rejected, or abused by their parents. However, on the basis of that association alone, we cannot conclude that bad parenting causes the antisocial behavior. The parent could have developed inappropriate behavior toward the child because the child may have been antisocial. Alternatively, both parent and child may have developed their behavior patterns because of a third factor such as their common gene pool.*

is assumed that personality is at least in part inherited, we could conclude that the similarity in the behavior of the parents and the children was determined by their shared genes rather than their social interactions.

We should also consider a set of investigations in which it was found that antisocial children had higher rates of physical ailments such as head and face injuries than normal children (Lewis & Shanok, 1979;

Lewis, Shanok, & Balla, 1979a, 1979b; Lewis, Shanok, Pincus, & Glaser, 1979; Shanok & Lewis, 1981). One explanation for these findings is that the physical traumas reflect the fact that the children were abused or neglected and that the abuse and neglect led to the antisocial behavior. Another explanation is that the physical traumas may have resulted in damage to the nervous system, which may in turn have contributed to the children's antisocial behavior (Pasamanick et al.,

TABLE 15.2   ADULTS DIAGNOSED AS EXHIBITING "BAD CONDUCT" (APD) EXPERIENCED MORE NEGLECT, REJECTION, AND ABUSE AS CHILDREN THAN ADULTS DIAGNOSED AS "NEUROTIC" OR "NORMAL"

	Adult Behavior		
	NORMAL (%)	NEUROTIC (%)	EXHIBITING BAD CONDUCT (%)
Ratings of Mothers			
Neglect in important areas	22	36	64
Inadequate parental control	18	24	46
Wish to be rid of child	6	24	54
Abandonment, repudiation of child	8	6	48
Physical cruelty	6	6	22
Negative evaluation of child	18	24	38
Babying, overhelping	34	42	20
Annoyance, impatience, etc.	32	34	16
Pressing for achievement	28	24	10
Ratings of Fathers			
Wish to be rid of child	4	0	26
Abandonment, repudiation of child	12	16	42
Passivity	30	30	10
Attention	40	28	12

Source: Adapted from Roff (1974).

1956). Third, it is possible that the sensation seeking that characterizes many children with the APD may have led them to engage in dangerous activities in which they were more likely to get hurt. If that was the case, the higher incidence of physical traumas may have been the *result* rather than the *cause* of the disorder. Thus again, a history of physical traumas provides us with another interesting piece for the background mosaic of the antisocial personality, but on the basis of the information we have examined so far, it is not clear exactly how that piece fits in.

In summary, numerous clinical observations and empirical investigations suggest that the childhoods of many persons with the APD are characterized by some form of bad parenting. However, it is unclear whether the bad parenting actually causes the APD, and our conclusions concerning the causes of the disorder will have to await the consideration of other data.

■ LEARNING EXPLANATIONS

Deficit in Classical Conditioning

Learning theorists have offered two explanations for the APD. The **deficit-in-classical-conditioning** explanation begins with the idea that anxiety is a classically conditioned response and goes on to suggest that persons with the primary type of the APD do not classically condition well and therefore do not develop classically conditioned anxiety. In other words, persons with the APD are not anxious because they have a deficit in the ability to develop classically conditioned anxiety responses.

It is important to recognize that the deficit-in-classical-conditioning explanation is limited to *classical* conditioning. It does not suggest that persons with the APD have an impairment in the ability to develop *operantly* conditioned responses. (Those two types of conditioning appear to occur in different parts of the brain.) Therefore, the ability of these persons to learn nonemotional responses is not impaired. Indeed, the clinical picture presented by persons with the APD suggests that they are of average or superior intelligence and that they know what is right and wrong but do not conform their behavior to the rules. Having made that distinction, we can now consider the research that is relevant to the deficit-in-classical-conditioning explanation.

Classical Conditioning. The first set of experiments to be considered was conducted to determine whether persons with the APD do in fact classically condition anxiety responses less well than normal per-

sons. In these experiments, persons who either did or did not have the APD participated in a series of conditioning trials in which they were presented with a tone, followed by a brief pause, and then a painful electric shock. The question was, are persons with the APD less likely to develop a conditioned anxiety response to the tone than other persons? In these experiments, anxiety was measured in terms of electrodermal responses measured during the pause following the tone. (Electrodermal responses involve increases and decreases in moisture on the hand, which are influenced by anxiety. You may have noticed that when you are anxious, your palms sweat.)

The results of at least five experiments indicate that persons who had the APD required more trials to learn (condition) the anxiety response and that they gave fewer anxiety responses than persons who did not have the disorder (Hare, 1965a; Hare & Craigen, 1974; Hare & Quinn, 1971; Lykken, 1957; Schachter & Latané, 1964). The results of one of these experiments are presented graphically in Figure 15.1.

In another investigation, the classical conditioning of 104 adolescents was measured, and the individu-

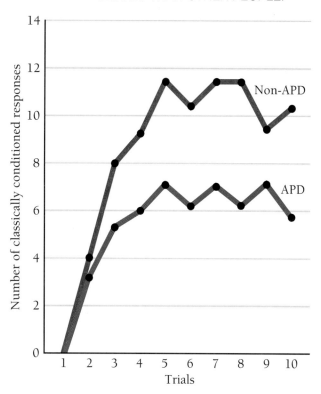

FIGURE 15.1   PERSONS WITH THE ANTISOCIAL PERSONALITY DISORDER (APD) CLASSICALLY CONDITION MORE SLOWLY THAN OTHER PEOPLE.

Source: Hare (1965a), p. 369, fig. 1-A.

als were followed up 10 years later to determine which of them had engaged in some form of antisocial (delinquent) behavior (Loeb & Mednick, 1976). If we assume that at least some of the antisocial behavior was due to the APD, it would be expected that the individuals who engaged in antisocial behavior would have demonstrated worse classical conditioning than individuals who did not engage in antisocial behavior. That is exactly what the investigators found; individuals who engaged in antisocial behavior had shown poor classical conditioning 10 years earlier. Overall, then, there is substantial and consistent evidence that people with the APD do not develop classically conditioned anxiety as well as other people. With that established, we must examine the question of whether a deficit in classical conditioning influences the *behavior* of people with the APD.

Avoidance Conditioning.
Before discussing the research in this area, it might be helpful to describe briefly the procedures involved in **avoidance conditioning** and discuss its relevance for understanding behavior in the APD. In experiments on avoidance conditioning, persons work on problems that involve making a series of responses and the persons are punished (usually with electrical shocks) each time they respond incorrectly. For example, an individual working on a "mental maze" (throwing a series of switches in a specific order) is given an electrical shock each time a mistake is made.

Performance in avoidance conditioning situations improves when, through the process of classical conditioning, anxiety is associated with the incorrect response and then that response is avoided in order to avoid anxiety. Avoidance conditioning experiments are relevant for studying the APD because if persons with the disorder are less likely to develop classically conditioned anxiety, they should also be less anxious about making incorrect responses and should therefore perform less well than people who do not have the disorder. In avoidance conditioning experiments, then, performance is an indirect measure of the ability of the individuals to develop classically conditioned anxiety responses. Actually, avoidance conditioning experiments provide a rather good analogue for numerous real-life situations in which you are punished for making an inappropriate response and hence in the future you avoid that response and use a more appropriate response instead. For example, if a person cheats on an examination and gets punished, the next time he or she thinks about cheating, anxiety will increase, and to avoid that, the person will not cheat.

The results of numerous experiments indicate that persons with the APD evidence slower or less avoidance conditioning than other persons (Hare, 1965b; Hare & Craigen, 1974; Lykken, 1957; Rosen & Schalling, 1971; Schachter & Latané, 1964; Schmauk, 1970). The results of one of these experiments are presented graphically in Figure 15.2. In that experiment, the participants sat in front of a box containing four switches. The box was programmed so as to constitute a complicated "mental maze" with 20 choice points. For each choice point, the participant had to press one of the four switches. One of the switches was designated as "correct" and advanced the participant to the next choice point, but the other switches were designated as "incorrect." Pressing an incorrect switch did not advance the participant and instead caused him or her to receive an electrical shock. Of course, the designation of correct and incorrect switches was different for different choice points. The results in Figure 15.2 indicate that as the 21 trials with the maze progressed, the individuals with the APD showed less avoidance of the shocked switches than the other individuals. It can

FIGURE 15.2   PERSONS WITH THE ANTISOCIAL PERSONALITY DISORDER (APD) DID NOT LEARN TO AVOID SHOCKED RESPONSES AS WELL AS OTHER PERSONS.

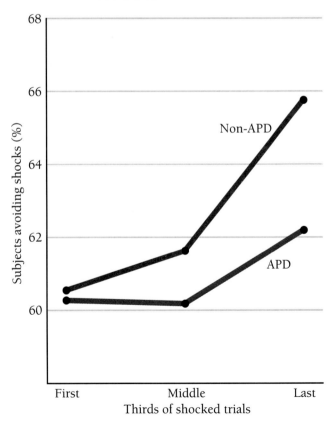

Source: Adapted from Schachter and Latané (1964), p. 248, fig. 2A.

be inferred from these results that the persons with the APD were less likely to develop the classically conditioned anxiety that underlies performance in avoidance conditioning.

The results of this experiment indicate that people who do and do not have the APD learn what is correct, but those with the APD do not learn to avoid incorrect responses that are punished. These results are of course consistent with the clinical picture of persons with the APD; they know what they should do, but they do not inhibit inappropriate responses. Overall, then, a considerable amount of evidence supports the deficit-in-classical-conditioning explanation for the lack of anxiety and consequent lack of inhibitions in persons with the APD.

Operantly Conditioned Avoidance of Anxiety

The explanation based on the **operantly conditioned avoidance of anxiety** begins with the premise that during a normal childhood, children are promptly punished for misbehaviors and that in an attempt to avoid the punishment and the anxiety associated with it, children stop misbehaving and instead behave appropriately. However, the operantly conditioned avoidance explanation suggests that during childhood, persons with the APD learn operant responses that they can use to *avoid the punishment* that should follow the inappropriate behavior, and thus they avoid the anxiety and eliminate the restraints against misbehavior (Maher, 1966).

Consider the following simple example: 4-year-old Billy is caught eating cookies before dinner, an act that his mother has expressly forbidden. When caught, but before his mother begins to punish him, Billy contritely admits that he knew that he was not supposed to eat the cookies, and he professes sorrow over the fact that he did not obey. Furthermore, he goes on to point out that the problem was that his mother is "such a *wonderful* cook" and "the cookies were *so good*," he just could not help himself! Billy also adds in the most endearing manner that in the future, he will try hard to avoid falling prey to temptation.

An interaction like this can have a number of effects that may be relevant to the development of the APD. If Billy can con his mother and thereby avoid the punishment, he will learn that he can misbehave without getting punished and that "fast talking" is an effective way of avoiding punishment. In other words, the misbehavior is not punished and the fast talking is rewarded by a reduction in anxiety when punishment is avoided. Even if the punishment is only postponed by the fast talking, the effectiveness of the punishment will be reduced because punishment is effective only if

it closely follows the misbehavior. Furthermore, even if the talking is not always effective, the intermittent nature of its effectiveness will actually contribute to the ultimate strength of the strategy. That is because responses that are rewarded *intermittently* are more resistant to extinction than responses that are rewarded 100% of the time (see Chapter 2).

Because individuals learn that they can get what they want without worrying about punishment, they do not learn to delay gratification. For example, they may buy things on credit knowing that they do not and will not have the money to pay for them, or they may take other people's possessions if their own are not readily at hand. Failure to learn to delay gratification results in impulsive behavior. Failure to learn to delay gratification may also contribute to emotional shallowness in responding to others because love, commitment, and respect for another individual are reflected in large measure by the degree to which we are willing to forgo something for the sake of the other individual. This can be seen in dramatic sacrifices made for others but is more often demonstrated in small acts such as curbing momentary irritability, tolerating minor annoyances, and respecting the rights of others. People who have not learned to delay gratification are unlikely to be able to empathize with the needs of others (which is an important part of loving) or to put off their own satisfaction so that they can respond to the needs of others.

The foregoing discussion has implied that the child learned the responses leading to the APD through trial and error, but that is not necessarily so. The same learning could be achieved through observation and modeling (Bandura, 1969). The opportunity for observing inappropriate behaviors would certainly exist because, as was pointed out earlier, people with the APD have often been raised by parents with the APD. Seeing parents misbehave and then talk themselves out of punishment would certainly provide a basis for the development of this pattern of behavior in children.

Unfortunately, although the operant conditioning explanation is based on well-established laws of learning, no research has been conducted to test directly whether this type of learning history in fact leads to the APD. That is because it would be unethical to attempt to condition an individual to use antisocial behavior.

Before concluding our discussion of the learning explanations for the APD, it might be helpful to compare the two explanations that have been put forward. The fundamental difference lies in the fact that the deficit-in-classical-conditioning explanation suggests that the person is *impaired in the ability to develop anxi-*

ety, whereas the operant conditioning explanation suggests that the person has the normal ability to develop anxiety but has *learned techniques to avoid the anxiety*. In both cases, the individual has a relative lack of anxiety, but the lack stems from very different processes. One problem for the deficit-in-classical-conditioning explanation is that it does not explain why the individual has a deficit, but that might be accounted for by the physiological explanation we will consider next.

PHYSIOLOGICAL EXPLANATION

The physiological explanation for the APD suggests that persons who suffer from the primary type of the disorder are *neurologically underaroused*. Neurological underarousal is used to account for the relative lack of anxiety seen in persons with the disorder.

Electrocortical Arousal

Electrocortical arousal refers to the levels of electrical activity in the brain, and this activity is measured by means of electroencephalogram (EEG) recordings (see Chapter 3). The electrocortical activity of persons with the APD has been of interest to researchers for a long time, and this area of investigation has produced some interesting and important findings. We will examine the prevalence and nature of the electrocortical abnormalities found in persons with the APD and will then consider the question of whether those abnormalities can be meaningfully related to the symptoms of individuals with the APD.

Numerous studies have shown that people with the antisocial personality disorder have a high incidence of EEG abnormalities. The abnormal EEGs seem to indicate a connection between reduced cortical arousal and antisocial personality development.

EEG Abnormalities. The EEGs of persons with the APD have been examined in at least 20 investigations, which have encompassed the records of almost 2,000 individuals, and thus we have a reasonable database from which to draw conclusions (see Holmes, 1991). Every one of those studies revealed a high incidence of **EEG abnormalities** among persons with the APD. Indeed, in 16 of the investigations, the incidence of EEG abnormalities among persons with the APD was in the range of 47% to 58%, a rate more than three times greater than the rate among normal individuals (approximately 15%; Ellingson, 1954). These studies provide evidence that persons with the APD have a higher incidence of abnormal EEG activity than other individuals.

Two specific abnormalities have been identified in the EEGs. The first is the presence of unusually high amounts of **slow-wave activity** (e.g., electrical impulses in the range of 8 to 12 cycles per second rather than 16 to 20 cps). Slow waves reflect a lower state of cortical arousal, and these findings have been the basis for the inference that persons with the APD suffer from **cortical underarousal**. The second type of abnormality is what is called **positive spiking**. Specifically, at intermittent points during the slow waves, some persons show sudden bursts of electrocortical activity. A number of investigators have suggested that positive spiking is more likely to occur in persons with the APD who are prone to act aggressively, and the investigators have implied that the bursts of aggression are reflections of the bursts of electrocortical activity. That causal link has not been confirmed yet.

Relationship of EEG Abnormalities to Behavior.
It is not enough to conclude simply that persons with the APD are more likely to evince abnormal EEGs than normal individuals because if the EEG abnormalities are relevant to the disorder, there should be some relationship between them and the behavior patterns seen in the disorder. In an attempt to identify the possible connections between abnormal EEGs and the behavior patterns seen in the APD, some investigators have pointed out that the abnormal EEGs that are observed in persons with the APD are very similar to the EEG patterns of young children, for whom slow waves and positive spiking are normal. This similarity has led to the suggestion that persons with APD suffer from **delayed cortical development** and that the delayed cortical development is responsible for their "childlike" behavior (e.g., egocentricity, impulsivity, inability to delay gratification).

Consistent with the delayed-development notion, it has been reported that EEG abnormalities among persons with the APD tend to decrease with age (Hill, 1952; Hill & Watterson, 1942) and that persons with the APD have typically been described as "burning out" when they get older (Robins, 1966). So far, however, a direct relationship between declines in EEG abnormalities and declines in the APD has not been reported.

A more specific explanation is that the EEG abnormalities seen in individuals with the APD reflect a **malfunction of the limbic system**, a system which plays an important role in the regulation of emotion. This hypothesis is based on two findings. First, the abnormal EEGs are most likely to be found at the temporal or posttemporal areas of the skull, and the limbic system is located under those areas. Second, the slow-wave activity suggests that the limbic system is underactive or underaroused, and such underarousal may account for the general lack of emotional arousal seen in persons with the APD. Also, the sudden bursts of activity (positive spiking) in those areas may account for the sudden and otherwise inexplicable emotional outbursts of persons with the APD.

The question arises whether reduced cortical arousal is the cause or the result of the APD. Fortunately, a number of experiments have shed light on that question. In one experiment, persons who did or did not have the APD participated in an avoidance conditioning experiment after being injected with either a placebo or epinephrine (Schachter & Latané, 1964). Epinephrine is a stimulant, and its administration to persons with the APD would increase their levels of cortical arousal, which would in turn be expected to increase their conditionability and improve their performance on the avoidance conditioning task.

The results revealed that after being injected with the placebo, as expected, the persons with the APD performed less well than the other persons. In contrast, after being injected with epinephrine, the persons with the APD performed as well as or better than the others, thus suggesting that the injection of the epinephrine (and the consequent increase in arousal) caused the persons with the APD to perform "normally." These results are presented in Figure 15.3. (It might be noted that when the people who did not have the APD were injected with epinephrine, they performed less well than they had when injected with a placebo, a difference that was probably due to the fact that epinephrine got them overaroused and thus impaired their functioning.) Similar results have been reported in another experiment, in which arousal was manipulated with noise rather than drugs (Chesno & Kilmann, 1975). These results provide support for the contention that differences in arousal cause the behavior seen in the APD rather than vice versa.

If increases in arousal decrease the behavior seen in the APD, then the question arises whether de-

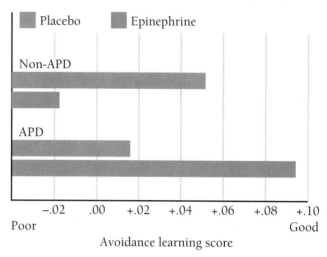

FIGURE 15.3 EPINEPHRINE IMPROVED AVOIDANCE CONDITIONING IN PERSONS WITH THE ANTISOCIAL PERSONALITY DISORDER (APD).

Source: Adapted from Schachter and Latané (1964), p. 251, fig. 3.

creases in arousal increase the behavior seen in the disorder. That interesting possibility was tested in an experiment in which university students took an important examination and thereafter were administered either a placebo or a drug that decreased cortical arousal (chlorpromazine) (Schachter & Latané, 1964). Then each student was allowed to score the examination taken earlier. The results indicated that students who had taken the arousal-decreasing drug cheated more frequently when scoring their examinations than the students who had taken the placebo. Indeed, the difference in cheating in the two conditions was almost 20%. If cheating is taken as an indication of the APD, this experiment provides evidence that cortical underarousal bears a direct causal relationship to the development of the disorder.

It is clear from the foregoing discussion that many persons with the APD show signs of electrocortical problems and that most of these problems involve cortical underarousal. Moreover, it has been demonstrated that increasing and decreasing arousal lead, respectively, to decreases and increases in the types of behavior associated with the disorder. These findings certainly point to a physiological basis for at least some cases of the APD. Therefore, we must go on to determine why some individuals suffer from cortical underarousal.

Genetics

In most of the studies that have focused on the heritability of the APD, criminal behavior was used as a

TABLE 15.3   MONOZYGOTIC (MZ) TWINS HAVE A HIGHER
CONCORDANCE RATE FOR CRIMINAL BEHAVIOR THAN
DIZYGOTIC (DZ) TWINS

STUDY	MONOZYGOTIC TWINS (%)	DIZYGOTIC TWINS (%)
Lange (1931)	77	12
Legra (1933)	100	0
Rosanoff et al. (1934)	68	18
Kranz (1936)	65	54
Stumpfl (1936)	61	37
Borgstrom (1939)	75	40
Yoshimasu (1965)	61	11
Hayashi (1967)	73	60
Christiansen (1968)	33	11
Dalgaard and Kringlen (1976)	22	18

Note. All DZ twin pairs contain siblings of the same sex.
Source: Adapted in part from Dalgaard and Kringlen (1976).

measure of the disorder. However, criminal behavior is not the only measure of the disorder, and insofar as it is not a good measure, the results of the research will be distorted.

Studies of Twins.   Investigators have compared the concordance rates for criminal behavior in monozygotic (MZ) and dizygotic (DZ) twins. The results of 10 such comparisons are summarized in Table 15.3. The results of every one of the studies in the table indicated that the concordance rate for criminality is higher among MZ twins than among DZ twins. If criminality is a reflection of the APD, then these studies suggest that the disorder is due at least in part to genetic factors.

Additional analyses conducted in one of the studies of twins revealed that the difference in concordance rates between MZ and DZ twins was greater in rural areas than in urban areas (Christiansen, 1968). That finding suggests that in rural areas, where there may be fewer social reasons for crime (e.g., fewer adolescent gangs, members of the communities are better known to one another), genetic factors play a greater role in determining who will commit a crime than they do in urban areas, where there may be more social reasons for crime. In other words, both social and genetic factors may contribute to crime, and where the social factors are minimized, the genetic factors may be more apparent. These findings offer additional evidence for the genetic basis for the APD.

Studies of Adoptees.   In two investigations, the researchers first identified groups of antisocial and nonantisocial individuals who had been adopted at birth and raised by adoptive parents. (The individuals in the two groups were similar on relevant demographic variables such as sex, age, social class, and neighborhood of rearing.) Then the researchers assessed the rates of antisocial behavior in both the biological and adoptive parents of the antisocial and nonantisocial adoptees. The results of both investigations indicated that the biological parents of antisocial individuals had higher rates of antisocial behavior than their adoptive parents, thus providing evidence for the hypothesis that there is a genetic factor in the development of antisocial behavior. These results are summarized in Table 15.4.

In two other investigations, the researchers identi-

TABLE 15.4   BIOLOGICAL PARENTS OF ANTISOCIAL OR CRIMINAL
INDIVIDUALS HAD HIGHER RATES OF ANTISOCIAL
BEHAVIOR THAN ADOPTIVE PARENTS

	BIOLOGICAL FATHERS (%)	ADOPTIVE FATHERS (%)
Schulsinger (1972)		
Psychopathic adoptees	9.3	1.9
Control adoptees	1.8	.0
Hutchings and Mednick (1974)		
Criminal adoptees	48.9	23.0
Control adoptees	27.9	9.7

Source: Adapted from Mednick and Hutchings (1978).

TABLE 15.5   ADOPTED CHILDREN WHO HAD ANTISOCIAL BIOLOGICAL
PARENTS WERE MORE LIKELY TO HAVE AN ANTISOCIAL
PERSONALITY DISORDER THAN ADOPTED CHILDREN
WHO DID NOT HAVE ANTISOCIAL BIOLOGICAL PARENTS

	ANTISOCIAL PERSONALITY (%)
Crowe (1974)	
Criminal mothers	13
Noncriminal mothers	0
Cadoret (1978b)	
Antisocial parent(s)	17
Nonantisocial parents	0

fied parents who were or were not antisocial and then determined the rates of antisocial behavior in their children who had been adopted away at birth. The results of those studies indicated that adopted children whose biological parents were antisocial were more likely to be diagnosed as having an antisocial personality disorder than adopted children whose biological parents were not antisocial. Those results are summarized in Table 15.5.

Taken together, the results of the studies of twins and the studies of adoptees provide strong evidence that genetic factors play a role in the development of antisocial behavior. However, it is essential to recognize that these results do not demonstrate that heredity accounts for all or even the majority of cases of antisocial behavior. For example, the concordance rate among monozygotic twins was not 100%.

XYY Syndrome.   Before concluding our discussion of the role of heredity in the APD, some comments should be made concerning what has become known as the **XYY syndrome**. Human beings generally have 46 chromosomes, and two of those chromosomes determine an individual's sex; women have two X chromosomes, whereas men have one X and one Y chromosome. In the mid-1960s, reports began to appear indicating that some men had an *extra Y chromosome* and that those men were more likely than other men to have committed violent crimes (Jacobs et al.,

1965). The studies that generated those findings suffered from a variety of methodological problems, but they sparked great interest because it appeared that a specific genetic basis for crime and violence had been found. Those speculations gained credibility and wide public attention when it was discovered that Richard Speck, a man who killed eight nurses one night in Chicago, had an extra Y chromosome.

Because of the potential importance of the XYY syndrome, an extensive investigation was conducted of the chromosome structure of virtually all of the tall men who were born in Copenhagen, Denmark, during the years 1944–1947 (Witkin et al., 1976). (Attention was focused on tall men because it was not practical to contact all men, and tall men are more likely to have the XYY structure.) Three types of men were identified: (a) those with the normal XY structure, (b) those with the XYY (extra male) structure, and (c) those with the XXY (extra female) structure. Government and military records were then used to obtain information concerning the criminal convictions and intelligence of the men. Table 15.6 contains a summary of the characteristics of these men.

The results of this investigation yielded three noteworthy findings. First, men with the XYY chromosome structure were indeed more likely to be convicted of crimes than men with the normal XY chromosome structure. However, men with the XXY chromosome structure also tended to be convicted of

TABLE 15.6   MEN WITH THE XYY CHROMOSOME STRUCTURE WERE CONVICTED OF MORE CRIMES BUT
WERE LESS INTELLIGENT AND HAD LESS EDUCATION THAN MEN WITH THE XY STRUCTURE

GROUP	CRIMINALITY (%)	INTELLIGENCE SCORE	EDUCATION INDEX
XY (4,083)	9.3	43.7	1.55
XYY (12)	41.7	29.7	.58
XXY (16)	18.8	28.4	.81

Notes. Numbers in parentheses indicate number of subjects in each group. "Intelligence Score" refers to a score on a standard military test and not IQ. "Education Index" scores reflect how many of the examinations subjects passed that were given in the 9th, 10th, and 13th years of school.
Source: Adapted from Witkin et al. (1976).

Speculations that men with an extra Y chromosome are more likely to commit violent crimes (the XYY Syndrome) came to public attention in the 1960s. Such speculations gained credibility when Richard Speck, a man who killed eight nurses one night in Chicago, was found to have an extra Y chromosome. However, subsequent scientific investigations have shown that men with this chromosome structure do not commit more violent crimes than men with other chromosome structures, and that the presence of an extra Y chromosome cannot be used to account for criminal behavior or the antisocial personality disorder.

more crimes, thus indicating that it is not the presence of an extra Y chromosome per se that is related to criminal convictions. Furthermore, when the nature of the crimes was examined, it was found that the men with the XYY chromosome structure did not commit more violent crimes than those committed by the men with the other chromosome structures.

Second, the men with the XYY and XXY chromosome structures had lower intelligence scores and lower levels of educational achievement than the men with the normal XY chromosome structure. This is important because it suggests that the higher levels of criminal convictions among men with the abnormal chromosome structures may not be due to "inherited criminality," as was originally suggested, but rather to lower levels of intelligence. Actually, men with the XYY chromosome structure may not commit more crimes than other men, but being less bright, they may just get caught more frequently.

Finally, it is worth noting that the XYY chromosome structure is very rare. Even in the high-risk population that was studied (tall men), the XYY structure was found in less than .3% of the men, thus suggesting that regardless of the underlying mechanism, it cannot account for much criminal behavior. Overall, then, it does not appear that the presence of an extra Y chro-

mosome can be used to account for criminal behavior or the APD.

Comment

It is important to recognize that no one explanation or set of evidence can account for all cases of the APD. That suggests that there are probably different forms of the disorder and that there may be more than one correct explanation for it.

Although a variety of very different explanations for the APD have been offered, the explanations do not necessarily conflict. Some may actually work together, or different explanations may account for different types of the disorder. For example, the deficit in classical conditioning may be due to cortical underarousal (i.e., low arousal may inhibit conditioning), and the underarousal may be due in turn to genetic factors. That group of explanations may account for the primary type of the disorder in which individuals do not have the ability to develop anxiety. Learning to avoid anxiety with operant responses may account for the secondary type of the disorder. Poor parenting may be associated with the APD because (a) the parents provide models that the children imitate, (b) the stressful childhood provides opportunities to learn to avoid anxiety, or (c) bad parenting is a symptom of the parents' APD, which is transmitted genetically to their children.

▮ TREATMENT

Because persons with the APD do not have any of the traditional symptoms of abnormal behavior (e.g., anxiety, depression, delusions, hallucinations), they are often not diagnosed as having a psychological problem and are therefore not brought in for treatment. Furthermore, because their behavior is often illegal, they are more likely to be punished than treated. Even when an individual is recognized as suffering from the APD, treatment is often not attempted because it is widely assumed that these people are difficult or impossible to treat. The notion is that at best you have to wait for the disorder to burn out. However, because of the serious problems these people create, it is essential that we examine the limited research that has been conducted on their treatment.

Psychodynamic Approach

The dominant psychodynamic explanation for the APD is that persons with the disorder have not had loving and behaviorally appropriate parental figures with whom they could identify and from whom they could learn appropriate behaviors. Therefore, most psychodynamically oriented therapists attempt to serve as supportive, strong, and behaviorally appropriate parental figures for their clients with the APD. The therapists provide support, affection, and understanding, but they also provide firm and consistent guidance. The goal is to help the client identify with the therapist and in so doing enable the client to take on the appropriate and mature characteristics of the therapist. In treatment, then, psychodynamically oriented therapists usually focus on developing *maturation through identification* rather than on solving problems through insights as they do with most other types of patients.

Because the verbal reports of clients are usually used to judge the effectiveness of psychotherapy and because clients with the APD are exceptionally adept at telling others what they want to hear, these clients often manifest what appear to be rapid improvements in psychotherapy. Unfortunately, these "improvements" are frequently followed by "relapses," and if the clients' *behaviors* rather than their *reports* are used as the measure of the effects of psychotherapy, there is no evidence that psychodynamic psychotherapy is of much utility in changing the behavior. Indeed, the reviews of the research on the effectiveness of psychotherapy for treating these individuals have consistently yielded negative conclusions, and there seems to be little reason for optimism (McCord & McCord, 1964; Suedfeld & Landon, 1978). Because persons with the APD have a poor history of response to treatment, many psychotherapists are reluctant to accept them for treatment.

Learning Approach

The major learning theory explanation for the APD is that persons with the disorder have a deficit in the ability to develop classically conditioned anxiety responses, and thus they do not learn to avoid inappropriate behaviors. Therefore, therapeutic interventions based on classical conditioning would be fruitless. However, it might be possible to use operant conditioning to develop appropriate responses. The problem with this approach is that persons with the APD are already able to get the rewards they desire through their inappropriate behaviors, and consequently there is little that the therapist can hold out as a reward or an incentive for appropriate behavior. As might be expected from the foregoing comments, very few reports have been published concerning the use of conditioning techniques for treating persons with the APD, and those that have appeared have not provided evidence for the utility of this approach (Hare, 1970; MacCulloch & Feldman, 1966; Vietor, 1967).

Physiological Approach

The physiological explanation for the APD suggests that it stems from cortical underarousal, and therefore persons with the disorder do not condition well and often engage in inappropriate behaviors to increase their levels of arousal. Based on that explanation, we might expect that clients could be treated with cortical stimulants that would increase susceptibility to conditioning and reduce the need for stimulation.

Some evidence supporting the positive effect of stimulants was presented earlier when we discussed how the administration of epinephrine facilitated the avoidance conditioning of persons with the APD so that they were able to perform like normals (Schachter & Latané, 1964). In addition, other evidence indicates that the administration of stimulants (e.g., amphetamines) is effective for reducing the general behavioral symptoms of the APD (Satterfield & Cantwell, 1975; Suedfeld & Landon, 1978). Unfortunately, the effects of stimulants are short-lived, and it is not feasible to keep individuals on stimulants for long periods of time. Overall, then, the results of the research concerning the effectiveness of drugs for treating the APD are encouraging and suggestive, but at present, the findings are limited in number and nature. In view of these qualifications, we cannot conclude that the APD can be treated or controlled with drugs.

Prognosis

It should be clear that we are not yet able to control or treat the APD. That conclusion, in combination with the fact that persons with the disorder do a great deal of harm, has led some frustrated and exasperated observers to suggest, only partly in jest, that all persons with the APD should be banished to a desert island. However, despite our apparent inability to treat the disorder, the prognostic picture is not completely gloomy, and persons with the disorder may not require as drastic a response as banishment.

The ray of hope in the otherwise gloomy prognosis is provided by the evidence indicating that many persons with the disorder "burn out" or "settle down" as they enter their late 30s or early 40s (Craft, 1969; Gibbens et al., 1955; Maddocks, 1970; Robins, 1966; Weiss, 1973). For example, one investigator found that of 94 persons with the disorder who were followed from childhood, 34% remitted their symptoms by the age of 40 (Robins, 1966). Similar findings have been reported by other investigators (Craft, 1969; Tong & McKay, 1959).

In one interesting study related to APD burnout, 521 prisoners who did or did not have the disorder were studied over a period of years to determine changes in their criminal behavior (Hare et al., 1988). Figure 15.4 presents the data concerning the percentage of men who were in prison during various 5-year age segments between the ages of 16 and 45. The men with the APD are most likely to be in prison during their 30s, but their rate of imprisonment drops to the level of the non-APD men by age 45. Although these findings are encouraging, it is important to note that the remission of symptoms does not occur with all persons and that even those who do remit their symptoms can cause considerable personal and legal havoc before burning out.

FIGURE 15.4   MEN WITH THE ANTISOCIAL PERSONALITY DISORDER (APD) ARE MOST LIKELY TO SPEND TIME IN PRISON DURING THEIR 30s, BUT APPARENTLY BECAUSE THE DISORDER "BURNS OUT," DURING THEIR 40s THEIR RATE RETURNS TO THAT OF MEN WHO DO NOT HAVE THE APD.

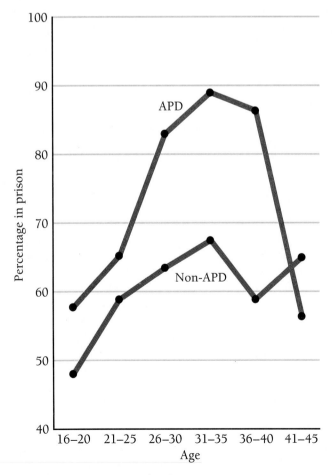

Source: Hare et al. (1988), p. 713, fig. 2.

• Other Personality Disorders

The remaining personality disorders can be organized into two groups. The first group contains the less serious disorders that involve the exaggeration of normal personality traits such as dependence, passivity, and narcissism. We will refer to the disorders in this group as **trait disorders**. The second group contains disorders that are more serious and involve symptoms like some of those found in paranoia and schizophrenia. Because these disorders fall in the gray area bordering on other serious disorders, we will refer to them as **marginal disorders**. For some of these disorders, the discussion will be limited to descriptions of the symptom patterns. That is because relatively little is known about the causes of those disorders or they are "mild forms" of disorders that we have discussed elsewhere.

▉ TRAIT DISORDERS

Traits are generally thought of as enduring ways in which individuals respond to other individuals and situations. For example, an individual with the trait of hostility will generally respond to others in antagonistic, belligerent, or contrary ways, and an individual with the trait of compulsivity will be orderly, methodical, and lacking in spontaneity. Traits lead to personality disorders when they interfere with personal functioning or cause distress. For example, an individual with a lot of hostility may drive others away and therefore become lonely and depressed. A person who is very compulsive may spend so much time planning that he or she never gets anything done. It is interesting to note that in many cases, the individual does not object to having the trait but does object to the effects of the trait. A friend of mine with the obsessive-compulsive personality disorder states adamantly that "there is nothing wrong with being highly organized" but later says, "I get anxious and depressed because I am always planning but never get anything done!" He does not seem to mind the trait, but he does not like its effects on his life.

Obsessive-Compulsive Personality Disorder

Individuals with the **obsessive-compulsive personality disorder** have high needs for perfection, order, and control, and their lives become dominated by getting organized and prepared. Problems arise because they get so bogged down with organization and details that they do not get started on the projects they plan. Also, their overattention to details prevents them from seeing the "big picture," so they may spend too much time on meaningless or relatively unimportant aspects of a problem they must solve. A student with the obsessive-compulsive personality disorder who has to write a paper may spend endless hours collecting material, organizing it into neat piles, and worrying about tiny problems for footnotes but may never clearly define the goal of the paper or never actually get around to writing it. The student spends all the available time preparing and never actually produces anything.

Persons with the obsessive-compulsive personality disorder do not have meaningful interpersonal relations because they are so tied up getting their work organized that they do not take time for friendships. Furthermore, because of their need for control, they often insist that others do things *their* way rather than allowing for the give-and-take that is necessary in a friendship. Also, their need for control makes these individuals personally stilted, stiff, and unable to feel or to express emotions that are necessary for warm, close relationships. In short, rather than "going with the flow" and being spontaneous in their interpersonal relations, these individuals live behind a dam where everything is controlled and emotionally flat.

Finally, persons with the obsessive-compulsive personality disorder are not particularly happy; they do not take time for pleasure or relaxation, and they are constantly worrying about missing some detail and failing.

A person with the obsessive-compulsive personality disorder has high needs for perfection, order, and control. Felix Unger, the fastidious member of The Odd Couple, *could have been diagnosed as suffering from a minor form of this disorder.*

The obsessive-compulsive personality disorder differs from the obsessive-compulsive anxiety disorder in that the major symptom in the personality disorder is a need for perfection and order, whereas the major symptom in the anxiety disorder is recurrent thoughts or actions. There is some overlap in the disorders in that the person with the personality disorder may persistently think or worry about being organized, but the persistent thoughts are focused on organization (rather than on violence, for example), and the personality disorder is less disruptive of normal living.

Avoidant Personality Disorder

Individuals with an **avoidant personality disorder** are exceptionally sensitive to potential social rejection and the humiliation that goes with it. Because of their concerns about rejection, these individuals avoid relationships unless they are guaranteed uncritical acceptance. They want affection, closeness, and acceptance, but they avoid the relationships that might satisfy those needs because of their stronger need to defend against rejection. In other words, avoidance is a defense; if they do not attempt to make friends, they cannot be rejected.

One young man with the avoidant personality disorder wanted desperately to have close friends with whom he could share experiences, but he was so afraid of rejection (it would prove him inadequate) that he never attempted to establish friendships. Instead, he focused his efforts on "achieving," with the hope that others would accept him because of his competence, but acceptance based on his achievements and competence did not satisfy his need for friendship. This very competent young man lived an isolated and unfulfilled existence.

Because individuals with the avoidant disorder cannot satisfy their need for closeness and constantly feel as though they will be rejected, they tend to have a low self-concept and to suffer from anxiety and depression. In addition to causing personal unhappiness, their avoidance of relationships can interfere with their occupational functioning. Due to their avoidance of social situations, in extreme cases this disorder blends into the social phobia discussed in Chapter 4. Overall, the behavior of the individual with an avoidance personality disorder is designed to reduce anxiety about rejection. The person simply concludes, "If I don't get close, I can't get rejected or hurt."

Dependent Personality Disorder

Individuals with the **dependent personality disorder** passively allow others to make major decisions for them. They are often easy to get along with because they will not do anything to jeopardize their relationships with the persons on whom they rely for major decisions. The inability of these individuals to make decisions can result in anxiety and depression and can interfere with their ability to get anything done if they are placed in roles involving responsibility or leadership. They may feel uncomfortable or helpless when alone, and they will go to great lengths to keep others around them.

One middle-level business manager with the dependent personality disorder got along well in the company because he always went along with the group. When votes were taken in meetings, he always looked both ways to see which direction the vote was going before casting his vote. He went along but did not advance in the company because he never contributed leadership or unique ideas. He was frustrated and depressed about his position, but too afraid to do anything about it. His disorder probably stemmed from a time when as a new person in the company, he offered a new idea and, from his perspective, got "stepped on."

This disorder is more frequently seen in women, but that may be due to the fact that the stereotype of women traditionally involves dependence. The cause of this disorder is not clear, but it probably stems from a lack of self-confidence. Overly dependent individuals seem to be saying to themselves, "I am probably going to be wrong, so if I do not initiate anything, I cannot be blamed or criticized."

Histrionic Personality Disorder

There are three notable characteristics of individuals with the **histrionic** (HIS-trē-ON-ik) **personality disorder**. First, such people are usually attractive, charming, appealing, and sexually seductive. However, although they try to charm and seduce everyone, if things start to get serious, they back off quickly. Freud speculated that the immature and inconsistent behavior of histrionic individuals resulted from their interest in but fear of sex. Like the moth and the flame, these individuals flutter around sex, but when things get hot, they back off.

Second, histrionic individuals like to be the center of attention and often act in overly dramatic and emotional ways to attract attention (crying, weeping, threatening to commit suicide). In the excitement and tragedies they generate, they always play the starring role, and others are relegated to supporting roles.

Third, despite their great shows of affect, histrionic individuals are emotionally very shallow, and their emotions may shift quickly from person to person or from positive to negative. Because of their emotional shallowness and lack of sincere consideration for oth-ers, their relationships tend to be stormy and short-lived.

Overall, then, these individuals are outgoing (especially with potential sexual partners), but their behavior is designed to gain them attention and assurance, and they can become extremely demanding, egocentric, dependent, vain, inconsiderate, and manipulative when things do not go their way. An individual with a histrionic personality disorder can be a lot of fun (especially to flirt with) at a party, but the relationship is best ended at the end of the party. At present, we do not have any firm evidence concerning the cause and treatment of the histrionic personality disorder, but fortunately, it is not a particularly serious disorder.

Narcissistic Personality Disorder

The archetype for the **narcissistic** (NAR-si-SIS-tik) **personality disorder** is Narcissus, the character in Greek

According to Greek mythology, Narcissus fell in love with his own reflection in a pond. Persons with the narcissistic personality disorder have a grandiose sense of their own importance, and are preoccupied with fantasies about their ultimate success, power, brilliance, or beauty.

mythology who fell in love with his reflection in a pond. Individuals with a narcissistic personality disorder have a grandiose sense of their own importance, and they are preoccupied with fantasies about their ultimate success, power, brilliance, or beauty. Because they think they are "special," they demand constant attention and admiration from everyone around them. These individuals see themselves as entitled to favors from others because of their importance, and consequently they take advantage of the people around them. If criticized rather than praised, they may respond with cool indifference, or their overblown egos may collapse like a punctured balloon. Also, because they are so self-centered, they have difficulty maintaining relationships. Legend has it that because Narcissus was so absorbed in himself, he spurned the love of Echo, who then went off to die alone in a cave. There may be a moral in that story for individuals who deal with persons who have the narcissistic personality disorder.

MARGINAL DISORDERS

The symptoms of the four personality disorders in this group overlap somewhat with the symptoms of the more serious disorders of paranoia, schizophrenia, and the mood disorders. In considering these personality disorders, then, we must note how they are similar to the other disorders but also how they are different. It is tempting to assume that these personality disorders are simply early stages or milder forms of the more serious disorders, but at present they are considered as distinct and separate disorders. Hence, it should not be assumed that individuals with these disorders will subsequently develop the more serious disorders.

Paranoid Personality Disorder

The dominant feature of the **paranoid personality disorder** is an *unwarranted suspiciousness* and *mistrust of people* that persists even in the face of strong evidence that there is no justification for the concerns. Because these individuals perceive threats as coming from everyone around them, they tend to be anxious, distant, humorless, and argumentative, and they often "make mountains out of molehills" when dealing with problems. Their lack of trust in others and their "protective" behaviors undermine their interpersonal relationships and may interfere with their job performance. However, these individuals often work very hard (they think they must to "keep ahead" of others), and if they are in a situation in which they can work

independently, they may do very well. This disorder is diagnosed more commonly in men, and it is not yet clear what causes it. The paranoid personality disorder differs from the delusional (previously called paranoid) disorder in that individuals with the delusional disorder have clearly formed delusions (see Chapter 12), whereas those with the paranoid personality disorder have only vague suspicions and mistrust.

Schizoid Personality Disorder

The primary symptom of individuals with the **schizoid** (SKIT-zoyd) **personality disorder** is a *lack of interest in other people or social relationships.* Not only do they not reach out to others, but they also rarely respond to others. For example, they are indifferent to the praise or criticism of others, and they rarely make reciprocal gestures such as smiling or nodding. Persons with the schizoid disorder are loners—physically, intellectually, and emotionally.

Individuals with the schizoid disorder also show very little emotion and hence appear aloof, humorless, cold, and emotionally flat. Although they show the social isolation and flat affect that are characteristic of schizophrenia, they do not show any evidence of a thought disorder (no hallucinations, delusions, or language problems), and therefore they cannot be considered to be suffering from schizophrenia.

Schizotypal Personality Disorder

The individual with the **schizotypal** (SKIT-zō-TĪ-pul) **personality disorder** has many more of the characteristics of schizophrenia than the person with the schizoid disorder, but the symptoms are not severe enough to justify the diagnosis of schizophrenia. These persons may have bizarre beliefs (e.g., they may think that they are clairvoyant or have mental telepathy), be socially inept and isolated, or engage in eccentric or peculiar behaviors (e.g., they may talk to themselves or have strange rituals and motor behaviors), and they may not pay any attention to their appearance. However, despite their symptoms, they stay just barely on the normal side of the fine line that separates normals from schizophrenia. For example, they may say, "I feel *as if* my dead mother were in the room with me," which is subtly different from saying, "My dead mother *is* in the room with me." In other words, the person with the schizotypal disorder has *illusions*, whereas the person with schizophrenia has *delusions*. Similarly, schizotypally disordered individuals also have odd speech patterns in that they are digressive and vague, but they do not suffer from the serious distortions ("word salads") seen in schizophrenia. The schizotypal personality disorder may be a mild form of schizophrenia.

Borderline Personality Disorder

The last major personality disorder we will discuss is the **borderline personality disorder**. Interest in this disorder is high, but the disorder is complex and not yet well understood. Originally, the term *borderline* was used to refer to individuals whose adjustment was on the borderline between normal and psychotic. For example, we would refer to individuals as having "borderline schizophrenia" if they were disturbed but not enough to be classified as suffering from schizophrenia. However, now the term *borderline* is used to refer to a specific personality disorder that is characterized primarily by *instability*. Unlike an individual with a mood disorder or schizophrenia who has one set of relatively stable symptoms, the individual with the borderline personality disorder shows *different symptoms at different times*. For the most part, the symptoms revolve around problems of mood, mild disturbances in thought processes, and impulsive self-injurious behavior. Together, those symptoms disrupt the individuals' interpersonal relationships. Although individuals with the borderline disorder show some of the symptoms seen in mood or schizophrenic disorders, their symptoms are usually not as severe as those shown by persons with full-blown mood or schizophrenic disorders. Overall then, persons with the borderline disorder seem to stand on the borderline between various disorders and move in and out of the fringes of the disorders.

Individuals with the borderline personality disorder usually show symptoms in four areas, as shown in Figure 15.5 (Zanarini, Gunderson, Frankenburg, & Chauncey, 1990). First, they show unstable *mood*. For example, they will plummet into *depression*, only to come out of it after a while. They usually do not go through manic phases as in the bipolar disorder, but instead they vacillate between normal or flat mood to moderate or severe depression. These individuals also go through periods of intense anger that can interfere with effective social functioning.

Second, individuals with the borderline personality disorder have intermittent periods during which they experience *thought disturbances*, but the disturbances are not as extreme as those seen in schizophrenia (Zanarini, Gunderson, & Frankenburg, 1990). That is, rather than suffering from full-blown hallucinations, individuals with the borderline personality disorder show "unusual perceptions" that include illusions and depersonalization. For example, one woman told me that sometimes she felt as though she could see through people and that other times she felt as

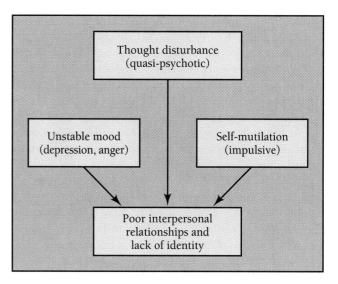

FIGURE 15.5   THERE ARE FOUR MAJOR SYMPTOM AREAS IN THE BORDERLINE PERSONALITY DISORDER.

though she were dead. Similarly, rather than having clear-cut delusions, persons with the borderline disorder reflect "odd" thinking that includes superstitiousness and magical beliefs. For example, a student reported that sometimes he felt like he could control events by thinking about them. Important phrases here are "as though" and "like"; the individuals did not completely believe that they were really dead or could control events, but they were approaching those conclusions. These thought disturbances are more like those seen in the schizotypal personality disorder than those in schizophrenia. Because these disturbances are not as extreme as those seen in schizophrenia, they are sometimes called **quasi-psychotic thought disturbances**.

The third notable symptom in the borderline disorder is intermittent *self-mutilating* and *suicidal* behavior (Winchel & Stanley, 1991). The suicidal behavior appears to stem from the combination of their depression and impulsiveness. The self-mutilation often involves acts like burning themselves with cigarettes, carving up their bodies with razor blades, making deep scratches with fingernails, sandpapering their skin, and pouring acid on themselves. It is notable that this behavior is not designed to result in death. Rather, the self-mutilation is often done in an emotionally detached way, and the patients report that they self-mutilate in an attempt to feel or experience themselves as "real." Concerning her self-mutilation, one patient reported to me, "If I bleed, I know I'm alive. If I cut myself up, I may feel some *something*." In another case, a woman carved the word *slut* into her stomach after having sex with a man. She said she did it to make herself feel bad about what she had done.

The fourth symptom is associated with *interpersonal relationships.* Individuals with the borderline personality disorder tend to have very intense relationships that are very unstable, so they vacillate between love and hate. Persons with the disorder do not simply drift in and out of friendships, but instead show abrupt, frequent, and dramatic changes between intense love and equally intense hate in any one relationship. The disruption of their interpersonal relationships may be a by-product of the other symptoms. That is, the fluctuations in their mood (especially their anger), their thought disturbances (especially paranoid thoughts about betrayal abandonment by others), and their impulsiveness make it difficult to maintain relationships with others.

Some of the symptoms of the borderline disorder are seen in other personality disorders, but the symptoms are seen more frequently and are more likely to occur in combination with one another in the borderline disorder. The frequency of these behaviors in the borderline personality disorder and other personality disorders is illustrated in Figure 15.6.

The instability in mood, thoughts, behavior, and interpersonal relationships that is seen in the borderline personality disorder has led theorists to suggest that individuals with this disorder have a problem with *identity.* That is, the instability reflects the lack of any real sense of self or self-direction, and indeed, these individuals often report a sense of being "empty." One woman reported that she felt as though there was a big hole inside of her. The word *unstable* is usually used to describe individuals with the borderline personality disorder, but that word does not do justice to their lives. Indeed, their personal and interpersonal lives are better described as *intermittently chaotic.*

It is noteworthy that the borderline personality disorder is diagnosed more frequently in women than men, but it is not yet clear whether that is due to an actual difference in the incidence of the disorder in men and women or to a bias in the use of the diagnosis (Castaneda & Franco, 1985). There is evidence that homosexual activity occurs more in individuals with the borderline disorder than in other individuals (Zubenko et al., 1987). The homosexuality may be a reflection the individuals' lack of identity. That is, they may be trying other roles or orientations in an attempt to find an identity or interpersonal closeness. In that case, the homosexuality may be more a case of transient behavior than a firmly established orientation.

Many explanations have been offered for the borderline personality disorder, but there is still no consensus concerning the cause. A major question concerning cause is whether this is *one disorder* or a *combination of disorders* as the schizoaffective disorder is a combination of schizophrenia and a mood disor-

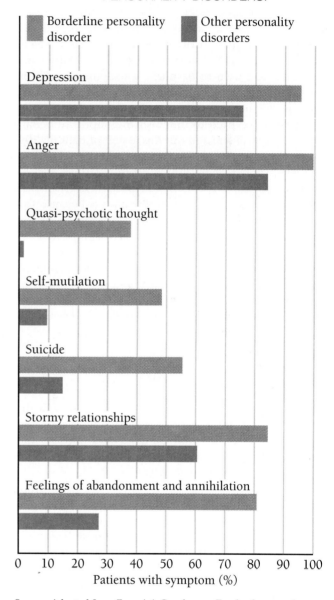

FIGURE 15.6 PROBLEMS WITH MOOD, COGNITIONS, SELF-MUTILATION, AND INTERPERSONAL RELATIONSHIPS ARE HIGHER IN INDIVIDUALS WITH THE BORDERLINE PERSONALITY DISORDER THAN IN INDIVIDUALS WITH OTHER PERSONALITY DISORDERS.

Source: Adapted from Zanarini, Gunderson, Frankenburg, and Chauncey (1990), p. 164, tab. 2.

der. One widely held explanation is that the borderline disorder may be a "low-grade" combination of schizophrenia (or the schizotypal disorder) and a mood disorder (primarily depression) that is further complicated by problems of impulse control.

The absence of a consensus concerning cause complicates the approach to treatment. Psychotherapy has been focused on a wide variety of problems (e.g., lack of adequate role models, sexual abuse), but from a practical standpoint, psychotherapy usually involves helping the individuals achieve a sense of self, find direction, and simply get through their tumultuous and chaotic lives. The therapy often involves support, counseling, and guidance to help the client get from day to day.

Drug therapy has been focused on the three suspected contributing disorders of schizophrenia, mood, and impulse control (Coccaro & Kavoussi, 1991; Teicher & Glod, 1989). Neuroleptic drugs such as Thorazine or Haldol are used to treat the schizophrenic component, antidepressants or lithium may be used to treat the unstable moods, and drugs that enhance serotonin activity may be used to diminish the impulsive behavior. (As you will learn in our discussion of conduct disorders in Chapter 16, impulsivity is often related to low levels of serotonin.) At the present time, the effects of the drug treatment can be best described as mixed, but it is not clear whether that is because the drugs are not particularly effective or because of the wide differences in patients with the diagnosis of borderline personality disorder. Unfortunately, we have a long way to go for an adequate description, understanding, and treatment of this important disorder. In Case Study 15.2, one of my students talks about her struggle with the borderline personality disorder.

Impulse Control Disorders

Before concluding our discussion of personality disorders, a comment should be made concerning a number of other disorders that are not technically personality disorders but are listed under the related heading of **impulse control disorders**. Under that heading, DSM-IV lists the **intermittent explosive disorder** (loss of control of aggressive impulses that cannot be better explained by other disorders), **kleptomania** (KLEP-tō-MĀN-ē-uh) (failure to resist the impulse to steal), **pyromania** (PĪ-rō-MĀN-ē-uh) (failure to resist the impulse to set fires), **pathological gambling** (uncontrolled gambling), and **trichotillomania** (TRIK-uh-TIL-uh-MĀN-ē-uh) (failure to resist the impulse to pull out one's own hair). These can be serious disorders, and you should be aware of them, but because they are relatively rare or relatively little is known about them, we will not discuss them here.

▪ SUMMARY

- -

Individuals with the antisocial personality disorder are often referred to as *psychopaths* or *sociopaths*. These individuals are characterized by (a) a general lack of anxiety, (b) hedonism, (c) shallow emotional attachments to other individuals, (d) well-developed social and verbal skills that they use to make their inappropriate behaviors appear reasonable and justifiable, (e) inability to benefit from punishment, (f) impulsivity, (g) sensation seeking, and in some cases, (h) senseless acts of extreme aggression. These individuals do not show any of the traditional signs of abnormal behavior. The antisocial personality disorder has its onset in early adulthood, and it appears to "burn out" around midlife.

Psychoanalytic theorists suggest that persons with the APD have not had the opportunity to develop an adequate superego or that they are fixated at an early stage of psychosexual development because they were exposed to bad parenting. There is evidence that the childhoods of these persons are often characterized by lack of love, rejection, abuse, and inconsistencies in parental responses.

Learning theorists suggest that the APD stems from a deficit in the ability to learn anxiety through classical conditioning, and there is evidence supporting that position. It has also been suggested that some persons with the APD may be able to develop anxiety, but they learn operant responses that permit them to avoid it. That theory has not been tested.

From a physiological standpoint, it is assumed that the lack of anxiety in persons with the APD is due to cortical underarousal. Support for that explanation is provided by research indicating that many persons with the APD show EEG abnormalities (slow waves) that reflect cortical underarousal and that by increasing and decreasing cortical arousal, we can decrease and increase the symptoms of the APD. There is also evidence that the concordance rate for the APD is higher among monozygotic than among dizygotic twins and that persons with the APD are more likely to have biological relatives with the disorder. Those findings suggest that the disorder is due in part to genetic factors.

The other personality disorders were grouped into two types, trait disorders and marginal disorders. The trait personality disorders include the following: (a) the obsessive-compulsive personality disorder, which involves high needs for order, perfection, and control; (b) the avoidant personality disorder, in which the individual is highly sensitive to social rejection and therefore avoids interpersonal relations in an attempt to avoid rejection; (c) the dependent personality disorder, in which the person allows others to make decisions and thereby avoids responsibility and blame; (d) the histrionic personality disorder, in which the person is seductive, works to be the center

Case Study 15.2

A STUDENT WRITES ABOUT THE SYMPTOMS OF HER BORDERLINE PERSONALITY DISORDER

Linda is a tall, attractive, and bright young woman. When she was a senior in high school, she received a scholarship to a six-year combined college-dental school program that would begin immediately after graduation. However, Linda did not graduate with her classmates. As they marched across the stage, she was confined to a mental hospital with a serious borderline personality disorder. For the next three years, Linda was in and out of a number of hospitals. She was finally able to enter college, and with support and treatment she was able to graduate. Her symptoms are better but certainly not gone. Here she writes about some of her symptoms.

CONCERNING HER FEELINGS AND SELF-MUTILATION

It is very hard for me to explain how I feel and how I felt. Feelings really overwhelm me. There are times when I felt like I would explode or burst because of the feelings. It was like my skin would crawl and I felt trapped. I felt like screaming or doing something to release the feelings. I usually chose to burn or cut myself. That was a release for me. When I saw the blood coming out, it was like seeing the hurt drip away. Other times when I would hurt myself it was because of the hatred I felt for myself.

From the very first time I hurt myself I loved the feeling. I don't think there are words to explain how it feels. There is so much involved. I felt very "out of control" with everything in my life, and the cutting and burning gave me a sense of control. The act of mutilating yourself is a very powerful thing. More than control, it gives you a sense of *being*. You *see* the blood or the burnt flesh and you know *you are real*.

I remember burning myself one time when I was feeling rejected and very alone. I felt a very intense and overwhelming pain inside, in my gut. The pain was emotional, not physical. I got in my car and just drove. I had tears in my eyes because I hurt so badly. I felt very spaced. That was always how I felt when I hurt myself. I was numb to the point of feeling outside of my body. It is like when you are dreaming. You can see yourself from the outside and all that is going on from that view. I felt very light, as if I were weightless. I drove to a parking lot. I did not go there with the intention of hurting myself, it just happened. I had a cigarette lighter in my car. I lit it and let the flame touch my flesh. I

burned a section of my arm that was about 2 inches by 3 inches. The skin blistered and burned. It gave me a warm feeling all over. It didn't hurt, it felt good. I'm not sure what made me stop, but tears came to my eyes after it was all over. Not because it hurt, but because of the release. I felt better when I was done. All of the pain was gone. Maybe the physical mutilation let me focus my attention on the outside, instead of on the internal pain. Whenever I hurt myself I had a feeling of renewal. It was like starting fresh without all of the emotions.

The cutting was a lot like the burning, but it seems like I cut myself when I was angry, especially at myself. When I cut myself deeply, I wasn't trying to kill myself, I just wanted to bleed. One time when I cut myself, I dripped the blood all over two pieces of paper and saved it. The blood did something for me. It was a high to see the blood. Maybe it made me feel "real" or may it was just a release—a release of the pain.

The release I experienced with the cutting was similar to what I felt with my bulimia. I consider my eating behavior a part of my self-destructive behavior. There was a period of time that I was bingeing and purging five to six times a day. It engulfed my whole life—it *became my life*. The bingeing made me feel kind of high and I felt like I could start fresh. I never did start fresh. I just kept eating to fill the emptiness and purging to release the emotions. I couldn't stop.

ABOUT MOOD

I felt depressed most of the time. Sometimes I felt like I couldn't go on in life. It's not that there was something so *wrong* with my life, but there was something *missing*. I still feel like that. It is like there is a huge hole inside of me. Sometimes when I am alone I can feel it—the emptiness inside of me. There's nothing there. I have tried many things to fill that void—food, alcohol, drugs, sex, relationships—but none of those things make it go away. *I want so badly to feel whole but I just don't.* I have wanted to kill myself because I don't think I will ever feel whole. More than really wanting to die, I just wanted to be in a coma-like state for a while and then wake up and have everything be better, like I was only having a bad nightmare. I really struggle with finding a meaning in my life—and finding me!

CONCERNING HER PARANOIA AND INTERPERSONAL RELATIONSHIPS

I felt like the whole world was against me. I thought people wanted to hurt me. I knew that everyone talked about me and hated me. I knew if "they" would just leave me alone I would be okay. I felt like people were hurting me on purpose. I thought if they only knew how much I already hurt inside, they would be sorry for pushing me to hurt more. I grew to hate everyone because of this. It was like a double-edged sword. I felt like no one loved or cared about me, but when they would try to get close, I would push them far away. It was a never-ending circle.

I have not been able to have any really stable relationships. Most of the men I have gotten involved with are "safe" in some way. They are really unavailable before I even get involved. I always have an out with these kinds of people. My last relationship was with a drug addict. As long as he had problems, I always had a good excuse to get out. When he was clean for eight months, I got out of the relationship. My biggest fear is rejection, so I do it first.

One time I jumped into a relationship with a man from out of state. I thought that we would just date for the summer and then he would go home. Well, he did go home but I went to visit him one weekend. The very next Friday I dropped out of college and moved into an apartment with him. I had always thought, "If I could only get to another place my life will be better." It was another desperate attempt to fill the emptiness. Well, it was a disaster and two months later I moved back but he came with me. Driving back in the U-Haul, I was so desperate that I drove straight through a dangerous ice-storm. I hated him so much at that point that I wanted to have a bad wreck and have him die. I had my seatbelt on so I felt relatively safe. I just wanted so badly for him to die. For 2½ years after that I went through loving him and wanting to marry him one day to hoping he would just overdose and die the next day. I loved him and I hated him.

I don't understand why I am like this; I wish I did. I think a part of it is that I don't have a grasp of who I am and what I want in life, so I am always chang-

ing my mind. One day a man is the love of my life and I want to marry him, and the next day I hate him. It is a lot like how I feel about *myself*.

HER SUMMARY

The best way to describe how I feel is to share something I wrote a few years ago when I was struggling the most:

> The way that I feel inside is so strange. I can't believe after all the tears I've cried I still feel the same. I want pain on the outside, I want to hurt myself, but I don't want pain on the inside. What will I gain? I don't know.

> Emptiness. That's what I feel. Yet there's so much inside. There's so much hurt. The hurt is what I want gone. I cut myself and let it out, I burn myself.

> I always run from the pain. I run and run. I never know what it is, I just run. Right now I want to run, far away where no one will find me, to a place where I will be safe.

> I don't like this feeling. I want it to end. I want to cut myself, what of me. It's like all of a sudden someone invaded my body. I'm different now than I was.

> I don't want to tell anyone because when I change back they will still watch me and I can't take that. I can't tell anyone how I feel. I am trapped here. There's no way to win, not even suicide. I'm stuck here to hurt and to feel all of this pain and all of this agony.

HER TREATMENT

Linda has taken Prozac (a bicyclic) for her depression, Haldol (a high-potency neuroleptic) for her psychotic-like symptoms, Tegretal (an anticonvulsant) that can be helpful for controlling her mood swings, and Ativan (a benzodiazepine) for her anxiety. With the medication and intensive psychotherapy and counseling, Linda was able to do well in college and graduate. She has come a long way, but as her comments indicate, she still has a way to go.

---

of attention, and is emotionally very shallow; and (e) the narcissistic personality disorder, which is characterized by self-centeredness and an exaggerated sense of self-worth.

The marginal personality disorders include the following: (a) the paranoid personality disorder,

which revolves around unwarranted suspiciousness and mistrust of others but does not involve clearly formed delusions; (b) the schizoid personality disorder, in which the individual shows a lack of social interest and very little emotion but no thought disorder; (c) the schizotypal personality disorder, in which the symptoms are similar to but not as severe as those seen in schizophrenia (e.g., persons have illusions but not delusions); and (d) the borderline personality disorder, in which the person shows a high degree of insta- bility in symptoms involving mood, thought disorder, and impulsivity in self-injurious behavior, all of which are associated with disruptions in interpersonal rela- tionships and a lack of personal identity.

KEY TERMS, CONCEPTS, AND NAMES

In reviewing and testing yourself on what you have learned from this chapter, you should be able to identify and discuss each of the following:

antisocial personality disorder
avoidance conditioning
avoidant personality disorder
borderline personality disorder
cortical underarousal
deficit in classical conditioning
delayed cortical development
dependent personality disorder
EEG abnormalities
electrocortical arousal
histrionic personality disorder
impulse control disorders
intermittent explosive disorder

kleptomania
malfunction of the limbic system
marginal disorders
moral insanity
narcissistic personality disorder
obsessive-compulsive personality
    disorder
operantly conditioned avoidance of
    anxiety
paranoid personality disorder
pathological gambling
personality disorders
positive spiking

primary type of the APD
psychopath
pyromania
quasi-psychotic thought disturbance
schizoid personality disorder
schizotypal personality disorder
secondary type of the APD
slow-wave activity
sociopath
trait disorders
trichotillomania
XYY syndrome

Chapter 16

Disorders of Infancy, Childhood, and Adolescence

· O U T L I N E ·

Charlie is 6 years old and is absolutely out of control. He cannot keep his attention on anything for more than a few seconds, and he is constantly squirming, fidgeting, running around, or interrupting people. He does not listen to instructions or ignores them. Because of his wild activity, he sometimes hurts children around him. When he was younger, his parents thought he was just an "active child," but they now know that he suffers from the *attention-deficit hyperactivity disorder.* It has been recommended that Charlie be given a drug called Ritalin that is effective for treating the disorder, but his parents are not sure they want to start a 6-year-old on drugs.

Evan is 5. He spends his days sitting cross-legged on the floor, rocking back and forth and staring into space. He is oblivious to what is going on around him. When he is touched or picked up, he is unresponsive and limp. This lack of response to others has been apparent since he was born; he just never cuddled like other infants. Evan has not developed any verbal behavior, but in a very mechanical way he will sometimes repeat words that are said to him. He is diagnosed as suffering from *autism,* and his prognosis is poor.

Ann is an attractive college freshman. She is bright, slim, and athletic, and she appears normal to her friends. In fact, many of her friends envy her "cute little body." What nobody knows is that Ann suffers from *bulimia.* Five or six times a week, Ann goes on uncontrollable eating binges during which she will stuff herself with tremendous amounts of food in a short period of time. She does this by going to three or four different drive-through fast-food restaurants. To relieve the abdominal pain caused by the binge and to avoid gaining weight, Ann forces herself to vomit all that she ate during the binge. This behavior pattern is upsetting to Ann, and she is often depressed, but somehow she cannot stop it. Because the vomiting brings gastric acid into her mouth, she is developing sore spots in her throat, and the enamel on her teeth is beginning to deteriorate.

Carolyn is 7 years old and is still wetting her bed at night, and therefore she is diagnosed as suffering from *enuresis.* Recently, her parents bought a pad that goes on her bed. When Carolyn urinates, the pad becomes damp and causes a bell to ring. That wakes Carolyn up, and she stops urinating. This treatment seems to be working, but the therapist cautioned that Carolyn might have relapses.

Tim is 14 and shows a variety of twitches and tics. His head sometimes jerks, and he often blinks and grimaces. Most surprising is that occasionally he blurts out words, usually vulgarities. He does not mean to do it, and he is embarrassed by it, but he cannot control it. Because of his strange behavior, most other children avoid him. His isolation and embarrassment are interfering with his social development. Tim suffers from a rare disorder known as *Tourette's disorder.*

In this chapter we will discuss a variety of disorders that are grouped together because they usually appear first during infancy, childhood, or adolescence. Interest in these disorders has increased greatly during the past 30 years. Indeed, DSM-I listed only six disorders of infancy, childhood, and adolescence, but DSM-IV lists over 30. Some of these disorders will disappear as the child grows older, but others will persist into adulthood if they are not treated. Disorders in this group range from relatively minor ones like tics to very serious ones like infantile autism. It will not be possible to discuss each disorder thoroughly, so we will focus on those that are most important or about which we know the most. However, we will review the symptoms of most of the remaining disorders.

Our discussion will be organized into four groups. First, we will examine the **disruptive behavior disorders**. Children with these disorders have problems with attention, hyperactivity, and antisocial behavior, and their behavior is disruptive for the people around them. Second, we will review the **developmental disorders**. Children with these disorders have problems with emotional and academic development. The effects of these disorders may be pervasive, as in the case of infantile autism, in which the individual's entire life is affected, or they may be very specific and influence only one skill, such as reading or arithmetic. Third, we will consider the **eating disorders.** Most notable in that group are anorexia and bulimia, which are serious and can be fatal. Fourth, we will review a group of unrelated disorders that includes problems with elimination (urination, defecation), anxiety, and tics. Mental retardation is also a disorder of infancy, childhood, and adolescence, but we will consider it in a separate chapter (Chapter 20).

• Disruptive Behavior Disorders

The two most important disruptive behavior disorders are the *attention-deficit hyperactivity disorder*, which involves overactivity, and the *conduct disorders*, which involve aggression and delinquency. The distinction between the two types of disorders is that the behavior of individuals with the attention-deficit hyperactivity disorder is out of control, whereas the behavior of individuals with conduct disorders is controlled but inappropriate.

ATTENTION-DEFICIT HYPERACTIVITY DISORDER

Children with the **attention-deficit hyperactivity disorder** are unable to focus their attention for any rea-

sonable length of time, and that leads to a variety of disruptive and impulsive behaviors. They are almost constantly running, climbing, and speaking out without regard to what is appropriate. In the long run, their inattention and inappropriate behaviors can result in serious personal, social, and academic problems. The attention-deficit hyperactivity disorder appears in children before the age of 7, it is 10 times more common among boys than girls, and it may occur in as many as 10% of elementary school children.

Symptoms

The major symptom of the attention-deficit hyperactivity disorder is the *inability to maintain attention*. Children with this disorder do not seem to listen to directions, are easily distracted, and often fail to finish tasks they begin. Because the children do not attend and do not think things through, they often act impulsively. They quickly shift from one activity to another, are likely to call out spontaneously in class, and have difficulty waiting their turn.

The other important symptoms in this disorder are *hyperactivity* and *impulsivity*. Children with the disorder

Children with the attention-deficit hyperactivity disorder are unable to focus their attention. They do not listen to directions, are easily distracted, and often fail to complete tasks. They often act impulsively, quickly shifting from one activity to another.

have a hard time sitting still or even staying seated, are constantly on the move, and act as though they were driven by a high-speed motor that never gets turned off. These children are very difficult to manage, and one or two of them can quickly make a classroom seem more like a zoo.

Secondary symptoms include serious academic difficulties that stem from the inability to study and their disruptive classroom behavior. The disorder also retards social development because even though children with the disorder are often liked as "class clowns," they do not develop close personal relationships.

Issues

Are Attention Problems a Disorder?
Some critics argue that rather than considering the symptoms as constituting a psychological disorder and treating the child with psychotherapy or medication, the behavior should simply be thought of as the result of poor training, and attention should be focused on the environmental factors that permit or even foster the misbehavior (e.g., permissive parents, inconsistent parents, poor school environments) (Conrad, 1975; Prior & Sanson, 1986; Ross & Ross, 1982; Zentall, 1975). However, the data that we will consider in the following sections generally lead to the conclusion that hyperactivity is a serious disorder and not simply misbehavior.

Are There Long-Term Effects?
A second controversy has to do with the long-term course of the disorder. Some theorists assume that the disorder is due to "delayed development" and is therefore only a temporary problem during childhood. Others assume that the disorder involves a serious underlying problem that will persist into adulthood. To determine whether there are long-term effects, investigators have conducted more than 30 studies in which they either followed up children with the disorder to see what they were like as adults or traced the histories of adults to see what they were like as children (Fischer et al., 1990; Lilienfeld & Waldman, 1990; Mannuzza et al., 1991). The results of those studies indicate that between 30% and 80% of children with attention-deficit hyperactivity disorders continue to show symptoms of the disorder in adolescence and adulthood. Case Study 16.1 is focused on a student of mine who suffers from the attention-deficit hyperactivity disorder. She does not have a particularly severe case, but as you will see, it does interfere with her life, and there is no doubt that her life would have been easier and more productive if she had been diagnosed earlier. The fact that attention-

deficit hyperactivity can be a long-term disorder contributes to the importance we must attach to it.

Explanations

Learning and cognitive theorists initially speculated that children with the attention-deficit hyperactivity disorder have simply *not learned effective strategies for controlling and focusing attention.* However, interest in that explanation has waned, and it is now widely believed that most cases of the disorder are due to *organic brain dysfunction.* Specifically, there is now evidence that the disorder involves *underactivity* in the areas of the brain that are responsible for the control of motor activity and attention (Zametkin et al., 1990). For example, recent findings indicate that individuals with the attention-deficit hyperactivity disorder show lower levels of metabolism in the brain than individuals who do not have the disorder, and that the greatest differences are in the premotor cortex and superior prefrontal cortex areas that control motor activity and attention. The differences in metabolism as measured with a PET scan are presented in Figure 16.1. The reduced metabolism probably reflects lower levels of activity in the areas of the brain that are responsible for *inhibition,* and when the inhibition is reduced, motor behavior and attention run wild. A parallel situation occurs when you drink alcohol: Alcohol is a depressant, and at low levels it depresses the inhibitory areas of the brain, thereby resulting in a loosening up of behavior (see Chapter 18). As we will see later, drugs that stimulate activity in the inhibitory areas of the brain are effective for reducing the attention-deficit hyperactivity disorder.

FIGURE 16.1 PERSONS WITH THE ATTENTION-DEFICIT HYPERACTIVITY DISORDER SHOW LOWER LEVELS OF BRAIN ACTIVITY THAN OTHER PERSONS.

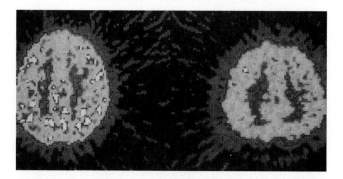

The image on the right is from a person with the disorder and the image on the left is from a person who does not have the disorder. Brighter yellow indicates more activity (glucose metabolism).
Source: Zametkin et al. (1990), p. 1365, fig. 4.

Case Study 16.1

A COLLEGE STUDENT WRITES ABOUT HER ATTENTION-DEFICIT HYPERACTIVITY DISORDER

I'm not your typical case of attention-deficit hyperactivity disorder because I wasn't diagnosed until my sophomore year in college and because I'm a female, but I've got it and it causes problems. Knowing that I have the disorder helps because now I know what is going on, but knowing does not help the symptoms.

The best way I can illustrate what it is like to have an attention-deficit disorder is to tell you that focusing on writing this case study is very difficult and frustrating! I've been trying for hours to come up with the next logical thought or sentence. It is taking me forever, and it is still disorganized. I keep drifting off the track. It is no wonder that I was called the "Space Queen" by one of my high school teachers.

It's difficult for me to stay on task, whether it's writing a paper, listening to a lecture, or reading a book. Because of this, I'm at an immediate disadvantage academically. It often takes me hours to get through one short textbook chapter, and writing a paper can take forever. My mind just keeps wandering—regardless of how interesting the topic may be.

Restlessness also contributes to the long length of time it takes me to complete a task. I have to take "study breaks" very frequently because I simply cannot sit still for long. When I am forced to remain in one place for a period of time, such as in a lecture, I'll generally be swinging my leg or tapping my foot.

Time is my biggest enemy: The fact that it takes me so long to do anything completely disrupts my life. The amount of time I use to perform anything is the largest disruption in my life. Because my distractions and restlessness make me slower at doing things, I always feel incompetent and rather stupid, which is why I struggle with a bad self-image.

Low self-esteem is a major component of my disorder. It takes me a long time to do anything, so I feel abnormal and like I'm not intelligent enough to finish assignments as quickly and easily as others. However, some of my problem with self-image is due to my social relationships that get fouled up because of my disorder. I'm typically labeled an "air head" (or "Space Queen") because my mind wanders. Frequently I only hear a portion of a conversation and, embarrassingly, I have to ask them to repeat it. That annoys people.

I've been taking Ritalin for about a year now. It helps, but its only a treatment, not a cure. It helps me focus and concentrate much better while I study, but it does not completely prevent me from daydreaming. Because Ritalin helps me focus my attention, I'm able to accomplish more in less time than I did before, so I feel a little better about myself. And because it is a stimulant, I feel more motivated to study.

While on the drug, I am also calmer and not so uptight or agitated in social situations. I don't take sarcastic comments or constructive criticism as personally as I did in the past. I feel that the drug has resulted in some very positive changes. My sister noticed a definite difference and improvement in my personality just days after I began using it. I haven't experienced any negative side effects except for an occasional dry mouth, feeling of thirst, and slight weight loss. But the positive effects far outweigh the negative side effects and I'm thankful for the difference it has made in my disorder and in my life.

Having identified brain dysfunction as a cause of the attention-deficit hyperactivity disorder, we must go on to identify the causes of the brain dysfunction. There are now data indicating that some cases of the disorder appear to be due to *infections* during the first 12 weeks of pregnancy or to **anoxia** (uh-NOK-sē-uh) (lack of oxygen) during the birth process (Gualtieri et al., 1982; Towbin, 1978). Probably most important among the environmental factors is the *ingestion of lead*. Lead ingestion occurs when children eat chips of paint containing lead or when they inhale air that is polluted with the emissions from automobiles run on gasoline containing lead (David et al., 1979; Marlowe et al., 1985; Needleman et al., 1979). The influence of lead ingestion in children is illustrated in Figure 16.2 (p. 380), which indicates that children who had higher levels of lead deposits in their teeth were more distractible, hyperactive, and impulsive.

Another environmental factor that was identified but overemphasized is *food additives* (coloring, preservatives, flavorings). It was originally suggested that hyperactivity was an allergic reaction and that as many as 50% of hyperactive children could be returned to normal levels of functioning when placed on an additive-free diet (Feingold, 1975, 1976). However, in better-controlled studies in which hyperactive children were given diets containing additives or placebos, it was found that additives accounted for only about 5% of the cases of increased hyperactivity (Conners, 1980; Marshall, 1989). The effects of food additives are not as powerful or pervasive as they were once thought to be, but we must not ignore any factor that accounts for

FIGURE 16.2   HIGH LEVELS OF LEAD IN CHILDREN
WERE ASSOCIATED WITH HIGH
LEVELS OF DISTRACTIBILITY,
HYPERACTIVITY, AND IMPULSIVITY.

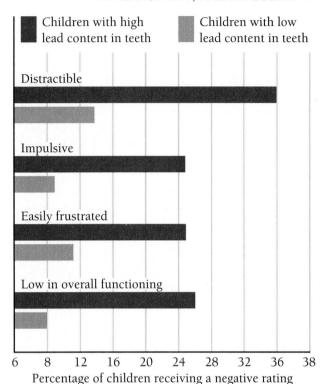

Source: Adapted from Needleman et al. (1979), p. 692, tab. 3.

even 5% of a disorder as serious as the attention-deficit hyperactivity disorder.

Genetic factors have also been implicated in the attention-deficit hyperactivity disorder, and three sets of findings deserve attention. First, it was found that biological relatives, especially male relatives, of hyperactive children were more likely to have been hyperactive as children than the adoptive relatives of hyperactive children (Cantwell, 1972; Morrison & Stewart, 1971, 1974). Some of those results are summarized in Table 16.1. Second, the activity levels of members of monozygotic twin pairs were more similar (correlation .96) than the activity levels of members of dizygotic twin pairs (correlation .59) (Willerman, 1973). Third, parents of children with the attention-deficit hyperactivity disorder tended to have problems with cognitive functioning even if they could not be diagnosed as suffering from an attentional deficit per se (August & Stewart, 1982). This combination of findings clearly suggests that genetic factors play a role in at least some cases of the attention-deficit hyperactivity disorder, but the exact mechanism by which the disorder is transmitted is complex and not yet understood (Cantwell, 1975a, 1975b).

Treatment

Both psychological and physiological approaches have been used to treat the attention-deficit hyperactivity disorder. Psychological approaches have revolved around teaching children **self-instruction** procedures that are designed to help them focus their attention and improve self-control (Kendall, 1984; Meichenbaum & Goodman, 1971). The underlying notion is that if children think through what they are going to do before doing it, they will slow down and act more appropriately. For example, while working on a problem, the children are given a "reminder card" with questions on it: "What's the problem?" "How can I do it?" "Am I using my plan?" "How did I do?" Children are also given "say it before you do it" exercises in which they are given a task but must verbalize what they are going to do before doing it. These training procedures are accompanied by rewards for thinking through and for appropriate subsequent behaviors. Unfortunately, this strategy has met with only limited success. The children seem to be able to gain some control in the clinic while supervised closely, but the effects do not generalize beyond the clinic.

TABLE 16.1   BIOLOGICAL RELATIVES OF CHILDREN WITH THE
ATTENTION-DEFICIT HYPERACTIVITY DISORDER WERE
MORE LIKELY TO HAVE THE DISORDER AS CHILDREN
THAN WERE ADOPTIVE RELATIVES OR RELATIVES OF
CONTROL CHILDREN

| | Relatives Who Had the Disorder as Children (%) | | |
	BIOLOGICAL	ADOPTIVE	CONTROL
Fathers	15.0	8.6	2.4
Uncles	11.7	1.8	.0
Mothers	5.1	2.9	2.4
Aunts	1.5	.0	.0

Source: Morrison and Stewart (1973), p. 890, tab. 4.

The physiological approach to treatment usually involves the administration of a drug marketed under the trade name **Ritalin (methylphenidate)**. A less widely used drug is **Dexedrine (dextroampheta-mine)**. Contrary to what you might expect, the drugs that are used to *calm* hyperactive children (and adults) are actually *stimulants* (Conners & Werry, 1979). Because the drugs have an effect that is the opposite to what is generally expected, the effect is widely referred to as the **paradoxical drug effect**. The drugs appear to work because they stimulate activity in the *inhibitory* areas of the brain, and that activity then reduces motor behavior and distractibility.

In one experiment, the investigators compared the effects of a placebo and three dosage levels of Ritalin on academic performance (arithmetic and reading scores), negative classroom behaviors (destruction of property, being out of seat, disturbing others, inappropriate talking, name-calling, swearing, teasing), and task behaviors (appropriate actions directed toward completing the assignment) (Pelham et al., 1985). The results indicate that the Ritalin was more effective than the placebo for increasing academic performance, increasing task behaviors, and reducing negative behaviors. Furthermore, moderate or higher levels of the drug were more effective than very low levels of the drug. These results are presented in Figures 16.3 and 16.4. The fact that higher levels were

FIGURE 16.4 METHYLPHENIDATE INCREASED TASK BEHAVIORS AND DECREASED NEGATIVE BEHAVIORS IN CHILDREN WITH THE ATTENTION-DEFICIT HYPERACTIVITY DISORDER.

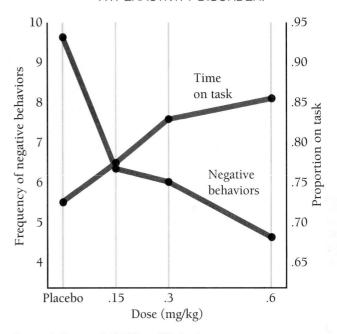

Source: Pelham et al. (1985), p. 950, fig. 2.

more effective can be used to explain the ineffectiveness of some drug treatment programs in which lower levels of the drugs were used.

Similar results have been reported in a variety of other investigations, and it appears that the drugs are at least somewhat effective for treating about 75% of the children with the attention-deficit hyperactivity disorder (see Solanto, 1984). Furthermore, the drugs are also effective for reducing the aggressive and antisocial behavior that often accompanies the disorder (Hinshaw et al., 1992; see also Hinshaw, 1991). In some experiments, the drugs resulted in improved *social* behavior but did not influence the performance on standardized *achievement* tests, and it was therefore argued that the effects of the drug were limited. The fact that the drugs influenced social behavior but not academic achievement is due to the fact that a 6- or 8-week drug treatment period would not be expected to influence the performance on tests that measure years of academic work; improvements on those tests could only be expected after long-term use of the drug.

It is noteworthy that the stimulant drugs have the same beneficial effects on the activity and attention levels of adults with the attention-deficit hyperactivity disorder (Klorman et al., 1984; Rapoport et al., 1980). However, when adults who do not have the disorder take the drug, they get "high." That is because the

FIGURE 16.3 METHYLPHENIDATE INCREASED ACADEMIC PERFORMANCE IN CHILDREN WITH THE ATTENTION-DEFICIT HYPERACTIVITY DISORDER.

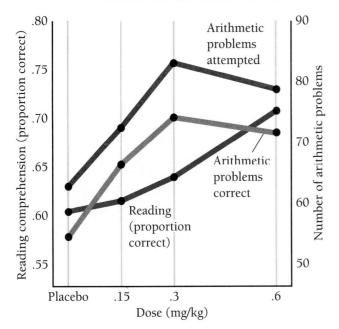

Source: Pelham et al. (1985), p. 950, fig. 1.

stimulant pushes adults with normal levels of brain activity to higher levels of activity. The fact that the drugs can create a high poses a problem because some parents abuse the drugs that are prescribed for their children.

Numerous experiments have been conducted to determine whether cognitive training is more or less effective than medication and whether the combination of cognitive training plus medication is more effective than either treatment alone (Abikoff & Gittelman, 1985; Brown et al., 1985; Cohen et al., 1981; Gittleman-Klein et al., 1976; Hinshaw et al., 1984a, 1984b; Horn et al., 1983; Pelham et al., 1980; Pelham et al., 1985; Pelham et al., 1986; Schroeder et al., 1983; Wolraich et al., 1978). It has generally been found that medication is more effective than cognitive training, and that the combination of cognitive training and medication was not superior to medication alone. Although it is now widely recognized that drugs are effective for overcoming the attention-deficit hyperactivity disorder, it is important to recognize that they are a *treatment* and not a *cure*. Therefore, it is sometimes necessary to keep individuals on a maintenance dose of the drug.

Two cautions should be mentioned with regard to the use of the drugs. First, we must be careful not to use the drugs unless they are really necessary. Surveys of teachers and parents indicate that they consider as many as 50% of all children as restless, distractible, or hyperactive (Lapouse & Monk, 1958; Schultz, 1974; Werry & Quay, 1971), but it is unlikely that all of those children suffer from the attention-deficit hyperactivity disorder, and it would be inappropriate to medicate them all. Nor should medication be used as a substitute for appropriate parenting and classroom discipline.

Second, we must be careful that children who do require medication are not given excessively high dosages. The drugs seem to be effective for treating the disorder because they limit the range of stimuli to which the individual will respond, but if the dosage level is extremely high, the individual will respond to only a very limited range of stimuli, and that may result in social withdrawal and repetitive or "mechanical" behaviors (Solanto & Conners, 1982; Wender, 1971). For example, after receiving a high dose of medication, one originally hyperactive child persisted in writing one homework assignment for 5 hours. In another case, a previously talkative and sociable child withdrew to a corner, where he read the same story over and over and refused to interact with others. In other words, excessively high levels of the drugs will result in abnormal behavior that is the opposite of the attention-deficit hyperactivity disorder, a symptom pattern called **response stereotypy** (STER-ē-ō-TI-pē).

The problems of drug overuse and excessively high dosages are not unique to the drug treatment of the attention-deficit hyperactivity disorder, and the potential problems associated with medication misuse should not be invoked as reasons for limiting the appropriate use of medication.

Finally, with regard to treatment, there is some evidence that the use of Ritalin might slow growth in children who are taking the drug (Klein et al., 1988). Evidence concerning this effect is inconsistent, and in some cases in which the drug did initially retard growth, the deficit was made up when the children were taken off the drug. At present, the potential side effect of methylphenidate on growth does not appear to have serious long-term consequences, but it is a controversial issue that requires additional attention.

CONDUCT DISORDERS

The second major type of disruptive behavior disorder consists of the **conduct disorders**. The symptoms of these disorders revolve around a persistent pattern of misbehavior in which the individual breaks rules and violates the rights of others. Such disorders occur in about 8% of the 10- and 11-year-olds in urban areas and in about 4% of the children in rural areas (Graham, 1979; Rutter et al., 1975). Boys are three times as likely to suffer from them as girls.

Conduct disorders are important not only because they cause problems when the individuals are children, but also because they are related to disruptive and criminal behavior later in life. For example, aggression in childhood is the best predictor of aggression in later life, and many children with conduct disorders go on to become criminals as adults (Quay, 1986). However, not all criminals displayed conduct disorders as chil-

Aggression expressed against other people, animals, or objects is the most obvious symptom of a conduct disorder.

dren, thereby indicating that criminal behavior stems from a number of causes of which conduct disorders is only one.

Symptoms

The symptoms of a conduct disorder include running away from home, lying, setting fires, truancy from school or work, breaking and entering, destroying other people's property, cruelty to animals or people, sexual misconduct, initiating physical fights, use of a weapon in a fight, and stealing (mugging, extortion, armed robbery). Probably the most salient symptom of a conduct disorder is aggression that is expressed against other people, animals, or objects.

The symptoms of the **oppositional defiant disorder** are similar to those seen in the conduct disorders, though less serious. Individuals with the oppositional defiant disorder are characteristically negativistic, defiant, argumentative, and hostile. They differ from persons with the other conduct disorders in that instead of acting out *against* others, they are actively *resistant* to others. Children with the oppositional defiant disorder are likely to lose their tempers, argue with adults, refuse to do as they are told, and intentionally do things to annoy others.

Explanations

Psychodynamic theorists believe that conduct disorders have their origin in the child's relationship with his or her parents. If parents are *overindulgent*, children grow up believing that they can do anything without the fear of punishment, whereas if parents are overly *restrictive* and *withholding*, children grow up believing that to meet their needs, they must take what they want regardless of the consequences. The crucial element is *frustration*, and in many cases frustration leads to aggression (Berkowitz, 1989; Dollard et al., 1939; Geen, 1990). However, it is also true that when faced with frustration, many individuals withdraw, so frustration is not a comprehensive explanation.

Learning theorists suggest that the inappropriate behaviors seen in conduct disorders are *learned through imitation and reward* (Bandura, 1983). Consistent with that explanation are numerous findings indicating that individuals who observe aggression in others subsequently perform more acts of aggression. Indeed, the evidence indicates that not only do observers of aggression perform more acts like the ones that they saw, but they also perform more aggressive acts in general. In one classic study, it was found that mothers who used more aggressive child-rearing behaviors had children who were more aggressive in general than mothers who used less aggressive methods

(Sears et al., 1957). That is, punishment seemed to foster aggression rather than suppress it. However, it is also possible that the link between aggression in the mothers and children was due to genetic factors, or that aggressive and unmanageable behavior in children brought out aggression in the parents (Bell, 1968; Frick et al., 1992).

Cognitive theorists believe that individuals with conduct disorders behave aggressively because *they perceive others as hostile and threatening;* that is, their behavior is a defensive response to what they see as a hostile world. There is now considerable evidence that chronically aggressive individuals do perceive others as hostile (Dodge & Coie, 1987; Dodge & Tomlin, 1987). In one study, aggressive and nonaggressive boys were shown a videotape in which one boy "accidentally" spilled paint on another boy's project (Dodge & Somberg, 1987). When asked about the accident, the aggressive boys were more likely than nonaggressive boys to perceive the accident as maliciously intentional and to report that they would respond with anger.

The physiological explanation for conduct disorders is focused on two factors, the first of which is *low levels of serotonin.* Serotonin is important because it plays a role in the inhibition of punished responses (Soubie, 1986). That is, if an animal has learned not to make a response because it will be punished, but then the animal's level of serotonin is lowered with a drug, the animal will disregard the possibility of punishment and make the response. This disregard for punishment is similar to what we see in the behavior of individuals with conduct disorders. Furthermore, there is now substantial evidence linking low levels of serotonin to aggression in humans. For example, in a study of young men in the military, it was found that 80% of the variability in their levels of aggression could be accounted for by their levels of serotonin; lower levels of serotonin were associated with higher levels of aggression (Brown et al., 1979). Similarly, in a prospective study of children and adolescents with conduct disorders, it was found that levels of serotonin measured at one time were correlated −.72 with levels of aggression two years later (Kruesi et al., 1992). That is, low levels of serotonin were linked to high levels of subsequent aggression.

The second physiological factor of interest is *high levels of* the male hormone *testosterone.* The link between aggression and testosterone was illustrated in a study of young prison inmates who differed in their levels of aggression and social dominance (Ehrenkranz et al., 1974). Those who were most aggressive (those who were probably suffering from conduct disorders) had the highest levels of testosterone, those with intermediate levels of aggression had intermediate levels of testosterone, and those with low lev-

FIGURE 16.5   HIGHER LEVELS OF AGGRESSION
WERE ASSOCIATED WITH HIGHER
LEVELS OF TESTOSTERONE.

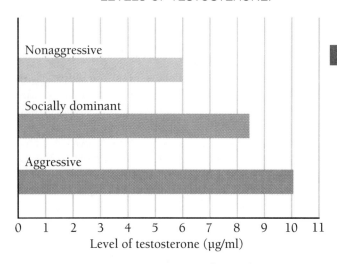

Source: Adapted from Ehrenkranz et al. (1974), p. 471, tab. 1.

els of aggression had the lowest levels of testosterone. Those findings are presented in Figure 16.5.

Given that low levels of serotonin and high levels of testosterone are related to the aggression seen in conduct disorders, the question arises, what leads to those deviant biochemical levels? Prolonged stress can influence levels of serotonin and testosterone (see Chapters 9 and 19), but most of the chronic differences in those levels are probably due to genetic factors. Consistent with that are the findings indicating that genetic factors play an important role in conduct disorders (e.g., Cadoret & Cain, 1980; Jarey & Stewart, 1985; Mednick, Gabrielli, & Hutchings, 1984). Specifically, biological children of parents with conduct disorders show high levels of conduct disorders even when they are adopted at birth and raised by parents who do not have conduct disorders.

Each of the explanations just described probably accounts for some cases of conduct disorders, but most cases probably result from the interaction of causes. That is, physiological factors may provide a predisposition to aggressive behavior, and frustration, the observation of models, or the perception of a threat may trigger or give form to aggressive acts.

• Developmental Disorders

Developmental disorders involve problems that interfere with emotional and academic development in infants and children. In this section, we will give careful attention to the very serious **pervasive developmen-**

tal disorder known as infantile autism. Later we will briefly consider the **learning disorders** associated with language, academic, and motor abilities.

■ INFANTILE AUTISM

Symptoms

Infantile autism is an exceptionally serious disorder that involves three primary symptoms. The first is a *lack of responsiveness to other people.* Children with autism appear to be off in their own world; they do not respond to others around them and seem even to be unaware of the presence of others. As infants, they do not cry when left alone, do not smile at others, and do not vocalize in response to others. When picked up, they are stiff or limp and do not cuddle against their parents' bodies as normal infants do. Later in life, these individuals do not relate to others, but neither do they get into conflicts with others. They are simply "on their own wavelength" and are unable to respond to other people in the way humans usually do.

The lack of interpersonal interest shown by children with autism was demonstrated in a study in which disturbed and normal children were allowed to look at human and nonhuman environmental stimuli (Hutt & Ounsted, 1966). When compared to the nonautistic children, those with autism spent more time gazing at environmental stimuli and less time gazing at human stimuli. These results are summarized in Figure 16.6. Children with autism also seem to prefer sameness with regard to environmental stimuli. Often they will rigidly keep things such as toys or clothing in careful order and become upset if there is any change in their daily routine.

The second symptom is an *impairment in verbal and nonverbal communication.* Even by the age of 5 or 6, many children with autism cannot use language at all. They are mute or will only make meaningless sounds that are not used to communicate with others. The absence of language is a very important factor in determining the child's prognosis. Specifically, if the child does not have language skills by the age of 5, there is a 75% chance that he or she will never make an adequate personal or social adjustment (Eisenberg & Kanner, 1956). The relationship between language ability and subsequent adjustment is not simply a matter of intelligence. When children with autism and other disturbed children with comparable IQs were followed up, the children with autism were less likely to show improvement (Rutter & Lockyer, 1967).

Children with autism who do talk will often show a variety of peculiar speech patterns. For example, they may simply repeat what is said to them. If you say,

FIGURE 16.6 CHILDREN WITH AUTISM PREFERRED TO LOOK AT NONHUMAN RATHER THAN HUMAN STIMULI.

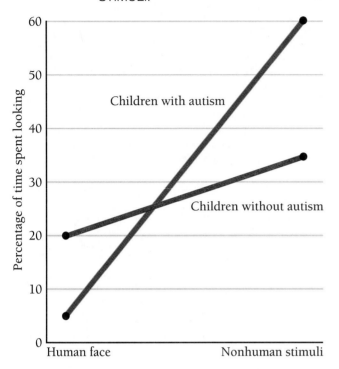

Source: Adapted from Hutt and Ounsted (1966), p. 349, fig. 4.

An important feature of the symptoms of autism is that they appear *very early.* Indeed, if a child is to be diagnosed as suffering from autism, the symptoms must be apparent before the child is 2½ years old. Parents who have some experience with infants and who know what to expect notice a problem with the child almost from the time of birth.

Autism is not an "either-or" disorder; there are degrees of severity. Individuals with less severe cases are generally referred to as **high-functioning** (Yirmiya & Sigman, 1991). High-functioning individuals show less disruption in social and cognitive functioning, and in many cases show normal levels of intelligence. With regard to performance on IQ tests, the high-functioning individuals do less well on subtests that measure social intelligence (e.g., arranging pictures to make a story) than they do on nonsocial subtests (e.g., arranging blocks to make a design).

In Case Study 16.2, you will find portions of an interview I had with the mother of a child with autism. In the interview she describes the child's behavior and her reactions.

"Hello, Jimmy," the child may say, "Hello, Jimmy." This response pattern is referred to as **echolalia** (EK-ō-LĀ-lē-uh) because the child repeats what is said without a sense of meaning, much as an echo comes back from a mountainside. In some cases, the echolalia is delayed, and the child will repeat the phrase hours later, completely out of context and with no apparent stimulus. Another unusual speech pattern is **pronoun reversal**, whereby the child will use *he, she,* or *you* for *I* or *me.* For example, a boy with autism who wants a cookie may say, "You want a cookie" or "He want a cookie."

The third symptom is a greatly *restricted repertory of activities and interests.* Children with autism may sit alone for hours with a fixed stare, or they may rock back and forth endlessly. In other cases, they may repeat certain behaviors such as spinning a toy over and over, or they may repeatedly go through ritualistic gestures with their fingers and hands. For example, they may move the fingers as if playing a piano, and they will do this for hours at a time. Some of these behaviors seem to be forms of self-stimulation. Often these children engage in self-mutilation behaviors such as scratching or hitting themselves. In one case a child who was not restrained banged his head 1,800 times in 8 days (Lovaas & Simmons, 1969).

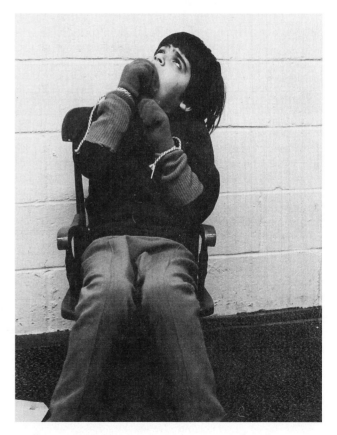

Children with autism show little response to other people, reduced ability to communicate, and restricted repertory of activities and interests. Some children with autism engage in self-mutilation. This boy has mittens tied over his hands to prevent him from scratching himself.

Case Study 16.2

Holmes: Can you tell me when you first noticed that something was wrong with Tom?

Mother: In retrospect, I think I always felt there was something wrong, even as early as the pregnancy. The pregnancy was technically normal—tests didn't show any problems—but it just wasn't like my other two pregnancies. He was always moving and kicking, and I just thought he was unhappy in the womb. Then right after he was born, I noticed a couple of things that were different from my other children. Tom had difficulty sucking at the breast, and he never seemed to be comforted when he was picked up or cuddled. In fact, picking him up seemed to upset him more; his muscles would become rigid, and he would scream at the top of his lungs. This worried my husband and me; we thought we were doing something wrong in the bonding process.

Holmes: Can you tell me about his reactions to other people?

Mother: Well, at first he would scream and twist if touched by anyone, but as he got older, he stopped showing that extreme reaction, but he didn't react positively either. He was just neutral and limp. However, when he was picked up by an unfamiliar person, he would have a severe negative reaction, a real tantrum.

Apart from that, he seemed to be in his own little world. When he was an infant, it was difficult to get his attention, and then it was impossible to hold it for more than a few seconds. He never played with other children or adults. Instead, he would do activities like looking in mirrors or at shiny objects for hours at a time. He also liked to spin the lids from jars over and over. One of his favorite things was to sit in front of the washing machine and watch the clothes go round and round. Sometimes he would sit in a corner and rock back and forth, or he would flap his arms and sing "da da de la da" over and over. For a while, we tried to force social interactions on him, hoping we could "break through." That never worked, and he would resist by banging his head on the floor and screaming. At around eight or nine, he started interacting with others a little, and now he will sometimes initiate a conversation or an activity. I'm not sure whether we had an influence or he finally matured a little.

Holmes: How about developmental tasks, things like smiling, walking, and talking? Did he start doing those things on schedule?

Mother: Tom did everything much later than other children. He didn't roll over until eight months, and he didn't walk until twenty-six months. When he finally did walk, he walked only on his toes until he was five. He started talking at around four, but even then he didn't talk; he just repeated what others were saying. We had a terrible time getting him toilet-trained. It wasn't until he was five that he could stay dry during the day, and he wet himself at night until he was twelve.

Holmes: Did Tom show any unusual behaviors other than his lack of social interest and delayed development?

Mother: One thing that has been a real problem is that he just cannot deal with change. To keep peace in the house, everything in his room—which is where he stayed most of the time—had to be kept exactly the same all the time. One time, I threw away an old beat-up wastebasket that had been in his room, and for two weeks he cried, demanding that it be returned. When he was moved from the fifth to the sixth grade, he refused to go to school for three weeks and became violent when we tried to drag him out of the house. As long as things were perfectly constant and no one tried to get into his little world, he would be all right. Well, I don't mean "all right," but he wouldn't become agitated or violent.

Holmes: You mentioned school. How's he been doing in school?

Mother: School has always been a struggle for us all. Just getting him to go has been tough, but on the whole, Tom has done pretty well. Most of the time, he has been in a special class for children with behavior disorders, so he gets more structure and more individualized instruction. Once he was "mainstreamed" into a regular typing class, but the change and additional stimulation were too much for him. He is now doing tenth-grade-level work, which is just about where he should be. For the past year, he has been in a special occupational program where he earns school credit for working three hours a day. First he worked in a veterinary clinic, where he did odd jobs. He loved being around the animals, but he couldn't handle the lack of structure—different chores all the time—so he started withdrawing and finally stopped going. Then he was switched to a fast-food restaurant where he had a consistent assignment, but for some reason that didn't work out either. I think there was too much activity and pressure to keep up.

Holmes: When was Tom first diagnosed as suffering from autism?

Mother: (*long pause; rubs her temples and slumps in her chair a little*) All along, we'd been very worried about Tom's development, and we'd taken him to a variety of specialists, but it was the language problem at age four—the delay and the echolalia—that convinced everyone that Tom was autistic. (*pause*) I will never forget the day the diagnosis was finally made. The possibility that he was autistic had been mentioned earlier, but we had always avoided confronting it. We kept looking somewhere else for a "better" explanation—something that could be cured. When the social worker told us the diagnosis, it was like we had been hit by a truck. We had seen the truck coming, but we had intentionally looked the other way. We had a son who was autistic—what were we going to do! First we got books and started reading about autism, but that made things worse because they said it was the parents' fault for being cold and distant. We felt terrible, but then the psychologist explained that those were old theories and that now it is believed that autism is due to some genetic problem or a problem during pregnancy. That didn't make the problem less serious, but it helped relieve some of our guilt. (*pause*)

We've come to accept the fact that Tom is different from other children. There are limits to what he can do and limits to what we can do for him. Autism isn't an either-or thing—there are degrees of it, and Tom's case isn't as severe as many others. He can live at home and function to some extent in the community.

Someday, when we aren't around to take care of him, he will probably have to be moved to some sort of sheltered living situation. I've grown to recognize that we have to accept people the way they are. We need to keep helping Tom, but we also need to accept him and his limitations. We think or hope he is happy, but a lot of the time it is hard to know what is going on in his world.

Issues

Prevalence and Demographic Factors.

Infantile autism occurs in about .04% of the population (Gilberg, 1984). It is four times more likely to occur in males than in females.

The results of early studies suggested that autism was more likely to occur in the upper socioeconomic classes and that the parents of autistic children were more likely to be professionals (Eisenberg & Kanner, 1956). However, more recent and better studies have consistently indicated that autism is not related to social class (Gilberg & Schaumann, 1982; Tsai et al., 1982). The initial findings relating autism to upperclass status were probably due to the fact that the studies were conducted in prestigious and expensive hospitals where the children of wealthy parents were more likely to be brought for treatment.

Infantile Autism Versus Schizophrenia in Childhood.

For many years, there was a controversy over whether autism was a separate disorder or simply an instance of schizophrenia in childhood. However, it is now generally agreed that infantile autism and schizophrenia in childhood are separate disorders (American Psychiatric Association, 1987). A variety of factors separate infantile autism from schizophrenia in childhood:

1. Children with autism rarely have a family history of schizophrenia, but persons with schizophrenia often have a family history of schizophrenia.
2. Children with autism often show a lack of intellectual development, but that is not the case with children who suffer from schizophrenia.
3. Children with autism have limited speech, whereas children with schizophrenia have normal speech ability but communicate bizarre ideas.
4. Autism is apparent almost at birth, whereas schizophrenia develops later.
5. Children with autism do not show the positive response to neuroleptic drugs, whereas most persons with schizophrenia do (see Chapter 14), thus suggesting a different underlying process.

With regard to the differences between autism and schizophrenia, it can be said that children with autism appear *unoriented* and *detached*, whereas children with schizophrenia appear *disoriented* and *confused*. Overall, autism and schizophrenia are thus considered separate disorders, and we should not assume that the causes and treatments for one can be applied to the other.

Explanations

Infantile autism poses one of the major unsolved mysteries of abnormal psychology. However, since the disorder was first identified in 1943 (Kanner, 1943), we have ruled out a number of erroneous explanations, and we are now developing better explanations for the disorder.

Psychodynamic Explanations.

Early psychodynamic explanations for autism focused on the role of parents' personalities and their styles of child rearing (see Werry, 1979). For example, it was suggested that the parents of autistic children were cold, formal, humorless, detached, highly rational, and objective (Bettelheim, 1967; Kanner, 1943). Supposedly, parents of that type did not provide their children with interpersonal warmth and nurturance, and it was assumed that the children then turned away from these "mechanical" parents and turned inward for comfort and stimulation. The psychodynamic explanations have lost most of their credibility and supporters because numerous investigations have revealed that the parents of autistic children do not differ from the parents of normal children or from parents of other types of disturbed children. That was found to be the case in terms of personality (Cox et al., 1975; Koegel et al., 1983; McAdoo & De Myer, 1978), infant care practices (De Myer et al., 1981), interaction patterns (Cantwell et al., 1979; Koegel et al., 1983), language patterns (Wolchik, 1983), and other variables.

Learning Explanations.

Learning theorists have attempted to explain autism by suggesting that the abnormal behaviors such as headbanging, uncooperativeness, tantrums, and mutism are often followed by rewards such as attention, food, and toys that are designed to distract the child and reduce the abnormal behavior (Ferster, 1961; Lovaas & Smith, 1989). However, rather than reducing the abnormal behavior, the rewards reinforce the behavior. At the same time, normal behaviors are ignored and hence not rewarded because they do not upset the people around the child. In other words, these theorists suggest that autistic behavior is taught by parents who reward the wrong behavior.

The learning explanation for autism has been tested indirectly with experiments in which attempts were made to eliminate autistic behavior by changing what behaviors were rewarded. The notion was that if autistic behavior was caused by rewarding the abnormal behavior, ceasing those rewards and rewarding normal behavior should eliminate the autism. Those experiments will be discussed in the section on therapy, but for now it should be noted that ignoring or punishing autistic behaviors and rewarding normal behaviors has been only somewhat effective in making children with autism more manageable, and it has not resulted in a cure or reversal of the autism (Lovaas et al., 1973). Furthermore, even if the new behaviors could be developed through learning, that does not necessarily mean that the old behaviors developed through learning. Because of these problems, interest in conditioning as the cause of autism has waned.

Physiological Explanations. Comparisons of children who do and do not have autism have revealed a variety of physiological differences. For example, it has been found that some individuals with autism have (a) lesions in the brain stem (Fein et al., 1981; Gilberg et al., 1983; Rosenblum et al., 1980), (b) enlarged ventricles and related abnormalities (Campbell et al., 1982; Damasio et al., 1980; Piven et al., 1990), (c) reversed cerebral asymmetry (which means that the right side of the brain is larger than the left side, the opposite of what is found in nonautistic individuals; Hier et al., 1979), (d) more active right than left hemispheres (Blackstone, 1978; James & Barry, 1983), and (e) biochemical imbalances that are not found in the brains of nonautistic children. The greater size and activity of the right hemisphere has been of particular interest because language functions are developed primarily on the left side, and language problems play a major role in autism.

The differences between individuals who do and do not suffer from autism in terms of brain structure and chemistry all strongly suggest that autism is due to some form of *brain dysfunction.* Unfortunately, we do not understand the nature of the dysfunction or how it

results in autistic behavior. However, we are beginning to understand that the dysfunction, whatever it is, is due primarily to biological hazards and genetics.

The biological hazards related to autism revolve around problems during pregnancy and birth. There is now substantial evidence that the mothers of children with autism experience more problems during pregnancy than mothers of normal children (Finegan & Quarrington, 1979; Kagan, 1981; Nelson, 1991; Torrey et al., 1975). These problems include bleeding, infectious or viral diseases, poisoning, and physical trauma. These hazards are most likely to result in autism when they occur during the first trimester of pregnancy, when the fetus is going through crucial stages of development and is particularly vulnerable.

With regard to the links between problems during pregnancy, brain dysfunction, and autism, it is relevant to note that children with autism are more likely than normal children to show minor **physical anomalies** (Campbell et al., 1978; Gualtieri et al., 1982). These physical anomalies include minor structural problems with the eyes, ears, mouth, hands, and feet. The notion is that hazards during pregnancy cause a variety of problems in the developing fetus, among which are structural anomalies and the brain damage that results in autism. (Note that by themselves, these anomalies do not interfere with functioning, and it is not unusual for one or two anomalies to occur in an otherwise normal child.)

There is also substantial evidence that children with autism experience more problems during the birth process than normal children. In one study, the birth records of 23 children with autism were compared to the birth records of their 15 normal siblings, and it was found that the children with autism had more difficulties in the birth process than their siblings did (Finegan & Quarrington, 1979).

It is also noteworthy that autism is most likely to occur in first pregnancies. Indeed, in one study of 38 children with autism, 94% had been born from a first pregnancy (Kagan, 1981). Mother's age during pregnancy has been shown to be related to autism (Gilberg, 1980; Gilberg & Gilberg, 1983; Tsai & Stewart, 1983). For example, in one study, it was found that 85% of the mothers who gave birth to children with autism were 5 years older than the average age for motherhood (30.7 vs. 26.0 years old).

Apart from problems with pregnancy and birth, there is also evidence that as many as 11% of individuals with autism suffer from rare diseases that could influence brain development and functioning (Ritvo et al., 1990). The 11% figure is much higher than what would be expected in a normal population because the diseases are generally very rare, and thus the high co-occurrence rate suggests a causative role. There is also evidence that individuals with autism are more likely to have problems with their immune systems, and the reduced effectiveness of the immune systems would make the individuals more vulnerable to infectious diseases that could influence the brain (e.g., Warren et al., 1990).

The evidence for the influence of biological hazards is impressive, but biological hazards alone cannot account for all cases of autism. Therefore, we must go on to consider the role that genetic factors play in the disorder. We cannot test for a genetic basis for autism by studying the offspring of individuals with autism because individuals with the disorder rarely marry and do not produce children. However, we can examine the rates for autism among siblings, and investigations of that type indicate that between 2% and 5% of the siblings of individuals with autism also suffer from the disorder (August et al., 1981; Folstein, 1991; Hanson & Gottesman, 1976; Minton et al., 1982; Ritvo et al., 1982; Rutter, 1967). Concordance rates of 2% and 5% are not high, but they are 50 to 125 times higher than the rate of autism in the general population (.04%), so they provide evidence that there is a genetic basis for at least some cases of autism.

Investigators have also found that the "normal" siblings of individuals with autism are more likely to suffer from cognitive impairments such as delayed speech development or reduced verbal abilities (Bartak et al., 1975; Folstein & Rutter, 1977; Minton et al., 1982; Rutter et al., 1971; Vaillant, 1963). For example, delayed language development was found in 25% of the siblings of individuals with autism, and the verbal IQ scores of the siblings were between 14 and 23 points lower than their performance IQ scores. (Differences between verbal and performance IQ scores of 15 points or more are suggestive of neurological dysfunction. For a discussion of these scores, see Chapter 3.) In other words, although they are not actually autistic, many of the siblings of autistic children appear to suffer from what might be thought of as mild symptoms of autism.

The genetic basis for autism has also been examined in studies of the concordance rates for autism in monozygotic and dizygotic twin pairs (see Fish & Ritvo, 1979; Folstein, 1991; Hanson & Gottesman, 1976; Smalley et al., 1988). In the best study of this type, it was found that the concordance rate among monozygotic twin pairs was 36%, while the concordance rate among dizygotic twins was 0% (Folstein & Rutter, 1977). Those results clearly indicate that at least some cases of autism have a genetic basis.

In the study just mentioned, the investigators also checked to see if the nonautistic members of twin pairs suffered from any cognitive impairments (speech development delayed until after the 3rd birthday, inferior verbal skills, abnormal articulation) that might reflect a mild form of autism (Folstein & Rutter, 1977). The results indicated that among monozygotic twin pairs, the concordance rate for autism in one twin and cognitive impairment in the other was 46%, while among dizygotic twin pairs, the rate was only 10%. When the autism-impairment concordance rate was combined with the autism-autism concordance rate, the overall concordance rate for cognitive disturbance among monozygotic twin pairs was 82%, versus only 10% among dizygotic twin pairs (see Table 16.2). These results suggest that there is a genetic basis for a range of impairment and that only for some individuals is the impairment severe enough to justify the diagnosis of autism.

As the evidence concerning the causes of autism mounts, it is becoming clear that both biological hazards and genetic factors must be considered. The fact that multiple factors must be considered was neatly demonstrated in an investigation in which both genetic and biological hazards were examined in 21 twin pairs (Folstein & Rutter, 1977). First it was determined that 32% of the cases of autism could be accounted for by genetic factors because there were four sets of monozygotic twins who were concordant for autism. (None of the dizygotic twin pairs was concordant.) Next, an examination of pregnancy and birth records

TABLE 16.2 THE CONCORDANCE FOR COGNITIVE IMPAIRMENT IS GREATER IN MONOZYGOTIC THAN DIZYGOTIC TWIN PAIRS

	Percentage of Twin Pairs	
	MONOZYGOTIC	DIZYGOTIC
Concordance for autism (both suffer from autism)	36	0
Concordance for cognitive impairment (one suffers from autism, the other a cognitive impairment)	46	10
Total concordance	82	10

Source: Data from Folstein and Rutter (1977).

revealed that 40% of the autistic children had been exposed to biological hazards during pregnancy or birth (e.g., delay in breathing, neonatal convulsions, congenital anomalies, low birth weight, narrow umbilical cord, neonatal apnea). It is particularly interesting that none of the monozygotic twins who were concordant for autism had experienced such hazards, a finding that strengthens the interpretation that those cases were due to genetic rather than biological factors. Taken together, the genetic and hazard factors accounted for 80% of the cases of autism. The task facing investigators now is to determine the cause of the remaining 20% of the cases.

Treatment

A variety of approaches have been used in attempts to treat childhood autism (Rutter, 1985), but none has been shown to be consistently effective. In the 1950s and early 1960s, a great deal of attention was devoted to intensive, long-term psychodynamic treatment, but there is virtually no evidence that it was effective, and that approach has now been generally abandoned.

An exciting development was introduced in the mid-1960s when behavior modification strategies were introduced. In those treatment programs, children with autism were rewarded for appropriate behaviors and punished for inappropriate or self-destructive behaviors (Lovaas et al., 1966; Lovaas & Simmons, 1969; Wolf et al., 1967). This can be an extremely difficult and prolonged task. For example, it may require thousands of trials in which a child is given bits of food for correct responses in order to teach the child simply to say one word, and then it is unlikely that the child will know what the word means or be able to use it in a sentence. Indeed, the child may be imitating rather than talking. These programs required a great deal of time, effort, and money, but the initial results were very encouraging, and a film of the progress made by autistic children in this program is still shown widely in college classes on psychology (Lovaas, 1969). At the end of that film, children who were once mute, echolalic, self-destructive, and unable to interact with others are shown to be behaving much more normally. The implication was that behavior modification procedures are effective for treating autistic children.

Regrettably, the original film and the related research reports may imply or promise more than what was actually accomplished. The results that were reported suffer from two serious problems that generally go unrecognized. The first is that the treatment effects simply did not last (Lovaas et al., 1973). Despite 6 hours of one-on-one treatment per day for a period of 14 months, the newly developed appropriate behaviors dropped out when the treatment was stopped, and the

old, inappropriate behaviors returned. This is illustrated for two children, Pam and Rick, in Figure 16.7. During the year of treatment (1964–1965), appropriate play increased and self-stimulation decreased, but when Pam and Rick were assessed 3 years later, these activities had returned to their original levels. At that time (1968), treatment was reinstituted, and for a brief time appropriate play and self-stimulation decreased. However, when the children were assessed again after another 2 years in which they were not treated (1970), the gains made in treatment had disappeared. Indeed, as indicated in the figure, 5 years after the end of training, Pam and Rick were showing less appropriate play and more self-stimulation than they had before treatment was begun.

The second problem is that the treatment did not actually result in the hoped-for behavior even during the treatment period. The behavior therapists suggest that the treatment increased social and affectionate behavior, and as an example they point out that after treatment, the previously withdrawn autistic children would run across the room with outstretched arms to their therapist in the hope of being picked up and hugged (Lovaas, 1969). However, what is not made clear in the film is that the children were barefooted and the behavior occurred in a room that had a shock-grid on the floor that would be used to administer

FIGURE 16.7 APPROPRIATE BEHAVIORS DECLINED AND INAPPROPRIATE BEHAVIORS RETURNED AFTER A BEHAVIOR MODIFICATION PROGRAM FOR AUTISTIC CHILDREN WAS ENDED.

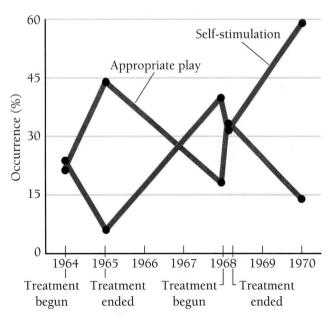

Source: Adapted from Lovaas et al. (1973), p. 149, fig. 8.

punishment to the children (Lovaas et al., 1965). The children ran across the room to be picked up by the therapist to avoid getting shocks to their feet and not in an attempt to get or express affection. It is also noteworthy that the purportedly affectionate behavior did not generalize to another room that did not have a shock grid on the floor. Unfortunately, then, the responses achieved with the behavior modification program were not always what they appeared to be, and the improved behavior did not last or generalize to other situations. A sad footnote to this attempt at treatment is that the children whom we saw treated in the film and for whom we had such high hopes were subsequently readmitted as full-time residents of psychiatric institutions.

The story does not end there because the investigators tried again with a more extensive program (Lovaas, 1987). In this second investigation treatment was started earlier (at about 3 years of age), was more intensive (more than 40 hours per week of one-on-one treatment), and lasted longer (at least 2 years), and the parents were actively involved in the treatment. The notion was that the children needed more treatment and that other people in the children's lives should be involved so as to enhance the generalization and maintenance of the newly learned behaviors. Treatment involved ignoring or punishing inappropriate behaviors (aggression, self-stimulation, noncompliance with instructions) and rewarding appropriate behaviors (attempts to talk, prosocial activities, compliance with instructions). When the children started kindergarten, treatment was reduced to 10 hours per week, and when they started first grade, the treatment was usually limited to consultation with parents. The second investigation also included a minimal treatment control condition (10 hours or less per week of one-on-one treatment).

The results indicated that 47% of the children in the treatment condition successfully passed through normal first grade in a public school and demonstrated a normal IQ, whereas none of the children in the control condition got through first grade or demonstrated a normal IQ (Lovaas, 1987). Symptoms of autism such as self-stimulation and abnormal speech were assessed before treatment began but not at the end of treatment, so we do not know the degree to which those behaviors were influenced. However, the investigator implied that if they had not been improved, the children would not have been able to complete first grade.

These results are certainly positive, but the investigation has come under severe criticism, and the results are surrounded in controversy (Lovaas et al., 1989; Schopler et al., 1989). For example, the critics pointed out that (a) the children were not randomly assigned to the treatment and control conditions, (b) no data on behavior were reported, (c) changes in IQ scores may reflect changes in compliance rather than changes in cognitive functioning, and (d) the children in the treatment condition may have been pushed through school by staff pressure. At present, it is hazardous to draw firm conclusions concerning this approach to treatment; the children in the treatment condition were more likely to complete first grade, but it is not clear how or why. In the absence of good data, we must be careful neither to hold out false hopes nor to abandon hope.

Before concluding our discussion of the behavioral approach to treatment, we should give some attention to the controversy over the use of punishment for suppressing inappropriate and potentially dangerous behaviors (Etzel et al., 1987; Guess et al., 1987; Kiernan, 1988; Lavigna & Donnellan, 1986; Wedell et al., 1987). Children with autism frequently engage in very serious self-injurious behaviors such as headbanging, which they might do hundreds of times a day, and there is no doubt that the use of **aversive procedures** such as slapping them, giving them painful electrical shocks, or spraying noxious substances in their faces can quickly bring those behaviors to a stop. However, the question is, is it ethical to use aversive procedures on children who are not in a position to object? Does the end justify the means?

Some people have argued that aversive procedures are not justified, and they have taken steps to outlaw them. For example, a bill was introduced in Congress in 1987 to withhold funding from any agency that used aversive procedures in the treatment of "any individual with a severe disability." The bill died in committee and has not been reintroduced. In another case, the state of Massachusetts attempted to suspend the operation of a treatment center where aversive procedures were used in the treatment of children with autism (Fuller, 1986). Opponents of aversive procedures argued that the procedures constituted "officially sanctioned child abuse." In response, the parents of a boy named Brendon filed a class-action suit in which they argued that by denying the use of aversive procedures, the state was denying Brendon and other children the *right to an effective treatment in the absence of an effective alternative.* They pointed out that over a period of 15 years, Brendon had been discharged as "untreatable" from a number of prestigious institutions for autistic children, but that while being treated with the aversive procedures at the Behavioral Research Institute, he had shown remarkable improvement. The judge found in favor of the parents and thereby permitted the use of the aversive procedures. Since that decision, there have been a number of other challenges to the use of aversive procedures, but

The prognosis for autistic children is poor; fewer than 25% make a satisfactory adjustment by adolescence or adulthood. Dustin Hoffman portrayed an autistic adult in the movie Rainman.

all have failed (UPI, 1987a, 1987b). Aversive procedures work, and although they seem harsh, they are more humane than letting people do serious harm to themselves. The key to their effective and ethical use is to apply only the amount that is necessary to suppress the inappropriate behaviors, and to institute a system of checks to ensure that the procedures are not misused.

A wide variety of drugs have been used in attempts to treat autism, including neuroleptics, antihistamines, antidepressants, stimulants, L-dopa, and megavitamins. Two experiments and a variety of clinical reports suggest that in some cases, the neuroleptic Haldol (see Chapter 14) may help reduce the hyperactivity, outbursts of rage, and sleeplessness that are sometimes present in autism (Anderson et al., 1984; Campbell et al., 1978; Engelhardt et al., 1970; see review by Gittelman & Kanner, 1986). The neuroleptic may have made the children somewhat easier to manage, but it did not reduce the core symptoms of the autism. None of the other drugs has proved to have any positive effects, and the stimulants (amphetamines) caused a worsening of the symptoms.

In view of the ineffectiveness of our treatments and the fact that in most cases the disorder does not diminish as the individual gets older, the prognosis for autistic children is poor. Fewer than 25% make a satisfactory adjustment by adolescence or adulthood (De Myer et al., 1981; Eisenberg & Kanner, 1956; Rutter & Lockyer, 1967), and between 40% and 70% continue to live in institutions (Lotter, 1978). The number of autistic individuals who live in institutions increases as they become older, a finding that is probably attributable to the fact that as the children get older, the parents are less able to cope with them (De Myer et al., 1981). Overall, it must be concluded that autism poses one of the most prominent and serious failures of psychology and psychiatry, and we can only hope that there will be a breakthrough in the future. At present, however, the picture is bleak.

LEARNING, COMMUNICATION, AND MOTOR SKILLS DISORDERS

Before concluding our discussion of developmental disorders, some comment should be made concerning a relatively new set of disorders called **learning, communication, and motor skills disorders**. These disorders are summarized in Table 16.3. Serious questions have been raised about whether these problems should be considered psychological disorders or

TABLE 16.3 LEARNING, COMMUNICATION, AND MOTOR SKILLS DISORDERS

Reading Disorder. Reading ability is markedly below what would be expected on the basis of the child's intellectual ability.

Mathematics Disorder. Mathematic ability is markedly below what would be expected on the basis of the child's intellectual ability.

Expressive Language Disorder. Use of language is markedly below what would be expected on the basis of the child's intellectual ability (e.g., poor vocabulary, overly simple sentences, limitation to the present tense).

Written Expression Disorder. Composition of written text is markedly below what would be expected on the basis of the child's intellectual ability (e.g., poor spelling and grammer).

Phonological Disorder. Consistent failure to use speech sounds as expected for age and dialect.

Stuttering. Consistent failure to speak without involuntary disruption or blocking.

Developmental Coordination Disorder. Performance in motor skills activities is markedly below what would be expected on the basis of the child's chronological age and intellectual ability.

Note: In all disorders, low ability must interfere with achievement and activities.

whether they might be more appropriately considered educational problems. Some critics have suggested that labeling these problems as psychological reflects a psychological or psychiatric "imperialism" whereby psychologists and psychiatrists are trying to gain control over problems that are beyond their traditional and appropriate scope. The decision about whether they are psychological or educational problems will ultimately rest on the determination of the cause or causes of the problems. For the most part, we currently know very little about their causes and treatment.

• Eating Disorders

ANOREXIA AND BULIMIA

Anorexia nervosa and *bulimia nervosa* are eating disorders that have reached epidemic proportions in the past 20 years. Both disorders are found primarily in young women, and they are serious enough to result in death. Because they are so widespread and serious, they deserve careful consideration.

Symptoms

Anorexia Nervosa. The major symptom of **anorexia nervosa** (AN-uh-REK-sē-uh nur-VŌ-suh) is the *refusal to maintain body weight* over a minimal normal weight for age and height. The maintenance of a weight that is 15% below expected is suggested to be diagnostic of anorexia.

Other symptoms include an intense *fear of gaining weight* or becoming fat and a *distortion of body image.* Regardless of how thin and emaciated these individuals become, they are still afraid of becoming fat, say they "feel fat," and therefore they continue their attempts to lose weight. Because of their distorted self-perception, persons with anorexia do not see themselves as too thin or as suffering from a serious disorder, and hence they do not seek help.

The last major symptom of anorexia in females is the *absence of at least three consecutive menstrual cycles.* This is known as **amenorrhea** (uh-MEN-uh-RĒ-uh). It is interesting to note that amenorrhea sets in before there is significant weight loss. The reason for that is not yet clear.

Individuals with anorexia have a number of secondary symptoms that stem from their inappropriate diets and weight loss. These include slow heart rate (bradycardia), low blood pressure (hypotension), low body temperature (hypothermia), and other problems associated with disturbances in metabolism. One woman with anorexia had a heart rate of only 28 beats per minute and had blood pressure so low it could not

Regardless of how emaciated individuals with anorexia may be, they still "feel fat" and may continue to lose weight.

be measured (Brotman & Stern, 1983). Finally, persons with anorexia often suffer from depression. Indeed, well over 50% also meet the criteria for a major depressive disorder (Eckert et al., 1982; Herzog, 1984).

The course of anorexia is quite variable. Some individuals experience a single episode followed by a complete recovery with no residual problems. Others have a number of serious episodes interspersed with concerns about weight and careful but not excessive dieting. In some persons, anorexia is a chronic condition that ultimately leads to death. A notable example of a fatal case was pop singer Karen Carpenter.

It is interesting to note that persons with anorexia do not lose their interest in food and in fact will sometimes go to great lengths to prepare elaborate meals for others, but they will not eat the meals themselves. One student of mine who suffered from anorexia frequently brought me rich and wonderful chocolate desserts but never ate any of them herself. She made the desserts for me after jogging a few miles, going to her aerobics class, and limiting her food intake for the day to a bowl of cereal and a few carrots.

Bulimia Nervosa.   The major symptom of **bulimia nervosa** (byoo-LIM-ē-uh nur-VŌ-suh) is *eating binges.* During an eating binge, the individual consumes very large amounts of food in a short period of time. Binges are usually done in secret and carefully planned so as to avoid detection because the individual knows that they are inappropriate and abnormal. The eating binge is often accompanied by a feeling of lack of control over the eating behavior. The binge ends when the individual can eat no more and develops abdominal pains. Immediately following the binge, the individual usually *purges* (voluntarily induces vomiting). The purge is used to reduce the abdominal pain and to avoid weight gain because people with bulimia are concerned about gaining weight. The binge-purge sequence is usually followed by guilt, self-criticism, and depression. Some persons with bulimia will also use laxatives, diuretics, diets, or exercise to control their weight. The binge, purge, and after-effects are physically painful, emotionally distressing, time-consuming, and expensive.

Secondary symptoms associated with bulimia include sore throat, swollen salivary glands, and destruction of tooth enamel as a consequence of frequent vomiting. Persons with bulimia also suffer from nutritional problems, dehydration, and intestinal damage. Depression is frequently associated with bulimia, and surveys have revealed that between 23% and 70% of these patients could be diagnosed as suffering from a major depression (Herzog, 1984; Strober, 1982; Walsh et al., 1985). One woman's struggle with bulimia is presented in Case Study 16.3.

Issues

Historical Trends.   Because anorexia and bulimia have attracted so much attention lately, it is widely thought that these are new disorders, but that is not the case. Cases of these eating disorders can be found in the records of the ancient Greeks, and the modern history of "fasting girls" began with publications in 1873 (Vandereycken & Lowenkopf, 1990). Even then the disorders were described as common, but they were subsumed under the diagnoses of *hysteria, neurasthenia* ("weak nerves"), and *sitophobia* ("fear of eating"), so they did not attract separate attention. A study of the incidence of anorexia over a 50-year period (1935–1984) in Rochester, Minnesota, revealed a steady rate for women aged 20 to 59 (Lucas et al., 1991). For women 10 to 19 years of age, there was a slight dip in the incidence in the 1950s and then a small increase in recent years. Some of the increase we are seeing now may simply reflect a greater willingness to admit to the disorders because the disorders are now recognized. Indeed, in some cases mothers whose daughters are being treated for these eating disorders admit somewhat sheepishly that they had similar problems when they were younger but that they never admitted the problems to anyone.

Gender and Age.   Women are much more likely than men to suffer from anorexia and bulimia, in a ratio of about 10 to 1 (Carlat & Camargo, 1991; Lucas et al., 1991). The disorders may have a somewhat earlier onset in women than men, a difference that may be due to the fact that women mature earlier than men.

Anorexia and bulimia are disorders primarily of late adolescence and early adulthood, with the most frequent age of onset being between 15 and 19 (Lucas et al., 1991; see Figure 16.8 [p. 396]). Fortunately, in most cases, the disorder burns out within a few years, although the individuals may experience some lingering concerns about weight. That is, the more serious symptoms of eating disorders appear to be time-limited.

Strategic Versus Other Eating Disorders.   Before discussing the causes of anorexia and bulimia, it is helpful to make a distinction between what appear to be two types of anorexia and bulimia. On the one hand, there are cases like the student in Case Study 16.3, in which the behavior appears to be *out of control* and *involuntary.* Just as the person with schizophrenia cannot voluntarily stop hallucinating, so these persons cannot control their inappropriate eating behaviors. On the other hand, there seem to be cases in which the persons show many of the symptoms of anorexia or bulimia, such as failure to maintain body weight or bingeing, but the behavior is *under voluntary control.* Many people diet excessively, numerous others abuse stimulants to curb appetite, and I know of women students who keep bottles of ipecac syrup hidden in their dresser drawers to use occasionally for purging when they have eaten too much. (Ipecac is a nonprescription medication designed to induce vomiting in children who have swallowed poison.) In these cases, however, the behavior is *voluntary, controllable,* and *designed to achieve a specific goal.* These behaviors might be called **strategic eating disorders** to distinguish them from the other eating disorders. There is now some research support for this clinically derived distinction. A factor analysis of the questionnaire responses of 313 individuals with eating disorders revealed one factor that involved loss of control and bingeing or vomiting as major components, and a second factor that involved concern with body shape, drive for thinness, and dieting behavior as major components (Tobin et al., 1991). The presence of these separate factors does not necessarily reflect the existence of distinct subtypes, but the existence of the factors is certainly suggestive.

Case Study 16.3

A STUDENT TALKS ABOUT HER BULIMIA AND HER DESPERATION

The following account was written by an honors student of mine who had suffered from anorexia while in high school and had suffered from bulimia for approximately 2 years before writing this.

"If I were to use one word to describe how it feels to be bulimic, I would use *desperate*. I experience many feelings while bingeing, purging, and waiting for the next cycle, but the most noticeable is desperation.

"Once I've decided to binge, I can't think of anything else. The first thing I have to do is get off by myself. I will lie to my friends and skip classes to get away. I usually tell my friends that I'm going to class or to study. I even leave for class early or late so no one will walk with me.

"After I figure out how I'm going to get off by myself, I think about money. What I eat when I binge depends on how much money I have. If I have quite a bit, I'll binge on whatever I crave regardless of cost. If I have only a little, I buy the cheapest things I can. Even if I'm broke, I will find a way to binge. At the sorority house, I will pack a big sack lunch. I've sold books for binge money, and I've borrowed from others. When all else fails, I'll even write a bad check.

"Next comes the actual binge. I usually eat at a number of places because I don't want anyone to know how much I actually eat. I almost always buy something I can carry out, and then I eat as I go from place to place. I do that because I have an irrational belief that as long as I am in the process of eating, the food is not being digested, but when I stop eating, my stomach will start working double time to get all the calories out of the food.

"This irrational belief leaves me feeling desperate to get rid of the food I've just eaten, and that leads to the purge. As soon as possible after eating, I travel from bathroom to bathroom purging. I don't want to spend too much time in any one bathroom because I'm afraid someone might walk in. I'm also afraid of leaving a noticeable odor. I think that I know every public bathroom in town, and I know when most of them are likely to be empty.

"My bingeing will take on different tones depending on why I am doing it. Sometimes it's just habit and I can't think of an alternative. In that case, I'm fairly calm and my actions have a determined, inevitable quality. It's almost like I'm in a trance. I purposefully move from place to place, and I don't get anxious about little inconveniences.

"More often, however, a specific event or emotion triggers a binge. It can be just about anything—fear, anger, depression. Whatever the reason for bingeing, the procedure takes on a frantic quality. I need to binge, and I need to do it immediately! I still take precautions so nobody knows what I'm doing, but I'm more likely to take some risks. The binge takes precedence over everything else. I eat faster, and I'm more likely to take laxatives if I don't think I've gotten rid of enough.

"Sometimes I feel relieved afterward, especially if it was an overwhelming or upsetting emotion that triggered the binge. If I'm bingeing out of habit, I usually feel depressed and might cry afterward wondering why I'm doing this to myself. Often I go right into another binge.

"It's not only when I'm bingeing that I feel desperate. In between binges, I am desperately searching for a strategy to stop the behavior. I've spent endless hours in the library and bookstores looking for an answer. I've read many diet books and tried their diets hoping that the structure of a diet will help me stop bingeing. I've read antidiet books, books on nutrition, and books on anorexia and bulimia. Ironically, I often read these books as I pig out. For me, bingeing, purging, and the desperate struggle have become a way of life."

Two other points should be noted with regard to the distinction between strategic and other eating disorders. First, the distinction is not currently "official" in that it is not made in DSM-IV; however, the distinction might be helpful when considering causes and treatments. Second, like many distinctions in abnormal psychology, this distinction might not reflect two separate types but instead could reflect the ends of a continuum.

Case Study 16.4 (p. 397) focuses on the eating behavior of Jane Fonda, who seems to have suffered from strategic anorexia and bulimia. Her experiences and behaviors are in sharp contrast to those of the young woman in Case Study 16.3, who described her behavior as uncontrolled and desperate.

Explanations

Psychodynamic Explanations.
Based on Freud's idea that eating can be a substitute for sex, it was suggested that the refusal to eat (anorexia) reflects the adolescent's anxiety about emerging sexual urges (Ross, 1977). In other words, it is thought that young

FIGURE 16.8   ANOREXIA OCCURS MOST
FREQUENTLY IN LATE
ADOLESCENCE AND EARLY
ADULTHOOD.

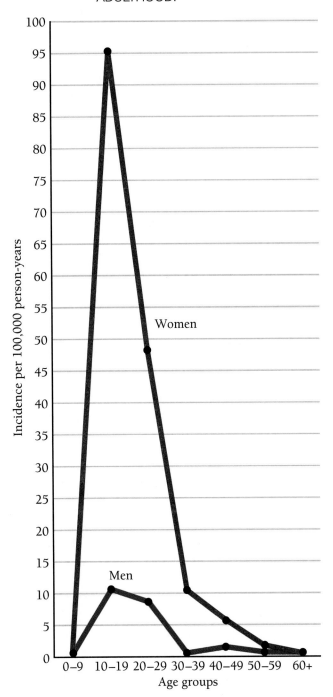

Source: Lucas et al. (1991), p. 919, tab. 2.

women with anorexia are symbolically avoiding sexuality by avoiding eating. In that regard, it is noteworthy that the starvation associated with anorexia does retard sexual development and can inhibit sexual drive.

It has also been suggested that women with anorexia were brought up in families in which there was a façade of happiness, but the families were actually characterized by competitiveness and striving for success (Bruch, 1982). Because the children could not meet the demands of the family, they developed a poor concept of self, became depressed, and used the refusal to eat as a way of passively rebelling and developing their own style of life.

Anorexia has also been explained by suggesting that the adolescent girl has strongly identified with the cultural standard that emphasizes slimness as beautiful. Gloria Vanderbilt pointed out that "you can never be too rich or too thin." Furthermore, the women in centerfold pictures and Miss America pageant winners have become progressively thinner over the decades (Garner et al., 1980). We are also constantly reminded of the importance of slimness by the numerous advertisements and articles pertaining to weight loss and dieting that appear in national magazines. Consistent with this emphasis on slimness, one study indicated that even though only 4% of girls between 12 and 18 years of age were medically overweight, 40% of them considered themselves overweight (Davies & Furham, 1986).

Finally, some psychodynamic theorists have suggested that bulimia is somehow related to childhood sexual abuse. In support of that hypothesis, many therapists report that their clients with eating disorders report memories of childhood sexual abuse. However, a review of the controlled research did not provide any evidence that reports of childhood sexual abuse were higher in women with eating disorders than they were in the general population, therefore leaving that explanation without controlled support (Pope & Hudson, 1992).

The various psychodynamic explanations for anorexia are derived from widely held theories of personality, but for the most part they are not supported by research findings, and therefore at present they can only be considered interesting speculations.

Learning Explanations.   Learning theorists suggest that anorexia may be brought on by rewards from the environment. Because "slim is in," individuals who are losing weight may get rewarded for being "lean and lovely," and that reinforces inappropriate diet behavior. If losing 5 lb is good, losing 25 lb must be even better. In women's dorms and sorority houses, it is not unusual for there to be weight-loss programs and even contests between groups, with the women losing the most weight getting attention, praise, and even prizes. The anorexic student who used to bring me desserts was particularly successful in this regard and was envied and consistently rewarded by her peers. Unfortu-

Case Study 16.4

JANE FONDA: A CASE OF STRATEGIC ANOREXIA AND BULIMIA

In the introduction of her first book on exercise, Jane Fonda (1981) talked about how for many years she binged, purged, and misused medication to control her weight. The bingeing apparently began at the age of 14, when she went away to boarding school. She and her classmates developed "a preoccupation with food," and she recalls bingeing on coffee ice cream by the gallon, pound cake by the pound, and brownies by the bagful. For the young Fonda, "eating binges were *de rigueur*" [required by fashion, etiquette, or custom]. The routine of eating binges became firmly established and was broken only by an occasional crash diet to slim down for a dance or a weekend away from school. In other words, bingeing was an activity, not a compulsion, and it could be stopped when necessary (e.g., to fit into a dress).

Fonda and her classmates discovered purging in a class on Roman civilization. It seems that during large feasts, the Romans would go to a room called a *vomitorium*, vomit up what they had eaten, and then return to the feast and start all over again. This was a great discovery for Fonda and her friends because, as she put it, they thought, "Ah-ha, here's a way to *not* have our cake and eat it too!" (p. 14). Fonda reports that she became addicted to the eat-and-binge cycle. Concerning its cause, she wrote, "I think it may be caused in large part by the combination of the social pressure to be thin and an almost infantile need to prove that you can be in control at least of your own body" (p. 14).

When she went to college, Fonda discovered another way to avoid weight: taking stimulants to curb appetite. She used Dexedrine and reports becoming addicted to the drug. She then experienced "a terrible sense of fatigue and depression" when she stopped taking it (see discussion of withdrawal symptoms in Chapter 18).

After college, Fonda worked as a model to support her acting lessons. She was thin but still concerned about gaining weight. She wanted to lose more weight because at the time, the extremely thin and angular look was the "ideal." The answer was more pills. She writes, "In boarding school I had discovered vomiting, in college Dexedrine, and as a model I learned about diuretics" (p. 15). Diuretics have the effect of reducing fluids in the body and thereby reducing weight. With diuretics, inches seemed to evaporate overnight, and Fonda took them for the next 20 years. Because her body adjusted to them (a process called tolerance; see Chapter 18), she had to keep increasing the dosage. The prescribed level was one pill every 3 days, but soon she was taking two or three pills a day. It wasn't until many years later that she learned that prolonged use of high levels of diuretics can be very dangerous unless the diuretics are accompanied by dietary supplements to replace the vitamins and minerals flushed out of the body with the fluids.

Clearly, for a long time, Fonda engaged in serious and potentially dangerous eating (and vomiting) patterns that might qualify as an eating disorder. These patterns started in her early teens, lasted well into adulthood, and involved bingeing, purging, and the inappropriate use of medication to reduce appetite and weight. As Fonda describes it, however, her behavior seems to have been goal-directed and voluntary. She wanted to achieve a culturally valued look (lean and lovely) that was essential for social acceptance and her profession. She used an inappropriate eating behavior to achieve her goal until she realized the danger and found alternatives. Her behavior had been "strategic," that is, effective for gaining acceptance and a professional goal, and over a long period of time had become a style of life. Although the pattern of her behavior was serious, it was quite different in nature from the irrational and uncontrolled starvation, bingeing, and purging seen in many persons with eating disorders.

---

nately, they did not realize that they were rewarding her for the symptoms of a potentially fatal disorder.

It is also possible that some cases of anorexia are due to a classically conditioned phobia for fatness or eating (Crisp, 1967). The thought of gaining weight may be anxiety provoking, and because eating leads to weight gain, anxiety may become associated with eating. The person then reduces that anxiety by avoiding eating. In fact, because not eating reduces the anxiety, the self-starvation is actually rewarded. One client told me that when she went through a cafeteria line, she would feel fine while in the salad section (nonfattening food) but would become increasingly anxious as she came closer and closer to the main course and dessert sections. She would therefore rush by those sections very quickly; her anxiety would subside when she got to the beverages, where she would take only water. The woman had developed a phobia for fattening foods, and she reduced her classically conditioned anxiety by avoiding them.

Learning theorists also suggest that the binge eating seen in bulimia is a brief but intensely pleasurable experience and that the bingeing is used to distract the individuals and help them briefly avoid anxiety (Heatherton & Baumeister, 1991). Many students "pig out" on foods like ice cream or french fries when under stress, and they find it pleasurable (rewarding). In one group of women with bulimia, tension was the most frequently mentioned factor that preceded a binge, and 66% of the subjects reported relief from the tension as a consequence of the binge (Abraham & Beumont, 1982). The purge may also be rewarding because it reduces the pains and weight gains that result from the binge.

Cognitive Explanations. Cognitive theorists hypothesize that individuals with anorexia have incorrect beliefs about their "weight problem" and that they exaggerate the consequences of gaining weight. The person starts out thinking, "I'm a little overweight," is concerned that the weight might become a problem, and embarks on a reasonable diet program. But as time goes by, the person begins exaggerating the seriousness of the "weight problem," focusing on any information suggesting that there is a problem, and ignoring information to the contrary. This selective attention leads to increasingly erroneous beliefs, severe dieting, and ultimately anorexia.

In one investigation, women who suffered from bulimia, women who dieted frequently, and women who neither suffered from bulimia nor dieted (controls) reported what they were thinking about every 30 minutes for 2 days (Zotter & Crowther, 1991). Inspection of the reports indicated that (a) the women with bulimia and the women who were dieting thought more about eating and weight than control women did, (b) the women with bulimia had more depression-related thoughts than the dieting and control women, and (c) the women with bulimia had more *distorted* thoughts about eating and weight (e.g., excessive weight, bad body shape) than the dieting and control women. Those findings, especially the ones reflecting distorted or erroneous thoughts, are consistent with the cognitive explanations.

Physiological Explanations. The physiological explanations for anorexia and bulimia revolve around a suspected malfunction of the **hypothalamus** (Hī-pō-THAL-uh-mus), the area of the brain that is responsible for appetite (Bemis, 1978). It appears that low levels of **serotonin** and **norepinephrine** (the neurotransmitters that are important for the functioning of the hypothalamus) may be responsible for the eating disorders. This explanation has its origins in early experiments with rats and monkeys in which it was found that if lesions were made in the lateral portions of the hypothalamus, the animals greatly reduced or ceased eating (Anand & Brobeck, 1951a, 1951b; Anand et al., 1955). It was also found that if the animals could be kept alive by artificial feeding techniques, many of them eventually recovered and began eating normally again, a pattern like that seen in humans with anorexia (Teitelbaum & Steller, 1954). In contrast, lesions made in the ventromedial hypothalamus resulted in excessive eating (Duggan & Booth, 1986). The parallel between animal and human behavior is provocative, but it does not necessarily prove that anorexia in humans is due to problems in the hypothalamus.

In working with humans, investigators were initially led to examine the relationship between eating disorders and low levels of serotonin and norepinephrine because eating disorders were almost always accompanied by depression. The reasoning was that because low levels of those neurotransmitters are related to depression, and because depression often co-occurs with eating disorders, low levels of those neurotransmitters might underlie both disorders.

Convincing evidence for the roles of serotonin and norepinephrine come from studies in which the investigators measured the levels of the neurotransmitters in individuals who were or were not suffering from eating disorders. (The neurotransmitters were usually measured indirectly by measuring metabolites in the cerebrospinal fluid.) For example, in one study the investigators measured the levels of neurotransmitters in patients who had a *high frequency of binges* (mean of 23 binges per week), patients who had a *low frequency of binges* (mean of 10 binges per week), and individuals who did not have eating disorders. Levels were measured at the time the patients were admitted for treatment and again 4 weeks later after eating patterns were stabilized with careful behavioral control (staff members accompanied the patients whenever they went to the bathroom or left the ward) (Jimerson et al., 1992). The results indicated that high-frequency bingers had lower levels of serotonin than the low-frequency bingers both at the time of admission and later when eating patterns were stabilized. These results are presented in Figure 16.9.

The low levels of serotonin in bulimia are particularly interesting not only because they might contribute to problems of appetite, but also because they are linked to decreases in inhibition (see Chapter 10). That is, the low levels of serotonin might contribute to the impulsive and excessive eating and subsequent purging seen in bulimia, behaviors that ordinarily would be inhibited. Finally, it is noteworthy that a drug that is used to reduce appetite in the treatment of obesity (Pondimin/fenfluramine) achieves that result by reducing serotonin activity (and can bring on depres-

FIGURE 16.9   HIGH-FREQUENCY BINGERS HAD LOWER LEVELS OF SEROTONIN (METABOLITE) THAN LOW-FREQUENCY BINGERS AT ADMISSION AND AFTER EATING WAS STABILIZED.

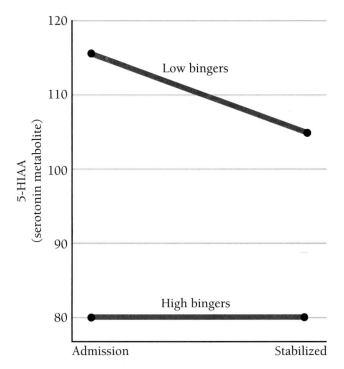

Source: Adapted from Jimerson et al. (1992), p. 134, fig. 1.

sion as a side effect). Overall then, there is considerable evidence linking neurotransmitters to eating behavior.

If low levels of serotonin and norepinephrine are related to eating disorders, then it would be expected that correcting those levels with drugs would correct the eating disorders. In fact, as we will see later when we discuss treatment, antidepressant drugs that increase the levels of serotonin and norepinephrine are indeed effective for treating eating disorders.

Low levels of serotonin and norepinephrine provide only half of the explanation, however, because we must also know what causes the levels of those neurotransmitters to be low. There are two possibilities, the first of which is *prolonged stress*. The results of numerous experiments have indicated that stress leads to reduced levels of serotonin and norepinephrine (see Chapter 9), so prolonged psychological stress could trigger the physiological process that leads to the eating disorder.

The second possibility is that the problem is due to *genetic factors*. Supporting this possibility are the re-

sults of investigations of anorexia in monozygotic (MZ) and dizygotic (DZ) twins. In two studies, the concordance rate for the disorder was high in MZ twin pairs (75% and 45%, respectively), whereas the concordance rate in DZ twin pairs was zero (Nowlin, 1983; Schepank, 1981).

At present we have some good explanations for eating disorders, but no one explanation accounts for all cases. As with other disorders we have discussed, it is probable that more than one explanation is correct and that different types of eating disorders have different causes. For example, strategic eating disorders may be accounted for best in terms of learning or erroneous cognitions, whereas involuntary eating disorders may be due to physiological factors. Different causes would require different approaches to treatment, and next we will consider the treatment of eating disorders.

Treatment

Alarm over the prevalence and seriousness of anorexia and bulimia among adolescents and young adults led to the development of what are generally referred to as eating disorder clinics. These are inpatient facilities that are usually part of a general hospital. The clinics differ in therapeutic orientation (e.g., psychodynamic, learning, eclectic), but most place a heavy reliance on external control of eating behavior. Diets are carefully prepared, food intake is closely monitored, and opportunities for purging are eliminated by controlling access to bathrooms and other areas where an individual might vomit. Such clinics are usually rather expensive ($800 per day), and clients usually stay for 90 days (the amount of time covered by health insurance). Of course, not all persons with anorexia and bulimia can be treated in eating disorder clinics, and many are treated in more typical outpatient clinics.

Psychodynamic-Based Treatments.   Psychodynamic treatments usually involve attempts to relieve depression and improve self-concepts because those factors are believed to be the causes of anorexia and bulimia. Numerous case studies involving this type of treatment have been reported, but there is no controlled evidence that the psychodynamic treatment is effective (e.g., Bruch, 1973; Holmgren et al., 1984; Sohlberg et al., 1987).

Learning-Based Treatments.   Therapists have also used the principles of learning and have provided rewards (e.g., visitors, television, tokens) for appropriate eating and weight gains (Azerrad & Stafford, 1969; Geller et al., 1978; Halmi et al., 1975; Mizes & Lohr,

1983). Unfortunately, the absence of controlled research makes it impossible to conclude that these techniques are effective.

Cognitive-Based Treatments.

A substantial amount of controlled research has been conducted to assess the effects of cognitive therapy on eating disorders, and a variety of positive results have been reported (see review by Craighead & Agras, 1991). In one experiment, 40 women who were suffering from bulimia were randomly assigned to either an immediate cognitive-behavioral treatment condition or to a delayed cognitive-behavioral treatment condition (Telch et al., 1990). Women in the immediate treatment condition participated in one 90-minute group therapy session per week for a 10-week period and then were followed up after another 10-week period. In contrast, women in the delayed treatment condition did not receive any treatment for the first 10-week period but then participated in the treatment program during the next 10-week period. In the treatment sessions, the women were taught first how to identify the patterns of eating, thinking, and mood that triggered binge-eating episodes. Then they were taught how to gradually develop alternative patterns that would lead to healthy, binge-free eating. Self-reports of binge eating were collected at the beginning of the project, after the first 10-week period (treatment or delay), and after the second 10-week period (treatment or follow-up). The results indicated that the women who were treated in the first 10-week period showed reductions in binges relative to the women whose treatment was delayed. Those results are presented in Figure 16.10. It was also found that the women who were treated in the second 10-week period showed reductions in binges like those shown earlier by the other women. These and other findings clearly indicate that changing thought patterns about eating and weight can alter the symptoms of eating disorders in many people.

Physiologically Based Treatments.

The physiological approach is founded on the notion that the disorders stem from low levels of norepinephrine or serotonin, and therefore treatment involves the use of drugs that increase the levels of those neurotransmitters. Because the neurotransmitters that are low in anorexia and bulimia are the same ones that are low in depression, the treatment of anorexia and bulimia involves the use of *antidepressant* drugs, namely, bicyclics, tricyclics, and MAO inhibitors (Pryor et al., 1990; see Chapter 11).

Substantial evidence has accumulated indicating that antidepressant drugs are effective for treating many cases of anorexia and bulimia (Fluoxetine Bu-

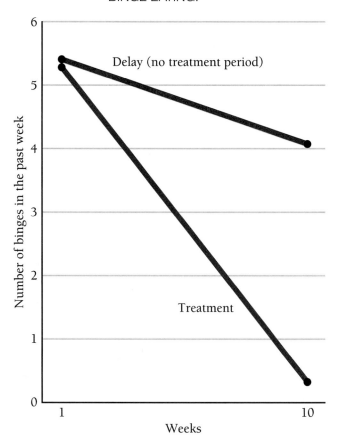

FIGURE 16.10   COGNITIVE-BEHAVIORAL THERAPY WAS EFFECTIVE FOR REDUCING BINGE EATING.

Source: Adapted from Telch et al. (1990), p. 632, tab. 1.

limia Nervosa Collaborative Study Group, 1992; Hughes et al., 1986; Marcus et al., 1990; Mitchell & Groat, 1984; Pope & Hudson, 1982, 1984; Pope et al., 1983; Walsh et al., 1982; Walsh et al., 1984; Walsh et al., 1991). For example, in one experiment 387 patients with bulimia were either put on a relatively *low level of Prozac* (20 mg per day), a relatively *high level of Prozac* (60 mg per day), or a *placebo* (Fluoxetine Group, 1992). Prozac was used because it blocks the reuptake of serotonin, thereby increasing the level of serotonin at the synapse (see Chapters 2 and 11). When reductions in vomiting were assessed, the high dose of Prozac was most effective, followed by the low dose and then the placebo. Those results are presented in Figure 16.11. Similar results were found when reductions in binge eating were considered.

In another experiment, patients suffering from bulimia were given either a tricyclic (Norpramin/desipramine) or a placebo for 6 weeks (Hughes et al., 1986). The patients taking the tricyclic experienced a 91% decrease in binge eating and a 30% decrease in depression. In contrast, the patients taking the place-

FIGURE 16.11   PROZAC (FLUOXETINE) WAS SUPERIOR TO A PLACEBO FOR REDUCING VOMITING IN WOMEN WITH BULIMIA.

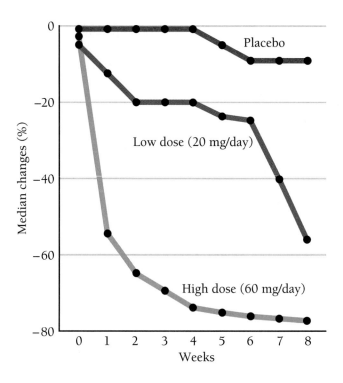

Source: Fluoxetine Bulimia Nervosa Collaborative Study Group (1992), p. 142, fig. 1.

bo showed only a 19% decrease in binge eating and only a 5% decrease in depression. Later, when the patients who originally took the placebo were given the tricyclic, they showed an 84% decrease in binge eating, thus offering additional support for the effects of the drug.

Other evidence concerning the effects of tricyclics comes from analyses of the levels of the drug found in the patients' blood. In 10 patients, the drug level in the blood was below the level that is thought to be necessary to be effective. Four of those patients had recovered, but the other six still had symptoms. When the dosage level was increased for the six patients who still had symptoms, four of them recovered completely, thus suggesting that when the drug did not work, in most cases it was probably due to an insufficient dose level.

Positive effects have also been found with MAO inhibitors (Walsh et al., 1984). However, one cautionary note should be sounded concerning the use of the MAOIs. I pointed out earlier that when taking these drugs, patients must control their diets carefully be-

cause the combination of the drugs and certain foods can be fatal (see Chapter 11). Unfortunately, many of the foods eaten while bingeing are on the restricted list, and thus we must be very careful in the use of MAO inhibitors for treating bulimia.

In many cases the drug effects appear to last as long as the patients stay on the drug. In one 2-year follow-up study of 20 women with bulimia who were treated with antidepressants, 85% either maintained or improved on their original response to the drug (Pope et al., 1985). Of the other three subjects, one relapsed after she ceased taking her medication, and two others showed only a partial return to their binge-eating symptoms. Other investigators have raised concerns about the long-term effectiveness of the drug treatment of eating disorders, and this is a topic on which future research must be focused (Walsh et al., 1991).

One other comment is warranted concerning the selection of medications. Some individuals with eating disorders are apprehensive about taking tricyclics because one side effect is weight gains. This problem can be overcome with Prozac, which normalizes eating patterns for many persons but which does not cause weight gain.

The experiments on the effects of bicyclics, tricyclics, and MAO inhibitors for treating eating disorders have shown that the drugs can be very effective, but note that no drug was effective for treating all patients. Therefore, it may be that there are subgroups of patients who are responsive to different types of drugs (as different types of depressive patients respond to different types of drugs) or that eating disorders stem from different causes, only one of which is physiological.

OTHER EATING DISORDERS

There are two other eating disorders, *pica* and *rumination*, but they are relatively rare and usually limited to infants or very young children. Although the symptom patterns have been described, little is known about the etiology of these disorders.

Pica

The major symptom of **pica** (PĪ-kuh) is the persistent eating of nonnutritive substances such as paint, plaster, hair, cloth, sand, bugs, leaves, pebbles, and animal droppings. For reasons that are not yet understood, the child prefers to eat nonnutritive substances over food. This symptom pattern can result in serious weight loss, malnutrition, poisoning, and intestinal problems.

Rumination

The word *rumination* comes from a Latin word meaning "to chew the cud," and the major symptom of the **rumination disorder** is the repeated regurgitation of food. The regurgitation does not involve typical vomiting activity (retching, nausea, disgust). Instead, the young child brings partially digested food up into the mouth and either spits it out or rechews it and reswallows it much as a cow chews its cud. The activity seems to result in considerable pleasure and satisfaction. The disorder can be serious because if the food is continually spit out, the child will suffer from malnutrition and may die. Fortunately, spontaneous remissions are thought to be common.

• Other Disorders

ELIMINATION DISORDERS

Symptoms

Enuresis (EN-yoo-RĒ-sis) is the voluntary or involuntary voiding of urine into the child's clothing or bed after the age at which the child should be able to control the flow of urine. An individual is said to suffer from enuresis if he or she voids inappropriately at least twice a week for 3 months after the age of 5.

Encopresis (EN-kō-PRĒ-sis) is the voluntary or involuntary passage of feces in inappropriate places such as in clothing or on the floor. To be diagnosed as suffering from encopresis, the child must be at least 4 years old because toilet training should be completed by that age, and inappropriate bowel movements must occur at least once a month for a period of 3 months so as to ensure that the symptoms are not just accidents. Both enuresis and encopresis are thought to be psychological, and therefore in making the diagnoses, physical disorders such as infections must be ruled out. Here we will focus on enuresis because it is a more widespread problem than encopresis and because more is known about it.

A distinction is made between *primary enuresis*, in which the individual has not had a dry period of longer than 1 year, and *secondary enuresis*, in which the individual has been dry for a period of at least a year and then begins to wet again. In the case of primary enuresis, the individual never gained control, whereas with secondary enuresis, control was achieved and then something happened to interfere with the control.

Enuresis is much more common than many people realize (see Figure 16.12). It is estimated that it occurs in 10% to 20% of 5-year-olds, 7% of 7-year-olds, and as many as 2% of individuals over the age of 14 (Doleys, 1983; Lovibond & Coote, 1969; Pierce, 1980; Verhulst et al., 1985). The disorder is more common in boys than girls (Rutter et al., 1973). Because it is so common, it has been suggested that wetting at age 5 or 6 is not abnormal and that the cutoff point for labeling it a disorder should be moved up to age 8. As some indication of the degree of the problem and the level of concern about it, it might be noted that just as there are summer camps for children who want to learn football, baseball, or horseback riding, there are now summer camps for kids with enuresis who want to learn bladder control.

Explanations

Psychodynamic Explanations. The psychodynamic explanations assume that enuresis stems from intrapsychic conflict. For example, Freud (1905/1953) suggested that it was a substitute for masturbation, which was forbidden. Other theorists posited that enuresis is a form of passive aggression stemming from the Oedipus attraction or that it results from a regression to an earlier stage of development in the face of conflict (Fenichel, 1945; Mowrer, 1950). These explanations do not have any empirical support.

More general psychodynamic theories suggest that stress inhibits the learning of bladder control or disrupts learning that may have already occurred (Couchells et al., 1981; Douglas, 1973; Morgan & Young, 1972; Shaffer, 1973; Stein & Susser, 1966). As evidence for the role of stress, theorists point out that in many cases, children with enuresis show other adjustment problems (Stehbens, 1970). In other words, stress leads to enuresis as well as other problems. Alternatively, it is possible that the other adjustment problems seen in children with enuresis are not a reflection of stress in general but rather a result of the enuresis. Consistent with that possibility, there is evidence that when the symptoms of enuresis are treated and reduced, the other problems also diminish (Baker, 1969; Baller, 1975; Starfield, 1972). Stress undoubtedly plays a role in many cases of enuresis, but whether it is a cause, an effect, or both has not yet been determined.

Learning Explanations. A widely held explanation for enuresis is that the individual has simply not yet learned the urine retention response (Lovibond & Coote, 1969). Evidence for this explanation comes from research indicating that the use of training procedures in which bladder control is taught are very ef-

FIGURE 16.12   LOSS OF BLADDER CONTROL AT LEAST ONCE A
MONTH IS A PROBLEM FOR MANY YOUNGSTERS.

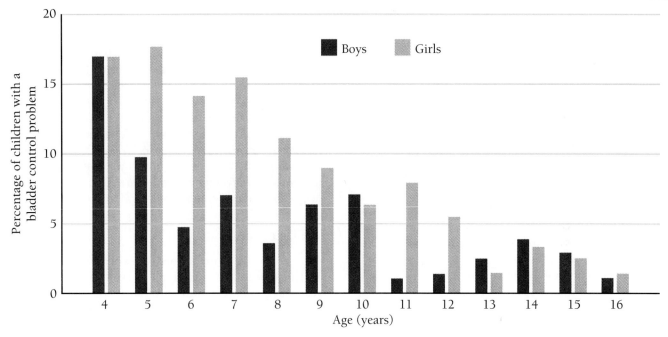

Source: Verhulst et al. (1985), p. 992, fig. 1.

fective for overcoming enuresis in many individuals. Those procedures and results will be considered in greater detail in our discussion of treatment.

Physiological Explanations. There are a number of physiological explanations for enuresis, the first of which is that the disorder stems from a maturational lag or delay in the normal development of the neurological system that governs bladder control (Troup & Hodgson, 1971). In other words, the neurological development necessary for bladder control may be delayed in some individuals, thereby preventing them from learning bladder control. Consistent with the developmental-lag hypothesis is the finding that almost all individuals do outgrow the disorder eventually.

A second physiological explanation is that the level of bladder pressure that is necessary to stimulate urination is lower in some children than in others. The lower pressure that is required for urination in children with enuresis may not be sufficient to wake them up if they are sleeping or alert them if they are awake, thus resulting in uncontrolled or unexpected urination (Yates, 1975).

A third physiological explanation is that children with enuresis sleep more deeply than other children, and their bladder tension is not sufficient to awaken them so that they can go to the toilet. The evidence

for differences in sleep patterns between children who do and do not have enuresis is contradictory at best. Moreover, the deep-sleep hypothesis has difficulty explaining problems with bladder control experienced by some children during waking hours (Gillin et al., 1982). For these reasons, this explanation has largely been rejected.

The exact physiological mechanism underlying enuresis is not clear, but we do have evidence linking genetic factors to enuresis. Numerous reports indicate that between 40% and 60% of children with enuresis have parents who had the same problem as children (Bakwin, 1961; Michaels & Goodman, 1934; Stockwell & Smith, 1940). In view of the stigma associated with bedwetting, it is likely that parents underreport the problem, and thus even the relationships that have been found may be understated. Furthermore, in one study of twins, there was a concordance rate of 70.4% for enuresis among monozygotic boys, but the rate was only 30.5% among dizygotic boys (Bakwin, 1971). The respective concordance rates for girls were 65.4% and 43.8%. The maturational lag and low-pressure hypotheses are viable explanations for primary enuresis in which the individual has never achieved bladder control, but by themselves, those hypotheses cannot account for secondary enuresis in which control is achieved and then lost. However, it is possible that individuals with secondary enuresis have the mechanisms necessary for bladder control but also have a predisposition for the disruption of those mechanisms when exposed to stress. In other words, like many other disorders we have discussed, secondary enuresis may be the result of a biological predisposition in combination with environmental factors such as stress. This interaction explanation seems to account for much of the data, but it is still speculative.

Treatment

Traditional psychotherapy has not been particularly effective for treating enuresis (Doleys, 1978), and at present the most popular approach to treatment involves what is known as the **bell-and-pad procedure**. With this procedure an electrically wired pad is placed beneath the sheet of the child's bed. When the child urinates in the bed, the fluid serves to close a circuit in the pad, which immediately sounds a bell that awakens the child, who then stops urinating in bed and goes to the toilet. (See Lovibond & Coote, 1969; Werry, 1967.)

A review of the research on the bell-and-pad technique suggests that it is effective with about 75% of the treated cases (Doleys, 1977). The problem is that among the individuals who are originally helped with this technique, about 40% relapse. However, if the treatment procedure is reinstituted, about 30% of the individuals regain bladder control.

There are two theories to explain the effectiveness of the bell-and-pad procedure. The classical conditioning explanation suggests that bladder tension becomes associated with the bell, awakening, and cessation of urination so that eventually the child wakes up and withholds urine when the bladder tension develops (Mowrer & Mowrer, 1938). The operant avoidance conditioning explanation suggests that being suddenly awakened by the bell is unpleasant, and the child learns to avoid that by withholding urination (Lovibond, 1963). At present, we do not understand why the bell-and-pad technique works, but from a practical standpoint, the important thing is that it does work.

A variety of drugs have also been used to treat enuresis, and the tricyclic antidepressants have been found to be somewhat effective (see review by Blackwell & Currah, 1973). The reason for their effectiveness is not clear, but the drugs probably inhibit the urination reflex. Some critics have suggested that enuresis is a "depressive equivalent" (a symptom of depression) and that the drugs are effective because they reduce depression. However, that seems unlikely because the drugs have an immediate effect on the enuretic disorder, whereas they take weeks to reduce depression (see Chapter 11).

■ TIC DISORDERS

In general, **tics** involve *involuntary recurrent motor movements*. The movements range from small twitches to large movements of major portions of the body. Some tics involve the muscles of the diaphragm and result in grunts, noises, and even words, but those are rare. Individuals with tics can consciously suppress the tics for short periods of time, but as soon as attention is turned away, the tics return. Tic disorders occur more frequently in males than in females, but generally they are rare. There are two types of tic disorders. The simple tic disorder involves only small to moderate muscle movements; Tourette's disorder involves larger muscle movements and vocal utterances.

Tic Disorder

Children with a **tic disorder** experience recurrent and involuntary contractions of skeletal muscles that result in jerking or twitching movements of the body or face. Eye blinks and facial twitches are most common. By themselves, tics are simple and usually not particularly serious, but they can lead to unfortunate secondary effects. Specifically, a child with a tic will often be the target of ridicule from peers, which may lead the child to feel ashamed and to withdraw socially. Tics can occur during only a brief transient period or may be a chronic problem.

Tourette's Disorder

Tourette's disorder involves tics like those in the tic disorder, but they often involve more and larger muscle groups, so the motor movements are more pronounced. More important, Tourette's disorder involves **vocal tics** that result in grunts, yelps, barks, and words. As many as 30% of the individuals with Tourette's disorder have a verbal tic that involves the involuntary uttering of obscenities (Comings, 1990). For example, in the absence of any reason for doing so, the individual might yell out words that most other people find shocking. This syndrome, known as **coprolalia** (kop-ruh-LĀ-lē-uh), can obviously be very disruptive of normal psychosocial functioning. The tics seen in Tourette's disorder can be voluntarily suppressed for short periods of time, but as soon as attention is diverted, they return.

The symptoms of Tourette's disorder are made worse by stress, and a vicious cycle can develop in which the symptoms result in social stress, which in turn increases the likelihood of the symptoms. The disorder usually appears around age 7, it is three times more likely to occur in males than females, and it lasts throughout adulthood (Comings, 1990). Individuals with Tourette's disorder often also show symptoms of the attention-deficit hyperactivity disorder and the obsessive-compulsive disorder (Comings & Comings, 1990).

Explanations

Psychodynamic theorists have speculated that tics reflect a breaking through of pent-up energy associated with unconscious conflicts and that tics that involve blinking of the eyes or turning away represent attempts by the individual to avoid conflicts (Fenichel, 1945). A more widely accepted explanation is that tics are due to an organic brain dysfunction (Bauer & Shea, 1984; Cohen & Leckman, 1984; Comings, 1990). More specifically, tics are probably due to excessively high levels of dopamine activity. In that regard, recall that dopamine is the neurotransmitter in the area of the brain responsible for motor activity and that it is involved in the involuntary twitching movements seen in tardive dyskinesia and Parkinson's disease (see Chapters 15 and 20).

Evidence linking Tourette's disorder to dopamine activity includes findings that drugs that increase dopamine activity exacerbate tics and drugs that reduce dopamine activity (neuroleptics such as Haldol) can be effective for treating tic disorders (Gittelman & Kanner, 1986; Kurlan, 1989; Zamula, 1988). It has been suggested that coprolalia can be explained by the fact that dopamine is also an important transmitter in the limbic system which is responsible for emotion; that is, the elevated emotion in combination with the elevated tic behavior might result in the spontaneous utterance of obscenities (Messiha & Carlson, 1983). A number of factors could contribute to the excessive dopamine activity, but primary among them is genetics (see review by Devor, 1990). For example, there is evidence that the incidence of the disorder is higher in family members with the disorder than it is in the general population (7.4% vs. .05%) and that the concordance rate is higher among monozygotic than dizygotic twins (Messiha & Carlson, 1983; Pauls et al., 1984; Shapiro & Shapiro, 1982).

SUMMARY

In this chapter, we discussed four groups of disorders that usually first appear during infancy, childhood, or adolescence. In the group of disruptive disorders, we first considered the attention-deficit hyperactivity disorder, which involves inattention, impulsivity, and hyperactivity. This problem first becomes apparent during early childhood, but the symptoms can persist into adolescence and adulthood. Learning and cognitive theorists believe that children with this disorder have not learned how to control or focus attention. Other theorists suggest that the disorder is due to organic brain dysfunction. Relationships have been found between this disorder and environmental factors (ingestion of lead, food additives), pregnancy and birth factors (infection, anoxia), and genetic factors. The most effective and widely used treatment involves administering stimulants (Ritalin, Dexedrine), which have the effect of helping the individual focus attention more effectively. The symptoms of the conduct disorders were also reviewed. Conduct disorders have been explained in terms of frustration resulting from child-rearing practices, observational learning of aggression, views of the world as hostile, and biological factors that include low levels of serotonin, high levels of testosterone, and genetics.

In the group of developmental disorders, we first examined infantile autism, a disorder that is apparent soon after birth and involves a lack of responsiveness to other people, impairment of communication skills, and a restricted repertoire of activities. The disorder probably stems from some yet undetermined organic cause, and problems during pregnancy or birth and genetic factors are associated with the disorder. At present, we do not have an effective treatment for autism. We also gave some brief attention to the symptoms of the learning, communication, and motor skills disorders. It was pointed out that there is some question as to whether these problems should even be considered psychological or psychiatric disorders.

Third, we discussed eating disorders, the most important of which are anorexia and bulimia. Anorexia involves a pervasive fear of becoming fat that results in excessive dieting and serious weight loss. Bulimia revolves around binge eating and purging. The disorders have been explained by suggesting that individuals with these disorders are reacting against a demanding and unpleasant family situation, taking the cultural preference for slimness to an extreme, suffering from a classically conditioned phobia for eating and fatness, exaggerating and overresponding to a purported weight problem, or suffering from a hypothalamic malfunction (low levels of serotonin or norepinephrine) that may be due to prolonged stress or genetic problems. Treatments involving changing cognitions and antidepressants appear to be the fastest and most effective treatments. We also briefly reviewed the symptoms of pica (eating of nonnutritive substances) and rumination (regurgitation) that occur in infants or very young children.

In the last group of disorders, we first discussed enuresis, which involves bedwetting. Wetting by itself is not a particularly serious problem, but the anxiety, lowered self-esteem, and social stigma associated with it can result in psychological problems. The best explanations for the disorder include failure to learn bladder control, physiological mechanisms that may be inherited, or a combination of those factors. The bell-and-pad treatment procedure is relatively effective. Finally, we explored tic disorders (the simple tic disorder and Tourette's disorder), which involve involuntary muscle movements and sometimes vocal tics.

KEY TERMS, CONCEPTS, AND NAMES

In reviewing and testing yourself on what you have learned from this chapter, you should be able to identify and discuss each of the following:

amenorrhea	echolalia	pica
anorexia nervosa	encopresis	play therapy
anoxia	enuresis	pronoun reversal
attention-deficit hyperactivity disorder	high-functioning individuals	response stereotypy
aversive procedures	hypothalamus	Ritalin (methylphenidate)
bell-and-pad procedure	infantile autism	rumination disorder
bulimia nervosa	learning, communication, and motor	self-instruction
conduct disorders	skills disorders	serotonin
coprolalia	norepinephrine	strategic eating disorders
developmental disorders	oppositional defiant disorder	tic disorder
Dexedrine (dextroamphetamine)	paradoxical drug effect	tics
disruptive behavior disorders	pervasive developmental disorder	Tourette's disorder
eating disorders	physical anomalies	vocal tics

Notes:

Chapter 17

Psychological Influences on Physical Disorders

• O U T L I N E •

Bill was an enthusiastic, aggressive, effective mid-level executive who was rapidly climbing the corporate ladder at a computer company. Bill always set high goals for himself, and while others complained about pressure, he sought it out. Because of the demands he placed on himself (in addition to those inherent in his job), Bill was always "on the run." He became impatient in meetings when others talked slowly or took time to state the obvious. When that happened, he would jump in and finish their sentences for them so they could "get on with it." Even while driving, he conducted business over his car phone. Bill was making progress, but it was brought to an immediate halt when, at the age of 43, he had a serious heart attack. The combined effects of stress and a poor diet had resulted in an almost total blockage of the arteries that provide blood for the muscles of the heart. Bill survived the attack, and now, with his usual enthusiasm and commitment, he is involved in a rehabilitation program. He has changed his diet, is on a rigorous program of aerobic exercise, and tries to "stop to smell the flowers" now and then.

Helen has been under a lot of stress during the past 6 months. Her mother was seriously ill and then died 3 months ago; 2 months ago, she and her husband moved from Chicago to Los Angeles; and now she is struggling with the problems of establishing herself in her new job as well as looking after their 3-year-old son. Lately she has been sick a lot: colds, sore throats, the flu. The prolonged stress may well have reduced the functioning of her immune system, making her less able to fight off infections.

Chris has been having severe pains in his stomach, and the other day, he coughed up some blood. He knew before he went to his physician what the problem was: ulcers. His father had them, so he knew the symptoms. His physician prescribed some medication that reduced the production of stomach acid, but also warned him that the medication was just a stopgap measure; he would have to reduce the stress in his life.

In this chapter, we will consider how psychological factors can cause or exacerbate physical disorders such as heart attacks, high blood pressure, strokes, headaches, asthma, muscle and joint pain, rashes, ulcers, colds, and even cancer. Physical disorders that are influenced by psychological factors were once referred to as **psychosomatic** or **psychophysiological disorders**, but those labels are no longer used officially. The realization that psychological factors contribute to many physical disorders has led to the development of the new area of **health psychology**, in which psychologists work to identify, prevent, and treat the psychological factors that lead to physical illnesses.

At the outset, we should distinguish between the disorders to be discussed here and the **somatoform disorders** that were discussed in Chapter 6. In somatoform disorders, *psychological factors cause symptoms of physical disorders, but there is no actual physical disorder* (e.g., no tissue damage). For example, an individual with a conversion disorder may have a paralyzed arm, but there is no actual damage to the nerves, muscles, or bones of the arm. In the disorders to be discussed now, psychological factors lead to *real physical disorders*. For example, prolonged psychological stress can cause the production of excess acid in the stomach, and the acid in turn causes ulcers (holes in the walls of the stomach).

The fact that psychological factors such as stress can influence physiological functioning provides an interesting balance for the findings reviewed earlier in this book that physiological factors such as neurotransmitters can influence psychological functioning. Clearly, the more we learn, the more we realize that there is a considerable degree of overlap and interaction between the psychological and physiological causes of psychological and physiological disorders. Our increased understanding of the interplay between psychological and physical factors has led us to abandon the once-popular notion of **mind-body dualism**, which suggests that the mind and body operate separately from each other.

STRESS AND PHYSIOLOGICAL RESPONSES

Stress is the psychological factor that underlies the development of most physical illnesses. We discussed stress in Chapter 2, so here I will simply review the steps that lead from stressors to stress to physical disorders (see Table 2.8). A *stressor* is a situation or problem that requires an *adjustment* that overtaxes us. Once we become aware of the situation or problem, we attempt to *cope* with it through constructive problem solving. If coping fails, the *stress response* is triggered. The stress response has both a *psychological component* (e.g., anxiety) and a *physiological component* (e.g., elevated heart rate). We may respond to the stress with *defense mechanisms* that may reduce the stress but do not solve the underlying problem. If the defense is not effective, the psychological and physiological components of stress will remain high. It is the prolonged elevation of the physiological component of stress that leads to the physical disorders we will discuss in this chapter. Specifically, the prolonged elevation of responses such as heart rate, blood pressure, and muscle tension and the production of excessive gastric acid can lead to physical disorders such as heart attacks, hypertension, headaches, and ulcers. Because the nervous system provides the link between the psychological stressors and the body's physiological responses, we will briefly review the organization and function of the nervous system before considering the body's responses.

System Organization and Function

The organization of the nervous system is summarized in Figure 17.1 (p. 412). The system is divided into two major parts, the **central nervous system** and the **peripheral nervous system**. The central nervous system consists of the *brain* and the *spinal cord*, and its major function is to *interpret information* and *initiate responses*. In contrast, the peripheral nervous system involves all of the nerve connections that are *not* in the brain and spinal cord, and its major function is to *carry information* to and from the central nervous system.

Psychological factors contribute to many physical disorders. For example, prolonged stress may eventually reduce the functioning of this individual's immune system.

FIGURE 17.1   THE NERVOUS SYSTEM IS ORGANIZED INTO TWO MAJOR
              DIVISIONS.

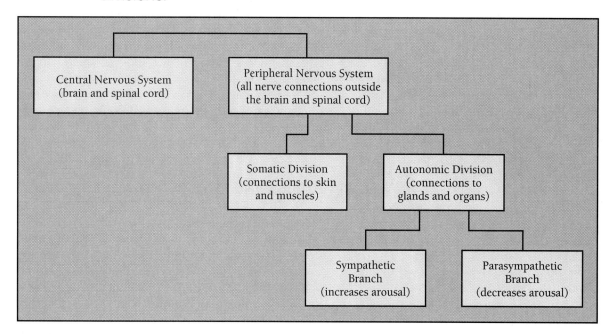

The peripheral nervous system is in turn divided into two divisions. The **somatic division** connects the central nervous system to the *muscles* and *skin*, and the **autonomic division** connects the central nervous system to various *glands* and *organs*. The autonomic division is of most interest in our study of stress because the increased activity of structures such as the adrenal glands and the heart play a crucial role in the physiological stress response.

The autonomic system is divided into the **sympathetic branch**, which is responsible for *increasing arousal*, and the **parasympathetic branch**, which is responsible for *decreasing arousal*. However, the two branches are connected, so activity in one branch eventually leads to activity in the other branch, and therefore a balance is usually achieved. For example, when confronted with a stressor, the sympathetic branch is activated and increases arousal by increasing the activity of various organs and glands (e.g., higher heart rate, more acid to the stomach). Activation of the sympathetic branch also leads to the activation of the parasympathetic branch, which then decreases arousal by decreasing activity of organs and glands (e.g., lower heart rate, less acid to the stomach). If the systems were not interconnected and one or the other system was allowed to run unchecked, arousal would soar out of control or we would lapse into a comatose state.

There are three additional points to recognize concerning the organization and function of the nervous system. First, stressors result in the intense and prolonged stimulation of the sympathetic branch of the autonomic system, thereby overwhelming the calming effect of the parasympathetic branch. As long as new and stressful stimulation is coming in, the sympathetic branch will be continually activated, and you will remain in a high state of arousal.

Second, the sympathetic branch responds as a unit, so when it is stimulated, there is a general, undifferentiated arousal. This is the reason that many of the components of the stress response may actually be irrelevant for a particular stressor. For example, an increase in heart rate may be necessary to supply blood to the muscles when you are confronted by an attacker and have to fight or run, but an increase in heart rate is irrelevant (and possibly even distracting) when you are confronted with a stressful intellectual problem (a difficult examination). The general physiological response to stressors may have been adaptive for our ancestors, whose biggest problem was running away from wild animals, but it is maladaptive today, when most stressors are of the cognitive or intellectual type. Because of the undifferentiated nature of the response to stress, the physical disorders that result from stress are often unrelated to the types of stress that bring them on. For example, getting high blood pressure is not functionally related to prolonged intellectual stress.

Third, the autonomic division is not under voluntary control (the autonomic division is *automatic*), so you cannot voluntarily control the arousal generated by the sympathetic branch. For example, when under stress, your heart may beat fast and your blood pressure may go up, but under most circumstances you cannot do much to control those responses.

Paths of Physiological Responding

The nervous system responds to a stressor via two paths, and they are summarized in Figure 17.2. When you cannot cope with a situation, a signal is sent to the **hypothalamus**, the area of the brain responsible for general arousal. The hypothalamus then sends signals along the two paths of the autonomic division of the peripheral nervous system. One path involves the stimulation of the **pituitary gland**, which in turn stimulates the **adrenal cortex** (the outside shell of the **adrenal glands**), causing **cortisol** to be released into the bloodstream. The release of cortisol results in increased levels of **glucose** (blood sugar), which provides the energy for action.

The second path involves the stimulation of the **brain stem** and parts of the **spinal cord**, which in turn stimulate the interior portion of the adrenal

FIGURE 17.2   THE PHYSIOLOGICAL RESPONSE TO STRESSORS FOLLOWS TWO PATHS.

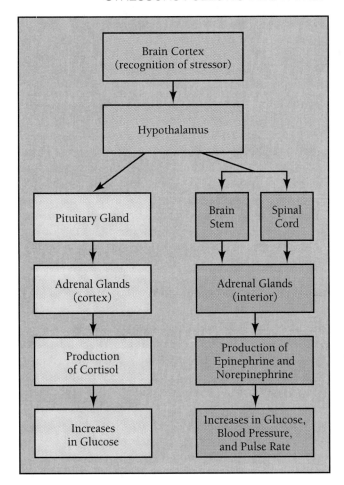

glands to secrete **epinephrine** (EP-i-NEF-rin) (sometimes called *adrenaline*) and **norepinephrine** in the bloodstream. Together, epinephrine and norepinephrine result in (a) increased levels of glucose, which provide more energy; (b) increased heart rate, which speeds the delivery of nutrients to cells; and (c) increased blood pressure, which stems from the fact that peripheral blood vessels constrict to force blood to the organs that need it most. Overall, the activity in both paths of the nervous system result in higher levels of physiological arousal, and this increased arousal leads to the physical symptoms and disorders we will consider in this chapter.

Circulating Versus Central Catecholamines

As just noted, epinephrine and norepinephrine play important roles in the stress response because they lead to increased heart rate and blood pressure. Epinephrine and norepinephrine are both **catecholamines**, and when they are in the bloodstream, they are referred to as **circulating catecholamines**.

You may recall that we discussed catecholamines in connection with depression and schizophrenia (see Chapters 9 and 13). Specifically, it was pointed out that low levels of norepinephrine lead to depression, and high levels of dopamine lead to schizophrenia. However, you should note that the catecholamines that lead to depression and schizophrenia are in the *brain* rather than the *circulatory system*, and therefore they are generally referred to as **central nervous system catecholamines**. Circulating catecholamines and central nervous system catecholamines are chemically the same, but they act in *different systems* and therefore can have *different effects*. Circulating catecholamines stimulate the cardiovascular system and increase heart rate and blood pressure, whereas central catecholamines stimulate the limbic system and elevate mood and cognitive arousal. Also, the levels of catecholamines in one system are not always related to the levels in the other system. For example, the levels of norepinephrine in the brain are usually not related to the levels of norepinephrine in the circulatory system. Be sure not to confuse circulating and central catecholamines; in our discussion of stress, we will focus on circulating catecholamines.

Just as individual differences in the production of central catecholamines lead individuals to be normal, depressed, or schizophrenic, so individual differences in the production of circulating catecholamines lead some individuals to be more responsive to stressors than other individuals. Those differences in the production of circulating catecholamines may predispose some persons to develop stressor-related physical disorders.

With this understanding of stress as a background, we can now begin our discussion of specific physical disorders that are affected by psychological factors. We will limit our discussion to cardiovascular diseases, headaches, ulcers, and illnesses related to the immune system. Those disorders are widespread and important and reflect different processes. Although these physical disorders are relatively common, many people do not really understand them. For example, the exact mechanisms of heart attacks and strokes are not widely understood, and few people understand what causes the pain in a migraine headache. Therefore, we will review the nature of each disorder before discussing the role that psychological factors play in its development. This will provide you with a better understanding of the disorders and will enable you to see how the physiological and psychological factors work together to cause and maintain the disorders.

CARDIOVASCULAR DISORDERS

In this section, we will discuss two related disorders, *coronary artery disease* and *hypertension*. These disorders are the leading causes of death in the United States because they contribute to heart attacks, strokes, kidney failure, and a wide variety of other serious problems.

Coronary Artery Disease

Coronary artery disease involves the buildup of fats (*cholesterol* and *triglycerides*) inside the arteries. That buildup results in a narrowing of the passage through which the blood must flow, consequently reducing blood flow. The reduction of blood flow can be serious because the major function of the circulatory system is to deliver oxygen and nutrients to the tissues throughout the body. As an artery becomes *occluded* (clogged and closed) because of the buildup of fats, blood flow to the tissues served by that artery is progressively reduced, and the tissues will die. The buildup of fats in blood vessels is called **atherosclerosis** (ATH-uh-rō-skluh-RŌ-sis). Figure 17.3 shows a cross section of a coronary artery that is almost completely occluded due to atherosclerosis.

Atherosclerosis often results in what is commonly called a *heart attack*. The heart consists of muscle called *myocardia*, and a heart attack occurs when the arteries that supply the myocardia with blood become occluded. When the myocardia are deprived of sufficient blood, they die, and the heart stops pumping. An area of tissue that has died is called an *infarct*, and therefore the technical term for a heart attack is a **my-**

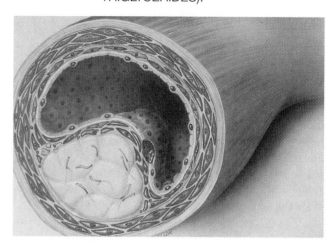

FIGURE 17.3   THIS CORONARY ARTERY IS ALMOST COMPLETELY OCCLUDED BY THE BUILDUP OF FATS (CHOLESTEROL AND TRIGLYCERIDES).

ocardial (Mī-ō-KAR-dē-ul) **infarction (MI)**. A heart attack is most likely to occur during periods of exercise or stress because then the heart must beat faster and its muscles require more blood.

An early sign of insufficient blood to the myocardia is a sharp pain around the heart. This pain is called **angina** (an-Jī-nuh), and it usually occurs with exercise. When individuals experience angina, they usually take a tablet containing **nitroglycerin** (Nī-trō-GLIS-uh-rin) that causes the artery to dilate temporarily and allow more blood through. However, that is only a short-term solution for the problem.

In addition to limiting blood supply because of a general narrowing of the arteries, atherosclerosis can lead to problems of blood supply in three other ways. First, when blood comes into contact with a rough cholesterol deposit on the wall of an artery, the blood tends to form a clot. Such a blood clot, called a **thrombus** (THROM-bus), can add to the blockage of the artery. Second, a thrombus may break off and be carried downstream to a smaller artery or capillary, where it will block the blood flow. When that occurs, the individual is said to have an **embolism** (EM-buh-LIZ-um), and the tissues farther downstream will be deprived of blood and die. Third, when fat deposits build up, the arteries become thick and brittle, and therefore they are more likely to rupture. Such ruptures are called **vascular accidents**. If an artery ruptures, the tissues it serves will be deprived of blood and die.

In this chapter, we will focus on problems associated with reduced blood flow to the heart, but it is important to recognize that all tissues need blood to live, and therefore the development of atherosclerosis has implications far beyond heart failure. For example, a general occlusion, a thrombus, an embolism, or a vascular accident in the brain can lead to a **cerebral infarction** (death of a part of the brain), or what is more commonly called a **stroke**. Cerebral infarctions are serious because a loss of tissue in the brain can result in the loss of the functions for which the tissue was responsible. That could involve a minor loss of memory, the loss of muscle control over activities like walking or talking, or the loss of some function that is essential to life itself. (Cerebral infarctions will be discussed in greater detail in Chapter 20.)

With the description of coronary artery disease as background, we can now consider how physiological and psychological factors interact to result in the disease.

Influence of Type A Behavior and Hostility

Numerous factors contribute to coronary artery disease and hypertension. They include genetics, diet (high intake of fats, cholesterol, triglycerides, and salt), carbon monoxide from cigarette smoking, and stress. Many of these factors are related to lifestyle and thus are psychological in nature. However, the psychological factor that has received most attention is the **Type A behavior pattern**, and it is on this that we will focus our attention.

As early as 1892, it was observed that the individual who is most likely to develop coronary artery disease is "vigorous in mind and body," is "keen and ambitious," and behaves as though his or her "engine is always at full speed ahead" (Osler, 1892). This observation was repeated in the late 1950s when two cardiologists noted that their patients who had heart attacks tended to be intense, competitive, concerned with achievement, aggressive, hostile, overcommitted, and driven by a sense of time urgency (Friedman & Rosenman, 1959, 1974). They termed this the *Type A behavior pattern* and contrasted it with the *Type B pattern*, which involves a more relaxed, leisurely, mellow approach to life that is not associated with the development of coronary artery disease.

An understanding of the Type A behavior pattern can be gleaned from an examination of how it is measured. One method is known as the **structured interview** technique (Rosenman, 1978). During the interview, the interviewer asks about a variety of behaviors that are related to the Type A pattern (e.g., "Do you often do two things at the same time?" "Do you eat and walk rapidly?" "Do you always feel in a hurry to get going and finish what you have to do?"). The answers to those questions help in diagnosing an individual with the Type A pattern, but of most importance is the way the individual responds during the interview. Compared to individuals with the Type B

Type A individuals are hostile, competitive, and feel a sense of time urgency. They also show higher heart rate and higher blood pressure in stressful situations and set higher goals for themselves than others.

pattern, those with the Type A pattern speak more vigorously, more rapidly, and louder; they answer faster and give shorter answers that are more to the point. In addition, Type A individuals are more alert, tense, and hostile and are more likely to try to hurry the interviewer and jump in and finish a sentence if the interviewer pauses (Chesney et al., 1981).

The Type A behavior pattern can also be measured with a number of paper-and-pencil questionnaires (Glass, 1977; Haynes et al., 1978). The questionnaires include items like this:

When waiting for an elevator, I
  (a) wait calmly until it arrives.
  (b) push the button again even if it has already been pushed.

These questionnaires are widely used because they are fast and easy, but they are not as effective for making the diagnosis as the structured interview.

Relationships with Cardiovascular Disease and Arousal.
The relationship between the Type A behavior pattern and coronary artery disease has been demonstrated in a number of major investigations. One such study was the Western Collaborative Group Study, in which a wide variety of risk factors such as smoking, blood pressure, cholesterol in the blood, lack of exercise, education, and personality were originally measured in 3,154 men between the ages of 39 and 59 (Rosenman et al., 1975; Rosenman, Brand, et al., 1976). An examination of the men 8½ years later revealed that when compared to men who originally showed the Type B behavior pattern, those who originally showed the Type A behavior pattern were more than twice as likely (a) to develop coronary artery disease (have occluded arteries), (b) to have a myocardial

infarction, and (c) to experience angina. It is important to note that the relationship between the Type A behavior pattern and coronary artery disease existed even after the effects of other risk factors such as smoking, blood pressure, and diet were controlled, clearly indicating that something about the Type A behavior itself led to the coronary problems. Other large-scale studies have yielded similar findings (see Matthews, 1988).

In addition, numerous laboratory investigations have been conducted in which Type A and Type B individuals were compared in terms of cardiovascular responses and behavior when exposed to stressful or challenging situations (see Glass, 1977; Holmes, 1983; Houston, 1983; Matthews, 1982). Those investigations produced two notable sets of findings.

First, it was found that Type A individuals show higher heart rates and higher blood pressures in stressful or challenging situations than Type B individuals. For example, in one experiment, college students who were either Type A or Type B worked on a task that was either easy or difficult while their blood pressure was monitored (Holmes et al., 1984). The task was described as an intelligence test, and it consisted of listening to a set of numbers being read and then attempting to repeat the set backward. In the easy condition, only three numbers had to be remembered and repeated, but in the difficult condition, the set consisted of seven numbers. The results indicated that Type A and Type B students showed comparable systolic blood pressure levels when working on the easy tasks, but the Type A students showed higher systolic blood pressure than Type B students when working on the difficult task. These results are presented in Figure 17.4.

The second notable finding was that Type A individuals set higher goals for themselves than Type B individuals and therefore force themselves to work harder. For example, in the preceding experiment, when students were asked to indicate whether they would like to work on harder or easier tasks in a second part of the experiment, Type A students chose more difficult tasks than Type B students (Holmes et al., 1984). In another experiment in which Type A and Type B individuals ran on a treadmill, Type A individuals ran until they were closer to their actual limits of physical exhaustion before giving up than Type B individuals (Carver et al., 1976).

The combination of increased arousal during challenge and increased challenge seeking would lead the Type A individuals to be more highly aroused more frequently than Type B individuals. That is important because heightened cardiovascular arousal is related to the development of coronary artery disease. (We will discuss the process that links arousal to coronary artery disease later.)

FIGURE 17.4   STUDENTS WITH THE TYPE A BEHAVIOR PATTERN SHOWED HIGHER SYSTOLIC BLOOD PRESSURE WHEN WORKING ON A DIFFICULT (STRESSFUL) TASK THAN STUDENTS WITH THE TYPE B BEHAVIOR PATTERN.

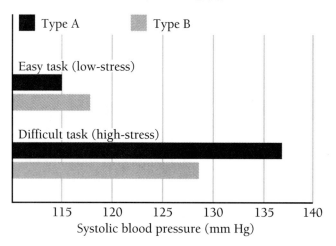

Source: Adapted from Holmes et al. (1984), p. 1326, fig. 1.

Type A Pattern or Hostility?   Investigators have recognized that the Type A behavior pattern consists of a number of components such as competitiveness, time urgency, and hostility, so research has focused on the roles played by the separate components of the pattern. That research indicates that the **hostility** component is the best predictor of coronary artery disease (Barefoot et al., 1983; Chesney & Rosenman, 1985; Houston et al., 1992; MacDougal et al., 1985; Matthews et al., 1977; Smith, 1992; Williams et al., 1980). In one study, the investigators followed up 255 physicians who had taken a test of hostility 25 years earlier when they were in medical school (Barefoot et al., 1983). The results indicated that physicians with hostility scores above the median were almost five times more likely to have a heart attack than those with scores below the median. The relationship between hostility and cardiovascular problems held up even when other risk factors such as smoking were controlled. These results are presented in Figure 17.5. (It might be noted that high hostility scores were also related to higher rates of death due to other factors such as cancer, accident, suicide, and gastrointestinal problems, thus suggesting that hostility may play a very broad role in human health.)

Hostility actually appears to be a better predictor of cardiovascular problems than the Type A pattern in general. The relationships of hostility and Type A to coronary artery disease were demonstrated in a study of more than 400 individuals who (a) took a simple

FIGURE 17.5   HIGH HOSTILITY AMONG STUDENTS
WAS FOUND TO BE RELATED TO
CORONARY HEART DISEASE 25
YEARS LATER.

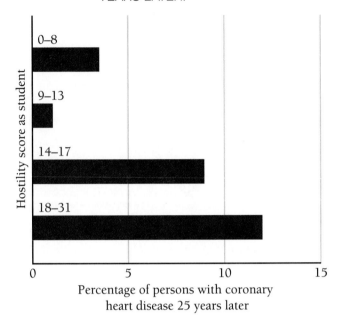

Source: Adapted from Barefoot et al. (1983), p. 60, fig. 1.

paper-and-pencil test of hostility, (b) participated in
the structured interview test of Type A behavior, and
(c) underwent extensive medical testing to determine
the degree to which their arteries were occluded
(Williams et al., 1980). The results of the investigation
revealed that among persons with low hostility scores,
only 48% had an occlusion, whereas among persons
with high hostility scores, 70% had an occlusion. Type
A patients were more likely to have occlusions than
Type B patients, but that relationship was probably
due to the fact that hostility is part of the Type A pattern.

A classic example of the relationship between
Type A or hostility and coronary artery disease is the
case of Mike Ditka. Ditka was known as a particularly
driven and hostile player on the Chicago Bears football team, and those characteristics were also apparent
when he coached the team. He was an effective coach
(the Bears won the Super Bowl in 1986), but the
media made much of his hostility. At age 49, he had a
serious heart attack (3 days after the Bears suffered a
shattering 30–7 loss to the New England Patriots). In
typical Type A manner, 2 weeks later, Ditka was back
on the sidelines. His assistant was coaching, but Ditka
was pacing up and back (probably muttering under his
breath), with his cardiologist right behind him.

Now that we have established that the Type A behavior pattern or the hostility component of the pat-

tern is related to the development of coronary artery
disease, we must go on to explain why the relationship
exists. Understanding the process is important if we
are to design effective intervention and treatment programs. We will consider two explanations for the relationship between Type A or hostility and coronary
artery disease, one that suggests that Type A or hostility causes coronary artery disease and another that suggests that Type A or hostility is only correlated with
coronary artery disease.

Type A or Hostility as a Cause.   We know that
Type A individuals show higher levels of arousal under
stress and seek out more stressful situations than Type
B individuals. We also know that hostile individuals experience more interpersonal conflict and receive less
social support, both of which can lead to increased
and prolonged levels of arousal (Smith, 1992). The
question is, does their higher, more frequent, and prolonged arousal lead to coronary artery disease? There
are four reasons to believe that it does. First, there is
evidence that *arousal due to stress is related to the production of cholesterol.* In one study, the cholesterol levels of corporate accountants and tax accountants were
assessed periodically between January and June (Friedman et al., 1958). The results indicated that the corporate accountants who were under fairly chronic stress
showed consistently elevated cholesterol levels, but the
tax accountants showed lower levels of cholesterol except for the period around April 15 when they were
under stress because of the rush to get tax forms filed.
That relationship is presented in Figure 17.6 (p. 418).
Similar increases in cholesterol have been observed in
students during the stress of final examinations (Dreyfuss & Czaczkes, 1959).

Second, there is evidence that the catecholamines
(e.g., epinephrine and norepinephrine) that are secreted in the bloodstream during stress lead to *greater
clumping of cholesterol particles* (Ardlie et al., 1966). In
other words, the catecholamines that are present during stress may cause particles of cholesterol to stick together, thus forming clots in the blood or on the
artery walls. Those clots could lead to occlusion of the
arteries.

Third, there is now evidence that elevated heart
rate (like that seen during stress) is related to *more
rapid accumulation of cholesterol on the artery walls.* This
was documented in an experiment in which the heart
rates of six monkeys in an experimental group were artificially lowered by destroying part of the nerve node
that controls heart rate (Beere et al., 1984). Eight
other monkeys in a control condition underwent the
same operation, but the node was not destroyed. After
the operation, the monkeys in both conditions were
fed a high-cholesterol diet for 6 months. Examination

FIGURE 17.6   CHOLESTEROL LEVELS INCREASE DURING PERIODS OF
STRESS, AS IN ACCOUNTANTS AT TAX-FILING TIME.

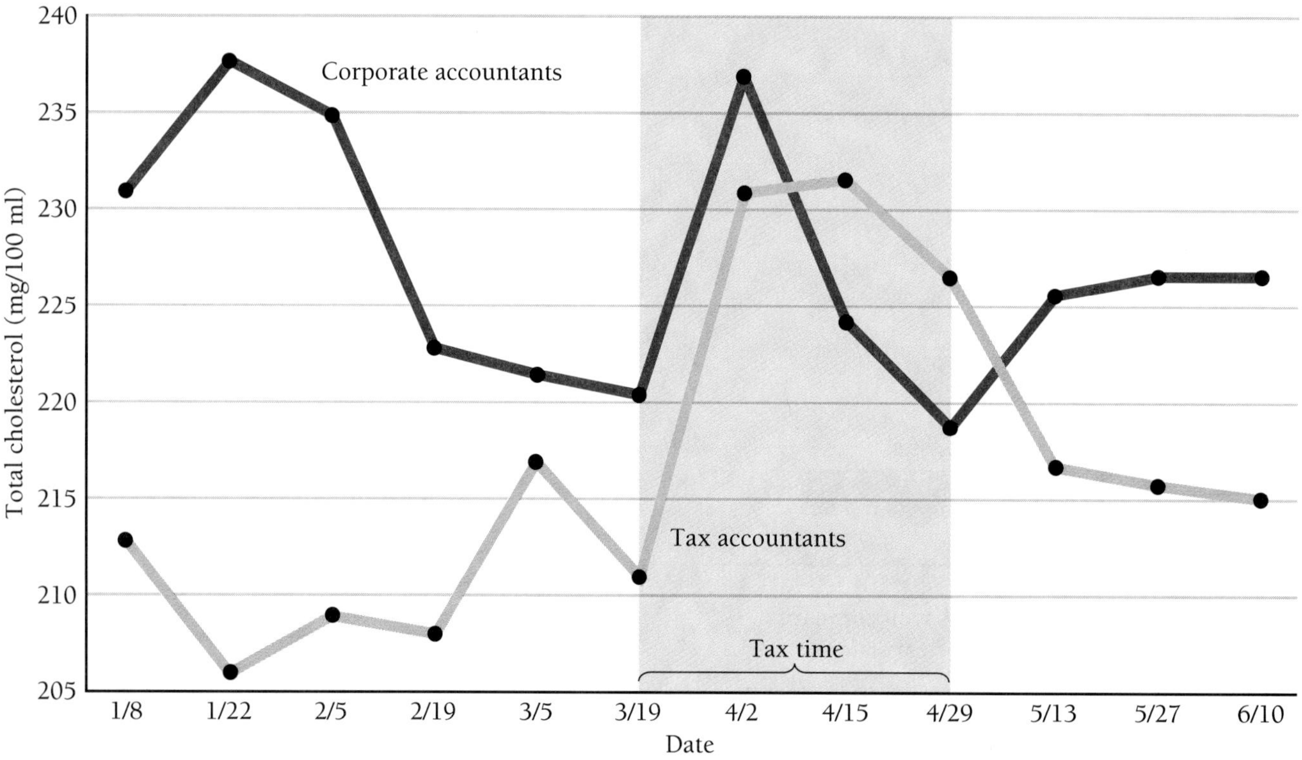

Source: Adapted from Friedman et al. (1958), p. 856, fig. 2.

of the coronary arteries of the monkeys at the end of the 6-month period revealed that the monkeys whose heart rates had been reduced showed occlusions of only 21.6%, but the monkeys whose heart rates had not been reduced showed occlusions of 55.9%. In other words, the monkeys with slower heart rates had occlusions that were 34.3% less extensive than the monkeys with higher heart rates. The higher heart rates led to greater occlusions because the brief reversal of blood flow that occurs between each beat of the heart provides an opportunity for cholesterol plaques to become attached to the walls of the arteries. More heartbeats lead to more blood flow reversals, which in turn lead to more plaque buildup on the artery walls.

Fourth and finally, the high blood pressure that is associated with high arousal results in *small lesions on the artery walls*, and cholesterol is likely to get caught in those lesions, thereby aiding the buildup that leads to an occlusion.

In summary, Type A or hostile individuals have higher and more frequently elevated levels of arousal, and those elevated levels of arousal lead to the development of coronary artery disease because they (a) increase the production of cholesterol, (b) increase the

clumping of cholesterol particles, (c) increase the likelihood that cholesterol will stick to the artery walls, and (d) increase the development of lesions in the arteries to which cholesterol can adhere. These findings suggest that arousal is the factor that links Type A behavior or hostility to coronary artery disease in a causal chain. These relationships are summarized on the left side of Figure 17.7.

Type A or Hostility as a Correlate.   The second explanation for the relationship between Type A behavior or hostility and coronary artery disease is that both the behavior and the disease are caused by a third factor, probably genetically determined high levels of catecholamines, and therefore the behavior and the disease are only *correlated* with each other. The notion is that (a) some individuals are genetically predisposed to produce high levels of circulating catecholamines, (b) the catecholamines result in high levels of physiological arousal, and (c) the high arousal leads both to the Type A behavior or hostility and to the coronary artery disease. This explanation is summarized graphically on the right side of Figure 17.7.

FIGURE 17.7   THERE ARE TWO EXPLANATIONS FOR THE RELATIONSHIP BETWEEN BEHAVIOR AND CORONARY ARTERY DISEASE.

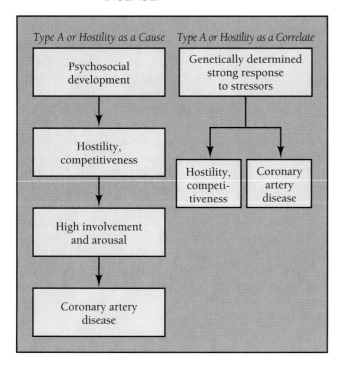

Support for the notion that genetics plays an important role comes from two sets of findings. First, there is evidence that the overall Type A behavior pattern is not inherited, but some of its components are inherited (Horn et al., 1976; Matthews & Krantz, 1976; Rahe et al., 1978; Rosenman, Rahe, et al., 1976). For example, when 93 pairs of middle-aged monozygotic (MZ) twins and 97 pairs of middle-aged dizygotic (DZ) twins were given a variety of personality measures, it was found that traits such as activity level, impulsiveness, dominance, and aggression showed evidence of inheritability (Rahe et al., 1978). Many of these genetically related traits are related to the Type A behavior pattern and hostility.

Second, there is evidence that genetic factors play an important role in determining an individual's cardiovascular response to stress (e.g., Carmelli et al., 1985; Carroll et al., 1985; Rose et al., 1982; Smith et al., 1987; see review by Rose, 1986). In these studies, MZ and DZ twins had their blood pressures measured while they were exposed to stress (e.g., they took intelligence tests or immersed their hands in freezing water). The results indicated that members of MZ twin pairs showed greater similarities in blood pressure responses to the stressors than did members of DZ twin pairs, and it was estimated that as much as 50% of the

variability in blood pressure responses to stress was due to genetic factors.

In summary, there is evidence that genetic factors contribute to hostility and to cardiovascular responsivity, and that suggests that rather than hostility causing cardiovascular problems, both may be due to genetic factors. However, it also seems likely that hostile or competitive individuals would be more likely to get into situations that lead to additional stress and cardiovascular arousal and problems. Overall, then, the relationship between personality factors and cardiovascular disorders is probably due to *both* the influence of personality (Type A and hostility) on arousal, which in turn leads to cardiovascular problems, and to genetic factors that lead to hostility and arousal, which then lead to coronary artery disease.

Hypertension

The other major cardiovascular disease involves high blood pressure, and it is called **hypertension** (HĪ-pur-TEN-shun). There are two types of hypertension, *essential* and *secondary*. **Essential hypertension** is high blood pressure *for which a physical cause has not been found*, and thus it is assumed that the elevated pressure is due to psychological factors. (Essential hypertension is sometimes referred to as *primary* hypertension.) In contrast, **secondary hypertension** is high blood pressure that stems from *known physiological causes* such as excessive salt in the diet, kidney malfunction, or atherosclerosis. It is called "secondary" because the elevated blood pressure is a side effect of some other physical disorder. In this chapter, we will be concerned mostly with essential hypertension.

Hypertension is a widespread and potentially serious disorder. It has been estimated that 1 out of every 6 adults has hypertension, and that 90% of those individuals suffer from essential hypertension. Many individuals are not aware that they have hypertension because it does not have any noticeable symptoms. With regard to its seriousness, hypertension has been shown to increase the risk of coronary artery disease, MIs, vascular accidents, and kidney failure.

There are two blood pressures, the *systolic* and the *diastolic*. The **systolic** (sis-TOL-ik) **blood pressure** is the high level of pressure that occurs immediately after each heartbeat when blood is suddenly forced through the system. In contrast, the **diastolic** (DĪ-uh-STOL-ik) **blood pressure** is the low level of pressure that occurs just before each heartbeat. Blood pressure is measured in terms of the height of a column of mercury that could be supported by the pressure. Normal systolic pressure is about 120 mm Hg (millimeters of mercury), and normal diastolic pressure is generally considered to be 80 mm Hg. When talking about blood pressure, we give the systolic pressure first and then the diastolic pressure, and thus we might say that an individual's pressure is "120 over 80" (written 120/80). Although 120/80 is considered "normal," pressure varies widely. Women generally have lower pressure, older individuals have higher pressure, and any one individual's pressure may go up and down during the day due to a variety of factors.

Individuals are usually diagnosed as suffering from hypertension if they have sustained blood pressure readings of 140/90 or higher (Pickering, 1968). However, both pressures need not be high for a problem to exist, and there is no agreement over whether the elevation of the systolic or diastolic pressure is more important. It might be noted that some individuals suffer from **hypotension** (HĪ-pō-TEN-shun), or low blood pressure. Hypotension is not a serious problem, but it can result in sudden dizziness when getting up quickly from a chair or a bed because for a brief period there is not enough pressure to get blood to the brain.

The development of essential hypertension involves two steps. First, stress results in a temporary increase in blood pressure (see Figure 17.2). Second, the increased blood pressure causes the arteries to stretch, and the stretch is detected by a set of sensors called **baroreceptors** (BAR-ō-rē-SEP-turz) that then send signals to the central nervous system to reduce blood pressure. Specifically, peripheral blood vessels are dilated, heart rate is reduced, and the strength of the heart's contraction is reduced, all of which serve to reduce pressure. However, if pressure is high for a prolonged period of time, the baroreceptors adjust to the higher level of pressure and signal the central nervous system only when the pressure goes even higher. In other words, after an extended increase in pressure, the baroreceptors reset themselves, and high pressure becomes the norm.

Psychological factors—specifically, the Type A behavior pattern and hostility—play an important role in the development of essential hypertension because those factors contribute to more frequent and more prolonged elevations in blood pressure, and those elevations increase the likelihood that the baroreceptors will be reset at higher levels. The long-term effects of individual differences in cardiovascular reactivity to stress was illustrated in a study in which the investigators followed up men who 15 years earlier had shown either high or low heart rate and blood pressure responses to a reaction time test that involved a threat of shock (Light et al., 1992). The results indicated that the men who had shown high blood pressure and heart rate *reactivity* 15 years earlier had developed higher *chronic* blood pressure and heart rate by the time of the follow-up than the men who earlier had shown low cardiovascular reactivity. Clearly, individual differences in the response to stress have long-term implications.

Treatment

An individual whose coronary arteries are approaching the point of occlusion might undergo **coronary bypass surgery**, which involves grafting in an unclogged piece of artery so that the blood can bypass the occluded area and hence get to the heart. Another operation that is frequently performed involves taking a tiny flexible tube with an inflatable balloon on the end and inserting it into the occluded artery. At the point of the occlusion, the balloon is inflated, forcing the fatty material against the side of the artery and making a larger passageway in the artery. This operation is called **angioplasty** (AN-jē-ō-PLAST-ē). More recently an operation has been developed in which a tube with a rotating knife blade is inserted into the occluded artery. When the blade spins, it chops up the obstructing material so it can be carried away in the bloodstream.

A variety of drugs are also being used in the treatment of cardiovascular disease. One type of drug that is widely used to treat hypertension is the **diuretic** (DĪ-yuh-RET-ik). Diuretics reduce the amount of fluid in the body, and when the fluid level is lower, there is less pressure in the cardiovascular system. Hypertension is also treated with drugs called **vasodilators** (VĀ-zō-dī-LĀ-turz) that cause the blood vessels to dilate, making more room in the system and thereby reducing the pressure.

Stress on the cardiovascular system can also be reduced with drugs known as **beta** (BĀ-tuh) **blockers** that reduce heart rate (e.g., propranolol, sold under the trade name Inderol). If heart rate is reduced, the heart's need for oxygen is reduced, and therefore the likelihood of heart attack is reduced. These drugs are called beta blockers because they block synaptic transmission at the beta receptors at the synapses of the sympathetic nervous system. Finally, a new group of drugs has been developed that are effective for reducing as much as 60% of the cholesterol buildup in arteries, and thus in some cases, atherosclerosis may be overcome with medication rather than surgery.

Prevention

Surgery and medication can be effective for treating existing problems, but unless appropriate preventive steps are taken, the problems will return. It is not uncommon to see patients coming in for a second or third angioplasty or even a second bypass operation.

Therefore, the key is *prevention*, and most prevention programs are nonmedical. Prevention is usually focused on two factors, *diet* and *stress*. First, attempts are made to change the person's diet so that the ingestion of fats is reduced, thereby reducing the basic building blocks of cholesterol and atherosclerosis. Second, attempts are made to teach the person how to control or reduce the stress in life because stress is a major contributor to cardiovascular disease. We will consider three strategies that are widely used in attempts to reduce stress.

Biofeedback Training.   Responses of the autonomic branch of the peripheral nervous system are generally not under voluntary control, and that makes it difficult to control the physiological responses to stress. For example, ordinarily you cannot voluntarily reduce your heart rate or blood pressure during periods of stress. However, some years ago, it was suggested that our inability to control autonomic responses was due to the fact that we had not had sufficient opportunities to learn such control. Feedback about performance is essential to learning (e.g., you cannot learn to decrease your blood pressure unless you know when it is going up and down), and thus we do not learn to control autonomic responses because ordinarily we do not get enough feedback about them. That speculation, in combination with the development of sophisticated electronic equipment that can provide individuals with instant feedback about changes in their autonomic responses, led to the development of **biofeedback training** procedures whereby individuals get feedback about their autonomic responses and then, ideally, learn to control them.

Blood pressure biofeedback has been widely publicized as an effective treatment for hypertension, and a number of investigators have reported that hypertensive patients who received biofeedback showed decreases in blood pressure of as much as 26 mm Hg. They also reported that after biofeedback training, individuals could maintain normal blood pressure without the aid of medication. However, in most studies, the changes in blood pressure of patients receiving biofeedback were not compared to changes in patients who did not receive treatment (no-treatment controls), so from those experiments we cannot determine whether biofeedback was actually effective. To correct that problem, a series of experiments was conducted in which some patients received blood pressure biofeedback training while others simply sat quietly for a comparable length of time. Surprisingly, the results of those experiments indicated that the biofeedback training was no more effective than sitting quietly (see Holmes, 1981). Thus despite widespread publicity and extensive clinical use of biofeedback training, there is no reliable controlled evidence that biofeedback is effective for treating hypertension.

Aerobic Exercise and Physical Fitness.   Until around 1970, rest was prescribed for individuals who had experienced a heart attack. The notion was that the heart was weakened and should not be strained. However, now it is generally agreed that **aerobic exercise** can aid in the treatment and prevention of cardiac disorders in a number of ways. (Aerobic exercises include jogging, swimming, cycling, and others that elevate heart rate to 70% of its maximum for at least 20 minutes. Your maximum heart rate is determined by subtracting your age from 220.) For example, aerobic exercise can reduce the buildup of cholesterol in arteries. That is the case because there are two types of cholesterol, one "bad" and one "good." The bad type is known as **LDL** (low-density lipoproteins), comes from fat in the diet, and builds up in the arteries. The good type is known as **HDL** (high-density lipoproteins), is produced when we exercise, and carries away the LDL before it can build up. In other words, by exercising, we increase the production of HDL, which reduces the buildup of LDL.

Aerobic exercise also serves to enlarge and strengthen the heart so that it can pump more blood more efficiently (i.e., the volume of blood pumped

Aerobic exercise can help reduce the buildup of cholesterol in the arteries and strengthen the heart. The relationship between aerobic fitness and improved cardiovascular responses during stress has been demonstrated in a number of studies.

with each beat is increased). The increased efficiency of the heart means that it will have to work less hard (beat slower and require less oxygen) under normal conditions and under stress.

The relationship between **aerobic fitness** and improved cardiovascular responses during stress has been demonstrated in a number of investigations (Holmes, 1993). For example, in one study the heart rates and blood pressures of students were measured while they rested and while they worked on a stressful intellectual task (subtracting by 7 as fast as possible from the number 3,584; McGilley & Holmes, 1988). The results indicated that during stress, the students who were in better aerobic condition had heart rates that were 29 beats per minute (bpm) lower than the less fit students. Those results are presented in Figure 17.8. During stress, the more fit students also had systolic blood pressures that averaged 13.8 mm Hg lower than that of the less fit students.

Exercise programs have also been demonstrated to be effective for physiological and psychological rehabilitation of individuals after a heart attack or bypass surgery. One experiment revealed that compared to patients who received routine medical care, patients who participated in an exercise program showed better cardiovascular functioning (lower heart rate and blood pressure, better performance on a treadmill), better self-concept, less employment-related stress, more enjoyment of leisure time, and greater sexual activity (Roviaro et al., 1984). Unfortunately, when the patients were examined again 7 years later, the patients who had been in the routine-care condition were doing better (e.g., less depressed, able to run farther on a treadmill) than the patients who had been in the exercise condition (McGilley et al., 1993). The problem was that the patients in the exercise condition thought they were "cured" when the program was over, so they stopped exercising, but the patients who received routine care were still concerned about themselves, so they slowly began to increase the amount they exercised, and that exercise led to improvements in their physical and psychological health. Clearly, exercise must be part of a change in lifestyle, not just a temporary treatment.

Social Support.   The results of a variety of investigations indicate that **social support** is associated with lower heart rate and blood pressure (Bland et al., 1991; Dressler, 1991; Gerin et al., 1992; Unden et al., 1991). For example, individuals who participate in more club activities and individuals who report more social support at home or at work show lower cardiovascular arousal when they come for physicals, and they also show lower arousal when cardiovascular measures are taken in social and work settings. Of course, it is possible that social support does not reduce arousal but that individuals who are less aroused attract more support (e.g., they may be less hostile). To determine whether social support actually leads to lower cardiovascular arousal, an experiment was conducted in which an accomplice of the experimenter argued with an individual while the individual's blood pressure was taken (Gerin et al., 1992). In a social-support condition, a third person defended the individual, whereas in a no-social-support condition, the third person did not come to the individual's defense. The results indicated that when individuals were given social support, they showed smaller increases in blood pressure and heart rate, thus confirming the link between social support and reduced cardiovascular arousal.

In addition to helping prevent the onset of cardiovascular disease, social support can also help prevent relapse after the disease has set in and has been treated with bypass surgery (Fontana et al., 1989; King et al., 1993; Kulik & Mahler, 1989). For example, patients who have high levels of social support experience less

FIGURE 17.8   AEROBICALLY FIT PERSONS
SHOWED SMALLER INCREASES IN
HEART RATE WHEN EXPOSED TO
STRESS THAN LESS AEROBICALLY
FIT PERSONS.

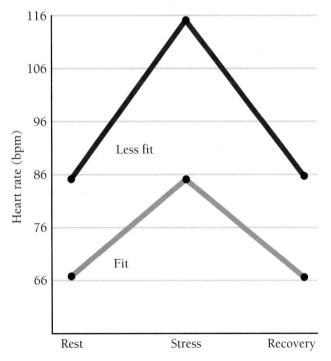

Source: Adapted from McGilley and Holmes (1988), p. 129, fig. 3.

angina, thus indicating that they have better blood supply to the heart than patients who have low levels of social support.

Stress Management Training.

Originally, **stress management training** programs were designed to make Type A individuals more like Type B individuals. In one investigation, individuals who had experienced MIs were randomly assigned either to a condition in which they participated in a standard cardiac rehabilitation program (i.e., they received instructions concerning diet and exercise) or to a condition in which they participated in the same rehabilitation program but also participated in group counseling sessions designed to reduce their Type A behavior patterns (Friedman et al., 1984; Friedman & Ulmer, 1984). The results indicated that the individuals who received counseling to reduce the Type A behavior showed reductions in Type A behavior as measured by both structured interviews and questionnaires. More important, the individuals who received the counseling were *less than half* as likely to have another MI as the individuals who participated in only the traditional rehabilitation program (annual recurrence rates of 3.0% and 6.6%, respectively).

The results suggest that it is possible to change the Type A behavior pattern, but achieving such a change is difficult, and the change may not be accompanied by changes in physiological reactivity (Roskies et al., 1986). Some of the difficulty associated with changing Type A behavior may be due to the fact that many individuals do not want to give up their Type A behaviors because those behaviors are very effective for achieving success (Mettlin, 1976). Indeed, in Western society, the Type A behavior pattern is generally admired and rewarded, and unless individuals are faced with imminent death from another MI, they are resistant to change their behavior patterns (Friedman & Ulmer, 1984).

Fortunately, it may not be necessary to change the entire behavior pattern because only a limited number of components of the Type A pattern are related to the development of cardiovascular problems. For example, anger and hostility are related to cardiac problems, but speed and impatience are not (Jenkins et al., 1974). Therefore, the goal now of many treatment programs is to help individuals avoid hostility or reduce the physiological arousal that accompanies it. These programs involve a variety of strategies including teaching individuals to (a) improve communication so that hostility can be avoided, (b) express their feelings so that tension is reduced, (c) use strategies for achieving goals that do not necessitate prolonged arousal, (d) establish rewards for achievements that do not re-

quire "workaholic" behaviors, and (e) use progressive muscle relaxation exercises to reduce arousal (e.g., Roskies & Avard, 1982; Roskies et al., 1978; Suinn, 1980).

Preliminary findings concerning the effects of these approaches are encouraging, but in most cases, their long-term effects on individuals with cardiovascular disorders is yet to be confirmed. To be maximally effective for preventing the development of cardiovascular disorders, these programs may have to be started relatively early in life because there are data indicating that the atherosclerotic process begins in childhood (McNamara et al., 1971). Finally, because of the difficulty of changing even a limited number of personality characteristics, some treatment and prevention problems are focused on simply teaching individuals how to avoid or control the specific stresses that lead to cardiovascular problems (Roskies, 1980).

In summary, cardiovascular disorders pose a variety of serious medical problems in Western society, and there is now substantial evidence that psychological factors are related to cardiovascular problems. The most important of those factors seems to be hostility. Hostility is correlated with and perhaps causes cardiovascular disorders because it is associated with increased levels of arousal, which lead to the cardiovascular disorders. The arousal levels that lead to cardiovascular disorders can be reduced with medication (beta blockers), aerobic exercise, and some stress management programs.

HEADACHES

Headaches are one of the most common causes of pain. It is estimated that between 10% and 30% of Americans suffer from chronic headaches. We will focus our attention on the *migraine* and *muscle tension* types of headaches because they pose the most serious and frequent problems.

Migraine Headaches

Migraine headaches result in very severe pain that can completely incapacitate an individual. Indeed, some patients describe the pain as like a burning rod being driven through the brain. There are two types of migraine headaches. The *classic* type afflicts about 2% of headache sufferers and consists of two phases. The first phase begins about 30 minutes before the actual headache starts, and the symptoms involve visual problems (e.g., flashing lights, blind spots), dizziness, and sometimes abdominal pain. These are called **prodro-**

mal symptoms (*prodromal* means "running before"), and they serve as a warning that a headache is about to begin. The headache begins in the second phase, and at first it involves a unilateral (one-sided) throbbing pain that usually occurs in the temporal or occipital areas (side or back of the head). In addition to the pain, the individual usually becomes nauseated and very sensitive to light and is most comfortable in a dark, cool place. As time goes on, the pain changes from throbbing to constant. The headache lasts for a few hours but usually less than 24.

The second type of migraine is the *common* type, and it afflicts about 12% of headache sufferers. The common migraine is not preceded by prodromal symptoms, and the pain is usually generalized rather than limited to one area of the head. However, the common migraine does involve the other symptoms (e.g., nausea, sensitivity to light) and is just as painful as the classic type. The severity of the pain associated with migraine headaches cannot be understated.

The prodromal symptoms of the classic migraine are due to an extreme *constriction* of the cranial arteries (the arteries that supply blood to the head). The constriction limits the blood supply, and that causes the symptoms. As the process progresses, the cranial arteries change from a state of constriction to a state of extreme *dilatation*. When the arteries dilate and increase in size, they put pressure on the surrounding pain-sensitive nerves, and it is that pressure that results in the pain of the headache. The initial throbbing nature of the pain is due to the hydraulic pulsations of blood through the dilated arteries. As the attack continues, the arteries become inflamed and rigid in their dilated state, and therefore the pain changes from throbbing to steady.

We know that migraine pain is due to extreme dilatation of the cranial arteries, but we do not yet clearly understand the factors that cause the arteries to dilate. It does appear, however, that genetic factors play a role in predisposing individuals to migraine headaches and that the genetic link is stronger for women. It also appears that estrogen is somehow connected to migraine headaches because the incidence of migraines in women drops sharply after menopause and the incidence of migraines in women who are taking estrogen supplements drops sharply when those supplements are reduced. Finally, over the years, there have been numerous speculations concerning the role of stress in precipitating migraine headaches, but as yet the effects of stress have not been confirmed.

Tension Headaches

Tension headaches, sometimes called **muscle contraction headaches**, are very common. The pain is constant (nonpulsating), usually occurs on both sides of the head, and most frequently occurs primarily in the frontal area (forehead) or the suboccipital area (back of the head just above the neck). The pain of tension headaches stems from the fact that the muscles in the afflicted area have been contracted for prolonged periods of time. Exactly how the pain is generated is not clear, but it is probably related to reduced blood flow and reduced energy stores that are associated with prolonged static contractions of the muscles. The prolonged muscle contractions are generally believed to stem from psychological stressors. For example, individuals who are attempting to deal with stressors may frown persistently, contracting the frontalis muscles, or they may hold their heads rigidly for long periods of time, causing prolonged contraction of the muscles at the base of the skull.

Treatment

Migraine.   The medical approach to the treatment of migraines involves the administration of stimulants such as *ergotamine tartrate* and *caffeine*. Stimulants are effective for reducing the pain because they result in constriction of the dilated arteries and therefore reduce the pressure on the surrounding pain-sensitive nerves. However, to be effective, the stimulants must be taken during the very early stage of the headache before the dilated arteries become rigid. If the attempt to constrict the arteries is made after they become rigid, the treatment will not be effective, and the individual will have to endure the pain until the headache runs its course.

The most widely publicized psychological treatment of migraine headaches involves *finger temperature biofeedback*, a treatment developed by accident. As the story goes, a woman had been participating in an experiment designed to determine whether increased blood flow to the hands could be achieved by repeating phrases such as "blood is flowing into my hands, and they are becoming warmer." To measure changes in blood flow, a temperature-sensitive sensor was placed on her finger and another one was placed on her forehead. Temperature was used as an indirect measure of blood flow because increased blood to an area will result in greater warmth there. For example, your hands become cold when you are tense because your peripheral blood vessels constrict and reduce the blood flow to the hands. During the training sessions, the woman was allowed to watch the temperature meter and by doing so got feedback about how well she was doing. One day, before coming in for one of her research sessions, the woman realized that she was about to have a migraine. However, rather than stay home, she went to the session, at which she practiced the hand-warming procedure, and much to her surprise, for some reason the migraine did not materialize. She commented on this to the investigator, who then speculated that by increasing the blood flow to her hand, the woman had decreased the blood flow to the cranial arteries. He went on to speculate that because of the reduced flow to the cranial arteries, those arteries were less likely to dilate, and the migraine was aborted. There quickly followed numerous other case studies relating finger temperature biofeedback to reduced migraines, and almost overnight, temperature biofeedback became the "hot" treatment for migraines. The notion was "warm your hands and cool your head" to avoid migraines. Unfortunately, subsequent controlled research has not provided any support for the efficacy of biofeedback for the treatment of migraine headaches (see Holmes, 1981; Holmes & Burish, 1984). For example, in one experiment, the individuals were given either true biofeedback or false biofeedback that did not accurately reflect skin temperatures (Mullinix et al., 1978). The results indicated that the individuals in the true biofeedback condition were better able to increase their finger temperatures, but they did not show greater reductions in headaches or medication usage than the individuals who received the false biofeedback. It was also found that the degree to which headaches did or did not improve was not correlated with the degree to which patients did or did not increase their finger temperature. In other words, the control of finger temperature (blood flow) was not related to the headache activity. Even more devastating were the findings of another investigation, in which it was demonstrated that with biofeedback, individuals can learn to relax and increase blood flow to the hands, but the changes in blood flow to the hands are not related to changes in blood flow to the cranial arteries (Largen et al., 1978). Furthermore, it now appears that the dilatation of the cranial arteries is not due to changes in blood flow. Overall, temperature biofeedback has not been found to be effective for treating migraine headaches, and for physiological reasons, it probably cannot be effective. Despite these findings, however, because of the publicity given to the results of the early case studies and the intuitive appeal of the approach, biofeedback is still widely advertised and used as a treatment for migraine headaches.

Tension.   Tension headaches are treated medically with tranquilizers or muscle relaxants (see Chapter 6). The psychological approach to treatment involves teaching individuals how to relax in general and how to relax the muscles of their faces, necks, and shoulders specifically. Two approaches have been used to teach relaxation, **progressive muscle relaxa-**

tion training and **electromyographic** (ē-LEK-trō-MĪ-ō-GRAF-ik) **(EMG) biofeedback training.** Progressive muscle relaxation training is a procedure in which individuals tense and then relax sets of muscles. This is done so that they can become familiar with the sensations and techniques that are associated with muscle relaxation, and with this increased awareness, they become more effective at achieving relaxation at will (see Chapter 6). By focusing the training on the muscles that are associated with tension headaches (forehead and neck), progressive muscle relaxation training can be an effective way to reduce the headaches (see reviews by Burish, 1981; Holmes & Burish, 1984).

In EMG biofeedback training, electrodes are used to detect muscle activity, and the individual is given immediate feedback about whether muscles are tensing or relaxing. A tone is usually used to provide the feedback; the tone goes higher when the muscles become tense and lower when they relax. By listening to the tone and trying to get it to go lower, the individual can learn to relax specific sets of muscles. There is a substantial amount of evidence that EMG biofeedback training is more effective than no treatment for reducing muscle tension headaches (see Holmes & Burish, 1984; Holmes, 1981). Those findings are encouraging, but it is important to note that in experiments in which the effects of EMG biofeedback training were compared to the effects of progressive muscle relaxation training, both techniques were *equally effective.* In other words, EMG biofeedback training is effective for reducing tension headaches, but not more effective than the cheaper and easier progressive muscle relaxation training, so muscle relaxation training is probably the treatment of choice.

In summary, at present, there is no strong evidence linking psychological factors to migraine headaches and no evidence that psychological approaches such as biofeedback are helpful for treating those headaches. But stress that leads to prolonged muscle contractions does appear to provoke muscle tension headaches, and those headaches can be treated effectively with either EMG biofeedback or progressive muscle relaxation training.

PEPTIC ULCERS

The word *ulcer* refers to any abnormal break in the skin or a mucous membrane. The ulcers from which most people suffer are **peptic ulcers**, which occur in the digestive system, and about 10% of Americans suffer from them. In addition to causing considerable pain, ulcers can be dangerous because they lead to internal bleeding and can result in death. Figure 17.9 is a photo of an ulcer.

Types and Causes

Peptic ulcers result from an imbalance between the level of *gastric acid* (primarily hydrochloric acid and pepsin) that is produced to break down foodstuffs, and the level of *mucus* that is produced to neutralize the acid and thereby protect the walls of the intestinal tract. If the acid level gets too high because too much acid is being produced or because not enough mucus is being produced, the acid will eat holes (ulcers) in the walls of the intestinal tract. The ulcers result in pain and vomiting, sometimes of blood (Weiner, 1991).

Peptic ulcers are divided into two types, depending on where in the digestive system they occur. **Duodenal** (DOO-uh-DĒ-nul) **ulcers** occur in the *duodenum*, which is the first part of the small intestine where food enters the intestine from the stomach. About 85% of duodenal ulcers are caused by *overproduction of gastric acid* rather than by underproduction of mucus.

Gastric ulcers occur in the stomach, and in contrast to duodenal ulcers, they are usually the result of *too little protective mucus* rather than too much gastric acid. (The exception is when food from the small intestine backs up into the stomach and brings additional acid with it.) In many cases, individuals develop gastric ulcers because they have ingested high levels of substances like aspirin or alcohol that reduce mucus, thus causing an acid–mucus imbalance.

FIGURE 17.9   PEPTIC ULCERS ARE HOLES IN THE WALL OF THE DUODENUM OR THE STOMACH.

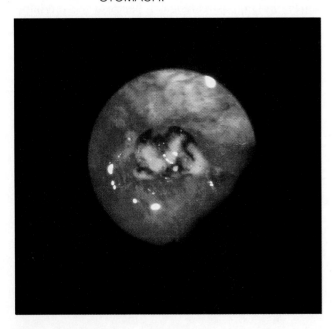

Stress.   A major reason for the overproduction of gastric acid is stress. Evidence for the influence of stress on the development of ulcers is provided by a study of air traffic controllers who worked in towers in what were characterized as high- or low-stress situations (Cobb & Rose, 1973). The results indicated that (a) the air traffic controllers had a higher incidence of ulcers than a control group of airmen, (b) the air traffic controllers developed their ulcers earlier than the airmen, and (c) the air traffic controllers who worked in the high-stress towers had a higher incidence of ulcers than those who worked in the low-stress towers. Other evidence for the effects of stress comes from the findings that the incidence of ulcers increases during wartime and is higher in urban than rural areas (Pflanz, 1971).

However, to say that stress leads to ulcers is an oversimplification because it appears that some types of stress are more likely to lead to ulcers than others. A considerable amount of research on rats indicates that *unpredictable* stress is more likely to lead to ulcers than predictable stress (Seligman, 1968; Weiss, 1968, 1970). For example, in one experiment, two groups of rats received the same number of electrical shocks, but for one group, the shocks were preceded by a brief warning signal, whereas for the other group, the shocks came without warning (Weiss, 1970). The results indicated that the rats in the unpredictable shock condition were more likely to develop ulcers and developed larger ulcers than the rats in the predictable shock condition.

The other characteristic that seems to be important is whether or not the stress is controllable, with uncontrollable stress leading to more ulcers. In one experiment, rats were randomly assigned to conditions in which they did or did not receive electric shocks that would be stressful. The rats who were shocked had different degrees of control over the shock. In one condition, they could avoid or terminate the shock if they pushed a lever, whereas the rats in the other condition could not do anything to avoid or terminate the shocks. The rats who could not control the shock were given shocks that were comparable to those received by rats who could control the shocks.

The investigation produced two noteworthy findings: First, in general, rats that were shocked developed larger ulcers than rats that were not shocked. That was to be expected because the shocked rats experienced more stress than the nonshocked rats. Second, among rats that were shocked, those that could not control the shock developed larger ulcers than those that could control the shock despite the fact that the rats in both conditions received shocks of the same levels.

It is usually concluded from these results that stress that is unpredictable or uncontrollable is more likely to lead to ulcers, but that conclusion requires two qualifications. First, it may not be the *nature* of the stress (i.e., unpredictable or uncontrollable) that is crucial but rather the *level* or *amount* of stress that is important. If a rat does not know when stress will come (i.e., unpredictable stress), the rat will be constantly under stress and thus under more stress than a rat that knows when the stress will come. Similarly, if a rat can control stress, the rat will know when the stress will end and thus will be under less stress than a rat that cannot control the stress. In other words, predictability and control may simply be factors that influence the amount of stress, and the amount of stress may be the crucial factor in the development of ulcers.

The second qualification is that when rats are stressed, they develop *gastric* ulcers, but over 80% of the ulcers in humans are *duodenal* ulcers. Because of this inconsistency in the types of ulcers produced in rats and humans, we cannot be absolutely sure that the results based on rats can be generalized to humans. Confirmation of the effects in humans will have to await future research.

Physiological Predisposition.

From the foregoing discussion, it seems clear that stress can lead to the development of ulcers, but it is equally clear that by itself, stress is not sufficient to cause ulcers. That is, many people who undergo stress do not develop ulcers. It now appears that in addition to being exposed to stress, the individuals who develop ulcers also have a physiological predisposition to produce high levels of gastric acid (Weiner, 1991).

Individual differences in the gastric response to stress and their relationship to ulcers was illustrated in an early study in which persons who did or did not have ulcers were exposed to the same level of stress, after which the levels of hydrochloric acid in their stomachs were measured (Mittelmann et al., 1942). The results indicated that when exposed to the stress, the individuals who had ulcers showed higher levels of the acid and more stomach churning than the individuals who did not have ulcers.

More convincing evidence concerning the interaction of acid production and the development of ulcers comes from a prospective study in which the investigators identified newly inducted army draftees who had either high or low levels of pepsinogen (a precursor of pepsin, which is one of the gastric acids) but who did not have ulcers (Weiner et al., 1957). When the men were followed up after 16 weeks of stressful basic training, it was found that 15% of the men with high levels of pepsinogen had developed ulcers, whereas none of the men with low levels of pepsinogen had done so. Other investigators have found similar results in civilian populations (e.g., Mirsky, 1958).

There is now strong evidence that the tendency to produce high levels of gastric acid in response to stress is genetically determined. On the animal level, by selectively breeding rats, investigators were able to develop a strain in which every rat who was exposed to stress developed ulcers (Sines, 1963). On the human level, studies of twins indicate that there is a 54% concordance rate for ulcers in monozygotic twins but only a 17% concordance rate in dizygotic twins (Eberhard, 1968). The genetically determined predisposition for high acid production, possibly in combination with the fact that some families are under higher stress than others, can be used to account for the finding that family members of a person with an ulcer are three times more likely to have ulcers than individuals in the general population (Fodor et al., 1968; McConnell, 1966).

In general, the research consistently indicates that a predisposition to produce high levels of gastric acid in combination with stress leads to the development of ulcers. This is another example of the diathesis-stress model used in earlier chapters to account for other disorders. Overall, then, rather than talking about the *stress-ulcer* relationship, we should talk about the *predisposition-stress-ulcer* relationship.

Treatment and Prevention

Medical treatment for ulcers sometimes involves surgically removing the portion of the stomach or intestine that is ulcerated. That obviously removes the ulcer, but because it does not remove the underlying problems (acid production and stress), the ulcers are very likely to return. Another medical procedure involves partially cutting the vagus nerve that stimulates acid production in the stomach, but this extreme treatment is rarely used. Other treatments include the use of antacid drugs to neutralize the excess gastric acid and the use of a drug (cimetidine) that blocks nerve transmission to the stomach and reduces the production of gastric acid by 70% to 80%. These are effective maintenance treatments and can be used for prolonged periods of time by individuals who normally produce excess gastric acid or are constantly under stress. However, because in many cases the excess acid is due to stress, the treatment of choice often involves various types of stress management training programs in which individuals are taught to avoid or control stress.

IMMUNOLOGICAL DISORDERS

We are constantly exposed to infectious and toxic agents such as bacteria, viruses, fungi, and parasites. If allowed to go unchecked, these agents can result in a wide variety of disorders, ranging from colds to cancer. Fortunately, the **immune system** fights these disease-causing agents. What is important for us here is that in recent years, we have learned that psychological factors play an important role in the functioning of the immune system. Here we will review how the immune system works, examine the role that psychological factors play in its functioning, and then consider the role that psychological factors play in two major diseases that are related to the immune system, cancer and rheumatoid arthritis.

Immune System Functioning

The disease-causing agents that enter the body are generally referred to as **antigens** (AN-ti-junz). The function of the immune system is to destroy antigens and thereby prevent disease. The major combatants in the war against antigens are the **white blood cells** that circulate throughout the body via the bloodstream. White blood cells are technically called **leukocytes** (LOO-kuh-sīts), from the Greek for "light-colored cells." Leukocytes are produced in the lymphoid tissues in the lymph nodes, bone marrow, spleen, and parts of the gastrointestinal tract.

There are three types of leukocytes, but most attention has been focused on the **lymphocytes** (LIM-fuh-sīts), which are produced in the lymph nodes and are particularly effective for destroying antigens. Lymphocytes are divided into two types, **B cells** and **T**

cells. B cells destroy antigens by surrounding them and secreting substances that break the antigens down (i.e., by poisoning them). T cells can be divided into three types: (a) **killer cells** that destroy antigens by engulfing them (eating them), (b) **helper cells** that identify antigens and signal the lymph nodes when it is necessary to produce more B and T cells (essentially, the helper cells serve as "scouts"), and (c) **suppressor cells** that cause a reduction in the production of B and T cells when they are not needed. The organization and functions of the immune system are presented graphically in Figure 17.10.

The degree to which the immune system is active and effective is referred to as the individual's level of **immunocompetence** (the thoroughness with which the immune system identifies and destroys antigens). High immunocompetence is characterized by high levels of B cells, killer T cells, and helper T cells and low levels of suppressor T cells. In the laboratory, immunocompetence is measured by artificially introducing a weak antigen into the blood and then testing to determine whether the numbers of disease-fighting lymphocytes increases. Because the number of leukocytes increases to fight infection, a physician performs a white blood cell count to determine whether a person has an infection. It is important to recognize that there are wide individual differences in immunocompetence; the less responsive the immune system, the more an individual will suffer from infections and diseases. Let us now take a look at the factors that influence immunocompetence.

FIGURE 17.10 THE CELLS OF THE IMMUNE SYSTEM FIGHT ANTIGENS (INVADING CELLS) IN A VARIETY OF WAYS.

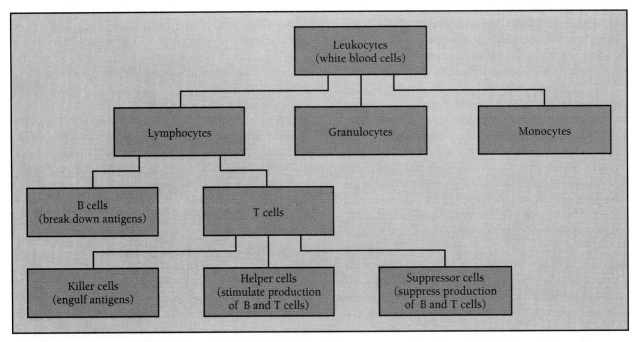

Psychological Factors and Immune System Functioning

Decreases in Immunocompetence.
Immunocompetence can be influenced by both physiological and psychological factors. A physiological factor that has attracted widespread attention is the **AIDS** (acquired immunodeficiency syndrome) virus, which kills lymphocytes instead of being killed by them. Specifically, the AIDS virus kills the helper T cells, and therefore the system is not stimulated to produce more killer cells when the body is invaded by antigens. In the absence of sufficient killer cells, the individual with AIDS dies of various infections, often pneumonia.

Of most importance for our discussion here is the fact that psychological factors can exert a strong influence on the functioning of the immune system (see Jemmott & Locke, 1984; Weisse, 1992). The influence of psychological factors first attracted attention when investigators reported that individuals who had been subjected to high levels of life stress were more likely to become physically ill in the following 2 or 3 months (see Cohen & Williamson, 1991; Dohrenwend & Dohrenwend, 1974). In one of the early studies in this area, the investigators measured the levels of life stress (e.g., family or financial problems) in a group of seamen before they left for an extended cruise, and then tracked the number of illnesses they experienced during the cruise (Rahe et al., 1970). The results indicated that the seamen who had experienced higher levels of life stress experienced more illnesses than those who had experienced lower levels of life stress. Those results are presented in Figure 17.11.

In studies linking life stress to illness, it is assumed that *high life stress leads to a decrease in immunocompetence,* which in turn leads to illness. Consistent with that speculation, there is now considerable evidence that stress decreases immunocompetence. For example, stressful final examinations led to lower immunocompetence among students, and the effect was greater among lonely students who lacked social support (Kiecolt-Glaser et al., 1984). Another study revealed that students had lower immunocompetence following a stressful period in school than following a vacation (Jemmott et al., 1983). It has also been demonstrated that individuals who are undergoing the prolonged stress of bereavement (death of a family member or loved one) show lower levels of immunocompetence than individuals who are not experiencing the stress of bereavement (Bartrop et al., 1977; Linn et al., 1982; Schleifer et al., 1983).

Immunocompetence has also been found to be related to depression: It is lower in depressed than nondepressed individuals (Denney et al., 1988; Kronfol et al., 1983; Schleifer et al., 1984), previously depressed patients who are now symptom-free show normal levels

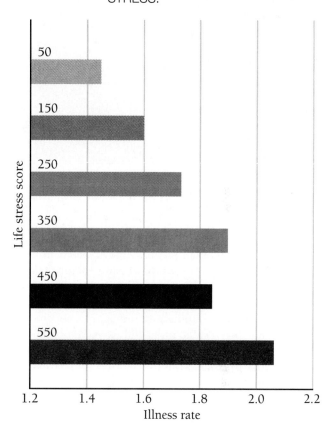

FIGURE 17.11 MEN WHO EXPERIENCED HIGH LIFE STRESS WERE MORE LIKELY TO GET SICK THAN MEN WHO DID NOT EXPERIENCE HIGH LIFE STRESS.

Source: Adapted from Rahe et al. (1970), p. 404, fig. 1.

of immunocompetence (Sengar et al., 1982), and the level of depression is related to the level of immunocompetence, with more depressed individuals showing lower immunocompetence (Denney et al., 1988; Kronfol et al., 1983; Linn et al., 1982). Depression is probably associated with lowered immunocompetence because depression reflects the presence of stress or because depression itself is a stressor (see Chapter 8). Finally, studies of U.S. and Soviet astronauts revealed that the stress of space flight resulted in lowered levels of immunocompetence (Taylor & Dardano, 1983; Taylor et al., 1986). Thus it can be concluded that psychological stress has the effect of reducing immunocompetence, which can in turn influence physical health.

Increases in Immunocompetence.
The finding that increases in psychological stress can lead to decreases in immunocompetence leads to the question of whether psychological treatments that reduce stress could increase immunocompetence in people who are exposed to stress. That possibility gained support from

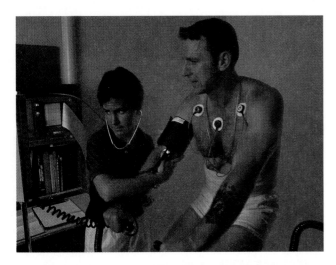

In addition to improving cardiovascular responsiveness to stress, aerobic exercise training is also an effective way to increase immunocompetence.

an experiment in which students participated in a series of stress reduction training sessions before taking an important examination (Kiecolt-Glaser et al., 1984). Levels of immunocompetence were assessed a month before the examination and again after the examination. The results indicated that the students showed generally lower immunocompetence after the exams than they had a month earlier (i.e., stress reduced immunocompetence), and there was a correlation between the number of training sessions the students attended and their levels of immunocompetence; students who attended more stress reduction training sessions showed higher immunocompetence. In another experiment, elderly individuals had their immune systems assessed before and after receiving relaxation training, social contact, or no treatment over a period of 1 month (Kiecolt-Glaser et al., 1985). Comparisons of the groups revealed that the individuals who received relaxation training showed increases in immunocompetence, whereas the individuals in the other conditions did not. Thus there is now some evidence that stress management techniques are effective for reducing the effects of stress on the immune system.

Another behavior strategy that is effective for increasing immunocompetence is aerobic exercise training. Ample evidence now indicates that an acute bout of strenuous aerobic exercise will increase the levels of various lymphocytes (e.g., Edwards et al., 1984; Hedfors et al., 1976, 1978, 1983; Landmann et al., 1984; Robertson et al., 1981).

The results of one study suggest that aerobic exercise and fitness may serve to facilitate immune system functioning and reduce illness (Roth & Holmes, 1985). In that study, the investigators identified stu-

dents who either were or were not experiencing high levels of life stress, and they then categorized the students according to high or low aerobic fitness. When the health records of the students were examined for the following 8-week period, it was found that the students who were not physically fit and who were under high stress showed high levels of illness, while the students who were physically fit and under high stress showed low levels of illness. In fact, the fit students under high stress showed illness levels that were comparable to those of students under low stress. In other words, aerobic fitness served to offset the effects of stress in the stress-illness relationship. These results are presented in Figure 17.12.

In a follow-up experiment, the investigators took students who were experiencing high life stress and assigned them to an aerobic exercise condition, a relaxation training condition, or a no-treatment control condition (Roth & Holmes, 1987). When the students were examined 2 months later, it was found that the students in the aerobic training condition were less depressed than the students in the other conditions, but there was not a difference in illness levels across the three conditions. From the findings of the two investigations, it was concluded that aerobic fitness is an effective means of avoiding stress-related illnesses, but persons must be fit at the time of the onset of the stress. In other words, aerobic fitness serves as a *prophylactic, not a cure.*

In summary, a wide variety of evidence links stress to reduced functioning of the immune system, and it is generally agreed that reduced immunocompetence

FIGURE 17.12 WHEN EXPOSED TO LIFE STRESS, AEROBICALLY FIT PERSONS WERE LESS LIKELY TO GET SICK THAN LESS AEROBICALLY FIT PERSONS.

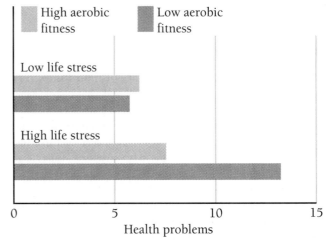

Source: Adapted from Roth and Holmes (1985), p. 169, fig. 1.

following stress is the mediating factor in the stress–illness relationship. Stress management and aerobic exercise programs have been shown to be effective behavioral strategies for increasing immunocompetence. With this material as background, we can now go on to consider two of the many diseases that are related to the immune system and that are influenced by psychological factors.

Cancer

Cancer is a group of diseases that involve the *abnormal reproduction of cells*. All cells are genetically programmed to reproduce themselves, but they are also programmed to stop reproducing. The cessation of cell reproduction is crucial because without it, we would never stop growing. A breakdown in the mechanism that stops cell reproduction leads to the abnormal growths we call tumors.

There are two types of tumors, **malignant** (muh-LIG-nunt) **tumors** and **benign** (bē-NĪN) **tumors**. There are two important differences between these types of tumors. First, malignant tumors can invade and choke out adjacent tissues, whereas benign tumors are self-contained and pose problems only when they put pressure on adjacent tissues. (Benign tumors range from serious brain tumors to inconsequential warts and moles.) Second, malignant tumors can shed cells that then travel to other parts of the body (via the bloodstream or lymphatic channels), where they establish new tumors. The process of shedding and spreading cells is called **metastasis** (muh-TAS-tuh-sis). If a malignant tumor is not controlled with surgery, medication, or radiation, it will eventually block or kill some tissue that is essential to life (e.g., brain, lungs, colon, kidney), and the individual will die. The probability of serious consequences is of course greatly increased if the tumor has metastasized.

Cancers occur when the genes that control cell reproduction are altered in structure by **spontaneous mutation** (damage in the process of cell division) or by exposure to foreign substances called **carcinogens** (kar-SIN-uh-jinz), substances capable of causing cancer. Well-known carcinogens include tobacco smoke, asbestos, and ultraviolet light.

The immune system is crucial for the control of cancer because the immune system can identify and destroy carcinogens that enter the body, and it can also identify and destroy cancerous tissues before they get out of control. We are all exposed to carcinogens, and some investigators have suggested that many or even all people develop cancers, but usually the immune system succeeds in holding them in check or eliminating them. However, problems arise if the level of carcinogens is so high that the immune system is overwhelmed or if the level of the immune system's functioning is reduced and therefore it cannot cope with the carcinogens.

The relationship between immune system functioning and the risk of developing cancer is clearly illustrated in the case of individuals who have organ transplants. The immune systems of transplant recipients would recognize the transplanted organ as foreign and therefore attack it (this is called *organ rejection*), so their immune systems must be suppressed with medication. Unfortunately, that suppression increases the likelihood that the individuals will develop cancer because the immune systems are no longer active enough to fight off carcinogens and abnormal tissues (Penn & Starzl, 1972).

Earlier in this chapter it was pointed out that psychological stress can reduce the functioning of the immune system, and therefore it is possible that psychological stress may contribute to the development of cancer. We will now examine the evidence concerning the relationships between psychological factors and cancer.

Psychological Factors Contributing to Cancer.

At the outset it should be noted that factors such as smoking, diet, alcohol consumption, and exposure to ultraviolet light all contribute to the development of cancer, and insofar as those factors are related to behavior, psychological processes are important in their control. Indeed, psychologists are involved in the development of programs to change behaviors ranging from smoking to sunbathing in the hope of reducing the incidence of cancer. In this chapter, however, we will focus on the suspected relationship between stress and cancer.

The possible relationship between stress and cancer has been studied in a number of ways. One way has been to use *retrospective reports* to compare the histories of stressful experiences in the lives of persons who did and did not have cancer (e.g., Cheang & Cooper, 1985; Ernster et al., 1979; Goodkin et al., 1986; Graham et al., 1971; Jacobs & Charles, 1980; Le Shan, 1966; Muslin et al., 1966; Schmale & Iker, 1966b). Typical of this type of research is a study in which the investigators interviewed 110 male patients who had lesions in their lungs that had not yet been diagnosed as cancerous (Horne & Picard, 1979). In the interviews, the patients were rated on 5-point scales in terms of childhood instability, job stability, marriage stability, lack of plans for the future, and recent significant losses (e.g., loss of job; death of spouse, parent, or sibling). Two years later, when final diagnoses of the patients' tumors were made, it was found that high scores on each of the scales except childhood instability were related to a greater likelihood that the patients' tumors were malignant. For example, 68% of the patients with malignant tumors had experienced a significant loss, compared to only 33% of the patients with benign tumors. When the sums of scores from all five scales were used, 80% of the patients with malignant tumors, but only 39% of the patients with benign tumors, had high scores. Finally, it is interesting to note that the patients' stress-related interview scores were more effective than information about their smoking behavior for predicting whether they had malignant or benign tumors. Unfortunately, although a number of studies like this one have revealed a relationship between stress and cancer, firm conclusions cannot be drawn from this group of studies because (a) the findings are sometimes inconsistent from study to study, (b) serious questions can be raised about the validity of the self-reports (the stress of having cancer may lead persons to exaggerate the stressful nature of previous experiences), and (c) it is possible that even if the cancer patients did experience more stress, the stress may have been the result of the undetected cancer rather than a cause of the cancer (see Cox & Mackay, 1982; Fox, 1978; Greer & Morris, 1978). A second way in which the relationship between stress and cancer has been studied is with *prospective studies* in which (a) data were collected on a group of individuals who were not suspected of having cancer, (b) the individuals were then followed up to determine who developed cancer, and finally, (c) those who did and did not develop cancer were compared in terms of the data that were collected earlier. In the largest project of this type, the students in 17 successive classes at Johns Hopkins Medical School (1948–1964) participated in intensive psychosocial evaluations while they were students and were followed up in terms of their health status years later (Duszynski et al., 1981; Shaffer et al., 1982; Thomas, 1976). Unfortunately, this approach has not produced many positive results, and the few that were found have not been corroborated by other investigators. Overall, this approach has yielded little, if any, support for the stress-cancer relationship.

Another line of investigation has involved studying the *personalities* of individuals who develop cancer, and this has led indirectly to evidence for the stress-cancer relationship. Originally, researchers attempted to identify a general "cancer-prone" personality, but they met with no success. However, the investigators did find three specific personality characteristics that were related to the development of cancer. Two of those characteristics are *depression* and *hopelessness* (Dattore et al., 1980; Schmale & Iker, 1966a, 1971; Shekelle et al., 1981; Whitlock & Siskind, 1979). In one prospective study, more than 2,000 healthy males were given the Minnesota Multiphasic Personality Inventory, and when they were followed up 17 years later, it was found that those who had had high scores on the Depression scale were twice as likely to have developed cancer (Shekelle et al., 1981).

A third personality factor that seems to be related to the development of cancer is the *suppression of emotion* (Dattore et al., 1980; Greer & Morris, 1978; Kissen, 1966; Kissen et al., 1969; Kneier & Tremoshok, 1984). The investigators in one study did a psychological evaluation of 160 women who were suspected of having breast cancer but who had not yet undergone tumor biopsies (Greer & Morris, 1978). When the women were followed up 5 years later, it was found that those whose tumors were cancerous had been judged earlier to be more likely to suppress anger than those whose tumors were benign.

The personality-cancer relationship has also been studied by examining the relationship between personality and *length of survival* (Blumberg et al., 1954; Derogatis et al., 1979; Pettingale, 1984; Pettingale et al., 1977; Schonfield, 1972). The results of this line of investigation have indicated that essentially the same characteristics that were associated with a greater likelihood of developing cancer (e.g., depression, hopelessness, suppresion of emotion) were also associated with short survival times. For example, in a study of women with breast cancer, those who were characterized as depressed, helpless, and hopeless were less likely to be disease-free 10 years later than women who were characterized as having a "fighting spirit" (Pettingale, 1984; Pettingale et al., 1977).

Overall, it appears that depression, hopelessness, and suppression of emotion may be related to the likelihood of developing cancer and to the length of survival after the diagnosis is made. The question that arises then is, why are these personality characteristics related to cancer? In attempting to answer that question, it should be noted that all three personality characteristics are associated with stress. Feelings of depression and hopelessness are caused by stress, or if the depression is caused by biological factors, the depression itself can be stressful. Furthermore, suppression of emotions prolongs stress, thus increasing its impact. It appears, then, that in studying the personality-cancer relationship, we may actually be studying the stress-cancer relationship.

The possible relationships of stress, personality, and cancer are presented graphically in Figure 17.13. Theory 1 in the figure suggests that stress leads to certain personality characteristics and to the development of cancer. In this theory, the relationship between personality and cancer stems from their common relationship with stress. You may recall from the discussion of research methodology in Chapter 3 that the correlation between two variables (in this case, personality and cancer) does not necessarily mean

FIGURE 17.13   STRESS, PERSONALITY, AND CANCER MAY BE
RELATED IN ONE OF TWO WAYS.

Theory 1: Stress leads to the development of certain personality
characteristics and to cancer, so personality characteristics
are indirectly related to cancer because of underlying stress.

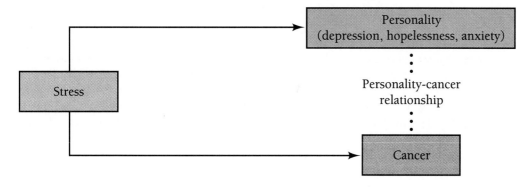

Theory 2: Certain personality characteristics lead to stress, and that
prolonged stress contributes to the development of cancer.

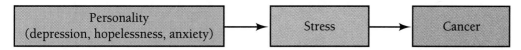

that there is a causal relationship between them because the relationship could be due to the effects of a third variable (in this case, stress). Theory 2 in the figure suggests that the possession of certain personality characteristics is stressful, and the stress of having those characteristics may contribute to the development of cancer.

The next question we must ask is, if stress is the crucial variable in the personality-cancer relationship, why do the results relating personality to cancer appear to be stronger than the results relating stress to cancer? The answer may be that there are many potential stressors and that different individuals may find different things stressful (e.g., the loss of a friend may be devastating for one person and merely unpleasant for another), and therefore it may be difficult to find relationships between specific events and cancer. However, the presence of depression and hopelessness may be a sign that a person has been stressed regardless of the specific stressor. Therefore, by looking at personality characteristics that reflect stress, we may be more likely to recognize stress than if we look at specific events that may or may not be stressful for a particular individual.

Before drawing any firm conclusions concerning the relationship between stress and cancer, we should examine the research in which stress was experimentally manipulated. Certainly, the most convincing way to establish a relationship between stress and cancer would be to conduct controlled experiments in which one group of individuals is exposed to extreme stress while another group is not and then compare the rates of cancer in the two groups. Although this approach would be ideal from a methodological standpoint, it would not be ethically acceptable to do such experiments on humans. However, numerous experiments of this type have been conducted with animals (see Justice, 1985; Riley, 1981; Sklar & Anisman, 1981).

In a typical experiment, half of the animals were injected with substances that could cause cancer, while the other half did not get the injections. Half of the animals in each group were then exposed to stress (random electrical shocks, forced swimming, cold), while the others were not, and then the rates of cancer development were measured in all groups. In a variety of experiments, it was found that the animals who received the cancerous injections and were exposed to the stress showed the highest or fastest rate of cancer development.

Those findings provide strong support for the stress-cancer relationship. However, not all of the experiments produced those findings, and it now appears that *stress may have different effects with different types of cancer* (Justice, 1985). Specifically, it has been suggested that in the case of *viral cancers* (cancers caused by viruses), the presence of stress may cause an increase in tumor growth, and the termination of stress may cause a decrease in tumor growth. However,

TABLE 17.1   EFFECTS OF STRESS ON THE DEVELOPMENT OF VIRAL
AND NONVIRAL TUMORS IN ANIMALS

	DURING STRESS	FOLLOWING STRESS
Viral tumors	Increased growth	Decreased growth
Nonviral tumors	Decreased growth	Increased growth

Note. Increases and decreases are relative to no-stress conditions.
Source: Adapted from Justice (1985), p. 110, fig. 1.

in the case of *nonviral cancers* (cancers due to factors other than viruses), the presence of stress may actually cause a decrease in tumor growth whereas the termination of stress may cause an increase in tumor growth. These relationships are summarized in Table 17.1.

These findings do not necessarily contradict the hypothesis that stress influences immune system functioning, which in turn influences the development of cancers, but they suggest that the process may be considerably more complex than was originally thought. In the case of nonviral cancers, which are thought to be more prevalent in humans, it appears that it is the *change* from stress to nonstress conditions that may be important, but the occurrence of stress is still crucial. Before firm conclusions can be drawn, however, additional research will be necessary to document the patterning in humans and clarify the underlying processes.

Psychological Treatment of the Cancer Patient.
In concluding our discussion of psychological factors and cancer, three brief comments are warranted concerning the psychological treatment of patients with cancer. First, because cancer frequently results in death, it is an exceptionally stressful disease and consequently can cause serious psychological problems. Therefore, psychologists often provide treatments that *help patients and their families cope with the stress.* The evidence suggests that these treatment programs can be very effective (Gordon et al., 1980; Trijsburg et al., 1992).

Second, the chemotherapy that many cancer patients must undergo results in numerous negative side effects such as pain, nausea, and vomiting, and psychologists have been active and effective in developing treatment programs that help *reduce the side effects* (see Carey & Burish, 1988; Redd & Andrykowski, 1982). For example, it has been demonstrated that muscle relaxation training is effective for reducing nausea, physiological arousal (pulse rate, blood pressure), anxiety, depression, and anger among cancer patients who are undergoing chemotherapy (Lyles et al., 1982).

Third, some attempts have been made to use psychological approaches for the *treatment of the cancer itself.* Specifically, some physicians and psychologists have advocated using relaxation training and visual imagery as adjuncts to the traditional medical treatments (Simonton & Simonton, 1975; Simonton et al., 1980). An important component of this treatment is the belief that individuals can voluntarily control their physiological processes by mental means, and therefore patients spend time imagining their white ("good") blood cells eating or in some way destroying the cancerous ("bad") cells.

This approach has received wide attention in the mass media, and advocates often cite cases of patients with "incurable" cancers who were cured through this approach to treatment. The case studies are often dramatic, but it is important to recognize that at present, *there is no controlled evidence that this approach to treatment is at all effective* (American Cancer Society, 1982). The cures that are reported are probably cases of spontaneous remission that occur occasionally (usually without the use of imagery), and the advocates of the approach who frequently appear on TV talk shows neglect to mention that thousands of persons have tried the approach with no effect.

Rheumatoid Arthritis

Arthritis is a disease that involves *pain in the joints.* It is the second most prevalent disease in the United States, following coronary heart disease. Although arthritis is rarely fatal, it can be exceptionally painful and often results in severe crippling. There are three major types of arthritis, each with a different basis for the pain. First, *osteoarthritis* results from the wearing away of the smooth lining of the joints, and as such it is a structural or mechanical problem. Second, *gout* stems from the presence of crystals in the joints (usually of the large toe). The crystals develop when the kidneys do not excrete enough uric acid from the body; thus gout is a problem of metabolism. Third, *rheumatoid arthritis* occurs when the immune system attacks substances that get into the joints and in the process does damage to the membrane that covers the joints. Exactly why this occurs is not clear, but the immune system may be overresponding to stress.

We will focus on **rheumatoid arthritis** (ROOM-uh-toyd ar-THRĪ-tis) because it is widely assumed that psychological factors play a role in its development.

About 1% of the population suffers from rheumatoid arthritis, and the ratio of female to male sufferers is 3:1. Most cases occur between the ages of 20 and 50, but a rare juvenile form occurs in young children. Rheumatoid arthritis usually affects the small joints in the hands, wrists, knees, and ankles.

Psychological Factors Contributing to Rheumatoid Arthritis. The cause of rheumatoid arthritis is not completely understood, but for many years, it has been speculated that psychological factors play a role in its development. Investigators first attempted to determine whether a specific personality type was associated with arthritis; that is, if an "arthritic personality" existed (see Anderson et al., 1985). A wide variety of personality characteristics were proposed (e.g., depression, hostility, inhibition), but after more than 40 years of research, there is still very little reliable evidence connecting specific personality characteristics to the disease. Furthermore, insofar as there are consistencies in the findings, most can be attributed to the fact that personality was measured after the onset of the disorder, and therefore the characteristics observed in the patients may be effects rather than causes of the disease. In one series of six investigations, it was found that patients with rheumatoid arthritis had higher scores on the Depression, Hysteria, and Hypochondriasis scales of the MMPI than other individuals, but an examination of those scales revealed that they contained disease-related items such as "I am in just as good physical health as most of my friends," "During the past few years I have been well," and "I have few or no pains" (Pincus et al., 1986). When the disease-related items were removed, the differences between the patients and controls disappeared. At present, then, there does not appear to be any reliable evidence that specific personality characteristics are related to the development of rheumatoid arthritis.

In contrast to the findings concerning personality, there is a growing body of evidence that *psychological stress* (e.g., financial problems, loss, marital conflict) is related to the development of rheumatoid arthritis (see Anderson et al., 1985; Weiner, 1977). In one study, extensive interviews dealing with life events were conducted with a group of patients who were believed to be developing rheumatoid arthritis and with an age-matched group of patients suffering from other medical problems (Baker, 1982). (Using patients who are just developing the disorder helped reduce the possibility that the presence of the disease influenced the patients' reports.) A year later, the patients who had a confirmed diagnosis of rheumatoid arthritis were compared to the general medical patients. The results indicated that 68% of the arthritic patients reported an important life stress in the year before the onset of their symptoms, whereas only 36% of the general medical patients reported such a stress.

Stress and Subtypes of Rheumatoid Arthritis. Although numerous studies have indicated a relationship between stress and the development of rheumatoid arthritis, in a variety of cases stress was not found to be a factor. One possible explanation for the inconsistency in the findings is that stress may be only one of a number of factors that can lead to the disease, and therefore only a subset of cases is related to stress. Support for that possibility comes from a number of studies in which the investigators identified what appear to be two forms of the disease, one stress-related and one not stress-related (Rimon, 1969; Rimon & Laakso, 1985). The characteristics of the two forms are listed in Table 17.2. What is most noteworthy is the fact that in one form, the symptoms are associated with stress and there is not a family history of the disease, whereas in the other form, the symptoms are not related to stress but there is a family history of the disorder. In other words, rheumatoid arthritis may be related to stress or to a genetic factor.

A 15-year follow-up of the patients who were used to make the original distinction between stress-related and non-stress-related rheumatoid arthritis revealed two interesting findings (Rimon & Laakso, 1985). First, the patients in the stress-related group were more likely to show a variable course in the disease. In other words, for these patients, the symptoms were sometimes better and sometimes worse, whereas the course of the disease for the other patients was constant and progressive. Second, the increases in symptomatology that were observed in the stress-related

TABLE 17.2   CHARACTERISTICS OF STRESS-RELATED AND NON-STRESS-RELATED FORMS OF RHEUMATOID ARTHRITIS

STRESS-RELATED FORM	NON-STRESS-RELATED FORM
Rapid onset of symptoms	Slow, insidious onset of symptoms
Varying severity of symptoms	Fairly constant symptoms
Little or no family history of rheumatoid arthritis	High proportion of family members with rheumatoid arthritis
Onset of symptoms associated with stress	Onset of symptoms not associated with stress

Source: Adapted from Rimon and Laakso (1985).

group were most likely to occur during times of major life stress, thus suggesting that for these patients, stress was the crucial factor in their disease. It is also interesting to note that five of the patients in the stress-related group who did not show changes in symptom severity over time were apparently under constant high levels of stress because of an alcoholic spouse.

Overall, these findings refine our understanding of rheumatoid arthritis and suggest that in at least one form, stress plays an important role in its development. The possible relationship between stress and rheumatoid arthritis is illustrated in the experience of a 34-year-old woman who describes her experience in Case Study 17.1.

Overall, there is now a substantial amount of evidence linking psychological stress to the development of rheumatoid arthritis, but we still do not understand the process involved. Most theorists assume that the effect is mediated by the immune system. It is possible that in these patients, stress results in an excessive response of the immune system that leads to the joint damage, but this is still very speculative. In most individuals, stress leads to a diminished response of the immune system, but there is now some evidence that the reverse can also be true, and it may be that persons who develop rheumatoid arthritis are somehow predisposed to that type of response.

SUMMARY

In this chapter, we considered the relationship between psychological factors and the development of various physical disorders. We began with a review of stress, which is the major psychological factor that contributes to physical disorders. After recognizing a stress, persons can cope with it (work to solve the problem) or defend against it (use strategies that reduce anxiety but do not solve the underlying problem). If coping and defenses are not effective for reducing the stress, physiological responses are triggered that result in increased arousal, and that increased physiological arousal leads to physical disorders.

Coronary artery disease involves the buildup of fats (cholesterol and triglycerides) inside the arteries (atherosclerosis), reducing blood flow. If blood flow to the muscles of the heart is reduced, the muscles do not get the oxygen they need and they die, resulting in a heart attack. The Type A behavior pattern, especially the hostility component of that pattern, has been shown to be related to (a) the development of coronary artery disease, (b) increased arousal (higher heart rate and blood pressure) in challenging or stress-

ful situations, and (c) the setting of higher personal goals. It is widely believed that Type A behavior or hostility causes coronary artery disease because it leads the individual to be more highly aroused in more situations, and the higher arousal leads to greater production, clumping, and accumulation of cholesterol on the walls of the arteries. Alternatively, it may be that Type A behavior or hostility and coronary artery disease are only correlated with each other and that the relationship is due to a genetically determined high level of arousal that leads to both the behavior and the disease. Coronary artery disease can be treated with various medical procedures (bypass surgery, angioplasty, medication), but prevention revolves around changes in diet, reductions in stress, or reduction of the response to stress via aerobic fitness, social support, or stress management.

Essential hypertension is chronically elevated blood pressure (140/90 or higher) for which there is no known physical cause. It appears that stress leads to increased pressure. If the increase is prolonged, the baroreceptors responsible for detecting excessively high pressure become reset, accepting high pressure as normal, and therefore the system does not react to reduce pressure.

Migraine and tension headaches are often attributed to stress, but stress has been linked only to tension headaches. Tension headaches can be treated effectively with EMG biofeedback training or muscle relaxation training.

Peptic ulcers (duodenal and gastric) are lesions in the digestive tract that stem from excessive acid or insufficient mucus. Stress leads to the production of excess acid, but this is mostly likely to occur in individuals who are genetically predisposed to the production of high levels of acid. Treatment and prevention revolve around reducing acid production with medication and reducing stress.

The immune system fights disease by producing leukocytes (white blood cells) that destroy antigens. Individuals who are experiencing a high level of stress are more likely to become physically ill because stress reduces immunocompetence. Cancer involves the abnormal reproduction of cells, which results in tumors. That process is often triggered by carcinogens and is more likely to occur if the immune system is suppressed and therefore less likely to destroy carcinogens. Evidence now suggests that persons who are depressed, lack hope, or suppress emotion are at greater risk for cancer and may survive less long once the disorder develops. Those personality characteristics are probably related to cancer because they reflect the effects of stress. Arthritis is also related to the functioning of the immune system, and there is also evidence linking the development of arthritis to stress.

Case Study 17.1

STRESS AND RHEUMATOID ARTHRITIS IN A PHYSICALLY ACTIVE 34-YEAR-OLD WOMAN: A PERSONAL ACCOUNT

I have always been healthy, physically active, and interested in sports. I ride my horse a couple of times a week, play golf and tennis frequently, and play on a softball team. Because of my interest in sports, 4 years ago I took all of my savings, borrowed some money, and opened a sporting goods store. More about that later; first let me tell you about the physical problems that developed.

One day about 3 years ago, I started having a pain and some swelling in my right wrist. It bothered me, but I didn't worry about it at first because I assumed that it stemmed from some tendinitis I had from a skiing accident a few years earlier. However, a few days later, I also began to have pain in my other wrist, and my fingers began swelling. Then I noticed that my feet and ankles were swollen, and I started having trouble putting on my shoes. The problem got worse very fast, and soon I couldn't open a bottle or a car door, couldn't shift my car, and couldn't bend my knees, which made fitting people for athletic shoes really tough. Things came to a head when I had to make a long drive and developed severe aches in all of my joints. My feet and knees hurt so badly that I had to stop every half hour to stretch and rest them. The next day, I went to my physician, who took some blood tests and told me that I had rheumatoid arthritis. Arthritis? Me? How could that be? Arthritis is for old people—how did I get it?

I went to a rheumatologist for a second opinion, but she came to the same diagnosis. In talking with me, the rheumatologist asked whether anyone in my family suffered from arthritis and whether I was under stress. No, no one else in the family suffered from arthritis, but yes, I was definitely under a tremendous amount of stress. The stress was associated with my new business. The problem was that I had paid a contractor $75,000 to remodel my store in a mall, but the contractor left town without paying the subcontractors who had done the work. I was left responsible for paying the $75,000 again. The store was making money, but not enough to pay off the start-up costs twice. I was trying to run the store, I was deep in debt, and I was being constantly harassed by creditors, lawyers, and vendors. I was struggling to keep my head above water, but I was slowly slipping under—and now I was rapidly developing a crippling case of rheumatoid arthritis.

I was put on some expensive medication to reduce the inflammation in my joints, and my physical activities were restricted so that I would not hurt my inflamed joints and cause permanent damage. I also did simple exercises with a physical therapist so that my joints wouldn't freeze up.

The medication held the symptoms in check, but I had to stay on the medication. And though the arthritis was under control, my business problems weren't, and finally I had to sell out and give up. It had been a terrible time; I was personally and financially devastated, but it was over and behind me. I decided to take a year off, come back to school, and try to figure out what to do next. I really enjoyed being back in school, and after a couple of months, I noticed that my joint pain was becoming less and less and I was getting more movement and flexibility. In consultation with my physician, I began slowly to reduce the amount of medication I was taking until I was completely off it. I have now been off the medication *and symptom-free* for a little over a year. I can't prove that the stress of the business failure caused the arthritis, but the arthritis came and went with the stress. I've got my fingers crossed that neither will come back—and the fact that I can cross my fingers tells you how well I'm doing!

The findings presented in this chapter indicate that psychological stress works with other factors (e.g., genetic predispositions, high levels of carcinogens) to contribute to the development of physical disorders. These findings complement earlier findings indicating that physiological factors contribute to psychological disorders, and together they highlight the interaction of psychological and physiological factors in the development of disorders.

KEY TERMS, CONCEPTS, AND NAMES

In reviewing and testing yourself on what you have learned from this chapter, you should be able to identify and discuss each of the following:

adrenal cortex	aerobic exercise	AIDS
adrenal glands	aerobic fitness	angina

angioplasty
antigens
arthritis
atherosclerosis
autonomic division (of peripheral nervous system)
baroreceptors
B cells
benign tumors
beta blockers
biofeedback training
brain stem
cancer
carcinogens
catecholamines
central nervous system
central nervous system catecholamines
cerebral infarction
circulating catecholamines
coronary artery disease
coronary bypass surgery
cortisol
diastolic blood pressure
diuretic
duodenal ulcers
electromyographic (EMG) biofeedback training
embolism
epinephrine

essential hypertension
gastric ulcers
glucose
HDL
health psychology
helper cells
hostility
hypertension
hypotension
hypothalamus
immune system
immunocompetence
killer cells
LDL
leukocytes
lymphocytes
malignant tumors
metastasis
migraine headache
mind–body dualism
muscle contraction headaches
myocardial infarction (MI)
nitroglycerin
norepinephrine
parasympathetic branch (of nervous system)
peptic ulcers
peripheral nervous system
pituitary gland

prodromal symptoms
progressive muscle relaxation training
psychophysiological disorders
psychosomatic disorders
rheumatoid arthritis
secondary hypertension
social support
somatic division (of peripheral nervous system)
somatoform disorders
spinal cord
spontaneous mutation
stress
stress management training
stroke
structured interview
suppressor cells
sympathetic branch (of nervous system)
systolic blood pressure
T cells
tension headaches
thrombus
Type A behavior pattern
vascular accidents
vasodilators
white blood cells

Notes:

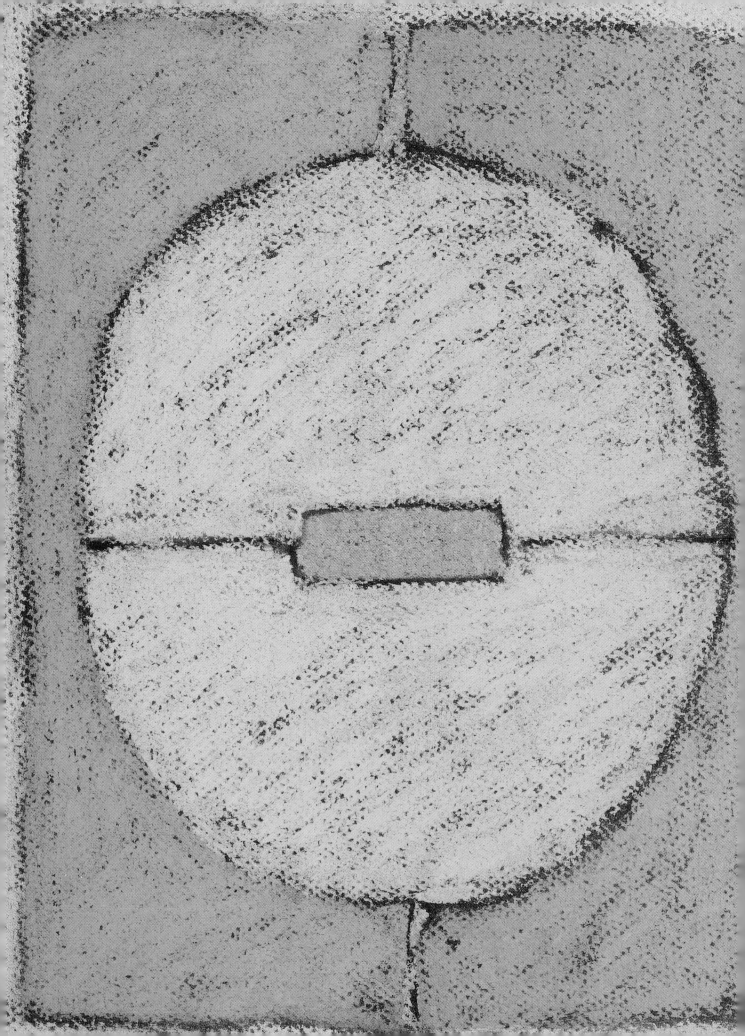

Chapter 18

Substance Dependence and Abuse

• O U T L I N E •

en Bias was a talented college basketball player who had just signed a multimillion-dollar contract to play for the world champion Boston Celtics. His future was bright when he shot some cocaine and died of cardiac arrest. Thousands of cases of heart attacks from unknown causes are undoubtedly due to cocaine use.

Ruth is a bright, anxious, tense, sensitive, and somewhat inhibited 34-year-old woman who rarely drinks alcohol. However, every few months, she goes on a binge. She buys a bottle of vodka, takes it home, and drinks until she passes out. After 8 or 10 hours, she comes to with a terrible hangover and is sick for a day or so. She is always ashamed of what she has done, and most people do not know about her problem. Ruth suffers from the binge type of alcoholism. The very high level of alcohol may serve briefly to reduce her high level of arousal.

John is an uninhibited, impulsive guy who often takes risks just for kicks, and consequently he has frequent scrapes with the law. John always seems to be drinking—always having a drink or having just finished one. He does not drink a lot at any one time, so he is rarely really drunk, but he is usually just a little high. John appears to have the persistent type of alcoholism. The low level of alcohol may have the effect of depressing the inhibitory areas of the brain, thereby resulting in a higher level of arousal for him.

After smoking marijuana, an engineer ran his train through a red signal light and hit another train. Seventeen people died. . . . A man with twice the legal limit of alcohol in his blood drove his pickup truck down the wrong side of the road and hit a school bus head on. He survived, but 27 schoolchildren were killed. . . . An autopsy revealed cocaine in the body of a pilot whose plane crashed, killing all passengers.

In a recent survey, more than 500,000 high school students and more than 35,000 elementary school students admitted using cocaine at least once a week, and those reports are probably on the conservative side. The prognosis for these children is bleak.

Cynthia used LSD occasionally with some of her friends, and the "trips" were usually pleasant and fun. However, twice she had really bad trips that were terrifying, and during one, she tried to kill herself. Because of the bad trips, she has stopped using LSD, but now she is having "flashbacks" (trips that occur when she does not take the drug). She never knows when a flashback will occur, and she feels out of control. She is now afraid to be alone because she does not know when she will need help.

Headline stories appear almost daily that document the fact that the misuse of drugs is one of the most serious problems facing Western civilization today. At this point, the "war on drugs" is not being won; if anything, we seem to be losing. Drug abuse was once primarily an adult problem, but now millions of children use drugs such as cocaine on an almost daily basis. This is a problem to which we must give very careful and thorough attention.

In this chapter, we will not take a moral stand concerning whether or not it is appropriate to use drugs. Instead, we will focus on understanding the effects of drugs and the reasons why some persons become dependent on them. Armed with that background, you will be able to make your own informed judgments concerning what is and what is not appropriate.

ISSUES ASSOCIATED WITH SUBSTANCE DEPENDENCE AND ABUSE

Definition and Nature of Psychoactive Drugs

The substances that we will consider in this chapter are generally referred to as **psychoactive drugs**. Stated simply, a psychoactive drug is any substance that alters your *mood* (e.g., makes you happy, sad, angry, depressed), alters your *awareness of the external environment* (e.g., time, location, conditions), or *alters your awareness of the internal environment* (e.g., dreams, images). For example, after taking a psychoactive drug, an individual may feel elated, be unaware of the passage of time, and may focus on fantasies rather than what is going on in the immediate environment.

Over the years, the term *psychoactive* has taken on numerous negative connotations. It often conjures up images of the "junkie," the person "spaced out on dope," the Wall Street broker or rock star sniffing coke, and the disheveled heroin addict slumped in a doorway. However, the term *psychoactive* does not imply good or bad, legal or illegal. Marijuana, cocaine, heroin, and LSD are all psychoactive substances, but so are sugar, caffeine, nicotine, alcohol, and codeine. Furthermore, although psychoactive drugs are often abused and can lead to serious problems, they also have many important and valuable uses, such as the use of depressants (Valium) to reduce anxiety or the use of narcotics (codeine) to control pain.

Factors Influencing Drug Effects

A number of factors other than the chemical makeup of a drug can influence its effects. Those factors deserve some attention before we go on.

Dose-Dependent Effects.   One of the first things to recognize is that the effects of drugs can vary with the quantity taken. In other words, the effects of drugs can be **dose-dependent**. First, dose level can influence how *much* of an effect will occur. This is obvious in the case of alcohol: A few beers can result in a slight slurring of speech; a few more in a greater slurring of speech. Second, dose level can influence the *type* of effects that will occur. Small doses of nicotine produce physiological stimulation, but larger doses result in physiological sedation that can be great enough to cause death.

Individual Differences.   The effects of many drugs are sometimes influenced by the personality of the individuals taking them. For example, a small dose of caffeine (the equivalent of two cups of coffee) can improve the intellectual performance of extroverted individuals (e.g., enable them to study better), but the same dose can impair the performance of introverted individuals (Revelle et al., 1976). That effect stems from the fact that extroverts are often neurologically underaroused, so the stimulating effect of the caffeine brings them up to an optimal level of arousal, but introverts are already at an optimal level of arousal, so the additional stimulation provided by the caffeine pushes them beyond the optimal level, and consequently their performance declines.

Individual differences in experience with drugs can also influence the effects of drugs. For example, individuals who are inexperienced in the use of marijuana do not report any effects of the drug even when physiological measures indicate that effects are occurring. In contrast, experienced users notice the effects right away.

The influence of genetic factors can be seen in the fact that there is a higher concordance rate for alcoholism among monozygotic (MZ) than dizygotic (DZ) twins (Goodwin 1985a, 1985b). In other words, genetic factors seem to predispose some individuals to become dependent on alcohol and other drugs.

Interaction Effects.   The effects of a drug can be drastically altered if it is taken in combination with another drug. Drugs taken together often interact, usually increasing the intensity of the effects; the degree of increase is often *more* than the sum of the two drugs taken separately. For example, the combination of Valium and alcohol results in much greater levels of physiological sedation than would be the case if the effects of each drug were simply added. Some individuals will intentionally take combinations of drugs to get stronger effects, but that can be very dangerous because the degree of the effect is hard to predict and the overall effect can prove fatal.

Tolerance and Cross-Tolerance. **Tolerance** refers to the fact that after repeated administrations of the same dose of a drug, *that dose level begins having less and less effect.* As this tolerance for the drug develops, the individual must take higher and higher levels of the drug to achieve the same effect. In ancient Greece, tolerance was used as a defensive strategy by individuals who thought that someone might attempt to poison them. The individuals would take increasing amounts of the poison an enemy might use so that they would eventually be immune to a dose given by an enemy. Today, many individuals who take drugs over prolonged periods develop very high levels of tolerance, and therefore they must take very high levels of the drugs to achieve the desired effects. That can have serious consequences because at high levels, the drugs may have dangerous side effects for which tolerance does not develop.

Cross-tolerance refers to the fact that when a drug of one type is taken, *tolerance can develop for other drugs of that type.* For example, taking morphine, which is an opiate, will reduce the effects of other opiates such as opium or heroin.

Because of the factors discussed in this section, any one drug can have different effects at different times for the same individual, and any one drug can have different effects in different individuals. Therefore, when attempting to explain a drug effect, it is important to understand not only the drug but also the individual, the situation, and the history of that individual's use of the drug.

Withdrawal and Dependence

Withdrawal refers to the fact that after a drug has been taken for a while, *physiological symptoms can occur when the drug is stopped or its level is reduced.* In some cases, withdrawal symptoms are relatively mild, such as the feelings of tension that occur when an individual stops smoking. In other cases, withdrawal symptoms are terrifying and can be fatal. For instance, withdrawal from alcohol or heroin can involve uncontrollable movements of the body (kicking, jerking), nausea, and serious delirium (hallucinations). Because the physiological symptoms of withdrawal can be so severe, anticipation of those symptoms often produce psychological symptoms such as fear and anxiety.

It is important to note that the symptoms of withdrawal can be quickly reduced or eliminated by taking another dose of the drug or by taking a dose of a different drug from the same class of drugs. The frightening symptoms of barbiturate withdrawal can be quickly eliminated with another dose of barbiturates or a dose of another depressant such as alcohol. Withdrawal symptoms play a crucial role in the development of drug dependence because the individual must continue taking the drug (getting a "fix") to avoid the withdrawal symptoms.

The effects of drugs are dose-dependent. For example, a drink or two might result in a slight slurring of speech. After several additional drinks, speech will be slurred even more.

Dependence occurs when the individual must *take the drug to avoid withdrawal symptoms.* Drinkers who need alcohol to avoid the "shakes" are drug-dependent. We usually think of dependence as a physiological phenomenon, but psychological dependence can also develop when individuals need drugs to achieve pleasure or avoid psychological unpleasantness. For example, hallucinogens such as LSD do not cause physiological dependence (they do not lead to physiological withdrawal symptoms), but some persons may become dependent on them as an escape from unpleasant or dull lives or as a means of obtaining pleasure. Dependence is thus most likely to result from the attempt to avoid unpleasant physiological symptoms of withdrawal, but it can also stem from persistent attempts to achieve pleasure and avoid psychological stress.

Diagnosis of Substance Dependence and Abuse

There are three major diagnoses related to the use of drugs. The first is **substance dependence**. The symptoms that lead to that diagnosis are (a) the need for higher levels of the drug to achieve the desired effects (i.e., tolerance), (b) the presence of withdrawal symptoms when substance use is reduced, (c) the taking of larger amounts of the substance than was intended, (d) unsuccessful attempts to cut down or control substance use, and (e) reduction of participation in normal social, occupational, and recreational activities caused by the use of the substance.

The second major diagnosis is **substance abuse**, and that diagnosis is made when the individual is not dependent on a drug but the use of the drug repeatedly leads to a serious impairments in the individual's functioning. Examples that would qualify for the diagnosis of substance abuse include a student who misses school occasionally due to a "crash" after taking a drug, a person who repeatedly drives while intoxicated, and an individual who alienates other people because of drug use.

The third diagnosis is **substance-induced psychotic disorder**. That diagnosis is used when an individual develops psychological symptoms such as hallucinations and delusions after taking too much of a drug. High doses of many drugs can cause those effects, but it commonly occurs when persons take amphetamines. This reaction is often referred to as a **toxic psychosis**: The individual experiences a psychosis because a toxic level of a drug is taken. Substance-induced disorders can be serious, but they dissipate as the drug wears off.

Types of Drugs

In this chapter, we will classify drugs in terms of their effects. With this approach, we can divide the drugs into four classes:

1. **Depressants**, which have a general *sedating* effect
2. **Narcotics**, which have a *dulling* effect on sensory experiences
3. **Stimulants**, which have a general *arousing* effect
4. **Hallucinogens** (huh-LOO-sin-ō-jenz), which have a *distorting* effect on sensory experiences

Types of drugs, their mode of action, their effects, and the names of specific drugs are summarized in Table 18.1.

In the rest of this chapter, we will first carefully examine the various types of drugs. For each, we will consider the background and effects of the drug, the physiological process that is responsible for the drug's effects, and the problems that are associated with misuse of the drug. This organization will enable you to make comparisons among drugs and will prepare you

TABLE 18.1   TYPES OF DRUGS, THEIR MODES OF ACTION, THEIR EFFECTS, AND EXAMPLES

DRUG CATEGORY	ACTION	EFFECTS	EXAMPLES
Depressants	Depress arousal centers	Sedation	Alcohol, barbiturates, benzodiazepines
Narcotics (opiates)	Decrease neural transmission	Dulling of senses	Opium, morphine, heroin, methadone
Stimulants	Increase neural transmission (but may also block transmission)	Arousal	Amphetamines, caffeine, cocaine, nicotine
Hallucinogens	Vary, depending on drug	Distortion	Cannabis (marijuana, hashish), LSD, mescaline, psilocybin

to understand the causes and treatments of substance abuse and dependence. After discussing the various types of drugs, we will examine the reasons why persons abuse and become dependent on drugs. Finally, we will consider the strategies that are used to overcome substance dependence and abuse.

DEPRESSANTS

Depressants *reduce physiological arousal, reduce psychological tension*, and help individuals *relax.* They are most frequently used to counteract the stress of daily living. Examples include a drink at the end of the day, a sleeping pill, and Valium taken when anxiety or muscle tension gets too high. Although depressants usually reduce arousal, large quantities consumed at one time can cause a brief high or "rush." There are three types of depressants: *alcohol, barbiturates,* and *benzodiazepines.*

Alcohol

You may be surprised that **alcohol** is a depressant because after a few drinks, many people become more

Alcohol depresses the inhibitory centers of the brain, causing an individual to become less inhibited and more expansive.

outgoing and expansive, less inhibited, and "high" rather than subdued. The uplifting effect of alcohol is due to the fact that at first alcohol depresses *inhibitory* centers of the brain, causing the individual to become less inhibited and more expansive. However, as the level of intoxication increases, the depression effect becomes more widespread and reduces activity in the areas of the brain that are responsible for *arousal,* and then sedation and sleep set in.

It should be noted that at least some of the disinhibiting effects of alcohol are due to *expectancies* about its effects. Many people believe that they will be a little "loose" after drinking, so some of their uninhibited behavior is due to how they expect they should behave. Evidence for this is provided by research indicating that individuals who drink nonalcoholic beverages that they think contain alcohol will act more aggressively, become more sexually aroused, and be less anxious (Lang et al., 1975; Wilson & Abrams, 1977; Wilson & Lawson, 1976). Because of expectancies, some individuals may actually get "drunk" on nonalcoholic beers and wine.

Apart from its elating and depressing effects, alcohol affects vision and balance and reduces muscle control, so speech becomes slurred and coordination decreases. It also impairs concentration and judgment, so individuals make poor decisions. The combination of impaired vision, lessened muscle control, and impaired cognitive functioning can lead to disastrous consequences, especially in the case of driving.

The alcohol we drink (technically called *ethyl alcohol* or *ethanol*) is produced by a process called *fermentation.* Fermentation occurs when sugar is dissolved in water and then microorganisms called yeasts convert the sugar into alcohol and carbon dioxide. The carbon dioxide bubbles off and leaves the alcohol and water. Fermentation of sugar from different sources leads to different types of beverages; fermentation of grapes leads to wine, and fermentation of grains leads to beer. Alcohol makes up between 3% and 12% of the volume of these beverages.

Because the yeasts that convert sugar into alcohol die in solutions that contain more than 10% or 15% alcohol, the fermentation process stops when the alcohol content is still relatively low. To produce beverages with alcohol content higher than 10% or 15%, the process of distillation is used. In distillation, the liquid containing alcohol is heated until the alcohol vaporizes, leaving the water behind. The vapor is then cooled and condensed to yield a liquid with a higher alcohol content. The familiar still in pictures of "moonshiners" was used for distillation. Distilling the alcohol from different sources leads to different drinks: Grapes produce brandy; grains, whiskey; molasses, rum; and potatoes, schnapps. (Gin and vodka are mixtures of pure alcohol, water, and flavoring.) Alcohol makes up between 40% and 50% of the volume of these drinks.

Mode of Action.
Alcohol is usually drunk and then absorbed from the digestive tract. Drinking alcohol before or during a meal will reduce the rate of absorption because most of the absorption occurs in the small intestine, and the alcohol will be delayed in getting there if it is mixed with food that is being digested in the stomach. Once alcohol is absorbed by the digestive tract, it is widely and evenly distributed to tissues throughout the body. Some of the alcohol goes to the tissues of the lungs and is vaporized into the air. That is why it is possible to use the alcohol content of expired air as an index of the amount of alcohol in other areas of the body. This is the basis for the *breathalyzer test* that is used for determining intoxication levels of persons suspected of driving while under the influence of alcohol.

Alcohol can also be consumed by inhalation. When inhaled, the alcohol vapors are absorbed by the lungs, dissolved in the blood, and then distributed throughout the body. The traditional brandy snifter is designed to facilitate the inhalation of alcohol vapors. The large base of the glass can be cupped in the hand so that the heat from the hand aids vaporization, and the small opening at the top of the glass concentrates the vapors so that they can be effectively inhaled. Brandy produces a substantial amount of vapor because it has a very high alcohol content.

Although we understand how alcohol is absorbed by the body and know the effects alcohol has on behavior, we do not yet fully understand the neurological processes that occur between absorption and behavior. We know that alcohol depresses inhibitory centers and later depresses arousal centers, but we do not yet know exactly how it does this. Understanding the process is complicated by the fact that alcohol is distributed widely in the body, and thus it probably has several sites or means for achieving its effects.

Problems of Misuse.
Tolerance for alcohol develops rapidly, and within a few weeks, dose levels must be increased by 30% to 50% to achieve the desired effect. The tolerance develops because drinking alcohol stimulates the production of substances in the body that destroy it, so the more alcohol that is consumed, the more is destroyed.

After a period of chronic consumption, cessation of alcohol intake leads to withdrawal symptoms that can be traumatic, severe, and even lethal. The first withdrawal symptoms include agitation and involuntary contraction of the muscles (the "shakes"). Next the individual experiences muscle cramps, nausea,

vomiting, and profuse sweating. In extreme cases, the withdrawal involves delirium (hallucinations) and seizures. This is referred to as *delirium tremens,* or *the "d.t.'s."* These symptoms can be very serious. Some years ago, about 10% of the patients who went through withdrawal from high levels of alcohol died, but with modern techniques of treatment, that problem has been eliminated. Withdrawal can be eased by giving the individual small amounts of other short-acting depressants (e.g., Valium), thereby permitting withdrawal with fewer symptoms.

Barbiturates and Benzodiazepines

Barbiturates reduce arousal, and they were the first type of tranquilizer available commercially (see Chapter 6). At low levels, barbiturates result in relaxation, light-headedness, and a loss of motor coordination. Higher doses bring on slurred speech, greater reductions in motor control, mild euphoria, and sleep. At very high doses, they cause a brief rush that is followed by relaxation or sleep. In some cases, barbiturates lead to aggression, an effect that probably occurs because they reduce inhibitions.

Benzodiazepines are the latest generation of tranquilizers. Well-known drugs of this type include Ativan (lorazepam), Librium (cholodiazepoxide), Valium (diazepam), and Xanax (alprazolam) (see Chapter 6). These drugs are misused by two different groups of individuals. One group consists of individuals who use them simply to reduce daily tensions and aid in sleep, but they use them too frequently or in excessively high dosages. This is a normal extension of the appropriate use of the drugs, and these users have unwittingly slipped across the fine line that separates appropriate use from abuse.

The other group of misusers consists of the "street" drug users. They use barbiturates and benzodiazepines to produce a brief rush, to achieve a state of relaxed euphoria, or to aid in "coming down" from a high caused by taking a stimulant. Barbiturates and benzodiazepines are very similar in many respects, but barbiturates are more powerful, more likely to be misused, and more likely to result in dependence, so we will focus our attention on them.

Mode of Action.
Barbiturates are quickly absorbed into the bloodstream from the digestive system and then pass rapidly into the brain, where they have their effects. However, after a very short period, they are redistributed to areas of the body that contain fat and are slowly released from there. Because of this pattern of absorption, storage, and release, barbiturates quickly achieve their major effects, but then the effects drop off and persist at a low level for some time. Barbitu-

rates differ in the speed with which effects occur, and those differences determine the clinical use of the drugs. Barbiturates that act fast but have relatively brief effects are used as anesthetics (hexobarbital), those with a less rapid onset but moderately long-lasting effects are used as sleeping pills (pentobarbital), and the long-lasting ones were once used to treat anxiety and epilepsy (phenobarbital). In most cases, barbiturates are taken orally, but injecting them directly into the bloodstream will quicken their effects and result in a brief period of very intense euphoria.

Barbiturates reduce arousal by *reducing neural transmission.* They do that in two ways. First, they enhance the effects of GABA, which is a substance that serves to inhibit neural transmission (see Chapters 5 and 6). Second, barbiturates block the effects of excitatory neurotransmitters, but the exact process is not yet well understood. Paradoxically, at very high levels, barbiturates *facilitate neural transmission,* and that effect is responsible for the rush. As the drug level drops, the rush turns to relaxation.

Problems of Misuse.

Prolonged use of barbiturates results in serious withdrawal symptoms. The symptoms begin between 12 and 36 hours after the drug is taken, depending on whether it was the fast- or slow-acting type. Symptoms vary considerably, but they usually include tension, tremors, loss of motor control, nausea, and often delirium that can include visual and auditory hallucinations. If the individual has been taking high doses, withdrawal can be very dangerous and actually lethal if it is done too quickly. In those cases, it may be necessary to begin giving the individual a less potent depressant (e.g., phenobarbital or even alcohol) for which the dose level can be controlled and slowly reduced. In less severe cases in which substitution is not necessary, the symptoms of withdrawal fade slowly over a 2-week period, but they can last for months in minor forms.

A serious problem associated with barbiturate use is death due to accidental overdose. Death stems from the fact that barbiturates cause a reduction in respiration, and at high doses, they may cause an individual to stop breathing completely. The possibility of accidental death increases with prolonged use because individuals develop a tolerance for barbiturates and therefore must take increasingly higher doses to achieve the desired effects. The amount that is necessary to kill also increases over time, but not as fast as the amount necessary to obtain the desired effects, so as time goes by, the amount necessary to get the effect approaches the lethal dose, thus reducing the room for error. This is illustrated in Figure 18.1. The possibility of overdose and death is greatly enhanced when

barbiturates are taken in combination with other depressants such as alcohol because the two depressants will work together to suppress respiration.

NARCOTICS

The term *narcotics* is often used to refer to illegal drugs, but technically it refers to a specific class of drugs derived from *opium.* These drugs are usually referred to as **opiates** (Ō-pē-its). Narcotics have the effect of dulling or numbing the senses and producing a sleeplike state. However, when high levels are delivered to the brain rapidly, opiates can cause a sudden high or rush. Opiates include *opium, morphine,* and *heroin.* There are also a number of synthetic (artificially produced) opiates such as Dolopine (methadone), which is used as a substitute for heroin in addiction treatment programs, and Demerol (meperidine) and Darvon (propoxyphine), which are used as analgesics (painkillers).

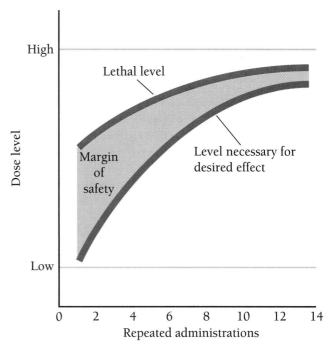

FIGURE 18.1   THE DOSE LEVEL NECESSARY FOR INTOXICATION RISES FASTER OVER TIME THAN THE LETHAL DOSE LEVEL, SO DEATH DUE TO OVERDOSE BECOMES EVER MORE LIKELY.

Source: Adapted from Wesson and Smith (1977), p. 35.

Opium

Opium (Ō-pē-um) is the sap of the poppy plant, and the name *opium* comes from a Greek word that means "sap." In the form of sap, opium can be chewed, and it will produce a prolonged state of mellow relaxation. The use of opium in this way dates at least as far back as 4000 B.C., and it is still chewed by the natives of Southeast Asian countries (Burma, Laos, and Thailand) where the poppies are grown. Opium can also be inhaled (smoked). Smoking it is an effective way of getting greater quantities to the brain faster, and it results in a deep, stuporous state that can be maintained for many hours. It has been described as a state of "divine enjoyment."

One of the most notorious uses of opium occurred in Chinese opium dens, where it was smoked in pipes and the smokers would languish for days in a stuporous state. The Chinese developed the technique of smoking opium in 1644 when the emperor forbade the practice of smoking tobacco. Eighty-five years later, the use of opium was also forbidden, but by then the practice was well established, and the use of opium flourished in China until 1949, when the People's Republic of China was formed, at which point all opium-related activity was stopped.

The use of opium was not limited to the Orient. In Britain during the 19th century, opium was incorporated into pills, candies, vinegars, and wines and was used extensively for both recreational and medicinal purposes. One notable use was in preparations such as Mrs. Winslow's Soothing Syrup, which was used to "dope" the children of working mothers while the mothers were away. Because of its widespread use, many individuals became addicted to it, including such literary notables as Byron, Shelley, Keats, Walter Scott, Elizabeth Barrett Browning, and Samuel Coleridge. In an attempt to break his addiction, Coleridge once hired a man to follow him and physically block his entry to any store in which he might buy opium. The use of opium reached epidemic proportions in Britain, and finally its nonprescription use was banned in 1868 with the Pharmacy Act. Opium was also used widely in the United States until 1914, when its nonmedical use was outlawed.

Morphine and Codeine

Morphine (MOR-fēn) is one of the active ingredients in opium, and it is extracted from the opium and used as a drug itself. It is dissolved in liquid and then injected into the bloodstream. After a brief high, it results

Smoking opium results in a stupor that can be maintained for hours. The Chinese developed the technique of smoking opium in 1644 when the emperor forbade smoking tobacco; opium became illegal in the People's Republic of China in 1949. Opium was widely abused in other forms both in England, where nonmedical use was banned in 1868, and in the United States, where nonmedical use was banned in 1914.

in a mellow state of relaxation. The name *morphine* comes from Morpheus, the Greek god of sleep. Morphine and other narcotics cause sleepy sensations, but unlike the depressants, they do not actually increase sleep and may decrease it. Morphine was widely used as an analgesic during the Civil War, and in extreme cases, it is still used for that purpose today.

Codeine (CŌ-dēn) is another but less powerful active ingredient of opium that is isolated and used by itself. It is widely used as an analgesic and is found in various prescription painkillers and cough medicines.

Heroin

Heroin (HĀR-uh-win) is also derived from opium, but it is a semisynthetic drug that is produced by adding chemical structures to the morphine molecule. The difference in chemical structure enables heroin to get to the brain faster, and once in the brain, it is changed back into morphine. The faster delivery makes heroin about 3 times more potent than morphine and 10

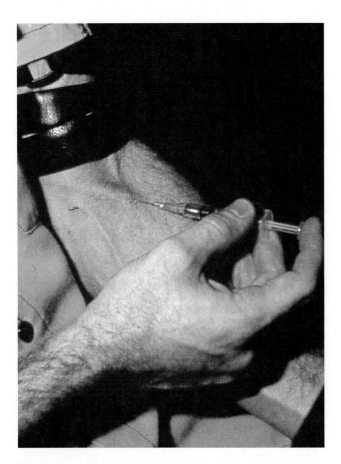

Heroin is a semisynthetic drug created by adding chemical structures to the morphine molecule. The different chemical structure enables heroin to get to the brain quickly where it is then changed back into morphine.

times more potent than opium. Heroin was invented in 1898 by the chemist who had invented aspirin, and it was initially advertised by the Bayer company as a safe, superior aspirin. The name *heroin* was derived from a German word meaning "concentrated power," and it certainly has that.

Heroin is usually used in powdered form. It is mixed with tobacco and smoked, inhaled directly into the nostrils ("snorting"), dissolved and injected under the skin ("skin popping"), or dissolved and injected directly into the veins ("mainlining"). Heroin can cause a rush that users say is similar to sexual orgasm. The rush lasts about 60 seconds and is followed by a 4- to 6-hour stuporous period during which bodily needs for food or sex are greatly diminished. This has been described as a pleasant time of relaxation, reverie, and mild euphoria. After the period of relaxation, the symptoms of withdrawal begin setting in. With increased use, tolerance for the drug develops, and larger and larger quantities are needed to achieve the effects.

Mode of Action

Opiates achieve their dulling or numbing effects by *reducing neural transmission*. The reduced transmission occurs because the opiates stimulate specific receptor sites on presynaptic neurons, and that stimulation inhibits the release of neurotransmitters.

Many of the positive medical effects of opiates can be traced to the fact that they reduce neurological activity in various parts of the central nervous system. For example, their analgesic effect is due to the fact that in the spinal cord, they inhibit the incoming nerve impulses that signal pain. Opiates also reduce the emotional aspects of pain by reducing neural transmission in the limbic system of the brain. Opiates are effective cough suppressants because they reduce activity in the cough center of the brain. (Codeine has been used in cough medicines for many years but is now being replaced with *dextromethorphan*, which is less addicting.) Opiates are also effective for reducing diarrhea because they disrupt and reduce activity in the intestines, and that slows the movement of digested materials. (A side effect of analgesics containing opiates is constipation.)

The fact that there are specific receptor sites for opiates led researchers to speculate that the body must produce its own opiates. In other words, it was reasoned that if there are naturally occurring opiate receptor sites, there must be naturally occurring opiates to fill them. The opiate-like substances were found in 1973 and named **endorphins** (en-DOR-finz), a term derived from the words *endogenous* (meaning "internally produced") and *morphine*. It is believed that endorphins are released during times of great stress, and like exogenous opiates, they serve to reduce synaptic transmission and reduce pain. It has been hypothesized that the "highs" that are occasionally experienced by distance runners when they are nearing exhaustion may be due to the release of endorphins that block pain and cause pleasure.

Problems of Misuse

The prolonged use of opiates leads to dependence and serious problems of withdrawal. The severity of the opiate withdrawal process varies with the amount of opiates that have been consumed, but in many cases, it is a terrifying and extremely uncomfortable experience that is greatly feared by most opiate users. The withdrawal process begins about 8 hours after the last ingestion of the drug, and the first symptom is general restlessness that can lead to severe agitation that may lead to violence. The individual has chills, hot flashes, and difficulty in breathing. Some individuals then fall into a deep sleep, but others have prolonged insomnia. Next the individual will experience a loss of motor control resulting in twitches, shaking, and kicking. These may be accompanied by painful muscle cramps, diarrhea, vomiting, and extreme sweating. During withdrawal, it is as though all of the systems that had been suppressed by the opiates are now turned on full blast and going wild; tranquility has turned to terror, and heaven has turned to hell. The process of withdrawal usually takes about 3 days, but it can be stopped immediately by another dose of opium and so when faced with the early symptoms of withdrawal, users will do almost anything to get more opiates.

Apart from withdrawal, the use of opiates, particularly heroin, can be extremely dangerous both physically and psychologically. The most extreme physical consequence of heroin use is death when a high dose causes a cessation of respiration. Overdose deaths occur because individuals take *too much* heroin; take heroin that is of *higher quality* than what they are used to, so more gets to the brain than it can handle; or take heroin *in combination with depressants* (e.g., alcohol, barbiturates) that also reduce respiration. The singer Janis Joplin died because she took heroin after drinking heavily. The likelihood of an overdose increases with time because the individual builds up a tolerance for opiates and therefore must take greater amounts to achieve the desired effects. The excessive use of opiates has other serious physical effects such as insomnia, severe constipation, and the decline of sex hormones, causing a reduction in secondary sexual characteristics and sexual performance.

STIMULANTS

Stimulants *increase arousal* and cause *states of euphoria* that are generally referred to as "highs." They have those effects because they *increase the levels of certain neurotransmitters* and thereby *increase the level of neurological activity in the limbic system*, a system that is responsible for pleasure. The two most powerful stimulants that are abused are the *amphetamines* and *cocaine*, but attention should also be given to *caffeine* and *nicotine*.

Amphetamines

When **amphetamines** (am-FET-uh-mēnz) are taken orally, they result in feelings of well-being, high spirits, high energy, vigor, elation, and reduced fatigue. Because amphetamines are absorbed slowly from the digestive system, when they are taken orally, the effects come on slowly but last between 3 and 6 hours. The high is then followed by a low or period of depression. When amphetamines are inhaled or injected into the bloodstream, they are delivered to the brain faster and in greater quantity, and therefore they produce a sudden rush. That rush is soon followed by a low or depression.

When used appropriately, the arousing effects of amphetamines have a number of beneficial effects such as reducing fatigue (pep pills), reducing appetite (diet pills), dilating air passages in the lungs to relieve asthma attacks, and treating the attention-deficit hyperactivity disorder (see Chapter 16). During World War II, amphetamines were given to the GIs so that they could fight longer and harder. The inappropriate use of amphetamines involves using them to "get high." Street users of amphetamines refer to them as "speed."

Mode of Action.   The arousing effects of amphetamines are due to the fact that they increase the level of neurotransmitters such as norepinephrine, serotonin, and dopamine at the synapses in the limbic system of the brain, which is responsible for pleasure. It is interesting to note that low levels of norepinephrine and serotonin result in depression, and small doses of stimulants were once used to treat depression (see Chapter 11).

Problems of Misuse.   Prolonged use of amphetamines leads to withdrawal symptoms of depression, listlessness, and fatigue. Apart from the problems of withdrawal, the use of amphetamines has three serious consequences. First, high doses cause dramatic increases in blood pressure that can result in cerebral infarctions (breaking of blood vessels in the brain; see Chapter 20), which in turn lead to brain damage and death. Second, high doses of amphetamines can result in **amphetamine psychoses**, substance-induced organic mental disorders in which the individual experiences delusional symptoms like those seen in paranoid schizophrenia, often revolving around feelings of persecution. The psychotic behavior stems from the fact that amphetamines stimulate the production of the neurotransmitter dopamine, and high levels of dopamine are related to schizophrenia (see Chapter 13). Although amphetamine psychoses can be serious, they dissipate as the drug wears off and therefore do not usually have long-term consequences. The third serious effect of high levels of amphetamines is that the individuals sometimes become dangerous to themselves or others. In other words, while under the influence of amphetamines, some persons become very aggressive or do foolish things that endanger their own lives. Some of these erratic behaviors may be due to delusions associated with the amphetamine psychoses.

Cocaine

Cocaine is the other major stimulant that is often abused. The effects of cocaine on mood are similar to those of amphetamines, but much more intense. The drug causes an intense high or rush that is characterized by feelings of exhilaration, energy, well-being, self-confidence, and being "on top of the world." The high lasts about 30 minutes and is followed by a period of mild depression.

Cocaine comes from the leaves of the coca plant, which is grown in South America, and its use has a long history. The Indians of Peru chewed coca leaves as early as 2500 B.C., and stone idols found in Colombia dating back to 500 B.C. have puffed-out cheeks suggesting that they were chewing coca leaves (an image not dissimilar from that of the modern baseball player with his wad of chewing tobacco). The Spanish, who conquered the Incas, did not chew the coca leaves but used them as rewards for the enslaved Indians. Giving the Indians coca leaves also reduced the cost of their upkeep because the coca reduced their appetites.

When cocaine was shipped back to Europe, its pleasant effects were quickly recognized by the young Sigmund Freud, who found cocaine to be helpful in dealing with his depression. In fact, Freud was so impressed with its effects that he wrote an article titled "Song of Praise" in which he extolled the virtues of cocaine. Fortunately, Freud soon ceased using the drug when he learned of its harmful effects. The value of cocaine was also proclaimed by writers of the period, such as Robert Louis Stevenson, who believed that it stimulated their creativity and enabled them to write better.

Probably the most widespread use of cocaine occurred between 1886 and 1906 when coca leaves were used in the recipe for Coca-Cola. The "classic" Coke was indeed "the real thing." Coca leaves are still used in Coca-Cola, but the cocaine has been removed, and the stimulant effect of Coca-Cola now comes from caffeine. In its original version with the cocaine base, Coca-Cola was thought to have health benefits, and therefore it was sold in drugstores. It is probably for that reason that soda fountains originally developed in drugstores.

Cocaine can be processed and used in a number of ways. The simplest way is to chew the coca leaves, as the Indians of South America still do. Like the amphetamines, cocaine is absorbed slowly from the digestive system, and therefore taking it orally results in a prolonged mild euphoria.

Most of the cocaine used in the United States is in the form of a powdered white salt called **cocaine hydrochloride** that has been diluted ("cut") with various substances. By inhaling ("sniffing," "snorting") the salt or dissolving it and injecting it into the bloodstream, high levels of cocaine can be gotten to the brain quickly, producing the rush. The strength of a rush is determined by the degree to which the cocaine has been diluted with other substances, and consequently a number of processes have been developed to purify cocaine so as to enhance the rush. One common procedure is to heat the cocaine hydrochloride until it forms a vapor that is free of the impurities with which it was diluted, and then the vapor can be inhaled. An even more refined and powerful form can be obtained by chemically separating the cocaine molecule from the hydrochloride. Freed from its hydrochloride base, the cocaine can then be burned, and the vapors of the pure cocaine can be inhaled. This is known as "free-basing." "Crack" is a highly concentrated form of cocaine.

Mode of Action. The cocaine rush results from the fact that cocaine increases the levels of various neurotransmitters (norepinephrine, serotonin, dopamine) by blocking their reuptake, and the higher levels of transmitters result in more neurological activity in the limbic system (pleasure center) of the brain. In contrast, at high levels, cocaine can block the conduction of nerve impulses along the axon and thereby reduce neurological activity. It is because of that blocking that injections of cocaine can be used as a local anesthetic. In fact, Novocain, which is often used as an anesthetic in dental procedures, is a synthetic form of cocaine that lacks the stimulant properties. With regard to its anesthetic properties, it is interest-

When cocaine is separated from its hydrochloride base, it can be burned and inhaled. This process, known as "freebasing," is practiced at all socioeconomic levels.

ing to note that inhaling cocaine hydrochloride is sometimes called a "freeze" because the cocaine anesthetizes the nose.

Problems of Misuse.

Cocaine use is not generally thought to lead to physiological dependence, but there is some controversy over that (Jones, 1984). There is no question, however, that individuals can develop an extremely strong psychological dependence on the drug, and in many respects that makes the question of physiological dependence irrelevant. Once dependent, individuals will do almost anything to get cocaine, and it is estimated that as much as half of the violent crime in the United States may be cocaine-related. As is the case with amphetamines, when cocaine wears off, the individual experiences a withdrawal symptom of depression. The depression can be eliminated with another dose of cocaine, but when that dose wears off, the depression will be deeper and more prolonged. The extreme pleasure associated with cocaine and the desire to avoid the depression that follows can lead individuals to high levels of use, which is

very expensive, and the cost of maintaining the "habit" can be personally and financially disastrous.

In addition to dependence and depression, there is now evidence that in some individuals cocaine can induce a psychosis that usually involves paranoid delusions (Satel & Edell, 1991; Satel et al., 1991). In individuals who already have disorders, the psychosis may last for months, whereas in others it will dissipate as the drug wears off. We do not know exactly why cocaine precipitates a psychosis, but the symptoms can be controlled with neuroleptic drugs (Gawin, 1989).

The use of cocaine also poses serious medical risks because it can block conduction of nerve impulses. This can be lethal, and it is now suspected that many emergency room cases of heart failure for "unknown reasons" may actually be cocaine-related. This problem is becoming more severe as more refined and more powerful forms of cocaine are becoming available.

Basketball star Len Bias (in the Maryland uniform) died of cardiac arrest after shooting cocaine.

An unfortunate combination of the psychological and medical effects of cocaine occurred in a case in which police were summoned to a house in which they found an irrational man who was brandishing a knife and threatening to kill the people around him. The police attempted to subdue the man, but while doing so, he suddenly fell dead. An autopsy revealed high levels of cocaine in the man's system. Apparently, the behavior that caused the police to be called was a toxic psychosis stemming from a cocaine injection, and his sudden death was the result of cardiac arrest due to the cocaine.

Another medical problem associated with the sniffing of cocaine is severe damage to the mucous membranes of the nose, sometimes resulting in the destruction of the inside of the nose. Because of the anesthetic effect of cocaine, the pain associated with the damage can be reduced with additional cocaine (the freeze), but that, of course, leads to even more damage.

Caffeine

Caffeine is the most prominent and strongest stimulant in a group of drugs called **methylxanthines** (METH-ul-ZAN-thēnz). Caffeine occurs naturally in coffee and tea, and it is also added to many cola drinks and over-the-counter drugs. The levels of methylxanthines found in various preparations are listed in Table 18.2.

The discovery of caffeine in coffee is often attributed to a herd of goats belonging to an Islamic monastery (Jacob, 1935). As the story goes, one day the goats wandered off and ate some berries from a *Coffea arabica* bush, and for the next 5 days, they frolicked continuously without showing any signs of fatigue. Having observed this, the abbot of the monastery sampled the berries late one evening, with the result that he was still wide awake and invigorated when it came time for midnight prayers. As the saying goes, "The rest is history."

It is interesting to note that at about the same time that opium dens were popular in England, the tradition of the coffeehouse was also getting started. In contrast to the opium dens, in which the customers were "doped" and lay semiconscious, in coffeehouses the patrons were stimulated and participated in animated discussions late into the night. These discussions frequently revolved around politics, and because there was concern that the coffeehouses were hotbeds of sedition and revolution, an attempt was made to outlaw them in 1675. The attempt failed, and the tradition of the coffeehouse continues to this day.

The arousing effect of caffeine is usually used for maintaining wakefulness. A 300-mg dose of caffeine (the equivalent of two or three cups of coffee) increases the time to fall asleep from 18 minutes to 66 minutes and decreases the time in sleep from 475 minutes to 350 minutes (Brenesova et al., 1975). Apart from maintaining wakefulness, the stimulating effects of caffeine can enhance performance on a wide variety of tasks (Weiss & Laties, 1962). However, it is important to recognize that caffeine does not improve the performance of rested individuals. Instead, it only serves to offset the effects of fatigue and enable tired individuals to perform at normal (or close to normal)

TABLE 18.2   LEVELS OF METHYLXANTHINES IN FREQUENTLY USED PRODUCTS

PRODUCT (mg)	CAFFEINE (mg)	OTHER METHYLXANTHINES
One cup of coffee		
Decaffeinated	1–2	
Instant	29–117	
Perked	39–168	
Drip	56–176	
One cup of tea	30–75	
One cup of cocoa		75–150 total
Coca-Cola (12 oz)	45	
Pepsi-Cola (12 oz)	30	
Chocolate bar		150–300 total
Analgesics (1 tablet)		
Anacin	22.7	
Dristan	16.2	
Excedrin	65.0	
Stimulants (1 tablet)		
No-Doz	100	
Vivarin	200	

levels. These effects seem to be stronger for physical or simple tasks (e.g., driving) than for complex intellectual tasks (e.g., solving mathematical equations).

Mode of Action.

Caffeine in coffee and tea is readily absorbed from the digestive system and reaches peak blood levels in 30 to 60 minutes. The process may take somewhat longer when the caffeine is taken in cola beverages. Caffeine remains active in the system for about 3½ hours. It is interesting to note that smoking cigarettes speeds the elimination of caffeine from the system, and therefore the frequent pattern of smoking and drinking coffee actually reduces the effect of the coffee. The process by which caffeine has its stimulating effect is not well understood, but it appears to revolve around the heightened release of norepinephrine, which increases arousal.

Problems of Misuse.

Ingestion of high levels of caffeine (500 to 800 mg per day) results in agitation, tension, irritability, insomnia, loss of appetite, increased heart rate, and headaches. In short, it results in the symptoms of an anxiety disorder. At extremely high levels (1,800 mg or more), it can result in a toxic psychosis with symptoms revolving around mania that can lead to violence. High levels of caffeine can also exacerbate existing psychological problems because it increases arousal and because it blocks the effects of antianxiety and antipsychotic medications (benzodiazepines and phenothiazines; Greden et al., 1978; Kulhanek et al., 1979; Paul et al., 1980).

Withdrawal symptoms occur even in persons who drink as few as five cups of coffee a day. The symptoms usually include tension, agitation, and muscle tremors. As with other drugs, the symptoms of caffeine withdrawal can be terminated with a dose of caffeine. A common and mild form of withdrawal can be seen in persons who are grouchy in the morning until they have their first cup of coffee. Their withdrawal symptoms (e.g., tension, agitation) set in because the persons did not get any caffeine while sleeping during the night. In most cases, abuse of caffeine does not result in the dire consequences that stem from abuse of many of the other substances discussed in this chapter, but the fact that it affects so many people makes it a serious problem.

Nicotine

Nicotine is derived from tobacco, and most people get nicotine from smoking. People use nicotine both when they are sluggish and want to increase arousal (e.g., after a meal or during a break) and also when they are tense and want to decrease arousal (e.g., during periods of stress). In other words, though classed as a stimulant, nicotine can serve as *both a stimulant and a depressant.* The fact that nicotine can play both roles increases its use. We will explore the reasons for nicotine's complicated and sometimes contradictory effects after we review its background.

Nicotine is naturally produced by the tobacco plant, which was originally cultivated and used by the Indians of North America. In 1492, when Columbus arrived in what is now the Bahamas, the natives presented him with some "dry leaves" that he concluded "must be a thing very much appreciated among them" (McKim, 1986). At first, the explorers did not understand the smoking behavior (they called it "drinking smoke") and found it repulsive. When one of the crew realized the pleasure of smoking and took up the habit he was tried and imprisoned for his "devilish habit." This conflict and lack of understanding between smokers and nonsmokers still goes on today, and although smokers are not imprisoned, numerous laws are being passed that limit where and when they may smoke.

Mode of Action.

Most people get nicotine from smoking cigarettes or cigars that consist of the dried (cured) leaves of the tobacco plant. When the tobacco is burned, nicotine vapors are absorbed by the lungs, and then the nicotine is passed into the bloodstream, where it is carried first to the heart and then to the brain. Because this is a very direct route, absorbing nicotine from the lungs results in a relatively strong and fast effect.

Increasing numbers of people are now also getting nicotine from the chewing of tobacco. Tobacco designed for chewing consists of the leaves of the tobacco plant that have been soaked in a solution of sugar and licorice and then dried. When the tobacco is chewed, nicotine is absorbed through the membranes of the mouth and passed to the bloodstream, and the tobacco is spit out. Absorption from the mouth results in less effect than absorption from the lungs.

A once-popular means of getting nicotine is to inhale it in the form of *snuff.* Snuff consists of very finely ground tobacco that is mixed with perfumes (e.g., menthol, lavender, cinnamon). Gentlemen used to carry small boxes of snuff and would occasionally place a small amount on the back of the hand and then sniff it into the nostrils.

Once in the brain, nicotine has an influence on both the central and the peripheral nervous systems. In the central nervous system, nicotine molecules fit into and stimulate numerous nerve centers, causing higher levels of neurological activity and arousal. For example, nicotine stimulates the area of the brain that is responsible for respiration and thereby increases breathing rate. It also stimulates the area of the brain

Snuff is finely ground tobacco mixed with perfume. It was once fashionable for gentlemen to inhale nicotine in this form.

stem that is responsible for vomiting, and it is for that reason that new smokers who have not yet developed a tolerance for nicotine get sick to their stomachs when they try smoking. That is also why nonsmokers become nauseated when they are around smokers and have to inhale tobacco smoke. With regard to the peripheral nervous system, nicotine stimulates the release of epinephrine into the bloodstream, which increases arousal in terms of responses such as heart rate and blood pressure (see Chapter 17).

At high levels, the effects of nicotine are *reversed*, and it blocks the stimulation of various nerves, therefore serving as a depressant. The blocking of nerve transmission can be very serious because some of the nerves that are blocked are responsible for respiration, and when those nerves are blocked, the individual can die of respiratory arrest. Each year, a number of children die because they eat tobacco and get too much nicotine into their systems.

Problems of Misuse. The stimulation produced by nicotine results in muscle tremors, increases in heart rate, increases in blood pressure, and constriction of the blood vessels in the skin. The limitation of blood flow to the skin is what is responsible for the cold hands of smokers (skin temperature is determined by the amount of blood in the area), and it is also responsible for the fact that the skin of smokers wrinkles and ages faster than that of nonsmokers.

Probably the most notable problems associated with nicotine revolve around withdrawal, the symptoms of which include tension, irritability, inability to concentrate, dizziness, drowsiness, nausea, constipa-

tion, muscle tremors, headaches, insomnia, and an increase in appetite that results in weight gain. The withdrawal symptoms usually last less than 6 months but can persist for years.

The physical symptoms of nicotine withdrawal are certainly not as severe as those of heroin withdrawal, but some individuals who have gone through both nicotine and heroin withdrawal report that psychologically it is as difficult to give up smoking as it is to give up heroin (McKim, 1986). Indeed, there is a growing body of evidence that nicotine withdrawal can lead to a wide variety of psychiatric symptoms such as depression and anxiety disorders (Breslau et al., 1992, 1993; Leibenluft et al., 1993). These symptoms occur in many individuals but are seen most often in those with a history of depression or anxiety. I am aware of one individual who began having hallucinations when she stopped smoking, but she could quickly stop the hallucinations by having a cigarette. Because another cigarette will reduce the unpleasant withdrawal symptoms immediately and because cigarettes are readily available, it is often very difficult to give up smoking.

Many of the relatively mild short-term effects of nicotine, such as increased heart rate and blood pressure, can result in very serious long-term problems such as coronary artery disease (see Chapter 17). Also, the process of getting nicotine through smoking can result in other serious problems such as cancer because the smoke introduces carcinogens into the body.

Before concluding our discussion of nicotine, we should return to the paradox mentioned earlier concerning the fact that nicotine can serve as both a stimulant and a depressant. This paradox is interesting in and of itself, but understanding it is also important in helping us understand why and in what situations individuals use nicotine. There are three reasons why nicotine can be both a stimulant and a depressant. The first is the *level of nicotine* that is taken. The effects of nicotine are dose-dependent; at low levels, nicotine stimulates nerve activity, and at high levels, it blocks that activity. However, dose level cannot account for all of the contradictory effects because the same dose level (e.g., one cigarette) will serve to arouse at one time and relax at another time.

The second explanation revolves around the *reduction of withdrawal symptoms*. The symptoms of nicotine withdrawal involve unpleasant increases in tension, but those symptoms can be quickly reduced by another dose of nicotine. Therefore, a habitual smoker who has not had a cigarette for a while and who is aroused because of withdrawal symptoms can reduce this arousal by taking another cigarette. The mild stimulating effect of the cigarette will be offset by the reduction in arousal that is due to the reduction in withdrawal symptoms.

A third explanation for the arousal-reducing effect of nicotine is strictly psychological. If an individual is tense, smoking a cigarette may be calming because it gives the individual something to do; that is, it serves as a temporary *distraction*. The very tense individual who is constantly lighting a cigarette, taking a puff or two, putting the cigarette out (or simply leaving it in the ashtray), and then lighting another is not getting more nicotine than the individual who smokes the cigarette all the way through, but the repeat lighter is certainly getting more breaks and distraction, and that may temporarily reduce arousal.

HALLUCINOGENS

The effect of the hallucinogens is to *distort* sensory experiences. In other words, while under the influence of hallucinogens, the things people see or hear are altered, changed, or deformed so that they appear different. These distortions can be termed *hallucinations* (perceptual experiences that do not have a basis in reality), hence the term *hallucinogen*. It is important to note, however, that a high dose of almost any drug can result in hallucinations. Consequently, the term *hallucinogen* should be used for drugs that produce hallucinations at low levels so that the hallucinations cannot be attributed to poisoning (McKim, 1986).

There are wide differences among the various drugs that are referred to as hallucinogens. Some people might argue that cannabis (marijuana) is technically not a hallucinogen because it does not cause hallucinations and because its mode of action is probably different from that of the other drugs in the group. However, cannabis is included here because it does alter sensory and cognitive experiences and its effects are closer to those of the more traditional hallucinogens than they are to the effects of other types of drugs. For the sake of clarity, in the following discussion, we will refer to cannabis by name and use the term *hallucinogen* to refer to the other drugs (e.g., LSD, mescaline).

Cannabis

Marijuana, *hashish*, and *hash oil* all come from the hemp plant, *Cannabis sativa*; the name for the underlying drug is **cannabis** (KAN-uh-bis). **Marijuana** (MA-ri-HWA-nuh) is simply the dried leaves of the cannabis plant, and it is the most common form in which cannabis is used. Marijuana is usually inhaled by smoking the leaves in the form of a cigarette (the "marijuana joint" or "reefer"), but it can also be taken orally by grinding the leaves and baking them in cookies and candy ("Alice B. Toklas brownies"). **Hashish** (ha-SHĒSH) is the dried resin from the top of the female plant, and it is usually in powder form. Like marijuana, hashish can be mixed with tobacco and smoked or baked in cookies and eaten, but because it is more concentrated, it has stronger effects than marijuana. An even more concentrated form of cannabis is **hash oil**, which is obtained by first mixing the hashish with alcohol, which extracts the active ingredients from the hashish. The alcohol is then boiled away, and the chaff from the hashish is strained off. What remains is a red oil that contains a high concentration of the active ingredients. Hash oil is used by putting a drop on a normal cigarette and then smoking it or by putting a drop on hot metal and inhaling the vapors.

Cannabis can affect mood, sensory experiences, and cognitive functioning, but its effects vary greatly from person to person and time to time. Probably the most common effect is to cause mood swings that range from a placid dreaminess or a floating sensation called "getting off" to euphoric gaiety referred to as a "high." The high brought on by cannabis is very different from the high achieved with the stimulants like amphetamines or cocaine. Rather than being a "rush" of excitement and arousal, the cannabis high involves mild euphoria and feelings of gaiety. During the high, everything seems funny or even hilarious. Cannabis usually results in a positive mood shift, but sometimes it results in depression or negative experiences. The negative mood shifts are relatively rare and mild, and they should not be confused with the "bad trips" that will be discussed later in connections with drugs like LSD.

Cannabis also affects sensory perceptions in that experiences seem richer, fuller, brighter, and more intense. Users describe the cannabis experience as like going from black-and-white to color TV, from mono to stereo sound, and from bland to spicy food. The sense of time is also distorted; time seems stretched out, and a 5-minute period seems to last 10 minutes or longer.

Finally, cannabis has a number of cognitive effects. The interpretation of experiences is changed so that the simplest things may appear very important, interesting, and profound. While under the influence of cannabis, individuals have what they think are great insights, and they believe themselves to be more creative. However, research has consistently shown that while on cannabis, individuals are *not* more insightful or creative and in fact are probably *less* so (Braden et al., 1974; Grinspoon, 1977). Other cognitive effects of cannabis include an increase in distractibility and a decline in short-term memory such that sometimes individuals start sentences but cannot finish them because they forget what they started to say.

It is interesting that cannabis may not have much effect the first times it is used. That is probably due in part to the fact that the novice user does not know how to take the drug effectively (e.g., the smoke is not held in the lungs long enough, so not enough is absorbed), but it may also be that it takes some experience to recognize and respond to the effects of the drug. Like exotic food, cannabis may be an acquired taste that takes time to develop. It is also relevant that the effects of the drug seem to be influenced to some degree by the mood of the other individuals with whom the drug is taken (Rossi et al., 1978). This suggests that cannabis may make individuals more susceptible to the influence of others.

Mode of Action. The active ingredients in cannabis are substances called **cannabinoids** (KAN-uh-bin-OIDZ). When cannabis is inhaled, the cannabinoids are quickly absorbed through the lungs, and the effects are noticed within a few minutes, with the peak effect occurring in 30 to 60 minutes. The effects of smoking cannabis can be enhanced by taking a deep draw on the cannabis cigarette and then holding the smoke in the lungs for 15 or 20 seconds before exhaling, thus allowing more time for absorption. Absorption of cannabinoids from the digestive system is much slower, and the effects of eating cannabis do not peak for 3 hours, but once started, the effects may last 5 hours or even longer.

The chemical basis for the effects of cannabis is very complex and not well understood. That is the case in part because cannabis contains more than 80 different cannabinoids that may contribute to the effects in different ways. Furthermore, burning cannabis (as is done when it is smoked) changes some of the cannabinoids and creates other ones, and when cannabis is eaten (as in brownies), new cannabinoids are formed during digestion and metabolism (Kephalis et al., 1976; Salimenk, 1976). Independent of what cannabinoids are responsible for the effects, we do not yet know how the effects are achieved in the brain, but it is assumed that they influence the limbic system.

Problems of Misuse. Controversies over the alleged benefits and dangers of cannabis use have been numerous. Proponents argue that when it is used in moderation, cannabis is an effective and safe relaxant and that its use is less serious than the use of alcohol or tranquilizers. Furthermore, they point out that cannabis has a number of medical applications, such as the reduction of the nausea and vomiting that often accompany chemotherapy for cancer. It may also be effective as an anticonvulsant and useful for treating glaucoma (a disorder consisting of increased pressure in the eyeball that can lead to blindness; Braude & Szara, 1976; Cohen & Stillman, 1976; Institute of Medicine, 1982). The fact that cannabis has medical uses but is an illegal drug has resulted in a number of court cases in which patients sought to have the drug made available on a prescription basis.

Critics have argued that the use of cannabis leads to increased violence, higher rates of abnormal behavior, the use of more dangerous drugs, and overall reductions in motivation. The assertions that cannabis leads to violence were widespread in the 1930s and were in large part responsible for the passage of laws such as the Marijuana Tax Act that restricted the use of cannabis. However, it was more recently concluded that "there is absolutely no systematic data to support the myth" that cannabis use leads to violence (McKim, 1986, p. 228). Indeed, long-term studies in controlled hospital settings have never provided evidence that cannabis use leads to violence. Instead, mood ratings indicated decreased feelings of hostility and increased feelings of friendliness when cannabis was used. The results of field studies are consistent with those of the laboratory studies (e.g., Tinklenberg, 1974).

The findings concerning the relationship between cannabis use and abnormal behavior are more complex. Studies conducted in the United States have not revealed that cannabis users are more likely to be diagnosed as suffering from abnormal behavior than nonusers, and there is no evidence that cannabis use causes psychoses in normal individuals (Grinspoon, 1977). However, there is some evidence that the drug can lead to disorders among individuals who *already have adjustment problems*, and it can *intensify existing schizophrenic and paranoid disorders* (Choptra & Smith, 1974). With regard to the intensification of existing problems, the comments of a person with a history of a serious delusional disorder are relevant (for background on this case, see Case Study 12.6). The individual is now functioning normally but made the following comments concerning the consequences of smoking cannabis:

I do not smoke marijuana because when I do, all of my paranoid symptoms come back. I have never experienced a "nice high" like many of my friends have. In an attempt to understand what happens, I have smoked alone with a tape recorder so I could record what happens. However, it all happens so fast that I freak out and go into a paranoid panic. I check the house for bugs and of course I turn the tape recorder off! All of the behaviors are present that I experienced during my rough moments without the drug—and that's no fun. I simply don't smoke marijuana anymore.

When considering the relationship between cannabis and mental disorders, it is important to take the dose level into consideration. At very high dosages, cannabis will result in abnormal behaviors in most persons, but that is true of many types of drugs, an effect known as *toxic psychosis*. An important point in this regard is that the symptoms of the disorder disappear when the drug wears off, and thus it does not appear that cannabis results in long-term disorders even when it is taken at high levels (Meyer, 1975). Overall, the controversies concerning the use of cannabis have moderated in the past few years, not necessarily because the critics changed their views but because attention has shifted to other drugs.

LSD, Psilocybin, and Mescaline

The remaining group of hallucinogens contains a wide variety of drugs, but probably the best known and most widely used are **LSD (lysergic acid)**, which is a synthetically produced drug; **psilocybin** (sī-luh-SĪ-bin), which is found in the *Psilocybe mexicana* mushrooms of Mexico; and **mescaline**, which comes from small button-like growths on the peyote cactus of Mexico and the southwestern desert of the United States.

These drugs come from very different sources and have very different modes of action, and the effects of any one drug may be quite variable from person to person and from time to time for any one person. However, they generally result in periods of dramatically changed sensory experiences. Colors are brighter, sounds are more intense, and shapes are often distorted. Because everything is so different, it is like taking a trip to a different world, much like Alice's trip to Wonderland, and for that reason, the period of the drug effect is called a "trip." Trips usually last between 4 and 8 hours.

The changes in perception and feelings of being transported lead to a variety of emotional experiences such as depersonalization and detachment. If the changed perceptions are pleasant, the trip can be enjoyable and exciting, but if the changed perceptions are unpleasant, the trip can be terrifying and traumatic. "Bad trips" get most of the public attention because they can lead to dangerous acts or hospitalization. However, even "good trips" can lead to serious consequences, as in the case of a young woman who thought she had supernatural powers and jumped out of a 12-story window in an attempt to fly. We do not understand what makes some trips enjoyable and others terrifying, but the individual's *mood* or *expectations* when beginning the trip appear to play some role.

In the 1960s, it was thought that hallucinogens caused brief periods of schizophrenia and that the hallucinogens and hallucinogenic experiences might be helpful for understanding schizophrenia. However, we now know that the causes and nature of the hallucinogenic experience are very different from schizophrenia, and consequently the use of hallucinogens to study schizophrenia has been abandoned. It was also once thought that hallucinogens might help people discover important personal insights about themselves, and therefore hallucinogens were sometimes used as an adjunct to psychotherapy. That also turned out to be erroneous. What seemed important to the drug user while taking the drug turned out to be silly, meaningless, or wrong when the drug wore off, and therefore that use of the drug was also abandoned. Finally, hallucinogens were used widely and are still used by some people for strictly recreational purposes.

Mode of Action. Hallucinogens are taken orally, absorbed through the digestive tract, and then carried to the brain via the bloodstream. Most hallucinogens are structurally similar to certain neurotransmitters in the brain (e.g., LSD and psilocybin are similar to serotonin, and mescaline is similar to norepinephrine), and it is assumed that once in the brain, they stimulate the postsynaptic receptor sites that are normally stimulated by the neurotransmitters they resemble (Jacobs, 1987; McKim, 1986). The fact that the hallucinogens generate such a wide variety of effects can probably be attributed to the fact that the nerves they stimulate are very basic and interconnect and stimulate many other nerve networks, thereby setting in motion a cascade of complex neurological activity. However, it is important to recognize that most of our present understanding of the mode of action of hallucinogens is based on speculations and assumptions rather than on empirically demonstrated relationships. Furthermore, there are some hallucinogens for which structurally similar neurotransmitters have not been found, and exactly how they achieve their effects is still a mystery.

Problems of Misuse.   The use of LSD, psilocybin, and mescaline has a number of negative consequences. First, during the trip, individuals may do things that are dangerous to themselves or others. An example of this is the woman who jumped off a building because she thought she could fly. Second, although the use of hallucinogens does not increase the likelihood of long-term psychoses, at least 5% of the individuals who use LSD experience **flashbacks**, which are sudden and uncontrollable recurrences of perceptual distortions like those experienced during the trip (Horowitz, 1969). These are particularly frightening because not having just taken the drug, the individuals do not understand what is happening or why. After experiencing a flashback, the individual may become chronically anxious, worry about having another one, and worry about losing control in a potentially dangerous situation. We do not yet know why flashbacks occur. Third, there is some evidence that LSD can result in chromosomal damage, and thus its use poses serious problems for children born to hallucinogen users. Finally, hallucinogens are generally not physiologically addictive, but some individuals become psychologically dependent on the drugs as a means of escaping from the tedium of their everyday lives.

This concludes our discussion of the various substances on which individuals become dependent. In the next section, we will examine the important question of why some individuals abuse and become dependent on drugs.

EXPLANATIONS FOR SUBSTANCE DEPENDENCE AND ABUSE

Accounting for substance abuse or dependence has always been a thorny problem, and explanations have ranged from the moral to the medical. The major conflict is over the question of whether drug abuse is *voluntary misbehavior* or an *illness*. The misbehavior explanation received some legal support in a Supreme Court decision concerning alcoholism. That case revolved around the fact that veterans must use their educational benefits within 10 years of completing their military service. However, two veterans who had not used their benefits asked for an extension based on the fact that they had been suffering from alcoholism, and therefore had not been able to use the benefits. The Veterans Administration denied their request on the grounds that alcoholism was "willful misconduct" and not an illness. When the men appealed the case to the Supreme Court, the justices concluded that they were not in a position to decide whether or not alcoholism was an illness, but they voted 4 to 3 to affirm the right of the Veterans Administration to label alcoholism "willful misconduct." Even the justices who considered alcoholism an illness agreed that "the consumption of alcohol is not regarded as wholly involuntary." This ruling lent credence to the misbehavior explanation for alcoholism, but it should be noted that the ruling was a *court opinion* and not a *scientific fact*. The justices admitted that they were not in a position to come up with a better conclusion, so they simply let stand the prevailing "misbehavior" opinion. Our task in this section will be to determine whether substance abuse and dependence are due to willful misconduct or whether there is a better explanation.

There are a number of explanations for substance dependence, and we will evaluate each of them. Initially, it may appear that the explanations are independent and compete with one another, but as we have found in our attempts to explain other disorders, it may be that there is a common element that is simply being viewed from different perspectives.

Exposure

Early theorists assumed that exposure to drugs and initial light usage would necessarily lead to drug abuse and dependence. It was that orientation that led early antidrug crusaders to predict that one puff on a marijuana cigarette would ultimately lead to opium dens and heroin addiction. Exposure to drugs is of course necessary if a problem is to develop. In 1949, when the People's Republic of China was founded, the government effectively eliminated access to opium and thereby eliminated its use and the widespread dependence on it.

Although exposure is *necessary* for dependence, exposure is not *sufficient* to explain dependence. Convincing evidence for that comes from the fact that among the soldiers who were addicted to heroin while in Vietnam, only 12% relapsed within 3 years of their return to the United States (Robins et al., 1974; Robins et al., 1975). The drugs were still available at home, but the life situations of the veterans had changed, so their patterns of drug usage changed. (For a review of other evidence contradicting the exposure explanation, see Alexander and Hadaway, 1982.)

Situational Factors

It is possible that exposure in combination with certain situational factors might lead to dependence. The crucial situational factors are usually thought to be those that cause some form of stress that might be reduced or eliminated by drugs. The individual in a stressful job may drink too much or take excessive numbers of sleeping pills. The individual who has nothing better to do may look for "kicks" with stimulants or take "trips" with hallucinogens. The individual trapped in the slums may abuse substances in attempts at temporarily escaping an intolerable situation.

The effects of situational factors on drug abuse were clearly demonstrated in experiments in which laboratory animals were given free access to drugs in their cages. The interesting finding was that animals that were housed alone in standard laboratory cages consumed 16 times more morphine than animals who were housed in a large colony of other animals (Alexander et al., 1978; Alexander et al., 1981; Hadaway et al., 1979). It appears that the restricted, isolated conditions of the standard cages may have been stressful for the mobile and social animals like rats and monkeys, and their drug use may have been a response to the stressful situation. The very high rate of substance abuse and dependence among soldiers serving in Vietnam may have been due to the high stress of that situation, and the lessening of stress on returning to the United States may account for the substantial drop-off in drug use among the veterans. Those who continued to abuse drugs may have been those for whom the conditions in the United States were also stressful (e.g., lack of jobs, broken homes).

From these results, it appears that situational factors do contribute to substance abuse and dependence, but situational factors do not account for all of the problems because there are many individuals who exist in boring, stressful, or otherwise unpleasant situations who do not turn to chemical substances for a solution. Why are only some persons affected? We will next consider factors that might predispose individuals to substance abuse and dependence.

Family Characteristics

Theorists have long suspected that family characteristics during childhood predispose individuals to later drug abuse. Often-cited factors are poor role models, lack of discipline, and stress in the form of family disorganization (divorce, separation, inappropriate punishment) from which the child might want to escape through the use of drugs. To determine whether family characteristics are related to alcoholism, numerous prospective investigations have been conducted in which families were studied, and then the children were followed up as adults and examined for alcoholism. A review of the results of those investigations revealed that children who went on to develop alcoholism (a) were raised in homes with more marital conflict, (b) received inadequate parenting, and (c) had parents who were more likely to be alcoholic, sexually deviant, or antisocial (see Zucker & Gomberg, 1986). The antisocial nature of the parents is probably

the crucial factor because all the other facets appear to be instances of antisocial behavior.

If the parents of children who became drug abusers are antisocial in personality, it is possible that they serve as bad role models for their children and that one of the inappropriate behaviors that the children learn is substance abuse. In that way, parental characteristics could cause substance abuse. Alternatively, it is also possible that the antisocial behavior of the parents and the antisocial behavior (drug abuse) of the children is due to a third factor, *shared genes.* In our discussion of the antisocial personality disorder in Chapter 15, it was pointed out that the disorder is due in large part to genetic factors, and therefore antisocial parents may contribute to antisocial behavior and drug abuse through gene transmission instead of or in addition to role modeling and parenting. We will consider these possibilities in greater detail later.

Personality

It was initially suggested that substance abusers had regressed to the oral stage of psychosexual development and were using drugs to satisfy unfulfilled needs (Fenichel, 1945). In the case of alcoholism, much was made of the fact that many individuals who suffer from alcoholism drink from a bottle (a breast substitute?) rather than a glass. However, little empirical support could be found for the regression explanation, so a search was begun for a combination of personality traits that was thought to comprise the *addictive personality* (see Nathan, 1988; Sutker & Allain, 1988). One problem in identifying the traits that lead to substance abuse is to separate traits that cause the drug abuse from those that result from the drug abuse. Does depression lead to alcoholism, or are persons who suffer from alcoholism depressed because of the problems caused by their drinking? We will have to answer this question with prospective studies in which individuals were studied as children and then followed up as adults.

Antisocial Behavior.   A unique addictive personality has not been found, but the research has generated two consistent findings that are important. The first is that *antisocial behavior* in childhood and adolescence is related to substance abuse in adulthood (see Nathan, 1988; Zucker & Gomberg, 1986). Specifically, children and adolescents who are frequently in trouble, show poor impulse control, do not value conventional institutions, and are independent, aggressive, and pleasure-seeking are more likely to abuse drugs as adults than children who do not have those characteristics.

The question then arises, what causes the antisocial behavior pattern of which substance abuse is a part? One possibility is that the behavior is learned from antisocial parents or other role models. For example, antisocial behavior and substance abuse would be more likely in environments in which the "big kids are snorting coke" and the most affluent people are "dealers."

A second possible explanation is that individuals who are antisocial and abuse drugs suffer from the antisocial personality disorder (see Chapter 15). In most cases, that disorder appears to be due to a low level of neurological arousal that results in a low level of anxiety, which in turn reduces inhibitions and permits antisocial behavior. The low level of neurological arousal may play a role in reducing restraints against drug abuse, but it may also contribute to drug abuse because underaroused persons may use drugs to raise (normalize?) their arousal levels. Indeed, when persons with the antisocial personality disorder abuse drugs, they are most likely to use stimulants.

Depression. The second personality factor that has been consistently related to substance abuse is *depression*. However, there is some question about whether the depression is a cause or an effect of substance abuse. In some cases, depressed persons use stimulants as an antidote for their depression, as Freud took cocaine, or they may take depressants to deaden their senses and thereby avoid their problems. In other cases, however, individuals become depressed because of the problems caused by their substance abuse (loss of jobs and friends).

Differences in Personality and Patterns of Abuse. The findings linking both antisocial behavior and depression to substance abuse may seem inconsistent at first because antisocial behavior is not usually associated with depression. The explanation for the inconsistency lies in the possibility that substance abuse may be associated with antisocial behavior or depression rather than the two in combination. In other words, there may be two different personality types related to substance abuse: antisocial behavior and depression.

Support for the notion that two different personality patterns may be linked independently to substance abuse was supported by the results of some recent research in which it was found that there are *two types of alcoholism* and that the different types are associated with *different personality characteristics* (see Cloninger, 1987). One type of alcoholism is characterized by *persistent drinking* at moderate to heavy levels. In those cases, it appears that the individual does not have the ability to abstain from using alcohol regularly. We will refer to this as the **persistent type of alcoholism**.

The persistent type of alcoholism is associated with impulsivity, lack of anxiety, risk taking, novelty seeking, independence, distractibility, and antisocial behavior. In other words, individuals with the persistent type of alcoholism are uninhibited and seem to suffer from at least a mild form of the antisocial personality disorder. These personality characteristics are generally associated with *neurological underarousal* (see Chapter 15), and it is assumed that the individuals use alcohol persistently but at low levels to increase their arousal to optimal or normal levels. Recall that at low levels, alcohol is a stimulant.

In contrast, the other type of alcoholism is characterized by *long periods of abstinence* during which the individual is able to control the drinking, but once drinking begins, the person *cannot stop*, and the drinking takes the form of a *binge*. We will call this the **binge type of alcoholism**.

Individuals with the binge type of alcoholism are characterized as anxious, inhibited, cautious, shy, dependent, depressed, and emotionally sensitive. It is assumed that these individuals are neurologically overaroused and that the high levels of alcohol they consume during a binge serve to reduce arousal. Recall that at high levels, alcohol is a depressant. The possibility that individuals with low or high levels of arousal may use different patterns of drinking (or different types of drugs) to normalize their levels of arousal is referred to as the **self-medication hypothesis** of substance dependence (Khantzian, 1985; Meisch, 1991). The characteristics associated with the persistent and binge types of alcoholism are summarized in Table 18.3. The persistent and binge types are usually discussed as though they were distinct types, but they are probably the end points of a continuum.

In summary, there is now consistent evidence linking the antisocial personality pattern and depression to substance abuse, and there is reason to believe that the link between personality and substance abuse may be due to underlying differences in arousal. Low levels of arousal lead to low levels of anxiety, uninhibited behavior, and the use of substances to increase arousal. In contrast, high levels of arousal lead to high levels of anxiety, inhibitions, and the use of substances to reduce arousal (Cloninger, 1987; Khantzian, 1985).

Anxiety Reduction

Learning theorists have long argued that the consumption of alcohol *reduces anxiety*, is *rewarding*, and therefore leads to more consumption (see Wilson, 1987). The anxiety reduction explanation was originally based on research with laboratory animals in which it was found that conflict and stress increased alcohol consumption and that the animals would come

TABLE 18.3   THERE APPEAR TO BE TWO TYPES OF ALCOHOLISM, AND THE TWO TYPES ARE ASSOCIATED WITH DIFFERENT PERSONALITY CHARACTERISTICS, AND DIFFERENT POSSIBLE UNDERLYING PROCESSES

	PERSISTENT TYPE	BINGE TYPE
Drinking Behavior	Early onset (before age 25)	Late onset (after age 25)
	Persistent	Periods of abstinence
	Moderate to heavy	Severe binges
	Cannot abstain	Cannot stop binges
Personality	Lack of anxiety	Anxious
	Impulsive	Inhibited
	Risk-taking	Cautious
	Novelty-seeking	Shy
	Independent	Dependent
	Distractible	Depressed
	Antisocial	Socially sensitive
Gender	Equally prevalent in men and women	More prevalent in women
Underlying Process	Persons are physiologically underaroused; frequent low doses of alcohol serve as stimulants that increase arousal.	Persons are physiologically overaroused; high doses of alcohol during binges serve as depressants that decrease arousal.

closer to a feared stimulus if they had been given alcohol (Conger, 1951; Freed, 1971; Wright et al., 1971). Similar results have been reported with humans (Sher & Levenson, 1982). It appears that alcohol can reduce anxiety, and the question we must answer here is why.

The first explanation is that alcohol reduces anxiety because it is a *physiological depressant*, and as such it can reduce the arousal we label as anxiety. In one study, males who either did or did not have a family history of alcoholism were exposed to stressful stimuli (electrical shocks) while sober or after drinking alcohol (Finn et al., 1990). For the men who had a family history of alcoholism, drinking alcohol greatly reduced their responsiveness to the stressful stimuli. In contrast, the alcohol did not affect the responsiveness of the men who did not have a family history of alcoholism. The results for heart rate are presented in Figure 18.2. These results clearly indicate that at least among individuals with a family history of alcoholism, alcohol can reduce arousal or anxiety.

The second explanation is that alcohol reduces anxiety because it *impairs cognitive functioning* (information processing) that is essential for recognizing the existence of a problem (Hull, 1981). You may have noticed that persons who have been drinking tend to focus on one or two ideas and ignore other ideas that may be more relevant or more important. If people do not attend to all of the relevant factors in their environment, they may not see or remember a problem that is anxiety-provoking. This effect seems to be strongest when there are a variety of things going on in the environment because in those situations, it is more difficult for the individual who has been drinking to process all of the information that is coming in (Steele et al., 1986; Steele & Josephs, 1988).

Third, alcohol may reduce anxiety because it *enhances positive feelings*. There is evidence that the stimulating effects of small doses of alcohol reduce anxiety because they lead to more feelings of energy, power, well-being, and confidence (McClelland et al., 1972; Yankofsky et al., 1986). In summary, alcohol can reduce anxiety through (a) physiological sedation, (b) cognitive interference or distraction, and (c) energization of positive feelings. All three types of anxiety reduction would be rewarding and could encourage drinking.

FIGURE 18.2   ALCOHOL REDUCED AROUSAL IN RESPONSE TO STRESSFUL STIMULATION IN MALES WITH A FAMILY HISTORY OF ALCOHOLISM.

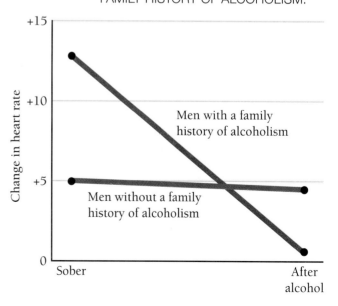

Source: Adapted from Finn et al. (1990), p. 83, fig. 2.

Expectations

It has also been suggested that at least some of the effects of alcohol (and other drugs) are due to users' *expectations*. Support for this possibility comes from a variety of experiments in which persons drank either (a) an alcoholic beverage they knew contained alcohol, (b) a placebo (nonalcoholic) beverage they thought contained alcohol, or (c) a nonalcoholic beverage they knew contained no alcohol. Among persons who thought that alcohol reduces inhibitions, those who drank the alcoholic or the placebo beverage were less inhibited and more aggressive than those who drank the nonalcoholic beverage (Cooper et al., 1992; Leigh, 1989; Wilson, 1987).

Some theorists have also used expectations to account for alcohol craving and uncontrolled drinking, behaviors that are usually attributed to physiological factors. Specifically, it has been suggested that individuals' craving for alcohol results from their expectancy that the alcohol will enable them to achieve some desired goal, such as anxiety reduction or less inhibition (Marlatt, 1985; Wise, 1988). Similarly, it is assumed that uncontrolled drinking (the belief that one drink will necessarily lead to another and eventually to a drunk) stems from the expectancy that one drink necessarily leads to another drink.

Support for the role of expectancies in uncontrolled drinking comes from studies in which persons were allowed to drink either alcoholic or placebo (nonalcoholic) beverages and their drinking was monitored (Berg et al., 1981; Marlatt et al., 1973). The results indicated that the best predictor of how much was drunk was not whether the beverages contained alcohol, but whether the participants thought they could control their drinking; those who did not think they could control their drinking drank more, regardless of whether the drink contained alcohol. The belief that drinking cannot be controlled may account for relapses after periods of abstinence (Marlatt, 1978; Rollnick & Heather, 1982). In other words, uncontrolled binge drinking may be a self-fulfilling prophecy.

One qualification should be noted concerning the research in which placebo drinks were used. It is impossible to do placebo research with heavy drinking because at high levels of consumption, the fact that drinks do not contain alcohol becomes obvious. Therefore, the research involving placebos has been limited to light drinking. This means that the findings based on placebos may not generalize to the heavy drinking that is usually associated with serious abuse.

Physiological Factors

The most widely held physiological explanation for substance abuse and dependence is that some individuals are predisposed to the problem because they have *different physiological needs* or because they *process drugs differently*. There are a variety of physiological differences between persons who do and do not have a history of alcoholism, but it is impossible to draw conclusions about the cause of alcoholism from those findings because the differences may be the result of the long-term use of alcohol (see Grant, 1987). To circumvent that problem, most attention is now being focused on differences between the children of parents who do or do not suffer from alcoholism (Pihl et al., 1990; Schuckit, 1987). The logic behind this approach is as follows: (a) Alcoholism is in large part an inherited disorder, (b) parents who suffer from alcoholism pass on to their children the physiological factors that lead to alcoholism, and (c) comparing the children of parents who do and do not suffer from alcoholism *before the children begin drinking* will make it possible to identify differences that exist before the effects of drinking set in.

This type of research has revealed that the sons of parents with alcoholism have *higher levels of neurological arousal* and show *greater reductions in neurological arousal after drinking alcohol* than the sons of parents who do not suffer from alcoholism. Specifically, it has been found that *before* drinking alcohol, sons of parents who suffered from alcoholism showed brain wave activity that indicated *higher arousal* (fewer of the slow-wave alpha EEG potentials that are associated with relaxation), but *after* drinking alcohol, they showed *greater decreases* in the brain wave activity that reflects arousal (increases in the slow-wave alpha EEG potentials). These findings suggest that some persons are genetically predisposed to abuse alcohol because they have unpleasantly high levels of arousal and because alcohol is particularly effective for reducing (normalizing?) their levels of arousal. This effect was also illustrated with heart rate in Figure 18.2. When compared to men who did not have a family history of alcoholism (were not genetically predisposed), those who did have a family history of alcoholism (were genetically predisposed) showed a greater heart rate response to stress when sober but a smaller response to stress after drinking alcohol (Finn et al., 1990).

It is becoming increasingly clear that the physiological processes that lead to alcoholism are determined in large part by genetic factors. For example, the results of more than 50 studies indicate that the rate of alcoholism among children of parents with the disorder is three to four times higher than among children of parents who do not suffer from the problem (see Goodwin, 1985a, 1985b; Schuckit, 1987). These results certainly suggest a genetic contribution, but firm conclusions cannot be drawn because in studies of families, we cannot separate the effects that are due to genetic and environmental factors.

It is becoming increasingly clear that the physiological processes leading to alcoholism are determined in large part by genetic factors, giving some people a genetic predisposition to alcoholism. Eugene O'Neill's Long Day's Journey Into Night *portrayed a family ravaged by alcoholism.*

The genetic-versus-environment problem was overcome in research in which the investigators examined the rates of alcoholism in adopted children whose biological parents either did or did not suffer from alcoholism (Searles, 1988). In one adoption study, the investigators examined two large groups of adoptees (Cadoret et al., 1986). The first group had biological relatives who had histories of either alcoholism or antisocial behavior, whereas the second group did not have biological relatives with either of those problems. When the adoptees were examined as adults, three interesting findings emerged: First, it was found that a biological family history of antisocial behavior was related to antisocial behavior in the adoptees and that the antisocial behavior in the adoptees was in turn related to the abuse of all types of drugs (stimulants, depressants, narcotics, and hallucinogens). That finding suggests that one route to drug abuse involves the inheritance of the antisocial personality disorder, which in turn leads to drug abuse. Some theorists have referred to this type of alcoholism as *secondary* or *psychopathic* alcoholism because it is mediated by the antisocial behavior (Cadoret et al., 1984; Schuckit, 1973).

The second finding of interest is that a biological family history of alcoholism was also related to the abuse of all types of drugs but not to any particular personality characteristic. This suggests that some individuals may have a biological predisposition to drug abuse that is independent of antisocial behavior or personality. This type of alcoholism is referred to as *primary* alcoholism because it is not mediated by personality factors (Cadoret et al., 1984; Schuckit, 1973).

The third noteworthy finding is that some of the adoptees who did not have a biological family history of antisocial behavior or alcoholism did develop drug abuse problems. Those adoptees were more likely than others to be raised in adoptive families in which there was parental discord (separation or divorce) or a disturbed parent. In other words, *situational* stress contributed to drug abuse independent of a biological family history of antisocial behavior or alcoholism. Overall, the results of this study suggest that there are three routes to substance abuse: (a) a genetic predisposition that is mediated by antisocial behavior, (b) a genetic predisposition that is independent of antisocial behavior, and (c) environmental stress.

Strong evidence for the role of genetic factors was recently provided by a study of 1,030 monozygotic (MZ) and dizygotic (DZ) female twin pairs (Kendler, Heath, et al., 1992). The results indicated that the concordance rate for MZ twin pairs was 46.9%, whereas the concordance rate for DZ twin pairs was 31.5%. Using these data, the authors estimated the inheritability of alcoholism to be about 60%. These findings are particularly interesting because they are based on women, whereas most other findings are based on men.

Before concluding this discussion of genetic factors, some comment should be made concerning how genetic and environmental factors *interact* to result in substance abuse and dependence. This interaction was illustrated in a study of the persistent and binge types of alcoholism. To test the genetic and environmental contributions to these two types of alcoholism, adoption studies were conducted in which adoptees were first classified as having a biological family history of the persistent type of alcoholism, a biological family history of the binge type of alcoholism, or no biological family history of alcoholism. The adoptees in those groups were then divided into those whose adoptive environments either did or did not involve alcohol abuse (Bohman et al., 1981; Cloninger, Bohman, & Sigvardsson, 1981; see review by Cloninger, 1987). By comparing the rates of alcoholism among the various groups, we can assess the separate and combined effects of genetic and environmental factors.

Two conclusions can be drawn from the data concerning persistent alcoholism. First, genetic factors alone are very important, whereas environmental factors alone are only moderately important. Specifically, when compared to individuals who did not have a genetic or an environmental background related to substance abuse, those with *only a genetic background* showed a rate of substance abuse that was almost *nine times higher* (16.9 vs. 1.9), while individuals with *only an environmental background* showed a rate that was only *two times higher* (4.1 vs. 1.9). Second, the *combination* of a genetic background plus an environmental background did not result in a rate of substance abuse that was much higher than what occurred with only a genetic background (17.9 vs. 16.9). These results are presented in Figure 18.3. Overall then, it appears that in persistent alcoholism, genetic factors play a dominant role while environmental factors contribute relatively little either alone or in combination with genetic factors.

Two conclusions can also be drawn from the data concerning the binge type of alcoholism. First, genetic factors alone are moderately important, whereas environmental factors alone are unimportant. Specifically, when compared to individuals who did not have a genetic or an environmental background related to substance abuse, those with *only a genetic background* showed a rate of substance abuse that was *1½ times higher* (6.7 vs. 4.3), while individuals with *only an environmental background* showed a rate that was essentially the *same* (4.2 vs. 4.3). Second, the *combination* of a ge-

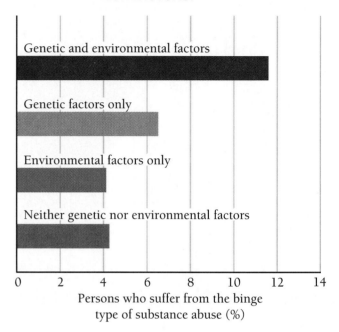

FIGURE 18.4 BINGE DRINKING APPEARS TO BE DUE TO A COMBINATION OF GENETIC AND ENVIRONMENTAL RISK FACTORS.

Persons who suffer from the binge type of substance abuse (%)

Source: Adapted from Cloninger (1987), p. 412, tab. 2.

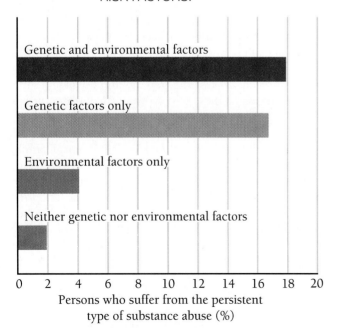

FIGURE 18.3 PERSISTENT DRINKING APPEARS TO BE DUE PRIMARILY TO GENETIC RISK FACTORS.

Persons who suffer from the persistent type of substance abuse (%)

Source: Adapted from Cloninger (1987), p. 413, tab. 3.

netic background plus an environmental background resulted in a rate of substance abuse that was higher than the rate caused by either factor alone. Specifically, the combination of genetic and environmental backgrounds resulted in a rate of alcoholism that was *nearly twice* what occurred with only a genetic background (11.6 vs. 6.7) and nearly *three times* what occurred with only an environmental background (11.6 vs. 4.2). These results are presented in Figure 18.4. Overall then, binge alcoholism appears to be influenced by both genetic and environmental factors, and those factors can work together to increase the rate of alcoholism.

The evidence for a genetic basis for alcoholism is quite strong. Indeed, based on family, twin, and adoption studies, it has been estimated that the overall heritability rate is about 64%, and it may be as high as 90% for primary alcoholism (Cloninger et al., 1983; Cloninger et al., 1984; Pickens et al., 1991). However, it is important to recognize that alcoholism is not a single disorder, and genetic factors undoubtedly play different roles in different forms of the disorder (McGue et al., 1992).

Before concluding our discussion of the genetics of alcoholism, it should be noted that there is a growing body of evidence that some forms of alcoholism are linked to a specific gene, known as *DRD2* (Uhl et al., 1992). That gene is responsible for the sensitivity of specific dopamine receptors (D/2 receptors). That is relevant because we know that blocking the activity of dopamine-mediated nerve tracks can reduce the self-administration of certain drugs in animals. Data linking alcoholism to the DRD2 gene are new and controversial, but they have been found in six different laboratories. If these findings prove to be reliable, they could lead to new understandings of some types of alcoholism.

In this discussion of physiological and genetic factors, we have focused primarily on alcoholism, but it is important to recognize that physiological and genetic factors also play important roles in the abuse of other substances. For example, studies of families and of twins have revealed that genetic factors play an important role in nicotine dependence (Breslau et al., 1993; Kendler et al., 1993). It may be that in contrast to the case with alcohol, genetic factors lead to a low level of arousal, which leads to depression and the need for stimulation via nicotine.

Comment

It is clear from the preceding sections of this chapter that a wide variety of factors have been considered in our attempt to understand the problem of substance abuse, and that each of the factors appears to play a role. However, it is also clear that among the factors that have been considered, physiological factors appear to play the most important role. That is, genetic factors appear to establish different levels of arousal and different responses to drugs that will influence the likelihood that the drugs will be used. Physiological factors are clearly important, but their role must be considered in context. For example, there is no evidence that physiological factors somehow take over or "commandeer" the individual and trigger uncontrollable drinking bouts (Goldman et al., 1991). Instead, it is undoubtedly the case that physiological factors establish needs for drugs and responses to drugs, and then personality and environmental factors determine whether the drugs will be used. A popular phrase associated with the treatment of substance abuse is "Just say no!" Saying no is certainly a solution, but it is important to recognize that for physiological reasons, *saying no is much harder for some individuals than it is for others*, and we must be sensitive to those differences. With this material as background, we can go on to discuss the treatment of substance abuse.

APPROACHES TO TREATMENT

Four strategies are employed for solving the substance abuse problem. The first involves *eliminating the availability* of drugs so that individuals cannot begin misusing them. This was the strategy used to rid China of the opium dens. It can be done effectively in closed or highly controlled societies, but it is very difficult to achieve in more open societies.

The second strategy is to use *severe penalties* for drug abuse. Proposed penalties include long prison sentences, mandatory execution of individuals involved in drug-related murders, and stiff fines. An interesting instance of a stiff fine is the confiscation of personal property associated with illegal drug use. This approach allows police officials to seize and then sell any property such as cars, boats, and planes in which even the smallest amount of drugs is found (a policy known as "zero tolerance"). In one case, a 133-ft, $2.5 million yacht was seized when .1 oz of marijuana was found on board. The penalty strategy breaks down because of problems with enforcement: insufficient numbers of police, long and expensive delays in prosecution, and lack of space in facilities to incarcerate all of the convicted offenders.

The third strategy is the *legalization of drug use.* This strategy essentially says, "If you can't beat 'em, join 'em," and making drug use legal at least eliminates the criminal element. Most drugs are easy and cheap to produce, and they are expensive only because they are illegal. If they were made legal, the profit and crime associated with them would be eliminated, and people who abused drugs could be identified, helped, or at least provided with safer drugs and procedures. This approach is used in England, where heroin addicts are registered and provided with heroin or a heroin substitute. Although this strategy may eliminate the crime associated with drug abuse, it does not reduce the drug abuse, and if drug abuse is tolerated, it is possible that increasing numbers of individuals will begin using drugs, which could have a negative overall effect on society. Some critics have charged that legalization of heroin use in England has resulted in increased numbers of heroin users.

The fourth strategy for dealing with drug abuse problems involves *psychological* and *physiological treatment.* There are four different approaches to such treatment: self-control, maintenance, blocking, and correction.

The *self-control approach* is based on the assumption that substance abuse is due to a "weakness of character," and the treatment involves using moral persuasion and social support to help the individual avoid the use of drugs. The self-control approach is

Persons who are dependent on heroin may be given methadone to help forestall withdrawal symptoms and begin the withdrawal process. However, the results of research on this method of treating heroin addiction are discouraging.

used by Alcoholics Anonymous and by Synanon, which is a program designed for persons addicted to opiates. Unfortunately, gaining and maintaining self-control is very difficult for substance abusers. In fact, Synanon claims that only 10% of the treated individuals maintain abstinence. Even that may be an overly optimistic figure because Synanon accepts only highly motivated clients who are most likely to improve. As noted earlier, physiological factors may make self-control very difficult for some individuals, so it is not surprising that this approach is often ineffective.

The *maintenance approach* involves giving persons a relatively harmless substitute for the substance on which they are dependent. In the case of heroin addiction, a substitute called **methadone** (Dolopine) is used. Methadone prevents the painful effects of withdrawal, and therefore the individuals do not need to resort to illegal behavior to get drugs to avoid the feared withdrawal.

This approach to treatment is based on two assumptions. The first is that the addiction probably cannot be cured and that its most serious effect is to force many persons into illegal behavior to support their habits. Providing addicted individuals with methadone eliminates their need to get opiates to avoid withdrawal and therefore indirectly protects society. The second assumption is that continued opiate use is due primarily to the fear of withdrawal rather than the pleasure derived from the drugs. The methadone does eliminate the withdrawal symptoms, but it does not provide the pleasurable sensations of heroin. Heroin could be used in maintenance therapy (as it sometimes is in

Britain), but there are three advantages in using methadone: (a) It can be taken orally and therefore avoids the problems associated with needles; (b) it puts off withdrawal symptoms for 24 hours rather than 8 hours, so it need be taken only once a day; and (c) it partially blocks the effects of heroin, so if heroin is taken to obtain a rush, its effects are somewhat diminished. Although addicted individuals can be kept on methadone indefinitely, the goal is to wean them slowly from the drug. This is difficult, however, because eventually withdrawal symptoms set in.

The results of research concerning the effects of methadone maintenance are discouraging. One explanation for the weak effects of the maintenance approach is that although methadone reduces the fear of withdrawal, it does not provide the pleasure that the heroin does. If continued opiate use is due even in part to the pleasure derived from the drug, methadone is doing only part of the job.

The use of patches for treating nicotine dependence is a form of treatment through maintenance. The patches deliver a constant low level of nicotine into the bloodstream, thereby eliminating the need to smoke. This approach is quite effective (see Fiore et al., 1992). Nicotine gum can also be effective for reducing the symptoms of withdrawal (Hughes et al., 1991; Killen et al., 1990). Of course, eventually the individual must be weaned off of the patch or the gum, and that can result in relapse. It is noteworthy that the combination of the patch plus social support appears to be most effective.

The *blocking approach* was developed because continued substance abuse may be due to the pleasure derived from taking the drugs. With the blocking

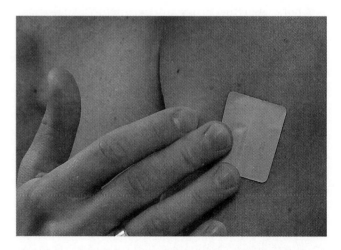

The use of patches for nicotine dependence is a form of treatment through maintenance. The patches deliver a low level of nicotine into the bloodstream, thereby eliminating the craving to smoke.

approach, individuals are given drugs that block the positive effects of the substances that are being abused or cause the individual to become nauseated (Kosten & Kosten, 1991). In the case of heroin addiction, the person is given an **opiate antagonist** (naloxone), which completely blocks the effects of heroin, thereby eliminating the pleasure it usually provides. Opiate antagonists work by fitting into the opiate receptors, thus blocking the opiates so that they cannot have their effect. Recently it was reported that opiate antagonists are also effective for treating alcoholism (O'Malley et al., 1992; Volpicelli et al., 1992). It appears that some of the pleasure derived from alcohol may be derived from the fact that alcohol stimulates the opiate system, so blocking that system can help reduce alcohol consumption. In a somewhat different approach to blocking, an individual suffering from alcoholism may be given a drug (disulfiram) that will cause nausea if alcohol is drunk, thus eliminating its positive effects. If the abused substances no longer provide pleasure, the users should cease taking them. The results of this type of treatment are mixed (Elkins, 1991). Individuals do stop taking the forbidden drugs while they are taking the antagonist, but once they stop taking the antagonist and know that they can again derive pleasure from the drugs, many individuals go back to using the forbidden drugs. However, in 1993, a more powerful version of disulfiram was patented that might be used in patches that would slowly release the medication into an individual's system. Patches might make it more difficult to stop taking the medication.

The fourth strategy in treatment involves *correcting* the problem that initially led to the abuse. In many cases, correction is difficult (changing an entire lifestyle) or not realistically possible (removing the individual from the social environment), or the problem may be physiological and not amenable to correction. In those cases, we may have to rely on substitutes and blocking agents to control rather than correct the problem.

Unfortunately, despite the claims made by advocates of various substance abuse programs, the data suggest that our current methods are not particularly effective in treating substance abuse problems.

SUMMARY

We began this chapter by pointing out that not all psychoactive drugs are necessarily bad and that a variety of factors can influence the effects of a drug. For example, the effects can be altered or even changed by the dose level and the characteristics of the person taking the drug. It was also pointed out that people develop tolerance for drugs and must take greater and greater amounts to achieve the desired effects. Taking different drugs in the same class can result in cross-tolerance. Withdrawal involves physiological symptoms that occur when a person stops taking a drug, and dependence is said to occur when an individual takes a drug to avoid the symptoms of withdrawal.

Drugs were organized into four types as a function of their effects. Depressants (alcohol, barbiturates, benzodiazepines) serve to reduce arousal and tension. Narcotics (opium, morphine, heroin), sometimes also called opiates, have the effect of dulling or numbing the senses. Stimulants (amphetamines, cocaine, caffeine, nicotine) increase arousal. Hallucinogens (cannabis, LSD, psilocybin, mescaline) are a heterogeneous group of drugs that distort sensory experiences. Persons abuse drugs to get a brief high or "rush," achieve a state of relaxation, or distract themselves with different sensory experiences.

Exposure to drugs is necessary for problems of abuse to develop, but exposure is not sufficient as an explanation for substance abuse. Situational factors such as stress are related to substance abuse, but they cannot account for all instances of abuse.

There is evidence that the parents of persons with substance abuse problems are likely to have antisocial personalities, but it is not clear whether the offspring develop substance abuse problems because of modeling or the sharing of genes. With regard to personality, it appears that persons who abuse drugs are likely to be depressed or show characteristics of the antisocial personality disorder. Furthermore, there is evidence that type of personality may be related to type of alcohol abuse; depressed persons tend to be binge drinkers, whereas antisocial persons tend to be persistent drinkers. Excessive drinking may also be related to the anxiety-reducing effects of alcohol and the expectations people have about the effects of alcohol.

It now appears that some persons may abuse drugs to "normalize" their levels of physiological arousal. People who are underaroused may take drugs to increase arousal to normal levels, and people who are overaroused may take drugs to decrease arousal to normal levels. A strong genetic link for substance abuse has been established. It may be that genetic factors influence arousal levels, which are then altered with drugs.

Treatment of substance abuse has been attempted by enhancing the abusers' self-control, substituting a less dangerous substance on which they can be maintained, chemically blocking the effects of the undesired drug so that it does not have pleasurable effects, or correcting the underlying problem.

KEY TERMS, CONCEPTS, AND NAMES

In reviewing and testing yourself on what you have learned from this chapter, you
should be able to identify and discuss each of the following:

alcohol	dose-dependent	opiate antagonist
amphetamine psychoses	endorphins	opiates
amphetamines	flashbacks	opium
barbiturates	hallucinogens	persistent type of alcoholism
benzodiazepines	hashish	psilocybin
binge type of alcoholism	hash oil	psychoactive drugs
caffeine	heroin	self-medication hypothesis
cannabinoids	LSD (lysergic acid)	stimulants
cannabis	marijuana	substance abuse
cocaine	mescaline	substance dependence
cocaine hydrochloride	methadone	substance-induced psychotic disorder
codeine	methylxanthines	tolerance
cross-tolerance	morphine	toxic psychosis
dependence	narcotics	withdrawal
depressants	nicotine	

Notes:

Chapter 19
Sexual Disorders

•OUTLINE•

Ken is worried about his sex life—or more accurately, his lack of sex life. There are a lot of good-looking women around and a couple have "put a move on him," but he just isn't interested in sex. Good friendships with women are fine, but unlike most of the other guys his age, he has little or no sexual desire. He knows he is not gay, but he worries about his lack of interest in women. Ken suffers from a *sexual dysfunction* known as a *desire disorder*.

Alice is a 33-year-old woman who has always enjoyed sex. The problem is that during intercourse, she cannot reach orgasm, regardless of how long the sexual activity is maintained. She is confused because she can achieve orgasm easily through masturbation. Alice does not blame her sexual partners and instead assumes that she has some "unconscious problem" about men. This is beginning to interfere with her relationships. Alice suffers from a very common and easily treated sexual dysfunction known as a *secondary orgasm disorder*.

Margaret and her husband love each other very much and would not think of hurting each other. However, for Margaret to become sexually aroused, it is necessary for her husband to slap her face and twist her arm behind her back until it hurts. He does not like doing it, but Margaret wants him to do it, and it is the only way she can become aroused, so they have gone through this ritual every time they have had sex for the past 8 years. Margaret suffers from *sexual masochism*.

Carl has had sexual relationships with a couple of women, but his favorite way of achieving sexual gratification is to dress in women's clothing and then masturbate. Wearing the women's clothing is very exciting for him, and he has three different outfits hidden in the bottom drawer of his dresser. This is an example of *transvestic fetishism*.

As long as Daniel can remember, he has wanted to be a girl. As a child, he preferred to play with girls, and when they played house, he wanted to be the mother. When the other boys in the neighborhood called him a sissy, he didn't care; he thought boys were disgusting. In adolescence, Daniel tried to "become a man," but it just didn't "feel right." Later he drifted back and forth across the sex-role line. He would try to play the traditional male role in public, but in private or with close friends, he took the role of a woman and was more comfortable. Now age 30, he says he is tired of "fighting the battle of who I am" and is being considered for sex reassignment surgery. He says, "On the outside I may have a penis, but inside I am a woman, and that is who I like being, so let's change the outside." Daniel has a *gender identity disorder*.

In this chapter, we will consider three types of disorders that are associated with sex. The first type is known as *sexual dysfunctions*. These disorders involve insufficient sexual *desire*, insufficient sexual *arousal*, and problems with *orgasm*. These deserve careful attention because they are very widespread and often misunderstood. The second type, labeled *paraphilias*, includes disorders in which individuals achieve sexual arousal through *inappropriate means*. For example, persons may gain sexual pleasure from exposing their genitals to others, dressing in the clothes of the opposite sex, or hurting their sexual partners. The third type is called the *gender identity disorder*. It revolves around *discomfort with one's physiologically determined sex*. For example, a male may believe that he would be more comfortable if he were a woman, or he may believe that he actually is a woman. The types of disorders are summarized in Table 19.1.

When discussing sexual disorders, we must distinguish between *illegal* and *abnormal* behaviors. Illegal behaviors are not necessarily abnormal, and vice versa. For example, oral sex is illegal in many states, but it is not defined as abnormal in DSM-IV. In contrast, wearing clothes of the opposite sex to gain sexual pleasure is not illegal, but it is defined as abnormal. In this chapter, we will focus on the abnormal behaviors.

It should also be noted that *homosexuality is not considered an abnormal behavior.* Homosexuality was identified as a disorder in the first two editions of the *Diagnostic and Statistical Manual*, and in the third edition it was considered a disorder only if it made the individual anxious or uncomfortable ("ego-dystonic homosexuality"). However, because of changes in social norms and strong political pressures, when DSM-III-R was published in 1987, homosexuality was not listed as a disorder.

Sexual disorders are usually not as debilitating as anxiety, depression, and schizophrenia, and therefore they are often seen as less serious for the individual involved. However, these disorders can be very disruptive because of the impact they can have on other people. This is particularly true when the disorders involve behaviors such as rape, sadism, or the sexual abuse of children. Because sexual disorders are very prevalent in our society and because some of them can pose a danger, it is important that we give them careful consideration.

• Sexual Dysfunctions

Sexual dysfunctions involve the *absence or failure of the sexual response at some point during the sexual response cycle.* The sexual response cycle can be divided into four phases:

1. The **appetitive phase**, in which the individual has fantasies about sexual activity and develops a desire for sexual activities
2. The **excitement phase**, which consists of subjective sexual pleasure and physiological changes (e.g., erection for males and vaginal lubrication for females)
3. The **orgasm phase**, which involves a peaking of subjective sexual pleasure with heightened physiological changes (e.g., ejaculation for the male and contraction of the wall of the vagina for females)
4. The **resolution phase**, which consists of a sense of general relaxation and well-being and a low level of physiological arousal; during this phase, males temporarily cannot respond with another erection or orgasm, but females can respond almost immediately to additional stimulation

Three dysfunction disorders have been identified. Each is associated with a different phase of the sexual response cycle.

1. The *desire disorder* is associated with the appetitive phase and involves a lack of sexual desire.
2. The *arousal disorder* is associated with the excitement phase and involves insufficient physiological arousal despite the presence of desire.
3. The *orgasm disorder* is associated with the orgasm phase and involves either failure to achieve an orgasm despite the presence of desire and arousal or premature orgasm.

TABLE 19.1 THERE ARE THREE TYPES OF SEXUAL DISORDERS

SEXUAL DYSFUNCTIONS	PARAPHILIAS	GENDER IDENTITY DISORDER
Desire disorder	Exhibitionism	Gender identity disorder
Arousal disorder	Fetishism	
Orgasm disorder	Transvestic fetishism	
	Frotteurism	
	Pedophilia	
	Sexual masochism	
	Sexual sadism	
	Voyeurism	

DESIRE DISORDERS

Desire disorders involve a *deficiency or lack of desire* for sexual activity. Individuals with desire disorders lack the sexual urge, have few sexual fantasies, and may therefore not seek sexual stimulation. However, if sexually stimulated, they can become sexually aroused. A summary of numerous surveys suggests that 1% to 15% of males and 1% to 35% of females suffer from desire disorders (Nathan, 1986).

Individuals differ greatly in terms of the degree to which they are upset by desire disorders. Some individuals are not upset by them; these individuals simply do not miss the sexual activities in which they are not interested. Others are very upset because they want the sexual pleasure they see portrayed on television and in movies, books, and commercials. Furthermore, for some individuals, the lack of desire is inconsistent with their cultural role (e.g., the "macho" male or the female "sex symbol"), and they become concerned about how they are perceived by others. In those cases, desire disorders can lead to depression because the individuals think they are missing out on something, or the disorders can lead to anxiety because the individuals think they are not measuring up. Finally, lack of sexual desire can cause depression and anxiety for the individuals' partners, who may assume that the lack of

Individuals differ greatly in terms of the degree to which they are upset by desire disorders. Al and Peg Bundy from television's Married with Children *make their lack of desire for each other a source of frequent jokes.*

desire is a reflection on them and their sexual attractiveness.

Psychological Explanations and Treatments

Psychological explanations for desire disorders generally fall into one of three categories. The first of these involves the *defensive suppression* of desire. For example, psychodynamic theorists have suggested that individuals with desire disorders have not adequately resolved their incestuous wishes for their mothers or fathers (Oedipal and Electra attractions) and that by suppressing their desires, they can avoid the forbidden attraction. It may also be that during childhood, they learned to equate sex with sin or to see sex as dirty; therefore their interest in sex is suppressed or repressed.

A second type of explanation revolves around the effects of *stress*. Proponents of this explanation suggest that individuals who are under stress must focus their attention and energy on the problem of coping with the stress, leaving little attention or energy available for sex.

The third explanation is *interpersonal* and revolves around the possibility that desire disorders may reflect a way of manipulating, punishing, or instilling feelings of inadequacy in one's partner. The notion is that the individual who wants to make the partner feel bad (as punishment for something) may develop desire disorders and then blame the lack of desire on the partner, thereby undermining the partner's feelings of worth and attractiveness.

Psychotherapy is a popular technique for treating desire disorders, but relatively little controlled research has been reported concerning its effectiveness. In one study, the investigators collected data from both members of 128 couples who participated in psychotherapy because one member of the couple had a desire disorder (Schover & Lo Piccolo, 1982). The couples were seen for at least 15 weekly sessions, and therapy consisted of "a combination of behavioral, cognitive-behavioral, Gestalt, and psychodynamic interventions to supplement the usual sex therapy format" (p. 182), which involved education and guided practice in sexual activities. The results were generally positive and indicated that after treatment, the clients reported increases in the frequency of intercourse and in overall sexual satisfaction. That was the case for both members of the couple regardless of which suffered from the desire disorder. Results related to increases in intercourse for cases in which the male suffered from a desire disorder are presented in Figure 19.1.

These results are encouraging, but three qualifications should be noted. First, because there was no placebo control condition against which to compare the responses of the treated clients, we cannot be sure whether it was the therapy per se or the positive expectations about effects that resulted in the improve-

FIGURE 19.1   PSYCHOTHERAPY WAS ASSOCIATED WITH INCREASED FREQUENCY OF INTERCOURSE AND SEXUAL SATISFACTION.

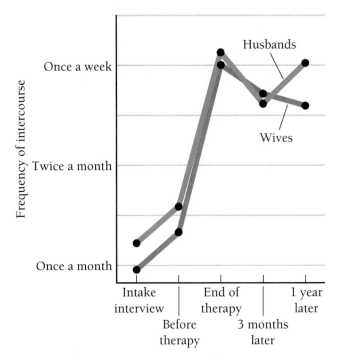

Source: Adapted from Schover and Lo Piccolo (1982), pp. 188–189, figs. 2 and 3.

ments. In that regard, it is interesting to note that the couples began reporting improvements *even before therapy began* (see changes between "Intake interview" and "Before therapy" in Figure 19.1). Second, even if the treatment was effective, in this investigation, there is no way to determine what component of the therapy was responsible for the effects. It might have been psychological insights, improvements in communication, new sexual techniques, or any of a number of other possibilities. Third, the 1-year follow-up results were based on fewer than one-third of the clients who entered the program, and it may be that clients who did not benefit did not participate in the follow-up sessions. If that is the case, the results may be biased in the positive direction. Overall, it appears that some individuals who participate in psychotherapy for desire disorders report improvements, but it is not clear how many people improve or what it is about the treatment that results in the improvement.

Physiological Explanations and Treatments

The physiological explanation for desire disorders is based on *hormone imbalances,* and treatment revolves around readjusting the balances. Before discussing this explanation and treatment, it will be helpful to describe briefly the physiological process responsible for normal desire.

The process begins in the hypothalamus, an area of the brain that is responsible for arousal in general. When the hypothalamus in a male is stimulated by some sex-related stimulus (e.g., a visual image, a touch, a scent), it secretes a **releasing hormone** that stimulates the pituitary gland, which in turn secretes hormones known as **gonadotropins** (gō-NAD-uh-TRŌ-pinz). (*Gonad* refers to any reproductive gland, such as testes or ovaries, and *tropin* means "alter or influence.") As the name implies, the gonadotropins stimulate the male's testes, which then produce **testosterone** (tes-TOS-tuh-rōn), the hormone responsible for the arousal of desire. Testosterone results in desire, but it also causes the hypothalamus to *reduce* the production of the releasing hormone that started the process. In other words, there is a negative feedback loop in the system so that the level of testosterone is maintained within a narrow range. If that were not the case, once stimulated, the system would run unchecked. The chemical process responsible for arousal in men is illustrated in Figure 19.2.

FIGURE 19.2   HORMONES INFLUENCE SEXUAL DESIRE IN MALES.

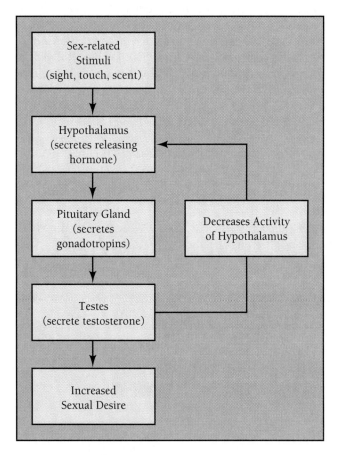

Hormones also influence sexual desire in women, but the process is more complex due to the involvement of other hormones and fluctuations associated with the menstrual cycle.

The chain of events is similar in a woman, but it is considerably more complex because the production of hormones varies greatly during a woman's monthly cycle and because additional hormones are involved. In general, however, in the woman, the gonadotropic hormones stimulate the ovaries to produce **proges-terone** (prō-JES-tuh-rōn). That hormone contributes to desire, and like testosterone in the male, it is involved in a negative feedback loop that reduces hypothalamic production of the releasing hormone that started the process.

When considering this system, it is important to recognize that it involves a number of different parts (hypothalamus, pituitary gland, sex organs) as well as a variety of hormones (releasing, gonadotropin, testosterone or progesterone), and all of the components must operate within narrow tolerances if the system is to work effectively. Any of the components of the system can be thrown off by spontaneous fluctuations, damage, disease, or external factors. In other words, the system is complex, there are numerous opportunities for malfunction, and any malfunction can result in altered sexual desire. Scientists are only now unraveling the subtleties of the sex hormone system.

Support for the notion that hormone imbalances can result in desire disorders comes from two sets of research results. First, there is ample evidence that *low levels of the sex hormones are associated with low sexual desire* (e.g., Bancroft, 1984a, 1984b; Lo Piccolo, 1983). For example, in one investigation, the sexual responses

FIGURE 19.3   MEN WITH LOW LEVELS OF TESTOSTERONE SHOWED LOW DESIRE RESPONSES TO FANTASY BUT NORMAL AROUSAL RESPONSES TO STIMULATION BY FILMS.

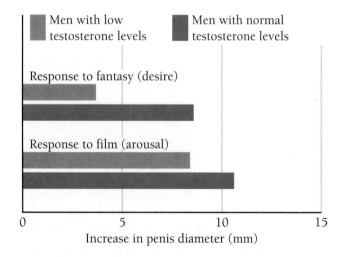

Source: Adapted from Bancroft (1984a), p. 6, fig. 2.

FIGURE 19.4   TESTOSTERONE REPLACEMENT THERAPY INCREASED MEN'S DESIRE RESPONSES (ERECTIONS) TO FANTASY.

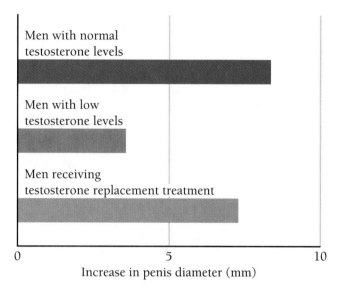

Source: Adapted from Bancroft (1984a), p. 6, fig. 2.

(erections) of men with normal or low levels of testosterone were compared when the men engaged in erotic fantasy and when they were exposed to an erotic film (Bancroft, 1984a). (Men with low levels of testosterone are described as *hypogonadal.*) The results of this investigation indicated that hypogonadal men showed much lower sexual arousal in response to fantasy, but only slightly lower sexual arousal when stimulated by the erotic film. In other words, the males with low hormone levels showed *less sexual desire,* but *unimpaired physical response to stimulation.* These results are presented in Figure 19.3.

Related to the findings linking lower hormone levels to lower desire is the finding that as men grow older and their levels of testosterone decline, they show lowered sexual desire and arousal (Schiavi et al., 1990). Once stimulated and aroused, the men report normal levels of enjoyment and satisfaction.

The second set of research findings supporting the hormone explanation for desire disorders comes from data indicating that *increasing the levels of the sex hormones increases sexual desire* (e.g., Bancroft, 1984a; Bancroft & Wu, 1983; Davidson, 1984; Davidson et al., 1979; Kwan et al., 1983). For example, in one investigation, hypogonadal males either were or were not injected with testosterone, after which their responses to sexual fantasy and erotic films were assessed (Bancroft, 1984a). The results of this investigation are presented in Figure 19.4. Inspection of the data indicates that the hypogonadal males who were given the testosterone showed higher levels of arousal while fantasizing about sex than the hypogonadal males who were not given the testosterone. In fact, the males who were given the testosterone showed a level of arousal during fantasy that was almost as high as that of normal males.

It should be noted that the link between low levels of hormones and desire disorders has been found in men but not in women. For example, in one study the levels of reproductive hormones (testosterone, estradiol, progesterone, prolactin, and luteinizing hormone) were measured every 4 days over the menstrual cycle in women who did or did not suffer from desire disorders, but no differences in hormone levels were found (Schreiner-Engel et al., 1989).

Now that we have established that low levels of sex hormones are related to low levels of sexual desire, at least in men, we must go on to examine possible causes for the low levels of sex hormones. Hormone levels can be influenced by many factors such as disease, age, and genetic background, but external influences are of most interest here. For many years, zoologists have known that subtle alterations in weather and amount of light can cause changes in the levels of gonadotropins produced in sheep, goats, and deer and that those changes in turn influence the animals' desire and mating behavior. In humans, turning the lights down low may not increase hormone levels, but recent evidence has clearly documented that *psychological stress can decrease hormone levels*. For example, when men who were under normal levels of stress were compared to men who were under high levels of stress during combat training or combat in Vietnam, it was found that the men under stress produced lower levels of testosterone (Rose et al., 1969). These findings are presented in Figure 19.5.

From the findings reported in this discussion, it is clear that physiological factors play an important role in determining sexual desire in humans. However, it is also clear that psychological factors can influence the physiological factors. In those cases the causal chain is as follows: Psychological stress leads to physiological changes, and then physiological changes lead to psychological symptoms.

In approaching the treatment of arousal disorders, it is essential to determine whether the disorder stemmed from a physiological problem (disease) or a psychological problem (stress). If the low levels of testosterone are due to low levels of production because of a physiological problem, then treatment may simply involve administering testosterone to bring his level up to normal, a procedure called **testosterone replacement therapy**. This procedure can be very effective. For example, the results reported in Figure 19.4 indicated that when hypogonadal men were administered testosterone, their levels of sexual arousal were almost as high as those of normal men.

In contrast, if the low levels of testosterone are due to the effects of stress, treatment can be directed at reducing stress. An interesting illustration of the effects of stress reduction on testosterone levels is provided by a study of men in officer candidate school (Kreuz et al., 1972). The testosterone levels of these men were measured during the first phase of the training, when stress was very high, and then again during the second phase of the training, when the men were "over the hump" and stress levels were greatly reduced. The levels of testosterone during the first and second phases of training for each of the men are presented in Figure 19.6 (p. 480). Inspection of those data indicate that testosterone levels went up when stress went down.

AROUSAL DISORDERS

Individuals with **arousal disorders** desire and participate in sexual activity, but once the activity is initiated, they *cannot achieve an adequate level of physiological arousal or cannot maintain the necessary level of arousal.* In males, the major symptom is the failure to achieve or maintain a complete erection. The prevalence of arousal disorders is estimated to be 10% to 20% in males, but we do not have sufficient data to estimate the prevalence in women (Nathan, 1986). Case Study 19.1 (p. 481) is an excerpt from an interview with a young man who came to a clinic because of an arousal disorder.

Diagnostic Procedures and Problems

Arousal disorders can stem from either psychological or physiological causes. One approach to determining

FIGURE 19.5 MEN UNDER STRESS SHOWED LOWER LEVELS OF TESTOSTERONE THAN MEN NOT UNDER STRESS.

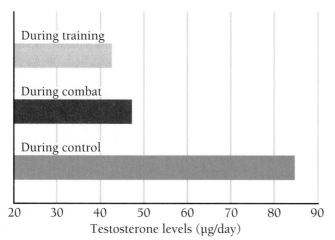

Source: Adapted from Rose et al. (1969), p. 425, fig. 3.

FIGURE 19.6   DECREASES IN STRESS WERE
ASSOCIATED WITH INCREASES IN
TESTOSTERONE.

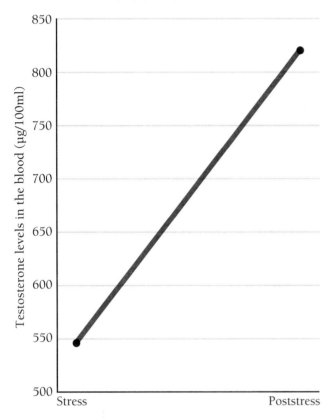

Source: Data from Kreuz et al. (1972), p. 480, tab. 1.

the cause in a particular case is to determine whether or not the individual is physiologically capable of arousal (Conte, 1986). A widely used technique for determining whether a male is capable of sexual arousal involves the measurement of **nocturnal penile tumescence** (tyoo-MES-ins). *Tumescence* refers to readiness for sexual activity (i.e., erection), and in physiologically normal males, this occurs occasionally during periods of rapid-eye-movement (REM) sleep. If the individual has erections during sleep, it can be assumed that he is physiologically capable of sexual arousal and that his problems in achieving or maintaining arousal while awake must be due to psychological factors.

Nocturnal penile tumescence is measured by placing a cuff on the penis. If an erection occurs, the cuff expands, breaking a series of small seals. In the morning, the seals can be checked to determine whether an erection occurred (Barlow, 1977; Karacan, 1982; Kaya et al., 1979).

Psychological Explanations and Treatments

There is widespread agreement that *anxiety* is the major psychological cause of arousal disorders. The notion is that anxiety over inadequacy prevents arousal or causes a premature drop in arousal (Barlow, 1977, 1986; Kaplan, 1981; Masters & Johnson, 1970; Wolpe, 1958). The question is, what process links anxiety to reduced arousal? In answering that question, it is important to recognize that anxiety is made up of two components, a cognitive component consisting of thoughts such as worry about failure and a physiological component consisting of increased somatic arousal such as increased heart rate and blood pressure. The cognitive component of anxiety is thought to be important for understanding arousal disorders because it leads to *distraction*, and distraction can in turn lead to a reduction of sexual arousal.

The role of distraction in reducing sexual arousal has been demonstrated in a variety of ways (Cerny, 1978; Geer & Fuhr, 1976; Henson & Rubin, 1971; Laws & Rubin, 1969). For example, it has been shown that individuals can voluntarily suppress sexual arousal while watching erotic films if they shift their attention to something else (i.e., watch the film but think about something else). Also, involuntary reductions in sexual arousal occur when subjects hear erotic material in one ear but distracting material (e.g., math problems) in the other ear.

The distracting thoughts that are most common among individuals with arousal disorders involve concerns about sexual performance and failure. In other words, it is assumed that problems with arousal are due to the fact that individuals worry about their sexual performance, those thoughts distract them, and then the distraction reduces arousal.

It is also worth noting that individuals with arousal disorders underestimate their levels of sexual arousal. That was demonstrated in an investigation in which males estimated their levels of sexual arousal while their actual levels of arousal were measured in terms of penile erection (Sakheim et al., 1984). The results indicated that males with psychologically based arousal disorders underestimated their arousal more than normal males or even males with physiologically based arousal disorders. Comparable results have been reported for females (Morokoff & Heinman, 1980). The tendency for individuals with arousal disorders to underestimate their arousal levels is important because their erroneous assumptions about their underarousal could contribute to their concerns and lead to additional distraction.

Treatment for psychologically based arousal disorders revolves around attempts to reduce anxiety by in-

Case Study 19.1

INTERVIEW WITH A MAN COMPLAINING OF AN AROUSAL DISORDER

The client was a handsome 34-year-old man. The early part of the interview did not offer any evidence of adjustment problems, and it was apparent that the client had an active and mature social life. The following discussion ensued when the interviewer turned the conversation to the problem that had brought the client to the clinic.

Client: Well, the problem is that— Well, I just have a hard time getting an erection when I get physically involved with a woman. It's not that I don't want sex—I really do. But somehow when we get right down to it . . . when the time comes to begin making love, I can't get an erection. I'm just limp.

Interviewer: Hmmm. Can you tell me a little more about it? Can you describe a typical situation in which you have a problem?

Client: (*pause*) Well, let's say I've gone out with a woman for a while and it comes to the point where one night things are getting physical. Everything goes great—I mean, I'm aroused and excited—and she is too, but then I just can't seem to go further. It's not that I don't stay excited; I'm really excited and enjoying what we're doing, but when it gets to the point at which I should have a good erection, it doesn't come.

Interviewer: Have you ever had an erection? For example, do you ever wake up in the morning with an erection, or can you get an erection with masturbation?

Client: Oh, yeah, I frequently wake up with an erection—that's normal—and I can masturbate. Sometimes it takes me a little while to get started, but I always get there.

Interviewer: How about with a woman? Do you ever get an erection with a woman?

Client: Yes. Sometimes when we just get started and we're just necking I'll get an erection for a while and then I think, "Great, this time we're going to make it," but then I lose it and can't get it back. It's really annoying.

Interviewer: Have you ever completed intercourse with a woman?

Client: Oh, sure. It didn't used to be a problem, but lately it just hasn't been working. It's a relatively recent problem. (*pause*) It gets kind of embarrassing. I get to a high point, and then I just can't go further. I usually hide what's happening—or not happening—and make up some excuse to, well, to bring things to an end. (*pause*) Not long ago, I dated a woman who caught on to what was going on, but she was pretty relaxed about the whole thing. She just laughed and said, "Don't worry. We'll get around it," and we just kept making out. She kept playing with me and eventually I came around, at least for a while. She seemed to know what she was doing.

Interviewer: Has anything changed for you that might be associated with the problem? Have you had any physical or psychological problems?

Client: (*sighs*) No, nothing that I can think of. When the problem started, I did a little reading about it. The articles I read said that anxiety was the problem and that the trick was not to let yourself get distracted by upsetting thoughts, so I worked real hard to concentrate my attention on what I was doing, how much I enjoyed the woman's body, and I tried not to think about the problem. (*sighs*) Great idea but tough to pull off. The problem is always there. Forcing yourself to concentrate on what you are doing is . . . well, by working to avoid the problem, you admit that there is a problem, and it doesn't seem to work for me. The work of concentrating is almost enough to wreck my arousal. (*sighs*) It's a mess—and it's frustrating as hell.

---

stilling more confidence in the client, and thereby reducing the cognitions that interfere with sexual arousal (Lo Piccolo & Stock, 1986). Cognitive therapists might also teach the client to focus on the positive aspects of sex and in so doing reduce distraction. Therapists and clients usually report success with these techniques, but so far we have little adequately controlled research to document the effectiveness of these approaches.

Physiological Explanations and Treatments

It was once assumed that over 90% of erectile failures were due to psychological problems, but more recent research indicates that as many as 50% or 60% of the problems may actually be due to various organic conditions (Fisher et al., 1979; Kaya et al., 1979).

Before discussing the physiological explanations for arousal disorders, a brief comment should be made concerning the physiology of sexual arousal. Sexual arousal can be initiated either in the brain by sexual thoughts and desires or in the genital area by stimulation of the sex organs and the area around them. In both cases, nerve impulses are sent to the lower portion (sacral section) of the spinal cord. From there, parasympathetic nerve impulses are sent to the male's penis or to the female's clitoris. (The clitoris is the major site of arousal for the female, and it will be described and discussed in greater detail later when we consider orgasm disorders.) The parasympathetic impulses cause a dilation of the **erectile tissues** in those organs. Erectile tissues consist of blood channels that are normally empty, but when stimulated, they dilate tremendously and fill with blood. Considerable pressure builds up in erectile tissues because blood flow out is restricted. Dilation and filling of the erectile tissues in the penis causes it to become enlarged and erect. In the female, the dilation and filling of erectile tissues results in a swelling and firming of the clitoris. For the female, the parasympathetic impulses also cause the secretion of mucus just inside the vaginal opening.

A number of physiological problems can reduce sexual arousal. For example, *neurological damage* to the hypothalamus, spinal cord, or connecting nerve pathways could result in the reduction or absence of the nerve stimulation that causes changes in blood flow. Unfortunately, because damage to the central nervous system is irreversible, arousal disorders due to nerve damage are usually permanent.

Reduced arousal can also stem from *blockage of the arteries* that supply blood to the penis or clitoris. If those arteries are blocked, the filling of the erectile tissues will be limited, and therefore arousal will be limited. This problem is more pronounced in men, probably because during midlife, men are more prone to the development of atherosclerosis (see Chapter 17). When the disorder is due to artery blockage, treatment is focused on enhancing blood supply, but in some cases a prosthetic device may be implanted in the penis (Metz & Mathiesen, 1979; Michal et al., 1977). The prosthetic device consists of an inflatable balloon that is implanted in the penis and connected to a pump. When an erection is desired, the pump is turned on, the balloon is inflated, and the penis becomes erect.

Finally, anxiety can lead to physiological effects that can reduce sexual arousal. Earlier it was pointed out that anxiety has both cognitive and physiological components and that the cognitive component reduces arousal because it leads to distraction. However, the physiological component of anxiety can also influence arousal because anxiety is associated with increased activity of the *sympathetic* branch of the autonomic nervous system. This is important because sexual arousal is associated with *parasympathetic* activity, and the sympathetic and parasympathetic are *antagonistic* (competing) reactions that lead to different types of activity. Most important, the parasympathetic activity leads to the *dilation* and filling of the peripheral and erectile tissues that is crucial to sexual arousal, but the sympathetic activity leads to *constriction* of these tissues and consequently to a drop in sexual arousal. Because sympathetic activity initially dominates parasympathetic activity, the sympathetic activity

associated with anxiety can overwhelm the parasympathetic activity and reduce or eliminate sexual arousal. In this case, a physiological factor (anxiety) causes a change in a physiological factor (reduced parasympathetic activity), which produces the arousal disorder.

The effects of chronic and acute stress (anxiety) on sexual arousal in males was demonstrated in a study of employed and unemployed men (Morokoff et al., 1987). In this study, it was assumed that unemployed men were under chronic stress and that employed men were not under stress. To manipulate acute stress, half of the men in each group were told that at the end of the laboratory session, they would be asked to give a short talk about their sexual behavior to a group of students. The men in the no-acute-stress condition were not led to believe that they would have to talk about their sexual behavior. During the laboratory session, the men watched an erotic film of a heterosexual couple making love, and while they watched the film, their sexual arousal was measured by assessing changes in penis diameter (erection). The results indicated that among men who were under chronic stress, the addition of the acute stress (expecting to talk about sex with students) resulted in a lower level of arousal in response to erotic stimulation than in other men. In other words, the combination of chronic and acute stress resulted in a reduction in arousal that might be interpreted as an arousal disorder.

ORGASM DISORDERS

Individuals with **orgasm disorders** desire and participate in sexual activity, become aroused, and maintain the arousal, but *they do not experience an orgasm or, in the case of males, they experience orgasm too soon.* Orgasm disorders pose problems because they deprive individuals of the pleasure they seek; even more important, they lead to feelings of inadequacy. Indeed, we used to refer to individuals who did not experience orgasm as sexually "inadequate" or "frigid." Those pejorative labels have been abandoned, but it is still common to talk about the "failure to achieve" orgasm, and that phrase reflects an underlying negative evaluation. Orgasm disorders occur in both men and women but are more common in women.

Explanations and Treatments of Orgasm Disorders in Women

In women, a distinction is made between the **primary orgasm disorder**, in which the woman has never experienced an orgasm through any means, and the **secondary orgasm disorder**, in which the woman can experience orgasm during masturbation but not during sexual intercourse. Together, these problems affect between 5% and 30% of women.

Traditionally, orgasm disorders in women have been explained in terms of anxieties and unconscious conflicts associated with sex. For example, it was assumed that a woman who did not experience orgasm was unable to "let go" sexually. The resistance was thought to be rooted in childhood experiences that led women to believe that sex was dirty or harmful. If women with orgasm disorders were not aware of such thoughts, it was assumed that they had *unconscious conflicts* about sexuality, probably revolving around unresolved attractions for their fathers or mothers.

The secondary orgasm disorder, in which women can experience orgasm with masturbation but not with intercourse, was sometimes explained by suggesting that the women were *fixated* at an early stage of psychosexual development. The notion was that we go through a number of psychosexual stages, and masturbation is associated with an earlier stage than intercourse. Therefore, it was assumed that the woman with a secondary orgasm disorder had not progressed far enough in her psychosexual development to experience orgasm with intercourse. Alternatively, it was suggested that a psychosocial crisis forced the woman to *regress* to an earlier stage of development at which orgasm may not have been an appropriate response (Fagan et al., 1986).

For many years, the concepts of anxiety, fixation, and regression were widely used to explain orgasm disorders, but the popularity of these explanations has waned since the late 1960s. That decline occurred not only because the explanations lacked empirical support and did not lead to effective treatment, but also because a more contemporary and parsimonious explanation was developed that did lead to effective treatment. It is now widely believed that many orgasm disorders are due to the fact that women or their sexual partners *simply do not know what should be done to achieve maximal stimulation*, or if they do know what should be done, *they do not do it*. In other words, failure to achieve orgasm may be due to lack of knowledge or inadequate sexual technique rather than underlying conflicts. Support for this explanation comes from the finding that teaching women more about their bodies and educating sexual partners about what type of stimulation is most arousing is a very effective method for overcoming orgasm disorders. To understand the problems that women may encounter in achieving an orgasm, it will be helpful to discuss briefly how stimulation does and does not occur during intercourse.

As the penis moves in the vagina during intercourse, the friction created by the penis rubbing against the walls of the vagina stimulates the sensitive penis, thereby maintaining the male's arousal and leading to his orgasm. In contrast, the movement of the penis in the vagina does not result in much direct sexual stimulation for the woman because the first two-thirds of the vagina has relatively few nerve endings and hence is not particularly sensitive to stimulation. Stated simply, intercourse is maximally effective for the attainment of the male's orgasm but is not particularly effective for achieving that goal for women. (In that regard, it is interesting to note that men and women require about the same amount of time to achieve orgasm through masturbation, but during intercourse, men experience orgasm much faster than women; Offir, 1982.)

It should be noted that some investigators believe that some women have a short, sexually sensitive area just inside the vagina known as the **G spot**, and stimulation of that area may lead to arousal and orgasm (Addiego et al., 1981; Alzate & Hoch, 1986; Goldberg et al., 1983; Ladas et al., 1982; Perry & Whipple, 1981). However, the existence of the G spot is not well documented, and its importance is a matter of some controversy.

The fact that the vagina is not particularly sensitive does not mean that intercourse is not pleasurable and cannot result in orgasm for the woman. Instead, the pleasure, arousal, and orgasm experienced by women during intercourse appear to be due primarily to the stimulation of the clitoris.

The **clitoris** (KLIT-uh-ris) is a pea-sized body located a small distance above the vaginal opening (see Figure 19.7 on p. 484). The clitoris is normally covered by a hood (a small flap of skin). Gently pulling the hood back reveals its tip, called the **glans** (like its counterpart on the penis). In contrast to the vagina, the clitoris contains many nerve endings (probably more than the larger penis), and it is exceptionally sensitive to stimulation. In fact, it is so sensitive that some women do not want it touched directly and prefer that it be stimulated indirectly by caressing the area around it, which serves to move the hood and thereby stimulate the glans.

Because the clitoris is easily manipulated and its manipulation results in sexual arousal, the clitoris plays an important role in achieving orgasm through masturbation. The clitoris also plays an important role in sexual arousal and orgasm during intercourse because as the penis moves in and out of the vagina, it causes the tissues around the vaginal opening to move, and that movement causes the hood over the clitoral glans to move, stimulating the glans and thereby providing pleasurable sensations and orgasm.

The clitoris is actually the end of the **clitoral shaft**, which extends back into the body and then di-

FIGURE 19.7   THE CLITORIS IS MADE UP OF ERECTILE TISSUE AND IS
THE PRIMARY AREA OF SEXUAL STIMULATION FOR
MOST WOMEN.

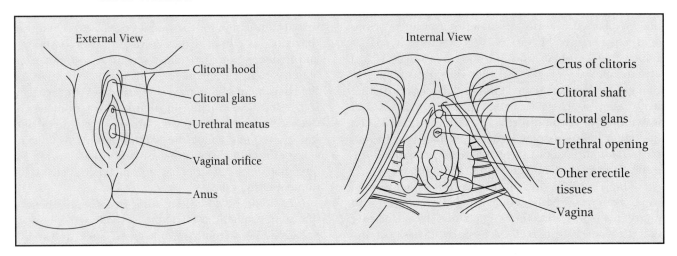

vides into two leglike structures (see Figure 19.7). The clitoral shaft contains erectile tissue like that in the penis, and during sexual excitement, the erectile tissue of the clitoris fills with blood, causing a swelling such that the clitoral shaft doubles or triples in size. The pressure caused by the increase in size results in greater sensitivity, which contributes to increased arousal. Because of the size and importance of the underlying structures, the tiny clitoris and glans have been referred to as the tip of an "erogenous iceberg."

Treatment for the primary orgasm disorder using the education or training approach can entail a number of steps. First, it may be necessary for the woman to learn more about her body and what gives her pleasure. This may involve sitting down with a mirror and visually exploring her body. That is followed by gentle touching, fondling, or massaging in the genital area to discover where and what type of stimulation is most effective for achieving sexual arousal. Such exploration and self-stimulation may have been avoided or forbidden by more traditional attitudes toward personal development and sexuality. In most cases, manual stimulation is sufficient to achieve arousal and orgasm, but sometimes a vibrator will be used as an adjunct. Essentially, the woman learns to achieve orgasm through masturbation. (This would not be necessary in the case of the secondary orgasm disorder, in which the woman can already achieve orgasm through masturbation.)

The next phase involves having the woman communicate to her partner what it is that arouses her. Because it is sometimes difficult to talk about those things, some therapists suggest that the woman take her partner's hand and gently guide him and show him the kind of stimulation she wants. Once the cou-

ple is comfortable with this form of genital stimulation, it is suggested that they attempt intercourse. Many therapists suggest that the first intercourse should be done with the woman on top because that way she has the major responsibility for movement and can better control the nature of the stimulation. Once orgasm has been achieved in this position, the couple is encouraged to experiment with other positions.

Education, self-exploration, self-stimulation, communication with the partner, and practice are all important steps in this therapy. However, couples must also develop attitudes of self-acceptance and responsibility for their own sexual pleasure. The woman must realize that *sex is not something that just happens* or is *done to her* but rather something in which she *actively participates* and *shares control* with her partner. Sometimes this type of therapy will be combined with coun-

Education is an important part of therapy for sexual dysfunctions.

seling designed to reduce interpersonal anxiety or tension, thereby facilitating communication and mutual acceptance.

This approach to the treatment of orgasm disorders is very effective, with success rates usually reported to be greater than 75% (see reviews by Marks, 1981; Master & Johnson, 1970; Offir, 1982). The proportion of women with the primary orgasm disorder who are subsequently able to experience an orgasm with masturbation may be as high as 95%.

It should not be concluded that overcoming an orgasm disorder is always a strictly mechanical or educational process. There is no doubt that anxiety about sex or interpersonal tensions with her partner can interfere with the woman's arousal and enjoyment of sex and can reduce the likelihood of an orgasm. However, it now seems that anxiety is less important than it was once thought to be, and in many cases, anxiety and interpersonal tension may be the *result* of problems with sex rather than their cause. For example, a woman who feels that her partner does not understand or is not sensitive to her needs may become tense or resentful in her sexual relationship, and that may disrupt her personal relationship with her partner. That disruption will interfere with communication and reduce the likelihood that the sexual problem will be resolved, and a vicious cycle may develop. In such cases, attention must sometimes be given to personal and interpersonal problems as well as education and technique.

Recently, I saw a greeting card that seems to reflect the more assertive and healthier approach that is being taken by women with regard to sex. On the front was a drawing of a woman saying, "Open this card." Inside it said, "Great, now that I know you can follow instructions, wanna play with my bod?"

Explanations and Treatments of Orgasm Disorders in Men

Only about 5% of males are unable to achieve orgasm (Nathan, 1986), and consequently relatively little attention has been given to this problem. In contrast, an orgasm disorder that occurs in about 35% of males is **premature ejaculation**. Unlike other orgasm disorders, which involve the failure to achieve orgasm, premature ejaculation involves reaching orgasm *too soon*. Specifically, ejaculation occurs after only minimal stimulation, meaning that the individual has an orgasm before he wishes it and before his partner has been sufficiently stimulated and satisfied.

Numerous explanations have been offered to account for premature ejaculation. For example, it has been attributed to (a) fear of women and what a woman might do during prolonged intercourse (e.g., castration; Schmidt & Cowie, 1983); (b) hostility on the part of the male, who is depriving the female of the pleasure of sex by terminating the act early (Stanley, 1981); (c) high levels of anxiety that contribute to heightened arousal; (d) the inability to perceive arousal accurately, making it impossible to exercise control (Kaplan, 1981); (e) abstinence from sexual activity, which results in higher arousal (Spiess et al., 1984); (f) hypersensitivity of the penis, leading to excessively high stimulation (Damrav, 1963); and (g) conditioning in situations that encouraged short ejaculatory times (e.g., places where return of parents or others was imminent, pay-by-the-hour motels, backseats of cars, "quickies" with prostitutes; Masters & Johnson, 1970). Unfortunately, the evidence for these explanations is limited at best, and we do not have a confirmed explanation for the disorder (see reviews by Lo Piccolo & Stock, 1986; Ruff, 1985).

Although we do not yet understand the cause of premature ejaculation, we have developed two effective treatments for the problem. The first is known as the **start-stop technique**. It involves stimulation of the penis, as would be done in masturbation, until a high level of arousal is achieved (the start phase). Then the stimulation is stopped before the level of arousal gets to the point of ejaculation. During the stop phase, the arousal subsides, and then the procedure is repeated. This is done three or four times on any one day and is usually practiced two or three times per week. Over time, the length of time between the start of stimulation and the point of ejaculation becomes longer. The prolongation of arousal before ejaculation in the practice sessions appears to generalize well to sexual activity with a partner.

The second treatment is known as the **start-squeeze technique** (Masters & Johnson, 1970). The start-squeeze technique is very similar to the start-stop technique except that when arousal gets high, instead of simply stopping the stimulation, the individual briefly squeezes the end of the penis. Doing so does not hurt, but it immediately reduces arousal and eliminates the urge to ejaculate. The squeeze simply appears to be a fast way to reduce arousal between periods of stimulation. Both the start-stop and start-squeeze techniques are very effective for treating premature ejaculation, and success rates as high as 90% to 98% have been reported (Kilmann & Auerbach, 1979). It is encouraging that these treatments are effective, but we still do not understand the cause of premature ejaculation or why these treatments are effective for overcoming the disorder (Lo Piccolo & Stock, 1986).

Having discussed problems with sexual functioning, we can now turn our attention to the paraphilias, in which individuals achieve arousal and pleasure through deviant means.

• Paraphilias

In general, **paraphilias** (PĀR-uh-FIL-ē-uz) revolve around *deviant means of achieving sexual arousal*. The major symptoms of paraphilias are recurrent sexual urges, fantasies, and arousal that are associated with (a) nonhuman objects such as articles of clothing, (b) suffering or humiliation, or (c) nonconsenting individuals such as children. The term *paraphilia* is derived from *para*, meaning "deviant," and *philia*, meaning "attraction."

We do not know how widespread paraphilias are because the behaviors are usually private and often occur without a partner or with a partner who consents and will not report the behavior. Furthermore, in some cases, the partner may not even be aware that the other individual's arousal stems from a paraphilia. For example, a woman having sex with a man may not realize that his arousal stems from her clothes or from fantasies about harming her rather than from her and her body.

Despite the fact that reports of paraphilias are relatively rare, it is believed that the prevalence of these disorders is high. That assumption is based in part on the fact that there are hundreds of catalogs for paraphilic paraphernalia such as whips, chains, handcuffs, and leather sex suits, and there are numerous magazines devoted to things such as child pornography and transvestism (dressing in the clothes of the opposite sex). It is generally assumed that with the exception of Sexual Masochism, paraphilias are found primarily in men.

Because many or most individuals with paraphilias go undetected, our understanding of these disorders is based on a very limited and possibly select subset of individuals, and we must therefore be very cautious in drawing conclusions from the existing data. For example, individuals with paraphilias are sometimes described as less intelligent and more likely to have other adjustment or legal problems, but it is likely that we have only caught and studied the more inept individuals.

Before concluding our discussion of paraphilias, three qualifications should be noted. First, sexual arousal that is associated with objects rather than human adults is not necessarily symptomatic of a disorder. Many men find women's underwear arousing, but that is not considered abnormal unless the clothing is preferred to women or the individual is distressed by the arousal. Second, for a diagnosis of paraphilia to be made, the behavior must have resulted in "recurrent, intense, sexual urges and sexually arousing fantasies" for "a period of at least six months" (American Psychiatric Association, 1987, p. 280). During that time, the individual must have acted on these urges or been "markedly distressed by them." In other words, occasional arousal or brief experimentation does not constitute a disorder and should not be a source of alarm. Third, in many cases, paraphilias such as fetishes (using objects of clothing as a part of the sex act) are relatively harmless when acted out with a consenting partner. In that case, the major problem is that the partner may not share the paraphilia and will therefore not find the behavior pleasurable.

Eight paraphilias are identified in DSM-IV. We will briefly describe each and then go on to consider their suspected causes and treatments.

TYPES OF PARAPHILIAS

Exhibitionism

Exhibitionism involves the *exposure of the genitals* to a stranger in an attempt to achieve sexual arousal. Exhibitionism does not involve further sexual activity with the stranger, and therefore exhibitionists do not pose a physical danger to others. The classic example of the exhibitionist is the "flasher" who suddenly opens his coat to expose himself to an unsuspecting woman. Some years ago, "streaking" (running nude in public places) was a frequent prank on college campuses, but it did not result in arousal (at least not for the streaker) and therefore would not be considered to be exhibitionism.

A variety of surveys suggest that about 60% of exhibitionists are married and that they do not differ from the general population in intelligence, educational level, or vocation. There is also evidence that they do not suffer from other forms of abnormal behavior at a rate greater than the general population (see review by Blair & Lanyon, 1981). An example of an exhibitionist is presented in Case Study 19.2.

Fetishism

The major symptom of **fetishism** is the *use of nonliving objects (fetishes)* to obtain sexual arousal. The most common fetish objects are articles of women's clothing such as bras, underpants, stocking, shoes, and boots. The individual will often masturbate while fondling, kissing, or smelling the fetish object. In other cases, the individual's sexual partner will wear the object during sexual encounters, thereby providing an arousing stimulus that enables the fetishist to participate in otherwise normal sexual behavior. The diagnosis of fetishism is not used when an individual gains sexual pleasure from the use of nonhuman objects such as vibrators that were designed to provoke sexual arousal. The diagnosis is also not made when articles of cloth-

Case Study 19.2

EXHIBITIONISM IN A 43-YEAR-OLD MAN

The client was a married, 43-year-old college-educated man of average appearance who was the manager of a small printing business. He was referred to the clinic by the court after his second arrest for exposing himself in public. On each occasion, he had exposed himself to an attractive woman. In his initial interview, he admitted that he had probably exposed himself as often as once a month for the past 20 years.

His acts of exhibitionism always occurred in public places such as busy streets, entrances to department stores, or subway platforms as the train pulled out. After exposing himself, he would run and quickly lose himself in the crowd.

The exposures were not spontaneous events but were carefully planned over a couple of days, and the planning was associated with increasing anticipation, excitement, and tension. Just before the exposure, he would have an erection, and by slipping his hand through an opening in the bottom of his coat pocket, he would unzip his pants and pull his penis and testicles forward and out of his pants. Then when he was directly in front of the woman,

he would open his coat and stand with his genitals exposed. After 2 or 3 seconds, he would pull his coat closed and run away. He would usually run two or three blocks, often dodging through stores and across streets. He described "the chase" as a "very exciting part of the whole thing." After the chase, he felt "exhausted but relaxed—you know, like you feel after good sex."

A psychological examination did not reveal anything particularly striking about the client. The only other unusual sexual behavior he reported involved going to a "male peep show" in the back of a porno bookstore a few times. His wife reported that he always seemed "completely normal." She commented that their sex life was "limited but OK." She repeatedly mused, "I can't figure this out. It just doesn't make sense." The patient's reaction was mixed. He seemed thoroughly ashamed and chagrined about being caught, but there was a tone of futility and hollowness in his promise that he would not do it again, an attitude shared by the clinic staff. To avoid prosecution, the client agreed to treatment.

---

ing are used for cross-dressing, as in the case of transvestism.

Transvestic Fetishism

Men suffering from **transvestic fetishism** gain sexual pleasure from *dressing in women's clothing*, a behavior defined as **cross-dressing**. Cross-dressing can range from wearing only one article of the women's clothing while alone to dressing completely in women's clothing and appearing that way in public. In some cases, the cross-dressing is so effective that it is difficult to distinguish a cross-dressed transvestite from a woman. However, the person's goal is not to "pass" but to achieve arousal.

A man with a transvestic fetish will often masturbate while dressed in women's clothes and will fantasize about other men being attracted to him while he is dressed in those clothes. In a very limited number of cases, homosexuals may cross-dress to attract other men, but the homosexuals do not gain sexual pleasure from the cross-dressing per se and are therefore not diagnosed as having a transvestic fetishism. Similarly, female impersonators may cross-dress as part of an act, but unless they gain sexual pleasure from the cross-dressing itself, they are not diagnosed as having a transvestic fetishism. Finally, it is important to recognize that the presence of transvestic fetishism does not necessarily preclude participation in normal sexual re-

lationships. Such a possibility is illustrated in Case Study 19.3.

Men suffering with a transvestic fetishism gain sexual pleasure from dressing in women's clothing.

Case Study 19.3

TRANSVESTIC FETISHISM IN A HAPPILY MARRIED MAN: HIS WIFE'S REPORT

Allan and I were married during the summer before our senior year in college. Married life was great. We had a cozy apartment close to campus, our classes and grades went well, and we really loved being married. It was wonderful—until one terrible afternoon in December. I had classes in the afternoon, but that day I didn't feel very well, so I cut my 2 o'clock chem lab and went home to the apartment. When I walked in, I got the shock of my life: *Allan was sitting on the bed dressed in my clothes: hose, skirt, blouse, and jewelry—the works!* He even had one of my bras under the blouse, but he couldn't snap it because it was too small. I couldn't believe it, and at first I just stood stock-still and stared.

As soon as Allan saw me, he jumped up and started to "explain." I became so upset, I don't remember everything he said, but I know he tried to tell me that he had a multiple personality. He said that I married the "straight" half and this was his "other half." He said that the half that married me didn't know about this and that everything was all right with that half. I didn't believe a word he was saying. I thought that he was making it up as an excuse. I didn't know what to think—I was in shock. There sat my husband dressed in my clothes—and he'd been doing it for months. I finally just broke down and cried; my neat little world was coming apart. Allan changed clothes and tried to comfort me, but I didn't want him to touch me. Finally, he went out for a walk so that I could be alone for a while.

By the time he came back, I had settled down emotionally, but I still didn't know what to do. He sat down and explained that he was ashamed of what he had done and that the story about having a multiple personality was just an excuse. He admitted that he had been secretly dressing in women's clothing since he was 12 or 14 but that he didn't know how it all started. It just did, and it had been going on for a long time. He told me that sometimes he just sat in the clothes and other times he masturbated. He seemed really ashamed of that. He said he never went out of the house dressed that way and that he never did it with anyone else. He told me he wasn't a homosexual. After a while, he told me that he loved me, that our sex had always been really good for him, that dressing in women's clothes was something that was just "separate from everything else," and that he was sorry. My feelings were confused; I loved Allan, but I felt weird with him. That night, he slept on the couch.

The next day, we went to a counselor at the university clinic. I didn't know what would happen. I thought that maybe there was some form of drug therapy or that we should consider divorce. The counselor was pretty calm about the whole thing, but he really didn't have much to say either. We saw him once a week for a couple of months. One thing that came from the sessions is that I learned that Allan's cross-dressing problem is a "stand-alone" problem, and it does not mean that there is anything else wrong with Allan. I was relieved about that. The other thing that happened in our sessions was that we came to view Allan's cross-dressing as a "mistake" or as an "alternative sexual behavior." The analogy was to an affair—it was an inappropriate indiscretion that could be stopped. You couldn't erase the past, but you could try to forget (forgive?) it and go on. That may be stretching the point a bit, but it is a way of thinking about it that helps us. It's been 2 years since that December afternoon. The topic of the cross-dressing is still a bit touchy, but usually I don't think about it, and Allan and I are very happy. Sometimes you just have to "go with the flow" and take things one step at a time. Allan had kind of an unusual affair, but it's over and behind us now.

Frotteurism

The diagnostic label **frotteurism** (frō-TUR-iz-um) is derived from the French word *frotter*, which means "to rub," and the disorder involves *rubbing against or touching a nonconsenting individual*. The rubbing is usually done in crowded public places such as stores or on public transportation where minor instances of rubbing can be attributed to simply bumping into the other person. In those situations, a male might rub his genitals against the thighs or buttocks of a woman. In more overt cases, the male may actually fondle the woman's genitalia or breasts and then flee when she realizes what is happening.

Pedophilia

Pedophilia (PED-uh-FIL-ē-uh) refers to a *sexual attraction to children* (*ped* comes from a Greek word meaning "child"). In most cases of pedophilia, the child is younger than 13 years old (prepuberty), and the molesting individual is a male 16 or older (postpuberty). Attraction to girls is reported to be twice as common as attraction to boys, but many individuals with pedophilia are attracted to both girls and boys.

The activities undertaken by the child molester include undressing the child and looking, exposing himself to the child, masturbating in the presence of the child, fondling the child, engaging in oral sex with the child, and penetrating the child's vagina, mouth, or anus with fingers or penis. In many cases, it is not necessary for the offending individual to use physical force because the child is not aware of the inappropriate nature of the activities and the offender presents them as "games." However, force is used in some cases, and sometimes elaborate ruses or threats of punishment are used to prevent the child from informing others of the activities.

Individuals who sexually molest children are often thought of as "marginal characters" or "dirty old men," but that is usually not the case. Child molestation is a very serious act reflecting a serious problem, but the typical child molester is an otherwise respectable, law-abiding individual who began the behavior while a teenager (Groth et al., 1982). Furthermore, most child molesters are not strangers to their victims, and in many cases, they are brothers, fathers, or uncles of the victims (Conte & Berliner, 1981). It is probably because child molesters do not fit the stereotype that many of them go undetected; no one suspects these otherwise normal individuals of engaging in such behavior, and reports by children, if any, are disregarded.

An important distinction has been made between molesters who have a *preference for children* and molesters who use children only as *substitutes for adult sexual partners* (Groth & Birnbaum, 1978; Groth et al., 1982; Howells, 1981). Those who prefer children to adults are usually unmarried, their victims are often males rather than females, and their offenses are generally planned and form a consistent part of their lives. In contrast, individuals who use children as substitutes are primarily attracted to adults as sexual partners. They have more or less normal heterosexual histories, and their use of children seems to be impulsive and associated with periods of life stress or rejection. As with most distinctions in psychology, the distinction between preference and substitute probably represents the two ends of a continuum rather than a dichotomy. However, the distinction highlights the fact that it is difficult or impossible to generalize about individuals who suffer from pedophilia (Lanyon, 1986).

Sexual Masochism

The diagnosis of **sexual masochism** (MAS-uh-KIZ-um) is used when an individual derives sexual pleasure from being *abused* or from *suffering*. The abuse may be verbal and involve humiliation, but it is more likely that the abuse is physical and involves being beaten, bound, and tortured. Masochistic activities may be used independently of other sexual acts, as when a person gains sexual pleasure from simply being hurt by another person, or the masochistic activities may be combined with sexual acts, as when an individual wants to be beaten during intercourse.

One woman client reported that she could become aroused only if her partner "treated me like a whore and pretended to rape me," and a male client could maintain arousal during intercourse only if his partner scratched or dug into his back with a sharp fork. For these individuals, being humiliated or experiencing pain was the only way they could achieve or maintain sexual arousal. In some cases, the masochism is played out only in fantasies. The fantasies may involve being raped or being held or bound by others so that there is no possibility of escape. The case of an otherwise well-adjusted individual with a sexual masochism disorder is presented in Case Study 19.4 (p. 490).

Sexual Sadism

Sexual sadism (SĀ-diz-um) is the flip side of sexual masochism in that an individual with this disorder derives sexual pleasure from *causing others to suffer* or from *fantasies about making others suffer*. Sadists may physically abuse their partners during sexual activity as a means of achieving arousal and satisfaction. An "ideal couple" might involve a sadist and a masochist. Case Study 19.5 (p. 491) involves a case of sexual sadism; we will return to this case later when we discuss treatment.

Voyeurism

The disorder known as **voyeurism** (VWA-YUR-iz-um) involves gaining sexual pleasure from *looking at other*

A huge industry is built on the needs of voyeurs.

Case Study 19.4

SEXUAL MASOCHISM IN AN OTHERWISE NORMAL MAN

One 26-year-old middle-class college-educated man routinely visited a prostitute who would remain dressed but undress him and then beat him with a rolled-up newspaper. The beating was only somewhat painful, but the slapping of the paper against his skin made a considerable amount of noise. Taking a beating like this resulted in intense sexual arousal, and as the beating became harder and faster, he would finally ejaculate.

The man's ability to attain sexual arousal in normal foreplay with a woman was very limited, and usually he became aroused only if he fantasized that after becoming aroused, he was going to be severely beaten by the woman. He never told his partners that his arousal was due to his fantasies. Because his normal sexual activities with women were relatively unsuccessful and because he did not want to tell his partners what they would have to do to really "turn him on," he limited most of his sexual activities to the prostitute whom he paid to "do what I needed."

The young man came to the clinic for a "checkup" to make sure that he did not have any other problem. He said that some years ago, he had come to terms with the fact that he "did things a little differently," but he wanted assurance that his "eccentricity" was not a sign of some other problem of which he was not aware. Despite a very thorough examination, no signs of any psychological disturbance could be found other than the masochism. The only relevant childhood experience he was able to recall was that he once became very upset when his older brother was severely spanked with a rolled-up newspaper. He was informed that no other problems were apparent, and he was offered treatment for the masochism. He declined treatment, pointing out, "It's not causing me any other problems, I'm not hurting anyone, I'm not doing anything illegal, and I'm enjoying myself. What I do is a little different, but so what?" He mused that it might be easier if he enjoyed normal sex but indicated that he did not want "to fix what is working pretty well for me." A follow-up call made a year later by a member of the clinic staff did not reveal any evidence of change in the young man's sexual behavior, attitude, or general adjustment.

---

people who are disrobing or nude. It is usually done without the observed individuals knowing, and the element of secrecy adds to the excitement. The "peeping Tom" who looks in a woman's window at night is the classic example of the voyeur. It is important to note that the voyeur does not seek contact or actual sexual activity with the individual he or she is watching. Instead, the simple act of looking and fantasizing about being with the individual is sufficient to achieve sexual pleasure, but in some cases the voyeur may masturbate while watching or later while recalling what was seen.

A huge industry is built on the needs of voyeurs. It includes pornographic magazines, movies, videotapes, strip shows, and "peep shows" where a man can sit alone in a small room and "peep" through a small window at a woman stripping. It should not be concluded that all such looking for sexual pleasure necessarily reflects a disorder. On the contrary, viewing is often an important component of normal sexual behavior. Viewing is considered to be a disorder only if the sexual behavior is limited to viewing or the viewing is preferred to normal sexual activities.

EXPLANATIONS AND TREATMENTS

Psychodynamic

The psychodynamic explanation for sexual sadism is based on Freud's idea that the two basic instincts are aggression and sex, and that the energies from these instincts are interchangeable so that aggression can trigger sexual arousal and sex can give rise to aggression (Bieber, 1974; Freud, 1920/1955). The transfer of arousal from aggression to sex can be used to account for cases in which sadistic acts such as whipping and beating are used to stimulate sexual arousal. In contrast, the transfer of arousal from sex to aggression can be used to explain instances in which sadism occurs after the individual is sexually aroused and sex is in progress. It is noteworthy that minor aggressive acts such as biting often occur at the height of normal sexual behavior, and that has been used as evidence for the sex-to-aggression transfer.

Although the transference of energy between aggression and sex is a normal process, according to psychodynamic theory it is most likely to occur in individuals who are not at the genital stage of psychosexual development and for whom the distinction between drives has not been made clear. Finally, psychodynamic theorists believe that the incidence of sadism is higher in men because they have higher innate levels of aggression, so aggressive acts are more likely to be stimulated (Freud, 1905/1953).

The explanation of masochism has posed a problem for most psychodynamic theorists because Freud asserted that humans were driven by the *pleasure principle* (see Chapter 2), but masochism involves the seeking of *pain* (Bieber, 1974; Freud, 1915/1955, 1919/1955, 1925/1955). However, in a paper titled

Case Study 19.5

SEXUAL SADISM IN A 47-YEAR-OLD MARRIED MAN

The patient was a 47-year-old man who was unable to obtain sexual satisfaction unless he hurt his wife. Throughout the 25 years of their marriage, the patient had frequently handcuffed his wife, shaved her head, stuck pins in her back, and hit her as a means of achieving ejaculation. Although his behaviors were often extreme, he never hurt his wife seriously enough for her to require medical attention, and because she never took legal action, the problem went undetected. In addition to the actual behavior, the patient was preoccupied with sadistic fantasies, which made it difficult for him to concentrate and work.

The patient was clearly aware of the inappropriate nature of his behavior, and after each occurrence, he was disgusted with himself and remorseful. To avoid the problem, when he felt the tension mounting, he would stay at the office late. Alternative means of obtaining sexual gratification were largely ineffective. Masturbation led to an erection, but he could achieve ejaculation only if he hurt his wife.

Source: Adapted from Berlin and Meinecke (1981), p. 605.

"Beyond the Pleasure Principle," Freud (1920/1955) suggested that masochism might be a manifestation of another instinct, the *death instinct*. Alternatively, it was suggested that masochism involved the defensive turning of the aggressive instinct inward onto the self. In other words, when it is too threatening to express aggression against another person, the aggression may be expressed against the self, and the result is masochism.

The traditional psychodynamic explanation for exhibitionism and transvestism is that they are attempts to deny the possibility of castration (Bak & Stewart, 1974). The notion is that the male is fixated at or has regressed back to the phallic stage of psychosexual development at which the dominant problem is concern about castration (see Chapter 2), and paraphilias reflect the male's attempts to deny the possibility that he could be castrated. For example, with exhibitionism, the male can convince himself and others that he has not been castrated, and with a transvestic fetishism (cross-dressing), he can deny the fact that women have been castrated because beneath the women's clothing he will find a penis.

The theme underlying these explanations for paraphilias is that the individuals are functioning at an immature level of psychosexual development (i.e., they are fixated at or have returned to an earlier stage of development) and that they are still struggling with a variety of basic conflicts. This is important because it leads to the notion that the paraphilias are only part of a larger personality disorder (Karpman, 1951; Loland & Balint, 1956). However, at present, there is no strong or consistent evidence that individuals with paraphilias have other major problems or that they suffer from underlying personality disorders (Forgac & Michaels, 1982; MacNamara & Sagarin, 1977; Prince & Bentler, 1972). For example, a survey of 504 subscribers to a magazine for transvestites revealed very little evidence that the individuals had other adjustment problems. The results of another study revealed that individuals who cross-dressed were not more likely to be convicted of criminal behavior than other persons, and it has also been found that exhibitionists scored within the normal range on all of the scales of the MMPI. Indeed, one of the striking features of individuals with paraphilias is that in all other respects they appear to be very normal. Friends, family, and colleagues are always stunned when the nice guy they have known for years gets caught "flashing" or is convicted of child molestation. In some cases, individuals with paraphilias do show signs of conflict and stress, but usually the conflicts and stress appear to be the *result* rather than the *cause* of the deviant sexual behaviors (Buhrich, 1981).

Because the psychodynamic explanation for paraphilias assumes that the disorders are due to some underlying personality disorder, treatment is focused on fostering emotional development and overcoming unconscious conflicts. However, at present, there is no controlled evidence that psychotherapy is effective for treating paraphilias, and therefore we must rely on case studies to provide support for the psychodynamic position (Berlin & Meinecke, 1981). Because of the limited support for the psychodynamic position, increasing attention is being focused on the learning, cognitive, and physiological explanations and treatments.

Learning and Cognitive

Learning theorists attribute paraphilias to *classical conditioning*, and they suggest that there are two ways in which conditioning can lead to paraphilias. First, paraphilias can develop when by chance, sexual arousal is paired with a particular object or activity. For example, a young boy may happen to experience sexual arousal while being punished. The pairing leads to an association between punishment and sexual arousal, and therefore in the future, when the young man is punished, he will experience sexual arousal. In this case, the pairing of punishment with sexual arousal could provide the basis for a sexual masochism disorder. Furthermore, because the sexual arousal is pleasurable (rewarding), the young man will actively seek out activities that involve punishment and lead to the sexual arousal. In other words, an *operantly conditioned* habit of using the paraphilic object or activity to gain sexual pleasure will be developed.

Support for the classical conditioning explanation comes from laboratory research in which paraphilias were developed by pairing sexual arousal with previously neutral stimuli (Rackman, 1966; Rackman & Hodgson, 1968). In one series of experiments, 10 male participants were first shown a slide of a pair of knee-length women's boots (a neutral stimulus) and then immediately thereafter they were shown a slide of a nude or scantily dressed woman (a source of sexual arousal). Sexual arousal was assessed with a device that measured changes in penis size. The results indicated that after the slide of the boots was paired a number of times with the slides of the nudes, every one of the males showed increased sexual arousal when they saw only the slide of the boots. In other words, after conditioning, simply seeing the boots resulted in an erection. Furthermore, for some of the participants, the effects of the conditioning generalized to related objects, and the participants showed sexual arousal when they were shown slides of a pair of high-heeled black shoes or a pair of gold sandals. In these experiments, then, paraphilias were developed in the laboratory through classical conditioning.

When considering this explanation, the question arises, how does the sexual arousal originally get paired with nonsexual stimuli? In answering that question, it should first be noted that emotions such as anger, anxiety, amusement, and sex all result in similar patterns of physiological arousal. Indeed, unless changes in the genital area are taken into account, it is usually impossible to determine what emotion an individual is experiencing by only measuring physiological arousal. One implication of the similarity of arousal across emotions is that arousal generated by one emotion can be transferred and can provide the basis for another emotion (Barclay, 1971; Schachter, 1964; Zillman, 1983). (This is similar to what Freud discussed with regard to sex and aggression, but it is not limited to sex and aggression.) The transfer is usually due to a *relabeling* of the arousal. For example, an individual who is fearful will experience arousal, but the arousal may be labeled as sex rather than fear, and therefore will be *experienced* as sex rather than fear. The transfer of arousal across emotions is referred to as **arousal transference**.

Evidence that arousal from other emotions can be transferred and lead to sexual arousal has been provided by a number of experiments on rats and humans (e.g., Barfield & Sachs, 1968; Berscheid & Walster, 1974; Dutton & Aron, 1974; Hoon et al., 1977; Redmond et al., 1982; Roviaro & Holmes, 1980). For example, it has been shown that males who had just been frightened by walking across a high, swaying suspension bridge showed more interest in a female experimenter and used more sexual themes in the stories they told in response to TAT cards than males who had just walked across a low, stable bridge (Dutton & Aron, 1974).

Arousal transference involving sex is apparently frequent among adolescents, for whom sex is relatively new and not yet well defined. For example, studies of adolescent boys indicate that approximately 50% experience an erection from some type of nonsexual but exciting stimulus such as an accident, a fire, being chased, or being punished (Bancroft, 1970; Ramsey, 1943). This arousal transference can be used to explain how some paraphilias get started. Consider the following possibility: A young boy becomes nonsexually aroused while being punished, the arousal is transferred (labeled as) sexual arousal, and therefore sexual arousal becomes associated with being punished. Because the sexual arousal is pleasurable, in the future, the boy seeks out situations in which he will be punished so that he can experience the pleasurable sexual arousal. The result is the paraphilia known as sexual masochism.

This learning explanation for paraphilias has led to a treatment strategy known as **aversion therapy** that involves pairing anxiety with the paraphilic object or activity so that in the future the object or activity will elicit anxiety in addition to or instead of sexual arousal (Barker, 1965; Cooper, 1964; Kushner, 1965; Marks & Gelder, 1967; Marks et al., 1970; Raymond & O'Keefe, 1965). In one study of aversion therapy, individuals with transvestic fetishes participated in two training sessions per day for a 2-week period (Marks & Gelder, 1967). During each session, the client wore a set of electrodes on his arm through which he could be given painful shocks by remote control. Shocks were administered when the client began putting on any article of woman's clothing or when he indicated that he was fantasizing about the woman's clothing. The results indicated that as training progressed, the clients became less and less likely to have erections while handling or thinking about the women's clothing. It is noteworthy that the training procedures did not reduce the clients' sexual responsiveness to appropriate sexual stimuli (e.g., slides of nude women). In other words, aversion therapy reduced the response to the women's clothing but not to women. The results of a follow-up study conducted 2 years later indicated that for most clients, the effects of the training were still apparent (Marks et al., 1970).

One client in the study became sexually aroused when he fantasized about "being tied up" (a mild sexual masochism disorder). Treatment involved administering a mild electrical shock whenever he indicated that he was having one of his masochistic fantasies. The effect of the training on the likelihood of the client's experiencing an erection when thinking about being tied up is illustrated in Figure 19.8. The degree to which a client experienced an erection while thinking about being tied up declined sharply with training and by the end of the third session was virtually eliminated.

Aversion therapy can be effective for two reasons. First, if the paraphilic object (or activity) can be made to elicit anxiety, it will be avoided. In other words, the therapist attempts to develop a classically conditioned *phobia* for the paraphilic object, and it is hoped that the client will then avoid the paraphilic object and return to normal sexual relationships. Second, if the paraphilic object can be made to elicit anxiety, the anxiety may interfere with and inhibit the sexual arousal.

A potential problem with aversion therapy is that clients may become anxious about paraphilic objects while in the therapist's office where they know the objects will be paired with negative consequences (e.g.,

FIGURE 19.8   AVERSION THERAPY WAS EFFECTIVE FOR REDUCING THE AROUSAL (ERECTION) RESPONSE TO THE FANTASY OF BEING TIED UP.

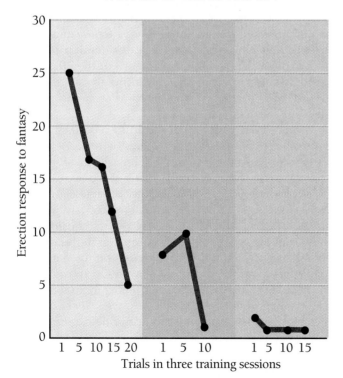

Trials in three training sessions

Source: Adapted from Marks and Gelder (1967), p. 715, fig. 2.

shock), but the clients may realize that the negative consequences will *not* occur when the objects are used in the privacy of their homes. In other words, clients may distinguish between situations, and the conditioned anxiety will not generalize.

A second learning explanation for paraphilias is also based on the concept of classical conditioning, but in this explanation it is assumed that for some reason the appropriate sexual partner is not available, and therefore the individual achieves sexual arousal or pleasure from some object that is associated with the desired but absent partner. In this explanation, the paraphilia is a *substitute*. For example, men find women arousing, and because articles of women's clothing are associated with the women, those objects could give rise to arousal and pleasure (generalization). Therefore, when the woman is not available, the male might use a woman-associated substitute object to achieve arousal and pleasure. Support for this explanation comes from the fact that most paraphilic objects are associated with women; men with paraphilias usually collect women's clothing, not garbage can covers, and when men with paraphilias dress inappropriately to gain sexual pleasure, they do so in women's clothing, not in animal costumes.

A crucial question concerning this explanation and the related approach to treatment is, why is the sexual partner not available? In most cases, a partner may not be available because women and sexual relationships are perceived as being threatening and are therefore avoided. With regard to that possibility, it is interesting to note that some individuals with paraphilias are characterized as timid and lacking in social skills. In those cases, social ineptitude may have resulted in failed social or sexual relationships, and that might have led the individuals to seek alternative sources of sexual gratification.

Treatment based on this explanation revolves around making members of the opposite sex more psychologically accessible. That is usually accomplished with some form of social skills training that will increase the likelihood of social success. Relaxation training (systematic desensitization) is also used to reduce the anxiety associated with members of the opposite sex (Bond & Hutchinson, 1960; Wolpe, 1958). Treatment based on social skills training and relaxation training may not be completely effective because, although it may make members of the opposite sex more approachable, the paraphilic behavior has a long history of reward (sexual gratification), and therefore the individual may not wish to give it up. Consequently, the most effective approach to treatment may involve social training and systematic desensitization to increase the accessibility of a normal sexual relationship, followed by aversion therapy to decrease the attraction of the paraphilic behavior. In other words, first make the appropriate sex object accessible, and then develop an avoidance of the inappropriate sex object.

Physiological

One popular explanation for paraphilias is that they result from *excessively high sex drive*. It is assumed that males with paraphilias have higher than normal levels of the male hormone testosterone. The underlying notion seems to be that the high level of drive somehow "spills over" into inappropriate sexual behavior or drives the individual to abnormal behavior. This explanation and the image of the "oversexed pervert" are widely held by the general public. However, the data supporting this explanation are very limited and inconsistent. For example, when men who did and did not have transvestic fetishes were compared on a variety of sex-related hormones, no differences were found (Buhrich et al., 1979).

If paraphilias are due to high sex drive, then reducing the drive with surgery (castration) or medication should be an effective treatment. Successes with these treatments have been used as evidence for the relationship between high drive and paraphilias. However, it is important to recognize that even if it were found that the reduction of sexual drive resulted in a reduction of paraphilias, that would not necessarily mean that the paraphilias stemmed from excessively high sex drive. Instead, it is possible that paraphilias are due to *misdirected* sex drive. Reducing the drive might reduce the paraphilias because it reduces sexual behavior in general, not necessarily because the drive was too high.

Independent of whether or not paraphilias are due to excessively high sex drive, we must carefully examine the treatments designed to reduce sex drive because they may be effective and because they have generated considerable controversy. The most drastic approach is *castration* (surgical removal of the testicles), which removes the source of testosterone. Use of this approach is limited to individuals such as rapists whose sexual behavior poses a serious danger to others. Castration does reduce sexual desire, but contrary to what many people believe, it does not necessarily eliminate sexual arousal and behavior. For example, 39 rapists who had been castrated and released from jails in Germany reported that after castration, they had greatly reduced frequencies of sexual thoughts, masturbation, and sexual intercourse, but 50% of the men reported that they were still able to have sexual intercourse (Heim, 1981). Overall, then, the main effect of castration may be to reduce the sexual desires that lead to the inappropriate sexual behavior.

While discussing the use of surgery to reduce sexual drive, it might be noted briefly that brain surgery has also been used to reduce the drive (Rieber & Sigusch, 1979; Schmidt & Schorsch, 1981). In operations performed in Germany, portions of the hypothalamus were destroyed in 75 patients. The operations were focused on the hypothalamus because that is the area of the brain responsible for arousal (recall our earlier discussion of desire disorders and Figure 19.2). Because the basis of the operation was questionable and the results equivocal and irreversible, this procedure has been abandoned.

The second approach to lowering sex drive involves the use of *medication*. The drugs that are used to reduce sex drive in males are known as **antiandrogens** (AN-tī-AN-druh-jenz) because the male hormones they reduce belong to a class of hormones known as **androgens** (AN-druh-jenz). The most frequently used antiandrogen is **MPA** (medroxyprogesterone acetate), which is widely known by its trade name, **Depo-Provera** (DEP-ō-prō-VĀR-uh) (Money, 1970). Depo-Provera is injected into a muscle, from which it is slowly released into the bloodstream. Because it is released slowly, patients undergoing treatment need to be given a shot only once or twice a week. Once in the bloodstream, Depo-Provera inhibits the release of sex-related hormones from the pituitary gland. That inhibition is important because ordinarily, the hormones from the pituitary gland stimulate the testes and cause the release of testosterone, which is responsible for sexual arousal. Depo-Provera thus reduces the male sex drive by reducing the release of the sex-related hormones.

The major side effects of Depo-Provera include drowsiness, weight gain, and increased blood pressure (Berlin & Krout, 1986). With regard to side effects, it should be noted that the drug is not a feminizing medication, and men who take it do not develop female sex characteristics such as breasts. All of the effects of Depo-Provera are eliminated within about 10 days after its discontinuance, and therefore its use does not have long-term effects.

Depo-Provera has often found to be effective for controlling inappropriate sex behavior (e.g., Berlin & Meinecke, 1981; Gange, 1981; Langevin et al., 1979; Money, 1970; Wincze et al., 1986). In one study in which patients were followed for between 5 and 15 years, it was found that only 3 of 20 treated patients relapsed (Berlin & Meinecke, 1981). In considering these findings, two important points should be noted. First, many of the findings were based on the patients' self-reports, and those reports may not be accurate because patients may be hesitant to report treatment failures that involve inappropriate (even illegal) sex behavior. Second, insofar as the drug does reduce inappropriate sexual behavior, its effects seem to be due primarily to the fact that it reduces subjective sexual *desire* rather than reducing physiological sexual *arousal* (Langevin et al., 1979; Wincze et al., 1986).

Case Study 19.6

USE OF DEPO-PROVERA FOR TREATING A CASE OF SEXUAL SADISM

The patient was a 47-year-old man who was obsessed with thoughts of sexual masochism and who had handcuffed, beaten, and stuck pins in his wife to achieve sexual satisfaction throughout their 25-year marriage. (This man's symptoms were described in greater detail in Case Study 19.5.) The patient voluntarily sought treatment when he became frightened that he might seriously harm or even kill his wife.

For 4 years, the patient was given Depo-Provera, which maintained the testosterone in his blood at below-normal levels. During the treatment period,

the patient did not report a single instance of sexual sadism, did not have any extramarital sexual relationships, and reported that conventional sexual activities became a regular part of his marriage. In addition, the patient reported that his sexual sadistic urges and obsessions were greatly reduced. In this case, then, the medication was effective for reducing the inappropriate sexual obsessions, urges, and behaviors.

Source: Adapted from Berlin and Meinecke (1981), p. 605.

The second point was demonstrated in a double-blind experiment in which exhibitionists were given either Depo-Provera or a placebo and then shown slides of nudes. While the subjects watched the nudes, they rated their levels of arousal, and at the same time, their actual levels of arousal were assessed by measuring changes in penis size. The results indicated that relative to subjects who were given the placebo, those who were given the Depo-Provera rated themselves as less sexually aroused but showed the same degree of erection. In other words, like castration, Depo-Provera appears to reduce the thoughts or desires that lead to sexual behavior, but if the individual is properly stimulated, he can become sexually aroused and active. This pattern of results is less than what was expected of the drug, but if the drug does reduce sexual desire, it may forestall inappropriate behaviors. Case Study 19.6 describes the use of Depo-Provera for treating a case of sexual sadism.

The use of antiandrogens to treat paraphilias is controversial, and some writers have questioned whether the procedures are ethical (e.g., Halleck, 1981). Some individuals, such as sadists, rapists, and child molesters, pose serious threats, and in the absence of other effective treatments for those individuals, medication may be appropriate. However, concerns are raised about the possibility of forcing medication on nondangerous individuals. Some abnormal sexual practices may be matters of preference or eccentricity and do not endanger others, and in those cases, medication may not be appropriate.

Recidivism, Psychotherapy, and New Laws

One of the most distressing findings concerning paraphilias is that the rate of **recidivism** (repeat offenses) is very high (Furby et al., 1989; Marshall et al., 1991; Rice et al., 1991; Rubinstein et al., 1993). For example, in one sample of individuals who had been convicted of sexual offenses such as child molestation and rape, it was found that 31% were later convicted for a sec-

ond sexual offense, and that individuals who received treatment for their disorder were just as likely to be convicted of another offense as those who did not receive treatment (Rice et al., 1991). The 31% recidivism rate is undoubtedly an underestimation of the actual rate because sex crimes often go unreported and because the individuals had to be actually convicted of the second offense, and such convictions are often difficult to obtain. The high rate of recidivism reflects the persistent nature of the disorder and the fact that thus far we have not developed effective psychological interventions.

Because of the general ineffectiveness of psychotherapy for treating sexual offenders and because of the fear these individuals engender in the public, **sexual-predator laws** have been passed that are designed to confine these individuals for periods beyond their usual criminal sentences. Specifically, if a jury finds that an individual is *likely* to commit another sexual offense *in the future*, the individual can be confined for an indeterminate length of time. This procedure is a drastic departure from our usual legal procedures in which an individual is confined *after* having committed an illegal act, not because it is suspected that he or she *might* commit an illegal act *in the future*. The justification for the law is understandable, but it raises serious constitutional questions. We will discuss this issue in greater detail in Chapter 21 when we discuss legal issues in general.

• Gender Identity Disorder

We must begin this discussion by making a distinction between **physiological sex identification**, which is the *objective knowledge of whether you are a male or female* based on the type of genitalia (penis, vagina) you possess, and **psychological gender identity**, which is the *subjective feeling of being a male or a female*. Most individuals have a gender identity that is consistent with

Unfortunately, the rate of repeat offenses is very high among individuals who commit sexual offenses such as child molestation and rape. One study showed that individuals who were treated for their disorders were just as likely to be convicted for another offense as those who did not receive treatment.

their physiological sex identification, but there are exceptions. For example, an individual may possess a penis, have all of the normal male secondary sex characteristics (e.g., deep voice and facial hair), and play a traditional male role in public but may feel that he is in fact a woman. When there is an inconsistency between an individual's physiological sex identification and his or her gender identity, the individual is diagnosed as suffering from a *gender identity disorder*.

The major symptom of a **gender identity disorder** is persistent and intense distress about one's physiological sex identification. Children with the disorder may actually insist that they are of the opposite sex. Young girls reject typical feminine behavior and dress, believe that they will grow a penis and not grow breasts or menstruate, and may refuse to urinate in a sitting position. Young boys may reject masculine behavior and dress, believe that they will grow up to be women, and believe that their genitals are disgusting and that it would be better not to have a penis or testes. During

adolescence and adulthood, individuals with the disorder are more realistic and realize that their physiological sex identification will not change, but they are still very uncomfortable with it. Some individuals with gender identity disorders dress as members of the opposite sex, but they do so because they are most comfortable in those clothes, not because doing so gives them sexual gratification as in the case of transvestic fetishism.

Individuals differ in the degree to which they experience an incongruence between their assigned sex and gender identities. For some individuals the incongruence is relatively mild and the individuals experience only "discomfort" with their assigned sex. In more severe cases, the individuals have the sense of actually belonging to the opposite sex (e.g., "a woman trapped in a man's body"). These individuals are often preoccupied with actually changing their primary and secondary sexual characteristics to those of the opposite sex.

A phrase that is often used when discussing sexual practices or disorders is "sexual preference," and the phrase is usually taken to imply that the individual has voluntarily or consciously *chosen* one type of sexual partner or identity over another. For example, it is implied that the individual with a gender identity disorder has chosen to identify with an opposite-sex role. However, one thing that becomes clear when working with individuals who have gender identity disorders is that *they do not feel that they have a choice about their sexual identities.* Individuals with the gender identity disorder often fight the cross-sex identity, but they usually fail in that fight and eventually give up and accept the cross-sex identity as their "fate." For these individuals, the expression "sexual imperative" seems more appropriate than "sexual preference."

The consequences of fighting the cross-sex identification are reflected in the results of a survey that was conducted on male transvestites whose behavior appeared to be part of a gender identity disorder. Fully 69% of the individuals surveyed reported that at one time or another they had gone through a "purge" in which they had destroyed or given away all of their feminine clothing. However, the pressure to cross-dress had become too great, and at the time of the survey, only 1% reported "trying to restrict myself and hope to stop it"; 22% expected to continue things "about as they are"; and 72% hoped "to be able to expand my activities more" or were "trying to develop my feminine self more fully" (Prince & Bentler, 1972, p. 915). It seems that just as individuals with anxiety cannot voluntarily reduce their arousal and individuals with schizophrenia cannot suppress their delusions, so persons with gender identity disorders may not be able to avoid or deny their cross-sex identification.

EXPLANATIONS AND TREATMENTS

Childhood Behavior Patterns

One clear and consistent finding is that individuals with gender identity problems showed cross-sex behavior patterns even as young children. Numerous studies have documented that as children, the males were described as "sissies" who preferred feminine activities and the females were described as "tomboys" who preferred masculine activities (e.g., Benjamin, 1966; Green, 1974, 1976, 1985; Prince & Bentler, 1972; Stoller, 1968).

In considering the early onset of these disorders, it is important to recognize that although virtually all adults with gender identity disorders were sissies or tomboys during childhood, *not all children who are sissies or tomboys have gender identity disorders as adults.* In fact, gender identity disorders are relatively rare, and although sissies and tomboys are more likely to develop the disorder, even among sissies or tomboys, the probability of the disorder later in life is low. For these reasons, *you should not assume that a young child who has interests and behaviors characteristic of the opposite sex is necessarily showing the early signs of a gender identity disorder.*

The finding that the symptoms of the gender identity disorder appear first in childhood has led some theorists to assume that the disorders stem from the training in *inappropriate gender roles during early childhood.* Specifically, it has been suggested that parents or other adults somehow foster the development of cross-sex behaviors, possibly because they wanted a child of the other sex. The father who wanted a son may treat his daughter like a son, taking her to football games or the office, thereby teaching her to be "one of the boys."

It has also been suggested that the disorder stems from the possibility that the child has *identified with the opposite sex parent* because the same-sex parent was not available for identification due to factors such as broken homes or hostility on the part of the same-sex parent. If a father is away much of the time or is so threatening that he cannot be approached, a young boy may spend most of his time with his mother and learn her gender role.

Explaining gender identity disorders in terms of inappropriate sex-role socialization is initially appealing, but three problems should be recognized. First, it is possible that parents respond to children in a cross-sex fashion because the children behave in a cross-sex manner. Fathers may get out and throw the football with their tomboy daughters because the daughters are good at it and enjoy it. In other words, the responses of the parents may be an *effect* rather than a *cause* of the children's behavior.

Second, for every case in which parents encouraged cross-sex behavior, there appears to be one (or more) cases in which frustrated parents did everything possible to *discourage* the cross-sex behavior. Fathers sometimes literally drag their feminine sons to sporting events to teach them to be men, and failing that, they bring them to the clinic for help.

Third and most important, there is no controlled evidence to support the inappropriate-socialization explanation, but there is some evidence that seems to contradict it. In one study, 60 "feminine" boys who showed "extensive cross-gender behavior" (early gender identity disorder) were compared to 50 normally "masculine" boys, and it was found that the feminine boys consistently differed from the masculine boys in interests and behaviors, but there were virtually no differences between the groups on demographic variables that would be expected to lead to differences in child-rearing experiences (Green, 1976). The feminine boys were more likely to avoid sports and rough-and-tumble play, cross-dress, relate better to girls than to boys, have a doll as a favorite toy, play house, take the feminine role when playing house, be sensitive to women's fashions, want to grow up to be like their mothers, and say that they would rather be a girl than a boy. In contrast, however, the groups did not differ in terms of parents' age, level of education, religion, political party, or ethnic group. Nor were there differences in number of children in the family, birth order in the family, or height or weight.

There may be some subtle confluence of psychological factors that leads to the development of the gender identity disorders, but if one exists, it has not yet been identified. Therefore, at present, we are left without an empirically verified psychological explanation for this group of disorders.

Hormone Imbalances During Fetal Development

A very different explanation for gender identity disorders is based on the possibility that during *fetal development,* these individuals were exposed to higher than average levels of *hormones related to the opposite sex.* There is a good deal of evidence that the physical sex characteristics and sexual behavior of many animals can be greatly influenced and even reversed by exposing the fetus to opposite-sex hormones. However, the question that arises is whether the hormones could also influence more subtle social behavior that is generally thought to be learned.

To test that possibility, investigators exposed one group of female monkeys to androgens (male hormones) while they were in the womb but did not do that to another group of monkeys, and then the social behavior of the monkeys was monitored as they grew up (Young et al., 1964). The results indicated that the monkeys who were exposed to the androgens behaved more like male monkeys than those who were not exposed to the androgens. For example, like male monkeys, the androgen-exposed females were more likely to threaten other monkeys, initiate play, and engage in more rough-and-tumble play patterns. Importantly, these masculine behaviors were strictly social and were not related to sexual behavior per se, thereby providing an interesting parallel for the behavior seen in humans with gender identity disorders.

The results with animals are interesting, but it must be asked whether the same effects would be found in humans, for whom it is believed that social factors play an important role in psychosexual development. There are a number of studies that are relevant when considering this question, only three of which will be considered here. Two of the studies focused on girls whose mothers had been given high levels of androgens while pregnant in attempts to avoid complications during pregnancy (Ehrhardt et al., 1968; Ehrhardt & Money, 1967). The results of both studies indicated that when compared to other girls, those who had been exposed in utero to the androgens were more likely to be described as "tomboys," participate in rough-and-tumble play, prefer boyish clothes, and aspire to culturally masculine ideals.

The third study was conducted on two groups of males whose mothers had been given high levels of estrogens (female hormones) during pregnancy (Yalom et al., 1973). One group was 16 years old at the time of the study, and the other group was 6 years old. These groups were compared to age-matched subjects whose mothers had not been exposed to the estrogens. Comparisons of the 16-year-olds indicated that those ex-posed to the estrogens were rated as less "masculine"; more feminine when throwing and catching a ball, swinging a bat, and running; less aggressive; and having fewer masculine interests. Ratings of the 6-year-olds revealed only that those who had been exposed to the estrogens were less assertive and less athletic. The finding that differences were less pronounced in the 6-year-olds can be attributed to the fact that because they were younger, normal sex-role development had not progressed as far, so possibilities for differences were more limited.

Taken together, the results of these and other investigations are consistent and provocative but not conclusive. Therefore, the hormone explanation for the gender identity disorders will have to await additional research.

Sex Reassignment Surgery

In an attempt to cope with their problem, some individuals with the gender identity disorder take on the gender role with which they feel comfortable. In other words, they behave socially like opposite-sex individuals, and for some this provides an acceptable, albeit imperfect, solution for their problem. Others seek a more drastic solution, **sex reassignment surgery**, or what is commonly called a *sex-change operation*. The first of the modern sex reassignment surgeries was the celebrated case of Christine Jorgensen in 1953 (Hamburger et al., 1953); since then, many such operations have been performed.

Surgery can be effective in making the individuals look like individuals of the opposite sex, but the operations are more than just cosmetic. In the case of the male-to-female change, it is possible to create an artifi-

Christine Jorgensen was the first person to receive sex reassignment surgery. The former GI later received a Woman of the Year award from the Scandinavian Societies of New York.

Case Study 19.7

MARILYN: AN APPLICANT FOR SEX REASSIGNMENT SURGERY

Marilyn presented herself as a rugged looking, tall male with masculine voice quality, gait, and mannerisms. She is the second youngest of six children. Her father died in an automobile accident 10 years ago at age 60. There is no family history of psychiatric contacts, alcoholism, or suicide. The family is described as deeply religious and supportive apart from one sister who refers to the patient as a "queer."

As early as Marilyn can remember, she wanted to be like "other guys." In fact, as a young child she prayed for a penis. When she entered grade school she became very upset when she wore dresses. Her family and school finally consented to her wearing overalls. Marilyn preferred boys' games to girls' activities, which led her peers to call her "half-boy, half-girl." Marilyn has lived as a male since she left school and currently manages a section of a large drugstore.

Marilyn reports a long-standing sexual attraction to females but disgust with her own genitals and breasts. She attempted heterosexual intercourse at age 17 which she describes as a dismal failure. She had a brief romance some 20 years ago with another female who left her to marry a male; that woman divorced her husband recently and is now living with Marilyn. Marilyn sought out sex reassignment surgery approximately 15 years ago, but she did not follow through on it due to the state of the surgical technology at that time.

Marilyn does not allow women to touch her breasts or vagina during sex play. She is adamant about not being a lesbian or interested in lesbian women. She feels that sex reassignment surgery will enhance her relationships with desired partners and enable her to live more comfortably as a male.

Source: Roback and Lothstein (1986), pp. 407–408.

---

cial vagina-like opening so that the individual can have intercourse and even experience orgasm. The change is further facilitated by the administration of female hormones, which result in the development of breasts and other female characteristics. The female-to-male change is more difficult and less successful because although it is now possible to construct a penis, it has not been possible to reroute blood flow to enable the individual to have an erection. Case Study 19.7 concerns a woman who applied for sex reassignment surgery.

Apart from appearance and sexual performance, the important question is, does sex reassignment surgery result in improved gender identity adjustment? Since 1975, there have been at least 14 studies in which data have been collected from individuals who underwent sex reassignment surgery, and they have generated three noteworthy findings (see Abramowitz, 1986). First, about two-thirds of the individuals who undergo sex reassignment surgery report improved adjustment after surgery. Second, although about three times as many males as females apply for the surgery and the male-to-female operation is cosmetically more effective, it appears that the female-to-male surgery is psychologically more effective. The reasons for that are not clear. Third, about 7% of the operations result in bad or tragic outcomes. Those outcomes are quite varied and may involve a psychotic episode, hospitalization, or suicide. Sometimes the individual requests another operation to restore the original sex.

Most positive conclusions about the effects of sex reassignment surgery must be accepted somewhat ten-

tatively because most of the studies did not involve comparisons with control (non-operated-on) individuals. Indeed, the results of a controlled study done at the Gender Identity Clinic of Johns Hopkins University raises serious questions about the success of the operations (Meyer & Reter, 1979). Although that study is open to some criticisms, it is better than most, and its results indicate that control individuals who were not operated on showed improvements in adjustment over the follow-up period that were comparable to improvements in individuals who underwent the operation (i.e., both groups improved). The controversy over the effects of sex reassignment surgery is similar to the early controversy over the effects of psychotherapy, and we will have to wait until more and better experiments are reported before drawing firm conclusions about the psychological consequences of the surgery.

SUMMARY

There are three types of sexual dysfunctions. The first is the desire disorder, which involves a general lack of interest in or desire for sexual activity. Psychological explanations for desire disorders include (a) a defensive avoidance of sex because it is thought to be dirty; (b) the effects of stress, which can consume necessary energy; and (c) interpersonal relations in which the individual punishes the partner by not responding. Psychotherapy seems to be effective for treating desire disorders, but it is not yet clear what it is about the therapy that is responsible for its effects. From a physiological standpoint, desire disorders are thought to be due to low levels of the hormones that are responsible for desire. There is evidence to support the hormone explanation, and there is also evidence that stress can reduce the hormone levels, so in at least some cases, an interaction between psychological and physiological factors can cause desire disorders. However, to this point, the evidence linking hormone levels to desire is limited to males.

Individuals with the arousal disorder desire sexual activity but cannot achieve or maintain the necessary level of physiological arousal. The most popular psychological explanation involves the influence of anxiety, which interferes with sexual arousal, and there is a substantial amount of evidence that the distraction that is associated with anxiety can reduce the response to sexual stimulation. Physiological explanations are focused on neurological problems and limitations in blood flow that could reduce sexual response. Attention has also been given to the possibility that anxiety, which is a sympathetic nervous system response, could interfere with sexual arousal, which is largely a parasympathetic nervous system response.

The orgasm disorder in women involves failure to achieve orgasm. Early explanations revolved around psychological inhibitions and fixation at early stages of psychosexual development. However, more recent explanations have focused on lack of understanding and inadequate sexual technique. An approach to treatment that is based on education and training has proved very effective for overcoming the disorder. Some males do not achieve orgasm, but a more common problem for them is premature ejaculation. Numerous explanations have been offered for this disorder, but so far its etiology has not been established. Fortunately, premature ejaculation can be effectively treated with the start-stop and start-squeeze techniques.

Paraphilias are disorders in which the individual obtains sexual pleasure through deviant means such as the experience of pain, punishment of others, or contact with nonhuman objects or nonconsenting partners. The paraphilias include exhibitionism (exposure of the genitals), fetishism (use of nonhuman objects), transvestic fetishism (cross-dressing), frotteurism (rubbing against nonconsenting persons), pedophilia (use of children), sexual masochism (pain to self), sexual sadism (inflicting pain on others), and voyeurism (looking at others).

Psychodynamic theorists attribute paraphilias to attempts to defend against castration and to the melding of sexual and aggressive drives. They also assume that paraphilias are simply manifestations of broader underlying personality disorders. Evidence for this explanation is based primarily on case studies, and thera-

py based on this approach has not proved particularly effective.

Learning theorists assume that paraphilias are due to classical conditioning; the paraphilic objects (or activities) are paired with sexual arousal so in the future the objects themselves elicit the arousal. Treatment based on this approach involves pairing anxiety with the paraphilic objects so that the anxiety will replace sexual arousal and the individual will avoid the objects. Laboratory evidence supports this explanation and treatment strategy. Paraphilias may also occur when individuals fear and avoid members of the opposite sex and then use the paraphilic objects as substitutes. In those cases, treatment is focused on extinction of fear of members of the opposite sex so that they will be more accessible and other objects will not be necessary to achieve arousal.

There is no clear physiological explanation for paraphilias, but it is often assumed that they stem from excessively high sexual drive. Physiological treatment revolves around reducing testosterone levels (and thereby sex drive) by means of castration or medication. These procedures do reduce sexual desires, and that may have the effect of reducing sexual behavior, but they do not necessarily eliminate the possibility of sexual activity. Recidivism rates for sexual offenders are high, and psychotherapeutic interventions do not appear to be helpful.

Individuals with gender identity disorders objectively know the physiological sex group to which they belong but feel more comfortable in the role of the opposite sex. In other words, there is an inconsistency between the individual's physiological sex identification and his or her gender identity. Gender identity disorders are usually first apparent during childhood, when the child shows cross-sex interests and characteristics (i.e., sissies and tomboys). The appearance of the disorder in childhood led some theorists to speculate that the problem stemmed from inappropriate gender-role training in childhood. So far, evidence for that explanation is based on case studies, but there are also many cases in which the parents apparently tried very hard without success to reverse cross-sex behavior and encourage sex-consistent behavior. It has also been speculated that exposure to high levels of opposite-sex hormones during fetal develop may cause gender identity disorders. Research with monkeys and humans has indicated that early exposure to opposite-sex hormones can lead to opposite-sex characteristics and behaviors, but a specific link to gender identity disorders has not yet been established. One form of treatment sought by some transsexuals is sex reassignment surgery. This surgery can be very effective from a cosmetic standpoint, but there is still controversy over its psychological value.

KEY TERMS, CONCEPTS, AND NAMES

In reviewing and testing yourself on what you have learned from this chapter, you should be able to identify and discuss each of the following:

androgens	frotteurism	recidivism
antiandrogens	gender identity disorder	releasing hormone
appetitive phase	glans	resolution phase
arousal disorder	gonadotropins	secondary orgasm disorder
arousal transference	G spot	sex reassignment surgery
aversion therapy	nocturnal penile tumescence	sexual dysfunctions
clitoral shaft	orgasm disorder	sexual masochism
clitoris	orgasm phase	sexual predator laws
cross-dressing	paraphilias	sexual sadism
Depo-Provera	pedophilia	start-squeeze technique
desire disorders	physiological sex identification	start-stop technique
erectile tissues	premature ejaculation	testosterone
excitement phase	primary orgasm disorder	testosterone replacement therapy
exhibitionism	progesterone	transvestic fetishism
fetishism	psychological gender identity	voyeurism

Chapter 20

Organic Mental Disorders and Mental Retardation

· O U T L I N E ·

mma is 68 years old, and her daughter describes her as "slipping a lot lately." Most notable has been her loss of memory for recent events. For example, Emma will carry on a normal conversation, but 15 minutes later she will begin discussing the same topic again as though it had not already been discussed. At other times, she will go to get something in another room, but halfway there she will forget why she is going. Emma realizes that she is losing control, and that makes her very nervous. Recently she has also experienced a lack of coordination in her left arm. Sometimes she will go for weeks or months without showing any decline, and then she will show a sudden drop in functioning. Emma is suffering from *senile dementia*, probably due to a *multi-infarct disorder*. In other words, the decline in her mental status is probably due to a series of small strokes.

A few years ago, Harlan's hands began shaking a little. Not long after that, he began having trouble doing things like writing. It seemed like he was losing control of some of his small muscles. As time went by, the effects became more widespread, and he began walking with a stiff, shuffling gait. Harlan was diagnosed as suffering from *Parkinson's disease*. He is now being treated with a drug called L-dopa. The drug is effective for controlling his symptoms, but sometimes it interferes with his cognitive performance, and he begins hallucinating.

Michael suffers from a moderate level of mental retardation due to *Down syndrome*. His abilities are very limited, but he is a lovable, good-natured, and playful child. There is no treatment for Down syndrome. When he is older, Michael will probably spend his days working in a sheltered workshop, but he will always require a great deal of care and supervision. His parents worry about who will take care of him after they are gone.

• Organic Mental Disorders and Dementia

Organic mental disorders involve physiological problems in the brain such as the deterioration, death, or malfunction of brain cells. Symptoms of organic mental disorders involve the loss of cognitive functions such as memory and the loss of muscular control. For many years, psychologists largely ignored these disorders. However, recently there has been renewed interest in them because they are becoming increasingly prevalent, they have a variety of psychological ramifications, and psychological techniques are helpful in diagnosing and treating them.

The most important symptom associated with organic mental disorders is **dementia** (di-MEN-shuh). Dementia refers to *an organically caused loss of intellectual abilities* that is great enough to interfere with social and occupational functioning. In most cases, the deficit involves a decline in memory, judgment, abstract reasoning ability, and other higher intellectual functions.

Dementia influences many abilities, but the primary problem seems to be with *memory*, and the decline in memory may be responsible for much of the declines in other abilities. Initially, individuals suffering from dementia are unable to remember small things such as names, telephone numbers, directions, or minor events. In some cases, they will not remember and therefore will repeat a conversation that occurred only minutes before. As time goes by, the loss of memory may influence personal habits, and hygiene can deteriorate because the individual does not remember what he or she is supposed to do. In the advanced stage, persons with dementia may be unable to remember major events in their lives (birthdays, deaths) or recognize family members, and they may even become lost in their own homes.

Individuals who suffer from dementia often develop a set of coping strategies that allows them to compensate somewhat for their loss of functioning. Probably the most common coping strategy is note writing. Individuals who are losing their memories will write notes to remind themselves of the things they cannot effectively store in memory. One 76-year-old woman who had lost much of her memory due to Alzheimer's disease took extensive notes while watching various television programs because during the commercial breaks she would forget what had happened and become very confused about the story line. She also left notes to herself all around the house reminding herself to do things: "Turn off the stove," "Lock the front door," "Put toothpaste on your brush," "Don't turn the knobs that control the color on the

Individuals who are losing their memories will often write notes to themselves as reminders.

television." Strategies like that can be very helpful in the early and middle stages of dementia, but in the final stages, not even they can make up for the intellectual loss.

In some cases, dementia can cause changes in the individual's personality or temperament. The extent and nature of the changes differ greatly from one person to another. As they begin to lose control, some people become irritable and difficult to manage; others essentially give up and become very compliant. Some individuals develop paranoid delusions. The delusions probably stem from the fact that these persons are losing control and do not understand what is happening around them, so they make up explanations. For example, an elderly man who cannot find his money may assume that someone is stealing it. In most cases, the changes in personality are a *secondary effect* of the dementia rather than part of the dementia per se.

The decline in functioning due to dementia is progressive, but the rate at which abilities decline varies considerably among individuals. Some individuals show a very slow decline, whereas others decline rapidly. There are also differences in the nature of the decline. Some disorders, such as Alzheimer's disease, involve a progressive deterioration of the brain, so the decline in memory and ability is generally smooth. With other disorders, such as the multi-infarct disorder, which involves numerous strokes that kill different parts of the brain at different times, the decline is steplike, and each stroke may involve a different ability. For example, a person may show a steady level of functioning and then a sudden drop in memory performance, followed by a plateau and then a sudden loss of some motor ability. The nature of the decline (smooth vs. steplike) is sometimes an important factor in determining the cause of the dementia.

ISSUES ASSOCIATED WITH ORGANIC MENTAL DISORDERS

Presenile Versus Senile Dementia

If the decline begins before the age of 65, it is referred to as **presenile dementia**, but if it begins after age 65, it is referred to as **senile dementia**. The age of onset of dementia is of course important for the individual suffering from the disorder, but it is also important for family members because in the case of disorders for which there is a genetic basis, early onset is associated with a greater likelihood that biological relatives will also suffer from the disorder.

Primary Versus Secondary Dementia

Primary dementia refers to a decline in intellectual functioning that is due to an *organic disorder of the brain*, whereas **secondary dementia** refers to a decline in intellectual function that is the result of *some other disorder*. For example, declines in abilities due to Alzheimer's disease are primary dementia, whereas the declines in functioning that are associated with depression are instances of secondary dementia. In one case, it was thought that a woman with Alzheimer's disease had gone through a period of particularly rapid deterioration or had had a stroke because she became listless, disoriented, and almost mute. However, a month later, she showed striking improvement. Because deterioration from organic causes could not be reversed, it was concluded that her temporary decline in functioning was due to a period of depression. Recent research indicates that it is difficult or impossible to distinguish between dementia that stems from mild Alzheimer's disease and from depression (Rubin et al., 1991). That poses a serious problem because almost 20% of the individuals admitted to nursing homes may suffer from severe undiagnosed depression (Rovner et al., 1991). Obviously, if the basis for the dementia were misdiagnosed, treatment would be focused on the wrong problem. In this chapter, we will focus on primary dementia.

Organic Mental Disorders Versus Other Psychiatric Disorders

Organic mental disorders were once thought of as distinctly different from other mental disorders such as anxiety, depression, and schizophrenia. That was because the organic disorders were thought to stem from *physiological causes*, whereas the other disorders were thought to stem from *psychological causes*. However, as we have learned in earlier chapters, many of the other disorders are now known to be caused at least in part by physiological factors (e.g., problems with neurotransmitters). It appears, then, that there may be more continuity between the organic and other disorders than was previously thought. Both types of disorders can have an organic basis, but in most cases, the major cause of organic mental disorders is a *deterioration* of the brain, whereas the major cause of the other disorders is usually a *malfunction* of the brain. However, there are exceptions to that rule, and deterioration can lead to malfunction. With this material as a general background, we will go on to consider five different organic mental disorders.

ORGANIC MENTAL DISORDERS

The five disorders that will be discussed here were selected because they are prominent disorders and because they stem from different types of causes. In considering each disorder, we will describe the physical and psychological symptoms and then discuss the causes of the symptoms.

Alzheimer's Disease: Brain Deterioration

Alzheimer's (OLTS-Hī-murz) **disease** is probably the most common cause of dementia among elderly people. It is three times more prevalent among women than men. In the early phases, the person is generally forgetful. The major problem is with *short-term memory*. In the middle phase, problems with short-term memory increase and may become so severe that the individual is unable to hold a memory long enough to transform it into purposeful action. That problem is known as **cognitive abulia** (uh-BYOO-lē-uh). (The word *abulia* refers to an abnormal lack of ability to act or make a decision.) For example, an individual may go into a room to do something but once in the room may completely forget why he or she is there. (That happens to all of us at times, but in Alzheimer's disease it is a persistent problem.)

In the final stage of the disorder, both short-term and long-term memory functions are lost. The individual is not only unable to recall what happened a few

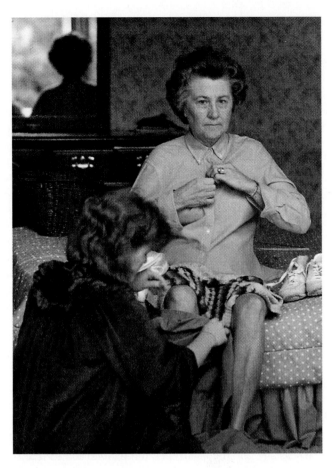

In the final stages of Alzheimer's disease, the memory loss suffered may be so severe that a patient may be unable to carry out basic self-care.

minutes earlier, but is also unable to recognize family members such as his or her own children. In this stage, people suffering from Alzheimer's disease are disoriented and may not be able to take care of themselves. Problems with other systems may also develop; for example, there may be a loss of motor control, meaning that the person can no longer control elimination processes.

In the early phases of the disorder, some individuals with Alzheimer's disease do not show obvious problems with memory, but they may develop paranoid delusions. For example, they may think that members of the family are plotting against them. We do not know why that pattern develops. It may be that the individual is beginning to experience some cognitive confusion and attributes the loss of control to external sources. In other words, instead of saying, "I can't find things because I am getting old and losing my memory," the individual might say, "I can't find things because other people are taking them or hiding them." If that is the case, the personality changes would be a secondary rather than a primary symptom of the neurological deterioration.

In all cases of Alzheimer's disease, the decline in cognitive functioning eventually becomes apparent and is the dominant symptom. However, because the disorder sets in gradually, its onset is hard to identify. It is commonly thought that death will occur 5 to 10 years after the start of the disorder, but it has not been demonstrated that the disorder is necessarily the cause of death. Given the late onset of Alzheimer's, it is quite possible that the patients would die within 5 to 10 years even if they did not have the disorder.

Alzheimer's disease is most likely to occur late in life (after age 65), but presenile cases do occur. One woman was afflicted in her early 50s, and within 3 years, the deterioration had reached the point at which she had difficulty talking because she could no longer remember words. The age of onset of Alzheimer's disease is related to the probability that biological relatives will also suffer from the disorder. The earlier the onset, the greater the likelihood that the patient's offspring will also develop the disorder.

Autopsies of individuals who suffered from Alzheimer's disease have revealed three types of brain deterioration. First, the neurons in the cortex appear to be tangled and in disarray. This is referred to as **neurofibrillary** (NYOO-rō-FIB-ruh-LER-ē) **tangling**, and it is illustrated in Figure 20.1. It is suspected that the tangled neurons result in disruptions in neurological functioning, which in turn causes the cognitive confusion that is associated with Alzheimer's disease. It is as though "all the wires got crossed." Second, the nerve endings in the brains of individuals with Alzheimer's disease show high levels of deterioration. The patches

FIGURE 20.1   BRAIN CELLS OF PERSONS WITH ALZHEIMER'S DISEASE ARE CHARACTERIZED BY NEUROFIBRILLARY TANGLING, PLAQUES, AND GRANULOVACUOLAR DEGENERATION.

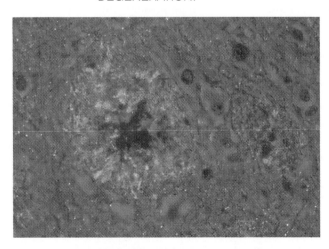

of deterioration are called **plaques** (plaks). The fact that the nerve ends are deteriorated probably serves to inhibit effective transmission of nerve impulses, which would interfere with cognitive functioning. Third, there may be small holes in the body of the nerve, which reflect general deterioration. This is called **granulovacuolar** (GRAN-yuh-lō-VAK-yoo-Ō-lur) **degeneration**. This type of deterioration seems to be limited to the area of the brain known as the *hippocampus*, which plays a major role in memory. In addition to causing problems with cognitive functioning, in some cases these types of neurological problems can cause other symptoms such as involuntary motor movements (twitches or facial grimaces) or slurring of speech. Whether or not motor behavior is influenced is determined by where in the brain the deterioration occurs.

Researchers have identified the structural problems associated with Alzheimer's disease (tangles, plaques, granulovacuolar degeneration), but they have not yet identified exactly what causes those problems. Numerous promising explanations are under investigation, but because most of them are still highly speculative, it would not be appropriate to focus on any one speculation here. However, it has been discovered that patients with Alzheimer's disease who have a family history of the disorder have a defect on *gene 21* (Saint George–Hyslop et al., 1987). It was also found that the area of the gene where the defect occurs is responsible for the production of amyloid proteins that are associated with abnormal tissue development (plaques, granulovacuolar degeneration) in the brain (Goldgaber et al., 1987; Selkoe et al., 1987; Tanzi et al., 1987). The location of the defect on gene 21 is particularly interesting because an extra gene 21 is associated with the form of mental retardation known as Down syndrome, and individuals with that syndrome have a high prevalence of Alzheimer's disease in later life. It should not be concluded that the genetic defect that has been isolated is responsible for all cases of Alzheimer's disease. It is possible that there may be more than one cause. In fact, it is possible that Alzheimer's symptoms may reflect a group of degenerative disorders rather than a single disease.

In general, a diagnosis of Alzheimer's disease can only be confirmed with an autopsy, and therefore in living patients a diagnosis of Alzheimer's disease is made by exclusion. In other words, when all other possible explanations for the dementia have been ruled out, it is assumed that the individual has Alzheimer's disease. The chromosomal problem that is responsible for cases of Alzheimer's disease that are due to heredity can be detected with a blood test, but the complicated nature of the test makes it impractical for general screening (Murrell et al., 1991).

Finally, a comment should be made concerning the so-called **nootropic** (Nō-uh-TRŌ-pik; "mind-acting") **drugs** (Piracetam, Oxiracetam) that have been proposed as a treatment for Alzheimer's disease. Early research on animals suggested that these drugs might reverse neurological problems associated with memory loss and learning disabilities. These findings sparked hope in relatives of individuals with Alzheimer's disease and received widespread attention. However, the effects in animals are questionable, and there is no reliable evidence that the drugs have any effects in humans (Bartus, 1990).

Case Study 20.1 reflects the early and middle phases of Alzheimer's disease in a woman as seen by her daughter, who, because of the genetic basis of the disease, may also be at risk.

Huntington's Disease: Brain Deterioration Due to a Single Dominant Gene

The major physical symptoms of **Huntington's disease** (also called **Huntington's chorea**) are *involuntary jerking and twisting movements of the body* along with facial grimacing. Intellectual symptoms include *problems with memory and a general decline in intellectual functioning*. The disorder usually sets in sometime around the age of 40, but symptoms can appear as early as age 25. Minor intellectual problems and moodiness may appear first, followed by minor motor disturbances such as small twitches and grimaces. As the disease progresses, the motor movements become more widespread and severe. The individual will have difficulty walking, talking, and even swallowing. Eventually there is a complete loss of bodily control. Death occurs about 15 years after the onset of the first symptoms. Fortunately, the disease is relatively rare. Woody Guthrie, the folksinger and songwriter ("This Land Is Your Land"), died of Huntington's disease; his wife chronicled his ordeal in a book titled *A Mighty Hard Road: The Woody Guthrie Story* (Yurchenco, 1970).

The symptoms of Huntington's disease are due to a progressive degeneration of the brain. The jerking and twisting movements occur primarily because the neurons that produce the inhibitory neurotransmitter **GABA** have been destroyed. Without GABA, the dopamine-related neurons associated with motor behavior become overactive, and therefore uncontrolled motor activity occurs. The dementia results from the general deterioration of the brain. Exactly why the brain begins to deteriorate is not known, but the process is somehow triggered by one dominant abnormal gene that is passed along to 50% of the offspring of a person who suffers from Huntington's disease.

Knowing about the genetic origins of Huntington's disease has both positive and negative aspects.

Case Study 20.1

A DAUGHTER TALKS ABOUT HER MOTHER'S EXPERIENCE WITH ALZHEIMER'S DISEASE AND HER CONCERNS ABOUT HER OWN FUTURE

My mother was once an active, healthy, charming, independent, and very intelligent woman. When my father died, Mother took a position with a small importing company, and in a short time she became the company's executive manager. After she retired, she led a very active social life. She had lots of friends, traveled a lot, did volunteer work, gardened, and gave splendid parties. In short, she really "had it together," and she was fun to be around.

Around age 68 or 69, however, Mother began to slow down. She stopped going out and ceased seeing friends. She spent most of her time at home reading or watching television. I really wasn't too concerned; after all, she was almost 70. After a while, however, her behavior seemed to deteriorate somewhat. She became very forgetful and sometimes seemed a little confused, although she covered it up well. I attributed most of these changes to the fact that she wasn't getting much social stimulation, and undoubtedly that did play a role. As time went on, however, her forgetfulness became very pervasive, and she had to leave notes for herself everywhere reminding her what to do (e.g., "Be sure to lock the door," "Remember to turn the oven off," "Feed the cat"). Most noticeable was the fact that when she read books or watched television, she would take extensive notes. I soon realized that without the notes, she would not be able to remember what had happened at that point in the story. As this got worse, I became concerned about her living alone, so I arranged for a woman who lived across the hall to look in on her a few times a day. Over the next year, Mother got by on her own, but she was doing less and less well. Because of my increasing concern, I made arrangements for her to have a complete checkup at the medical center.

Four days after her examination, I was called in for a conference with the physician, neurologist, psychologist, and social worker who had seen her. The physician came right to the point and said that there were three things I needed to know. First, he said that mother was in excellent physical condition (90th percentile for her age group on most measures) and that she would probably live another 15 years. Second, he said that it was their judgment that Mother was suffering from a serious and rapidly progressing case of Alzheimer's disease. He said—these are his words—that at the rate her disease was advancing, *she will be a vegetable in 5 years.* I had been prepared for bad news, but that really stunned me. He went on to point out that given Mother's life expectancy and the speed with which the Alzheimer's was progressing, she would need *total* care for an *extended* period of time, and therefore I was going to have to face a very substantial financial responsibility. I had barely taken that in when he made his third point: "Finally, I have to tell you that Alzheimer's is inherited, and it is highly probable that you will develop the disease. You should take that into account in making financial plans for your own future." Clearly, *I was facing serious problems.*

The first thing I had to do was find a place for Mother to live. Because she could still take care of herself, she didn't need to live in a nursing home, and I was fortunate to find a "minimal care" facility that was operated by the Catholic church. Originally, the building had been a college dormitory, but it had been converted to a home for elderly persons when the college no longer needed it. Residents have individual rooms, which they furnish with their own furniture. The homelike rooms are good-sized and have wash basins, but like in many old dorms, the residents share bathroom facilities on each floor. Meals are provided in a dining room just as in a college dorm. Residents must be relatively healthy because there is no nursing care. However, the staff will remind residents to take medication as needed. All of the staff members are caring and wonderful, and the facility has been a Godsend.

Of course, Mother did not want to move out of her own home, and as she left, she said to her neighbor, "I'll never have another happy day in my life. It's over." I almost broke down and cried, but the move had to be made.

Over the next 2 years, Mother began showing a slow and progressive deterioration. After the first year, she had almost no short-term memory. While talking with her on the phone one evening, for example, I asked her to check to make sure she had clean socks in her dresser drawer. She put down the phone to go to the dresser, but before she got there she forgot what she was supposed to do, and then she forgot that she was on the phone, so she just went and sat in her chair, leaving the phone off the hook. I had to hang up, call to the front desk, and have them send someone up to hang the phone up so I could call back.

She also started having trouble with aphasia (the loss of ability to use certain words). One evening on the phone, she said, "It's broken." I asked, "What's broken, Mother?" but she couldn't tell me. She just couldn't find the word. Finally, in frustration she said, "You know, the thing on the wall." "Where on the wall, Mother?" "Next to the window." "Do you mean the clock, Mother?" "Yes, the clock's broken and not working." Sometimes talking with mother is like playing 20 questions because she just can't find the words she needs. She gets very frustrated and sometimes just gives up.

As time went by, Mother became less and less aware of what was happening around her. On a number of occasions I noticed that Mother would become very confused for a couple of days, and when the confusion cleared up, she would not be functioning as well as she had before. I think she may be having little strokes. The Alzheimer's is causing the slow deterioration, and the strokes are probably responsible for the sudden drops in ability.

As her level of functioning has declined, Mother has withdrawn and interacts less and less with other residents. She goes to meals and goes "through the motions" of social interaction, but I don't think she really understands what is going on around her. Most of the time now, she simply sits in her room, hunched forward, looking at the floor. Sometimes the television is on, but it doesn't make much difference because she really can't follow it anymore. The *TV Guide* that used to be heavily marked with reminders about what to watch now lays unopened on the floor.

One of the saddest things is that at times Mother is aware of the fact that she has lost control. One day I told her that I thought she was looking good, and after a moment's pause, she frowned and said in a weak little voice, "Oh, maybe I look good, but I'm not really good. I get all mixed up about everything. I don't know what to do. I don't know what's happening." Sometimes she seems absolutely terrified. It tears me apart to see her like that. Sometimes I think it might be better if she lost that one last visage of insight.

I've heard that some people become hostile or paranoid as they go through this deterioration, but I'm very fortunate in that so far Mother has remained very sweet, affectionate, and considerate. She always says she is "fine," but I know that she is worried and very unhappy. The other day, she told one of the other residents that she wishes she were dead and would like to jump out of her window but can't open it.

We've had a couple of crises recently. About 3 months ago, I was called at my office and told that Mother had put all of her clothes in a pile outside her door, stating that she was leaving. When I got there 20 minutes later, I found Mother sitting on her bed weeping with her head in her hands. She knew that she had done something wrong, but she could not remember what it was, and she was frightened. I put the clothes away, and the incident passed. Two weeks ago, I was called early in the morning and told that I had to come over right away. Mother had not come down for breakfast, and when the staff had gone to her room to check on her, they found her disoriented, mute, and incontinent. She had soiled herself and was wandering around half dressed. After cleaning her up, I took her to the medical center. A checkup did not reveal any physical problem; indeed, she was pronounced "physically very healthy." When the tests were done that afternoon, some of the confusion had cleared up, so I took her back to her room. The crisis passed, but Mother's level of functioning did not return to what it had been. She is much more confused and less verbal, and for some reason she can't seem to change clothes by herself anymore. Now every evening I have to stop by and help her get ready for bed and put out her clothes for the next day. With this help, she can get by, but the woman who administers the home says that she doesn't think they will be able to keep Mother much longer. I have begun looking for a facility that can provide more care.

I'm struggling with three rough problems. First, it's a terrible experience to watch Mother go through this. I love her, she has done so much for me, and now there's so little I can do for her as she slowly loses control. It's tearing me apart emotionally.

Second, I'm not sure how I am going to handle all of this financially. It's clear that soon Mother will have to be moved to a nursing home, but nursing home care is terribly expensive, it isn't covered by insurance, and Mother might need it for years and years. This could wipe me out financially. I'm not sure how I'm going to handle it, and if I can't, what will happen? What will happen to Mother when we can't afford the care she needs?

Last, I worry about what is ultimately going to happen to me. Sometimes when I see Mother confused and slumped in her chair staring at the floor, I see myself 20 years from now. It's like looking into a horrible crystal ball. Is this going to happen to me? Is this my future I'm looking at slumped alone in the chair? If it is, who is going to look after me when I lose control, become incontinent, and can't dress myself? Will I waste away like that—and be alone with no one to help? It's frightening. . . .

On the positive side, the spread of the disorder can be limited if persons who already have the disorder or are likely to develop it (children of patients with Huntington's disease) are advised not to have children. On the negative side, Huntington's is a terrifying disease, and knowing about the genetic link can provoke a great deal of anxiety in the children of patients with the disease. They must live their early lives watching their parents experience a devastating deterioration and knowing that they have a 50% chance of meeting the same fate. For that reason, it is understandable that these individuals often suffer from anxiety and depression and may be suicidal (McHugh & Folstein, 1975). The psychological symptoms can be exacerbated when the early symptoms begin to appear and the individual knows what torture he or she is about to experience.

Sometimes individuals suffering from Huntington's disease will be misdiagnosed as suffering from some other disorder such as schizophrenia. That is most likely to happen if the family history of the disorder is not known. However, as time passes and the muscular symptoms become more pronounced, the true problem will be recognized. At present, there is no effective treatment or cure for Huntington's disease.

Parkinson's Disease: Effects of Low Levels of Dopamine

The physical symptoms of **Parkinson's disease** involve *tremors; impairment of fine motor movements,* which can cause a stiff or shuffling gait; and rigidity of the face and other parts of the body. Some individuals with Parkinson's disease become depressed and withdrawn and appear overly controlled. Those psychological symptoms may be a direct result of the disorder, but it is more likely that they stem from anxiety about the symptoms and attempts to control them. The disorder is relatively common, affecting at least 500,000 people in the United States at any given time (Duvoisin, 1984). It is usually diagnosed in individuals over the age of 50.

Parkinson's disease is due in part to the destruction of the **substantia nigra** (sub-STAN-shē-uh NĪ-gruh; "dark matter"), a dark gray area of the midbrain that is responsible for motor movements. A secondary effect of the loss of the substantia nigra is a drop in the production of dopamine, and the resulting imbalance in neurotransmitters is thought to be responsible for some of the other motor symptoms. It is not clear what causes the destruction of the substantia nigra, but it could result from infections, infarctions, tumors, or drugs.

The drug **L-dopa** is effective for reducing, if not eliminating, the symptoms in approximately 80% of the individuals who suffer from Parkinson's disease

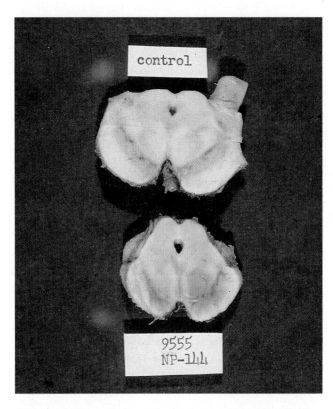

Parkinson's disease is the result of a deterioration of the substantia nigra. The deterioration causes a drop in the production of dopamine, which then leads to the motor symptoms patients experience.

(Bauer et al., 1982). L-dopa interacts with an enzyme and is converted into dopamine. The increased levels of dopamine that result are nearer to normal levels and thereby reduce the symptoms. Thus L-dopa is effective for *treating* but not for *curing* Parkinson's disease.

You may recall from our earlier discussion that schizophrenia stems from high levels of dopamine activity and that the neuroleptic drugs that are used to treat schizophrenia reduce dopamine activity (see Chapters 13 and 14). At high levels, those drugs may decrease schizophrenia, but they can also bring on the symptoms of Parkinson's disease because of an excessive reduction of dopamine activity. Not surprisingly, high levels of L-dopa used to treat Parkinson's disease can result in excessively high levels of dopamine activity and bring on the symptoms of schizophrenia. In treating these disorders, then, it is necessary to achieve the delicate balance of a dopamine level that is neither too low nor too high.

Multi-Infarct Dementia: Death of Brain Tissue Due to Lack of Blood

Blood provides the nourishment that cells must have to survive, and if the supply of blood is cut off, the cells will die. For example, if the heart muscles do not get enough blood, the result is a myocardial infarction—the muscular layer of the wall of the heart dies (see Chapter 17). When the blood supply to part of the brain is cut off, that part of the brain dies, and the individual is said to have had a **cerebral infarction.** The common term for a cerebral infarction is **stroke.**

If the infarction affects a part of the brain that is essential to life, the individual will die. If the infarction affects a part of the brain that is responsible for motor or cognitive functioning, the individual will live but will lose the ability that was associated with that part of the brain. For example, an infarction in the motor area will result in paralysis; an infarction in an area that is responsible for language will result in the inability to use words. The case of a professor in a large midwestern university provides a particularly poignant example of the language difficulties that sometimes follow a cerebral infarction. After his first infarction, he developed aphasia, which posed problems when he lectured. (Aphasia is the loss of ability to use or understand words that one ordinarily knows.) He was a nationally recognized expert on Shakespeare and had not forgotten anything he knew about Shakespeare, but he could not remember Shakespeare's name. His lectures would go something like this: "Yesterday, I began lecturing about the sonnets of . . . of . . . oh, you know, the chap who wrote *Hamlet.*" Over time, he developed a list of important words that he could not bring to mind, and when he drew a blank during a lecture, he would quickly go down his "cheat sheet" to find the word or name he needed. Unfortunately, he suffered several more cerebral infarctions and has completely lost his ability to communicate.

Because tissues in the central nervous system (brain and spinal cord) cannot replace themselves, once the tissues are dead, they are gone forever. Fortunately, however, sometimes other areas of the brain may take over the functions of the dead areas. Therefore, with time and retraining, approximately 20% of stroke victims regain their abilities (20% die and 60% have some residual impairment; Lishman, 1978).

Many individuals have one massive cerebral infarction that kills them or leaves them with large and sudden disabilities (e.g., major paralyses, lack of language), but other individuals have a series of small infarctions, each of which destroys a small area of the brain. Over time, these small infarctions can result in the loss of a large part of the brain and in considerable dementia. This is known as **multi-infarct dementia** (i.e., dementia that results from multiple small infarcts). Other parts of the brain may take over some of the lost functions, but the speed with which functions are lost exceeds the rate at which they can be taken over, and thus there is a net loss over time.

With time and retraining, approximately 20% of stroke victims regain abilities lost due to their strokes.

Two things about the symptom pattern in multi-infarct dementia distinguish it from other dementias. First, the decline in abilities is *uneven* rather than smoothly progressive. This is because a sudden loss in function following an infarction is followed by a plateau until the next infarction. The sudden loss of function may be large or small, and it may influence any one of a number of abilities. Overall, this results in an uneven and erratic rate of decline in abilities. The second distinguishing feature of multi-infarct dementia is that it usually results in the loss of *specific abilities* (loss of language, loss of memory, paralysis of parts of the body) rather than a general deterioration of function. In other words, the loss of abilities is "patchy" rather than general. The patchy nature of the loss is due to the fact that specific areas of the brain are destroyed by the infarcts. However, over time many infarcts will result in a widespread loss of functions, and therefore the deterioration will appear to be more general. In some persons, the loss of abilities can be very frightening and result in high levels of anxiety.

Cerebral infarctions stem from four factors. The first is a progressive narrowing and eventual blockage of the blood vessels because of the buildup of fatty material on the walls of the blood vessels. This is known as **atherosclerosis**, and it results in a reduced blood flow to parts of the brain, which in turn leads to the death of those parts of the brain. Second, infarcts occur because blood vessels lose their elasticity and rupture when their blood pressure increases. When a rupture occurs, the blood flow to the area of the brain served by that artery is interrupted. The process by which the vessels lose their elasticity is known as **arteriosclerosis** (ar-TĒ-rē-ō-skluh-RŌ-sis). This is the "hardening of the arteries" that is often referred to when discussing cerebral problems in older individuals. The third cause of infarcts also involves a rupture, but in this case the rupture occurs when the wall of a blood vessel develops a weak spot, swells, and finally breaks. Such a weak spot is called an **aneurysm** (AN-yur-IZ-um). Fourth, a clump of atherosclerotic plaque may develop and suddenly clog an artery, thereby reducing blood flow. That is known as an **embolism** (EM-bul-IZ-um).

Once the syndrome of multi-infarcts begins, there is little that can be done to arrest it, but numerous things can be done to prevent or reduce the likelihood of its beginning. Among those things are diets that lower low-density cholesterol to reduce atherosclerosis, and controlling blood pressure with medication or aerobic exercise (see Chapter 17) to reduce the likelihood of rupturing blood vessels.

General Paresis: Destruction of the Brain Due to an Infection

The symptoms of **general paresis** (puh-RĒ-sis), or what is widely called *syphilis of the brain*, include delusions of grandiosity, depression, and a general dementia manifested most clearly as an impairment of memory. As the disorder progresses, the delusions and depression fade, and the dementia becomes the dominant symptom. In the advanced stages, the patient becomes apathetic and incoherent. Death usually occurs approximately 5 years after the onset of the disorder. In the early stage of general paresis, a patient might be misdiagnosed as suffering from schizophrenia because of the delusions and the decline in general functioning.

General paresis is due to a syphilitic infection of the brain. The symptoms stem from the fact that the brain tissue is destroyed by a microorganism known as a **spirochete** (SPĪ-rō-KĒT), specifically, *Treponema pallidum.* The spirochete usually enters the body during sexual contact, but it can enter through any break in the skin. Most attention is focused on the effects of the infection of the brain, but the infection can destroy organs throughout the body. Fortunately, the spirochete can be killed and the disease process arrested with large doses of penicillin. Of course, the treatment does not restore destroyed brain tissue.

General paresis was once widespread, but it is less common now because it can be effectively treated with penicillin, and a test is available to identify carriers. However, some recent evidence suggests that the incidence of the disorder is increasing because individuals are becoming lax about prevention.

This concludes our discussion of organic brain disorders, and we can now turn our attention to another serious problem, mental retardation. The fact that mental retardation is discussed in the same chapter as organic brain disorders should not be taken to suggest that retardation is necessarily due to organic problems. Many cases are due to organic causes, but retardation can also stem from sociocultural factors.

• Mental Retardation

It is estimated that more than 6 million people in the United States have IQs in the retarded range (under 70). *That is as many people who live in New York City,* and it makes mental retardation one of our most widespread health problems. If individuals with borderline IQs (between 70 and 85) are included, the number of afflicted individuals rises to well over 40 million— more than *twice the combined populations of the cities of New York, Los Angeles, Chicago, Houston, Philadelphia, Detroit, Dallas, San Diego, and Phoenix!* Stated in another way, 1 out of every 6 U.S. citizens suffers from some level of mental retardation. The personal, social, and economic impact of mental retardation is especially great because it is usually a chronic and irreversible condition. In view of the extent of mental retardation and its seriousness, it is essential that we give it careful consideration.

DSM-IV sets out three criteria that must be met to reach a diagnosis of **mental retardation**:

1. The individual must have "significantly subaverage general intellectual functioning." Technically, that is defined as an IQ of 70 or below.
2. The individual must have "deficits or impairments in adaptive functioning" that result from or are associated with the low intelligence. Impairments in adaptive functioning are defined as the inability to meet the standards of the individual's age group (e.g., inability to care for oneself, ineffective interpersonal skills).
3. The disorder must set in before the age of 18. If an individual functions normally until the age of 18 and only thereafter shows a decline, the individual is diagnosed as suffering from some form of dementia rather than retardation.

The line between normal ability and retardation is not always clear or consistent because it is often difficult to measure IQ exactly. Also, what is demanded of an individual in terms of adaptability varies widely from one situation to another. For example, the demands for adaptation for a secretary in an urban office may be much higher than those for a farm laborer. An individual may move back and forth across the line between normality and retardation, depending on the circumstances of testing and demands of life situations.

There are three major causes of mental retardation: genetic factors, physical factors stemming from the environment such as problems during pregnancy and diet, and psychosocial factors such as an impoverished environment. We will consider some of the difficult and sometimes controversial issues associated with mental retardation, and then examine the types of retardation that stem from genetic, physical, and psychosocial factors.

ISSUES ASSOCIATED WITH MENTAL RETARDATION

Levels of Retardation

There are four **levels of retardation**. Just as the line between normality and retardation is not clear, the lines between the various levels of retardation are not clear, but for general descriptive purposes, it is helpful to identify ranges of retardation, as described in Table 20.1.

Problems with Measuring Intelligence

IQ scores are usually the major factor in determining whether an individual is suffering from mental retardation. However, there are three potentially serious problems with using traditional IQ tests for measuring retardation. First is the possibility that traditional IQ

TABLE 20.1   THERE ARE FOUR LEVELS OF MENTAL RETARDATION

Mild Mental Retardation (IQ = 50–70)
This is roughly equivalent to what was once called "educable." This group constitutes the largest segment of persons with retardation—about 85%.
Education and Training Potential.   People with this level of retardation typically develop social and communication skills during preschool years, have minimal impairment in sensorimotor areas, and are often indistinguishable from normal children until a later age. They can acquire academic skills up to about the sixth-grade level.
Long-Term Outlook.   During their adult years, they usually achieve minimal self-support but may need help in unusual circumstances or under stress. At present, virtually all people with mild retardation can live successfully in the community, independently or in supervised apartments or group homes.

Moderate Mental Retardation (IQ = 34–50)
This is roughly equivalent to what used to be referred to as the "trainable" level of retardation. The term *trainable* should not be used because it implies that these persons cannot benefit from educational programs. This group constitutes about 10% of the retarded population.
Education and Training Potential.   These individuals can learn to communicate during the preschool years. They may profit from vocational training and, with moderate supervision, can take care of themselves. They can profit from social and occupational training but are unlikely to progress beyond the second-grade level in academic subjects. They may learn to travel independently in familiar places.
Long-Term Outlook.   During adolescence, their retardation may interfere with peer relationships. In adulthood, they may be able to contribute to their own support by performing unskilled or semiskilled work under supervision in sheltered workshops or in the competitive job market. They need supervision and guidance when under stress. They adapt well to life in the community, usually in supervised group homes.

Severe Mental Retardation (IQ = 20–35)
This group constitutes 3% to 4% of the retarded population.
Education and Training Potential.   During preschool, they display poor motor development and acquire little or no communicative speech. During school age, they may learn to talk and can be trained in elementary hygiene skills. They profit to only a limited extent from training in such things as the alphabet and simple counting. They can be taught to sight-read words such as *men, women,* and *stop.*
Long-Term Outlook.   In their adult years, they may be able to perform simple tasks under close supervision. Most adapt well to life in the community, in group homes, or with their families.

Profound Mental Retardation (IQ = below 20)
This group constitutes 1% to 2% of the retarded population.
Education and Training Potential.   As children, these people display minimal capacity for sensorimotor functioning. A highly structured environment with constant aid and supervision by a caregiver is required for optimal development. Motor development and self-care and communication skills may improve if appropriate training is provided.
Long-Term Outlook.   Many of these people live in the community, in group homes, in intermediate care facilities, or with their families. Most attend day programs, and some can perform simple tasks under close supervision in a sheltered workshop.

Source: Adapted from American Psychiatric Association (1987), pp. 32–33, and (1994), pp. 41–42, and 46.

About 85% of persons with mental retardation are mildly retarded and are able to achieve minimal self-support.

tests are not effective for measuring the abilities of poor children or children from ethnic groups who have different cultural experiences. Evidence for this is provided by a study in which it was found that IQ scores were related to academic achievement for white students but not for African-American or Mexican-American students (Goldman & Hartig, 1976). Apparently, the IQ scores were not related to achievement in the Mexican-American students because the tests were biased against the cultural backgrounds of those students. Another study revealed that African-American students who suffered from retardation had lower IQ scores than white students who suffered from retardation, but there were no differences between the white and African-American students on measures of social functioning (Adams et al., 1973). Again, it appears that the traditional IQ tests did not adequately measure the intelligence of the African-American students. These studies demonstrate that traditional measures of IQ may be irrelevant or invalid for diagnosing retardation in members of groups with different cultural backgrounds.

A second problem is that the traditional IQ tests may not measure abilities that are relevant for the "real world," and therefore the retardation they measure may be limited to the schoolroom (Ginsberg, 1972). In this regard, it is interesting to note that when **Alfred Binet** (bē-NĀ) (1857–1911) developed the first widely used IQ test in 1905, the test was explicitly designed to predict how well students would do in school. Thus an IQ test may indicate that an individual is retarded in terms of the types of tasks performed in school, but that does not necessarily mean that he or she is retarded with regard to tasks that may be important outside of school.

A third problem is that most intelligence tests were standardized on individuals with normal intelligence, and very little attention was given to individuals with lower levels of intelligence. Unlike units of distance or weight that are the same when they are measured in large and small amounts (an inch is the same length when it is part of a mile as when it is part of a foot), intelligence at low levels may be somehow different from intelligence at high levels. If that is the case, the ways of measuring intelligence in normal individuals may not be appropriate for measuring intelligence in individuals who suffer from retardation.

A fourth but somewhat less important problem stems from the fact that in some cases, individuals with retardation suffer from a variety of physical and emotional problems in addition to their retardation, and those problems may interfere with their performance on the test and distort the results. The level of performance that results from the combination of retardation and other problems may reflect individuals' current *functional* levels of ability (i.e., what they are able to do given all their problems), but it does not reflect what they would be able to do intellectually if their other problems were treated. In that sense, then, the IQ test may provide an unrealistically low estimate of the abilities of some individuals.

All the potential problems mentioned here can serve to invalidate the measurement of intelligence and alter the diagnosis of retardation. However, note that DSM-IV explicitly requires that the assessment of IQ be based on one or more of the individually administered general intelligence tests (see Chapter 3) rather than on paper-and-pencil tests. Individually administered tests usually involve up to 2 hours of interactions between the client and a highly trained test administrator, and the test administrator should be able to recognize when a problem is interfering with a client's performance so that allowances can be made or the test can be disregarded (see Chapter 3). Note also that the diagnosis of mental retardation requires that the individual perform poorly on an intelligence test and *also demonstrate an inability to function adequately*. Therefore, even if the IQ test provides a low but invalid measure of the individual's capacity, that by itself will not result in the diagnosis. The individual must also show problems in daily functioning.

Problems with Classification and Declassification

Being classified or labeled "mentally retarded" can pose problems for children. Those who are labeled as retarded may be separated from their peers and taught in special classes, and that may lead them to think negatively of themselves. In addition, other persons may expect or demand less of individuals who are classed as retarded. If individuals think negatively of themselves and others expect less of them, their performance levels may actually drop. In one series of experiments in which teachers were given false information about the intelligence levels of their students, it was found that the students who were randomly assigned to the "low intelligence" group got lower grades and actually performed less well than the children assigned to the "high intelligence" group (Rosenthal & Jacobson, 1968). That effect was probably due to the fact that the teacher had different expectations for the different groups of students, and the students met their teacher's expectations. In other words, the label "mentally retarded" may become a self-fulfilling prophecy and may contribute to or result in retardation.

Recently, there has been movement in the direction of **declassification** of individuals labeled as retarded. In a number of legal cases, it was argued that members of minority groups were erroneously classified as retarded because their abilities had not been measured accurately by traditional IQ tests. The courts agreed and ruled that the children must be reclassified as normal. The court-ordered reclassification eliminates the potential problems associated with being labeled as retarded. However, at the same time, the declassification deprives some children of special educational opportunities designed to help them overcome their educational difficulties (Reschly, 1981). Ironically, although it is the individuals whose retardation is due to psychosocial factors (impoverished environments and poor schools) who are hurt most by labeling, they are also the individuals who are hurt most if they are not given special attention to counteract their cultural experiences and attitudes. There does not seem to be a simple solution to this problem.

Mental Defect or Delayed Development?

There is no doubt that *severe* retardation is due to **mental defects** such as damaged chromosomes or brain damage. That is, there is some problem with the structure or functioning of the brains of individuals who suffer from severe retardation. However, there is some controversy over the cause of *mild* retardation. Some theorists believe that even mild retardation is due to some specific mental defect (Milgram, 1969). They explain the fact that we have not yet found the actual defects by suggesting that the defects are very small and subtle.

In contrast, other theorists believe that *mild* retardation is due to **delayed development** (Zigler, 1969; Zigler & Balla, 1982). These theorists suggest that individuals go through stages of cognitive development and that for some reason, the intellectual development of some individuals is retarded at some early stage. (It is interesting to note that the term *retarded* implies that there is a *delay* in development rather than a *defect*.) The delay could stem from (a) growing up in a culturally impoverished environment, (b) attitudes about achievement ("I can't do it, so I won't try"), (c) lack of motivation ("I don't care about doing it, so I won't try"), or (d) lack of parental encouragement ("You're dumb, so don't bother to try").

The answer to the question of whether mild retardation is due to a defect or to a delay in development has important implications in terms of what should be done for individuals who suffer from retardation. If retardation is due to a defect, treatment should be focused on teaching individuals ways of *compensating* for the problem because it cannot be corrected. For example, individuals might be given vocational training designed to provide them with income-producing skills that do not require a high degree of intelligence. By contrast, if retardation is due to a delay in development, treatment should be focused on *correcting* the problem. For example, individuals might be placed in a program in which they are exposed to exercises and experiences that will enable them to grow intellectually and change their attitudes about themselves and their abilities.

The answer to the defect-or-delay controversy also has implications for the prevention of retardation. If it is assumed that retardation is due to delayed development, it is important that we expose children to cultural opportunities and positive attitudes. Indeed, the Head Start program was founded on the assumption that retardation was due to delays in development, and the program was designed to prevent or offset those delays. Delayed development is certainly a more optimistic explanation because it suggests that with proper experiences, mild retardation can be prevented or effectively treated.

A variety of attempts have been made to resolve the defect-versus-delayed-development controversy. The results have been mixed, and it is probably safest to conclude that mild retardation can be due to a defect or a delay in development. Attention should be given to both possibilities when considering prevention and treatment. The problem may not be to determine which explanation is correct in general but rather to determine which explanation is correct for a particular individual.

With an understanding of these issues as background, we can now go on to consider the causes and types of mental retardation. We will discuss types of retardation that result from genetic, physical, and psychosocial factors.

RETARDATION DUE TO GENETIC FACTORS

Retardation due to genetic factors accounts for only about 25% of the cases of mental retardation, but most often, genetic factors result in the most severe forms of retardation. In addition to being more severely retarded, persons whose retardation is due to genetic factors are often more easily identifiable because they look different.

Down Syndrome: The Effect of an Extra Chromosome

Down syndrome results in a moderate to severe level of general retardation (IQs range from 35 to 49). Individuals suffering from Down syndrome are easily recognizable because they have almond-shaped eyes that slant upward, a small nose with a low bridge, and a furrowed tongue that protrudes because the mouth is

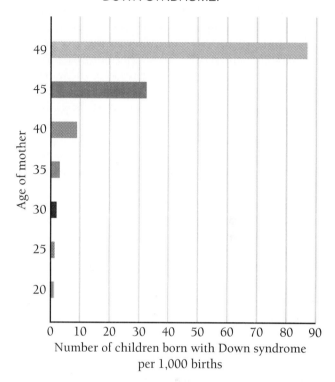

FIGURE 20.2 OLDER MOTHERS ARE MORE LIKELY TO GIVE BIRTH TO CHILDREN WITH DOWN SYNDROME.

Sources: Hook (1982); Hook and Chambers (1977); Hook and Fabia (1978); Hook and Lindsjo (1978).

Down syndrome results in a moderate to severe level of retardation. The facial features of persons with the disorder include almond-shape eyes that slant upward, a small nose with a narrow bridge, and a small tongue that protrudes because the mouth is small and has a low roof. The syndrome is the result of the individual having an extra number 21 chromosome.

small and has a low roof. Their hands are usually small with short stubby fingers, and as adults these individuals are often short and stocky. Because the eyes of individuals with Down syndrome give them a somewhat Asiatic appearance, the disorder was originally referred to as "Mongolism." This syndrome occurs in about 1 of every 1,000 live births and is therefore one of the most common causes of retardation.

In most cases, Down syndrome is due to the fact that the individual has an *extra number 21 chromosome*, a problem known as **trisomy** (TRĪ-sō-mē) **21** (Pueschel & Thuline, 1983). We know that the extra chromosome 21 is responsible for Down syndrome, but we do not yet know how it has its effect.

One important finding concerning Down syndrome is that older women are more likely to give birth to infants with the disorder. In fact, the number of Down syndrome births per 1,000 live births increases from .58 in mothers who are 20 years old to 87.93 in mothers who are 49. Figure 20.2 dramatizes this increase in the rate of Down syndrome births. We do not yet understand why mother's age is associated with the syndrome. It is possible that because older women's eggs have been held in "suspended animation" for longer, they have been exposed to more environmental agents or stresses that disrupt them. It is also possible that the hormonal changes that occur in midlife influence the process (Crowley et al., 1982; Mikkelsen & Stene, 1970; Smith & Wilson, 1973).

There is also evidence that father's age can be related to the disorder (Erickson & Bjerkedal, 1981; Regal et al., 1980). However, whereas the risk greatly increases after the mother passes her mid-30s, the risk on the father's side does not increase until he passes his mid-50s.

The presence of an extra chromosome 21 in an unborn fetus can be detected with a test known as **amniocentesis** (AM-nē-ō-sen-TĒ-sis). This test is performed during the 14th or 15th week of pregnancy. It involves inserting a hollow needle through the abdominal wall and into the uterus of the pregnant woman and then withdrawing a small amount of the fluid in which the fetus is developing. The fetal cells that are withdrawn with the fluid are cultivated ("cultured") for 3 weeks and then examined to determine whether they have extra number 21 chromosomes. If they do, it is likely that the infant will have Down syndrome, and the parents may choose to end the pregnancy. There is some risk associated with amniocentesis because the fetus may be injured when the needle is inserted into the uterus. Therefore, the test is routinely recommended only for older women who are at high risk for giving birth to a child with Down syndrome.

Although individuals with Down syndrome are seriously retarded, they are usually good-natured, happy, affectionate, socially well adjusted, and playful in a "clownish" way (Brink & Grundling, 1976; Gibbs & Thorpe, 1983; Moore, 1973). But as they age, they are more likely to suffer from Alzheimer's disease and other disorders that add appreciably to the problems of their care (Miniszek, 1983).

Fortunately, some persons with Down syndrome are only moderately retarded and with careful guidance can make a somewhat normal adjustment. In Case Study 20.2, a mother talks about her moderately retarded daughter who has Down syndrome.

Phenylketonuria (PKU): A Genetic Problem with Metabolism

Phenylketonuria (FĒ-nil-KĒ-tun-YOO-rē-uh), usually abbreviated **PKU**, results in a severe level of retardation with IQ rarely higher than 40 or 50. Many persons with this disorder are so retarded that they cannot walk or talk. They are also likely to be irritable, unpredictable, and hyperactive, and they are generally unresponsive to other persons (Robinson & Robinson, 1976). Furthermore, they often show aimless motor behavior such as arm waving, rocking, and unusual finger movements. This combination of emotional and

motor symptoms is similar to the symptom pattern seen in children with autism (see Chapter 16), and therefore some children with PKU are misdiagnosed as suffering from autism. Persons who suffer from PKU are likely to have blond hair, blue eyes, and very fair skin. PKU occurs in approximately 1 of every 15,000 live births (Carter, 1975).

PKU results from a low level of an enzyme that is necessary to break down the amino acid **phenylalanine** (FĒ-nil-AL-uh-nīn). If the phenylalanine is not broken down, it forms **phenylpyruvic** (FĒ-nil-pī-ROO-vik) **acid**, which destroys the brain (Jervis, 1939, 1947). In other words, when the enzyme level is low, the acid level builds up and destroys the brain. The destruction of the brain results in mental retardation and inappropriate behavior. The low level of the critical enzyme that ultimately leads to brain damage is due to a recessive gene that is carried by as many as 1 individual in 50 (Rosenthal, 1970). If two individuals with the gene give birth to a child, there is a 25% chance that the child will have PKU.

Although an infant with PKU is born with an inability to break down phenylalanine, at birth the acid levels have not had time to build up and begin destroying the brain. Therefore, if the disorder is diagnosed early and steps are taken to treat the problem, the effects of the disorder can be reduced or eliminated. Screening for PKU is done with a simple urine or blood test when the infant is only a few days old. Infants found to have PKU are put on a diet that is low in phenylalanine, thereby preventing the buildup of the phenylpyruvic acid and preventing the destruction of the brain. The sooner the low-phenylalanine diet is begun, the less severe the retardation will be. Indeed, if the diet is begun early in infancy and is maintained for at least 6 years, the retardation will be minimal (Berry et al., 1967; Tredgold & Soddy, 1970). There is one difficulty with a low-phenylalanine diet, however: Phenylalanine is found in almost all foods that contain protein. This means that there is very little that the child can eat without being deprived of protein, which is essential for growth. To get around the problem, the child must eat synthetically developed foods that contain protein but not phenylalanine (Lofenalac, PKU-Aid, Phenylfree). Unfortunately, those foods are expensive, they usually do not taste good, and it is often difficult to get the child to eat them. Overall, then, PKU can and must be treated, but the process can be difficult. Because the disorder can be corrected if the diet is begun early, it is especially tragic when it is misdiagnosed (usually as autism) and treatment is delayed. If the treatment is delayed more than a couple of years, severe and irreversible damage occurs.

One more important fact concerning PKU should be mentioned: Women who had PKU as children but

Case Study 20.2

A MOTHER TALKS ABOUT HER 15-YEAR-OLD DAUGHTER WHO HAS DOWN SYNDROME

I am the mother of a 15-year-old daughter with Down syndrome. Kimberly is currently attending junior high school and is in the 9th grade, enjoying all the ordinary things that teenage girls enjoy. Her passions are rock music and movie stars. She is looking forward to being able to work next summer and earn some money (probably to buy more music tapes) and to eventually move into her own apartment, just like her brother did when he graduated from high school.

When Kimberly was born, the city had numerous support programs for developmentally disabled children and their families, but the problem was finding the programs. The medical community and social service offices were not coordinated, and therefore new parents in the hospital with a disabled child could not get all the information they needed to help them adjust to this dramatic change in their lives. Trying to deal with the shock of having a child that was not "normal" and not being able to find support services was traumatic for both my husband and me. All our pediatrician told me was that I did not have to take her home if I didn't want to, that there were institutions available. I remember thinking that she is only a baby, and a baby only needs love and care and a family. There was no way that I was going to put her in an institution. Fortunately, my mother lived across the street from a family that had a son with Down syndrome, and she immediately brought as much information as she could to the hospital.

Adequate support is critical at this time because the parents in this situation go through a grieving process—grieving for the normal child that they did not have. The hopes and dreams that you have for your children must be adjusted to encompass your special child, and this takes time. I believe that it is important to recognize this process, for it helps us finally to accept the situation and move positively toward the future.

We found that at first we were able to plan ahead for only a short period of time, and we did not look too far down the road. When Kim was a baby, for instance, my hopes were only that she be able to go to a preschool. When she was 3 years old, we started thinking about what would be available for her when she was 5. We also learned not to let our own thoughts and objectives create limits for Kim. When she was 3, it never occurred to me that she would ever be reading at the third- or fourth-grade level and that she would be interested in the things that she is interested in today.

We were fortunate to be in a school district in which she had the opportunity to be "mainstreamed" into some normal classrooms, and for many classes that was successful. In one case, however, I think Kim realized that she was not comfortable in a normal classroom, and she seemed much happier when we returned her to her special education classroom. She is currently attending special education classes but is mainstreamed into regular physical education, art, and music classes and enjoys participating in all of them. She is learning, in a somewhat structured environment, to participate in the real world.

Kim's wants and desires are not that different from those of normal teenagers, but trying to meet those wants and desires is. As parents of a child with Down syndrome—or any disability, for that matter—we usually have to go to bat for our child in order for her to have some experiences that ordinary children take for granted. It is normal for seventh and eighth graders to gather with their friends on Friday or Saturday night, and Kim wants to do the same thing, but she doesn't always have the capacity to handle the situation. We also have to be careful that other people do not take advantage of her. Fortunately, we have been able to work with the city's Parks and Recreation Department to develop some structured weekend activities in which Kim and her friends can participate successfully and safely.

Kim wants to drive a car when she is 16, which is not too far away, and we haven't quite figured out how to deal with that. Our stock answer is that if she can pass the written driving test like everyone else, she can get her learner's permit. That's the same answer that we give to her younger sister. In essence, we are trying, and have always tried, to treat Kimberly as normally as possible and to expect the same responsibilities from her that we do from the other children. The hard part is to give her enough leeway to try so that she (and we) can learn her limits, but to do so without being too lax and assuming that she can handle everything. When Kim was only 2 months old, a good friend told me that I shouldn't put limits on what I thought Kim was capable of becoming. I have never forgotten her advice, and I know that Kim has far exceeded anything that I could have imagined when she was only a few months old.

As a parent of a disabled child who is soon to be an adult, I am learning that it is important for Kim to learn to cope with the real world. I want her to be able to go to movies, go to the store, go on a date if she wants, and do ordinary things independently, without having people stare at her and think she is weird. I want her to learn to dress nicely, to keep her hair combed and her face washed. I want her to care that her clothes match and that she looks presentable. I want her to move out of the house when it is appropriate, just as I want my other children to do the same thing. Our hopes and dreams for Kim are the same as our hopes and dreams for our other children: that she will build a life for herself beyond the family; that she will have her own job, own home, and some independence; that she can cope with the world around her and be happy. I want people around her to accept that she has the same rights to these goals and happiness that anyone else does. Our fears are that she will be rejected because of her disability, that there will not be anyone to watch out for her when we are gone, and that necessary services for people with developmental disabilities will disappear.

---

were effectively treated are likely to give birth to brain-damaged children. That is because the mothers still have high levels of phenylalanine, which can damage the fetus while it is developing in the womb. This was not a problem before we knew how to treat PKU because females with PKU became so retarded as children that they were institutionalized and did not reproduce. In view of the problem posed for the children of women with PKU both in terms of passing the recessive gene on and in terms of the dangerous fetal environment they provide their children, these women should give serious consideration to not having children (Carter, 1975; Pueschel & Goldstein, 1983).

Other Types of Retardation Due to Genetic Factors

Many other types of retardation stem from genetic problems, but most of them are rare. However, some brief attention should be given to three of the more notable types.

Turner's Syndrome.

Turner's syndrome (or **gonadal dysgenesis**) is limited to women and only sometimes results in general retardation. When retardation does occur, it is usually associated primarily with deficits in *space-form perception* rather than in verbal abilities (Bock & Kolakowski, 1973). The problem with space-form perception influences their ability to see relationships between objects and how things fit together. The disorder is due to the fact that the woman is missing one of the two female chromosomes (X instead of XX). As you might expect from the cause, physical symptoms consist primarily of a lack of secondary sex characteristics after puberty. That can be treated with female hormones, but the treatment does not help the deficits in cognitive abilities.

Klinefelter's Syndrome.

In contrast to Turner's syndrome, **Klinefelter's syndrome** is limited to men and results from the presence of extra female chromosomes. Instead of having an XY chromosome configuration (one female and one male chromosome), which is normal for males, the individual will have an XXY or XXXY configuration. In some cases, the man may have as many as five female chromosomes. This genetic problem causes retardation in only about half the cases, but the severity of the problem increases as the number of extra X chromosomes increases (Forssman, 1970).

Cretinism (Hypothyroidism).

The most notable physical characteristic of **cretinism** (or **hypothyroidism**) in adults is very short stature (dwarfism), which is sometimes associated with obesity, a protruding abdomen, stubby fingers, dry skin, and sparse and brittle hair. Cretinism is frequently but not always associated with retardation, which can range from moderate to severe. In infants, cretinism can be detected by a low heart rate, low respiratory rate, and low body temperature.

Cretinism is usually due to a recessive gene that interferes with the production of **thyroxin** (THI-ROK-sin) by the thyroid gland. Thyroxin is responsible for maintaining a proper metabolic rate, and if there is too little thyroxin (hence the term *hypothyroidism*), metabolism and development are slowed. This low metabolism is responsible for the low heart rate, low respiratory rate, and low body temperature. Although the low level of the thyroxin is usually due to a genetic problem, it can also result from radiation (X-rays) during pregnancy that interferes with the normal development of the thyroid gland. It can also be caused by an iodine deficiency in the mother during pregnancy, but that cause has been largely eliminated in countries where iodine is added to table salt.

If detected early and treated with thyroid medication (thyroxin obtained from animals), the problem can often be cured or reduced. The treatment reverses the progression of the disease following birth but cannot repair any damage that might have occurred before birth.

RETARDATION DUE TO PHYSICAL FACTORS IN THE ENVIRONMENT

A variety of physical factors such as infections, drugs, temperature, pressure, nutrition, injuries, and abuse can damage the brain. These factors can have their influence while the fetus is in the womb (*prenatal* period), during the birth process (*perinatal* period), and during the first few years following birth (*postnatal* period). The retardation that results from these factors is usually less severe than that caused by genetic factors, but it is still very serious. Attention to such retardation is important because in most cases it can be avoided.

Fetal Alcohol Syndrome: Effects of Maternal Drinking During Pregnancy

We now know that the consumption of alcohol by pregnant women can result in a variety of problems in their offspring, and this has come to be known as **fetal alcohol syndrome**, sometimes abbreviated **FAS**. One of the symptoms is mental retardation, which can range from mild to severe. Other cognitive symptoms can include attentional difficulties and hyperactivity (see Chapter 16). Physical abnormalities include microcephaly (small brain), distortions of the face, and cardiac abnormalities. Not all of these symptoms are always present, and they appear in different combinations.

Symptoms of children with fetal alcohol syndrome can include mental retardation, attentional difficulties, hyperactivity, small brain, distortions of the face, and cardiac abnormalities.

Fetal alcohol syndrome may affect as many as 1 in 750 live births, and between 26% and 76% of the children born to alcoholic women suffer from fetal alcohol syndrome, making alcohol one of the most common causes of physically based mental retardation (Streissguth et al., 1978). Furthermore, many victims of fetal alcohol syndrome grow up to abuse alcohol as adults, thereby producing another generation of sufferers. This serious and widespread form of mental retardation is all the more tragic because it can be prevented so easily.

Alcohol is not the only drug that can have detrimental effects on fetal development. Many other drugs (e.g., tranquilizers) taken by pregnant women can also result in deformities and retardation in their offspring, and pregnant women must be cautious about taking almost any medication.

Rubella (German Measles): Effects of Infection During Pregnancy

The symptoms of a pregnant woman suffering from a case of **rubella** (roo-BEL-uh) (**German measles**) consist only of a low-grade fever and a slight skin rash. However, her infection can cause an inflammation of her fetus's brain, which in turn leads to a degeneration of the brain tissue. Different parts of the brain are destroyed, depending on its stage of development when the inflammation occurs, and thus the effects of rubella may differ from one child to another. Retardation may be mild or very severe, and there may also be defects involving sight, hearing, and heart function. The likelihood of mental retardation is 50% if the infection occurs in the first month of pregnancy but declines thereafter. As with most other forms of retardation, there is no treatment for the disorder once it occurs, but it can be effectively prevented by vaccination of future mothers.

Lead Poisoning: Effects of Exposure During Pregnancy and Early Childhood

Exposure to lead early in life can disrupt neurological development and cause mental retardation. The retardation may be of only moderate severity, but this form of retardation is very widespread and therefore a serious problem. Children develop lead poisoning when they eat chips of paint that contain lead, play in dirt in contaminated industrial areas, or inhale lead in the air (automobile or industrial pollutants). The poisoning can also occur during fetal development when pregnant women are exposed to lead.

The effects of exposure to lead on IQ were demonstrated in a study in which lead concentrations were assessed in pregnant women and later in their offspring (Baghurst et al., 1992). Exposure to the lead stemmed from the fact that the individuals were living in a city with a large lead-smelting plant and where there were high levels of lead in the air. IQ was measured when the children were 7 years old. The results indicated that high and low levels of maternal lead were linked to differences in IQ of almost 10 points (99.8 vs. 108.5, respectively), and that high and low levels of lead in the children at age 7 were linked to differences in IQ of more than 10 points (98.7 vs. 109.6).

RETARDATION DUE TO PSYCHOSOCIAL FACTORS

Severe forms of mental retardation constitute only a small proportion of the cases of mental retardation; they are found in equal proportions in all levels of society, and they stem from physiological problems. In contrast, moderate forms of mental retardation are much more prevalent; they are more likely to be found in the lower social classes, and in most cases they are presumed to be due to psychological or social factors. The severe forms of retardation can be linked to specific causes and broken into distinctly different types (e.g., Down syndrome, PKU), but moderate retardation is usually not linked to specific causes and is not broken into different types. We will consider some of the psychosocial factors that may contribute to moderate levels of mental retardation. In most cases, the psychosocial factors that are thought to be related to retardation are associated with differences in social class.

The influence of socioeconomic status and cultural background on intellectual ability was illustrated in an early study in which various abilities were assessed in Chinese, Jewish, Puerto Rican, and African-American children who came from middle- and lower-class backgrounds (Stodolsky & Lesser, 1967). Some of the results are presented in Figure 20.3, and they reveal two findings. First, children from the lower class generally performed less well than children from the middle class, and second, children from different ethnic backgrounds showed different patterns of ability. Those findings provide strong evidence for the effects of class and culture on intellectual abilities.

The effects of psychosocial factors were also dramatically illustrated in the case of a child who was locked in an attic until she was 6 years old (Davis, 1947). When she was found, her IQ was estimated to be only 25, but within 3 years, she was functioning at the appropriate level for her age. This child's retardation was more extreme than what is usually thought to stem from psychosocial factors, but, of course, the psychosocial factors to which she was exposed were more extreme than what most children experience. Case

FIGURE 20.3   CHINESE AND JEWISH CHILDREN SHOWED DIFFERENT PATTERNS OF ABILITIES, AND CHILDREN FROM THE LOWER CLASS PERFORMED LESS WELL THAN CHILDREN FROM THE MIDDLE CLASS.

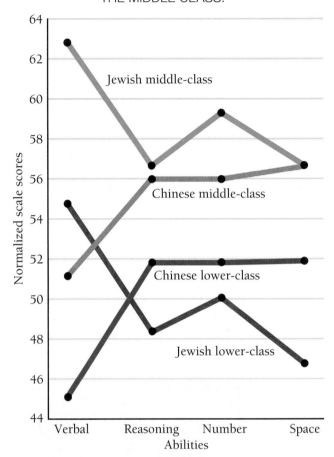

Source: Data from Stodolsky and Lesser (1967), p. 568, figs. 2 and 3.

Study 20.3 focuses on an individual whose retardation stems from psychosocial factors.

The findings in Figure 20.3 and the case of the confined child provide strong support for the relationship between psychosocial factors and intellectual abilities. The question is, what specific psychosocial factors influence intellectual development? Despite years of research, the answer to that question remains controversial, but we will mention some of the factors that are generally thought to be important. In most cases, these factors are associated with social class, which is probably why members of the lower class are more likely to suffer from moderate retardation.

1. *Limited Psychosocial Environments.* Enriched social environments are thought to contribute to enhanced brain development and superior cognitive skills. Unfortunately, lower-class children have fewer toys to play

Case Study 20.3

THE CONTRIBUTION OF PSYCHOSOCIAL FACTORS TO MILD RETARDATION

Lester was raised in a severely blighted, tough, urban ghetto. His father deserted the family soon after Lester was born, so he, his mother, and his two older sisters lived on welfare. Occasionally his mother worked as a cleaning woman and was paid "under the table," but for the most part they had to subsist on public assistance. In the first 8 years of Lester's life, the family moved six times because the buildings in which they were living were condemned, set on fire, or unheated in winter or because the family was evicted for not paying rent. Lester's diet during his early childhood consisted largely of soft drinks, donuts, and junk food. His major activities consisted of watching television and roaming the streets at all hours of the day and night.

Elementary school started badly. He was not prepared for the limitations it placed on him (despite his young age, he was used to doing what he wanted when he wanted), and he could not see any value in what he was supposed to learn. Even at age 6, in his world, "street-wise" was better than "book-wise." He told his teacher, "Letters 'n them don't git ya nothin'." Because of his lack of interest and the frequent disruptions he caused, he alienated his teacher. Within 3 months, he and his teacher had implicitly arrived at a standoff: He came to school (or usually did) because he had to, but once there, he did nothing, and as long as he did not cause trouble, the teacher ignored him. He wasted away the days doodling, napping, or goofing off. Because he was not an overt troublemaker, he was not disliked, and he was passed along from grade to grade without having learned anything.

His entrance into high school changed little except that when he did not feel like going to school, he simply "cut." Letters to his mother were useless, and threats of suspension were empty because he did not want to be in school anyway. Lester was not alone in coming to and going from school as he wished; on a typical day, almost half the students would be absent from any one of his classes. The only class in which he showed any consistent interest and ability was auto shop, where he became adept at fine-tuning automobiles. Lester did not graduate, but it is not clear from the records whether he ever formally dropped out. Apparently, he just drifted out of school and no one bothered to try to bring him back.

When he was 17, Lester was picked up by the police on suspicion of auto theft, and as part of the pretrial assessment, he was sent to a juvenile detention center, where he was given an individual intelligence test. The results revealed that his overall IQ was only 62. Follow-up was never done because he was released when the case was dropped.

Today Lester is functionally illiterate. He cannot effectively read or write, and his math skills are limited to simple addition and subtraction. Socially, he is pleasant and gets along well with just about anyone. He works as a "gofer" in a local automobile repair shop. When he is not running errands, he acts as a helper for one of the mechanics, who is teaching him the business. In this hands-on situation, Lester is learning quickly, but ultimately his progress will be limited by the fact that he cannot read the repair manuals.

---

with, their homes contain fewer objects of any kind, and they are less likely to be taken on trips to places like museums or zoos (Deutsch et al., 1967).

2. *Language Habits.* Verbal behavior plays an important role both in the assessment of intelligence and in daily functioning, and therefore language habits are a crucial factor in mental retardation. Members of minority groups often learn forms of nonstandard English with which they can communicate with other members of their group but do not enable them to communicate with individuals who are using standard English. In some cases, the nonstandard English is as difficult for standard English speakers to understand as a foreign language. Apart from nonstandard English, lower-class children often learn very restricted language patterns that limit their thinking processes and reduce their problem-solving abilities.

3. *Child-Rearing Style.* A variety of studies have demonstrated that relative to middle-class mothers,

lower-class mothers are more authoritarian and allow their children fewer opportunities for self-exploration. They are also less likely to explain things, are more critical, talk less with their children, and use shorter and less complex sentences with fewer abstract words. These interactions do not foster critical thinking or academic challenges.

4. *Motivation.* Motivation is crucial for effective intellectual performance, but lower-class children are not encouraged to do well in school and do not see school performance as relevant or important. In some cases, lower-class individuals see themselves as locked into their situation and develop feelings of helplessness. In other words, they do not see themselves as in control but rather as controlled by external factors, so they give up and do not try (Battle & Rotter, 1963). This view of control has been documented in children as young as 3 years old (Stephens & Delys, 1973).

5. *Schooling.* There are often important differences

between the facilities that are available to students from different classes or racial groups. Also important is the nature of the teaching or interaction that goes on in the classroom. There is evidence that in classrooms consisting solely of African-Americans, 50% to 80% of the classroom time is devoted to disciplining children, versus 30% in all-white classrooms (Deutsch et al., 1967).

As we noted earlier, teachers' expectations about how well students will do and the attention they give them may also play a role. In the classic study in this area, teachers were told that some of their students would probably bloom by the end of the year but others would not (Rosenthal & Jacobson, 1968). At the end of the year, all of the students were given an IQ test, and it was found that the students who the teachers were led to believe would bloom in fact had higher scores even though the children had been randomly assigned to the bloomer and nonbloomer groups. A related study revealed that children who were not expected to do well were generally ignored by the teacher, and the reduced attention could certainly result in lowered performance (Rist, 1970). These detrimental effects of expectations can be serious, and therefore it may be fortunate that not all investigators found the effects (Elashoff & Snow, 1971).

6. *Poor Physical or Medical Care.* Individuals in the lower class often receive poorer prenatal and postnatal care than individuals in the middle class, and those differences in care can lead to retardation. Strictly speaking, infection, trauma, prematurity, and nutrition are not psychosocial factors, but they are associated with psychosocial factors (economic class) and therefore deserve mention in this context.

Overall, then, social class is related to a variety of psychological as well as physical factors that contribute to mental retardation.

It is important to recognize that in most cases, the evidence linking the psychosocial factors to mental retardation is correlational, and therefore we cannot definitely say that psychosocial factors cause retardation. However, because it seems highly likely that they do cause retardation and because their effects are reversible, it is important that we continue to focus attention and efforts on psychosocial factors as causes of retardation.

there were almost 200,000 retarded persons in public institutions, many more were in private facilities, and others were kept behind closed doors at home. The notion was that persons who suffered from retardation could not care for themselves and needed protection. It also seems likely that many parents were ashamed of their retarded children and attempted to hide them. Since then, however, great strides have been taken to modify, if not reverse, that position and to bring the retarded out into the mainstream of society. Indeed, between 1967 and 1984, the number of retarded persons in public institutions decreased by 55%.

This change in the treatment of retarded persons was motivated by two factors. First, it was suggested that if retarded persons were exposed to normal living conditions, they were more likely to develop more normal behavior patterns than if they were left to languish in institutions. This is known as the principle of **normalization** (Landesman & Butterfield, 1987). The principle of normalization does not deny that intellectual limitations influence the behavior of retarded persons, but it suggests that the intellectual limitations are only *part* of the problem. In an attempt to overcome the problems caused by experiential limitations, it was proposed that efforts be made to integrate retarded persons into the mainstream of society.

The second factor in the deinstitutionalization of retarded persons was economics. The average yearly cost per institutionalized person is well over $40,000, and costs are rising sharply. The cost to the federal and state governments is over $4 billion per year. In addition, there are the enormous costs of private hospitalization and many hidden costs associated with keeping retarded persons at home (e.g., a potential wage earner has to stay home to care for the person).

Both normalization and economic pressures led to deinstitutionalization, but not always successfully. In some cases, retarded persons were taken out of institutions only to be ignored and left alone in deplorable circumstances. In other cases, with specialized programs, normalization worked. Case Study 20.4 describes one effective program for helping retarded persons in the community. In this case, not only did the community help the retarded persons, but the retarded persons also made a meaningful contribution to the community.

PERSONS WITH RETARDATION IN THE COMMUNITY

Until the late 1960s, most persons who suffered from mental retardation were kept in large institutions where they were essentially "warehoused." In 1967,

SUMMARY

We began this chapter with a discussion of organic mental disorders. These disorders stem from physiological problems in the brain such as the deterioration or death of cells. The major symptom in these disor-

Case Study 20.4

COTTONWOOD: A COMMUNITY PROGRAM THAT IS "GOOD BUSINESS" AND A WHOLE LOT MORE

Cottonwood, Inc., is a community-based program for individuals who suffer from mental retardation in Lawrence, Kansas, a university town of about 60,000 people. Cottonwood serves two major functions. First, it provides supervised home living for its clients. It does this through 10 group homes that are scattered throughout the city. Rather than being "institutional," these homes are indistinguishable from other homes in the area. Most people are not even aware that the houses are group home facilities. Between four and six residents and a home supervisor live in each home. During the times when the residents are not working, the supervisor provides training in nutrition, grocery shopping, cooking, grooming, hygiene, clothing care, housekeeping, home maintenance, money management, leisure skills, and social skills. Residents pay a monthly fee to cover rent, utilities, and food, and they are responsible for the care and maintenance of the homes. As residents develop the necessary skills, they progress to a semi-independent living arrangement in which they have their own apartments, but they are still given up to 5 hours a week of training and guidance that is tailored to their particular needs.

Cottonwood's second major function is to provide occupational training and opportunities for its clients. There are three levels of training. First, approximately 30 clients work in the "sheltered workshop" program. In this program, clients are brought to the Cottonwood building, where, with close supervision and training, they work on projects involving light manufacturing, packaging, collating, and the preparation of bulk mailings. These are not meaningless or "makework" projects. Instead, Cottonwood has contracted for real work on a competitive basis with local businesses, and the clients are paid for their work. Because the projects are let on a competitive basis, and because the Cottonwood clients may work somewhat more slowly than other people, the wages paid to the clients may be somewhat lower than those paid to others. The important point is that the Cottonwood clients become productive, contributing members of society and are paid on a fair basis. Everyone wins.

The second level of job training and experience involves supervised group work in the community. For example, companies such as Quaker Oats often need a work force to complete a particular project, and a group from Cottonwood will take on the job. In those cases, Cottonwood transports its clients to and from the work site and provides on-site supervisors for them. This real-world work is an important experience for Cottonwood's clients because they can use their nonretarded coworkers as role models. In one case, a client stopped carrying his Snoopy lunch box when he saw that everyone else was carrying a plain black lunch box. The clients want to fit in, and with normal models available, they quickly learn how. Having the clients on the production line is also an important experience for the other workers who learn to overcome their stereotypes about persons with retardation and come to accept them.

Some clients go on to normal independent and competitive community employment. Typical employment involves work in fast-food restaurants, janitorial services, housecleaning jobs (especially in hotels and motels), and some light industry.

Employing retarded persons is not charity. As one executive after another says, *"It's just good business."* Indeed, the experiences of employers across the country consistently indicate that retarded workers are often more reliable, happier, and more likely to remain in the job than their nonretarded coworkers. The Cottonwood clients find their jobs to be challenging and interesting, and that makes them good employees. With this approach, everyone wins: Retarded persons get meaningful jobs and a chance to grow, employers get an excellent work force, and the economy is helped because people who were once consumers of tax dollars become producers of tax dollars. Cottonwood's logo is a "thumbs up" sign, and that is appropriate because they are making it work for everyone. It's good business *and a whole lot more.*

---

ders is dementia, which is an organically based loss of intellectual abilities. The most prominent symptom of dementia is the loss of memory, but declines in judgment, abstract reasoning, and higher intellectual functions also occur. Physical symptoms such as loss of motor control (jerking movements or paralysis) also play a role in some organic mental disorders. Dementia that sets in before the age of 65 is called presenile dementia; if it occurs after age 65, it is called senile dementia. It is important to distinguish between primary dementia, which is due to an organic problem, and secondary dementia, which results from some other disorder such as depression.

Although all organic mental disorders have an organic basis, the disorders differ from one another in terms of symptoms and the nature of the organic prob-

The move toward deinstitutionalization of retarded people has led to efforts to integrate them into mainstream society. Community-based programs that involve group homes and supervised work situations have been effective in many cases.

lem. Alzheimer's disease involves a general dementia (though memory problems are most prominent) and is due to a general deterioration of the brain. The disorder is most likely to occur in women over the age of 60 or 65 and is widespread. The major symptoms of Huntington's disease are involuntary motor movements (jerking and twisting of the body and facial grimacing) and general dementia. The symptoms usually occur initially around the age of 40. The disease is due to one abnormal dominant gene, and thus there is a strong genetic link for the disorder.

Parkinson's disease involves uncontrollable fine muscle movements and rigidity. Parkinson's disease is widespread, usually occurs around the age of 50, and is due to low levels of the neurotransmitter dopamine. Unlike most of the other organic mental disorders, in many individuals, the symptoms of Parkinson's disease can be controlled with medication (L-dopa).

Multi-infarct dementia occurs when the individual has a series of cerebral infarctions (strokes) that destroy areas of the brain. Symptoms include the loss of cognitive or motor functions, depending on where the infarctions occur. The loss of functions is irregular rather than smooth because the infarctions occur at irregular intervals.

The symptoms of general paresis (syphilis of the brain) are delusions, depression, and general dementia. The disorder results from the destruction of the brain by a microorganism (a spirochete). General paresis can be effectively treated with penicillin. Unfortunately, the symptoms of most (but not all) organic mental disorders are irreversible because damage is done to the cells of the central nervous system, which do not regenerate. These are serious disorders, and

the problems they pose are going to become greater as a greater proportion of the population becomes older due to increased life expectancies.

In the second part of this chapter, we focused on mental retardation, which is an exceptionally widespread problem. Depending on the definition that is used, between 6 and 41 million people in the United States suffer from mental retardation. There are four levels of retardation: mild, moderate, severe, and profound. IQ scores are usually the major measure of retardation, but we must be cautious in their use because standard IQ tests may not accurately measure the abilities of minority group members, may not measure real-world abilities, and may not provide accurate measures of intelligence at very low levels. Classifying or labeling individuals as mentally retarded may result in self-fulfilling prophecies, but if we treat retarded individuals as though they were not retarded, they may not get some of the special training they need to overcome or compensate for their problem. It is acknowledged that profound and severe levels of retardation are due to physiological defects, but there is controversy over whether mild retardation is due to defects or delays in development that may be due to psychosocial factors.

Genetic factors account for only about 25% of the cases of mental retardation, but they are the most serious cases. Down syndrome is a serious and irreversible form of retardation that results from an extra chromosome 21. Phenylketonuria (PKU) stems from a genetically determined high level of acid that destroys the brain, but the level of acid can be controlled with diet, and if the diet is begun early enough, the retardation can be avoided or minimized. Other notable types of retardation due to genetic factors include Turner's syndrome, which occurs when one female chromosome is missing; Klinefelter's syndrome, which occurs when there are one or more extra female chromosomes; and cretinism (hypothyroidism), which results from reduced production of the thyroid hormone thyroxin, which slows metabolism.

Retardation can also be caused by physical factors in the environment that affect the brain during the prenatal, perinatal, or postnatal periods. Alcohol consumption by pregnant women can result in fetal alcohol syndrome, in which retardation can be minimal or severe. A case of rubella (German measles) in a pregnant woman can result in a form of retardation. In that disorder, the mother's infection causes an inflammation in the brain of the fetus that destroys brain cells and results in the retardation. Exposure to lead during the prenatal period or early childhood can cause mild levels of retardation.

A wide range of psychosocial factors are suspected as causes of mild retardation. These include the psychosocial environment, language habits, child-rearing style, motivation, schooling, and poor physical and medical care. The fact that these factors differ across social class is used to explain why mild forms of retardation are more prevalent in the lower classes than in the middle or upper classes.

KEY TERMS, CONCEPTS, AND NAMES

- -

In reviewing and testing yourself on what you have learned from this chapter, you should be able to identify and discuss each of the following:

Alzheimer's disease	GABA	phenylketonuria (PKU)
amniocentesis	general paresis (syphilis of the brain)	phenylpyruvic acid
aneurysm	granulovacuolar degeneration	plaques
arteriosclerosis	Huntington's disease (chorea)	presenile dementia
atherosclerosis	Klinefelter's syndrome	primary dementia
Binet, Alfred	L-dopa	rubella (German measles)
cerebral infarction	levels of retardation	secondary dementia
cognitive abulia	mental defect	senile dementia
cretinism (hypothyroidism)	mental retardation	spirochete
declassification (of persons with mental retardation)	multi-infarct dementia	stroke
	neurofibrillary tangling	substantia nigra
delayed development	nootropic drugs	thyroxin
dementia	normalization	trisomy 21
Down syndrome	organic mental disorders	Turner's syndrome (gonadal dysgenesis)
embolism	Parkinson's disease	
fetal alcohol syndrome (FAS)	phenylalanine	

PART 6

Issues of Law, Patient Care, and Prevention

• OUTLINE •

Chapter 21

Legal Issues

• O U T L I N E •

Andrew was arrested for stealing a car. Before his trial, his attorney discovered that Andrew had a serious thought disorder that made it difficult or impossible for Andrew to understand the legal proceedings or to testify accurately. (Andrew was probably suffering from schizophrenia.) When this was confirmed by a psychologist, the judge ruled that Andrew was *incompetent to stand trial.* That ruling postponed the trial, and Andrew was committed to a hospital for treatment until he was judged competent. The incompetence ruling protected Andrew from an unfair trial, but there was still a problem because his confinement for treatment might be longer than his confinement would be if he stood trial and was convicted.

Leslie believed that the man next door was building a nuclear device in his basement and that he was going to use it to blow up the Capitol. One night, while listening to a commercial on TV, she received a "secret message from the president" instructing her to kill the man next door and thereby save civilization. The next morning, she shot the man with a .38 as he left for work. She knew that killing was wrong, but this was "self-defense for the world—I had no choice." At her trial, her attorney argued that Leslie's behavior had been a result of a "mental disease or defect," and therefore under the laws of the state, she should be found *not guilty by reason of insanity.* The jury agreed, and Leslie was committed to a hospital for treatment rather than to a prison for punishment. It is interesting to note that if Leslie had been tried in a nearby state where the laws were different, she would have been found guilty regardless of her mental state because she knew that killing another person was wrong. After a year and a half in the hospital, Leslie was released.

In a fit of passion, Donald bludgeoned to death a man who had made a pass at his wife. At his trial a year later, Donald testified that he had been so upset at the time of the killing that he would have hit the man even if a police officer had been standing there and he knew that he would be caught. The defense argued that at the time of the killing, Donald was *temporarily insane,* but he was normal now. The defense suggested that Donald should be found not guilty by reason of insanity and released. After all, they argued, if he is normal now, there is no point in confining him for treatment. The prosecution argued that it is difficult enough to determine a person's mental state at the present, much less a year ago, and that a convincing case had not been made for insanity. Apart from that, one might wonder whether without treatment, Donald might become insane again the next time he became upset.

Martha has been a patient in a huge state hospital for 6 years. She was committed to the hospital against her will after a neighbor reported to the police that Martha was talking about killing herself, and a panel of psychiatrists agreed that she was a "danger to herself." Martha has petitioned the court for release on the grounds that "talk therapy" once a week is not doing her any good. The court is in a difficult position because the law requires that patients be treated or released, but there is no rule for determining what is appropriate treatment.

Lois is suffering from severe depression and is suicidal. Psychotherapy and drugs have had little or no effect, and it appears that she will have to be hospitalized for a long time. Faced with that, it has been decided to try electroconvulsive (shock) therapy. Lois has refused the treatment. However, Lois can be given the electroconvulsive therapy against her will because she is *involuntarily committed* to the hospital and because not using the treatment would result in greatly increased costs to the hospital.

Craig signed himself into the hospital voluntarily when he thought he was "losing control" of his thoughts. After being in the hospital a week, he feels somewhat better, but he does not like the drugs he is being given, and he generally dislikes the hospital. Two days ago, he told the ward nurse that he wanted to sign out of the hospital and go home. She gave him the appropriate forms to fill out and told him that there would be a 48-hour waiting period before he could be discharged. During the waiting period, the hospital staff decided that Craig needed to be hospitalized, so they changed his status from voluntary to involuntary commitment. Now he cannot leave the hospital. He is furious and argues that if he had not come in voluntarily, he would not be there and that if he were a medical patient with cancer, they would let him leave. He claims his right of equal protection is being violated, and he wants out.

In earlier chapters, we examined the nature and treatment of various types of abnormal behavior. In this chapter, we will take a different perspective and examine a variety of legal issues related to abnormal behavior. Specifically, we will consider (a) the rules that are used to determine whether individuals are competent to stand trial, (b) the rules that are used to determine whether individuals are insane and not responsible for their actions, (c) the procedures that are used to commit individuals to mental hospitals voluntarily and involuntarily, and (d) the rights of hospitalized mental patients.

We must give careful attention to these issues because they influence the protection that is afforded to disturbed individuals. They also influence the protection that is provided for other members of society who may be threatened by disturbed individuals. In 1980, John Hinckley, Jr., attempted to assassinate the president of the United States. In his defense, he claimed that he was insane. Should he have been treated and released, or should he have been punished for the crime as another citizen would be punished? Joyce Brown lived next to a heat vent on a New York City street and sometimes burned money given to her by passersby. Should she have been committed to a hospital against her will, or should she have been allowed to continue living on the street as she wished? These are

some of the questions we will attempt to answer in this chapter. The issues linking abnormal behavior and the law are complex because of the delicate balance that must be achieved between the need to protect the rights of disturbed individuals and the need to avoid violating the rights of other members of society.

COMPETENCE TO STAND TRIAL

It is important that individuals who are accused of crimes be given the best opportunity to defend themselves in court. Individuals who cannot adequately defend themselves because they suffer from mental disorders can be declared **incompetent to stand trial**, and their trials will be postponed. To be declared incompetent to stand trial, it must be determined that the individual *cannot understand the proceedings or cannot contribute to his or her defense* (e.g., communicate effectively with the defense attorney, provide adequate testimony; Roesch & Golding, 1980; Schwitzgebel & Schwitzgebel, 1980). For example, a person with schizophrenia whose thought processes were so disturbed that he or she could not understand what was being said or could not respond appropriately would be declared incompetent to stand trial. The incompetence

The embezzlement trial of television evangelist Jim Bakker was stalled when his attorney claimed he was incompetent to stand trial. After 3 days of evaluation, Bakker was ruled competent to stand trial.

defense is an extension of the notion that an individual should not be tried in absentia. In other words, defendants must be physically and mentally present at their trials. The decision concerning whether an individual is competent to stand trial is made by a judge, who usually obtains recommendations from experts such as psychiatrists and psychologists (*Dusky* v. *United States*, 1960; *Pate* v. *Robinson*, 1966). In a review of a large number of defendants whose competence had been evaluated, it was found that individuals were most likely to be judged incompetent if they showed psychotic behavior such as hallucinations, delusions, disturbed behavior, or disturbed mood that would interfere with their ability to participate in their defense (Nicholson & Kugler, 1991).

It is important to note that *incompetence does not relieve the individual of responsibility for an illegal act.* Instead, it simply allows the trial to be *postponed* until he or she can participate appropriately. During the postponement, the defendant is confined in a hospital or prison for the criminally insane. This confinement is for the purpose of treating the individual so that eventually he or she will be competent to stand trial.

There are three potential problems with the use of the incompetence defense. First, some individuals attempt to *fake* incompetence as a means of stalling the legal proceedings against them. At the Nuremberg war crimes trial, Rudolf Hess successfully feigned amnesia well enough to fool the psychiatric panel and delay his trial by months. Fortunately, experts are usually able to detect attempts to fake incompetence, and even if the attempts are successful, they only postpone the trial and do not get the individual off.

The second problem is that it is possible for individuals to be *confined longer for the treatment of the incompetence than they would be confined if they stood trial for their crimes and were convicted.* That does not seem fair. The results of one investigation revealed that the average length of incarceration for incompetence was almost 6 years, which is much longer than the time most criminals spend in jail for serious crimes (McGarry & Bendt, 1969). In one institution, three individuals were found who had been incarcerated for incompetence but then overlooked for 17, 39, and 42 years, respectively.

Obviously, confinement for that long is inappropriate, and the Supreme Court has now ruled that the confinement must not be longer than what is necessary to treat the individual and render him or her competent to stand trial, and that if it is unlikely that the individual will ever become competent, the individual must either be committed to a hospital or released (*Jackson* v. *Indiana*, 1972). Apart from the problem posed by the fact that confinement because of incompetence may be longer than imprisonment for the crime, there is always the possibility that after a prolonged confinement for incompetence, the individual will be found not guilty of the crime.

The third problem occurs when the system is *misused* by law enforcement officials. When dealing with individuals who are a nuisance but who do not commit serious crimes, law enforcement officials may arrest the individuals and then have them declared incompetent as a means of getting them off the streets for longer periods than are justified by their illegal acts. In those cases, what was originally developed as a defense becomes a tool for prosecution. This type of confinement is particularly onerous because unlike other pretrial confinements, incarceration for incompetence does not permit release on bail.

In summary, the concept of incompetence to stand trial was established to protect disturbed individuals from unfair trials, but the implementation of the incompetence plea has problems and can be abused, so it must be used carefully. With this as background, we can go on to consider the question of whether disturbed individuals are legally responsible for illegal acts they commit.

■ THE INSANITY DEFENSE

In our society, it is generally agreed that individuals are in control of their behavior, and therefore they are responsible for their behavior and should be punished if they do something that is illegal. However, if for some reason individuals cannot control their behavior, it is not appropriate to hold them responsible or punish them for their behavior. That line of reasoning led to the **insanity defense**. Stated most broadly, the insanity defense asserts that *individuals who cannot behave appropriately because of mental disorders should not be held responsible for their behavior and should not be punished for their illegal behavior.*

If an individual is judged to be "not guilty by reason of insanity," he or she is committed to a hospital for treatment rather than to a prison for punishment. When the authorities agree that the individual no longer suffers from the disorder that led to the criminal behavior, the individual is released and does not have to go to prison. The insanity plea is very controversial, and we must give it careful consideration because it has a variety of important implications.

General Issues

Before discussing the rules that are used to determine whether or not an individual is insane, we should briefly mention three related issues. First, note that the term *insanity* is a *legal* term and not a psychological or medical one. This is relevant because it means that whether or not an individual is judged to be insane is determined by the laws of a given state rather than by what is labeled as abnormal in DSM-IV. For example, under some laws, an individual could be hallucinating, delusional, and diagnosed as suffering from schizophrenia, but if he or she knew the difference between right and wrong, the individual would be judged to be sane.

Second, different states employ different rules for determining whether an individual is insane. Because of these differences, in one state an individual might be declared not guilty by reason of insanity and be treated rather than punished, but in another state the same individual would be judged guilty and punished rather than treated.

Third, there are wide differences of opinion concerning how strict or lenient the rule for determining insanity should be. On the one hand, some critics argue that insanity should be defined very narrowly so that individuals who willfully commit crimes will be punished. The most conservative position is that all humans are always responsible for their behavior, and the insanity defense should be abolished. Indeed, it

has been abolished in Utah, Montana, and Idaho. On the other hand, other people contend that insanity should be defined broadly so as to avoid the possibility of punishing disturbed individuals who need treatment. The most liberal position is that anyone who commits an illegal act is suffering from some sort of problem and should be rehabilitated rather than punished. As will become apparent in the subsequent discussion, the rules that are used for defining insanity differ widely, and as you read about each, you should consider which rule you think is most appropriate. After all, insanity is determined by laws, and someday you may be asked to vote to determine how insanity will be defined in your state.

Rules for Defining Insanity

There are basically three rules for defining insanity. We will consider each rule, along with its strengths and weaknesses. The rules will be considered in chronological order so that you can see how the concept is evolving. An understanding of these rules is important because they determine whether individuals who commit serious crimes such as murder will be punished, treated, or simply set free (Wettstein et al., 1991).

The M'Naghten Rule: Knowledge of Right Versus Wrong. This rule is named for Daniel M'Naghten, who in 1843 murdered the secretary of the British prime minister. M'Naghten actually meant

In 1843 Daniel M'Naghten murdered a public official but the British court ruled that he was not guilty by reason of insanity. Outrage over this verdict resulted in a new standard for determining insanity, the M'Naghten rule. That rule holds that an individual can be declared insane if at the time of the crime the individual did not know what he or she was doing or did not know the act was wrong.

to kill the prime minister but mistook the male secretary for his intended victim. During the trial, it was discovered that M'Naghten thought that the prime minister was plotting against him and that "the voice of God" had instructed him to kill the prime minister. Because M'Naghten's behavior had resulted from delusions of persecution and hallucinations rather than evil intent, he was found not guilty by reason of insanity. Instead of being punished, he was committed to a mental hospital, where he remained for the rest of his life.

There was widespread public outrage over the fact that an individual who had willfully committed murder was not punished. Most important, Queen Victoria was infuriated by the insanity verdict. Numerous attempts had been made on the lives of members of the royal family, and she thought that the failure to punish M'Naghten would encourage more such attempts. As a consequence, the queen demanded that a tougher test of insanity be developed. The test that was subsequently developed in the House of Lords came to be known as the **M'Naghten** (mik-NOT-un) **rule**. It holds that an individual can be declared insane if at the time of the crime he or she *did not know what he or she was doing* or *did not know that it was wrong*.

The M'Naghten rule has been severely criticized because it is based entirely on the individual's knowledge of *right versus wrong* and therefore it ignores all of the other mental abnormalities that can contribute to behavior. For example, it does not take into consideration the possibility that the individual knew that the act was wrong but could not exercise control because of overpowering emotions (so-called "crimes of passion" or "irresistible impulses"). Furthermore, it does not take into consideration the possibility that the individual knew that the act was wrong but had to commit it because of hallucinations or delusions. A person suffering from schizophrenia might know that killing is wrong but believe that it must be done in self-defense because the other person is sending brain-killing X-ray waves. The critics of the M'Naghten rule argue that overwhelming emotions and mental aberrations such as hallucinations and delusions are at least as important as the simple knowledge of right versus wrong, and that therefore the M'Naghten rule is too narrow.

In some states that employ the M'Naghten rule, an additional rule has been introduced that takes into account the influence of an **irresistible impulse** (sudden overwhelming emotion) that can lead to illegal behavior (*Smith* v. *United States*, 1929). The irresistible impulse rule is sometimes known as the **elbow rule** because it essentially asks, *would this individual have committed the crime if a police officer had been standing at his or her elbow, thereby ensuring that he or she would be caught?* The notion is that if the police were standing next to you so that you certainly would be caught, and if you still committed the illegal act, you must be out of control and should be judged to be insane.

Problematic as the M'Naghten rule may be, it stood unchallenged for over 100 years, and it is still used in some states today.

The Durham Rule: Product of Mental Disease or Defect.

The second major rule is named for Monte Durham, who had been in and out of mental hospitals and prisons before he was charged with breaking into a house in 1951. At his trial, Durham pleaded not guilty by reason of insanity, but the judge rejected the plea because he did not think that it had been established that Durham did not know the difference between right and wrong or that Durham was subject to an irresistible impulse (*Durham* v. *United States*, 1954). Because the insanity defense was rejected, Durham was convicted. However, Durham's lawyer appealed the conviction on the grounds that the M'Naghten rule was obsolete and not based on a modern understanding of human behavior (i.e., the M'Naghten rule focused only on knowledge of right and wrong). The appeal was successful, the conviction was overturned, and Durham was retried using a new rule for determining insanity. In passing down his decision in Durham's retrial, the judge wrote:

The legal and moral traditions of the western world require that those who of their own free will and with evil intent commit acts which violate the law shall be criminally responsible for those acts. Our traditions also require that where those acts stem from and are the product of mental disease or defect . . . moral blame shall not attach . . . and hence there will not be criminal responsibility.

This rule broadened the concept of insanity by indicating that any illegal behavior that resulted from a *mental disease or defect* could be considered the product of insanity. This rule became known as the **Durham rule**, and it was adopted by the U.S. federal courts in 1954.

Critics of the Durham rule argue that the "mental disease or defect" rule is too broad and that almost anyone could claim insanity under it. What is a mental disease or defect? Is an individual with alcoholism suffering from a mental disease or defect and therefore not responsible for illegal acts? How about someone with a migraine headache?

The American Law Institute Rule: Lack of Substantial Capacity to Appreciate and Conform Conduct.

After drinking wine all day, Archie Brawner went to a party where he got into a fight. He left the party, got a gun, returned, and in a rage fired the gun through a door and killed a man. At the trial, the defense argued that Brawner suffered from a psychiatric problem and should be declared insane. Because of the general discontent with the M'Naghten and Durham rules, the court adopted a new rule that had been developed by the American Law Institute, and therefore it is called the **American Law Institute rule**. The first part of the rule reads as follows:

A person is not responsible for criminal conduct if at the time of such conduct as a result of mental disease or defect he lacks substantial capacity either to appreciate the criminality (wrongfulness) of his conduct or to conform his conduct to the requirements of law.

Some of the phrases used in this rule are intentionally vague to leave the jury some flexibility in interpreting the rule and determining who is sane and insane. For example, the word *appreciate* can be interpreted in the narrow sense of "knowing," thereby allowing the rule to be used like the M'Naghten rule (the insane person does not know that the act is wrong). Alternatively, *appreciate* can be used in the broader sense of "understanding," which could be influenced by things such as delusions and hallucinations. When that broader interpretation is used, the rule can be used like the Durham rule (the insane person's act must be the product of a mental disease or defect).

The use of the phrase "lacks substantial capacity" also allows jurors flexibility because they can decide whether there was enough (substantial) lack of knowledge or mental disease to result in the act. In other words, the jury could find that the defendant is somewhat disturbed but not disturbed enough to justify a decision of not guilty by reason of insanity. Finally, by stating that the insane person cannot "conform his conduct to the requirements of law," the rule allows the use of the irresistible impulse rule (an insane person with an irresistible impulse cannot conform his behavior). Because of the flexibility built into the rule, different individuals can give it different interpretations, and therefore fewer individuals find a basis for criticizing it.

The second part of the American Law Institute rule reads: "The terms 'mental disease or defect' do not include an abnormality manifested only by repeated criminal or otherwise antisocial conduct." This provision explicitly precludes habitual criminals from using repeated criminal activities as evidence of a mental disease or defect. This provision also precludes an individual with an antisocial personality disorder (a psychopath) from pleading insanity because, as we learned earlier, one of the major signs of that disorder is repeated criminal behavior (see Chapter 15).

One problem with the original American Law Institute rule was that "mental disease" was not defined adequately. That was rectified in the Brawner case, when it was ruled that "mental disease or defect includes any abnormal condition of the mind which substantially *affects mental or emotional processes* and substantially *impairs behavior controls*" (*United States* v. *Brawner*, 1972). Like the rest of the American Law Institute rule, this definition of mental disease is very flexible. The American Law Institute rule was originally adopted widely in the United States, but as we will see later, many states have now abandoned it for a stricter rule.

To recap, with the M'Naghten rule, insanity was defined very narrowly (knowledge of right versus wrong); then with the Durham rule, it was defined very broadly (mental disease or defect); and finally with the American Law Institute rule, insanity was defined rather vaguely (lacks substantial capacity to appreciate or conform; mental disease is any process that substantially impairs behavior controls). The result of this evolution is that there is now some flexibility in the application of the concept of insanity.

Practical Problems with the Insanity Defense

Independent of the philosophical problems of whether there should be an insanity defense and how broadly or narrowly it should be defined, there are a number of practical problems and questions associated with

The decision concerning competence to stand trial is put in the hands of experts, but the more complex decision concerning insanity is left to untrained jurors.

implementing the insanity defense. One problem revolves around the fact that the decision concerning whether an individual is insane or not is determined by the vote of a jury. This is problematic because jurors may not have the technical knowledge or training that is necessary to make informed judgments concerning insanity. Leaving the decision concerning sanity to jurors might be like asking 12 individuals with no training in medicine to decide whether an individual with a pain on the right side of the abdomen has strained a muscle, has appendicitis, or is faking. After reading this book, you will probably be more knowledgeable about abnormal behavior than most juries, but would you be comfortable judging whether an individual has a mental disease or defect, or would you rather leave that decision to an expert? In that regard, it is interesting to note that the decision concerning competence to stand trial is put in the hands of experts (psychologists and psychiatrists), whereas the more complex decision concerning sanity is left to untrained jurors. Should the decision concerning insanity be left to a panel of independent experts?

Related to the fact that juries make the decision is the fact that in many cases, the jury must rely on opinions of expert witnesses, and often those witnesses disagree. What are juries to do when faced with expert witnesses who disagree?

Another problem revolves around the fact that in making a decision about insanity, we must determine the nature of the individual's state of mind *at the time the act was committed.* It is difficult enough to determine an individual's mental condition at the present time, and it may be almost impossible to determine what it was like days, weeks, or even years earlier.

There is also the related problem of treating the individual who was insane at the time of the act but is sane now. How do you treat an individual for a disorder he or she no longer has? Is the individual simply to be turned loose? Will the public stand for that? What is to prevent the "temporary insanity" from coming back and leading the individual to commit another crime?

Still another problem is that persons who are found not guilty by reason of insanity are incarcerated until they are "cured," but in many cases, the resulting period of incarceration is longer than what would have occurred if they had been found to be sane and simply sent to prison. Is that appropriate?

Finally, in most cases, the individual is presumed sane until proven insane. In our system of justice, the burden of proof is on the prosecution, and therefore we may ask whether the person should be presumed to be insane until proven sane.

Some of the problems associated with judging insanity are illustrated in Case Study 21.1, of John W.

In 1980 John Hinckley, Jr., attempted to assassinate President Ronald Reagan in an effort to impress actress Jodie Foster. He was judged not guilty by reason of insanity and sent to a hospital for treatment.

Hinckley, Jr., who attempted to assassinate President Ronald Reagan and then pleaded insanity. Hinckley's symptoms were somewhat vague and can lead to different diagnoses (e.g., was he suffering from schizophrenia or only the schizoid personality disorder; was he depressed or only dysthymic?). Because his symptoms can be interpreted in various ways, there is room for disagreement about whether or not he was insane (e.g., did his symptoms impair his behavioral control?). It is important to understand the facts and issues of this case because it will undoubtedly provide a legal benchmark and point of controversy for many years to come. In some respects, the Hinckley case will have an effect in America like the M'Naghten case had in England. As you read this case, you might try to arrive at your own diagnosis for John Hinckley and determine for yourself whether or not he was insane. (Read Case Study 21.1 before continuing in the text.)

Rule Changes in Response to the Hinckley Verdict

When Hinckley was found not guilty by reason of insanity, there was a considerable backlash against the use of the insanity defense. In some states, the insanity defense was simply abolished; in others, there were long debates about possible modifications of the rules. The American Psychiatric Association recommended the basis for insanity should not include the inability to conform behavior to the requirements of the law (Insanity Defense Work Group, 1983). In essence, that change returned the basis for insanity to the M'Naghten rule (knowledge of right versus wrong), and the

(text resumes on p. 543)

Case Study 21.1

JOHN W. HINCKLEY, JR.: AN INSANITY DEFENSE AFTER ATTEMPTING TO ASSASSINATE PRESIDENT RONALD REAGAN

JOHN HINCKLEY'S BACKGROUND

John Hinckley, Jr., was born in Ardmore, Oklahoma, in 1955, the youngest of three children. His father was a prosperous businessman. When John was 5, the family moved to Dallas, Texas, where he started attending school. In elementary school, he quarterbacked the football team, starred in basketball, became an avid Beatles fan, and appeared to be a well-adjusted child. When John was in the sixth grade, the family moved to an affluent and prestigious suburb (the home had its own swimming pool and even a soft-drink machine), and it was then that things seemed to change for John. As his mother put it, he was no longer the "kingpin"—he was the manager of the football team rather than the quarterback, he took up solitary activities such as playing the guitar, and he developed "his own little withdrawn personality."

After John graduated from high school, the family moved to Evergreen, Colorado, and John went to Lubbock, Texas, where he enrolled as a freshman at Texas Tech. During the following summer and fall, he lived in Dallas, a period he described this way: "I stayed by myself in my apartment and dreamed of future glory in some undefined field, perhaps music or politics." He returned to Texas Tech for the spring and fall semesters, but after that, his life became chaotic and disjointed. For example, he lived in at least 17 different places between his junior year in college and the time 4 years later when he attempted to assassinate the president. Because of space limitations, we cannot deal with those years in detail, but some facts are particularly noteworthy.

Midway through the spring semester of his junior year, John dropped out of school and sold his car to finance a trip to California, where he planned to sell songs he had been writing. Six weeks later, a letter he wrote to his parents was filled with optimism, but the tide soon turned, and when he wrote a month later, he said: "Through a series of sorry circumstances, I am in trouble. For the past 2 and a half weeks I have literally been without food, shelter and clothing." He asked for money, which his parents sent. On the positive side, he wrote about an encouraging contact with United Artists and a girlfriend named Lynn Collins. In fact, however, no contact had been made with United Artists, and Lynn Collins did not exist.

One fact about the period in California that later took on great significance was that John saw the movie *Taxi Driver* 15 times. The major character in the film is Travis Bickle, a lonely New York taxi driver. Travis meets a girl named Betsy, who works for a presidential candidate, but after their first date, she walked out on him, leaving him heartbroken. Travis goes to kill the candidate for whom Betsy works but is scared off by the Secret Service men. Later Travis encounters a 12-year-old prostitute named Iris (played by Jodie Foster), whom he decides to rescue. When Travis attacks Iris's pimp, he is shot and wounded, and the newspapers portray him as a hero. Some time later, by chance, Travis picks up Betsy in his cab, and because of his notoriety, she shows renewed interest in him.

John Hinckley apparently identified with the lonely Travis and subsequently took on many of his characteristics (dressed as he did, drank peach brandy, bought and played with guns, and began taking pills of various sorts). The film and his identification with Travis also led him to an intense interest in Jodie Foster, whom he saw as needing to be loved and rescued.

After returning from California, John worked for a while as a busboy and later returned to Texas Tech. While in school, he complained of a variety of physical ailments such as a sore eye, sore throat, earache, and light-headedness. He also became interested in the National Socialist (American Nazi) party and later wrote that "at the age of 23, I was an all-out anti-semite and white racist." In September 1979, he started publishing a newsletter for the American Front, an organization that he described as "an alternative to the minority-kissing Republican and Democrat parties." John called himself the "national director" and listed members in 37 states, but in fact there was no organization and he had made the whole thing up. The next year, he founded a mail-order company called Listalot from which people could buy lists of different types, but the lists were fictitious.

Off and on during this time, John sought help for more physical symptoms and was given a prescription for an antihistamine. Later he complained of hearing problems, dizzy spells, heart palpitations, and an "anxiety attack." The physician who saw him for those symptoms wrote in the record: "Patient showed a flat affect throughout examination and depressive reaction." An antidepressant (Surmontil) was prescribed. When John wrote to his sister, he said: "My nervous system is about shot. I take heavy medication for it which doesn't seem to do much good except make me very drowsy. By the end of the summer, I should be a bone fide basket case." After more visits to the physician, a tranquilizer (Valium) was prescribed.

John returned to Colorado to house-sit while his parents were away, and at that time, he began seeing a psychologist (Darrell Benjamin), who was a consultant on personnel matters for John's father. The psychologist regarded John as very immature and suggested that John formulate a plan for his life. Consistent with that suggestion, John worked out an agreement with his parents whereby he could sell some stock to finance a course in writing at Yale. He left for New Haven but did not register for class. Instead, he called Jodie Foster on the phone twice (she was a student at Yale) and then, after only 5 days, flew back to Colorado. Of that time he wrote: "My mind was on the breaking point. A relationship I had dreamed about went absolutely nowhere. My disillusionment with EVERYTHING was complete." After 4 days in Colorado, he flew to Lubbock and then to Washington, D.C., where he wrote to his sister, "Yale is such a disappointment. These past weeks have been strange times. I keep getting hit over the head by reality. It doesn't feel good."

This was followed by a series of trips to Columbus, Dayton, New Haven, Lincoln, Nashville, Chicago, New York, and Dallas. Some of these trips involved the stalking of President Jimmy Carter, whom John planned to shoot, but he decided against that. Before one flight between Nashville and New York, airport security guards found three pistols in John's suitcase. He was fined $62.50, held 5 hours, and then released.

At the end of this frenzy of traveling, John took an overdose of the antidepressant that had been prescribed for him, but he survived, and at his parents' insistence, he began seeing a psychiatrist named John Hopper. Between weekly sessions with Dr. Hopper in Colorado, John started making trips to Washington, New York, and New Haven. Sometimes he traveled under the assumed name of John Hudson. On trips to New Haven, he left notes, poems, and presents for Jodie Foster at her dormitory at Yale. One note read: "Just wait. I'll rescue you very soon. Please cooperate." Another said: "I love you six trillion times. Don't you maybe like me just a little bit? (You must admit I am different.) It would make all of this worthwhile."

On March 6, 1980, John ran out of money and called home for help. His father arranged for him to fly to Colorado and met John at the airport. Dr. Hopper, John's psychiatrist, advised the elder Hinckley, "Give John a hundred dollars and tell him good-bye," so Hinckley gave his son $210 and sent him off on his own. John spent the next couple of weeks living in motels. On March 25, his mother drove him to the airport. Of the trip to the airport she recalled,

> It was so hard to see John go, because I felt in my mind that once again John might be leaving and maybe he might try to take his own life. . . . He looked so bad, and so sad, and so absolutely in total despair and I was frightened, and I didn't know what he was going to do. . . . [At the airport,] John got out of the car and I couldn't even look at him. And he said, "Well, Mom, I want to thank you for everything. I want to thank you for everything you have ever done for me."

John flew to Hollywood but the next day took a bus to Washington, D.C., where he arrived on the afternoon of March 29 and registered at the Park Central Hotel.

THE SHOOTING

On the morning of March 30, 1980, John took a Valium and went to McDonald's for breakfast. On the way back, he bought a copy of the *Washington Star*, in which he noticed the president's schedule. Back in his room, John took a shower and took some Valium to help him calm down. He then loaded his .22 caliber pistol, specifically using exploding-head Devastator bullets. Next he wrote a letter to Jodie Foster. In that letter, he wrote of his plan to kill the president. He also wrote of his love for her and the reason for attempting to kill the president:

> As you well know by now I love you very much. Over the past seven months I've left you dozens of poems, letters and love messages in the faint hope that you could develop an interest in me. . . . I honestly did not wish to bother you with my constant presence. I know the many messages left at your door and in your mailbox were a nuisance, but I felt that it was the most painless way for me to express my love for you. . . . I will admit to you that the reason I'm going ahead with this attempt now is because I just cannot wait any longer to impress you. I've got to do something now to make you understand, in no uncertain terms, that I am doing all of this for your sake! By sacrificing my freedom and possibly my life, I hope to change your mind about me. This letter is being written only an hour before I leave for the Hilton Hotel. Jodie, I'm asking you to please look into your heart and at least give me the chance, with this historical deed, to gain your respect and love. I love you forever.

John then went to the Washington Hilton, where the president was scheduled to speak at 1:45. He waved as the president went in and then waited for him to come out. The president came out at 2:25, surrounded by aides and protectors. In response to a call from the crowd, the president turned, and as he did, John Hinckley crouched like a marksman and fired six shots in rapid succession. The first bullet hit the president's press secretary in the face and entered his brain. The second hit a policeman in the back. The third went over the president's head. The fourth hit a Secret Service agent in the chest. The fifth bullet hit the glass of the president's limousine, and the sixth ricocheted off the limousine and entered the president's chest, where it glanced off a rib and came to rest in a lung only inches from his heart. John Hinckley was wrestled to the ground by a Secret Service agent who reported that Hinckley "was still clicking the weapon," now empty, as they went down.

THE TRIAL

The trial opened in May 1982 and lasted until mid-June. The facts of the attempted assassination were clear and indisputable. Indeed, they were recorded by a television news cameraman, and the trial was begun with a showing of the videotape. John Hinckley had attempted to assassinate the president; the question was, *was he sane or insane at the time of the attempt?* Because the assassination was attempted in the District of Columbia, where the Brawner rule is used to determine sanity or insanity, the crucial question was, did John Hinckley, Jr., lack substantial capacity to appreciate the wrongfulness of his act or conform his conduct to the requirements of the law? The prosecution and defense waged a legal tug-of-war using teams of experts in an attempt to pull the jury in one direction or another.

THE DEFENSE

The defense attorneys first called John Hopper, the psychiatrist who had treated John Hinckley after the attempted suicide and who had suggested that the family turn John out on his own. Hopper testified that John's problems during late adolescence and early adulthood were "typical" of an unsuccessful son in a successful family. In other words, Hopper did not see John as particularly disturbed. That testimony would have played into the hands of the

prosecution, which was to argue that John was not insane, but the defense attorneys cleverly turned the testimony around. First, they suggested that Hopper was mistaken in his judgment. As support for that, they pointed out that despite the fact that John had had 22 therapy sessions with Hopper, Hopper knew nothing of John's extensive trips around the country, intense interest in the movie *Taxi Driver*, arrest in Nashville, or numerous other relevant facts about John's life. Then the defense attorneys used the fact that Hopper had been misled to suggest that John was so clever at disguising his problems that he was able to fool even a trained psychiatrist. The conclusion to be drawn by the jury was that they should not also be misled by John's superficial appearance of normality.

The defense also called William Carpenter, another psychiatrist, who testified that it was his judgment that John Hinckley was suffering from a major depression and from schizophrenia. It was Carpenter's opinion that because schizophrenia is a serious disorder that results in breaks from reality and delusions of reference, John Hinckley was not responsible for his acts.

Another important and controversial defense witness was David Bear, a psychiatrist who had special expertise in brain structure. Bear brought two things to the defense. First, he pointed out the role the movie *Taxi Driver* had played in John's symptoms. He pointed out that it was normal for a young man to fall in love with an actress, but he said that after being rejected by Jodie Foster, it was abnormal of Hinckley to continue pursuing her and to believe that she was a "prisoner at Yale" and that he had to "rescue" her. Bear asserted that Iris's renewed interest in Travis after he shot the pimp suggested to John that violence is rewarded by the attention of a woman and that John's fantasies about Travis and Iris had taken over his mind. According to Bear, John was essentially acting out the movie script. He had to rescue Jodie/Iris, and he could get her attention and love through violence. That, Bear concluded, "was psychosis."

Second, Bear testified about the results of a CT scan that was done on John's brain (see Chapter 3). Bear testified that the brains of many persons with schizophrenia are characterized by widened sulci (folds on the surface of the brain; see Chapter 13) and that John Hinckley's CT scan indicated that his brain had widened sulci. The implication was that the CT scan provided evidence that John Hinckley was suffering from schizophrenia. On cross-examination, the prosecutor tried to make the point that widened sulci is not a perfect sign of schizophrenia (i.e., some normal individuals have widened sulci) and that the CT scan could not be used to "confirm" a diagnosis of schizophrenia because the diagnosis had not been made in the first place. There was considerable controversy over whether the CT scan should be allowed as evidence, but eventually the judge ruled that it would be allowed. That ruling set an important precedent because never before had evidence of that type been allowed.

The defense also called Ernst Prelinger, a psychologist from Yale, as a witness. Prelinger testified that on the Wechsler Adult Intelligence Scale, John had an overall IQ of 113. More important, Prelinger reported that on the MMPI, John had abnormally high scores on all but one of the scales that measured abnormal behavior (e.g., schizophrenia, depression, anxiety) and that there was no evidence that he was faking his responses.

In summary, the defense argued that there was both psychological and physiological evidence that John Hinckley was suffering from schizophrenia and that his schizophrenia had rendered him unable to appreciate the wrongfulness of his act.

THE PROSECUTION

The major expert witness for the prosecution was a psychiatrist named Park Dietz. Dietz had led the team of government psychiatrists that produced a 628-page report concerning Hinckley's mental status, and Dietz was on the stand for 5 days testifying about the conclusions. It was Dietz's conclusion that Hinckley was suffering from a dysthymic disorder (a mild form of depression that falls between normal depression and the more serious major depressive disorder; see Chapter 8) and that he had three types of personality disorders: schizoid, narcissistic, and a combination of the borderline and passive-aggressive types.

In essence, the prosecution witnesses agreed with those of the defense with regard to the general *nature* of John's problems, but they saw the problems as *less serious*. They saw John as suffering from *dysthymia* rather than depression and as having a *schizoid* or *borderline* personality disorder rather than schizophrenia. In their report, the team of psychiatrists for the prosecution concluded that "Mr. Hinckley's history is clearly indicative of a person who did not function in a usual, reasonable manner. However, there is no evidence that he was so impaired that he could not appreciate the wrongful-

ness of his conduct or conform his conduct to the requirements of the law." Dietz argued that rather than suffering from schizophrenia, John was a lazy, fame-seeking, spoiled loner who lied and cheated to get what he wanted from his parents. As evidence of John's need for attention, Dietz pointed out that following the shooting, John had asked if reports of his assassination attempt would preempt the Academy Awards show that was scheduled for that night.

The other witness for the prosecution was Sally Johnson, a psychiatrist who had spent more time interviewing John Hinckley than anyone else. Johnson testified that Hinckley suffered from numerous personality disorders, but she did not consider them psychotic, nor did she think that they prevented Hinckley from being responsible for his acts.

In summary, the prosecution argued that John Hinckley was an immature and disturbed individual but that he was not suffering from schizophrenia and his level of disturbance was not enough to interfere with his ability to appreciate the wrongfulness of his act or conform his behavior to the law.

THE VERDICT

After months of testimony, Judge Barrington Parker gave the jury its instructions. As part of those instructions, he told the jury that mental illness was defined as "any abnormal condition of the mind" that "substantially affects mental or emotional processes and substantially impairs [a person's] behavior controls." The judge then made two important points: First, he told the jury that the burden was on the prosecution to prove that John Hinckley was *not* insane at the time of the assassination attempt. In other words, John was *insane until proven sane*, and if there was any reasonable doubt about his sanity, the jury had to bring in a verdict of not guilty by reason of insanity. Second, the judge addressed the effect of finding John not guilty by reason of insanity. The judge pointed out that if found to be insane, John would be committed to Saint Elizabeth's Hospital and that within 50 days, a hearing would have to be held to determine whether he could be released. In essence, he warned the jury that if they found John insane, he would not be punished and might soon be eligible for release.

After 4½ days of deliberation, the jury returned its verdict: on all counts, not guilty by reason of insanity. John W. Hinckley, Jr., was remanded to Saint Elizabeth's Hospital, where he remains to this day.

Source: Caplan (1984).

change was accepted by the U.S. Congress, so it now applies in all U.S. federal courts. It was also adopted by about half of the state courts. Knowledge of right versus wrong is certainly a more restrictive definition of insanity, but it is noteworthy that returning to that rule has not resulted in a dramatic decline in the use or success (acquittal rate) of the insanity defense (McGreevy et al., 1991).

One alternative rule that was proposed is the **mentally ill but guilty** rule. Under that rule, there would be two trials. The first would determine whether the defendant was sane or insane, and the second would determine whether the defendant was innocent or guilty. If found to be both insane and guilty, the individual would first be sent to a mental hospital for treatment until sane and then to prison to be punished for the crime. This procedure was developed to satisfy both supporters and opponents of the insanity defense, but you cannot satisfy both without some logical contradiction. How can you agree that an individual was insane and therefore not responsible for his or her behavior, and then punish the individual for the behavior for which you had agreed he or she was not responsible?

Other proposed changes involve making the defense prove insanity rather than making the prosecution prove sanity (that is already the case in some states) and barring psychiatrists and psychologists from testifying so that the judgment would be left entirely to the jury.

In recent years, the insanity defense has been invoked in trials that received widespread publicity in the media. Most cases still hinge on the effects of psychotic symptoms such as hallucinations and delusions, but increasing numbers of defendants are using a multiple personality disorder as a defense (Serban, 1992). Those defendants allege either that they are incompetent to stand trial because they do not know what their other personality did, so they cannot defend themselves, or that they are insane because they are not responsible for the actions of their other personality. A second currently popular defense involves the posttraumatic stress disorder. Defendants who use that defense allege that their crimes (usually shooting sprees) are defensive reactions that occur during a "flashback." These are usually linked to military experiences in Vietnam, but some defendants have claimed that growing up in dangerous slums caused posttraumatic stress disorders, leading to flashbacks and hence to the crimes. These defenses have been referred to as "trendy alibis," and although they receive a lot of attention, there is no evidence that they are more effective than other insanity defenses (Appelbaum et al., 1993).

In conclusion, most people probably believe that it is better to treat than punish individuals whose illegal behavior is due to a mental disorder. However, it is exceptionally difficult to formulate a generally acceptable rule for determining who is insane. Furthermore, because the attitudes about insanity change with the political climate and events, the debate over the insanity defense will continue. It is important that you understand the issues and appreciate the implications of the various options so that you can make an informed decision if you must confront the question of insanity. What rule would you use for determining insanity, and whose responsibility should it be to determine whether an individual is sane or insane?

VOLUNTARY AND INVOLUNTARY HOSPITALIZATION

It is generally believed that many psychological disorders can be treated most effectively in a hospital, and that many disturbed individuals must be confined in hospitals for their own safety and for the safety of others. Because of these beliefs, disturbed individuals are often hospitalized, many of them against their will. We will now consider the difficult question of who can be hospitalized voluntarily and involuntarily.

Voluntary Hospitalization

Anyone who feels in need of help can apply for **voluntary admission** to a mental hospital. The individual will be examined by an admitting psychiatrist or a psychologist, and if the symptoms are judged to be serious, the individual will be admitted for at least a period of evaluation. However, now that hospitals are facing serious economic cutbacks, individuals will not be admitted unless it is really necessary, and they may not be held as long as was once the case.

When considering voluntary hospitalization, it is important to realize that voluntary admission does not necessarily mean voluntary release. After voluntarily signing into a mental hospital, an individual may decide to leave. However, to be discharged, the patient must sign a form requesting discharge and then wait a required period of time (often 72 hours). If the hospital staff believes that the patient should not leave the hospital, commitment proceedings will be initiated during the waiting period so that by the end of the waiting period, the patient will have been *involuntarily* committed and is then unable to leave.

It is interesting that the conversion of a voluntary admission to an involuntary commitment is not done with medical patients who want to terminate treatment. A medical patient who wishes to leave must sign a form indicating that he or she is doing so "against medical advice" but is nevertheless permitted to go. Hospitals generally prefer to have mental patients sign themselves in voluntarily because it gets the treatment off in a spirit of cooperation and freedom, but that spirit can be short-lived if the patient decides to leave.

A recent Supreme Court decision has raised concerns about the validity of some voluntary admissions because it may be that some individuals are *not legally competent to make the decision concerning admission.* The case revolved around a man named Darryl Burch who was found walking along a highway, bruised, bloodied, disoriented, and thinking he was "in heaven." He was taken to a mental hospital where he was given voluntary commitment papers to sign, which he did. He was then held for 5 months, during which he was not given a hearing concerning his willingness to stay in the hospital because he had admitted himself voluntarily. When his symptoms were brought under control and he was released, he filed a suit alleging that he had been deprived of his liberty without due process because he had been admitted as a voluntary patient when he was incompetent to give his informed consent to such an admission (*Zinermon* v. *Burch*, 1990; Winick, 1991). When interpreted narrowly, this decision could mean that patients who want to admit themselves voluntarily would first have to be examined for competence; if they were found to be competent, they could sign in voluntarily, but if they were found to be incompetent, they would have to be committed involuntarily. This could add an expensive and time-consuming step to the admission procedure.

Involuntary Hospitalization

Many individuals in mental hospitals have been hospitalized against their will. That is known as **involuntary commitment**. The act of committing individuals to mental hospitals against their will must be done carefully because in doing so we are depriving the individuals of their civil liberties; indeed, we are depriving them of their freedom. There are two justifications for committing an individual to a mental hospital against his or her will: the *protection of the individual* and the *protection of society.*

Protection of the Individual (*Parens Patriae*).

It is generally agreed that the state has the right and responsibility to protect and provide for the well-being of people within its jurisdiction. That right and that responsibility are referred to as the doctrine of *parens patriae* (PAR-enz PĀ-trē-ī; Latin for "parent of the country"), which under English law held that the king was "the general guardian of all his infants, idiots, and lunatics." There are three situations under the doctrine

Disturbed individuals are sometimes hospitalized against their will. The justifications for this include protection of the individual and protection of society. Committing individuals against their will must be done carefully because it deprives them of their civil liberties. Many have argued that involuntary commitment of homeless people has occurred because the homeless disturbed other people rather than because they were disturbed.

of *parens patriae* in which the state has the right to commit an individual to a mental hospital:

1. If the individual *needs treatment*
2. If the individual is *dangerous to himself or herself*
3. If the individual *cannot take care of himself or herself*

Most people agree that individuals meeting one or more of these requirements need hospitalization. For example, suicidal individuals are dangerous to themselves, need treatment, and in many cases should be hospitalized at least until the crisis has passed. However, problems arise when the disturbed individuals do not think they need treatment but the authorities think they do. Suicidal individuals usually think they know what is best and do not want to be hospitalized.

In court decisions it has been stressed that individuals should not be committed to hospitals involuntarily if they are capable of making their own decisions on the matter. In one case, the court ruled that unless it could be proved that a mentally ill individual is unable to make an appropriate decision about hospitalization because of the mental illness, the individual should be allowed to decide about hospitalization (*Lessard* v. *Schmidt*, 1972). The problem with this ruling is that if an individual's judgment concerning hospitalization is different from that of an authority, it is assumed that the individual's judgment is wrong and that the person cannot make an appropriate decision. Therefore the individual will be hospitalized involuntarily. In essence, the ability to make an appropriate decision about hospitalization is operationally defined as agreeing with the authorities on the decision. This places the potential patient in a catch-22 situation: *He or she has the right to make the decision about hospitalization only as long as that decision is the same as that of the authorities.*

There is also a potential legal problem with committing individuals to mental hospitals under the doctrine of *parens patriae*. We do not involuntarily hospitalize individuals with medical disorders such as cancer, so if we involuntarily hospitalize individuals with mental disorders, we may be violating their **right to equal protection**, a right guaranteed by the 14th Amendment to the U.S. Constitution. In other words, individuals who suffer from mental disorders must not be treated differently from individuals who suffer from medical disorders. Because of these problems, the states of Pennsylvania, Michigan, Washington, Alabama, West Virginia, and Kentucky no longer permit involuntary hospitalization on the basis of *parens patriae*.

Protection of Society (Police Power of the State).

Involuntary commitment may also be justified under the **police power of the state** if the individual is considered dangerous to others (*Humphrey* v. *Cady*, 1972; *Jackson* v. *Indiana*, 1972). Most persons would probably agree that individuals who are dangerous to others should be confined. However, a problem arises because the results of numerous studies indicate that psychologists and psychiatrists are not particularly accurate at predicting who is dangerous (Diamond, 1974; Ennis & Litwack, 1974; Kozol et al., 1972; Monahan, 1973, 1976, 1978, 1984; Rofman et al., 1980; Steadman, 1973; Steadman & Keveles, 1972, 1978; A. A. Stone, 1975). If we cannot predict who is dangerous, we may commit individuals who do not need to be committed and thereby unjustifiably deprive them of their freedom.

In one study, 967 criminally insane patients who were assumed to be dangerous were released from prison hospitals, and the investigators followed them up to determine their rate of dangerous acts (Steadman & Keveles, 1972). Although the patients were released because of a change in the law rather than because they were judged to be "cured," after 4 years, only 2.7% of them had behaved dangerously and were back in a hospital or in prison. In other words, 97.3% of the individuals who had been incarcerated because they were supposedly dangerous did not commit dangerous acts when they were released. That finding is particularly noteworthy because these individuals were originally hospitalized because they had committed a dangerous act, and therefore we might expect them to be more likely to commit another dangerous act.

These results are very striking, but some question can be raised about their interpretation. It can be argued that the period of hospitalization helped the patients (if only to make them older and more docile), and thus it was because of the hospitalization that the patients were no longer dangerous (Monahan, 1978). That is a possibility, but it seems unlikely, and at present, the weight of evidence is that we are not able to predict dangerousness accurately. In view of our inability to predict who will be dangerous, serious concerns have been raised about the use of predicted dangerousness as a justification for involuntary hospitalization.

There has been recent movement toward requiring that the danger posed by the individual be "imminent" rather than at some unspecified time in the future. Because we are probably better able to assess an individual's current mental and emotional state of mind than we can predict what he or she will be like sometime in the future, we may be better able to predict imminent danger than danger in general.

A potential legal problem is also associated with hospitalizing individuals who are only suspected of being dangerous because doing so may violate their right to equal protection. Mentally ill individuals who are suspected of being dangerous are confined, but individuals who are not mentally ill and are suspected of being dangerous (e.g., a suspected "hit man" for the Mafia) are not confined. Furthermore, mentally ill individuals who might be dangerous in the *future* are confined, but others who are not mentally ill cannot be locked up until it has been proved that they have *already* committed a dangerous act. Thus it appears that in many cases mentally ill individuals are not treated equally under the law, and it must be asked whether it is fair to treat them more harshly than we treat suspected criminals.

In recent years, questions about the appropriate use of involuntary commitment have arisen with regard to the treatment of homeless people in cities such as New York and Washington. In those cities, sweeps were occasionally conducted in which individuals who were living in doorways or over heating grates were picked up and taken to mental hospitals against their will. City officials justified the sweeps by saying that the commitments were for the good of the individuals involved, but civil libertarians argued that the homeless people were not a danger to anyone and were able to take care of themselves, albeit in a somewhat different manner than most other people. In short, the critics

Joyce Brown lived on the streets until she was hospitalized against her will. In a court hearing she effectively argued that she was not disturbed but had an eccentric lifestyle. She was hospitalized for 84 days. Later she lectured on her case at the Harvard Law School.

argued that the street people were being taken off the street and committed to hospitals because they *disturbed other people* rather than because *they were disturbed*. This problem is illustrated in Case Study 21.2. This case study should be read before the following commentary.

The case of Joyce Brown illustrates a number of the problems and issues we have discussed in this book. First, how do we define "abnormal"? From a personal perspective, Brown was neither distressed nor disabled, but from a cultural perspective, she was deviant. The case also illustrates the point that behavior must be considered in a context. Burning or throwing money away certainly sounds "crazy," but doing so in an attempt to convince people who are forcing it on you that you have all you need and do not want more may not be crazy. More germane to the concerns of this chapter is the question of the protection of the rights of individuals. Brown's right to live as she wished must be protected, but at the same time, we must be sensitive to the concerns of people visiting businesses (restaurants) in the area who might be offended by her.

There is also the question of how we determine whether a person presents a danger to self or others. Joyce Brown was forcibly taken off of the street, pur-

portedly for her own good, but in fact she was physically healthy, and life on the street was the life she preferred. She was also picked up because of concern that others would attack her, but in our society we usually incarcerate the *attackers*, not the *person they attack*. The case of Joyce Brown illustrates all of these problems and questions, but it does not solve or answer any of them. What decision would you have made about Joyce Brown?

Finally, as with all case studies, it is important that we not generalize from Brown to all homeless people. Many are not on the street by choice, many have been literally thrown out of hospitals in which they would rather be living and getting treatment, and many are not able to function effectively, so they desperately cling to—and sometimes fall from—a thin ledge of existence.

Before concluding this discussion of involuntary commitment, a comment should be made concerning the possibility of **involuntary outpatient commitment** (Mulvey et al., 1987). With this procedure, the individual would not be confined to a hospital but would be required to attend outpatient therapy. This is a middle-ground approach that does not deprive individuals of their basic freedom and saves the state the cost of hospitalization, but at the same time it ensures that individuals receive the treatment and supervision they need. Involuntary outpatient commitment could not be used with all patients (e.g., clearly dangerous individuals would not be eligible), but it might be an appropriate and advantageous approach for many.

It should be clear from the foregoing discussion that our attempts to help disturbed individuals and to protect society through involuntary hospitalization are fraught with legal, logical, and practical problems. At best, the system is an imperfect series of compromises designed to protect the rights of all. As with other such compromises, sometimes the protection of one individual's rights infringes on the rights of another, and we must constantly be sensitive to the needs of all and work to maintain the delicate balance between protection and infringement.

Procedures for Involuntary Hospitalization

We have learned that the grounds for involuntary hospitalization are need for treatment, danger to self, inability to care for self, and danger to others. The question we must consider now is, what procedures are used to commit an individual to a hospital? Stated more personally, what would someone have to do to get you hospitalized against your will?

There are wide differences in procedures from state to state, but in most states, the procedure is very

Case Study 21.2

THE STRANGE CASE OF THE WOMAN WHO BURNED MONEY

The case of the woman who burned money began on Thursday, October 29, 1987, when the *New York Times* carried a front-page story under the headline "Mentally Ill Homeless Taken off New York Streets." The article explained how vans carrying a psychiatrist, a nurse, and a social worker had been dispatched to begin a "vigorous campaign to remove severely mentally ill homeless people from Manhattan streets, parks and byways" so that the city could "forcibly provide them with medical and psychiatric care."

The first person to be picked up and taken to the Bellevue Hospital Center was described as "a disheveled woman in her 40's who lived for nearly a year against the wall of a restaurant . . . and often defecated in her clothes." The mayor had visited the woman once 6 months earlier, and in a speech to the American Psychological Association he said, "She lies there all year around, and she defecates in her clothing when she is not lucid, and when she is lucid she defecates on the sidewalk."

A more complete picture of the woman was provided by a companion article with the title "Burning Dollars on the Sidewalk." The woman, who was thought to be named Ann Smith (but was sometimes called Joyce), had been living on the sidewalk on Second Avenue near 65th Street, where she kept warm by sitting in front of a 1- by 3-ft heat vent from a restaurant. Local merchants and residents had shown sympathy for her and had often left her food or given her money. A florist had given her flowers. "She liked them," he said, "but was troubled that they die." The article went on to point out that one of the most confusing aspects of this "troubled person" was her inconsistency between begging and belligerence, belligerence that often involved throwing away or burning money that she had been given. A woman from the restaurant reported, "She asks for a quarter and then when you give her three quarters, she is going to throw the other two away. . . . I don't know why. It's very strange. A lot of people were worried about her. . . . They stop and give her money, but sometimes she won't take it. 'I don't need your money,' she yelled." The florist reported that "around Christmas time, that's the only woman I know who rips up $100 and $50 bills. . . . She rips them up in teeny little pieces." His coworker added, "She likes to burn them."

At a news conference the next day, the mayor called the roundup program a "breakthrough" that "should have been started five years earlier." However, resistance was developing among civil libertarians, who believed that the rights of the people being picked up were being violated. A staff attorney with the New York Civil Liberties Union said he had received a call from the first person picked up (Ann Smith) who wanted help getting out of Bellevue. (In New York, involuntarily committed patients must be given a hearing within 5 days.) Of Smith he said, she was "lucid and extremely articulate and extremely angry. . . . She was aware of her rights and felt strongly that they had been violated." When concerns were raised about people being forced to come in against their will, in one case in handcuffs, the director of the project commented, "People say, 'We don't want to come.' With the police with us, we say, 'You must come, we want to help you.' I don't think voluntarily is the word, but cooperatively."

The next development in the case was on Monday, November 2, when it was reported that in a telephone interview from a psychiatric ward at Bellevue, Ann Smith had said, "I like the streets, and I am entitled to live the way I want to live. . . . I know that there are people and places I can go to if I don't choose to be on the streets. . . . In this day and age, in the '80s in the United States of America, where everyone comes to be free, my rights are being violated." With regard to her burning of money, she said that she did it because she was sometimes insulted that people threw money at her. She was angry about a press release distributed by city hall describing her as "dirty, disheveled and malodorous . . . delusional, withdrawn and unpredictable." In fact, her comments did not sound like those of the derelict described in the press release. Smith asked the reporter to visit her at Bellevue, but despite the fact that legally Smith was entitled to visitors and had been visited by a neighborhood resident, hospital officials barred the reporter, assigned a security guard to follow him through the public areas of the hospital, and then barred Smith from making additional phone calls. These restrictions were justified by suggesting "that the kind of media attention that is being requested by members of the press would be detrimental to her condition."

On Monday, November 2, a 5-hour hearing was conducted in a courtroom at Bellevue to determine whether New York City had the right to take Ann Smith off the street and treat her in a psychiatric ward against her will. Psychiatrists for the city testified that she was suffering from chronic schizophrenia, ran in front of cars, lived in her own feces, was so sick that she was completely unaware of her illness, and had to be hospitalized for her own good because she was a danger to herself and might be assaulted by others.

The defense attorneys challenged those allegations and argued that Smith (who was now giving her name as Billy Boggs) was only an "eccentric" who wanted to live on the streets and be left alone. They also pointed out that on five occasions during the past year, Smith (Boggs) had been taken to other psychiatric hospitals, but on each occasion, she had not been admitted because there was no evidence that she was a danger to herself. On cross-examination, the city officials admitted that they had no evidence that Smith (Boggs) had ever harmed herself. Furthermore, during the cross-examination, the defense attorney read hospital records in which it was stated that Smith (Boggs) "had a delusion that she was unfairly incarcerated." The attorney then asked whether he would also be judged to have a delusion if he felt that Smith had been incarcerated unfairly. The psychiatrist on the stand said no.

A particularly noteworthy fact about the hearing was that throughout the proceedings, Smith (Boggs) was well groomed and attentive, and "much like any defendant, she penciled notes to her lawyer during testimony." In addition, as in her earlier comments, she was consistently articulate, lucid, and knowledgeable. She certainly did not fit the stereotype of the disoriented homeless person or appear to be "so sick that she was completely unaware of her illness," as alleged earlier.

The next surprising turn of events occurred on the second day of the hearing, when three women identified Ann Smith as Joyce Brown and reported that for 10 years she had been a secretary for the Human Rights Commission in Elizabeth, New Jersey. The women who identified her were her sisters, and they had recognized her from an artist's sketch that had been used on a television news broadcast. The women had been searching hospitals, morgues, and police stations for their sister since she had disappeared a year earlier after a family fight.

The sisters explained that Brown had been raised in a middle-class family in Livingston, New Jersey, had graduated from high school and business college, and then had worked as a secretary for 19 years. Over several years, she had used cocaine and heroin and eventually lost her job. She then moved in with her family, but she became abusive and was asked to leave. Next she lived in shelters in Newark but, according to her sisters, was asked to leave those when she became abusive. Brown was briefly hospitalized, and her sisters lost contact with her when she was released. At the hearing, Brown's sisters asked that she be confined for treatment.

On the third day of the hearing, Brown defended her life on the street and her right to continue living there. She argued that she was a "professional" homeless person who was able to care for herself on the streets and was longing to get "back to the streets." She explained that she could live effectively on a budget of $7 a day and that she would easily panhandle between $8 and $10 per day. Local businesses allowed her to use their rest rooms and the air from the heating vent kept her warm, so all of her needs were taken care of. She described how she talked with passersby such as executives, lawyers, and doctors about movies, restaurants, current events, and their families. When asked if she could care for herself, she replied, "That's what I have been doing all along, and I have done a good job. . . . My mental health is good, and my physical health is good." She explained that she used false names to help her evade her sisters, who were looking for her and wanted to put her in a hospital.

When asked about tearing up money, she replied that she only did it when people insisted on throwing money at her when she already had enough for the day. "If money is given to me and I don't want it, of course I am going to destroy it. . . . I've heard people say: 'Take it. It will make me feel good.' But I say: 'I don't want it. I don't need it.' Is it my job to make them feel good by taking their money?"

Brown said that the only time she became abusive was when the city workers from Project Help kept offering her help she did not need and then "swooped down" and took her to the hospital. "Every time I was taken before, I was treated like a criminal. . . . I didn't need their food. I didn't need their conversation. I didn't need them around."

In his closing argument, Brown's defense attorney said that the city had not provided any evidence that Brown had hurt herself or was dangerous to others, and he added that she was skilled in living on the streets. The attorney for the city rebutted, "Decency and the law and common sense do not require us to wait until something happens to her. It is our duty to act before it is too late."

If you had been the judge, what would you have decided in this case? Was Brown disturbed, unable to care for herself, and a danger to others, or had she chosen an unconventional lifestyle in which she functioned effectively and posed no threat to others? Was she disturbed, or was she simply disturbing to others?

The judge ruled against Brown. She was involuntarily committed to the psychiatric ward at Bellevue Hospital Center for 84 days. Upon her release, Harvard University invited her to speak. After her lecture at Harvard, she returned to the streets.

Source: *The New York Times*, October 29–November 7, 1987.

simple. The process starts when a police officer, a mental health professional, or simply another citizen alleges to the police or a judge that the individual is dangerous to self or others. Note that no real evidence is necessary other than the opinion of the individual filing the complaint, and often that individual has no training, knowledge, or expertise concerning abnormal behavior.

Once the allegation is made, the police pick the individual up and take him or her to a mental hospital, where a brief examination is conducted by at least one physician. Often this examination lasts only a few minutes, and it may be conducted by a physician who is not necessarily a psychiatrist. That examination usually leads to **emergency (involuntary) hospitalization** so that additional observations and examinations can be conducted. The probability of emergency hospitalization once the process begins is very high because physicians do not want to take chances and let individuals go who might hurt themselves or others. Depending on the state, the emergency hospitalization can be as short as 24 hours (Texas) or as long as 20 days (New Jersey). Some states require judicial approval of emergency commitments, but that approval is usually only a formality because it is unlikely that a judge who is not trained in psychology or psychiatry will reverse the recommendation of the physician. In some states, a preliminary hearing must be conducted within 48 hours of the commitment to determine whether there is probable cause for continued detention of the individual. At the end of the emergency hospitalization period, the individual must (a) agree to voluntary hospitalization, (b) be committed on a regular basis for an indeterminate length of time, or (c) be released.

Clearly, it is quite easy to have an individual committed and detained for a considerable length of time. Indeed, in many cases, suspected criminals are more likely to be released or are released sooner than individuals who are suspected of having mental disorders.

RIGHTS OF HOSPITALIZED MENTAL PATIENTS

Now that we understand the principles and procedures that govern hospitalization, we can go on to consider the rights that individuals have once they are hospitalized. We will review the court decisions that provide the bases for the rights of mental patients. We will also briefly review the cases that led to the decisions so that you will have some understanding of the circumstances and problems that necessitated the legal actions.

Right of the "Least Restrictive Alternative"

At one time, treatment meant total hospitalization, but it is now recognized that there is a continuum of treatment options that differs in the degree to which the patient is confined. Those options include (a) total hospitalization in a closed ward, (b) hospitalization in an open ward where patients have the right to leave and go to other parts of the hospital, (c) day hospitalization in which patients spend the day in the hospital but spend the night at home, (d) night hospitalization in which patients spend the evening and night in the hospital but spend the day at work or at home, and (e) outpatient care in which patients live at home and come to a clinic only for treatment sessions. Recognition of these options is important because the courts have consistently ruled that if individuals are committed for treatment, they have the right to be treated in the **least restrictive alternative** that will serve the purpose of the treatment (*Lake* v. *Cameron*, 1966; *Lessard* v. *Schmidt*, 1974; *Shelton* v. *Tucker*, 1960; *Welsch* v. *Litkins*, 1974; *Wyatt* v. *Stickney*, 1971, 1972). Not only does this mean that they should be treated outside of the hospital if that is feasible, but if they must be hospitalized, they must be treated in the least restrictive ward possible (*Covington* v. *Harris*, 1969).

Because it was traditionally assumed that individuals needed to be in a hospital, in the past we probably overhospitalized disturbed individuals. One study conducted in Texas revealed that 60% of the hospitalized patients could be treated effectively at home and therefore did not need to be in the highly restrictive hospitals (Kittrie, 1960). The appropriate use of the least restrictive alternative for treatment should eliminate that problem.

Right to Receive Treatment

You may have assumed that individuals who were hospitalized against their will would at least be treated so that they could improve and someday be released. Unfortunately, that has not necessarily been the case, and many patients who might have benefited from treatment languished in mental hospitals for years, essentially untreated.

Four important legal decisions have concerned patients' rights to treatment. We will consider those decisions in chronological order so that you can see how the laws concerning the right to treatment are evolving.

The Right to Treatment. Charles C. Rouse was charged with carrying a dangerous weapon, but when tried, he was found not guilty by reason of insanity and was therefore involuntarily committed to a mental hospital. After 4 years of confinement during which he was not treated, Rouse applied for a discharge, arguing that the crime for which he had been charged carried a maximum prison sentence of only 1 year and that he was therefore being held too long without treatment (*Rouse* v. *Cameron*, 1966). When the case was taken to the court of appeals, it was ruled that "the purpose of involuntary hospitalization is treatment, not punishment. . . . Absent treatment, the hospital is transform[ed] . . . into a penitentiary where one could be held indefinitely for no convicted offense" (p. 453). The judge also indicated that "the hospital need not show that the treatment will cure or improve him but only that there is a bona fide *effort* to do so" (p. 456). This case provided an important step in establishing patients' right to treatment in that the ruling required that at least an effort has to be made to treat hospitalized patients.

Standards for Treatment Staff.

The next step in the evolution of the right to treatment occurred when a suit was filed against the Alabama Commissioner of Mental Health, Dr. Stonewell Stickney, on behalf of Ricky Wyatt and more than 8,000 other involuntarily committed mental patients in Alabama (*Wyatt* v. *Stickney*, 1971, 1972). The suit charged that the patients were not receiving adequate treatment, and it asked that the court take over the supervision of the treatment programs. There was good evidence to support the charge of inadequate treatment; at the time, the Alabama state mental hospitals averaged *one physician for every 2,000 patients*! Assuming that the physicians did nothing but see patients 8 hours a day, 52 weeks a year, that would mean that each patient would receive approximately 1 minute of therapy a week!

In ruling on this case, the judge first reaffirmed the right to treatment, and then went on to specify the numbers and types of staff members who must be available to provide treatment. He ruled that for every 250 patients, there had to be at least 2 psychiatrists, 4 psychologists, 3 general physicians, 7 social workers, 12 registered nurses, and 90 attendants. This standard was much higher than the one that was then in use in Alabama, but it was still substantially lower than what was recommended by the American Psychiatric Association as the minimum standard.

Determination of Appropriate Treatment.

Once it was ruled that patients had a right to treatment and the minimum number of staff members was specified, the question arose, what is appropriate treatment? This question was raised in the case of Nicholas Romeo, a profoundly retarded 33-year-old man with an IQ between 8 and 10. His mother brought suit against the superintendent of the hospital in which Nicholas was a patient because Nicholas had injured himself on at least 63 occasions in one 29-month period (one of

his symptoms was self-mutilation), and she did not think that he was being treated adequately. In response, the judge ruled that Nicholas did have a right to reasonable care and safety, but the judge went on to conclude that because judges are not trained in psychology and psychiatry, they are not in a position to determine what treatment is most effective for various patients. Therefore, it was ruled that decisions concerning what treatment is appropriate should be left to professionals (*Youngberg* v. *Romeo*, 1981). That seems reasonable, but by allowing professionals to determine what is appropriate, the court opened the door to a wide variety (and possibly low levels) of treatment because standards may differ from one professional or hospital to another.

When Is Confinement Not Justified?

When Kenneth Donaldson was 49 years old, he was committed to the Florida state hospital at Chattahoochee on his father's allegation that he was delusional. After a brief hearing before a county judge, Donaldson was found to be suffering from paranoid schizophrenia and was committed to the hospital for "care, maintenance, and treatment." A progress note written in his hospital file shortly after he was hospitalized indicated that he was "in remission," which meant that he was no longer showing the symptoms of his disorder. Despite that, he was not released from the hospital.

After Donaldson has been hospitalized against his will for almost 20 years, he petitioned for release. He argued that he should be released because (a) he was not dangerous or mentally ill, (b) he was not receiving treatment, and (c) there were people in the community who were willing to take him in and give him a job. In responding, the Supreme Court ruled that "a State cannot constitutionally confine . . . a nondangerous individual who is capable of surviving safely in freedom by himself or with the help of willing and responsible family members or friends" (*O'Connor* v. *Donaldson*, 1975). With this ruling, the Court said that individuals who are not dangerous and who can live effectively outside of a hospital cannot be held in hospitals against their will.

It is important to recognize that in this case, the Court did not address the question of whether patients who are not being treated have a right to be released; it simply said that *nondangerous patients cannot be kept in the hospital if they can function outside the hospital.* The Supreme Court will rarely go further than what is necessary to rectify the wrong in the case that is being heard, and in the case of Donaldson, the Court could order his release and thereby solve his problem because confinement was not necessary. The Court did not then have to consider the question of Donaldson's right to treatment. With this case, then, the issue of patients' right to treatment did not move forward or backward. That point is often misunderstood, and consequently, the *O'Connor* v. *Donaldson* case is often erroneously mentioned in discussions of the right to treatment when in fact it is only relevant to the question of whether patients who can function outside may be kept in the hospital.

In the four cases we have considered, we have seen that the Court (a) recognized that hospitalized mental patients have a right to treatment (*Rouse* v. *Cameron*, 1966), (b) set the minimum number of staff members that must be available to treat patients (*Wyatt* v. *Stickney*, 1971, 1972), (c) said that it was the responsibility of professionals to determine what type and how much treatment was appropriate (*Youngberg* v. *Romeo*, 1981), and (d) declared that nondangerous individuals cannot be confined if they are able to function independently outside the hospital (*O'Connor* v. *Donaldson*, 1974). In summary, the Court originally moved into the important but murky area of treatment when it established the right to treatment and specified the personnel necessary to provide minimal treatment, but then it backed away when it came to specifying what procedures constituted appropriate treatment. Little has changed since the Donaldson decision, but the law is a dynamic body that changes when new cases are brought up, and it is likely that we will see a further evolution of the right to treatment in the future.

The court rulings we have discussed here specify what should be done with regard to the commitment, treatment, and release of hospitalized patients. However, there is often a considerable difference between what the law requires and what in fact occurs, and most mental patients are not in a good position to defend their rights. That is in part the case because mental patients usually do not know their rights and hence simply accept what seems to be their fate. In an attempt to make sure that patients know their rights with regard to treatment, it is now required that a statement of their rights be posted prominently in hospitals. That statement is presented in Figure 21.1.

Posting a notice of the patients' right to treatment is a step in the right direction, but it is a small and rather passive step, and its impact is questionable. Patients may not see the notice, and even if they do, they may not understand it. It should also be noted that in many cases, the hospital (or state) is not required to provide an attorney to help patients. That is in sharp contrast to the case of prisoners, who are guaranteed legal counsel. In other words, criminals are treated better than hospitalized mental patients. Furthermore, if patients believe that their rights are being violated and complain, there is often no one to listen, or if people do listen, they do not take the patients seriously. Why should they? The patients are "crazy"—if they were not crazy, they would not be in the hospital. It is

FIGURE 21.1   THIS NOTICE OF MENTAL PATIENTS' RIGHTS MUST BE POSTED IN HOSPITALS.

NOTICE TO PATIENTS

The United States Supreme Court recently ruled that a mental patient who has been involuntarily hospitalized, who is not dangerous to himself or others, who is receiving only custodial care, and who is capable of living safely in the community has a constitutional right to liberty—that is, has a right to be released from the hospital. The Supreme Court's opinion is available for patients to read.

If you think that the Supreme Court ruling may have a bearing on your present status, please feel free to discuss the matter with your hospital staff. In addition, if you wish to talk with an attorney about the meaning of the Supreme Court decision and how it may apply to you, the Superintendent has a list of legal organizations that may be of assistance. The staff will be glad to aid anyone who wishes to contact a lawyer.

Source: National Institutes of Mental Health.

a catch-22, so the patients and their rights are often ignored, and the patients languish in hospitals untreated.

Most of our discussion so far has focused on the legal principles involved in the right to treatment; no attention has been given to the practical implications associated with the implementation of those principles. When faced with a mandate to treat all hospitalized patients, states are confronted with a potentially overwhelming financial burden. What is to be done when there are not sufficient financial resources to treat all of the hospitalized patients? Should disturbed patients whom we cannot afford to treat be released from the hospitals to fend for themselves in the community? Will the professionals who have the responsibility for defining treatment redefine as "adequate" whatever can be afforded and thereby again turn hospitals into holding bins, human warehouses, or prisons? These practical issues are as important as the principles, and we will consider them in some detail in the next chapter when we consider deinstitutionalization and community care.

Right to Refuse Treatment

We have established that patients have the right to be treated. But do they also have the right to refuse treatment? For example, if you were hospitalized, would you have the right to refuse psychotherapy? Would you have the right to refuse psychosurgery if it were recommended?

In our society, individuals are generally free to decide what is best for them, and this implies that patients have the right to refuse treatment if they do not think that the treatment is appropriate. However, there are three situations in which mental patients may not have the right to refuse treatment. First, they may not have the right to refuse treatment if they are declared *incompetent*. The notion is that the incompetent individual is unable to understand or evaluate what is going to be done and is therefore unable to make an informed judgment about whether the treatment is appropriate. If an individual is declared incompetent, the power to make the decision about treatment may be shifted to a parent or guardian, but in most cases, whoever is empowered to make the decision simply accepts the recommendation of the psychiatrist or psychologist in charge.

Second, individuals may not have the right to refuse treatment if they are *involuntarily committed* to a hospital. For example, depressed individuals who are suicidal may not have the right to refuse antidepressant medication, and paranoid individuals who are dangerous to others who they think are plotting against them may not have the right to refuse neuroleptic (antipsychotic) medication. In those cases, the necessity to protect the individual or society takes precedence over the individual's right to refuse treatment.

Third, even a competent and voluntarily committed individual may not have the right to refuse treatment if the refusal results in *increased costs* for the community. For example, an individual may not have the right to refuse group psychotherapy or medication if the only option is more expensive individual psychotherapy.

However, there are two situations in which patients do have the right to refuse treatment. First, patients have the right to refuse treatment if the treatment *violates their religious beliefs*. This was affirmed when a circuit court ruled in favor of a patient who objected to taking drugs because she was a Christian Scientist (*Winters* v. *Miller*, 1971). The ruling was based on the First Amendment, which guarantees the right to the free expression of religion.

Second, an individual has the right to refuse a particular treatment if another *equally effective but less obtrusive treatment is available*. For example, if it could be demonstrated that for a given patient psychotherapy was as effective as electroconvulsive therapy, the patient could refuse the electroconvulsive therapy.

Overall, the underlying principle is that a patient has the right to refuse treatment unless such refusal is not in the best interest of the patient or places an additional burden or danger on society. The problem comes in deciding who is in the appropriate position to decide what is best for the patient and when society is at risk. In two cases, it was ruled that because of the negative side effects of some medications, even involuntarily committed patients could refuse to take them (*Rennie* v. *Klein*, 1979; *Rogers* v. *Okin*, 1979). To help the patients make informed decisions about medication, it was ruled that lists of the side effects of medications had to be posted in the hospitals. This resulted in widespread refusal to take the medications and a consequently serious deterioration of the patients' condition.

In an attempt to correct the practical problems caused by the ruling that patients could refuse to take medication, one of the cases was reconsidered by the court. After that hearing, it was ruled that when the good of the patient or society is in question, the judgment of mental health professionals must take precedence over the judgment of patients (*Rennie* v. *Klein*, 1983). Theoretically, psychologists and psychiatrists are the experts, and they are in the best position to make such judgments, but granting the decision power to experts robs the patient of his or her rights. There is no simple solution to this problem, and the best that can be done is monitor carefully what is done for (or to) patients so that experts will not abuse their power and patients will not make foolish decisions. Finally, it should be noted that if a patient refuses a treatment that would facilitate release from the hospital, the patient cannot then demand to be released because treatment is inadequate.

Some of the problems posed by the courts' decision to grant patients the right to refuse treatment are illustrated in Case Study 21.3. The case involves a patient with the bipolar disorder who was in a private hospital and who refused medication. (For background on treatment of the bipolar disorder, see Chapter 11.)

Other Rights

The rights to receive and refuse treatment are certainly important because they may determine what is done for patients and how long patients stay in the hospital, but a number of other rights must be protected as well so that the patients' stay in the hospital will not be unduly uncomfortable.

Physical Environment. With regard to the physical environment, it has been ruled, for example, that for each patient there should be at least 40 sq ft in the day room and 10 sq ft in the dining room. Patients must also be provided with curtains or screens in their sleeping quarters to ensure privacy, and there must be

Case Study 21.3

DELAY OF EFFECTIVE TREATMENT AND INCREASED COST OF CARE

Ms. A was a 55-year-old woman who was admitted for her fifth hospitalization to a private psychiatric hospital. She was diagnosed as suffering from a manic episode of a bipolar disorder. Ms. A was held in an intensive treatment ward but was frequently placed in seclusion because of outbursts in which she hit others and burned herself with cigarettes. During the first week of hospitalization, Ms. A was started on lithium, but the treatment was discontinued because she refused it. No attempt was made to force her to take the medication because of potential legal implications, and consequently she remained unmedicated for 19 days. After 37 days in the hospital, a commitment hearing was held, and the court authorized both commitment and treatment. Once she was committed, she was no longer able to refuse treatment, and therefore she was immediately given lithium. Within a month, she showed significant improvement, and 2 weeks later, she was discharged.

Ms. A's hospital bill was $25,137. Because of the delay in getting effective treatment started, it was estimated that the cost was $11,550 higher than it would have been if she had accepted the lithium immediately. (Because 80% of the patient's hospital expenses were paid by an insurance company, much of the expense associated with the patient's refusal to take medication was borne by the public.) The family also incurred additional costs of $1,017 for legal fees and the consultation of an independent psychiatrist. In addition to these financial costs, there is also the cost to other patients of having a highly disturbed and disruptive patient on the ward and the emotional cost to the family of the prolonged illness of a loved one.

Because of cases such as this, the hospital in which the patient was hospitalized established a policy whereby if a potentially dangerous patient refuses treatment, and if after outside legal consultation the family concurs with the patient's decision, the patient is referred to a public mental hospital.

Source: Adapted from Perr (1981).

---

one toilet for every eight patients (*Wyatt* v. *Stickney*, 1971, 1972).

Personal Clothing. It has also been ruled that a patient has the right to wear his or her own clothing unless the clothing is determined to be dangerous or otherwise inappropriate in terms of the treatment program. Some patients who are likely to try to escape from an open ward are required to wear hospital gowns so that they can be easily spotted if they try to leave, and patients who are suicidal may not be allowed to wear belts or other articles of clothing that they could use to hang themselves. A patient who thinks he is Superman would probably not be allowed to go around the hospital in a red-and-blue cape because that would condone his delusion. Furthermore, believing that he can fly with his cape on, the patient might jump off a high wall.

Patient Labor. The question of whether patients should be forced to work in the hospital is a difficult one. On the one hand, being involved in productive work can provide a much-needed boost in self-concept, and work done in the hospital may reduce the cost of running the hospital. On the other hand, if patients are committed involuntarily and then compelled to work, that is essentially slavery (involuntary servitude), which is prohibited by the 13th Amendment to the Constitution.

Two important decisions have been passed down by the courts in an attempt to strike a balance between work and slavery. First, it was ruled that mental patients may be required to do work that contributes to the operation of the institution so long as the work has

The question of whether a patient should be forced to work in a hospital is difficult. Being involved in productive work can boost self-concept. But a patient who has been involuntarily committed and then forced to work is essentially being subjected to involuntary servitude, a violation of the 13th Amendment to the Constitution.

some therapeutic value. The problem is in defining what work is therapeutic. It could be argued that forcing patients to scrub floors is inappropriate, but it can also be argued that scrubbing floors is a normal and necessary activity and that in doing so, patients learn to take responsibility and may even develop a sense of accomplishment and pride.

Second, a more recent court decision placed a serious limitation on patient work programs when it was ruled that patients may not perform work "for which the hospital is under contract with an outside organization" (*Wyatt* v. *Stickney*, 1971). This means that if a hospital has contracted with an outside company to do maintenance work or prepare food, patients cannot participate in those activities even if doing so is therapeutic. It appears that this ruling was designed for the economic benefit of commercial firms that do business with the hospital rather than the psychological benefit of the patients who are confined in the hospital. The ruling has had some unfortunate consequences. For example, in one hospital in a rural area, the patients grew all of their own food, a practice that filled their days, gave them considerable self-satisfaction, and substantially offset the expense of their hospitalization. However, a local grocery company brought considerable political pressure to bear and got a contract to supply the hospital with food. Today, the patients sit idly on benches and watch others plow the fields, and hospital costs have soared. Clearly, numerous pressures and concerns must be weighed and a delicate balance must be achieved if patient work is to be effective.

Civil Rights.   The protection of civil rights is very important in our society, and simply being hospitalized as a mental patient cannot be used as grounds for the restriction of civil rights. For example, patients have the right to manage their personal and financial affairs, make contracts, marry, divorce, vote, and make a will (*Wyatt* v. *Stickney*, 1971, 1972). However, those rights can be restricted if the individual is judged incompetent, and in those cases, a court-appointed guardian will take responsibility for looking after the welfare of the individual.

THE PUBLIC'S RIGHT TO PROTECTION

Most of our attention in this chapter has been focused on the rights of patients, but the right to safety of others must not be ignored. The right to safety was discussed briefly when I pointed out that one of the

reasons for involuntary hospitalization of patients was public safety (police powers of the state). However, the right to safety has been extended to include the right to be protected if a patient who is *not hospitalized* poses a threat. This right grew out of a case in California in which a young male student told his therapist about his fantasies about killing a young woman named Tanya Tarasoff who had rejected his advances. The therapist was concerned, and he informed the campus police, who questioned the young man but then released him when he promised that he would stay away from Ms. Tarasoff. However, the therapist did not inform Ms. Tarasoff of the potential danger. The student discontinued therapy, and a few weeks later he stabbed Ms. Tarasoff to death. Ms. Tarasoff's parents filed suit, alleging that the therapist was negligent for not warning their daughter about the danger. In what has come to be known as the **Tarasoff ruling**, the Supreme Court of California concluded that when a therapist *knows* or *should know* that a patient presents a serious risk of violence to another individual, the therapist "incurs an obligation to use reasonable care to protect the intended victim against such danger" (*Tarasoff* v. *Regents*, 1976; supra note 8). To discharge that obligation, the therapist must (a) warn the intended victim or others who are likely to warn the intended victim, (b) notify the police, or (c) take other reasonable steps to protect the intended victim. This is often called the "duty to warn" principle, but in fact the court ruled only that a therapist take reasonable care to protect individuals, and reasonable care may or may not involve warning. Therefore, this is more accurately referred to as the **"duty to protect" principle**.

This principle continues to evolve as cases are brought to the courts, and at this time there are a number of ambiguities and inconsistencies from state to state. One inconsistency involves the question of whether the patient must name a specific person in the threat. For example, individuals who were harmed when John Hinckley, Jr., attempted to assassinate President Reagan sued Hinckley's therapist, alleging that he should have known that Hinckley was dangerous. However, their suits were dismissed because no specific threats were made against specific persons. In contrast, there is a case in which a former patient with a history of violent behavior began shooting people at random with a shotgun he had just bought. When a woman who was blinded in the attack and whose husband was killed filed suit against the man's therapist, the court ruled in her favor because the history of violence supposedly made the future violence foreseeable despite the fact that the patient did not make a specific threat.

The duty to protect usually does not extend to cases of suicide. For example, when Tammy Bellah committed suicide and her parents sued her therapist for not doing something to protect Tammy from herself, the court ruled against the suit. However, there are cases in which the duty to protect has been extended to property. In one case, during therapy a patient threatened to burn down his father's barn and in fact later did so. When the father filed suit, the court concluded that the therapist was in fact liable because he had not warned the father. Obviously, there is a need for increased clarity and consistency in the application of the duty to protect.

The duty to protect raises questions about the confidentiality of the information disclosed to a therapist, and court rulings have been inconsistent with regard to whether a patient has grounds for suit if a therapist discloses information about the threat posed by the patient. Questions about the protection of confidentiality can pose problems for patients who may feel inhibited about talking freely with their therapists. Questions about confidentiality can also pose problems for therapists who could be sued for breaches in confidentiality but could also be sued for failure to protect if they do not breach confidentiality. Despite the inconsistencies in the legal rulings, the code of ethics of the American Psychological Association is clear: *Protection of others takes precedence over the right to confidentiality.*

■ SUMMARY

A variety of laws have been developed to protect individuals who are suffering from mental disturbances. First of all, if an individual is to be tried for a crime but is unable to understand the proceedings or is unable to aid in his or her defense, the individual can be declared incompetent to stand trial, and the trial must be postponed until the individual is competent. Incompetence does not absolve the individual of responsibility; it only postpones the trial. Second, an individual who has committed a crime may plead not guilty by reason of insanity. An individual who is judged not guilty by reason of insanity is not considered responsible for the illegal act and is treated rather than punished.

There are three rules for determining whether an individual is insane. They are the M'Naghten rule (knowledge of right versus wrong), the Durham rule (product of mental disease or defect), and the Ameri-

can Law Institute rule (lacks substantial capacity to appreciate wrongfulness and to conform conduct). Different rules are used in different states.

Numerous controversies rage over the concept and implementation of the insanity defense. For example, opinion differs about how conservative or liberal the law should be, who should make the decision about whether a defendant is insane, how we should assess temporary insanity after the fact, and whether a person should be considered sane until proven insane or vice versa. Because of these controversies, the laws and procedures are in a state of flux, and new procedures are being developed (e.g., the verdict of mentally ill but guilty).

Individuals who believe that they need help can voluntarily sign themselves into hospitals, and in so doing, they retain the right to leave the hospital after giving appropriate notice. There are two bases for the involuntary commitment of individuals to hospitals. The first of these is the protection of the individual (*parens patriae*). Under this doctrine, individuals can be committed if they (a) need treatment, (b) are dangerous to themselves, or (c) cannot take care of themselves. Second, individuals can also be involuntarily committed for the protection of society (under the police power of the state). Problems associated with involuntary commitment revolve around the right to equal protection (physically ill patients are not hospitalized against their will) and the difficulty of judging when a person is dangerous.

Once hospitalized, patients have the right to live in the least restrictive environment possible, the right to be treated, the right to be released if they are not treated, and in some circumstances the right to refuse treatment. In addition, patients have the right to a reasonable living environment, and in most cases they have the right to wear their own clothing. Furthermore, they cannot be exploited as cheap labor, and their civil rights are protected.

Finally, the public has a right to protection from potentially dangerous patients who are not hospitalized. The laws are inconsistent concerning when therapists must take action to protect others and when the actions to protect others might violate the patients' right to confidentiality. However, ethical principles indicate that the public's safety takes precedence over the patients' right to confidentiality.

With this material as background, in Chapter 22, we will examine what life is like in mental hospitals, consider whether patients can be treated effectively in the community rather than in hospitals, and determine whether it is possible to prevent the development of abnormal behavior.

KEY TERMS, CONCEPTS, AND NAMES

In reviewing and testing yourself on what you have learned from this chapter, you should be able to identify and discuss each of the following:

American Law Institute rule
Durham rule
"duty to protect" principle
elbow rule
emergency (involuntary)
   hospitalization
incompetent to stand trial

insanity defense
involuntary commitment
involuntary outpatient commitment
irresistible impulse
least restrictive alternative
mentally ill but guilty
M'Naghten rule

parens patriae
police power of the state
right to equal protection
Tarasoff ruling
voluntary admission

Court Decisions Referred To in This Chapter

Covington v. *Harris*, 419 F.2d 617 (D.C. Cir. 1969).
Durham v. *United States*, 214 F.2d 862 (D.C. Cir. 1954).
Dusky v. *United States*, 362 U.S. 402 (1960).
Humphrey v. *Cady*, 405 U.S. 504 (1972).
Jackson v. *Indiana*, 406 U.S. 715 (1972).
Lake v. *Cameron*, 364 F.2d 657 (D.C. Cir. 1966).
Lessard v. *Schmidt*, 349 F. Supp. 1078 (E.D. Wisc. 1972), vacated and remanded on other grounds, 94 S.Ct. 713 (1974).
O'Connor v. *Donaldson*, 422 U.S. 563 (1975), affecting 493 F.2d 507 (5th Cir. 1974).
Pate v. *Robinson*, 384 U.S. 375 (1966).
Rennie v. *Klein*, No. 77-2624 (N.J. Sept. 14, 1979).
Rennie v. *Klein*, 720 F.2d 266 (3d Cir. 1983).

Rogers v. *Okin*, 478 F. Supp. 1342 (I.D. Mass. 1979).
Rouse v. *Cameron*, 373 F.2d 451 (D.C. Cir. 1966).
Shelton v. *Tucker*, 364 U.S. 479 (1960).
Smith v. *United States*, 148 F.2d 665 (1929).
Tarasoff v. *Regents of the University of California*, 551 P.2d 334 (1976).
United States v. *Brawner*, 471 F.2d 969 (D.C. 1972).
Welsch v. *Litkins*, 373 F. Supp. 487 (D. Minn. 1974).
Winters v. *Miller*, 446 F.2d 65, 71 (2d Cir. 1971).
Wyatt v. *Stickney*, 325 F. Supp. 781 (M.D. Ala. 1971).
Wyatt v. *Stickney*, 344 F. Supp. 343 (M.D. Ala. 1972).
Youngberg v. *Romeo*, 457 U.S. 307 (1981).
Zinermon v. *Burch*, 110 S. Ct. 975 (1990).

Notes:

Chapter 22

Hospitalization, Community Care, and Prevention

• OUTLINE •

Mark is 49 years old. He is diagnosed as having schizophrenia, and he has been in and out of hospitals for the past 20 years. His last hospitalization lasted 7 years and ended not because he had shown improvement but because of a new program designed to get patients out of the hospital and treat them in the community. Because of his "crazy" behavior, neither Mark's parents nor his sisters will let him live in their homes, so he now lives on welfare in a barren one-room apartment in a run-down part of the city. Treatment consists of going to a nearby clinic once a week to get medication that he is supposed to take four times a day. Frequently, however, he gets confused or forgets to take his medication, and then he becomes disoriented. When that happens, he is usually picked up by the police, who take him to the hospital, where he is given a high dose of medication, held for a few hours, and then released. Because he cannot care for himself adequately, Mark is underweight and at serious risk for disease. Mark has not committed suicide and has not been rehospitalized, so he is considered to be a "success."

Linda has been in the hospital for almost 2 years. Originally, she did not like being hospitalized and wanted to be released. However, when the possibility of being discharged came up about a year ago, she became very anxious about "making it on the outside," and her symptoms became worse. She was not discharged. Since then, she has begun "settling in" and "blending into the woodwork." She has become a "good patient"; her personal grooming has deteriorated somewhat, but she is compliant, and her behavior rarely attracts attention. Each time she is given a brief examination, she demonstrates enough symptoms to justify keeping her in the hospital, but not so much as to require any additional attention or a change in wards.

Christine is a psychologist in a community mental health center. Her primary responsibility is doing psychotherapy with individuals who are living in the surrounding community. Most of her clients came to the clinic for help before their problems became so serious that hospitalization was necessary. When problems do become serious, clients at the center can be hospitalized for intensive care during the day, but they are sent home at night. Christine's goal is to help the clients at whatever stage they are at, but to do so without breaking their contacts with their friends and families in the community. In addition to seeing clients, Christine also runs workshops for various community and business groups in which she talks about the early signs of mental health problems, teaches stress management techniques, and informs people about the various free services that are available such as support groups and crisis centers. With these workshops, Christine helps people not only with early detection but also with the prevention of mental health problems.

The state legislature faced a problem last term. Costs of education had gone up drastically, and numerous roads needed to be repaired or completely rebuilt, but tax income was flat, and funds from the federal government's revenue-sharing program had been reduced. One possible means of cutting costs was to reduce the number of patients in the state mental hospital. Each patient was costing the state tens of thousands of dollars per year, so considerable yearly savings could be achieved. The legislators argued that the cut-back in funds for the hospital system was not simply an economic strategy. Instead, getting patients out of the old hospitals and treating them in the community was a step in the direction of modern mental health practices. This was humane progress, not just economics. At the end of the legislative session, one other relevant bill was passed. It gave cities the right to pass zoning ordinances prohibiting the establishment of "halfway houses" in residential areas. Most cities immediately adopted the protective ordinances. A month later, a discharged patient stood on the front steps of a hospital and asked, "But where do I go?" No one heard because the door to the hospital was already closed, and no one was waiting in the community.

For many years disturbed individuals were thought of as patients, they were treated in large hospitals, and little was done for them until their problems became serious. To some extent, that is still true, but in the late 1960s, a program was begun that was designed to get disturbed individuals out of the hospitals and treat them while they lived at home. Furthermore, we began to focus attention on preventing the development of abnormal behavior rather than only treating it after it became serious. In this chapter, we will first describe the traditional mental hospital and discuss what a patient's life is like in the hospital. Then we will consider the deinstitutionalization movement which is designed to get patients out of the hospitals. Next we will review the types of care that are available for disturbed individuals who are living in the community. Finally, we will consider the programs that have been established to prevent the development of abnormal behavior.

TRADITIONAL MENTAL HOSPITALS

In Chapter 21 we examined the circumstances under which disturbed individuals can be hospitalized either voluntarily or involuntarily. Here we will consider important personal and practical questions: What is life like in mental hospitals? How do patients adjust to life in mental hospitals? Are mental hospitals effective places for treating abnormal behavior?

At the outset it should be recognized that psychiatric patients are hospitalized in a wide variety of facilities, ranging from huge mental hospitals with thousands of patients to small psychiatric units in general medical hospitals. Some facilities are very pleasant, but most are rather unpleasant, and many are simply deplorable. Some hospitals have homelike qualities, and others are like college dormitories, but unfortunately many have the characteristics of prisons. Because of the diversity in facilities, it is difficult to

characterize the "typical" mental hospital, but I will try to convey some idea of what psychiatric hospitals are like and the effects they have on patients.

Physical Setting

Most psychiatric hospitals are organized by wards. Each ward usually has its own day room, nursing station, isolation room, sleeping facilities, and staff. There are generally between 20 and 100 patients on a ward.

Wards often differ in terms of types of patients they have or the functions they serve. For example, in a large hospital, there may be an **admitting ward**, where new patients live while they are being diagnosed, and **intensive treatment wards**, where patients are given all that the hospital has to offer in an attempt to get them out before their problems become chronic. Large hospitals may also have separate wards

Hospitalized patients spend most of their waking time in a day room.

for chronic patients who have not responded to treatment and who will probably never recover. Those wards are often referred to as **domiciliaries** (DOM-uh-SIL-ē-er-ēz) or "back wards." Essentially, no treatment other than medication is attempted on those wards; the patients are simply maintained ("warehoused") there until they die.

Wards are also usually organized by age so that children and adolescents are separated from adults, and some wards are devoted to only one type of patient, such as those with eating disorders (anorexia, bulimia) or substance abuse problems (alcoholism, drug addiction). In the case of a small psychiatric unit that is part of a general hospital, there are not enough patients or facilities for specialized wards, so all patients are grouped together on one ward.

Less disturbed patients and those who are not likely to escape are often assigned to **open wards**, where the doors are not locked and the patients are free to go to other parts of the hospital whenever they wish. More disturbed patients are assigned to **closed wards**, where the doors are locked and may be guarded by an attendant.

The **day room** is probably the most important part of any ward because it is where the patients spend most of their waking hours. By law, the day room must be large enough so that each patient has a space at least 6½ ft by 6½ ft. Day rooms are generally rather barren, drab, and utilitarian, with a minimum of furniture. Patients spend most of their time in the day room simply sitting or watching endless hours of television.

Another important part of the ward is the **nurses' station**, which is usually a glass-enclosed office where the nurses spend most of their time and where patients' records and medications are kept. The nurses supervise the patients from the station, and in some hospitals it is comparable to the guard tower in a prison.

Most wards also have an **isolation room** (often referred to as the "quiet room") in which patients can be confined temporarily if they become upset, agitated, destructive, or abusive. Most isolation rooms are cell-like rooms that contain only a mattress so that patients will not have anything with which to hurt themselves. In most cases, patients are forcibly confined to the isolation room when they are being disruptive or self-destructive, but sometimes patients will voluntarily use it as a retreat.

Adjoining the day room are the patients' sleeping rooms, each housing one to five patients. In most cases, patients are not allowed to go to their sleeping rooms during the day, so they will often sleep or nap in the day room.

Other important hospital facilities include a dining room (usually a cafeteria), often a snack bar (or at least an area with vending machines for candy), and an area for occupational, art, or music therapy. The hospital may also have recreational areas and work areas to which the patients can go or be taken. Finally, somewhere near the ward will be the offices of the psychologists, psychiatrists, social workers, and various administrators who are responsible for the treatment and care of the patients. Unfortunately, in most hospitals, the offices of the treatment staff are some distance from the ward, a factor that symbolically separates treatment from daily living and separates the treatment staff from the patients.

Before concluding this discussion of hospital facilities, a comment should be made about **day** or **night hospitalization** versus full-time hospitalization. Most patients live in the hospital on a 24-hour-a-day basis, but some are admitted for only the daytime or the nighttime. With this approach, patients who have some place to go during the day are admitted to the night program. They come in at about dinnertime, receive treatment during the evening, spend the evening, sleep in the hospital, and leave in the morning. These people use the hospital like most people use their homes. In contrast, patients who have a supportive environment in which they can spend the night participate in the day hospital program. They come to the hospital in the morning, receive treatment during the day, and go home in the late afternoon or early evening. They go to the hospital like most people go to work.

The day or night hospital procedure has two advantages: First, patients can maintain better contact with the outside world if they are not hospitalized all the time, and second, the hospital can serve twice as

Most wards have an isolation room in which patients can be temporarily confined if they become agitated, destructive, or abusive.

many patients. Unfortunately, despite the fact that the day or night procedure is less expensive and has been consistently shown to be as effective as or even more effective than full-time hospitalization, the day or night procedure is not widely used (Herz et al., 1971; Penk et al., 1978).

The atmosphere in most hospitals is bleak and lonely at best. The physical facilities are usually gloomy, and although there may be many patients, they are often emotionally isolated from one another and hence alone in the crowd. Furthermore, patients are usually strictly segregated from staff, which increases the feelings of separation and abandonment among patients. Indeed, many staff members walk past patients as if they were inanimate objects rather than human beings who are overwhelmed with problems.

Staff

Every mental hospital has a variety of staff members with different responsibilities. **Psychologists** do individual and group therapy and often play a prominent role in diagnosing specific disorders and formulating treatment plans. **Psychiatrists** also do individual psychotherapy and sometimes group therapy. Because psychiatrists are trained in medicine, they also take responsibility for the various physical treatments such as drugs and electroconvulsive (shock) therapy.

Because psychologists and psychiatrists spend most of their time in their offices dealing with individual patients, they are rarely in the ward, and therefore the day-to-day running of the ward is primarily in the hands of **psychiatric nurses**. Nurses become extremely important and powerful individuals in patients' lives because it is usually the nurses' reports that determine what happens to the patients. For example, if a nurse reports that a patient is agitated, the patient may be given a sedative, sent to the isolation room, or confined to the ward. In contrast, positive reports from a nurse can result in movement to a better ward, home visits, and other privileges.

There are numerous stories about head nurses such as Nurse Ratched in the book *One Flew over the Cuckoo's Nest* (Kesey, 1962) who rule their wards like monarchs rule kingdoms, and there is more than a grain of truth in the stories about their legendary power. However, it is important to recognize that of all of the professionals who deal with the patients in the hospital, the nurses are probably in the best position to know and evaluate the patients. The psychiatrists and psychologists may see the patients for an hour or two each week and talk with them about their innermost feelings, but the nurses must deal with the patients on a daily basis when they are tired, hungry, frustrated, unable to sleep at night, and rejected by their peers and families.

Although nurses have more contact with the patients than other professionals, that should not be taken to mean that they necessarily have a lot of contact. One study revealed that nurses came out of the nurses' station an average of only 11.5 times in an 8-hour shift, and that included the times they came out to leave the ward (Rosenhan, 1973). In that study, it was impossible to determine the amount of time the nurses actually spent with the patients because the contacts were too brief.

The members of the hospital staff who have the most contact with the patients are the **psychological technicians** (formerly called *ward attendants*) who actually spend most of their time on the ward rather than in offices or at nursing stations. The technicians are important because they are often the patients' only ongoing contacts with normal individuals. Also, because the technicians are not professional staff, the patients can often relate to them better, and they sometimes become friends. In some circumstances, the contact between attendants and patients can be very intense. This is especially true if the patient is put on "suicide watch," because then the technician must stay within a few feet of the patient on a 24-hour-a-day basis regardless of what the patient is doing.

Concerning the relationship between patients and technicians, one patient commented:

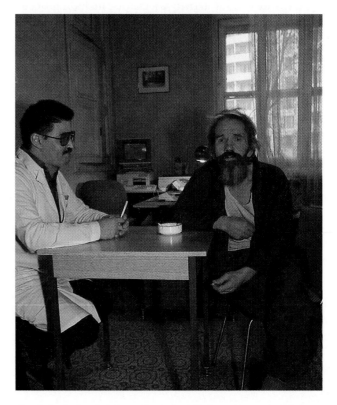

Psychological technicians (formerly called ward attendants) have more contact with patients than other hospital staff.

Mike is the only real friend I have left. He's the only guy I can talk to. The nurses, hell, they just come out to yell at me. The only time they know I'm alive is when I'm doing something wrong or when it's time to shove more medicine down me. The goddamned doctors just play useless word games in their offices and try to screw my head around. They don't know what's going on. How could they? They almost never see me. Mike knows me and keeps me straight.

Although the technicians are low on the power hierarchy, they do have considerable power because their reports about patients' behavior often provide the basis for the impressions that are formed by the nurses, psychologists, and psychiatrists who ultimately make the decisions about the patients. In the war against mental disorders, then, the psychiatrists and psychologists are the generals, the nurses are the lieutenants, and the psychological technicians are the foot soldiers who are on the front line.

Social workers also play important roles for hospitalized patients because they maintain the link between the patient and his or her family. The social worker also plays a crucial role in helping with the transitions into and out of the hospital and will also often work closely with the patient during the posthospitalization period when the patient is struggling with practical problems like finding a place to live, getting a job, paying bills, and gaining custody of children. In some cases, social workers also do group and individual psychotherapy.

Finally, various activity therapists, including **occupational therapists, art therapists,** and **music therapists,** often work with hospitalized patients. It is not expected that knitting a potholder, finger painting, or learning to play a musical instrument will cure schizophrenia. However, it is hoped that the social interaction associated with the activities will provide the opportunity to talk about problems, try out new social roles, and increase contact with reality. In other words, the activities themselves are not a cure, but they may be a medium in which more normal behavior can be developed.

It should now be clear that on the ward there is often very little contact between patients and the professional staff. The question then arises, what happens when there is contact? In one study, persons who were pretending to be patients (pseudopatients) approached staff members with questions like "Could you tell me when I will be eligible for grounds privileges?" "Could you tell me when I will be presented at the staff meeting?" or "Could you tell me when I am likely to be discharged?" (Rosenhan, 1973). The results indicated that the staff members stopped to talk only 2% to 4% of the time. Fully 71% of the time, psychiatrists simply looked away and walked past. Those results are summarized in Table 22.1.

Furthermore, when staff members did respond to the questions asked by patients, the answers they gave were often not really answers. For example:

Pseudopatient: Pardon me, Doctor. Could you tell me when I'm eligible for grounds privileges?
Physician: Good morning, Dave. How are you today? (*moves off without waiting for a response*)

If a patient responded that way to a question from a staff member, the response would be considered "inappropriate" and taken as evidence that the patient was out of contact with reality and needed continued hospitalization.

The nature of the contact (or lack thereof) between the professional staff and the patients in mental hospitals is unfortunate, but it should not be concluded that the behavior of the staff necessarily reflects a lack of concern or commitment. In most cases, the lack of contact between staff and patients stems from the fact that the staff is overworked. Furthermore, it is personally stressful and threatening to work with disturbed individuals on a daily basis. As the old saying goes, "There but for the grace of God go I," and that can be very threatening. It may be that the interpersonal distance that the staff maintains is to some extent a defensive strategy. Just as surgeons cover their patients' faces when they operate to separate "the person" from "the operation," so staff members in mental hospitals may place emotional screens between themselves and patients.

TABLE 22.1   HOSPITAL STAFF MEMBERS AVOIDED RESPONDING WHEN ASKED QUESTIONS BY PSEUDOPATIENTS ON A PSYCHIATRIC WARD

TYPE OF RESPONSE	FROM PSYCHIATRIST (%)	FROM NURSE OR ATTENDANT (%)
Moved on, head averted	71	88
Made eye contact	23	10
Paused to chat	2	2
Stopped to chat	4	.5

Source: Rosenhan (1973), p. 255, tab. 1.

Patienthood

Mental hospitals differ from general medical hospitals in that they provide a total community in which individuals can live for long periods. Researchers who study social institutions point out that mental hospitals are more like the military or prisons than they are like other hospitals, and they refer to these types of organizations as **total institutions** (Goffman, 1961). Before we go on to consider the research on how patients adjust to hospitalization, it might be helpful to consider the experience of hospitalization from the patient's point of view. Case Study 22.1 (p. 566) was written by a college student who was admitted to a psychiatric ward of a general medical hospital after she attempted suicide by taking an overdose of sleeping medication. Her comments are particularly interesting because they reflect changes in her attitudes about hospitalization and her ambivalence about the experience.

An important feature of total institutions is that the persons inside the institution are rigidly stratified, and those at the bottom (enlisted persons, prisoners, mental patients) have no power. Persons at the bottom of the hierarchy are told what to wear, with whom they may talk, when they may eat, and exactly how they will behave. In mental hospitals, they are even told *what is real* and *what to feel.* Finally, the staff in a mental hospital is especially powerful because the staff determines when or even if the individual will ever be released.

At first, many patients reject the control of the staff and do not accept the role of "mental patient." New patients often make comments like "I'm just here for a couple of days of rest because I was under a lot of stress. I'm not a mental patient like the other people here." However, in time patients come to accept their role—for better or for worse. For some patients, hospitalization is an opportunity to get help, a positive experience. For many, however, it is not positive. Their self-confidence is eroded, they recognize that they are completely dependent on the staff for everything, and they accept the role of "sick, dependent mental patient." They are patients, and to behave otherwise would only provide the staff with more justification for concluding that they are out of contact with reality and more justification for holding them in the hospital longer.

The development of dependence in patients makes them much easier to deal with (which is why some institutions implicitly foster the dependence), but dependence results in some unwanted side effects. As patients become more dependent on the hospital, they become less competent socially and vocationally, and they experience a general loss in self-esteem. These factors decrease the patients' ability to function independently and reduce the likelihood that they will be able to leave the institution. Not only do the patients become less *able* to leave, but after some time, they do not *want* to leave because they no longer have confidence that they can "make it on the outside." This personal deterioration is due not to the patients' disorders but to their experience of being institutionalized. This surrendering of personal control and acceptance of dependence on the hospital is referred to as the **institutionalization syndrome,** and it can be as debilitating as the disorder that originally brought the patient to the hospital. Overall, then, the experience of hospitalization can have a negative effect on patients that is independent of their disorders. If we want individuals to become self-assured and independent, confinement in a mental hospital may not be the best place to begin.

Patients are powerless in the institution, but they do learn to manipulate the system and thereby gain some indirect control over their circumstances. For example, if they want attention, they may act disturbed because the disturbed patients get more attention from the staff. Alternatively, if better-adjusted patients are getting privileges, they may act less disturbed. This method of gaining some control is referred to as **impression management,** and its effects were clearly demonstrated in a study in which "newcomers" (patients who had been in the hospital for less than 3 months) and "old-timers" (patients who had been in the hospital for more than 3 months) were asked to fill out a questionnaire about symptoms (Braginsky et al., 1966). For half of the patients, the questionnaire was labeled as a test of "mental illness," and the patients were told that those who got high scores would probably have to stay in the hospital. For the other half of the patients, the same questionnaire was labeled as a test of "self-insight," and the patients were told that those who got high scores would probably be released soon.

The results are very interesting: The old-timers responded so that they would have to stay in the hospital (high "mental illness" and low "self-insight"), but newcomers responded so that they would be released (low "mental illness" and high "self-insight"). These findings have two important implications. First, old-timers did not want to leave the hospital, a finding that reflects the institutionalization syndrome. Second, both old-timers and newcomers manipulated the impressions others received in an attempt to achieve what they wanted (i.e., continuance in the hospital or release).

Some patients are so good at impression management that they can even fool highly trained professionals. In one experiment, patients with schizophrenia who had been in a hospital for 2 years or more were assigned to a "discharge" condition or to an "open ward" condition (Braginsky & Braginsky, 1967). Patients in

Case Study 22.1

PSYCHIATRIC HOSPITALIZATION AFTER A SUICIDE ATTEMPT: A COLLEGE JUNIOR TALKS ABOUT HER EXPERIENCE

The first thing I remember was being in the emergency room of the hospital. All I could do was lie there. I wanted to tell them that I was all right, that everything would be fine if they would just let me die, but Mom and Dad were talking to a nurse, and I couldn't make myself move. They told me later that I rocked back and forth and moaned a lot, but I don't remember.

A few hours later, a male nurse from the psychiatric ward came to my room and asked if I would sign a form to enter myself into the hospital voluntarily. I remember that it took me several minutes to figure out that I was supposed to sign my name—or at least it seemed like several minutes. My next thought was that later I was going to be really sorry that I signed myself in.

When I awoke in the morning, I was in a hospital room in a regular medical ward, and they were getting ready to take me up to the psychiatric ward. When I realized what was going on, I pleaded with my parents to take me home. The thought of spending time on a psychiatric ward was scary!

When the nurse took me up to the ward to show me around, I was really worried. I was worried that they would make me stay there, which they did. The psychiatric ward was different from the rest of the hospital. People walked around in street clothes, and adults sat in the lounge watching TV and playing games. I kept waiting for someone to start screaming or for someone to appear in a straitjacket.

They assigned me to a room by myself, but first they took away everything I had. I found out later that they removed anything with which I could hurt myself. It took 2 days for me to get back my curling iron and my contact cooker. I wasn't allowed a razor, and they looked through everything that anyone brought me.

They gave me a phone only on the condition that I promise not to try to hurt myself. They said that if I did try to hurt myself, they would put me in a hospital where they'd tie me down and keep me that way. I decided on the phone. I was so embarrassed when they told me that it would be a while before they would trust me to eat with the other patients in the cafeteria or to do anything by myself. Because I was a suicide risk, I was put on "special observation," which meant that someone sat right next to me *at all times.* Also, when I was in the bathroom, they knocked on the door every few seconds and made me answer.

I told Mom not to tell my [college] roommates or anyone where I was. I was afraid they wouldn't want to know or, worse yet, wouldn't care. Mom told them anyway, but I was visited only twice by my roommates. I can understand that; it's hard to talk to someone who is not allowed to have sharp objects around and who you think is crazy. I suppose it was also frightening for them to be on the ward.

The first few days were bad. I felt out of touch and like a person who was stuck someplace he wasn't supposed to be but couldn't convince anyone of it. When I was escorted around the halls for a walk, I looked at the other patients and wondered what it was like to be a psychiatric patient. It was scary and embarrassing to realize that I was one.

My boyfriend came to visit me every day and always called. I don't think I could have maintained contact without him. He was the only person, except for the people on the floor, who saw me as an individual with problems, not as a *social disease.* My parents were uncomfortable at first. They stumbled when they talked and wouldn't look at me. I hated myself for putting them through it, but I blamed them for letting me live. Gradually, though, I was glad I was there. My mom was terrific. She was cheerful and optimistic. She told me not to worry about school, that I deserved a break. She sympathized with me and made me feel like it was OK to admit I had problems. My dad didn't handle it as easily. He wouldn't come to see me alone because the one time he did, we had nothing to say. He wouldn't talk about what was wrong, why I was there, or what help I was getting. I think he kind of tried to see it as a normal hospital stay.

I was on the ward for about a week when they finally took me off "special observation" and put me in a double room and allowed me to eat with the others. They told me that I was expected to mingle and talk with others in the ward, in group meetings, and with my counselors. I didn't want to talk. I didn't see the use of telling my problems to people who were already mentally ill. What good was that going to do anyone? Also, I was ashamed. Normal people do not lose control. Every time I tried to talk in group therapy, all I could do was cry. I just lost control, and I hated myself and them for making me do it.

After about 2 weeks in the hospital, I begged my doctor to let me out. He did on Thanksgiving Day. Sometimes I wish that he'd made me stay longer, but I can't ask to go back because asking to go in is worse than being put there because then you're admitting you have a problem. It's even harder for people to understand when a person admits that he has a problem. Then they say he's begging for attention. I'm not so sure that's wrong, either. I don't know.

When I got back to school, I felt like everyone was looking at me, saying, "Look, I can tell she's been in a mental hospital." I was scared to come back. I didn't want to be put into a group of people who were singled out for the rest of their lives. I still get nervous every time someone says, "What were you doing last semester?" I don't want to talk about it or think about it. I still wish it had never happened. I needed to go to the hospital, and it helped, but I wish it had never happened.

---

the discharge condition were told that they were going to be interviewed by a person who "is interested in examining patients to see whether they might be ready for discharge." In contrast, patients in the open-ward condition were told that the interviewer "is interested in examining patients to see whether they should be in open or closed wards." The interviews were tape-recorded and later scored by three psychiatrists in terms of the amount of abnormality the patients showed and the amount of hospital control the patients needed. The results indicated that the patients in the discharge condition led the psychiatrists to believe that they had high levels of abnormality and high needs for hospital control. Patients in the open-ward condition led the psychiatrists to believe that they had low levels of abnormality and low needs for hospital control. Those results are summarized in Figure 22.1. In other words, the long-term patients could manipulate the impressions of highly trained experts so that the patients could get what they wanted (i.e., stay in the hospital but on a good ward). The individuals may have been patients, but they were not stupid.

Another important factor to consider is how patients get "lost" in the hospital. In Chapter 21 we noted instances in which individuals had been admitted to a hospital and were then somehow overlooked for as long as 42 years (McGarry & Bendt, 1969). It is usually assumed that patients get lost in the system because there are so many patients and so few staff members. However, it also appears that some patients intentionally keep a low profile so as to lose themselves in the system (Braginsky et al., 1969). These patients have been called "invisible patients," and studies of them have shown that they are not necessarily more or less disturbed than other patients. Instead, it appears that they have accepted their role as mental patients, decided that the hospital is a good and safe place to be, and adopted a lifestyle that does not give them much exposure to the staff. Their notion seems to be "out of sight, less likely to be discharged." Evidence for the fact that this strategy works comes from the finding that invisible patients are not more disturbed than other patients but are less likely to be discharged.

In our discussion of hospitalization, two seemingly contradictory views have been presented. On the one hand, it was pointed out that most mental hospitals are distinctly unpleasant places in which to live. The physical facilities are drab, patients are restricted and powerless, and life is monotonous and dehumanizing. On the other hand, the evidence suggests that many mental patients want to stay in the hospitals. Patients present themselves as sicker than they are so as not to be discharged, and the results of numerous surveys indicate that as many as 80% of mental patients have favorable attitudes about hospitals, sometimes seeing them as desirable or even liberating places in which to live (Brady et al., 1959; Imre, 1962; Imre & Wolf, 1962; Rosenblatt & Mayer, 1974; Shiloh, 1968).

The difference between the views of hospitals held by outsiders and those held by patients can be accounted for in terms of the reference points of the two groups. For many patients, the hospital may provide better living conditions or a more psychologically secure environment than they face outside, whereas outsiders probably have better living conditions or a more psychologically secure environment than they face outside, whereas outsiders probably have better alternatives, making the hospital seem relatively unattractive (Mayer & Rosenblatt, 1974). It is important to recognize this difference and take the patients' perspective when attempting to understand their behavior. For ex-

FIGURE 22.1   LONG-TERM PATIENTS WERE ABLE TO INFLUENCE PSYCHIATRISTS' RATINGS SO THAT THE PATIENTS COULD STAY IN THE HOSPITAL OR ON AN OPEN WARD.

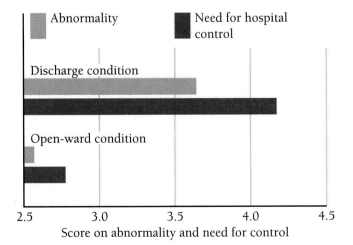

Source: Adapted from Braginsky and Braginsky (1967).

ample, we might assume that patients would work to get out of hospitals, but that is not necessarily so. In fact, there is evidence that some patients' preference for living in the hospital leads them to stay longer and to return sooner (Drake & Wallach, 1979).

When struggling with the question of whether he should leave the hospital, one patient wrote a poem using a cave as a metaphor for the hospital (Hayward & Taylor, 1956):

Yes, I want the cave,
There, I know here I am.
I can grope, in the dark,
    and feel the cave walls.
And the people, there, know I'm there,
    and they step on me, by mistake,—
I think, I hope.
But outside—
Where am I?

Effectiveness of Hospitalization

The negative effects of hospitalization (i.e., the institutionalization syndrome) have been known for many years. However, it was generally assumed that the positive effects of hospitalization outweighed the negative effects and that patients who were treated in hospitals were more likely to improve than patients who were treated elsewhere. Those assumptions have been seriously challenged, and we need to consider carefully the question of whether hospitalization is in fact better than treatment elsewhere (Kiesler, 1982a, 1982b; Kiesler & Sibulkin, 1988).

In 10 experiments, disturbed individuals were randomly assigned to hospital treatment or to some alternative care—day care, drugs with outpatient psychotherapy, or adequate housing without any specific treatment (see Kiesler, 1982a). The results of these experiments are startling: *In no case was hospitalization found to be more effective than the alternative care, and in almost every case the alternative care had more positive effects.* For example, in one experiment, first-admission patients who were diagnosed as suffering from schizophrenia were randomly assigned either to a good mental hospital where they received traditional treatment including psychotherapy, drugs, occupational therapy, and ward meetings, or they were assigned to a small, homelike facility run by a nonprofessional staff where the patients and staff shared the responsibility for maintenance and food preparation (Mosher et al., 1975; Mosher & Menn, 1978). Follow-up evaluations of the patients after 1 year and 2 years revealed that those who had been assigned to the homelike facility were less disturbed and more likely to be employed. Among patients who were discharged, those from the homelike facility were more likely to be living alone or with

peers, whereas those from the hospital were more likely to be living with parents or relatives. Furthermore, the patients from the homelike facility were 20% less likely to be rehospitalized.

In another experiment, patients with acute schizophrenia were assigned to either regular inpatient treatment or outpatient treatment in which they received drug therapy and counseling (Levenson et al., 1977). There were no dramatic differences between the success rates of the two groups, but the patients who received the outpatient treatment tended to do better, and their treatment cost only one-sixth what the inpatient treatment cost ($565 vs. $3,330). In summary, the 10 experiments on this question indicated that alternative care outside a hospital was as effective as or even more effective than treatment in a hospital—and it cost less. The results of these experiments raise serious questions about the use of hospitals for treating abnormal behavior. So let us examine two alternatives to hospitalization: deinstitutionalization and community care.

◼ DEINSTITUTIONALIZATION

Not long ago, the superintendent of a large state mental hospital told me that one of his major goals was to "build more flower gardens." When I looked surprised, he explained that the hospital had embarked on an ambitious program of returning patients to the community for care, and that as the hospital population became smaller, the buildings that had once housed patients were torn down. The foundations of the demolished buildings were then filled with earth, flowers, trees, and shrubs. Indeed, when I looked out his office window, I saw a series of large rectangular gardens, each surrounded by a low wall formed by the top of the foundation of the original building. Where patients once languished, petunias now flourished. As we will see, however, in some cases, the bulldozing of buildings and planting of petunias may have been premature.

Not all former hospital buildings are being turned into flower beds, but the **deinstitutionalization** of mental patients has been widespread, and the number of patients in hospitals was reduced by about 75% between 1950 and 1980. The numbers of patients in state and county mental hospitals during those years are presented graphically in Figure 22.2. Two changes in the curve are notable. First, the curve begins to flatten out and then decline slightly in the late 1950s and early 1960s. That change was due to the introduction of antipsychotic medication (neuroleptic drugs) that reduced the symptoms of many disturbed individuals

The deinstitutionalization program has been partially responsible for the large drop in numbers of hospitalized patients. Between 1950 and 1980, the United States saw a 75% decrease in the number of hospitalized patients.

and enabled them to live in the community. Second, in the late 1960s, the curve goes into a steep decline such that the total number of patients declines by over 25,000 per year, a change that reflects the deinstitutionalization movement. The number of patients is

FIGURE 22.2   THE NUMBER OF PATIENTS IN MENTAL HOSPITALS DECLINED DRAMATICALLY BETWEEN 1950 AND 1980.

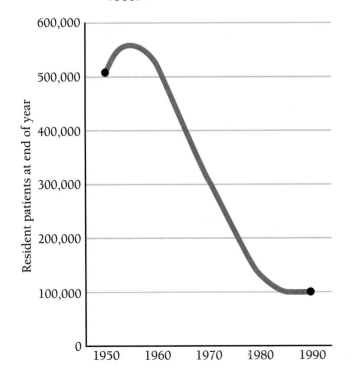

still being reduced, but the decline has slowed recently, probably because we may be getting down to the "hard core" of chronic patients who are extremely difficult to release.

The reduction of the number of patients in hospitals is certainly striking, but it is even more dramatic when you realize that the reduction has occurred while the general population was increasing. The success of the deinstitutionalization movement is reflected in the fact that a feasibility study conducted in the state of Vermont led to the recommendation that the state hospital be abolished (Carling et al., 1987). In other words, it was recommended that Vermont have a state mental health system with *no state hospital.*

There are three major reasons behind the movement to treat individuals in the community rather than in hospitals: (a) to avoid the negative aspects of hospitals, (b) to capitalize on the positive aspects of communities, and (c) to cut costs. We will consider each of these reasons and then examine the problems posed by deinstitutionalization.

Negative Aspects of Hospitals

The first reason that is usually given for deinstitutionalization can be summarized with the statement "You can't make a normal adjustment in an abnormal environment." The notion is that the major goal of treatment is to help disturbed individuals make a better adjustment, but the concept of adjustment implies *adjustment to something.* In most cases, we adjust to the standards or models around us, but the hospital environment does not provide a good standard for adjustment. That being the case, a hospital would be the worst place to make a normal adjustment because the individuals with whom patients interact most are other patients who are behaving in abnormal ways. It is unlikely that a patient who was attempting to deal with his or her own problems would be able to make a good adjustment when surrounded by other patients who thought they were Napoleon, heard the voice of God in the bathroom, or believed they had radioactive saliva and whose behaviors included constant pacing, suicide attempts, and urinating on the floor.

Furthermore, hospitalization is not conducive to normal adjustment because it fosters the surrender of personal responsibility and undermines self-confidence. That is so because in most hospitals, things are done *to* or *for* patients rather than *by* patients. The institutionalization syndrome that we discussed earlier is due in large part to the patients' adjustment to the norms and standards of the hospital. Thus because hospitals have negative effects on patients, it seems reasonable to get the patients out of the hospital. However, as we will see later, in some cases, the circumstances into which we are releasing the patients may be worse than the hospitals.

Positive Aspects of Communities

The second reason for moving patients out of the hospital and into the community is the belief that patients can be cared for more effectively in the community. Most notable in this regard is that if individuals are treated in the community rather than at some distant hospital, it is not necessary for them to be separated from their friends, family, and coworkers, from whom they can obtain valuable social support. Furthermore, if they are treated while living in the community, the patients can work actively to overcome sources of stress rather than being isolated from them and only talking about them. In addition, if patients are treated in the community, they can avoid the difficult transition from the hospital back to the community. That transition usually comes at a time when the patients' adjustment is still fragile; they are unsure about their ability to function in the outside world (after all, that is where they "broke down"), and the stress of the transition can result in a relapse.

Economics

The third factor behind the deinstitutionalization movement is simple economics. Mental hospitals are very expensive to operate. In addition to the direct costs of treatment (therapists and medication), there are numerous indirect costs such as food, building construction, building maintenance, and extensive support staffs that include everyone from nurses to groundskeepers. The indirect costs of hospitalization easily exceed the costs of treatment, but by treating patients in the community, all indirect costs can be eliminated, and considerable savings can be achieved. It could also be argued that treating patients in the community might also result in greater savings later because treatment in the community is more effective for reducing relapses, therefore reducing the cost of rehospitalization.

Unfortunately, the savings achieved by deinstitutionalization are not always as great as they appear at first. That is because very disturbed individuals who are discharged from state hospitals often go to other facilities such as privately operated nursing homes. The costs of institutionalizing the patients in those facilities are usually higher and are usually paid for by private insurance companies or by the federal government through the Medicare program. In other words, the costs are not saved but simply *shifted* from state governments to private industry and the federal government.

Problems with Deinstitutionalization

When the deinstitutionalization movement began in the mid-1960s, the motivating factor was improved care of disturbed individuals. It was believed that patients could be served better in the community than in the hospital. However, when the boom economy of the 1960s slowed down and budget deficits began to appear, priorities changed, and the cost-cutting value of deinstitutionalization became more important. Unfortunately, financially pressed legislatures not only took the savings created by closing hospitals, but they also attempted to save money by cutting back or stopping the funding for community-based treatment programs. As a result, many deinstitutionalized patients were left stranded. Not only had the door to the hospital been closed behind them, but the door to community care was now also shut.

The closing of mental hospitals is usually presented as a "progressive, modern movement" toward more humane treatment of patients in communities, and few people stop to ask what happens to the patients after they are released. Ignored is the fact that getting patients out of the hospital is only half of the deinstitutionalization program, and if alternative care is not provided outside of the hospital, we are probably being more inhumane than humane. In many cases, deinstitutionalized patients end up living on welfare in run-down areas of the cities that have become known as "psychiatric ghettos." Other former patients join the ranks of the homeless and live on the streets. In an attempt to avoid or hide such problems in their areas, some officials have given discharged patients one-way bus tickets to distant cities in other states.

It should also be noted that the failure to link community care with the closing of hospitals posed problems not only for former patients who were turned out but also for potential patients who were never able to get in when the need first arose and for whom community care was not available.

The existence of psychiatric ghettos and increasing numbers of disturbed individuals living on the streets caused a backlash against deinstitutionalization, and some efforts were made to reinstitutionalize patients, such as the program in New York City that resulted in the institutionalization of Joyce Brown, the woman who burned money (see Case Study 21.2). However, because of the high costs of hospitalization, those attempts have been tokens at best. The program in New York City involved setting aside only 28 beds for a city with 8.5 million inhabitants. Furthermore, reinstitutionalization does not solve the problem; it just reintroduces the problems that deinstitutionalization was designed to overcome.

Do not conclude that community care is entirely unavailable, because that is not the case. Care is available, but there does not appear to be enough care or the right type of care to meet the need. Next we will consider the types of community care that are available.

COMMUNITY CARE

The release of patients from the mental hospitals does not necessarily imply that the patients are cured or even completely treated. Thus an important component of deinstitutionalization involves providing adequate treatment programs in the community, known as **community care**. The idea of systematically treating disturbed individuals in the community is not new. It can be traced back to the town of Gheel in Belgium in the 13th century (Aring, 1974). As legend has it, in A.D. 600 a pagan king decapitated his beautiful daughter, Dymphna, when she refused to marry him. The townspeople thought the king was mentally ill and that his behavior was the work of the Devil. Because Dymphna had been able to resist the Devil, it was assumed that God had granted her special powers to fight the evil forces that led to mental illness. When her story spread, people who were struggling with mental disorders came to Gheel in the hope of being inspired to fight the Devil more effectively and be cured. A number of miraculous cures were documented, and Dymphna was canonized by the Catholic church in 1247.

In 1600 in the town of Gheel, Belgium, a pagan king executed his daughter, Dymphna, for refusing to marry him. The townspeople thought the king was mentally ill and that his behavior was the work of the Devil. Because his daughter had resisted the Devil, people thought she had special powers to fight the evil forces that caused mental illness. Disturbed individuals flocked to the town of Gheel, and the community developed a tradition of caring for these individuals.

(Dymphna is still the patroness of individuals with epilepsy and mental illness.)

Due to the publicity, hundreds of disturbed individuals began coming to Gheel seeking cures, and in 1430 a small hospital was built. However, because so many people came, and because many who were not cured stayed on, the number of disturbed individuals quickly swelled beyond the capacity of the hospital. In an attempt to accommodate all of the disturbed people, the townspeople began taking them into their homes. The church initially administered the program, but in 1852 the responsibility was shifted to the state, which then "certified" families as qualified to provide housing and care. Being certified became a matter of pride, social standing, and tradition that was handed down for generations.

Through the years, Gheel has provided a model of community tolerance and care for disturbed individuals. It is interesting that the tradition of community care in Gheel grew from necessity when facilities and funds were not sufficient for institutional care. Similar limitations in facilities and funds also play important roles in the current movement toward community care, but today the disturbed individuals are not being welcomed with the same compassion and enthusiasm as they were in Gheel.

Community treatment programs revolve around *outpatient clinics, community mental health centers, halfway houses,* and *home care visits.* When reading about the facilities and programs for community care, keep in mind that they are designed both for former patients who have been discharged from hospitals and for other disturbed individuals who do not yet need hospitalization.

Outpatient Clinics

As the name implies, **outpatient clinics** are nonresidential treatment facilities to which patients go for therapy while living in the community. Outpatient clinics have long been an important part of mental hospitals. After a hospitalized patient has improved enough to be released, treatment is continued in the outpatient clinic. However, the problem with outpatient clinics is that they are usually located in large hospitals, and because those hospitals often serve large areas, the clinics are not conveniently located for many patients. Patients who have to travel a great distance to get to an outpatient clinic once or twice a week are likely to drop out of treatment. That is unfortunate because treatment and support during the transitional period when patients are moving back into the community are crucial. Without such aftercare, gains made in the hospital may be lost, and the patients may have to be rehospitalized. Thus outpatient clinics play an important role in community care, but their role is often limited by geographic problems.

Community Mental Health Centers

Community mental health centers were designed to overcome the location problem of hospital-based outpatient clinics. As the name implies, they are smaller clinics that are conveniently located in the communi-

ties in which potential users live. However, community mental health centers were designed to be much more than just convenient, and their development stemmed from what in the 1960s was a new approach to mental illness. A brief review of the legislative history that led to the development of community mental health centers will help you understand the goals they were designed to meet.

In 1955, Congress established the Joint Commission on Mental Illness and Health to examine the treatment of mental patients in the United States. After 6 years of study, the commission concluded that patients in large mental hospitals were more likely to receive *custodial care* than *treatment,* and that even when treatment was provided, it was *not readily available* to many individuals who needed it because the hospitals were located too far from where the patients lived. The commission also recommended that more attention be devoted to the *prevention* of mental illness.

In response to the commission's report, President Kennedy sent to Congress the Community Mental Health Centers Act, proposing that the large, centrally located state and federal mental hospitals be phased out and replaced by many community mental health centers. These centers were to be designed to serve four functions:

1. *Outpatient Therapy with Day Hospitalization.* Patients could come in once or twice a week for treatment and, when necessary, stay at the centers during the day but return home at night. The hope was that by making treatment readily available near where the individuals lived, disturbed individuals would be more likely to come in for help before their problems became so serious that full-time hospitalization was necessary.

2. *Short-Term Inpatient Hospitalization in Emergency Cases.* By hospitalizing the patients near where they lived, social support from friends and relatives could be maintained, and the difficult transition from a distant hospital back to the community could be avoided. The community mental health centers were not designed to have their own inpatient facilities; instead, they were to use the facilities of local general hospitals that had small psychiatric wards. Only as a last resort were individuals who required long-term care to be sent to large central hospitals.

3. *24-Hour-a-Day Emergency Services.* People would be able to get help immediately over the phone or on a walk-in basis whenever it was necessary. When an individual is in the middle of a crisis, it does not help much to say, "Well, we can see you a week from Tuesday at two-thirty." People in crisis need help *immediately,* and early intervention may keep the problem from getting worse. Essentially, the concept of the medical emergency room was applied to the treatment of psychological problems.

4. *Educational and Consultation Services.* The goal of these services, offered to both individuals and other agencies in the community, was not treatment but *prevention.* For example, in the community in which I live, the staff of the local community mental health center routinely provides lectures and seminars for various companies on topics such as stress management and the early identification of personal problems. Also, staff members are quick to step in to provide help when potential problems arise. Once when a firefighter was killed while battling a fire, the staff of the community mental health center immediately set up group and individual counseling sessions for all of the members of the fire department to help them deal with the stresses associated with the death of their comrade.

Thus the goals of the community mental health centers are summed up in their name: They provide help in the individuals' *community* and promote *mental health* by using the resources in the community, catching problems early, and working toward prevention.

Another potential value of community mental health centers is that they may be more "culturally sensitive" than the large hospital-based treatment facilities (Rogler et al., 1987). Traditionally, the mental health services that are provided by large hospitals are aimed at the middle class and are based on a middle-class lifestyle. In many cases, however, *Roseanne* might be a better model than *The Brady Bunch* for understanding the life of a client, and because community mental health centers are "where the clients are," the centers may be more sensitive to the problems of the populations they serve. With that sensitivity, they may also be more attractive to members of minority groups and therefore will be used more effectively than traditional facilities.

The community mental health center program has met with mixed success. On the positive side, the centers are located in the neighborhoods where their clients live, and they do make outpatient treatment, day hospitalization, short-term inpatient treatment, and 24-hour crisis intervention readily available to members of the community. In addition to being physically accessible, the centers are also financially accessible because fees are based on a sliding scale that takes the family's income and expenses into account. On the negative side, the success of the program has been limited because there are not enough centers to meet the need. When President Kennedy originally proposed them, he suggested that there be one center for every 100,000 persons. With today's population, that would mean 2,415 centers, but almost 30 years later, only

about 1,000 have been established. Furthermore, in many centers, the staff are so busy providing primary care for disturbed individuals that they have very little time to devote to the problem of prevention. In other words, they are so busy bailing out the psychological boat that they do not have time to solve the problem by fixing the crack in the hull. Overall, however, community mental health centers have had a significant impact on the delivery of mental health services, and there is no doubt that they will continue to play an important role.

Halfway Houses

Up to this point we have talked about patients as though they either did or did not have to be in a hospital. However, many patients do not need the intensive care provided by hospitals, but do need a semistructured environment in which to live. Other patients may need a supportive environment in which to live while making the transition from hospital to community life. As the name implies, **halfway houses** provide places for patients to live that are halfway between hospitalization and independent life in the community.

A halfway house is usually a large older home that has been converted into a number of small living units. Cooking and eating are usually done as a group so that costs can be kept low, work can be shared, and residents do not become socially isolated. Halfway houses are usually staffed by paraprofessionals, often a married couple who manage the house and supervise the residents in exchange for rent and possibly a small wage. Like the other residents, the paraprofessionals usually have other jobs.

Most halfway houses are not designed for long-term use by residents. Rather, they serve only as transitional living and care facilities while the residents are readjusting to life in the community. While living in the halfway house, the residents get settled into jobs and social groups before moving out on their own. In the halfway house, the residents can get support from the paraprofessionals and the other residents. Residents who have been out of the hospital longer can serve as models for newer residents, and later the newer residents will take on those responsibilities when the older residents move out.

Home Care

All of the treatment programs we have discussed so far require that the client go to the treatment facility, but some programs are now being established in which the caregivers go to the client. Going to the client is sometimes necessary because the client is too disturbed to come in for treatment. This approach is not unique to the care of psychologically disturbed persons; for years, there have been visiting-nurse programs for medical patients who were not sick enough for full-time hospitalization but too sick or otherwise unable to go to the hospital for outpatient care. Psychological and medical house calls may be somewhat expensive, but they are cheaper than hospitalizing patients, and if the patients are not going to be hospitalized, house calls may be the only way some patients will get treatment.

Many (but not all) of the individuals who are helped by these programs are homeless and living on the streets. Unlike the program in New York that was discussed earlier in which the goal was to get the people off the streets and into hospitals, the goal of these programs is to treat the people where they are. With these programs, it is hoped that in time the homeless will move off the streets, but into homes, not hospitals. Case Study 22.2 highlights a community program in Baltimore called COSTAR in which psychiatric nurses work in the community providing medical, psychological, and social support for disturbed individuals.

Public Acceptance of Patients in the Community

Most people agree that whenever possible, it is preferable to treat nondangerous patients in the community rather than in hospitals. However, a problem arises when people have to face the possibility of having mental patients live in *their* communities. Numerous surveys have indicated that most people have negative attitudes about or are afraid of mentally ill individuals, and it has been estimated that as many as half of all psychiatric facilities that were planned for residential areas were blocked by community opposition (Piasecki, 1975). In one city in New York, the residents went so far as to pass a law making it illegal for mental patients to live within the city limits. (A mental patient was defined as anyone who was taking antipsychotic medication.)

People have negative attitudes about mental patients and oppose their presence in the community, but the question arises whether the presence of patients in a community is even noticeable. To answer that question, one group of investigators conducted a survey of 180 individuals living in 12 residential neighborhoods in New York City (Rabkin et al., 1984). Six of the neighborhoods contained a treatment facility such as a large outpatient clinic, a halfway house, or a single-room-occupancy hotel known to attract former mental patients. The community residents who were surveyed in those areas lived within one block of the treatment facility. The other six neighborhoods were comparable in all respects but did not contain a treat-

ment facility; residents in those areas were used as controls.

The results revealed two interesting findings: First, when residents were asked to rate problems in their community (e.g., burglary, unemployment, and "crazy people in the street"), there were no differences between the responses of residents in the treatment and control areas. In other words, the presence of patients in the neighborhood did not influence the residents' perception of the quality of life in the neighborhood. Second, when residents were asked about the presence of treatment facilities in their neighborhoods, 77% of the residents in the treatment areas were unaware of the presence of the facility despite the fact that they lived within one block of it. Of the residents living near a facility, 23% reported being aware of it—but then, 13% of the residents living in the control areas incorrectly reported the presence of a treatment facility in their neighborhood. If 13% is taken as the error rate (the percentage of people with erroneous beliefs about the existence of a facility in their neighborhood), it could be concluded that only 10% of the individuals living within one block of a large psychiatric treatment facility were aware of its existence.

These results do not offer any evidence that the presence of a treatment facility for mental patients has a negative impact on the quality of a community, and they reveal that only very few people even become aware of treatment facilities in their community. Unfortunately, such facts do little to change people's emotionally based attitudes. Would you be in favor of having a mental patient treatment facility in your neighborhood?

It is interesting that some of the stigma associated with treatment facilities is related to the names we give the facilities. "Mental hospital" and "hospital for the criminally insane" certainly sound ominous to both the public and patients. In one state mental hospital in which I worked that was labeled a "mental health center," nurses often threatened disruptive patients by saying, "If you keep acting that way, we are going to transfer you from this *mental health center* to a *mental hospital!*" The patients quickly complied with whatever the nurse wanted. The effects of labels on the public's response to treatment facilities was documented when the name of one mental hospital was changed to the Madison Center. Immediately after the name change, the local residents passed a bond issue to provide additional funding, and children began walking on the sidewalk in front of the building rather than crossing the street to avoid coming near it (Roberts & Roberts, 1985).

Thus as in Gheel 500 years ago, economic necessity is once again giving birth to the community care of

Case Study 22.2

TAKING HELP TO THE HOMELESS MENTALLY ILL: THE EXAMPLE OF COSTAR

In Baltimore, as elsewhere, it was recognized that many individuals are too disturbed to come in for treatment. One scenario runs as follows: A disturbed individual is hospitalized temporarily, put on a maintenance dosage of medication that enables him or her to function in the community, and is then released with the expectation that he or she will return to the hospital (or outpatient clinic) for medication as needed. However, for some reason, the patient stops taking the medication and consequently relapses. Once relapsed, the patient becomes too disoriented to return to the hospital. Then the disturbed patient is likely to wind up on the street because he or she cannot pay the rent, is rejected by his or her family, or is so disoriented that he or she cannot coexist with others in a normal environment.

In an attempt to reach out and treat such individuals, the Johns Hopkins Hospital and the city of Baltimore established the Community Support, Treatment, and Rehabilitation (COSTAR) program, in which psychiatric nurses work with the patients in the community—on the streets and in their homes. This program differs from most other programs in that it relies primarily on psychiatric nurses rather than social workers, and therefore patients can be given medical attention in addition to psychological treatment.

The case of a 41-year-old woman named Sinora provides a good example of the kinds of problems that the patients have and the kinds of treatments that are used. Sinora was diagnosed as suffering from chronic schizophrenia, and she must take her antipsychotic medication every day or her condition will seriously deteriorate. However, living on the streets as she did, she often forgot her medication, so she became very disoriented and eventually had to be rehospitalized. To circumvent this problem, every day Sinora is visited by a nurse who gives her the medication and makes sure she takes it, but that is not all the nurse does. When Sinora was first found, she was unable to take care of herself, and the nurse had to begin by helping her eat and even bathing her because Sinora frequently soiled herself. The nurse explains, "You start right where they are. . . . Often they'll stumble and go back down, but we all do. Everybody has the right to do that." Over the course of 2 years, the nurse has kept Sinora on her medication, helped her find housing, taught her good grooming and hygiene, taught her how to keep house and shop economically, and helped her budget her money, and she is now taking Sinora to a job-training center. This is real progress, progress that could not be made without daily contact. The nurse commented, "By seeing Sinora every morning for 15 or 20 minutes or maybe a half hour, she and I can sit down and plan her day, see what problems have come up, and solve them before they get to be big problems."

By seeing Sinora every day and doing things like having a meal with her in a fast-food restaurant, the nurse can consistently monitor Sinora's emotional state so that the medication can be adjusted if necessary. The nurse is also able to observe Sinora's behavior in the reality of day-to-day living so that real problems can be identified and solved. This is more effective than trying to work with a patient in the artificial environment of a hospital, where you can only talk about what goes on.

COSTAR even handles Sinora's welfare checks, budgeting the funds carefully over each month. This can be difficult because initially the client may not trust the nurse or understand what is being done. However, with assisted budgeting, as with other aspects of the program, the clients are encouraged to participate in treatment; the treatment is not forced on them from the outside.

Is the COSTAR program successful? The answer depends on how you measure success. It is unlikely that clients like Sinora will ever be completely "normal," and they will probably always require a visit once a week or every other week if not every day. However, their ability to function on their own has been greatly increased, and with some assistance, many clients do very well. For example, recall that Sinora is now living in stable housing and is getting job training, so eventually she may be at least somewhat self-supporting. That is a long way from being a disoriented schizophrenic living on the street. An initial evaluation of the program revealed that in the year following admission to the COSTAR program, patients were much less likely to require hospitalization than they were in the preceding year when they were not in the program. Apart from the human benefit in terms of quality of life, keeping clients out of the hospital results in a substantial financial saving that more than offsets the costs of the labor-intensive visiting program.

Does Sinora think the program is successful? When asked about COSTAR, Sinora said, "I'm glad COSTAR found me so they could give me my right medicines. I don't never want to be put away no more, Mister. I'm tired of it."

Source: Giansante (1988).

disturbed individuals. However, unlike Gheel, in many cases the community care is given grudgingly at best, and often people want the care to be given in someone else's community.

The Need for Asylums

Community care is a laudable idea, and in many respects it is very successful. When it is not successful, the shortcomings often stem from problems of implementation rather than from flaws in the ideas. However, even if community care were operating at the optimal level that could be realistically expected, there would probably still be a need for mental hospitals. The reason is that individuals who are in great crisis or who are suffering from absolutely overwhelming symptoms (e.g., hideous hallucinations or dangerous delusions) may briefly need a place of refuge, a place to recoup before taking up the battle again. This was demonstrated during times of war when soldiers broke down under great stress. If they were given a few days away from the battle, they were able to recoup and return to the front line. For some individuals, the same may be true during some of life's battles.

What may be needed in some cases is best described by the term *asylum*. The use of that term may seem somewhat paradoxical because it is usually associated with the early institutions for mentally ill individuals, institutions that were characterized by chaos and bedlam (see Chapter 1). Technically, however, the term refers to "a place of refuge and protection," and synonyms include *sanctuary, shelter,* and *refuge.* It was that sort of environment that the early mental health workers were trying to establish and that they thought would cure mental illness. Our mental health forebears may have been incorrect in their belief that asylums were effective for *curing* mental illness, but an asylum in the true sense of the word may be an important brief initial step in the process of treatment and recovery. In our enthusiasm for getting individuals out of impersonal and often deleterious large mental hospitals and keeping them in the community, it is important that we not forget that sometimes individuals who are under great stress can sometimes benefit from a brief respite, from an *asylum.*

◼ COST OF TREATMENT

An issue that runs throughout this chapter is the *cost of treatment,* so at this point it will be helpful if we review some of the figures and financial issues associated with psychiatric care.

Cost

It is difficult to provide overall figures concerning costs because different disorders entail different costs, costs can vary with the quality of treatment, and there are regional differences in costs. However, the following figures will provide you with some rough estimates of costs.

Inpatient Hospitalization. The typical cost of hospitalization in private hospital is often as high as $1,000 a day, and in many cases that figure may not include such "extras" as psychological testing, psychotherapy, physical exams, medication, laboratory work, other treatments such as ECT, or the services of other professionals such as social workers. Those additional costs can easily add hundreds of dollars a day. In many cases, the cost of psychiatric hospitalization is comparable to medical or surgical hospitalization, but there is one very important difference between the two: Whereas medical or surgical hospitalization usually lasts for a few days or a week, *psychiatric hospitalization can last for months.* Being in a psychiatric hospital for 1 month could easily cost well over $40,000, so it is clear that the cost of psychiatric hospitalization can be overwhelming.

When attempting to understand these high costs, it is essential to recognize that the private hospitals are usually run to make a profit, and because there is relatively little competition in the area, there is little necessity to keep costs down and considerable incentive to keep them high. State hospitals do not provide an alternative to private hospitalization because the state hospitals are being phased out.

In some instances, hospitalization is essential for the welfare of the patient and the community, but in many cases individuals are hospitalized to keep beds full and profits up. Indeed, one recent study revealed that nearly 40% of psychiatric hospital care days were unnecessary, and that about 75% of the admissions for substance abuse were unnecessary (American Psychological Association, 1993). At one hospital I know of, patients who are being treated for eating disorders are usually discharged after about 58 or 59 days. Why not earlier or later? The answer is that patients' insurance benefits run out after 60 days! In other words, it appears that in many cases patients are kept in the hospital or released not as a function of their mental condition but as a function of their financial condition. Such abuse is possible because patients and family members are frightened by psychiatric disorders, and they are not in a position to judge what treatment or how much treatment is necessary. Unfortunately, individuals rarely get second opinions concerning the treatment of psychiatric disorders.

Day Hospitalization and Outpatient Treatment.

Day hospitalization rates can run $200 to $300 a day—still high but a considerable saving compared to staying overnight, when little treatment would be provided anyway. Of course, all of the extras like therapy must be added to the base figure. Outpatient treatment is probably the most cost-effective. Psychotherapy outside of the hospital usually costs between $75 and $125 an hour. In addition to psychotherapy, many patients now receive other treatments such as electroconvulsive therapy on an outpatient basis.

Drugs.

In most cases, drugs are a relatively inexpensive mode of treatment. For example, a month's supply of Valium costs about $30 (generic form: $9), and Prozac, which is one of the more expensive antidepressants, costs about $70 a month. Many patients rely on Haldol to control the symptoms of their schizophrenia, and it costs about $260 a month (generic form: $60). However, there are some drugs that are very expensive. For example, Clozaril (along with the necessary weekly blood tests) can cost about $650 per month. Of course, to the cost of drugs we must add the expense of regular consultations with a physician during which the effectiveness of the drug can be evaluated and dosage levels changed if necessary.

Drugs cost less than most other treatments, but we ought not conclude that drugs should be used simply because they are less expensive. Treatments should be chosen on the basis of their effectiveness for the disorder in question.

Insurance and Cost Control

The cost of treatment is usually covered by health insurance, but because those costs are simply passed on to the consumer in the form of higher premiums, there is now a strong movement to cut costs. One means of cutting costs is called **managed health care**. In those programs, you buy a policy for all of your health care needs (physical and psychological) from one organization, and then whenever you have a problem, you see a **primary-care physician** who is responsible for deciding whether you need treatment. If this physician decides that you need treatment, you are referred to one of the specialists in the organization. Costs are reduced in managed-care programs because there is an emphasis on prevention and early detection, which is less expensive than treatment after a problem has developed. Costs are also controlled because the primary-care physician who evaluates your needs will not refer you for unnecessary treatments.

Some psychologists and psychiatrists have raised concerns about the role of psychiatric treatment in managed-care programs. They suggest that in attempts to reduce costs, some psychiatric disorders may not be covered by the insurance policies, patients may be less likely to be referred for benefits that do exist, and the amount of treatment that is budgeted may not be sufficient to overcome the problem. One of my colleagues complained that primary-care physicians underestimate the seriousness of many psychiatric problems, so the physicians do not refer the individuals for treatment, and when the physicians do refer individuals for treatment, they approve only a few weeks of treatment when adequate treatment may in fact take years.

There is no doubt that there have been serious abuses of the psychiatric component of the health care system and that there is a real need to overcome those problems and reduce costs in general. The challenge is to screen potential patients carefully and to identify the most cost-effective treatment. However, even the most cost-effective treatment can be very expensive. Case Study 22.3 (p. 578) illustrates the very high cost of drug treatment for one patient.

PREVENTION OF ABNORMAL BEHAVIOR

We will never have enough mental health professionals to treat all disturbed individuals, and therefore our only real hope for eradicating abnormal behavior is to establish effective prevention programs. Actually, it may be more efficient, cheaper, and more humane to focus more efforts on prevention than treatment. In this section we will consider the problems, programs, and progress associated with our attempts at prevention.

Before discussing specific prevention programs, two obvious but often overlooked issues should be mentioned. First, when working to prevent abnormal behavior, we must concentrate on the factors that we think cause the abnormal behavior. That is probably obvious, but what may be missed is the fact that for any one disorder, there are usually many suspected causes (psychodynamic, learning, cognitive, physiological). The question then arises is, on which suspected cause should we focus? Do we attempt to develop defenses against intrapsychic conflicts, reduce stress, change learned thought patterns, or eliminate specific genes?

Most intervention programs revolve around stress reduction. The implicit notion is that stress leads to abnormal behavior or that stress will be most likely to trigger abnormal behavior in individuals who are predisposed to such behavior (the diathesis-stress hypothesis). That seems reasonable, but it should be recognized that in focusing on stress reduction, we have ignored a variety of other potential causes. Therefore if our attempts at prevention are not com-

Case Study 22.3

THE COST OF BETTY'S DRUGS: $353 A WEEK

This case study is based on Betty, the woman who suffers from schizophrenia and who we discussed in Case Studies 12.2 and 14.4. You will recall that Betty has suffered from a very severe case of schizophrenia for about 20 years, and that she has been hospitalized numerous times. However, Betty is now taking a number of drugs that are effective for reducing many of her symptoms. Those drugs, plus a good deal of social support from friends and the staff at a local mental health center, make it possible for Betty to live outside of the hospital. Unfortunately, the drugs do not eliminate the symptoms, and she is still plagued by a variety of delusions (the police are after her) and hallucinations (monks and demons telling her to kill herself, rats on the floor, people dissolving into blobs of blood). Struggling with her symptoms poses one serious problem for Betty, but she faces another—paying for her drugs. Here is a list of the drugs and treatments that Betty must take along with the weekly costs.

DRUG OR TREATMENT	WEEKLY COST ($)
Clozaril (antipsychotic)	220
Zoloft (antidepressant)	14
Oxybutynin chloride (antispasmodic for bladder control, to counter a side effect of the other drugs)	7
Ativan (antianxiolytic)	13
Klonopin (antianxiolytic)	28
Chloral hydrate (sleeping pill)	1
Blood test for granulocytosis	20
Psychiatric consultation (to monitor symptoms, drugs)	50
Total	353

The cost of Betty's treatment comes to $18,356 per year. How does Betty pay for this? Betty is a very bright woman with a graduate degree in library science who once had a career as a librarian, but because of her symptoms, she is unable to work. Therefore, Betty must live on Social Security disability benefits of $160 per week, which is *less than half of her weekly medical bill.* Fortunately, Betty qualifies for Medicaid assistance, which will pay her medical bills *after she pays the annual deductible of $2,321.* Spread over the year, the deductible comes to $45 a week, so Betty has $115 a week to cover *all* of her expenses (rent, utilities, food, clothing, etc.). Sometimes Betty is simply not able to pay the deductible fee for the drugs, in which case she cannot get the drugs. Usually her pharmacist will give her credit and let her go into debt, but there are limits. One time Betty had no money and was within 2 days of running out of Clozaril. Without the drug, Betty's condition would immediately deteriorate, she would not be able to function in the community, and she would have to be placed in a state hospital (assuming that a space could be found). Hospitalization in the state hospital would cost the government about $40,000 per year, so the cost of the Clozaril is a bargain, but with deficits mounting, the government may not be able to afford either. Then what will happen? Clearly, the cost of treatment can be an overwhelming financial burden both for the individual and for the government. And remember, in many cases, this is a lifelong burden. What would you do if you were faced with this?

Note. The costs described here do not include those of the mental health service that provides a case manager who helps Betty deal with daily problems.

---

pletely successful, it may be that the program was focused on the wrong cause. For example, programs that are focused on stress reduction will not be successful in preventing disorders that are due to strictly physiological problems.

The second issue that should be noted is that regardless of what we think causes abnormal behavior, there are practical, technical, and ethical limits on what we can actually do to prevent abnormal behavior. For example, we may believe that abnormal behavior results from intrapsychic conflict, but it is not feasible to give every child intensive psychotherapy so that they can develop defenses against such conflict. Or we may believe that abnormal behavior is due to genetic problems, but it is neither ethical nor technically possible to use selective mating or surgery to eliminate specific genes. Therefore, when we design intervention programs, we must focus on the *possible*, and insofar as our prevention programs are constrained by practical, technical, and ethical factors, we must expect limitations on the effectiveness of the programs. In summary, when developing prevention programs, we must give careful attention to the questions of what causes abnormal behavior and how or whether we can intervene in the causal chain. Having recognized these issues and limitations, we can go on to discuss the various types of intervention programs that have been tried.

There are three types of prevention, and each type is associated with a different phase of the development of abnormal behavior:

1. *Primary prevention* is aimed at *eliminating the causes* of abnormal behavior.
2. *Secondary prevention* is designed to *catch problems early* so that they do not become serious.
3. *Tertiary prevention* is focused on *reducing relapses* in recovered clients.

Let us examine the programs and problems that are associated with these three types of prevention.

Primary Prevention

Primary prevention is designed to *eliminate the causes* of abnormal behavior. Attempts at primary prevention include such things as improved prenatal and postnatal care, day care for children and the elderly, educational programs to reduce substance abuse, reductions in environmental poisons (e.g., lead in paint and exhaust fumes), improvements in diet, increases in exercise, prevention of head injuries with better athletic helmets and greater use of seat belts, improved housing that allows for privacy and reduces stress, and the reduction of poverty in an attempt to reduce the stress it brings. Sometimes these programs are not thought of as mental health programs because they have other, more immediate physical health and safety benefits. However, the programs do have important "downstream" effects on mental health because they reduce brain damage and stress that lead to abnormal behavior.

One primary prevention program was designed to provide poor, young, unmarried pregnant women with better prenatal care and preparation for motherhood (Olds, 1982). These women usually get very poor prenatal care and give birth to babies who are underweight and suffer from neurological difficulties that lead to serious problems later. In addition, these women are likely to neglect or abuse their babies, causing additional problems for the children. The intervention program involved having a nurse visit the women to teach them proper diet and to help them obtain medical and financial assistance available in the community. The nurse also provided social support for the women and helped them establish relationships

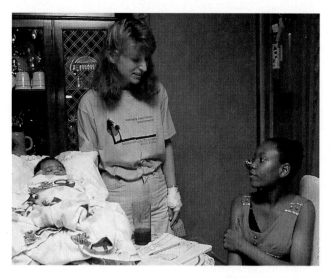

One effective primary intervention program is designed to provide poor, young, unmarried women with better prenatal and postnatal care. The goal is to help improve the health of the newborn and provide support for the mother, thus reducing many of the physical complications and emotional stresses that can lead to abnormal behavior.

with others in the community so that they would have someone to turn to when problems arose. Visits by the nurse continued after birth so that the mothers could be taught about infant development, care, and safety.

An evaluation of the effects of the program revealed that compared to mothers who were not visited, mothers who were visited made better use of community services, gave birth to heavier babies, were less likely to neglect or abuse their babies, and provided their babies with more appropriate playthings. In addition, the visited unmarried mothers were less likely to get pregnant again and were more likely to hold a job. These immediate effects are impressive, but it is likely that we can expect even more important effects in the future because the children of visited mothers will probably show fewer serious adjustment problems in adolescence and adulthood. A long-term follow-up will be necessary to verify that possibility, but it is clear that the children of visited mothers got a better start.

The implementation of primary prevention programs that focus on problems like air pollution, poverty, and safety is often more within the domain of politics than psychology, but psychologists are actively involved in the development and administration of the programs. Indeed, since the mid-1960s, psychology has had a subspecialty known as **community psychology**. Practitioners in that area often work in governments rather than clinics and direct their efforts toward changing communities rather than changing clients.

The establishment of primary prevention programs is certainly encouraging, but unfortunately many of the problems on which the programs are focused have proved to be very difficult to solve, and consequently successes have been limited. For example, despite massive federal programs, we have not been able to eliminate poverty. Also, advances that were being made were reduced by changes in budgetary priorities. For example, prenatal and postnatal care is crucial for warding off brain damage and various behavior problems, but funds for such care were cut in the face of the need to balance the federal budget. Advocates of prenatal and postnatal care argued that in the long run, cutting the programs would lead to higher costs because the expense of supporting a mentally retarded individual for a lifetime is much higher than the cost of providing prenatal and postnatal care. In essence, they argued that we can pay *hundreds* of dollars for prenatal care now or pay *hundreds of thousands* of dollars for institutionalization later. Thus, because some problems proved to be difficult to solve and because of reductions in funding, much of the early optimism about the effects of primary prevention has faded. This is not to deny that great strides have been made, but the dream of a Camelot of mental health turned out to be as elusive as the mythical kingdom itself.

Secondary Prevention

Because primary prevention has not been completely successful, we must fall back onto a second line of defense. That defense is known as **secondary prevention**, and it is aimed at *solving problems in their early stages so that they will not lead to more serious problems.* With secondary prevention, we identify individuals who are at high risk for developing disorders, and then attempt to provide them with coping strategies and support that will reduce the impact of the disorder-causing factors. In other words, rather than eliminating the causes of abnormal behavior, the strategy is to build up the defenses of individuals who are most likely to be exposed to the causes. This is similar to vaccination in medicine: Since we cannot kill all of the germs that cause an illness, we inoculate the individuals who are most likely to be exposed to the germs. Our efforts are focused on high-risk individuals because our resources are limited and because for most diseases, it is neither feasible nor necessary to inoculate everyone.

Efforts at secondary prevention include training programs for young children who are at high risk for developing abnormal behavior, support groups for persons facing particular problems, and crisis intervention programs for individuals going through potentially overwhelming stresses.

Early Childhood Interventions. Many theorists believe that the development of abnormal behavior can be reduced if children who are at high risk are provided with warm, supportive emotional environments and are taught effective strategies for coping with problems. This approach makes intuitive sense, but three impediments must be recognized. First is the problem of identifying high-risk children. Probably the best strategy for doing that is to use family history. Throughout this book, it has been pointed out that the children of disturbed parents are at higher risk than other children. However, for most disorders, the risk rate for individuals with a family history of the disorder is only about 10% higher than for individuals who do not have a family history of the disorder. In other words, family history may be our best predictor of risk, but it is not a particularly good predictor. In the absence of a good risk predictor, we will miss treating many children who might benefit from the help.

A second problem revolves around compliance with the treatment program. When programs are provided for high-risk children, the dropout rate is often as high as 80%. In view of the difficulty we have in getting people to wear automobile seat belts, it is not surprising that we have difficulty getting them to wear "psychological seat belts" when the benefits are less clear and the effort required is greater.

A third problem stems from the fact that with many disorders, we do not know exactly what causes the problem (or there is disagreement over what causes the problem), and hence it is not clear what a prevention program should include. What would you do for an individual who was at high risk for the development of schizophrenia? The problems of identification, compliance, and nature of treatment make the development of effective prevention programs difficult—but not impossible, and we will now examine programs that have been developed for schizophrenia and school behavior problems.

In a number of places, children who were at high risk for schizophrenia were identified and then provided with a preventive program (e.g., Schulsinger et al., 1975). However, so far there are no reports concerning the long-term effects of the programs. This does not necessarily mean that the programs have been ineffective. It may simply be that because schizophrenia does not develop until early or middle adulthood, not enough time has gone by for the effects to appear. But some evidence suggests that early intervention programs may *not* be effective for reducing serious disorders such as depression and schizophrenia. For example, you may recall that adoption studies revealed that the children of disturbed parents who were adopted and raised by normal parents had about the same rates of abnormal behavior as the children who were not adopted and were raised by the disturbed parents. In other words, those results suggest that at least for the disorders that have a strong genetic basis, moving the children to a better psychological environment may not substantially reduce the likelihood of the disorder.

However, not all problems are due to genetic factors, and intervention programs might be effective for disorders that are due to other factors. Furthermore, it could be argued that the early intervention programs are more effective than simply a "normal" family environment. In summary, we do not yet have a conclusive answer to the question of whether early intervention programs are effective for reducing disorders such as schizophrenia in children who are at high risk.

In contrast to the case with schizophrenia, data suggest that early interventions can be effective for reducing less serious troubles such as school behavior problems (e.g., Durlak, 1980; Kirschenbaum et al., 1980; Yu et al., 1986). School behavior problems are of concern themselves, but they are also of interest because in some cases, they are thought to be early signs of more serious problems that will appear later. The notion is that if we can overcome the school problems, we will be able to avoid the more serious problems later.

In one prevention project, 119 first, second, and third graders with school behavior problems were assigned to one of three conditions: (a) a *behavioral* treatment condition in which assistants in the classroom gave the children tokens (candy or small toys) and praise for appropriate target behaviors, (b) a *relationship* treatment condition in which assistants developed warm and trusting nondirective therapeutic relationships with the children and helped the children express feelings and conflicts, and (c) a *no-treatment* control condition (Durlak, 1980). Before and after the 10-week program, teachers rated the children on behaviors such as acting out and shyness or withdrawal. A comparison of those ratings indicated that the children in the behavioral treatment condition showed substantial reductions in problem behaviors, while the children in the relationship and no-treatment conditions showed minimal or no improvement. These changes are presented in Figure 22.3.

Results indicating that we can reduce school behavior problems are encouraging, but we must be cautious in making interpretations concerning the long-term prevention of more serious problems. Programs like the one discussed here can reduce current, relatively minor problems, and that is important, but so far there is no evidence that the programs reduce the incidence of more serious problems later. Long-

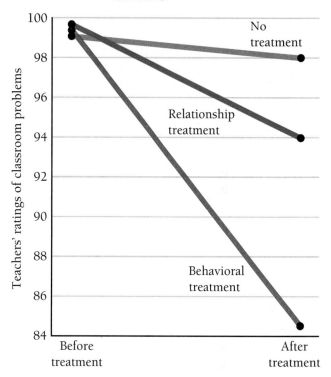

FIGURE 22.3 BEHAVIORAL TREATMENT WAS MORE EFFECTIVE THAN RELATIONSHIP-BASED TREATMENT OR NO TREATMENT FOR REDUCING CLASSROOM BEHAVIOR PROBLEMS.

Source: Adapted from Durlak (1980), p. 333, tab. 1.

term follow-up evaluations of the treated children are necessary, but none has yet been reported. At present then, we do not have any evidence that early intervention programs for children at high risk are effective in terms of secondary prevention.

Support Groups.   Another approach to secondary prevention involves the use of **support groups** for individuals who are facing specific stressful problems that could lead to abnormal behavior. Support groups are small groups of people who share a common problem (e.g., bereavement, being a single parent, illness) and meet to share their experiences and to help one another deal with the problem.

Support groups are very popular today. In fact, in one university town of approximately 60,000 people, there were almost 60 different active support groups, and it is estimated that nationally, 12 million people participate in roughly 500,000 support groups. Name your problem, and there is probably a group for you, and there is now a national self-help clearinghouse to

Support groups are often helpful to individuals who face specific stressful problems. Participants can benefit by sharing their experiences with others who face similar problems.

help you find the group. Probably the best known of the support groups is Alcoholics Anonymous. Case Study 22.4 reflects the experiences of people who are in a support group for persons with muscular dystrophy.

Support groups seem to derive their value from four factors. The first is *emotional support*. In the midst of a crisis, someone is there to hold you, figuratively and sometimes literally. The parents of a child who has just died unexpectedly are likely to be emotionally devastated and not believe that they will ever get through the experience. However, others in a support group who have "been there" can provide much-needed emotional support during the crisis. Similarly, a member of Alcoholics Anonymous will sit through the night with a struggling alcoholic who is fighting the urge to drink.

Second, support groups demonstrate to members that they are *not alone* in having the problem. Knowing that someone is there to help is important, but knowing that you are not the only person with the problem also helps. One member of Alcoholics Anonymous who had not had a drink in 2 years said that the first thing she learned was that

> I was not alone, that there was a roomful of people working toward what I was working toward. . . . AA showed me that I wasn't so different. I had always thought I was dropped here by aliens. Until AA, nobody understood how I felt at 3 A.M. sitting by myself with a bottle. (Hurley, 1988, p. 67)

Third, support groups can provide good *role models*. Newer members can see that "you do get through it" and "there is a life after this experience."

Finally, support groups provide *information*. Members tell one another about other sources of help and how to cope with various problems. They also warn one another about what to expect in the future so as not to be caught off guard by a new phase of the problem.

Most support groups do not involve professionals or even paraprofessionals. Professionals such as physicians, psychologists, social workers, and child care specialists might be called on occasionally to talk about a particular problem, but for the most part, support groups involve *peers helping peers*. That is important because not only do peers provide good role models, but reliance on peers also greatly reduces the cost of support groups. Indeed, support groups usually operate free of charge. Sometimes support groups are referred to as "*self*-help groups," but in many respects that is a misnomer because in the group, individuals help one another. Probably better names would be "mutual-help groups" or "mutual-help and information groups." Whatever they are called, the groups provide emotional support for the present, a sense of belonging, hope for the future, role models, and valuable information. As such, these groups probably do a lot to reduce stress and limit the development of abnormal behavior.

Crisis Intervention.   Support groups are designed to provide prolonged help for relatively chronic problems. However, sometimes acute crises arise that require immediate short-term help. Examples of such crises include the death of a loved one, rape, suicide attempts, and financial problems. In those situations, many individuals turn to **crisis intervention centers**

Case Study 22.4

A SUPPORT GROUP FOR PERSONS WITH MUSCULAR DYSTROPHY: COMMENTS OF GROUP MEMBERS

Muscular dystrophy (MD) is an inherited disease that involves the progressive deterioration of the muscles. During the early phases, persons with the disorder may lose the ability to walk and have to rely on a wheelchair. Later they may lose all muscle control and even go blind. Because the consequences of MD are so dire and because there is no treatment for the disorder, having MD can be a very stressful experience.

In my community there is a support group for persons with MD. Eight or 10 people get together once a week at the home of one of them. The group was originally organized by a professor who has MD, but everyone shares in the leadership. Members include students, professionals, and blue-collar workers. Here are some of their responses when I asked about what the group meant to them.

> For me, the most important thing the group does is let me feel and express really strong emotions that I couldn't express anywhere else. Knowing that you've got MD and knowing what might happen to you can be really frightening. It can also make you angry—why me? In the group, it's OK to have strong feelings and to express them. Others do it too. It's good to get those feelings out, especially with other people who understand what you are going through. Our support group is strong because we cry together—and because we curse together!

> The group helps me maintain my self-esteem. It's really hard to maintain your self-esteem when you are losing control of your body, have to live in a wheelchair, and may be going blind. It's easy to see yourself as "one down," not as good as others, or not having a future. But group members constantly tell you, "You're important to us," "We need you," "We care about you," "You're important in our lives," and "You have a contribution to make." With that boost from the group, I get the guts to go on. Without the group, I would have given up on myself long ago.

> We don't share only bad things. It's important to get the bad things out, but it's also important to share some laughs. We have a thing we call "Laugh Together." Group members videotape or tape-record things that make them laugh and feel really good, and then we play the tapes at the meetings. We also share "take-home laugh tapes." You have to balance the crying with a little laughing, and we share and help each other with both.

> I learn a lot from the people in the group. I learn what to expect if my disease progresses, and I learn practical ways of dealing with the problems. People with MD can tell you more about the disease and how to cope than your doctor can. They're living with it on a daily basis. With the tips they give me and with them showing me that they can live with this thing, I think I'll make it.

that provide services like telephone hot lines and 24-hour-a-day walk-in counseling.

The nature of a typical crisis center is reflected in Case Study 22.5 (p. 584). This case study was written by an undergraduate student of mine who is a volunteer worker in the crisis center.

Tertiary Prevention

Unfortunately, we are often unable to eliminate the causes of abnormal behavior, and we sometimes fail in our attempts to head off the development of such behavior. When those preventive strategies fail, individuals develop various disorders that must be treated, and that gives rise to tertiary prevention, the third line of defense against abnormal behavior. **Tertiary** (TUR-shē-ER-ē) **prevention** involves working to *prevent relapses* in individuals who have had disorders. (The word *tertiary* simply means "third type.")

Because treatment is usually focused on correcting the problem that led to the disorder, most treatments are designed both to eliminate current

symptoms and to prevent relapses. Therefore, most of our discussions of treatment so far have implicitly involved tertiary prevention. For example, if through treatment we resolve conflicts, improve the individual's ability to cope with stress, or correct chemical imbalances, we not only reduce current symptoms but also, it is hoped, prevent their return. A frequently used measure of the effectiveness of treatment is *relapse rate* (the length of time an individual can remain symptom-free or at least out of treatment after therapy has ended).

Because most of our discussions of treatment have involved strategies for tertiary prevention, little else needs to be said here other than to highlight the fact that although causes of disorders may be eliminated through treatment, this does not necessarily mean that the causes will not return. In too many cases, individuals who have been effectively treated (even cured) think they can go back to their old ways, but that is not the case. Just as the individual who has been effectively treated for pneumonia must continue to avoid germs, so the individual who has been effectively treated for a

Case Study 22.5

AN UNDERGRADUATE TALKS ABOUT HER EXPERIENCES WORKING AT A CRISIS CENTER

When most people think about a phone-in crisis center, they probably think immediately about suicide calls, but that is only a very small part of what goes on. The crises come in all shapes and sizes and at all times of the day and night. Sometimes the work at our center is pretty intense, but at other times it can be fairly laid-back. People call to talk about relationships, loneliness, frustrations at work, and just about everything else. Our job is not to tell them how to handle these problems; we give them information and help them sort things out. The idea is to enable them to help themselves.

The center in which I work as a volunteer is in a large old three-story house that's located between the university campus and the downtown area of the city. The first floor of the house has a room with three phones and two old couches, and it is here that the volunteers spend most of their time. Most night shifts are busy until about 2 or 3 in the morning, and then those couches come in really handy to crash on. Of course, there are some nights when you can kiss sleep good-bye completely. There are rooms on both the first and second floors where we can go with people who come in and want to talk. The second and third floors have sleeping accommodations for 10 or 12 people, but those are used only for emergencies, not for long-term stays.

People volunteer to work at the center for a lot of different reasons. Some have had crises and want to return the help they received during those times, and others, like me, are just interested in what goes on at such a center. Regardless of what originally drew us to the center, we all share one motivation: We care about people and want to be able to express that in an active way.

Before starting work, the 15 people in my training group took part in over 60 hours of training. We were taught about community services and resources so that we could make effective referrals, and we were given a lot of training in counseling skills. Most of that came through role playing and watching experienced staff members while they worked. We also spent a lot of time hashing through information and our own feelings about issues such as drug use, sexuality, suicide, and rape. Through those discussions, I learned a lot about the topics and myself. As for my skills as a counselor, I'm certainly no professional, but I know a lot more about how to find and give help than I did before.

Nights in the center can be really hectic. One night not long ago, I came in the back door at about 20 before midnight and found the two staff members on the phone and the front doorbell ringing. I answered the door and found a family of five who'd just driven into town from Texas. They'd been driving all day and, having no money, needed a place to stay for a few days. I explained that we offer only emergency housing and that they would have to start looking for other accommodations the next day. (We don't encourage or allow people to stay for more than a few days. Independence is the goal, not dependence.) After explaining a few guidelines—smoking is permitted only on the first floor, short cleanup chores were expected in the morning in exchange for staying—I showed them to a bedroom.

When I got downstairs, one of the phones was ringing. The caller was a young woman wanting to know the effects of some pills she'd found. I looked up the drug in one of the reference books we have and told her that the drug as an antihistamine with slight sedative effects. She thanked me and then went on to tell me that she'd found the pills on her roommate's dresser. She wanted to know what they were because her roommate had been acting funny lately and she was worried about her. We talked for another half hour or so about her relationship with her roommate and the frustration and sadness connected with the whole situation. She'd called for the drug info, but I think that the real issue was something different. It often seems to work that way.

I had only a few minutes to record the call in the log, say hello to my shift partner, and say good-bye to the two departing staffers from the previous shift before the next call came in. It was from a man who started off by saying, "Life's really slowing down for me." His sleepy voice seemed to echo his sentiments, and he told me that he'd now been unemployed for about 3 months and he and his wife had separated. He missed his kids. I recognized this caller as someone who'd called before, depressed. We talked for a few minutes about his feelings of loneliness and worthlessness, and then I ventured a question about his sleepy voice. He admitted that he'd been drinking heavily and that he'd taken a few pills too. I told him that I was concerned about the effects of both the alcohol and the pills, and he replied that he thought it was OK, especially because he wouldn't mind not waking up in the morning. We then talked about his suicidal feelings, and he expressed a lot of his hurt and depression, but at the same time, he said he didn't really want to die. Because he was sounding sleepier and sleepier, I asked him if he would feel comfortable calling a

584

friend to take him to the emergency room to make sure the alcohol and pills weren't doing permanent damage. He was fairly open to both my concern and his ambivalence about suicide and agreed to call a friend. I encouraged him to call back the next day and let us know how he was doing. It's rare that we do a "crisis outreach" (driving to the person), even for suicide calls. This call is an example of how we encourage people to use their own resources such as friends to help them.

Our next caller was a police officer requesting that we send a rape counselor to the hospital. Paul, my shift partner, called one of the staffers who is specially trained in rape counseling and asked her to go to the hospital.

The call immediately following that was from a woman at the Women's Transition Center, a shelter mainly for abused women. She was calling to let us know that one of their volunteers was coming to meet a woman who'd been beaten up by her husband earlier in the evening. Our place serves as a neutral meeting ground for the shelter's volunteers to meet with women in transition (leaving an abusive situation, divorce, etc.) before taking them to the shelter's secret location. (The location of the Women's Transition Center is kept under wraps so that angry husbands and others cannot find the women.)

While we were waiting for the staff member from the shelter, Paul got a call from a "regular" (a person who calls us a lot). Some of these folks are trying to work through frustrating situations, but usually the reason they call is loneliness. While Paul talked with the regular, I took a call from a person wanting to know where he could get a free blood test. It turned out that the blood test he really wanted was for HIV antibodies (the antibodies that indicate the presence of the AIDS virus), so I looked up the information in our files under "AIDS" and recommended that he contact the Health Department for the cheapest, most confidential setting. Then we talked for a while about some of the AIDS myths that are floating around and about the pressures he felt because he is gay.

It was then about 2:30, and as I was finishing up the call about AIDS, Paul answered a knock at the front door. He expected it to be the volunteer from the women's shelter, but it turned out to be two men and a woman, all rather inebriated. When I ar-

rived in the entry hall, our late-night visitors were trying to convince Paul to let the woman spend the night at the center to "sleep it off." Paul was explaining to them that we generally don't serve as a flophouse, but they were in an argumentative mood and couldn't understand why we were refusing them a place to stay. While this was going on, the woman who had been beaten up by her husband arrived to meet the person from the women's shelter. It was a bit tricky for a moment because the woman was kind of skittish, having just left a violent situation. Walking in on a group of drunk people who were talking angrily couldn't have helped her much, so I took her off to another part of the house. Paul soon convinced the three drunken characters to leave, and as they were going out the front door, there was a knock at the back door. It was a relief to find it was just the staff member from the women's shelter.

Paul and I spent the next hour talking through the various calls and visitors and writing up our log reports. Talking over what goes on with my shift partner helps me work through contacts that were disturbing or that I feel I didn't handle well. It also gives me a chance to offer support for what my partner is doing. Because everything is kept confidential within the center, we really rely on each other for encouragement and support.

The two women left for the women's shelter around 3:45, and then Paul and I slept on the couches until about 7:30, when I was awakened by a phone call. The caller wanted to talk about what she was going to do that day and needed a listening ear and some support as she made plans to continue her job search and write some letters. I recognized this woman as someone who'd recently been released from the state hospital and who was reentering community life. She apologized for waking me up, and we laughed a little about her escapades earlier in the kitchen as she'd tried to make an omelet. I told her before she hung up that it was good to talk with her, and I meant it. Working at this center has given me a real sense of what's important when working with people: Whatever type of crisis they're in—whether it's suicide or a burned omelet—let them know that they're understood and that someone cares. It's that kind of human contact that makes this work so fulfilling.

psychological problem must be sensitive to the factors that brought on the problem (e.g., conflict, stress, physiological factors). In other words, in working with

clients, we must avoid letting them think that once a problem is solved, they can ignore it in the future. Instead, in many cases, we must build cautions about the future into our initial treatments, and we must provide follow-up treatment programs for recovered clients.

SUMMARY

We began this chapter with a description of mental hospitals. We focused on the physical facilities, organization, staff, and lifestyle of hospitals. We also discussed how patients adjust to life in the hospital and how they can manage the impressions the staff have of them so that the patients can get what they want. Surprisingly, many patients want to stay in the hospital and act in ways that will keep them there. A number of experiments have indicated that treatment as an inpatient in a mental hospital is no more effective for overcoming abnormal behavior than treatment in the community.

Attention shifted next to the deinstitutionalization movement that has resulted in a 75% reduction in the number of patients in mental hospitals. This movement was designed (a) to avoid the problems posed by hospitalization (e.g., the institutionalization syndrome, the difficulty of making a normal adjustment in an abnormal environment), (b) to capitalize on the positive aspects of community living (e.g., social support, eliminating the difficult transition back to the community), and (c) to reduce treatment costs. Although deinstitutionalization has been effective for reducing the number of hospitalized patients, questions have been raised over whether treatment was transferred to the community or whether patients were discharged and then abandoned.

Concerning treatment in the community, we discussed (a) outpatient clinics that usually operate in large centrally located hospitals; (b) community mental health centers that are conveniently located in the community and provide walk-in treatment, day care treatment, and prevention programs; (c) halfway houses in which former patients can live while making the transition from the hospital back into the community; and (d) home care programs in which the treatment is taken to disturbed clients in the community rather than expecting them to come to the clinic for treatment. The public generally approves of the concept of community care of disturbed individuals but usually does not want the treatment facilities or the disturbed individuals in their communities. We concluded the discussion of community care by pointing out that during periods of overwhelming stress, some individuals may benefit from a brief escape—a refuge or asylum.

Next we discussed the cost of treatment. Hospitalization can cost as much as $1,000 per day. Day hospitalization, outpatient treatment, and especially drug treatment can be much less expensive, but the treatment of choice must be based on cost-effectiveness, not cost per se. Costs of treatment are being reduced through health care management programs, but concerns have been raised over whether psychiatric treatment will be dealt with appropriately in those programs.

Finally, we discussed the attempts that are being made to prevent the development of abnormal behavior. Primary prevention involves eliminating factors such as pregnancy and birth problems, poverty, poor housing, cultural stress, poor parenting, and pollution that cause abnormal behaviors. We have been effective in reducing some of these causes, but some of our efforts have had to be curtailed because of reduced funding. Secondary prevention is designed to catch problems in an early stage and solve them before they result in serious abnormal behavior. Examples of secondary prevention programs include training for children who are at high risk for the development of abnormal behavior, support groups that help individuals deal effectively with particular problems, and crisis intervention programs that help individuals through rough periods. Tertiary prevention efforts are focused on recovered patients. The goal is to reduce relapses by increasing support and providing follow-up care.

KEY TERMS, CONCEPTS, AND NAMES

In reviewing and testing yourself on what you have learned from this chapter, you should be able to identify and discuss each of the following:

admitting ward	day hospitalization	isolation room
art therapist	day room	managed health care
asylum	deinstitutionalization	music therapist
closed ward	domiciliaries	night hospitalization
community care	halfway house	nurses' station
community mental health center	impression management	occupational therapist
community psychology	institutionalization syndrome	open ward
crisis intervention center	intensive treatment ward	outpatient clinic

primary-care physician

primary prevention

psychological technician (ward
    attendant)

psychiatric nurse

psychiatrist

psychologist

secondary prevention

social worker

support group

tertiary prevention

total institution

Glossary

Active phase Phase in the course of schizophrenia when the symptoms are clearest and most pronounced.

Acute stress disorder An anxiety disorder lasting a month that is triggered by a stressor. Of interest because it may provide the basis for a later posttraumatic stress disorder.

Admitting ward Ward of a mental hospital to which new patients are admitted while diagnoses and treatment plans are being made.

Adoptee studies (in genetics) A method by which the genetic contribution to a disorder is measured by studying the prevalence of the disorder among the biological children of people with the disorder who are raised by their biological parents or by adoptive parents who do not have the disorder.

Adrenal glands Glands located above the kidneys; the outer cortex produces cortisol, and the interior portion facilitates the production of epinephrine and norepinephrine during stress.

Aerobic fitness A measure of physical fitness based on the efficiency with which the body processes oxygen.

Agitated depression Depression characterized by high levels of aimless activity such as pacing.

Agoraphobia Disorder characterized by fear of being in public places from which escape might be difficult if the individual suddenly becomes anxious.

Agranulocytosis A disease involving the immune system that is sometimes a side effect of taking Clozaril.

AIDS (acquired immune deficiency syndrome) A disease in which a virus kills lymphocytes instead of being killed by them, thereby reducing the person's ability to fight infections.

Alcohol A major depressant developed through fermentation.

All-or-none principle The principle whereby stimulation of a nerve cell either does or does not cause it to fire.

Alzheimer's disease A type of dementia in which the major symptom is the loss of short-term memory followed by the loss of long-term memory.

Amenorrhea Cessation of menstruation, often associated with anorexia.

American Law Institute rule A somewhat flexible rule for defining insanity that incorporates aspects of the M'Naghten and Durham rules.

Amine hypothesis Hypothesis suggesting that a disorder (e.g., depression) is caused by a problem with a neurotransmitter (e.g., a catecholamine).

Amines A class of neurotransmitters.

Amnesia (dissociative) A loss of memory due to psychological factors.

Amniocentesis A test in which cells of a developing fetus are sampled and studied to determine whether development is normal. Frequently used to test for the presence of Down syndrome.

Amphetamine psychoses Abnormal behavior (usually revolving around delusions) resulting from high doses of amphetamines.

Amphetamines A class of stimulants.

Amygdala Area of the brain responsible for aggression; part of the limbic system.

Analogue research Research in which variables or populations similar but not identical to those of interest are studied. Often used to avoid technical or ethical problems.

Anal stage The second of the stages of psychosexual development. Important for the development of needs for cleanliness, order, and other habits.

Androgens Hormones that result in male characteristics.

Aneurysm A weak spot in an artery that bursts, causing a heart attack or stroke.

Anger turned inward One of Freud's explanations for depression.

Angina Pain around the heart and left shoulder caused by reduced blood supply to the heart muscles.

Angioplasty Surgical procedure in which a flexible tube with a balloon on the end is inserted into an artery that has been narrowed by the buildup of plaque. The balloon is inflated to compress the plaque against the sides of the artery to permit greater blood flow.

Anna O. A patient of Josef Breuer's whose treatment played an important role in Freud's early theorizing about abnormal behavior.

Anorexia nervosa An eating disorder, the major symptom of which is the refusal to eat enough to maintain appropriate body weight.

Anoxia Lack of oxygen; if it occurs during birth, brain damage can result.

Antiandrogens Drugs that suppress androgens and are sometimes used in the treatment of sexual disorders. The best known is Depo-Provera.

Antidepressant Medication used to treat depression. The best-known types are tricyclics and MAO inhibitors.

Antigens "Foreign" substances in the body that result in increased activity of the immune system.

Antipsychotic drugs Drugs used to treat disorders such as schizophrenia. Also called *neuroleptics.*

Antisocial personality disorder Personality disorder in which the individual lacks anxiety (or a conscience) and consequently engages in antisocial behavior.

Anxiety An emotional response characterized by apprehension, tension, physiological arousal (e.g., elevated heart rate, blood pressure, and muscular tension), and restlessness.

Anxiety disorders Group of disorders including anxiety states and phobic disorders.

Anxiety states Disorders in which anxiety is excessively high, diffused, and not limited to specific situations. (Contrast with *phobic disorders.*)

Arousal disorder Sexual dysfunction in which the individual cannot achieve or maintain sexual arousal despite the presence of sexual desire.

Arousal transference The idea that arousal can be transferred across different emotions such as fear.

Arteriosclerosis The process by which arteries lose their elasticity ("hardening of the arteries").

Arthritis (rheumatoid) Disorder characterized by pain in the joints that is caused by the destruction of the membrane that covers the joints.

Associative intrusions Inappropriate associations that interfere with normal thought processes (see, for example, *clang associations*). Thought to be important in the thought disorder associated with schizophrenia.

Associative network theory of memory The theory that related memories are stored in networks and that the stimulation of a network will result in the recall of the memories in that network.

Atherosclerosis Cardiovascular disease characterized by the buildup of fats on the walls of blood vessels, which reduces blood flow.

Attention-deficit hyperactivity disorder Disorder of childhood in which the major symptoms are the inability to maintain attention and a high level of activity.

Atypical neuroleptics Drugs that are used to treat schizophrenia that are selective in the blocking of dopamine receptors sites and which increase the level of serotonin at synapses.

Autonomic division Division of the peripheral nervous system involving connections to glands and organs.

Aversion therapy Treatment based on classical conditioning in which unpleasant consequences (shock, nausea) are paired with a stimulus or an activity (fetish object, drinking) so that eventually the stimulus or activity will elicit anxiety and be avoided.

Avoidance conditioning Procedure whereby a stimulus is paired with negative consequences, and thus through a combination of classical and operant conditioning, the individual learns to avoid the stimulus.

Avoidant personality disorder Personality disorder in which the individual is especially sensitive to social rejection and humiliation and therefore avoids other people.

Avoidant thinking Strategy by which a person avoids anxiety by intentionally not thinking about an anxiety-provoking object or situation.

Axis I: Major Clinical Syndromes When making diagnoses, used to identify the major disorders (e.g., anxiety state, schizophrenia).

Axis II: Personality Disorders When making diagnoses, used to identify disorders of personality.

Axis III: General Medical Conditions When making diagnoses, used to indicate whether there are any medical conditions that might influence the disorder.

Axis IV: Psychosocial and Environmental Problems When making diagnoses, used to indicate whether there are any social or enviromental stressors that might influence the disorder.

Axis V: Global Assessment of Functioning When making diagnoses, current and highest level of functioning in the past year are rated so that potential for improvement can be assessed.

Axon The arm of a nerve cell down which the impulse travels.

Barbiturates A type of depressant drug; an early form of tranquilizer.

Baroreceptors Stretch-sensitive receptors around arteries coming from the heart that detect increases in blood pressure. Important in the development of hypertension.

B cell Type of lymphocyte that breaks down antigens.

Behavioral contagion A process by which inhibitions related to certain behaviors are reduced by observing another person perform the behavior without negative consequences.

Behaviorism An explanation for behavior developed by John B. Watson based on classical and operant conditioning and in which attention is given only to observable factors.

Bell-and-pad procedure Procedure for treating enuresis. A moisture-sensitive pad is placed on the mattress, and when a child urinates during sleep, the pad detects the urine and rings a bell, which awakens the child.

Belle indifférence, La Attitude of indifference toward what appear to be serious physical symptoms shown by some persons with conversion disorders.

Benign tumors Noncancerous tumors. They do not invade adjacent tissues and do not shed cells that spread to other parts of the body. (Contrast with *malignant tumors.*)

Benzodiazepines A class of drugs that are used to treat anxiety. They reduce anxiety by increasing levels of GABA. The best-known drug of this type is Valium.

Beta blockers A class of drugs that are used to reduce heart rate.

Bicyclics A type of antidepressant drug, the chemical structure of which has the form of two circles (see also *Prozac*).

Binet, Alfred Developer of one of the first tests of intelligence. It was used to predict academic performance.

Binge type of alcoholism Drinking pattern characterized by relatively short periods of uncontrolled high levels of drinking separated by periods of nondrinking. (Contrast with *persistent type of alcoholism.*)

Biofeedback training Procedure in which an individual is given immediate feedback about changes in some physiological response (e.g., heart rate, blood pressure, muscle tension) so that the person can learn to control the response.

Biological traumas Prenatal and perinatal complications that can lead to abnormal behavior such as schizophrenia.

Bipolar disorder Mood disorder in which mood fluctuates between mania and depression. Formerly called the *manic-depressive disorder.*

Bleuler, Eugen Early theorist who coined the term *schizo-*

phrenia and suggested that the disorder stemmed from a breakdown in associations.

Blocking agents Drugs that have their effect (reducing neural transmission) by blocking the receptor sites on the postsynaptic neuron so that the neuron cannot be stimulated.

Body dysmorphic disorder A somatoform disorder in which the individual is preoccupied with some imagined defect in his or her appearance.

Borderline personality disorder Personality disorder characterized by serious instability. The diversity of symptoms seen in this disorder suggests that it borders on or overlaps with numerous other disorders.

Breuer, Josef An early colleague of Sigmund Freud. Probably best known because of his patient Anna O.

Brief psychotic disorder A disorder usually involving florid symptoms of schizophrenia. It sometimes stems from overwhelming stress, and the symptoms remit after a few hours to 4 weeks.

Bulimia nervosa An eating disorder, the major symptom of which is binge eating followed by self-induced purges (e.g., vomiting or excessive use of laxatives).

Burned-out phase Stage of schizophrenia in which persons who have suffered for many years no longer show the major symptoms of the disorder but show great personal deterioration, due perhaps in part to their institutionalization and social isolation.

Caffeine A stimulant, the strongest in a group known as methylxanthines.

Cancer Disease involving the inappropriate reproduction of cells.

Cannabinoids The active ingredients in cannabis (marijuana).

Cannabis A mild hallucinogen; marijuana.

Cannon-Bard theory of emotion Theory that suggests that emotions lead to physiological responses.

Carcinogens Factors that can cause cancer, often by altering gene structures.

Case study research Research based on the intensive study of one individual. Generalizations and conclusions concerning cause are hazardous.

Catatonic schizophrenia A rare type of schizophrenia usually characterized by lack of motor movement or "waxy flexibility."

Catecholamines A class of neurotransmitters that includes norepinephrine and dopamine.

Catharsis A release of tension, often by talking about a problem.

Central nervous system Division of the nervous system comprising the brain and spinal cord.

Cerebral infarction Death of brain cells due to lack of blood supply. Some forms of dementia in elderly persons are due to multiple cerebral infarctions. Also known as *stroke.*

Charcot, Jean-Martin Early physician who thought that somatoform (hysterical) disorders were due to a weak nervous system and who treated them with suggestion (hypnosis).

Checklists of symptoms An alternative to using diagnostic labels for describing persons.

Children's Apperception Test (CAT) A projective test like the TAT designed especially for children.

Circulating catecholamines Catecholamines (epinephrine, norepinephrine) released into the bloodstream as part of the stress response. They stimulate higher arousal and can cause clumping of cholesterol.

Clang associations Associations based on a rhyme (*bug, dug, clown, frown*) that can result in the intrusion of new thoughts. Clang associations are thought to influence the thought disorders of persons with schizophrenia.

Classical conditioning Conditioning in which a neutral stimulus (e.g., a bell) is consistently paired with a particular response (salivation) such that in time the previously neutral stimulus will elicit the response. The process was originally identified by Pavlov.

Client-centered psychotherapy A form of psychotherapy derived from the humanistic position in which the goal is to establish a nurturant environment in which the client can grow personally.

Clinical psychologist *See* **Psychologist (clinical)**.

Clinical significance A research finding that is of practical as opposed to statistical significance.

Clitoris A highly sensitive body of tissues located above the vaginal opening. Its stimulation is important for reaching orgasm.

Closed ward Ward of a mental hospital reserved for highly disturbed patients who are not allowed to leave the ward.

Clozaril (clozapine) An atypical neuroleptic that relieves negative as well as positive symptoms with fewer side effects than other neuroleptics.

Cocaine (cocaine hydrochloride) Stimulant derived from the leaves of the coca plant. Can reduce pain by blocking nerve impulse down the axon. Causes a "high" by reducing reuptake of neurotransmitters.

Codeine One of the active ingredients in opium (less powerful than morphine).

Cognitive abulia Inability to hold a memory long enough to transform it into purposeful action; seen in Alzheimer's disease.

Cognitive anxiety Symptoms of anxiety associated with arousing thoughts rather than somatic arousal.

Cognitive diathesis-stress hypothesis The notion that negative cognitions in combination with stress lead to depression.

Cognitive flooding Technique for treating anxiety in which the person is directed to think about the objects or situations that elicit anxiety. When the thoughts are not followed by the expected dire consequences, it is believed that the anxiety response will extinguish.

Cognitive perspective The view that problems with information processing are responsible for abnormal behavior.

Cognitive processes Processes related to thinking; important to abnormal behavior insofar as thinking influences behavior.

Cognitive restructuring Strategy for treating abnormal behavior in which the goal is to alter behavior by altering the way the person thinks about factors related to the behavior.

Cognitive rigidity Failure to consider alternatives, often seen in persons who are suicidal.

Cognitive set A predisposition to notice or interpret things in a specific way. Negative cognitive sets are associated with depression.

Cognitive therapy Approach to treatment in which an attempt is made to change the way a person thinks about situations (i.e., change cognitive sets) and thereby change behavior.

Community care Strategy whereby persons suffering from abnormal behavior are treated in the community on an outpatient basis rather than in a hospital.

Community mental health center Small, conveniently located, usually nonresidential treatment center. Its goal is to provide early, easily accessible care and prevention programs.

Community psychology Branch of clinical psychology concerned with changing communities as a means of preventing abnormal behavior.

Comorbidity The co-occurrence of two or more disorders in an individual at one time.

Compensation Defense mechanism in which the individual works especially hard to overcome a weakness that provokes anxiety.

Compulsion An irresistible impulse to engage repeatedly in some act, usually maladaptive.

Computerized axial tomography (CT scan) A type of X-ray of the brain taken from the top and showing successive "slices" of the brain.

Concordance rate The rate of co-occurrence of a disorder in specific pairs of persons, usually monozygotic or dizygotic twins.

Conditioned stimulus A previously neutral stimulus that after classical conditioning occurs is able to elicit the conditioned response.

Conduct disorders Group of disorders involving extreme misbehavior; should be differentiated from the antisocial personality disorder.

Confounding The changing of more than one independent variable in an experiment such that it cannot be determined which variable is responsible for changes in the dependent variable.

Conflict-anxiety-defense-symptoms sequence The sequence of events that Freud believed led to abnormal behavior.

Control condition The condition in an experiment in which everything is identical to the experimental condition except that the independent variable is not manipulated.

Controlled experimental research Research involving experimental and control conditions. Conclusions concerning cause can be drawn from this type of research.

Conversion disorder Disorder in which the individual has one or more major physical symptoms for which an organic basis cannot be found. Symptoms usually impair functioning.

Coping strategies Constructive, adaptive means of dealing with stress.

Coprolalia The speaking or yelling of obscenities that sometimes occurs as part of Tourette's disorder.

Coronary artery disease Disease process in which blood flow to the muscles of the heart is reduced due to buildup of plaque (cholesterol) on the walls of the arteries.

Coronary bypass surgery Surgery in which a piece of artery is grafted onto another artery so that blood flow can bypass an occluded area.

Correlational research Research based on correlations. Conclusions concerning causation cannot be drawn from this type of research.

Correlation coefficient (*r*) Statistic that reflects the degree to which two (or more) variables covary (increase or decrease together).

Cortical atrophy Deterioration of the cortex of the brain.

Cortical underarousal Low levels of arousal in areas of the brain responsible for emotion. Thought to be important in the development of the antisocial personality disorder.

Cortisol Hormone produced by the adrenal gland during stress that in turn causes an increase in the productions of glucose.

Counterconditioning *See* **Systematic desensitization**.

Covert suicide Suicide disguised to appear as an accident or natural death.

Craft palsies Early term used to refer to *conversion disorders* that interfered with occupational functioning.

Cretinism (hypothyroidism) Slowed metabolism and development due to a recessive gene that interferes with the production of thyroxin. Symptoms include short stature and mental retardation.

Crisis intervention center Health care center offering programs designed to reduce stress during crises and thereby avoid the development of abnormal behavior.

Cross-dressing Dressing in the clothes of the opposite sex to gain sexual gratification.

Cross-tolerance Development of tolerance for one drug resulting in tolerance for another drug in the same class.

Current self Current level of functioning as discussed by humanists. Contrasted with the ideal (actualized) self toward which humans strive.

Cyclothymic disorder Less severe form of the bipolar disorder.

Dancing manias Mass psychogenic illnesses involving jerking movements, most frequently noted in the 14th and 15th centuries.

Day hospitalization Strategy whereby patients are treated in the hospital during the day but sent home at night.

Day room Room in a hospital where patients spend their days, usually watching television.

Death instinct Freud's proposed counterbalance to the life instinct; sometimes used to explain suicide.

Declassification (of persons with mental retardation) A movement to cease labeling persons as retarded because of the unreliability of the diagnosis and the fact that there is a stigma attached to it.

Defense mechanisms Strategies by which persons reduce anxiety without dealing with the cause of the anxiety (e.g., repression, displacement).

Deficit in classical conditioning The idea that persons with the antisocial personality disorder are limited in their ability to develop classically conditioned responses and therefore do not develop anxiety.

Deinstitutionalization A movement begun in the late 1960s to move patients out of hospitals and treat them in the community.

Delayed cortical development The idea that the low level of cortical arousal in persons with the antisocial personality disorder (which is similar to that seen in young children) is due to a delay in development.

Delayed development The idea that mental retardation is due to slowed development rather than to a mental defect.

Delusion A bizarre belief that is held despite strong evidence to the contrary; a symptom often seen in schizophrenia.

Delusional disorder A disorder in which the only symptom is a delusion, usually of persecution; formerly called *paranoid disorder*.

Demand characteristics The pressures in a situation to behave in a specific way (e.g., like a patient while in a hospital).

Dementia An organically caused loss of intellectual abilities.

Dementia praecox A term once used to describe schizophrenia, referring to an early deterioration of cognitive abilities.

Demonology An early belief that abnormal behavior was due to possession by demons.

Dendrites   Treelike structures that radiate outward from the body of a nerve cell.

Denial   A defense mechanism in which the person reinterprets an anxiety-provoking situation by redefining it as nonthreatening.

Dependence   The need to take a drug to avoid withdrawal symptoms.

Dependent personality disorder   A personality disorder in which the individual allows other persons to make decisions for him or her.

Dependent variable   The variable in an experiment that is influenced by the independent variable.

Depersonalization disorder   A dissociative disorder in which for brief periods individuals experience distortions of the self (e.g., feeling as if their extremities have changed in size or they are out of their bodies).

Depo-Provera   An antiandrogen drug used to reduce sexual desire.

Depressants   A class of drugs, which includes alcohol, barbiturates, and benzodiazepines, the major effect of which is to reduce neurological activity.

Depression   An emotional response characterized by feelings of hopelessness and sadness, low self-esteem, pessimism, reduced motivation, slowed thought processes, psychomotor retardation or agitation, and disturbances of sleep, appetite, and sexual arousal.

Depression with postpartum onset   Depression that occurs shortly after a woman gives birth.

Depression with seasonal pattern   The diagnostic label for the *seasonal affective disorder (SAD).*

Desire disorder   A sexual dysfunction characterized by a lack of sexual desire; if stimulated sufficiently, however, the individual can achieve sexual arousal.

Developmental approach to personality   The idea that persons go through stages of psychosexual development (oral, anal, phallic, latency, genital).

Developmental disorders   A group of disorders beginning in infancy or childhood, including the pervasive disorder of autism and specific developmental disorders (language, academic, and motor skills).

Deviance from cultural norms   One of the factors that is sometimes used to define abnormal behavior.

Dexamethasone suppression test (DST)   A test used to determine whether depression is endogenous or exogenous.

Dexedrine (dextroamphetamine)   A stimulant, sometimes used to treat the attention-deficit hyperactivity disorder.

Diastolic blood pressure   The level of pressure in the circulatory system between beats of the heart; usually 80 mm Hg.

Diathesis-stress hypothesis   The idea that a person may be predisposed to develop a disorder and that the disorder will become manifest when the person is exposed to a triggering stress.

Diazepam (Valium)   A benzodiazepine that is widely used to treat anxiety.

Disability   One of the factors that is sometimes used to define abnormal behavior.

Disorganized schizophrenia   The type of schizophrenia showing the most psychological disorganization and lacking a systematic set of delusions.

Displacement   A defense mechanism with two forms. In object displacement, an emotion is transferred from one object to another because the expression of the emotion with the original object is threatening. In drive displacement, an unacceptable drive is converted into an acceptable one.

Disruptive behavior disorders   A group of disorders of infancy, childhood, and adolescence including the attention-deficit hyperactivity disorder and the conduct disorders.

Dissociative disorders   A group of disorders involving a disturbance of the integrative function of memory, identity, and consciousness. Disorders include amnesia, fugue, multiple personality, and depersonalization.

Dissociative identity disorder   The diagnostic label that has replaced *multiple personality disorder.*

Distraction   A strategy for reducing anxiety by diverting attention away from the anxiety-provoking factor; also a process thought to be responsible for the thought disturbance in schizophrenia.

Distress   One of the factors that is sometimes used to define abnormal behavior.

Disturbed thought processes   A syndrome characterized by disruption in mental functions, including hallucinations and delusions.

Diuretic   A drug given to reduce blood pressure by reducing the volume of bodily fluids.

Dix, Dorothea   An early reformer who worked to raise funds for mental hospitals.

Dizygotic (fraternal) twins   Nonidentical twins who do not have identical sets of genes.

Domiciliaries   Wards in psychiatric hospitals that are used simply to hold patients who do not respond to treatment.

Dopamine   A neurotransmitter. High levels of dopamine activity are associated with schizophrenia; low levels are associated with Parkinson's disease.

Dopamine explanation for schizophrenia   The notion that schizophrenia is due to excessive levels of dopamine activity.

Dose-dependent   Having different effects at different dose levels.

Dose-response relationship   The fact that a drug can have different effects at different dosage levels.

Double-bind hypothesis   A hypothesis that suggests that schizophrenia stems from childhood experiences in which persons receive contradictory messages and then give irrelevant responses to avoid giving wrong responses.

Double-blind procedure   A procedure used in experimental research in which neither the subject nor the experimenter knows whether the subject has been exposed to the experimental procedure or the control procedure. This approach reduces bias.

Down syndrome   Mental retardation caused by an extra number 21 chromosome.

Draw-A-Person Test   A projective test in which personality interpretations are based on the client's drawing of persons.

Dream interpretation   A technique used in psychoanalysis to uncover unconscious material, involving analysis of the latent and manifest content of dreams.

Drive displacement   A process (sometimes a defense) by which an individual converts one drive into another.

Drug prophylaxis   The practice of keeping a patient on a maintenance dose of a drug to prevent relapse.

DSM-IV   The fourth edition of the *Diagnostic and Statistical Manual of Mental Disorders,* published by the American Psychiatric Association in 1994.

Duodenal ulcers   Holes in the lining of the duodenum (first part of small intestine) caused by high levels of gastric acid.

Durham rule A rule specifying that if a criminal act was "the product of mental disease or defect," the perpetrator can be judged to be insane and hence not responsible for the behavior.

"Duty to protect" principle A rule that says that therapists have the duty to warn individuals if they are in danger from a person in therapy.

Dysthymic disorder A less severe version of the unipolar disorder.

Eating disorders A group of disorders including anorexia, bulimia, pica, and rumination.

Echolalia A symptom of infantile autism in which the child repeats whatever is said to him or her.

Ego The executive or mediating component in Freud's structural approach to personality.

Ego-dystonic Anxiety-provoking or repulsive to the ego.

Ego psychology A revision of Freud's theory, suggested by his followers, that emphasizes cognitive processes over drives.

Elbow rule Used to identify crimes that result from an irresistible impulse. Would the person have committed the crime if a police officer had been standing at his or her elbow?

Electra attraction Freud's term for the attraction a young girl feels toward her father.

Electroconvulsive therapy (ECT) A treatment for depression in which an electrical charge is passed through the brain, causing convulsions.

Electrocortical arousal The level of electrical activity in the brain; measured with the electroencephalograph.

Electroencephalograph (EEG) A device for measuring the electrical activity of the brain.

Electromyographic (EMG) biofeedback training A procedure in which persons are given feedback concerning muscle activity and use the feedback to learn to relax muscles or regain control of muscles after a stroke or an accident.

Embolism A clot that blocks blood flow through an artery.

Emergency (involuntary) hospitalization Hospitalization because the person is thought to be a danger to self or others.

Encopresis An elimination disorder in which the symptom is the inability to control bowel movements.

Endogenous depression Depression due to physiological factors.

Endorphins Opiate-like substances produced by the body that serve to reduce synaptic transmission and reduce pain.

Enuresis An elimination disorder in which the symptom is the inability to achieve bladder control.

Epinephrine A circulating catecholamine. Also called *adrenaline.*

Erectile tissue Tissue in the penis and clitoris that fills with blood during sexual arousal.

Essential hypertension High blood pressure due to psychological factors. Also known as *primary hypertension.*

Exhibitionism A paraphilia in which pleasure is derived from exposing the genitals.

Exogenous depression Depression due to psychosocial factors.

Experimental condition The condition in an experiment in which the independent variable is manipulated.

Experimental research A research strategy in which an independent variable is manipulated in an experimental condition but not in the control condition, and consequent effects on the dependent variable are measured.

Extinction Elimination of a classically conditioned response by the repeated presentation of the conditioned stimulus without the unconditioned stimulus or elimination of an operantly conditioned response by no longer presenting the reward after the response.

Extrapyramidal symptoms Motor behaviors such as twitches that are sometimes a side effect of neuroleptic drugs.

Factitious disorder Faking symptoms for some personal reason.

False memories Memories that are not true but have been implanted by suggestion, are thought to be true, and sometimes influence behavior.

Family psychotherapy A treatment strategy whereby an attempt is made to overcome problems in the family (e.g., stress) that contribute to disorders.

Family studies (in genetics) A means of determining the genetic contribution to a disorder by studying the degree to which biologically related relatives (as contrasted with nonbiologically related relatives) have the disorder.

Fear hierarchy A list of feared objects or situations, ranked from least to most feared, that is used in systematic desensitization.

Fetal alcohol syndrome (FAS) Mental retardation that results from a mother's drinking alcohol while pregnant.

Fetishism A paraphilia in which sexual gratification is derived from a nonhuman object (e.g., a shoe).

Fixated Remaining at one stage of psychosexual development and consequently showing abnormal behavior for one's age.

Flashback Recurrence of an LSD experience without current ingestion of the drug; occurs in persons who have taken LSD repeatedly on previous occasions.

Flooding A technique for treating anxiety in which the individual is asked to imagine a fear-provoking (phobic) stimulus. Negative consequences do not follow, thus permitting the fear response to extinguish.

Free association A technique in which an individual talks about whatever comes to mind without censoring thoughts; developed by Freud and used in psychoanalysis to expose unconscious thoughts.

Freud, Anna Daughter of Sigmund Freud who carried on her father's work but emphasized the role of the ego and defenses.

Freud, Sigmund Founder of the psychoanalytic approach to personality and abnormal behavior.

Frontal lobes Areas of the brain in which integration of thoughts and feelings takes place. High and low levels of activity in the frontal lobes can lead to symptoms of schizophrenia.

Frotteurism A paraphilia in which sexual gratification is derived from rubbing against another person.

Fugue Dissociative disorder in which the individual moves to another location and develops a new identity.

GABA A neurotransmitter (gamma-aminobutyric acid) that is important for the functioning of inhibitory neurons. Low levels of GABA are associated with high levels of anxiety.

Gastric ulcers Holes in the lining of the stomach due to low levels of protective mucus.

Gender identity disorder Disorder in which the individual has persistent and intense distress about his or her physiological sex identification.

Generalization The phenomenon whereby once classical conditioning has occurred, a stimulus similar to the conditioned stimulus can elicit the response.

Generalized anxiety disorder A disorder in which the individual is anxious regardless of the stimulus situation. Anxiety is said to be "free-floating."

General paresis (syphilis of the brain) Deterioration of the brain and resulting mental retardation due to infection by the spirochete.

Genital stage The last of Freud's stages of psychosexual development.

Glans The tip of the clitoris.

Glove anesthesia A conversion disorder in which the person loses feeling in the hand.

Glucose A sugar that is used for energy throughout the body.

Gonadotropins Hormones released by the pituitary gland that stimulate the testes to produce testosterone, resulting in sexual arousal.

Granulovacuolar degeneration A condition involving small holes in the bodies of nerves that result in a general deterioration. Seen in persons with Alzheimer's disease.

Group psychotherapy An approach to treatment in which several clients are seen simultaneously by one therapist.

G spot An area in the vagina that is allegedly highly sensitive to stimulation.

Habit strength intrusions Intrusions based on sets of words that are frequently used together (e.g., "reach out and touch someone") and may trigger inappropriate new thoughts.

Haldol (haloperidol) A widely used neuroleptic.

Halfway house A small residential facility in which persons live while making the transition from hospital to community.

Hallucinations Sensory experiences (e.g., sounds, feelings, smells) that have no basis in reality.

Hallucinogens Drugs such as LSD that cause perceptual distortions.

Halstead-Reitan Neuropsychology Battery A test used to identify the extent and nature of impairment due to brain damage.

Hashish The dried resin from the top of the female marijuana plant. Has stronger effects than marijuana.

Hash oil A concentrated form of hashish.

HDL (high-density lipoprotein) The "good" type of cholesterol, which carries LDL (low density lipoprotein) away before it can occlude an artery.

Health psychology An area of psychology devoted to the influence of psychological factors on health and illness.

Helper cells Cells in the immune system that identify antigens and signal the lymph nodes to produce killer cells.

Heroin A semisynthetic narcotic based on opium. Rapidly delivered to the brain, where it is changed into morphine.

High-potency neuroleptics Neuroleptic drugs that are very effective for blocking dopamine but can cause serious side effects.

Hippocampus Area of the brain that is crucial for processing information and may be deformed in schizophrenia; part of the limbic system.

Hippocrates An early Greek physician who proposed that abnormal behavior stemmed from an imbalance of humors (fluids) in the body.

Histrionic personality disorder A disorder characterized by seductiveness, need for attention, and emotional shallowness.

Hopelessness An attitude of despair that is symptomatic of depression and suicide.

Hormones Fluids secreted by glands into the bloodstream that influence behavior, usually through stimulation.

Hostility The important factor in the Type A behavior pattern in terms of the development of coronary artery disease.

House-Tree-Person Test A projective test in which inferences about personality are based on how a person draws a house, a tree, and a person.

Humanistic-existential perspective The view that abnormal behavior results from the failure to achieve our ideal selves or from our awareness that we could cease to exist and must take responsibility.

Humors (bodily fluids) In medieval psychology and physiology, four fluids in the body, the proportions of which were thought to determine a person's behavior, temperament, and health.

Huntington's disease (chorea) Disorder involving involuntary jerking and twisting movements along with declines in memory and intellectual functioning. Results from a progressive deterioration of the brain caused by one dominant gene.

Hypersomnia Excessive sleep.

Hypertension High blood pressure, usually defined as systolic pressure over 140 mm Hg or diastolic pressure over 90 mm Hg.

Hyperventilation Rapid shallow breathing that can lead to feelings of light-headedness and anxiety.

Hypochondriasis A somatoform disorder characterized by excessive concern over minor physical ills.

Hypofrontality hypothesis A hypothesis that the negative symptoms of schizophrenia are due to low levels of activity in the frontal lobes of the brain.

Hypotension Low blood pressure.

Hypothalamus Area of the brain responsible for bodily processes such as eating, drinking, sleeping, and sexual behavior.

Hysterical disorders (hysteria) An earlier term for what today are referred to as somatoform and dissociative disorders.

Iatrogenic disorders Disorders that are introduced inadvertently in the course of treatment of other disorders.

Id In Freud's structural approach to personality, the source of all energy and drives.

Ideal self The self toward which the humanists believe all people strive; self-actualization.

Identification Defense mechanism in which an individual takes on the characteristics of another person so as to be like that person.

Immune system The bodily system that fights disease. Psychological stress can suppress its operation.

Immunocompetence Degree of responsiveness of the immune system.

Implosion therapy Psychotherapy for anxiety based on flooding.

Impulse control disorders A group of personality disorders that includes kleptomania, pyromania, and pathological gambling.

Incompetent to stand trial Ruling when an individual cannot understand the charges or cannot effectively participate in his or her own defense. Trial is then postponed until the person is judged competent.

Incomplete Sentences Test Projective test in which inferences about personality are based on how a person completes sentences (e.g., "What I hate most is . . .").

Independent variable The variable that is manipulated and whose effects are studied in an experiment.

Indole amines A class of neurotransmitters that includes serotonin.

Infantile autism A developmental disorder of infancy and childhood that appears shortly after birth and involves a lack of responsiveness to others, impairment in verbal and nonverbal skills, and a greatly restricted repertory of activities and interests.

Information processing   The process by which the sensory memory, short-term memory, long-term memory, and memory networks influence the storage and retrieval of information.

Inhibitory neurons   Neurons the firing of which inhibits the firing of other neurons. Low levels of inhibitory neuron activity are associated with anxiety.

Insanity defense   Legal judgment that specifies that a person is not responsible for a criminal act for psychological reasons.

Institutionalization syndrome   A set of behaviors (usually asocial) associated with long-term residence in an institution rather than with a disorder per se.

Intellectualization   A defense mechanism that reduces stress by focusing on objective, nonemotional aspects of a threatening situation.

Intensive treatment ward   Hospital ward to which new patients may be assigned for intensive treatment before their disorders become chronic.

Intermittent explosive disorder   A type of impulse control disorder that involves a loss of control of aggressive impulses that cannot be explained by other disorders.

Intermittent schedule of reward   A schedule whereby rewards for correct responses are given less than 100% of the time. This increases resistance to extinction.

Interpersonal withdrawal   An explanation for abnormal behavior (especially schizophrenia) that suggests that because of the stress of interpersonal relationships, the individual withdraws, and the subsequent lack of feedback concerning behavior results in inappropriate behavior.

Introversion   A behavior pattern characterized by limited social interaction and high interpersonal anxiety.

In vitro exposure   Exposure to a (feared) stimulus through imagination during (desensitization) therapy. (Contrast with *in vivo exposure.*)

In vivo exposure   Actual exposure to a (feared) stimulus during therapy (flooding). (Contrast with *in vitro exposure.*)

Involuntary commitment   Commitment to a mental hospital against the patient's will because the patient is considered a danger to self or others.

Involuntary outpatient commitment   Procedure whereby persons may be required by the court to participate in outpatient treatment as an alternative to involuntary hospitalization.

Involutional depression   Depression associated with old age; no longer used as formal diagnostic condition separate from other depressions.

Irresistible impulse   A basis for an insanity plea. See also *elbow rule.*

Isolation room   A room in a hospital to which a patient can go for quiet or to which a patient can be sent if being disruptive.

James-Lang theory of emotion   The notion that the labeling of physiological arousal leads to emotions.

Killer cells   T-cell lymphocytes that break down antigens.

Kleptomania   The inability to resist the impulse to steal.

Klinefelter's syndrome   Mental retardation in men resulting from the presence of one or more extra X (female) chromosomes.

Kraepelin, Emil   Early theorist who suggested that schizophrenia had an early onset, consisted of progressive and irreversible intellectual deterioration, and was caused by physiological factors. Coined the term *dementia praecox.*

Lapses of attention   Part of the explanation offered by cognitive theorists for the disturbed thought processes seen in schizophrenia.

Latency stage   Fourth of the stages of psychosexual development suggested by Freud.

Latent content   The symbolic or hidden meaning in dreams.

LDL (low density lipoprotein)   The "bad" type of cholesterol that occludes arteries.

L-dopa   A drug that increases dopamine levels and is used to treat Parkinson's disease but that can also bring on the symptoms of schizophrenia.

Learned helplessness   The idea that when one cannot control outcomes, one develops feelings of helplessness, which lead to depression.

Learning perspective   The position that abnormal behavior is learned through classical and operant conditioning.

Least restrictive alternative   A legal ruling requiring that mental patients not be subjected to greater restrictions during treatment than absolutely necessary.

Leukocytes   White blood cells, the major component of the immune system.

Libido   Freud's term for psychological energy; often used to refer to sexual energy.

Limbic system   A group of structures in the midbrain that are responsible primarily for arousal (e.g., mood, appetite, sex, sleep, aggression).

Lithium carbonate   A drug that is effective for treatment of the bipolar disorder and in some cases the unipolar disorder.

Little Albert   A young child in whom John Watson classically conditioned a fear of furry objects.

Long-term memory   The part of the information-processing system where memories are stored for long periods in networks.

Loss   Concept that Freud thought crucial to the development of depression.

Lower-limit drug therapy   The idea that the dose levels of drugs should be occasionally lowered to determine whether the patient can get by with less.

Low-potency neuroleptics   Early antipsychotic drugs that are somewhat less effective for blocking dopamine activity than more recent drugs. (Contrast with *high-potency neuroleptics* and *atypical neuroleptics.*)

LSD (lysergic acid diethylamide)   A hallucinogen.

Luria-Nebraska   A widely used neuropsychological test.

Lymphocytes   A group of leukocytes that includes B cells and T (killer, helper, and suppressor) cells.

Magnetic resonance imaging (MRI)   A technique for obtaining images of internal organs such as the brain.

Malignant neuroleptic syndrome   A potentially fatal side effect of neuroleptics.

Malignant tumor   A cancerous growth that can shed cells, which spread the growth to other parts of the body.

Malingering   Faking symptoms for external incentives.

Managed health care   An insurance program in which the individual contracts with a group of specialists for treatment but is screened for treatment by a primary care physician.

Mania   Excessive activity, flight of thought, and grandiosity, seen in one phase of the bipolar disorder.

Manic-depressive disorder   Earlier name for what is now referred to as the *bipolar disorder.*

Manifest content   The apparent or obvious content of dreams.

Mantra   A syllable, usually a nonword, that is repeated or chanted as part of meditation.

MAO inhibitors (MAOIs)   A class of antidepressant drugs that increase the levels of neurotransmitters by inhibiting the activity of chemical agents (monoamine oxidizers) that would destroy the neurotransmitters.

Marginal disorders   Personality disorders that are similar to more serious disorders such as schizophrenia and paranoia.

Marijuana   Cannabis.

Maslow, Abraham   A humanistic theorist who suggested that people strive for self-actualization.

Mass hysteria   Earlier name for *mass psychogenic illness.*

Mass psychogenic illness   Occurrence of a somatoform disorder (e.g., fainting, nausea) in a large number of people at one time; formerly called *mass hysteria.*

Maternity blues   Mild depression that briefly afflicts many women shortly after they give birth.

Meditation   A strategy for relaxation based primarily on distraction through the use of a mantra.

Melatonin   A hormone that has been implicated in the seasonal affective disorder.

Mental defect   Belief that mental retardation is due to a defect in the brain rather than delayed development.

Mentally ill but guilty   A relatively new court ruling under which the individual is found to be mentally ill and is treated; once treatment is completed, the perpetrator is punished for the crime that was committed while disturbed.

Mental retardation   Disorder involving significantly subaverage intellectual functioning and deficits or impairments in adaptive behavior that begin before age 18.

Meprobamate (Equanil, Miltown)   A major tranquilizer, primarily a muscle relaxant.

Mescaline   A hallucinogen.

Mesmer, Franz Anton   Early physician who treated persons with somatoform disorders through suggestion; considered the father of hypnosis.

Mesmerism   Hypnosis.

Metabolism   A process by which a substance is changed or broken down into other substances.

Metabolism of neurotransmitters   Process that reduces the levels of neurotransmitters at the synapse. Counteracted with MAO inhibitors.

Metabolites   The end products of metabolism.

Methadone   A drug that can forestall the withdrawal symptoms of heroin dependence and can reduce the effects of heroin. Used in the treatment of heroin dependence.

Methylxanthines   A group of stimulants, among which the strongest is caffeine; found in coffee, tea, and chocolate.

MHPG   A metabolite of norepinephrine. Changing levels in the urine are associated with changes in mood.

Migraine headache   A severe headache caused by dilatation of the extracranial arteries, which places pressure on surrounding pain-sensitive nerves.

Milieu therapy   Activities such as art, music, crafts, and discussion conducted in a hospital.

Mind–body dualism   The notion that the mind and the body operate independently; discredited by evidence linking psychological factors to physical illnesses.

Minnesota Multiphasic Personality Inventory (MMPI)   A widely used objective personality test containing more than 500 questions.

Mitral valve prolapse   Incomplete closing of the valve between the left ventricle and the left atrium, permitting some backflow of blood when the heart beats. Sometimes associated with anxiety, but causal relationship is not clear.

M'Naghten rule   A rule for insanity based on the person's knowledge of right versus wrong.

Modeling   Learning by observing and imitating others.

Monozygotic (identical) twins   Twins who have identical gene structures.

Mood disorders   A group of disorders that includes the unipolar, dysthymic, bipolar, and cyclothymic disorders.

Mood disorder with psychotic features   A disorder that involves both serious problems with mood (depression or mania) and delusions.

Moral anxiety   One of the two types of anxiety (the other was neurotic) that Freud thought resulted in abnormal behavior.

Moral insanity   Early term for the *antisocial personality disorder.*

Morphine   One of the active ingredients in opium. Also extracted and used as a narcotic itself.

Mourning   The feeling of sadness and loss following the death of a loved one. Freud saw a connection between mourning and depression.

MPA   See *Depo-Provera.*

Multi-infarct dementia   Dementia that results from many small cerebral infarcts (strokes).

Multiple-baseline experimental research   A research technique in which treatments are introduced and then withdrawn a number of times, and changes in behavior are noted. Contrast this with research in which one group receives the treatment and another does not, and then the behavior of the two groups is compared.

Multiple personality disorder   A dissociative disorder in which the individual has two or more separate personalities, usually sharply contrasting. Officially called the *dissociative identity disorder.*

Muscle contraction headache   A headache caused by the prolonged contraction of the muscles in the neck extending to the head. Also called *tension headache.*

Myocardial infarction (MI)   Death of heart muscle due to insufficient blood supply; also called *heart attack.*

Myth of mental illness   The notion that rather than reflecting an illness, abnormal behavior is simply different, wrong, or reasonable as a response to an unreasonable environment.

Narcissistic personality disorder   Disorder in which the person has a grandiose sense of importance and is preoccupied with fantasies about success, power, or beauty.

Narcotics   A class of drugs derived from opium, including opium, morphine, and heroin, that have the effect of numbing the senses.

Negative cognitive sets   Thought structures reflecting the tendency to see things in a bad light and to expect the worst. Cognitive theorists assume that these sets are related to the development of depression.

Negative symptoms   Symptoms such as poverty of speech, flat affect, inability to experience pleasure, and lack of motivation seen in schizophrenia. Thought to be due to structural problems in the brain or low levels of activity in the frontal lobes. (Contrast with *positive symptoms.*)

Neo-Freudian theories   Theories based on modifications of Freud's theories.

Nerve fiber   A group of nerve cells that all serve the same function.

Nerve impulse   An electrical impulse that travels down a nerve.

Neural transmission The transfer of a nerve impulse from cell to cell across the synapse by a chemical process.

Neurofibrillary tangling A tangling of nerves in the brain associated with Alzheimer's disease.

Neuroleptics Drugs used to treat psychotic disorders.

Neuron A nerve cell.

Neuropsychological testing Testing to determine the nature, extent, and sometimes the location of brain damage.

Neurotic anxiety One of the two types of anxiety (moral anxiety was the other) that Freud believed led to abnormal behavior.

Neurotransmitters Chemicals (e.g., norepinephrine, dopamine, serotonin) released by presynaptic neurons that travel across the synapse and stimulate postsynaptic neurons. High or low levels influence the levels of neurological activity and result in abnormal behavior.

Nicotine Stimulant found primarily in tobacco. Use results in strong dependence.

Night hospitalization Procedure in which patients spend their nights in a hospital where they receive treatment but spend their days in the community or at work.

Nocturnal penile tumescence Erections that occur during sleep. Their occurrence is used to rule out physiological factors as a cause of arousal disorders in men.

Noncontinuous drug therapy Drug therapy in which the patient is occasionally taken off the drug to determine whether the drug is still necessary.

Nonspecific (common) factor explanation An explanation for the finding that most therapies are effective, the notion being that all of the therapies share a factor that contributes to improvement.

Nootropic drugs Drugs once thought to help with the problems of memory in Alzheimer's disease.

Norepinephrine A neurotransmitter that plays a role in depression.

Nurses' station An office in a hospital ward (often enclosed in glass) where nurses remain when not attending to patients.

Object displacement A defense in which the individual shifts the feelings or responses for one object (person) to another.

Objective testing Tests of personality that can be scored objectively (e.g., true or false, multiple choice). The Minnesota Multiphasic Personality Inventory is often used for objective testing.

Observational learning Learning based on observing the behavior of others; see also *modeling*.

Obsession The repeated, uncontrollable thinking of a thought.

Obsessive-compulsive personality disorder Disorder characterized by obsessions, compulsions, or both.

Oedipus attraction Freud's term for the attraction a young boy feels toward his mother.

Open ward A ward where patients are free to come and go at will (though they may not necessarily leave the hospital).

Operant conditioning Learning based on the fact that desired responses are followed by rewards and undesired responses are followed by punishment.

Opiate antagonist A drug (e.g., naloxone) that blocks the effects of heroin, thereby eliminating the pleasure it can induce.

Opiates A group of drugs derived from opium (also called narcotics). Examples include opium, morphine, and heroin.

Opium A narcotic that is also the basis for morphine and heroin.

Oppositional defiant disorder Disorder of childhood in which the person is negativistic, defiant, argumentative, hostile, and generally resistant to others.

Oral stage First of the stages of psychosexual development identified by Freud. Pleasure is associated with the mouth, and the infant has no sense of separateness from the external world.

Organic mental disorders Disorders, usually involving dementia, for which the organic cause is known.

Orgasm disorder Sexual dysfunction involving the failure to achieve orgasm by women and premature ejaculation by men.

Outpatient clinic Facility in which patients are treated while living in the community.

Pain disorder A somatoform disorder, the major symptom of which is pain that has no physiological basis.

Panic attacks Intense periods of anxiety that appear to come "out of the blue." May be induced by injections of sodium lactate.

Panic disorder An anxiety disorder, the major symptom of which is panic attacks.

Panic disorder with agoraphobia A disorder in which the individual develops agoraphobia as a result of having experienced panic attacks outside the home.

Paradoxical drug effect The fact that stimulant drugs can have a calming effect on persons with the attention-deficit hyperactivity disorder.

Paranoid personality disorder Disorder characterized by unwarranted suspiciousness and mistrust of people. Differs from delusion disorder (paranoia) in its absence of clearly formed delusions.

Paranoid schizophrenia Schizophrenia characterized by delusions of persecution.

Paraphilias Sexual disorders that involve deviant means of achieving sexual arousal. Examples include masochism, fetishism, and exhibitionism.

Paraprofessionals Persons who do not have professional training or degrees in psychotherapy but treat (often successfully) individuals suffering from psychological disorders.

Parasympathetic branch Branch of the autonomic nervous system responsible for reducing arousal.

Parens patriae The principle that the state has the right and responsibility to protect and provide for the well-being of its citizens; the basis for involuntary hospitalization.

Parkinson's disease Disease characterized by loss of muscle control (early or mild forms involve frequent twitches) that results from low levels of dopamine. Treatment with L-dopa can be effective but may provoke symptoms of schizophrenia.

Pathological gambling A type of impulse control disorder.

Pavlov, Ivan Russian physiologist who first identified classical conditioning.

Peak experiences Brief periods of self-actualization described by humanists.

Pedophilia A paraphilia in which the individual gains sexual gratification from sexual activities with children.

Peptic ulcers Breaks in the lining of the digestive system.

Performance intelligence An intelligence test score based on the ability to perform various tasks such as putting a puzzle together and arranging colored blocks to create a design.

Perinatal complications Problems during birth (e.g., lack of oxygen) that cause brain damage and lead to abnormal behavior.

Peripheral nervous system Components of the nervous system outside the brain and spinal cord. Branches include the autonomic and the somatic.

Persecutory delusions Delusions that people are plotting against the person; seen in the delusional disorder and sometimes in schizophrenia.

Persistent type of alcoholism Drinking pattern characterized by continued low levels of drinking. Thought to be due to low levels of arousal that might be normalized by small amounts of alcohol. (Contrast with *binge drinking*.)

Personality disorders Disorders involving behaviors that are less deviant than most of the behaviors associated with many other disorders. Examples include the antisocial, obsessive-compulsive, dependent, narcissistic, paranoid, and borderline personality disorders.

Pervasive developmental disorder A type of serious disorder of infancy and childhood; includes autism.

Phallic stage Third stage of psychosexual development described by Freud. Most notable during this phase are Oedipal or Electra attractions.

Phenomenological approach Approach to understanding behavior based on the idea that knowledge is gained through experience rather than through thought and intuition.

Phenylalanine Amino acid that if not broken down forms phenylpyruvic acid, which destroys the brain in infants and results in a type of mental retardation known as phenylketonuria.

Phenylketonuria (PKU) Mental retardation due to high levels of phenylpyruvic acid, which destroys the brain.

Phenylpyruvic acid *See* **Phenylalanine.**

Phobic disorder An anxiety disorder in which the individual has an inappropriate fear of a specific object or situation.

Physical anomalies Abnormalities such as misshapen head, ears, or hands that reflect problems with fetal development and are often associated with other disorders such as mental retardation or autism.

Physiological perspective The position that abnormal behavior is the result of problems with synaptic transmission, brain structure, and hormones.

Physiological sex identification An individual's objective knowledge (based on genitalia) of being male or female. (Contrast with *psychological gender identity*.)

Pica An eating disorder characterized by the persistent ingestion of nonnutritive substances such as dirt, hair, or cloth.

Pinel, Philippe Early reformer in France who took mental patients out of their chains.

Placebo effect Phenomenon whereby the expectation that a treatment will have a specific effect may produce the effect even if the treatment is technically inactive.

Pleasure principle Freud's notion that one of the factors underlying behavior is the desire for pleasure, which in most cases involves drive reduction.

Police power of the state The notion that the state has the right to protect citizens from individuals who are dangerous; used as a basis for involuntary hospitalization of persons believed to be dangerous to others.

Positive spiking Sudden abnormal bursts of EEG activity, often seen in persons with the antisocial personality disorder and speculated to be associated with outbursts of aggression.

Positive symptoms Symptoms such as hallucinations, delusions, and disturbances of thought that are seen in schizophrenia and are believed to be due to problems with neural transmission. (Contrast with *negative symptoms*.)

Positron emission tomography (PET scan) A means of graphically portraying chemical processes in the brain. Radioactive agents bind to chemicals (e.g., glucose), permitting the location of the chemicals to be tracked by measuring the radioactivity in various areas of the brain.

Postamphetamine depression Depression resulting when a person ceases taking amphetamines.

Postpartum depression *See* **Depression with postpartum onset.**

Postsynaptic neuron Neuron that is stimulated when a nerve impulse is transmitted across a synapse.

Posttraumatic stress disorder An anxiety disorder, the major symptom of which is the reexperiencing of feelings associated with an earlier traumatic event (e.g., war, natural disaster, physical attack).

Preconscious Level of consciousness involving memories of which one is not usually aware but which can be brought to awareness with some effort (e.g., names of friends from long ago). (Contrast with *conscious mind* and *unconscious*.)

Predisposing factors Genetic, physiological, or psychological factors that make an individual more likely to develop a disorder.

Prefrontal lobotomy Operation in which the frontal lobes of the brain are removed or separated from the rest of the brain.

Premature ejaculation The orgasm disorder in men that involves reaching orgasm too soon.

Premenstrual dysphoric disorder A mood disorder that involves excessive depression and stress prior to the onset of menstruation.

Prenatal complications Problems during fetal development (e.g., mother's illness, exposure to hormones) that influence brain development and lead to abnormal behavior.

Presenile dementia A deterioration of cognitive functioning that occurs before the age of 65. (Contrast with *senile dementia*.)

Presynaptic neuron Neuron that fires and then releases a neurotransmitter into the synapse so that the next (postsynaptic) nerve can be stimulated.

Primary dementia Deterioration of cognitive functioning due to an organic disorder of the brain (e.g., strokes).

Primary depression Depression that is not the result of another disorder, drug, or treatment. (Contrast with *secondary depression*.)

Primary type of the APD Type of the antisocial personality disorder in which the individual seems incapable of developing anxiety rather than effectiveness at avoiding anxiety. (Contrast with *secondary type of the APD*.)

Primary orgasm disorder Disorder in which a woman does not experience orgasm during masturbation or intercourse.

Primary prevention Attempting to prevent disorders by eliminating their cause.

Primary process Fantasies used to satisfy needs; identified by Freud.

Priming The notion that a memory network can be activated by using a thought or feeling in that network and thereby increase the likelihood that other memories or feelings in the network will be activated.

Prodromal phase Phase of a disorder before the major symptoms become apparent.

Prodromal symptoms Symptoms that precede the onset of a disorder. Prodromal symptoms of a classic migraine include visual problems, dizziness, and sometimes abdominal pain.

Progesterone Hormone associated with feminine characteristics.

Progressive muscle relaxation Procedure in which a person is taught to relax muscles, usually beginning with the head and working down to the feet.

Projection Defense mechanism whereby a person attributes his or her undesirable traits to others; also the basis of projective tests.

Projective tests Tests in which clients are shown ambiguous stimuli (e.g., inkblots, pictures of people) and asked to talk about them.

Pronoun reversal Speech characteristic seen in children with autism in which they reverse genders of pronouns.

Propanediols Drugs initially used to treat disturbed persons. Benefits seem to be due to their sedating effects rather than to any effects on underlying problems.

Prozac (fluoxetine) A bicyclic antidepressant drug that blocks the reuptake of serotonin and is effective for treating depression and the obsessive-compulsive disorder.

Pseudocyesis A conversion disorder involving symptoms of pregnancy; formerly called *hysterical pregnancy*.

Psilocybin A hallucinogen.

Psychiatric nurse A nurse with specific training in the care and treatment of persons with mental disorders.

Psychiatrist A physician (MD) with advanced training in the care and treatment of persons with mental disorders.

Psychoactive drug Any substance that alters mood, awareness of the external environment, or awareness of the internal environment.

Psychoanalysis A treatment developed by Freud that focuses primarily on identifying unconscious causes of abnormal behavior through the use of such techniques as free association.

Psychoanalyst A psychotherapist who is trained in and uses the technique of psychoanalysis.

Psychoanalytic theory Theory of human behavior developed primarily by Freud.

Psychodynamic perspective on abnormal behavior The position that abnormal behavior is the result of unconscious conflicts.

Psychological gender identity The subjective feeling of being male or female. If in conflict with one's physical sex identification, a gender identity disorder results.

Psychologist (clinical) A person with advanced training (PhD, PsyD) in the care and treatment of persons with mental disorders.

Psychomotor stimulants Drugs that increase the production of neurotransmitters and thereby increase mood and activity. Depression may result when these drugs are withdrawn, so they are rarely used to treat depression.

Psychopath Early and still widely used term for a person with what is now called the *antisocial personality disorder*; term often implies a physiological basis for the disorder.

Psychopharmocology The study of the effects of drugs on behavior.

Psychosexual stages The oral, anal, phallic, latency, and genital stages, which Freud thought important in the development of personality.

Psychosomatic disorders A term once used to describe physical disorders (e.g., ulcers) that were caused by psychological factors.

Psychosurgery Procedure in which parts of the brain are removed or destroyed in an attempt to treat mental disorders. (See also *prefrontal lobotomy*.)

Psychotherapy A treatment for disorders that explores causes and solutions for mental disorders by talking.

Pyromania An inpulse control disorder in which the individual cannot resist setting fires.

Quasi-experimental research Research in which rather than manipulating the independent variable, the investigator uses naturally occurring situations in which there are differences in the independent variable (e.g., studying persons in stressful jobs rather than creating stress for persons). Often used to avoid ethical problems in research.

Quasi-psychotic thought disturbance A thought disorder that is less serious than that seen in schizophrenia that occurs in the borderline personality disorder.

Random assignment Procedure in which in experimental research subjects are assigned to conditions on a nonsystematic basis.

Rapid cycling The tendency to go thorough the phases of the bipolar disorder quickly.

Rational-emotive therapy Cognitive therapy in which the client is forced to reexamine erroneous beliefs and develop new, more appropriate ones.

Rationalization A defense in which the individual gives a good reason but not the real reason for a behavior and thereby avoids anxiety.

Reaction formation A defense in which the individual does or feels the opposite of what is expected and thereby avoids anxiety.

Recidivism Relapse; a return to former patterns of behavior.

Receptor sites Areas on a postsynaptic neuron that when stimulated by neurotransmitters cause the neuron to fire.

Regression Defense mechanism characterized by the retreat to an earlier stage of development.

Relaxation response A type of meditation.

Releasing hormone Hormone released by the hypothalamus during sexual arousal that stimulates the pituitary gland.

Reliability The notion that test results or research findings obtained at one time can be found again at another time or by another tester/investigator.

Repression Defense mechanism whereby threatening memories are stored in the unconscious.

Residual phase Phase in the course of schizophrenia that follows the active phase in which symptoms have diminished and become less clear.

Residual schizophrenia A mild disorder that occurs after at least one schizophrenic episode and is characterized by some of the symptoms of schizophrenia, which are generally muted.

Resistance Blocking or talking about trivial issues in psychotherapy (or analysis) when the client is faced with anxiety-provoking material. Can be used as a sign that an important issue has been encountered.

Response stereotypy Abnormal repetitive behaviors that result when persons with the attention-deficit hyperactivity disorder are given too high a dose of stimulant medication.

Retarded depression Depression characterized by slowed movements and thoughts. (Contrast with *agitated depression*.)

Retrograde amnesia Loss of memory for recent events that extends progressively to more distant events. Sometimes associated with electroconvulsive therapy, especially when bipolar electrode placement is used.

Reuptake Absorption of neurotransmitters by the presynaptic neurons. The process is inhibited by bicyclic and tricyclic drugs.

Reversed cerebral asymmetry The fact that in some persons with schizophrenia, the right side of the brain (in right-handed persons) is heavier than the left side of the brain. The opposite is usually true in persons who do not suffer from schizophrenia.

Rewards   Factors that can be used to reinforce a behavior.

Rheumatoid arthritis   *See* **Arthritis**.

Right to equal protection   Constitutional right under the Fourteenth Amendment that may be violated with mental patients (as when they are hospitalized involuntarily).

Ritalin (methylphenidate)   A stimulant used to treat the attention-deficit hyperactivity disorder.

Rorschach   A projective test consisting of 10 cards, each with one inkblot.

Rubella (German measles)   An infectious disease that if experienced by a woman during pregnancy can cause an inflammation of the brain of the fetus, which can in turn lead to degeneration of the brain and mental retardation.

Rumination disorder   An eating disorder of childhood involving repeated regurgitation of food.

Rush, Benjamin   Early reformer in the area of mental disorders; known as the "father of American psychiatry."

Schizoaffective disorder   Disorder involving the symptoms of both schizophrenia and depression.

Schizoid personality disorder   A personality disorder characterized by a lack of interest in other people and little emotion. Lack of hallucinations, delusions, or problems with thought processes distinguish this from schizophrenia.

Schizophrenia   A serious disorder involving a decline in functioning, hallucinations, delusions, and/or disturbed thought processes. Symptoms must persist for at least 6 months.

Schizophrenic deficit   The impairment in intellectual functioning seen in schizophrenia, due to a disturbance in thought processes.

Schizophreniform disorder   Disorder involving the symptoms of schizophrenia that lasts only 1 to 6 months.

Schizophrenogenic mother   A mother who is both attentive and rejecting, once thought to contribute to the development of schizophrenia.

Schizotypal personality disorder   Disorder involving many of the symptoms of schizophrenia, but not severe enough to result in a diagnosis of schizophrenia (e.g., patient says, "I feel as if I am hearing voices," not "I am hearing voices").

Scientist-practitioner model   An approach to the training of psychologists in which they are trained to be both scientists who do research and practitioners who treat disturbed individuals.

Seasonal affective disorder (SAD)   A mood disorder characterized by depression during periods of less daylight and sometimes by mania during periods of increased daylight. Offically called *depression with seasonal pattern.*

Season-of-birth effect   The fact that individuals who later develop schizophrenia are more likely to be born in late winter.

Secondary dementia   Dementia as a side effect of some other disorder (e.g., depression) rather than due to an organic disorder.

Secondary depression   Depression as a side effect of medication or another disorder.

Secondary hypertension   High blood pressure that results from some known physical cause.

Secondary mania   Mania as a side effect of medication or another disorder.

Secondary orgasm disorder   Sexual dysfunction in which a woman is able to achieve orgasm through masturbation but not through intercourse.

Secondary prevention   Attempting to solve problems at an early stage before they result in serious disorders.

Secondary process   Freud's term for thinking and problem solving.

Secondary type of the APD   Form of the antisocial personality disorder in which the individual is capable of experiencing anxiety but has learned to avoid it.

Selective attention   The process in which individuals focus attention on what they believe is most important, thereby possibly missing other important material.

Selective recall   The fact that recall is influenced by factors such as priming and mood, thereby possibly distorting what is recalled.

Self-actualization   A state of development described by humanists in which individuals rise above their own needs and can freely give of themselves.

Self-efficacy   An attitude reflecting self-confidence and positive expectancies.

Self-fulfilling prophecy   A result that occurs largely because the individual expects it (e.g., failure because of the expectancy of failure).

Self-medication hypothesis   The notion that individuals take drugs in an attempt to normalize their levels of arousal.

Semantic intrusions   Associative intrusions involving multiple-meaning words (e.g., hearing the word *date* in a conversation about fruits, the disturbed person takes it in its interpersonal-relationship sense).

Senile dementia   Dementia that begins after the age of 65.

Sensory deprivation   Limitation of all sensory inputs (sound, sight, touch, smell), once thought to contribute to schizophrenia. The psychological effects are now known to be due in large part to demand characteristics.

Sensory memory   The component of the information-processing system in which incoming stimuli are first registered before some are sent to the short-term memory.

Serotonin   A neurotransmitter, low levels of which result in depression, aggression, or both.

Sex reassignment surgery   Procedure whereby an individual with the gender identity disorder is surgically altered to have the appearance and some of the functions of the opposite sex.

Sexual dysfunctions   A group of sex-related disorders including the desire, arousal, and orgasm disorders.

Sexual masochism   A paraphilia in which the individual gains sexual gratification from pain.

Sexual predator laws   Laws that make it possible to confine an individual who is considered at risk of committing a sexual crime.

Sexual sadism   A paraphilia in which the individual gains sexual gratification from harming another person.

Shared psychotic disorder   A delusional disorder that develops in a second person as a consequence of his or her association with a person who has a delusional disorder. Formerly called *folie à deux.*

Short-term memory   The component of the information-processing system in which thinking is done and information is processed for storage in the long-term memory.

Side effects   Additional, unintended effects of a treatment (e.g., dry mouth in the use of antidepressants).

Situation redefinition   Reconceputalization of a threatening situation as nonthreatening (e.g., a test is regarded as an opportunity for learning). Also called *denial.*

Skinner, B. F.   American scientist who contributed to the understanding and use of operant conditioning.

Slow-wave activity   Brain-wave activity found primarily in the temporal lobes of persons with the antisocial personality disorder.

Social phobia   Disorder characterized by fear of behaving in an embarrassing way and of being criticized; results in avoidance of people.

Social support   Emotional support from others, which has been shown to reduce the effects of stress.

Social worker   A professional who works with patients and their families, often with the goal of facilitating the patients' return and adjustment to the community.

Sociogenic model   The notion that schizophrenia is caused by social stresses.

Sociopath   Early term for a person with what is now called the *antisocial personality disorder*. Implicit in the term is the belief that the disorder stems from social psychological factors (e.g., child rearing).

Sodium lactate   A substance that can set off a panic attack if injected into persons with a history of naturally occurring panic attacks.

Soft signs (of brain damage)   Problems with muscular or visual coordination that may reflect diffuse or minimal brain damage that is often not otherwise detectable.

Somatic anxiety   Anxiety reflected primarily in physiological symptoms such as rapid heartbeat, sweating, and rapid breathing.

Somatic division   The part of the peripheral nervous system involving connections with the muscles and skin.

Somatization disorder   A somatoform disorder involving the report of a large number of physical symptoms for which no physical cause can be found.

Somatoform disorders   A class of disorders, including the somatization, hypochondriasis, conversion, idiopathic pain, and dysmorphic disorders.

Specific patient explanation   An explanation for the finding that all therapies appear to be somewhat effective because different therapies are effective for different patients.

Specific phobia   Disorder involving any irrational fear other than agoraphobia or social phobia.

Sphygmomanometer   Device used to measure blood pressure.

Spirochete   A microorganism (*Treponema pallidum*) responsible for general paresis (syphilitic infection that results in brain damage).

Spontaneous recovery   Spontaneous remission of symptoms or the spontaneous return of a classically conditioned response after extinction procedures.

Spontaneous remission   Disappearance of a disorder without treatment; often seen with depression.

Stanford-Binet   An individual intelligence test administered to schoolchildren.

Start-squeeze technique   An effective technique for treating premature ejaculation.

Start-stop technique   An effective technique for treating premature ejaculation.

State anxiety   Anxiety that is limited to one particular situation (e.g., tests) as opposed to being continually present. (Contrast with *trait anxiety*.)

Statistically significant   A research finding that is reliable.

Stimulants   A group of substances, including amphetamines, cocaine, caffeine, and nicotine, that have the effect of increasing neurotransmission.

Stimulus overload   In schizophrenia, the experience of being overwhelmed by external and internal stimulation. Contributes to problems with thought processes.

Strategic eating disorders   Eating disorders that stem from a goal such as losing weight for a particular event rather than from a more serious or pervasive problem.

Stress   The psychological and physiological response to overtaxing changes; results in responses such as anxiety, depression, and elevated physiological arousal.

Stress management training   Procedures for teaching persons to deal with stress, such as muscle relaxation, coping strategies, and time management.

Stressor   A factor that elicts the stress response.

Stroke   *See* **Cerebral infarction**.

Structural abnormalities of the brain   Factors such as enlarged ventricles, cortical atrophy, and subcortical entropy that are associated with schizophrenia.

Structural approach to personality   Freud's description of personality in terms of the id, ego, and superego.

Structured interview   An interview that is limited to a specific set of questions.

Sublimation   A defense mechanism in which the individual channels pent-up sexual energy into some other activity.

Substance abuse   Disorder in which persons are not dependent on a substance (drug) but engage in maladaptive behavior as a result of their taking the drug.

Substance dependence   Disorder involving the loss of control of the use of substances (drugs) and/or the onset of withdrawal symptoms when the substance is not taken.

Substance-induced psychotic disorder   A psychotic disorder that stems from high levels of a drug.

Substantia nigra   Large, dark-colored area of the midbrain responsible for motor activity. Destruction of the substantia nigra and the associated drop in the production of dopamine are responsible for the motor symptoms of Parkinson's disease.

Suicide   The voluntary ending of one's own life.

Suicide gestures   Behaviors that are intended to look like attempts of a person to take his or her own life but are actually designed to communicate distress or to manipulate others.

Superego   In Freud's structural approach to personality, the conscience or moral arm of society, developed by identification with the parent.

Support group   A group of persons with similar problems who meet to give one another social support and exchange information and coping strategies.

Suppression   A defense mechanism consisting of conscious attempts to stop or avoid thinking about a threat.

Suppressor cells   T lymphocytes that reduce the activity of the immune system in the absence of antigens.

Sympathetic branch   Branch of the autonomic nervous system responsible for increases in arousal.

Synapse   Gap between neurons, crossed by neurotransmitters in the process of neural transmission.

Systematic desensitization   A treatment procedure in which a relaxation response is paired with an anxiety-provoking stimulus in an attempt at counterconditioning.

Systolic blood pressure   The high level of blood pressure that occurs immediately after each beat of the heart; usually around 120 mm Hg.

Tarasoff ruling   A legal decision that therapists have a duty to protect people if a client poses a danger to those people.

Tardive dyskinesia   Disorder involving involuntary muscle contractions (initially of the face and head) due to long-term use of high levels of neuroleptic drugs.

T cells Special-purpose lymphocytes, including killer, helper, and suppressor cells.

Temporal lobe epilepsy Disorder involving erratic firing of neurons in the temporal lobe that can bring on seizures. The episodes are sometimes preceded by hallucinations.

Temporal lobes Areas of the brain where memories for visual and auditory experiences are stored; stimulation of the temporal lobes can result in hallucinations.

Tension headache *See* **Muscle contraction headache**.

Terminal button Vessel at the end of the axon from which neurotransmitters are released.

Tertiary prevention Attempts to prevent relapses in persons who have responded successfully to treatment.

Testosterone Hormone produced by the testes (when stimulated by gonadotropins), responsible for sexual desire in males.

Testosterone replacement therapy Administration of testosterone as a treatment for the desire disorder in males.

Thematic Apperception Test (TAT) A projective test consisting primarily of drawings of people. Clients are asked to make up stories about what is going on in the pictures.

Thorazine (chlorpromazine) Early neuroleptic that is still widely used in the treatment of schizophrenia.

Thorndike, Edward L. American scientist who studied operant conditioning.

Thought content intrusions The inclusion of new and irrelevant thoughts, contributing to the disturbed thought processes seen in schizophrenia.

Thrombus A clot that blocks the blood flow through an artery.

Thyroxin Hormone produced by the thyroid gland, the underproduction of which leads to cretinism (hypothyroidism).

Tic disorder A disorder involving recurrent and involuntary contractions of muscles resulting in jerking of the body or face. Includes Tourette's disorder, which involves vocal tics.

Time-limited psychotherapy Psychotherapy intended to last only a specified number of sessions.

Token economy A treatment approach in which patients are rewarded with tokens when they show appropriate behaviors. Tokens can later be exchanged for food, improved living conditions, and privileges.

Tolerance Phenomenon whereby a specific dose level of a drug has less effect after repeated administrations.

Total institution An institution such as the military, a prison, or a mental hospital that can control all aspects of a person's life.

Tourette's disorder A tic disorder involving involuntary movements of large muscles; often includes vocal tics such as grunts, yelps, barks, and words (sometimes obscenities).

Toxic psychosis A psychosis that results from high levels of medication.

Trait anxiety Anxiety that is a pervasive personality trait rather than a response to a specific situation. (Contrast with *state anxiety*.)

Trait disorders A group of personality disorders that revolve around a trait that interferes with personal functioning or causes distress. Examples include the obsessive-compulsive, dependent, passive-aggressive, and sadistic disorders.

Tranquilizers Drugs that serve to reduce arousal and associated tension.

Transcendental meditation A widely practiced form of meditation in which the individual allegedly transcends normal consciousness.

Transference Process in psychotherapy (or analysis) in which the client redirects toward the therapist feelings about someone in the client's life.

Transorbital lobotomy Psychosurgery during which a knife is inserted into the frontal lobes through the eye socket and then swung back and forth.

Transvestic fetishism A paraphilia in which the individual gains sexual pleasure from dressing in the clothes of the opposite sex.

Trichotillomania An impulse control disorder in which the individual cannot resist the urge to pull out his or her hair.

Tricyclics A group of drugs widely used to treat depression.

Trisomy 21 Possession of an extra number 21 chromosome; the condition results in Down syndrome.

Tyramine A substance that interacts with MAOIs to cause a hypertensive crisis.

Tuke, William Quaker who opened a retreat for mental patients.

Turner's syndrome (gonadal dysgenesis) Disorder limited to women that sometimes results in mental retardation revolving around space-form relationships; caused by the absence of one female (X) chromosome.

Twin studies (in genetics) A technique in which the concordance rate of a disorder is compared in monozygotic and dizygotic twins in an effort to determine the genetic and environmental effects.

Type A behavior pattern Behavior characterized by urgency, competitiveness, overcommitment, and hostility.

Unconditioned stimulus A stimulus that can elicit a response without prior conditioning (e.g., meat elicits salivation).

Unconscious Area of the mind in which threatening memories that are not retrievable are stored (repressed).

Undifferentiated schizophrenia Catch-all category for all persons with schizophrenia who do not fit into other categories.

Unipolar disorder A mood disorder of which depression is the major symptom.

Unstructured interview An interview that does not follow a specific set of questions. (Contrast with *structured interview*.)

Validity The notion that a test measures what it is supposed to measure.

Vasodilators Drugs that cause the dilation of blood vessels and thereby reduce blood pressure.

Ventricles Cavities in the brain.

Verbal conditioning Procedure whereby the use of particular words or statements can be increased by following them with rewards (attention). Suggested as a process that might occur in psychotherapy.

Verbal intelligence Intelligence based on a person's ability to define words, provide information, explain similarities, do arithmetic problems, and remember lists of numbers.

Vicarious conditioning Conditioning that occurs when one individual observes another being conditioned.

Vocal tics Grunts, noises, and sometimes words that are produced by uncontrollable contractions of the diaphragm.

Voluntary admission Self-admission to a hospital, which carries with it the right to leave after appropriate notice unless admission status is changed to involuntary commitment.

Voyeurism A paraphilia in which an individual gains sexual gratification from looking at others who are nude or disrobing.

Watson, John B. American scientist who pioneered the idea that conditioning provided the basis of fears. His most famous case was Little Albert.

Wechsler Adult Intelligence Scale (WAIS) An individual intelligence test for adolescents and adults.

Wechsler Intelligence Scale for Children, Third Edition (WISC-III) An individual intelligence test for schoolchildren.

Wechsler Preschool-Primary Scale of Intelligence (WPPSI) An individual intelligence test for preschool children.

White blood cells *See* **Leukocytes**.

Withdrawal Group of symptoms such as nausea and vomiting that occur when a person stops taking a drug.

Word salads Jumbled words used by some persons with schizophrenia.

XYY syndrome A genetic condition in which a male has an extra male (Y) chromosome; once thought to be associated with violent antisocial behavior.

References

Abikoff, H., & Gittelman, R. (1985). Hyperactive children treated with stimulants. *Archives of General Psychiatry, 42,* 953–961.

Abraham, S. F., & Beumont, P. J. (1982). How patients describe bulimia or binge eating. *Psychological Medicine, 12,* 625–635.

Abramowitz, S. I. (1986). Psychosocial outcomes of sex reassignment surgery. *Journal of Consulting and Clinical Psychology, 54,* 183–189.

Abramson, L. Y., & Sackeim, H. A. (1977). A paradox in depression: Uncontrollability and self-blame. *Psychological Bulletin, 84,* 838–851.

Abramson, L. Y., Seligman, M. E., & Teasdale, J. D. (1978). Learned helplessness in humans: Critique and reformulation. *Journal of Abnormal Psychology, 87,* 49–74.

Adams, J., McIntosh, E., & Weade, B. L. (1973). Ethnic background, measured intelligence, and adaptive behavior scores in mentally retarded children. *American Journal of Mental Deficiency, 78,* 1–6.

Addiego, F., Belzer, E. G., Comolli, J., Moger, W., Perry, J. D., & Wipple, B. (1981). Female ejaculation: A case study. *Journal of Sex Research, 17,* 13–21.

Addonizio, G. (1991). The pharmacologic basis of neuroleptic malignant syndrome. *Psychiatric Annals, 21,* 152–156.

Adler, A. (1927). *The practice and theory of individual psychology.* Orlando, FL: Harcourt Brace.

Agren, H. (1982). Depressive symptom patterns and urinary MHPG excretion. *Psychiatry and Research, 6,* 185–196.

Alexander, B. K., Beyerstein, B. L., Hadaway, P. F., & Coambs, R. B. (1981). The effect of early and later colony housing on oral ingestion of morphine in rats. *Pharmacology, Biochemistry, and Behavior, 15,* 571–576.

Alexander, B. K., Coambs, R. B., & Hadaway, P. F. (1978). The effect of housing and gender on morphine self-administration in rats. *Psychopharmacology, 58,* 175–179.

Alexander, B. K., & Hadaway, P. F. (1982). Opiate addiction: The case for an adaptive orientation. *Psychological Bulletin, 92,* 367–381.

Alexander, L. (1953). *Treatment of mental disorder.* Philadelphia: Saunders.

Allen, M. G., Cohen, S., Pollin, W., & Greenspan, S. I. (1974). Affective illness in veteran twins: A diagnostic review. *American Journal of Psychiatry, 131,* 1234–1239.

Allison, R. B. (1984). Difficulties diagnosing the multiple personality syndrome in a death penalty case. *International Journal of Clinical and Experimental Hypnosis, 32,* 102–117.

Allison, R. B., & Schwartz, T. (1980). *Minds in many pieces: The making of a very special doctor.* New York: Rawson, Wade.

Alloy, L. B. (1982). The role of perceptions and attributions for response-outcome noncontingency in learned helplessness: A commentary and discussion. *Journal of Personality, 50,* 441–479.

Alloy, L. B., & Abramson, L. Y. (1979). Judgment of contingency in depressed and nondepressed students: Sadder but wiser? *Journal of Experimental Psychology: General, 108,* 441–485.

Altamura, A. C., Percudani, M., Guercetti, G., & Invernizzi, G. (1989). Efficacy and tolerability of fluoxetine in the elderly: A double-blind study versus amitryptiline. *International Journal of Psychopharmacology, 4,* 103–106.

Alzate, H., & Hoch, Z. (1986). The "G spot" and "female ejaculation": A current appraisal. *Journal of Sex and Marital Therapy, 12,* 211–220.

Amenson, C. S., & Lewinsohn, P. M. (1981). An investigation into the observed sex differences in prevalence of unipolar depression. *Journal of Abnormal Psychology, 90,* 1–13.

American Cancer Society. (1982). Unproven methods of cancer management. *CA-A Journal for Clinicians, 32,* 58–61.

American Psychiatric Association. (1952). *Diagnostic and statistical manual of mental disorders.* Washington, DC: Author.

American Psychiatric Association. (1968). *Diagnostic and statistical manual of mental disorders* (2nd ed.). Washington, DC: Author.

American Psychiatric Association. (1980). *Diagnostic and statistical manual of mental disorders* (3rd ed.). Washington, DC: Author.

American Psychiatric Association. (1987). *Diagnostic and statistical manual of mental disorders* (3rd ed., rev.). Washington, DC: Author.

American Psychiatric Association. (1994). *Diagnostic and statistical manual of mental disorders* (4th ed.). Washington, DC: Author.

American Psychiatric Association, Task Force on Electroconvulsive Therapy. (1978). *Electroconvulsive therapy.* Washington, DC: American Psychiatric Association.

American Psychological Association (1993). Evidence grows of abuse by psychiatric hospitals. *APA Monitor, 24* (1), 20.

American Psychological Association, Task Force on Laboratory Tests in Psychiatry (1987). The dexamethasone suppression test: An overview of its current status in psychiatry. *American Journal of Psychiatry, 144,* 1253–1262.

Anand, B. K., & Brobeck, J. R. (1951a). Hypothalamic control of food intake in rats and cats. *Yale Journal of Biology and Medicine, 24,* 123.

Anand, B. K., & Brobeck, J. R. (1951b). Localization of a feeding center in the hypothalamus of the rat. *Proceedings of the Society for Experimental Biology and Medicine, 77,* 323–324.

Anand, B. K., Dua, S., & Schoenberg, K. (1955). Hypothalamic control of food intake in rats and monkeys. *Journal of Physiology (London), 127,* 143–152.

Anderson, K. O., Bradley, L. D., Young, L. D., & McDaniel, L. K. (1985). Rheumatoid arthritis: Review of psychological factors related to etiology, effects, and treatment. *Psychological Bulletin, 98,* 358–387.

Anderson, L. T., Campbell, M., Grega, D. M., Perry, R., Small, A. M., & Green, W. H. (1984). Haloperidol in the treatment of infantile autism: Effects on learning and behavior symptoms. *American Journal of Psychiatry, 141,* 1195–1202.

Andreasen, N. C. (1982). Negative symptoms in schizophrenia: Definition and reliability. *Archives of General Psychiatry, 39,* 784–788.

Andreasen, N. C. (1988). Brain imaging: Applications in psychiatry. *Science, 239,* 1381–1388.

Andreasen, N. C., Nasrallah, H. A., Dunn, V., Olsen, S. C., Grove, W. M., Ehrhardt, J. C., Coffman, J. A., & Crossett, J. H. (1986). Structural abnormalities in the frontal system in schizophrenia. *Archives of General Psychiatry, 43,* 136–144.

Andreasen, N. C., & Olsen, S. C. (1982). Negative v. positive schizophrenia: Definition and validation. *Archives of General Psychiatry, 39,* 789–794.

Andreasen, N. C., Rezai, K., Alliger, R., Swayze, V. W., Flaum, M., Kirchner, P. Cohen, G., & O'Leary, D. S. (1992). Hypofrontality in neuroleptic-naive patients and in patients with chronic schizophrenia: Assessment with xenon 133 single-photon emission computed tomography and the Tower of London. *Archives of General Psychiatry, 49,* 943–958.

Andreasen, N. C., Smith, M. R., Jacoby, C. G., Kennert, J. W., & Olsen, S. C. (1982). Ventricular enlargement in schizophrenia: Definition and prevalence. *American Journal of Psychiatry, 139,* 292–296.

Andrews, G., Tennant, C., Hewson, D., & Vaillant, G. (1978). Life event stress, social support, coping style and risk of psychological impairment. *Journal of Nervous and Mental Disease, 166,* 307–316.

Angrist, B. M., & Gershon, S. (1970). The phenomenology of experimentally induced amphetamine psychosis: Preliminary observations. *Biological Psychiatry, 2,* 97–107.

Angrist, B. M., Lee, H. K., & Gershon, S. (1974). The antagonism of amphetamine-induced symptomatology by a neuroleptic. *American Journal of Psychiatry, 131,* 817–819.

Angrist, B. M., Sathananthan, G., & Gershon, S. (1973). Behavioral effects of L-dopa in schizophrenic patients. *Psychopharmacologia, 31,* 1–12.

Anisman, H. (1978). Aversively motivated behavior as a tool in psychopharmacological analysis. In H. Anisman & G. Binami (Eds.), *Psychopharmacology of aversively motivated behavior.* New York: Plenum.

Ansbacher, H. L., & Ansbacher, R. R. (1956). *The individual-psychology of Alfred Adler.* New York: Basic Books.

Appelbaum, P. S., Jick, R. Z., Grisso, T., Givelber, D., Silver, E., & Steadman, H. J. (1993). Use of posttraumatic stress disorder to support an insanity defense. *American Journal of Psychiatry, 150,* 229–234.

Appleby, I. L., Klein, D. F., Schar, E. J., & Levitt, M. (1981). Biochemical indices of lactate-induced panic: A preliminary report. In D. F. Klein & K. Rabkin (Eds.), *Anxiety: New research and changing concepts* (pp. 411–423). New York: Raven Press.

Ardlie, N. G., Glew, G., & Schwartz, C. J. (1966). Influence of catecholamines on nucleotide-induced platelet aggregation. *Nature, 212,* 415–417.

Arieti, S. (1974). An overview of schizophrenia from a predominantly psychological approach. *American Journal of Psychiatry, 131,* 241–249.

Aring, C. D. (1974). The Gheel experience. *JAMA, 230,* 998–1002.

Arkonak, O., & Guze, S. B. (1963). A family study of hysteria. *New England Journal of Medicine, 268,* 239–242.

Asberg, M., Träskman, L., & Thoren, P. (1976). 5-HIAA in the cerebrospinal fluid: A biochemical suicide predictor? *Archives of General Psychiatry, 33,* 1193–1197.

August, G. J., & Stewart, M. A. (1982). Is there a syndrome of pure hyperactivity? *British Journal of Psychiatry, 140,* 305–311.

August, G. J., Stewart, M. A., & Holmes, C. S. (1983). A four-year follow-up of hyperactive boys with and without conduct disorder. *British Journal of Psychiatry, 143,* 192–198.

August, G. J., Stewart, M. A., & Tsai, L. (1981). The incidence of cognitive disabilities in the siblings of autistic children. *British Journal of Psychiatry, 138,* 416–422.

Avery, D. H., Bolte, M. A., Dager, S. R., Wilson, L. G., Weyer, M., Cox, G. B., & Dunner, D. L. (1993). Dawn simulation treatment of winter depression: A controlled study. *American Journal of Psychiatry, 150,* 113–117.

Avery, D. H., & Lubrano, A. (1979). Depression treated with imipramine and ECT: The De Carolis study reconsidered. *American Journal of Psychiatry, 136,* 559–562.

Ayllon, T. (1963). Intensive treatment of psychotic behavior by stimulus satiation and food reinforcement. *Behaviour Research and Therapy, 1,* 53–61.

Azerrad, J., & Stafford, R. L. (1969). Restorative eating behavior in anorexia nervosa through operant conditioning and environmental manipulation. *Behaviour Research and Therapy, 7,* 165–171.

Baastrup, P. C., Paulsen, J. C., Schou, M., Thomsen, K., & Amdisen, A. (1970). Prophylactic lithium: Double-blind discontinuation in manic depressive and recurrent depressive disorders. *Lancet, 2,* 326–330.

Bacher, N. M., & Ruskin, P. (1991). Addition of fluoxetine to treatment of schizophrenic patients. *American Journal of Psychiatry, 148,* 274–275.

Baghurst, P. A., McMichael, A. J., Wigg, N. R., Vimpani, G. V., Robertson, E. F., Roberts, R. J., & Tong, S. (1992). Environmental exposure to lead and children's intelligence at the age of seven years. *New England Journal of Medicine, 327,* 1279–1284.

Bak, R. C., & Stewart, W. A. (1974). Fetishism, transvestism, and voyeurism: A psychoanalytic approach. In S. Arieti (Ed.), *American handbook of psychiatry* (Vol. 3, pp. 352–363). New York: Basic Books.

Baker, B. L. (1969). Symptom treatment and symptom substitution in enuresis. *Journal of Abnormal Psychology, 74,* 42–49.

Baker, F. M. (1991). Cocaine psychosis. *Journal of the National Medical Association, 81,* 987–1000.

Baker, G. H. (1982). Life events before the onset of rheumatoid arthritis. *Psychotherapy and Psychosomatics, 38,* 173–177.

Bakwin, H. (1961). Enuresis in children. *Journal of Psychosomatic Research, 8,* 89–100.

Bakwin, H. (1971). Enuresis in twins. *American Journal of Diseases in Children, 121,* 221–225.

Baller, W. R. (1975). *Bed-wetting: Origin and treatment.* Elmsford, NY: Pergamon Press.

Bancroft, J. (1970). Disorders of sexual potency. In O. Hill (Ed.), *Modern trends in psychosomatic medicine* (pp. 246–259). Norwalk, CT: Appleton & Lang.

Bancroft, J. (1984a). Hormones and human sexual behavior. *Journal of Sex and Marital Therapy, 10,* 3–22.

Bancroft, J. (1984b). Testosterone therapy for low sexual interest and erectile dysfunction in men: A controlled study. *British Journal of Psychiatry, 14,* 146–151.

Bancroft, J., & Wu, F. C. (1983). Changes in erectile responsiveness during androgen therapy. *Archives of Sexual Behavior, 12,* 59–66.

Bandura, A. (1969). *Principles of behavior modification.* Austin, TX: Holt, Rinehart and Winston.

Bandura, A. (1977). Self-efficacy: Toward a unifying theory of behavioral change. *Psychological Review, 84,* 191–215.

Bandura, A. (1983). Psychosocial mechanisms of aggression. In R. G. Geen & E. I. Donnerstein (Eds.), *Aggression: Theoretical and empirical reviews, Vol. 1: Theoretical and methodological issues.* Dallas, TX: Academic Press.

Bandura, A., & Rosenthal, T. (1966). Vicarious classical conditioning as a function of arousal level. *Journal of Personality and Social Psychology, 3,* 54–62.

Bandura, A., & Walters, R. H. (1963). *Social learning and personality development.* New York: Ronald Press.

Barclay, A. (1971). Linking sexual and aggressive motives: Contributions to "irrelevant" arousals. *Journal of Personality, 39,* 481–492.

Barefoot, J. C., Dahlstrom, W. G., & Williams, R. B. (1983). Hostility, CHD incidence and total mortality: A 25-year follow-up study of 255 physicians. *Psychosomatic Medicine, 45,* 59–63.

Barfield, R., & Sachs, B. (1968). Sexual behavior: Stimulation by painful electric shock to skin in male rats. *Science, 161,* 392–395.

Barker, J. C. (1965). Behavior therapy for transvestism: A comparison of pharmacological and electrical aversion techniques. *British Medical Journal, 111,* 268–276.

Barlow, D. H. (1977). Assessment of sexual behavior. In R. A. Ciminero, K. S. Calhoun, & H. E. Adams (Eds.), *Handbook of behavioral assessment* (pp. 461–508). New York: Wiley.

Barlow, D. H. (1986). Causes of sexual dysfunction: The role of anxiety and cognitive interference. *Journal of Consulting and Clinical Psychology, 54,* 140–148.

Barr, C. E., Mednick, S. A., & Munk-Jorgensen, P. (1990). Exposure to influenza epidemics during gestation and adult schizophrenia. *Archives of General Psychiatry, 47,* 869–874.

Barsky, A. J. (1992). Psychiatric comorbidity in DSM-III-R hypochondriasis. *Archives of General Psychiatry, 49,* 101–108.

Bartak, L., Rutter, M., & Cox, A. (1975). A comparative study of infantile autism and specific developmental receptive language disorders: 1. The children. *British Journal of Psychiatry, 126,* 127–145.

Barthell, C. N., & Holmes, D. S. (1968). High school yearbooks: A nonreactive measure of social isolation in graduates who later became schizophrenic. *Journal of Abnormal Psychology, 73,* 313–316.

Barton, J. L., Mehta, S., & Snaith, R. P. (1973). The prophylactic value of extra ECT in depressive illness. *Acta Psychiatrica Scandinavica, 49,* 386–392.

Bartrop, R., Luckhurst, E., Lazarus, L., Kiloh, L., & Penney, R. (1977). Depressed lymphocyte function after bereavement. *Lancet, 1,* 834–836.

Bartus, R. T. (1990). Drugs to treat age-related neurodegenerative problems. *Journal of the American Geriatrics Society, 38,* 680–695.

Bassuk, E. L., & Schoonover, S. C. (1977). *The practitioner's guide to psychoactive drugs.* New York: Plenum.

Bateson, G., Jackson, D. D., Haley, J., & Weakland, J. (1956). Toward a theory of schizophrenia. *Behavioral Science, 1,* 251–264.

Battle, E. S., & Rotter, J. B. (1963). Children's feelings of personal control as related to social class and ethnic group. *Journal of Personality, 31,* 482–490.

Bauer, A. M., & Shea, T. M. (1984). Tourette syndrome: A review and educational implications. *Journal of Autism and Developmental Disorders, 14,* 69–80.

Bauer, R. B., Stevens, C., Reveno, W. S., & Rosenbaum, H. (1982). L-dopa treatment of Parkinson's disease: A ten-year follow-up study. *Journal of the American Geriatrics Society, 30,* 322–325.

Baum, A., Gatchel, R. J., & Schaeffer, M. A. (1983). Emotional, behavioral, and physiological effects of chronic stress at Three Mile Island. *Journal of Consulting and Clinical Psychology, 51,* 565–572.

Baxter, L. R., Phelps, M. E., Mazziotta, J. C., Schwartz, J. M., Gerner, R. H., Selin, C. E., & Sumida, R. M. (1985). Cerebral metabolic rates for glucose in mood disorders. *Archives of General Psychiatry, 42,* 441–447.

Beck, A. T. (1967). *Depression: Clinical, experimental, and theoretical aspects.* New York: HarperCollins.

Beck, A. T. (1976). *Cognitive therapy and the emotional disorders.* New York: International Universities Press.

Beck, A. T., Brown, G., Berchick, R. J., Stewart, B. L., & Strer, R. (1990). Relationship between hopelessness and ultimate suicide: A replication with psychiatric outpatients. *American Journal of Psychiatry, 147,* 190–195.

Beck, A. T., & Emery, G. (1985). *Anxiety disorders and phobias: A cognitive perspective.* New York: Basic Books.

Beck, A. T., Rush, A. J., Shaw, B. F., & Emery, G. (1979). *Cognitive therapy of depression.* New York: Guilford Press.

Beck, A. T., Steer, R., Kovacs, M., & Garrison, B. (1985). Hopelessness and eventual suicide: A 10-year prospective study of patients hospitalized with suicidal ideation. *American Journal of Psychiatry, 142,* 559–563.

Beck, A. T., Ward, C. H., Mendelson, M., Mock, J. E., & Erbaugh, J. K. (1961). An inventory for measuring depression. *Archives of General Psychology, 4,* 561–571.

Beck, A. T., Ward, C. H., Mendelson, M., Mock, J. E., & Erbaugh, J. K. (1962). Reliability of psychiatric diagnosis: 2. A study of consistency of clinical judgments and ratings. *American Journal of Psychiatry, 119,* 351–357.

Beck, A. T., Weissman, A., Lester, D., & Trexler, L. (1974). The measurement of pessimism: The hopelessness scale. *Journal of Consulting and Clinical Psychology, 42,* 861–865.

Beckman, H., & Goodwin, F. K. (1980). Urinary MHPG in subgroups of depressed patients and normal controls. *Neuropsychobiology, 6,* 91–100.

Bedau, H. A., & Radelet, M. L. (1987). Miscarriages of justice in potentially capital cases. *Stanford Law Review, 40,* 21–179.

Beere, P. A., Glagov, S., & Zarins, C. K. (1984). Retarding effect of lowered heart rate on coronary atherosclerosis. *Science, 226,* 180–182.

Bell, R. A. (1968). A reinterpretation of the direction of effects in studies of socialization. *Psychological Review, 75,* 81–95.

Bellack, A. S., & Muesler, K. T. (1992). Social skills training for schizophrenia? *Archives of General Psychiatry, 49,* 76.

Bellak, L. (1954). *The Thematic Apperception Test and the Children's Apperception Test in clinical use.* Philadelphia: Grune & Stratton.

Belmaker, R., Pollin, W., Wyatt, R. J., & Cohen, S. (1974). A follow-up of monozygotic twins discordant for schizophrenia. *Archives of General Psychiatry, 30,* 219–222.

Belsher, G., & Costello, C. G. (1991). Do confidants of depressed women provide less social support than confidants of nondepressed women? *Journal of Abnormal Psychology, 100,* 516–525.

Bemis, K. M. (1978). Current approaches to the etiology and treatment of anorexia nervosa. *Psychological Bulletin, 85,* 593–617.

Benjamin, H. (1966). *The transsexual phenomenon.* New York: Julian Press.

Bennet, I. (1960). *Delinquent and neurotic children.* London: Tavistock/Routledge.

Bennett, D., & Holmes, D. S. (1975). Influence of denial (situation redefinition) and projection on anxiety associated with threat to self-esteem. *Journal of Personality and Social Psychology, 32,* 915–921.

Bennett, D., Holmes, D. S., & Frost, R. O. (1978). Effects of instructions, biofeedback, cognitive mediation, and reward on the control of heart rate and the application of that control in a stressful situation. *Journal of Research in Personality, 12,* 416–430.

Benson, H. (1975). *The relaxation response.* New York: Morrow.

Bentall, R. P. (1990). The illusion of reality: A review and integration of psychological research on hallucinations. *Psychological Bulletin, 107,* 82–95.

Berg, G., Laberg, J. C., Skutle, A., & Ohman, A. (1981). Instructed versus pharmacological effects of alcohol in alcoholics and social drinkers. *Behaviour Research and Therapy, 19,* 55–66.

Berger, P. A., & Rexroth, K. (1980). Tardive dyskinesia: Clinical, biological, and pharmacological perspectives. *Schizophrenia Bulletin, 6,* 102–116.

Bergin, A. E., & Lambert, M. J. (1978). The evaluation of therapeutic outcomes. In S. L. Garfield & A. E. Bergin (Eds.), *Handbook of psychotherapy and behavior change* (pp. 139–189). New York: Wiley.

Berkowitz, L. (1989). Frustration-aggression hypothesis: Examination and reformulation. *Psychological Bulletin, 106,* 59–73.

Berlin, F., & Krout, E. (1986). Pedophilia: Diagnostic concepts, treatment, and ethical considerations. *American Journal of Forensic Psychiatry, 7,* 13–30.

Berlin, F., & Meinecke, C. (1981). Treatment of sex offenders with antiandrogenic medication: Conceptualization, review of treatment modalities, and preliminary findings. *American Journal of Psychiatry, 138,* 601–607.

Berman, K. F., Torrey, E. F., Daniel, D. G., & Weinberger, D. R. (1992). Regional cerebral blood flow in monozygotic twins discordant and concordant for schizophrenia. *Archives of General Psychiatry, 49,* 927–934.

Berry, H. K., Sutherland, B. S., Umbarger, B., & O'Grady, D. (1967). Treatment of phenylketonuria. *American Journal of Diseases of Childhood, 113,* 2–5.

Berscheid, E., & Walster, E. (1974). A little bit about love. In T. Huston (Ed.), *Foundations of interpersonal attraction* (pp. 355–381). Dallas, TX: Academic Press.

Bertelsen, A. (1979). A Danish twin study of manic-depressive disorders. In M. Schou & E. Stromgren (Eds.), *Origin, prevention and treatment of affective disorder* (pp. 227–239). London: Academic Press.

Bertelsen, A., Havald, B., & Hauge, M. (1977). A Danish twin study of manic-depressive disorders. *British Journal of Psychiatry, 130,* 330–351.

Bertilsson, L. (1978). Mechanism of action of benzodiazepines: The GABA hypothesis. *Acta Psychiatrica Scandinavica, 274,* 19–26.

Bettelheim, B. (1967). *The empty fortress.* New York: Free Press.

Beutler, L. E. (1991). Have all won and must all have prizes? Revisiting Luborsky et al.'s verdict. *Journal of Consulting and Clinical Psychology, 59,* 226–232.

Beutler, L. E., Crago, M., & Arizmendi, T. G. (1986). Research on therapist variables in psychotherapy. In S. L. Garfield & A. E. Bergin (Eds.), *Handbook of psychotherapy and behavior change* (pp. 257–310). New York: Wiley.

Bexton, W. H., Heron, W., & Scott, T. (1954). Effects of decreased variation in sensory environment. *Canadian Journal of Psychology, 8,* 70–77.

Bianchi, G. N. (1973). Patterns of hypochondriasis: A principal components analysis. *British Journal of Psychiatry, 122,* 541–548.

Bieber, I. (1974). Sadism and masochism: Phenomenology and psychodynamics. In S. Arieti (Ed.), *American handbook of psychiatry* (Vol. 3, pp. 316–333). New York: Basic Books.

Bihari, K., Pato, M. T., Hill, J. L., & Murphy, D. L. (1991). Neurologic soft signs in obsessive-compulsive disorder. *Archives of General Psychiatry, 48,* 278.

Billings, A. G., Cronkite, R. C., & Moos, R. H. (1983). Social-environmental factors in unipolar depression: Comparisons of depressed patients and nondepressed controls. *Journal of Abnormal Psychology, 92,* 119–133.

Billings, A. G., & Moos, R. H. (1981). The role of coping responses and social resources in attenuating the impact of stressful life events. *Journal of Behavioral Medicine, 4,* 139–157.

Biran, M., & Wilson, G. T. (1981). Treatment of phobic disorders using cognitive and exposure methods: A self-efficacy analysis. *Journal of Consulting and Clinical Psychology, 49,* 886–899.

Blackstone, E. (1978). Cerebral asymmetry and the development of early infantile autism. *Journal of Autism and Childhood Schizophrenia, 8,* 339–353.

Blackwell, B., & Currah, J. (1973). The psychopharmacology of nocturnal enuresis. In I. Kolvin, R. MacKeith, & S. Meadow (Eds.), *Bladder control in enuresis.* London: Heinemann.

Blair, C. D., & Lanyon, R. I. (1981). Exhibitionism: Etiology and treatment. *Psychological Bulletin, 89,* 439–463.

Bland, S. H., Krogh, V., Winkelstein, W., & Trevisan, M. (1991). Social network and blood pressure: A population study. *Psychosomatic Medicine, 53,* 598–607.

Blaney, P. H. (1977). Contemporary theories of depression. *Journal of Abnormal Psychology, 86,* 203–233.

Blaney, P. H. (1986). Affect and memory: A review. *Psychological Bulletin, 99,* 229–246.

Bleuler, E. (1936). *Textbook of psychiatry* (A. Brill, Trans.). New York: Macmillan.

Bleuler, E. (1950). *Dementia praecox* (J. Zinkin, Trans.). New York: International Universities Press.

Bliss, E. L. (1980). Multiple personality. *Archives of General Psychiatry, 37,* 1388–1397.

Bliss, E. L. (1984). A symptom profile of patients with multiple personalities, including MMPI results. *Journal of Nervous and Mental Disease, 171,* 197–202.

Blom, B. E., & Moore, M. C. (1978). *Mental Health Audit Criteria Series: Psychotropic drug therapies.* Chicago: Interqual.

Bloom, B. L. (1992). Computer-assisted psychological intervention: A review and commentary. *Clinical Psychology Review, 12,* 169–197.

Bloom, L., Houston, B. K., Holmes, D. S., & Burish, T. G. (1977). The effectiveness of attentional diversion and situation redefinition for reducing stress due to a nonambiguous threat. *Journal of Personality and Social Psychology, 11,* 83–94.

Blumberg, E. M., West, P. M., & Ellis, F. W. (1954). A possible relationship between psychological factors and human cancer. *Psychosomatic Medicine, 16,* 277–286.

Bock, R. D., & Kolakowski, D. (1973). Further evidence of sex-linked major-gene influence on human spatial visualizing ability. *American Journal of Genetics, 25,* 1–14.

Bohman, M., Sigvardsson, S., & Cloninger, C. R. (1981). Maternal inheritance of alcohol abuse. *Archives of General Psychiatry, 38,* 965–969.

Bollen, K. A., & Phillips, D. P. (1981). Suicidal motor vehicle fatalities in Detroit: A replication. *American Journal of Sociology, 81,* 404–412.

Bollen, K. A., & Phillips, D. P. (1982). Imitative suicides: A national study of the effects of television news stories. *American Sociological Review, 47,* 802–809.

Bond, I. K., & Hutchinson, H. C. (1960). Application of reciprocal inhibition therapy to exhibitionism. *Canadian Medical Association Journal, 83,* 23–25.

Bond, P. A., Jenner, J. A., & Sampson, D. A. (1972). Daily variation of the urine content of 3-methoxy-4-hydroxyphenylglycol in two manic-depressive patients. *Psychological Medicine, 2,* 81–85.

Borgstrom, C. A. (1939). Eine Serie von Kriminellen Zwillingen. *Archiv für Rassen- und Gesellschaftsbiologie, 33,* 334–343.

Boring, E. G. (1940). Was this analysis a success? *Journal of Abnormal and Social Psychology, 35,* 4–10.

Borkovec, T., & Sides, K. (1979). Critical procedural variables related to the physiological effects of progressive relaxation: A review. *Behavior Research and Therapy, 17,* 119–126.

Bornstein, P. E., Clayton, P. J., Halikas, J. A., Maurice, W. L., & Robins, E. (1973). The depression of widowhood after thirteen months. *British Journal of Psychiatry, 122,* 561–566.

Bostock, T., & Williams, C. L. (1975). Attempted suicide: An operant formulation. *Australian and New Zealand Journal of Psychiatry, 9,* 107–110.

Bower, E. M., Shellhamer, T. A., & Daily, J. M. (1960). School characteristics of male adolescents who later became schizophrenic. *American Journal of Orthopsychiatry, 30,* 712–729.

Bower, G. H. (1981). Mood and memory. *American Psychologist, 36,* 129–148.

Bower, G. H. (1987). Commentary on mood and memory. *Behaviour Research and Therapy, 25,* 443–455.

Bowlby, J. (1952). *Maternal care and mental health*. Geneva: World Health Organization.

Bowlby, J. (1973). *Attachment and loss*. New York: Basic Books.

Boyd, J. H., & Weissman, M. M. (1982). Epidemiology. In E. S. Paykel (Ed.), *Handbook of affective disorders* (pp. 109–125). New York: Guilford Press.

Bradbury, T. N., & Miller, G. A. (1985). Season of birth in schizophrenia: A review of evidence, methodology, and etiology. *Psychological Bulletin, 98,* 569–594.

Braden, W., Stillman, R. C., & Wyatt, R. J. (1974). Effects of marijuana on contingent negative variation and reaction times. *Archives of General Psychiatry, 31,* 537–541.

Brady, E. U., & Kendall, P. C. (1992). Comorbidity of anxiety and depression in children. *Psychological Bulletin, 111,* 244–255.

Brady, J. P., Zeller, W. W., & Reznikoff, M. (1959). Attitudinal factors influencing outcome of treatment of hospitalized psychiatric patients. *Journal of Clinical and Experimental Psychopathology, 20,* 326–334.

Braff, D. L., Grillon, C., & Geyer, M. A. (1992). Gating and habituation of the startle reflex in schizophrenic patients. *Archives of General Psychiatry, 49,* 206–215.

Braginsky, B. M., & Braginsky, D. D. (1967). Schizophrenic patients in the psychiatric interview: An experimental study of their effectiveness at manipulation. *Journal of Consulting Psychology, 21,* 543–547.

Braginsky, B. M., Braginsky, D. D., & Ring, K. (1969). *Methods of madness: The mental hospital as a last resort*. Austin, TX: Holt, Rinehart and Winston.

Braginsky, B. M., Grosse, M., & Ring, K. (1966). Controlling outcomes through impression management: An experimental study of the manipulative tactics of mental patients. *Journal of Consulting Psychology, 30,* 295–300.

Bramel, D., Bell, J., & Margulis, S. (1965). Attributing danger as a means of explaining one's fear. *Journal of Experimental Social Psychology, 1,* 267–281.

Brandsma, J. M., & Ludwig, A. M. (1974). A case of multiple personality: Diagnosis and treatment. *International Journal of Clinical and Experimental Hypnosis, 22,* 216–233.

Braucht, G. (1979). Interactional analysis of suicidal behavior. *Journal of Consulting and Clinical Psychology, 47,* 653–669.

Braude, M. C., & Szara, S. (1976). *Pharmacology of marijuana* (Vol. 2). Dallas, TX: Academic Press.

Braun, B. G. (1983a). Neurophysiologic changes in multiple personality due to integration: A preliminary report. *American Journal of Clinical Hypnosis, 26,* 84–92.

Braun, B. G. (1983b). Psychophysiologic phenomena in multiple personality and hypnosis. *American Journal of Clinical Hypnosis, 26,* 124–137.

Braun, B. G. (1984). Hypnosis creates multiple personality: Myth or reality? *International Journal of Clinical and Experimental Hypnosis, 32,* 191–197.

Breggin, P. R. (1979). *Electroshock: Its brain-disabling effects*. New York: Springer.

Brehm, S. S., & Smith, T. W. (1986). Social psychological approaches to psychotherapy and behavior change. In S. L. Garfield & A. E. Bergin (Eds.), *Handbook of psychotherapy and behavior change* (pp. 69–116). New York: Wiley.

Breier, A., & Astrachan, B. M. (1984). Characterization of schizophrenic patients who commit suicide. *American Journal of Psychiatry, 141,* 206–209.

Breier, A., Buchanan, R. W., Elkashef, A., Munson, R. C., Kirkpatrick, & Gellad, F. (1992). Brain morphology and schizophrenia: A magnetic resonance imaging study of limbic, prefrontal cortex, and caudate structures. *Archives of General Psychiatry, 49,* 921–926.

Breier, A., Schreiber, J. L., Dyer, J., & Pickar, D. (1991). National Institute of Mental Health longitudinal study of chronic schizophrenia. *Archives of General Psychiatry, 48,* 239–246.

Brenesova, V., Oswald, I., & Loudon, J. (1975). Two types of insomnia: Too much waking or not enough sleep. *British Journal of Psychiatry, 126,* 439–445.

Breslau, N., Davis, G. C., Andreski, P., & Peterson, E. (1991). Traumatic events and posttraumatic stress disorder in an urban population of young adults. *Archives of General Psychiatry, 48,* 216–222.

Breslau, N., Kilbey, M. M., & Andreski, P. (1992). Nicotine withdrawal symptoms and psychiatric disorders: Findings from an epidemiological study of young adults. *American Journal of Psychiatry, 149,* 464–469.

Breslau, N., Kilbey, M. M., & Andreski, P. (1993). Nicotine dependence and major depression: New evidence from a prospective investigation. *Archives of General Psychiatry, 50,* 31–35.

Brewer, C. (1978). Post-abortion psychosis. In M. Sandler (Ed.), *Mental illness in pregnancy and the puerperium*. Oxford: Oxford University Press.

Brewin, C. R. (1985). Depression and causal attributions: What is their relation? *Psychological Bulletin, 98,* 297–309.

Brink, M., & Grundling, E. M. (1976). Performance of persons with Down's syndrome on two projective techniques. *American Journal of Mental Deficiency, 81,* 265–270.

Bromberg, W. (1959). *The mind of man: A history of psychotherapy and psychoanalysis*. New York: HarperCollins.

Brotman, A. W., & Stern, T. A. (1983). Case study of cardiovascular abnormalities in anorexia nervosa. *American Journal of Psychiatry, 140,* 1227–1228.

Brown, F. (1942). Heredity in the psychoneuroses. *Journal of the Royal Society of Medicine, 35,* 785–790.

Brown, G. L., & Goodwin, F. K. (1986). Human aggression and suicide. *Suicide and Life-Threatening Behavior, 16,* 223–240.

Brown, G. L., Goodwin, F. K., Ballenger, J. C., et al. (1979). Aggression in humans correlates with cerebrospinal fluid amine metabolites. *Psychiatry Research, 1,* 131–139.

Brown, G. W., & Birley, J. L. T. (1968). Crises and life changes and the onset of schizophrenia. *Journal of Health and Social Behavior, 9,* 203–214.

Brown, G. W., & Harris, T. O. (1978). *Social origins of depression: A study of psychiatric disorders in women*. New York: Free Press.

Brown, G. W., Harris, T. O., & Peto, J. (1973). Life events and psychiatric disorders: 2. Nature of causal link. *Psychological Medicine, 3,* 159–176.

Brown, R. T., Wayne, M. E., & Medenis, R. (1985). Methylphenidate and cognitive therapy: A comparison of treatment with hyperactive boys. *Journal of Abnormal Child Psychology, 13,* 69–88.

Bruch, H. (1973). *Eating disorders: Obesity, anorexia nervosa, and the person within.* New York: Basic Books.

Bruch, H. (1982). Anorexia nervosa: Therapy and theory. *American Journal of Psychiatry, 139,* 1531–1538.

Buchsbaum, M. S., Haier, R. J., Potkin, S. G., Nuechterlein, K., Bracha, H. S., Katz, M., Lohr, J., Wu, J., Lottengerg, S., Jerabek, P. A., Trenary, M., Tafalla, R., Reynolds, C., & Bunney, W. E. (1992). Frontostriatal disorder of cerebral metabolism in never-medicated schizophrenics. *Archives of General Psychiatry, 49,* 935–942.

Buck, J. N. (1948). The H-P-T test. *Journal of Clinical Psychology, 4,* 151–158.

Buhrich, N. (1981). Psychological adjustment in transvestism and transsexualism. *Behavior Research and Therapy, 19,* 407–411.

Buhrich, N., Theile, H., Yaw, A., & Crawford, A. (1979). Plasma testosterone, serum FSH, and serum LH levels in transvestism. *Archives of Sexual Behavior, 8,* 49–53.

Bunch, J. (1972). Recent bereavement in relation to suicide. *Journal of Psychosomatic Research, 16,* 361–366.

Bunney, W. E., Jr. (1978). Psychopharmacology of the switch process in affective illness. In K. Killam, A. Di Mascio, & M. Lipton (Eds.), *Psychopharmacology: A generation of progress* (pp. 1249–1259). New York: Raven Press.

Bunney, W. E., Jr., & Davis, J. M. (1965). Norepinephrine in depressive reactions. *Archives of General Psychiatry, 13,* 483–494.

Bunney, W. E., Jr., & Murphy, D. L. (1976). Neurobiological considerations on the mode of action of lithium carbonate in the treatment of affective disorders. *Pharmacopsychiatry, 9,* 142–147.

Burckhardt, G. (1891). Über Rindenexcisionen als Beitrag zur operativen Therapie die Psychosen. *Algemeine Zeitschrift für Psychiatrie, 47,* 463–468.

Burish, T. G. (1981). EMG biofeedback in the treatment of stress-related disorders. In C. K. Prokop & L. A. Bradley (Eds.), *Medical psychology: Contributions to behavioral medicine* (pp. 395–421). Dallas, TX: Academic Press.

Burrows, G. D., Davies, B., Fail, L., Poynton, C., & Stevenson, H. (1976). A placebo-controlled trial of diazepam and oxprenolol for anxiety. *Psychopharmacology, 50,* 177–179.

Buss, A. H., & Lang, P. J. (1965). Psychological deficit in schizophrenia: 1. Affect, reinforcement, and concept attainment. *Journal of Abnormal Psychology, 70,* 2–24.

Busto, U., Sellers, E. M., Naranjo, C. A., Cappell, H., Sanchez-Craig, M., & Sykora, K. (1986). Withdrawal reaction after long-term therapeutic use of benzodiazepines. *New England Journal of Medicine, 315,* 854–859.

Butler, G., & Mathews, A. (1983). Cognitive processes in anxiety. *Advances in Behaviour Research and Therapy, 5,* 51–62.

Cade, J. F. (1949). Lithium salts in the treatment of psychotic excitement. *Medical Journal of Australia, 2,* 349–352.

Cadoret, R. J. (1978a). Evidence of genetic inheritance of primary affective disorder in adoptees. *American Journal of Psychiatry, 135,* 463–466.

Cadoret, R. J. (1978b). Psychopathology in adopted-away offspring of biologic parents with antisocial behavior. *Archives of General Psychiatry, 35,* 176–184.

Cadoret, R. J., & Cain, C. (1980). Sex differences in predictors of antisocial behavior in adoptees. *Archives of General Psychiatry, 37,* 1171–1175.

Cadoret, R. J., Troughton, E., O'Gorman, T. W., & Heywood, E. (1986). An adoption study of genetic and environmental factors in drug abuse. *Archives of General Psychiatry, 43,* 1131–1136.

Cadoret, R. J., Troughton, E., & Widmer, R. (1984). Clinical differences between antisocial and primary alcoholics. *Comprehensive Psychiatry, 25,* 1–8.

Calev, A., Nigal, D., Shapira, B., Tubi, N., Chazan, S., Ben-Yehuda, Y., Kugelmass, S., & Lerer, B. (1991). Early and long-term effects of electroconvulsive therapy and depression on memory and other cognitive functions. *Journal of Nervous and Mental Disease, 179,* 526–533.

Cameron, N. (1944). Experimental analysis of schizophrenic thinking. In J. S. Kasanin (Ed.), *Language and thought in schizophrenia.* New York: Norton.

Campbell, D., & Beets, J. (1978). Lunacy and the moon. *Psychological Bulletin, 85,* 1123–1129.

Campbell, D. T., & Stanley, J. C. (1963). Experimental and quasi-experimental designs for research and teaching. In N. L. Gage (Ed.), *Handbook of research on teaching.* Skokie, IL: Rand McNally.

Campbell, M., Geller, B., Small, A. M., Petti, T., & Ferris, S. (1978). Minor physical anomalies in young psychotic children. *American Journal of Psychiatry, 135,* 573–575.

Campbell, M., Rosenbloom, S., Perry, R., George, A., Kricheff, I., Anderson, L. T., Small, A. M., & Jennings, S. (1982). Computerized axial tomography in young autistic children. *American Journal of Psychiatry, 139,* 510–512.

Cannon, T. D., Mednick, S. A., & Parnas, J. (1989). Genetic and perinatal determinants of structural brain deficits in schizophrenia. *Archives of General Psychiatry, 46,* 883–889.

Cantwell, D. P. (1972). Psychiatric illness in the families of hyperactive children. *Archives of General Psychiatry, 27,* 414–417.

Cantwell, D. P. (1975a). Genetics of hyperactivity. *Journal of Child Psychology and Psychiatry, 16,* 261–264.

Cantwell, D. P. (1975b). Genetic studies of hyperactivity in children. In R. Fieve, D. Rosenthal, & H. Brill (Eds.), *Genetic research in psychiatry.* Baltimore: Johns Hopkins University Press.

Cantwell, D. P., Baker, L., & Rutter, M. (1979). Families of autistic and dysphasic children: 1. Family life and interaction patterns. *Archives of General Psychiatry, 36,* 682–687.

Caplan, L. (1984). *The insanity defense and the trial of John W. Hinckley, Jr.* Boston: Godine.

Carey, G. (1982). Genetic influences on anxiety neurosis and agoraphobia. In R. Mathew (Ed.), *The biology of anxiety* (pp. 36–50). New York: Brunner/Mazel.

Carey, G., & Gottesman, I. I. (1981). Twin and family studies of anxiety, phobic, and obsessive disorders. In D. F. Klein & J. G. Rabkin (Eds.), *Anxiety: New research and changing concepts.* New York: Raven Press.

Carey, M. P., & Burish, T. G. (1988). Etiology and treatment of the psychological side effects associated with cancer chemotherapy: A critical review and discussion. *Psychological Bulletin, 104,* 307–325.

Carlat, D. J., & Camargo, C. A. (1991). Review of bulimia nervosa in males. *American Journal of Psychiatry, 148,* 831–843.

Carling, P. J., Miller, S., Daniels, L., & Randolph, F. L. (1987). A state mental health system with no state hospital: The Vermont feasibility study. *Hospital and Community Psychiatry, 38,* 617–619.

Carlson, G. A., Kotin, J., Davenport, Y. B., & Adland, M. (1974). Follow-up of 53 bipolar manic depressive patients. *British Journal of Psychiatry, 124,* 134–139.

Carlsson, A. (1978). Antipsychotic drugs, neurotransmitters, and schizophrenia. *American Journal of Psychiatry, 135,* 164–172.

Carlsson, A., & Lindquist, M. (1963). Effect of chlorpromazine or haloperidol on the formation of 3-methroxyramine and normetaneprine in mouse brains. *Acta Pharmacologica et Toxicologica, 20,* 140–144.

Carmelli, D., Chesney, M. A., Ward, M. M., & Rosenman, R. H. (1985). Twin similarity in cardiovascular stress response. *Health Psychology, 4,* 413–423.

Caroff, S. N., Man, S. C., Lazarus, A., Sullivan, K., & MacFadden, W. (1991), Neuroleptic malignant syndrome: Diagnostic issues. *Psychiatric Annals, 21,* 147.

Carone, B. J., Harrow, M., & Westermeyer, J. F. (1991). Posthospital course and outcome in schizophrenia. *Archives of General Psychiatry, 48,* 247–253.

Carpenter, W. T., & Heinrich, D. W. (1983). Early intervention, time-limited, targeted pharmacotherapy of schizophrenia. *Schizophrenia Bulletin, 9,* 533–545.

Carroll, B. J. (1982). The dexamethasone suppression test for melancholia. *British Journal of Psychiatry, 140,* 292–304.

Carroll, D., Hewitt, J. K., Last, K. A., Turner, J. R., & Sims, J. (1985). A twin study of cardiac reactivity and its relationship to parental blood pressure. *Physiology and Behavior, 34,* 103–106.

Carson, R. C. (1984). The schizophrenias. In H. Adams & P. Sutker (Eds.), *Comprehensive handbook of psychopathology* (pp. 441–438). New York: Plenum.

Carter, C. H. (Ed.). (1975). *Handbook of mental retardation syndromes.* Springfield, IL: Thomas.

Carver, C. S., Coleman, A. E., & Glass, D. C. (1976). The coronary-prone behavior pattern and the suppression of fatigue on a treadmill test. *Journal of Personality and Social Psychology, 33,* 460–466.

Carver, C. S., & Ganellen, R. J. (1983). Depression and components of self-punitiveness: High standards, self-criticism, and overgeneralization. *Journal of Abnormal Psychology, 92,* 330–337.

Casey, R. J., & Berman, J. S. (1985). The outcome of psychotherapy with children. *Psychological Bulletin, 98,* 388–400.

Casper, R. C., Redmond, E., Katz, M. M., Schaffer, C. B., Davis, J. M., & Koslow, S. H. (1985). Somatic symptoms in primary affective disorder. *Archives of General Psychiatry, 42,* 1098–1104.

Cassiday, K. L., McNally, R. J., & Zeitlin, S. B. (1992). Cognitive processing of trauma cues in rape victims with post-traumatic stress disorder. *Cognitive Therapy and Research, 16,* 283–295.

Castaneda, R., & Franco, H. (1985). Sex and ethnic distribution of borderline personality disorder in an inpatient sample. *American Journal of Psychiatry, 142,* 1202–1203.

Centers for Disease Control. (1986). *Youth suicide surveillance.* Washington, DC: U.S. Public Health Service.

Cerletti, U., & Bini, L. (1938). L'elettroshock. *Archivio Generale di Neurologia Psichiatria e Psicoanalisi, 19,* 266–268.

Cerny, J. A. (1978). Biofeedback and the voluntary control of sexual arousal in women. *Behavior Therapy, 9,* 847–855.

Chang-Liang, R., & Denney, D. R. (1976). Applied relaxation training in self-control. *Journal of Counseling Psychology, 23,* 183–189.

Chapman, L. J., Chapman, J. P., & Miller, G. A. (1964). A theory of verbal behavior in schizophrenia. In B. A. Maher (Ed.), *Progress in experimental personality research* (Vol. 1, pp. 49–77). Dallas, TX: Academic Press.

Chapman, L. J., Chapman, J. P., & Miller, G. A. (1984). A theory of verbal behavior in schizophrenia: Postscript. In B. A. Maher (Ed.), *Contributions to the psychopathology of schizophrenia.* Dallas, TX: Academic Press.

Cheang, A., & Cooper, C. L. (1985). Psychosocial factors in breast cancer. *Stress Medicine, 1,* 61–66.

Chesney, M. A., Eagleston, J. R., & Rosenman, R. H. (1981). Type A behavior: Assessment and interventions. In C. K. Prokop & L. A. Bradley (Eds.), *Medical psychology: Contributions to behavioral medicine* (pp. 19–36). Dallas, TX: Academic Press.

Chesney, M. A., & Rosenman, R. H. (1985). *Anger and hostility in cardiovascular and behavioral disorders.* Washington, DC: Hemisphere.

Chesno, F., & Kilmann, P. (1975). Effects of stimulation intensity on sociopathic avoidance learning. *Journal of Abnormal Psychology, 84,* 144–150.

Chew, P. K., Phoon, W. H., & Mae-Lim, H. A. (1976). Epidemic hysteria among some factory workers in Singapore. *Singapore Medical Journal, 17,* 10–15.

Choptra, I. C., & Smith, J. W. (1974). Psychotic reaction following cannabis use in East Indians. *Archives of General Psychiatry, 30,* 24–27.

Christiansen, K. O. (1968). Threshold of tolerance in various population groups illustrated by results from the Danish criminologic twin study. In A. V. S. de Reuck & R. Poter (Eds.), *The mentally abnormal offender* (pp. 109–120). Boston: Little, Brown.

Clark, D. M., & Teasdale, J. D. (1985). Constraints on the effects of mood on memory. *Journal of Personality and Social Psychology, 48,* 1595–1608.

Clarke, R. V., & Lester, D. (1989). *Suicide: Closing the exits.* New York: Springer.

Clayton, P., Desmarais, L., & Winokur, G. (1968). A study of normal bereavement. *American Journal of Psychiatry, 125,* 168–178.

Cleckley, J. (1941). *The mask of sanity.* St. Louis, MO: Mosby.

Cleckley, J. (1976). *The mask of sanity* (5th ed.). St. Louis, MO: Mosby.

Cloitre, M., & Liebowitz, M. R. (1991). Memory bias in panic disorder: An investigation of the cognitive avoidance hypothesis. *Cognitive Therapy and Research, 15,* 371–386.

Clomipramine Collaborative Study Group. (1991). Clomipramine in the treatment of patients with obsessive-compulsive disorder. *Archives of General Psychiatry, 48,* 730–738.

Cloninger, C. R. (1987). Neurogenetic adaptive mechanisms in alcoholism. *Science, 236,* 410–416.

Cloninger, C. R., Bohman, M., & Sigvardsson, S. (1981). Inheritance of alcohol abuse: Cross-fostering analysis of adopted men. *Archives of General Psychiatry, 36,* 861–868.

Cloninger, C. R., Bohman, M., Sigvardsson, S., & von Korring, A. (1984). Psychopathology in adopted-out children of alcoholics. In M. Glanter (Ed.), *Recent developments in alcoholism.* New York: Plenum.

Cloninger, C. R., Martin, R., Clayton, P., et al. (1981). Blind follow-up and family study of anxiety neurosis: Preliminary analysis of the St. Louis 500. In D. F. Klein & J. G. Rabkin (Eds.), *Anxiety: New research and changing concepts.* New York: Raven Press.

Cloninger, C. R., Reich, T., & Yokoyama, S. (1983). Genetic diversity, genome organization, and investigation of the etiology of psychiatric diseases. *Psychiatric Developments, 3,* 225–246.

Clum, G. A., & Knowles, S. L. (1991). Why do some people with panic disorders become avoidant? A review. *Clinical Psychology Review, 11,* 295–313.

Cobb, S., & Rose, R. M. (1973). Hypertension, peptic ulcer and diabetes in air traffic controllers. *JAMA, 224,* 489–492.

Coccaro, E. F., & Kavoussi, R. J. (1991). Biological and pharmacological aspects of borderline personality disorder. *Hospital and Community Psychiatry, 42,* 1029–1033.

Cochrane, R., & Robertson, A. (1975). Stress in the lives of parasuicides. *Social Psychiatry, 10,* 161–172.

Cohen, A., Barlow, D., & Blanchard, E. (1985). Psychophysiology of relaxation-associated panic attacks. *Journal of Abnormal Psychology,* 94, 96–101.

Cohen, B. M., Lipinski, J., Pope, H., Harris, P., & Altesman, R. (1980). Neuroleptic blood levels and therapeutic effect. *Psychopharmacology, 70,* 191–194.

Cohen, D. J., & Leckman, J. F. (1984). Introduction to special section on Tourette's syndrome. *Journal of the American Academy of Child Psychiatry, 23,* 123–125.

Cohen, J. D., & Servan-Schreiber, D. (1992). Introduction to nerual network models in psychiatry. *Psychiatric Annals, 22,* 113–118.

Cohen, M., Badal, D., Kilpatric, A., Reed, W., & White, P. (1951). The high familial prevalence of neurocirculatory asthenia (anxiety neurosis, effort syndrome). *American Journal of Human Genetics, 3,* 126–158.

Cohen, N. J., Sullivan, S., Minde, K. K., Novak, C., & Helwig, C. (1981). Evaluation of the relative effectiveness of methylphenidate and cognitive behavior modification in the treatment of kindergarten-aged hyperactive children. *Journal of Abnormal Child Psychology, 9,* 43–54.

Cohen, S., Chiles, J., & MacNaughton, A. (1990). Weight gain associated with clozapine. *American Journal of Psychiatry, 147,* 503–504.

Cohen, S., & Stillman, R. C. (1976). *The therapeutic potential of marijuana.* New York: Plenum.

Cohen, S., & Williamson, G. M. (1991). Stress and infectious disease in humans. *Psychological Bulletin, 109,* 5–24.

Cohen, S. L., & Fiedler, J. E. (1974). Content analysis of multiple messages in suicide notes. *Suicide and Life-Threatening Behavior, 4,* 75–95.

Colby, C. A., & Gotlib, I. H. (1988). Memory deficits in depression. *Cognitive Therapy and Research, 12,* 611–627.

Cole, J. O. (1982). Antipsychotic drugs: Is more better? *McLean Hospital Journal, 7,* 61–87.

Cole, J. O., Goldberg, S. C., & Davis, J. M. (1966). Drugs in the treatment of psychosis: Controlled studies. In P.

Solomon (Ed.), *Psychiatric drugs* (pp. 153–180). Philadelphia: Grune & Stratton.

Cole, J. O., Goldberg, S. C., & Klerman, G. L. (1964). Phenothiazine treatment in acute schizophrenia. *Archives of General Psychiatry, 10,* 246–261.

Coleman, R. E. (1975). Manipulation of self-esteem as a determinant of mood of elated and depressed women. *Journal of Abnormal Psychology, 84,* 693–700.

Colligan, M. J., Pennebaker, J. W., & Murphy, L. R. (1982). *Mass psychogenic illness: A social psychological analysis.* Hillsdale, NJ: Erlbaum.

Collins, A. M., & Loftus, E. F. (1975). A spreading-activation theory of semantic processing. *Psychological Bulletin, 82,* 407–428.

Comings, D. E. (1990). *Tourette's syndrome and human behavior.* Duarte, CA: Hope Press.

Comings, D. E., & Comings, B. G. (1984). Tourette's syndrome and attention deficit disorder with hyperactivity: Are they genetically related? *Journal of the American Academy of Child Psychiatry, 23,* 126–133.

Comings, D. E., & Comings, B. G. (1990). A controlled family history study of Tourette's syndrome: I. Attention-deficit hyperactivity disorder and learning disorders. *Journal of Clinical Psychiatry, 51,* 275–280.

Congdon, M. H., Hain, J., & Stevenson, I. (1961). A case of multiple personality illustrating the transition from role playing. *Journal of Nervous and Mental Disease, 132,* 497–504.

Conger, J. J. (1951). The effects of alcohol on conflict between behavior in the albino rat. *Quarterly Journal of Studies on Alcohol, 12,* 1–29.

Conners, C. K., (1980). *Food additives and hyperactive children.* New York: Plenum.

Conners, C. K., & Werry, J. S. (1979). Pharmacotherapy. In H. C. Quay & J. S. Werry (Eds.), *Psychopathological disorders of children* (2nd ed., pp. 336–386). New York: Wiley.

Conrad, P. (1975). The discovery of hyperkinesis: Notes on the medication of deviant behavior. *Social Problems, 23,* 12–21.

Conte, H. R. (1986). Multivariate assessment of sexual dysfunction. *Journal of Consulting and Clinical Psychology, 54,* 149–157.

Conte, J. R., & Berliner, L. (1981). Sexual abuse of children: Implications for practice. *Social Casework, 62,* 601–606.

Cook, M., Mineka, S., Wolkenstein, B., & Laitsch, K. (1985). Observational conditioning of snake fear in unrelated rhesus monkeys. *Journal of Abnormal Psychology, 94,* 591–610.

Cook, T. D., & Campbell, D. T. (1979). *Quasi-experimentation: Design and analysis issues for field settings.* Skokie, IL: Rand McNally.

Coons, P. M. (1988). Psychophysiological aspects of multiple personality disorder. *Dissociation, 1,* 47–53.

Coons, P. M., Milstein, V., & Marley, C. (1982). EEG studies of two multiple personalities and a control. *Archives of General Psychiatry, 39,* 823–825.

Cooper, A. J. (1964). A case of fetishism and impotence treated by behavior therapy. *British Journal of Psychiatry, 109,* 649–652.

Cooper, M. L., Russell, M., Skinner, J. B., Frone, M. R., & Mudar, P. (1992). Stress and alcohol use: Moderating effects of gender, coping, and alcohol expectancies. *Journal of Abnormal Psychology, 101,* 139–152.

Coryell, W., Endicott, J., & Keller, M. (1991). Major depression in a nonclinical sample. *Archives of General Psychiatry, 49,* 117–125.

Coryell, W., Endicott, J., & Keller, M. (1992). Rapidly cycling affective disorder: Demographics, diagnosis, family history, and course. *Archives of General Psychiatry, 49,* 126–131.

Coryell, W., & Tsuang, M. T. (1986). Outcome after 40 years in DSM-III schizophreniform disorder. *Archives of General Psychiatry, 43,* 324–328.

Costa, E., & Greengard, P. (1975). *Mechanisms of action of benzodiazepines.* New York: Raven Press.

Costello, C. G. (1982). Fears and phobias in women: A community study. *Journal of Abnormal Psychology, 91,* 280–286.

Couchells, S. M., Johnson, S. B., Carter, R., & Walker, D. (1981). Behavioral and environmental characteristics of treated and untreated enuretic children and matched nonenuretic controls. *Journal of Pediatrics, 99,* 812–816.

Covi, L., Lipman, R., Derogatis, L. R., Smith, J. E., & Pattison, J. H. (1974). Drugs and group psychotherapy in neurotic depression. *American Journal of Psychiatry, 131,* 191–198.

Covington v. Harris, 419 F.2d 617 (D.C. Cir. 1969).

Coward, D. M., Imperato, A., Urwyler, S., & White, T. G. (1989). Biochemical and behavioural properties of clozapine. *Psychopharmacology, 99,* S6–S12.

Cox, A., Rutter, M., Newman, S., & Bartak, L. (1975). A comparative study of infantile autism and specific developmental language disorders: 2. Parental characteristics. *British Journal of Psychiatry, 126,* 146–159.

Cox, T., & Mackay, C. (1982). Psychosocial factors and psychophysiological mechanisms in the aetiology and development of cancer. *Social Science and Medicine, 16,* 381–396.

Coyne, J. C. (1976a). Depression and the response of others. *Journal of Abnormal Psychology, 85,* 186–193.

Coyne, J. C. (1976b). Toward an interactional description of depression. *Psychiatry, 39,* 14–27.

Coyne, J. C., Aldwin, C., & Lazarus, R. S. (1981). Depression and coping in stressful episodes. *Journal of Abnormal Psychology, 90,* 439–447.

Coyne, J. C., & Gotlib, I. H. (1983). The role of cognition in depression: A critical appraisal. *Psychological Bulletin, 94,* 472–505.

Craft, M. J. (1969). The natural history of psychopathic disorder. *British Journal of Psychiatry, 115,* 39–44.

Craighead, L. W., & Agras, W. S. (1991). Mechanisms of action in cognitive-behavioral and pharmacological interventions for obesity and bulimia nervosa. *Journal of Consulting and Clinical Psychology, 59,* 115–125.

Craske, M. G., & Barlow, D. H. (1989). Nocturnal panic. *Journal of Nervous and Mental Disease, 177,* 160–167.

Creese, I. (1985). Dopamine and antipsychotic medications. In R. E. Hales & A. Frances (Eds.), *Psychiatry update: The American Psychiatric Association annual review* (Vol. 4). Washington, DC: American Psychiatric Press.

Crisp, A. H. (1967). The possible significance of some behavioral correlates of weight and carbohydrate intake. *Journal of Psychosomatic Research, 11,* 117–131.

Crowe, R. R. (1974). An adoption study of antisocial personality. *Archives of General Psychiatry, 31,* 785–791.

Crowe, R. R., Pauls, D. L., Slymen, D., & Noyes, R. (1980). A family study of anxiety neurosis. *Archives of General Psychiatry, 37,* 77–79.

Crowe, R. R., Noyes, R., Pauk, D., & Sylman, D. (1983). A family study of panic disorder. *Archives of General Psychiatry, 40,* 1065–1069.

Crowley, P. H., Hayden, T. L., & Gulitai, D. K. (1982). Etiology of Down syndrome. In S. M. Pueschel & J. E. Rynders (Eds.), *Down syndrome: Advances in biomedicine and the behavioral sciences.* Cambridge, MA: Ware Press.

Cutrona, C. (1983). Causal attributions and perinatal depression. *Journal of Abnormal Psychology, 92,* 161–172.

Da Costa, J. M. (1871). On irritable heart. *American Journal of Medical Science, 61,* 17–52.

Dager, S., Saai, A. K., Comess, K. A., & Dunner, D. L. (1988). Mitral valve prolapse and the anxiety disorders. *Hospital and Community Psychiatry, 39,* 517–527.

Dalgaard, O. S., & Kringlen, E. (1976). A Norwegian twin study of criminality. *British Journal of Criminology, 16,* 213–232.

Dalton, K. (1971). Prospective study into puerperal depression. *British Journal of Psychiatry, 118,* 689–692.

Damasio, H., Maurer, R. G., Damasio, A. R., & Chui, H. (1980). Computerized tomographic scan findings in patients with autistic behavior. *Archives of Neurology, 37,* 504–510.

Damrav, F. (1963). Premature ejaculation: Use of ethyl amino benzoate to prolong coitus. *Journal of Urology, 89,* 936–939.

Danker-Brown, P., & Baucom, D. H. (1982). Cognitive influences on the development of learned helplessness. *Journal of Personality and Social Psychology, 43,* 793–801.

Dasgupta, K., & Hoover, C. E. (1990). Additional cases of suicidal ideation associated with fluoxetine. *American Journal of Psychiatry, 147,* 1570–1571.

Dattore, P. J., Shontz, F. C., & Coyne, L. (1980). Premorbid personality differentiation of cancer and noncancer groups: A test of the hypothesis of cancer proneness. *Journal of Consulting and Clinical Psychology, 48,* 388–394.

David, O. J., Clark, J., & Voeller, K. (1979). Lead and hyperactivity. *Lancet, 2,* 900–903.

Davidson, J. M. (1984). Response to "Hormones and human sexual behavior" by John Bancroft, MD. *Journal of Sex and Marital Therapy, 10,* 23–27.

Davidson, J. M., Camargo, C. A., & Smith, E. R. (1979). Effects of androgens on sexual behavior in hypogonadal men. *Journal of Clinical Endocrinology and Metabolism, 48,* 955–958.

Davies, E., & Furham, A. (1986). The dieting and body shape concerns of adolescent females. *Journal of Child Psychology and Psychiatry, 27,* 417–428.

Davis, H., & Unruh, W. R. (1981). The development of the self-schema in adult depression. *Journal of Abnormal Psychology, 90,* 125–133.

Davis, J. M. (1976a). Overview: Maintenance therapy in psychiatry: 2. Affective disorders. *American Journal of Psychiatry, 133,* 1–13.

Davis, J. M. (1976b). Recent developments in the drug treatment of schizophrenia. *American Journal of Psychiatry, 133,* 208–214.

Davis, J. M., Schaffer, C. B., Killian, G. A., Kinard, C., & Chan, C. (1980). Important issues in the drug treatment of schizophrenia. *Schizophrenia Bulletin, 6,* 70–87.

Davis, K. (1947). Final note on a case of extreme isolation. *American Journal of Sociology, 57,* 432–457.

Degreef, G., Ashari, M., Bogerts, B., Bilder, R. M., Jody, D. N., Alvir, J. M. J., & Lieberman, J. A. (1992). Volumes of ventricular system subdivisions measured from magnetic resonance images in first-episode schizophrenic patients. *Archives of General Psychiatry, 49,* 531–537.

De Leon-Jones, F., Maas, J. W., Dekirmenjian, H., & Sanchez, J. (1975). Diagnostic subgroups of affective disorders and their urinary excretion of catecholamine metabolites. *American Journal of Psychiatry, 132,* 1141–1148.

d'Elia, G., & Raotma, H. (1975). Is unilateral ECT less effective than bilateral ECT? *British Journal of Psychiatry, 126,* 83–89.

DeMyer, M. K., Hingtgen, J. N., & Jackson, R. K. (1981). Infantile autism reviewed: A decade of research. *Schizophrenia Bulletin, 7,* 388–451.

Denney, D. R., Stephenson, L. A., Penick, E., & Weller, R. (1988). Lymphocyte subclasses and depression. *Journal of Abnormal Psychology, 97,* 499–502.

Derogatis, L. (1993). *The symptom checklist series.* Minneapolis: NSC Assessments.

Derogatis, L. R., Abeloff, M. D., & Melisaratos, N. (1979). Psychological coping mechanisms and survival time in metastatic breast cancer. *JAMA, 242,* 1504–1508.

De Rubeis, R. J., Evans, M. D., Hollon, S. D., Garvey, M. J., Grove, W. M., & Tuason, V. B. (1990). How does cognitive therapy work? Cognitive change and symptoms change in cognitive therapy and pharmacotherapy for depression. *Journal of Consulting and Clinical Psychology, 58,* 862–869.

Detera-Wadleigh, S. D., Berrettini, W. H., Goldin, L. R., Boorman, D., Anderson, S., & Gershon, E. S. (1987). Close linkage of c-Harvey-ras-1 and the insulin gene to affective disorder is ruled out in three North American pedigrees. *Nature, 325,* 808–809.

Deutsch, M. (1967). The disadvantaged child. New York: Basic Books.

Devanand, D. P., Verma, A. K., Tirumalasetti, F., & Sackeim, H. A. (1991). Absence of cognitive impairment after more than 100 lifetime ECT treatments. *American Journal of Psychiatry, 148,* 929–932.

DeVeaugh-Geiss, J., Moroz, G., Biederman, J., Cantwell, D. P., Fontaine, R., Greist, J., Reichler, R., Katz, R., & Landau, P. (1992). Clomipramine hydrocholoride in childhood and adolescent obsessive-compulsive disorder: A multicenter trial. *Journal of the American Academy of Child and Adolescent Psychiatry, 31,* 45–49.

Devor, E. J. (1990). Untying the Gordian knot: The genetics of Tourette's syndrome. *Journal of Nervous and Mental Disease, 178,* 669–679.

Diamond, B. L. (1974). Psychiatric prediction of dangerousness. *University of Pennsylvania Law Review, 123,* 439–452.

Di Mascio, A., Weissman, M. M., Prusoff, B. A., Neu, C., Zwilling, M., & Klerman, G. L. (1979). Differential symptom reduction by drugs and psychotherapy in acute depression. *Archives of General Psychiatry, 36,* 1450–1456.

Doane, J. A., Falloon, R. H., Goldstein, M. J., & Mintz, J. (1985). Parental affective style and the treatment of schizophrenia. *Archives of General Psychiatry, 42,* 34–42.

Dobson, K. S. (1989). A meta-analysis of the efficacy of cognitive therapy for depression. *Journal of Consulting and Clinical Psychology, 57,* 414–419.

Dodge, K. A., & Coie, J. D. (1987). Social-information-processing factors in reactive and proactive aggression in children's peer groups. *Journal of Personality and Social Psychology, 53,* 1146–1158.

Dodge, K. A., & Somberg, D. R. (1987). Hostile attributional biases among aggressive boys are exacerbated under conditions of threats to the self. *Child Development, 58,* 213–224.

Dodge K. A., & Tomlin, A. M. (1987). Utilization of self-schemas as a mechanism of interpretational bias in children. *Social Cognition, 5,* 280–300.

Dohrenwend, B. P., & Egri, G. (1981). Recent stressful life events and episodes of schizophrenia. *Schizophrenia Bulletin, 7,* 12–23.

Dohrenwend, B. S., & Dohrenwend, B. P. (1974). *Stressful life events.* New York: Wiley.

Doleys, D. M. (1977). Behavioral treatments for nocturnal enuresis in children: A review of the recent literature. *Psychological Bulletin, 84,* 30–54.

Doleys, D. M. (1978). Assessment and treatment of enuresis and encopresis in children. In M. Hersen, R. Eisler, & P. Miller (Eds.), *Progress in behavior modification.* Dallas, TX: Academic Press.

Doleys, D. M. (1983). Enuresis and encopresis. In T. H. Ollendick & M. Hersen (Eds.), *Handbook of child psychopathology.* New York: Plenum.

Dollard, J., Doob, L., Miller, N., Mower, O., & Sears, R. (1939). *Frustration and aggression.* New Haven, CT: Yale University Press.

Donaldson, S. R., Gelenberg, A. J., & Baldessarini, R. J. (1983). The pharmacologic treatment of schizophrenia: A progress report. *Schizophrenia Bulletin, 9,* 504–526.

Douglas, J. W. (1973). Early disturbing events and later enuresis. In I. Kolvin, R. C., MacKeith, & S. Meadow (Eds.), *Bladder control and enuresis* (pp. 109–117). Philadelphia: Lippincott.

Drake, R. E., & Wallach, M. A. (1979). Will mental patients stay in the community? A social psychological perspective. *Journal of Consulting and Clinical Psychology, 47,* 285–294.

Dressler, W. W. (1991). Social support, lifestyle incongruity, and arterial blood pressure in a southern black community. *Psychosomatic Medicine, 53,* 608–620.

Dreyfuss, F., & Czaczkes, J. W. (1959). Blood cholesterol and uric acid of healthy medical students under stress of an examination. *Archives of Internal Medicine, 103,* 708–711.

Duggan, J. P., & Booth, D. A. (1986). Obesity, overeating, and rapid gastric emptying in rats with ventromedial hypothalamic lesions. *Science, 231,* 609–611.

Duncan-Jones, P., & Henderson, S. (1978). The use of a two-phase design in a prevalence survey. *Social Psychiatry, 13,* 231–237.

Durham v. United States, 214 F.2d 862 (D.C. Cir. 1954).

Durkheim, E. (1951). *Suicide* (J. A. Spaulding & G. Simpson, Trans.). New York: Free Press. (Originally published 1897)

Durlak, J. A. (1979). Comparative effectiveness of paraprofessional and professional helpers. *Psychological Bulletin, 86,* 80–92.

Durlak, J. A. (1980). Comparative effectiveness of behavioral and relationship group treatment in the secondary prevention of school maladjustment. *American Journal of Community Psychology, 8,* 327–339.

Durlak, J. A. (1981). Evaluating comparative studies of paraprofessional and professional helpers: A reply to Nietzel and Fisher. *Psychological Bulletin, 89,* 566–569.

Dusky v. United States, 362 U.S. 402 (1960).

Duszynski, K. R., Shaffer, J. W., & Thomas, C. B. (1981). Neoplasm and traumatic events in childhood: Are they related? *Archives of General Psychiatry, 38,* 327–331.

Dutton, D. G., & Aron, A. P. (1974). Some evidence for heightened sexual attraction under conditions of high anxiety. *Journal of Personality and Social Psychology, 30,* 510–517.

Duvoisin, R. C. (1984). *Parkinson's disease.* New York: Raven Press.

Dyck, M. J. (1991). Positive and negative attitudes mediating suicide ideation. *Suicide and Life-Threatening Behavior, 21,* 360–373.

Eaves, G., & Rehm, A. J. (1984). Cognitive patterns in symptomatic and remitted unipolar major depression. *Journal of Abnormal Psychology, 93,* 31–40.

Eberhard, G. (1968). Personality in peptic ulcer: Preliminary report of a twin study. *Acta Psychiatrica Scandinavica, 203,* 131.

Eckert, E. D., Goldberg, S. C., Halmi, K. A., Casper, R. C., & Davis, J. M. (1982). Depression in anorexia nervosa. *Psychological Medicine, 12,* 115–122.

Edwards, A. J., Bacon, T. H., Elms, C. A., Verardi, R., Felder, M., & Knight, S. C. (1984). Changes in the populations of lymphoid cells in human peripheral blood following physical exercise. *Clinical and Experimental Immunology, 58,* 420–427.

Egeland, J. A., Gerhard, D. S., Pauls, D. L., Sussex, J. N., Kidd, K. K., Allen, C. R., Hostetter, A. M., & Housman, D. E. (1987). Bipolar affective disorders linked to DNA markers on chromosome 11. *Nature, 325,* 783–787.

Ehrenkranz, J., Bliss, E., & Sheard, M. (1974). Plasma testosterone: Correlations with aggressive behavior and social dominance. *Psychosomatic Medicine, 36,* 469–476.

Ehrhardt, A., Epstein, R., & Money, J. (1968). Fetal androgens and female gender identity in the early-treated andrenogenital syndrome. *Johns Hopkins Medical Journal, 122,* 160–167.

Ehrhardt, A., & Money, J. (1967). Progestin-induced hermaphroditism: IQ and psychosexual identity in a study of ten girls. *Journal of Sex Research, 3,* 53–100.

Eisenberg, L., & Kanner, L. (1956). Early infantile autism, 1943–1955. *American Journal of Orthopsychiatry, 26,* 556–566.

Elashoff, J. D., & Snow, R. E. (1971). *Pygmalion reconsidered.* Worthington, OH: Jones.

Elkin, I., Parloff, M. B., Hadley, S. W., & Autry, J. H. (1985). NIMH Treatment of Depression Collaborative Research Program: Background and research plan. *Archives of General Psychiatry, 42,* 305–316.

Elkin, I., Shea, M. T., Watkins, J. T., Imber, S. D., Sotsky, S. M., Collins, J. F., Glass, D. R., Pilkonis, P. A., Leber, W. R., Kocherty, J. P., Fiester, S. J., & Parloff, M. B. (1989). National Institute of Mental Health Treatment of Depression Collaborative Research Program. *Archives of General Psychiatry, 46,* 971–982.

Elkins, R. (1991). An appraisal of chemical aversion (emetic therapy) approaches to alcoholism treatment. *Behavioral Research and Therapy, 29,* 387–411.

Ellingson, R. J. (1954). The incidence of EEG abnormality among patients with mental disorders of apparently nonorganic origin: A critical review. *American Journal of Psychiatry, 111,* 263–275.

Ellis, A. (1962). *Reason and emotion in psychotherapy.* Secaucus, NJ: Lyle Stuart.

Ellis, A., & Grieger, R. (1977). *Handbook of rational emotive therapy* (Vol. 1). New York: Springer.

Ellis, A., & Grieger, R. (1986). *Handbook of rational emotive therapy* (Vol. 2). New York: Springer.

Emmelkamp, P. M. (1982). *Phobic and obsessive-compulsive disorders: Theory, research, and practice.* New York: Plenum.

Emmelkamp, P. M. (1986). Behavior therapy with adults. In S. L. Garfield & A. E. Bergin (Eds.), *Handbook of psychotherapy and behavior change.* New York: Wiley.

Engel, G. (1970). Conversion symptoms. In C. MacBryde & R. Blacklow (Eds.), *Signs and symptoms: Applied pathologic physiology and clinical interpretation.* Philadelphia: Lippincott.

Engelhardt, D., Polizos, P., & Margolis, R. A. (1970). *Psychological syndromes responsive to pharmacotherapy: Autism and schizophrenic behavior.* Paper presented at the Symposium on Psychopharmacology in Children, Framingham, MA.

Enna, S. J., & De France, J. F. (1980). Clycine, GABA and benzodiazepine receptors. In S. J. Enna & H. I. Yamamura (Eds.), *Neurotransmitter receptors* (Pt. 1, pp. 43–70). London: Chapman & Hall.

Ennis, B. J., & Litwack, T. R. (1974). Psychiatry and the presumption of expertise: Flipping coins in the courtroom. *California Law Review, 62,* 693–752.

Erickson, J. D., & Bjerkedal, T. O. (1981). Down syndrome associated with father's age in Norway. *Journal of Medical Genetics, 18,* 22–28.

Ernster, V. L., Sacks, S. T., Selvin, S., & Petrakis, N. L. (1979). Cancer incidence by marital status: U.S. third national cancer survey. *Journal of the National Cancer Institute, 63,* 567–578.

Estes, W. K. (1991). Cognitive architectures from the standpoint of an experimental psychologist. *Annual Review of Psychology, 42,* 1–28.

Etzel, B. C., Hineline, P. N., Iwata, B. A., Johnston, J. M., Lindsley, O. R., McGrale, J. E., Morris, E. K., & Pennypacker, H. S. (1987). The ABA Humanitarian Awards for Outstanding Achievement in Pursuit of the Right to Effective Treatment. *Behavior Analyst, 10,* 235–237.

Etzersdorfer, E., Sonneck, G., & Nagel-Fuess, S. (1992). Newspaper reports and suicide. *New England Journal of Medicine, 327,* 502–550.

Evans, R. L. (1981). New drug evaluations: Alprazolam. *Drug Intelligence and Clinical Pharmacy, 15,* 633–637.

Exner, J. E. (1978). *The Rorschach: A comprehensive system: Vol. 2. Current research and advanced interpretation.* New York: Wiley.

Eysenck, H. J. (1961). The effects of psychotherapy. In H. J. Eysenck (Ed.), *Handbook of abnormal psychology* (pp. 697–725). New York: Basic Books.

Eysenck, M. W., Mogg, K., May, J., Richards, A., & Mathews, A. (1991). Bias in interpretation of ambiguous sentences related to threat in anxiety. *Journal of Abnormal Psychology, 100,* 144–150.

Faedda, G. L., Tondo, L., Teicher, M. H., Baldessarini, R. J., Gelbard, H. A., & Floris, G. F. (1993). Seasonal mood disorders: Patterns of seasonal recurrence in mania and depression. *Archives of General Psychiatry, 50,* 17–23.

Fagan, P. J., Meyer, J. K., & Schmidt, C. W. (1986). Sexual dysfunction with an adult developmental perspective. *Journal of Sex and Marital Therapy, 12,* 243–257.

Fahy, T. A. (1988). The diagnosis of multiple personality disorder: A critical review. *British Journal of Psychiatry, 153,* 597–606.

Falconer, D. S. (1960). *Introduction to quantitative genetics.* New York: Ronald Press.

Falloon, I. R., Boyd, J. L., McGill, C. W., Williamson, M., Razani, J., Moss, H. B., Gilderman, A. M., & Simpson, G. M. (1985). Family management in the prevention of morbidity of schizophrenia. *Archives of General Psychiatry, 42,* 887–896.

Faraone, S. V., Kremen, W. S., & Tsuang, M. T. (1990). Genetic transmission of major affective disorders: Quantitative models and linkage analyses. *Psychological Bulletin, 108,* 109–127.

Farberow, N. L., & Simon, M. D. (1969). Suicide in Los Angeles and Vienna: An intercultural study of two cities. *Public Health Reports, 84,* 389–403.

Farberow, N. L., & Simon, M. D. (1975). Suicide in Los Angeles and Vienna. In N. L. Farberow (Ed.), *Suicide in different cultures* (pp. 185–204). Baltimore: University Park Press.

Farberow, N. L., & Shneidman, E. S. (1961). *The cry for help.* New York: McGraw-Hill.

Farde, L., Wiesel, F., Halldin, C., & Sedvall, G. (1988). Central D2-dopamine receptor occupancy in schizophrenic patients treated with antipsychotic drugs. *Archives of General Psychiatry, 45,* 71–76.

Faris, R. (1934). Cultural isolation and the schizophrenic personality. *American Journal of Sociology, 40,* 155–169.

Faris, R., & Dunham, R. M. (1939). *Mental disorders in urban areas: An ecological study of schizophrenia and other psychoses.* Chicago: University of Chicago Press.

Fein, D., Skoff, B., & Mirsky, A. (1981). Clinical correlates of brainstem dysfunction in autistic children. *Journal of Autism and Developmental Disorders, 11,* 305–315.

Feingold, B. F. (1975). *Why your child is hyperactive.* New York: Random House.

Feingold, B. F. (1976). Hyperkinesis and learning disabilities linked to the ingestion of artificial food colors and flavors. *Journal of Learning Disabilities, 9,* 551–559.

Fenichel, O. (1945). *The psychoanalytic theory of neuroses.* New York: Norton.

Ferster, C. B. (1961). Positive reinforcement and behavioral deficits of autistic children. *Child Development, 32,* 437–456.

Ferster, C. B. (1973). A functional analysis of depression. *American Psychologist, 28,* 857–870.

Finegan, J., & Quarrington, B. (1979). Pre-, peri-, and neonatal factors and infantile autism. *Journal of Child Psychology and Psychiatry, 20,* 119–128.

Fink, M. (1979). *Convulsive therapy: Theory and practice.* New York: Raven Press.

Fink, M., Taylor, M. A., & Volavka, J. (1970). Anxiety precipitated by lactate. *New England Journal of Medicine, 281,* 1429.

Finn, P. R., Zeitouni, N. C., & Pihl, R. O. (1990). Effects of alcohol on physiophysiological hyperreactivity to nonaversive and aversive stimuli in men at high risk for alcoholism. *Journal of Abnormal Psychology, 99,* 79–85.

Fiore, M. C., Jorenby, D. E., Baker, T. B., & Kenford, S. L. (1992). Tobacco dependence and the nicotine patch. *JAMA, 268,* 2687–2694.

Fischer, M. (1971). Psychoses in the offspring of schizophrenic monozygotic twins and their normal co-twins. *British Journal of Psychiatry, 118,* 43–52.

Fischer, M. (1973). Genetic and environmental factors in schizophrenia: A study of schizophrenic twins and their families. *Acta Psychiatrica Scandinavica* (Suppl. 238).

Fischer, M., Barkley, R. A., Edelbrock, C. S., & Smallish, L. (1990). The adolescent outcome of hyperactive children diagnosed by research criteria: II. Academic, attentional, and neuropsychological status. *Journal of Consulting and Clinical Psychology, 58,* 580–588.

Fish, B., & Ritvo, E. R. (1979). Psychoses of childhood. In J. D. Noshpitz (Ed.), *Basic handbook of child psychiatry* (pp. 249–304). New York: Basic Books.

Fisher, C., Schiavi, R. C., Edwards, A., Davis, D. M., Reitman, M., & Fine, J. (1979). Evaluation of nocturnal penile tumescence in the differential diagnosis of sexual impotence. *Archives of General Psychiatry, 36,* 431–437.

Fluoxetine Bulimia Nervosa Collaborative Study Group. (1992). Flouxetine in the treatment of bulimia nervosa. *Archives of General Psychiatry, 49,* 139–147.

Fodor, O., Vestea, S., & Urcan, S. (1968). Hydrochloric acid secretion capacity of the stomach as an inherited factor in the pathogenesis of duodenal ulcer. *American Journal of Digestive Diseases, 13,* 260–265.

Folkman, S., & Lazarus, R. S. (1980). Coping in an adequately functioning middle-aged population. *Journal of Health and Social Behavior, 19,* 219–239.

Folland, S. S. (1975). *Suspect toluene exposure at a boot factory.* Internal report, Tennessee Department of Health.

Folstein, S. E. (1991). Etiology of autism: Genetic influences. *Journal of Child Psychology and Psychiatry, 31,* 99–119.

Folstein, S. E., & Rutter, M. (1977). Infantile autism: A genetic study of 21 twin pairs. *Journal of Child Psychology and Psychiatry, 18,* 297–321.

Fonda, J. (1981). *Jane Fonda's workout book.* New York: Simon & Schuster.

Fontana, A. F., Kerns, R. D., Rosenberg, R. L., & Colonese, K. L. (1989). Support, stress, and recovery from coronary heart disease: A longitudinal causal model. *Health Psychology, 8,* 175–193.

Forgac, G. E., & Michaels, E. J. (1982). Personality characteristics of two types of male exhibitionists. *Journal of Abnormal Psychology, 91,* 287–293.

Forssman, H. (1970). Klinefelter's syndrome. *British Journal of Psychiatry, 117,* 35–37.

Fox, B. H. (1978). Premorbid psychological factors as related to cancer incidence. *Journal of Behavioral Medicine, 1,* 45–133.

Frank, E. (1991). Interpersonal psychotherapy as a maintenance treatment for patients with recurrent depression. *Psychotherapy, 28,* 259–266.

Frank, E., Kupfer, D. J., & Perel, J. M. (1989). Early recurrence in unipolar depression. *Archives of General Psychiatry, 46,* 771–775.

Frank, E., Kupfer, D. J., Perel, T. M., Cornes, C. L., Jarrett, D. J., Mallinger, A., Tase, M. E., McEachran, A. B., & Grochocini, V. J. (1990). Three-year outcomes for maintenance therapies in recurrent depression. *Archives of General Psychiatry, 47,* 1093–1099.

Frank, E., Kupfer, D. J., Wanger, E. F., McEachran, A. B., & Cornes, C. L. (1991). Efficacy in interpersonal psychotherapy as a maintenance treatment for recurrent depression: Contribution factors. *Archives of General Psychiatry, 48,* 1053–1059.

Frank, J. D. (1982). Therapeutic components shared by all psychotherapies. In J. H. Harvey & M. M. Parks (Eds.), *Psychotherapy research and behavior change* (Vol. 1). Washington, DC: American Psychological Association.

Freed, E. X. (1971). Anxiety and conflict: Role of drug-dependent learning in the rat. *Quarterly Journal of Studies on Alcohol, 32,* 13–29.

Freedman, B. J. (1974). The subjective experience of perceptual and cognitive disturbances in schizophrenia. *Archives of General Psychiatry, 30,* 333–340.

Freedman, B. J., & Chapman, L. J. (1973). Early subjective experience in schizophrenic episodes. *Journal of Abnormal Psychology, 82,* 46–54.

Freeman, T. (1971). Observations on mania. *International Journal of Psychoanalysis, 52,* 479–486.

Fremming, G. H. (1951). *The expectation of mental infirmity in a sample of the Danish population* (Occasional Papers on Eugenics No. 7). London: Eugenics Society.

Freud, A. (1946). *The ego and the mechanisms of defense.* New York: International Universities Press.

Freud, S. (1953). Three esays on the theory of sexuality. In J. Strachey & A. Freud (Eds.), *The standard edition of the complete psychological works of Sigmund Freud* (Vol. 7, pp. 125–331). London: Hogarth Press. (Originally published 1905)

Freud, S. (1955). Beyond the pleasure principle. In J. Strachey & A. Freud (Eds.), *The standard edition of the complete psychological works of Sigmund Freud* (Vol. 18, pp. 7–64). London: Hogarth Press. (Originally published 1920)

Freud, S. (1955). A child is being beaten. In J. Strachey & A. Freud (Eds.), *The standard edition of the complete psychological works of Sigmund Freud* (Vol. 17, pp. 179–204). London: Hogarth Press. (Originally published 1919)

Freud, S. (1955). The economic problems of masochism. In J. Strachey & A. Freud (Eds.), *The standard edition of the complete psychological works of Sigmund Freud* (Vol. 19). London: Hogarth Press. (Originally published 1925)

Freud, S. (1955). Instincts and their vicissitudes. In J. Strachey & A. Freud (Eds.), *The standard edition of the complete psychological works of Sigmund Freud* (Vol. 14, pp. 109–140). London: Hogarth Press. (Originally published 1915)

Freud, S. (1955). Mourning and melancholia. In J. Strachey & A. Freud (Eds.), *The standard edition of the complete psychological works of Sigmund Freud* (Vol. 14, pp. 237–243). London: Hogarth Press. (Originally published 1911)

Freud, S. (1957). The interpretation of dreams. In J. Strachey & A. Freud (Eds.), *The standard edition of the complete psychological works of Sigmund Freud* (Vol. 4, pp. 1–338). London: Hogarth Press. (Originally published 1900)

Freud, S. (1959). Inhibitions, symptoms and anxiety. In J. Strachey & A. Freud (Eds.), *The standard edition of the complete psychological works of Sigmund Freud* (Vol. 20, pp. 87–174). London: Hogarth Press. (Originally published 1926)

Frick, P. J., Lahey, B. B., Loeber, R., Stouthamer-Lober, M., Christ, M. A., & Hanson, K. (1992). Familial risk factors to oppositional defiant disorder and conduct disorder: Parental psychopathology and maternal parenting. *Journal of Consulting and Clinical Psychology, 60,* 49–55.

Frieberg, J. (1975, August). Electroshock therapy: Let's stop blasting the brain. *Psychology Today,* pp. 18–23.

Friedman, A. S. (1975). Interaction of drug therapy with marital therapy in depressed patients. *Archives of General Psychiatry, 32,* 619–637.

Friedman, M., & Rosenman, R. H. (1959). Association of specific overt behavior pattern with blood and cardiovascular findings: Blood cholesterol level, blood clotting time, incidence of arcus senilis and clinical coronary artery disease. *JAMA, 169,* 1286–1296.

Friedman, M., & Rosenman, R. H. (1974). *Type A behavior and your heart.* New York: Knopf.

Friedman, M., Rosenman, R. H., & Carroll, V. (1958). Changes in the serum cholesterol and blood clotting time in men subjected to cyclic variation of occupational stress. *Circulation, 17,* 852–861.

Friedman, M., Thoresen, C. E., Gill, J. J., Powell, L. H., Ulmer, D., Thompson, L., Price, V. A., Rabin, D. D., Breall, W. S., Dixon, T., Levy, R., & Bourg, E. (1984). Alteration of Type A behavior and reduction in cardiac recurrences in postmyocardial infarction patients. *American Heart Journal, 108,* 237–248.

Friedman, M., & Ulmer, D. (1984). *Treating Type A behavior and your heart.* New York: Knopf.

Fromm-Reichmann, F. (1948). Notes on the development of treatment of schizophrenics by psychoanalytic psychotherapy. *Psychiatry, 11,* 263–273.

Fromm-Reichmann, F. (1954). Psychotherapy of schizophrenia. *American Journal of Psychiatry, 111,* 410–419.

Frost, R., Goolkasian, G., Ely, R., & Blanchard, F. (1982). Depression, restraint and eating behavior. *Behaviour Research and Therapy, 20,* 113–122.

Frost, R., Graf, M., & Becker, J. (1979). Self-devaluation and depressed mood. *Journal of Consulting and Clinical Psychology, 47,* 958–962.

Frost, R. O., & Green, M. (1982). Velten Mood Induction Procedure effects: Duration and post-experimental removal. *Personality and Social Psychology Bulletin, 8,* 341–348.

Frost, R. O., Morgenthau, J. E., Riessman, C. K., & Whalen, M. (1986). Somatic response to stress, physical symptoms and health service use. *Behaviour Research and Therapy, 24,* 569–576.

Fry, P. (1989). Mediators of perceptions of stress among community-based elders. *Psychological Reports, 65,* 307–314.

Fuchs, C. Z., & Rehm, L. P. (1977). A self-control behavior therapy program for depression. *Journal of Consulting and Clinical Psychology, 45,* 206–215.

Fuller, B. (1986). *Parents sue agency head for $15 million* [Press release]. United Press International, Aug. 7, A.M. cycle.

Furby, L., Weinrott, M. R., & Blackshaw, L. (1989). Sex offender recidivism: A review. *Psychological Bulletin, 105,* 3–30.

Furst, S. S., & Ostow, M. (1979). The psychodynamics of suicide. In L. D. Hankoff & B. Einsidler (Eds.), *Suicide: Theory and clinical aspects* (pp. 165–178). Acton, MA: Publishing Sciences Group.

Gaist, P. A., Obarzanek, E., Skwerer, R., Duncan, G., Connie, C., Shultz, P. M., & Rosenthal, N. E. (1990). Effects of bright light on resting metabolic rate in patients with seasonal affective disorder and control subjects. *Biological Psychiatry, 28,* 989–996.

Galin, D., Diamond, R., & Braff, D. (1977). Lateralization of conversion symptoms: More frequent on the left. *American Journal of Psychiatry, 134,* 578–580.

Gange, P. (1981). Treatment of sex offenders with MPA. *American Journal of Psychiatry, 138,* 644–646.

Ganzini, L., McFarland, B. H., & Cutler, D. (1990). Prevalence of mental disorders after catastrophic financial loss. *Journal of Nervous and Mental Disease, 178,* 680–685.

Garb, H. N. (1985). The incremental validity of information used in personality assessment. *Clinical Psychology Review, 4,* 641–655.

Gardner, D. L., & Cowdry, R. W. (1985). Alprazolam-induced dyscontrol in borderline personality disorder. *American Journal of Psychiatry, 142,* 98–100.

Garfield, S. L. (1986). Research on client variables in psychotherapy. In S. L. Garfield & A. E. Bergin (Eds.), *Handbook of psychotherapy and behavior change* (pp. 213–256). New York: Wiley.

Garner, D. M., Garfinkel, P. E., Schwartz, D., & Thompson, M. (1980). Cultural expectations of thinness in women. *Psychological Reports, 47,* 483–491.

Gawin, F. H. (1989). Neuroleptic reduction of cocaine-induced paranoia but not euphoria. *Psychopharmacology, 91,* 142–143.

Geen, R. G. (1990). *Human aggression.* Pacific Grove, CA.: Brooks/Cole.

Geer, J. H., & Fuhr, R. (1976). Cognitive factors in sexual arousal: The role of distraction. *Journal of Consulting and Clinical Psychology, 44,* 238–243.

Gelenberg, A. (1983). Laryngopharyngeal dystonias. *Massachusetts General Hospital Biological Treatments in Psychiatry Newsletter, 6,* 3.

Gelernter, C. S., Uhde, T. W., Cimbolic, P., Arnkoff, D. B., Vittone, B. J., Tancer, M. E., & Bartko, J. J. (1991). Cognitive-behavioral and pharmacological treatments of social phobia. *Archives of General Psychiatry, 48,* 938–945.

Geller, M. I., Kelly, J. A., Traxler, W. T., & Marone, I. J.

(1978). Behavioral treatment of an adolescent female's bulimic anorexia: Modification of immediate consequences and antecedent conditions. *Journal of Clinical Child Psychology, 14,* 138–141.

Gerin, W., Pieper, C., Levy, R. & Pickering, T. G. (1992). Social support in social interaction: A moderator of cardiovascular reactivity. *Psychosomatic Medicine, 54,* 324–336.

Gerner, R. H., & Hare, T. A. (1981). CSF GABA in normal subjects and patients with depression, schizophrenia, mania, and anorexia nervosa. *American Journal of Psychiatry, 137,* 1098–1101.

Gershon, E. S., Miron, B., & Leckman, J. F. (1975). Genetic models of the transmission of affective disorders. *Journal of Psychiatric Research, 12,* 301–317.

Giansante, L. (1988). *The Morning Show,* National Public Radio, Feb. 5.

Gibbens, T. C., Pond, D. A., & Stafford-Clark, D. (1955). A follow-up study of criminal psychopaths. *British Journal of Delinquency, 5,* 126–136.

Gibbs, M. V., & Thorpe, J. G. (1983). Personality stereotype of non-institutionalized Down's syndrome children. *American Journal of Mental Deficiency, 87,* 601–605.

Gilberg, C. (1980). Maternal age and infantile autism. *Journal of Autism and Developmental Disorders, 10,* 293–297.

Gilberg, C. (1984). Infantile autism and other childhood psychoses in a Swedish urban region: Epidemiological aspects. *Journal of Child Psychology and Psychiatry, 25,* 35–43.

Gilberg, C., & Gilberg, I. C. (1983). Infantile autism: A total population study of reduced optimality in the pre-, peri-, and neonatal period. *Journal of Autism and Developmental Disorders, 13,* 153–166.

Gilberg, C., Rosenhall, U., & Johansson, E. (1983). Auditory brainstem responses in childhood psychosis. *Journal of Autism and Developmental Disorders, 13,* 181–195.

Gilberg, C., & Schaumann, H. (1982). Social class and infantile autism. *Journal of Autism and Developmental Disorders, 12,* 223–228.

Gilbert, R. M. (1976). Caffeine, a drug of abuse. In R. J. Gibbins, Y. Israel, H. Kalant, R. Popham, W. Schmidt, & R. Smart (Eds.), *Research advances in alcohol and drug problems* (Vol. 3). New York: Wiley.

Gillin, J. C., Rapoport, J. L., Mikkelsen, E. J., Langer, D., Vansleiver, C., & Mendelson, W. (1982). EEG sleep patterns in enuresis: A further analysis and comparison with controls. *Biological Psychiatry, 17,* 947–953.

Ginsberg, H. (1972). *The myth of the deprived child.* Englewood Cliffs, NJ: Prentice Hall.

Gist, R., & Welch, Q. B. (1989). Certification change versus actual behavior change in teenage suicide rates, 1955–1979. *Suicide and Life-Threatening Behavior, 19,* 277–288.

Gittelman, R., & Kanner, A. (1986). Psychopharmacotherapy. In H. C. Quay & J. S. Werry (Eds.), *Psychopathological disorders of childhood* (3rd ed., pp. 455–494). New York: Wiley.

Gittelman-Klein, R., Klein, D. F., Abikoff, H., Katz, S., Gloisten, A., & Kates, W. (1976). Relative efficacy of methylphenidate and behavior modification in hyperactive children: An interim report. *Journal of Abnormal Child Psychology, 4,* 461–472.

Glass, D. C. (1977). *Behavior patterns, stress, and coronary disease.* Hillsdale, NJ: Erlbaum.

Glazer, H. I., & Weiss, J. M. (1976). Long-term interference effect: An alternative to "learned helplessness." *Journal of Experimental Psychology: Animal Behavioral Processes, 2,* 202–213.

Goetzl, U. J., Green, R., Shybrow, P., & Jackson, R. (1974). X-linkage revisited (a further family study of manic-depressive illness). *Archives of General Psychiatry, 31,* 665–672.

Goff, D. C., Brotman, A. W., Waites, M., & McCormick, S. (1990). Trial of fluoxetine added to neuroleptics for treatment-resistant schizophrenic patients. *American Journal of Psychiatry, 147,* 492–494.

Goffman, E. (1961). *Asylums: Essays on the social situation of mental patients and other inmates.* Garden City, NY: Doubleday.

Gold, B. I., Bowers, M. B., Roth, R. H., & Sweeney, D. W. (1980). GABA levels in CSF of patients with psychiatric disorders. *American Journal of Psychiatry, 137,* 362–364.

Goldberg, D. C., Whipple, B., Fishkin, R. E., Waxman, H., & Fink, P. J. (1983). The Grafenberg spot and female ejaculation: A review of initial hypotheses. *Journal of Sex and Marital Therapy, 9,* 27–37.

Goldberg, S., Frosch, W., Drossman, A., Schooler, N., & Johnson, G. (1972). Prediction of response to phenothiazines in schizophrenia: A cross-validation study. *Archives of General Psychiatry, 26,* 367–373.

Golden, C. J., Hammecke, T., & Purisch, A. (1978). Diagnostic validity of a standardized neuropsychological battery derived from Luria's neuropsychological test. *Journal of Consulting and Clinical Psychology, 46,* 1258–1265.

Goldfried, M. R., & Trier, C. S. (1974). Effectiveness of relaxation as an active coping skill. *Journal of Abnormal Psychology, 83,* 348–355.

Goldgaber, D., Lerman, M., McBride, O., Saffiotti, U., & Gajdusek, D. (1987). Characterization and chromosomal localization of a cDNA encoding brain amyloid of Alzheimer's disease. *Science, 235,* 877–880.

Golding, J. M., Smith, R., & Kashner, M. (1991). Does somatization disorder occur in men? *Archives of General Psychiatry, 48,* 321–235.

Goldman, H. H., Adams, N. H., & Taube, C. A. (1983). Deinstitutionalization: The data demythologized. *Hospital and Community Psychiatry, 34,* 129–134.

Goldman, M. S., Brown, S. A., Christiansen, B. A., & Smith, G. T. (1991). Alcoholism and memory: Broadening the scope of alcohol-expectancy research. *Psychological Bulletin, 110,* 137–146.

Goldman, R. D., & Hartig, L. K. (1976). The WISC may not be a valid predictor of school performance for primary grade minority children. *American Journal of Mental Deficiency, 80,* 583–587.

Goldstein, M. J. (1980). Family therapy during the aftercare treatment of acute schizophrenia. In J. S. Strauss, M. Bowers, T. W. Dowey, S. Fleck, S. Jackson, & I. Levine (Eds.), *The psychotherapy of schizophrenia.* New York: Plenum.

Goldstein, M. J., & Rodnick, E. H. (1975). The family's contribution to the etiology of schizophrenia: Current status. *Schizophrenia Bulletin, 14,* 48–63.

Goodkin, K., Antoni, M. H., & Blaney, P. H. (1986). Stress and hopelessness in the promotion of cervical intraepithelial neoplasia to invasive squamous cell carcinoma of the cervix. *Journal of Psychosomatic Research, 30,* 67–76.

Goodman, S. H., & Emory, E. K. (1992). Perinatal complications in births to low socioeconomic status schizophrenic and depressed women. *Journal of Abnormal Psychology, 101,* 225–229.

Goodwin, A., & Williams, J. (1982). Mood-induction research: Its implications for clinical depression. *Behavior Research and Therapy, 20,* 373–382.

Goodwin, D. W. (1985a). Alcoholism and genetics. *Archives of General Psychiatry, 42,* 171–174.

Goodwin, D. W. (1985b). Genetic determinants of alcoholism. In J. H. Mendelson & N. K. Mello (Eds.), *The diagnosis and treatment of alcoholism* (pp. 65–88). New York: McGraw-Hill.

Goodwin, J. (1980). The etiology of combat-related post-traumatic stress disorders. In T. Williams (Ed.), *Post-traumatic stress disorders of the Vietnam veteran.* Cincinnati, OH: Disabled American Veterans.

Gordon, R. E., Kapostins, E. E., & Gordon, K. K. (1965). Factors in postpartum emotional adjustment. *Obstetrics and Gynecology, 25,* 158–166.

Gordon, W., Friedenbergs, I., Diller, L., Hibbard, M., Wolf, C., Levine, L., Lipkins, R., Ezrachi, O., & Lucido, D. (1980). Efficacy of psychosocial interventions with cancer patients. *Journal of Consulting and Clinical Psychology, 48,* 743–759.

Gorman, J. M. (1984). The biology of anxiety. In L. Grinspoon (Ed.), *Psychiatry update: The American Psychiatric Association annual review* (Vol. 3, pp. 467–482). Washington, DC: American Psychiatric Association.

Gorman, J. M., Goetz, R. R., Fyer, M., King, D. L., Fyer, A. J., Liebowitz, M. R., & Klein, D. F. (1988). The mitral valve prolapse-panic disorder connection. *Psychosomatic Medicine, 50,* 114–122.

Gorman, J. M., Liebowitz, M. R., Fyer, A. J., Dillon, D., Davies, S., Stein, J., & Klein, D. F. (1985). Lactate infusions in obsessive-compulsive disorders. *American Journal of Psychiatry, 142,* 864–866.

Gotlib, I. H., & Robinson, L. A. (1982). Responses to depressed individuals: Discrepancies between self-report and observer-rated behavior. *Journal of Abnormal Psychology, 91,* 231–240.

Gotlib, I. H., Whiffen, V. E., Wallace, P. M., & Mount, J. H. (1991). Prospective investigation of postpartum depression: Factors involved in onset and recovery. *Journal of Abnormal Psychology, 100,* 122–132.

Gottesman, I. I. (1991). *Schizophrenia genesis.* New York: Freeman.

Gottesman, I. I., & Shields, J. (1966). Schizophrenia in twins: 16 years, consecutive admissions to a psychiatric clinic. *British Journal of Psychiatry, 112,* 809–818.

Gottesman, I. I., & Shields, J. (1972). *Schizophrenia and genetics: A twin study advantage point.* Dallas, TX: Academic Press.

Gottesman, I. I., & Shields, J. (1976). A critical review of recent adoption, twin, and family studies of schizophrenia: Behavioral genetics perspectives. *Schizophrenia Bulletin, 2,* 360–401.

Gould, M. S., Wallenstein, S., & Davidson, L. (1989). Suicide clusters: A critical review. *Suicide and Life-Threatening Behaviors, 19,* 17–29.

Graham, J. R. (1990). *MMPI-2: Assessing personality and psychopathology.* New York: Oxford University Press.

Graham, P. (1979). Epidemiological studies. In H. C. Quay & J. S. Werry (Eds.), *Psychopathological disorders of childhood* (2nd ed., pp. 185–209). New York: Wiley.

Graham, S., Snell, L. M., Graham, J. B., & Ford, L. (1971). Social trauma in the epidemiology of cancer of the cervix. *Journal of Chronic Diseases, 24,* 711–725.

Grant, I. (1987). Alcohol and the brain: Neuro-psychological correlates. *Journal of Consulting and Clinical Psychology, 55,* 310–324.

Greden, J. F., Fontaine, P., Lubetsky, M., & Chamberlin, K. (1978). Anxiety and depression associated with caffeinism among psychiatric inpatients. *American Journal of Psychiatry, 135,* 963–966.

Green, A. R., & Costain, D. W. (1981). *Pharmacology and biochemistry of psychiatric disorders.* New York: Wiley.

Green, R. (1974). *Sexual identity conflict in children and adults.* New York: Basic Books.

Green, R. (1976). One-hundred ten feminine and masculine boys: Behavioral contrasts and demographic similarities. *Archives of Sexual Behavior, 5,* 425–446.

Green, R. (1985). Gender identity in childhood and later sexual orientation: Follow-up of 78 males. *American Journal of Psychiatry, 142,* 339–341.

Greenblatt, D. J., & Shader, R. I. (1978). Pharmacotherapy of anxiety with benzodiazepines and b-adrenergic blockers. In M. Lipton, A. Di Mascio, & K. Killam (Eds.), *Psychopharmacology: A generation of progress* (pp. 1381–1390). New York: Raven Press.

Greenblatt, D. J., & Shader, R. I. (1974). *Benzodiazepines in clinical practice.* New York: Raven Press.

Greenblatt, M., Grosser, G. H., & Wechsler, H. (1964). Differential response of hospitalized depressed patients to somatic therapy. *American Journal of Psychiatry, 120,* 935–943.

Greenspan, J., Schildkraut, J. J., Gordon, E. K., Baer, L., Arnoff, M. S., & Durell, J. (1970). Catecholamine metabolism in affective disorders: 3. MHPG and other catecholamine metabolites in patients treated with lithium carbonate. *Journal of Psychiatric Research, 7,* 171–183.

Greer, S., & Morris, T. (1978). The study of psychological factors in breast cancer: Problems of method. *Social Science and Medicine, 12,* 129–134.

Griffith, J., Cavanaugh, J., Held, J., & Oates, J. (1972). Dextroamphetamine: Evaluation of psychomimetic properties in man. *Archives of General Psychiatry, 26,* 97–100.

Griffth, R. W., & Saameli, K. (1975). Clozapine and agranulocytosis. *Lancet, 2,* 657.

Grinspoon, L. (1977). *Marijuana reconsidered.* Cambridge, MA: Harvard University Press.

Grinspoon, L., Ewalt, J., & Shader, R. I. (1968). Psychotherapy and pharmacotherapy in chronic schizophrenia. *American Journal of Psychiatry, 124,* 67–75.

Grinspoon, L., Ewalt, J., & Shader, R. I. (1972). *Schizophrenia: Pharmacotherapy and psychotherapy.* Baltimore: Williams & Wilkins.

Grob, G. N. (1991). Origins of DSM-I: A study in appearance and reality. *American Journal of Psychiatry, 148,* 421–431.

Gross, M. (1979). Pseudoepilepsy: A study in adolescent hysteria. *American Journal of Psychiatry, 136,* 210–213.

Gross, M., Lewis, E., & Hastey, J. (1974). Acute alcohol withdrawal syndrome. In B. Kissen & H. Begleiter (Eds.), *The biology of alcoholism* (Vol. 3, pp. 191–264). New York: Plenum.

Grossman, F. K., Eichler, L. S., & Winickoff, S. A. (1980). *Pregnancy, birth, and parenthood.* San Francisco: Jossey-Bass.

Groth, A. N., & Birnbaum, H. J. (1978). Adult sexual orientation and attraction to underage persons. *Archives of Sexual Behavior, 7,* 175–181.

Groth, A. N., Hobson, W. F., & Gary, T. S. (1982). The child molester: Clinical observations. In J. Conte & D. A. Shore (Eds.), *Social work and child sexual abuse* (pp. 129–144). New York: Haworth Press.

Gruenewald, D. (1971). Hypnotic techniques without hypnosis in the treatment of a dual personality. *Journal of Nervous and Mental Disease, 153,* 41–46.

Grunhaus, L., Gloger, S., Birmacher, B., Palmer, C., & Ben-David, M. (1983). Prolactin response to the cold pressor test in patients with panic attacks. *Psychiatry Research, 8,* 171–177.

Gualtieri, T., Adams, A., Shen, D., & Loiselle, D. (1982). Minor physical anomalies in alcoholic and schizophrenic adults and hyperactive and autistic children. *American Journal of Psychiatry, 139,* 640–642.

Guess, D., Hemstetter, E., Turnbull, H. R., & Knowlton, S. (1987). Use of aversive procedures with persons who are disabled: A historical review and critical analysis. *Monograph for the Association for Persons with Severe Handicaps* (Whole No. 2).

Guttmacher, L. B., Murphy, D. L., & Insel, T. R. (1983). Pharmacologic models of anxiety. *Comprehensive Psychiatry, 24,* 312–326.

Haaga, D. A. F., Dyck, M. J., & Ernst, D. (1991). Empirical status of cognitive theory of depression. *Psychological Bulletin, 110,* 215–236.

Haberlandt, W. (1967). Aportación a la genetica del suicidio. *Folia Clin Int, 17,* 319–322.

Hadaway, P. F., Alexander, B. K., Coambs, R. B., & Beyerstein, B. (1979). The effect of housing and gender on preference for morphine-sucrose solutions in rats. *Psychopharmacology, 66,* 87–91.

Haefely, W. E. (1977). Synaptic pharmacology of barbiturates and benzodiazepines. *Agents and Actions, 7,* 353–359.

Hagnell, O., Lanke, J., Rorsman, B., & Ojesjo, L. (1982). Are we entering an age of melancholy? Depressive illnesses in a prospective epidemiological study over 25 years: The Lundby Study, Sweden. *Psychological Medicine, 12,* 279–289.

Hale, W. D., & Strickland, B. R. (1976). Induction of mood states and their effect on cognitive and social behaviors. *Journal of Consulting and Clinical Psychology, 44,* 155.

Halford, W. K., & Hayes, R. (1991). Psychological rehabilitation of chronic schizophrenic patients: Recent findings on social skills training and family psychoeducation. *Clinical Psychology Review, 11,* 23–44.

Halleck, S. (1981). The ethics of antiandrogen therapy. *American Journal of Psychiatry, 138,* 642–643.

Halmi, K. A., Powers, P., & Cunningham, S. (1975). Treatment of anorexia nervosa with behavior modification. *Archives of General Psychiatry, 32,* 92–96.

Hamburger, C., Sturup, G. K., & Kahl-Iversen, E. (1953). Transvestism: Hormonal, psychiatric and surgical treatment. *JAMA, 152,* 391–396.

Hamilton, E. W., & Abramson, L. Y. (1983). Cognitive patterns and major depressive disorder: A longitudinal study in a hospital setting. *Journal of Abnormal Psychology, 92,* 173–184.

Hammen, C. L. (1991). Generation of stress in the course of unipolar depression. *Journal of Abnormal Psychology, 100,* 555–561.

Hammen, C. L., Ellicott, A., Gitlin, M., & Jamison, K. R. (1989). Sociotropy/autonomy and vulnerability to specific life events in patients with unipolar depression and bipolar disorders. *Journal of Abnormal Psychology, 98,* 154–160.

Hammen, C. L., & Peters, S. D. (1978). Interpersonal consequence of depression: Responses to men and women enacting a depressed role. *Journal of Abnormal Psychology, 87,* 322–332.

Hanback, J. W., & Revelle, W. (1978). Arousal and perceptual sensitivity in hypochondriacs. *Journal of Abnormal Psychology, 87,* 523–530.

Hanksworth, H., & Schwarz, T. (1977). *The five of me.* New York: Pocket Books.

Hanson, D. R., & Gottesman, I. I. (1976). The genetics, if any, of infantile autism and childhood schizophrenia. *Journal of Autism and Childhood Schizophrenia, 6,* 209–234.

Harding, C. M., Brooks, G. W., Ashikaga, T., Strauss, J. S. & Breier, A. (1987a). The Vermont longitudinal study of persons with severe mental illness: I. Methodology, study sample, and overall status 32 years later. *American Journal of Psychiatry, 144,* 718–726.

Harding, C. M., Brooks, G. W., Askikage, T., Strauss, J. S., & Brier, A. (1987b). The Vermont longitudinal study of persons with severe mental illness: II. Long-term outcome of subjects who retrospectively met DSM-III criteria for schizophrenia. *American Journal of Psychiatry, 144,* 727–735.

Hare, R. D. (1965a). Acquisition and generalization of a conditioned-fear response in psychopathic and non-psychopathic criminals. *Journal of Psychology, 59,* 367–370.

Hare, R. D. (1965b). Temporal gradient of fear arousal in psychopaths. *Journal of Abnormal Psychology, 70,* 442–445.

Hare, R. D. (1970). *Psychopathy: Theory and research.* New York: Wiley.

Hare, R. D., & Craigen, D. (1974). Psychopathy and physiological activity in a mixed-motive game situation. *Psychophysiology, 11,* 197–203.

Hare, R. D., McPherson, L. M., & Forth, A. E. (1988). Male psychopaths and their criminal careers. *Journal of Consulting and Clinical Psychology, 56,* 710–714.

Hare, R. D., & Quinn, M. J. (1971). Psychopathy and autonomic conditioning. *Journal of Abnormal Psychology, 77,* 223–235.

Harlow, H. F. (1959). Love in infant monkeys. *Scientific American, 54,* 244–272.

Harris, B. (1979). Whatever happened to Little Albert? *American Psychologist, 34,* 151–160.

Harris, E. L., Noyes, R., Crowe, R. R., & Chaudhry, D. R. (1983). Family study of agoraphobia. *Archives of General Psychiatry, 40,* 1061–1064.

Harris, R. L., Ellicott, A. M., & Holmes, D. S. (1986). The timing of psychosocial transitions and changes in women's lives: An examination of women aged 45 to 60. *Journal of Personality and Social Psychology, 51,* 409–416.

Hartmann, H. (1958). *Ego psychology and the problem of adaptation.* New York: International Universities Press.

Hartmann, H. (1964). *Essays on ego psychology: Selected problems in psychoanalytic theory.* New York: International Universities Press.

Hattie, J. A., Sharpley, C. F., & Rogers, H. J. (1984). Comparative effectiveness of professional and paraprofessional helpers. *Psychological Bulletin, 95,* 534–541.

Harvald, B., & Hauge, M. (1965). Hereditary factors elucidated by twin studies. In J. V. Neal, M. W. Shaw, and W. J. Shull (Eds.), *Genetics and the epidemiology of chronic diseases,* (pp. 45–61). Washington, DC: U.S. Department of Health and Human Services.

Hawk, A. B., Carpenter, W. T., & Strauss, J. S. (1975). Diagnostic criteria and five-year outcome in schizophrenia. *Archives of General Psychiatry, 32,* 343–347.

Hayashi, G. (1967). A study of juvenile delinquency in twins. In H. Misuda (Ed.), *Clinical genetics in psychiatry* (pp. 373–378). Tokyo: Ogaku Shain.

Haynes, S. G., Levine, S., Scotch, N., Feinleib, M., & Kannel, W. B. (1978). The relationship of psychosocial factors to coronary heart disease in the Framingham Study: 1. Methods and risk factors. *American Journal of Epidemiology, 107,* 362–383.

Hayward, M. L., & Taylor, J. E. (1956). A schizophrenic patient describes the action of intensive psychotherapy. *Psychiatry Quarterly, 30,* 211–248.

Heath, E. S., Adams, A., & Wakeling, P. L. (1964). Short courses of ECT and simulated ECT in chronic schizophrenia. *British Journal of Psychiatry, 110,* 800–807.

Heatherton, T. F., & Baumeister, R. F. (1991). Binge eating as escape from self-awareness. *Psychological Bulletin, 110,* 86–108.

Hebb, D. O. (1949). *Organization of behavior.* New York: Wiley.

Hedfors, E., Bibfeld, P., & Wahren, J. (1978). Mobilization to the blood of human non-T and K lymphocytes during physical exercise. *Journal of Clinical and Laboratory Immunology, 1,* 159–162.

Hedfors, E., Holm, G., Ivansen, M., & Wahren, J. (1983). Physiological variation of blood lymphocyte reactivity: T-cell subsets, immunoglobulin production, and mixed-lymphocyte reactivity. *Clinical Immunology and Immunopathology, 27,* 9–14.

Hedfors, E., Holm, G., & Ohnell, B. (1976). Variations of blood lymphocytes during work studied by cellsurface markers, DNA synthesis and cytotoxicity. *Clinical and Experimental Immunology, 24,* 328–335.

Hefez, A. (1985). The role of the press and the medical community in the epidemic of "mysterious gas poisoning" in the Jordan West Bank. *American Journal of Psychiatry, 142,* 833–837.

Heim, N. (1981). Sexual behavior of castrated sex offenders. *Archives of Sexual Behavior, 10,* 11–19.

Heimberg, R. G., Dodge, C. S., Hope, D. A., Kennedy, C. R., & Zollo, L. J. (1990). Cognitive behavioral group treatment for social phobia: Comparison with a credible placebo control. *Cognitive Therapy and Research, 14,* 1–23.

Helgason, T. (1961). Frequency of depressive states in Iceland as compared to the other Scandinavian countries. *Acta Psychiatrica Scandinavica, 162* (Suppl.), 81–90.

Helzer, J. E., & Winokur, G. (1974). A family interview study of male manic-depressives. *Archives of General Psychiatry, 31,* 73.

Henson, D. E., & Rubin, H. B. (1971). Voluntary control of eroticism. *Journal of Applied Behavior Analysis, 4,* 37–44.

Herrington, R. N., & Lader, M. H. (1981). Lithium. In H. Van Praag, M. H. Lader, O. Rafaelsen, & E. Sachar (Eds.), *Handbook of biological psychiatry: Vol. 5. Drug treatment in psychiatry: Psychotropic drugs* (pp. 61–72). New York: Dekker.

Herz, M. I., Endicott, J., Spitzer, R. L., & Mesnikoff, A. (1971). Day versus inpatient hospitalization: A controlled study. *American Journal of Psychiatry, 127,* 1371–1382.

Herz, M. I., Glazer, W. M., Mostert, M. A., Sheard, M A., Szymanski, H. V., Hafez, H., Mirza, M., & Vana, J. (1991). Intermittent vs maintenance medication in schizophrenia. *Archives of General Psychiatry, 48,* 333–339.

Herzog, D. B. (1984). Are anorexic and bulimic patients depressed? *American Journal of Psychiatry, 141,* 1594–1597.

Heston, L. L. (1966). Psychiatric disorders in foster-home-reared children of schizophrenic mothers. *British Journal of Psychiatry, 112,* 819–825.

Hier, D., Le May, M., & Rosenberger, P. (1979). Autism and unfavorable left-right asymmetries of the brain. *Journal of Autism and Developmental Disorders, 9,* 153–159.

Higley, J. D., Mehlman, P. T., Taub, D. M., Higley, S. B., Suomi, S. J., Linnoila, M., & Vickers, J. H. (1992). Cerebrospinal fluid monoamine and adrenal correlates of aggression in free-ranging rhesus monkeys. *Archives of General Psychiatry, 49,* 436–441.

Hilgard, E. R., & Marquis, D. G. (1961). *Conditioning and learning* (rev. ed.). Norwalk, CT: Appleton & Lang.

Hill, D. (1952). EEG in episodic psychotic and psychopathic behavior: A classification of data. *Electroencephalography and Clinical Neurophysiology, 4,* 419–442.

Hill, D., & Watterson, D. (1942). Electroencephalographic studies of psychopathic personalities. *Journal of Neurology and Psychiatry, 5,* 47–65.

Hinshaw, S. P. (1991). Stimulant medication and the treatment of aggression in children with attention deficits. *Journal of Clinical Child Psychology, 20,* 301–312.

Hinshaw, S. P., Heller, T., & McHale, J. P. (1992). Covert antisocial behavior in boys with attention-deficit hyperactivity disorder: Validation and effects of methylphenidate. *Journal of Consulting and Clinical Psychology, 60,* 274–281.

Hinshaw, S. P., Henker, B., & Whalen, C. K. (1984a). Cognitive-behavioral and pharmacologic interventions for hyperactive boys: Comparative and combined effects. *Journal of Consulting and Clinical Psychology, 52,* 739–749.

Hinshaw, S. P., Henker, B., & Whalen, C. K. (1984b). Self-control in hyperactive boys in anger-inducing situations: Effects of cognitive-behavioral training and of methyl-phenidate. *Journal of Abnormal Child Psychology, 12,* 55–77.

Hiroto, D. S. (1974). Locus of control and learned helplessness. *Journal of Experimental Psychology, 102,* 187–193.

Hiroto, D. S., & Seligman, M. E. P. (1975). Generality of learned helplessness in man. *Journal of Personality and Social Psychology, 31,* 311–327.

Hirsch, S. R., & Leff, J. P. (1975). *Abnormalities in parents of schizophrenics.* London: Oxford University Press.

Hirst, W. (1982). The amnesic syndrome: Descriptions and explanations. *Psychological Bulletin, 91,* 435–460.

Hodgkinson, S., Sherrington, R., Gurling, H., Marchbanks, R., Reeders, S., Mallet, J., McInnis, M., Petursson, H., & Brynjolfsson, J. (1987). Molecular genetic evidence for heterogeneity in manic depression. *Nature, 325,* 805–806.

Hoffman, R. E. (1992). Attractor neural networks and psychotic disorders. *Psychiatric Annals, 22,* 119–124.

Hogarty, G. E., Anderson, C. M., Reiss, D. J., Kornblith, S. J., Greenwald, D. P., Javna, C. D., & Madonia, M. J. (1986). Family psychoeducation, social skills training, and maintenance chemotherapy in the aftercare treatment of schizophrenia. *Archives of General Psychiatry, 43,* 633–642.

Hogarty, G. E., Anderson, C. M., Reiss, D. J., Kornblith, S. J., Greenwald, D. P., Ulrich, R. F., & Carter, M. (1991). Family psychoeducation, social skills training, and maintenance chemotherapy in the aftercare treatment of schizophrenia: II. Two-year effects of a controlled study on relapse and adjustment. *Archives of General Psychiatry, 48,* 340–347.

Hogarty, G. E., Goldberg, S., & the Collaborative Study Group. (1973). Drugs and social therapy in the aftercare of schizophrenic patients. *Archives of General Psychiatry, 28,* 54–63.

Hogarty, G. E., Goldberg, S., & Schooler, N. (1974). Drugs and social therapies in the aftercare of schizophrenic patients: 3. Adjustment of nonrelapsed patients. *Archives of General Psychiatry, 31,* 609–618.

Hogarty, G. E., Goldberg, S., Schooler, N., & Ulrich, R. F. (1974). Drugs and social therapy in the aftercare of schizophrenic patients: 2. Two-year relapse rates. *Archives of General Psychiatry, 31,* 603–608.

Hogarty, G. E., Schooler, N., Ulrich, R. F., Mussare, F., Ferro, P., & Herron, E. (1979). Fluphenazine and social therapy in the aftercare of schizophrenic patients: Relapse analyses of a two-year controlled study of fluphenazine decanoate and fluphenazine hydrochloride. *Archives of General Psychiatry, 36,* 1283–1294.

Holahan, C. K., Holahan, C. J., & Belk, S. S. (1984). Adjustment in aging: The roles of life stress, hassles, and self-efficacy. *Health Psychology, 3,* 315–328.

Holen-Hoeksema, S. (1991). Responses to depression and their effects on the duration of depressive episodes. *Journal of Abnormal Psychology, 100,* 569–582.

Hollander, E., Liebowitz, M. R., & Gorman, J. M. (1988). Anxiety disorders. In J. A. Talbott, R. E. Hales, & J. M. Gorman (Eds.), *American Psychiatric Press textbook of psychiatry.* Washington, DC: American Psychiatric Press.

Hollander, E., Schiffman, E., Cohen, B., Rivera-Stein, M. A., Rosen, W., Gorman, J. M., Fyer, A. J., Papp, L., & Liebowitz, M. R. (1990). Signs of central nervous system dysfunction in obsessive-compulsive disorder. *Archives of General Psychiatry, 47,* 27–32.

Hollingshead, A. B., & Redlich, F. C. (1958). *Social class and mental illness.* New York: Wiley.

Hollister, L. E., Overall, J. E., Kimball, I., & Pokorny, A. D. (1974). Specific indications for different classes of phenothiazines. *Archives of General Psychiatry, 30,* 94–99.

Hollon, S. D., & Beck, A. T. (1979). Cognitive therapy of depression. In P. C. Kendall & S. D. Hollon (Eds.), *Cognitive-behavioral interventions: Theory, research, and procedures* (pp. 153–203). Dallas, TX: Academic Press.

Hollon, S. D., Shelton, R. C., & Loosen, P. T. (1991). Cognitive therapy and pharmacotherapy for depression. *Journal of Consulting and Clinical Psychology, 59,* 88–99.

Holmes, D. S. (1967). Verbal conditioning or problem solving and cooperation? *Journal of Experimental Research in Personality, 2,* 289–295.

Holmes, D. S. (1968). Dimensions of projection. *Psychological Bulletin, 69,* 248–268.

Holmes, D. S. (1971). The conscious self-appraisal of achievement motivation: The self-peer rank method revisited. *Journal of Consulting and Clinical Psychology, 36,* 23–26.

Holmes, D. S. (1978). Projection as a defense mechanism. *Psychological Bulletin, 85,* 677–688.

Holmes, D. S. (1981). Existence of classical projection and the stress-reducing function of attributive projection: A reply to Sherwood. *Psychological Bulletin, 90,* 460–466.

Holmes, D. S. (1983). An alternative perspective concerning the differential physiological responsivity of persons with Type A and Type B behavior patterns. *Journal of Research in Personality, 17,* 40–47.

Holmes, D. S. (1984a). Defense mechanisms. In R. J. Corsini (Ed.), *Encyclopedia of psychology* (pp. 347–350). New York: Wiley.

Holmes, D. S. (1984b). Meditation and somatic arousal: A review of the experimental evidence. *American Psychologist, 39,* 1–10.

Holmes, D. S. (1985a). Self-control of somatic arousal: An examination of meditation and biofeedback. *American Behavioral Scientist, 28,* 486–496.

Holmes, D. S. (1985b). To meditate or rest, that is the question! *American Psychologist, 40,* 722–725.

Holmes, D. S., (1985c). To meditate or rest? The answer is, rest. *American Psychologist, 40,* 728–731.

Holmes, D. S. (1987). The influence of meditation versus rest on physiological arousal: A second examination. In M. A. West (Ed.), *The psychology of meditation* (pp. 81–103). Oxford: Oxford University Press.

Holmes, D. S. (1991). *Abnormal psychology.* New York: HarperCollins.

Holmes, D. S. (1993). Aerobic fitness and the response to psychological stress. In P. Seraganian (Ed.), *Exercise psychology: The influence of physical exercise on psychological processes.* New York: Wiley.

Holmes, D. S., & Burish, T. G. (1984). Effectiveness of biofeedback for treating migraine and tension headaches: A review of the evidence. *Journal of Psychosomatic Research, 27,* 515–532.

Holmes, D. S., & Houston, B. K. (1974). Effectiveness of situation redefinition and affective isolation for reducing stress. *Journal of Personality and Social Psychology, 29,* 212–218.

Holmes, D. S., & McCaul, K. D. (1989). Laboratory research on defense mechanisms. In R. Neufeld (Ed.), *Advances in investigation of psychological stress* (pp. 161–192). New York: Wiley.

Holmes, D. S., & McGilley, B. M. (1987). Influence of a brief aerobic training program on heart rate and subjective response to stress. *Psychosomatic Medicine, 49,* 366–374.

Holmes, D. S., McGilley, B. M., & Houston, B. K. (1984). Task-related arousal of Type A and Type B persons: Level of challenge and response specificity. *Journal of Personality and Social Psychology, 46,* 1322–1327.

Holmes, D. S., & Roth, D. L. (1985). Association of aerobic fitness with pulse rate and subjective responses to psychological stress. *Psychophysiology, 22,* 525–529.

Holmes, D. S., & Roth, D. L. (1989). The measurement of cognitive and somatic anxiety. Unpublished manuscript, Univ. of Kansas.

Holmes, D. S., Solomon, S., Cappo, B. M., & Greenberg, J. L. (1983). Effects of transcendental meditation versus resting on physiological and subjective arousal. *Journal of Personality and Social Psychology, 44,* 1245–1252.

Holmes, D. S., & Tyler, J. (1968). Direct versus projective measurement of achievement motivation. *Journal of Consulting and Clinical Psychology, 32,* 712–717.

Holmgren, S., Sohlberg, S., Berg, E., Johansen, B. M., Norring, C., & Rosmark, B. (1984). Phase I treatment for the chronic and previously treated anorexia bulimia nervosa patient. *International Journal of Eating Disorders, 3,* 17–35.

Hook, E. B. (1982). Epidemiology of Down syndrome. In S. M. Pueschel & J. E. Rynders (Eds.), *Down syndrome: Advances in biomedicine and the behavioral sciences.* Cambridge, MA: Ware Press.

Hook, E. B., & Chambers, G. M. (1977). Estimated rates of Down's syndrome in live births by one-year maternal age intervals for mothers aged 20 to 49 in a New York State study. In D. Bergsma, R. B. Lowry, B. K. Trimble, & M. Feingold (Eds.), *Numerical taxonomy of birth defects and polygenic disorders* (pp. 123–141). New York: Liss.

Hook, E. B., & Fabia, J. J. (1978). Frequency of Down syndrome by single-year maternal age interval: Results of a Massachusetts study. *Teratology, 17,* 223–228.

Hook, E. B., & Lindsjo, A. (1978). Down syndrome in live births by single-year maternal age interval in a Swedish study: Comparison with results from a New York study. *American Journal of Human Genetics, 30,* 19–27.

Hooley, J. M., & Teasdale, J. D. (1989). Predictors of relapse in unipolar depressives: Expressed emotion, marital distress, and perceived criticism. *Journal of Abnormal Psychology, 98,* 229–235.

Hoon, P., Wincze, J., & Hoon, E. (1977). A test of reciprocal inhibition: Are anxiety and sexual arousal in woman mutually inhibitory? *Journal of Abnormal Psychology, 86,* 65–74.

Hopkins, J., Marcus, M., & Campbell, S. B. (1984). Postpartum depression: A critical review. *Psychological Bulletin, 95,* 498–515.

Horenstein, D., Houston, B. K., & Holmes, D. S. (1973). Relationship between clients', therapists', and judges' evaluations of the progress of psychotherapy. *Journal of Counseling Psychology, 20,* 149–153.

Horn, A. S., & Snyder, S. H. (1971). Chlorpromazine and dopamine: Conformational similarities that correlate with antischizophrenic activity of phenothiazine drugs. *Proceedings of the National Academy of Sciences, 68,* 2325–2328.

Horn, J. M., Plomin, R., & Rosenman, R. H. (1976). Heritability of personality traits in adult male twins. *Behavior Genetics, 6,* 17–30.

Horn, W. F., Chatoor, I., & Conners, C. K. (1983). Additive effects of Dexedrine and self-control training: A multiple assessment. *Behavior Modification, 7,* 383–402.

Horne, R. L., & Picard, R. S. (1979). Psychosocial risk factors for lung cancer. *Psychosomatic Medicine, 41,* 503–514.

Horowitz, M. J. (1969). Flashbacks: Recurrent intrusive images after the use of LSD. *American Journal of Psychiatry, 126,* 147–151.

Houser, V. P. (1978). The effects of drugs on behavior controlled by aversive stimuli. In D. E. Blackman & D. J. Sanger (Eds.), *Contemporary research in behavioral psychopharmacology* (pp. 69–157). New York: Plenum.

Houston, B. K. (1972). Control over stress, locus of control, and response to stress. *Journal of Personality and Social Psychology, 21,* 249–255.

Houston, B. K. (1983). Psychophysiological responsivity and the Type A behavior pattern. *Journal of Research in Personality, 17,* 22–39.

Houston, B. K., Chesney, M. A., Black, G. W., Cates, D. S., & Hecker, M. H. (1992). Behavioral clusters and coronary heart disease risk. *Psychosomatic Medicine, 54,* 447–461.

Houston, B. K., & Holmes, D. S. (1974). Effectiveness of avoidant thinking and reappraisal in coping with threat involving temporal uncertainty. *Journal of Personality and Social Psychology, 30,* 382–388.

Howells, K. (1981). Adult sexual interest in children: Considerations relevant to theories of etiology. In M. Cook & K. Howells (Eds.), *Adult sexual interest in children* (pp. 55–94). London: Academic Press.

Howes, M. J., & Hokanson, J. E. (1979). Conversational and social responses to depressive interpersonal behavior. *Journal of Abnormal Psychology, 88,* 625–634.

Hughes, J. R., Gust, S. W., Skoog, K., Kenan, R. M., & Fenwick, J. W. (1991). Symptoms of tobaco withdrawal: A replication and extension. *Archives of General Psychiatry, 48,* 52–59.

Hughes, P. L., Wells, L. A., Cunningham, C. J., & Ilstrup, D. M. (1986). Treating bulimia with desipramine. *Archives of General Psychiatry, 43,* 182–186.

Hull, J. (1981). A self-awareness model of the causes and effects of alcohol consumption. *Journal of Abnormal Psychology, 90,* 586–600.

Hullin, R. P., MacDonald, R., & Allsop, M. N. (1972). Prophylactic lithium in recurrent affective disorders. *Lancet, 2,* 1044–1047.

Humphrey v. Cady, 405 U.S. 504 (1972).

Humphry, D. (1992). Rational suicide among the elderly. *Suicide and Life-Threatening Behavior, 22,* 125–129.

Hurley, D. (1988, January). Getting help from helping. *Psychology Today,* pp. 63–67.

Hutchings, B., & Mednick, S. A. (1974). Registered criminality in the adoptive and biological parents of registered male criminal adoptees. In R. R. Fieve, D. Rosenthal, & H. Brill (Eds.), *Genetic research in psychiatry.* Baltimore: Johns Hopkins University Press.

Hutt, C., & Ounsted, C. (1966). The biological significance of gaze aversion with particular reference to the syndrome of infantile autism. *Behavioral Science, 11,* 346–361.

Iacono, W. G., & Beiser, M. (1992). Are males more likely than females to develop schizophrenia? *American Journal of Psychiatry, 149,* 1070–1074.

Imber, S. D., Pilkonis, P. A., Sotsky, S. M., Elkin, I., Watkins, J. T., Collins, J. F., Shea, M. T., Leber, W. R., & Glass, D. R. (1990). Mode-specific effects among three treatments for depression. *Journal of Consulting and Clinical Psychology, 58,* 352–359.

Imlah, N. W., Ryan, E., & Harrington, J. A. (1965). The influence of antidepressant drugs on the response to ECT and subsequent relapse rates. *Neuropsychopharmacology, 4,* 438–442.

Imre, P. D. (1962). Attitudes of volunteers toward mental hospitals compared to patients and personnel. *Journal of Clinical Psychology, 18,* 516.

Imre, P. D., & Wolf, S. (1962). Attitudes of patients and personnel toward mental hospitals. *Journal of Clinical Psychology, 18,* 232–234.

Ingram, R. E. (1984). Toward an information-processing analysis of depression. *Cognitive Therapy and Research, 8,* 443–478.

Ingram, R. E., & Kendall, P. C. (1987). The cognitive side of anxiety. *Cognitive Therapy and Research, 11,* 523–536.

Inouye, E. (1965). Similar and dissimilar manifestations of obsessive-compulsive neuroses in monozygotic twins. *American Journal of Psychiatry, 21,* 1171–1175.

Inouye, E. (1972). Genetic aspects of neurosis: A review. *International Journal of Mental Health, 1,* 176–189.

Insanity Defense Work Group. (1983). American Psychiatric Association statement on the insanity defense. *American Journal of Psychiatry, 140,* 681–688.

Institute of Medicine. (1982). *Marijuana and health.* Washington, DC: National Academy Press.

Ironside, R., & Batchelor, I. R. (1945). The ocular manifestations of hysteria in relation to flying. *British Journal of Ophthalmology, 29,* 88–98.

Isen, A., & Gorgoglione, J. (1983). Some specific effects of four affect-induction procedures. *Personality and Social Psychology Bulletin, 9,* 136–143.

Isen, A., Shalker, T., Clark, M., & Karp, L. (1978). Affect, accessibility of material in memory, and behavior: A cognitive loop? *Journal of Personality and Social Psychology, 36,* 1–12.

Ivanoff, A., & Jang, S. J. (1991). The role of hopelessness and social desirability in predicting suicidal behavior: A study of prison inmates. *Journal of Consulting and Clinical Psychology, 59,* 394–399.

Jackson, B. (1972). Treatment of depression by self-reinforcement. *Behavior Therapy, 3,* 298–307.

Jackson v. Indiana, 406 U.S. 715 (1972).

Jacob, H. E. (1935). *Coffee: The epic of a commodity.* New York: Viking Penguin.

Jacob, T. (1975). Family interaction in disturbed and normal families: A methodological and substantive review. *Psychological Bulletin, 82,* 33–65.

Jacobs, A., Burnton, M., & Mellville, M. M. (1965). Aggressive behavior, mental subnormality, and the XYY male. *Nature, 208,* 1351–1352.

Jacobs, B. L. (1987). How hallucinogenic drugs work. *American Scientist, 75,* 386–391.

Jacobs, S. C., & Myers, J. (1976). Recent life events and acute schizophrenic psychosis: A controlled study. *Journal of Nervous and Mental Disease, 162,* 75–87.

Jacobs, T. J., & Charles, E. (1980). Life events and the occurrence of cancer in children. *Psychosomatic Medicine, 42,* 11–24.

Jacobsen, C. F., Wolfe, J. B., & Jackson, T. A. (1935). An experimental analysis of the functions of the frontal association areas in primates. *Journal of Nervous and Mental Disease, 82,* 1–14.

Jacobson, E. (1938). *Progressive relaxation.* Chicago: University of Chicago Press.

Jacobson, N. S. (Ed.). (1988). Defining clinically significant change [Special issue]. *Behavioral Assessment, 10*(2).

Jacobson, N. S., & Truax, P. (1991). Clinical significance: A statistical approach to defining meaningful change in psychotherapy. *Journal of Consulting and Clinical Psychology, 59,* 12–19.

Jakob, H., & Beckmann, H. (1986). Prenatal developmental disturbances in the limbic allocortex in schizophrenics. *Journal of Neural Transmission, 65,* 303–326.

James, A., & Barry, R. (1983). Developmental effects in the cerbral lateralization of autistic, retarded, and normal children. *Journal of Autism and Developmental Disorders, 13,* 43–56.

James, N., & Chapman, C. J. (1975). A genetic study of bipolar affective disorder. *British Journal of Psychiatry, 126,* 449–456.

Jamison, K. K., & Akiskal, H. S. (1983). Medication compliance in patients with bipolar disorder. *Psychiatric Clinics of North America, 6,* 175–192.

Janicak, P. G., Davis, J. M., Gibbons, R. D., Ericksen, S., Chang, S., & Gallagher, P. (1985). Efficacy of ECT: A meta-analysis. *American Journal of Psychiatry, 143,* 297–302.

Janowsky, D. S., El-Yousef, M. K., Davis, J. M., & Sekerke, J. (1973). Provocation of schizophrenic symptoms by intravenous administration of methylphenidate. *Archives of General Psychiatry, 28,* 185–191.

Jarey, M. L., & Stewart, M. A. (1985). Psychiatric disorder in the parents of adopted children with aggressive conduct disorder. *Neuropsychobiology, 13,* 7–11.

Jarvis, G. K., Boldt, M., & Butt, J. (1991). Medical examiners and manner of death. *Suicide and Life-Threatening Behavior, 21,* 115–133.

Jeans, R. F. (1976). Independently validated case of multiple personality. *Journal of Abnormal Psychology, 85,* 249–255.

Jemmott, J. B., Borysenko, J. Z., Borysenko, M., McClelland, D. C., Chapman, R., Meyer, D., & Benson, H. (1983). Academic stress, power motivation, and decrease in secretion rate of salivary secretory immunoglobulin A. *Lancet, 1,* 1400–1402.

Jemmott, J. B., & Locke, S. E. (1984). Psychosocial factors, immunologic mediation, and human susceptibility to infectious diseases: How much do we know? *Psychological Bulletin, 95,* 78–108.

Jenkins, C. D., Rosenman, R. H., & Zyzanski, S. J. (1974). Prediction of clinical coronary heart disease by a test for the coronary-prone behavior pattern. *New England Journal of Medicine, 290,* 1271–1275.

Jenner, P., Sheehy, M., & Marsden, C. D. (1983). Noradrenaline and 5-hydroxytryptamine modulation of brain dopamine function: Implications for the treatment of Parkinson's disease. *British Journal of Clinical Pharmacology, 15* (Suppl.), 277s–289s.

Jervis, G. A. (1939). The genetics of phenylpyruvic oligophrenia. *Journal of Mental Science, 85,* 719–762.

Jervis, G. A. (1947). Studies of phenylpyruvic oligophrenia: The position of the metabolic error. *Journal of Biological Chemistry, 169,* 651–656.

Jimerson, D. C., Lesem, M. D., Kay, W. H., & Brewerton, T. D. (1992). Low serotonin and dopamine metabolite concentrations in cerebrospinal fluid form bulimic patients with frequent binge episodes. *Archives of General Psychiatry, 49,* 132–138.

Johnson, J. G., & Bornstein, R. F. (1991). Does daily stress independently predict psychopathology? *Journal of Social and Clinical Psychology, 10,* 58–74.

Johnson, M. H., & Magaro, P. A. (1987). Effects of mood and severity on memory processes in depression and mania. *Psychological Bulletin, 101,* 28–40.

Johnstone, E. C., Crow, T. J., Firth, C. D., Husband, J., & Kreel, L. (1976). Cerebral ventricular size and cognitive impairment in chronic schizophrenia. *Lancet, 2,* 924–926.

Joiner, T. E., Alfano, M. S., & Metalsky, G. I. (1992). When depression breeds contempt: Reassurance seeking, self-esteem, and rejection of depressed college students by their roommates. *Journal of Abnormal Psychology, 101,* 165–173.

Jones, F. D., Maas, F. J., Dekirmenjian, H., & Fawcett, J. A. (1973). Urinary catecholamine metabolites during behavioral changes in a patient with manic-depressive cycles. *Science, 179,* 300–302.

Jones, M. C. (1924). The elimination of children's fears. *Journal of Experimental Psychology, 7,* 382–390.

Jones, R. T. (1984). The pharmacology of cocaine. In J. Grabowski (Ed.), *Cocaine: Pharmacology, effects, and treatment of abuse.* Rockville, MD: National Institute on Drug Abuse.

Judd, L. L., McAdams, L., Budnick, B., & Braff, D. L. (1992). Sensory gating deficits in schizophrenia. *American Journal of Psychiatry, 149,* 488–493.

Junginger, J., Barker, S., & Coe, D. (1992). Mood theme and bizarreness of delusions in schizophrenia and mood psychosis. *Journal of Abnormal Psychology, 101,* 287–292.

Justice, A. (1985). Review of the effects of stress on cancer in laboratory animals: Importance of time of stress application and type of tumor. *Psychological Bulletin, 98,* 108–138.

Kagan, V. (1981). Nonprocess autism in children: A comparative etiopathogenic study. *Soviet Neurology and Psychiatry, 14,* 25–30.

Kallman, F. J. (1954). Genetic factors in depression. In P. H. Hoch & J. Zubin (Eds.), *Depression* (pp. 1–24). Philadelphia: Grune & Stratton.

Kane, J. M. (1983). Low-dose medication strategies in the maintenance treatment of schizophrenia. *Schizophrenia Bulletin, 9,* 528–532.

Kane, J. M., Honigfeld, G., Singer, J., & Meltzer, H. (1988). Clozapine for the treatment-resistant schizophrenic. *Archives of General Psychiatry, 45,* 789–796.

Kane, J. M., Honigfeld, G., Singer, J., & Meltzer, H. (1989). Clozapine for the treatment-resistant schizophrenic: Results of a US multicenter trial. *Psychopharmacology, 99,* S60–S63.

Kane, J. M., Rifkin, A., Woerner, M., Reardon, G., Starantakos, S., Schiebel, D., & Ramos-Lorenzi, J. (1983). Low-dose neuroleptic treatment of outpatient schizophrenics. *Archives of General Psychiatry, 40,* 893–896.

Kanfer, R., & Zeiss, A. M. (1983). Depression, interpersonal standard setting, and judgments of self-efficacy. *Journal of Abnormal Psychology, 92,* 319–329.

Kanner, A. D., Coyne, J. C., Schaefer, C., & Lazarus, R. S. (1981). Comparison of two modes of stress management: Daily hassles and uplifts versus major life events. *Journal of Behavioral Medicine, 4,* 1–40.

Kanner, L. (1943). Autistic disturbances of affective content. *Nervous Child, 2,* 217–240.

Kanofsky, J. D., Sandyk, R., & Kay, S. R. (1990). Anatomical abnormalities in the brains of monozygotic twins discordant for schizophrenia. *New England Journal of Medicine, 323,* 547.

Kaplan, H. S. (1981). *The new sex therapy: Active treatment of sexual dysfunctions.* New York: Brunner/Mazel.

Karacan, I. (1982). Nocturnal penile tumescence as a biological marker in assessing erectile dysfunction. *Psychosomatics, 23,* 349–360.

Karacan, I., & Williams, R. L. (1970). Current advances in theory and practice relating to postpartum syndromes. *Psychiatry in Medicine, 1,* 307–328.

Karlsson, J. L. (1966). *The biologic basis of schizophrenia.* Springfield, IL: Thomas.

Karon, B., & Vanden Bos, G. (1972). The consequences of psychotherapy for schizophrenic patients. *Psychotherapy: Theory, Research and Practice, 9,* 111–119.

Karpman, B. (1951). The sexual psychopath. *JAMA, 146,* 721–726.

Kasa, K., Otsuki, S., Yamamoto, M., Sato, M., Kuroda, H., & Ogawa, N. (1982). Cerebrospinal fluid, aminobutyric acid and homovanillic acid in depressive disorders. *Biological Psychiatry, 17,* 877–883.

Kassin, S. M., & Wrightsman, L. S. (1994). Confession evidence. In S. M. Kassin & L. S. Wrightsman (Eds.), *The psychology of evidence and trial procedure.* Newbury Park, CA: Sage.

Kay, D. W., Fahy, T., & Garside, R. F. (1970). A seven-month double-blind trial of amitriptyline and diazepam in ECT-treated depressed patients. *British Journal of Psychiatry, 117,* 667–671.

Kaya, N., Moore, C., & Karacan, I. (1979). Nocturnal penile tumescence and its role in impotence. *Psychiatric Annals, 9,* 426–431.

Kazdin, A. E. (1991). Effectiveness of psychotherapy with children and adolescents. *Journal of Consulting and Clinical Psychology, 59,* 785–798.

Kazdin, A. E., & Wilcoxon, L. A. (1976). Systematic desensitization and nonspecific treatment effects: A methodological evaluation. *Psychological Bulletin, 83,* 729–758.

Keck, P. E., McElroy, S. L., & Pope, H. G. (1991). Epidemiology of neuroleptic malignant syndrome. *Psychiatric Annals, 21,* 148–151.

Kellermann, A. L., Rivara, F. P., Somes, G., Reay, D. T., Francisco, J., Banton, J. B., Prodzinski, J., Fligner, C., & Hackman, B. B. (1992). Suicide in the home in relation to gun ownership. *New England Journal of Medicine, 327,* 467–472.

Kellner, R., Uhlenhuth, E. H., & Glass, R. (1978). Clinical evaluation of antianxiety agents: Subject-own-control designs. In M. Lipton, A. Di Mascio, & K. Killam (Eds.), *Psychopharmacology: A generation of progress* (pp. 1391–1400). New York: Raven Press.

Kelly, D., Mitchell-Heggs, N., & Sherman, D. (1971). Anxiety and the effects of sodium lactate assessed clinically and psyciologically. *British Journal of Psychiatry, 119,* 129–141.

Kenardy, J., Evans, L., & Oei, T. P. (1992). The latent structure of anxiety symptoms in anxiety disorders. *American Journal of Psychiatry, 149,* 1058–1061.

Kendall, P. C. (1984). Cognitive-behavioral self-control therapy for children. *Journal of Child Psychology and Psychiatry, 25,* 173–179.

Kendall, P. C. (Ed.). (1992). Comorbidity and treatment implications. *Journal of Consulting and Clinical Psychology, 60,* 833–908.

Kendler, K. S., Heath, A. C., Neale, M. C., Kessler, R. C., & Eaves, L. J. (1992). A population-based twin study of alcoholism in women. *JAMA, 268,* 1877–1882.

Kendler, K. S., Gruenberg, A. M., & Strauss, J. S. (1982). An independent analysis of the Copenhagen sample of the Danish adoption study of schizophrenia: The relationship between childhood withdrawal and adult schizophrenia. *Archives of General Psychiatry, 39,* 1257–1261.

Kendler, K. S., Neale, M. C., Kessler, R. C., Heath, A. C., & Eaves, L. J. (1992a). Generalized anxiety disorder in women: A population-based twin study. *Archives of General Psychiatry, 49,* 267–272.

Kendler, K. S., Neale, M. C., Kessler, R. C., Heath, A. C., & Eaves, L. J. (1992b). A population-based twin study of major depression in women. *Archives of General Psychiatry, 49,* 257–266.

Kendler, K. S., Neale, M. C., MacLean, C. J., Heath, A. C., Eaves, L. J., & Kessler, R. C. (1993). Smoking and major depression. *Archives of General Psychiatry, 50,* 36–43.

Kennedy, J. L., Giuffra, L. A., Moises, H. W., Cavalli-Sforza, L. L., Pakstis, A. J., Kidd, J. R., Castiglione, C. M., Sjogren, B., Wetterberg, L., & Kidd, K. K. (1988). Evidence against linkage of schizophrenia to markers on chromosome 5 in a northern Swedish pedigree. *Nature, 336,* 167–170.

Kent, H., & Rosanoff, A. J. (1910). A study of association in insanity. *American Journal of Insanity, 67,* 317–390.

Kephalis, T. A., Kburus, J., Michael, C. M., Miras, C. J., & Padidakis, D. P. (1976). Some aspects of cannabis smoke chemistry. In G. G. Nahas (Ed.), *Marijuana: Chemistry, biochemistry and cellular effects* (pp. 39–50). New York: Springer.

Kesey, K. (1962). One flew over the cuckoo's nest. New York: Viking Penguin.

Kety, S. S., Rosenthal, D., Wender, P. H., Schulsinger, F., &

Jacobsen, B. (1975). Mental illness in the biological and adoptive families of adopted individuals who have become schizophrenic: A preliminary report based on psychiatric interviews. In R. R. Fieve, D. Rosenthal, & H. Brill (Eds.), *Genetic research in psychiatry.* Baltimore: Johns Hopkins University Press.

Keyes, D. (1981). *The minds of Billy Milligan.* New York: Bantam.

Khantzian, E. J. (1985). Self-medication hypothesis of addictive disorders. *American Journal of Psychiatry, 142,* 1259–1263.

Khot, V., & Wyatt, R. J. (1991). Not all that moves is tardive dyskinesia. *American Journal of Psychiatry, 148,* 661–666.

Kiecolt-Glaser, J. K., Garner, W., Speicher, C., Penn, G. M., Holliday, J., & Glaser, R. (1984). Psychosocial modifiers of immunocompetence in medical students. *Psychosomatic Medicine, 46,* 7–14.

Kiecolt-Glaser, J. K., Glaser, R., Williger, D., Stout, J., Messick, G., Sheppard, S., Ricker, D., Romisher, S. C., Briner, W., Bonnell, G., & Donnerberg, R. (1985). Psychosocial enhancement of immunocompetence in a geriatric population. *Health Psychology, 4,* 25–41.

Kiernan, C. (1988). Child abuse: A case for change? *British Journal of Special Education, 15,* 140–142.

Kiersch, T. A. (1962). Amnesia: A clinical study of ninety-eight cases. *American Journal of Psychiatry, 119,* 57–60.

Kiesler, C. A. (1982a). Mental hospitals and alternative care: Noninstitutionalization as potential public policy for mental patients. *American Psychologist, 37,* 349–360.

Kiesler, C. A. (1982b). Public and professional myths about mental hospitalization: An empirical reassessment of policy-related beliefs. *American Psychologist, 37,* 1323–1340.

Kiesler, C. A., & Sibulkin, A. E. (1988). *Mental hospitalization: Myths and facts about a national crisis.* Newbury Park, CA: Sage.

Killen, J. D., Fortmann, S. P., Newman, B., & Varady, A. (1990). Evaluation of a treatment approach combining nicotine gum with self-guided behavioral treatments for smoking relaapse prevention. *Journal of Consulting and Clinical Psychology, 58,* 85–92.

Kilmann, P. R., & Auerbach, R. (1979). Treatments of premature ejaculation and psychogenic impotence: A critical review of the literature. *Archives of Sexual Behavior, 8,* 81–100.

Kiloh, L. G. (1982). Electroconvulsive therapy. In E. S. Paykel (Ed.), *Handbook of affective disorders* (pp. 262–275). New York: Guilford Press.

King, K. B., Reis, H. T., Porter, L. A., & Norsen, L. H. (1993). Social support and long-term recovery from coronary artery surgery: Effects on patients and spouses. *Health Psychology, 12,* 56–63.

King, R. A., Riddle, M. A., Chappell, P. B., Hardin, M. T., Anderson, G. M., Lombroso, P., & Scahill, L. (1991). Emergence of self-destructive phenomena in children and adolescents during fluoxetine treatment. *Journal of the American Academy of Child and Adolescent Psychiatry, 30,* 179–186.

Kirschenbaum, D. S., De Voge, J. B., Marsh, M. E., & Steffen, J. J. (1980). Multimodal evaluation of therapy versus consultation components in a large inner-city intervention program. *American Journal of Community Psychology, 8,* 587–692.

Kirsling, R. A. (1986). Review of suicide among elderly persons. *Psychological Reports, 59,* 359–366.

Kissen, D. M. (1966). The significance of personality in lung cancer in men. *Annals of the New York Academy of Science, 125,* 820–826.

Kissen, D. M., Brown, R. I. F., & Kissen, M. A. (1969). A further report on personality and psychosocial factors in lung cancer. *Annals of the New York Academy of Science, 164,* 535–545.

Kittrie, N. N. (1960). Compulsory mental treatment and the requirements of "due process." *Ohio State Law Journal, 21,* 28–51.

Klatskin, E. H., & Eron, L. D. (1970). Projective test content during pregnancy and postpartum adjustment. *Psychosomatic Medicine, 32,* 487–493.

Klein, D. F. (1982). Medication in the treatment of panic attacks and phobic states. *Psychopharmacology Bulletin, 18,* 85–90.

Klein, D. F., & Rosen, B. (1973). Premorbid asocial adjustment and response to phenothiazine treatment among schizophrenic patients. *Archives of General Psychiatry, 29,* 480–485.

Klein, D. N. (1990). Depressive personality: Reliability, validity, and relation to dysthymia. *Journal of Abnormal Psychology, 99,* 412–421.

Klein, R. G., Landa, B., Mattes, J. A., & Klein, D. F. (1988). Methylphenidate and growth in hyperactive children: A controlled withdrawal study. *Archives of General Psychiatry, 45,* 1127–1130.

Klein, S. B. (1987). *Learning.* New York: McGraw-Hill.

Klerman, G. L. (1976). Age and clinical depression: Today's youth in the 21st century. *American Journal of Psychiatry, 139,* 302–306.

Klerman, G. L. (1979). The age of melancholy. *Psychology Today,* pp. 36–42, 88.

Klerman, G. L. (1990). Treatment of recurrent unipolar major depressive disorder. *Archives of General Psychiatry, 47,* 1158–1162.

Klerman, G. L., & Barrett, J. E. (1973). The affective disorders: Clinical and epidemiological aspects. In S. Gershon & B. Shopsin (Eds.), *Lithium: Its role in psychiatric research and treatment* (pp. 201–236). New York: Plenum.

Klerman, G. L., Di Mascio, A., Weissman, M., Prusoff, B. A. & Paykel, E. S. (1974). Treatment of depression by drugs and psychotherapy. *American Journal of Psychiatry, 131,* 186–191.

Klerman, G. L., Lavori, P. W., Rice, J., Reich, T., Endicott, J., Andreasen, N. C., Keller, M. B., & Hirschfield, R. M. (1985). Birth-cohort trends in rates of major depressive disorder among relatives of patients with affective disorder. *Archives of General Psychiatry, 42,* 689–693.

Klerman, G. L., & Schechter, G. (1982). Drugs and psychotherapy. In E. S. Paykel (Ed.), *Handbook of affective disorders* (pp. 329–337). New York: Guilford Press.

Klopfer, B. (1962). *The Rorschach technique: An introductory manual.* San Diego, CA: Harcourt Brace.

Klorman, R., Bauer, L. O., Coons, H. W., Lewis, J. L., Peloquin, L. J., Perlmutter, R. A., Ryan, R. M., Salzman, L. F., &

Strauss, J. (1984). Enhancing effects of methylphenidate on normal young adults' cognitive processes. *Psychopharmacology Bulletin, 20,* 3–9.

Kluft, R. P. (1982). Varieties of hypnotic interventions in the treatment of multiple personality. *American Journal of Clinical Hypnosis, 24,* 230–240.

Kneier, A. W., & Temoshok, L. (1984). Repressive coping reactions in patients with malignant melanoma as compared to cardiovascular disease patients. *Journal of Psychosomatic Research, 28,* 145–155.

Koch, J. L. (1891). *Die psychopathischen Minderwertigkeiten.* Ravensburg, Germany: Maier.

Kocsis, J. H., & Stokes, P. (1979). Lithium maintenance: Factors affecting outcome. *American Journal of Psychiatry, 136,* 563–566.

Koegel, R. L., Schreibman, L., O'Neill, R. E., & Burke, J. C. (1983). The personality and family-interaction characteristics of parents of autistic children. *Journal of Consulting and Clinical Psychology, 51,* 683–692.

Kohn, M. L. (1973). Social class and schizophrenia: A critical review and reformulation. *Schizophrenia Bulletin, 1,* 60–79.

Kohn, M. L., & Clausen, J. A. (1955). Social isolation and schizophrenia. *American Sociological Review, 20,* 265–273.

Kolb, L. C. (1973). *Modern clinical psychiatry.* Philadelphia: Saunders.

Kormos, H. R. (1978). The nature of combat stress. In C. R. Figley (Ed.), *Stress disorders among Vietnam veterans.* New York: Brunner/Mazel.

Korn, M. L., Brown, S., Apter, A., & Van Praag, H. M. (1990). Serotonin and suicide: A functional/dimensional viewpoint. In D. Lester (Ed.), *Current concepts in suicide.* Philadelphia: Charles Press.

Kornfeld, A. D. (1989). Mary Cover Jones and the Peter Case: Social learning versus conditioning. *Journal of Anxiety Disorders, 3,* 187–195.

Koss, M. P., & Butcher, J. N. (1986). Research on brief psychotherapy. In S. L. Garfield & A. E. Bergin (Eds.), *Handbook of psychotherapy and behavior change* (pp. 627–667). New York: Wiley.

Kosten, T. A., & Kosten, T. R. (1991). Pharmacological blocking agents for treating substance abuse. *Journal of Nervous and Mental Disease, 179,* 583–592.

Kozol, H., Boucher, R., & Garofalo, R. (1972). The diagnosis and treatment of dangerousness. *Crime and Delinquency, 18,* 371–392.

Kraepelin, E. (1971). *Dementia praecox and paraphrenia* (R. M. Barclay & G. M. Robertson, Trans.). New York: Krieger. (Originally published 1919)

Kraft, D. P., & Babigian, H. M. (1976). Suicide by persons with and without psychiatric contacts. *Archives of General Psychiatry, 33,* 209–215.

Kramer, B. A. (1985). Use of ECT in California. *American Journal of Psychiatry, 142,* 1190–1192.

Kramer, M. A. (1957). A discussion of the concepts of incidence and prevalence as related to epidemiologic studies of mental disorders. *American Journal of Public Health, 47,* 826–840.

Kranz, H. (1936). *Lebensschicksale Krimineller Zwillinge.* Berlin: Springer.

Krauthammer, C., & Klerman, G. L. (1979). The epidemiology of mania. In B. Shopsin (Ed.), *Manic illness* (pp. 11–28). New York: Raven Press.

Kreuz, L. E., Rose, R. M., & Jennings, J. R. (1972). Suppression of plasma testosterone levels and psychological stress: A longitudinal study of young men in officer candidate school. *Archives of General Psychiatry, 26,* 479–482.

Kringlen, E. (1967). Heredity and social factors in schizophrenic twins: An epidemiological-clinical study. In J. Romano (Ed.), *The origins of schizophrenia.* New York: Excerpta Medica Foundation.

Kringlen, E. (1968). An epidemiological-clinical twin study on schizophrenia. In D. Rosenthal & S. S. Kety (Eds.), *The transmission of schizophrenia.* Elmsford, NY: Pergamon Press.

Kronfol, Z., Silva, J., Greden, J., Deminski, S., Gardner, R., & Carroll, B. (1983). Impaired lymphocyte function in depressive illness. *Life Sciences, 33,* 241–247.

Kruesi, M. J., Hibbs, E. D., Zahn, T. P., Keysor, C. S., Hamburger, S. D., Bartko, J. J., & Rapoport, J. L. (1992). A 2-year prospective follow-up study of children and adolescents with disruptive behavior disorders. *Archives of General Psychiatry, 49,* 429–435.

Kulhanek, F., Linde, O. K., & Meisenberg, G. (1979). Precipitation of antipsychotic drugs in interaction with coffee or tea. *Lancet, 2,* 1130.

Kulik, J. A., & Mahler, H. I. (1989). Social support and recovery from surgery. *Health Psychology, 8,* 221–238.

Kurlan, R. (1989). Tourette's syndrome: Current concepts. *Neurology, 39,* 1625–1630.

Kushner, M. (1965). The reduction of a long-standing fetish by means of aversive conditioning. In L. P. Ulmann & L. Krasner (Eds.), *Case studies in behavior modification.* Dallas, TX: Holt, Rinehart and Winston.

Kwan, M., Greenleaf, W. J., Mann, J., Crapo, L., & Davidson, J. M. (1983). The nature of androgen action on male sexuality: A combined laboratory–self-report study on hypogonadal men. *Journal of Clinical Endocrinology and Metabolism, 57,* 557–562.

Kwon, S., & Oel, T. P. S. (1992). Differential causal roles of dysfunctional attitudes and automatic thoughts in depression. *Cognitive Therapy and Research, 16,* 309–328.

Lacey, J. I. (1950). Individual differences in somatic response patterns. *Journal of Comparative and Physiological Psychology, 43,* 599–604.

Lacey, J. I. (1967). Somatic response patterning and stress: Some revisions of activation theory. In M. H. Appley & R. Trumball (Eds.), *Psychological stress.* New York: McGraw-Hill.

Ladas, A. K., Whipple, B., & Perry, J. D. (1982). *The G spot.* Dallas, TX: Holt, Rinehart and Winston.

Lader, M. H. (1978). Benzodiazepines: The opium of the masses? *Neuroscience, 81,* 159–165.

Laing, R. D. (1964). Is schizophrenia a disease? *International Journal of Social Psychiatry, 10,* 184–193.

Laird, J. D., Wagener, J., Halal, M., & Szegda, M. (1982). Remembering what you feel: Effects of emotion on memory. *Journal of Personality and Social Psychology, 42,* 81–89.

Lake v. Cameron, 364 F.2d 657 (D.C. Cir. 1966).

Lam, R. W., Buchanan, A., Clark, C. M., & Remick, R. A. (1991). Ultraviolet versus non-ultraviolet light therapy for seasonal affective disorder. *Journal of Clinical Psychiatry, 52*, 213–216.

Lambert, M. J., Shapiro, D. A., & Bergin, A. E. (1986). The effectiveness of psychotherapy. In S. L. Garfield & A. E. Bergin (Eds.), *Handbook of psychotherapy and behavior change* (pp. 157–211). New York: Wiley.

Landesman, S., & Butterfield, E. C. (1987). Normalization and deinstitutionalization of mentally retarded individuals. *American Psychologist, 42*, 809–816.

Landmann, R. M., Muller, F. B., Perini, C., Wesp, M., Erne, P., & Buhler, R. R. (1984). Changes of immunoregulatory cells induced by psychological and physical stress: Relationship to plasma catecholamines. *Clinical and Experimental Immunology, 58*, 127–135.

Lang, A. R., Goechner, D. J., Adressor, V. J., & Marlatt, G. A. (1975). Effects of alcohol on aggression in male social drinkers. *Journal of Abnormal Psychology, 84*, 508–518.

Lang, P. J., & Buss, A. H. (1965). Psychological deficit in schizophrenia: 2. Interference and activation. *Journal of Abnormal Psychology, 70*, 77–106.

Lang, P. J., & Luoto, K. (1962). Mediation and associative facilitation in neurotic, psychotic, and normal subjects. *Journal of Abnormal and Social Psychology, 64*, 113–120.

Lange, J. (1931). *Crime as destiny.* London: Allen & Unwin.

Langevin, R., Paitich, D., Hucker, S., Newman, S., Ramsay, G., Pope, S., Geller, G., & Anderson, C. (1979). The effect of assertiveness training, Provera, and sex of therapist in the treatment of genital exhibitionism. *Journal of Behavioral and Experimental Psychiatry, 10*, 275–282.

Langner, T. S., & Michael, S. T. (1963). *Life stress and mental health.* Encino, CA: Glencoe.

Lanyon, R. I. (1986). Theory and treatment of child molestation. *Journal of Consulting and Clinical Psychology, 54*, 176–182.

Lapouse, R., & Monk, M. A. (1958). An epidemiologic study of behavior characteristics in children. *American Journal of Public Health, 48*, 1134–1144.

Largen, J. W., Mathew, R. J., Dobbins, K., Meyer, J. S., & Claghorn, J. L. (1978). Skin temperature self-regulation and noninvasive regional cerebral blood flow. *Headache, 18*, 203–210.

Larmore, K., Ludwig, A. M., & Cain, R. L. (1977). Multiple personality: An objective case study. *British Journal of Psychiatry, 131*, 35–40.

Lavigna, G., & Donnellan, A. (1986). *Alternatives to punishment: Solving behavior problems with non-aversive strategies.* New York: Irvington Publishers.

Laws, D. R., & Rubin, H. B. (1969). Instructional control of an autonomic sexual response. *Journal of Applied Behavioral Analysis, 2*, 93–99.

Lawson, J. S., McGhie, A., & Chapman, J. (1967). Distractibility in schizophrenia and organic cerebral disease. *British Journal of Psychiatry, 113*, 527–535.

Lazarus, A. A. (1968). Learning theory and the treatment of depression. *Behaviour Research and Therapy, 6*, 83–89.

Lazarus, R. S., & Folkman, S. (1984). *Stress, appraisal, and coping.* New York: Springer.

Leershen, C. (1984, January 9). John Madden on a roll. *Newsweek*, pp. 66–67.

Leff, J. P. (1976). Schizophrenia and sensitivity to the family environment. *Schizophrenia Bulletin, 2*, 566–574.

Leff, J. P., Hirsch, S. R., Gaind, S. R., Rodhe, P. D., & Stevens, B. S. (1973). Life events and maintenance therapy in schizophrenic relapse. *British Journal of Psychiatry, 123*, 659–660.

Leff, J. P., & Wing, J. K. (1971). Trial of maintenance therapy in schizophrenics. *British Medical Journal, 2*, 599–604.

Legra, A. M. (1933). Psychose und Kriminalität bei Zwillingen. *Zeitschrift für die gesamte Neurologie und Psychiatrie, 144*, 198–222.

Leibenluft, E., Fiero, P. L., Bartko, J. J., Moul, D. E., & Rosenthal, N. E. (1993). Depressive symptoms and the self-reported use of alcohol, caffeine, and carbohydrates in normal volunteers and four groups of psychiatric outpatients. *American Journal of Psychiatry, 150*, 294–301.

Leigh, B. C. (1989). In search of the Seven Dwarves: Issues of measurement and meaning in alcohol expectancy research. *Psychological Bulletin, 105*, 361–373.

Lenzenweger, M. F., Dworkin, R. W., & Wethington, E. (1989). Models of positive and negative symptoms in schizophrenia: An empirical evaluation of latent structures. *Journal of Abnormal Psychology, 98*, 62–70.

Lerer, B., Weiner, R. D., & Belmaker, R. (1984). *ECT: Basic mechanisms.* Washington, DC: American Psychiatric Association.

Lerner, Y., Lwow, E., Leviton, A., & Belmaker, R. (1979). Acute high-dose parenteral haloperidol treatment of psychosis. *American Journal of Psychiatry, 136*, 1061–1064.

Le Shan, L. (1966). An emotional life-history pattern associated with neoplastic disease. *Annals of the New York Academy of Sciences, 125*, 780–793.

Lessard v. Schmidt, 349 F. Supp. 1078 (E.D. Wis. 1972); 94 S.Ct. 713 (1974).

Lester, D. (1988). *The biochemical basis of suicide.* Springfield, IL: Thomas.

Lester, D. (1989). Suicide as a positive act. In D. Lester, *Can we prevent suicide?* (pp. 11–18). New York: AMS.

Lester, D. (1990). The effects of the detoxification of domestic gas in Switzerland on the suicide rate. *Acta Psychiatria Scandinavica, 82*, 383–384.

Lester, D. (1991). Suicide across the life span: A look at international trends. In A. A. Leenaars (Ed.), *Life span perspectives of suicide.* New York: Plenum.

Levenson, A. J., Lord, C. J., Sermas, C. E., Thornby, J. I., Sullender, W., & Comstock, B. A. (1977). Acute schizophrenia: An efficacious outpatient treatment approach as an alternative to full-time hospitalization. *Diseases of the Nervous System, 38*, 242–245.

Levin, A. P., Schneier, F. R., & Liebowitz, M. R. (1989). Social phobia: Biology and pharmacology. *Clinical Psychology Review, 9*, 129–140.

Levitt, E. E., & Lubin, B. (1975). *Depression.* New York: Springer.

Lewin, B. (1951). *The psycho-analysis of elation.* London: Hogarth.

Lewine, R. R. J. (1981). Sex differences in age of symptom onset and first hospitalization. *American Journal of Orthopsychiatry, 50*, 316–322.

Lewinsohn, P. M. (1974). A behavioral approach to depression. In R. J. Friedman & M. M. Katz (Eds.), *The psychology of depression: Contemporary theory and research* (pp. 157–179). Washington, DC: Winston/Wiley.

Lewinsohn, P. M., Duncan, E. M., Stanton, A. K., & Hautzinger, M. (1986). Age at first onset for nonbipolar depression. *Journal of Abnormal Psychology, 95,* 378–383.

Lewinsohn, P. M., Mischel, W., Chaplin, W., & Barton, R. (1980). Social competence and depression: The role of illusory self-perceptions. *Journal of Abnormal Psychology, 89,* 203–212.

Lewinsohn, P. M., Rodhe, P. D., Seeley, J. R., & Hops, H. (1991). Comorbidity of unipolar depression: I. Major depression with dysthymia. *Journal of Abnormal Psychology, 100,* 205–213.

Lewinsohn, P. M., Steinmetz, J. L., Larson, D. W., & Franklin, J. (1981). Depression-related cognitions: Antecedent or consequence? *Journal of Abnormal Psychology, 90,* 213–219.

Lewinsohn, P. M., Zeiss, A. M., & Duncan, E. M. (1989). Probability of relapse after recovery from an episode of depression. *Journal of Abnormal Psychology, 98,* 107–116.

Lewis, D. O., & Shanok, S. S. (1979). Medical histories of psychiatrically referred delinquent children: An epidemiologic study. *American Journal of Psychiatry, 136,* 231–233.

Lewis, D. O., Shanok, S. S., & Balla, D. A. (1979a). Parental criminality and medical histories of delinquent children. *American Journal of Psychiatry, 136,* 288–292.

Lewis, D. O., Shanok, S. S., & Balla, D. A. (1979b). Perinatal difficulties, head and face trauma, and child abuse in the medical histories of seriously delinquent children. *American Journal of Psychiatry, 136,* 419–423.

Lewis, D. O., Shanok, S. S., Pincus, J. H., & Glaser, G. H. (1979). Violent juvenile delinquents. *Journal of the American Academy of Child Psychiatry, 15,* 307.

Lieberman, J. A., Johns, C. A., Kane, J. M., Rai, K., Pisciotta, A. V., Saltz, B., & Howard, A. (1988). Clozapine-induced agranulocytosis: Non–cross reactivity with other psychotrophic drugs. *Journal of Clinical Psychiatry, 49,* 271–277.

Liebowitz, M. R., Fyer, A. J., Gorman, J. M., Dillon, D., Davies, S. O., Stein, J. M., Cohen, B. S., & Klein, D. F. (1985). Specificity of lactate infusions in social phobia versus panic disorders. *American Journal of Psychiatry, 142,* 947–949.

Liebowitz, M. R., Gorman, J. M., Fyer, A. J., Levitt, M., Dillon, D., Levy, G., Appleby, I. L., Anderson, S., Palij, M., Davies, S. O., & Klein, D. F. (1985). Lactate provocation of panic attacks: 2. Biochemical and physiological findings. *Archives of General Psychiatry, 42,* 709–719.

Liebowitz, M. R., Schneier, F., Campeas, R., Hollander, E., Hatterer, J., Fyer, A. J., Gorman, J. M., Papp, L., Davies, S. O., Gully, R., & Klein, D. F. (1992). *Archives of General Psychiatry, 49,* 290–300.

Liem, J. H. (1980). Family study of schizophrenia: An update. *Schizophrenia Bulletin, 6,* 429–455.

Light, K. C., Dolan, C. A., Davis, M. R., & Sherwood, A. (1992). Cardiovascular responses to an active coping challenge as predictors of blood pressure patterns 10 to 15 years later. *Psychosomatic Medicine, 54,* 217–230.

Lilienfeld, S. O., & Waldman, I. D. (1990). The relation between childhood attention-deficit hyperactivity disorder and adult antisocial behavior reexamined: The problem of heterogeneity. *Clinical Psychology Review, 10,* 699–725.

Lindner, R. (1944). *Rebel without a cause: The hypnoanalysis of a criminal psychopath.* Philadelphia: Grune & Stratton.

Linehan, M. M., Goodstein, J. L., Nielsen, S. L., & Chiles, J. A. (1983). Reasons for staying alive when you are thinking of killing yourself: The Reasons for Living Inventory. *Journal of Consulting and Clinical Psychology, 51,* 276–286.

Linn, B., Linn, M., & Jensen, J. (1982). Degree of depression and immune responsiveness. *Psychosomatic Medicine, 44,* 128–129.

Lishman, W. A. (1978). *The psychological consequences of cerebral disorder.* Oxford: Blackwell.

Litz, B. T. (1992). Emotional numbing in combat-related posttraumatic stress disorder: A critical review and reformulation. *Clinical Psychology Review, 12,* 417–432.

Litz, B. T., & Keane, T. M. (1989). Information processing in anxiety disorders: Application to the understanding of posttraumatic stress disorder. *Clinical Psychology Review, 9,* 243–257.

Lloyd, C., Zisook, S., Click, M., Jr., & Jaffe, K. E. (1981). Life events and response to antidepressants. *Journal of Human Stress, 7,* 2–15.

Lobitz, W. C., & Post, R. D. (1979). Parameters of self-reinforcement and depression. *Journal of Abnormal Psychology, 88,* 33–41.

Loeb, J., & Mednick, S. A. (1976). Asocial behavior and electrodermal response patterns. In K. O. Christiansen & S. A. Mednick (Eds.), *Crime, society, and biology: A new look.* New York: Gardner Press.

Loehlin, J. C., & Nichols, R. C. (1976). *Heredity, environment, and personality.* Austin: University of Texas Press.

Loftus, E. F. (1992). *The reality of repressed memories.* Psi Chi Lowell Lewis Distinguished Lecture, American Psychological Association, Washington, DC.

Loftus, E. F., & Palmer, J. C. (1974). Reconstruction of automobile destruction: An example of the interaction between language and memory. *Journal of Verbal Learning and Verbal Behavior, 13,* 585–589.

Loland, S., & Balint, M. (1956). *Perversions: Psychodynamics and therapy.* New York: Random House.

Lombroso, C. (1911). *Crime: Its causes and remedies.* Boston: Little, Brown.

Lo Piccolo, J. (1983). The prevention of sexual problems in men. In G. Albee, S. Gordon, & H. Leitenberg (Eds.), *Promoting sexual responsibility and preventing sexual problems* (pp. 39–65). Burlington, VT: University Press of New England.

Lo Piccolo, J., & Stock, W. E. (1986). Treatment of sexual dysfunction. *Journal of Consulting and Clinical Psychology, 54,* 158–167.

Loranger, A. W. (1984). Sex difference in age at onset of schizophrenia. *Archives of General Psychiatry, 41,* 157–161.

Loranger, A. W., & Levine, P. M. (1978). Age at onset of bipolar affective illness. *Archives of General Psychiatry, 35,* 1345–1348.

Lord, C. G., Ross, L., & Leeper, M. R. (1979). Biased assimilation and attitude polarization: The effects of prior theories on subsequently considered evidence. *Journal of Personality and Social Psychology, 37,* 2098–2109.

Lotter, V. (1978). Follow-up studies. In M. Rutter & E. Schopler (Eds.), *Autism: Reappraisal of concepts and treatment.* New York: Plenum.

Lovaas, O. I. (1969). *Behavior modification: Teaching language to psychotic children* [Film]. Norwalk, CT: Appleton & Lang.

Lovaas, O. I. (1987). Behavioral treatment and normal educational and intellectual functioning in young autistic children. *Journal of Consulting and Clinical Psychology, 55,* 3–9.

Lovaas, O. I., Berberich, J. P., Perloff, B. F., & Schaeffer, B. (1966). Acquisition of imitative speech in schizophrenic children. *Science, 151,* 705–707.

Lovaas, O. I., Koegel, R. L., Simmons, J. Q., & Long, J. S. (1973). Some generalizations and follow-up measures on autistic children in behavior therapy. *Journal of Applied Behavior Analysis, 6,* 131–165.

Lovaas, O. I., Schaeffer, B., & Simmons, J. Q. (1965). Experimental studies in childhood schizophrenia: Building social behaviors by use of electric shock. *Journal of Experimental Studies in Personality, 1,* 99–109.

Lovaas, O. I., & Simmons, J. Q. (1969). Manipulation of self-destruction in three retarded children. *Journal of Applied Behavior Analysis, 2,* 143–157.

Lovaas, O. I, & Smith, T. (1989). A comprehensive behavioral theory of autistic children: Paradigm for research and treatment. *Journal of Behavior Therapy and Experimental Psychiatry, 20,* 17–29.

Lovaas, O. I., Smith, T., & McEachin, J. J. (1989). Clarifying comments on the Young Autism Study: Reply to Schopler, Short, and Mesibov. *Journal of Consulting and Clinical Psychology, 57,* 165–167.

Lovibond, S. H. (1963). The mechanism of conditioning treatment of enuresis. *Behaviour Research and Therapy, 1,* 17–24.

Lovibond, S. H., & Coote, M. (1969). Enuresis. In C. G. Costello (Ed.), *Symptoms of psychopathology.* New York: Wiley.

Luborsky, L., Mellon, J., von Ravensway, P., Childress, A. R., Levine, F. J., Alexander, K., Crits-Christoph, P., Cohen, K. D., Hole, A. V., & Ming, S. (1985). A verification of Freud's grandest clinical hypothesis: The transference. *Clinical Psychology Review, 5,* 231–246.

Luborsky, L., Singer, B., & Luborsky, L. (1975). Comparative studies of psychotherapies: Is it true that "everyone has won and all must have prizes"? *Archives of General Psychiatry, 32,* 995–1008.

Lucas, A. R., Beard, C. M., O'Fallon, W. M., & Kurland, L. T. (1991). 50-year trends in the incidence of anorexia nervosa in Rochester, Minn.: A population-based study. *American Journal of Psychiatry, 148,* 917–922.

Luchins, D. J., Weinberger, D. R., & Wyatt, R. J. (1982). Schizophrenia and cerebral asymmetry detected by computer tomography. *American Journal of Psychiatry, 139,* 753–757.

Ludwig, A. M., Brandsma, J. M., Wilbur, C. B., Benfeldt, F., & Jameson, D. H. (1972). The objective study of a multiple personality, or are four heads better than one? *Archives of General Psychiatry, 26,* 298–310.

Luria, Z., & Osgood, C. E. (1976). A postscript to "The three faces of Evelyn." *Journal of Abnormal Psychology, 85,* 276–285.

Luxenberger, H. (1930). Vorlaufiger Bericht über psychiatrische Sereinuntersuchungen an Zwillingen. *Z. Ges. Neurol. Psychiat., 116,* 297–347.

Lykken, D. T. (1957). A study of anxiety in the sociopathic personality. *Journal of Abnormal and Social Psychology, 55,* 6–10.

Lyles, J. N., Burish, T. G., Krozely, M. G., & Oldham, R. K. (1982). Efficacy of relaxation training and guided imagery in reducing the adversiveness of cancer chemotherapy. *Journal of Consulting and Clinical Psychology, 50,* 509–524.

Lyons, M. J., Kremen, W. S., Tsuang, M. T., & Faraone, S. V. (1989). Investigating putative genetic and environmental forms of schizophrenia: Methods and findings. *International Review of Psychiatry, 1,* 259–275.

Maas, J. W. (1975). Catecholamines and depression: A further specification of the catecholamine hypothesis of the affective disorders. In A. J. Friedhoff (Ed.), *Catecholamines and behavior* (pp. 119–133). New York: Plenum.

Maas, J. W., Fawcett, J. A., & Dekirmenjian, H. (1972). Catecholamine metabolism, depressive illness, and drug response. *Archives of General Psychiatry, 26,* 246–262.

MacCrimmon, D., Cleghorn, J., Asarnow, R., & Steffy, R. (1980). Children at risk for schizophrenia. *Archives of General Psychiatry, 37,* 671–674.

MacCulloch, M. J., & Feldman, M. P. (1966). Personality and the treatment of homosexuality. *Acta Psychiatrica Scandinavica, 43,* 300–317.

MacDougal, J. M., Dembroski, T. M., Dimsdale, J. E., & Hackett, T. P. (1985). Components of Type A, hostility, and anger-in: Further relationships to angiographic findings. *Health Psychology, 4,* 137–152.

Machon, R. A., Mednick, S. A., & Schulsinger, F. (1987). Seasonality, birth complications and schizophrenia. *British Journal of Psychiatry, 151,* 122–124.

Machover, K. (1949). *Personality projection in the drawing of the human figure.* Springfield, IL: Thomas.

MacKieth, R. (1972). Is maturation delay a frequent factor in the origins of primary nocturnal enuresis? *Developmental Medicine and Child Neurology, 14,* 217–223.

MacLeod, C., & Mathews, A. (1988). Anxiety and the allocation of attention to threat. *Quarterly Journal of Experimental Psychology, 40A,* 653–670.

MacLeod, C., Mathews, A., & Tata, P. (1986). Attentional bias in emotional disorders. *Journal of Abnormal Psychology, 95,* 15–20.

MacMahon, B., & Pugh T. (1965). Suicide in the widowed. *American Journal of Epidemiology, 81,* 23–31.

MacNamara, D. E., & Sagarin, E. (1977). *Sex, crime, and the law.* New York: Free Press.

Maddocks, P. D. (1970). A five-year follow-up of untreated psychopaths. *British Journal of Psychiatry, 116,* 511–515.

Madigan, R. J., & Bollenbach, A. (1982). Effects of induced mood in retrieval of personal episodic and semantic memories. *Psychological Reports, 50,* 147–157.

Maguire, G. P., Lee, E. G., Bevington, D. J., Kuchemann, C. S., Crabtree, R. J., & Cornell, C. E. (1978). Psychiatric problems in the first year after mastectomy. *British Medical Journal, 1,* 963–965.

Maher, B. A. (1966). *Principles of psychopathology: An experimental approach.* New York: McGraw-Hill.

Maher, B. A. (1968). The shattered language of schizophrenia. *Psychology Today,* pp. 30–33, 60.

Maher, B. A. (1972). The language of schizophrenia: A review and interpretation. *British Journal of Psychiatry, 120,* 4–17.

Maher, B. A. (1983). A tentative theory of schizophrenic utterance. In B. A. Maher & W. Maher (Eds.), *Progress in experimental personality research* (Vol. 12, pp. 1–52). Dallas, TX: Academic Press.

Maher, B. A. (1988a). Anomalous experience and delusional thinking: The logic of explanations. In T. F. Oltmanns & B. A. Maher (Eds.), *Delusional beliefs* (pp. 15–33). New York: Wiley.

Maher, B. A. (1988b). Delusions as the product of normal cognitions. In T. F. Oltmanns & B. A. Maher (Eds.), *Delusional beliefs* (pp. 333–336). New York: Wiley.

Mahesh Yogi, M. (1963). *The science of being and art of living.* London: Allen & Unwin.

Maier, S. F., & Seligman, M. E. P. (1976). Learned helplessness: Theory and evidence. *Journal of Experimental Psychology: General, 103,* 3–46.

Maier, S. F., Seligman, M. E. P., & Solomon, R. (1969). Pavlovian fear conditioning and learned helplessness: Effects on escape and avoidance behavior of the CS-US contingency and voluntary responding. In B. Campbell & R. Church (Eds.), *Punishment and aversive behavior* (pp. 299–342). Norwalk, CT: Appleton & Lang.

Maldonado, G., & Kraus, J. F. (1991). Variation in suicide occurrence by time of day, day of week, and lunar phase. *Suicide and Life-Threatening Behavior, 21,* 174–187.

Males, M. (1991a). Reply to Kim Smith, Ph.D., on "Teen suicide and changing cause-of-death certification, 1953–1987." *Suicide and Life-Threatening Behavior, 21,* 402–405.

Males, M. (1991b). Teen suicide and changing cause-of-death certification, 1953–1987. *Suicide and Life-Threatening Behavior, 21,* 245–259.

Manji, H. K., Hsiao, J. K., Risby, E. D., Oliver, J., Rudorfer, M. V., & Potter, W. Z. (1991). The mechanisms of action of lithium: I. Effects of serotoninergic and noradrenergic systems in normal subjects. *Archives of General Psychiatry, 48,* 505–512.

Manley, P. C., McMahon, R. J., Bradley, C. F., & Davidson, P. O. (1982). Depressive attributional style and depression following childbirth. *Journal of Abnormal Psychology, 91,* 245–254.

Mann, J. J., & Kapur, S. (1991). The emergence of suicidal ideation and behavior during antidepressant pharmacotherapy. *Archives of General Psychiatry, 48,* 1027–1033.

Mann, J. J., McBride, P. A., Brown, R. P., Linnoila, M., Leon, A. C., De Meo, M., Mieczkowski, T., Myers, J. E., & Stanley, M. (1992). Relationship between central and peripheral serotonin indexes in depressed and suicidal psychiatric inpatients. *Archives of General Psychiatry, 49,* 442–446.

Mannuzza, S., Klein, R. G., Bonagura, N., Malloy, P., Giampino, T. L., & Adilli, K. A. (1991). Hyperactive boys almost grown up. *Archives of General Psychiatry, 48,* 77–83.

Manuck, S. B., Harvey, S. H., Lechleiter, S. L., & Neal, K. (1978). Effects of coping on blood pressure responses to threat of aversive stimulation. *Psychophysiology, 15,* 544–549.

Mao, C. C., Marco, E., Revuelta, A., Bertilsson, L., & Costa, E. (1977). The turnover rate of γ-aminobutyric acid in the nuclei of telencephalon: Implications in the pharmacology of antipsychotics and of a minor tranquilizer. *Biological Psychiatry, 12,* 359–371.

Marcus, A. D. (1991). Murder trials induce Prozac defense. *Wall Street Journal,* February 7, Section B, page 8.

Marcus, D. K., & Mardone, M. E. (1992). Depression and interpersonal rejection. *Clinical Psychology Review, 12,* 433–449.

Marcus, M. D., Wing, R. R., Ewing, L., Kern, E., McDermott, M., & Gooding, W. (1990). A double-blind, placebo-controlled trial of fluoxetine plus behavior modification in the treatment of obese binge-eaters and non-binge-eaters. *American Journal of Psychiatry, 147,* 876–881.

Margraf, J., Ehlers, A., & Roth, W. T. (1986). Sodium lactate infusions and panic attacks: A review and critique. *Psychosomatic Medicine, 48,* 23–51.

Margraf, J., Ehlers, A., & Roth, W. T. (1988). Mitral valve proplapse and panic disorder: A review of their relationship. *Psychosomatic Medicine, 50,* 93–113.

Markowitz, J., Brown, R., Sweeney, J., & Mann, J. J. (1987). Reduced length and cost of hospital stay for major depression in patients treated with ECT. *American Journal of Psychiatry, 144,* 1025–1029.

Marks, I. M. (1981). Review of behavioral psychotherapy: 2. Sexual disorders. *American Journal of Psychiatry, 138,* 750–756.

Marks, I. M., & Gelder, M. G. (1967). Transvestism and fetishism: Clinical and psychological changes during faradic aversion. *British Journal of Psychiatry, 113,* 711–729.

Marks, I. M., Gelder, M. G., & Bancroft, J. (1970). Sexual deviants two years after electric aversion. *British Journal of Psychiatry, 117,* 173–185.

Marks, J. (1978). *The benzodiazepines: Use, overuse, misuse, abuse.* Baltimore: University Park Press.

Marlatt, G. A. (1978). Craving for alcohol, loss of control, and relapse: A cognitive-behavioral analysis. In P. E. Nathan, G. A. Marlatt, & T. Loberg (Eds.), *Alcoholism: New directions in behavior research and treatment* (pp. 271–314). New York: Plenum.

Marlatt, G. A. (1985). Cognitive factors in the relapse process. In G. A. Marlatt & J. Gordon (Eds.), *Relapse prevention* (pp. 128–200). New York: Guilford Press.

Marlatt, G. A., Demming, B., & Reid, J. (1973). Loss-of-control drinking in alcoholics. *Journal of Abnormal Psychology, 81,* 233–241.

Marlowe, M., Cossairt, A., Moon, C., Errera, J., McNeel, A., Peak, R., Ray, J., & Schroeder, C. (1985). Main and interaction effects of metallic toxins on classroom behavior. *Journal of Abnormal Child Psychology, 13,* 185–198.

Marshall, P. (1989). Attention deficit disorder and allergy: A neurochemical model of the relation between the illnesses. *Psychological Bulletin, 106,* 434–446.

Marshall, W. L., Jones, R., Ward, T., Johnston, P., & Barbaree, H. E. (1991). Treatment outcome with sex offenders. *Clinical Psychology Review, 11,* 465–485.

Martin, A. (1923). History of dancing mania. *American Journal of Clinical Medicine, 30,* 265–271.

Marx, E. M., Williams, J. M. G., & Claridge, G. C. (1992). Depression and social problem solving. *Journal of Abnormal Psychology, 101,* 78–86.

Marzuk, P. M., Leon, A. C., Tardiff, K., Morgan, E. B., Stajic, M., & Mann, J. J. (1992). The effect of access to lethal methods of injury on suicide rates. *Archives of General Psychiatry, 49,* 451–458.

Masand, P., Gupta, S., & Dewan, M. (1991). Suicidal ideation related to fluoxetine treatment. *New England Journal of Medicine, 324,* 420.

Maslow, A. (1970). *Motivation and personality.* New York: HarperCollins.

Masson, J. M. (1984). *The assault on truth: Freud's suppression of the seduction theory.* Harmondsworth, England: Penguin.

Masters, W., & Johnson, V. (1970). *Human sexual inadequacy.* Boston: Little, Brown.

Matarazzo, J. D. (1986). Computerized clinical psychological test interpretations. *American Psychologist, 41,* 14–24.

Mathews, A. (1990). Why worry? The cognitive function of anxiety. *Behaviour Research and Therapy, 28,* 455–568.

Mathews, A., May, J., Mogg, K., & Eysenck, M. (1990). Attentional bias in anxiety: Selective search or defective filtering? *Journal of Abnormal Psychology, 99,* 166–173.

Matthews, G. R., & Antes, J. R. (1992). Visual attention and depression: Cognitive biases in the eye fixations of dysphoric and the nondepressed. *Cognitive Therapy and Research, 16,* 359–371.

Matthews, K. A. (1982). Psychological perspectives on the Type A behavior pattern. *Psychological Bulletin, 91,* 293–323.

Matthews, K. A. (1988). Coronary heart disease and Type A behaviors: Update on and alternative to the Booth-Kewley and Friedman (1987) quantitative review. *Psychological Bulletin, 104,* 373–380.

Matthews, K. A., Glass, D. C., Rosenman, R. H., & Bortner, R. W. (1977). Competitive drive, pattern A, and coronary heart disease: A further analysis of some data from the Western Collaborative Group Study. *Journal of Chronic Diseases, 30,* 489–498.

Matthews, K. A., & Krantz, D. S. (1976). Resemblances of twins and their parents in pattern A behavior. *Psychosomatic Medicine, 38,* 140–144.

Matthews, K. A., Wing, R. R., Kuller, L. H., Meilahn, E. N., Kelsey, S. F., Costello, E. J., & Caggiula, A. W. (1990). Influences of natural menopause on psychological characteristics and symptoms of middle-aged healthy women. *Journal of Consulting and Clinical Psychology, 58,* 345–351.

Mattick, R. P., Andrews, G., Hadzi-Pavlovic, D., & Christensen, H. (1990). Treatment of panic and agoraphobia: An integrative review. *Journal of Nervous and Mental Disease, 178,* 567–576.

Mavissakalian, M., & Michelson, L. (1983). Self-directed in vivo exposure practice in behavioral and pharmacological treatments of agoraphobia. *Behavior Therapy, 14,* 506–519.

Mavissakalian, M., & Perel, J. M. (1989). Imipramine dose-response relationship in panic disorder with agoraphobia. *Archives of General Psychiatry, 46,* 127–131.

Mavissakalian, M., & Perel, J. M. (1992a). Clinical experiments in maintenance and discontinuation of imipramine therapy in panic disorder with agoraphobia. *Archives of General Psychiatry, 49,* 318–323.

Mavissakalian, M., & Perel, J. M. (1992b). Protective effects of imipramine maintenance treatment in panic disorder with agoraphobia. *American Journal of Psychiatry, 149,* 1053–1057.

May, P. R. (1968). *Treatment of schizophrenia.* New York: Science House.

May, P. R., Tuma, A. H., Yale, C., Potepan, P., & Dixon, W. J. (1976). Schizophrenia: A follow-up study of results of treatment: 2. Hospital stay over two to five years. *Archives of General Psychiatry, 33,* 481–486.

May, P. R., Van Putten, T., Yale, C., Potepan, P., Jenden, D. J., Fairchild, M., Goldstein, M., & Dixon, W. J. (1976). Predicting individual responses to drug treatment in schizophrenia: A test dose model. *Journal of Nervous and Mental Disease, 162,* 177–183.

Mayer, J. E., & Rosenblatt, A. (1974). Clash in perspective between mental patients and staff. *American Journal of Orthopsychiatry, 44,* 432–441.

Maynert, E. W., & Levi, R. (1964). Stress-induced release of brain norepinephrine and its inhibition by drugs. *Journal of Pharmacology and Experimental Therapeutics, 143,* 90–95.

Mayou, R. (1979). The course and determinants of reactions to myocardial infarction. *British Journal of Psychiatry, 134,* 588–594.

McAdoo, W. G., & De Myer, M. K. (1978). Personality characteristics of parents. In M. Rutter & E. Schopler (Eds.), *Autism: A reappraisal of concepts and treatment.* New York: Plenum.

McCann, I. L., & Holmes, D. S. (1984). Influence of aerobic exercise on depression. *Journal of Personality and Social Psychology, 46,* 1142–1147.

McClelland, D. C., Davis, W. N., Kalin, R., & Wanner, E. (1972). *The drinking man.* New York: Free Press.

McConnell, R. B. (1966). *Genetics of gastro-intestinal disorders.* London: Oxford University Press.

McCord, W., & McCord, J. (1964). *The psychopath.* New York: Van Nostrand.

McCord, W., McCord, J., & Zola, I. (1959). *Origins of crime.* New York: Columbia University Press.

McGarry, A. L., & Bendt, R. H. (1969). Criminal vs Civil commitment of psychotic offenders: A seven-year follow-up. *American Journal of Psychiatry, 125,* 1387–1394.

McGhie, A., & Chapman, J. (1961). Disorders of attention and perception in early schizophrenia. *British Journal of Medical Psychology, 34,* 103–116.

McGilley, B. M., & Holmes, D. S. (1988). Aerobic fitness and response to psychological stress. *Journal of Research in Personality, 22,* 129–139.

McGilley, B. M., Holmes, D. S., & Holmsten, R. D. (1993). Influence of exercise rehabilitation on coronary patients: A six-year follow-up. Unpublished manuscript. Univ. of Kansas.

McGlashan, T. H., & Fenton, W. S. (1992). The positive-negative distinction in schizophrenia. *Archives of General Psychiatry, 49,* 63–72.

McGreevy, M. A., Steadman, H. J., & Callahan, L. A. (1991).

The negligible effects of California's 1982 reform of the insanity defense test. *American Journal of Psychiatry, 148,* 744–750.

McGue, M., Pickens, R. W., & Svikis, D. S. (1992). Sex and age effects on the inheritance of alcohol problem: A twin study. *Journal of Abnormal Psychology, 101,* 3–17.

McGuffin, P., & Mawson, D. (1980). Obsessive-compulsive neurosis: Two identical twin pairs. *British Journal of Psychiatry, 137,* 285–287.

McGuigan, F. J. (1966). Covert oral behavior and auditory hallucinations. *Psychophysiology, 3,* 73–80.

McHugh, P. R., & Folstein, M. F. (1975). Psychiatric syndromes of Huntington's chorea: A clinical and phenomenological study. In D. F. Benson & D. Blumer (Eds.), *Psychiatric aspects of neurological disease.* Philadelphia: Grune & Stratton.

McHugh, P. R., & Goodell, H. (1971). Suicidal behavior: A distinction in patients with sedative poisoning seen in a general hospital. *Archives of General Psychiatry, 25,* 456–464.

McInnes, R. (1937). Observations on heredity in neurosis. *Journal of the Royal Society of Medicine, 30,* 895–904.

McIntosh, J. L. (1992). Epidemiology of suicide in the elderly. *Suicide and Life-Threatening Behavior, 22,* 15–35.

McKim, W. A. (1986). *Drugs and behavior.* Englewood Cliffs, NJ: Prentice Hall.

McLean, P. D., & Hakstian, A. R. (1979). Clinical depression: Comparitive efficacy of outpatient treatments. *Journal of Consulting and Clinical Psychology, 47,* 818–836.

McLean, P. D., & Hakstian, A. R. (1990). Relative endurance of unipolar depression treatment effects: Longitudinal follow-up. *Journal of Consulting and Clinical Psychology, 58,* 482–488.

McLeod, J. D., Kessler, R. C., & Landis, K. R. (1992). Speed of recovery from major depressive episodes in a community sample of married men and women. *Journal of Abnormal Psychology, 101,* 277–286.

McNally, R. J. (1990). Psychological approaches to panic disorder: A review. *Psychological Bulletin, 108,* 403–419.

McNally, R. J., & Foa, E. B. (1987). Cognition and agoraphobia: Bias in the interpretation of threat. *Cognitive Therapy and Research, 11,* 567–581.

McNally, R. J., Riemann, B. C., & Kim, E. (1990). Selective processing of threat cues in panic disorder. *Behaviour Research and Therapy, 28,* 407–412.

McNamara, S. S., Molot, M. A., Stremple, J. F., & Cutting, R. T. (1971). Coronary artery disease in combat casualties in Vietnam. *JAMA, 216,* 1185.

Mednick, S. A. (1958). A learning theory approach to research in schizophrenia. *Psychological Bulletin, 55,* 316–327.

Mednick, S. A., Cudeck, R., Griffith, J. J., Talovic, S. A., & Schulsinger, F. A. (1984). The Danish High-Risk Project: Recent methods and findings. In N. F. Watt, E. J. Anthony, L. C. Wynne, & J. E. Rolf (Eds.), *Children at risk for schizophrenia.* Cambridge: Cambridge University Press.

Mednick, S. A., Gabrielli, W. F., & Hutchings, B. (1984). Genetic influences in criminal convictions: Evidence from an adoption cohort. *Science, 224,* 891–894.

Mednick, S. A., & Hutchings, B. (1978). Genetic and psychophysical factors in asocial behavior. In R. D. Hare &

D. Schalling (Eds.), *Psychopathic behavior: Approaches to research* (pp. 239–254). New York: Wiley.

Mednick, S. A., Machon, R. A., & Huttunen, M. O. (1990). An update on the Helsinki influenza project. *Archives of General Psychiatry, 47,* 292.

Mednick, S. A., Machon, R. A., Huttunen, M. O., & Bonett, D. (1988). Adult schizophrenia following prenatal exposure to an influenza epidemic. *Archives of General Psychiatry, 45,* 189–192.

Mednick, S. A., Parnas, J., & Schulsinger, F. A. (1987). The Copenhagen High-Risk Project, 1962–86. *Schizophrenia Bulletin, 13,* 485–495.

Mednick, S. A., & Schulsinger, F. A. (1968). Some premorbid characteristics related to breakdown in children with schizophrenic mothers. In D. Rosenthal & S. S. Kety (Eds.), *The transmission of schizophrenia.* Elmsford, NY: Pergamon Press.

Meduna, L. von (1935). Die Konvolsionstherapie der Schizophrenie. *Psychiatrisch-neurologische Wochenschrift, 37,* 317–319.

Meduna, L. von (1938). General discussion of the cardiazol therapy. *American Journal of Psychiatry, 94* (Suppl.), 46.

Meehan, P., Lamb, J. A., Saltzman, L. E., & O'Carroll, P. W. (1992). Attempted suicide among young adults: Progress toward a meaningful estimate of prevalence. *American Journal of Psychiatry, 149,* 41–44.

Mehta, D., Mehta, S., Petit, J., & Shriner, W. (1979). Cardiac arrhythmias and haloperidol. *American Journal of Psychiatry, 136,* 1468–1469.

Meichenbaum, D. (1972). Cognitive modification of test-anxious college students. *Journal of Consulting and Clinical Psychology, 39,* 370–379.

Meichenbaum, D. (1975). Self-instruction methods. In F. H. Kanfer & A. P. Goldstein (Eds.), *Helping people change* (pp. 357–392). Elmsford, NY: Pergamon Press.

Meichenbaum, D., & Goodman, J. (1971). Training impulsive children to talk to themselves: A means for developing self-control. *Journal of Abnormal Psychology, 77,* 115–126.

Meisch, R. A. (1991). Studies of drug self-administration. *Psychiatric Annals, 21,* 196–205.

Melia, P. I. (1970). Prophylactic lithium: A double-blind trial in recurrent affective disorders. *British Journal of Psychiatry, 116,* 621–624.

Mellman, T. A., & Uhde, T. W. (1989). Electroencephalographic sleep in panic disorder. *Archives of General Psychiatry, 46,* 178–184.

Meltzer, H. Y., Bastani, B., Kwon, K. Y., Ramirez, L. F., Burnett, S., & Sharpe, J. (1989). A prospective study of clozapine in treatment-resistant schizophrenic patients. *Psychopharmacology, 99,* S68–S72.

Meltzer, H. Y., Bastani, B., Ramirez, L. F., & Matsubara, S. (1989). Clozapine: New research on efficacy and mechanism of action. *European Archives of Psychiatry and Neurological Sciences, 238,* 332–339.

Mendlewicz, J., & Rainer, J. D. (1977). Adoption study supporting genetic transmission in manic-depressive illness. *Nature, 268,* 327–329.

Menninger, K. A. (1938). *Man against himself.* Orlando, FL: Harcourt Brace.

Messiha, F. S., & Carlson, J. C. (1983). Behavioral and clinical profiles of Tourette's disease: A comprehensive overview. *Brain Research Bulletin, 11,* 195–204.

Mettlin, C. (1976). Occupational careers and the prevention of coronary-prone behavior. *Social Science and Medicine, 10,* 367–372.

Metz, P., & Mathiesen, F. R. (1979). External iliac "steal syndrome" leading to a defect in penile erection and impotence. *Vascular Surgery, 13,* 70–72.

Meyer, J., & Reter, D. (1979). Sex reassignment: Follow-up. *Archives of General Psychiatry, 36,* 1010–1015.

Meyer, R. E. (1975). The psychiatric consequences of marijuana use. In J. R. Tinklenberg (Ed.), *Marijuana and health hazards* (pp. 133–152). Dallas, TX: Academic Press.

Michaels, J. E., & Goodman, S. E. (1934). Incidence and intercorrelations of enuresis and other neuropathic traits in so-called normal children. *American Journal of Orthopsychiatry, 4,* 79–106.

Michal, V., Kramar, R., Pospichal, J., & Hejhal, L. (1977). Arterial epigastricocavernous anastomosis for the treatment of sexual impotence. *World Journal of Surgery, 1,* 515–524.

Michelson, L. K., & Marchione, K. (1991). Behavioral, cognitive, and pharmacological treatments of panic disorder with agoraphobia: Critique and synthesis. *Journal of Consulting and Clinical Psychology, 59,* 100–114.

Mikkelsen, M., & Stene, J. (1970). Genetic counseling in Down's syndrome. *Human Heredity, 20,* 457–464.

Miles, J. E., McLean, P. D., & Maurice, W. L. (1976). The medical student therapist: Treatment outcome. *Canadian Psychiatric Association Journal, 21,* 467–472.

Milgram, N. A. (1969). The rational and irrational in Zigler's motivational approach to mental retardation. *American Journal of Mental Deficiency, 73,* 527–532.

Miller, A. (1949). *Death of a salesman.* New York: Viking Penguin.

Miller, D. H., Clancy, J., & Cummings, E. (1953). A comparison between unidirectional current, non-convulsive electrical stimulation given with Reiter's machine, standard alternating current electroshock (Cerletti method), and pentothal in chronic schizophrenia. *American Journal of Psychiatry, 109,* 617–620.

Miller, I. W., & Norman, W. H. (1979). Learned helplessness in humans: A review and attributional theory model. *Psychological Bulletin, 86,* 93–118.

Miller, M. P., Murphy, P. J., & Miller, T. P. (1978). Comparison of electromyographic feedback and progressive relaxation training in treating circumscribed anxiety-stress reactions. *Journal of Consulting and Clinical Psychology, 46,* 1291–1298.

Miller, P., & Ingham, J. G. (1976). Friends, confidants, and symptoms. *Social Psychiatry, 11,* 51–58.

Miller, S. D., & Triggiano, P. J. (1992). The psychophysiological investigation of multiple personality disorder: Review and update. *American Journal of Clinical Hypnosis, 35,* 47–61.

Miller, W. R. (1975). Psychological deficit in depression. *Psychological Bulletin, 82,* 238–260.

Mindham, R. H. S. (1973). An evaluation of continuation therapy with tricyclic antidepressants in depressive illness. *Psychological Medicine, 3,* 5–17.

Mindham, R. H. S. (1982). Tricyclic antidepressants and

amine precursors. In E. S. Paykel (Ed.), *Handbook of affective disorders* (pp. 231–245). New York: Guilford Press.

Mineka, S. (1985). Animal models of anxiety-based disorders: Their usefulness and limitations. In A. H. Tuma & J. Maser (Eds.), *Anxiety and anxiety disorders* (pp. 199–244). Hillsdale, NJ: Erlbaum.

Mineka, S., Davidson, M., Cook, M., & Keir, R. (1984). Observational conditioning of snake fear in rhesus monkeys. *Journal of Abnormal Psychology, 93,* 355–372.

Miniszek, N. A. (1983). Development of Alzheimer's disease in Down syndrome individuals. *American Journal of Mental Deficiency, 87,* 377–385.

Minkoff, K., Bergman, E., Beck, A. T., & Beck, R. (1973). Hopelessness, depression, and attempted suicide. *American Journal of Psychiatry, 130,* 455–459.

Minton, J., Campbell, M., Green, W., Jennings, S., & Samit, C. (1982). Cognitive assessment of siblings of autistic children. *Journal of the American Academy of Child Psychiatry, 21,* 256–261.

Mirsky, I. A. (1958). Physiologic, psychologic, and social determinants of the etiology of duodenal ulcer. *American Journal of Digestive Diseases, 3,* 285–314.

Mishler, E. G., & Waxler, N. E. (1968a). *Family processes and schizophrenia: Theory and selected experimental studies.* New York: Science House.

Mishler, E. G., & Waxler, N. E. (1968b). *Interaction in families: An experimental study of family processes and schizophrenia.* New York: Wiley.

Mitchell, J. E., & Groat, R. (1984). A placebo-controlled, double-blind trial of amitriptyline in bulimia. *Journal of Clinical Psychopharmacology, 4,* 186–193.

Mittelmann, B., Wolff, H. G., & Scharf, M. (1942). Emotions in gastroduodenal functions. *Psychosomatic Medicine, 4,* 5–61.

Mizes, J. S., & Lohr, J. M. (1983). The treatment of bulimia (binge-eating and self-induced vomiting): A quasi-experimental investigation of the effects of stimulus narrowing, self-reinforcement and self-control relaxation. *International Journal of Eating Disorders, 2,* 59–65.

Monahan, J. (1973). The psychiatrization of criminal behavior. *Hospital and Community Psychiatry, 24,* 105–107.

Monahan, J. (1976). The prevention of violence. In J. Monahan (Ed.), *Community mental health and the criminal justice system.* Elmsford, NY: Pergamon Press.

Monahan, J. (1978). Prediction research and the emergency commitment of dangerous mentally ill persons: A reconsideration. *American Journal of Psychiatry, 135,* 198–201.

Monahan, J. (1984). The prediction of violent behavior: Toward a second generation of theory and policy. *American Journal of Psychiatry, 141,* 10–15.

Money, J. (1970). Use of an androgen-depleting hormone in the treatment of sex offenders. *Journal of Sex Research, 6,* 165–172.

Monnelly, E. P., Woodruff, R. A., & Robins, L. N. (1974). Manic depressive illness and social achievement in a public hospital sample. *Acta Psychiatrica Scandinavica, 50,* 318–325.

Monroe, S. M., Imhoff, D. F., Wise, B. D., & Harris, J. E. (1983). Prediction of psychosocial symptoms under high-risk psychosocial circumstances: Life events, social support, and symptom specificity. *Journal of Abnormal Psychology, 92,* 338–350.

Monroe, S. M., & Simons, A. D. (1991). Diathesis-stress theories in the context of life stress research: Implications for the depressive disorders. *Psychological Bulletin, 110,* 406–425.

Moore, B. C. (1973). Some characteristics of institutionalized mongoloids. *Journal of Mental Deficiency Research, 17,* 46–54.

Moran, L. J. (1953). Vocabulary knowledge and usage among normal and schizophrenic subjects. *Psychological Monographs, 67* (370).

Moran, L. J., Mefferd, R. B., Jr., & Kimble, J. P. (1964). Idiodynamic sets in word association. *Psychological Monographs, 78* (579).

Morgan, R. T., & Young, G. C. (1972). The conditioning treatment of childhood enuresis. *British Journal of Social Work, 2,* 503–509.

Morokoff, P. J., Baum, A., McKinnon, W. R., & Gilland, R. (1987). Effects of chronic unemployment and acute psychological stress on sexual arousal in men. *Health Psychology, 6,* 545–560.

Morokoff, P. J., & Heinman, J. R. (1980). Effects of erotic stimuli on sexually functional and dysfunctional women: Multiple measures before and after therapy. *Behaviour Research and Therapy, 18,* 127–137.

Morrison, J. R., & Stewart, M. A. (1971). A family study of the hyperactive child syndrome. *Biological Psychiatry, 3,* 189–195.

Morrison, J. R., & Stewart, M. A. (1973). The psychiatric status of the legal families of adopted hyperactive children. *Archives of General Psychiatry, 28,* 888–891.

Morrison, J. R., & Stewart, M. A. (1974). Bilateral inheritance as evidence for polygenicity in the hyperactive child syndrome. *Journal of Nervous and Mental Disease, 158,* 226–228.

Mosher, L. R., & Keith, S. J. (1980). Psychosocial treatment: Individual, family, and community support approaches. *Schizophrenia Bulletin, 6,* 10–41.

Mosher, L. R., & Menn, A. Z. (1978). Community residential treatment for schizophrenia: Two-year follow-up. *Hospital and Community Psychiatry, 29,* 715–723.

Mosher, L. R., Menn, A. Z., & Matthews, S. M. (1975). Soteria: Evaluation of a home-based treatment for schizophrenia. *American Journal of Orthopsychiatry, 45,* 455–467.

Motto, J. A. (1977). Estimation of suicidal risk by the use of clinical models. *Suicide and Life-Threatening Behavior, 74,* 237–245.

Motto, J. A., Heilbron, D. C., & Juster, R. P. (1985). Development of a clinical instrument to estimate suicide risk. *Archives of General Psychiatry, 42,* 680–686.

Mowrer, O. H. (1950). *Learning theory and personality dynamics.* New York: Ronald Press.

Mowrer, O. H., & Mowrer, W. A. (1938). Enuresis: A method for its study and treatment. *American Journal of Orthopsychiatry, 8,* 436–447.

Mucha, T. F., & Reinhardt, R. F. (1970). Conversion reactions in student aviators. *American Journal of Psychiatry, 127,* 493–497.

Muijen, M., Silverstone, T., Mehmet, A., & Christie, M. (1988). A comparative clinical trial of fluoxetine, mianserin and placebo in depressed outpatients. *Acta Psychiatrica Scandinavica, 78,* 384–390.

Mullan, M. J., & Murray, R. M. (1989). The impact of molecular genetics on our understanding of the psychoses. *British Journal of Psychiatry, 154,* 591–595.

Mullaney, J. A. (1984). The relationship between anxiety and depression: A review of some principal component analytic studies. *Journal of Affective Disorders, 7,* 139–148.

Mullinix, J. M., Norton, B. J., Hack, S., & Fishman, M. (1978). Skin temperature biofeedback and migraine. *Headache, 17,* 242–244.

Mulvey, E. P., Geller, J. L., & Roth, L. H. (1987). The promise and peril of involuntary outpatient commitment. *American Psychologist, 42,* 571–584.

Murphy, G. (1923). Types of word-associations in dementia praecox, manic-depressives, and normal persons. *American Journal of Psychiatry, 2,* 539–571.

Murphy, G. E., Simons, A. D., Wetzel, R. D., & Lustman, P. J. (1984). Cognitive therapy and pharmacotherapy: Singly and together in the treatment of depression. *Archives of General Psychiatry, 41,* 33–41.

Murphy, J. (1976). Psychiatric labeling in cross-cultural perspective. *Science, 191,* 1019–1028.

Murphy, J. M., Olivier, D. C., Monson, R. R., Sobol, R. M., Federman, E. B., & Leighton, A. H. (1991). Depression and anxiety in relation to social status. *Archives of General Psychiatry, 48,* 223–229.

Murray, H. A. (1943). *Thematic Apperception Test.* Cambridge, MA: Harvard University Press.

Murrell, J., Farlow, M., Ghetti, B., & Benson, M. D. (1991). A mutation in the amyloid precursor protein associated with hereditary Alzheimer's disease. *Science, 254,* 97–99.

Muscettola, G., Potter, W. Z., Pickar, D., & Goodwin, F. (1984). Urinary 3-methoxy-4-hydroxyphenylglycol and affective disorders. *Archives of General Psychiatry, 41,* 337–342.

Muslin, H. L., Gyarfas, K., & Pieper, W. J. (1966). Separation experience and cancer of the breast. *Annals of the New York Academy of Science, 125,* 802.

Myers, J. K., Weissman, M. M., Tischler, G. L., Holzer, C. E., Leaf, P. J., Orvaschel, H., Anthony, J. C., Boyd, J. H., Burke, J. D., Kramer, M., & Stoltzman, R. (1984). Six-month prevalence of psychiatric disorders in three communities. *Archives of General Psychiatry, 41,* 959–967.

Myerson, A (1940). Review of mental disorders in urban areas: An ecological study of schizophrenia and other psychoses. *American Journal of Psychiatry, 96,* 995–997.

Natale, M. (1977). Effects of induced elation-depression on speech in the initial interview. *Journal of Consulting and Clinical Psychology, 45,* 45–52.

Natale, M., & Hantas, M. (1982). Effect of temporary mood states on selective memory about the self. *Journal of Personality and Social Psychology, 42,* 927–934.

Nathan, P. E. (1988). The addictive personality is the behavior of the addict. *Journal of Consulting and Clinical Psychology, 56,* 183–188.

Nathan, S. G. (1986). The epidemiology of the DSM-III psychosexual dysfunctions. *Journal of Sex and Marital Therapy, 12,* 267–281.

National Institute of Mental Health. (1976, April 20). Rising suicide rate linked to economy. *Los Angeles Times*, sec. 8, pp. 2, 5.

Neal, A. M., & Turner, S. M. (1991). Anxiety disorders with African Americans: Current status. *Psychological Bulletin, 109*, 400–410.

Neale, J. M. (1971). Perceptual span in schizophrenia. *Journal of Abnormal Psychology, 77*, 196–204.

Neale, J. M., & Oltmanns, T. F. (1980). *Schizophrenia*. New York: Wiley.

Needleman, H. L., Gunnoe, C., Leviton, A., Reed, R., Peresie, H., Maher, C., & Barrett, P. (1979). Deficits in psychologic and classroom performance of children with elevated dentine lead levels. *New England Journal of Medicine, 300*, 689–695.

Nelson, K. B. (1991). Prenatal and perinatal factors in the etiology of autism. *Pediatrics, 87*, 761–766.

Nelson, R. E., & Craighead, W. E. (1977). Selective recall of positive and negative feedback, self-control behaviors, and depression. *Journal of Abnormal Psychology, 86*, 379–388.

Nelson, R. E., & Craighead, W. E. (1981). Tests of a self-control model of depression. *Behavior Therapy, 12*, 123–129.

Nicholson, R. A., & Kugler, K. E. (1991). Competent and incompetent criminal defendants: A quantitative review of comparative research. *Psychological Bulletin, 109*, 355–370.

Nies, A., & Robinson, D. S. (1982). Monoamine oxidase inhibitors. In E. S. Paykel (Ed.), *Handbook of affective disorders* (pp. 246–261). New York: Guilford Press.

Nietzel, M. T., & Fisher, S. G. (1981). Effectiveness of professional and paraprofessional helpers: A comment on Durlak. *Psychological Bulletin, 89*, 555–565.

Nowlin, N. S. (1983). Anorexia nervosa in twins: Case report and review. *Journal of Clinical Psychiatry, 44*, 101–105.

Noyes, R., Clancy, J., Crowe, R. R., Hoenk, P., & Slymen, D. J. (1978). The familial prevalence of anxiety neurosis. *Archives of General Psychiatry, 35*, 1057–1059.

Noyes, R., Clarkson, C., Crowe, R. R., Yates, W. R., & McChesney, C. M. (1987). A family study of generalized anxiety disorder. *American Journal of Psychiatry, 144*, 1019–1024.

Nurnberger, J. I., & Gershon, E. S. (1982). Genetics. In E. S. Paykel (Ed.), *Handbook of affective disorders* (pp. 126–145). New York: Guilford Press.

Nyback, H. J., Borzecki, Z., & Sedvall, G. (1968). Accumulation and disappearance of catecholamines formed from tyrosine-C in mouse brain: Effect of some psychotrophic drugs. *European Journal of Pharmacology, 4*, 395–402.

Oakes, W. F. (1982). Learned helplessness and defensive strategies: A rejoinder. *Journal of Personality, 50*, 515–525.

Oakes, W. F., & Curtis, N. (1982). Learned helplessness: Not dependent upon cognitions, attributions, or other such phenomenal experiences. *Journal of Personality, 50*, 387–408.

O'Connor v. Donaldson, 493 F.2d 507 (5th Cir. 1974); 422 U.S. 563 (1975).

Ödegård, O. (1972). The multifactorial theory of inheritance in predisposition of schizophrenia. In A. K. Kaplan (Ed.), *Genetic factors in schizophrenia*. Springfield, IL: Thomas.

Offir, C. W. (1982). *Human sexuality*. Orlando, FL: Harcourt Brace.

Ofshe, R. J. (1992). Inadvertent hypnosis during interrogation: False confession due to dissociative state; misidentified multiple personality and the satanic cult hypothesis. *International Journal of Clinical and Experimental Hypnosis, 40*, 125–155.

O'Hara, M. W., Rehm, L. P., & Campbell, S. B. (1982). Predicting depressive symptomatology. *Journal of Abnormal Psychology, 91*, 457–461.

O'Hara, M. W., Schlechte, J. A., Lewis, D. A., & Varner, M. W. (1991). Controlled prospective study of postpartum mood disorders: Psychological, environmental, and hormonal variables. *Journal of Abnormal Psychology, 100*, 63–73.

O'Hara, M. W., Schlechte, J. A., Lewis, D. A., & Wright, E. J. (1991). Prospective study of postpartum blues. *Archives of General Psychiatry, 48*, 801–806.

O'Hara, M. W., Zekoski, E. M., Philipps, L. H. C., & Wright, E. J. (1990). Controlled prospective study of postpartum mood disorders: Comparison of childbearing and nonchildbearing women. *Journal of Abnormal Psychology, 99*, 3–15.

Olds, D. (1982). The Prenatal/Early Infancy Project: An ecological approach to prevention of developmental difficulties. In J. Belsky (Ed.), *In the beginning*. New York: Columbia University Press.

Olinger, L. J., Kuiper, N. A., & Shaw, B. F. (1987). Dysfunctional attitudes and stressful life events: An interactive model of depression. *Cognitive Therapy and Research, 11*, 25–40.

Ollendick, T. H. (1986). Behavior therapy with children and adolescents. In S. L. Garfield & A. E. Bergin (Eds.), *Handbook of psychotherapy and behavior change* (pp. 525–564). New York: Wiley.

Oltmanns, T. F., & Maher, B. A. (1988). *Delusional beliefs*. New York: Wiley.

O'Malley, S. S., Jaffee, A. J., Chang, G., Schottenfeld, R. S., Meyer, R. E., & Rounsaville, B. (1992). Naltrexone and coping skills therapy for alcohol dependence: A controlled study. *Archives of General Psychiatry, 49*, 881–887.

Opler, L. A., Kay, S. R., Rosado, V., & Lindenmayer, J. P. (1984). Positive and negative syndromes in chronic schizophrenic inpatients. *Journal of Nervous and Mental Disease, 172*, 317–325.

Orbach, I., Bar-Joseph, H., & Dror, N. (1990). Styles of problem solving in suicidal individuals. *Suicide and Life-Threatening Behavior, 20*, 56–64.

Orlinsky, D. E., & Howard, K. I. (1986). Process and outcome in psychotherapy. In S. L. Garfield & A. E. Bergin (Eds.), *Handbook of psychotherapy and behavior change* (pp. 311–384). New York: Wiley.

Orne, M. T. (1962). On the social psychology of the psychological experiment: With particular reference to demand characteristics and their implications. *American Psychologist, 17*, 776–783.

Orne, M. T., Dinges, D. F., & Orne, E. C. (1984). On the differential diagnosis of multiple personality in the forensic context. *International Journal of Clinical and Experimental Hypnosis, 32*, 118–169.

Orne, M. T., & Scheibe, K. E. (1964). The contribution of nondeprivation factors in the production of sensory deprivation effects: The psychology of the panic button. *Journal of Abnormal and Social Psychology, 68,* 3–12.

Osgood, C. E., & Luria, Z. (1954). A blind analysis of a case of multiple personality using the semantic differential. *Journal of Abnormal and Social Psychology, 49,* 579–591.

Osgood, C. E., Luria, Z., & Smith, S. W. (1976). A blind analysis of another case of multiple personality using the semantic differential technique. *Journal of Abnormal Psychology, 85,* 256–270.

Osler, W. (1892). *Lectures on angina and allied states.* Norwalk, CT: Appleton & Lang.

O'Sullivan, C. S., & Durso, F. T. (1984). Effect of schema-incongruent information on memory for stereotypical attributes. *Journal of Personality and Social Psychology, 47,* 55–70.

Palmer, R. L. (1981). *Electroconvulsive therapy: An appraisal.* New York: Oxford University Press.

Pardes, H., Kaufmann, C. A., Pincus, H. A., & West, A. (1989). Genetics and psychiatry: Past discoveries, current dilemmas, and future directions. *American Journal of Psychiatry, 146,* 435–443.

Partridge, G. E. (1928). A study of 50 cases of psychopathic personality. *American Journal of Psychiatry, 7,* 953–973.

Pasamanick, B., Rogers, M. E., & Lilienfeld, A. M. (1956). Pregnancy experience and the development of behavior disorders in children. *American Journal of Psychiatry, 112,* 613–618.

Pate v. Robinson, 384 U.S. 375 (1966).

Patsiokas, A., Clum, G., & Luscomb, R. (1979). Cognitive characteristics of suicide attempters. *Journal of Consulting and Clinical Psychology, 47,* 478–484.

Paul, G. L., & Lentz, R. J. (1977). *Psychosocial treatment of chronic mental patients.* Cambridge, MA: Harvard University Press.

Paul, S. M., Marangos, P. J., Goodwin, F. K., & Slotnick, P. (1980). Brain-specific benzodiazepine receptors and putative endogenous benzodiazepine-like compounds. *Biological Psychiatry, 15,* 407–428.

Pauls, D. L., Bucher, K., Crowe, R. R., & Noyes, R. (1980). A genetic study of panic disorder pedigrees. *American Journal of Human Genetics, 32,* 639–644.

Pauls, D. L., Kruger, S. D., Leckman, J. F., Cohen, D. J., & Kidd, K. K. (1984). The risk of Tourette's syndrome and chronic multiple tics among relatives of Tourette's syndrome patients obtained by direct interview. *Journal of the American Academy of Child Psychiatry, 23,* 134–137.

Pavy, D. (1968). Verbal behavior in schizophrenia: A review of recent studies. *Psychological Bulletin, 70,* 164–178.

Paykel, E. S., Emms, E. M., Fletcher, J., & Rassaby, E. S. (1980). Life events and social support in puerperal depression. *British Journal of Psychiatry, 136,* 339–346.

Paykel, E. S., Prusoff, B. A., & Myers, J. K. (1975). Suicide attempts and recent life events: A controlled comparison. *Archives of General Psychiatry, 32,* 327–333.

Paykel, E. S., & Tanner, J. (1976). Life events, depressive relapse, and maintenance treatment. *Psychological Medicine, 6,* 481–485.

Payne, R. W. (1962). An object classification test as a measure of over-inclusive thinking in schizophrenic patients. *British Journal of Social and Clinical Psychology, 1,* 213–221.

Payne, R. W., & Friedlander, A. (1962). A short battery of simple tests for measuring overinclusive thinking. *Journal of Mental Science, 108,* 362–367.

Payne, R. W., Matussek, P., & George, E. I. (1959). An experimental study of schizophrenic thought disorder. *Journal of Mental Science, 105,* 627–652.

Pearlin, L., & Schooler, C. (1978). The structure of coping. *Journal of Health and Social Behavior, 19,* 2–21.

Pearlson, G. D., Kim, W. S., Kubos, K., Moberg, P., Jayaram, G., Bascom, M., Chase, G., Goldfinger, A., & Tune, L. (1989). Ventricle–brain ratio, computed tomographic density, and brain area in 50 schizophrenics. *Archives of General Psychiatry, 46,* 690–697.

Pelham, W. E., Bender, M. E., Caddel, J., Booth, S., & Moorer, S. H. (1985). Methylphenidate and children with attention deficit disorder. *Archives of General Psychiatry, 42,* 948–952.

Pelham, W. E., Schnedler, R. W., Bologna, N., & Contreras, A. (1980). Behavioral and stimulant treatment of hyperactive children: A therapy study with methylphenidate probes in a within-subject design. *Journal of Applied Behavior Analysis, 13,* 221–236.

Pelham, W. E., Schnedler, R. W., Miller, J., Ronnei, M., Paluchowski, C., Burdow, M., Marks, D., Nilsson, D., & Bender, M. E. (1986). The combination of behavior therapy and psychostimulant medication in the treatment of hyperactive children: A therapy outcome study. In L. Bloomingdale (Ed.), *Attention deficit disorders.* Jamaica, NY: Spectrum.

Penfield, W. (1955). The permanent record of the stream of consciousness. *Acta Psychologica, 11,* 47–69.

Penfield, W., & Perot, P. (1963). The brain's record of auditory and visual experience. *Brain, 86,* 595–696.

Penk, W. E., Charles, H. L., & Van Hoose, T. A. (1978). Comparative effectiveness of day hospital and inpatient psychiatric treatment. *Journal of Consulting and Clinical Psychology, 46,* 94–101.

Penn, I., & Starzl, T. E. (1972). Malignant tumors arising de novo in immunosuppressed organ transplant recipients. *Transplantation, 14,* 407–417.

People v. Buono, Calif. 81-A354231 (1983).

Perls, F. S. (1970). Four lectures. In J. Fagan & I. L. Shepherd (Eds.), *Gestalt therapy now: Therapy, techniques, applications.* Palo Alto, CA: Science and Behavior Books.

Perr, I. N. (1981). Effects of the Rennie decision on private hospitalization in New Jersey: Two case reports. *American Journal of Psychiatry, 138,* 774–778.

Perris, C. (1982). The distinction between bipolar and unipolar affective disorders. In E. S. Paykel (Ed.), *Handbook of affective disorders.* New York: Guilford Press.

Perry, J. D., & Whipple, B. (1981). Pelvic muscle strength of female ejaculators: Evidence in support of a new theory of orgasm. *Journal of Sex Research, 17,* 22–39.

Peterson, C., Schwartz, S. M., & Seligman, M. E. P. (1981). Self-blame and depressive symptoms. *Journal of Personality and Social Psychology, 41,* 253–259.

Peterson, C., & Seligman, M. E. P. (1984). Causal explanations as a risk factor for depression: Theory and evidence. *Psychological Review, 91,* 347–374.

Petterson, U. (1974). *Manik depressiv sjukdom.* Doctoral dissertation, Karolinska Institute, Stockholm.

Pettingale, K. W. (1984). Coping and cancer prognosis. *Journal of Psychosomatic Research, 28,* 363–364.

Pettingale, K. W., Greer, S., & Tee, D. E. H. (1977). Serum IgA and emotional expression in breast cancer patients. *Journal of Psychosomatic Research, 21,* 395–399.

Petty, F., & Sherman, A. D. (1984). Plasma GABA levels in psychiatric illness. *Journal of Affective Disorders, 6,* 131–138.

Pflanz, M. (1971). Epidemiological and sociocultural factors in the etiology of duodenal ulcer. *Advances in Psychosomatic Medicine, 6,* 121–151.

Philipps, L. H. C., & O'Hara, M. W. (1991). Prospective study of postpartum depression: 4½-year follow-up of women and children. *Journal of Abnormal Psychology, 100,* 151–155.

Phillips, D. P. (1974). The influence of suggestion on suicide: Substantive and theoretical implications of the Werther effect. *American Sociological Review, 39,* 340–354.

Phillips, D. P. (1977). Motor vehicle fatalities increase just after publicized suicide stories. *Science, 196,* 1464–1465.

Phillips, D. P. (1979). Suicide, motor vehicle fatalities, and the mass media: Evidence toward a theory of suggestion. *American Journal of Sociology, 84,* 1150–1174.

Phillips, K. A. (1991). Body dysmorphic disorder: The distress of imagined ugliness. *American Journal of Psychiatry, 148,* 1138–1149.

Phillips, K. A., Gunderson, J. G., Hirschfeld, R. M., & Smith, L. E. (1990). A review of the depressive personality. *American Journal of Psychiatry, 147,* 830–837.

Piasecki, J. (1975). *Community response to residential services for the psychosocially disabled.* Paper presented at the first annual conference of the International Association for Psychosocial Rehabilitation Services, Horizon House Institute, Philadelphia.

Pickar, D., Owen, R. R., & Litman, R. E. (1991). New developments in the pharmacotherapy of schizophrenia. In A. Tasman & S. Goldfinger (Eds.), *American Psychiatric Press Review of Psychiatry* (Vol. 10). Washington, DC: American Psychiatric Press.

Pickar, D., Owen, R. R., Litman, R. E., Konicki, E., Gutierrez, R., & Rapaport, M. H. (1992). Clinical and biologic response to clozapine in patients with schizophrenia. *Archives of General Psychiatry, 49,* 345–353.

Pickar, D., Sweeney, D. R., Maas, J. W., & Heninger, G. R. (1978). Primary affective disorder, clinical state change, and MHPG excretion: A longitudinal study. *Archives of General Psychiatry, 35,* 1378–1383.

Pickens, R. W., Svikis, D. S., McGue, M., Lykken, D. T., Heston, L. L., & Clayton, P. J. (1991). Heterogeneity in the inheritance of alcoholism. *Archives of General Psychiatry, 48,* 19–28.

Pickering, G. (1968). *High blood pressure.* London: Churchill.

Pierce, C. M. (1980). Enuresis. In H. I. Kaplan, A. Freedman, & B. Sadock (Eds.), *Comprehensive textbook of psychiatry* (3rd ed., pp. 2780–2787). Baltimore: Williams & Wilkins.

Pigott, T., Pato, M. T., Bernstein, S. E., Grover, G. N., Hill, J. L., Tolliver, T. J., & Murphy, D. L. (1990). Controlled comparisons of clomipramine and fluoxetine and the treatment of obsessive-compulsive disorder. *Archives of General Psychiatry, 47,* 926–932.

Pihl, R. O., Peterson, J., & Finn, P. (1990). Inherited predisposition to alcoholism: Characteristics of sons of male alcohollics. *Journal of Abnormal Psychology, 99,* 291–301.

Pincus, T., Callahan, L. F., Bradley, L. A., Vaughn, W. D., & Wolfe, F. (1986). Elevated MMPI scores for hypochondriasis, depression, and hysteria in patients with rheumatoid arthritis reflect disease rather than psychological status. *Arthritis and Rheumatism, 29,* 1456–1466.

Pinel, P. (1806). *A treatise on insanity* (D. Davis, Trans.). New York: Hafner.

Pitt, B. (1968). "Atypical" depression following childbirth. *British Journal of Psychiatry, 114,* 1325–1335.

Pitt, B. (1973). Maternity blues. *British Journal of Psychiatry, 122,* 431–433.

Pitt, B. (1982). Depression and childbirth. In E. S. Paykel (Ed.), *Handbook of affective disorders* (pp. 361–378). New York: Guilford Press.

Pitts, F. N., & Allen, R. E. (1979). Biochemical induction of anxiety. In W. E. Fann, I. Karacan, A. D. Pokorny, & R. L. Williams (Eds.), *Phenomenology and treatment of anxiety* (pp. 125–140). Englewood Cliffs, NJ: Prentice Hall.

Pitts, F. N., & McClure, J. N. (1967). Lactate metabolism in anxiety neurosis. *New England Journal of Medicine, 277,* 1328–1336.

Piven, J., Berthier, M. L., Starkstein, S. E., Nehme, E., Pearlson, G., & Folstein, S. (1990). Magnetic resonance imaging evidence for a defect of cerbral cortical development in autism. *American Journal of Psychiatry, 147,* 734–739.

Plomin, R., De Fries, J. C., & McClearn, G. E. (1990). *Behavioral genetics: A primer.* New York: Freeman.

Pokorny, A. D. (1968). Myths about suicide. In H. Resnik (Ed.), *Suicidal behaviors.* Boston: Little, Brown.

Pope, H. G., Aizley, H. G., Keck, P. E., & McElroy, S. L. (1991). Neuroleptic malignant syndrome: Long-term follow-up of 20 cases. *Journal of Clinical Psychiatry, 52,* 208–212.

Pope, H. G., & Hudson, J. I. (1982). Treatment of bulimia with antidepressants. *Psychopharmacology, 78,* 176–179.

Pope, H. G., & Hudson, J. I. (1984). *New hope for binge eaters: Advances in the understanding and treatment of bulimia.* New York: HarperCollins.

Pope, H. G., & Hudson, J. I. (1992). Is childhood sexual abuse a risk factor for bulimia nervosa? *American Journal of Psychiatry, 149,* 455–463.

Pope, H. G., Hudson, J. I., Jonas, J. M., & Yurgelun-Todd, D. (1983). Bulimia treated with imipramine: A placebo-controlled, double-blind study. *American Journal of Psychiatry, 140,* 554–558.

Pope, H. G., Hudson, J. I., Jonas, J. M., & Yurgelun-Todd, D. (1985). Antidepressant treatment of bulimia: A two-year follow-up study. *Journal of Clinical Psychopharmacology, 5,* 320–327.

Post, F. (1982). Affective disorders in old age. In E. S. Paykel (Ed.), *Handbook of affective disorders* (pp. 393–402). New York: Guilford Press.

Prichard, J. C. (1835). *A treatise on insanity.* London: Sherwood, Gilbert & Piper.

Prien, R. F., Klett, C. J., & Caffey, E. M. (1974). Lithium prophylaxis in recurrent affective illness. *American Journal of Psychiatry, 131,* 198–203.

Prien, R. F., Kupfer, D. J., Mansky, P. A., Small, J. G., Tuason, V. B., Voss, C. B., & Johnson, W. E. (1984). Drug therapy in the prevention of recurrences in unipolar and bipolar disorders. *Archives of General Psychiatry, 41,* 1096–1104.

Prince, M. (1908). *The dissociation of personality.* White Plains, NY: Longman.

Prince, V., & Bentler, P. M. (1972). Survey of 504 cases of transvestism. *Psychological Reports, 31,* 903–917.

Prior, M., & Sanson, A. (1986). Attention deficit disorder with hyperactivity: A critique. *Journal of Child Psychology and Psychiatry, 27,* 307–319.

Pryor, T., McGilley, B., & Roach, N. E. (1990). Psychopharmacology and eating disorders: Dawning of a new age. *Psychiatric Annals, 20,* 1–11.

Pueschel, S. M., & Goldstein, A. (1983). Genetic counseling. In J. L. Matson & J. A. Mulick (Eds.), *Handbook of mental retardation* (pp. 259–270). Elmsford, NY: Pergamon Press.

Pueschel, S. M., & Thuline, H. C. (1983). Chromosome disorders. In J. L. Matson & J. A. Mulick (Eds.), *Handbook of mental retardation* (pp. 121–142). Elmsford, NY: Pergamon Press.

Putnam, F. W. (1989). *Diagnosis and treatment of multiple personality disorder.* New York: Guilford Press.

Putnam, F. W., Guroff, J. J., Silberman, E. K., Barban, L., & Post, R. M. (1986). The clinical phenomenology of multiple personality disorder: Review of 100 recent cases. *Journal of Clinical Psychiatry, 47,* 285–293.

Quay, H. C. (1986). Conduct disorders. In H. C. Quay & J. S. Werry (Eds.), *Psychopathological disorders of childhood* (3rd ed., pp. 35–72). New York: Wiley.

Quitkin, F., Rabkin, J. G., Ross, D., & McGrath, P. J. (1984). Duration of antidepressant drug treatment. *Archives of General Psychiatry, 41,* 238–245.

Quitkin, F., Rifkin, A., & Klein, D. F. (1975). Very high dose vs standard dosage fluphenazine in schizophrenia. *Archives of General Psychiatry, 32,* 1276–1281.

Rabkin, J. G., Muhlin, G., & Cohen, P. W. (1984). What neighbors think: Community attitudes toward local psychiatric facilities. *Community Mental Health Journal, 20,* 304–312.

Rackman, S. (1966). Sexual fetishism: An experimental analogue. *Psychological Record, 16,* 293–296.

Rackman, S. (1989). The return of fear: Review and prospect. *Clinical Psychology Review, 9,* 147–168.

Rackman, S., & Hodgson, S. (1968). Experimentally induced "sexual fetishism": Replication and development. *Psychological Record, 18,* 25–27.

Radloff, L. S. (1975). Sex differences in depression: The effects of occupational and marital status. *Sex Roles, 1,* 249–265.

Radloff, L. S. (1977). The CES-D Scale: A self-report depression scale for research in the general population. *Applied Psychological Measurement, 1,* 385–401.

Radloff, L. S., & Rae, D. S. (1979). Susceptibility and precipitating factors in depression: Sex differences and similarities. *Journal of Abnormal Psychology, 88,* 174–181.

Rahe, R. H., Hervig, L., & Rosenman, R. H. (1978). Heritability of Type A behavior. *Psychosomatic Medicine, 40,* 478–486.

Rahe, R. H., Mahan, J. L., & Arthur, R. J. (1970). Prediction of near-future health change from subjects' preceding life changes. *Journal of Psychosomatic Research, 14,* 401–406.

Raleigh, M. J., McGuire, M. T., Brammer, G. L., & Yuwiler, A. (1984). Social and environmental influences on blood serotonin concentrations in monkeys. *Archives of General Psychiatry, 41,* 405–410.

Ramsey, G. (1943). The sexual development of boys. *American Journal of Psychiatry, 56,* 217.

Rapee, R. M. (1991). Generalized anxiety disorder: A review of clinical features and theoreteical concepts. *Clinical Psychology Review, 11,* 419–440.

Rapoport, J. L., Ryland, D. H., & Kriete, M. (1992). Drug treatment of canine acral lick: An animal model of obsessive-compulsive disorder. *Archives of General Psychiatry, 49,* 517–521.

Ravaris, C. L., Nies, A., Robinson, D. S., Ives, J. O., Lamborn, K. R., & Korson, L. (1976). A multi-dose, controlled study of phenelzine in depression-anxiety states. *Archives of General Psychiatry, 33,* 347–350.

Ravaris, C. L., Robinson, D. S., Ives, J. O., Nies, A., & Bartlett, D. (1980). Phenelzine and amitriptyline in the treatment of depression. *Archives of General Psychiatry, 37,* 1075–1080.

Raymond, M. J., & O'Keefe, K. (1965). A case of pin-up fetishism treated by aversion conditioning. *British Journal of Psychiatry, 111,* 579–581.

Raz, S., & Raz, N. (1990). Structural brain abnormalities in the major psychoses: A quantitative review of the evidence from computerized imaging. *Psychological Bulletin, 108,* 93–108.

"A Recovering Patient." (1986). "Can we talk?" The schizophrenic patient in psychotherapy. *American Journal of Psychiatry, 143,* 68–70.

Redd, W. H., & Andrykowski, M. A. (1982). Behavioral intervention in cancer treatment: Controlling aversion reactions to chemotherapy. *Journal of Counseling and Clinical Psychology, 50,* 1018–1029.

Redl, F., & Wineman, D. (1951). *Children who hate.* New York: Free Press.

Redmond, D., Kosten, T., & Peiser, M. (1982). Spontaneous ejaculation associated with anxiety: Psychophysiological considerations. *American Journal of Psychiatry, 140,* 1163–1166.

Rees, D., & Lutkins, S. G. (1971). Parental depression before and after childbirth. *Journal of the Royal College of General Practitioners, 21,* 26.

Regal, R. R., Cross, P. K., Lamson, S. H., & Hook, E. B. (1980). A search for evidence for a paternal age effect independent of a maternal age in birth certificate reports of Down's syndrome in New York State. *American Journal of Epidemiology, 112,* 650–655.

Regier, D. A., Myers, J. K., Kramer, L. N., Robins, L. N., Blazer, D. G., Hough, R. L., Eaton, W. W., & Locke, B. Z. (1984). The NIMH Epidemiological Catchment Area program. *Archives of General Psychiatry, 41,* 934–941.

Rehm, L. P. (1977). A self-control model of depression. *Behavior Therapy, 8,* 787–804.

Rehm, L. P., Fuchs, C. Z., Roth, D. M., Kornblith, S. J., & Romano, J. M. (1979). A comparison of self-control and assertion skills treatment of depression. *Behavior Therapy, 10,* 429–442.

Reiss, D., Plomin, R., & Hetherington, M. (1991). Genetics and psychiatry: An unheralded window on the environment. *American Journal of Psychiatry, 148,* 283–291.

Rennie v. Klein, No. 77-2624 (N.J. Sept. 14, 1979); 720 F.2d 266 (3d Cir. 1983).

Reschly, D. (1981). Psychological testing in educational classification and placement. *American Psychologist, 36,* 1094–1102.

Revelle, W., Amaral, P., & Turriff, S. (1976). Introversion/extroversion, time stress, and caffeine: Effect on verbal performance. *Science, 192,* 149–150.

Rice, E. M., Quinsey, V. L., & Harris, G. T. (1991). Sexual recidivism among child molesters released from a maximum security psychiatric institution. *Journal of Consulting and Clinical Psychology, 59,* 381–386.

Richards, D. (1973). Depression after hysterectomy. *Lancet, 2,* 430.

Richman, J. (1992). A rational approach to rational suicide. *Suicide and Life-Threatening Behavior, 22,* 130–141.

Rickels, K., & Snow, L. (1964). Meprobamate and phenobarbital sodium in anxious neurotic psychiatric medical clinic outpatients: A controlled study. *Psychopharmacologia, 5,* 339–348.

Rickels, K., Case, W. G., Schweizer, E., Garcia-Espana, F., & Fridman, R. (1991). Long-term benzodiazepine users 3 years after participation in a discontinuation program. *American Journal of Psychiatry, 148,* 757–761.

Rieber, I., & Sigusch, V. (1979). Psychosurgery on sex offenders and sexual "deviants" in West Germany. *Archives of Sexual Behavior, 8,* 523–528.

Rifai, A. H., Reynolds, C. F., & Mann, J. J. (1992). Biology of elderly suicide. *Suicide and Life-Threatening Behavior, 22,* 48–61.

Rifkin, A., Klein, D. F., Dillon, D., & Levitt, M. (1981). Blockade by imipramine or desipramine of panic induced by sodium lactate. *American Journal of Psychiatry, 138,* 676–677.

Riley, V. (1981). Psychoneuroendocrine influences on immunocompetence and neoplasia. *Science, 212,* 1100–1109.

Rimon, R. (1969). A psychosomatic approach to rheumatoid arthritis: A clinical study of 100 female patients. *Acta Rheumatologica Scandinavica, 13* (Suppl.), 1–154.

Rimon, R., & Laakso, R. (1985). Life stress and rheumatoid arthritis. *Psychotherapy and Psychosomatics, 43,* 38–43.

Risby, E. D., Hsiao, J. K., Manji, H. K., Bitran, J., Moses, F., Zhou, D. F., & Potter, W. Z. (1991). The mechanisms of action of lithium: II. Effects of adenylate cyclase activity and β-adrenergic receptor binding in normal subjects. *Archives of General Psychiatry, 48,* 513–524.

Rist, R. C. (1970). Student social class and teacher expectations: The self-fulfilling prophecy in ghetto education. *Harvard Educational Review, 40,* 411–451.

Ritter, E., & Holmes, D. S. (1968). Behavioral contagion: Its occurrence as a function of differential restraint reduction. *Journal of Experimental Research in Personality, 3,* 242–246.

Ritvo, E. R., Mason-Brothers, A., Freeman, B. J., Pingree, C.,

Jenson, W. R., McMahon, W. M., Petersen, P. B., Jorde, L. B., Mo, A., & Ritvo, A. (1990). The UCLA–University of Utah epidemiologic survey of autism: The etiologic role of rare diseases. *American Journal of Psychiatry, 147,* 1614–1621.

Ritvo, E. R., Ritvo, A., & Brothers, A. (1982). Genetic and immunohematologic factors in autism. *Journal of Autism and Developmental Disorders, 12,* 109–114.

Roback, H. B., & Lothstein, L. M. (1986). The female midlife sex change applicant: A comparison with younger transsexuals and older male sex change applicants. *Archives of Sexual Behavior, 15,* 401–415.

Roberts, A. H. (1985). Biofeedback: Research, training, and clinical roles. *American Psychologist, 40,* 938–941.

Roberts, J., & Roberts, T. (1985). Taking the center to market. *Community Mental Health Journal, 21,* 264–281.

Robertson, A. J., Ramesar, K. C., Potts, R. C., Hibbs, J. H., Browning, M. C., Brown, R. A., Hayes, P. C., & Beck, J. S. (1981). The effect of strenuous physical exercise on circulating blood lymphocytes and serum cortisol levels. *Journal of Clinical and Laboratory Immunology, 5,* 53–57.

Robin, A. (1962). Psychological changes of normal parturition. *Psychiatric Quarterly, 36,* 129–150.

Robins, C. J., & Block, P. (1989). Cognitive theories of depression viewed from a diathesis-stress perspective: Evaluations of the models of Beck and of Abramson, Seligman, and Teasdale. *Cognitive Therapy and Research, 13,* 297–313.

Robins, E., & Guze, S. B. (1972). Classification of affective disorders: The primary-secondary, the endogenous-reactive, and the neurotic-psychotic concepts. In T. A. Williams, M. M. Katz, & J. A. Shields (Eds.), *Recent advances in the psychobiology of the depressive illnesses* (pp. 283–293). Washington, DC: U.S. Government Printing Office.

Robins, E., & O'Neal, P. (1958). Culture and mental disorder: A study of attempted suicide. *Human Organization, 49,* 7–11.

Robins, L. N. (1966). *Deviant children grown up.* Baltimore: Williams & Wilkins.

Robins, L. N., Davis, D. H., & Nurco, D. N. (1974). How permanent was Viet Nam drug addiction? In M. H. Green & R. L. Du Pont (Eds.), *The epidemiology of drug abuse* (NIDA Journal Suppl., Pt. 2, Vol. 64). Washington, DC: U.S. Government Printing Office.

Robins, L. N., Helzer, J. E., & Davis, D. H. (1975). Narcotic use in Southeast Asia and afterwards. *Archives of General Psychiatry, 32,* 955–961.

Robins, L. N., Helzer, J. E., Weissman, M. M., Orvaschel, H., Gruenberg, E., Burke, J. D., & Reigier, D. A. (1984). Lifetime prevalence of specific psychiatric disorders in three sites. *Archives of General Psychiatry, 41,* 949–958.

Robinson, L. A., Berman, J. S., & Neimeyer, R. A. (1990). Psychotherapy for the treatment of depression: A comprehensive review of controlled-outcome research. *Psychological Bulletin, 108,* 30–49.

Robinson, N. M., & Robinson, H. B. (1976). *The mentally retarded child.* New York: McGraw-Hill.

Roesch, R., & Golding, S. L. (1980). *Competence to stand trial.* Urbana: University of Illinois Press.

Roff, M. (1974). Childhood antecedents of adult neurosis, severe bad conduct, and psychological health. In D. Ricks,

A. Thomas, and M. Roff (Eds.), *Life history research in psychopathology* (Vol. 3). Minneapolis: University of Minnesota Press.

Rofman, E. S., Askinazi, C., & Fant, E. (1980). The prediction of dangerous behavior in emergency commitment. *American Journal of Psychiatry, 137,* 1061–1064.

Rogers, C. R. (1951). *Client-centered therapy.* Boston: Houghton Mifflin.

Rogers v. Okin, 478 F. Supp. 1342 (I.D. Mass. 1979).

Rogler, L. H., Malgady, R. G., Costantino, G., & Blumenthal, R. (1987). What do culturally sensitive mental health services mean? *American Psychologist, 42,* 565–570.

Rohde, P. D., Lewinsohn, P. M., & Seeley, J. R. (1991). Comorbidity of unipolar depression: II. Comorbidity with other mental disorders in adolescents and adults. *Journal of Abnormal Psychology, 100,* 214–222.

Rokeach, M. (1964). *The three Christs of Ypsilanti.* New York: Knopf.

Rollnick, S., & Heather, N. (1982). The application of Bandura's self-efficacy theory to abstinence-oriented alcoholism treatment. *Addictive Behaviors, 7,* 243–250.

Rorschach, H. (1942). *Psychodiagnostics: A diagnostic test based on perception* (P. Lemkau & B. Kronenberg, Trans.). Philadelphia: Grune & Stratton.

Rosanoff, A. J., Handy, L. M., & Plesset, I. R. (1935). The etiology of manic-depressive syndromes with special reference to their occurrence in twins. *American Journal of Psychiatry, 91,* 725–762.

Rosanoff, A. J., Handy, L. M., & Rosanoff, I. (1934). Criminality and delinquency in twins. *Journal of Criminal Law and Criminality, 24,* 923–934.

Rose, R. J. (1986). Familial influences on cardiovascular reactivity. In K. A. Matthews, S. M. Weiss, T. Detre, T. M. Dembroski, B. Falkner, S. Manuck, & R. Williams (Eds.), *Handbook of stress, reactivity, and cardiovascular disease* (pp. 259–272). New York: Wiley.

Rose, R. J., Bourne, P. G., Poe, R. O., Mougey, E. H., Collins, D. R., & Mason, J. W. (1969). Androgen responses to stress: 2. Excretion of testosterone, epitestosterone, androsterone, and etiochoanolone during basic combat training and under threat of attack. *Psychosomatic Medicine, 31,* 418–436.

Rose, R. J., Miller, J. Z., & Grim, C. E. (1982). Familial factors in blood pressure response to laboratory stress: A twin study. *Psychophysiology, 19,* 583.

Rosen, A., & Schalling, D. (1971). Probability learning in psychopathic and non-psychopathic criminals. *Journal of Experimental Research in Personality, 5,* 191–198.

Rosen, D. H. (1970). The serious suicide attempt: Epidemiological and follow-up study of 886 patients. *American Journal of Psychiatry, 127,* 764–770.

Rosenbaum, M. (1980). The role of the term *schizophrenia* in the decline of diagnoses of multiple personality. *Archives of General Psychiatry, 37,* 1383–1385.

Rosenblatt, A., & Mayer, J. E. (1974). Patients who return: A consideration of some neglected influences. *Journal of the Bronx State Hospital, 2,* 71–81.

Rosenblum, S. M., Arick, J. R., Krug, D. A., Stubbs, E. G., Young, N. B., & Pelson, R. O. (1980). Auditory brainstem evoked responses in autistic children. *Journal of Autism and Developmental Disorders, 10,* 215–225.

Rosenhan, D. L. (1973). On being sane in insane places. *Science, 179,* 250–258.

Rosenman, R. H. (1978). The interview method of assessment of the coronary-prone behavior pattern. In T. M. Dembroski, S. M. Weiss, J. L. Shields, S. G. Haynes, & M. Feinleib (Eds.), *Coronary-prone behavior.* New York: Springer.

Rosenman, R. H., Brand, R. J., Jenkins, C. D., Friedman, M., Straus, R., & Wurm, M. (1975). Coronary heart disease in the Western Collaborative Group Study: Final follow-up experience of 8½ years. *JAMA, 233,* 872–877.

Rosenman, R. H., Brand, R. J., Sholtz, R. I., & Friedman, M. (1976). Multivariate prediction of coronary heart disease during 8.5-year follow-up in the Western Collaborative Group Study. *American Journal of Cardiology, 37,* 903–910.

Rosenman, R. H., Rahe, R. H., Borhani, N. O., & Feinleib, M. (1976). Heritability of personality and behavior. *Acta Geneticae Medicae et Gemellologiae, 25,* 221–224.

Rosenthal, D. (1961). Sex distribution and the severity of illness among samples of schizophrenic twins. *Journal of Psychiatric Research, 1,* 26–36.

Rosenthal, D. (1970). *Genetic theory and abnormal behavior.* New York: McGraw-Hill.

Rosenthal, D., Wender, P. H., Kety, S. S., Schulsinger, F., Weiner, J., & Ostergaard, L. (1968). Schizophrenics' offspring reared in adoptive homes. In D. Rosenthal & S. S. Kety (Eds.), *The transmission of schizophrenia.* Elmsford, NY: Pergamon Press.

Rosenthal, D., Wender, P. H., Kety, S. S., Welner, J., & Schulsinger, F. (1971). The adopted-away offspring of schizophrenics. *American Journal of Psychiatry, 128,* 307–311.

Rosenthal, N. E., Sack, D. A., Gillin, J. C., Lewy, A. J., Goodwin, F. K., Davenport, Y., Mueller, P. S., Newsome, D. A., & Wehr, T. A. (1984). Seasonal affective disorder: A description of the syndrome and preliminary findings with light therapy. *Archives of General Psychiatry, 41,* 72–80.

Rosenthal, R., & Jacobson, L. (1968). *Pygmalion in the classroom.* Austin, TX: Holt, Rinehart and Winston.

Roskies, E. (1980). Considerations in developing a treatment program for the coronary-prone (Type A) behavior pattern. In P. O. Davison & S. M. Davidson (Eds.), *Behavioral medicine: Changing health life-styles* (pp. 299–333). New York: Brunner/Mazel.

Roskies, E., & Avard, J. (1982). Teaching healthy managers to control their coronary-prone (Type A) behavior. In K. R. Blankstein & J. Polivy (Eds.), *Self-control and self-modification of emotional behavior.* New York: Plenum.

Roskies, E., Seradganian, P., Oseasohn, R., Hanley, J. A., Cullu, R., Martin, N., & Smilga, C. (1986). The Montreal Type A Intervention Project: Major findings. *Health Psychology, 5,* 45–69.

Roskies, E., Spevack, M., Surkis, A., Cohen, C., & Gilman, S. (1978). Changing the coronary-prone (Type A) behavior pattern in a non-clinical population. *Journal of Behavioral Medicine, 1,* 201–216.

Ross, C. A. (1989). *Multiple personality disorder: Diagnosis, clinical features, and treatment.* New York: Wiley.

Ross, C. A., Joshi, S., & Currie, R. (1990). Dissociative experiences in the general population. *American Journal of Psychiatry, 147,* 1547–1552.

Ross, C. A., Miller, S. D., Reagor, P., Bjornson, L., Fraser, G. A., & Anderson, G. (1990). Structured interview data on 102 cases of multiple personality disorder from four centers. *American Journal of Psychiatry, 147,* 596–601.

Ross, C. A., Norton, R., & Wozney, K. (1989). Multiple personality disorder: An analysis of 236 cases. *Canadian Journal of Psychiatry, 34,* 413–418.

Ross, D. M., & Ross, S. A. (1982). *Hyperactivity: Research, theory, and action.* New York: Wiley-Interscience.

Ross, J. L. (1977). Anorexia nervosa: An overview. *Bulletin of the Menninger Clinic, 41,* 418–436.

Rossi, A. M., Kuehnle, J. C., & Mendleson, J. H. (1978). Marijuana and mood in human volunteers. *Pharmacology, Biochemistry and Behavior, 8,* 447–453.

Roth, D. L., & Holmes, D. S. (1985). Influence of physical fitness in determining the impact of stressful life events on physical and psychological health. *Psychosomatic Medicine, 47,* 164–173.

Roth, D. L., & Holmes, D. S. (1987). Influence of aerobic exercise training and relaxation training on physical and psychological health following stressful life events. *Psychosomatic Medicine, 49,* 355–365.

Roth, S. (1979). A revised model of learned helplessness in humans. *Journal of Personality, 48,* 103–133.

Roth, W. T., Margraf, J., Ehlers, A., Taylor, C. B., Maddock, R. J., Davies, S., & Agras, W. S. (1992). Stress reactivity in panic disorder. *Archives of General Psychiatry, 49,* 301–310.

Rotter, J. B., & Rafferty, J. E. (1950). *Manual for the Rotter Incomplete Sentences Blank, College Form.* New York: Psychological Corporation.

Rouillon, F., Phillips, R., Serrurier, D., Ansart, E., & Gérard, M. J. (1989). Rechutes de dépression unipolaire et efficacité de la maprotiline. *Encéphale, 15,* 527–534.

Rouse v. Cameron, 373 F.2d 451 (D.C. Cir. 1966).

Roviaro, S., & Holmes, D. S. (1980). Arousal transference: The influence of fear arousal on subsequent sexual arousal for subjects with high and low sex guilt. *Journal of Research in Personality, 14,* 307–320.

Roviaro, S., Holmes, D. S., Holmsten, D. (1984). Influence of a cardiac rehabilitation program on the cardiovascular, psychological, and social functioning of cardiac patients. *Journal of Behavioral Medicine, 7,* 61–81.

Rovner, B. W., German, P. S., Brant, L. J., Clark, R., Burton, L., & Folstein, M. F. (1991). Depression and mortality in nursing homes. *JAMA, 265,* 993–996.

Roy, A. (1978). Vulnerability factors and depression in women. *British Journal of Psychiatry, 113,* 106–110.

Roy, A. (1982). Risk factors for suicide in psychiatric patients. *Archives of General Psychiatry, 39,* 1089–1095.

Roy, A. (1983). Family history of suicide. *Archives of General Psychiatry, 40,* 971–974.

Roy, A. (1990). Possible biologic determinants of suicide. In D. Lester (Ed.), *Current concepts of suicide.* Philadelphia: Charles Press.

Roy, A., Segal, N., Centerwall, B., & Robinette, D. (1991). Suicide in twins. *Archives of General Psychiatry, 48,* 29–32.

Rozensky, R. H., Rehm, L. P., Pry, G., & Roth, D. (1977). Depression and self-reinforcement behavior in hospitalized patients. *Journal of Behavior Therapy and Experimental Psychiatry, 8,* 35–38.

Rubin, E. H., Kincherf, D. A., Grant, E. A., & Storandt, M. (1991). The influence of major depression on clinical psychometric assessment of senile dementia of the Alzheimer type. *American Journal of Psychiatry, 148,* 1164–1171.

Rubinstein, M., Yeager, C. A., Goodstein, C., & Lewis, D. O. (1993). Sexually assaultive male juveniles: A follow-up. *American Journal of Psychiatry, 150,* 262–265.

Rudd, M. D. (1989). The prevalence of suicidal ideation among college students. *Suicide and Life-Threatening Behavior, 19,* 173–183.

Rudestam, K. E. (1971). Stockholm and Los Angeles: A cross-cultural study of the communication of suicidal intent. *Journal of Consulting and Clinical Psychology, 36,* 82–90.

Ruff, G. A. (1985). Premature ejaculation: Past research progress, future directions. *Clinical Psychology Review, 5,* 627–639.

Rush, A. J., Beck, A. T., Kovacs, M., & Hollon, S. D. (1977). Comparative efficacy of cognitive therapy and imipramine in the treatment of depressed patients. *Cognitive Therapy and Research, 1,* 17–37.

Rush, B. (1812). *Medical inquiries and observations upon the diseases of the mind.* Philadelphia: Kimber & Richardson.

Rutter, M. (1967). Psychotic disorders in early childhood. *British Journal of Psychiatry* (Special Publ. No. 1), 133–158.

Rutter, M. (1974). The development of infantile autism. *Psychological Medicine, 4,* 147–163.

Rutter, M. (1985). The treatment of autistic children. *Journal of Child Psychology and Psychiatry, 26,* 193–214.

Rutter, M., Bartak, L., & Newman, S. (1971). Autism: A central disorder of cognition and language? In M. Rutter (Ed.), *Infantile autism: Concepts, characteristics and treatment.* London: Churchill-Livingstone.

Rutter, M., Cox, A., Tupling, C., Berger, M., & Yule, W. (1975). Attainment and adjustment in two geographical areas: 1. Prevalence of psychiatric disorder. *British Journal of Psychiatry, 126,* 493–509.

Rutter, M., & Lockyer, L. (1967). A five to fifteen year follow-up study of infantile psychosis: 1. Description of sample. *British Journal of Psychiatry, 113,* 1169–1182.

Rutter, M., Yule, W., & Graham, P. (1973). Enuresis and behavioral deviance: Some epidemiological considerations. In I. Kolvin, R. MacKeith, & S. Meadow (Eds.), *Bladder control in enuresis.* London: Heinemann.

Sacchetti, E., Vita, A., Guarneri, L., & Cornarcchia, M. (1991). The effectiveness of fluoxetine, clomipramine, nortriptyline and desipramine in major depressives with suicidal behavior: Preliminary findings. In G. Cassano & H. Akiska (Eds.), *Serotonin-related psychiatric syndromes: Clinical and therapeutic links.* London: Royal Society of Medicine Services.

Sachar, E. (1982). Endocrine abnormalities in depression. In E. S. Paykel (Ed.), *Handbook of affective disorders* (pp. 191–201). New York: Guilford Press.

Sackeim, H. A. (1985). The case for ECT. *Psychology Today,* pp. 37–40.

Sacks, H. (1940). Was this analysis a success? Comment. *Journal of Abnormal and Social Psychology, 35,* 11–16.

Saint George–Hyslop, P., Tanzi, R. E., Polinsky, R., Haines, J., Nee, L., Watkins, P. C., Myers, R., Feldman, R., Pollen, D., Drachman, D., Growdon, J., Bruni, A., Foncin, J., Salmon,

D., Frommelt, P., Amaducci, L., Sorbi, S., Piacentini, S., Stewart, G., Hobbs, W., Conneally, P., & Gusella, J. F. (1987). The genetic defect causing familial Alzheimer's disease maps on chromosome 21. *Science, 235,* 885–890.

Sakheim, D. K., Barlow, D. H., Beck, J. G., & Abrahamson, D. J. (1984). The effects of an increased awareness of erectile cues on sexual arousal. *Behaviour Research and Therapy, 22,* 151–158.

Salimenk, C. A. (1976). Pyrolysis of cannabinoids. In G. G. Nahas (Ed.), *Marijuana: Chemistry, biochemistry, and cellular effects* (pp. 31–38). New York: Springer.

Sanderson, W. C., Di Nardo, P. A., Rapee, R. M., & Barlow, D. H. (1990). Syndrome comorbidity in patients diagnosed with a *DSM-III-R* anxiety disorder. *Journal of Abnormal Psychology, 99,* 308–312.

Sanger, D. J., & Blackman, D. E. (1976). Effects of chlordiazepoxide, ripazepam and d-amphetamine on conditioned acceleration timing behavior in rats. *Psychopharmacology, 48,* 209–215.

Sanger, D. J., & Blackman, D. E. (1981). Rate dependence and the effects of benzodiazepines. In T. Thompson, P. Dews, & W. A. McKim (Eds.), *Advances in behavioral pharmacology* (Vol. 3, pp. 1–20). Dallas, TX: Academic Press.

Sarason, I. G. (1980). Introduction to the study of test anxiety. In I. G. Sarason (Ed.), *Test anxiety: Theory, research, and applications.* Hillsdale, NJ: Erlbaum.

Satel, S., & Edell, W. S. (1991). Cocaine-induced paranoia and psychosis proneness. *American Journal of Psychiatry, 148,* 1708–1711.

Satel, S., Southwick, S. M., & Gawin, F. H. (1991). Clinical features of cocaine-indiced paranoia. *American Journal of Psychiatry, 148,* 495–498.

Satterfield, J. H., & Cantwell, D. P. (1975). Psychopharmacology in the prevention of antisocial and delinquent behavior. *International Journal of Mental Health, 4,* 277–335.

Schaar, K. (1974). Suicide rate high among women psychologists. *APA Monitor, 5,* 1, 10.

Schachter, S. (1964). The interaction of cognitive and physiological determinants of emotional state. In L. Berkowitz (Ed.), *Advances in experimental social psychology* (Vol. 1, pp. 49–80). Dallas, TX: Academic Press.

Schachter, S., & Latané, B. (1964). Crime, cognition and the autonomic nervous system. In M. R. Jones (Ed.), *Nebraska symposium on motivation* (pp. 221–275). Lincoln: University of Nebraska Press.

Schachter, S., & Singer, J. E. (1962). Cognitive, psychological and physiological determinants of emotional state. *Psychological Review, 69,* 379–399.

Schepank, H. G. (1981). Anorexia nervosa: Zwillings Kasuistik über ein seltens Krankheitsbild. In A. Heigl-Evers & H. G. Schepank (Eds.), *Ursprunge seelisch bedingter Krankheiten* (Vol. 2.) Gottingen, Germany: Verlag für Medizinische Psychologie/Vandenhoeck und Ruprecht.

Schiavi, R. C., Schreiner-Engel, P., Mandeli, J., Schanzer, H., & Cohen, E. (1990). Healthy aging and male sexual function. *American Journal of Psychiatry, 147,* 766–771.

Schildkraut, J. J. (1965). The catecholamine hypothesis of affective disorders: A review of supporting evidence. *American Journal of Psychiatry, 122,* 509–522.

Schildkraut, J. J. (1973). Norepinephrine metabolites as biochemical criteria for classifying depressive disorders and predicting responses to treatment: Preliminary findings. *American Journal of Psychiatry, 130,* 695–698.

Schildkraut, J. J., Keeler, B. A., Grab, E. L., Kantrowich, J., & Hartmann, E. (1973). MHPG excretion and clinical classification in depressive disorders. *Lancet, 1,* 1251–1252.

Schildkraut, J. J., & Kety, S. S. (1967). Biogenic amines and emotion. *Science, 156,* 21–30.

Schildkraut, J. J., Orsulak, P. J., Schatzberg, A. F., Gudeman, J. E., Cole, J. O., Rohde, W. A., & La Brie, R. A. (1978). Toward a biochemical classification of depressive disorders: 1. Differences in urinary excretion of MHPG and other catecholamine metabolites in clinically defined subtypes of depression. *Archives of General Psychiatry, 35,* 1427–1433.

Schleifer, S. J., Keller, S. E., Meyerson, A. T., Raskin, M. J., Davis, K. L., & Stein, M. (1984). Lymphocyte function in major depressive disorder. *Archives of General Psychiatry, 41,* 484–486.

Schmale, A. H., & Iker, H. P. (1966a). The affect of hopelessness and the development of cancer. *Psychosomatic Medicine, 28,* 714–721.

Schmale, A. H., & Iker, H. P. (1966b). The psychological setting of uterine cervical cancer. *Annals of the New York Academy of Science, 25,* 807–813.

Schmale, A. H., & Iker, H. P. (1971). Hopelessness as a predictor of cervical cancer. *Social Science and Medicine, 5,* 95–100.

Schmauk, F. J. (1970). Punishment, arousal, and avoidance learning in sociopaths. *Journal of Abnormal Psychology, 76,* 325–335.

Schmidt, C. W., & Cowie, D. (1983). Common male sexual disorders: Impotence and premature ejaculation. In J. M. Meyer, C. W. Schmidt, & T. N. Wise (Eds.), *Clinical management of sexual disorders* (pp. 173–196). Baltimore: Williams & Wilkins.

Schmidt, E. H., O'Neal, P., & Robins, E. (1954). Evaluation of suicide attempts as a guide to therapy. *JAMA, 155,* 549–557.

Schmidt, G., & Schorsch, E. (1981). Psychosurgery of sexually deviant patients: Review and analysis of new empirical findings. *Archives of Sexual Behavior, 10,* 301–323.

Schmidt, P. J., & Rubinow, D. R. (1991). Menopause-related affective disorders: A justification for further study. *American Journal of Psychiatry, 148,* 844–852.

Schofield, W. (1964). *Psychotherapy: The purchase of friendship.* Engelwood Cliffs, NJ: Prentice Hall.

Schofield, W., & Balian, L. A. (1959). A comparative study of the personal histories of schizophrenic and nonpsychiatric patients. *Journal of Abnormal and Social Psychology, 59,* 216–225.

Schonfield, J. (1972). Psychological factors related to delayed return to an earlier lifestyle in successfully treated cancer patients. *Journal of Psychosomatic Research, 16,* 41–46.

Schooler, C., & Spohn, H. E. (1982). Social dysfunction and treatment failure in schizophrenia. *Schizophrenia Bulletin, 8,* 85–98.

Schopler, E., Short, A., & Mesibov, G. (1989). Relation of behavioral treatment to "normal functioning": Comments on Lovaas. *Journal of Consulting and Clinical Psychology, 57,* 162–164.

Schotte, D., & Clum, G. (1982). Suicide ideation in a college population: A test of a model. *Journal of Consulting and Clinical Psychology, 50,* 690–696.

Schotte, D., & Clum, G. (1987). Problem-solving skills in suicidal psychiatric patients. *Journal of Consulting and Clinical Psychology, 55,* 49–54.

Schotte, D., Cools, J., & Payvar, S. (1990). Problem-solving deficits in suicidal patients: Trait vulnerability or state phenomenon? *Journal of Consulting and Clinical Psychology, 58,* 562–564.

Schou, M., Mellerup, E. T., & Rafaelsen, O. J. (1981). Mode of action of lithium. In H. M. Van Praag, M. H. Lader, O. J. Rafaelsen, & E. Sachar (Eds.), *Handbook of biological psychiatry: Pt. 4. Brain mechanisms and abnormal behavior* (pp. 805–824). New York: Dekker.

Schover, L., & Lo Piccolo, J. (1982). Treatment effectiveness for dysfunctions of sexual desire. *Journal of Sex and Marital Therapy, 8,* 179–197.

Schreiber, F. R. (1973). *Sybil.* New York: Warner Books.

Schreiner-Engle, P., Schiavi, R. C., White, D., & Ghizzani, A. (1989). Low sexual desire in women: The role of reproductive hormones. *Hormones and Behavior, 23,* 221–234.

Schroeder, S. R., Lewis, M. H., & Lipton, M. A. (1983). Interactions of pharmacotherapy and behavior therapy among children with learning and behavioral disorders. In K. Gadlow & I. Bialer (Eds.), *Advances in learning and behavioral disabilities* (Vol. 2, pp. 179–225). Greenwich, CT: JAI Press.

Schuckit, M. A. (1973). Alcoholism and sociopathy: Diagnostic confusion. *Quarterly Journal of Studies on Alcohol, 34,* 157–164.

Schuckit, M. A. (1987). Biological vulnerability to alcoholism. *Journal of Consulting and Clinical Psychology, 55,* 301–309.

Schulsinger, F. (1972). Psychopathy, heredity and environment. *International Journal of Mental Health, 1,* 190–206.

Schulsinger, F., Kety, S. S., Rosenthal, D., & Wender, P. H. (1979). A family study of suicide. In M. Schou & E. Stromgren (Eds.), *Origin, prevention and treatment of affective disorder* (pp. 227–287). London: Academic Press.

Schulsinger, F., Mednick, S. A., Venables, P. H., Ramon, A. C., & Bell, B. (1975). Early detection and prevention of mental illness: The Mauritius project. *Neurophychobiology, 1,* 166–179.

Schultz, E. (1974). Prevalence of behavioral symptoms in rural elementary school children. *Journal of Abnormal Child Psychology, 2,* 17–24.

Schultz, R., Braun, B. G., & Kluft, R. P. (1989). Multiple personality disorder: Phenomenology of selected variables in comparison to major depression. *Dissociation, 2,* 45–51.

Schwartz, G. E., Davidson, R. J., & Goldman, D. (1978). Patterning of cognitive and somatic processes in the self-regulation of anxiety. *Psychosomatic Medicine, 40,* 321–328.

Schwarz, J. R. (1981). *The hillside strangler: A murderer's mind.* New York: New American Library.

Schwitzgebel, R. L., & Schwitzgebel, R. K. (1980). *Law and psychological practice.* New York: Wiley.

Scott, T., Bexton, W. H., & Doane, B. (1959). Cognitive effects of perceptual isolation. *Canadian Journal of Psychology, 13,* 200–209.

Scovern, A. W., & Kilmann, P. R. (1980). Status of electroconvulsive therapy: Review of the outcome literature. *Psychological Bulletin, 87,* 260–303.

Seager, C. P., & Bird, R. L. (1962). Imipramine with electrical treatment in depression: A controlled trial. *Journal of Mental Science, 108,* 704–707.

Searles, J. S. (1988). The role of genetics in the pathogenesis of alcoholism. *Journal of Abnormal Psychology, 97,* 153–167.

Sears, R. R., Maccoby, E. E., & Levin, H. (1957). *Patterns of Child Rearing.* Evanston, IL: Row, Peterson.

Segal, Z. V., Shaw, B. F., Vella, D. D., & Katz, R. (1992). Cognitive and life stress predictors of relapse in remitted unipolar depressed patients: A test of the congruency hypothesis. *Journal of Abnormal Psychology, 101,* 26–36.

Seidman, L. J. (1983). Schizophrenia and brain dysfunction: An integration of recent neurodiagnostic findings. *Psychological Bulletin, 94,* 195–238.

Seligman, M. E. P. (1968). Chronic fear produced by unpredictable shock. *Journal of Comparative and Physiological Psychology, 66,* 402–411.

Seligman, M. E. P. (1975). *Helplessness: On depression, development, and death.* New York: Freeman.

Selkoe, D. J., Bell, D. S., Podlisny, M. B., Price, D. L., & Cork, L. C. (1987). Conservation of brain amyloid proteins in aged mammals and humans with Alzheimer's disease. *Science, 235,* 873–877.

Sendbuehler, J. M. (1977). Suicide and attempted suicide among the aged. *Canadian Medical Association Journal, 117,* 418–419.

Sendbuehler, J. M., & Goldstein, S. (1977). Attempted suicide among the aged. *Journal of the American Geriatric Society, 25,* 245–248.

Sengar, D., Waters, B., Dunne, J., & Bouer, J. (1982). Lymphocyte subpopulations and mitogen response to lymphocytes in manic-depressive disorders. *Biological Psychiatry, 17,* 1017–1022.

Serban, G. (1992). Multiple personality: An issue for forensic psychiatry. *American Journal of Psychotherapy, 46,* 269–280.

Shaffer, D. (1973). The association between enuresis and emotional disorder: A review of the literature. In I. Kolvin, R. MacKeith, & S. Meadow (Eds.), *Bladder control in enuresis.* London: Heinemann.

Shaffer, J. W., Duszynski, K. R., & Thomas, C. B. (1982). Youthful habits of work and recreation and later cancer among physicians. *Journal of Clinical Psychology, 38,* 893–900.

Shakow, D. (1963). Psychological deficit in schizophrenia. *Behavioral Science, 8,* 275–305.

Shakow, D., & Jellinek, E. M. (1965). Composite index of the Kent-Rosanoff free association test. *Journal of Abnormal Psychology, 70,* 403–404.

Shanok, S. S., & Lewis, D. O. (1981). Medical histories of female delinquents. *Archives of General Psychiatry, 38,* 211–213.

Shapiro, A. (1980). A contribution to a history of the placebo effect. *Behavioral Science, 5,* 109–131.

Shapiro, A., & Morris, L. (1978). Placebo effects in medical and psychological therapies. In S. L. Garfield & A. E. Bergin (Eds.), *Handbook of psychotherapy and behavior change.* New York: Wiley.

Shapiro, D. A., & Shapiro, D. (1982). Meta-analysis of comparative therapy outcome studies: A replication and refinement. *Psychological Bulletin, 92,* 581–604.

Shapiro, D. H. (1980). *Meditation.* Hawthorne, NY: Aldine.

Shaw, E. D., Stokes, P. E., Mann, J. J., & Manevitz, A. Z. (1987). Effects of lithium carbonate on the memory and motor speed of bipolar outpatients. *Journal of Abnormal Psychology, 96,* 64–69.

Shea, M. T., Widiger, T. A., & Klein, M. H. (1992). Comorbidity of personality disorders and depression: Implications for treatment. *Journal of Consulting and Clinical Psychology, 60,* 857–868.

Shekelle, R. B., Raynor, W. J., Ostfeld, A. M., Garron, D. C., Bieliauskas, L. A., Liu, S. C., Maliza, C., & Paul, O. (1981). Psychological depression and 17-year risk of death from cancer. *Psychosomatic Medicine, 43,* 117–125.

Shelton v. Tucker, 364 U.S. 479 (1960).

Sher, K. J., & Levenson, R. W. (1982). Risk for alcoholism and individual differences in the stress-response-dampening effect of alcohol. *Journal of Abnormal Psychology, 91,* 350–367.

Sherrington, R., Bynjolfsson, J., Petursson, H., Potter, M., Dudleston, K., Barraclough, B., Wasmuth, J., Dobbs, M., & Gurling, H. (1988). Localization of a susceptibility locus for schizophrenia on chromosome 5. *Nature, 336,* 164–167.

Shiloh, A. (1968). Sanctuary or prison? Responses to life in a mental hospital. *Trans-Action, 6,* 28.

Shneidman, E. S. (1979). An overview: Personality, motivation, and behavior theories. In L. D. Hankoff & B. Einsidler (Eds.), *Suicide: Theory and clinical aspects* (pp. 143–163). Acton, MA: Publishing Sciences Group.

Shneidman, E. S., & Farberow, N. L. (Eds.). (1957). *Clues to suicide.* New York: McGraw-Hill.

Shoham-Salomon, V., & Hannah, M. T. (1991). Client-treatment interaction in the study of differential change processes. *Journal of Consulting and Clinical Psychology, 59,* 217–225.

Shutts, D. (1982). *Lobotomy: Resort to the knife.* New York: Van Nostrand.

Siever, L. J., & Davis, K. L. (1985). Overview: Toward a dysregulation hypothesis of depression. *American Journal of Psychiatry, 142,* 1017–1031.

Silver, M. A., Bohnert, M., Beck, A. T., & Marcus, D. (1971). Relation of depression to attempted suicide and seriousness of intent. *Archives of General Psychiatry, 25,* 573–576.

Silver, R. L., Wortman, C. B., & Klos, D. S. (1982). Cognitions, affect, and behavior following uncontrollable outcomes: A response to current human helplessness research. *Journal of Personality, 50,* 480–514.

Simon, G. E., Katon, W. J., & Sparks, P. J. (1990). Allergic to life: Psychological factors in environmental illness. *American Journal of Psychiatry 147,* 901–906.

Simons, A. D., Garfield, S. L., & Murphy, G. E. (1984). The processes of change in cognitive therapy and pharmacotherapy for depression: Changes in mood and cognition. *Archives of General Psychiatry, 41,* 45–51.

Simonton, O. C., Mathews-Simonton, S. S., & Sparks, T. F. (1980). Psychological intervention in the treatment of cancer. *Psychosomatics, 21,* 226–233.

Simonton, O. C., & Simonton, S. S. (1975). Belief systems and management of the emotional aspects of malignancy. *Journal of Transpersonal Psychology, 7,* 29–47.

Sines, J. O. (1963). Physiological and behavioral characteristics of rats selectively bred for susceptibility to stomach ulcer development. *Journal of Neuropsychiatry, 4,* 396–398.

Sinyor, D., Schwartz, S. G., Peronnet, F., Brisson, G., & Seraganian, P. (1983). Aerobic fitness level and reactivity to psychosocial stress: Physiological, biochemical, and subjective measures. *Psychosomatic Medicine, 45,* 205–217.

Sirois, F. (1982). Perspectives in epidemic hysteria. In M. J. Colligan, J. W. Pennebaker, & L. R. Murphy (Eds.), *Mass psychogenic illness* (pp. 217–236). Hillsdale, NJ: Erlbaum.

Sizemore, C. C., & Pittillo, E. S. (1977). *I'm Eve.* Garden City, NY: Doubleday.

Skinner, B. F. (1953). *Science and human behavior.* New York: Macmillan.

Sklar, L. S., & Anisman, H. (1981). Stress and cancer. *Psychological Bulletin, 89,* 369–406.

Slater, E. (1953). *Psychotic and neurotic illness in twins* (Medical Research Council Special Report Series No. 278). London: Her Majesty's Stationery Office.

Slater, E., & Glithero, E. (1965). A follow-up of patients diagnosed as suffering from hysteria. *Journal of Psychosomatic Research, 9,* 9–13.

Slater, E., & Shields, J. (1969). Genetical aspects of anxiety. In M. H. Lader (Ed.), *Studies of anxiety* (pp. 62–71). Ashford, England: Headley Brothers.

Slater, J., & Depue, R. A. (1981). The contribution of environmental events and social support to serious suicide attempts in primary depressive disorder. *Journal of Abnormal Psychology, 90,* 275–285.

Sloane, R. B., Staples, F. R., Cristol, A. H., Yorkson, N. J., & Whipple, K. (1975). *Psychotherapy versus behavior therapy.* Cambridge, MA: Harvard University Press.

Small, G. W., & Nicholi, A. (1982). Mass hysteria among school children. *Archives of General Psychiatry, 39,* 721–724.

Small, G. W., Propper, M. W., Randolph, E. T., & Spencer, E. (1991). Mass hysteria among student performers: Social relationship as a symptom predictor. *American Journal of Psychiatry, 148,* 1200–1205.

Smalley, S. L., Asarnow, R. F., & Spence, A. (1988). Autism and genetics: A decade of research. *Archives of General Psychiatry, 45,* 953–961.

Smeraldi, E., Negri, F., & Melica, A. M. (1978). A genetic study of affective disorders. *Acta Psychiatrica Scandinavica, 56,* 382–398.

Smith, B., & Sechrest, L. (1991). Treatment of aptitude × treatment interactions. *Journal of Consulting and Clinical Psychology, 59,* 233–244.

Smith, D. W., & Wilson, A. A. (1973). *The child with Down's syndrome (mongolism).* Philadelphia: Saunders.

Smith, J. C. (1976). Psychotherapeutic effects of transcendental meditation with controls for expectation of relief and daily sitting. *Journal of Consulting and Clinical Psychology, 44,* 630–637.

Smith, J. S., & Kiloh, L. G. (Eds.). (1977). *Psychosurgery and society*. Elmsford, NY: Pergamon Press.

Smith, M. L., Glass, G. V., & Miller, T. I. (1980). *The benefits of psychotherapy*. Baltimore: Johns Hopkins University Press.

Smith, T. W. (1992). Hostility and health: Current status of a psychosomatic hypothesis. *Health Psychology, 11,* 139–150.

Smith, T. W., Turner, C., Ford, M., Hunt, S., Barlow, G., Stutts, B., & Williams, R. (1987). Blood pressure reactivity in adult male twins. *Health Psychology, 6,* 209–220.

Smith v. United States, 148 F.2d 665 (1929).

Snow, R. E. (1991). Aptitude-treatment interaction as a framework for research on individual differences in psychotherapy. *Journal of Consulting and Clinical Psychology, 59,* 205–216.

Snyder, M., & White, P. (1982). Moods and memories: Elation, depression, and the remembering of events of one's life. *Journal of Personality and Social Psychology, 50,* 149–167.

Snyder, S. H. (1976). The dopamine hypothesis of schizophrenia. *American Journal of Psychiatry, 133,* 197–202.

Sohlberg, S., Rosmark, B., Norring, C., & Holmgren, S. (1987). Two year outcome in anorexia nervosa/bulimia: A controlled study of an eating control program combined with psychoanalytically oriented psychotherapy. *International Journal of Eating Disorders, 6,* 243–255.

Solanto, M. V. (1984). Neuropharmacological basis of stimulant drug action in attention deficit disorder with hyperactivity: A review and synthesis. *Psychological Bulletin, 95,* 387–409.

Solanto, M. V., & Conners, C. K. (1982). A dose-response and time-action analysis of autonomic and behavioral effects of methylphenidate in attention deficit disorder with hyperactivity. *Psychophysiology, 19,* 658–667.

Soloff, P. H., George, A., Nathan, R. S., Schulz, P. M., & Perel, J. M. (1987). Behavioral dyscontrol in borderline patients treated with amitriptyline. *Psychopharmacological Bulletin, 23,* 177–181.

Solomon, S., Holmes, D. S., & McCaul, K. D. (1980). Behavioral control over aversive events: Does control that requires effort reduce anxiety and physiological arousal? *Journal of Personality and Social Psychology, 39,* 729–736.

Sorenson, S. B., Rutter, C. M., & Sneshensel, C. S. (1991). Depression in the community: An investigation into age of onset. *Journal of Consulting and Clinical Psychology, 59,* 541–546.

Sotsky, S. M., Glass, D. R., Shea, M. T., Pilkonis, P. A., Collins, J. F., Elkin, I., Watkins, J. T., Imber, S. D., Leber, W. R., Moyer, J., & Oliveri, M. E. (1991). Patient predictor of response to psychotherapy and pharmacotherapy: Findings in the NIMH Treatment of Depression Collaborative Research Program. *American Journal of Psychiatry, 148,* 997–1008.

Soubie, P. (1986). Reconciling the role of central serotonin neurons in human and animal behavior. *Behavioral and Brain Sciences, 9,* 319–364.

Spanos, N. P. (1986). Hypnosis, nonvolitional responding, and multiple personality: A social psychological perspective. In B. A. Maher & W. Maher (Eds.), *Progress in experimental personality research* (Vol. 14). Dallas, TX: Academic Press.

Spanos, N. P., Weekes, J. R., & Bertrand, L. D. (1985). Multiple personality: A social psychological perspective. *Journal of Abnormal Psychology, 94,* 362–367.

Speer, D. C. (1992). Clinically significant change: Jacobson and Truax (1991) revisited. *Journal of Consulting and Clinical Psychology, 60,* 402–408.

Spielberger, C. D. (1971). Anxiety as an emotional state. In C. D. Spielberger (Ed.), *Anxiety: Current trends in theory and research*. Dallas, TX: Academic Press.

Spiess, W. F., Geer, J. H., & O'Donohue, W. T. (1984). Premature ejaculation: Investigation of factors in ejaculatory latency. *Journal of Abnormal Psychology, 93,* 1521–1522.

Spirito, A., Brown, L., Overholser, J., & Fritz, G. (1989). Attempted suicide in adolescence: A review and critique of the literature. *Clinical Psychology Review, 9,* 335–363.

Spoont, M. R. (1992). Modulatory role of serotonin in neural information processing: Implications for human psychopathology. *Psychological Bulletin, 112,* 330–350.

Srole, L., Langner, T. S., Michael, S. T., Opler, M. K., & Rennie, T. A. C. (1962). *Mental health in the metropolis: The midtown Manhattan study*. New York: McGraw-Hill.

Stack, S. (1990). Media impacts on suicide. In D. Lester (Ed.), *Current concepts of suicide*. Philadelphia: Charles Press.

Stahl, S. M., & Lebedun, M. (1974). Mystery gas: An analysis of mass hysteria. *Journal of Health and Social Behavior, 15,* 44–50.

Stampfl, T. G., & Lewis, D. J. (1967). Essentials of implosive therapy: A learning-theory-based psychodynamic behavioral therapy. *Journal of Abnormal Psychology, 72,* 496–503.

Stampfl, T. G., & Lewis, D. J. (1968). Implosive therapy: A behavioural therapy? *Behaviour Research and Therapy, 6,* 31–36.

Stanley, E. (1981). Premature ejaculation. *British Medical Journal, 282,* 1521–1522.

Stanley, M., & Stanley, B. (1989). Biochemical studies in suicide victims: Current findings and future implications. *Suicide and Life-Threatening Behavior, 19,* 30–42.

Starfield, B. (1972). Enuresis: Its pathogenesis and management. *Clinical Pediatrics, 11,* 343–350.

Steadman, H. J. (1973). Follow-up on Baxstrom patients returned to hospitals for the criminally insane. *American Journal of Psychiatry, 3,* 317–319.

Steadman, H. J., & Keveles, G. (1972). The community adjustment and criminal activity of Baxstrom patients, 1966–1970. *American Journal of Psychiatry, 129,* 304–310.

Steadman, H. J., & Keveles, G. (1978). The community adjustment and criminal activity of Baxstrom patients. *American Journal of Psychiatry, 135,* 1218–1220.

Steele, C. M., & Josephs, R. A. (1988). Drinking your troubles away: 2. An attention-allocation model of alcohol's effect on psychological stress. *Journal of Abnormal Psychology, 95,* 196–205.

Steele, C. M., Southwick, L., & Pagano, R. (1986). Drinking your troubles away: The role of activity in mediating alcohol's reduction of psychological stress. *Journal of Abnormal Psychology, 95,* 173–180.

Stehbens, J. A. (1970). Enuresis in schoolchildren. *Journal of School Psychology, 8,* 145–151.

Stein, Z. A., & Susser, M. W. (1966). Nocturnal enuresis as a phenomenon of institutions. *Developmental Medicine and Child Neurology, 8,* 677–685.

Stengel, E. (1964). *Suicide and attempted suicide.* New York: Viking Penguin.

Stephens, J. H., & Kamp, M. (1962). On some aspects of hysteria: A clinical study. *Journal of Nervous and Mental Disease, 134,* 305–315.

Stephens, M. W., & Delys, P. (1973). External control expectancies among disadvantaged children at preschool age. *Child Development, 44,* 670–674.

Stern, D. B. (1977). Handedness and the lateral distribution of conversion reactions. *Journal of Nervous and Mental Disease, 164,* 122–128.

Stewart, M. A., Cummings, C., Singer, S., & de Blois, C. S. (1981). The overlap between hyperactive and unsocialized aggressive children. *Journal of Child Psychology and Psychiatry, 22,* 35–45.

Stiles, W. B., Shapiro, D. A., & Elliott, R. (1986). "Are all psychotherapies equivalent?" *American Psychologist, 41,* 165–180.

Stockwell, L., & Smith, C. K. (1940). Enuresis: A study of causes, types, and therapeutic results. *American Journal of Diseases of Children, 59,* 1013–1033.

Stodolsky, S., & Lesser, G. (1967). Learning patterns in the disadvantaged. *Harvard Educational Review, 37,* 546–593.

Stoll, A. L., Tohen, M., & Baldessarini, R. J. (1992). Increasing frequency of the diagnosis of obsessive-compulsive disorder. *American Journal of Psychiatry, 149,* 638–640.

Stoller, R. (1968). *Sex and gender.* New York: Science House.

Stone, A. A. (1975). *Mental health and law: A system in transition.* Rockville, MD: National Institute of Mental Health Center for Studies of Crime and Delinquency.

Stone, E. A. (1975). Stress and catecholamines. In A. J. Friedhoff (Ed.), *Catecholamines and behavior* (pp. 31–72). New York: Plenum.

Strauss, J. S., & Carpenter, W. T. (1972). The prediction of outcome in schizophrenia: 1. Characteristics of outcome. *Archives of General Psychiatry, 27,* 739–746.

Strauss, J. S., Carpenter, W. T., & Bartko, J. J. (1974). The diagnosis and understanding of schizophrenia: 2. Speculations on the processes that underlie schizophrenic symptoms and signs. *Schizophrenia Bulletin, 11,* 61–76.

Strauss, J. S., Kokes, F. R., Ritzler, B. A., Harder, D. W., & Van Ord, A. (1978). Patterns of disorder in first-admission psychiatric patients. *Journal of Nervous and Mental Disease, 166,* 611–623.

Streissguth, A. P., Herman, C. S., & Smith, D. W. (1978). Intelligence, behavior, and dysmorphogenesis in the fetal alcohol syndrome: A report on 20 patients. *Journal of Pediatrics, 92,* 363–368.

Strickland, B. R., Hale, W. D., & Anderson, L. K. (1975). Effect of induced mood states on activity and self-reported affect. *Journal of Consulting and Clinical Psychology, 43,* 587.

Strober, M. (1982). The significance of bulimia in juvenile anorexia nervosa: An exploration of possible etiological factors. *International Journal of Eating Disorders, 1,* 28–43.

Stumpfl, F. (1936). *Die Ursprunge des Verbrechens.* Leipzig: Thieme.

Sud, A., & Sharma, H. (1989). Test anxiety, intrusive thoughts, and attentional process. *Journal of Personality and Clinical Studies, 5,* 139–145.

Suddath, R. L., Christison, G. W., Torrey, E. F., Casanova, M. F., & Weinberger, D. R. (1990). Anatomical abnormalities in the brains of monozygotic twins discordant for schizophrenia. *New England Journal of Medicine, 322,* 789–794.

Suedfeld, P., & Landon, P. B. (1978). Approaches to treatment. In R. D. Hare & D. Schalling (Eds.), *Psychopathic behavior: Approaches to research* (pp. 347–376). New York: Wiley.

Suinn, R. M. (1980). Pattern A behaviors and heart disease: Intervention approaches. In J. M. Ferguson & C. B. Taylor (Eds.), *The comprehensive handbook of behavioral medicine* (Vol. 1, pp. 5–28). Jamaica, NY: Spectrum.

Sullivan, H. S. (1962). *Schizophrenia as a human process.* New York: Norton.

Suppes, T., Baldessarini, R. J., Faedda, G. L., & Tohen, M. (1991). Risk of recurrence following discontinuation of lithium treatment in bipolar disorder. *Archives of General Psychiatry, 48,* 1082–1088.

Susser, E. S., & Lin, S. P. (1992). Schizophrenia after prenatal exposure to the Dutch hunger winter of 1944–1945. *Archives of General Psychiatry, 49,* 983–989.

Sutcliffe, J. P., & Jones, J. (1962). Personal identity, multiple personality and hypnosis. *International Journal of Clinical and Experimental Hypnosis, 39,* 281–300.

Sutker, P. B., & Allain, A. N. (1988). Issues in personality conceptualization of addictive behaviors. *Journal of Consulting and Clinical Psychology, 56,* 172–182.

Swann, W. B., Wenzlaff, R. M., Krull, D. S., & Pelham, B. W. (1992). Allure of negative feedback: Self-verification strivings among depressed persons. *Journal of Abnormal Psychology, 101,* 293–306.

Swedo, S. E., Leonard, H. L., Kruesi, M. J. P., Rettew, D. C., Listwak, S. J., Berrettini, W., Sipetic, M., Hamburger, S., Gold, P. W., Potter, W. Z., & Rapoport, J. L. (1992). Cerebrospinal fluid neurochemistry in children and adolescents with obsessive-compulsive disorder. *Archives of General Psychiatry, 49,* 29–36.

Sweeney, P. D., & Gruber, K. L. (1984). Selective exposure: Voter information preferences and the Watergate affair. *Journal of Personality and Social Psychology, 46,* 1208–1221.

Szasz, T. S. (1961). *The myth of mental illness.* New York: HarperCollins.

Szasz, T. S. (1970). *The manufacture of madness.* New York: Macmillan.

Tanzi, R. E., Gusella, J. F., Watkins, P. C., Burns, G. A., Saint George–Hyslop, P., Van Keuren, M. L., Patterson, D., Pagan, S., Kurnit, D. M., & Neve, R. L. (1987). Amyloid B protein gene: cDNA, mRNA distribution, and genetic linkage near the Alzheimer locus. *Science, 235,* 880–884.

Tarasoff v. Regents of the University of California, 551 P.2d 334 (1976).

Tarsh, M. J. (1978). Severe obsessional illness in dizygotic twins treated by leucotomy. *Comprehensive Psychiatry, 19,* 165–169.

Taylor, G. R., & Dardano, J. R. (1983). Human cellular immune responsiveness following space flight. *Aviation, Space, and Environmental Medicine, 54* (Suppl. 1), S55–S59.

Taylor, G. R., Neale, L. S., & Dardano, J. R. (1986). Immunological analyses of U.S. space shuttle crew members. *Aviation, Space, and Environmental Medicine, 57,* 213–217.

Teasdale, J. D. (1983). Negative thinking in depression: Cause, effect or reciprocal relationship? *Advances in Behavior Research and Therapy, 5,* 3–25.

Teasdale, J. D. (1988). Cognitive vulnerability to persistent depression. *Cognition and Emotion, 2,* 247–274.

Teasdale, J. D., & Bancroft, J. (1977). Manipulation of thought content as a determinant of mood and corrugator electromyographic activity in depressed patients. *Journal of Abnormal Psychology, 86,* 235–241.

Teasdale, J. D., & Fogarty, S. J. (1979). Differential effects of induced mood on retrieval of pleasant and unpleasant events from episodic memory. *Journal of Abnormal Psychology, 88,* 248–257.

Teicher, M. H., & Gold, C. A. (1989). Pharmacotherapy of patients with borderline personality disorder. *Hospital and Community Psychiatry, 40,* 887–889.

Teicher, M. H., Gold, C. A., & Cole, J. O. (1990). Emergence of intense suicidal preoccupation during fluoxetine treatment. *American Journal of Psychiatry, 147,* 207–210.

Teitelbaum, P., & Steller, E. (1954). Recovery from the failure to eat produced by hypothalamic lesions. *Science, 120,* 894–895.

Telch, C. F., Agras, W. S., Rossiter, E. M., Wilfrey, D., & Kenardy, J. (1990). Group cognitive-behavioral treatment for the nonpurging bulimic: An initial evaluation. *Journal of Consulting and Clinical Psychology, 58,* 629–635.

Telch, M. J., Lucas, J. A., & Nelson, P. (1989). Nonclinical panic in college students: An investigation of prevalence and symptomology. *Journal of Abnormal Psychology, 98,* 300–306.

Tellegen, A., Lykken, D. T., Bouchard, T. J., Wilcox, K., Segal, N., & Rich, S. (1988). Personality similarity in twins reared apart and together. *Journal of Personality and Social Psychology, 54,* 1031–1039.

Tennant, C., & Babbington, P. (1978). The social causation of depression: A critique of the work of Brown and his colleagues. *Psychological Medicine, 8,* 565–575.

Tennen, H. (1982). A review of cognitive mediators in learned helplessness. *Journal of Personality, 50,* 526–541.

Tennen, H., Drum, P. E., Gillen, R., & Stanton, A. (1982). Learned helplessness and the detection of contingency: A direct test. *Journal of Personality, 50,* 426–442.

Tennen, H., Gillen, R., & Drum, P. E. (1982). The debilitating effect of exposure to noncontingent escape: A test of the learned helplessness model. *Journal of Personality, 50,* 409–425.

Termal, M., Termal, J. S., Quitkin, F. M., McGrath, P. J., et al. (1989). Light therapy for seasonal affective disorder: A review of efficacy. *Neuropsychopharmacology, 2,* 1–22.

Thigpen, C. H., & Cleckley, H. M. (1954). A case of multiple personality. *Journal of Abnormal and Social Psychology, 49,* 139–151.

Thigpen, C. H., & Cleckley, H. M. (1957). *The three faces of Eve.* New York: Fawcett.

Thigpen, C. H., & Cleckley, H. M. (1984). On the incidence of multiple personality disorder. *International Journal of Clinical and Experimental Hypnosis, 32,* 63–66.

Thomas, C. B. (1976). Precursors of premature disease and

death: The predictive potential of habits and family attitudes. *Annals of Internal Medicine, 85,* 653–685.

Tietze, C., & Lewitt, S. (1972). Joint program for the study of abortion: Early medical complications of legal abortion. *Studies in Family Planning, 3,* 97–122.

Tillich, P. (1952). *Courage to be.* New Haven, CT: Yale University Press.

Tinklenberg, J. R. (1974). Marijuana and human aggression. In L. L. Miller (Ed.), *Marijuana: Effects on human behavior* (pp. 339–358). Dallas, TX: Academic Press.

Tobin, D. L., Johnson, C., Steinberg, S., Staats, M., & Dennis, A. B. (1991). Multifactorial assessment of bulimia nervosa. *Journal of Abnormal Psychology, 100,* 14–21.

Tohen, M., Waternaux, C. M., & Tsuang, M. T. (1990). Outcome in mania. *Archives of General Psychiatry, 47,* 1106–1111.

Tong, J. E., & McKay, G. W. (1959). A statistical follow-up of mental defectives of dangerous and violent propensities. *British Journal of Delinquency, 9,* 276.

Torgersen, S. (1979). The nature and origin of common phobic fears. *British Journal of Psychiatry, 119,* 343–351.

Torgersen, S. (1983). Genetic factors in anxiety disorders. *Archives of General Psychiatry, 40,* 1085–1089.

Torrey, E. F. (1988). Nowhere to go: The tragic odyssey of the homeless mentally ill. New York: HarperCollins.

Torrey, E. F., Hersh, S. P., & McCabe, K. D. (1975). Early childhood psychosis and bleeding during pregnancy. *Journal of Autism and Childhood Schizophrenia, 5,* 287–297.

Torrey, E. F., Rawlings, R., & Waldman, I. N. (1988). Schizophrenic births and viral diseases in two states. *Schizophrenia Research, 1,* 73–77.

Toufexis, A. (1988, June 20). Why mothers kill their babies. *Time,* pp. 81–82.

Towbin, A. (1978). Cerebral dysfunctions related to perinatal organic damage: Clinical-neuropathologic correlates. *Journal of Abnormal Psychology, 87,* 617–635.

Tredgold, A. F., & Soddy, K. (1970). *Tredgold's mental retardation.* Baltimore: Williams & Wilkins.

Trijsburg, R. W., van Kippenberg, F. C., & Rijpma, S. E. (1992). Effects of psychological treatment on cancer patients: A critical review. *Psychosomatic Medicine, 54,* 489–517.

Troup, C. W., & Hodgson, N. B. (1971). Nocturnal functional bladder capacity in enuretic children. *Journal of Urology, 105,* 129–132.

Troutman, B. R., & Cutrona, C. E. (1990). Nonpsychotic postpartum depression among adolescent mothers. *Journal of Abnormal Psychology, 99,* 69–78.

Trower, P., & Gilbert, P. (1989). New theoretical conceptions of social anxiety and social phobia. *Clinical Psychology Review, 9,* 19–36.

Trzebiatowska-Trzeciak, O. (1977). Genetical analysis of unipolar and biopolar endogenous affective psychoses. *British Journal of Psychiatry, 131,* 478–485.

Tsai, L., & Stewart, M. (1983). Etiological implications of maternal age and birth order in infantile autism. *Journal of Autism and Developmental Disorders, 13,* 57–65.

Tsai, L., Stewart, M., Faust, M., & Shook, S. (1982). Social class distribution of fathers of children enrolled in the

Iowa Autistic Program. *Journal of Autism and Developmental Disorders, 12,* 211–221.

Tuckman, J., Kleiner, R., & Lavell, M. (1959). Emotional content of suicide notes. *American Journal of Psychiatry, 116,* 59–63.

Turkington, C. (1986). Brief examines volition. *APA Monitor, 17*(5), 22.

Turner, R. J., & Wagonfeld, M. O. (1967). Occupational mobility and schizophrenia: An assessment of the social causation and social selection hypothesis. *American Sociological Review, 32,* 104–113.

Turner, S. M., & Beidel, D. C. (1989). Social phobia: Clinical syndrome, diagnosis, and comorbidity. *Clinical Psychology Review, 9,* 3–18.

Turner, S. M., Beidel, D. C., & Nathan, R. S. (1985). Biological factors in obsessive-compulsive disorders. *Psychological Bulletin, 97,* 430–450.

Turner, S. M., Beidel, D. C., & Stanley, M. A. (1992). Are obsessional thoughts and worry different cognitive phenomena? *Clinical Psychology Review, 12,* 257–270.

Tye, N. C., Iversen, S. D., & Green, A. R. (1979). The effects of benzodiazepines and serotonergic manipulations on punished responding. *Neuropharmacology, 18,* 689–654.

Tyrer, P., Lee, I., & Alexander, J. (1980). Awareness of cardiac function in anxious, phobic, and hypochondrical patients. *Psychological Medicine, 10,* 171–174.

Tyrer, S., & Shopsin, B. (1982). Symptoms and assessment of mania. In E. S. Paykel (Ed.), *Handbook of affective disorders* (pp. 12–23). New York: Guilford Press.

Uhl, G. R., Persico, A. M., & Smith, S. S. (1992). Current excitement with D/2 dopamine receptor gene alleles in substance abuse. *Archives of General Psychiatry, 49,* 157–160.

Ullman, L. P., & Krasner, L. (1969). *A psychological approach to abnormal behavior.* Englewood Cliffs, NJ: Prentice Hall.

Unden, A., Orth-Gomer, K., & Elofsson, S. (1991). Cardiovascular effects of social support in the workplace: Twenty-four-hour ECG monitoring of men and women. *Psychosomatic Medicine, 53,* 50–60.

United States v. Brawner, 471 F.2d 969 (D.C. 1972).

Vaillant, G. E. (1963). Twins discordant for early infantile autism. *Archives of General Psychiatry, 9,* 163–167.

Valenstein, E. S. (Ed.). (1980). *The psychosurgery debate.* New York: Freeman.

VandenBos, G. R., & Pino, C. D. (1980). Research on outcome of psychotherapy. In G. R. Vanden Bos (Ed.), *Psychotherapy: Practice, research, policy* (pp. 23–69). Newbury Park, CA: Sage.

Vandereycken, W., & Lowenkopf, E. L. (1990). Anorcxia nervosa in 19th-century America. *Journal of Nervous and Mental Disease, 178,* 531–535.

Van Praag, H. M. (1986). Affective disorders and aggression disorders: Evidence for a common biological mechanism. *Suicide and Life-Threatening Behavior, 16,* 103–132.

Van Putten, T. (1975). Why do patients with manic-depressive illness stop their lithium? *Comprehensive Psychiatry, 16,* 179–183.

Van Putten, T., & May, P. (1976). Milieu treatment for schizophrenics. In L. West & D. Flinn (Eds.), *Treatment of schizophrenia.* Philadelphia: Grune & Stratton.

Van Scheyen, J. D., & Van Kammen, D. P. (1979).

Clomipramine-induced mania in unipolor depression. *Archives of General Psychiatry, 36,* 560–565.

Vaughn, C. E., & Leff, J. P. (1976). The influence of family and social factors on the course of psychiatric illness: A comparison of schizophrenic and depressed neurotic patients. *British Journal of Psychiatry, 129,* 125–137.

Vaughn, C. E., Snyder, K. S., Jones, S., Freeman, W. B., & Falloon, R. H. (1984). Family factors in schizophrenic relapse: Replication in California of British research on expressed emotion. *Archives of General Psychiatry, 41,* 1169–1177.

Veith, I. (1965). *Hysteria: The history of a disease.* Chicago: University of Chicago Press.

Velten, E. (1968). A laboratory task for induction of mood states. *Behaviour Research and Therapy, 6,* 473–482.

Venables, P. H. (1964). Input dysfunction in schizophrenia. In B. A. Maher (Ed.), *Progress in experimental personality research* (Vol. 1). Dallas, TX: Academic Press.

Verhulst, F. C., van der Lee, J. H., Akkerhuis, G. W., Sanders-Woudstra, J. A. R., Timmer, F. C., & Donkhorst, I. D. (1985). The prevalence of nocturnal enuresis: Do DSM-III criteria need to be changed? *Journal of Child Psychology and Psychiatry and Allied Disciplines, 26,* 989–993.

Vietor, W. P. (1967). Conditioning as a form of psychotherapy in treating delinquents: Some data from the literature. *Excerpta Criminologica, 7,* 3–6.

Volavka, J., Cooper, T., Czobor, P., Bitter, I., Meisner, M., Laska, E., Gastanaga, P., Krakowski, M., Chow, J., Growner, M., & Douyon, R. (1992). Haloperidol blood levels and clinical effects. *Archives of General Psychiatry, 49,* 354–361.

Volpicelli, J. R., Alterman, A. I., Hayashida, M., & O'Brien, C. P. (1992). Naltrexone in the treatment of alcohol dependence. *Archives of General Psychiatry, 49,* 876–880.

Vonnegut, M. (1975). *The Eden express.* New York: Praeger.

Waddington, J. L., Weller, M. P. I., Crow, T. J., & Hirsch, S. R. (1992). Schizophrenia, genetic retrenchment, and epidemiologic renaissance. *Archives of General Psychiatry, 49,* 990–994.

Wagner, E. E., & Heise, M. R. (1974). A comparison of Rorschach records of three multiple personalities. *Journal of Personality Assessment, 38,* 308–331.

Walsh, B. T., Hadigan, C. M., Devlin, M. J., Gladis, M., & Roose, S. P. (1991). Long-term outcome of antidepressant treatment for bulimia nervosa. *American Journal of Psychiatry, 148,* 1206–1212.

Walsh, B. T., Roose, S. P., Glassman, A. H., Gladis, M., & Sadik, C. (1985). Bulimia and depression. *Psychosomatic Medicine, 47,* 123–131.

Walsh, B. T., Stewart, J. W., Roose, S. P., Gladis, M., & Glassman, A. H. (1984). Treatment of bulimia with phenelzine. *Archives of General Psychiatry, 41,* 1105–1109.

Walsh, B. T., Stewart, J. W., Wright, L., Harrison, W., Roose, S. P., & Glassman, A. H. (1982). Treatment of bulimia with monoamine oxidase inhibitors. *American Journal of Psychiatry, 139,* 1629–1630.

Ward, C. H., Beck, A. T., Mendelson, M., Mock, J. E., & Erbaugh, J. K. (1962). The psychiatric nomenclature: Reasons for diagnostic disagreement. *Archives of General Psychiatry, 7,* 198–205.

Warner, M. D., Peabody, C. A., & Boutros, N. N. (1990). A

survey of neuroleptic malignant syndrome. *Journal of Nervous and Mental Disease, 178,* 664–665.

Warren, L. W., & McEachren, L. (1983). Psychosocial correlates of depressive symptomatology in adult women. *Journal of Abnormal Psychology, 92,* 151–160.

Warren, R. P., Yonk, L. J., Burger, R. A., Cole, P., Odell, J. D., Warren, W. L., White, E., & Singh, V. K. (1990). Deficiency of suppressor-inducer T cells in autism. *Immunological Investigations, 19,* 245–251.

Watkins, J. G. (1984). The Bianchi (L.A. Hillside Strangler) case: Sociopath or multiple personality? *International Journal of Clinical and Experimental Hypnosis, 32,* 67–101.

Watson, C. G., Tilleskjor, C., Kucala, T., & Jacobs, L. (1984). The birth seasonality effect in nonschizophrenic psychiatric patients. *Journal of Clinical Psychology, 40,* 884–888.

Watson, J. B., & Rayner, R. (1920). Conditioned emotional reactions. *Journal of Experimental Psychology, 3,* 1–14.

Watt, N. (1978). Patterns of childhood social development in adult schizophrenics. *Archives of General Psychiatry, 35,* 160–165.

Watt, N., Stolorow, R., Lubensky, A., & McClelland, D. (1970). School adjustment and behavior of children hospitalized as schizophrenic as adults. *American Journal of Orthopsychiatry, 40,* 637–657.

Wedell, K., Welton, J., Evans, B., & Goacher, A. (1987). Policy and provision under the 1981 Act. *British Journal of Special Education, 14,* 50–53.

Wegner, J. T., Catalano, F., Gibralter, J., & Kane, J. M. (1985). Schizophrenics with tardive dyskinesia. *Archives of General Psychiatry, 42,* 860–865.

Wehr, T. A., & Rosenthal, N. E. (1989). Seasonality and affective illness. *American Journal of Psychiatry, 146,* 829–839.

Wehr, T. A., Sack, D. A., Rosenthal, N. E., & Cowdry, R. W. (1988). Rapid cycling affective disorder: Contribution factors and treatment responses in 51 patients. *American Journal of Psychiatry, 145,* 179–184.

Weinberger, D. R. (1987). Implications of normal brain development for the pathogenesis of schizophrenia. *Archives of General Psychiatry, 44,* 660–669.

Weiner, H. (1977). *Psychobiology and human disease.* New York: Elsevier.

Weiner, H. (1991). From simplicity to complexity (1950–1990): The case of peptic ulceration: I. Human studies. *Psychosomatic Medicine, 53,* 467–490.

Weiner, H., Thaler, M., Reiser, M. F., & Mirsky, I. A. (1957). Etiology of duodenal ulcer: 1. Relation of specific psychological characteristics to rate of gastric secretion. *Psychosomatic Medicine, 17,* 1–10.

Weiner, R. (1982). Another look at an old controversy. *Contemporary Psychiatry, 1,* 61–62.

Weiss, B., & Laties, V. G. (1962). Enhancement of human performance by caffeine and the amphetamines. *Pharmacological Review, 14,* 1–36.

Weiss, G., Kruger, E., Danielson, V., & Elman, M. (1975). Effects of long-term treatment of hyperactive children with methylphenidate. *Canadian Medical Association Journal, 112,* 159–165.

Weiss, J. M. (1968). Effects of coping responses on stress. *Journal of Comparative and Physiological Psychology, 24,* 409–414.

Weiss, J. M. (1970). Somatic effects of predictable and unpredictable shock. *Psychosomatic Medicine, 32,* 397–408.

Weiss, J. M. (1973). The natural history of antisocial attitudes: What happens to psychopaths? *Journal of Geriatric Psychiatry, 6,* 236–242.

Weiss, J. M., Glazer, H. I., & Pohoresky, L. A. (1976). Coping behavior and neurochemical change in rats: An alternative explanation for the original "learned helplessness" experiments. In G. Serban & A. King (Eds.), *Animal models in human psychobiology.* New York: Plenum.

Weisse, C. S. (1992). Depression and immunocompetence: A review of the literature. *Psychological Bulletin, 111,* 475–489.

Weissman, M. M., (1974). The epidemiology of suicide attempts, 1969–1971. *Archives of General Psychiatry, 30,* 737–746.

Weissman, M. M. (1979a). The myth of involutional melancholia. *JAMA, 242,* 742–744.

Weissman, M. M. (1979b). The psychological treatment of depression: Research evidence for the efficacy of psychotherapy alone, in comparison and in combination with pharmacotherapy. *Archives of General Psychiatry, 36,* 1261–1269.

Weissman, M. M., & Klerman, G. L. (1977). Sex differences in the epidemiology of depression. *Archives of General Psychiatry, 34,* 98–111.

Weissman, M. M., & Myers, J. K. (1978). Affective disorders in a United States urban community: The use of research diagnostic criteria in an epidemiologic survey. *Archives of General Psychiatry, 35,* 1304–1311.

Weissman, M. M., Prusoff, B. A., Di Mascio, A., Neu, C., Goklaney, M., & Klerman, G. L. (1979). The efficacy of drugs and psychotherapy in the treatment of acute depressive episodes. *American Journal of Psychiatry, 136,* 555–558.

Wekstein, L. (1979). *Handbook of suicidology: Principles, problems, and practice.* New York: Brunner/Mazel.

Welsch v. Litkins, 373 F. Supp. 487 (D. Minn. 1974).

Wender, P. H., Rosenthal, D., Kety, S. S., Schulsinger, F., & Weiner, J. (1974). Cross-fostering: A research strategy for clarifying the role of genetic and experiential factors in the etiology of schizophrenia. *Archives of General Psychiatry, 30,* 121–128.

Wender, P. H. (1971). *Minimal brain dysfunction in children.* New York: Wiley-Interscience.

Werry, J. S. (1967). Enuresis nocturna. *Medical Times, 95,* 985–991.

Werry, J. S. (1979). The childhood psychoses. In H. C. Quay & J. S. Werry (Eds.), *Psychopathological disorders of childhood.* New York: Wiley.

Werry, J. S., & Quay, H. C. (1971). The prevalence of behavior symptoms in younger elementary school children. *American Journal of Orthopsychiatry, 41,* 136–143.

West, M. A. (1987). *The psychology of meditation.* Oxford: Oxford University Press.

Westermeyer, J. F., Harrow, M., & Marengo, J. T. (1991). Risk of suicide in schizophrenia and other psychotic and nonpsychotic disorders. *Journal of Nervous and Mental Disease, 179,* 259–266.

Wettstein, R. M., Mulvey, E. P., & Rogers, R. (1991). A prospective comparison of four insanity defense standards. *American Journal of Psychiatry, 148,* 21–27.

Wetzel, R. (1977). Factor structure of Beck's Suicide Intent Scales. *Psychological Reports, 40,* 295–302.

Wheeler, L. (1966). Toward a theory of behavioral contagion. *Psychological Review, 73,* 179–192.

Wheeler E. D., White, P. D., Reed, E. W., & Cohen, M. E. (1948). Familial incidence of neurocirculatory asthenia ("anxiety neuroses," "effort syndrome"). *Journal of Clinical Investment, 27,* 562.

Whiffen, V. E. (1992). Is postpartum depression a distinct diagnosis? *Clinical Psychology Review, 12,* 485–508.

Whitlock, F. A. (1967). The aetiology of hysteria. *Acta Psychiatrica Scandinavica, 43,* 144–162.

Whitlock, F. A., & Siskind, M. (1979). Depression and cancer: A follow-up study. *Psychological Medicine, 9,* 747–752.

Widiger, T. A., Frances, A. J., Harris, M., Jacobsberg, L. B., Fyer, M. R., & Manning, D. (1991). Comorbidity among axis II disorders. In J. M. Oldham (Ed.), *Personality disorders: New perspectives on diagnostic validity.* Washington, DC: American Psychiatric Press.

Wilcox, J. A. (1986). Perinatal distress and infectious disease as risk factors for catatonia. *Psychopathology, 19,* 196–199.

Wilcox, J. A., & Nasrallah, H. A. (1987a). Perinatal distress and prognosis of psychotic illness. *Neuropsychobiology, 17,* 173–175.

Wilcox, J. A., & Nasrallah, H. A. (1987b). Perinatal insult as a risk factor in paranoid and nonparanoid schizophrenia. *Psychopathology, 20,* 285–287.

Wilcoxon, L. A., Schrader, S. L., & Nelson, R. E. (1976). Behavioral formulations of depression. In W. E. Craighead, A. E. Kazdin, & M. J. Mahoney (Eds.), *Behavior modification: Principles, issues, and applications.* Boston: Houghton Mifflin.

Willerman, L. (1973). Activity level and hyperactivity in twins. *Child Development, 44,* 288–293.

Williams, D. H. (1986). The epidemiology of mental illness in Afro-Americans. *Hospital and Community Psychiatry, 37,* 42–49.

Williams, J. B. (1985a). The multiaxial system of DSM-III: Where did it come from and where should it go? 1. Its origins and critiques. *Archives of General Psychiatry, 42,* 175–180.

Williams, J. B. (1985b). The multiaxial system of DSM-III: Where did it come from and where should it go? 2. Empirical studies, innovations, and recommendations. *Archives of General Psychiatry, 42,* 181–186.

Williams, R. B., Haney, T. L., Lee, K. L., Kong, Y., Blumenthal, J. A., & Whalen, R. E. (1980). Type A behavior, hostility, and coronary atherosclerosis. *Psychosomatic Medicine, 42,* 539–549.

Williams, S. L., & Rappoport, A. (1983). Cognitive treatment in the natural environment for agoraphobics. *Behavior Therapy, 14,* 299–313.

Wilson, A. A. (1903). A case of double consciousness. *Journal of Mental Service, 49,* 640–658.

Wilson, G. T. (1987). Cognitive studies in alcoholism. *Journal of Consulting and Clinical Psychology, 55,* 325–331.

Wilson, G. T., & Abrams, D. (1977). Effects of alcohol on social anxiety and physiological arousal: Cognitive versus pharmacological processes. *Cognitive Therapy and Research, 1,* 195–210.

Wilson, G. T., & Lawson, D. M. (1976). The effects of alcohol on sexual arousal in women. *Journal of Abnormal Psychology, 85,* 489–497.

Winchel, R. M., & Stanley, M. A. (1991). Self-injurious behavior: A review of the behavior and biology of self-mutilation. *American Journal of Psychiatry, 148,* 306–317.

Wincze, J., Bansal, S., & Malamud, M. (1986). Effects of MPA on subjective arousal, arousal to erotic stimulation, and nocturnal penile tumescence in male sex offenders. *Archives of Sexual Behavior, 15,* 293–305.

Winefield, H. R. (1987). Psychotherapy and social support: Parallels and differences in the helping process. *Clinical Psychology Review, 7,* 631–644.

Wing, J. K. (1975). Impairment in schizophrenia: A rational basis for social treatment. In R. Wirt, G. Winokur, & M. Roff (Eds.), *Life history research in psychopathology.* Minneapolis: University of Minnesota Press.

Wing, J. K., Mann, S. A., Leff, J. P., & Nixon, J. M. (1978). The concept of a "case" in psychiatric population surveys. *Psychological Medicine, 8,* 203–217.

Winick, B. J. (1991). Voluntary hospitalization after *Zinermon* v. *Burch. Psychiatric Annals, 21,* 584–589.

Winokur, A., Clayton, P., & Reich, T. (1969). *Manic depressive illness.* St. Louis, MO: Mosby.

Winokur, A., & Rickels, K. (1981). Combination of drugs and psychotherapy in the treatment of psychiatric disorders. In H. M. Van Praag, M. H. Lader, O. J. Rafaelsen, & E. Sachar (Eds.), *Handbook of biological psychiatry: Pt. 6. Practical applications of psychotropic drugs and other biological treatments* (pp. 181–213). New York: Dekker.

Winokur, G. (1973). Depression in the menopause. *American Journal of Psychiatry, 130,* 92–93.

Winokur, G., & Clayton, P. (1967). Family history studies: Two types of affective disorders separated according to genetic and clinical factors. In J. Wortis (Ed.), *Recent advances in biological psychiatry* (Vol. 9, pp. 35–50). New York: Plenum.

Winokur, G., Morrison, J., Clancy, J., & Crowe, R. R. (1972). The Iowa 500: 2. A blind family history comparison of mania, depression, and schizophrenia. *Archives of General Psychiatry, 27,* 462–464.

Winslow, R. (1990, May 14). Sandoz Corp.'s Clozaril treats schizophrenia but can kill patients. *Wall Street Journal,* pp. 1, 14.

Winters, K. C., & Neale, J. M. (1985). Mania and low self-esteem. *Journal of Abnormal Psychology, 94,* 282–290.

Winters v. Miller, 446 F.2d 65, 71 (2d Cir. 1971).

Wise, R. A. (1988). The neurobiology of craving: Implications for the understanding and treatment of addiction. *Journal of Abnormal Psychology, 97,* 118–132.

Witkin, H. A., Mednick, S. A., Schulsinger, F., Bakkestrom, E., Christiansen, K. O., Goodenough, D. R., Hirschhorn, K., Lundsteen, C., Owen, D. R., Philip, J., Rubin, D. B., &

Stocking, M. (1976). Criminality in XYY and XXY men. *Science, 193,* 547–555.

Wittenborn, J. R. (1951). Symptom patterns in a group of mental hospital patients. *Journal of Consulting Psychology, 15,* 290–302.

Wittenborn, J. R. (1962). The dimensions of psychosis. *Journal of Nervous and Mental Disease, 134,* 117–128.

Wolchik, S. (1983). Language patterns of parents of young autistic and normal children. *Journal of Autism and Developmental Disorders, 13,* 167–180.

Wolf, M., Risley, T., Johnston, M., Harris, F., & Allen, E. (1967). Application of operant conditioning procedures to the behaviour problems of an autistic child: A follow-up and extension. *Behaviour Research and Therapy, 5,* 103–112.

Wolf, T. M., Elston, R. C., & Kissling, G. E. (1989). Relationship of hassles, uplifts, and life events to psychological well-being of freshman medical students. *Behavioral Medicine, 15,* 37–45.

Wolfe, S., & Victor, M. (1972). The physiological basis of the alcohol withdrawal syndrome. In N. Mellow & J. Mendelson (Eds.), *Recent advances in the study of alcoholism* (pp. 188–199). Washington, DC: U.S. Government Printing Office.

Wolkin, A., Sanfilipo, M., Wolf, A. P., Angrist, B., Brodie, J. D., & Rotrosen, J. (1992). Negative symptoms and hypofrontality in chronic schizophrenia. *Archives of General Psychiatry, 49,* 959–965.

Wolpe, J. (1958). *Psychotherapy by reciprocal inhibition.* Stanford, CA: Stanford University Press.

Wolpert, E. A., Goldberg, J. F., & Harrow, M. (1990). Rapid cycling in unipolar and bipolar affective disorders. *American Journal of Psychiatry, 147,* 725–728.

Wolraich, M., Drummond, T., Salomon, M., O'Brien, M., & Sivage, C. (1978). Effects of methylphenidate alone and in combination with behavioral modification procedures on the behavior and academic performance of hyperactive children. *Journal of Abnormal Child Psychology, 6,* 149–161.

Wong, D. F., Wagner, H. N., Dannals, R. F., Links, J. M., Frost, J. J., Ravert, H. T., Wilson, A. A., Rosenbaum, A. E., Gjedde, A., Douglass, K. H., Petronis, J. D., Folstein, M. F., Toung, J. K. T., Burns, H. D., & Kuhar, M. J. (1984). Effects of age on dopamine and serotonin receptors measured by positron tomography in the living human brain. *Science, 226,* 1393–1396.

Wong, D. F., Wagner, H. N., Tune, L. E., Dannals, R. F., Pearlson, G. D., Links, J. M., Tamminga, C. A., Broussolle, E. P., Ravert, H. T., Wilson A. A., Toung, J. K. T., Malat, J., Williams, J. A., O'Tuma, L. A., Snyder, S. H., Kuhar, M. J., & Gjedde, A. (1986). Positron emission tomography reveals elevated D2 dopamine receptors in drug-naive schizophrenics. *Science, 234,* 1558–1563.

Woodruff, R. A., Robins, L. N., Winokur, G., & Reich, T. (1971). Manic depressive illness and social achievement. *Acta Psychiatrica Scandinavica, 47,* 237–249.

Wright, J. M. von, Pekanmaki, L., & Malin, S. (1971). Effects of conflict and stress on alcohol intake in rats. *Journal of Studies on Alcohol, 32,* 420–441.

Wyatt v. Stickney, 325 F. Supp. 781 (M.D. Ala. 1971); 344 F. Supp. 343 (M.D. Ala. 1972).

Wynne, L. C., Tookey, M. L., & Doane, J. (1979). Family studies. In L. Bellak (Ed.), *Disorders of the schizophrenic syndrome.* New York: Basic Books.

Yalom, I. D., Green, R., & Fish, N. (1973). Prenatal exposure to female hormones. *Archives of General Psychiatry, 28,* 554–561.

Yalom, I. D., Lunde, D. T., Moos, R. H., & Hamburg, D. A. (1968). "Postpartum blues" syndrome: A description and related variables. *Archives of General Psychiatry, 18,* 16–27.

Yankofsky, L., Wilson, G. T., Adler, J., Hay, W., & Vrana, S. (1986). The effect of alcohol on self-evaluation, awareness of negative interpersonal feedback, and perceptions of control and power. *Journal of Studies on Alcohol, 47,* 26–33.

Yates, A. J. (1975). *Theory and practice in behavior therapy.* New York: Wiley.

Yirmiya, N., & Sigman, M., (1991). High-functioning individuals with autism: Diagnosis, empirical findings, and theoretical issues. *Clinical Psychology Review, 11,* 669–683.

Yonker, K. A., Kando, J. C., Cole, J. O., & Blumenthal, S. (1992). Gender differences in pharmacokinetics and pharmacodynamics of psychotropic medication. *American Journal of Psychiatry, 149,* 587–595.

Yoshimasu, J. (1965). Criminal life curves of monozygotic twin-pairs. *Acta Criminologica (Japan), 31,* 5–6.

Young, R. C., & Klerman, G. L. (1992). Mania in late life: Focus on age at onset. *American Journal of Psychiatry, 149,* 867–878.

Young, W. C., Goy, R. W., & Phoenix, C. H. (1964). Hormones and sexual behavior. *Science, 143,* 212–218.

Youngberg v. Romeo, 457 U.S. 307 (1981).

Yu, P., Harris, G. E., Solovitz, B. L., & Franklin, J. L. (1986). A social problem-solving intervention for children at high risk for later psychopathology. *Journal of Clinical Child Psychology, 15,* 30–40.

Yurchenco, H. (1970). *A mighty hard road: The Woody Guthrie story.* New York: McGraw-Hill.

Zametkin, A. J., Nordahl, T. E., Gross, M., King, A. C., Stemple, W. E., Rumsey, J., Hamburger, S., & Cohen, R. M. (1990). Cerebral glucose metabolism in adults with hyperactivity of childhood onset. *New England Journal of Medicine, 323,* 1361–1366.

Zamula, E. (1988). Taming Tourette's tics and twitches. *FDA Consumer Report, 22,* 104–110.

Zanarini, M. C., Gunderson, J. G., & Frankenburg, F. R. (1990). Cognitive features of the borderline personality disorder. *American Journal of Psychiatry, 147,* 57–63.

Zanarini, M. C., Gunderson, J. G., Frankenburg, F. R., & Chauncey, D. L. (1990). Discriminating borderline personality disorder from other axis II disorders. *American Journal of Psychiatry, 147,* 161–167.

Zeisset, R. M. (1968). Desensitization and relaxation in the modification of psychiatric patients' interview behavior. *Journal of Abnormal Psychology, 73,* 13–24.

Zentall, S. S. (1975). Optimal stimulation as the theoretical basis of hyperactivity. *American Journal of Orthopsychiatry, 45,* 549–563.

Zerbin-Rudin, E. (1969). Zur Genetik der depressiven Erkränkungen. In H. Hippius & H. Selbach (Eds.), *Das depressive Syndrom.* Munich: Urban & Schwarzenberg.

Zerbin-Rudin, E. (1972). Genetic research and the theory of

schizophrenia. *International Journal of Mental Health, 1,* 42–62.

Zerbin-Rudin, E. (1979). Genetics of affective psychoses. In M. Schou & E. Stromgren (Eds.), *Origin, prevention, and treatment of affective disorders* (pp. 185–197). Dallas, TX: Academic Press.

Ziegler, F. J., Imboden, J. B., & Meyer, E. (1960). Contemporary conversion reactions: A clinical study. *American Journal of Psychiatry, 116,* 901–909.

Ziegler, E. (1969). Development versus difference theories of mental retardation and the problem of motivation. *American Journal of Mental Deficiency, 73,* 536–555.

Zigler, E., & Balla, D. (1982). *Mental retardation: The developmental-difference controversy.* Hillsdale, NJ: Erlbaum.

Zigler, E., & Phillips, L. (1961). Psychiatric diagnosis: A critique. *Journal of Abnormal and Social Psychology, 3,* 607–618.

Zillman, D. (1983). Transfer of excitation in emotional behavior. In J. T. Cacioppo & R. E. Petty (Eds.), *Social psychophysiology: A sourcebook* (pp. 215–240). New York: Guilford Press.

Zinermon v. Burch, 110 S.Ct. 975 (1990).

Zipursky, R. B., Lim, K. O., Sullivan, E. V., Brown, B. W., & Pfefferbaum, A. (1992). Widespread cerebral gray matter volume deficits in schizophrenia. *Archives of General Psychiatry, 49,* 195–205.

Zis, A. P., & Goodwin, F. K. (1982). The amine hypothesis. In E. S. Paykel (Ed.), *Handbook of affective disorders.* New York: Guilford Press.

Zotter, D. L., & Crowther, J. H. (1991). The role of cognitions in bulimia nervosa. *Cognitive Therapy and Research, 15,* 413–426.

Zubenko, G. S., George, A. W., Soloff, P. H., & Schulz, P. (1987). Sexual practices among patients with borderline personality disorder. *American Journal of Psychiatry, 144,* 748–752.

Zubin, J., & Spring, B. J. (1977). Vulnerability: A new view of schizophrenia. *Journal of Abnormal Psychology, 86,* 103–126.

Zucker, R., & Gomberg, E. (1986). Etiology of alcoholism reconsidered: The case for a biopsychosocial process. *American Psychologist, 41,* 783–793.

Credits

Text and Tables

Chapter 22 Page 568, poem reprinted from L. M. Hayward and J. E. Taylor, *Psychiatric Quarterly*, 1956, pp. 241–242.

Figures and Illustrations

P. 5, The Granger Collection, New York / p. 6, Ets J. E. Bulloz / p. 7 (top), National Library of Medicine, Bethesda, Maryland / p. 7 (bottom), The Granger Collection, New York / p. 8, The Freud Museum, London / p. 9, Ken Heyman/Black Star / p. 19 (left), Michael Newman/Photo Edit / p. 19 (right), Innervisions / p. 20, Lew Merrim/Monkmeyer Press Photo Service / p. 22, Lonnie Major/ALLSPORT USA / p. 25, The Granger Collection, New York / p. 26, Bob Daemmrich/Stock Boston / p. 30, Bob Daemmrich/Stock Boston / p. 34, Secchi-Lecague/Roussel-Uclaf/ CNRI/SPL/Photo Researchers / p. 38, PhotoFest / p. 52, Bob Daemmrich/Stock Boston / p. 53, David Young-Wolff/Photo Edit / p. 57, Mimi Forsythdale/Monkmeyer Press Photo Service / p. 59, Howard Sochurek / p. 66, Martin Rogers/Tony Stone Images / p. 67, Peter Byron/Monkmeyer Press Photo Service / p. 79, Stephen P. Allen/Gamma-Liaison / p. 80 (left), Erika Stone / p. 80 (right), Dratch/The Image Works / p. 83 (left), AP/Wide World / p. 83 (right), AP/Wide World / p. 84, Innervisions / p. 86, Ed Wojtas/Globe Photos, Inc. / p. 91, Frank Siteman/ Monkmeyer Press Photo Service / p. 103, Juliana Force Purchase/From the collection of Whitney Museum of American Art / p. 107, Custom Medical Stock Photo. All Rights Reserved. / p. 118, Ann Chwatsky/The Picture Cube / p. 119, Rapelye/Art Resource, NY / p. 123, Mark Antman/The Image Works / p. 125, Comstock Inc. / p. 132, Richard Hutchings/Photo Researchers / p. 135, Sandy Roessler/The Stock Market / p. 149, The Bettmann Archive / p. 150, The Bettmann Archive / p. 153, *Atlanta Constitution*/Sygma / p. 154, AP/Wide World / p. 158, UPI/ Bettmann / p. 160, John Anderson / p. 170, Innervisions / p. 173, THE SERVANT, 1988, Claudio Brave, Private Collection, Courtesy Marlborough Gallery, New York / p. 179, Ann McQueen/Stock Boston / p. 180, PhotoFest / p. 181, Phillip Davies/New York *Newsday/Los Angeles Times* Photo / p. 189, Dick Young/Unicorn Stock Photos / p. 190, Tony Freeman/Photo Edit / p. 192 (top), The Image Works / p. 192 (bottom), Jock Pottle/Design Conceptions / p. 193, Lester Sloan/Woodfin Camp & Associates / p. 196, Charles Gatewood/The Image Works / p. 218, UCLA School of Medicine, Courtesy of Drs. Michael E. Phelps and John C. Mazziotta / p. 220, P. Chauvel/Sygma / p. 223, Kevin Haislip/Gamma-Liaison / p. 227, Ben Weaver / p. 229, Owen Franken/Stock Boston / p. 232, AP/Wide World / p. 240, Stacy Pickerell/Tony Stone Images / p. 242, Innervisions / p. 250, Will McIntyre/Photo Researchers / p. 253, Steve Goldberg/Monkmeyer Press Photo Service / p. 266 (top), From Redding S. Sugg, Jr., *A Painter's Psalm: The Mural in Walter Anderson's Cottage*, Memphis State University Press, © 1978 by Redding S. Sugg, Jr. / 266 (bottom), Eunice Harris/Photo Researchers / p. 268 (top left), Elizabeth Moudine, "Elizabeth and the Beasts" / p. 268 (top right), Author unknown, Courtesy Holmes / p. 268 (bottom left), Elizabeth Moudine, "Death Tree" / p. 268 (bottom right), Elizabeth Moudine, "From Hell to Heaven" / p. 272, Mary Ellen Mark / p. 279, Nine Network, Australia/Gamma-Liaison / p. 287, Lee Sniker/The Image Works / p. 294, Bob Daemmrich/The Image Works / p. 295 (left), Mel Gordon Edrington/The Image Works / p. 295 (right), U.S. Army Photo / p. 298, PhotoFest / p. 302, Poulides/Thatcher/Tony Stone Images / 311 (all), Howard Sochurek / p. 314, NIMH / p. 323, Sven Martson/Comstock Inc. / p. 325, Bob Daemmrich/Stock Boston / p. 328, James Newberry / p. 333, Jerry Cooke/Photo Researchers / p. 350, AP/Wide World / p. 354, Shooting Star / p. 358, Howard Sochurek / p. 362, AP/Wide World / p. 365, Shooting Star / p. 366, SuperStock, Inc. / p. 377, Nancy Aceuedoel/Monkmeyer Press Photo Service / p. 378, Dr. Zmetkin/NIMH / p. 382, Mary Ellen Mark / p. 385, Joel Gordon Photography / p. 392, MGM/Shooting Star / p. 393, George S. Zimbel/Monkmeyer Press Photo Service / p. 411, Art Pahlke / p. 414, Diane Nelson/Custom Medical Stock Photo. All Rights Reserved. / p. 415, Tom McCarthy/Unicorn Stock Photos / p. 418, Michael L. Abramsom/Woodfin Camp & Associates /p. 421, Sam Sargent/Gamma-Liaison / p. 426, Dr. Beer-Gabel/CNRI/SPL/Photo Researchers / p. 430, Four by Five Inc./Superstock / p. 446, Charles Gatewood/The Image Works / p. 449, Burt Glinn/Magnum Photos / p. 450, Sygma / p. 453 (left), Camerique/H. Armstrong Roberts / p. 453 (right), UPI/ Bettmann / p. 456, The Bettmann Archive / p. 465, PhotoFest / p. 468 (top), Forsyth/Monkmeyer Press Photo Service / p. 468 (bottom), Mulvehill/The Image Works / p. 476, Danny Feld / Shooting Star / p. 484, Kevin Horan/Picture Group / p. 487, Woodfin Camp & Associates / p. 489, Rafael Macia/Photo Researchers / p. 496, Amy Guip / p. 498, UPI/Bettmann / p. 505, Frieda Leinwand / p. 507 (top), Lynn Johnson/Black Star / p. 507 (bottom), Cecil Fox/SS/Photo Researchers / p. 511, Custom Medical Stock Photo. All Rights Reserved. / p. 512, Charles Gupton/Stock Boston / p. 515, P. Davidson/The Image Works / p. 517, Lawrence Migdale/Stock Boston / p. 521, George Steinmetz / p. 526, Greenlar/The Image Works / p. 534, UPI/ Bettmann / p. 535, The Granger Collection, New York / p. 537, John Neubauer/Photo Edit / p. 538, AP/Wide World / p. 542, The Picture Collection, The New York Public Library / p. 544, Elsa Peterson / p. 546, Gamma-Liaison / p. 553, Paul Fusco/Magnum Photos / p. 561, Paul Fusco/Magnum Photos / p. 562, V. Vyatkin/Novosti/SOVFOTO / p. 563, V. Vyatkin/Novosti/ SOVFOTO / p. 569, Courtesy Camarillo State Mental Hospital / p. 579, Dorothy Littell Greco/Stock Boston / p. 582, Jim Wilson/Woodfin Camp & Associates.

Name Index

Abikoff, H., 382
Abraham, S. F., 398
Abramowitz, S. I., 499
Abrams, D., 446
Abramson, L. Y., 172, 197, 199
Adams, J., 515
Addiego, F., 483
Addonizio, G., 339
Adler, A., 22
Agras, W. S., 400
Agren, H., 202
Akiskal, H. S., 257
Alexander, B. K., 460, 461
Alexander, L., 239–240
Allain, A. N., 461
Allen, M. G., 204
Allen, R. E., 106
Allison, R. B., 156, 159
Alloy, L. B., 172, 201
Altamura, A. C., 247
Alzate, H., 483
Amenson, C. S., 176
American Cancer Society, 434
American Medical Association (AMA), 14
American Psychiatric Association (APA), 48,
    49, 87, 178, 352, 387, 486, 515
American Psychological Association, 36,
    555, 576
Anand, B. K., 398
Anderson, K. O., 435
Anderson, L. T., 392
Andreasen, N. C., 59, 282, 310, 311
Andrews, G., 192
Andrykowski, M. A., 434
Angrist, B. M., 308, 309
Anisman, H., 201, 433
Ansbacher, H. L., 22
Ansbacher, R. R., 22
Antes, J. R., 198
Appelbaum, P. S., 543
Appleby, I. L., 106
Ardlie, N. G., 417
Arieti, S., 293
Aring, C. D., 571
Arkonak, O., 161
Aron, A. P., 492
Asberg, M., 230
Astrachan, B. M., 230
Auerbach, R., 485
August, G. J., 380, 389
Avard, J., 423
Avery, D. H., 250, 252

Ayllon, T., 330
Azzerrad, J., 399

Baastrup, P. C., 256
Babbington, P., 192
Babigian, H. M., 225
Bacher, N. M., 309
Baghurst, P. A., 521
Bak, R. C., 491
Baker, B. L., 402
Baker, G. H., 435
Bakwin, H., 403
Balian, L. A., 294
Balint, M., 491
Balla, D. A., 354, 516
Baller, W. R., 402
Bancroft, J., 198, 478, 492
Bandura, A., 27, 99, 130, 357, 383
Barclay, A., 492
Barefoot, J. C., 416, 417
Barfield, R., 492
Barker, J. C., 492
Barlow, D. H., 106, 480
Barr, C. E., 315
Barrett, J. E., 214
Barry, R., 388
Barsky, A. J., 60
Bartak, L., 389
Barthell, C. N., 294
Barton, J. L., 250
Bartrop, R., 429
Bartus, R. T., 508
Bassuk, E. L., 256
Bastani, B., 308, 336
Batchelor, I. R., 148
Bateson, G., 296
Battle, E. S., 523
Baucom, D. H., 200
Bauer, A. M., 405
Bauer, R. B., 511
Baum, A., 66, 191
Baumeister, R. F., 398
Baxter, L. R., 218
Beck, A. T., 48, 56, 104, 133, 196, 228, 229,
    242, 243
Beckman, H., 202
Bedau, H. A., 31
Beere, P. A., 417
Beets, J., 224
Beidel, D. C., 80
Beiser, M., 285
Bell, R. A., 353, 383
Bellack, A. S., 327

Bellak, L., 57
Belmaker, R., 294
Belsher, G., 192
Bendt, R. H., 534, 567
Benjamin, H., 497
Bennet, I., 353
Bennett, D., 41, 133
Benson, H., 134
Bentler, P. M., 491, 496, 497
Berg, G., 464
Berger, P. A., 338
Bergin, A. E., 126
Berkowitz, L., 383
Berlin, F., 491, 494, 495
Berliner, L., 489
Berman, K. F., 310
Berry, H. K., 518
Berscheid, E., 492
Bertilsen, A., 204, 218
Bertilsson, L., 105
Bescherat, J., 25
Bettelheim, B., 387
Beumont, P. J., 398
Beutler, L. E., 126, 254
Bexton, W. H., 299
Bianchi, G. N., 161, 162
Bieber, I., 490
Bihari, K., 108
Billings, A. G., 190, 192, 193
Bini, L., 249
Biran, M., 128, 130
Bird, R. L., 251
Birley, J. L. T., 294
Birnbaum, H. J., 489
Blackman, D. E., 139, 231
Blackstone, E., 388
Blackwell, B., 404
Blair, C. D., 486
Bland, S. H., 422
Blaney, P. H., 198, 199
Bleuler, E., 155, 267, 284, 285, 306
Bliss, E. L., 156
Block, P., 199
Blom, B. E., 256
Bloom, B. L., 54
Bloom, L., 41
Blumberg, E. M., 432
Bock, R. D., 520
Bohman, M., 465
Bollen, K. A., 221, 226
Bollenbach, A., 198
Bond, I. K., 493

Subject Index

Acceptance, 192
Acetylcholine, 339
Acrophobia, 80
Activation of memory, 28
Active phase of schizophrenia, 272
Acute stress disorder, 78, 86
Addictive personality, 461
Admitting wards, 561
Adolescence. *See* Attention-deficit hyperactivity disorder (APD); Eating disorders
Adolescent suicide, 220–221, 227
Adoptee studies, 68, 204, 218–219, 231, 313, 360–361, 380, 465
Adrenal cortex, 413
Adrenal glands, 413
Aerobic fitness, 193, 421–422, 430–431
Age
    antisocial personality disorder and, 352
    anxiety disorders and, 89, 90
        bipolar disorder and, 214
        depression and, 175–177, 179, 214
        eating disorders and, 394
        schizophrenia and, 285
        suicide and, 220
Aggression, 36, 231, 247, 382–384, 490
Agitated depression, 169
Agoraphobia, 76–81, 89, 127, 128, 139
Agranulocytosis, 336
AIDS (acquired immunodeficiency syndrome) virus, 429
Alcohol, 378, 443, 445–447
Alcoholics Anonymous, 468, 582
Alcoholism, 442, 443, 445, 460, 461
    binge type of, 462, 463, 465
    genetic and environmental factors and, 464–467
    persistent type of, 462, 463, 465
    physiological perspective on, 464–467
Algophobia, 80
All-or-none principle, 34
Alzheimer's disease, 36, 505–510
Amenorrhea, 392
American Law Institute rule, 536–537
Amine hypotheses, 34, 201–203
Amines, 201
Amnesia
    dissociative, 153
    faking, 155
Amniocentesis, 518
Amphetamine psychoses, 452
Amphetamines, 202, 248, 308, 392, 445, 451–452

Amygdala, 312
Amytal (amobarbital), 136
Anafranil (clomipramine), 138
Analgesics, 448, 450
Analogue research, 66
Anal stage of psychosexual development, 19–20, 97
Androgens, 494, 497–498
Aneurysm, 513
Anger turned inward, 189
Angina, 414, 416
Angioplasty, 420
Animal research, 9, 23–26, 66, 99, 108, 199–201, 205, 246, 417–418, 426–427, 433, 434, 461, 497–498, 508
Anna O., case of, 8
Anorexia nervosa, 150, 377
Anoxia nervosa, 379, 393–401
Antiandrogens, 494, 495
Antidepressants, 107, 108, 137–139, 182, 238–239, 244–251, 257–258, 370, 400–401, 404
Antigens, 428, 429
Antihistamines, 10, 392
Antipsychotics, 10, 308–309, 332–338, 370, 392, 405, 568
Antisocial personality disorder (APD), 159, 348
    cognitive symptoms, 349–350
    diagnostic criteria, 350–353
    genetic factors and, 359–362, 461
    historical background, 353–353
    learning perspective on, 355–358
    learning therapy for, 363
    mood symptoms, 349
    motor symptoms, 350
    physiological perspective on, 358–362
    physiological treatment of, 363
    prevalence and duration of, 352
    primary versus secondary disorders, 352
    psychodynamic perspective on, 353–355
    psychodynamic treatment of, 362–363
    substance dependence and abuse and, 461–462
Anxiety, 20–22
    arousal disorders and, 480, 482
    cognitive versus somatic, 90–91
    depression and, 77, 203–204
    extinction of, 127–130
    versus fear, 89–90
    inhibition of, 130–132
    lack of, 349, 353

mitral valve prolapse and, 107
normal versus abnormal, 86
schizophrenia and, 77
trait versus state, 90
Anxiety disorders
    classification of, 78
    cognitive perspective on, 101–105
    cognitive symptoms, 77
    cognitive therapy for, 133–136
    demographic characteristics and, 89–90
    diagnosis of, 87
    genetic factors and, 108–110
    humanistic-existential perspective on, 110–111
    learning perspective on, 98–101
    learning therapy for, 127–133
    mood symptoms, 77
    motor symptoms, 77–78
    physiological perspective on, 105–110
    physiological treatment of, 136–141
    prevalence of, 86
    psychodynamic perspective on, 97–98
    psychodynamic treatment of, 117–127
    somatic symptoms, 77
Anxiety reduction, alcohol and, 462–463
Anxiety states, 78
    acute stess disorder, 78, 86
    generalized anxiety disorder, 82, 87, 105, 136, 137
    obsessive-compulsive disorder, 61, 78, 84–86, 97, 107–108, 136, 137, 364–365, 405
    panic disorder, 76, 80–83, 86, 87, 89, 136, 137, 139
    posttraumatic stress disorder, 7, 54, 76, 78, 82–85
APD. *See* Antisocial personality disorder (APD)
Aphasia, 512
Appetitive phase of sexual response cycle, 475
Arousal disorders, 475, 479–482
Arousal transference, 492
Arteriosclerosis, 512–513
Arthritis, 434
Art therapists, 564
Art therapy, 323
Assisted suicide, 232
Associations, 32
Associative intrusions, 305–307
Associative network theory, 28–29, 196
Astraphobia, 80

Negative Symptoms)/Episodic With No Interepisode Residual Symptoms/Continuous (specify if: With Prominent Negative Symptoms)
Single Episode In Partial Remission (specify if: With Prominent Negative Symptoms)/Single Episode In Full Remission
Other or Unspecified Pattern
.30 Paranoid Type
.10 Disorganized Type
.20 Catatonic Type
.90 Undifferentiated Type
.60 Residual Type
295.40 Schizophreniform Disorder
Specify if: Without Good Prognostic Features/With Good Prognostic Features
295.70 Schizoaffective Disorder
Specify type: Bipolar Type/Depressive Type
297.1 Delusional Disorder
Specify type: Erotomanic Type/Grandiose Type/Jealous Type/Persecutory Type/Somatic Type/Mixed Type/Unspecified Type
298.8 Brief Psychotic Disorder
Specify if: With Marked Stressor(s)/Without Marked Stressor(s)/With Postpartum Onset
297.3 Shared Psychotic Disorder
293.xx Psychotic Disorder Due to . . . [Indicate the General Medical Condition]
.81 With Delusions
.82 With Hallucinations
——.— Substance-Induced Psychotic Disorder (refer to Substance-Related Disorders for substance-specific codes)
Specify if: With Onset During Intoxication/With Onset During Withdrawal
298.9 Psychotic Disorder NOS

MOOD DISORDERS (317)

Code current state of Major Depressive Disorder or Bipolar I Disorder in fifth digit:
1 = Mild
2 = Moderate
3 = Severe Without Psychotic Features
4 = Severe With Psychotic Features
Specify: Mood-Congruent Psychotic Features/Mood-Incongruent Psychotic Features
5 = In Partial Remission
6 = In Full Remission
0 = Unspecified
The following specifiers apply (for current or most recent episode) to Mood Disorders as noted:
[a]Severity/Psychotic/Remission Specifiers/[b]Chronic/[c]With Catatonic Features/[d]With Melancholic Features/[e]With Atypical Features/[f]With Postpartum Onset
The following specifiers apply to Mood Disorders as noted:
[g]With or Without Full Interepisode Recovery/[h]With Seasonal Pattern/[i]with Rapid Cycling
Depressive Disorders
296.xx Major Depressive Disorder
.2x Single Episode[a,b,c,d,e,f]
.3x Recurrent[a,b,c,d,e,f,g,h]
300.4 Dysthymic Disorder
Specify if: Early Onset/Late Onset
Specify: With Atypical Features
311 Depressive Disorder NOS

Bipolar Disorders
296.xx Bipolar I Disorder
.0x Single Manic Episode[a,c,f]
Specify if: Mixed
.40 Most Recent Episode Hypomanic[g,h,i]
.4x Most Recent Episode Manic[a,c,f,g,h,i]
.6x Most Recent Episode Mixed[a,c,f,g,h,i]
.5x Most Recent Episode Depressed[a,b,c,d,e,f,g,h,i]
.7 Most Recent Episode Unspecified[g,h,i]
296.89 Bipolar II Disorder[a,b,c,d,e,f,g,h,i]
Specify (current or most recent episode): Hypomanic/Depressed
301.13 Cyclothymic Disorder
296.80 Bipolar Disorder NOS
293.83 Mood Disorder Due to . . . [Indicate the General Medical Condition]
Specify type: With Depressive Features/With Major Depressive-Like Episode/With Manic Features/With Mixed Features
——.— Substance-Induced Mood Disorder (refer to Substance-Related Disorders for substance-specific codes)
Specify type: With Depressive Features/With Manic Features/With Mixed Features
Specify type: With Onset During Intoxication/With Onset During Withdrawal
296.90 Mood Disorder NOS

Anxiety Disorder (393)

300.01 Panic Disorder Without Agoraphobia
300.21 Panic Disorder With Agoraphobia
300.22 Agoraphobia Without History of Panic Disorder
300.29 Specific Phobia
Specify type: Animal Type/Natural Environment Type/Blood-Injection-Injury Type/Situational Type/Other Type
300.23 Social Phobia
Specify if: Generalized
300.3 Obsessive-Compulsive Disorder
Specify if: With Poor Insight
309.81 Posttraumatic Stress Disorder
Specify if: Acute/Chronic
Specify if: With Delayed Onset
308.3 Acute Stress Disorder
300.02 Generalized Anxiety Disorder
293.89 Anxiety Disorder Due to . . . [Indicate the General Medical Condition]
Specify if: With Generalized Anxiety/With Panic Attacks/With Obsessive-Compulsive Symptoms
——.— Substance-Induced Anxiety Disorder (refer to Substance-Related Disorders for substance-specific codes)
Specify if: With Generalized Anxiety/With Panic Attacks/With Obsessive-Compulsive Symptoms/With Phobic Symptoms
Specify if: With Onset During Intoxication/With Onset During Withdrawal
300.00 Anxiety Disorder NOS

SOMATOFORM DISORDERS (445)

300.81 Somatization Disorder
300.81 Undifferentiated Somatoform Disorder

300.11 Conversion Disorder
Specify type: With Motor Symptom or Deficit/With Sensory Symptom or Deficit/With Seizures or Convulsions/With Mixed Presentation
307.xx Pain Disorder
.80 Associated With Psychological Factors
.89 Associated With Both Psychological Factors and a General Medical Condition
Specify if: Acute/Chronic
300.7 Hypochondriasis
Specify if: With Poor Insight
300.7 Body Dysmorphic Disorder
300.81 Somatoform Disorder NOS

FACTITIOUS DISORDERS (471)

300.xx Factitious Disorder
.16 With Predominantly Psychological Signs and Symptoms
.19 With Predominantly Physical Signs and Symptoms
.19 With Combined Psychological and Physical Signs and Symptoms
300.19 Factitious Disorder NOS

DISSOCIATIVE DISORDERS (477)

300.12 Dissociative Amnesia
300.13 Dissociative Fugue
300.14 Dissociative Identity Disorder
300.6 Depersonalization Disorder
300.15 Dissociative Disorder NOS

SEXUAL AND GENDER IDENTITY DISORDERS (493)

Sexual Dysfunctions
The following specifiers apply to all primary Sexual Dysfunctions:
Lifelong Type/Acquired Type
Generalized Type/Situational Type
Due to Psychological Factors/Due to Combined Factors
Sexual Desire Disorders
302.71 Hypoactive Sexual Desire Disorder
302.79 Sexual Aversion Disorder
Sexual Arousal Disorders
302.72 Female Sexual Arousal Disorder
302.72 Male Erectile Disorder
Orgasmic Disorders
302.73 Female Orgasmic Disorder
302.74 Male Orgasmic Disorder
302.75 Premature Ejaculation
Sexual Pain Disorders
302.76 Dyspareunia (Not Due to a General Medical Condition)
306.51 Vaginismus (Not Due to a General Medical Condition)
Sexual Dysfunction Due to a General Medical Condition
625.8 Female Hypoactive Sexual Desire Disorder Due to . . . [Indicate the General Medical Condition]
608.89 Male Hypoactive Sexual Desire Disorder Due to . . . [Indicate the General Medical Condition]
607.84 Male Erectile Disorder Due to . . . [Indicate the General Medical Condition]
625.0 Female Dyspareunia Due to . . . [Indicate the General Medical Condition]
608.89 Male Dyspareunia Due to . . . [Indicate the General Medical Condition]